# MEDIEVAL LATIN

An Introduction and Bibliographical Guide

ADVISORY COMMITTEE

Giles Constable

Bert Hall

Pamela O. Long

David J. McGonagle (*ex officio*)

Richard Sharpe

Daniel Sheerin

Faith Wallis

Olga Weijers

Haijo J. Westra

Jan M. Ziolkowski


PROJECT ASSISTANTS

Paige E.C. Crittenden
(November 1992–May 1994)

William F. Fahey
(November 1992–April 1993)

Laurence Pittenger
(June–August 1994, February–July 1995)

# MEDIEVAL LATIN

An Introduction and Bibliographical Guide

Edited by F.A.C. MANTELLO, *Department of Greek and Latin, The Catholic University of America,* and A.G. RIGG, *Centre for Medieval Studies, University of Toronto*

The Catholic University of America Press • Washington, D.C.

Copyright © 1996
The Catholic University of America Press
All rights reserved
Printed in the United States of America

The paper used in this publication meets the minimum requirements of American National
Standards for Information Science—Permanence of Paper for Printed Library materials,
ANSI z39.48–1984.
∞

**Library of Congress Cataloging-in-Publication Data**

Medieval Latin : an introduction and bibliographical guide /
    edited by F.A.C. Mantello and A.G. Rigg.
       p. cm.
    Includes bibliographical references (p. ) and indexes.
    1. Latin philology, Medieval and modern—Handbooks, manuals,
etc. 2. Latin language, Medieval and modern—Handbooks,
manuals, etc. 3. Latin philology, Medieval and
modern—Bibliography. 4. Latin language, Medieval and
modern—Bibliography. 1. Mantello, Frank Anthony Carl,
1945- . 11. Rigg, Arthur George, 1937- .
    PA2802.M43 1996
    016.477—dc20
    95-11339
    ISBN 0-8132-0841-6 (cloth : alk. paper)
    ISBN 0-8132-0842-4 (pbk. : alk. paper)

In memory of Martin Rawson Patrick McGuire, 1897–1969,
and Hermigild Dressler, O.F.M., 1908–1991

# CONTENTS

# ACKNOWLEDGMENTS

This handbook owes much to the support, assistance, and goodwill of others. The National Endowment for the Humanities generously funded those who produced and published it, and The Catholic University of America subsidized many additional project expenses and granted a period of leave from normal academic duties. Professor William McCarthy cheerfully converted dozens of computer files to a common word-processing format and provided much valuable electronic expertise. Mrs. B.L. Gutekunst, head of the Humanities Library at The Catholic University of America, permitted books that do not usually circulate to be removed for consultation from her divisional library. Dr. Catherine Brown Tkacz was extremely helpful during the early stages of preparing the application to the N.E.H. Professors Siegfried Schulz and George Gingras found time to produce English translations of German and French contributions to the volume. Professors John Lynch and Norman Zacour were kind enough to revise a draft of the chapter submitted by Professor John Gilchrist just before his tragic death in an automobile accident. In addition to offering much general encouragement and specific bibliographic assistance, Professor Thomas Halton provided, in his *Classical Scholarship: An Annotated Bibliography* (1986), compiled with Stella O'Leary, the system of letter and number codes adopted as the organizational schema for this handbook. Professor Michael Lapidge was consulted during the earliest phase of the project and commented astutely on the selection of contributors. Dr. David McGonagle, director of The Catholic University of America Press, strongly supported the project et every stage, even when the resulting guide began to expand unreasonably. Susan Needham, staff editor at the press, was equally encouraging and helpful. We are also very much indebted to Laurence Pittinger, William Fahey, and especially Paige Crittenden, who as project assistants spent countless hours verifying bibliographic references and performing many other tasks. Laurence's exacting care is particularly evident in the indices, which he compiled, and Paige's searches at the Library of Congress resulted in many bibliographic "discoveries."

We acknowledge warmly the assistance of our advisory committee, whose members played an important role in the planning of the guide and the choice of contributors. Two committee members, Dr. Richard Sharpe and Professor Jan Ziolkowski, in addition to preparing substantial contributions of their own, took time from other pressing responsibilities to examine various submissions with expert and searching eyes. We have benefited greatly from their scholarship, vigilance, and advice, and also from the criticisms, suggestions, and kind assistance of many others.

We would like to single out Monica Blanchard, Adam Cohen, Peter Goodman, and Professors Sidney Griffith, Molly Myerowitz Levine, John Petruccione, Linda Safran, and Daniel Sheerin for special thanks, and we are equally grateful for the careful work of copy editor Susan Thornton.

Our greatest debt is to the scholars in eight countries whose combined efforts have made this guide a reality. Almost all of them endured without complaint our editorial cavils, reminders about deadlines, and requests to expand, condense, and otherwise revise their work and to respond to comments and queries. All of them have had to wait far too long for their contributions to appear in print.

Finally, it is a privilege to recognize the pioneering work of our predecessors by dedicating this book to the memory of Martin Rawson Patrick McGuire (1897–1969) and Hermigild Dressler (1908–1991).

# PART ONE

# A   &bull;   INTRODUCTION

## AA   &bull;   MEDIEVAL LATIN, PAST AND PRESENT

Trust ye me, all langage well nygh is but rude beside latyne tonge.
*Barbarus (mihi crede) est sermo fere omnis preter latinum.** 

The Latin language has existed for some 3,000 years and has exerted an influence that is nothing less than astonishing. Its classical form, the literary language of the Roman Republic and Empire and the vehicle of a great literature, is still taught in schools and universities. Its vulgar or popular forms were the precursors of the Romance languages—Italian, Spanish, French, Portuguese, Catalan, Provençal, Sardinian, Romansh, Rumanian, and their many dialects. Its medieval form was Europe's lingua franca, offering the incomparable advantage of a living language common to the whole of Western Christendom and transcending local linguistic variations. Its revived "classical" form was the learned language of humanism and of early modern Europe until late in the seventeenth century. The present "deadness" of Latin can in no way obscure its historical role as the West's culturally preeminent instrument of thought and expression for well over 1,500 years. What is perhaps most remarkable about its survival is that it continued to be learned and used for literary, scholarly, liturgical, administrative, and many mundane purposes long after it had ceased to be anyone's native language.

The Latin used in the Middle Ages is the subject of this guide. Here interpreted broadly to include late antiquity and therefore to extend from c. A.D. 200 to 1500, this 1,300-year epoch was a period of profound linguistic change, of fluid interaction of languages: Latin responded to the influence of the classical literary tradition, Christianity, and the developing vernacular idioms, and these new languages were simultaneously receptive to the influence of Latin, borrowing not only lexical material but also themes, images, rhetorical devices, compositional techniques, and texts to be translated.

Though sometimes confused with Vulgar Latin, the colloquial language of Roman soldiers, colonists, and farmers, Medieval Latin is in fact the direct descendant of the literary, learned Latin of the classical period. As a literary language it resisted linguistic change more forcefully than its spoken counterpart, because it was formally taught by schoolmasters who drew upon an established and revered literary

---

*From fol. 11v of a fifteenth-century collection of 387 short English prose passages with model translations into Latin, assembled as exercises for the boys of Magdalen Grammar School, Oxford, and preserved in Arundel MS 249 of the British Library, London. See chapter DL.

heritage and sought to inculcate standards of correctness. Its conservatism did not, however, mean that it was hostile to innovations; like all living languages it was constantly being exploited for new purposes that required linguistic flexibility. Its writers, who were primarily male and clerical and nearly bilingual in Latin and their own vernaculars, produced over many centuries a vast body of texts and documents in all areas of human life. They wrote every imaginable kind of Latin, from simple, unadorned, expository prose to sophisticated rhythmical verse, latinizing words as necessary from common speech and in other ways testing the limits of the language. For many, Latin was an essential professional tool; others chose it as the only way of ensuring that their works would be widely read. In all the inherited classical literary genres, Medieval Latin authors produced works of power and imagination, imitating and reshaping Roman models, while also incorporating many new elements and responding creatively to entirely new influences. They did not merely transmit the traditions of antiquity.

Medieval Latin's most conspicuous feature, its astonishingly rich mixture of old and new Latin words and of old Latin words with new meanings, reflects the extent to which it resisted lexical purism and the rigid classical distinction between prose and poetic vocabulary. The Christianization of Latin in late antiquity, the most important factor in its postclassical development, imposed a new and extensive terminology in areas of ritual, belief, and administration, while the language, syntax, and themes of the Vulgate Bible penetrated all literary genres. Abstract thought pulled the language in fresh directions, forcing it to become, in the hands of the Schoolmen, a dialectical instrument of remarkable flexibility and originality. Other developments, including changes in the processes of government, the birth of universities, the growth of legal systems, the establishment and expansion of religious orders, the rediscovery of Aristotle, contributed many new terms. Its prestige—some would say tyranny!—required that almost all activities, scholarly and mundane, be described or documented in Latin. Its influence extended even to the compulsory cataloguing of everyday objects in contracts and wills.

Despite its richness and diversity and the excellence of much of its literature, Medieval Latin has often been dismissed, by austere classicists and others, as a debased form of Classical Latin—*infima latinitas* ("the lowest form of latinity," "kitchen Latin")—and a cloud of disparagement and prejudice has obscured its vital role in the transmission of Western culture. Scholars have acknowledged its profound cultural impact and its centrality in medieval life, but its importance as a linguistic and literary phenomenon was not fully recognized until modern times.

The rehabilitation of Medieval Latin began in the nineteenth century, assisted by the establishment of various editing and lexicographical enterprises and by the remarkable growth in recent years of interdisciplinary programs in medieval studies. Before these programs were initiated, Medieval Latin was studied most intensively at German universities, particularly Munich, to which American scholars traveled in the early years of this century for instruction from Ludwig Traube (1861–1907). Medieval Latin thereafter found a place in graduate curricula—it has never done well at the undergraduate level—at Harvard, Chicago, Toronto, and The Catholic University of America, followed more recently by other North American institutions when interdepartmental medieval studies programs were established. These programs bring together medievalists, both faculty and students, in such areas as Medieval Latin and vernacular languages and literatures, history, philosophy, theology, music, art and architecture, liturgy, law, and science and technology. Their aim is to reconstruct and study a distant but not completely alien civilization in all its parts, including the language that united its various cultures and subcultures. More and more institutions in North America are offering graduate degrees in medieval studies; many others provide medieval curricula through traditional departments such as classics, English, history, or Romance languages; several more offer certification or graduate minors. The consolidation of these programs, and the acknowledgment that Latin is the key to understanding medieval society and culture, has led in a few cases to the formal appointment of medieval latinists to serve the needs of graduate students in medieval studies. The proliferation of institutes, graduate centers, programs, and committees concerned with teaching the Middle Ages clearly reflects a growing interest in the study of the medieval period and its preeminent language; this enthusiasm is apparent also in the annual listing of scholarship in the bibliography *Medioevo latino,* which reveals that thousands of publications relevant to the field are now appearing every year.

## Select Bibliography

T. Brooke, T.P. Cross, and J.S.P. Tatlock, "The Study of Medieval Latin in American Universities," in *Modern Philology* 21 (1923–24) 309–15 [AA1].

G.R. Coffman, "The Committee on Mediaeval Latin Studies," in *Modern Philology* 21 (1923–24) 304–9 [AA2].

F.G. Gentry and C. Kleinhenz, eds., *Medieval Studies in North America: Past, Present, and Future* (1982) [AA3].

L.R. Lind, *Medieval Latin Studies: Their Nature and Possibilities* (1941) [AA4].

C.J. McDonough, "Medieval Latin Philology in the U.S.A. and Canada," in *La Filologia medievale e umanistica greca e latina nel secolo XX: Atti del congresso internazionale, Roma, Consiglio nazionale delle ricerche, Università La Sapienza, 11–15 dicembre 1989,* 2 vols. (1993) 579–600 [AA5].

W.D. Paden, ed., *The Past and Future of the Middle Ages: Medieval Literature in the 1990s* (1994) [AA6].

J. Van Engen, ed., *The Past and Future of Medieval Studies* (1994) [AA7].

**AB** ◦ BACKGROUND, AIMS,
AND STRUCTURE OF THE
PRESENT GUIDE

Like its predecessor, Martin McGuire's *Introduction to Medieval Latin Studies: A Syllabus and Bibliographical Guide* (The Catholic University of America Press, 1964), and the revision by Hermigild Dressler (1977), the present book has been designed as an aid for the graduate student who is beginning to work with Medieval Latin texts and documents. The editors will be very pleased if other readers also find it useful.

Work on the present handbook began in 1988, initiated by Dr. David J. McGonagle, director of The Catholic University of America Press, who had contributed to the preparation of the revised edition of McGuire's *Introduction.* The supply of this edition had been exhausted, and he wished to meet demand for the work with an updated version. This was to have the same goal as its predecessor: to provide within a single volume an "orientation in a field that presents special difficulties by its very vastness, to say nothing of other problems" (prefatory note). By providing only the briefest summary outlines rather than full-fledged "introductions," by being highly selective in his choice of topics and in his bibliographies, and by virtually excluding the period from c. 1100 to the close of the Middle Ages, McGuire was able, in 152 pages, to produce a highly useful vade mecum for graduate students, especially those working under his direction in a graduate course he had initiated at The Catholic University of America in 1929, "Introduction to Medieval Latin Studies." In Dressler's hands the original work grew to over 400 pages, as it was extended, rearranged, sometimes rewritten, and provided with fuller and more recent bibliographies. Predictably, both editions of McGuire's *Introduction* were faulted both for leaving things out and for trying to offer too much ("Qui trop embrasse mal étreint"). As the present editors contemplated how best to update the lecture notes and bibliographies assembled by McGuire and Dressler (see [BA26]), it was at once apparent that even an introductory coverage of a field that is at once so broad and so narrow as Medieval Latin was no longer within the expertise of one or two scholars or even a very well-informed small team of editors.

It was decided that the new McGuire-Dressler should be a collaborative effort and less a reedition of its predecessor, with supplementary or updated bibliography, than a replacement for it, with a fresh approach, organization, and format (the editions of 1964 and 1977 were photocopied typescripts). The editors also determined that coverage should extend to the beginnings of humanism and should seek to examine systematically developments in both the language and the literature of Medieval Latin.

A number of organizational models for the proposed replacement were considered, all of which assumed the commissioning of experts to write introductory essays accompanied by bibliographies that were to be limited but reasoned selections of fundamental works. Ultimately we adopted an outline that attempted to distinguish broadly between linguistic developments and Medieval Latin literary and quasi-literary works organized by genre. Professor Daniel Sheerin of the University of Notre Dame, whose advice was sought during the preliminary stages of the project, recommended that a fresh anthology of Medieval Latin, keyed to the new guide, annotated, and equipped with its own glossary, also be prepared as a companion volume. This collection, scheduled for publication along with the guide by CUA Press, was to bring together the representative texts, documents, and other Latin materials submitted by the guide's contributors and often specifically referred to in its essays.

Following consultations with staff of the program for Reference Materials of the National Endowment for the Humanities, a detailed proposal to publish two books, a new guide and a new anthology, was submitted for consideration to The Catholic University of America Press. The director obtained four favorable external evaluations of the proposal, and on 1 May 1990 the editorial committee of the press gave its approval. An application for N.E.H. funding was also successful.

The proposal included a plan to establish for the project an advisory committee of medieval latinists, lexicographers, and other scholars. These experts reviewed early detailed descriptions of the project and several assisted in developing guidelines to govern the final format of the guide and in refining the working list of contents first drafted by the editors. They identified potential contributors and many were also kind enough to write chapters for the book. Professors Wallis and Hall provided the rationale behind the contents and organization of the chapters concerned with medieval science and with technology and crafts, for both of which sections they agreed to compose brief, general introductions. The resulting guide is thus the joint effort of the contributors, the members of the advisory committee, and the editors.

Our original goal was to produce a manual of approximately 600 printed pages, including bibliographies and indices. Specific limits were established for each submission. As a consequence, however, of granting considerable latitude to our contributors, of asking some to expand their coverage of certain subjects, of increasing the number of subjects, and of adding items to bibliographies, the guide in its final form is longer than anticipated. We tried to include bibliographical references through 1991, but in some cases it was possible to add more recent publications. To save space, we have, with some exceptions, not recorded the place of publication for works printed after 1800.

We decided to divide the subject matter into two large sections (Parts Two and Three in the Contents), preceded by an introduction and a reasonably full listing of general reference and research tools (Part One). We believed it was important to try to take into account both linguistic and literary developments, and to expand the range of the volume to include fields of specialization not traditionally defined as Medieval Latin studies. After considerations of such general philological topics as pronunciation, orthography, morphology and syntax, word formation and lexicography, metrics, prose styles and *cursus,* etc., Part Two offers introductions to a wide range of different types of Latin, with an indication of their sources and examples of their specialized terminology and other characteristic linguistic features. There are chapters here on such topics as biblical, liturgical, administrative, legal, scientific, and documentary Latin, with mention also of the Latin used by the Schoolmen, in musical and grammatical treatises, etc. Part Three, arranged according to genre or type, is concerned with literary developments, but has been expanded to include some other forms of communication (e.g. historiography, hagiography, and the large body of writings associated with the *cura animarum*) not usually defined as literature or belles lettres. This part concludes with chapters on translations from and into Latin. Both Parts Two and Three are prefaced by general introductions to the language (chapter CA) and the literature (chapter GA) of Medieval Latin.

There will no doubt be objections to this practical bipartite division into "language" and "literature": some scholars have in fact sought to abolish the distinction between literary and other uses of language, and such concepts as "philology," "literature," "genre," "science," or "technology" may be inappropriate for discussions of works written in the Middle Ages, when knowledge was not neatly pigeonholed into types. Some topics, such as the Vulgate, treated here as a critical linguistic phenomenon, could have been placed just as appropriately within the guide's survey of literature (Part Three). A similar objection may be raised against the modern disciplinary labels used for the medieval sciences and crafts. The editors hope, however, that the highly schematic organization adopted for this guide will make it more useful and accessible as a research tool. Such a schema appeared in any case to reflect accurately enough the highly specialized and fragmented nature of Medieval Latin studies today. This artificial division into specialized categories will, however, oblige readers with broad interests to consult more than one chapter, and they will be aware at once of various overlaps.

Since the guide has been prepared primarily for beginning graduate students, the editors wished to bring together information that might facilitate the reading and interpretation of various kinds of Latin texts and documents. The essays have therefore been written as introductions for nonspecialists, and we have tried to restrict bibliographical references to significant or representative Latin sources (especially those mentioned in the essays) and to such modern works as dictionaries and related compilations, lexicographical studies, important bibliographies and other reference tools, and monographs and articles (especially those in English) of recognized value. It was very difficult, however, to impose a consistent structure on the contributions, and differences in approach and treatment will be apparent throughout the volume. These differences were unavoidable in a collaborative work of this kind and reflect the preferences and training of individual contributors, many of whom have very strong opinions about what kind of information is needed by novices and how it should be conveyed. Collaboration has resulted also in some inevitable duplication of information, as well as in disagreements and differences of opinion. In the case of the select bibliographies accompanying each essay, contributors had the choice of appending or omitting descriptive or evaluative comments; they were also asked to assemble their bibliographies in lists or in the form of bibliographical essays, with items linked together, or to use some appropriate combination of both these methods. Since the editors wished to eliminate the usual kinds of footnote citations, some authors have identified relevant texts or studies within their essays, or referred ahead to the numbered entries in their bibliographies, intending such references to serve almost as footnotes.

Despite the best efforts of contributors and editors, there are doubtless short-comings in the essays and in the choice of references cited. It should also be noted that systematic verification of so many bibliographical entries has proved extremely difficult, and many errors have no doubt passed undetected. We have attempted to keep track of the most recent reprints of books, but series information and modern translations of primary works have been recorded only infrequently. The editors apologize for any errors and inconsistencies and shall be pleased to receive corrections and to be told of other ways in which the volume can be improved. It is our hope that this guide will provide its readers with a body of useful information about Medieval Latin and at the same time identify specific areas that are still underdeveloped and ripe for research, both basic (editions, translations, catalogues, and other tools of access) and analytical.

As indicated above, this guide was to have as its sequel a new anthology of Medieval Latin, which, it was hoped, would enhance the general usefulness of the present volume for the instruction of beginning graduate students. Work on this anthology was well advanced when the Press regretfully determined that it was feasible at this time to proceed only with the publication of the guide. The editors are exploring the possibility of establishing a site on the *World-Wide Web* for the anthology materials.

AC ❖ ORGANIZATION

A glance at the Contents will reveal that this guide has three parts and five major divisions. To these divisions have been assigned the first eight letters of the alphabet. The fourth division (D–E–F) has two additional letters (E and F) to accommodate separate series of chapters concerned specifically with the latinity of medieval *Science* (EA–EM) and *Technology and Crafts* (FA–FM); the fifth division (G–H) includes a separate set of chapters (HA–HD) on medieval translations from and into Latin. At the end of the book are two indices of authors and texts mentioned in the bibliographies.

PART ONE
1. A    Introduction [AA–AD]
2. B    General Reference and Research Tools [BA–BH]
PART TWO
3. C    Medieval Latin Philology [CA–CH]
4. D–E–F    Varieties of Medieval Latinity [DA–DL], [EA–EM], [FA–FM]
PART THREE
5. G–H    Varieties of Medieval Latin Literature [GA–GW], [HA–HD]
INDICES I AND II

Within the five divisions are topical chapters or sections, each assigned a double-letter code that consists of one of the eight letters indicated above (A through H) followed by some other letter: thus the letters "BB" identify the chapter on "Latin Dictionaries and Related Works" in division "B," "General Reference and Research Tools," and the letters "CE" refer to the chapter on "Metrics" in division "C," "Medieval Latin Philology." These codes take the place of the usual chapter and section numbers. When chapters and sections have bibliographies, each of the entries in these bibliographies is assigned a number preceded by the two-letter code of the chapter or section in which it appears. These entry codes (e.g. [BB1], [BB2], [BB3], etc.; [CE1], [CE2], [CE3], etc.) are used for cross-references and in the indices. Readers should note that they will sometimes find bibliographic items relevant to their interests in the listings of division "B," "General Reference and Research Tools," as well as in the select bibliographies of individual chapters. The contents of the bibliographies are accessible through the indices, where references are exclusively to the entry codes. Section "AD" of the Introduction includes a list of bibliographic abbreviations used in the essays and bibliographies.

# ABBREVIATIONS

## General Abbreviations

| | |
|---|---|
| A.D. | *anno/annis Domini* |
| AF | Anglo-French |
| Ak. | Akademie |
| app. | appendix |
| AN | Anglo-Norman |
| AS | Anglo-Saxon |
| B.C. | before Christ |
| bk(s). | book(s) |
| B.L. | British Library (London) |
| B.N. | Bibliothèque Nationale (Paris) |
| c. | *circa,* about, approximately |
| cf. | *confer,* compare |
| ch(s). | chapter(s) |
| CL | Classical Latin |
| corr. | corrected (by) |
| d. | died |
| diss./Diss. | dissertation |
| ed./ed(s). | edition/edited by, editor(s) |
| e.g. | *exempli gratia,* for example |
| *Ep.* | *Epistola,* Letter |
| *et al.* | *et alii/aliae,* and others |
| etc. | *et cetera,* and so forth, and other places |
| f(f). | and the following |
| fasc(s). | fascicle(s) |
| fem. | feminine |
| fig(s). | figure(s) |
| fl. | *floruit,* flourished |
| fol(s). | folio(s) |
| *ibid.* | *ibidem,* in the same place |
| *id.* | *idem,* the same |
| i.e. | *id est,* that is |
| intro. | introduction (by) |

| | |
|---|---|
| LL | Late Latin |
| masc. | masculine |
| ME | Middle English |
| ML | Medieval Latin |
| MS(S) | *manuscriptum/ -a,* manuscript(s) |
| n(n) | note(s) |
| neut. | neuter |
| no(s). | number(s) |
| n.s. | new series |
| OE | Old English |
| OF | Old French |
| phil.-hist. | philologisch-historische |
| p(p)/p(p). | page(s) |
| pl. | plural |
| pl(s). | plate(s) |
| P.R.O. | Public Record Office (London) |
| pt(s)/pt(s). | part(s) |
| r | recto |
| r/repr. | reprint/reprint, reprinted (by) |
| rev. | revised (by), revision |
| sc. | *scilicet,* namely |
| sec. | section |
| ser. | series |
| sg. | singular |
| Sitz. | Sitzungsberichte |
| St. | Saint |
| supp(s). | supplement(s) |
| s.v(v). | *sub verbo/ verbis,* under the word/words |
| tr(s). | translated by, translator(s) |
| v | verso |
| v/vol(s). | volume(s) |
| Wiss. | Wissenschaften |

## Abbreviations of Books of the Latin Bible

For convenience *all* the biblical books are listed here in the alphabetical order of the abbreviations adopted for their names in the Stuttgart Vulgate: *Biblia sacra iuxta Vulgatam versionem,* ed. R. Gryson *et al.,* 4th rev. ed. (Stuttgart 1994); see [DA50]. The figures within parentheses indicate the number of chapters in each of the books.

| | |
|---|---|
| *Abd* | Abdias (Obadiah), *Abdias propheta* (1) |
| *Act* | Acts of the Apostles, *Actus Apostolorum* (28) |
| *Agg* | Aggeus (Haggai), *Aggeus propheta* (2) |
| *Am* | Amos, *Amos propheta* (9) |
| *Apc* | Apocalypse (Revelation), *Apocalypsis Iohannis* (22) |
| *Bar* | Baruch, *Liber Baruch* (6) |

| | |
|---|---|
| *Col* | Colossians, *Epistula Pauli ad Colossenses* (4) |
| 1 *Cor* | 1 Corinthians, *Epistula I Pauli ad Corinthios* (16) |
| 2 *Cor* | 2 Corinthians, *Epistula II Pauli ad Corinthios* (13) |
| *Ct* | Canticle of Canticles (Song of Songs, Song of Solomon), *Canticum Canticorum* (8) |
| *Dn* | Daniel, *Danihel propheta* (14) |
| *Dt* | Deuteronomy, *Liber Deuteronomii* (34) |
| *Ecl* | Ecclesiastes, *Liber Ecclesiastes* (12) |
| *Eph* | Ephesians, *Epistula Pauli ad Ephesios* (6) |
| 1 *Esr* | Esdras (Ezra), *Liber I Ezrae* (10) |
| 2 *Esr* (*Ne*) | Esdras (Ezra), *Liber II Ezrae;* Nehemias (Nehemiah), *Liber Nehemiae* (13) |
| *Est* | Esther, *Liber Hester* (16) |
| *Ex* | Exodus, *Liber Exodi* (40) |
| *Ez* | Ezechiel (Ezekiel), *Hiezechiel propheta* (48) |
| *Gal* | Galatians, *Epistula Pauli ad Galatas* (6) |
| *Gn* | Genesis, *Liber Genesis* (50) |
| *Hab* | Habacuc (Habakkuk), *Abacuc propheta* (3) |
| *Hbr* | Hebrews, *Epistula Pauli ad Hebraeos* (13) |
| *Iac* | James, *Epistula Iacobi* (5) |
| *Idc* | Judges, *Liber Iudicum* (21) |
| *Idt* | Judith, *Liber Iudith* (16) |
| *Ier* | Jeremias (Jeremiah), *Hieremias propheta* (52) |
| *Io* | John, *Evangelium secundum Iohannem* (21) |
| 1 *Io* | 1 John, *Epistula I Iohannis* (5) |
| 2 *Io* | 2 John, *Epistula II Iohannis* (1) |
| 3 *Io* | 3 John, *Epistula III Iohannis* (1) |
| *Iob* | Job, *Liber Iob* (42) |
| *Ioel* | Joel, *Iohel propheta* (3) |
| *Ion* | Jonas (Jonah), *Iona propheta* (4) |
| *Ios* | Josue (Joshua), *Liber Iosue* (24) |
| *Is* | Isaias (Isaiah), *Isaias propheta* (66) |
| *Iud* | Jude, *Epistula Iudae* (1) |
| *Lam* | Lamentations, *Lamentationes* (*Threni*) (5) |
| *Lc* | Luke, *Evangelium secundum Lucam* (24) |
| *Lv* | Leviticus, *Liber Levitici* (27) |
| *Mal* | Malachias (Malachi), *Malachi propheta* (4) |
| *Mc* | Mark, *Evangelium secundum Marcum* (16) |
| 1 *Mcc* | 1 Machabees (Maccabees), *Liber I Macchabeorum* (16) |
| 2 *Mcc* | 2 Machabees (Maccabees), *Liber II Macchabeorum* (15) |
| *Mi* | Micheas (Micah), *Micha propheta* (7) |
| *Mt* | Matthew, *Evangelium secundum Mattheum* (28) |
| *Na* | Nahum, *Naum propheta* (3) |
| *Nm* | Numbers, *Liber Numerorum* (36) |
| *Os* | Osee (Hosea), *Osee propheta* (14) |
| 1 *Par* | 1 Paralipomenon (Chronicles), *Liber I Paralipomenon* (29) |
| 2 *Par* | 2 Paralipomenon (Chronicles), *Liber II Paralipomenon* (36) |
| *Phil* | Philippians, *Epistula Pauli ad Philippenses* (4) |

| | |
|---|---|
| *Phlm* | Philemon, *Epistula Pauli ad Philemonem* (1) |
| *Prv* | Proverbs, *Liber Proverbiorum* (31) |
| *Ps* | Psalms, *Liber Psalmorum* (150) |
| 1 *Pt* | 1 Peter, *Epistula I Petri* (5) |
| 2 *Pt* | 2 Peter, *Epistula II Petri* (3) |
| 1 *Rg* (1 *Sm*) | 1 Kings, *Liber I Regum;* 1 Samuel, *Liber I Samuhelis* (31) |
| 2 *Rg* (2 *Sm*) | 2 Kings, *Liber II Regum;* 2 Samuel, *Liber II Samuhelis* (24) |
| 3 *Rg* (1 *Rg*) | 3 (1) Kings, *Liber III (I) Regum* (22) |
| 4 *Rg* (2 *Rg*) | 4 (2) Kings, *Liber IV (II) Regum* (25) |
| *Rm* | Romans, *Epistula Pauli ad Romanos* (16) |
| *Rt* | Ruth, *Liber Ruth* (4) |
| *Sap* | Wisdom, *Liber Sapientiae Salomonis* (19) |
| *Sir* (*Ecli*) | Sirach (Ecclesiasticus), *Liber Iesu filii Sirach* (*Liber Ecclesiastici*) (52) |
| *So* | Sophonias (Zephaniah), *Sofonias propheta* (3) |
| *Tb* | Tobias (Tobit), *Liber Tobiae* (14) |
| 1 *Th* | 1 Thessalonians, *Epistula I Pauli ad Thessalonicenses* (5) |
| 2 *Th* | 2 Thessalonians, *Epistula II Pauli ad Thessalonicenses* (3) |
| 1 *Tim* | 1 Timothy, *Epistula I Pauli ad Timotheum* (6) |
| 2 *Tim* | 2 Timothy, *Epistula II Pauli ad Timotheum* (4) |
| *Tit* | Titus, *Epistula Pauli ad Titum* (3) |
| *Za* | Zacharias (Zechariah), *Zaccharias propheta* (14) |

## Bibliographic Abbreviations

(N.B.: For abbreviations used to refer to the works of Classical Latin authors, please see the *Oxford Latin Dictionary* [*OLD*], pp. ix–xxi.)

| | |
|---|---|
| *A&A* | *Antike und Abendland* (Berlin 1945–) |
| *AASS* | *Acta Sanctorum quotquot toto urbe coluntur, vel a catholicis scriptoribus celebrantur* (Antwerp, etc. 1643–; 67 vols. had appeared by 1940); reprints: v1–43 (Venice 1734–70); v1–60 (Paris and Rome 1863–70); see [BG1] v1:16–17; vols. are numbered only within each month, and therefore references are to month, volume within the month, and page(s). |
| *AB* | *Analecta Bollandiana* (Brussels 1882–) |
| *AFH* | *Archivum Franciscanum Historicum* (Quaracchi/Grottaferrata 1908–) |
| *AFP* | *Archivum Fratrum Praedicatorum* (Rome 1931–) |
| *AHDL* | *Archives d'histoire doctrinale et littéraire du moyen âge* (Paris 1926–) |
| *AKG* | *Archiv für Kulturgeschichte* (Cologne, etc. 1903–) |
| *ALMA* | *Archivum Latinitatis Medii Aevi* [*Bulletin Du Cange*] (Paris, etc. 1924–) |
| *AM* | *Acta Musicologica* (Leipzig 1931–) |
| *AMS* | *Albertus Magnus and the Sciences: Commemorative Essays 1980*, ed. J.A. Weisheipl (Toronto 1980) |
| *AntJ* | *The Antiquaries Journal* (London/New York, etc. 1921–) |
| *AP* | *Les arts poétiques du XIIe et du XIIIe siècle: Recherches et documents* |

| | |
|---|---|
| | *sur la technique littéraire du moyen âge,* ed. E. Faral (Paris 1924, r1982) |
| *APh* | *L'année philologique: Bibliographie critique et analytique de l'Antiquité gréco-latine* (Paris 1924/26–); see [BA1]. |
| *ASE* | *Anglo-Saxon England* (Cambridge/New York 1972–) |
| *BCC* | *Bibliotheca chemica curiosa,* ed. J.-J. Manget, 2 vols. (Geneva 1702, r1976–77) |
| *BECh* | *Bibliothèque de l'École des chartes* (Paris 1839/40–) |
| *BHL* | *Bibliotheca hagiographica latina antiquae et mediae aetatis,* 2 vols. (Brussels 1898–1901, r1949) and 2 supps. (Brussels 1911, 1986) |
| *Blaise* | A. Blaise, *Dictionnaire latin-français des auteurs du moyen âge/Lexicon latinitatis medii aevi, praesertim ad res ecclesiasticas investigandas pertinens* (Turnhout 1975) |
| *BPhM* | *Bulletin de philosophie médiévale* (Louvain 1964–) |
| *BSLC* | G. Sanders and M. Van Uytfanghe, *Bibliographie signalétique du latin des chrétiens,* CCLP 1 (Turnhout 1989) |
| *CamSoc* | Publications of the *Camden Society* (London 1838–); see [BG20]. |
| *CCSL* | *Corpus Christianorum: Series Latina* (Turnhout 1954–); see [BG24]. |
| *CCCM* | *Corpus Christianorum: Continuatio Mediaevalis* (Turnhout 1966–); see [BG24]. |
| *CCLP* | *Corpus Christianorum: Lingua Patrum* (Turnhout 1989–) |
| *CD* | *Comparative Drama* (Kalamazoo, MI 1967–) |
| *CHFMA* | *Les classiques de l'histoire de France au moyen âge* (Paris 1923–) |
| *CHLMP* | *The Cambridge History of Later Medieval Philosophy from the Rediscovery of Aristotle to the Disintegration of Scholasticism, 1100–1600,* ed. N. Kretzmann *et al.* (Cambridge, etc. 1982) |
| *CIVICIMA* | Publications of *Le comité international du vocabulaire des institutions et de la communication intellectuelles au moyen âge* (Turnhout 1988–); see [BB67]. |
| *CLP* | F.J.E. Raby, *A History of Christian-Latin Poetry from the Beginnings to the Close of the Middle Ages,* 2nd ed. (Oxford 1953, r1966) |
| *CPh* | *Classical Philology* (Chicago 1906–) |
| *CRM* | Solinus, *Collectanea rerum memorabilium,* ed. T. Mommsen, 2nd ed. (Berlin 1895, r1958) |
| *CSEL* | *Corpus Scriptorum Ecclesiasticorum Latinorum* (Vienna/Leipzig/Prague 1866–); see [BG29]. |
| *CTC* | *Catalogus translationum et commentariorum: Mediaeval and Renaissance Latin Translations and Commentaries. Annotated Lists and Guides,* ed. P.O. Kristeller, F.E. Cranz, *et al.* (Washington 1960–); see [BA13]. |
| *DA* | *Deutsches Archiv für Erforschung des Mittelalters* (Marburg 1950–); see [BA14]. |
| *DACL* | *Dictionnaire d'archéologie chrétienne et de liturgie,* 15 vols. in 30 (Paris 1903–53); see [BD47]. |
| *DDA* | Theophilus, *De diversis artibus,* ed. and tr. C.R. Dodwell (Oxford/New York 1961, r1986); tr. J.G. Hawthorne and C.S. Smith (Chicago 1963, r1976) |

| | |
|---|---|
| *DHVS* | *Documents pour l'histoire du vocabulaire scientifique* (Besançon/Nancy 1980–) |
| *Didas.* | Hugh of St. Victor, *Didascalicon: De studio legendi,* ed. C.H. Buttimer (Washington 1939); tr. J. Taylor (New York 1961, r1991) |
| *DMA* | *The Dictionary of the Middle Ages,* 13 vols. (New York 1982–89); see [BD5]. |
| *DOP* | *Dumbarton Oaks Papers* (Washington, etc. 1941–) |
| *DSAM* | *Dictionnaire de spiritualité, ascétique et mystique,* 17 vols. (Paris 1932–95); see [BD50]. |
| *Du Cange* | C. Du Fresne, Sieur Du Cange, *Glossarium ad scriptores mediae et infimae latinitatis* (Paris 1678); see [CD15–16]. |
| *DVJSLW* | *Deutsche Vierteljahrsschrift für Literaturwissenschaft und Geistes-geschichte* (Stuttgart, etc. 1923–) |
| *EHR* | *The Economic History Review* (Oxford, etc. 1927–) |
| *EL* | *Ephemerides liturgicae* (Rome, etc. 1887–) |
| *EMV* | P. Klopsch, *Einführung in die mittellateinische Verslehre* (Darmstadt 1972) |
| *Etym.* | Isidore, *Etymologiarum sive originum libri XX,* ed. W.M. Lindsay, 2 vols. (Oxford 1911, r1985); repr. (with corrections and Spanish translation) J. Oroz Reta and M.-A. Marcos Casquero, 2 vols. (Madrid 1982–83); bk. 2, ed. and tr. P.K. Marshall (Paris 1983); bk. 9, ed. M. Reydellet (Paris 1984); bk. 12, ed. and tr. J. André (Paris 1986); bk. 17, ed. and tr. J. André (Paris 1981) |
| *FMS* | *Frühmittelalterliche Studien* (Berlin 1967–) |
| *FSI* | *Fonti per la storia d'Italia [per il medio evo]* (Rome 1887–) |
| *GIF* | *Giornale italiano di filologia* (Rome 1948–) |
| *GRBS* | *Greek, Roman and Byzantine Studies* (Durham, NC, etc. 1958–) |
| *GSMH* | R.C. Van Caenegem and F.L. Ganshof, *Guide to the Sources of Medieval History* (Amsterdam/New York/Oxford 1978); see [BA16]. |
| *HBS* | Publications of the *Henry Bradshaw Society* (London 1891–); see [BG42]. |
| *HGL* | *L'héritage des grammairiens latins de l'Antiquité aux Lumières: Actes du Colloque de Chantilly, 2–4 septembre 1987,* ed. I. Rosier (Paris/Louvain 1988) |
| *HL* | *Humanistica Lovaniensia* (Leuven/The Hague 1928–); see [CH2]. |
| *HMES* | L. Thorndike, *A History of Magic and Experimental Science,* 8 vols. (New York 1923–58, r1964) |
| *HTech* | *A History of Technology,* ed. C. Singer *et al.,* 8 vols. (Oxford 1954–84); v2: *The Mediterranean Civilizations and the Middle Ages, c. 700 B.C. to c. 1500 A.D. (1956)* |
| *IMB* | *International Medieval Bibliography* (Leeds 1967–); see [BA25]. |
| *Inst.* | Cassiodorus, *Institutiones divinarum et humanarum lectionum,* ed. R.A.B. Mynors (Oxford 1937, r1961); tr. L.W. Jones (New York 1946, r1969) |
| *JBAC* | *Jahrbuch für Antike und Christentum* (Münster/W. 1958–) |
| *JMH* | *Journal of Medieval History* (Amsterdam 1975–) |
| *JMLat* | *The Journal of Medieval Latin* (Turnhout 1991–) |
| *JPMMS* | *Journal of the Plainsong & Mediaeval Music Society* (Englefield |

|  | Green, Eng. 1978–91); continued by *Plainsong & Medieval Music* (Cambridge 1992–) |
|---|---|
| *JS* | *Journal des Savants* (Paris 1816–) |
| *Lewis-Short* | C.T. Lewis and C. Short, *A Latin Dictionary* (Oxford 1879; many reprintings); see [CD19]. |
| *LL* | E. Löfstedt, *Late Latin* (Oslo, etc. 1959) |
| *LLER* | R. Wright, *Late Latin and Early Romance in Spain and Carolingian France* (Liverpool 1982) |
| *LLM* | *La lexicographie du latin médiéval et ses rapports avec les recherches actuelles sur la civilisation du moyen-âge,* Colloque international du Centre National de la Recherche Scientifique no. 589 (Paris, 18–21 October 1978), organized by Y. Lefèvre (Paris 1981); see [BB42]. |
| *LM* | *Lexikon des Mittelalters* (Munich/Zurich 1977–); see [BD7]. |
| *MA* | *Le Moyen Age: Revue d'histoire et de philologie* (Brussels, etc. 1988–) |
| *MAev* | *Medium Aevum* (Oxford 1932–) |
| *MAP* | *Mélanges Auguste Pelzer: Études d'histoire littéraire et doctrinale de la scolastique médiévale offertes à Monseigneur Auguste Pelzer à l'occasion de son soixante-dixième anniversaire* (Louvain 1947) |
| *MBMRF* | *Münchener Beiträge zur Mediävistik und Renaissance-Forschung* (Munich 1967–) |
| *MEL* | *Medioevo latino: Bollettino bibliografico della cultura europea dal secolo VI al XIV* (Spoleto 1980–); see [BA30]. |
| *MGG* | *Die Musik in Geschichte und Gegenwart: Allgemeine Enzyklopädie der Musik,* ed. F. Blume, 17 vols. (Kassel 1949–86), including supps. and *Register;* new edition in progress, ed. L. Finscher (1994–) |
| *MGH* | *Monumenta Germaniae Historica* (Hannover/Leipzig/Berlin, etc. 1826–); see [BG55]. |
| .AA | *Auctores antiquissimi* |
| .EPP | *Epistolae* |
| .Poetae | *Poetae Latini medii aevi* |
| .SRG | *Scriptores rerum Germanicarum in usum scholarum separatim editi* |
| .SRM | *Scriptores rerum Merovingicarum* |
| *MIC* | *Monumenta iuris canonici* (New York/Vatican City 1965–); see [BG56]. |
| *MittStud* | B. Bischoff, *Mittelalterliche Studien: Ausgewählte Aufsätze zur Schriftkunde und Literaturgeschichte,* 3 vols. (Stuttgart 1966–81) |
| *MiscC* | *Miscellanea Cassinese* (Badia de Montecassino 1897–) |
| *MiscM* | *Miscellanea Mediaevalia* (Berlin 1962–) |
| *MJbK* | *Münchner Jahrbuch der bildenden Kunst* (Munich 1906–) |
| *MLJ* | *Mittellateinisches Jahrbuch* (Cologne 1964–) |
| *MM* | *The Mariner's Mirror* (London 1911–) |
| *MP* | *Mittellateinische Philologie: Beiträge zur Erforschung der mittelalterlichen Latinität,* ed. A. Önnerfors (Darmstadt 1975); see [CC18]. |
| *MPLM* | D. Norberg, *Manuel pratique de latin médiéval* (Paris 1968, r1980) |
| *MS* | *Mediaeval Studies* (Toronto 1939–) |
| *MSI* | *Medieval Studies: An Introduction,* ed. J.M. Powell, 2nd ed. (Syracuse, NY 1992) |

| | |
|---|---|
| *MTIS* | *Music Theory and Its Sources: Antiquity and the Middle Ages*, ed. A. Barbera (Notre Dame, IN 1990) |
| *NCE* | *New Catholic Encyclopedia*, 18 vols. (New York/Washington 1967–88); see [BD107]. |
| *NGDMM* | *The New Grove Dictionary of Music and Musicians*, ed. S. Sadie, 20 vols. (London/Washington 1980, r1980 with minor corrections) |
| *NH* | Pliny the Elder, *Naturalis historia*, ed. and tr. H. Rackham *et al.*, 10 vols., Loeb Classical Library (Cambridge, MA/London 1938–63) |
| *NHDM* | *The New Harvard Dictionary of Music*, ed. D.M. Randel (Cambridge, MA 1986); rev. of W. Appel, *Harvard Dictionary of Music*, 2nd ed. (Cambridge, MA 1969) |
| *Niermeyer* | J.F. Niermeyer and C. Van de Kieft, *Mediae latinitatis lexicon minus* (Leiden 1954–76, r1993); see [CD22]. |
| *NKGWG* | *Nachrichten von der königlichen Gesellschaft der Wissenschaften zu Göttingen*, phil.-hist. Klasse (Göttingen 1894–1923) |
| *NOHM* | *The New Oxford History of Music*, 10 vols. (London/New York 1954–90, r1994); v1: *Ancient and Oriental Music*, ed. E. Wellesz (1957); v2: *The Early Middle Ages to 1300*, rev. ed. (1990), by R. Crocker and D. Hiley, of *Early Medieval Music, up to 1300* (1955); v3: *Ars Nova and the Renaissance, 1300–1540*, ed. A. Hughes and G. Abraham (1960) |
| *OLD* | P.G.W. Glare, *Oxford Latin Dictionary* (Oxford 1968–82); see [CD18]. |
| *OPHP* | *The Oxford Poems of Hugh Primas and the Arundel Lyrics*, edited from Bodleian Library MS. Rawlinson G.109 and British Library MS. Arundel 384 by C.J. McDonough, *TMLT* 15 (Toronto 1984) |
| *PAPS* | *Proceedings of the American Philosophical Society* (Philadelphia 1838–) |
| *PFS* | R.H. and M.A. Rouse, *Preachers, Florilegia and Sermons: Studies on the Manipulus florum of Thomas of Ireland* (Toronto 1979) |
| *PIMA* | P. Dronke, *Poetic Individuality in the Middle Ages: New Departures in Poetry, 1000–1150*, 2nd ed. (London 1986) |
| *PL* | *Patrologia Latina*, 222 vols. (Paris 1841–64); see [BG51]. |
| *PM* | P. Lehmann, *Die Parodie im Mittelalter*, 2nd ed. (Stuttgart 1963) |
| *PMLA* | *Publications of the Modern Language Association of America* (Baltimore 1884/85–) |
| *Poli.* | John of Salisbury, *Policraticus*, ed. C.C.J. Webb, 2 vols. (Oxford 1909, r1965); tr. C.J. Nederman (Cambridge/New York 1990); bks. 1–4, ed. K.S.B. Keats-Rohan, *CCCM* 118 (Turnhout 1993) |
| *PRML* | T. Janson, *Prose Rhythm in Medieval Latin from the 9th to the 13th Century* (Stockholm 1975); see [CF24]. |
| *R&R* | *Renaissance and Renewal in the Twelfth Century*, ed. R.L. Benson *et al.* (Oxford/Cambridge, MA 1982, r1991) |
| *RB* | *Revue Bénédictine* (Abbaye de Maredsous, Denée, Belgium 1890–) |
| *RBPhH* | *Revue belge de philologie et d'histoire/Belgisch tijdschrift voor philologie en geschiedenis* (Brussels 1922–) |
| *REAug* | *Revue des études augustiniennes* (Paris 1955–) |
| *RecAug* | *Recherches augustiniennes* (Paris 1958–); supp. to *REAug* |
| *REL* | *Revue des études latines* (Paris 1923–) |

| | |
|---|---|
| *RHC* | *Recueil des historiens des croisades,* 16 vols. (Paris 1841–1906, r1967); see [BG67]. |
| *RLAC* | *Reallexikon für Antike und Christentum: Sachwörterbuch zur Auseinandersetzung des Christentums mit der antiken Welt,* ed. T. Klauser *et al.* (Stuttgart 1950–) |
| *RMA* | J.J. Murphy, *Rhetoric in the Middle Ages: A History of Rhetorical Theory from Saint Augustine to the Renaissance* (Berkeley, CA 1974) |
| *RMAL* | *Revue du moyen âge latin* (Lyons 1945–) |
| *RomRev* | *Romanic Review* (New York 1910–) |
| *RPL* | *Res Publica Litterarum* (Lawrence, KS 1978–) |
| *RQ* | *Renaissance Quarterly* (New York 1967–) |
| *RSer* | *Rolls Series* [*Rerum Britannicarum medii aevi scriptores*]: *Chronicles and Memorials of Great Britain and Ireland during the Middle Ages,* 253 vols. (London 1858–96, r1964); see [BG69]. |
| *RSPT* | *Revue des sciences philosophiques et théologiques* (Paris 1907–) |
| *SAP* | Thomas de Chobham (Thomas of Salisbury), *Summa de arte praedicandi,* ed. F. Morenzoni, *CCCM* 82 (Turnhout 1988) |
| *SAr* | *Sudhoffs Archiv* (Wiesbaden 1966–) |
| *SBMS* | *A Source Book in Medieval Science,* ed. E. Grant (Cambridge, MA 1974) |
| *SChr* | *Sources chrétiennes* (Paris 1941–); see [BG73]. |
| *SE* | *Sacris erudiri: Jaarboeck voor Godsdienstwetenschappen* (Brugge, etc. 1948–) |
| *SelSoc* | Publications of the *Selden Society* (London 1888–); see [BG72]. |
| *SF* | C.D. Lanham, *Salutatio Formulas in Latin Letters to 1200: Syntax, Style, and Theory* (Munich 1975) |
| *SLP* | F.J.E. Raby, *A History of Secular Latin Poetry in the Middle Ages,* 2nd ed., 2 vols. (Oxford 1957) |
| *SM* | *Studi medievali* (Spoleto 1904–13, 1928–52 [n.s.], 1960– [3rd ser.]) |
| *SMA* | *Science in the Middle Ages,* ed. D.C. Lindberg (Chicago 1978) |
| *SO* | *Symbolae Osloenses* (Oslo, etc. 1922–) |
| *Souter* | A. Souter, *A Glossary of Later Latin to 600 A.D.* (Oxford 1949) |
| *StA* | *Studia Anselmiana* (Rome 1977–) |
| *STMS* | *Science and Technology in Medieval Society,* ed. P.O. Long (New York 1985) |
| *SurSoc* | Publications of the *Surtees Society* (Edinburgh/Durham/London 1835–) |
| *TA* | J.M. Ziolkowski, *Talking Animals: Medieval Latin Beast Poetry, 750–1150* (Philadelphia 1993) |
| *TAPhS* | *Transactions of the American Philosophical Society* (Philadelphia 1771–) |
| *TC* | *Technology and Culture* (Chicago 1959–) |
| *TH* | *Textile History* (Newton Abbot, Devon, England 1968–) |
| *TLL* | *Thesaurus Linguae Latinae* (Munich 1899–); see [CD17] and [BC106]. |
| *TLLTCE* | T. Hunt, *Teaching and Learning Latin in Thirteenth-Century England,* 3 vols. (Cambridge/Rochester, NY 1991); v1: texts, v2: glosses, v3: indexes |
| *TMLT* | *Toronto Medieval Latin Texts* (Toronto 1972–); see [BG80]. |

| | |
|---|---|
| *TPhS* | *Transactions of the Philological Society* (Oxford 1854–) |
| *TSMAO* | *La typologie des sources du moyen âge occidental* (Turnhout 1972–); see [BA78–131]. |
| *VC* | *Vigiliae Christianae: A Review of Early Christian Life and Language* (Amsterdam 1947–) |
| *VMK* | *Veröffentlichungen der Musikhistorischen Kommission* (Munich 1976–) |
| *ZDADL* | *Zeitschrift für deutsches Altertum und deutsche Literatur* (Berlin 1841–) |
| *ZRPh* | *Zeitschrift für romanische Philologie* (Tübingen 1877–) |

## Signs Used in Etymologies

&lt;   derived from
&gt;   whence derived
*   assumed (i.e. a hypothetical word, or a word no longer extant)

# B · GENERAL REFERENCE AND RESEARCH TOOLS

Assembled in division "B," in the eight sections (BA through BH) whose titles and contents are listed here, are reference works of various kinds that may assist in the reading and interpretation of Medieval Latin texts or in the identification of publications that may usefully be consulted by medieval latinists. These works include bibliographical, biographical, linguistic, encyclopedic, computerized, technical, and other aids, and they supplement, with some duplication for the sake of convenience, the reference and research tools listed in the individual bibliographies of the chapters of this volume. Section BG is a select listing of the standard collections where late antique and Medieval Latin texts have been published.

For Medieval Latin handbooks, manuals, guides, and modern anthologies please see the bibliographies of chapters CA and GA; modern literary histories are listed in chapter GA. A selection of earlier literary histories, i.e. the works of antiquarian bibliographers and historians of religious orders and scholarly authors, is part of section BC.

BA  Bibliographical Guides and Surveys
   *(a) Standard Bibliographical Tools for Medieval Latinists*
   *(b) Specialized Medieval Bibliographies*

BB  Latin Dictionaries and Related Works
   *(a) Standard Latin Lexica, Classical and Postclassical*
   *(b) Specialized Lexica and Lexicographical Works*
   *(c) Medieval Glosses and Glossaries*

BC  Repertories of Authors, Texts, and Initia
   *(a) Literary Histories to 1900*
   *(b) Modern Repertories*

BD  Encyclopedias, Encyclopedic Dictionaries, and Related Works
   *(a) General Reference Works*
   *(b) National Biographical Dictionaries*
   *(c) Other Reference Works*

BE  Computer Resources
   *(a) Orientation, Applications*
   *(b) Databases, CD-ROMs, etc.*
   *(c) Electronic Discussion Groups*

BF  Other Basic Reference and Research Aids
   *(a) Dictionaries*
   *(b) Guides to Libraries and Archives*
   *(c) Guides to Scholars and Academic Institutions*
   *(d) Historical Atlases*
   *(e) Other Reference Works*

BG  Principal Series and Collections of Latin Texts

BH  Periodicals

# BA ❋ BIBLIOGRAPHICAL GUIDES AND SURVEYS

This section brings together works whose object is to provide lists, sometimes with descriptive or critical notes, of sources, studies, translations, and other publications (including manuscript catalogues) of general medieval interest or of importance for the study of a particular medieval author or subject. Some entries include the Middle Ages (or a part thereof) within larger bibliographical surveys or are pertinent because they list works that influenced, or were influenced by, medieval developments, or because they are otherwise useful to medievalists.

## (a) Standard Bibliographical Tools for Medieval Latinists

*L'année philologique: Bibliographie critique et analytique de l'Antiquité gréco-latine* [*APh*], ed. J. Marouzeau *et al.* (1924/26–): comprehensive, annual, bibliographical guide for classical studies, with much information useful to the medievalist; two main parts: "Auteurs et Textes" (listed alphabetically) and "Matières et Disciplines" (with several divisions, each with subdivisions); includes occasional annotations and references to reviews; continuation of Marouzeau's *Dix années de bibliographie classique . . . 1914–1924*, 2 vols. (1927–28, r1969), which itself continues S. Lambrino, *Bibliographie de l'Antiquité classique, 1896–1914*, v1 (1951) [**BA1**]; see also the *DCB* ([**BE32**]) [**BA2**]; the "Bibliographische Beilage" in every other issue of *Gnomon: Kritische Zeitschrift für die gesamte klassische Altertumswissenschaft* (1925–), and the associated computer file, *Gnomon Bibliographische Datenbank* (updated annually) [**BA3**]; and T.P. Halton and S. O'Leary, *Classical Scholarship: An Annotated Bibliography* (1986) [**BA4**].

*Bibliografia della lingua latina (1949–91)* (1993), assembled by F. Capaiuolo: conceived as a continuation of J. Cousin, *Bibliographie de la langue latine, 1880–1948* (1951) [**BA5**], with chapters on linguistics (I), the origin and history of Latin (II–III), orthography and pronunciation (V), phonology (VI), morphology (VII), syntax (VIII), style (X), and lexicography (XII), and sections on "Il latino delle province," "La diffusione del latino," "Tardo latino," "Il latino cristiano, il latino delle Chiesa," "La lingua delle iscrizioni," "Latino volgare e latino parlato (lingua d'uso)," "Dal latino al romanzo," and "L'informatica e la lingua latina"; chap. XII lists dictionaries, "indici, lessici e concordanze degli autori," and studies/lexica of technical terminology ("Lingue tecniche e settori linguistici speciali"); reviews are noted [**BA6**].

*Bibliographia patristica/Internationale patristische Bibliographie,* ed. W. Schnee-melcher *et al.* (1959–): comprehensive, annual listing, covering the years to the seventh century in the West and the eighth century in the East; arranged under nine headings, including *auctores,* with index of modern authors [BA7].

*Bibliographie internationale de l'humanisme et de la renaissance* (1966–): comprehensive, annual guide (of the Fédération internationale des sociétés et instituts pour l'étude de la Renaissance) to publications (books and articles) in all the fields of fourteenth-, fifteenth-, and sixteenth-century studies; arrangement is by section, with publications listed alphabetically by author in each; index of authors, places, and subjects; continues annual bibliographical listing (1948–65) in *Bibliothèque d'humanisme et renaissance: Travaux et documents* [BA8].

*Bibliographie linguistique/Linguistic Bibliography* (1939–): annual, international bibliography, with an index of authors, books, and articles in the field of languages and dialects; after chapters listing "general works" and studies concerned with "general linguistics and related disciplines" the classification is by linguistic group and language, with sections on Classical and Postclassical Latin; reviews are noted; v1 (1949) covers the period from 1939 to 1947 [BA9].

*Bibliotheca lexicologiae medii aevi,* ed. F.A. Tremblay, 10 vols. (1988–89): printed version of a vast, computerized assemblage in ten volumes of bibliographical items touching on all aspects of Medieval Latin "lexicology" (the study of words, their form, history, meaning, and use) from the fifth to the sixteenth century: v1, the classics and education in the Middle Ages; v2–4, lexicons and grammars in the Middle Ages; v5, the rise of the vernacular languages; v6, the influence of Vulgar Latin; v7-v8.1, lexicographical manuscripts; v8.2-v10 provide (a) lists of reference works, scholarly journals, and bibliographical resources, and (b) indexes of authors, titles, locations of manuscript repositories, abbreviations used for periodicals and standard reference tools, dates of manuscripts (by century) and of cited publications, and incipits of relevant medieval manuscripts; all entries are numbered and also classified by "descriptor" [BA10]. This *Bibliotheca* is part of a larger bibliographical enterprise, the *Thesaurus Bibliographiae Graecae et Latinae,* of the Service international de bibliographie en antiquité classique [*SIBAC*] (Université du Québec à Trois-Rivières); the *Thesaurus* also includes R. LaRue *et al., Clavis scriptorum graecorum et latinorum* [*CSGL*], 4 vols. (1985) (see [BC74]) [BA11].

*Cahiers de civilisation médiévale, Xe–XIIe siècles: Bibliographie* (1958–): each of the volumes of this journal issued from 1958 to 1968 includes a bibliography; thereafter the bibliographies appeared as unnumbered special issues; these list both books and articles for the period indicated, with an emphasis on the Western Middle Ages; annual index of authors, with separate index of names, places, texts, etc. for v1–5 (1958–62) [BA12].

*Catalogus translationum et commentariorum: Mediaeval and Renaissance Latin Translations and Commentaries. Annotated Lists and Guides* [*CTC*], ed. P.O. Kristeller, F.E. Cranz, *et al.* (1960–): descriptive lists, with bibliographical references, (a) of the Latin *translations* of ancient Greek authors (who wrote before A.D. 600, including patristic writers, but excluding those of Byzantium), and (b) of the Latin *commentaries* on Greek and Latin authors (who wrote before A.D. 600, excluding expositions of Aristotle; the Bible; medical, legal, and canonistic writings; and Medieval Latin authors); coverage extends through A.D. 1600 and arrangement is by author [BA13].

*Deutsches Archiv für Erforschung des Mittelalters* [*DA*] (1950–); previously (1937–44) entitled *Deutsches Archiv für Geschichte des Mittelalters:* semiannual, annotated listing of articles and books on medieval subjects, arranged topically; annual indexes of authors and subjects [BA14].

*Dissertation Abstracts International: Abstracts of Dissertations Available on Microfilm or as Xerographic Reproductions* (1969–): for description, and descriptive listing of other bibliographies of theses and dissertations, see [BA29] pp21–22; see also *Dissertation Abstracts Ondisc,* a database regularly updated and covering more than one million doctoral dissertations and masters' theses from 1861 to the present [BA15].

*Guide to the Sources of Medieval History* [*GSMH*], compiled by R.C. Van Caenegem and F.L. Ganshof (1978): a carefully schematized and annotated introduction to, and bibliographical survey of, the narrative sources of medieval history and of related auxiliary sciences, organized in five parts: a discussion and classification of sources by genre or type (pt1) is followed by an introduction to libraries and archives (pt2) and by orientations in the great collections and important repertories of sources (pt3), reference works for historians (pt4), and auxiliary disciplines (pt5); with index of names and titles [BA16].

*Index translationum: Répertoire international des traductions/International Bibliography of Translations* (1932–40, 1948–): annual listing of translations published worldwide, with index of authors/works translated; the *Cumulative Index to English Translations: 1948–1968,* 2 vols. (1973), covers the first 21 volumes of the second series [BA17]; see also C.P. Farrar and A.P. Evans, eds., *Bibliography of English Translations from Medieval Sources* (1946), and its supp., ed. M.A.H. Ferguson (1974) [BA18]. *The Literatures of the World in English Translation: A Bibliography,* ed. G.B. Parks and R.Z. Temple (1967–), includes "Latin Literature to A.D. 450" and "Medieval Latin Literature A.D. 450–1450" in v1, *The Greek and Latin Literatures,* pp201–335 [BA19]. Recent English translation series include *Translated Texts for Historians* (1985–), which focuses on the period from A.D. 300 to 800 and on sources in Latin, Greek, and Syriac [BA20], and the bilingual *Cambridge Medieval Classics* (1994–) (see [BG19]) [BA21].

*Internationale Bibliographie der Festschriften/International Bibliography of Festschriften,* ed. O. Leistner (1976), with subject index [BA22]; see also H.F. Williams, ed., *An Index of Mediaeval Studies Published in Festschriften, 1865–1946, with Special Reference to Romanic Material* (1951) [BA23].

*International Guide to Medieval Studies: A Quarterly Index to Periodical Literature,* 12 vols. (1961/62–72/73): surveys (with frequent annotations and subject and author indexes) of published articles in medieval history (social, economic, political, and ecclesiastical), science, arts and crafts, language and literature, from the sixth to the fourteenth century; produced by American Bibliographic Service (Darien, CT) [BA24].

*International Medieval Bibliography* [*IMB*] (1967–): comprehensive listing, published semiannually (except for 1967 and 1969), of articles, review articles, notes, and similar publications (but not monographs or short reviews) from hundreds of journals, festschriften, proceedings of conferences, and collected essays; covers all medieval fields (A.D. 450–1500), which are arranged by topic (subdivided geographically, with authors listed alphabetically within each area); (modern) author index and general index containing entries for subjects and names of persons, places, manuscripts, and texts; v1 reproduces file cards issued in 1967; for the computerized version, the *IMB on CD-ROM,* see [BE38] [BA25].

*Introduction to Medieval Latin Studies: A Syllabus and Bibliographical Guide,* 2nd ed., by M.R.P. McGuire and H. Dressler (1977): this continues to be a useful compendium of information, with 16 topical outlines and accompanying bibliographies that focus on important linguistic issues, followed by 21 separate select bibliographies that cover standard reference tools and a wide range of subjects and disciplines fundamental for research in Medieval Latin studies; see remarks in sec. AB of this guide [BA26].

*Latin Manuscript Books Before 1600: A List of the Printed Catalogues and Unpublished Inventories of Extant Collections,* by P.O. Kristeller; 4th ed. rev. and enlarged by S. Krämer, *MGH.Hilfsmittel* 13 (1993): indispensable guide to publications that are regularly surveyed in *MEL* (see [BA30]) under the rubric "Cataloghi di manoscritti"; sections *A* and *B,* arranged alphabetically by author, editor, or title, list (*A*) bibliographies and important studies of general paleographical or codicological interest, and (*B*) works (especially catalogues) describing manuscripts in more than one city; section *C,* arranged alphabetically by city, lists catalogues and inventories of individual libraries; the brief section *D* (pp937–41) is an alphabetical listing of guides to libraries and archives (see also [BF75–79]) [BA27].

*The Medieval Literature of Western Europe: A Review of Research, Mainly 1930–1960,* ed. J.H. Fisher (1966): critical surveys by specialists, with index of proper names (pp411–32); includes chapter on Medieval Latin by A.C. Friend (pp3–33) [BA28].

*Medieval Studies: A Bibliographical Guide,* ed. E.U. Crosby, C.J. Bishko, and R.L. Kellogg (1983): valuable one-volume guide of 1,131 pages, with about 9,000 entries (usually annotated), arranged by subject in 138 chapters; indices of authors/editors and topics (pp1059–1131) and extensive list of serials (pp1027–57) [BA29].

*Medioevo latino: Bolletino bibliografico della cultura europea dal secolo VI al XIV* [*MEL*], ed. C. Leonardi *et al.* (1980–): extensive, annual listing of publications in all aspects of medieval studies, divided into authors/texts and topics ("Discipline," "Filologia e Letteratura," "Generi Letterari," "Istituzioni," "Storia della Cultura della Spiritualità," "Storia della Medievistica" [since 1986], "Opere di Consultazione," "Congressi Miscellanee," all subdivided); includes references to reviews and indices of authors, manuscripts, etc.; v1–12 (1980–91) have the subtitle *Bolletino bibliografico della cultura europea dal secolo VI al XIII;* v1 indexes the literature for 1978 but includes numerous items from prior years [BA30]; a version of *MEL* on CD-ROM is in progress.

*Mittellateinisches Jahrbuch* [*MLJ*] (1964–): since 1980 this journal has usually contained a section, "Forschungsmitteilungen," on current research; *MLJ* also includes such surveys as K. Liman, "Mittellateinische Studien in Polen 1945–1979," in v19 (1984) 1–36 and v20 (1985) 1–48 [BA31].

*MLA International Bibliography of Books and Articles on the Modern Languages and Literatures* (1922–): comprehensive, annual listing—by language, topic, period, and individual author—of books and articles concerning European languages and literatures from the Middle Ages to the present; includes Medieval Latin; North American scholarship listed exclusively from 1921 to 1955, with international publications added thereafter; author indexes provided from 1964; electronic version also available [BA32]. A companion volume is the *MLA Directory of Periodicals: A Guide to Journals and Series in Languages and Literatures* (1978/79–), 7th ed. (1993–95), which, in its clothbound edition, contains listings for 3,277 journals and series; these identify editors and provide addresses, telephone/fax numbers, and other information, including submission requirements and descriptions of scope, languages accepted, etc. [BA33]. For a full listing of periodicals see [BF98].

*Progress of Medieval and Renaissance Studies in the United States and Canada,* 1–25 (1923–60): variously titled: "Canada" was added in 1933, "Renaissance" in 1940; includes lists of medieval and renaissance scholars and their publications as well as papers, projects, and doctoral dissertations [BA34].

*Quarterly Check-list of Medievalia: International Index of Current Books, Monographs, Brochures & Separates* (1958–78): lists (with annual index of authors, editors, and translators) non-periodical publications (books, reprints, translations) relating to Western Europe and Byzantium to the sixteenth century; produced by American Bibliographic Service (Darien, CT) as a companion bibliography to [BA24]) [BA35].

*Repertorium bibliographicum,* 2 vols. in 4 (1826–36, r1948 and 1966): standard, comprehensive listing of incunabula, assembled by L. Hain, with supp. by W.A. Copinger, 2 pts. in 3 (1895–1902, r1950), and *Appendices ad Hainii-Copingeri Repertorium bibliographicum: Additiones et emendationes* by D. Reichling, 7 vols. with supp. (1905–11 and 1914, r1953) [BA36]; see also the *Gesamtkatalog der Wiegendrucke* (1925–40, 1972–) [BA37] and, for early English editions, *A Short-Title Catalogue of Books Printed in England, Scotland, & Ireland and of English Books Printed Abroad, 1475–1640* [STC], compiled by A.W. Pollard and G.R. Redgrave (1926, r1969); rev. and enlarged by W.A. Jackson and F.S. Ferguson and completed by K. Pantzer, 2 vols. (1976–86) [BA38]. For other such catalogues of early printed editions see [BA13] v7:XVIII–XX; see also *ISTC* [BE35].

*Romanische Bibliographie* (1965–; published annually since 1979): comprehensive, international bibliography; a continuation of the bibliographical supplement (1878–1964) of *Zeitschrift für romanische Philologie* [ZRPh]; lists books and articles concerning all the Romance languages and literatures, with attention also to Latin (Vulgar, Christian, Medieval, etc.); each issue consists of three volumes that cover, without annotations, *festschriften,* proceedings of conferences, collections, etc. (v1); linguistics (v2); and literature (v3); the three volumes are indexed as a set in v1 [BA39].

*Serial Bibliographies for Medieval Studies* (1969): annotated guide, compiled by R.H. Rouse, to 283 bibliographies, with indexes of titles and editors; pt1 lists general and national/regional bibliographies and includes Byzantine, Islamic, and Judaic Studies; pt2 is organized by subject and includes Latin and the vernacular languages; archives and manuscripts; heraldry; numismatics; art and archaeology; Church history (including monasticism and the religious orders); economics and agriculture; geography and cartography; law and institutions; sociology, anthropology, and folklore; biblical studies and exegesis; liturgy and hagiography; pedagogy; theology and philosophy; music; science, technology, and medicine [BA40]. A similar guide, for literatures (including Classical and Postclassical Latin), is W.A. Wortman, *A Guide to Serial Bibliographies for Modern Literatures* (1982) [BA41].

*Speculum* (1926–): since 1973 the January issue of this journal has included a "Bibliography of Editions and Translations in Progress of Medieval Texts," compiled by L.L. Gioia and arranged alphabetically by title, author, or subject; a brief bibliography of medieval periodical literature published in North America also appeared in each issue from 1934 (v9.1) until 1972 (v47) [BA42].

*The Year's Work in Modern Language Studies* (1929/30–): signed and indexed (by author and subject) bibliographical essays about books and articles published during a given year on Medieval Latin and Neo-Latin, Romance, Germanic, Slavonic, and Celtic (since 1974) languages and literatures; the period 1940–49 is covered in v11 [BA43].

## (b) Specialized Medieval Bibliographies

Bibliographical guides—selective or inclusive—to publications in particular medieval fields, topics, themes, or chronological periods, or to individual authors and texts, or to some combination of subject, writer, and time span, are very numerous; only a small selection can be mentioned here. Such tools may list or review sources and/or studies; provide descriptions, critical evaluations, and references to reviews; or cover the medieval period only as part of a larger chronological survey. Many are published in periodicals that include regular listings (and reviews) of scholarship in particular fields; some journals are published exclusively for this purpose.

Specialized bibliographical resources are listed in the standard guides of section (a), and many have also been added to the bibliographies of the chapters of this volume. They may be most conveniently surveyed in [BA25], [BA29], [BA40], and [BA30] (under the rubric "Bibliografie"). Item [BA16] provides an extensive, annotated listing of guides to Medieval Latin narrative sources and documents, which may be updated by reference to [BA25] and [BA29–30].

A number of especially useful subject bibliographies are the following:

**1. Garland Bibliographies.** Several annotated bibliographical guides of use to medievalists have appeared in series—*Garland Medieval Bibliographies* (1990–), *[Garland] Bibliographies of the History of Science and Technology* (1982–), *Garland Folklore Bibliographies* (1981–), *Garland Reference Library of the Humanities* (1975–)—initiated by Garland Publishing (Hamden, CT); some of these volumes provide select bibliographies for medieval topics exclusively, while others include the Middle Ages as part of larger chronological surveys; many Garland bibliographies are assigned numbers in more than one series [BA44].

J.A. Alford and D.P. Seniff, *Literature and Law in the Middle Ages: A Bibliography of Scholarship* (1984) [BA45].

J.M. Bak *et al.*, *Medieval Narrative Sources: A Chronological Guide (with a List of Major Letter Collections)* (1987) [BA46].

S.E. Berger, *Medieval English Drama: An Annotated Bibliography of Recent Criticism* (1990) [BA47]: supplements and continues C.J. Stratman, *Bibliography of Medieval Drama,* 2nd ed. rev. and enlarged, 2 vols. (1972) [BA48].

L.N. Braswell, *Western Manuscripts from Classical Antiquity to the Renaissance: A Handbook* (1981) [BA49].

P. Carnes, *Fable Scholarship: An Annotated Bibliography* (1985) [BA50].

E.U. Crosby, C.J. Bishko, and R.L. Kellogg, *Medieval Studies: A Bibliographical Guide* (1983): see [BA29] [BA51].

J.W. Dauben, *The History of Mathematics from Antiquity to the Present: A Selective Bibliography* (1985) [BA52].

L.K. Davidson and M. Dunn-Wood, *Pilgrimage in the Middle Ages: A Research Guide* (1993) [BA53].

M. Dunn and L.K. Davidson, *The Pilgrimage to Santiago de Compostela: A Comprehensive, Annotated Bibliography* (1994) [BA54].

S.E. Farrier, *The Medieval Charlemagne Legend: An Annotated Bibliography* (1993) [BA55].

C.D. Ferguson, *Europe in Transition: A Select, Annotated Bibliography of the Twelfth-Century Renaissance* (1989) [BA56].

E. Gardiner, *Medieval Visions of Heaven and Hell: A Sourcebook* (1993) [BA57].

R.M. Gascoigne, *A Historical Catalogue of Scientists and Scientific Books from the Earliest Times to the Close of the Nineteenth Century* (1984) [BA58].

W.D. Hines, *English Legal History: A Bibliography and Guide to the Literature* (1990) [BA59].

C. Kallendorf, *Latin Influences on English Literature from the Middle Ages to the Eighteenth Century: An Annotated Bibliography of Scholarship, 1945–1979* (1982) [BA60].

N.H. Kaylor, Jr., *The Medieval Consolation of Philosophy: An Annotated Bibliography* (1992) [BA61].

B.G. Kohl, *Renaissance Humanism, 1300–1550: A Bibliography of Materials in English* (1985) [BA62].

C. Kren, *Medieval Science and Technology: A Selected, Annotated Bibliography* (1985) [BA63]; *eadem, Alchemy in Europe: A Guide to Research* (1990) [BA64].

V.M. Lagorio and R. Bradley, *The 14th-Century English Mystics: A Comprehensive Annotated Bibliography* (1981) [BA65].

W. Mieder, *International Proverb Scholarship: An Annotated Bibliography* (1982); *Supplement,* 2 vols. (1990–93) [BA66].

P.M. Molloy, *The History of Metal Mining and Metallurgy: An Annotated Bibliography* (1986) [BA67].

J.P. Oleson, *Bronze Age, Greek, and Roman Technology: A Select, Annotated Bibliography* (1986) [BA68].

J.E. Salisbury, *Medieval Sexuality: A Research Guide* (1990) [BA69].

M.L. Switten, *Music and Literature in the Middle Ages: An Annotated Bibliography* (1990) [BA70].

**2. Toronto Medieval Bibliographies** (1971–). This is a series of select bibliographies designed to orient (a) new students beginning their studies in a particular field, (b) more advanced students requiring guidance in unfamiliar areas of study, and (c) librarians seeking to assemble basic collections; items are frequently annotated; presentation varies from volume to volume [BA71].

L.E. Boyle, *Medieval Latin Palaeography: A Bibliographical Orientation* (1984) [BA72].
G. Constable, *Medieval Monasticism: A Select Bibliography* (1976) [BA73].
A. Hughes, *Medieval Music, The Sixth Liberal Art,* rev. ed. (1980) [BA74].
R.E. Kaske, A. Groos, and M.W. Twomey, *Medieval Christian Literary Imagery: A Guide to Interpretation* (1988) [BA75].
J.J. Murphy, *Medieval Rhetoric: A Select Bibliography,* 2nd ed. (1989) [BA76].
R.W. Pfaff, *Medieval Latin Liturgy: A Select Bibliography* (1982) [BA77].

**3. La typologie des sources du moyen âge occidental** [*TSMAO*] (1972–). This is an ongoing series of brief guides (68 in 1994), with bibliographies, to primary sources of all kinds, classified by genre; covers the period from A.D. 500 to 1500 and includes Muslim Spain; additional pages updating some of the first 39 fascicles were published in 1985, followed by a *Table of Fascicles 1–50* by the general editor, L. Genicot, in 1992; fascicles are published when they are completed and include the following titles, listed here alphabetically by author [BA78].

M.-A. Arnould, *Les relevés de feux,* no. 19 (1976, 1985) [BA79].

B.C. Bazàn, J.F. Wippel, G. Fransen, and D. Jacquart, *Les questions disputées et les questions quodlibétiques dans les facultés de Théologie, de Droit et de Médecine,* nos. 44–45 (1985) [BA80].

D.P. Blok, *Ortsnamen,* no. 54 (1988) [BA81].

R. Boyer *et al., L'épopée,* no. 49 (1988) [BA82].

C. Bremond, J. Le Goff, and J.-C. Schmitt, *L'"exemplum",* no. 40 (1982) [BA83].

A.-D. von den Brincken, *Kartographische Quellen: Welt-, See- und Regionalkarten,* no. 51 (1988) [BA84].

M.G. Briscoe and B.H. Jaye, *Artes praedicandi, artes orandi,* no. 61 (1992) [BA85].

P. Brommer, *"Capitula episcoporum": Die bischöflichen Kapitularien des 9. und 10. Jahrhunderts,* no. 43 (1985) [BA86].

M. Camargo, *Ars dictaminis, ars dictandi,* no. 60 (1991) [BA87].

G. Constable, *Letters and Letter-Collections,* no. 17 (1976) [BA88].

N. Coulet, *Les visites pastorales,* no. 23 (1977, 1985) [BA89].

A. Derolez, *Les catalogues de bibliothèques,* no. 31 (1979) [BA90].

G. Despy, *Les tarifs de tonlieux,* no. 19 (1976) [BA91].

A. De Vogüé, *Les régles monastiques anciennes (400–700),* no. 46 (1985) [BA92].

P. Dinzelbacher, *"Revelationes",* no. 57 (1991) [BA93].

J. Dubois, *Les martyrologes du moyen âge latin,* no. 26 (1978, 1985) [BA94].

R. Favreau, *Les inscriptions médiévales,* no. 35 (1979, 1985) [BA95].

R. Fossier, *Polyptiques et censiers,* no. 28 (1978) [BA96].

L. Fowler-Magerl, *Ordines iudiciarii and Libelli de ordine iudiciorum (from the middle of the twelfth to the end of the fifteenth century),* no. 63 (1994) [BA97].

G. Fransen, *Les décrétales et les collections de décrétales,* no. 2 (1972, 1985) [BA98]; *id., Les collections canoniques,* no. 10 (1973, 1985) [BA99].

C. Gaier, *Les armes* (1979, 1985), no. 34 [BA100].

L. Genicot, *Introduction,* no. 1 (1972) [BA101]; *id., Les actes publics,* no. 3 (1972, 1985) [BA102]; *id., Les généalogies,* no. 15 (1975, 1985) [BA103]; *id., La Loi,* no. 22 (1977, 1985) [BA104]; *id., L'architecture: Considérations générales,* no. 29 (1978) [BA105].

P. Godding, *La jurisprudence,* no. 6 (1973) [BA106].

P. Grierson, *Les monnaies,* no. 21 (1977) [BA107].

A. Graboïs, *Les sources hébraïques médiévales,* v1: *Chroniques, lettres et "responsa",* no. 50 (1987); v2: *Les commentaires exégétiques,* no. 66 (1993) [BA108].

R. Halleux, *Les textes alchimiques,* no. 32 (1979) [BA109].

M. Heinzelmann, *Translationsberichte und andere Quellen des Reliquienkultes,* no. 33 (1979) [BA110].

M. Huglo, *Les livres de chant liturgique,* no. 52 (1988) [BA111].

N. Huyghebaert, *Les documents nécrologiques,* no. 4 (1972); updating (1985) by J.-L. Lemaître [BA112].

D. Kelly, *The Arts of Poetry and Prose,* no. 59 (1991) [BA113].

K.H. Krüger, *Die Universalchroniken,* no. 16 (1976, 1985) [BA114].

M. McCormick, *Les annales du haut moyen âge,* no. 14 (1975) [BA115].

A.-G. Martimort, *Les "Ordines", les ordinaires et les cérémoniaux,* no. 56 (1991) [BA116]; *id., Les lectures liturgiques et leurs livres,* no. 64 (1992) [BA117].

R. Newhauser, *The Treatises of Vices and Virtues in Latin and the Vernacular*, no. 68 (1993) [BA118].

J. Pacquet, *Les matricules universitaires*, no. 65 (1992) [BA119].

M. Pastoureau, *Les armoiries*, no. 20 (1976, 1985) [BA120]; *id.*, *Les sceaux*, no. 36 (1981) [BA121]; *id.*, *Jetons, méreaux et médailles*, no. 42 (1984) [BA122].

G. Philippart, *Les légendiers et autres manuscrits hagiographiques*, nos. 24–25 (1977, 1985) [BA123].

O. Pontal, *Les statuts synodaux*, no. 11 (1975) [BA124].

E. Poulle, *Les sources astronomiques: Textes, tables, instruments*, no. 39 (1981) [BA125].

J. Richard, *Les récits de voyages et de pèlerinages*, no. 38 (1981, 1985) [BA126].

M. Sot, "*Gesta episcoporum, gesta abbatum*", no. 37 (1981, 1985) [BA127].

J. Szövérffy, *Latin Hymns*, no. 55 (1989) [BA128].

C. Thiry, *La plainte funèbre*, no. 30 (1978, 1985) [BA129].

G. Van Dievoet, *Les coutumiers, les styles, les formulaires et les "artes notariae"*, no. 48 (1986) [BA130].

C. Vogel, *Les "libri paenitentiales"*, no. 27 (1978); updating (1985) by A.J. Frantzen [BA131].

**4. Non-Series Bibliographies.** Bibliographical guides published recently *outside* the three series mentioned above include the following, selected as a small representative sample:

W. Affeldt *et al.*, *Frauen im Frühmittelalter: Eine ausgewählte, kommentierte Bibliographie* (1990) [BA132].

E.J. Ashworth, *The Tradition of Medieval Logic and Speculative Grammar from Anselm to the End of the Seventeenth Century: A Bibliography from 1836 Onwards* (1978) [BA133].

D.H. Banks, *Medieval Manuscript Bookmaking: A Bibliographical Guide* (1989) [BA134].

F. Bérard *et al.*, *Guide de l'épigraphiste: Bibliographie choisie des épigraphies antiques et médiévales*, 2nd ed. (1989) [BA135].

C.T. Berkhout and J.B. Russell, *Medieval Heresies: A Bibliography, 1960–1979* (1981) [BA136].

M. Brennan, *Guide des études érigéniennes: Bibliographie commentée des publications 1930–1987/A Guide to Eriugenian Studies: A Survey of Publications 1930–1987* (1989) [BA137].

A. Ferreiro, *The Visigoths in Gaul and Spain*, A.D. 418–711: *A Bibliography* (1988) [BA138].

E.B. Graves, *A Bibliography of English History to 1485* (1975): revision and expansion of C. Gross, *The Sources and Literature of English History from the Earliest Times to about 1485*, 2nd ed. (1915) [BA139].

W.B. Horner, *Historical Rhetoric: An Annotated Bibliography of Selected Sources in English* (1980): includes ch. (pp43–108), by L.M. Reinsma, on the Middle Ages [BA140].

R. Ingardia, *Thomas Aquinas: International Bibliography* (1993): continues T.L. Miethe and V.J. Bourke, *Thomistic Bibliography, 1940–1978* (1980), and V.J. Bourke, *Thomistic Bibliography, 1920–1940* (1945) [BA141].

W.E. Kleinbauer, *Early Christian and Byzantine Architecture: An Annotated Bibliography and Historiography* (1992) [BA142].

K. Koerner, "Medieval Linguistic Thought: A Comprehensive Bibliography," in *Studies in Medieval Linguistic Thought Dedicated to Geoffrey L. Bursill-Hall on the Occasion of His Sixtieth Birthday on 15 May 1980,* ed. K. Koerner *et al.* (1980) 265–96 [BA143].

T. Kohlhase and G.M. Paucker, *Bibliographie gregorianischer Choral* (1990) [BA144].

M. Lapidge and R. Sharpe, *A Bibliography of Celtic-Latin Literature, 400–1200* (1985) [BA145].

C.H. Lohr, *Commentateurs d'Aristote au moyen-âge latin: Bibliographie de la littérature secondaire récente/Medieval Latin Aristotle Commentators: A Bibliography of Recent Secondary Literature* (1988) [BA146].

J.E. López Pereira, "El latín medieval en España: su bibliografía," in *Euphrosyne* 15 (1987) 369–71 [BA147]; *id.,* "Quarant'anni di contributi della filologia spagnola allo studio del Medioevo Latino," tr. N. Messina, in *Schede medievali* 16–17 (1989) 33–53 [BA148].

F. de Place, *Bibliographie pratique de spiritualité cistercienne médiévale* (1987) [BA149].

J.T. Rosenthal, *Anglo-Saxon History: An Annotated Bibliography, 450–1066* (1985) [BA150].

P. Russel, "Recent Work in British Latin," in *Cambridge Medieval Celtic Studies* 9 (1985) 19–29 [BA151].

M.M. Sheehan and J. Murray, *Domestic Society in Medieval Europe: A Select Bibliography* (1990) [BA152].

E. Van der Vekene, *Bibliotheca bibliographica historiae sanctae Inquisitionis: Bibliographisches Verzeichnis des gedruckten Schrifttums zur Geschichte und Literatur der Inquisition,* 3 vols. (1982–92) [BA153].

G. Watson, ed., *The New Cambridge Bibliography of English Literature,* v1: 600–1660 (1974): includes writings in Latin [BA154].

J.W. Zophy, *An Annotated Bibliography of the Holy Roman Empire* (1986) [BA155].

The standard Latin dictionaries and glossaries, including Medieval Latin lexica of specific national regions, are listed in the bibliography of chapter CD. Some specialized lexical aids and studies are also mentioned in the bibliographies of individual chapters in this volume and in section BE. For an overview of modern developments in the field see [CD52]; A.-M. Bautier, "La lexicographie du latin médiéval: Bilan international des travaux," in [BB42] 433–53 [BB1]; and M.L. Angrisani Sanfilippo, "Lessicografia mediolatina," in *Cultura e scuola* 20.78 (1981) 76–87 [BB2].

A useful listing of lexical aids and concordances is H. Quellet, *Bibliographia indicum, lexicorum et concordantiarum auctorum Latinorum/Répertoire bibliographique des index, lexiques et concordances des auteurs latins* (1980) [BB3]; this replaces P. Faider, *Répertoire des index et lexiques d'auteurs latins* (1926, r1971) [BB4], and may be supplemented by reference to [BA6] and [BA30]. A number of concordances (see, e.g., [BB45] and [BB62]), have appeared in the series *Alpha-Omega*, in Reihe "B": *Indizes, Konkordanzen, statistische Studien zur mittellateinischen Philologie* (Hildesheim 1969–). Volumes in series "A" (1965–) provide indices and concordances primarily for classicists (see, e.g., [BB54]) [BB5].

The journal most closely associated with, and containing many contributions to, Medieval Latin lexicography is *Archivum Latinitatis Medii Aevi* [*ALMA*], published since 1924 and also known as *Bulletin Du Cange* (v25 [1955] 221–399: general indices for v1–25) [BB6]. The *Archiv für lateinische Lexikographie und Grammatik mit Einschluss des alteren Mittellateins*, ed. E. von Wolfflin (1831–1908), 15 vols., was published from 1884 to 1908 [BB7]. Extensive listings of general lexicographical and glossarial works; of lexica, indices, and concordances of individual authors, texts, and subjects; and of studies of vocabulary, language, and style are part of [BA5–6] and [BA10] v2:469–643, v3. Studies of aspects of medieval latinity (including vocabulary) are also mentioned in chapter CC.

Computer processing of volumes in the *Series Latina* and *Continuatio Mediaevalis* of the *Corpus Christianorum* collection of Brepols Publishers (see [BE30]) has produced two lexical tools entitled *Thesaurus Patrum Latinorum* [*TPL*]. The first is the *Instrumenta lexicologica latina* (1982–), two parallel series (A and B), published in fascicles and microfiche editions, that provide lists, concordances, indices, and indications of frequency of all the forms of words (A) and *lemmata* (B) in selected texts of *CCSL* and *CCCM;* the fascicles bear the numbers of the corresponding volumes in these series. The second tool is the *Thesauri* (1986–), also with two series (*A* and *B*), which treats, in print and on microfiche, groups of texts or individual works, e.g. writings of Augustine (*Thesaurus Augustinianus*), Bernard of Clairvaux, John Cassian, Marius Victorinus, Gregory the Great, Jerome; the *Sentences* of Peter Lombard, the *Cronica* of Salimbene [BB8]. See also [BE31].

## (a) Standard Latin Lexica, Classical and Postclassical

Listed here are general works not referred to in chapter CD or elsewhere in this volume. For the standard Latin dictionaries commonly used outside anglophone countries see [BA6] 448–50.

A. Bacci, *Lexicon vocabulorum quae difficilius latine redduntur*, 4th ed. (1963): an aid for translating modern-day terms into Latin (see also [BB11–13] and [BB20]) [BB9].

L. Diefenbach, *Glossarium latino-germanicum mediae et infimae aetatis e codicibus, manuscriptis et libris impressis* (1857, r1968): a supp. to the dictionary of Du Cange [CD15]; Diefenbach's *Novum glossarium latino-germanicum mediae et infimae aetatis* followed in 1867 (r1964) [BB10].

C. Egger, *Lexicon recentis latinitatis*, v1: A–L (1992) [BB11]; *id.*, *Lexicon nominum virorum et mulierum*, 2nd ed. (1963) [BB12]; *id.*, *Lexicon nominum locorum* (1977) and *Supplementum referens nomina latina-vulgaria* (1985) [BB13].

A. Ernout and A. Meillet, *Dictionnaire étymologique de la langue latine: Histoire des mots,* 4th ed. (3rd printing), with addenda and corrigenda by J. André (1980) [BB14].

E. Forcellini (1688–1768), ed., *Totius latinitatis lexicon,* 4 vols. (Padua 1771); rev. ed. by F. Corradini and J. Perin (6 vols., 1864–1926, including Perin's two-volume *Onomasticon totius latinitatis;* r1940 and 1965); see also R. Busa, *Totius latinitatis lemmata quae ex Aeg. Forcellini Patavina editione 1940 a fronte, a tergo atque morphologice opera IBM automati ordinaverat Robertus Busa* (1988) [BB15].

E. Habel and F. Gröbel, *Mittellateinisches Glossar,* 2nd ed. (1959, r1989 with new intro.) [BB16].

W.H. Maigne d'Arnis, *Lexicon manuale ad scriptores mediae et infimae latinitatis, ex glossariis Caroli Dufresne, D. Ducangii, D.P. Carpentarii, Adelungii, et aliorum, in compendium accuratissime redactum, ou Recueil de mots de la basse latinité, dressé pour servir à l'intelligence des auteurs, soit sacrés, soit profanes, du moyen âge* (1858 and 1890, r1977) [BB17].

C. Schmidt, *Petit supplément au Dictionnaire de Du Cange* (1906, r1970) [BB18].

A. Sleumer and J. Schmid, *Kirchenlateinisches Wörterbuch,* 2nd ed. (1926, r1990): Latin-German dictionary drawn chiefly from liturgical, biblical, and canonical sources [BB19].

H. Tondini and T. Mariucci, *Lexicon novorum vocabulorum . . . e libellis Latinitatis his decem superioribus annis in vulgus editis* (1964), with "Indiculus vocum Anglicarum," pp267–93 [BB20].

F. Wagner, *Lexicon Latinum seu . . . universae phraseologiae corpus congestum,* 2nd ed. expanded and translated from German into French by A. Borgnet (1878, r1965): with indices "vocum barbarum" and "vocum quae in foro militari, civilique sacroque obtinent" [BB21].

A. Walde, J.B. Hofmann, and E. Berger, *Lateinisches etymologisches Wörterbuch*, 5th ed., 3 vols. (1982) [**BB22**].

## (b) Specialized Lexica and Lexicographical Works (very selective)

J. André, *Étude sur les termes de couleur dans la langue latine* (1949) [**BB23**].

M. Bambeck, *Boden und Werkwelt: Untersuchungen zum Vokabular der Galloromania aufgrund von nichtliterarischen Texten, mit besonderer Berücksichtigung mittellateinischer Urkunden* (1968) [**BB24**].

E. Benveniste, *Le vocabulaire des institutions indo-européennes*, 2 vols. (1969); tr. E. Palmer: *Indo-European Language and Society* (1973) [**BB25**].

C.D. Buck, *A Dictionary of Selected Synonyms in the Principal Indo-European Languages: A Contribution to the History of Ideas* (1949, r1988) [**BB26**].

J.-M. Clément, *Lexique des anciennes règles monastiques occidentales*, 2 vols. (1978): lists all important words in the 31 known Western monastic rules (excluding Benedict, the *Regula Magistri*, the *Pachomiana latina*, and Basil/Rufinus) of the period before Benedict of Aniane [**BB27**].

F. Del Giudice and S. Beltrani, *Dizionario giuridico romano* (1993) [**BB28**].

K.E. Demandt, *Laterculus notarum: Lateinisch-deutsche Interpretationshilfen für spätmittelalterliche und frühneuzeitliche Archivalien*, 4th ed. (1986) [**BB29**].

C. De Meo, *Lingue tecniche del latino*, 2nd ed. (1986) [**BB30**].

A. Epe, *Index verborum Ruodliebianus* (1980) [**BB31**].

F. Graham, *Dictionary of Roman Military Terms* (1981) [**BB32**].

A. Haemmerle, *Alphabetisches Verzeichnis der Berufs- und Standesbezeichnungen vom ausgehenden Mittelalter bis zur neueren Zeit* (1933, r1966) [**BB33**].

M. Hammarström, *Glossarium till Finlands och Sveriges latinska medeltidsurkunder jämte språklig inledning* (1925) [**BB34**].

C.R. Jensen, *Parish Register Latin: An Introduction* (1988): Latin-English glossary, pp258–312 [**BB35**].

R.M. Karras, "The Latin Vocabulary of Illicit Sex in English Ecclesiastical Court Records," in *JMLat* 2 (1992) 1–17 [**BB36**].

R. Klinck, *Die lateinische Etymologie des Mittelalters* (1970) [**BB37**].

H. Kloster, *Imitatio: Concordance in Latin to the Imitation of Christ. Topical Concordance and Systematic Presentation of Books I–III of the Imitation* (1978) [**BB38**].

G. Köbler, *Wörterverzeichnis zu den Diplomata regum Francorum e stirpe merowingica* (1983) [**BB39**]; id., *Wörterverzeichnis zu den Concilia aevi Merovingici* (1977) [**BB40**].

J. Leclercq, *Études sur le vocabulaire monastique du moyen âge* (1961) [**BB41**].

*La lexicographie du latin médiéval et ses rapports avec les recherches actuelles sur la civilisation du moyen-âge* [*LLM*], Colloque international du Centre National de la Recherche Scientifique no. 589 (Paris, 18–21 October 1978), organized by Y. Lefèvre (1981): important collection of papers touching on many subfields of lexicographical research and on methodology [**BB42**].

B. Löfstedt, *Studien über die Sprache der langobardischen Gesetze: Beiträge zur frühmittelalterlichen Latinität* (1961) [**BB43**].

V. Lomanto and N. Marinone, *Index grammaticus: An Index to the Latin Grammar Texts*, 3 vols. (1990): index to an on-line computerized concordance based on [DI1] [**BB44**].

J.E. López Pereira *et al.*, *Corpus historiographicum latinum hispanum, saeculi VIII–XII: Concordantiae* (1993) [**BB45**].

K. Luggauer, *Juristenlatein: 2500 juristisch-lateinische Fachausdrucke und Fachzitate*, 4th ed. (1987) [**BB46**].

J. Luque Moreno *et al.*, *Scriptores latini de re metrica: Concordantiae-Indices* (1987–); v4 (1987): *Isidorus Hispalensis* ; v11 (1993): *Augustinus* [**BB47**].

R. Maltby, *A Lexicon of Ancient Latin Etymologies* (1991): helpful for "the identification and understanding of word-play in Latin poetry, both Classical and Mediaeval" [**BB48**].

P. Miquel, *Le vocabulaire latin de l'expérience spirituelle dans la tradition monastique et canoniale de 1050 à 1250* (1989) [**BB49**].

P. Mastandrea and L. Tessarolo, *De fine versus: Repertorio di clausole ricorrenti nella poesia dattilica latina, dalle origini a Sidonio Appollinare*, 2 vols. (1993) [**BB50**].

C. Mayer *et al.*, *Augustinus-Lexicon* (1986–) [**BB51**].

P. Monteil, *Beau et laid en latin: Étude de vocabulaire* (1964) [**BB52**].

I. Opelt, *Die lateinischen Schimpfwörter und verwandte sprachliche Erscheinungen: Eine Typologie* (1965) [**BB53**].

C. Opsomer, *Index de la pharmacopée latine du Ier au Xe siècle*, 2 vols. (1989) [**BB54**].

H. Pétré, *Caritas: Étude sur le vocabulaire latin de le charité chrétienne* (1948) [**BB55**].

R. Pichon, *Index verborum amatoriorum* (1902, r1966) [**BB56**].

P. Pierrugues, *Glossarium eroticum linguae latinae* (1826, r1965) [**BB57**].

E. Quicherat, *Thesaurus poeticus linguae latinae ou Dictionnaire prosodique et poétique de la lange latine, contenant tous les mots employés dans les ouvrages ou les fragments qui nous restent des poètes latins*, rev. and corr. E. Chatelain, 7th ed. (1922, r1967) [**BB58**].

C. Schrader-Muggenthaler [and S. Watson], *The New Historical Dictionary: German Latin Translations, Latin English Translations* (1991): for the professional genealogist [**BB59**].

P. Sella, *Glossario latino-emiliano* (1937) [**BB60**]; id., *Glossario latino-italiano, stato della Chiesa: Veneto, Abruzzi* (1944, r1965) [**BB61**].

H.E. Stiene and J. Grub, *Verskonkordanz zur Alexandreis des Walter von Châtillon* (1985) [**BB62**].

D. Sperber, *A Dictionary of Greek and Latin Legal Terms in Rabbinic Literature* (1984) [**BB63**].

D.C. Swanson, *The Names in Roman Verse: A Lexicon and Reverse Index of All Proper Names of History, Mythology, and Geography Found in the Classical Roman Poets* (1967) [**BB64**]; supplements O. Grandenwitz, *Laterculi vocum latinarum* (1904, r1966), confined to common nouns [**BB65**].

W. Weidler, P.A. Grun, and K.H. Lampe, *Latein für den Sippenforscher*, 2nd ed., 2 vols. (1965–69) [**BB66**].

O. Weijers, ed., Publications of *CIVICIMA* (= Le comité international du vocabulaire des institutions et de la communication intellectuelles au moyen âge): v1, *Actes du colloque "Terminologie de la vie intellectuelle au moyen âge" (Leyde/La Haye 20–21 septembre 1985)* (1988); v2, *Vocabulaire du livre et de l'écriture au moyen âge: Actes de la table ronde, Paris, 24–26 septembre 1987* (1989); v3, *Méthodes et instruments du travail intellectuel au moyen âge: Études sur le vocabulaire* (1990); v5, *Vocabulaire des écoles et des méthodes d'enseignement au moyen âge: Actes du colloque, Rome, 21–22 octobre 1989* (1992); v6, *Vocabulaire des collèges universitaires (XIIIe–XVIe siècles): Actes du colloque, Leuven, 9–11 avril 1992* (1993); v4, O. Weijers, *Dictionnaires et répertoires au moyen âge: Une étude du vocabulaire* (1991);

v7, *La formation du vocabulaire scientifique et intellectuel dans le monde arabe*, ed. D. Jacquart (1994) [**BB67**].

(c) **Medieval Glosses and Glossaries** (very selective; see also the bibliography of chapter CG.)

A. Castro, *Glosarios latino-españoles de la edad media* (1936, r1991) [**BB68**].

R. Damme, *Das Stralsunder Vokabular: Edition und Untersuchung einer mittel-niederdeutsch-lateinischen Vokabularhandschrift des 15. Jahrhunderts* (1989) [**BB69**].

G. Goetz *et al.*, *Corpus glossariorum latinorum*, 7 vols. (1888–1923, r1965): v1, *De glossariorum latinorum origine et fatis* (1923) [**BB70**].

K. Grubmüller, B. Schnell, *et al. Vocabularius ex quo*, 5 vols. (1988–89): edition of a popular fifteenth-century German-Latin glossary compiled as an aid to biblical and other studies, and drawing upon the works of Hugutio of Pisa, John of Genoa, William Brito, and Papias; item [**BB85**] is another glossary published in the same series, *Texte und Textgeschichte* (Tübingen 1980–) [**BB71**].

J.H. Hessels, *An Eighth-Century Latin–Anglo-Saxon Glossary Preserved in the Library of Corpus Christi College, Cambridge* (1890) [**BB72**]; *id.*, *A Late Eighth-Century Latin–Anglo-Saxon Glossary Preserved in the Library of the Leiden University* (1906) [**BB73**].

H.-W. Klein, A. Labhardt, and M. Raupach, *Die Reichenauer Glossen*, 2 vols. (1968–72) [**BB74**].

G. Köbler, *Althochdeutsch-lateinisches Wörterbuch*, 2nd ed. (1984) [**BB75**]; *id.*, *Althochdeutsch-neuhocdeutsch-lateinisches Wörterbuch*, 3rd ed., 2 vols. (1991–92) [**BB76**]; *id.* (with A. Quak), *Altniederdeutsch-lateinisches Wörterbuch* (1973) [**BB77**]; *id.*, *Lateinisch-germanistiches Lexikon*, 2nd ed. (1983) [**BB78**].

F.A. Leoni, *Tre glossari longobardo-latini* (1981) [**BB79**].

W.M. Lindsay *et al.*, *Glossaria latina iussu Academiae Britannicae edita*, 5 vols. (1926–31, r1965) [**BB80**].

L. de Man, *Middeleeuwse systematische glossaria* (1964) [**BB81**].

J.D. Pheifer, *Old English Glosses in the Épinal-Erfurt Glossary* (1974) [**BB82**].

M. Roques, *Recueil général des lexiques français du moyen âge (XIIe–XVe siècle)*, 2 vols. (1936–38) [**BB83**].

T.W. Ross and E. Brooks, Jr., *English Glosses from British Library Additional Manuscript 37075* (1984) [**BB84**].

P. Schmitt, *"Liber ordinis rerum": (Esse–essencia-Glossar)*, 2 vols. (1983) [**BB85**].

K. Siewert, *Glossenfunde: Volkssprachiges zu lateinischen Autoren der Antike und des Mittelalters* (1989) [**BB86**].

## BC • REPERTORIES OF AUTHORS, TEXTS, AND INITIA

The reference works listed here provide help in the identification of, and/or information about, Latin authors and texts. These aids include (a) a selection of literary histories of antiquarian bibliographers and historians of religious orders and scholarly authors, and (b) some modern guides—especially bio-bibliographies, first-line indices, and other repertoria of various kinds—-to Latin (and other) writers and their works and to anonymous texts. More general encyclopedic works with biographical and bibliographical information are listed in chapter BD. Items recorded in sections BA and BE and in the bibliographies of individual chapters in this volume provide similar assistance. Publications are regularly listed in *MEL* [BA30] in the sections entitled "Repertori ed enciclopedie," "Incipitari," "Incipitari ed explicitari." See also [BA49] pp99–129 and, for studies and catalogues of manuscripts of Medieval Latin texts, [BA27]. Important lists of Medieval Latin authors and works have been published as part of the various lexicographical projects outlined in chapter CD; fasc. 3 [D–E] (1986), for example, of the *Dictionary of Medieval Latin from British Sources* (see [CD33]), includes (ppxi–lxi) a bibliography, compiled by D.R. Howlett and R. Sharpe, of Anglo-Latin authors and texts; this supersedes previous listings and is supplemented by two additional pages in fasc. 4 [F–G–H] (1989). Similarly, the Polish Medieval Latin dictionary [CD40] includes a *Fasciculus extra ordinem editus* (1969), part of which (ppX–XLIII) is an *Index librorum operumque excerptorum*.

### (a) Literary Histories to 1900

N. Antonio (1617–84), *Bibliotheca hispana vetus, sive, Hispani scriptores qui ab Octaviani Augusti aevo ad annum Christi MD. floruerunt*, 2 vols., 3rd ed. (Madrid 1788) [BC1].

J. Bale (1495–1563), *Scriptorum illustrium Maioris Brytanniae catalogus*, 2 vols. (Basel 1557–59, r1971): expansion of his *Illustrium Majoris Britanniae scriptorum . . . summarium* (Ipswich 1548); 2nd ed. in 2 pts. (Basel 1557–59) [BC2]; *id.*, *Index Britanniae scriptorum*, ed. R.L. Poole and M. Bateson (1902, r1990 with new intro.) [BC3].

W. Cave (1637–1713), *Scriptorum ecclesiasticorum historia literaria a Christo nato usque ad saeculum XIV*, editio novissima, 2 vols. (Oxford 1740–43, Basel 1741–45) [BC4].

T. Dempster (1579?–1625), *Historia ecclesiastica gentis Scotorum* (London 1627) [BC5].

J.A. Fabricius (1668–1736), *Bibliotheca latina mediae et infimae aetatis* (including supplementary vol. by C. Schoettgen), 2nd ed., 6 vols. in 3 (Padua 1754); 3rd ed. (1858–59, r1962) [BC6].

J. François (1722–91), *Bibliothèque générale des écrivains de l'Ordre de Saint Benoît*, 4 vols. (Bouillon 1777–78, r1961 with "note liminaire sur les bibliographies bénédictines") [BC7].

K. Gesner (1516–65), *Bibliotheca universalis; sive, Catalogus omnium scriptorum locupletissimus in tribus linguis, Latina, Graeca & Hebraica* (Tiguri 1545, r1966); *Appendix bibliothecae universalis* (Tiguri 1555, r1966) [BC8].

*Histoire littéraire de la France* (1733–), begun by the Benedictines of the Congregation of St. Maur (v1–12 [1733–63]) and then (from v13 [1814]) edited by the Académie des Inscriptions et Belles-Lettres [BC9].

C.G. Jöcher (1694–1758), *Allgemeines Gelehrten-Lexicon*, 4 vols. (Leipzig 1750–51, r1960–61) and 7 supplementary vols. (1784–1897, r1960–61) [BC10].

J. Leland (1506?–52), *Commentarii de scriptoribus Britannicis*, ed. A. Hall, 2 vols. (Oxford 1709) [BC11].

P. Leyser (1690–1728), *Historia poetarum et poematum medii aevi* (Halle 1721, r1969) [BC12].

J. Pits (1560–1616), *Relationum historicarum de rebus anglicis tomus primus* (Paris 1619) [BC13].

J. Quétif (1618–98) and J. Echard (1644–1724), *Scriptores ordinis praedicatorum recensiti notisque historicis et criticis illustrati*, 2 vols. (Paris 1719–21, r1959–61); see [BC70] [BC14].

T. Tanner (1674–1735), *Bibliotheca Britannico-Hibernica; sive De scriptoribus qui in Anglia, Scotia, et Hibernia ad saeculi XVII initium floruerunt . . . commentarius* (London 1748, r1963) [BC15].

J. von Trittenheim (Trithemius, 1462–1516), *De scriptoribus ecclesiasticis* (Basel 1494) [BC16]; id., *Carmelitana bibliotheca, sive Illustrium aliquot Carmelitanae religionis scriptorum, & eorum operum cathalogus* (Florence 1593) [BC17].

L. Wadding (1588–1657), *Scriptores ordinis minorum* (Rome 1650, r1967 and 1978) [BC18].

J. Ware (1594–1666), *De scriptoribus Hiberniae* (Dublin 1639, r1967) [BC19].

T. Wright (1810–77), *Biographia britannica literaria; or, Biography of Literary Characters of Great Britain and Ireland, arranged in Chronological Order*, 2 vols. (1842–46) [BC20].

## (b) Modern Repertories

J. Allenbach *et al.*, *Biblia patristica: Index des citations et allusions bibliques dans la littérature patristique*, 5 vols. and supp. (1975–82) [BC21].

H. Barré, *Les homéliaires carolingiens de l'école d'Auxerre: Authenticité, inventaire, tableaux comparatifs, initia* (1962): incipits on pp137–344 [BC22].

C. Baur, *Initia patrum graecorum*, 2 vols. (1955) [BC23].

L. Berkowitz and K.A. Squitier, *Thesaurus Linguae Graecae Canon of Greek Authors and Works*, 3rd ed. (1990): see [BE43] [BC24].

L. Bertalot and U. Jaitner-Hahner, *Initia humanistica latina: Initienverzeichnis lateinischer Prosa und Poesie aus der Zeit des 14. bis 16. Jahrhunderts* (1985–): v1, *Poesie*; v2.1, *Prosa A-M* [BC25].

J.-G. Bougerol, "*Initia latinorum sermonum ad laudes S. Francisci*," in *Antonianum* 57 (1982) 706–90 [BC26].

A.M. Brady and B. Cleeve, *A Biographical Dictionary of Irish Writers,* rev. ed. (1985): pt2 lists writers in Irish and Latin [BC27].

E. Brouette, A. Dimier, and E. Manning, *Dictionnaire des auteurs cisterciens,* 2 vols. (1975–79): 2,063 entries; *Tables,* ed. S. Balzat-Brouette (1979); "Supplément," in B. Chauvin, *Mélanges à la mémoire du Père Anselme Dimier,* 3 vols. in 6 (1982–87), v2.3:275–80 [BC28].

J. Buchanan-Brown, *Cassell's Encyclopaedia of World Literature,* rev. ed., 3 vols. (1973) [BC29].

G.L. Bursill-Hall, *A Census of Medieval Latin Grammatical Manuscripts* (1981): incipits at pp295–359 [BC30]; *id., Medieval Priscian Commentaries: Introduction and Bibliography,* in *Historiographia Linguistica* 16 (1989) 89–130 [BC31].

U. Chevalier, *Répertoire des sources historiques du moyen âge:* pt1, *Bio-bibliographie,* 2 vols., 2nd ed. (1905–7, r1960); pt2, *Topo-bibliographie,* 2 vols. (1894–1903, r1959) [BC32].

J.-M. Clément, *Initia patrum latinorum,* 2 vols. (1971–79): incipits from the 65 vols. of *CCSL* and *CCCM* published from 1970 to 1978 [BC33].

*Colophons de manuscrits occidentaux des origines au XVIe siècle,* ed. Bénédictins du Bouveret (Saint-Benoit de Port-Valais, Bouveret, Switzerland), 6 vols. (1965–82) [BC34].

M.O. Cosenza, *Biographical and Bibliographical Dictionary of the Italian Humanists and of the World of Classical Scholarship in Italy, 1300–1800,* 2nd ed., 6 vols. (1962–67) [BC35]; *id., Checklist of Non-Italian Humanists, 1300–1800* (1969) [BC36].

E. Dekkers and E. Gaar, *Clavis patrum latinorum . . . a Tertulliano ad Bedam,* 3rd ed. (1995) [BC37].

M.C. Díaz y Díaz, *Index scriptorum latinorum medii aevi hispanorum,* 2 vols. (1958–59) [BC38].

A.B. Emden, *A Biographical Register of the University of Cambridge to 1500* (1963) [BC39]; *id., A Biographical Register of the University of Oxford to A.D. 1500,* 3 vols. (1957–59) [BC40]; *id., A Biographical Register of the University of Oxford, A.D. 1501 to 1540* (1974) [BC41].

E. Follieri, *Initia hymnorum ecclesiae Graecae,* 5 vols. in 6 (1960–66) [BC42].

A. Franklin, *Dictionnaire des noms, surnoms et pseudonymes latins de l'histoire littéraire du moyen âge [1100 à 1530]* (1875, r1966) [BC43].

J.W. Fuchs, O. Weijers, and M. Gumbert-Hepp, "Index fontium," in *Lexicon latinitatis Nederlandicae medii aevi* (see [CD39]), v1:9–65, 65*–65****; v3: "addenda et corrigenda ad indicem fontium" [BC44].

M. Geerard, *Clavis patrum graecorum,* 5 vols. (1974–87); v5 (by M. Geerard and F. Glorie): *Indices, initia, tabulae* [BC45]; *id., Clavis apocryphorum Novi Testamenti* (1992) [BC46].

L. Genicot, P. Tombeur, *et al., Index scriptorum operumque latino-belgicorum medii aevi: Nouveau répertoire des oeuvres médiolatines belges* (1973–): pt1, *VIIe–Xe siècles,* ed. A. Stainier (1973); pt2, *XIe siècle,* ed. P. Fransen and H. Maraite (1976); pt3, *XIIe siècle,* ed. M. McCormick: v1–2, *Oeuvres hagiographiques* (1977) and *Oeuvres non-hagiographiques* (1979) [BC47].

D. Glen, *The Poetry of the Scots: An Introduction and Bibliographical Guide to Poetry in Gaelic, Scots, Latin, and English* (1991) [BC48].

P. Glorieux, *Répertoire des maîtres en théologie de Paris au XIIIe siècle,* 2 vols. (1933–34) [BC49]; *id., La Faculté des arts et ses maîtres au XIIIe siècle* (1971) [BC50].

L. Goovaerts, *Écrivains, artistes, et savants de l'Ordre de Prémontré: Dictionnaire bio-bibliographique*, 4 vols. (1899–1920) [BC51].

V. Gortan and V. Vratović, *Hrvatski latinisti: Croatici auctores qui latine scripserunt*, 2 vols. (1969) [BC52].

R. Goulet, *Dictionnaire des philosophes antiques* (1989–) [BC53].

M. Grant, *Greek and Latin Authors, 800 B.C.–A.D. 1000: A Biographical Dictionary* (1980): with chronological list in app. B of authors by century [BC54].

R. Grégoire, *Les homéliaires du moyen âge: Inventaire et analyse des manuscrits* (1966) [BC55].

A. Gruys, *Cartusiana: Un instrument heuristique/A heuristic instrument/Ein heuristischer Apparat*, 3 pts. (1976–78): pt1, *Bibliographie générale: Auteurs cartusiens*; pt2, *Maisons*; pt3, *Supplément: Addenda et corrigenda, Index* [BC56].

J. Hackett, *Medieval Philosophers* (1992) [BC57].

K. Hallinger, P. Becker, *et al.*, *Initia consuetudinis Benedictinae: Consuetudines saeculi octavi et noni* (1963), Corpus consuetudinum monasticarum 1 [BC58].

B. Hauréau, *Notices et extraits de quelques manuscrits latins de la Bibliothèque Nationale*, 6 vols. (1890–93, r1967 in 3 vols.) [BC59]; id., *Initia operum scriptorum latinorum medii potissimum aevi ex codicibus, manuscriptis, et libris impressis*, 8 vols. (1973–74): repr. of H.'s handwritten index (4,600 pages); v7–8, assembled by A. Schmeller and G. Meyer, are an app.: *Schedarium initia amplectens praesertim ex codicibus Monacensibus, Gottingensibus, Bruxellensibus . . . collecta* (1974) [BC60].

J. Heckel, *Initia iuris ecclesiastici Protestantium* (1950) [BD61].

R. Hiestand, *Initien- und Empfängerverzeichnis zu Italia Pontificia I–X, MGH.Hilfsmittel* 6 (1983) [BC62]; id., *Initienverzeichnis und chronologisches Verzeichnis zu den Archivberichten und Vorarbeiten der Regesta pontificum Romanorum, MGH.Hilfsmittel* 7 (1983) [BC63].

"Hispanorum index scriptorum latinorum medii posteriorisque aevi," in *Euphrosyne* 12 (1983–84) 273–306 [BC64].

D. Huisman *et al.*, *Dictionnaire des philosophes*, 2nd ed. (1993) [BC65].

*Index scriptorum novus mediae latinitatis ab anno DCCC usque ad annum MCC qui afferuntur in Novo Glossario ab Academiis consociatis iuris publici facto*, 2nd ed. (1973); supp. (1989) [BC66].

"Indice provvisorio degli spogli italiani per il dizionario latino dell'alto medioevo"/"Index latinitatis italicae medii aevi antiquioris per litterarum ordinem digestus," in *ALMA* 6 (1931) I–V, 1–96; J. Praga, "Index auctorum latinitatis italicae medii aevi antiquioris: Supplementum dalmaticum," in *ALMA* 16 (1942) 61–63 [BC67].

M.-H. Jullien and F. Perelman, *Clavis scriptorum latinorum medii aevi*, sec. 1 (*Auctores Galliae*), pt1 (*735–987*) (1994) [BC68].

Š. Jurić, *Iugoslaviae scriptores latini recentioris aetatis*, ed. Z. Herkov *et al.* (1968–) [BC69].

T. Kaeppeli, *Scriptores ordinis praedicatorum medii aevi* (1970-93), 4 vols.: replacement for [BC14] [BC70].

L.A. Kennedy, *A Catalogue of Thomists, 1270–1900* (1987) [BC71].

P. Kibre, *Hippocrates Latinus: Repertorium of Hippocratic Writings in the Latin Middle Ages*, rev. ed. (1985) [BC72].

J. Kuzmík, *Lexicon auctorum, fontium et scriptorum librorum cum relationibus slovacis antiqui mediique aevi* (1983) [BC73].

R. LaRue *et al.*, *Clavis scriptorum graecorum et latinorum/Répertoire des auteurs grecs et latins/Repertoire of Greek and Latin Authors/Repertorium der griechischen und lateinischen Autoren,* 4 vols. (1985); see [BA11] [BC74].

H.B. Lincoln, *The Latin Motet: Indexes to Printed Collections, 1500–1600* (1993) [BC75].

D.C. Lindberg, *A Catalogue of Medieval and Renaissance Optical Manuscripts* (1975) [BC76].

A.G. Little, *Initia operum latinorum quae saeculis XIII. XIV. XV. attribuuntur, secundum ordinem alphabeti disposita* (1904, r1958): over 9,000 incipits [BC77].

C.H. Lohr, "Medieval Latin Aristotle Commentaries," in *Traditio* 23 (1967) 313–413 (A–F), 24 (1968) 149–245 (G–I), 26 (1970) 135–216 (J), 27 (1971) 251–351 (J–M), 28 (1972) 281–396 (N–Ri), 29 (1973) 93–197 (Ro–W), 30 (1974) 119–44 ("supplementary authors"); "Addenda et corrigenda," in *Bulletin de philosophie médiévale* 14 (1972) 116–26; *id., Latin Aristotle Commentaries* (1988–), v2: *Renaissance Authors* (1988) [BC78]: see also [BA146].

F. Lot *et al.,* "Index scriptorum operumque latino-gallicorum medii aevi (500–1000)," in *ALMA* 14 (1939) 113–230; "Index . . . medii aevi saec. XI (1000–1108)," in *ALMA* 16 (1942) 5–59; "Vitae, passiones, miracula, translationes sanctorum Galliae necnon alia opera hagiographica saec. XI in Gallia exarata (a. 1000–1108)," in *ALMA* 17 (1943) 5–26; "Notes complémentaires aux listes d'écrivains et de textes latins de France du XIme siècle" (by A. Boutemy), in *ALMA* 17 (1943), 27–40; "Additions et corrections aux indices scriptorum operumque (Pour la France jusqu'en l'an 1000)," in *ALMA* 20 (1950) 5–64; "Index scriptorum operumque latino-gallicorum saeculi XI: Addenda et corrigenda," in *ALMA* 21 (1951) 173–92 [BC79].

J. Machielsen, *Clavis patristica pseudepigraphorum medii aevi* (1990–) [BC80].

G. de Martel, *Répertoire des textes latins relatifs au livre de Ruth (VIIe–XVe s.)* (1990) [BC81].

G.E. Mohan, "Incipits of Logical Writings of the XIIIth–XVth Centuries," in *Franciscan Studies* 12 (1952) 349–489 [BC82]; *id.,* "Initia operum Franciscalium (XIII–XV s.)," in *Franciscan Studies* 35 (1975) 1*–92* (A–C), 36 (1976) 93*–177* (D–H), 37 (1977) 180*–375* (I–Q), 38 (1978) 377*–498* (R–V) [BC83].

A. Pelzer, *Répertoire d'incipit pour la littérature latine philosophique et théologique du moyen âge,* 2nd ed. (Rome 1951): repr. with additions by J. Ruysschaert, in A. Pelzer, *Études d'histoire littéraire sur la scolastique médiévale,* ed. A. Pattin and E. Van de Vyver (1964) 35–69 [BC84].

A. Potthast, *Bibliotheca historica medii aevi: Wegweiser durch die Geschichtswerke des europäischen Mittelalters bis 1500,* 2nd ed., 2 vols. (1896, r1954): standard guide to printed medieval sources for the period from A.D. 375 to 1500; updated version is being published as *Repertorium fontium historiae medii aevi, primum ab Augusto Potthast digestum, nunc cura collegii historicorum e pluribus nationibus emendatum et auctum* (1962–), which contains notices on historical sources of all kinds—narrative, descriptive, juridical, conciliar, epistolary, literary, etc. [BC85].

K. Reinhardt and H. Santiago-Otero, *Biblioteca bíblica ibérica medieval* (1986–) [BC86].

*Répertoire bio-bibliographique des auteurs latins, patristiques et médiévaux,* Institut de recherche et d'histoire des textes/Chadwyck-Healey, France (1987): 492 microfiches and guide; reproduces a card catalogue (closed in 1984) listing manuscripts, editions, and studies of Latin works from late antiquity to 1500 [BC87].

*Répertoire des fins de textes latins classiques et médiévaux,* Institut de recherche et d'histoire des textes/Chadwyck-Healey, France (1987): 223 microfiches and introduction [BC88].

*Répertoire d'incipit de sermons latins: Antiquité tardive et moyen-âge,* Institut de recherche et d'histoire des textes/Chadwyck-Healey, France (1988): 273 microfiches and guide [BC89].

J.C. Russell, *Dictionary of Writers of Thirteenth Century England* (1936, r1971) [BC90].

R. Russell, *Italian Women Writers: A Bio-Bibliographical Sourcebook* (1994) [BC91].

P. Salmon, *Analecta liturgica: Extraits des manuscrits liturgiques de la Bibliothèque Vaticane: Contribution à l'histoire de la prière chrétienne* (1974): incipits at pp329–44 [BC92].

[H.M. Schaller], *Initienverzeichnis zu August Potthast, Regesta pontificum Romanorum (1198–1304), MGH.Hilfsmittel 2* (1978) [BC93].

F.W.J. von Schelling (1775–1854), *Initia philosophiae universae* (1820–21), ed. H. Fuhrmans (with commentary) (1969) [BC94].

P. and J. Schlueter, *An Encyclopedia of British Women Writers* (1988) [BC95].

C.B. Schmitt and D. Knox, *Pseudo-Aristoteles Latinus: A Guide to Latin Works Falsely Attributed to Aristotle Before 1500* (1985) [BC96].

J.B. Schneyer, *Wegweiser zu lateinischen Predigtreihen des Mittelalters* (1965) [BC97].

R. Sharpe *et al., Corpus of British Medieval Library Catalogues: List of Identifications* (1993): to be updated and reissued as the series progresses [BC98].

P. Sicard, "Repertorivm Sententiarvm qvae in saecvli XII Hvgonis de Sancto Victore opervm codicibvs invenivntur (I)," in *SE* 32 (1991) 171–221 [BC99].

P.V. Spade, *The Mediaeval Liar: A Catalogue of the Insolubilia-Literature* (1975) [BC100].

W. Stammler *et al., Die Deutsche Literatur des Mittelalters: Verfasserlexikon,* 5 vols. (1931–55); 2nd ed. by K. Rue, G. Keil, *et al.* (1978–): includes Medieval Latin works of significance to the development of German literature [BC101].

Dom Stanislas (1853–1920), *Scriptores sacri ordinis Cartusiensis* (1993–) [BC102].

A. Steffen, "*Index operum latinorum medii aevi quae in hodiernis finibus Luxemburgensis ducatus scripta fuerunt,*" in *ALMA* 9 (1934) 252–55 [BC103].

F. Stegmüller, *Repertorium commentariorum in Sententias Petri Lombardi,* 2 vols. (1947); see also V. Doucet, *Commentaires sur les Sentences: Supplément au répertoire de M. Frédéric Stegmueller* (1954), and J. Van Dyk, "Thirty Years since Stegmüller: A Bibliographical Guide to the Study of Medieval Sentence Commentaries since the Publication of Stegmüller's *Repertorium Commentariorum in Sententias Petri Lombardi* (1947)," in *Franciscan Studies* 39 (1979) 255–315 [BC104].

F. Stegmüller *et al., Repertorium biblicum medii aevi,* 11 vols. (1950–80): alphabetical listing of all commentaries on the Bible, with extant manuscripts [BC105].

*Thesaurus Linguae Latinae: Index librorum scriptorum inscriptionum ex quibus exempla afferuntur,* editus iussu et auctoritate Consilii ab Academiis Societatibusque diversarum nationum electi, 2nd ed. (1990) [BC106].

B. de Troeyer, *Bio-bibliographia franciscana neerlandica ante saeculum XVI,* 3 vols. (1974) [BC107].

*Tusculum-Lexikon griechischer und lateinischer Autoren des Altertums und des Mittelalters,* ed. W. Buchwald, A. Holweg, and O. Prinz, 3rd ed. (1982); tr. (with additions) J.D. Berger and J. Billen: *Dictionnaire des auteurs grecs et latins de l'antiquité et du moyen âge* (1991) [BC108].

H. Van der Werf, *Integrated Directory of Organa, Clausulae, and Motets of the Thirteenth Century* (1989) [BC109].

M. Vattasso, *Initia patrum aliorumque scriptorum ecclesiasticorum latinorum ex Mignei Patrologia et ex compluribus aliis libris,* 2 vols. (1906–8, r1968) [BC110].

M. Vilallonga i Vives, *La Literatura llatina a Catalunya al segle XV: Repertori bio-bibliografic* (1993) [BC111].

F. Volpi and J. Nida-Rumelin, *Lexikon der philosophischen Werke* (1988) [BC112].

V. Volpi, *DOC: Dizionario delle opere classiche. Intestazioni uniformi degli autori, elenco delle opere e delle parti componenti, indici degli autori, dei titoli e delle parole chiave della letteratura classica, medievale e bizantina,* 3 vols. (1994) [BC113].

H.L.D. Ward and J.A. Herbert, *Catalogue of Romances in the Department of Manuscripts in the British Museum,* 3 vols. (1883–1910, r1961–62) [BC114].

D.E.R. Watt, *A Biographical Dictionary of Scottish Graduates to A.D. 1410* (1977) [BC115].

O. Weijers, *Le travail intellectuel à la Faculté des arts de Paris: Textes et maîtres (ca. 1200–1500),* v1: *Répertoire des noms commençant par A–B* (1994) [BC116].

H. Wiegand, *Hodoeporica: Studien zur neulateinischen Reisedichtung des deutschen Kulturraums im 16. Jahrhundert, mit einer Bio-Bibliographie der Autoren und Drucke* (1984) [BC117].

K.M. Wilson, *An Encyclopedia of Continental Women Writers,* 2 vols. (1991) [BC118].

A. Zawart, *The History of Franciscan Preaching and of Franciscan Preachers (1209–1927): A Bio-Bibliographical Study* (1928) [BC119].

ENCYCLOPEDIAS, ENCYCLOPEDIC DICTIONARIES, AND RELATED WORKS

Listed here is a small selection of multivolume encyclopedias, and of encyclopedic dictionaries, handbooks, and related works, intended primarily for the medievalist or containing substantial amounts of information (often with bibliographies) about, or important for the study of, medieval authors, texts, topics, places, and institutions. Also included are several national biographical dictionaries with entries on medieval writers and other figures. Excluded are standard encyclopedic works of general reference, such as *Chambers Encyclopedia, Brockhaus Enzyklopädie,* and *Encyclopaedia Britannica,* although many of these have excellent scholarly articles, with bibliographies, on medieval literature and history. Prosopographical works, which list lay and ecclesiastical dignitaries, officials, and institutions, are also excluded (with the exception of [BD82] and [BD123]), and works mentioned in the bibliographies of the other chapters of this volume are not listed again here.

On encyclopedic and other reference tools for all the fields of medieval studies, see [BA29]; on biographical dictionaries see [BA16] pp306–8 (national collections) and R.B. Slocum, *Biographical Dictionaries and Related Works: An International Bibliography of more than 16,000 Collective Biographies,* 2nd ed., 2 vols. (1986), with author, title, and subject indexes [BD1]; on prosopography see [BA16] 301–5; *Medieval Lives and the Historian: Studies in Medieval Prosopography,* ed. N. Bulst and J.-P. Genet (1986) [BD2]; and *Medieval Prosopography,* a semiannual periodical publication of the Medieval Institute, Kalamazoo, MI [BD3].

### (a) General Reference Works

*Dictionary of Medieval Civilization,* by J.H. Dahmus (1984): this and the summarized accounts in [BD6] and [BD8] are useful for ready reference [BD4].

*The Dictionary of the Middle Ages* [*DMA*], ed. J.R. Strayer *et al.,* 12 vols. and index (= v13: 565 pp.; errata: pp607–12) (1982–89) [BD5].

*The Illustrated Encyclopedia of Medieval Civilization,* by A. Graboïs (1980) [BD6].

*Lexikon des Mittelalters* [*LM*], ed. R. Auty *et al.* (1977–): has reached v6 (*Lukasbilder bis Plantagenêt*) [BD7].

*The Middle Ages: A Concise Encyclopaedia,* ed. H.R. Loyn (1989) [BD8].

*Reallexikon der germanischen Altertumskunde*, ed. J. Hoops, 4 vols. (1911–19); 2nd ed. by H. Jankuhn *et al.* (1968–) [BD9].

*Reallexikon für Antike und Christentum: Sachwörterbuch zur Auseinandersetzung des Christentums mit der antiken Welt* [*RLAC*], ed. T. Klauser *et al.* (1950–) [BD10].

## (b) National Biographical Dictionaries

*Allgemeine deutsche Biographie*, 56 vols. (1875–1912, r1967–71); supplemented by *Neue deutsche Biographie* (1953–) [BD11].

*Biographie nationale*, 44 vols. (1866–1986): for Belgium [BD12].

*Biographie nationale du pays de Luxembourg depuis ses origines jusqu'à nos jours*, ed. J. Mersch, 22 vols. (1947–75) [BD13].

*Biographisches Lexikon zur Geschichte der böhmischen Länder*, ed. H. Sturm (1974–) [BD14].

*Biographisches Lexikon zur Geschichte Südosteuropas*, ed. M. Bernath and F. von Schroeder (1970–) [BD15].

*A Concise Dictionary of Irish Biography*, ed. J.S. Crone, rev. ed. (1937) [BD16].

*Dansk Biografisk Lexikon*, 19 vols. (1887–1905), 27 vols. (1933–44), 16 vols. (1979–84) [BD17].

*Dictionary of National Biography*, ed. L. Stephen and S. Lee, 63 vols. and 3 supplementary vols. (1885–1901); errata and index (1903–4); supps. (1912–), including *Missing Persons*, ed. C.S. Nicholls *et al.* (1993): for England. *A New Dictionary of National Biography*, ed. H.C.G. Matthew, is in preparation [BD18].

*The Dictionary of Welsh Biography down to 1940*, ed. J.E. Lloyd and R.T. Jenkins (1959): English translation, with additions and corrections, of Welsh work of 1953 [BD19].

*Dictionnaire de biographie française* (1933–), ed. J. Balteau *et al.* [BD20].

*Dizionario biografico degli Italiani*, ed. A.M. Ghisalberti (1960–); index to v1–10 (1973) [BD21].

*Nieuw Nederlandsch Biografisch Woordenboek*, ed. P.C. Molhuysen *et al.*, 10 vols. (1911–37); based on *Biographisch Woordenboek der Nederlanden*, 21 vols. in 17 (1852–78, r1969) [BD22].

*Norsk Biografisk Leksikon*, 19 vols. (1923–83) [BD23].

*Svenskt Biografiskt Lexikon*, ed. B. Boethius *et al.* (1918–) [BD24].

## (c) Other Reference Works

*An Annotated Index of Medieval Women*, ed. A. Echols and M. Williams (1992): some 1,500 women from the period 800 to 1500 [BD25].

*Ausführliches Lexikon der griechischen und römischen Mythologie*, ed. W.H. Roscher, 6 vols. in 9, and 4 supps. (1884–1937, r1965–78): supps. include O. Gruppe, *Geschichte der klassischen Mythologie und Religionsgeschichte während des Mittelalters im Abendland und während der Neuzeit* (1921, r1965) [BD26].

*La Bible et les saints: Guide iconographique*, ed. G. Duchet-Suchaux and M. Pastoureau, 2nd ed. (1994); tr. D.R. Howell (1994) [BD27].

*A Biographical Dictionary of the Byzantine Empire*, ed. D.M. Nicol (1991) [BD28].

*A Calendar of Saints: The Lives of the Principal Saints of the Christian Year*, ed. J. Bentley (1986) [BD29].

*Cambridge Dictionary of Science and Technology*, ed. P.M.B. Walker (1988, r1992) [BD30].

*The Cambridge History of the Bible*, ed. P.R. Ackroyd, G.W.H. Lampe, and S.L. Greenslade, 3 vols. (1963–70) [BD31].

*A Catholic Dictionary of Theology*, ed. H.F. Davis *et al.* (1962–) [BD32].

*Catholicisme hier, aujourd'hui, demain* (1948– ) [BD33].

*A Companion to the Medieval Theatre*, ed. R.W. Vince (1989) [BD34].

*Diccionario de historia de España, desde sus orígenes hasta el fin del reinado de Alfonso XIII*, 2nd ed., 3 vols. (1970) [BD35].

*Dicionário de história de Portugal*, ed. J. Serrão, 6 vols. (1975–78, r1981) [BD36].

*Diccionario de historia eclesiástica de España*, ed. Q. Aldea Vaquero *et al.*, 4 vols. (1972–75); *Suplemento* 1 (1987) [BD37].

*A Dictionary of Biblical Interpretation*, ed. R.J. Coggins and J.L. Houlden (1990) [BD38].

*Dictionary of British Portraiture*, ed. R. Ormond and M. Rogers, 4 vols. (1979–81); v1: *The Middle Ages to the Early Georgians: Historical Figures Born before 1700;* index in v4 [BD39].

*A Dictionary of Christian Antiquities*, ed. W. Smith and S. Cheetham, 2 vols. (1875–80, r1968) [BD40].

*A Dictionary of Christian Biography, Literature, Sects and Doctrines*, ed. W. Smith and H. Wace, 4 vols. (1877–87, r1984): coverage from the apostolic period to the Carolingian [BD41].

*A Dictionary of Christian Spirituality*, ed. G.S. Wakefield (1983) [BD42].

*Dictionary of Medieval Knighthood and Chivalry: Concepts and Terms* (1986); *Dictionary of Medieval Knighthood and Chivalry: People, Places, and Events* (1988), both by B.B. Broughton [BD43].

*Dictionary of Saints*, ed. J.J. Delaney (1980) [BD44].

*Dictionary of Scientific Biography*, ed. C.C. Gillispie, 18 vols. including supps. (v15, 17–18) and index (v16) (1970–90) [BD45].

*Dictionary of the History of Science*, ed. W.F. Bynum, E.J. Browne, and R. Porter (1981, r1983) [BD46].

*Dictionnaire d'archéologie chrétienne et de liturgie* [*DACL*], ed. F. Cabrol and H. Leclercq, 15 vols. in 30 (1903–53): comprehensive coverage of all aspects of religious life from the early Christian era to the Carolingian period [BD47].

*Dictionnaire de la Bible*, ed. F. Vigouroux *et al.*, 5 vols. in 10 (1895–1912); supps. (1928– ) [BD48].

*Dictionnaire des ordres religieux et des familles spirituelles*, ed. G.-M. Oury (1988) [BD49].

*Dictionnaire de spiritualité, ascétique et mystique: Doctrine et histoire* [*DSAM*], ed. M. Viller *et al.*, 17 vols. (1932–95) [BD50].

*Dictionnaire des symboles: Mythes, rêves, coutumes, gestes, formes, figures, couleurs, nombres*, ed. J. Chevalier and A. Gheerbrant, rev. ed. (1982); tr. J. Buchanan-Brown (1994) [BD51].

*Dictionnaire de théologie catholique, contenant l'exposé des doctrines de la théologie catholique, leurs preuves et leur histoire*, ed. A. Vacant, E. Mangenot, *et al.*, 15 vols. in 30 (1903–50); *Table analytique*, v1–9 [A–L] (1929); *Tables générales*, 3 vols. (1951–72) [BD52].

*Dictionnaire d'histoire de l'enseignement*, ed. D. Demnard and D. Fourment (1981) [BD53].

*Dictionnaire d'histoire et de géographie ecclésiastiques* [*DHGE*], ed. A. Baudrillart *et al.* (1912–) [**BD54**].

*Dictionnaire encyclopédique de la Bible*, ed. P.-M. Bogaert *et al.* (1987) [**BD55**].

*Dizionario degli istituti di perfezione*, ed. G. Pelliccia and G. Rocca (1974–) [**BD56**].

*Dizionario degli scrittori greci e latini*, ed. F. Della Corte, 3 vols. (1988) with index in v3 [**BD57**].

*Dizionario patristico e di antichità cristiana*, ed. A. Di Berardino, 3 vols. (1983–88); tr. A. Walford: *Encyclopedia of the Early Church*, 2 vols. (1992) [**BD58**].

*Emblemata: Handbuch zur Sinnbildkunst des XVI. und XVII. Jahrhunderts*, ed. A. Henkel and A. Schöne (1967); supp. (1976) [**BD59**].

*Enciclopedia cattolica*, 12 vols. (1948–54) [**BD60**].

*Enciclopedia dell'arte medievale* (1991–) [**BD61**].

*Enciclopedia filosofica*, 2nd ed., 6 vols. (1967); 2nd ed. repr. and updated in 8 vols. (1982) [**BD62**].

*Enciclopedia virgiliana*, 5 vols. in 6 (1984–1991) [**BD63**].

*Encyclopaedia Biblica: A Critical Dictionary of the Literary, Political and Religious History, the Archaeology, Geography, and Natural History of the Bible*, ed. T.K. Cheyne and J.S. Black, 4 vols. (1899–1903); 2nd ed. (1914) in one vol. [**BD64**].

*Encyclopaedia Judaica*, ed. C. Roth, G. Wigoder, *et al.*, 16 vols. (1971–72); 2nd corr. ed. in 17 vols. (1982?); see also the *Jewish Encyclopedia*, 12 vols. (1901–6) [**BD65**].

*The Encyclopaedia of Islam*, ed. M.T. Houtsma *et al.*, 4 vols. in 7, plus supp. (1913–38, r1987); new ed. (1960–), with *Index of Proper Names to Volumes I–VII and to the Supplement, Fascicules 1–6* (1993) and *Index of Subjects* . . . (1994); see also the *Shorter Encyclopaedia of Islam*, ed. H.A.R. Gibb and J.H. Kramers (1953, r1991): deals primarily with religion and law [**BD66**].

*An Encyclopaedia of Philosophy*, ed. G.H.R. Parkinson *et al.* (1988) [**BD67**].

*Encyclopaedia of Religion and Ethics*, ed. J. Hastings *et al.*, 13 vols. (1908–26, r1961) [**BD68**].

*An Encyclopaedia of the History of Technology*, ed. I. McNeil (1988, r1990) [**BD69**].

*An Encyclopaedic Dictionary of Heraldry*, ed. J. Franklyn and J. Tanner (1970) [**BD70**].

*Encyclopedia of Early Christianity*, ed. E. Ferguson *et al.* (1990) [**BD71**].

*Encyclopedia of Medieval Church Art*, by E.G. Tasker, ed. J. Beaumont (1993) [**BD72**].

*The Encyclopedia of Military History: From 3500 B.C. to the Present*, ed. R.E. and T.N. Dupuy, 4th ed. (1993): 4th ed. published in U.S.A. as *The Harper Encyclopedia* . . . [**BD73**].

*The Encyclopedia of Philosophy*, ed. P. Edwards, 8 vols. in 4 (1967, r1972) [**BD74**].

*The Encyclopedia of Witchcraft and Demonology*, ed. R.H. Robbins (1959) [**BD75**].

*Encyclopédie philosophique universelle*, ed. A. Jacob *et al.* (1989–): v1, *L'univers philosophique* (1989); v2, *Les notions philosophiques: Dictionnaire* (1990), in 2 pts. (*A–L, M–Z*); v3, *Oeuvres philosophiques: Dictionnaire* (1992), in 2 pts. (pt1: *Philosophie occidentale: IIIe millénaire av. J.-C.–1889*); v4, *Les textes philosophiques* (forthcoming) [**BD76**].

*Enzyklopädie des Märchens: Handwörterbuch zur historischen und vergleichenden Erzählforschung*, ed. K. Ranke, H. Bausinger, *et al.* (1977–) [**BD77**].

*Garland Encyclopedias of the Middle Ages* (1993–): v1, *Medieval Scandinavia: An Encyclopedia*, ed. P. Pulsiano *et al.* (1993); v2, *Medieval France: An Encyclopedia*, ed. W.W. Kibler, G. Zinn, *et al.* (1994) [**BD78**].

*Glossar zur frühmittelalterlichen Geschichte im östlichen Europa*, ed. J. Ferluga *et al.* (1973–); series *A:* Latin sources; series *B:* Greek sources; series *C:* Slavic sources [**BD79**].

*Handbuch der Geschichte der Philosophie,* ed. W. Totok, 6 vols. (1964–90); v2: *Mittelalter* (1973) [BD80].

*Handwörterbuch des deutschen Aberglaubens,* ed. H. Bächtold-Stäubli and E. Hoffmann-Krayer, 10 vols. (1927–42, r1987 with new intro.) [BD81].

*Hierarchia catholica medii aevi,* 2nd ed., 2 vols. (1913–14, r1960), ed. K. Eubel: v1, *Ab anno 1198 usque ad annum 1431 perducta;* v2, *Ab anno 1431 usque ad annum 1503 perducta* [BD82].

*Historisches Wörterbuch der Philosophie,* ed. J. Ritter *et al.* (1971–) [BD83].

*The Holy Roman Empire: A Dictionary Handbook,* ed. J.W. Zophy (1980) [BD84].

*Kulturhistorisk leksikon for nordisk middelalder fra vikingetid til reformationstid,* 22 vols. (1956–78) [BD85].

*Lexicon abbreviaturarum: Dizionario di abbreviature latine ed italiane,* ed. A. Cappelli, 3rd rev. and corr. ed. (1929); many reprintings, including, most recently, that of 1993; supplemented by A. Pelzer, *Abbréviations latines médiévales* (1964, r1966 ["deuxième edition"] and 1982); English translation of Cappelli's introduction (ed. of 1929) by D. Heimann and R. Kay: *The Elements of Abbreviation in Medieval Latin Paleography* (1982); an electronic dictionary of Medieval Latin abbreviations, entitled *Abbreviationes,* which permits searches for words to match, exactly or closely, given abbreviations, and vice versa, has also been developed [BD86].

*Lexicon antiquitatum Slavicarum,* ed. W. Kowalenko *et al.* (1961–): until A.D. 1200 [BD87].

*Lexikon der biblischen Personen, mit ihrem Fortleben in Judentum, Christentum, Islam, Dichtung, Musik und Kunst,* ed. M. Bocian *et al.* (1989) [BD88].

*Lexikon der christlichen Ikonographie,* ed. E. Kirschbaum, G. Bandmann, and W. Braunfels, 8 vols. (1968–76) [BD89].

*Lexikon der Geschichte der Naturwissenschaften: Biographien, Sachwörter und Bibliographien* (1959–) [BD90].

*Lexikon der Heiligen und Päpste,* ed. C. Fichtinger, 2nd ed. (1984) [BD91].

*Lexikon der Heraldik,* ed. G. Oswald (1985) [BD92].

*Lexikon der Liturgie,* ed. G. Podhradsky, 2nd ed. (1962); tr. R. Walls and M. Barry: *New Dictionary of the Liturgy,* ed. L. Sheppard (1967) [BD93].

*Lexikon der mittelalterlichen Zahlenbedeutungen,* ed. H. Meyer and R. Suntrup (1987) [BD94].

*Lexikon der Namen und Heiligen,* ed O. Wimmer and H. Melzer, 6th ed. (1988) [BD95].

*Lexikon der Päpste,* ed. R. Fischer-Wollpert, 2nd ed. (1988) [BD96].

*Lexikon der romanistischen Linguistik,* ed. G. Holtus *et al.* (1988–) [BD97].

*Lexikon der Zaubermärchen,* ed. W. Scherf (1982) [BD98].

*Lexikon für Theologie und Kirche,* 2nd ed. by J. Höfer and K. Rahner, 10 vols. and *Register* (1957–67); 3rd ed. by W. Kasper, K. Baumgartner, *et al.* (1993–) [BD99].

*Lexikon zur Geschichte der Kartographie von den Anfängen bis zum ersten Weltkrieg,* ed. I. Kretschmer *et al.,* 2 vols. (1986) [BD100].

*Liturgish Woordenboek,* ed. L. Brinkhoff, 2 vols. (1958–68) [BD101].

*Marienlexikon,* ed. R. Baümer and L. Scheffczyk, 6 vols. (1988–94) [BD102].

*Motif-Index of Folk Literature: A Classification of Narrative Elements in Folk-Tales, Ballads, Myths, Fables, Mediaeval Romances, Exempla, Fabliaux, Jest-Books, and Local Legends,* by S. Thompson, 6 vols., rev. ed. (1955–58, r1966); electronic edition on computer laser optical disk (1993) [BD103].

*Die Musik in Geschichte und Gegenwart: Allgemeine Enzyklopädie der Musik* [*MGG*], ed. F. Blume, 17 vols. (1949–86), including supps. and *Register;* new edition in progress, ed. L. Finscher (1994–) [**BD104**].

*Neues Lexikon christlicher Symbole,* ed. D. Forstner and R. Becker (1991) [**BD105**].

*The New Arthurian Encyclopedia,* ed. N.J. Lacy *et al.,* 2nd ed. (1991) [**BD106**].

*New Catholic Enyclopedia* [*NCE*], 18 vols., including index (v15) and 3 supplementary vols. (1967–88): with its predecessor, *The Catholic Encyclopaedia,* 15 vols. and index (1907–14), a valuable work of reference for questions touching any aspect of Catholicism [**BD107**].

*A New Dictionary of Liturgy and Worship,* ed. J.G. Davies (1986) [**BD108**].

*Nuovo dizionario di Mariologia,* ed. S. De Fiores and S. Meo, 2nd ed. (1986) [**BD109**].

*The Oxford Classical Dictionary,* ed. N.G.L. Hammond and H.H. Scullard, 2nd ed. (1970, r1984) [**BD110**].

*Oxford Dictionary of Byzantium,* ed. A.P. Kazhdan *et al.,* 3 vols. (1991) [**BD111**].

*The Oxford Dictionary of Popes,* ed. J.N.D. Kelly (1986, r1988) [**BD112**].

*The Oxford Dictionary of Saints,* ed. D.H. Farmer, 3rd ed. (1992) [**BD113**].

*The Oxford Dictionary of the Christian Church,* ed. F.L. Cross and E.A. Livingstone, 2nd ed. (1974, r1983 with corrections and revisions, r1988) [**BD114**].

*The Oxford Guide to Classical Mythology in the Arts, 1300–1990s,* by J.D. Reid and C. Rohmann, 2 vols. (1993) [**BD115**].

*Paulys Realencyclopädie der classischen Altertumswissenschaft,* ed. G. Wissowa, 49 vols. in 58 (1894–1980); see also *Der kleine Pauly: Lexikon der Antike auf der Grundlage von Pauly's Realencyclopädie,* ed. K. Ziegler and W. Sontheimer, 5 vols. (1964–75, r1979) [**BD116**].

*Philosophisches Wörterbuch,* ed. H. Schmidt and G. Schischkoff, 22nd ed. (1991) [**BD117**].

*Realencyklopädie für protestantische Theologie und Kirche,* ed. J.J. Herzog and A. Hauck, 3rd ed., 24 vols. (1896–1913, r1969) [**BD118**].

*Die Religion in Geschichte und Gegenwart: Handwörterbuch für Theologie und Religionswissenschaft,* 7 vols. including index, 3rd. ed. (1957–65) [**BD119**].

*Sachwörterbuch der Mediävistik,* ed. P. Dinzelbacher *et al.* (1992) [**BD120**].

*Sacramentum Mundi: An Encyclopedia of Theology,* ed. K. Rahner *et al.,* 6 vols. (1968–70) [**BD121**].

*The Saints of Scotland,* ed. E.S. Towill, 3rd rev. ed. (1994) [**BD122**].

*Series episcoporum ecclesiae catholicae quotquot innotuerunt a beato Petro apostolo* and *Supplementum,* ed. P.B. Gams (1873–86, r1957); replacement in progress: *Series episcoporum ecclesiae catholicae occidentalis ab initio usque ad annum MCXCVIII,* ed. S. Weinfurter and O. Engels (1982–); this includes *Series V, Germania:* v1, *Archiepiscopatus Coloniensis,* ed. S. Weinfurter and O. Engels (1982); v2, *Archiepiscopatus Hammaburgensis sive Bremensis,* ed. S. Weinfurter and O. Engels (1984); *Series VI, Britannia, Scotia et Hibernia, Scandinavia:* v1, *Ecclesia Scoticana,* ed. D.E.R. Watt *et al.* (1991); v2, *Archiepiscopatus Lundensis,* ed. H. Kluger (1992); see also *Les évêques d'Albi, de Cahors et de Rodez des origines à la fin du XIIe siècle,* ed. J. Dufour (1989) [**BD123**].

*Theologische Realenzyklopädie,* ed. H.R. Balz, G. Krause, and G. Müller (1977–); *Register zu Band 1–17* (1990); *Abkurzungsverzeichnis,* 2nd ed. (1994) [**BD124**].

*Wörterbuch der Mystik,* ed. P. Dinzelbacher (1989) [**BD125**].

BE   •   COMPUTER RESOURCES

It is impossible to keep pace with developments in this increasingly important and rapidly changing field. Computer technology supports the compilation of bibliographies, *incipitaria,* inventories, lexica, concordances, and linguistic analyses, and provides convenient access to databases, discussion lists, on-line library catalogues, electronic texts and journals (such as *Bryn Mawr Medieval Book Review:* BMMR-L), digitized images, and a wide range of other resources. Important centers for the creation and development of large databases and other computer applications are the Centre de traitement electronique des documents [CETEDOC] of the Université Catholique de Louvain (Louvain-la-Neuve, Belgium), and the Section d'informatique of the institut de recherche et d'histoire des textes, Centre National de la Recherche Scientifique [IRHT-CNRS], in Paris.

Electronic projects are reported in publications noticed in *MEL* [BA30], under the rubric "Elaborazione elettronica dei dati," and may be surveyed in such journals as *Le médiéviste et l'ordinateur* (1979–) [BE1]; *Revue de l'Organisation internationale pour l'étude des langues anciennes par ordinateur* (1966–; see [BA6] 151–57) [BE2]; *Computers and the Humanities* (1966–; see, e.g., v24 [1990]) [BE3]; *Revue: Informatique et statistique dans les sciences humaines* (1983–; see, e.g., v25 [1989]) [BE4]; *Computers and Medieval Data Processing/Informatique et études médiévales* (1971–; inactive since 1987)[BE5]; and *History & Computing* (1989–) [BE6]. A third source of information is the published proceedings of round tables, workshops, and conferences, such as the International Conferences on Computers and the Humanities and on Literary and Linguistic Computing. For surveys of developments and resources in all the fields of medieval studies see *The Humanities Computing Yearbook 1988* (1988) and *1989–90* (1991) [BE7] and [BE18].

The best guide to the *Internet,* a system of computer networks that links research institutions throughout the world, is that of E. Krol, *The Whole Internet: User's Guide & Catalog,* 2nd ed. (1994) [BE8]. The preferred system for transferring texts, images, and sounds over the *Internet* is the ever-expanding *World Wide Web,* whose files have precise, searchable locations, are delivered to users by "servers" around the world, and are displayed by means of such software programs as *Netscape, Mosaic,* and *Lynx.* See D. Everhart, "Entering the Web: An Introduction to the World Wide Web for Medievalists," in *Medieval Academy News* 122 (Sept. 1995) 4–5. The *Labyrinth* project, initiated in May 1994 at Georgetown University, Washington, DC, offers a means of accessing electronic resources in medieval studies [BE9].

A *Directory of Electronic Journals, Newsletters, and Academic Discussion Lists* has been published annually since 1991; see the 5th edition (1995) [BE10] and the brief listing of academic discussion groups in section (c) below. These groups are probably the best source of information about computer resources and projects in the various fields of medieval studies. See also the semiannual *Gale Directory of Databases* (1993–), 2 vols., available electronically through online services: v1, *Online Databases;* v2, *CD-ROM, Diskette, Magnetic Tape, Handheld, and Batch Access Database Products* [BE11].

## (a) Orientation, Applications

C. Bourlet, C. Doutrelepont, and S. Lusignan, *Ordinateur et études médiévales: Bibliographie I* (1982) [BE12].

M. Folkerts and A. Kühne, eds., *The Use of Computers in Cataloging Medieval and Renaissance Manuscripts: Papers from the International Workshop in Munich, 10–12 August 1989* (1990): eleven papers on the exploitation of new technologies for indexing and studying manuscripts [BE13]; considerable overlap with *Bibliographic Access to Medieval and Renaissance Manuscripts: A Survey of Computerized Data Bases and Information Services,* ed. W.M. Stevens (1992) [BE14]; see review of both collections by J.J. O'Donnell in *Speculum* 68 (1993) 1118–19 [BE15].

L. Fossier, ed., *Le médiéviste et l'ordinateur: Actes de la table ronde (Paris, CNRS, 17 novembre 1989)* (1990) [BE16].

L. Fossier *et al.,* eds., *Informatique et histoire médiévale: Communications et débats de la table ronde CNRS, organisée par l'École française de Rome et l'Institut d'histoire médiévale de l'Université de Pise (Rome, 20–22 mai 1975)* (1977) [BE17].

A. Gilmour-Bryson, ed., *Computer Applications to Medieval Studies* (1984): includes a survey (pp1–22), by the editor, of applications since 1974 [BE18].

J. Hamesse, ed., *Méthodologies informatiques et nouveaux horizons dans les recherches médiévales: Actes du colloque international de Saint-Paul-de-Vence, 3–5 septembre 1990* (1992) [BE19].

J. Hamesse and A. Zampolli, eds., *Computers in Literary and Linguistic Computing: Proceedings of the Eleventh International Conference/L'ordinateur et les recherches littéraires et linguistiques: Actes de la XIe conférence internationale, Université Catholique de Louvain (Louvain-la-Neuve), 2–6 avril 1984* (1985) [BE20].

A. Hughes, *Late Medieval Liturgical Offices: Resources for Electronic Research* (1994): with three computer diskettes [BE21].

B. Juhl, "*Ex Machina:* Electronic Resources for the Classics," in *Choice* 32.8 (1995) 1249–61: valuable overview, with description of many tools of interest to medievalists [BE22].

*Méthodes quantitatives et informatiques dans l'étude des textes: En hommage à Charles Muller. Colloque international CNRS, Université de Nice, 5–8 juin 1986/Computers in Literary & Linguistic Research* (1986) [BE23].

R. Metz *et al.,* eds., *Historical Information Systems: Session B–12b: Proceedings, Tenth International Economic History Congress, Leuven, August, 1990* (1990) [BE24].

A. Schwob, K. Kranich-Hofbauer, and D. Suntinger, eds., *Historische Edition und Computer: Möglichkeiten und Probleme interdisziplinärer Textverarbeitung und Textbearbeitung* (1989) [BE25].

K.-F. Werner, ed., *L'histoire médiévale et les ordinateurs/Medieval History and Computers: Rapports d'une table ronde internationale, Paris, 1978* (1981) [BE26].

## (b) Databases, CD-ROMs, etc. (very selective)

*Bibliographic Information Base in Patristics/ Base d'information bibliographique en patristique* [*BIBP*]: a computerized bibliographical service for scholars of patristic literature and related fields (archaeology, iconography, epigraphy, papyrology, codicology, Church history, theology, liturgy, spirituality, monasticism, biblical exegesis, hagiography, etc.), with processing and storage of information at Université Laval (Québec) [BE27].

*Biographical Database for Late Antiquity:* computerized collection of information concerning many thousands of individuals attested to have lived between c. A.D. 260 and 640 [BE28].

*CANTUS: Indices of the Chants in Manuscript and Early Printed Sources of the Divine Office in Database Form:* ongoing project, initiated by Ruth Steiner of the School of Music at The Catholic University of America, Washington, DC [BE29].

*Cetedoc Library of Christian Latin Texts* [*CLCLT*]: database, on computer laser optical disk (1991), with updates (*CLCLT*–2 [1994]), of full texts of works edited in the *Series Latina* and *Continuatio Mediaevalis* of the *Corpus Christianorum* collection (see [BG24]), to which have been added the *Vulgate* and other essential texts not yet published in the *Corpus;* includes the complete works of Augustine, Bernard of Clairvaux, Gregory the Great, Jerome, and many other Latin authors [BE30].

*Cetedoc Index of Latin Forms* [*CILF*]: database, or *Thesaurus formarum totius latinitatis,* planned to contain all the Latin words in the Cetedoc databank, from antiquity to the present (and therefore including Medieval Latin from 735 to 1500); available on CD-ROM (1996); permits the study and comparison of the latinity of individual authors and periods by identifying unique and common forms, etc.; see also [BB8] [BE31].

*The Database of Classical Bibliography* [*DCB*]: computer file (v1, 1995), on laser optical disks, of the contents of *L'année philologique* [*APh*], v47–58 (1967–87; 185,238 bibliographic records), with other volumes (and contributed non-*APh* bibliographical notices) to be added in scheduled updates; see also [BA1] [BE32].

*Datenbank mittelalterlicher Personen und Personengruppen:* database of personal names drawn from obituaries and *libri memoriales,* designed for research on medieval names and groups [BE33].

*Handschriften des Mittelalters* [*HdM*]: database of incipits, with cross-references, collected from manuscript catalogues of German collections [BE34].

*Incunable Short Title Catalogue* [*ISTC*]: database (now being compiled at the British Library) with international coverage of materials (books, pamphlets, etc.) printed with movable type prior to 1501; information—author, title, printer, place and date of publication, location, etc.—drawn from published catalogues and other records, including (initially) F.R. Goff, *Incunabula in American Libraries: A Third Census of Fifteenth-Century Books Recorded in North American Collections* (1964, r1973 with annotations, corrections, etc.) and its *Supplement* (1972); see also [BA36–38] [BE35].

*The Index of Christian Art:* largest archive in the world for the study of medieval iconography (both Western and Eastern), founded in 1917, with information recorded on file cards cross-referenced to photographs; from 1989 the data have been entered in a computerized database, searchable by field(s), with subjects listed, described, and accompanied by information on styles, media, dates, patrons, locations, textual associations, etc. [BE36].

*In Principio: Incipit Index of Latin Texts/Incipitaire des textes latins:* a collection on computer laser optical disks of Latin incipits, based on those compiled since 1937 on card files in the Latin section of the Institut de recherche et d'histoire des textes (Paris) and covering the whole of Latin literature through the Renaissance; periodic updates planned (*In Principio*–3 [1995]); cooperation with the Hill Monastic Manuscript Library (St. John's College, Collegeville, MN), where 350,000 incipits have been collected, has been initiated [BE37].

*International Medieval Bibliography on CD-ROM* [*IMB*]: a project to produce, beginning in November 1995, an electronic version of one of the standard bibliographical listings of scholarship in all aspects of medieval studies (see [BA25]) [BE38].

*The Medieval and Early Modern Data Bank* [*MEMDB*]: a project designed to accommodate an expanding collection of historical information, specifically metrological, monetary, price, and wage information, including currency exchange rates [BE39].

*Patrologia Latina Database* [*PLD*]: a project undertaken by Chadwyck-Healey to produce an edition of all of Migne's *PL* (see [BG51])—texts and supplementary materials—on compter laser optical disks (1992–); five CD-ROMs are planned [BE40].

*PHI CD-ROM #5.3:* computer laser optical disk (1991), produced by the Packard Humanities Institute (Los Altos, CA) and containing complete texts of most Latin authors to A.D. 200 (file 1) and six versions of the Bible, including the *Septuagint* and the *Vulgate* (file 2) [BE41].

*Royal Irish Academy Archive of Celtic-Latin Literature* [*ACLL*]: a project of the Royal Irish Academy (which is producing a computer-based *Dictionary of Medieval Latin from Celtic Sources*) and Brepols Electronic Publishing designed to establish a permanent electronic database (*ACLL*–1 [1995]) containing all Celtic-Latin texts from the period A.D. 400–1200; a complement to *CLCLT* ([BE30]) [BE42].

*Thesaurus Linguae Graecae* [*TLG*]: electronic repository (computer laser optical disk, 1992), developed at the University of California, Irvine, of ancient and Byzantine Greek literature to the sixth century A.D., into which have been loaded the texts listed in [BC24]; current work will expand the database to include texts up to the end of the Byzantine Empire [BE43].

*Thesaurus Musicarum Latinarum* [*TML*]: *A Comprehensive Database of Latin Music Theory of the Middle Ages and the Renaissance:* see [DJ3] [BE44].

*Thomae Aquinatis opera omnia cum hypertextibus in CD-ROM* [BE45].

## (c) Electronic Discussion Groups (very selective)

Ancient Mediterranean: ANCIEN-L
Ancient and Medieval Numismatics: NUMISM-L
Arthurian Studies: ARTHURNET, CAMELOT
Biblical Greek: B-GREEK
Byzantine Studies: BYZANS-L
Classical Greek and Latin: CLASSICS
Early Christian Studies, A.D. 100–500: ELENCHUS
Greek and Latin Languages, Lexicography, and Electronic Texts: LEXI

Humanities and Computers: HUMANIST
Late Antiquity: LT-ANTIQ
Latin: Classical, Medieval, and Humanist: LATIN-L
Medieval Art: MEDART-L
Medieval Feminist Studies: MEDFEM-L
Medieval Gay Studies: MEDGAY-L
Medieval History: MEDIEV-L
Medieval Literacy: MEDLITERACY-L
Medieval Languages and Literatures: MEDTEXTL
Medieval Philosophy and Socio-Political Thought: MDVLPHIL
Medieval, Renaissance, and Baroque Music: EARLYM-L, MED-AND-REN-
    MUSIC
Medieval Science: MEDSCI-L
Middle Ages, A.D. 283–1500: MEDIEV-L
Rare books and Special Colections: EXLIBRIS
Renaissance and Reformation Studies: FICINO
Rhetoric: H-RHETOR

# OTHER BASIC REFERENCE AND RESEARCH AIDS

Listed here is a selection of vernacular and other dictionaries—including standard, medieval, and etymological dictionaries—and of other works of reference useful to medieval latinists.

## (a) Dictionaries

### French and Anglo-Norman

*Anglo-Norman Dictionary*, ed. W. Rothwell, L.W. Stone, *et al.* (1977–92) [BF1].

*Dictionnaire de la langue française*, ed. E. Littré, 7 vols., *édition integrale* (1956–58) [BF2].

*Dictionnaire de l'ancien français jusqu'au milieu du XIVe siècle*, ed. A.J. Greimas, 2nd ed. (1980) [BF3].

*Dictionnaire de l'ancienne langue française, et de tous ses dialects du IXe siècle au XVe siècle*, ed. F. Godefroy, 10 vols. (1881–1902, r1983) [BF4].

*Französisches etymologisches Wörterbuch: Eine Darstellung des galloromanischen Sprachschatzes*, ed. W. von Wartburg (1922–, r1948–78); *Beiheft: Ortsnamenregister, Literaturverzeichnis, Übersichtskarte*, 2nd ed. (1950); *Supplement zur 2. Aufl. des bibliographischen Beiheftes* (1957) [BF5].

*Le Grand Robert de la langue française: Dictionnaire alphabétique et analogique de la langue française*, 2nd ed. by A. Rey, 9 vols. (1986); CD-ROM version (1989) [BF6].

*Lexique français moderne-ancien français*, ed. R.P. De Gorog (1973) [BF7].

*Tobler-Lommatzch: Altfranzösisches Wörterbuch*, ed. A. Tobler and E. Lommatzch (1925–) [BF8].

### Provençal

*Lexique roman, ou Dictionnaire de la langue des troubadors, comparée avec les autres langues de l'Europe latine*, ed. M. Raynouard, 6 vols. (1836–44, r1928?–); supplemented by *Provenzalisches Supplement-Wörterbuch: Berichtigungen und Ergänzungen zu Raynouards Lexique roman*, ed. E. Lévy, 8 vols. (1892–1924, r1973) [BF9].

*Petit dictionnaire provençal-français*, ed. E. Lévy (1909, r1973) [BF10].

### Italian

*Dizionario etimologico della lingua italiana,* ed. M. Cortelazzo and P. Zolli, 5 vols. (1979–88) [BF11].

*Dizionario etimologico italiano,* ed. C. Battisti and G. Alessio, 5 vols. (1950–57, r1968) [BF12].

*Grande dizionario della lingua italiana,* ed. S. Battaglia and G.B. Squarotti (1961–); indices (1973–) [BF13].

### Spanish, Portuguese, Catalan

*Diccionari català-valencià-balear,* ed. A.M. Alcover, F. de B. Moll, *et al.,* 2nd ed., 10 vols. (1950–68, r1988) [BF14].

*Diccionari etimològic i complementari de la llengua catalana,* ed. J. Corominas *et al.,* 3rd ed. (1980–) [BF15].

*Diccionario crítico etimológico de la lengua castellana,* ed. J. Corominas, 4 vols. (1954–57, r1974); rev. ed. by J. Corominas and J.A. Pascual, *Diccionario crítico etimológico castellano e hispánico,* 6 vols. (1980–91) [BF16].

*Diccionario del español medieval,* ed. B. Müller (1987–) [BF17].

*Diccionario histórico de la lengua española* (1960–) [BF18].

*Diccionario medieval español, desde las glosas emilianenses y silenses (s. X) hasta el siglo XV,* ed. M. Alonso Pedraz, 2 vols. (1986) [BF19].

*Dicionário da lingua portuguesa, especialmente dos periodos medieval e clássico,* ed. A. Magne (1950–) [BF20].

*Dicionário etimológico da língua portuguesa,* ed. J.P. Machado, 3rd ed., 5 vols. (1977) [BF21].

*Grande dicionário da língua portuguesa,* ed. A. Moreno, C. Júnior, and J.P. Machado, 10th ed., 12 vols. (1949–59): revision and expansion of work of Antonio de Morais Silva (1755–1824) [BF22].

*Tentative Dictionary of Medieval Spanish,* ed. R.S. Boggs, 2 vols. (1946) [BF23].

### English

*An Anglo-Saxon Dictionary,* ed. J. Bosworth and T.N. Toller, 2 vols. (1882–98) with supps. (1921, 1972; r1992 together) [BF24].

*A Chronological English Dictionary Listing 80,000 Words in Order of Their Earliest Known Occurrence,* ed. T. Finkenstaedt *et al.* (1970) [BF25].

*A Concise Anglo-Saxon Dictionary,* ed. J.R.C. Hall, 4th ed. (1960, r1984) with supp. by H.D. Meritt [BF26].

*Dictionary of Old English* (1986–): a new lexicon of the language from its earliest appearance in written records, c. 600; now being published on microfiche by the Pontifical Institute of Mediaeval Studies for the Dictionary of Old English Project (Centre for Medieval Studies, University of Toronto); see also *A Microfiche Concordance to Old English: The List of Texts and Index of Editions* (1980), *A Microfiche Concordance to Old English: The High-Frequency Words* (1985), and *Abbreviations for Latin Sources and Bibliography of Editions* (published with the fourth fasc. [1992]) [BF27].

*An Etymological Dictionary of the English Language,* ed. W.W. Skeat, new ed. (1910, r1978) [BF28].

*Middle English Dictionary,* ed. H. Kurath, S.M. Kuhn, and R.E. Lewis (1952–) [BF29].

*A Middle-English Dictionary Containing Words Used by English Writers from the*

*Twelfth to the Fifteenth Century,* ed. F.H. Stratmann, new ed. (1891, r1978) by H. Bradley [**BF30**].

*The Oxford Dictionary of English Etymology,* ed. C.T. Onions *et al.* (1966, r1985 with corrections) [**BF31**].

*The Oxford English Dictionary, being a corrected re-issue with an introduction, supplement, and bibliography of A new English dictionary on historical principles* [*OED*], ed. J.A.H. Murray *et al.*, 13 vols. (1933, r1961); *Supplement,* ed. R.W. Burchfield, 4 vols. (1972–86); 2nd ed. prepared by J.A. Simpson and E.S.C. Weiner, 20 vols. (1989); *Additions series,* 2 vols. (1993); CD-ROM versions of first ed. (1988) and second ed. (1992); see D.L. Berg, *A Guide to the Oxford English Dictionary* (1993) [**BF32**].

## Celtic

*The Concise Scots Dictionary,* ed. M. Robinson (1985) [**BF33**].

*Dictionary of the Irish Language, Based Mainly on Old and Middle Irish Materials* (1913–): consists to date of fascs. and supps., the latter published as *Contributions to a Dictionary of the Irish Language;* compact ed. in 1 vol. (1983) [**BF34**].

*A Dictionary of the Older Scottish Tongue from the Twelfth Century to the End of the Seventeenth,* ed. W.A. Craigie, A.J. Aitken, *et al.* (1931–) [**BF35**].

*Dictionary of the Welsh Language,* ed. D.S. and J.H.S. Evans, 5 pts. [A–Enyd] (1887–96): never finished [**BF36**].

*A Dictionary of the Welsh Language,* ed. R.J. Thomas *et al.* (1950–) [**BF37**].

*An Etymological Dictionary of the Scottish Language,* ed. J. Jamieson, 2 vols. (1808); supp., 2 vols. (1825); new ed., 4 vols. (1879–82), by J. Longmuir and D. Donaldson; supp. (1887) [**BF38**].

*An Irish-English Dictionary,* ed. P.S. Dinneen, rev. ed. (1927, r1934 with additions, r1979) [**BF39**].

*Lexique étymologique de l'irlandais ancien,* ed. J. Vendryes *et al.* (1959–) [**BF40**].

*Spurrell's English-Welsh Dictionary,* ed. J.B. Anwyl, 11th ed. (1937) [**BF41**].

## German and Dutch

*Althochdeutscher Sprachschatz oder Wörterbuch der althochdeutschen Sprache,* ed. E.G. Graff, 6 vols. and index (by H.F. Massmann) (1834–46, r1963) [**BF42**].

*Althochdeutsches Wörterbuch,* ed. R. Schützeichel, 4th ed. (1989) [**BF43**].

*Althochdeutsches Wörterbuch auf Grund der von Elias v. Steinmeyer hinterlassenen Sammlungen,* ed. E. Karg-Gasterstädt and T. Frings (1952–) [**BF44**].

*Altsächsisches Wörterbuch,* ed. F. Holthausen, 2nd ed. (1967) [**BF45**].

*Deutsches Rechtswörterbuch: Wörterbuch der älteren deutschen Rechtssprache* (1914–); *Quellenheft* (1912); *Quellen-Ergänzungsheft* (1930–) [**BF46**].

*Deutsches Wörterbuch von Jacob und Wilhelm Grimm,* 16 vols. in 32 (1854–1960; r1984, including [v33] *Quellenverzeichnis* [1966–71]); rev. and expanded edition (1965–) [**BF47**].

*Etymologisches Wörterbuch der deutschen Sprache,* ed. F. Kluge and A. Götze, 22nd ed. (1989) by E. Seebold; translation of 4th German ed. by J.F. Davis: *An Etymological Dictionary of the German Language* (1891) [**BF48**].

*Middelnederlandsch Woordenboek,* ed. E. Verwijs, J. Verdam, *et al.*, 11 vols. (1885–1929, 1927–52 [v10], 1941 [v11]) [**BF49**].

*Mittelhochdeutsches Wörterbuch,* ed. G.F. Benecke, W. Müller, and F.H.T. Zarncke, 4 vols. in 5 (1854–66, r1990); supplemented by *Mittelhochdeutsches Handwörter-buch*, ed. M. Lexer, 3 vols. (1872–78, r1974) [BF50].

*Mittelniederdeutsches Handwörterbuch*, ed. A. Lasch, C. Borchling, and G. Cordes (1956–) [BF51].

*Mittelniederdeutsches Wörterbuch*, ed. K. Schiller and A. Lübben, 6 vols. (1875–81, r1969) [BF52].

*Nederlands etymologisch Woordenboek*, ed. J. de Vries (1971) [BF53].

*Trübners deutsches Wörterbuch*, ed. A. Götze *et al.*, 8 vols. in 9 (1939–57) [BF54].

*Vergleichendes Wörterbuch der gotischen Sprache*, ed. S. Feist, 3rd ed. (1939); tr. W.P. Lehmann: *A Gothic Etymological Dictionary* (1986) [BF55].

*Woordenboek der Nederlandsche taal* (1882–) [BF56].

### Icelandic, Norwegian, Danish, and Swedish

*Altnordisches etymologisches Wörterbuch*, ed. J. de Vries, 2nd ed. (1962) [BF57].

*Etymologisk Ordbog over det norske og det danske Sprog*, ed. H. Falk and A. Torp, 2 vols. (1903–6, r1994); tr. H. Davidsen: *Norwegisch-dänisches etymologisches Wörterbuch*, 2 vols. (1910–11, r1960) [BF58].

*An Icelandic-English Dictionary*, ed. R. Cleasby and G. Vigfusson, 2nd ed. (1957, r1962) with supp. (pp781–833) by W.A. Craigie [BF59].

*Islandisches etymologisches Wörterbuch*, ed. A. Jóhannesson (1956) [BF60].

*Lexicon poeticum antiquae linguae septentrionalis/Ordbog over det norsk-islandske skjaldesprog. Oprindelig forfattet af Sveinbjörn Egilsson*, ed. F. Jónsson, 2nd ed. (1931) [BF61].

*Nynorsk etymologisk Ordbok*, ed. A. Torp (1919) [BF62].

*Ordbog til det ældre danske sprog (1300–1700)*, ed. K.O.H.T. Kalkar, 6 vols. (1881–1976) [BF63].

*Ordbok öfver svenska medeltids-språket*, ed. K.F. Söderwall, 2 vols. in 3 (1884–1918); supp. in 35 pts. (1926–73) [BF64].

*Svensk etymologisk Ordbok*, ed. E. Hellquist, 3rd ed., 2 vols. (1957) [BF65].

*Vergleichendes und etymologisches Wörterbuch des altwestnordischen, altnorwegisch-islandischen, einschliesslich der Lehn- und Fremdwörter sowie der Eigennamen*, ed. F. Holthausen (1948) [BF66].

### Greek

*Dictionnaire étymologique de la langue grecque, étudiée dans ses rapports avec les autres langues indo-européens*, ed. E. Boisacq, 4th ed. (1950) [BF67].

*Dictionnaire étymologique de la langue grecque: Histoire des mots*, ed. P. Chantraine, 4 vols. (1968–80) [BF68].

*Glossarium ad scriptores mediae et infimae graecitatis*, ed. Charles Du Fresne, Sieur Du Cange, 2 vols. (Lyons 1688, r1958) [BF69].

*A Greek-English Lexicon*, ed. H.G. Liddell and R. Scott, 8th ed. (1897); rev. ed. [9th] by H.S. Jones, R. McKenzie, *et al.*, 10 pts. (1925–40); supps. by E.A. Barber *et al.* (1968) and R. Renehan (1975, 1982); among other contributions published since 1940, the supp. of 1968 incorporates revised addenda and corrigenda of the 9th ed. [BF70].

*Greek Lexicon of the Roman and Byzantine Periods (from B.C. 146 to A.D. 1100)*, ed. E.A. Sophocles, 2nd corr. ed. (1887, r1914, r1983) [BF71].

*A Greek-English Lexicon of the New Testament and Other Early Christian Literature*, ed. W. Bauer, tr. F.W. Gingrich and F.W. Danker, 2nd ed. (1979) [BF72].

*Griechisches etymologisches Wörterbuch,* ed. H. Frisk, 3 vols. (1960–72) [BF73].
*A Patristic Greek Lexicon,* ed. G.W.H. Lampe (1961–68, r1991) [BF74].

## (b) Guides to Libraries and Archives (See [BA27] 937–41.)

*International Directory of Archives/Annuaire international des archives* (1992) [BF75].
R.C. Lewanski, *European Library Directory: A Geographical and Bibliographical Guide* (1968) [BF76].
M. Vásquez de Parga *et al., International Bibliography of Directories and Guides to Archival Repositories, Archivum* 36 (1990) [BF77].
*World Guide to Libraries/Internationales Bibliotheks-Handbuch,* 11th ed. (1993) [BF78].
*World Guide to Special Libraries,* 2nd ed., 2 vols. (1990) [BF79].

## (c) Guides to Scholars and Academic Institutions (See [BA29] 17–20.)

*Commonwealth Universities Yearbook* (1914–), 4 vols.: roster of 230,000 faculty and administrators at universities and colleges of the [British] Commonwealth, arranged alphabetically by country; information about each institution's history, facilities, courses, degrees, etc. is included; faculty are listed by department and in an index (v4) of personal names; 70th ed. (1994) [BF80].
*Répertoire international des médiévistes/International Directory of Medievalists,* 8th ed. (1995): alphabetical listing of 17,777 medievalists in 72 countries, with names, institutional addresses, fields of specialization, and indexes by country and discipline; prepared by the Fédération internationale des instituts d'études médiévales [F.I.D.E.M.]/International Federation of Institutes of Medieval Studies [BF81].
*The World of Learning* (1947–): annual, international listing, arranged alphabetically by country, of academies, learned societies, research institutes, libraries and archives, museums and art galleries, universities and colleges, and other institutions of higher education; 44th ed. (1994), with index of institutions on pp1991–2094 [BF82].

## (d) Historical Atlases (See [BA16] 314–18.)

*Historic Towns: Maps and Plans of Towns and Cities in the British Isles, with Historical Commentaries, from Earliest Times to 1800,* ed. M.D. Lobel and W.H. Johns (1969–) [BF83].
D. Matthew, *Atlas of Medieval Europe* (1983, r1989) [BF84].
*The National Trust Historical Atlas of Britain: Prehistoric and Medieval Britain* (1993) [BF85].
J.S.C. Riley-Smith, *The Atlas of the Crusades* (1990) [BF86].

## (e) Other Reference Works

J. Berlioz *et al., Identifier sources et citations,* L'atelier du médiéviste 1 (1994) [BF87].
W. Fitzgerald, *Ocelli Nominum: Names and Shelf Marks of Famous/Familiar Manuscripts* (1992) [BF88].
E.B. Fryde *et al., Handbook of British Chronology,* 3rd ed. (1986) [BF89].

O. Leistner and H. Becker, *Internationale Titelabkürzungen von Zeitschriften, Zeitungen, wichtigen Handbüchern, Wörterbüchern, Gesetzen, Institutionen usw/International Title Abbreviations of Periodicals, Newspapers, Important Handbooks, Dictionaries, Laws, Institutions etc.*, 5th ed., 2 vols. (1993) [**BF90**].

H. Lengenfelder, ed., *International Bibliography of Specialized Dictionaries/Fachworterbücher und Lexika: Ein internationales Verzeichnis*, 6th ed. (1979) [**BF91**].

O. Meyer and R. Klauser, *Clavis mediaevalis: Kleines Wörterbuch der Mittelalterforschung* (1962): explanations of technical terms encountered in medieval studies [**BF92**].

*Personennamen des Mittelalters: PMA: Ansetzungs- und Verweisungsformen gemäß den RAK* [= *Regelm für die alphabetische Katalogisierung*, Band 6], 2 vols. (1989) [**BF93**].

S.M. Schwertner, ed., *Internationales Abkürzungsverzeichnis für Theologie und Grenzgebiete: Zeitschriften, Serien, Lexika, Quellenwerke mit bibliographischen Angaben/International Glossary of Abbreviations for Theology and Related Subjects: Periodicals, Series, Encyclopaedias, Sources with Bibliographical Notes*, 2nd ed. (1992) [**BF94**].

E.P. Sheehy *et al.*, eds., *Guide to Reference Books*, 10th ed. (1986): annotated and indexed listing of reference works in the humanities, social and behavioral sciences, history and area studies (including the Middle Ages and Renaissance), and science, technology, and medicine, each subdivided by field; *Supplement to the Tenth Edition* (covering the period 1985–90) by R. Balay and E.P. Sheehy (1992) [**BF95**].

D.J. Shove and A. Fletcher, *Chronology of Eclipses and Comets, A.D. 1–1000* (1984, r1987) [**BF96**].

R.L. Storey, *Chronology of the Medieval World: 800–1491* (1973, r1994): continues H.E.L. Mellersh, *Chronology of the Ancient World, 10,000 B.C. to A.D. 799* (1976, r1994) [**BF97**].

*Ulrich's International Periodicals Directory*, 33rd ed., 5 vols. (1994–95) [**BF98**].

A.J. Walford *et al.*, eds., *Walford's Guide to Reference Material*, 5th rev. ed. (1989–91): 21,994 annotated entries in 3 vols.: *Science and Technology* (v1), *Social and Historical Sciences, Philosophy and Religion* (v2), and *Generalia, Language and Literature, the Arts* (v3); 6th ed. in progress (1993–) [**BF99**].

J.S. Wellington, *Dictionary of Bibliographic Abbreviations Found in the Scholarship of Classical Studies and Related Disciplines* (1983) [**BF100**].

• PRINCIPAL SERIES AND
COLLECTIONS OF LATIN TEXTS

Listed here is a selection of important series and collections (in one or more volumes) wherein are printed Latin texts from late antiquity and the Middle Ages. This list includes only a small number of the great repertories of national historical texts and documents and of sources for the history of the Church and the Crusades; these are best surveyed in [BA16], [BA29], and especially the *Repertorium fontium historiae medii aevi* (see [BC85]), VI: *Series collectionum* (Rome 1962) and supp. (with addenda and corrigenda to VI) (Rome 1977) [BG1]. The *Repertorium* lists and annotates (in Latin) some 1,250 important source collections of all kinds. Medieval Latin texts and documents are often published in series sponsored by official government bodies, academies and universities, religious orders and communities, and national, regional, and local historical and literary societies. Frequently such sources are printed in one or more volumes within larger series that include studies and editions of vernacular works and extend beyond the Middle Ages. Several well-known collections (e.g. *Acta Sanctorum, Analecta hymnica medii aevi, Corpus iuris canonici, Corpus iuris civilis*) are noted in individual chapters of this volume and are not mentioned here. The best list and index of the Latin texts and records published in collections or series by the numerous historical societies of England and Wales have been compiled by E.L.C. Mullins, *Texts and Calendars: An Analytical Guide to Serial Publications* (London 1958, r1978 with corrections) and *Texts and Calendars II: An Analytical Guide to Serial Publications 1957–1982* (1983) [BG2]. For the standard modern anthologies of Medieval Latin texts, most of which were designed for the classroom, see the bibliographies of chapters CA and GA.

L. D'Achéry (1609–85), *Veterum aliquot scriptorum qui in Galliae bibliothecis, maxime Benedictinorum, latuerant spicilegium,* 13 vols. (Paris 1655–77); 2nd ed. (with indices): *Spicilegium sive collectio veterum aliquot scriptorum qui in Galliae bibliothecis delituerant,* 3 vols. (Paris 1723, r1965): collection of miscellaneous texts—chronicles, sermons, charters, letters, etc. [BG3].

G. Alberigo *et al., Conciliorum oecumenicorum decreta,* 3rd ed. (Bologna 1973); ed. N.P. Tanner (with translation): *Decrees of the Ecumenical Councils,* 2 vols. (London/Washington 1990) [BG4]; see [DF50].

*Analecta Franciscana sive chronica aliaque varia documenta ad historiam Fratrum Minorum spectantia* (Quaracchi/Florence 1885–) [BG5].

*Auctores Britannici Medii Aevi* (London 1969–): sponsored by the British Academy [BG6].

*Auteurs latins du moyen âge* (*Collection A.L.M.A.*) (Paris 1981–): recent series of critical texts, with translations and annotations, sponsored by the Association Guillaume Budé and the Centre Lenain de Tillemont; under the direction of J. Fontaine and F. Dolbeau [BG7].

*Bannatyne Club:* Edinburgh historical society (1823–61) that sponsored the publication of 116 vols. (Edinburgh 1823–1867) concerned with the history of Scotland, including several medieval texts [BG8].

*Beiträge zur Geschichte der Philosophie des Mittelalters: Texte und Untersuchungen,* ed. C. Baeumker *et al.,* 26 vols. (Münster/W. 1891–1927); continued by *Beiträge zur Geschichte der Philosophie und Theologie des Mittelalters,* v27–43 (Münster/W. 1928–90); n.s. (Münster/W. 1970–) [BG9].

*Biblioteca della Società storica subalpina* (Pinerolo/Turin 1899–): includes editions, in two series, of cartularies, charters, statutes, and other archival documents from northwest Italy [BG10].

*Bibliotheca Franciscana ascetica medii aevi* (Quaracchi/Florence/Grottaferrata 1904–) [BG11].

*Bibliotheca Franciscana scholastica medii aevi* (Quaracchi/Florence/Grottaferrata 1903–) [BG12].

*Bibliotheca latina medii et recentioris aevi,* ed. C.F. Kumaniecki (Warsaw/Bratislava 1960–): sponsored by the Polish Academy of Sciences [BG13].

*Bibliotheca scriptorum Graecorum et Romanorum Teubneriana* (Leipzig 1849–): includes editions of several patristic and Medieval Latin writers; 11 vols. were also published (Leipzig 1875–1912) as part of the *Bibliotheca scriptorum medii aevi Teubneriana* [BG14].

*Bibliotheca scriptorum medii recentisque aevorum* (Budapest/Leipzig 1930–) [BG15].

*Bibliothèque des Écoles françaises d'Athènes et de Rome* (Paris 1877–): the second and third series (Paris 1883–/Paris 1899–) comprise editions of papal registers and letters of the thirteenth and fourteenth centuries [BG16].

*Bibliothèque des textes philosophiques* (Paris 1932–): includes editions of Medieval Latin works [BG17].

*Bibliothèque Thomiste* (Paris 1921–): includes editions of Thomistic and other scholastic texts [BG18].

*Cambridge Medieval Classics* (Cambridge/New York 1994–): a new series of editions, with facing-page English translations and annotations, of prose, poetic, and dramatic works in Latin and Greek from the period between A.D. 350 and 1350; v1: *Nine Medieval Latin Plays* [*Sponsus, Officium stelle, Tres filie, Tres clerici, Verses pascales de tres Maries, Versus de pelegrino, Danielis ludus, Ordo virtutum, Ludus de passione*], ed. and tr. P. Dronke [general editor of the series] (1994); v2: *Hugh Primas and the Archpoet,* ed. and tr. F. Adcock (1994); v3: *Johannes de Hauvilla, Architrenius,* ed. and tr. W. Wetherbee (1994) [BG19].

*Camden Society* [*CamSoc*] (London 1838–): founded in 1838, this society was merged in 1897 with the Royal Historical Society; editions of British historical and other sources, including texts in Medieval Latin, have been published: there are five Camden series: *Old Series* (1838–72), *New Series* (1872–1901), *Third Series* (1900–63), *Fourth Series* (1964–92), *Fifth Series* (1993–) [BG20].

*Canterbury and York Society* (London/Oxford 1907–): founded in 1904, this society sponsors editions of English episcopal registers and other records [BG21].

*Les classiques de l'histoire de France au moyen âge* [*CHFMA*] (Paris 1923–) [BG22].

*Collection de textes pour servir à l'étude et à l'enseignement de l'histoire,* 51 vols. (Paris 1886–1929) [BG23].

*Corpus Christianorum* (Turnhout 1953–), (1) *Series Latina [CCSL]* (1954–): critical editions of Christian Latin texts from Tertullian (d. 240) to Bede (d. 735), planned to comprise about 250 vols.; (2) *Continuatio Mediaevalis [CCCM]* (1966–): Latin texts from the eighth to the fifteenth century; (3) *Series Graeca* (1977–): critical editions chiefly of the post-Nicene Fathers, intended to complete [BG30]; (4) *Series Apocryphorum [CCSA]* (1983–): critical editions of the apocrypha of the New Testament. The *CCSL* and *CCCM* were initiated to provide a "new Migne" (see [BG51]). See also [BB8] and [BE30] [BG24].

*Corpus consuetudinum monasticarum,* ed. K. Hallinger *et al.* (Siegburg 1963–) [BG25].

*Corpus latinum commentariorum in Aristotelem graecorum* (Louvain/Paris 1957–) [BG26].

*Corpus philosophorum medii aevi:* includes (1) *Aristoteles Latinus,* ed. G. Lacombe, A. Birkenmajer, M. Dulong, E. Franceschini, L. Minio-Paluello, and G. Verbeke (Bruges/Paris/Rome 1939–); (2) *Plato Latinus,* ed. R. Klibansky *et al.* (London 1940–) [BG27].

*Corpus scriptorum de musica* (Rome 1950–): published by the American Institute of Musicology [BG28].

*Corpus Scriptorum Ecclesiasticorum Latinorum [CSEL]* (Vienna/Leipzig/Prague 1866–): critical editions of Latin texts from late antiquity; see R. Hanslik, *100 Jahre Corpus scriptorum ecclesiasticorum latinorum* (1964) [BG29]; corresponding collection of Greek texts: *Die griechischen christlichen Schriftsteller der ersten (drei) Jahrhunderte* (Leipzig/Berlin 1897–) [BG30].

E. Du Meril (1801–71), *Poésies populaires latines antérieures au douzième siècle* (Paris 1843, r1969) [BG31]; *id., Poésies populaires latines du moyen âge* (Paris 1847, r1969) [BG32]; *id., Poésies inédites du moyen âge, précédées d'une histoire de la fable ésopique* (Paris 1854, r1969) [BG33].

*Editiones Heidelbergenses: Heidelberger Ausgaben zur Geistes- und Kulturgeschichte des Abendlandes* (Heidelberg 1946–) [BG34].

*España sagrada,* 56 vols. (Madrid 1747–1879, 1918, 1957–61): basic repertory of sources for Spanish ecclesiastical history; initiated by E. Florez (1702–73) [BG35].

*Études de philosophie médiévale* (Paris 1922–): includes editions [BG36].

*Florilegium patristicum tam veteris quam medii aevi auctores complectens,* 44 vols. (Bonn 1904–41) [BG37].

*Fonti per la storia d'Italia [per il medio evo] (FSI)* (Rome 1887–) [BG38].

*Franciscan Institute Publications* (St. Bonaventure, NY): several series, including *Text Series* (1951–); *Works of St. Bonaventure* (1955–); *Opera philosophica et theologica Guillelmi de Ockham* (1967–); *Adam Wodeham Series* (1991–) [BG39].

M. Gerbert (1720–93), *Scriptores ecclesiastici de musica sacra potissimum,* 3 vols. (St. Blasien 1784, r1963); rev. M. Bernhard, *Clavis Gerberti: Eine Revision von Martin Gerberts Scriptores ecclesiastici de musica sacra potissimum (St. Blasien 1784)* (1989–), and continued by C.E.H. de Coussemaker, *Scriptorum de musica medii aevi nova series,* 4 vols. (Paris 1864–76, r1963); see also the series *Greek and Latin Music Theory* (Lincoln, NE 1984–) [BG40].

H. Hagen, *Carmina medii aevi maximam partem inedita ex bibliothecis Helveticis collecta* (Bern 1877, r1975?) [BG41].

*Henry Bradshaw Society [HBS]* (London 1891–): founded in 1890, this society sponsors editions of "rare liturgical texts" [BG42].

O. Lehmann-Brockhaus, *Schriftquellen zur Kunstgeschichte des 11. und 12. Jahrhun-*

derts für Deutschland, Lothringen und Italien, 2 vols. (Berlin 1938, r1971); id., *Lateinische Schriftquellen zur Kunst in England, Wales und Schottland, vom Jahre 901 bis zum Jahre 1307*, 5 vols. (Munich 1955–60) [**BG43**].

*Liturgiegeschichtliche Quellen* (Münster/W. 1918–): continued by *Liturgiegeschichtliche Quellen und Forschungen* (v23–31) and *Liturgiewissenschaftliche Quellen und Forschungen* (v32–) [**BG44**].

J. Mabillon (1632–1707), *Veterum analectorum tomus I [–IV] complectens varia fragmenta & epistolia scriptorum ecclesiasticorum, tam prosa, quam metro, hactenus inedita*, 4 vols. (Paris 1675–85); rev. ed.: *Vetera analecta sive collectio veterum aliquot operum & opusculorum omnis generis, carminum, epistolarum, diplomatum, epitaphiorum, & c.*, ed. L.F.J. de la Barre (Paris 1723, r1967) [**BG45**].

G.D. Mansi (1692–1769), ed., *Sacrorum conciliorum nova et amplissima collectio*, 31 vols. (Florence/Venice 1759–98): great general collection of conciliar texts (with other sources); rev. ed. with continuation, 54 vols. in 59 (1901–27, r1960–61) [**BG46**].

E. Martène (1654–1739) and U. Durand (1682–1771), *Thesaurus novus anecdotorum*, 5 vols. (Paris 1717, r1966): miscellaneous collection of sources (letters, chronicles, conciliar *acta*, theological treatises, etc.) [**BG47**]; id., *Veterum scriptorum et monumentorum historicorum, dogmaticorum, moralium amplissima collectio*, 9 vols. (Paris 1724–33, r1966) [**BG48**].

Matthias Flacius Illyricus (1520–75), *Varia doctorum piorumque virorum de corrupto ecclesiae statu poemata* (Basel 1557) [**BG49**].

*Medieval Classics/ [Nelson's] Medieval Texts/Oxford Medieval Texts:* modern editions of narrative and literary sources published first by Thomas Nelson and Sons Ltd. (London/Edinburgh 1949–) and then by Oxford University Press (Oxford 1967–); Latin text and English translation on facing pages [**BG50**].

J.-P. Migne (1800–75), *Patrologiae cursus completus sive bibliotheca universalis . . . omnium ss. patrum*, (1) *Patrologia Latina [PL]*, 222 vols. [the last volume is numbered "221," but there is a 185 bis] (Paris 1841–64); and (2) *Patrologia Graecolatina [PG]*, 167 vols. (Paris 1857–66): justly famous and indispensable collection of Christian texts, extending in the Latin series to the end of the pontificate of Innocent III (1216), and in the *PG* to the fifteenth. Marred by misprints and the inevitable use of old and inferior editions; for revisions see P. Glorieux, *Pour revaloriser Migne: Tables rectificatives* (1952). A subject index—*Elucidatio in 235 tabulas Patrologiae latinae, auctore Cartusiensi* (Rotterdam 1952)—helps in the use of Migne's valuable but complicated indices (*PL* 218–21). For an electronic edition of *PL* see [**BE40**]; for the *initia* of the texts in *PL* see [**BC110**]. A five-volume supplement to *PL*, vols. 1–96—*Patrologiae cursus completus. Series latina: Supplementum [PLS]* (Paris 1958–74), ed. A. Hamman—provides corrections for users of the original series as well as editions of additional patristic texts; indices in v5. There is an two-volume *Index locupletissimus* for *PG* by T. Hopfner (Paris 1928–45); for the initia see [**BC23**]. In [**BG1**] v1:421–29, 435–54 are alphabetical lists of the authors in both series [**BG51**]. On the indefatigable J.-P. Migne see H. Leclercq, *DACL* v11.1:941–57 [**BG52**], and R.H. Block, *God's Plagiarist: Being an Account of the Fabulous Industry and Irregular Commerce of the Abbé Migne* (1994) [**BG53**].

*Mittellateinische Studien und Texte*, ed. K. Langosch (Leiden/Cologne 1965–) [**BG54**].

*Monumenta Germaniae Historica [MGH]* (Hannover/Leipzig/Berlin, etc. 1826–): indispensable ongoing collection of critical texts, studies, and auxiliary works concerned with medieval Germany and the Frankish kingdom from A.D. 500 to 1500 and divided into several series; see [BG1] v1:466–79 and supp. (pp87–91) and [BA16] 220–23 for contents, and D. Knowles, *Great Historical Enterprises* (1963) 65–97, on the establishment and early history of the *MGH;* version of *MGH* on CD-ROM initiated in 1995 [BG55].

*Monumenta iuris canonici* [*MIC*], publications of the Vatican Library and the Institute of Medieval Canon Law at the University of California, Berkeley (New York/Vatican City 1965–), in three series: A (*Corpus glossatorum,* 1969–), B (*Corpus collectionum,* 1973–), C (*Subsidia,* 1965–) [BG56].

*Monumenta ordinis Fratrum Praedicatorum historica* (Louvain/Rome/Stuttgart 1896–) [BG57].

*Monumenta Poloniae historica:* (1) old series, 6 vols. (Lvov/Cracow 1864–93); (2) *series nova* (Cracow/Warsaw 1946–) [BG58].

L.A. Muratori (1672–1750), ed., *Rerum Italicarum scriptores ab anno aerae Christianae quingentesimo ad millesimum quingentesimum,* 25 pts. in 28 vols. (Milan 1723–51): fundamental collection of Italian medieval narrative sources; *Indices chronologici* by C. Cipolla and A. Manno (1885, r1977) [BG59].

J. Öberg, *Two Millennia of Poetry in Latin: An Anthology of Works of Cultural and Historic Interest,* 4 vols. (London 1987–), with text in Latin and English on facing pages: v1 (1987), *The Late Classical Period and the Early Middle Ages;* v2, *The High Middle Ages;* v3, *The Italian Renaissance;* v4, *The Modern Age* [BG60].

*Opuscula et textus historiam Ecclesiae eiusque vitam atque doctrinam illustrantia:* (1) *series liturgica,* ed. R. Strapper and A. Rücker, 9 vols. (Münster/W. 1933–40); (2) *series scholastica* [*et mystica*], ed. M. Grabmann *et al.* (Münster/W. 1926–) [BG61].

*Orbis Romanus: Biblioteca di testi medievali a cura dell'Università cattolica del Sacro Cuore* (Milan 1933–) [BG62].

*Les philosophes belges: Textes et études,* 15 vols. (Louvain 1901–41); *Philosophes médiévaux* (Louvain 1948–) [BG63].

J.-B. Pitra (1812–89), *Spicilegium Solesmense complectens sanctorum patrum scriptorumque ecclesiasticorum anecdota hactenus opera, selecta e graecis orientalibusque et latinis codicibus,* 4 vols. (Paris 1852–58), with continuations: *Analecta sacra Spicilegio Solesmensi parata,* 8 vols. (Paris 1876–91), and *Analecta novissima Spicilegii Solesmensis altera continuatio,* 2 vols. (Paris 1885–88) [BG64].

*Publications in Mediaeval Studies:* sponsored by the University of Notre Dame (South Bend, IN) (Notre Dame/London 1936–) [BG65].

*Quellenschriften für Kunstgeschichte und Kunsttechnik des Mittelalters und der Renaissance* [*und die Neuzeit*] (Vienna 1871–) [BG66].

*Recueil des historiens des croisades* [*RHC*], 16 vols. (Paris 1841–1906, r1967), published by the Academie des Inscriptions et Belles-Lettres in five series, including *Historiens occidentaux* in 5 vols. (1844–95); a complimentary series, *Documents relatifs à l'histoire des croisades,* was initiated in 1946 [BG67].

*Recueil des historiens des Gaules et de la France/Rerum Gallicarum et Francicarum scriptores,* 24 vols. in 25 (Paris 1738–1904, r1965–67): fundamental collection of sources (chronicles, letters, *acta,* accounts, etc.) extending to the end of the Capetian period [BG68].

*Rerum Britannicarum medii aevi scriptores: Chronicles and Memorials of Great Britain and Ireland during the Middle Ages* [*RSer*]: official series of chiefly narrative sources—99 works in 253 vols. (London 1858–96, r1964)—published under the direction of the Master of the Rolls (hence "Rolls Series"); see David Knowles, [BG55] 101–34 [BG69].

*Rerum ecclesiasticarum documenta. Series maior: Fontes* (Rome 1956–): editions of liturgical texts, including the *Corpus antiphonalium officii,* ed. R.-J. Hesbert and R. Prévost, 6 vols. (1963–79) [**BG70**].

*Scriptores Latini Hiberniae* (Dublin 1955–): editions with facing-page English translations, published under the direction of the Dublin Institute for Advanced Studies [**BG71**].

*Selden Society* [*SelSoc*] (London 1888–): society founded in 1887 to promote the study of the history of English law and to publish legal sources [**BG72**].

*Sources chrétiennes* [*SChr*] (Paris 1941–): critical editions of Latin, Greek, and other works, with facing-page French translations [**BG73**].

*Sources d'histoire médiévale* (Paris 1965–): published by the Institut de recherche et d'histoire des textes of the Centre National de la Recherche Scientifique [**BG74**].

*Stromata patristica et mediaevalia,* ed. C. Mohrmann and J. Quasten, 5 vols. (Utrecht/Antwerp 1950–56) [**BG75**].

*Studies and Texts* (Toronto 1955–): published by the Pontifical Institute of Mediaeval Studies [**BG76**].

*Studi e testi* (Rome/Vatican City 1900–): a series of the Biblioteca Apostolica Vaticana; the first 99 vols. are indexed in v100 (1942, r1973), and v101–99 in v200 (1959) [**BG77**].

*Textes philosophiques du moyen âge* (Paris 1955–) [**BG78**].

*Thesaurus mundi: Bibliotheca scriptorum latinorum mediae et recentioris aetatis* (Zurich/Lugano/Padua 1950–) [**BG79**].

*Toronto Medieval Latin Texts* [*TMLT*] (Toronto 1972–): series of inexpensive, annotated texts, each usually based on one manuscript only, published for the Centre for Medieval Studies by the Pontifical Institute of Mediaeval Studies; General Editor: A.G. Rigg [**BG80**].

*Vite dei santi,* ed. C. Mohrmann, 4 vols. (Milan 1974–89): editions with Italian translations; v1, *Vita di Antonio,* ed. G.J.M. Bartelink, 4th ed. (1987); v2, *La Storia Lausiaca,* ed. G.J.M. Bartelink (1974); v3, *Vita di Cipriano, Vita di Ambrogio, Vita di Agostino,* ed. A.A.R. Bastiaensen, 3rd ed. (1989); v4, *Vita di Martino, Vita di Ilarione, In Memoria di Paola,* ed. A.A.R. Bastiaensen and J.W. Smit (1975) [**BG81**]. These editions are also part of the series *Scrittori greci e latini,* which includes the related volume, *Atti e passioni dei martiri,* ed. A.A.R. Bastiaensen *et al.* (Milan 1987, r1990) [**BG82**].

# BH • PERIODICALS

Extensive lists of journals that focus on the Middle Ages or whose scope includes *medievalia* are regularly part of issues of the *International Medieval Bibliography* [*IMB*] (see [BA25] and [BE38]) and *Medioevo Latino* [*MEL*] (see [BA30]); items numbered [BA26], [BA29], and [BA33] in this guide also provide lists of serials. New periodicals include the following: *Antiquité tardive/Late Antiquity* (Paris 1993–) [BH1]; *Bibliographie annuelle du moyen-âge tardif* (Paris 1991–) [BH2]; *Early Medieval Europe* (Harlow, Essex 1992–) [BH3]; *Exemplaria* (Binghamton, NY 1989–) [BH4]; *The Haskins Society Journal* (London 1989–) [BH5]; *Medieval Philosophy & Theology* (Notre Dame, IN 1991–94 [vols. 1–4]; New York 1996– [vols. 5–]) [BH6]; *Mediaevistik: Internationale Zeitschrift für interdisziplinäre Mittelalterforschung* (Frankfurt am Main/NY 1988–) [BH7]; *Revista d'historia medieval* (Valencia 1990–) [BH8]; and *The Journal of Medieval Latin: A Publication of the North American Association of Medieval Latin* [*JMLat*] (Turnhout 1991–) [BH9], the only periodical, apart from *Mittellateinisches Jahrbuch* [*MLJ*] (Cologne 1964–) [BH10], devoted entirely to Medieval Latin.

# PART TWO

# C · MEDIEVAL LATIN PHILOLOGY

## CA · INTRODUCTION

BY A.G. RIGG

What do we mean by Medieval Latin? How does it differ from Classical Latin and Vulgar Latin? How did the dialect of a small area of Italy come to be the principal medium for intellectual discourse for nearly 1,500 years? What does it mean that the language almost universally used for writing was not one normally used for speaking? When did Medieval Latin come to an end, and why?

The citizens of ancient Rome spoke the dialect of the region of Latium in central Italy. As the city's power increased, its language spread, first throughout Italy and then into the conquered and colonized areas of Gaul (on both sides of the Alps) and Spain. The colonists—soldiers, farmers, and administrators—did not speak with the Ciceronian clarity and elegance familiar to students of pure "Golden Age" Latin; they spoke demotic (that is, people's) Latin. The extent of the linguistic split between the literary language and its spoken form is uncertain; the difference may have been no more than that between the English of a high court judge and that of a laborer, or even between an individual's formal and informal styles. This demotic language, for which there is testimony in inscriptions, is known as Vulgar Latin. It was the ancestor of the vernacular Romance languages—Italian, French, Spanish, Portuguese, Catalan, Provençal, Romanian, and others—but it is not what we mean by Medieval Latin. Formal Latin, conservative in its grammar and usages, was taught in schools (which preserved it from change) and was also used for writing; it is what we mean when we refer to Classical Latin. The gap between Vulgar Latin (whose development properly belongs to the study of Romance philology) and Classical Latin widened, until the latter seems to have been no more than the written form of the spoken language: a citizen of Seville might speak an early form of "Spanish" but record his words in Latin, although the spelling of the latter would bear little relation to the spoken form. Something like this has happened to English: our spelling system is based, in part, on pronunciations that have not been used since the fourteenth century (when the *kn* in *knife* and the *gh* in *right* and *through* actually represented sounds).

It was from the formal Classical Latin that Medieval Latin emerged. The literary language, unlike Vulgar Latin, was preserved from most of the ordinary changes that contribute to linguistic change, mainly because the basis of teaching was an established literary heritage of texts and authorities. It was codified in written grammars, was preserved in the texts of ancient authors such as Cicero and Virgil, was the language of record, and was taught in schools. It was the kind of Latin at which Charlemagne's reforms aimed, and was also the Latin that spread into non-Romance-speaking countries like Ireland, England, Germany, and Scandinavia. In theory, this kind of Latin, since it was taught from books, was immune to change; in practice, there were some changes, which are surveyed in this book.

The success of Latin as an almost universal language of Western Europe until the end of the Middle Ages was due to several factors and took place in several stages. When the Roman Empire officially adopted Christianity, its language—Latin—automatically became the official language of the Church. As missionaries spread the new faith throughout Europe, into both Romance and non-Romance countries, they took Latin with them, in the form of ritual, service books, manuals of pastoral care, and of course the Bible. The official status of Latin was enhanced as papal authority increased, and with it the ecclesiastical bureaucracy. Moreover, the educational system was geared to Latin. In ancient Rome itself, the formal teaching of Latin (particularly forensic oratory) was the basis of all education, and this practice was extended throughout the Empire. To be a citizen of the Roman Empire, or at least to participate in its administration, meant learning Latin. With Christianity, the educational system passed into the hands of the clergy, who ensured that literacy effectively meant Latin. Although *cleric* and *clerk* now designate different people, they were at one time the same word.

When society felt the need to record legal transactions (such as property transfers) in writing, it turned to the clergy to inscribe them. Normally, the clergy chose Latin for the purpose. In Anglo-Saxon England, some documents are in Old English, and after the Norman Conquest (when English was relegated to third position) French was often used. Usually, however, Latin was the language of record: it had been the preeminent instrument of thought and expression since antiquity and could exploit the phrasing of the Roman legal tradition. Especially, it had an established grammar and orthography, standards the vernaculars lacked until the sixteenth century or even later. Formal teaching in English grammar is, for example, a relatively recent development. This is why English changed considerably between 700 and 1400 and why the author of *Beowulf* would have found even Chaucer's English totally incomprehensible.

The use of Latin for the writing of history, philosophy, and treatises about the natural sciences is hardly surprising, since the authors of such texts continued a tradition from ancient Rome. Modern readers are sometimes surprised by the use of Latin for belles lettres, particularly poetry, and especially lyric poetry; we have, since the nineteenth century, been accustomed to look for "sincerity" and a "personal voice," and it seems strange that medieval writers should try to "express themselves" in a language they learned only at school. This is our misunderstanding: medieval authors sought to weave a texture of allusions (from religious or secular sources) and for this purpose Latin had an immensely long tradition, something that the vernaculars entirely lacked. We have more reason to be surprised at the use of Latin for technology—weaving, shipbuilding, architecture, farming, coining, handicrafts, etc.—since, clearly, medieval laborers, tradesmen, and artisans did not talk Latin in the field or workshop. In fact, the manifestations of technological Latin are mainly to be found in legal contexts or educational ones (that is, the Latin of technology is a product of the record clerk or the schoolteacher, not the practitioner).

Until the fourteenth century (at the earliest) the vernacular languages were held in very low esteem. Modern linguists now recognize that Black American and African dialects are distinct forms of English, with coherent morphological and syntactic structures. Nevertheless, at least at the moment, it is unlikely that they will be used to draft legal documents or to express theoretical ideas in science, economics, or politics: the standard forms of American or British English have the prestige of antiquity and the virtue of stability, just as Latin had in the Middle Ages. The high status of Latin and the low status of the vernacular go hand in hand, and reinforce each other. As the laity could not (until the rise of a middle class) read at all, let alone write, it hardly mattered that texts and documents were written in a language they could not understand. This caused a systematic exclusion of the non-literate, non-Latin classes: the clergy controlled communications and legal transactions. It also led to snobbery: one fifteenth-century writer (no doubt an English speaker) referred to English as the language of the plowman. Anyone with any pretensions to education and literacy throughout the Middle Ages was, almost by definition, nearly bilingual in Latin and his or her own vernacular, although no one spoke Latin as a native tongue.

## The Nature of Medieval Latin

Medieval Latin, then, was the descendant of Classical Latin, the formal branch of the language of ancient Rome. As such, it was very conservative; as is mentioned elsewhere in this volume, Cicero himself would have been able to read most Medieval Latin with little difficulty, once he had accustomed himself to a few differences in spelling and some new vocabulary. The reason for this conservatism is that Latin was learned as a second language and its usage was inevitably referred to the authority of grammar books. Children learn their first language by ear and imitation; from the moment they begin to speak they quickly learn to generalize and to generate complex expressions, even from words they have heard only once. For example, they make plural nouns by adding /s/ or /z/, comparative adjectives by adding /er/, past tenses by adding /t/ or /d/ or /ed/; they produce compound tenses by using forms of the verb *be* and the present participle in -*ing* or by using forms of *shall* and *will*, and they negate by prefacing the verb with *do* or *did* and adding *not* to it. They learn all this from their parents or nurses and siblings, and later from companions; by age six they can probably form any sentence they need. At first they may generalize incorrectly, producing, for example, *fighted* (for *fought*), *brung* (for *brought*, by analogy with *sung*), *seed* (for *saw*), but the weight of custom quickly enables them to accommodate irregularities. In societies where there is no teaching of grammar (such as medieval England), analogy may overcome precedence; this is why we have *climbed* (Old English *clamb*), *wept* (OE *wēop*), *ships* (OE *scipu*), *brothers* (OE *brothru*).

Latin, however, was always learned from instruction, from teachers and texts (often with accompanying commentaries and glosses); there was no linguistic community that could agree on a newly generalized form. Thus Latin retained its five declensions of nouns, its four conjugations of verbs, and its three genders. Whereas French absorbed the neuter into the masculine (*hoc cor*, French *le coeur*), Medieval Latin retained the neuter. Whereas French developed a new future tense in -*rai*, Latin retained the -*bo*, -*am* patterns of Classical Latin. The grammar book was a constant point of reference, in the way that dictionaries are now used to perpetuate traditional spellings. The main grammar books—the *Ars minor* and *Ars maior* of Donatus and the *Institutiones grammaticae* of Priscian—were those that had been designed to describe Latin of the classical and late classical periods, and so perpetuated the usages of those eras.

Nevertheless, despite conservative teaching methods, there was change: if there had not been, there would have been no need for the present book. Even in the classical period there had been changes: the "freezing" of the language took place only with the grammars of the fourth and fifth centuries. Parasyllabic nouns of the third declension adopted accusatives -*em* and -*es* (for older -*im*, -*is*); the subjunctive came to be used with *cum* even when no causal relationship was implied; prepositions were used more and more to give precision to case endings; prepositional phrases (even redundant ones, like *abhinc*) continued to be formed; vocabulary increased either by suffixing (nouns in -*tio*, -*itas*, -*culum;* adjectives in -*bilis;* verbs in -*to*, etc.) or by borrowing, especially from Greek. The poet Horace accepted Greek borrowings, though he disliked hybrid formations (a prejudice which, for some reason, was applied by some grammarians to borrowings by English!). Medieval Latin would become particularly tolerant of Graecisms, neologisms, and words taken from vernacular languages; there was no standard authority against which to check the status of a word, and so there was no lexical purism or hostility to innovations.

Such changes—analogical extension, suffixing, adoption of foreign words—are endemic to all living languages. The usual causes include careless pronunciation (which results in the loss or weakening of inflections or other unstressed syllables, as in *Wednesday*), overuse of words (which results in the constant need for reemphasis, as in words denoting excess, like *much, very, terribly*), and, paradoxically, a desire for greater precision (which led to the development in English of compound tenses).

As Medieval Latin was not a living language in the ordinary sense, the changes which it suffered were of a different type, though they have some parallels in the vernacular languages. It changed because it was being used constantly for new purposes in an ever-changing world.

1. The effect of Christianity was both early and almost universal and cannot be overstated; through this the vocabulary and syntax of an originally Hebrew and Greek Bible penetrated ordinary Latin. For the cleric or monk, the greatest exposure to Latin came in the daily rituals of Christianity, and by this route the idioms and phrases of the Vulgate Bible became part of the ordinary language (for example, the use of *quod, quoniam,* and *quia,* all meaning "that," to introduce indirect speech). The administration and rituals of the Church required a new and specialized vocabulary; at first, care was taken to avoid the pagan connotations of Roman religion, but later *pontifex* came to be an acceptable term for bishop. Some words need particular care: *frater* may mean "brother" (sibling), "brother-monk," or (later) "friar."

2. Speculation about the nature of divinity was not a Roman habit, so Christianity had to develop terms like *trinitas, persona,* etc. Similarly, Romans were not given much to philosophical abstraction (beyond moral platitudes), and, through the rediscovery of Aristotle, a new vocabulary and (occasionally) syntax began to appear. Other abstract sciences—physics, astronomy, astrology, alchemy, mathematics—owed much of their vocabulary (indeed, their very names) to Greek or Arabic. In some scientific and philosophical treatises, especially translations, the syntax was sometimes influenced by the original language.

3. The Middle Ages were technologically very inventive; they bequeathed us the clock and new techniques in agriculture, shipbuilding, weaponry, weaving, dyeing,

architecture, etc. When terminology in these areas was needed—usually for the purpose of making an inventory or will—a Latin-trained clerk would need an appropriate word; few clerks were classicists and most were too busy to seek out a word from an ancient source; they would instead simply latinize the word the workmen themselves used.

4.  Workaday Latin was also needed to record legal transactions and court depositions. Standard transactions, like wills and land transfers, had their own well-established formulae, and scribes could hardly go wrong. When there was some narrative, however, as in a witness's report, the clerk had to write consecutive prose and sometimes became confused; it is in such cases that we find misuse of inflections.

5.  The topic of ungrammatical Latin raises a related issue. In some parts of pre-Carolingian Europe, notably Merovingian Gaul, the old educational system had completely collapsed but the habit of using Latin for documents had not died out. In such areas the Latin can only be described as barbaric. This type of Latin can hardly be called a language, as it is no longer a system with agreed rules.

Languages can occur in several forms. There is a "common language" understandable by all members of the linguistic community—the language in which, say, a judge, a biochemist, and a teenager communicate with each other. In Medieval Latin this would correspond to the general Christianized Classical Latin mentioned in (1) above. Then there are the specialized languages in which, say, biochemist talks to biochemist; these correspond to the special kinds of latinity that arose from the needs of (2) and (3) above. There are also other varieties of language within the common language, namely chronological and regional dialects. Chronologically, English is divided, for convenience, into Old English, Middle English, Early Modern English, and Present Day English. Geographically, English can be subdivided almost infinitely: within the British Isles (evident in pronunciation, vocabulary, morphology, and syntax) there are Scottish, Northern, Welsh, cockney (London), and Western; outside Britain there are American, South African, West Indian, Australian, and many others.

In Medieval Latin, however, chronological and regional developments were always subject to arrest and reform according to traditional grammar. Charlemagne's educational reforms arrested the decline of latinity in many parts of Europe, and the eventual rise of humanism removed even the biblically sanctioned deviations from Classical Latin syntax, substituting classical authority. Two features of orthography, *e* for both *ae* and *oe* (and occasional back-spellings of *ae* for *e*), and *ci* for *ti* after a vowel, were widely prevalent from about 1100 to 1450, but eventually even these yielded to humanist respelling. Sometimes a Latin spelling may reflect a chronological development in the corresponding vernacular: in Middle English, after about 1100, a double consonant came to indicate a preceding short vowel (since a double consonant caused a preceding long vowel to shorten); in the late fourteenth century *er* was lowered to *ar* in some words (accounting for *parson* beside *person*); both these spellings occasionally occur in contemporary Latin. Nevertheless, they are aberrations, and most scribes tend to spell in the traditional way.

Similarly, spellings occasionally represent local pronunciations. For Classical Latin *ignis,* southern France and Italy sometimes have *inis,* but northern France and England have *ingnis;* in neither case, however, are such spellings universal, even within their areas. Obviously, when a word is borrowed into Latin from a vernacular, it will normally be from the vernacular spoken by the author or scribe (except, perhaps, for sailing and trading terms, which would have a wider currency).

Regional (and for that matter chronological) developments are hard to discern in syntax or phrasing, though many attempts have been made to find the vernacular "substratum" of an author's latinity. Generally, one needs an accumulation of evidence; *ad* meaning "at," *habeo* used to form the perfect tense, *volo* used to indicate futurity, and *eo* ("go") plus infinitive to indicate intention, might together indicate an English author, but each alone would be insufficient evidence. What does emerge, however, is that the historian of Medieval Latin as a language needs to be aware of parallel developments in the vernacular languages, in pronunciation, spelling, syntax, and vocabulary.

In summary, the only form of Medieval Latin that could be called "common," in the sense of an agreed language of communication amongst all users of the Middle Ages, is the Latin described by the early grammarians with an admixture of Christian features (in vocabulary and syntax). Otherwise, there are simply local, specialized, or individual variations.

Medieval Latin did not "end"; it was gradually replaced by what we call Humanistic Latin or "Neo-Latin" (see ch. CH). Under the influence of such writers as Lorenzo Valla (d. 1457), the old bases of linguistic authority were changed from the fourth-century grammarians and Christian Latin to the ancient classical authors, especially Cicero. Naturally, individual idiosyncrasies of spelling, syntax, and morphology were eradicated, and such standard features of Medieval Latin as *e* for Classical Latin *ae* and *oe*, or *ci* for *ti*, disappeared. The arrival of Neo-Latin can be detected in spellings such as *aemulus* and *ratio*, but mainly by the absence of constructions such as *dixit quod, dixit quia, dixit quoniam*. The lexicon was gradually purified to include only words used by classical authors, except that in Church Latin and in scientific and technological Latin there was (and still is) some latitude. In verse, rhyme was eschewed by the humanists, but it survived for a long time in monumental inscriptions.

The pace at which this happened varied from country to country. In England the humanist movement began in earnest with the arrival of Italian scholars at the beginning of the reign of Henry VI (1422–61, 1470–71). Interestingly, the *Life of Henry V* (1413–22) by Tito Livio Frulovisi, written with classical spellings, was retranslated back into Medieval Latin by one of its scribes! The pronunciation of Latin, however, was not reformed until the end of the nineteenth century, and this reform took two directions. Schools and universities adopted the "restored" Classical Latin pronunciation; the Roman Catholic Church and its educational institutions adopted an Italianate pronunciation, whose dissemination was especially promoted by Pope Pius X (1903–14).

## Select Bibliography

### Vulgar Latin

C. Battisti, *Avviamento allo studio del latino volgare* (1949) [CA1].
G. Calboli, ed., *Latin vulgaire—latin tardif. II: Actes du IIème colloque international*

*sur le latin vulgaire et tardif, Bologne, 29 août–2 septembre 1988* (1990); see also the acts of the first colloquium in [CA7] [CA2].

M.C. Díaz y Díaz, *Antologia del latín vulgar*, 2nd ed. (1962) [CA3].

C.H. Grandgent, *An Introduction to Vulgar Latin* (1907, r1962): with app. of texts [CA4].

R.A. Haadsma and J. Nuchelmans, *Précis de latin vulgaire*, 2nd ed. (1966): with app. of texts [CA5].

J. Herman, *Le latin vulgaire*, 2nd ed. (1970) [CA6].

J. Herman, ed., *Latin vulgaire, latin tardif: Actes du Ier colloque internationale sur le latin vulgaire et tardif, Pecs, 2–5 semptembre 1985* (1987) [CA7].

J.B. Hofmann, *Lateinische Umgangssprache*, 3rd ed. (1951, r1978) [CA8].

H.F. Muller, *A Chronology of Vulgar Latin* (1929, r1970) [CA9].

H.F. Muller and P. Taylor, *A Chrestomathy of Vulgar Latin* (1932, r1990) [CA10].

L.R. Palmer, *The Latin Language*, 2nd ed. (1961, r1988): see ch. 6, "Vulgar Latin" [CA11].

V. Pisani, *Testi latini arcaici e volgari, con commento glottologico*, 2nd ed. (1960) [CA12].

V. Väänänen, *Introduction au latin vulgaire*, 3rd ed. (1981): with app. of texts [CA13].

## Introductions to Late Latin, Christian Latin, and Medieval Latin

A. Blaise, *Manuel du latin chrétien* (1955, r1986); tr. G.C. Roti: *A Handbook of Christian Latin: Style, Morphology, and Syntax* (1992) [CA14].

V. Blanco García, *Latín medieval: Introducción a su estudio y antología* (1944) [CA15].

R.A. Browne, *British Latin Selections A.D. 500–1400* (1954): anthology with long philological introduction (ppxiii–lxi) [CA16].

G. Caliò, *Il latino cristiano* (1965) [CA17].

G. Cremaschi, *Guida allo studio del latino medievale* (1959) [CA18].

A. De Prisco, *Il latino tardoantico e altomedievale* (1991) [CA19].

J. Fontaine, "Latinité tardive et médiévale: Mutations et renaissances du Ve au XVe siècle," in *Rome et nous: Manuel d'initiation à la littérature et à la civilisation latines: 18 études*, ed. G. Serbat (1977) 255–64 [CA20].

O. García de la Fuente, *Introducción al latín bíblico y cristiano* (1990) [CA21].

F. Kerlouégan *et al.*, *Initiation au système de la langue latine: Du latin classique aux langues romanes, Ier siècle avant J.C.–VIII siècle après J.C.* (1975) [CA22].

K. Langosch, *Lateinisches Mittelalter: Einleitung in Sprache und Literatur*, 3rd ed. (1975) [CA23].

L. Leone, *Latinità cristiana: Introduzione allo studio della latinità cristiano* (1978) [CA24].

E. Löfstedt, *LL* (1959) [CA25].

V. Loi, *Origini e caratteristiche della latinità cristiana* (1978) [CA26].

M.R.P. McGuire, "The Origin, Development, and Character of Christian Latin," and "The Origin, Development, and Character of Mediaeval Latin," in *Teaching Latin in the Modern World*, ed. id. (1960) 37–68, 118–40 [CA27].

M.R.P. McGuire and H. Dressler, *Introduction to Medieval Latin: A Syllabus and Bibliographical Guide*, 2nd ed. (1977); see [BA26] [CA28].

D. Norberg, *MPLM* [CA29].

H.P.V. Nunn, *An Introduction to Ecclesiastical Latin*, 3rd ed. (1951, r1963) [CA30].

A. Önnerfors, ed., *MP* (see [CC18]) [CA31].

V. Paladini and M. De Marco, *Lingua e letteratura mediolatina,* 2nd ed. (1980) [ca32].

G. Pepe, *Introduzione allo studio del medioevo latino,* 4th ed. (1969) [ca33].

K. Strecker, *Einführung in das Mittellatein,* 3rd ed. (1939); tr. R.B. Palmer, *Introduction to Medieval Latin* (1957, r1976): the only guide to Medieval Latin available in English, with many additions by the translator to Strecker's bibliographical entries; French translation by P. Van de Woestijne, *Introduction à l'étude du latin médiéval,* 3rd ed. rev. (1948) [ca34].

L. Traube, *Einleitung in die lateinische Philologie des Mittelalters,* ed. P. Lehmann, *Vorlesungun und Abhandlungen von Ludwig Traube,* v2 (1911, r1965) [ca35].

Other studies, both introductory and focusing on various aspects and problems of Vulgar and Postclassical Latin, are listed in [ca19] 231–49 [ca36].

## Theories of the Substrate

J.R. Craddock, *Latin Legacy versus Substratum Residue: The Unstressed "Derivational" Suffixes in the Romance Vernaculars of the Western Mediterranean* (1969), ch. 1: "The Substratum Theory and the Mediterranean Hypothesis: A Summary of Their Origin and Growth" (pp18–47) [ca37].

E. Löfstedt, *LL,* pp51–58: discusses the difficulty of establishing a substrate in German and Scandinavian Latin [ca38].

C. Mohrmann, *Het Middeleeuws Latijn als Substraat van westeuropese Cultuur* (1956) [ca39].

E. Vandvik, "National Admixture in Medieval Latin," in *SO* 23 (1944) 81–101: tries to demonstrate vernacular Scandinavian influence in Medieval Latin documents; some of the examples are doubtful [ca40].

CB   •   # ORTHOGRAPHY AND PRONUNCIATION

BY A.G. RIGG

## Orthography

In comparison with medieval vernacular languages, the spelling of Medieval Latin was relatively stable and conservative. Divergences from Classical Latin practice cause few problems, once the main points are understood.

Until the seventeenth and eighteenth centuries the letter forms *i/j* and *u/v* were not used, as now, to distinguish vowels and consonants: *u* was normal for both the vowel /u/ and the consonant /v/; *v*, if used at all, is in initial place for both /u/ and /v/, e.g. *vnde*. Two *u*'s are sometimes written as a *w*, as in *wlt* (= *uult* [*vult*]). Similarly, *j* is simply a positional variant of *i* (which may be both the vowel and the consonant): it is sometimes used initially (*juuenis* = *iuvenis*) and as the second element of *ii* (*filij* = *filii; vij* = *vii* [seven]).

Some phonetic changes were almost universal across Europe and were reflected in the orthography. Classical Latin *ae* (*æ*) and *oe* (*œ*) appear regularly as *e* after c. 1100, sometimes with an intermediate stage of *e*-cedilla or "hooked" *e* (*ę*), in which the hook is a vestigial *a*, e.g. *letus* = *laetus, puelle* = *puellae, celum* = *coelum*. Before a vowel, *-ti-* is usually spelled *-ci-*, e.g. *racio* = *ratio*, except after *s* and *x*, e.g. *mixtio*. Often Classical Latin *y* appears as *i*, e.g. *lira* = *lyra*.

Other common spelling oddities (by classical standards) reflect local pronunciations and traditions. Single consonants for double ones, especially in Italian-Latin, are frequent (*asumpti* = *assumpti*), and vice versa (*stillus* = *stilus* = *stylus*). In England, following Middle English practice, a double consonant may indicate a preceding short vowel, e.g. *commitor* = *comitor*. In French-Latin, *x* sometimes appears for *s* (*melox* = *melos*), and vice versa (*iusta* = *iuxta*). Loss of initial *h-* is common (*ac* = *hac, abet* = *habet*), and *h* is added where it is not present in Classical Latin (*honus* = *onus, hostium* = *ostium*), sometimes to indicate diaeresis (*trahicio* = *traicio*). Confusion in pretonic and posttonic vowels is common (*discendo* = *descendo, sepero* = *separo*), though scribes are usually careful with inflected endings. In languages in which *m* was a plosive, it is sometimes followed by *p* before another consonant (thus *ympnus* = *hymnus, yemps* = *hiems, dampnum* = damnum). Pronunciation of *-gn-* varied and the spellings reflected this; thus *ignis* appears as *innis* in an Italian manuscript, but as *ingnis* in English ones.

In many countries, especially the Romance-speaking ones and England, *c* before *e* or *i* was assibilated to /s/, and this is frequently reflected in spellings, e.g. *cessio = sessio, cilicium = silicium; sc* was similarly assibilated, giving rise to such spellings as *silicet* (= *scilicet*), *sedula/cedula* (= *schedula*). One also finds *z* for *di* in words like *zabulus* (= *diabolus*) and *zeta* (= *dieta = diaeta*). The unvoicing of final -*d* is seen in many common forms: *haut* (= *haud*), *set* (= *sed*), and *nequit* (= *nequid*, and conversely *nequid = nequit*). In some languages, especially Spanish, there was little or no distinction between /v/ and /b/, with a resulting confusion in spelling between, for example, the perfect and future tenses (-*auit* [= -*avit*] and -*abit*).

There was also sometimes a tendency to interchange *ph* and *f* (*fisis = physis, phisiculare = fissiculare*), and before a back vowel (*a, o, u*) *c* often appears as *ch* or *k*, e.g. *charus = carus*, either after the model of French *charité* (charity) or by assimilation to Greek *charis* (hence *karissimi*). As *ct* was often simplified to *t*, we see *autor* (= *auctor*) and conversely *arctus* (= *artus*). Similar simplification accounts for *st* and *xt* for *xst* (*esto/exto = exsto*), and vice versa. We also commonly find *qu* for *quu* (*equs = equus*, which may also = *aequus*).

Some spelling variations arise from lexical associations or confusions. Thus *redditus* "income" (from *reddere*) is often spelled *reditus* (as if from *redire* and in our sense of "return on capital"). The spelling *actor* for *auctor* suggests a role for an author that is not simply that of "amplifier." The place-name element *Jer-* is often spelled *Hiero-* by association with the Greek prefix for "holy." The *Ih-* in *Ihesus* (*Jhesus*), however, arises from the spelling of *Jesus* in Greek capital letters (ΙΗΣΟΥΣ). Proper names are naturally liable to variation, e.g. *Hadrianus/Adrianus,* and biblical names usually appear in the form used in the Vulgate, e.g. *Dalida, Nabugodonosor, Salamon* for Delilah, Nebuchadnezzar, Solomon. Variants of classical names include *Jubiter* (= Juppiter), *Adriane* (= Ariadne), *Occianus* (= Oceanus).

## Pronunciation

In 1528 Erasmus lamented that the divergence of Latin pronunciations across Europe was so wide that this once universal language was no longer mutually intelligible among nations. This situation points back to a growing divergence in pronunciations throughout the Middle Ages. The reconstruction of these pronunciations is difficult, and we can never be sure of more than a set of broad phonemic contrasts. We can be sure only that two common pronunciations are inappropriate: that of Classical Latin, and the practice outlined for ecclesiastical Latin in the *Liber usualis* of 1896.

The principal division is between those countries whose native languages were derived from Latin (Italy, Spain, Portugal, France) and the Germanic countries (Germany, Austria, England, and the Flemish area of the Netherlands). In the former, the Romance countries, there was a strong tendency to regard Latin as merely the "correct" formal spelling of the vernacular (just as we accept the spelling "night," despite its phonetic irrelevance); in this case the spelling would not be the basis for pronunciation. This has been argued for Spain before the reforms of Charlemagne in the late eighth century, but a series of French-Latin puns, first published in 1583, suggests that much the same was true for later France. Against this view, however, is the fact that from the fourth to the fourteenth century Latin verse was composed according to classical rules, which required the observation of long and short vowels and the articulation of all syllables; a knowledge of classical or quasi-classical pronunciation was necessary for the scansion of verse. We must accept that in schools, after the Carolingian reforms, more careful pronunciation must have been taught, running alongside a more informal style in spoken and sung Latin.

In Germanic countries, there was no question of perceiving Latin as the formal equivalent of the vernacular, and pronunciation was probably learned letter by letter. Much would depend, therefore, on the perception of the value of the letter, just as in modern English *i* may be perceived as the sound in "pin" or in "pine," or *gh* may be understood as it is pronounced in "tough" or in "through." In the Middle Ages, an English speaker would perceive *g* before a front vowel (e.g. *gero*) as /j/ or /dʒ/ (as in "judge"), but a German would see /g/ (as in "good"). An English speaker would see *gn* as /ŋgn/ (and perhaps spell it accordingly), a French speaker as /ɲ/ (as in "bunion"), and an Italian as /n/. An English speaker would see an /s/ in *bestia*, but a French speaker would, after French loss of *s* between *e* and *t* (as in *bête*), ignore it. Perceptions would also vary according to date, and thus, in England, lengthening in open syllables would mean that before 1200 the first *e* of *bene* would be short, but long after 1200. (A further puzzle in the pronunciation of Anglo-Latin is that from the Norman Conquest to the later fourteenth century instruction in school was frequently given in French, with the result that Latin may have been given a French flavor, though of course we do not know the quality of the French accents employed in the task. It is quite likely that Anglo-Latin /s/ for *c* and /dʒ/ for *g* before front vowels was the result of French influence.)

It would be impossible here to provide a chart of the value of all Latin vowels and consonants for the whole of Western Europe from the fourth to the fourteenth century. The reader is referred to the bibliography below. The types of evidence used in the reconstruction of pronunciation are as follows:

1. Disyllabic rhymes are very frequent in both quantitative and rhythmical verse from the eleventh century (see ch. CE) and are very useful for the pronunciation of consonants. They are less useful for vowels, as poets (often deliberately) rhymed long and short vowels.

2. Puns between Latin and English and French are found in the sixteenth and seventeenth centuries and can be used (with great caution) as evidence for earlier periods.

3. Loanwords from Latin in the vernacular reveal the way in which a Latin word was pronounced at the time of the borrowing, e.g. English *judicial* from *iudicialis*.

4. Frequent deviations from classical spelling, such as those listed above, provide good evidence; apparent spelling errors, unless mere slips of the pen, are also a good guide.

5. A knowledge of sound changes in the relevant vernaculars is useful. It is certain, for example, that the long vowels in fourteenth-century Anglo-Latin shared in the "Great Vowel Shift" of the fifteenth century, producing the sounds heard in modern legal Latin. Against this, one must always allow for the possibility of a reformed "classical" pronunciation.

6. Sixteenth- and seventeenth-century scholars frequently wrote about the pronunciation of Latin, often to criticize it. Their evidence can be used to reconstruct pronunciations of earlier times.

## Select Bibliography

W.S. Allen, *Vox Latina: A Guide to the Pronunciation of Classical Latin,* 2nd ed. rev. (1989): with an app. on the pronunciation of Latin in England [CB1].

M. Bonioli, *La pronuncia del latino nelle scuole dall'antichità al Rinascimento,* v1 (1962) [CB2].

F. Brittain, *Latin in Church: The History of Its Pronunciation,* rev. ed. (1955) [CB3].

H. Copeman, *Singing in Latin or Pronunciation Explor'd,* rev. ed. (1992): the only complete guide to most European countries [CB4].

G.H. Fowler, "Notes on the Pronunciation of Medieval Latin in England," in *History,* n.s., 22 (1937–38) 97–109 [CB5].

T.J. McGee, with A.G. Rigg and D.N. Klausner, eds., *Singing Early Music: The Pronunciation of European Languages in the Late Middle Ages and Renaissance* (1996): chapters by A.G. Rigg (Anglo-Latin) and H. Copeman (Latin in France, Italy, Spain, Portugal, Germany, and the Netherlands); a CD recording is provided with the book [CB6].

P.M. Ranum, *Méthode de la pronunciation latine dite vulgaire ou à la française: Petit méthode à l'usage des chanteurs et des récitants d'après le manuscrit de dom Jacques Le Clerc* (1991) [CB7].

V. Scherr, *Aufführrungspraxis Vokalmusik: Handbuch der lateinischen Aussprache: klassisch, italienisch, deutsch: mit ausführlicher Phonetik des italienischen* (1991) [CB8].

R. Wright, *LLER:* mainly on pre-Carolingian Spain, but the principles are important for all periods [CB9].

N.B.: The present writer's remarks on pronunciation in "Latin Language," in *DMA* 7:350–95 [CB10], are very general, based mainly on England and France; he has also changed his mind on some points, particularly *gn* and *qu.*

# CC  &#42;  MORPHOLOGY AND SYNTAX

BY A.G. RIGG

## Morphology

Spoken languages, especially when they are (as they were in the Middle Ages) unrestrained by the teaching of grammar, are prone to the influence of analogy in grammatical forms. The pressure of analogy is to replace unusual forms by common ones. In French, -*s* has been extended as a mark of plurality to nouns and adjectives, replacing the historically expected forms (e.g. *filiae bonae* > *filles bonnes*). In English, -*s* has been extended to most noun plurals, replacing earlier forms (e.g. Middle English *eyen*, present-day English *eyes*) to the extent that plurals with alien suffixes (*data, media, graffiti*) are often not recognized as plurals. In fairly recent times the past tenses *spake* and *bare* have been replaced by *spoke* and *bore* (with the *o* of the past participle). Analogical extension probably occurs when children are learning to generalize syntactic rules to the whole language.

The situation in Latin was quite different. The first thing to be learned (as students still know to their cost) is the inflections—the complex systems of noun, pronoun, and adjective declensions and of verb conjugations. There was no pressure to change the inflections (for example, to extend the first conjugation -*āre* system to other verbs, or to make all nouns conform to the second declension in -*us*). Any deviations from the learned pattern were seen as errors, as, for example, in a report of a Latin examination conducted by Odo Rigaldus (d. 1275), archbishop of Rouen, who castigated such inflectional errors as *inane* (vocative plural), *ferebatur* (active voice), and *ferturus* (future participle).

Individual writers, of course, occasionally forgot their grammar and produced forms that a teacher (then and now) would regard as errors. The fourteenth-century writer Richard Rolle (d. 1349) regularly writes *sentiui* (Classical Latin *sensi*) as though it followed the model of *audiui*. Mining documents (see ch. FK) treat *fodio, -ere* (mixed conjugation) first like a fourth conjugation verb (active infinitive *fodire*) and then like a second conjugation one (passive infinitive *foderi*). Aelfric's *Life of Athelwold*, written in 1006, has (ch. 16) *expulsit* (formed on *pulsus*, by analogy with *fulsit*) and (ch. 21) *poposcebat* (an amalgam of *poscebat* and *poposcerat*). New deponents (e.g. *monachor*, "be a monk") are sometimes found; conversely, some deponents are treated as passives, as in *Athelwold* (ch. 13): *ortamur ingredi*, "we are being encouraged to enter." Past participles of deponents are also often passive (as in Rather of Verona: *nactus, largitus*), following the Classical Latin precedence of *confessus*, "having been acknowledged." It is not unusual to see masculine dative singular *isto, illo* (Classical Latin *isti, illi*), feminine dative singular *une* (CL *uni*), masculine dative singular *toto* (CL *toti*), or -*e* for the ablative singular of parasyllabic nouns (CL -*i*). In one text of c. 1270, Classical Latin *verres,* third declension, has been reclassified as second declension ("*verri cum verris*"). Changes of gender also occur (*Carmina Burana* 145.5.3: *thymus,* CL *thymum*). Such forms should not be dismissed and emended by editors as though they were the result of slips by inattentive scribes: they are genuine, if ephemeral (and erroneous), linguistic phenomena. They are not, however, systemic: they do not enter a general morphology of Medieval Latin.

Sometimes suffixes were misunderstood and liable to reclassification. The neuter plural of the present participle (-*entia*) sometimes gave rise to a first declension feminine noun (*essentia,* "being"). Greek neuter nouns in -*ma* (genitive -*matis*) were sometimes treated as first declension feminines (accusative -*mam*). Many writers and scribes did not know enough Greek to recognize an accusative singular in -*ea,* a genitive singular in -*eos,* or a genitive plural in -*on* (which could easily be misunderstood as a neuter singular in -*ikon*). Compare the replacement in present-day English of the Italian plural *libretti* by the anglicized *librettos.*

In general, however, there is nothing in the inflectional system of Medieval Latin (apart from -*e* for Classical Latin *ae* and, conversely, *ae* for *e,* an accident of pronunciation) that would have disconcerted a Roman writer of the classical period.

The treatment of proper names not derived from Classical Latin varies, in names from the Bible and from the medieval vernacular languages. If a form can easily be assimilated to a Classical Latin pattern, it is: *Eva* and *Maria* are feminine first declension; *Salamon* is masculine third declension, like *Plato, -onis.* Some are indeclinable: *David, Nabugodonosor, Naboth.* Sometimes the form is unpredictable: *Adam* has a genitive *Adae* (*Ade*). Treatment of vernacular Germanic names is also unpredictable; sometimes they are provided with feminine -*a* and masculine -*us* terminations, assimilating them to the first and second declensions (*Atheldrida,* "Audrey"; *Alfredus,* "Alfred"), but they are often treated as indeclinable. Aelfric in his *Life of Athelwold* usually latinizes names, but the mother of King Edred (ch. 7) is *uenerabilis regina Eadgiuu.* Frankish names in -*o* (*Frodo, Dudo*) are treated like *Plato.*

The modern reader is sometimes faced with a dilemma in translating Medieval Latin surnames, especially in England after the Norman Conquest, when there were two vernaculars in use, English and French. For example, is *Johannes filius Stephani* "John Fitzstephen" or "John Stephenson"? Is *Stephanus* "Stephen" or "Etienne"? Is *Johannes Faber* "John Smith" or "Jean Le Fèvre"? Should Irish and Welsh patronymics, expressed in Latin by *filius* plus the genitive, be rendered in English by *O', Mac,* or *ap*? Modern practice varies.

The morphology of place names is even more arbitrary. Some are neuter (*Eboracum,* "York"); many are given feminine terminations in -*ia,* perhaps originally seen as an adjectival ending agreeing with *urbs* or *prouincia* understood (e.g. *Cantuaria,* "Canterbury"; *Abandonia,* "Abingdon"). Note the unusual locative *Parisius,* "at Paris." Adjectives derived from placenames are formed in -*ensis* (*Eboracensis,* "of York"). It is common to translate transparent elements: *Fons Clericorum,* "Clerkenwell."

## Syntax

In comparison with the development of the vernacular languages, Medieval Latin syntax shows relatively few changes from its classical ancestor. In the vernaculars, the widespread loss of inflectional endings caused massive dislocation and restructuring: the loss of case endings in both Romance languages and English caused dependence on prepositions and on a more fixed word order. In Latin, however, as noted above, the inflectional system remained intact and there was no internal pressure on the structure of the language. Such changes as there were came from two sources: tendencies already at work in Classical Latin and external forces, often in combination.

1. Already in Classical Latin the subjunctive was extended into all *cum* clauses, even simple temporal ones. In Medieval Latin it was sometimes extended into *dum* clauses, even when they mean "while," e.g. *Athelwold* (ch. 2): *felix eius genitrix, dum in utero eum haberet, huiuscemodi somnium . . . uidit.*

2. It is a short step from the Classical Latin use of the instrumental gerund (*fugiendo vincimus*) to the Medieval Latin gerund in the ablative of attendant circumstances, e.g. *ambulando loquebamur,* "we talked while walking," which becomes as common as the Classical Latin use of the present participle (*ambulantes loquebamur*). Some uses of the gerund and gerundive seem confused, e.g. Bede (d. 735), *Historia ecclesiastica* 3.13: *Tunc benedixi aquam, et astulam roboris praefati inmittens obtuli egro potandum* (one would expect *potandam* or *ad potandum*).

3. In Classical Latin the perfect passive is formed by *esse* and the past participle (*iussus est,* "he was ordered"); in Medieval Latin the verb *esse* sometimes regains its literal tense, so that *amata est* can mean "she is loved"; consequently, to form the past, past tenses of *esse* are needed (*amata erat/fuit*); this is a natural consequence of the adjectival nature of the past participle.

4. In Classical Latin the infinitive is a neuter indeclinable verbal noun (*hoc ridere meum,* "this laughter of mine"), but it is used only in the nominative or accusative cases. In Medieval Latin its nominal uses are extended; sometimes it is used after a preposition (*pro velle,* "in accordance with one's wish"; *pro posse,* "according to one's ability"); sometimes it is even found in the ablative (*meo videre,* "in my view"). In philosophy, as is well known, the infinitive *esse* is commonly used as a noun ("being"). In Classical Latin the infinitive of purpose is usually found only after verbs of motion, but in some medieval authors it is used more generally.

5. In Classical Latin the past participle is sometimes (though rarely) used predicatively after *habere: domitas habere libidines,* "to have one's desires tamed," i.e. "to have tamed one's desires." From this it is an easy step to the French *Je l'ai tué,* "I have killed him." English developed *I have killed him* in the same way, not from French influence but from the senses inherent in *have* and the past participle. When Medieval Latin uses such constructions (*habere* plus perfect participle to form a transitive perfect tense), it is probably in imitation of the vernacular rather than of the rare Classical Latin construction.

Most of the syntactic developments in Medieval Latin arise from the fact that all its users were, by birth, speakers of a vernacular language. While they might learn the inflections of Latin, their mental syntactic structures were English, French, German,

Italian, and so on. Thus they frequently expressed themselves in structures that reflected their native habits, even when using Latin words and inflections.

6. Classical Latin lacked definite and indefinite articles ("the," "a," "an"), though Greek had a definite article. Many medieval writers, accustomed to distinguishing between "man," "the man," and "a man" (French *le/la, un/une*), used forms of *ille* or *ipse* for the definite article and *quidam* for the indefinite; *ipse* is used to translate the Arabic definite article. The definite article usually points to something or someone already mentioned or known to the listener or reader, and so *predictus, prenominatus, memoratus* (all meaning "aforementioned") often mean little more than "the." In grammatical writings, forms of *hic* are used to indicate gender (*hic vir, hec puella, hoc verbum*); this may have been preferred to forms of *ille* as *hic* could be abbreviated to a single letter with a suprascript *i* or *o* or bar through the ascender.

7. Medieval Latin usage of the reflexives *se* and *suus* is often careless by classical standards, e.g. in the *Historia destructionis Troiae* (1287) of Guido delle Colonne: *Quem ut uidit rex, illari uultu suscepit et ab eo causam aduentus sui est gestis honorificis sciscitatus* (that is, the king asked Jason for the reason for Jason's arrival), and *Quem Medea tenui sono uocis furtiuis uerbis alloquitur ut veniente noctis umbraculo securus ad eam accedat* (that is, Medea invited Jason to visit her, not a third person). Another example is from *Flores historiarum* 2.85: *Ipsa die . . . tradidit Deus regem Scotiae Willelmum in manus suas* (that is, into the hands of Henry II, so that *suas* refers neither to God nor to William but to someone mentioned in the previous sentence). Uncertainty over *suus* may account for the frequent use of *proprius* in the same sense, e.g. *Aethelwold* (ch. 2): *quod [vexillum] inclinando se honorifice circundedit fimbriis propriis inpregnatam* ("the banner, bending itself down, respectfully surrounded the pregnant woman with its streamers").

8. In Classical Latin, reported statements (after verbs of saying, thinking, discovering, etc.) are usually expressed by the accusative and infinitive construction: *Dixi me abiturum esse* ("I said that I was going to leave"), *Comperiit Caesarem iam abisse* ("He discovered that Caesar had already left"). In Greek, such clauses are introduced by the particle/conjunction ὅτι, followed by a finite verb; in the Latin Vulgate Bible, this conjunction is rendered by *quod, quia,* or *quoniam,* e.g. *Act* 4:13: *comperto quod homines essent sine litteris; Act* 3:17: *scio quia per ignorantiam fecistis; Act* 3:22: *Moyses quidem dixit: Quoniam prophetam suscitabit vobis Dominus Deus vester.* This use of *quod, quia,* and *quoniam* to introduce indirect speech quickly spread in Medieval Latin. It was reinforced by the common Classical Latin use of *quod* to begin a noun clause ("the fact that . . .") and later by the influence of the vernacular languages: English introduces such clauses by *that* and French by *que* (itself derived from *quod*), thus increasing the tendency away from the accusative and infinitive construction. There was considerable doubt about whether to use the indicative or the subjunctive in such clauses; the quotations from the *Actus Apostolorum* cited above use both (*fecistis, suscitabit, essent*). Compare also Bede, *Historia ecclesiastica* 3.13: *antistes Acca solet referre quia . . . crebro eum (= Uilbrordum) audierit de mirandis . . . narrare,* but *ibid.* 3.14: *Scio . . . quia non multo tempore uicturus est rex.*

9. Even in Classical Latin, prepositions were being used to give specificity to overworked case endings: duration of time is sometimes expressed by *per* as well as by the simple accusative; specification was particularly necessary with the ablative, which had subsumed the cases of both separation and instrumentality, and *cum* is

sometimes used to indicate the instrument. This tendency continued in Medieval Latin: many medieval vernaculars had begun to lose their own case endings (notably English and French) and relied more heavily on prepositions. Some usages deserve comment: *ad* often means "at," e.g. Bede, *Historia ecclesiastica* 3.13: *quae ad reliquias eiusdem reuerentissimi regis . . . gesta fuerint* ("which had been done at the relics of this most reverent king"). Sometimes *ad* is used for the simple dative after verbs of speaking. The range of *de* is extended to include many functions of the genitive and of English "of" and French "de": *capellanus de Colston* ("a chaplain of Colston"), *Bartholomeus de Florentia;* a specifying genitive: *tentas de lardo* ("pledgets of lard"); two phrases in Bede's *Historia ecclesiastica* seem to understand *aliquid* (resembling French *de,* "some," though there can hardly be a connection): 3.13: *Habeo quidem de ligno, in quo caput eius . . . infixum est* ("Indeed I have some of the wood on which his head was fixed"); 3.15: *misit de oleo in pontum* ("he threw some oil in the sea"). *Iuxta* and *secundum* can both mean "according to (an author)." *Infra* often has the sense of *intra,* e.g. Geoffrey of Monmouth, *Historia Britonum* (ch. 18): *Brutus . . . naues munit, mulieres et paruulos infra eas iubet manere* ("Brutus . . . orders the women and children to stay inside them"). Prepositional phrases and compounds were common in Classical Latin, but their number increased greatly: e.g. *abinde,* "thereafter, from there" (cf. CL *abhinc, deinde*); *ab olim,* "from long ago"; *ad modicum,* "a little"; *ad tunc,* "then"; *ad statim,* "immediately"; *de facili,* "easily"; *de raro,* "rarely"; *ex tunc,* "from then"; *in brevi,* "briefly"; *in antea,* "before"; *per sic ut/quod,* "on condition that."

10. Verbs do not always govern the same cases as in Classical Latin: Isidore, *Etym.* 1.3.4, has *utor* and the accusative: *Hebraei viginti duo elementa litterarum . . . utuntur;* *iubeo* sometimes has the dative; *noceo, doceo,* and *impero* sometimes have the accusative. Impersonal verbs of feeling such as *pudet, penitet, piget,* etc., vary in the case of the person.

11. Conjunctions are much as in Classical Latin. *Licet* becomes very common for "although," introducing clauses (in the subjunctive) and modifying nouns, adjectives, and adverbs. To introduce purpose or final clauses (in addition to Classical Latin *ut* or *qui* and subjunctive) Medieval Latin uses *quatinus* and *quo* (which in Classical Latin required a comparative) and the subjunctive. *Quominus* is often used for "lest" (Classical Latin *ne*) for negative purpose and does not have to be introduced by a verb of preventing. *Quod,* "that" (for Classical Latin *ut*), is very commonly used to introduce result clauses after *sic, ita, in tantum,* etc.

12. Some auxiliary verbs extend their syntactic range. *Habeo* may be used to form the perfect tense (see no. 5 above) and also, as sometimes in Classical Latin, with infinitive to express "have to, be obliged to." In imitation of English "will," *volo* plus infinitive sometimes forms a future tense. *Valeo* is more common than in Classical Latin as an auxiliary equivalent to *possum,* "be able."

13. Some Medieval Latin writers were inexact in their use of tenses; this imprecision was encouraged in Germanic areas, since Germanic languages (e.g. Old English) used the past tense to cover the past, whether imperfect, perfect, or pluperfect. Two passages from the *Cnutonis gesta regis* (*Encomium Emmae*) illustrate this:

> 2.11: Tunc uictores sua leti uictoria, transacta iam nocte plus media, pernoctant quod supererat inter mortuorum cadauera. ("Then the victors . . . spend what remained of the night . . . .")

2.20: Ingressus monasteria et susceptus cum magna honorificencia, humiliter incedebat, et mira cum reuerentia, in terram defixus lumina, et ubertim fundens lacrimarum ut ita dicam flumina, tota intentione sanctorum expetiit suffragia. (". . . he was walking humbly and . . . sought the support of the saints.")

This imprecision is also seen in uses of the subjunctive: *Athelwold* (ch. 11): *nisi fouea eum susciperet, totus quassaretur* ("if the ditch had not caught him, he would have been entirely crushed"). In dependent clauses the moods and tenses often shift alarmingly, as in *Athelwold* (ch. 26):

En fateor plane quod non facile mihi occurrit scribere quanta uel qualia sanctus Athel-uuoldus *perpessus sit* pro monachis et cum monachis, et quam benignus *extitit* erga stu-diosos et oboedientes, aut quanta in structura monasterii *elaboraret*, . . . aut quam per-uigil *erat* in orationibus, et quam benigne *ortabatur* fratres ad confessionem.

14.   Sometimes we see a nominative absolute construction instead of the ex-pected ablative, e.g. *Gospel of Nicodemus* 16.3:

Tunc Annas et Cayfas sequestratos eos ab inuicem interrogantes singillatim, unanimiter ueritatem dixerunt uidisse se Iesum ascendentem in caelum. ("Then, Annas and Caiphas questioning them [the Jews] . . . , they [the Jews] said the truth, that they had seen Jesus ascending into heaven.")

Sometimes the ablative absolute is used inappropriately, as in these quotations from commentaries in two British Library manuscripts (Harley 1808 and Cotton Claudius D.VII):

Quo reuerso omnes aduersarios suos occidit et fugauit. ("When he [Ethelbert] had re-turned, he [Ethelbert] killed all his enemies . . . .")

Arthuro letaliter uulnerato, Constantino cognato suo filio Cadoris ducis Cornubie dyadema Britannie concessit. ("When Arthur had been fatally wounded, he [Arthur] gave the crown . . . to Constantine . . . .")

15.   The ablative absolute, with the noun element a *quod* clause ("the fact that . . ."), developed especially in bureaucratic Latin, so that *considerato quod . . .* means "the fact that . . . having been considered, considering the fact that . . ."; similarly, *dato quod* ("given that . . .") (see ch. DC). The verb *excipio* in Medieval Latin came to mean "to take out of consideration," particularly in the past participle, e.g. Bede, *Historia ecclesiastica* 3.17: *nil propriae possessionis, excepta ecclesia sua et adiacentibus agellis, habens* ("having no property of his own, except his church and the adjacent fields"); from this arose another quasi conjunction, *excepto quod,* "except for the fact that." Some other legal and semilegal expressions give rise to new English prepositions: *du-rante bello,* "while the war lasts, during the war"; *pendente lite,* "while the suit is in process, pending the (outcome of) the litigation."

16.   It is mainly in vocabulary that we see the specialized languages of professions, trades, and crafts, but there is one legal syntactic idiom of interest: *facit ad* is used to indicate the support given by a *quod* clause (subject of *facit*) to a proposition gov-erned by *ad: faciat ad predicta quod statim tangam in ultima responsione* ("let what I shall say immediately in the final reply give support to what has been said above"); *ad quod bene facit quod scribit Augustinus* ("this is fully supported by what Augustine writes").

Of the syntactic usages listed previously, some are natural developments of Classical Latin syntax; some seem to have been prompted or at least encouraged by vernacular usages. The latter form part of the "substratum theory," that Latin was modified according to the native language of the speaker or writer. Sometimes a substratum is fairly clear, but more often a Medieval Latin development can be seen to be endemic to Indo-European languages. The development of the definite article happens in such widely different languages as Classical Greek and late Old English. The perfect in *have* and the past participle arises independently in French and English and is also inchoate even in Classical Latin. The use of "prepositions" to clarify the function of case endings happened independently in English and French in response to the weakening of the endings, but was already at work in Classical Latin. Nearly every substrate idiom that has been proposed can be shown to have some antecedent in Classical Latin. For instance, *habeo* plus infinitive, "be obliged to," seems certain to arise from English "have to," but in fact has parallels in Classical Latin. Sometimes Latin texts that have been translated from other languages render their sources somewhat literally, but even here conclusions must be drawn carefully: in translations from Arabic, *ipse* is used to translate the Arabic definite article, but as *ipse* (along with *ille* and *iste*) was coming into use as a definite article in French and English Latin, an Arabic influence is not absolutely certain.

### Ungrammatical Latin

Although the forms and usages described above might distress a modern classicist, they are quite common—sometimes even the norm—for most Latin writings of the Middle Ages. The degree of classicism would depend merely on the extent to which a writer was familiar with, and eager to imitate, classical style. The medieval usages would not even be noticed by, let alone horrify, the normal educated medieval reader—any more than a modern American notices "Americanisms" in English. There are some texts, however, in which the rules of concord, case, tense, and mood are disregarded so completely that they can be described as almost grammarless. Often their information has simply been latinized by someone who knew some Latin—enough to give the impression that what the author wished to report was now encoded in the universal language, but not enough to satisfy normal linguistic criteria. Both care and flexibility are needed in the translation of such texts. They are valuable reminders that not everyone in the Middle Ages who could read and write was ipso facto a latinist: in some cases (as in pre-Carolingian Germany) the fault lay with community standards, but any age could produce a poor latinist; perhaps the clerk who failed the Latin examination mentioned above went on to write documents in this fashion.

### Summary

Medieval Latin was a synthetic language in an analytic world. In a synthetic language, the functions and relationship of words are indicated by inflections, and since Latin was always learned from teachers and books it retained its synthetic nature artificially. Nevertheless, in the Middle Ages it existed in a world of analytic languages, in which the meaning of a sentence is indicated primarily by word order rather than by inflections. As Latin was not just read and written but also spoken (in monaster-

ies and universities), its synthetic nature was constantly under pressure from its analytic users. Very slowly—unless checked—it began to imitate the linguistic structures of its speakers. In extreme reaction to this tendency, some writers, especially
schoolteachers, affected a very tortuous and elaborate style. On a different level, the
syntax of Latin (as the language of record) became rigid and formulaic, in order to
codify and perpetuate certain types of utterance, such as land transfers, letters of appointment, and the like: as in modern do-it-yourself forms for wills, all the user had
to do was to insert names and the other variables. (For this type of expression, see
chs. DC–DG).

Paradoxically, it was the rise of the vernaculars that led to the "classicization" of
Latin. As French, Italian, English, etc., became the normal languages of communication in government, law, religion, and science, and as literacy increased among lay
people, Latin retreated into the schoolroom. It became the object of scrutiny and
scholarship rather than a tool of normal communication; thus, free from the pressures to change, it was in a position to be "purified" by the humanists. As Medieval
Latin had never had a codified grammar, it was to the established standards of Classical Latin that the humanists returned. Although some medievalisms remained in
the writings of some humanists (see ch. CH), Latin style and syntax gradually began
to aim at the model of Cicero, and it is on the latinity of the late Roman Republic and
early Empire that modern grammars of Latin have been based.

## Select Bibliography

By "grammar," in the present context, we mean a book describing grammatical
forms (mainly inflections) and syntactical patterns or "rules"—books such as B.H.
Kennedy, *The Revised Latin Primer,* ed. and rev. J. Mountford (1962, r1976) [cc1], or
B.L. Gildersleeve and G. Lodge, *Gildersleeve's Latin Grammar,* 3rd ed. (1895; numerous reprintings) [cc2], or J.B. Greenough *et al., Allen and Greenough's New Latin
Grammar* (1888, r1983) [cc3]. In this sense of the word, no one has yet written a comprehensive grammar of Medieval Latin. In my opinion, no attempt to do so will be
made, or should be made—not because it would be extremely difficult, but because
it would give a shape to the idea of a single language, something that never existed.
A grammar implies a language that was shared by a definable community, but the
medieval "community" that used Latin was spread all across Europe and lasted for
over 1,000 years. The spoken and written forms of this community varied considerably, by date, region, and function. The only agreed common denominator was a
written standard, but any attempt to describe this "written standard" would at best
reflect the grammars of Donatus and Priscian from the fourth and sixth centuries
(see ch. DI), which themselves reflected the literary language of what we call "Classical Latin." Later deviations in morphology and syntax from this "standard"—between 500 and 1400—came from a variety of sources, from the idioms of the Vulgate
and Christian Latin (see ch. DA), from new forms of expression peculiar to specific
linguistic areas (administration, philosophy, theology, technology, science, etc.), but
above all from simple failure to observe the old rules. Such deviations were not mutually recognized, and so did not constitute a language, though a few specialist

philologists noted them. Generally speaking, if medieval writers of Latin had been so sensitive to language as to notice deviations from ancient grammar as described by Donatus and Priscian, they would not (like modern linguists) record them as new developments but would simply mark them as solecisms or blunders—unless, of course, they were biblical, and so above the rules of mortal grammarians.

Several books and studies purport to give a linguistic history of Medieval Latin. Some concentrate on developments in Vulgar Latin that led to the vernacular Romance languages (e.g. D. Norberg, *MPLM* [cc4]). This approach is perfectly legitimate, but does not address the ordinary Latin that arose from the learned tradition, e.g. the latinity of papal letters, Bernard of Clairvaux (d. 1153), Walter Map (d. 1209–10), and so on. The only successful enterprises in the description of Medieval Latin grammar are studies of the usage of specific authors or in limited collections of documents or texts from a particular period or region, e.g. P.L.D. Reid, *Tenth-Century Latinity: Rather of Verona* (1981) [cc5]. A small selection of similar studies is listed here, and the reader is also referred to the bibliographies on specific topics in this volume.

M.A. Adams, *The Latinity of the Letters of Saint Ambrose* (1927) [cc6].

J. Bastardas Perera, *Particularidades sintácticas del latín medieval (cartularios españoles de los siglos VIII al XI)* (1953) [cc7].

M. Bonnet, *Le latin de Grégoire de Tours* (1890, r1968) [cc8].

P.B. Corbett, *The Latin of the Regula Magistri, with Particular Reference to Its Colloquial Aspects* (1958) [cc9].

D.R. Druhan, *The Syntax of Bede's Historia ecclesiastica* (1938) [cc10].

G.H. Freed, *The Latinity of the Vitae Sancti Bonifatii Archiepiscopi Moguntini* (1926) [cc11].

H.J.E. Goelzer, *Étude lexicographique et grammaticale de la latinité de Saint Jérôme* (1884) [cc12].

M. Henshaw, *The Latinity of the Poems of Hrabanus Maurus* (1936) [cc13].

P. Hoonhout, *Het Latijn van Thomas van Celano, Biograf van Sint Franciscus* (1947) [cc14].

C.C. Mierow, "Medieval Latin Vocabulary, Usage, and Style: as Illustrated by the *Philobiblon* (1345) of Richard de Bury," in *CPh* 25 (1930) 343–57 [cc15].

L.B. Mitchell, *The Latinity of John de Trokelowe and of Henry of Blaneford* (1932) [cc16].

E.M. Newman, *The Latinity of the Works of Hrotsvit of Gandersheim* (1939) [cc17].

A. Önnerfors, ed., *MP:* reprinted studies, including O. Haag, "Die Latinität Fredegars" [1898], pp13–87; D. Norberg, "Die Entwicklung des Lateins in Italien von Gregor dem Großen bis Paulus Diaconus" [1958], pp88–105; U. Westerbergh, "Über die Sprache des Chronicon Salernitanum" [1956], pp106–91; E. Voigt, "Die Sprache im 'Ysengrimus' des Nivard von Gent" [1884] pp192–211; U. Kindermann, "Sprache und Stil in der 'Consolatio de morte amici' des Laurentius von Durham" [1969] pp231–241; F. Blatt, "Einleitung zu einen Wörterbuch über die Latinität Saxos" [1957] pp242–60; P. Klopsch, "Die Sprache des Pseudo-Ovidischen Gedichts 'De vetula'" [1967] pp261–82. Includes very useful, indexed bibliography (pp425–55, 456–62 [index]) of studies of medieval latinity by region, author, text [cc18]. For a recent bibliography of "Hibernian Latin" see T. Halton, "Early Christian Ireland's Contacts with the Mediterranean World to c. 650," in *Cristianesimo e specificità regionali nel Mediterraneo latino (sec.*

*IV–VI): XXII Incontro di studiosi dell'antichità cristiana, Roma, 6–8 maggio 1993*
(1994) 616–17 [cc19].

G.W. Regenos, *The Latinity of the Epistolae of Lupus of Ferrières* (1936) [cc20].

L.F. Sas, *The Noun Declension System in Merovingian Latin* (1937) [cc21].

P. Taylor, *The Latinity of the Liber historiae Francorum* (1924) [cc22].

J. Vielliard, *Le latin des diplômes royaux et chartes privées de l'époque mérovingienne*
(1927) [cc23].

Many other such studies have been published in the series *Latinitas Christiano-rum Primaeva: Studia ad sermonem Latinum Christianum pertinentia* (Nijmegen 1932–) [cc24], and in The Catholic University of America's *Patristic Studies* (Washington 1922–), e.g. [cc6] [cc25], and its *Studies in Medieval and Renaissance Latin Language and Literature* (Washington 1933–), e.g. [cc10] [cc26].

# CD • VOCABULARY, WORD FORMATION, AND LEXICOGRAPHY

## BY RICHARD SHARPE

The word hoard of Medieval Latin has never been effectively compassed in a dictionary. The reasons for this are various. First among them is the geographical spread of Latin, as a spoken and written language in the Romance language area, as a second language where the first language had no Latin basis, and as a strictly learned language used as an international medium. Another reason is the readiness of Medieval Latin to admit new words or to readmit words fallen from use, to change the meaning of words, and to form new words from Latin building blocks. This openness extended to words from the first languages of those who used Latin as a second language, whether that was Irish or Finnish or Hungarian. The way in which Latin was used allowed for new formations or loans to be created almost at will, giving a very wide range of words between those permanently part of the word hoard and mere nonce words. Third, Latin has a very long history, and throughout the Middle Ages the texts of earlier generations were read and studied; taste could lead at one period to novelty and experiment in the use of words, and at another to a preference for the vocabulary of older and more respected authors. Fourth, the medieval use of Latin for a thousand years, through so much of Europe and for all literate purposes, produced a vast body of texts, preserving examples of all the richness and variety of the language. This would not in itself be an obstacle to the making of a comprehensive dictionary, if the language itself were not so fluid and versatile; but because of its openness to new word formations within Latin and new borrowings from outside, Medieval Latin requires that the compilers of dictionaries go through texts of all types, on all subjects, from all areas and all periods. It is not surprising, therefore, that a comprehensive dictionary has eluded us. Almost none of the modern dictionaries covers the whole alphabet, but for basic purposes it is possible to get by with a good dictionary of Classical Latin [CD17–19] and a selective dictionary of Medieval Latin [CD22]. Some skill is involved in getting the best out of any dictionary.

The classical language has a limited word hoard—the vocabulary used by approved authors over a period of less than 300 years, from Lucretius to the younger Pliny. From the end of the classical period very many words not used by classical authors are seen in the works of a wide range of authors. Some of these usages can be found in preclassical writers such as Plautus, but they were avoided by those authors preserved as the classical canon. Thus *delicia* or *facetia* are used in the singular by

Plautus and by Aulus Gellius, but in the classical period both words are used only in the plural form; medieval usage commonly retained the plural *deliciae,* but *facetia* became normal. In Late Latin, therefore, one aspect of the changing word hoard is the use in polite literature of colloquialisms, avoided by the best authors for several generations but always there in ordinary use. The formation of new words by the productive use of prefixes and suffixes had probably been going on in ordinary Latin through the classical period, but it becomes visible only at the point when the literary language shakes off the formal constraints of classical taste. The eleventh-century manuscript of Tacitus's *Annales* offers a single example of *exspectabilis* (*Ann.* 16.21), where editors, no doubt correctly, prefer *spectabilis;* the word is not otherwise recorded before Tertullian, and the prosthetic *e-* (perceived as *ex-*) before *s* + consonant is a vulgarism in Late Latin (cf. French *école* < *sc(h)ola*), introduced into the text of Tacitus only by a later copyist.

From the fifth century to the eighth century in the area where Latin was normally spoken, Late Latin was highly productive of new words. Phonetic changes were also under way, part of the process that led to a diversity of Romance languages, and some of these are evident in written Latin. Again, the invasion of the Roman world by Germanic peoples brought new institutions and new words for them, borrowed from the different Germanic vernaculars. Common words such as *feuum* (only later *feodum*), *uadium, warniso,* and *werra* entered the Latin word hoard in this period.

Within one or two generations around the end of the eighth century and the beginning of the ninth, Latin came to be perceived as different from the Romance vernaculars; as the spoken languages established their own orthography to reflect their different forms and sounds, so the boundaries of Latin became firmer [CD42–43]. During the ninth, tenth, and eleventh centuries, new formations and loanwords are less conspicuous as a feature of the ordinary language, though a new avenue was opened for literary borrowings, often from Greek, to emphasize the learned character of Latin as distinct from the vernacular languages derived from Latin. From the end of the eleventh century, gradually, a change becomes apparent in the language. Latin was used by a widening range of writers for a widening range of purposes, so that more registers of Latin writing become visible in the twelfth century. By the thirteenth century this is very marked.

It is possible to detect a different attitude to word formation and the borrowing of words in the different registers. To pick out only three examples, one may say that stylish prose—papal and episcopal letters, for example—continues the habits of the best twelfth-century writers, drawing on ancient and patristic authors for their vocabulary. Academic prose has become linguistically more mundane, but the Schoolmen produced countless new latinate words and usages to meet their new needs. So, for example, *ens,* "a being," has the appearance of being the present participle of Classical Latin *sum, esse,* but it was always used as a noun; this in turn was made more abstract by the addition of *-itas,* Medieval Latin *entitas,* "the quality that makes a being a being." And as Classical Latin *qualitas* derived from *qualis,* so Medieval Latin *quidditas* was derived from *quid.* The increasing use of the written word for everyday needs in the thirteenth century meant that more and more Latin was written by clerks of very limited education, who relied much more heavily on the vernacular and especially on the close relationship between French and Latin.

In previous centuries deeds had often been written by such people, but deeds by their nature made limited demands on vocabulary. The writing of domestic and agricultural accounts or the recording of proceedings in the courts demanded a very wide vocabulary, and this produced a heavy traffic in new formations. This is very conspicuous in England from about 1200. Some of these new words can very easily be described as loanwords, from English, for example, into Latin. But in thirteenth-century England, French, and more specifically Anglo-French, was the first language of many clerks, and the formation of Latin words from French cannot always be seen strictly as a loan. The connection between Latin and French was sufficiently perspicuous that many writers could find the correct Latin stem in the French word and add a Latin suffix to it. So, for example, Late Latin *cambium, excambium* (that same prosthetic *e-*), gave Old French *cange, change, escange, eschange,* "exchange, change"; from the eleventh century on we find the word latinized as *cangium, changia* [sic], *escangium, excangium, scangium;* and alongside these forms, the knowledge of the Latin stem *camb-* reasserts itself, *escambium, eschambium, exchambium, scambium,* and similar forms. The form *eschambium* is essentially Medieval Latin *excambium* influenced by French, *escangium* is Latin formed from French, and *excangium* is the latter influenced again by Latin. In this last form, the writer knows that where French words begin *esc-* or *esch-* Latin has *ex-*, but he does not recall the more correct Latin *excambium.*

All of this sets a demanding agenda for the lexicographer, but before going on to consider how the task has been handled, I propose briefly to consider how dictionaries themselves developed in the Middle Ages [CD44–48].

Dictionaries as we know them were invented in medieval Europe, but they have their origin in two separate traditions that go back to the ancient world. Glossaries, explaining the meaning of difficult words as they occurred in texts, were compiled for Latin speakers learning to read Greek texts; and for both languages specialist glossaries of medical terms and such like were in circulation. Glossaries of this kind fall out of use in the sixth century. The second tradition was the aspect of grammar that sought to understand the inner meaning of words from their etymology and by this means to relate words derived (or thought to be derived) from the same origin. A third tradition, not directly connected but often overlapping with that of lexicography, produced encyclopedias. In the early Middle Ages the most important was the *Etymologiae* of Isidore of Seville, which was written in the 630s and came to be very widely distributed. Isidore actually devoted the whole of bk. 10 to a dictionary organized etymologically in the grammatical tradition.

In the early Middle Ages, glossaries served an elementary need for people learning to use Latin. In those parts of Europe where Vulgar Latin continued to be spoken, schools were concerned to teach correct Latin grammar, but in the British Isles and Germany teaching had to begin at a more elementary level. A teacher might gloss a text, writing the meaning of difficult words between the lines, and the most elementary glossaries are no more than collections of such glosses—individual words from the text together with the gloss, copied out in order as they occur in the text so that the glossary could be used by another reader. Such "batch glosses" [CD1] soon led to glossaries arranged according to their initial letter, words beginning with *A, B,* and so on, in the order of the alphabet. Between the seventh and the thirteenth centuries glossaries evolved very slowly towards full alphabetical order [CD2].

The tenth-century Latin–Latin/English glossary in British Library MS Harley 3376 [CD3] illustrates several aspects of how glossaries developed. Words are mostly arranged by the first three letters, *ere-, eri-, eru-, erp-,* but not in full alphabetical order, and some words are out of sequence: *erga* and *ergenna* are 30 entries apart. Some of these keywords are in the inflected forms as they occurred in the texts from which the glosses were extracted, as *erugine .i. rubigine.* Others are entered under the form chosen to illustrate the inflection of the word—nominative singular, present infinitive, or whatever. This form is termed the lemma, and *erigor* stands as the lemma for all the inflected forms of the word which together make up the lexeme or unit of vocabulary. The glosses, in both Latin and English, sometimes translate the word specifically as appropriate to the context from which it has been taken and sometimes in a wider, more general way, but there is no attempt to show the range of different meanings of a word. Some of these glosses are derived from batch glossaries on individual texts, some from earlier more general glossaries, but there is no system.

The first fully recognizable dictionary was compiled in Italy before 1050, Papias's *Elementarium doctrinae rudimentum* [CD4]. He sets out his principles very precisely in a long preface. His alphabetical order is based on the first three letters, though he is aware that spelling could be inconsistent, as between *hyena* and *iena.* He adds some important new features. First, he recognizes that the lemma cannot always indicate the grammatical status of a lexeme, so he adds an indication of gender, declension, or conjugation; he also proposes to mark long vowels in cases where this is not obvious. He is also the first to mention authors or texts as the authorities from which words are taken. Papias's book proved very successful, and more than a hundred manuscript copies survive.

The grammatical tradition, on the other hand, was concerned to show that a particular root could produce a verb, an agent noun, a verbal noun, participles used as adjectives, and so on; with prefixes its meaning could be changed in a variety of ways. This principle of *deriuatio* was pushed beyond obvious connections to associate words of similar form and meaning but with no philological connection: scientific etymology is a nineteenth-century development. The earliest example of a treatise on *deriuationes* was put together by Osbern Pinnock, a monk of Gloucester, in the mid-twelfth century [CD5]. It is much less easy to use than Papias, but it aspires to understand the basis of meaning by showing the etymological relationship between different lexemes. These are grouped in paragraphs hung on primary words; these paragraphs are arranged in no particular order except as essays on each letter of the alphabet. For each letter there is an exotically phrased preface, a series of *deriuationes,* and then *repetitiones,* lists of words and meanings with very little attempt at alphabetical order. Two features of Osbern's work are significant in the progress of lexicography. He replaced Papias's symbols for gender, declension, etc., with a system based on the termination of inflected forms; so, for example, the first and second conjugation verbs *dico, -are* and *dico, -ere* are given as "dico, cas" and "dico, cis." More importantly, he includes quotations from authorities to illustrate the use or meaning of words, and his reading was influenced by the desire to make his collection as full as possible. Thus he quotes Plautus several hundred times as evidence for preclassical Latin words that were no longer in active use; he is the first medieval author to show any familiarity with Plautus, and his interest lay in using him as a quarry for rare words [CD6].

Osbern's work is known from about thirty medieval copies, including an early one from Dore Abbey, now in Hereford Cathedral Library, MS P.v.5 (twelfth/thirteenth century), which was annotated in the early thirteenth century by a reader,

John of Bath; the work lent itself to expansion. Indeed, before the end of the twelfth century Hugutio of Pisa had merged some of the methods of Papias and Osbern into a new dictionary [CD7]. It is perhaps surprising that Hugutio did not take over the *ABC*-order of Papias but used only a rudimentary *A*-order, and added further difficulty by incorporating additional words out of sequence. In spite of these drawbacks Hugutio's work proved very successful, and some two hundred manuscript copies are known today. To overcome difficulties in consulting the work, Petrus de Alingio and others in the thirteenth century compiled alphabetical finding lists sometimes copied with Hugutio. In due course a complete revision of the work was produced in 1286, the *Catholicon* of Ioannes Balbus Ianuensis (John of Genoa), which used full alphabetical order [CD9]. Although manuscript copies of this are not as common as those of Hugutio, the *Catholicon* served as the basis for future work and was the first Latin dictionary to be printed, at Mainz in 1459/60, perhaps by Gutenberg.

The works of Papias, Osbern, Hugutio, and John of Genoa were not intended for readers in the first stages of learning Latin. They were treatises on the language which could be used for reference by intermediate students. Archbishop John Pecham, for example, in 1284 ordered that copies of Papias and Hugutio be provided at Merton College in Oxford so that the scholars could extend their Latin vocabulary (*RSer* 67.3:813). He also required a copy of William Brito's more advanced *Expositiones difficiliorum uerborum,* compiled in the 1260s, which uses the dictionaries and a wide range of classical, patristic, and modern authorities to explain some 2,500 words from the Latin Bible [CD10].

For the elementary learner a different sort of guide was necessary, and in the twelfth and thirteenth centuries we see a wide distribution of textbooks used for elementary purposes [CD11]. Among these there stand out a few that were designed to introduce a broad range of vocabulary, organized by subject but presented as continuous prose. Such works, written by Adam of Balsham, Alexander Neckam, and John of Garland, served as pegs for glosses explaining the Latin words in the vernacular. They provided students and clerks with a great deal of everyday Latin vocabulary (see ch. DL). Towards the end of the Middle Ages simple vocabulary lists, often organized by subject, seem to have become more popular as the elementary aids in acquiring a sufficient knowledge of Latin vocabulary for these purposes [CD12]. Lexical aids, whether continuous text with gloss or simple glossaries, stand far apart from the medieval lexicographical tradition. They can also be a snare for the modern lexicographer, because words often pass from glossary to glossary without ever appearing in ordinary use. Latham's *Word-List* [CD34] stigmatizes such forms with a double dagger. We should not assume that students really learned all the wide vocabulary offered in such works.

The sixteenth and seventeenth centuries saw great changes in the status of Latin. Medieval Latin came to be despised as "rusty" (*rubiginosus*), and the dictionaries, from Ambrogio Calepino onwards, were intended to help users of Latin write "better" Latin. The truly medieval element was left to the antiquaries [CD13–14]. The dictionary which dominated the field in Medieval Latin for two hundred and fifty years was compiled by a learned French aristocrat, Charles Du Fresne, Sieur Du Cange (1610–88) [CD15–16], whose work was closely associated with the Benedictine historical scholars at Saint-Germain, Dom Jean Mabillon and his colleagues and successors. Du Cange was primarily concerned with medieval society and institutions; though he used the form of a dictionary rather than an encyclopedia, his interests were historical rather than linguistic. Thus the entries for *annus* and *moneta* are in fact essays on chronology and numismatics. Even by the standards of the seventeenth century, his work was very weak on the philological side, but his reading was voluminous and the usefulness of the result was the basis of its success. He himself published a revised and augmented text, and in the eighteenth century one of Mabillon's successors, Dom Pierre Carpentier, produced a four-volume supplement to the six volumes of Du Cange's glossary. In the nineteenth century the glossary and supplement were merged to produce the dictionary most familar to modern medievalists as "Du Cange." By then lexicography was developing into a much more rigorous discipline; by the time Du Cange was last reset in the 1880s it was clearly obsolete, but the task of replacing it with a modern dictionary of Medieval Latin was too daunting even for that age of enterprise.

Two features of modern lexicography, which advanced greatly in the nineteenth century, were etymology—establishing by philological methods the origins of words—and historical semantics—the classification of senses in a way that illustrates the changing meanings of a word and its extension into new senses. Modern methods also require that a good dictionary be based on a systematic reading of the texts that provide its linguistic foundation. This may be achieved by sampling rather than by comprehensive excerpting, but, before relying on any dictionary, the user needs to know on what range of texts it is founded.

The foundations of the modern dictionaries were laid in the 1920s; decisions taken then have determined the shape of our reference books even today. Proposals for a new Medieval Latin dictionary had been made in the 1880s [CD49–51], but it was only in 1920 that a scheme was adopted for a collaborative project involving the national academies of the countries of Europe. It evolved as a three-tier project: each country should produce a dictionary based on its national sources; overarching these there should be a single dictionary for the period of greatest unity in Medieval Latin usage, a period which was eventually agreed as A.D. 800 to 1200; for the more technical branches of knowledge there should be specialist dictionaries. Different countries set to work with little coordination, so that now we have a range of national dictionaries based on quite different principles [CD25–41]. The Italian dictionary, very restricted in scale, focused only on the earlier Middle Ages; the German dictionary, though based on an extensive body of sources, excluded texts from the end of the thirteenth century. And naturally, progress was better where the task was smaller. The only national dictionaries that have reached completion even now are those based on sources from Finland and Croatia, both small-scale tasks. Of the larger-scale projects, the furthest advanced are those of Poland and the Netherlands. The German dictionary is far behind, and there are no dictionaries even in progress that attempt to survey the Latin vocabulary of medieval France, Italy, or Spain. Only the British dictionary attempts to cover the whole of the Middle Ages, from Late Latin authors such as Gildas and Aldhelm to the humanists in the late fifteenth and early sixteenth centuries. It is fortunate that the French language was so important in medieval England, because the British dictionary is the best available source for the interaction between Latin and the Romance vernaculars in the later Middle Ages. The supranational dictionary, *Novum glossarium mediae latinitatis* [CD24], began publication in 1957 with a draft of the letter *L;* and work has now proceeded as far as the letter *P.* Among all the available dictionaries, it is still very difficult to get an overview for words that do not begin with a letter near the start of the alphabet. For words towards the end of the alphabet there is almost nothing available, more than seventy years after the commencement of the project.

To get the best out of dictionaries, the user must be reasonably well acquainted with the way they are put together. The first need is to decide which dictionary will best serve one's purposes. For reading a text written in Germany before the end of the thirteenth century or in medieval England, obviously the national dictionary will answer any questions about the meaning of words, providing full illustration so that one can form a sense of the semantic range of the word. For words too late in the alphabet, then the classical dictionaries and a dictionary such as *Niermeyer* [CD22] may serve. For other purposes, it may be more appropriate to consider the examples quoted in all the national dictionaries, looking for whether a word is in universal use or is peculiar to a particular area. The user needs enough linguistic knowledge to recognize where a different national dictionary will be useless or where it may be better to go to the dictionary of the underlying vernacular language. For words towards the end of the alphabet, there are few dictionaries available, and the answering of complex semantic questions will depend on going directly to the primary sources.

Medieval Latin presents some problems to the lexicographer that are quite different from those of Classical Latin.

First, there may be a problem in how to spell the lemma under which words should be entered. Papias recognized this problem in citing the straightforward medieval spelling *iena* alongside Classical Latin *hy(a)ena*. Initial *h-* was not regarded as a letter—it can come and go at will; but this may produce some confusion in the reader's mind between, for example, Classical Latin *hora* and CL *ora*, CL *hostium* and CL *ostium*. By the twelfth century the diphthongs *ae* and *oe* had both become simply *e*; so in the infinitive and in some tenses CL *caedere* and CL *cedere* become homographs. In such cases classical orthography will be the guide to choosing the lemma. Similarly, Medieval Latin *caenouectorium*, "dung-cart, wheel-barrow," will be so spelt, even though it is nowhere recorded until after the diphthong *ae* had become *e*, because to do otherwise would be to divorce it from its root, CL *caenum*, "mud, filth." The question of whether the letters *i* and *j* or *u* and *v* should be differentiated will affect the placing of words. The medieval fluctuation between *c-* and *ch-* likewise, or the indifference to whether certain words should be written with *f* or *ph*, can drastically affect the order of entries. The dictionary compiled in the Netherlands has adopted some practical solutions: the diphthongs *ae* and *oe* are so printed but alphabetized as *e*, *h-* is disregarded, *y* is treated as *i*, *c-* and *ch-* are merged, *ph-* is merged with *f-*, and so on. This produces a sequence that is logical but not alphabetical; for example, ¹*cestus*, ²*caestus*, *caesura*, *ceterus*, ¹*coetus*, ²*cetus*, *ceu*, *keurmede*, *cyaneus*, *ciara*, *chiasma*, *chiasmus*. The British dictionary, on the other hand, tries to follow etymology. Both systems in their different ways require the user to understand the variables of medieval spelling (see ch. CB).

Papias's other example, the writing of Classical Latin *uerbena* as *berbena*, reflects a phonetic rather than an orthographic variation; indeed, it represents what one can almost call a dialectal variation in Late Latin. The treatment of *w-* in Late Latin as *g-* or *gu-* in Medieval Latin is a more significant variation, for it represents a real phonetic development. Late Latin *uadium*, "pledge, wage," was borrowed from Germanic early enough for the sound \w\ to be represented by Latin *u*; words entering Latin later will be written with *uu* or *w*, and still later with *gu* or (in England) *g*. So *warda* can be written *guarda* or *garda* at different dates, and English has preserved the word in both forms, "ward" and "guard." In choosing where to enter such words, the lexicographer may have regard to the date at which the word is first used or to etymological relationships—with possibly different results. In the British dictionary such words are treated under *W* as a matter of policy, though cross-references are provided from all the recorded spellings.

The same word may be written in quite different spellings, quite different words may be spelled the same. In reading a text, sense will usually determine whether "oram" is from *hora* or *ora*. This is a matter of spelling, but there are also true homographs, different words always spelled the same. Etymology can differentiate homographs, even where medieval authors were unaware of the difference: thus Medieval Latin *flos, -ris,* "flowers, menstrual flow," was probably regarded as the same word as Classical Latin *flos,* "flower," which had a wide range of other meanings; but this has arisen from the similarity of Old French *flor,* "flower," < CL *flos,* and OF *flor,* "flux, discharge," < CL *fluor.* Pairs of this kind can also arise erroneously, for example: [CD33], s.v. 2 *hereditare,* c1112 "spreuerii, falcones, et ostorii ibi hereditantes"; *hereditantes* here means "nesting," a mistaken latinization from Anglo-French *eir,* "heir," when the clerk was seeking to latinize AF *eire,* "nest," from which came Medieval Latin *aëriare* (of which there are no examples before the thirteenth century).

Classical Latin *galea,* "helmet," is obviously a different word from Medieval Latin *galea,* "galley." Because of the way in which Medieval Latin picks up words from its immediate surroundings, it is of more importance to look to the nearest possible source of the word rather than to its ultimate source. There is another word, Medieval Latin *galida,* which has the same sense as ML *galea,* "galley"; both words first appear in Crusade contexts in the twelfth century and may be presumed to derive from a Middle Eastern language. *Galida* is probably closest to that; Old French tends to lose *-d-,* whence OF *galee,* from which Medieval Latin *galea* and Middle English *galei* were both derived. On the basis of immediate source, therefore, ML *galida* and ML *galea* are different lemmata. It is very common to find pairs comprising a Latin word (of whatever period) and a medieval usage latinized from the Old French derivative of the original word: so CL *cauea* > OF *cage* > ML *cagia;* CL *fetus* > Provençal *fedon,* alongside which we find ML *feto* > OF *feon, faon,* "fawn" > ML *feo, fao.*

The link between the French word and its Latin source may be invisible. The common word, ML *homagium,* was formed from OF *homage,* which in turn can be derived from Late Latin *\*hominaticum;* this is only arrived at by putting together the obvious stem *homo, hominis,* and the suffix *-aticus,* which became *-age* in French. Knowledge of the relationship to *homo* gave rise to more etymological forms in Medieval Latin, *hominagium* and *homanagium* (cf. AF *omenage*), though these are rare in comparison. Medieval Latin *homagium* was part of the permanent word hoard; *hominagium* may have been an occasional formation by someone conscious of the Latin root. The rare form *feodelitas* is similar but reflects a false etymology: the writer is latinizing from AF *fedeilte,* OF *fealte,* "fealty," < CL *fidelitas;* not recognizing the true derivation, users have associated the word with feudal tenure and guessed at *feodum* as the root.

The capacity to form Latin words at will could produce a wide diversity of forms. An extreme case of this is *garillum,* "barricade," common in England; it has no obvious etymology in Latin, though the immediate source must be Anglo-French *garoil,* of which a single example is recorded in the *Anglo-Norman Dictionary* [DL5], though the word must have been in common use. In Latin use the word has no consistent form, varying in spelling, phonetics, declension, and gender; its users clearly had no sense of this as part of the Latin word hoard, but "borrowed" the word from Anglo-French over and over again, producing a different form almost every time. The variation in sound and spelling reflects the variety of Anglo-French; the variation in gender and declension shows that the word has no stable place in Latin; but in spite of thirty or so forms, these represent a single lemma. Here the number of examples required in a dictionary is out of all proportion to the semantic simplicity of the word.

In England ad hoc borrowing of this kind was extremely common in the thirteenth and fourteenth centuries. Until the late thirteenth century words most often come from French, thereafter from Middle English, though the Middle English source may itself have been borrowed from French. By the end of the fourteenth century, it was acceptable simply to use the vernacular word in a Latin context with hardly a gesture towards the provision of a Latin termination. Instead of writing the word in full, it was common to write the English word, ending with a mark of suspension: [CD33], s.v. *groundsella*, **1388** *cum pinnacione grunsill' diuersarum domorum,* **1389** *pro iij peciis meremii emptis pro gronnesellis pro reparacione domus.* The word here, Middle English *groundsille, gronsel,* "groundsel," has no recognizable Latin termination; even *gronnesellis* could be a simple English plural in *-is* rather than a Latin ablative. In a case such as this, it is open to doubt whether the word should be treated as latinized at all, though with the more common examples some users may have provided a termination while others have not. So, for example: **1390** *in stipendio carpen<tan>cium grunsullam;* one example has led to the treatment of the word as a Latin *a*-stem in the dictionary. It is extremely difficult in cases such as *garillum* or *groundsella* to decide on the spelling of the lemma in the dictionary.

Words entering Medieval Latin in this way, raising questions about their status and form in the language, are for the most part relatively straightforward from the semantic point of view. Most of the words with a really wide range of meanings had been part of the language since the classical period, though they may have branched out in different directions over the centuries. There are some words, such as prepositions or the very common verbs, that will always be difficult to treat in a dictionary, and for which the entries will often be difficult to use. The extreme example in modern English is the verb "to set," which runs to 154 numbered senses in the *Oxford English Dictionary* [BF32] (and the last of these, with the adverb "up," has more than fifty subdivisions). In Medieval Latin *ad* and *de*, for example, or *esse, facere, habere,* not only have the complexity of the classical words but have developed many new senses or uses. Other words may ramify in sense, sometimes without clear semantic connections, and it is advisable to become familiar with how a large entry may be handled in a historical dictionary. I have already mentioned Classical Latin *flos;* other words with many senses in Medieval Latin are CL *gratia*, LL *grossus*, CL *hora*. Some words may demand elaborate treatment even where their semantic range is not great: CL *homo*, for example, or especially ML *homagium*, where most of the extensive entry is devoted to illustrating the contexts in medieval society where homage was required.

Wherever the evidence allows, the makers of dictionaries will choose examples that make clear the meaning of a word in its context, that show its grammatical construction, and, in a good medieval dictionary, that place the word in its historical as well as linguistic context. Reading the quotations is an essential part of making full use of a dictionary, and it is often helpful to go to the dictionary principally for the examples of a familiar word. The dictionary entry for *horologium,* for example, not only illustrates the technological variety of medieval clocks but leads the user to many sources to find fuller information. Consulting the appropriate entries in a dictionary can open up innumerable lines of inquiry.

No amount of knowledge of the foundations and methods of the available dictionaries can lead to the right results unless the user also has sound linguistic judgment. There are various perils. One is to assume that the text may be wrong. Another is to presume that the dictionary has overlooked some meaning or usage. And the third, and most widespread, is to use the dictionary to prop up a tendentious reading of the text. It is true that there are errors in the transmission of texts, some of them no more than errors of transcription or proofreading in the printed editions, and there are also errors even in the best dictionaries. But it requires good judgment to pinpoint such mistakes, and one should not be hasty in making these assumptions. One should also beware not to form an opinion as to what an obscure passage means without reference to *all* the information in the dictionary for a particular word. The fact that one sense offered may suit a desired interpretation does not mean it is the appropriate sense: a usage attested only in the thirteenth century and later cannot safely be applied to a tenth-century text, for example, and one confined to agricultural accounts is unlikely to fit a theological treatise. And one must always resist any temptation to knock the dictionary senses into the sense one would like. Inappropriate attestations and near-misses in sense do not help elucidate a text. One must acquire an understanding of how Latin works, backed up by the evidence of the dictionaries, and not try to force a passage into a sense that goes against the linguistic grain. Only with confidence in such a policy does it become safe to begin identifying the errors of others. Far more people are misled by wishful thinking than by blunders in their texts and dictionaries.

## Select Bibliography

### Glossaries, Dictionaries, and Lexical Aids

#### (a) Medieval and Early Modern Works

A.S. Napier, ed., *Old English Glosses, Chiefly Unpublished* (1900, r1989): prints a number of batch glosses [CD1].

L.W. Daly, *Contributions to a History of Alphabetization in Antiquity and the Middle Ages* (1967) [CD2].

R.T. Oliphant, ed., *The Harley Latin-Old English Glossary* (1966) [CD3].

Papias, *Elementarium doctrinae rudimentum* (c. 1040–53) (Milan 1476; Venice 1485, 1491, and 1496; r1966); a new ed. was begun by V. De Angelis, *A* fasc. 1–3 (1977–80) [CD4].

Osbern Pinnock of Gloucester, *Panormia siue Liber deriuationum* (c. 1150–70), ed. A. Mai: *Thesaurus novus latinitatis, sive Lexicon vetus e membranis nunc primum erutum,* Classici auctores e Vaticanis codicibus editi 8 (1836); Osbern's preface to Hamelin is printed and the notes of John of Bath discussed by R.W. Hunt, "The Lost Preface to the *Liber deriuationum* of Osbern of Gloucester," in *Mediaeval and Re-*

*naissance Studies* 4 (1958) 267–82. A new ed. by F. Bertini and others is in preparation [CD5]. R. Sharpe, "London, British Library, MS Royal 15 C. XI and Osbern of Gloucester's Use of Plautus," in *Scriptorium* 45 (1991) 93–98, provides a test of Osbern's efficiency at excerpting this source [CD6].

Hugutio of Pisa, *Magnae deriuationes* (c. 1190), has never been printed; the manuscripts are surveyed by A. Marigo, *I codici manoscritti delle Deriuationes di Uguccione Pisano* (1936) [CD7]. See also C. Riessner, *Die "Magnae derivationes" des Uguccione da Pisa und ihre Bedeutung für die romanische Philologie* (1965) [CD8].

John of Genoa, *Catholicon* (1286) (Mainz 1460, r1971); a new ed. by A. Della Casa is in preparation [CD9].

William Brito, *Expositiones vocabulorum Biblie* (c. 1250–70), ed. L.W. and B.A. Daly, 2 vols. (1975) [CD10].

T. Hunt, *TLLTCE:* provides basic texts of the *De utensilibus* of Adam of Balsham (Adam of Petit Pont) (v1:172–76), the *De nominibus utensilium* of Alexander Neckam (v1:181–90; N.B.: the last page of text was omitted from the printed book and must be obtained as an erratum slip from the publisher), and the *Dictionarius* of John of Garland (v1:196–203); the vernacular glosses are printed in v2, and there are word indexes in v3. The first volume lays the foundations for a study of these texts in their wider context [CD11].

T. Wright and R.P. Wülcker, *Anglo-Saxon and Old English Vocabularies,* 2 vols., 2nd ed. (1884) [CD12].

T. Blount, *Nomo-Lexicon: A Law-Dictionary* (London 1670, r1970), was meant as a guide to the special terminology of the common law, much of it belonging to the twelfth to fourteenth centuries [CD13]; H. Spelman, *Glossarium Archaiologicum* (London 1664; 3rd ed., London 1687), was expressly designed to help the student of medieval institutions and customs [CD14].

C. Du Fresne, Sieur Du Cange, *Glossarium ad scriptores mediae et infimae latinitatis,* 3 vols. (Paris 1678); supp. (Lyon 1688); new extended ed., 6 vols. (Paris 1733–36), repr. several times; P. Carpentier's supp., 4 vols. (Paris 1766); new ed. by G.A.L. Henschel, 7 vols. (Paris 1840–50), repr. by L. Favre in 10 vols. (Niort 1883–87, with subsequent reprintings); addenda and corrigenda by various compilers: see, e.g., *ALMA* 1 (1924) 223–31; 2 (1925) 15–29, 51–52; 3 (1927) 12–21; 22 (1951–52) 89–156; *L'antiquité classique* 10 (1941) 95–113; 11 (1942) 67–85 [CD15]. For a biography of Du Cange, a critical assessment of his *Glossarium,* and an account of its publication history, supps., etc., see the articles by M. Esposito and H. Leclercq: "Du Cange," in *DACL* 4.2:1654–60; "Latin. 1. Le *Glossarium,*" in *DACL* 8.1:1422–52 [CD16].

## (b) Modern Latin Dictionaries

### 1. Classical, Late, and Medieval Latin

The *Thesaurus Linguae Latinae* [*TLL*] (Munich 1899–) is by far the most comprehensive dictionary of Classical and Late Latin, being based on an exhaustive excerpting of classical texts and a thorough use of authors down to the end of the sixth century; *A–M* (1900–66), *O–* (1968–81); work now proceeding on *P*. It is a monoglot dictionary, with definitions and editorial comments in Latin; its systematic classification is easy to follow once understood, but it is confusing to the reader who expects a historical-semantic approach. Preparation of a computerized version of the *TLL* is under way at the University of California at Irvine [CD17].

An excellent one-volume dictionary for Classical Latin is the *Oxford Latin Dictionary* [*OLD*], ed. P.G.W. Glare (Oxford 1968–82); its semantic classification is often subtle but always clear, its definitions very precise [CD18]. Still useful is C.T. Lewis and C. Short, *A Latin Dictionary* (Oxford 1879; reprinted many times); this was based on an older Latin-German dictionary; its classification, its definitions, and its typography leave much to be desired, but it is generally accurate, is easily accessible, and has the advantage of covering both Classical and Late Latin (with occasional leaps into the later Middle Ages, e.g. *gunna*, s.v. *canon*) [CD19].

For Late Latin see A. Souter, *A Glossary of Later Latin to 600 A.D.* (Oxford 1949) [CD20], and A. Blaise, *Dictionnaire latin-français des auteurs chrétiens, revu specialement pour le vocabulaire théologique par Henri Chirat* (Turnhout 1954, r1967?) [CD21].

The best one-volume dictionary for Medieval Latin is the *Mediae latinitatis lexicon minus,* ed. J.F. Niermeyer and C. Van de Kieft (Leiden 1954–76, r1993); it is selective, reflecting Niermeyer's reading in chronicles, documents, and legal texts from the period down to about 1100; classification is simple, there is little attempt at etymology, and definitions are given in French and English; serviceable for the historian reading the kind of texts on which it is based [CD22]. There is also A. Blaise, *Dictionnaire latin-français des auteurs du moyen-âge/ Lexicon latinitatis medii aevi, praesertim ad res ecclesiasticas investigandas pertinens* (Turnhout 1975) [CD23].

*Novum glossarium mediae latinitatis ab anno DCCC usque ad annum MCC,* ed. F. Blatt, Y. Lefèvre, *et al.* (Copenhagen 1957–): *L* (1957), *MN* (1959–69), *O* (1975–80), *P–panis* (1980), *paniscardus–parrula* (1987), *pars–passerulus* (1989), *passibilis–pazzu* (1993) [CD24].

## 2. National Lexica of Medieval Latin

AUSTRIA, GERMANY, SWITZERLAND: *Mittellateinisches Wörterbuch bis zum ausgehenden 13. Jahrhundert,* ed. O. Prinz, J. Schneider, *et al.* (Munich 1959–); fasc. 19 (*conductus–coniugium*) (1991) [CD25].

BELGIUM: *Thesaurus linguae scriptorum operumque Latino-Belgicorum medii aeui,* v1: *Le vocabulaire des origines à l'an mil,* ed. P. Tombeur, 4 vols. and 146 microfiches (Brussels 1986) [CD26].

CATALUNYA: *Glossarium mediae latinitatis Cataloniae,* ed. M. Bassols de Climent *et al.,* v1: A–D (Barcelona 1960–85); all work on the project ended with fasc. 9 (*dotalis–dux*) (1985) [CD27].

CROATIA: *Lexicon latinitatis medii aeui Iugoslauiae,* ed. M. Kostrenčić *et al.,* 2 vols. (Zagreb 1968–78) [CD28]; see also F. Semi, *Glossario del latino medioevale istriano* (Venice 1990) [CD29].

CZECH REPUBLIC: *Latinitatis medii aeui lexicon Bohemorum,* ed. E. Kamínková *et al.* (Prague 1977–); fasc. 14 (*heliodromus–*) (1992) [CD30].

DENMARK: *Lexicon mediae latinitatis Danicae,* ed. F. Blatt, B. Friis Johansen, *et al.* (Aarhus 1987–); fasc. 4 (*euitatio–increpito*) (1992) [CD31].

FINLAND: *Glossarium latinitatis medii aeui Finlandicae,* ed. R. Hakamies (Helsinki 1958) [CD32].

GREAT BRITAIN: *Dictionary of Medieval Latin from British Sources,* ed. R.E. Latham, D.R. Howlett, *et al.* (London 1975–); fasc. 4 (*F–G–H*) (1989) [CD33]. R.E. Latham, *Revised Medieval Latin Word-List from British and Irish Sources* (London 1965, r1989), provides a concise supplement to [CD19], with entries for new words or senses giving a brief definition and a range of dates but without examples [CD34].

HUNGARY: *Lexicon latinitatis medii aeui Hungariae,* ed. J. Harmatta and I. Boronkai (Budapest 1987–); v2, fasc. 3 (*conor–czwkarum*) (1991) [CD35]. This is intended to supersede the old national dictionary, *Glossarium mediae et infimae latinitatis regni Hungariae,* ed. A. Bartal (Leipzig/Budapest 1901, r1970) [CD36].

IRELAND: *Dictionary of Medieval Latin from Celtic Sources,* ed. A.J.R. Harvey (work began in 1975) [CD37].

ITALY: *Latinitatis Italicae medii aeui inde ab a. CDLXXVI usque ad a. MXXII lexicon imperfectum,* ed. F. Arnaldi *et al.,* published in *ALMA* between 1936 and 1964, collected in three vols. 1939, 1951, [1967]; repr. Turin 1970. Addenda, fasc. 1 (*a–axon*), in *ALMA* 35 (1967) 5–46; fasc. 9 (*la–mediator*), in *ALMA* 50 (1990–91) 5–32 [CD38].

THE NETHERLANDS: *Lexicon latinitatis Nederlandicae medii aeui,* ed. J.W. Fuchs, O. Weijers, *et al.* (Leiden 1969–); fasc. 42 (*odoromentum–oxus*) (1994) [CD39].

POLAND: *Lexicon mediae et infimae latinitatis Polonorum,* ed. M. Plezia *et al.* (Wroclaw/Cracow 1953–); fasc. 54 (*perdecet–persuadeo*) (1993) [CD40].

SWEDEN: *Glossarium mediae latinitatis Sueciae,* ed. U. Westerbergh and E. Odelman (Stockholm 1968–); v2, fasc. 4 (*phalanga–pyxis*) (1992) [CD41].

For other dictionaries and related works see chs. BB and BF (Vernacular Dictionaries).


## Studies

Important studies of the early development of Latin and the vernaculars are R. Wright, *LLER* [CD42], and M. Banniard, *Viva Voce: Communication écrite et communication orale du IVe au IXe siècle en occident latin* (1992) [CD43].

Recent studies of Latin lexicography in the Middle Ages include L.W. Daly and B.A. Daly, "Some Techniques in Mediaeval Latin Lexicography," in *Speculum* 39 (1964) 229–39 [CD44]; C. Buridant, "Lexicographie et glossographie médiévales: Esquisse de bilan et perspectives de recherche," in *LLM* 9–46 [CD45]; C. Buridant, ed., *La Lexicographie au moyen âge* (1986) [CD46]; O. Weijers, "Lexicography in the Middle Ages," in *Viator* 20 (1989) 139–54 [CD47]; O. Weijers, ed., *Dictionnaires et répertoires au moyen âge: Une étude de vocabulaire,* CIVICIMA 4 (1991) [CD48].

J.H. Hessels, "On the Need of a New Mediaeval Latin Dictionary," in *TPhS* (1895–98) 419–83 (with lists of words from *Lex Salica* and from Bracton) [CD49]; *id.,* "Irminon's Polyptychum AD 811–826," in *TPhS* (1899–1902) 471–552 [CD50]; *id.,* "The Polyptychum of the Abbey of Saint-Rémi at Rheims A.D. 848 to 861," in *TPhS* (1899–1902) 553–650 [CD51].

R. Sharpe, "Modern Dictionaries of Medieval Latin," in *Bilan et perspectives des études médiévales en Europe: Actes du 1er congrès européen d'études médiévales, Spoleto, 27–29 mai 1993,* ed. J. Hamesse (1995) 289–304 [CD52].

CE  •  **METRICS**

BY A.G. RIGG

There are, fundamentally, two different systems of versification in Medieval Latin: (1) those meters derived from classical quantitative practice, with or without the embellishment of rhyme, and (2) those based on stress accent, resulting either from the rhythmical reading of Classical Latin meters (with some new combinations) or from musical settings. Rhythmical verse is usually arranged in stanzas and commonly called "lyric."

## Quantitative Verse

(a) **Dactylic Verse.** The most popular verse forms throughout the Middle Ages remained, as in Classical Latin, the dactylic hexameter and elegiac couplet. Variations from the length of syllables in Classical Latin arise from several sources:

1. There is lengthening at the caesura, so that a naturally short vowel may be treated as long for the sake of the meter.
2. Shortening of a final vowel, particularly -ō and -ī, is very common.
3. Although medieval poets usually observe the length of vowels that signal morphemes, e.g. nominative fem. sg., neut. pl. in -ă, ablative fem. sg. in -ā, and paradigms such as vĕnio-vēni, they had no dictionaries to tell them the quality of a root vowel, and occasionally depart from Classical Latin practice. Some poets knew such subtleties: in the thirteenth century Henry of Avranches asked for papal permission to change amphimacers (metrical feet, now usually called cretics, each consisting of a short syllable between two long syllables, i.e. -˘-, as in *caritas*) to anapests (˘˘-). Serlo of Wilton (d. 1181) and others wrote "differential verses" to help distinguish words such as *plāco* and *plăceo*.
4. Finally, of course, there was simple incompetence, but this is rare.

(b) **Dactylic Verse with Rhyme.** Rhymes appear from about the fifth century, especially in hymns, but are usually only vocalic, i.e. between vowels. Rhyming became quite common, although it was avoided by the Carolingian poets. From the mid-eleventh century, disyllabic rhyme, of both vowel and consonant, becomes common, not just as an ornament but as a structural feature. Lines with final rhyme only, usually in couplets or quatrains, are known as *caudati* ("tailed").

The most frequent form is the leonine hexameter, rhyming between the strong caesura and the end of the line:

> Que monachi querunt patrio mea iure fuerunt.

The same rhyme in couplets produces *unisoni* ("single sounds"). Collaterals (*ventrini*) are couplets in which caesura rhymes with caesura and end with end:

> Flandria dulce solum super omnes terra beata
> tangis laude polum duce magno glorificata.

In *cancellati* (also known as *serpentini* or *cruciferi,* "cross-shaped"), the caesura of the first line rhymes with the end of the second, and vice versa:

> Crux cancellauit musam michi metra nouantem
> Forma triumphantem cruce regem significauit.

Such patterns are also found in elegiac couplets.

Weak caesura rhymes include *trinini salientes* ("jumping threesomes"):

> Stella maris que sola paris sine coniuge prolem
> iusticie clarum specie super omnia solem.

Rhymes coinciding with the foot rather than the caesura include, most commonly, *dactylici tripertiti:*

> Hora novissima tempora pessima sunt, vigilemus.
> ecce minaciter imminet arbiter ille supremus.

Rhyming hexameters remained popular, especially in lapidary verse, until well after the Renaissance.

(c) **Classical Non-rhyming Lyric Meters.** Meters such as sapphics, alcaics, asclepiads, glyconics, and others, using *metra* such as the iamb, trochee, choriamb, or anapest, were never common; they were written by the Carolingian poets and are occasionally found up to the eleventh century, but thereafter they appear only in the works of metrical specialists and teachers. They were known partly from Horace's *Odes* but especially from Boethius's *De consolatione Philosophiae* and Martianus Capella's *De nuptiis Mercurii et Philologiae.*

(d) **Quantitative Hymn Meters.** Iambic and trochaic meters were popular with early hymn writers such as Ambrose and Prudentius. Most common was the iambic dimeter, as in Ambrose's

> Aeterne rerum conditor
> noctem diemque qui regis,

and the iambic dimeter catalectic, as in Prudentius's

> Ades pater supreme
> quem nemo vidit unquam.

The trochaic tetrameter catalectic (trochaic septenarius), important for later developments, was also common, as in Prudentius's

Da puer plectrum choreis ut canam fidelibus
dulce carmen et melodum gesta Christi insignia.

Although such meters were familiar through the hymnal, they found few imitators in later Medieval Latin hymnology, where rhythm and rhyme were preferred.

## Rhythmical Verse

Rhythmical verse depends not on the length of the syllable but on its accent. In
the prose reading of a word, the stress falls on the penultimate syllable if the penultimate is long (*amábat*), but on the antepenultimate if the penultimate is short
(*amavéritis*). The regular combination of stressed and unstressed syllables, usually in
rising (iambic ˇ ´) or falling (trochaic ´ ˇ) pairs, produced an enormous range of new
verse forms in the later Middle Ages. Rhythmical lines are described by the number
of syllables in the line, together with the notation "p" or "pp": "p" indicates a line or
half-line with paroxytonic stress, that is, one in which the stress at the end falls on
the penultimate syllable; "pp" indicates a line with proparoxytonic stress, with the final stress on the antepenultimate syllable. Thus the line

Apparebit repentína dies magni dómini

is described as 8p + 7pp. Elision is rare in rhythmical verse, and vowels followed by
*m* are not elided. Hiatus is quite acceptable. Space does not permit the illustration of
more than a few forms.

(a) **Combinations of 8p + 7pp.** If the trochaic septenarius is read rhythmically,
it produces two half-lines of 8p and 7pp. When the first half-line is repeated, this gives
rise to the celebrated Victorine Sequence (named for Adam of St. Victor [d. c. 1180]),
rhyming *aabccb*. This was the most common rhythmical hymn meter of the later
Middle Ages, e.g.,

Stabat mater dolorosa
iuxta crucem lacrimosa
    dum pendebat filius,
cuius animam gementem
contristantem et dolentem
    pertransiuit gladius.

Sometimes the stanza is lengthened progressively through a hymn by increasing the
number of *a* and *c* lines.

(b) **Rhythmical Asclepiads.** The prose reading of the lesser asclepiad of Classical Latin, as in Horace's

Māecēnās ătăvīs ēdītĕ rēgĭbŭs,

produced two half-lines of 6pp + 6pp. In quatrains, rhyming finally *aaaa,* this became a very popular verse form, especially for satirical verse:

A tauro torrida   lampade Cynthii
fundente iacula   feruentis radii

> umbrosas nemoris   latebras adii
> explorans gratiam   lenis Favonii.

Sometimes there is also internal rhyme.

(c) **Goliardics.** A meter that owes nothing to Classical Latin antecedents is the Goliardic stanza, four lines of 7pp + 6p, rhyming *aaaa*. It was very popular for satirical and light-hearted verse:

> Meum est propositum   in taberna mori
> ut sint vina proxima   morientis ori.
> Tunc cantabunt laetius   angelorum chori:
> Sit Deus propitius   huic potatori.

Walter of Châtillon (d. 1202/3) and some followers wrote a Goliardic stanza *cum auctoritate,* with the final line taken from a Classical Latin poet. In this example the last line is from Juvenal's first satire:

> Missus sum in vineam   circa horam nonam;
> suam quisque nititur   vendere personam.
> Ergo quia cursitant   omnes ad coronam:
> semper ego auditor   tantum nunquamne reponam?

Sometimes there is also internal rhyme, leading editors (especially of hymns) to lay out the stanzas in eight short lines.

(d) **Sequences.** Many metrical forms owe their origin to music. In the liturgy, between the reading of the Epistle and the Gospel, melodies developed extending the final -*a* of the Alleluia. In time these melodies were fitted with words (known as *prosae* or *sequentiae*) to be sung by the choir, with alternating stanzas and concluding with a shared stanza. In time, with the introduction of rhyme, extremely elaborate rhyme schemes developed and stanzas might be fifteen or twenty (short) lines in length. Although apparently of religious origin, the sequence was often used for secular verse, occasionally satirical but most often amatory.

In the eleventh-century *Cambridge Songs,* some poems are headed with the tune to which they are to be sung, e.g. *Modus Ottinc,* meaning that the poem is to be sung to the "Otto tune"; the implication is that new words have been written for an old tune. In the fourteenth century a bishop of Ossory, Richard Ledrede (d. 1360), adapted what seem to be dance tunes for sacred purposes and headed his lyrics with the opening words of the songs (often in the vernacular) to which the new hymns were to be sung.

Finally, however, it must be stressed that although many literary historians tend to emphasize the lyric meters (because they are uniquely medieval), the predominant metrical forms for medieval poets writing in Latin were the well-established quantitative dactylic meters.

## Select Bibliography

See first A.G. Rigg, "Latin Meter," in *DMA* 7:371–76 [CE1], and *id.*, *A History of Anglo-Latin Literature, 1066–1422* (1992), app.: Metre (pp313–29) [CE2].

P. Klopsch, *EMV:* has much on variations in dactylic verse [CE3].

W. Meyer, *Gesammelte Abhandlungen zur mittellateinischen Rythmik,* 3 vols. (1905–36, r1970): a series of essays, fundamental but terminologically outdated [CE4].

D. Norberg, *Introduction à l'étude de la versification latine médiévale* (1958): the standard work [CE5]; *id., L'accentuation des mots dans le vers latin du moyen âge* (1985) [CE6]; *id., Les vers latins iambiques et trochaiques au moyen âge et leurs répliques rythmiques* (1988) [CE7].

A. Orchard, *The Poetic Art of Aldhelm* (1994) [CE8].

D.S. Raven, *Latin Metre: An Introduction* (1965): on classical meters and especially valuable on the quantitative lyrics [CE9]; see also G.B. Nussbaum, *Vergil's Metre: A Practical Guide for Reading Latin Hexameter Poetry* (1986) [CE10].

D. Schaller, "Bauformeln für akzentrhythmische Verse und Strophen," in *MLJ* 14 (1979) 9–21: presents an alternative system of notation for rhythmical verse [CE11]. For an application of Schaller's system, see C.J. McDonough, *OPHP* [CE12].

O. Schumann, *Lateinisches Hexameter-Lexicon: Dichterisches Formelgut von Ennius bis zum Archipoeta,* 6 vols., *MGH.Hilfsmittel* 4.1–6 (1979–83), with *Stellenregister* (1989) by D. Kottke *et al.*: an index of hexameter formulae [CE13].

Illustrations of medieval verse forms can be found readily in Evrard (Eberhard) of Bremen's *Laborintus* (composed between 1212 and 1280), in E. Faral, *AP* 336–77 [CE14], and in John of Garland's *Parisiana poetria,* ed. and tr. T. Lawler (1974), especially in the final book, where there is a set of poems in Horatian meters [CE15].

*See also* [BB50], [BB58].

CF   &bull;   # PROSE STYLES AND *CURSUS*

BY TERENCE O. TUNBERG

## Prose Styles

Much remains to be learned about Medieval Latin prose styles. It is clear, however, that most of the stylistic and formal elements typical of literary medieval prose owe a great deal to the Latin Church fathers of late antiquity. In fact, the Christian authors of the late Roman Empire developed a variety of styles for different purposes, ranging from the homiletic style sometimes called *sermo humilis* (a term also used to describe the language of the Latin Scriptures themselves), which is characterized by rather simple diction, loose syntax, and paratactic structure, to an elaborate grand style designed to appeal to the educated elite. But patristic Latin of all stylistic levels is especially distinguished by the deliberate departure from the canons of classical vocabulary, and the pervasive use of images and diction derived from the Scriptures. (See [CF10] pp25–66, [CF31], [CF39].) Employment of scriptural language and vocabulary remains a constant feature of Latin prose throughout the Middle Ages.

After the collapse of the Western Roman Empire in the later fifth century, the grammatical level of Latin written in many parts of Europe deteriorated. In Merovingian Gaul, for example, as knowledge of the literary language decreased, many writers of Latin depended on fixed formulae. Nevertheless, even during these centuries there were always some writers capable of expressing themselves in literary Latin, such as Gregory the Great (d. 604) in Italy, Gregory of Tours (d. 594/95) in Gaul, and Isidore of Seville (d. 636) in the Spanish peninsula. (See [CF11]; [CF18]; [CF19]; [CF34], especially pp364–68; [CF37].)

During the same period a distinctive latinity seems to have developed in Ireland, where there had been no Roman civil administration and Latin was introduced entirely as the language of Christianity. (See [CF29], [CF37] pp43–49, [CF49].) Perhaps the best known examples of this Hiberno-Latin are the strange texts called *Hisperica famina*, which are thought to have been composed sometime in the seventh century, perhaps as school compositions or rhetorical models. The style of the *Hisperica famina* is especially characterized by the prevalence of neologisms, words transliterated or derived from Greek, Celtic, or Irish words, as well as ordinary words invested with unusual meanings [CF6]. Irish monks themselves founded centers of Latin writing in Britain and on the Continent (such as Luxeuil and Bobbio), but the extent to which Irish latinity affected the styles of Latin prose cultivated in these areas is still a matter of debate. (See [CF6], [CF26], [CF52].)

By the late seventh century Latin studies were active in England also, and the most important testimony to the vitality of Anglo-Latin prose in this period is the works of Bede (d. 735) and Aldhelm (d. 709/10). While Bede's prose is noteworthy for its economy and clarity [CF1], Aldhelm's style represents an opposite extreme. Although Aldhelm's periods are skilfully structured, they are intricate and long-winded. He favors rhyme, alliteration, and interlaced word order and makes constant use of his immense vocabulary for amplification. Since this vocabulary includes a large proportion of archaisms and Greek words derived from glossaries, the term *hermeneutic* is often used to describe the writing of Aldhelm and those who adopted a similar mode of expression. Aldhelm was much imitated by his successors, and his influence on Anglo-Latin prose and poetry persisted until the Norman Conquest. A number of writers on the Continent also show traces of the hermeneutic style, including Liutprand of Cremona (d. 972) and Odo of Cluny (d. 944). (See [CF26], [CF37] pp43–49, [CF52].)

Although the latinity of many eighth- and ninth-century texts still appears rather crude if measured by later medieval standards [CF34], several scholars have noticed that the Latin written in many parts of Europe during this period tends to conform more closely than earlier medieval texts to the grammatical norms of the language as used by Christian writers of late antiquity. (See [CF34] pp372–77, [CF37] pp50–67.) In part this may have been a result of the reforms in clerical education and centralization of administration associated with Charlemagne. The Carolingian era also saw a revival of interest in a variety of ancient texts, both pagan and Christian. Thus it can hardly be a coincidence that the influence of literary models other than the Scriptures and the Church fathers becomes more noticeable as a stylistic phenomenon in this period. Perhaps the most quoted example of this is the *Vita Karoli* by Einhard (d. 840), which owes much to Suetonius's *Vita Augusti*. (See [CF32] v1, [CF34] pp369–88.)

There is widespread agreement among modern authorities that the eleventh and twelfth centuries represent a high point in the history of Medieval Latin literary prose. The leading authors of this period, many of whom were monks, such as Bernard of Clairvaux (d. 1153) and Peter the Venerable (d. 1156), emphasized symmetry and parallelism in the structure of their ample sentences through the use of such devices as isocolon (clauses of equal length), anaphora (repetition of the same word at the beginning of successive clauses), and end rhyme. In many cases, especially by the mid-twelfth century, the harmony of formal prose is enhanced by the practice of ending sentences and clauses with accentual rhythms, or *cursus,* a topic which we shall explore in more detail shortly. Although none of these devices was new, the best authors of the eleventh and twelfth centuries combined them in a characteristic fashion, and deployed them with a consistency of skill unequaled in the literary products of earlier medieval centuries. (See [CF33] pp541–48, [CF35] v2:347–67, [CF43] pp55–87.)

The aforementioned features represent the culmination of the prevailing tradition of Latin prose since the time of the Church fathers. But also in the eleventh, and especially in the twelfth century, several other trends in the writing of Latin prose received further development. Some authors of this period share a tendency towards classicism. Sometimes, as in the case of William of Poitiers (d. c. 1087/1101), whose primary model is said to have been Sallust, this classicism merely takes the form of avoiding the parallelism of sound and structure favored by the leading monastic authors of the time. In the case of other writers, such as Meinhard of Bamberg (d. 1088), the classicizing tendency is discernible not only in structure, but also in vocabulary and, to a very limited extent, in syntax. Some twelfth-century authors, like John of Salisbury (d. 1180), habitually incorporate large segments of ancient texts almost verbatim into their own prose, while others tend to limit themselves to apposite allusions, quotations, and echoes. Sustained and pervasive imitation, in which the imitator has so absorbed the language and style of the model as to make it his or her own vehicle of expression, is extremely rare or perhaps nonexistent in Latin prose written before the Renaissance. Imitation in the eleventh and twelfth centuries remains at the level of decoration, and most classicizing prose is still wholly medieval in structure, syntax, and vocabulary. (See [CF33] pp546–50, [CF36], [CF52].)

This kind of prose seems to have declined in importance during the last third of the twelfth century. By this date another manner of writing, which was probably a by-product of new developments in scholarship and learning, was becoming much more influential. The leading teachers in the newer disciplines of medicine, theology, and canon and civil law developed a much less elaborate prose, of which the most salient features are a technical vocabulary and a simple sentence structure that could easily conform to the requirements of dialectic. This sort of latinity became the hallmark of scientific and philosophical works in the later Middle Ages, but its influence is also visible in many Latin works produced outside the academic environment, especially in the thirteenth and fourteenth centuries. (See [CF22–23], [CF34] pp389–406.)

Other writers, however, especially some of the professors of *dictamen* (the art of composing letters and public documents) and those employed in chanceries, developed an artifical and highly ornamented style which can accurately be designated "manneristic." The mannerist, as defined by E.R. Curtius, "prefers the artificial and affected" and "wants to surprise, to astonish, to dazzle" ([CF13] p282). The manneristic trend, which apparently won favor in France during the latter part of the twelfth century, was probably one of the formative elements in the extravagant epistolary style adopted by Peter of Vinea, one of the most famous members of the court of the emperor Frederick II (d. 1250). The letters of Peter of Vinea had an extensive circulation, and seem to have become one of the primary models for chancery style during the later Middle Ages. Unlike most prose authors of the thirteenth century, Peter has been the subject of several stylistic studies. His letters are permeated with imagery and vocabulary derived from Scripture, civil law, and, to a lesser extent, the Roman poet Ovid. The epistolary manner of Peter of Vinea and others influenced by him is noteworthy for long periods, amplification, extensive use of sound-figures, and systematic application of *cursus,* many varieties of *annominatio* (word play), hyperbaton (separation of words which are grammatically linked), and far-fetched or even obscure metaphors. All these devices are calculated to give a majestic effect when the document is read (usually aloud). (See [CF12], [CF41], [CF47].) This manneristic strain in later medieval prose can be considered as the descendant, whether direct or indirect, of a manneristic tradition of writing Latin which had earlier medieval exponents, such as Aldhelm, and can be traced back to such late antique authors as Sidonius Apollinaris (d. 479), or perhaps even to Apuleius (fl. second century A.D.). (See [CF10] pp133–67, [CF13] pp273–301, [CF31], [CF52].)

Style was one of the subjects addressed by medieval teachers of Latin composition, and several methods of classifying prose styles existed by the early thirteenth century. The doctrine of the three *genera dicendi*—*grave, medium,* and *tenue*—has its roots in the three styles of speaking set forth in bk. 4 of *Ad Herennium* (4.8.11–16), an anonymous rhetorical textbook written probably in the first century B.C. that enjoyed immense popularity in the Middle Ages. In medieval grammar and rhetoric the three styles, which could apply to prose or verse, were sometimes exemplified by the three works of Virgil, the *Aeneid, Georgics,* and *Eclogues.* Moreover, each style came to be identified with certain human occupations, as well as types of animals and vegetation. (See [CF2] 1.6, pp7, 297–99; [CF4] pp86–89; [CF44].)

Another method of classifying styles, elaborated by Geoffrey of Vinsauf and John of Garland in the early thirteenth century, used prose rhythm as the essential criterion and defined four basic styles: the *stilus Tullianus,* which lacks accentual rhythm, but employs much rhetorical embellishment; the *stilus Gregorianus,* or the style of the papal curia; the *stilus Hilarianus,* which, as described by the theorists, appears to imitate a rhythmical hymn structure; and the *stilus Ysidorianus,* distinguished by isocolon and rhyme. Apart from the "Hilarian" style, of which few, if any, medieval examples are extant, this classification corresponds in a very approximate fashion to three of the principal types of prose actually written in the twelfth century. The "Tullian" style matches the classicizing trend, the "Isidorian" suggests the style of the great monastic writers, and the "Gregorian" would seem to denote the practice of chanceries, which observed the rules of *dictamen* and used the form of *cursus* in vogue in the papal curia. (See [CF7] pp104–9, 256–58; [CF33] pp564–65.) The *dictamen* professor Bene of Florence (d. before 1242) defines only three styles, but his simpler classification is also based on prose rhythm. (See [CF2] 1.15.12–16, p19.) Prose rhythm, therefore, was obviously an important consideration for these theorists, and modern scholars seem to agree, insofar as they regard accentual rhythm as one of the essential features of polished medieval prose.

## *Cursus*

The phrase "prose rhythm," when used in a wider sense, can denote nothing more than the ordering of the components of the sentence into a harmonious whole. (See [CF33] p543, especially n27.) In a stricter sense, however, it refers to the habit of terminating sentences and clauses with rhythmical units known as *clausulae,* a practice which is already conspicuous in the prose of Cicero and other ancient Latin writers. The *clausulae* of ancient prose, like the metrical schemes of ancient verse, are defined by the quantity of syllables. After the third century A.D., however, many authors employed the so-called *cursus mixtus,* in which the ictus of metrical patterns was made to coincide with word accent. In this system of prose rhythm, therefore, both word accent and quantitative meter were factors. *Cursus mixtus,* in turn, evolved into the medieval Latin prose rhythm called *cursus* by modern scholars, which was based entirely on word accent. (See [CF20], [CF39–40].) Although the term *cursus* actually occurs in medieval texts, it usually means something like "flow of speech," and the use of this word to refer specifically to systems of *clausulae* seems to be a modern scholarly adaptation. (See [CF24] pp63–68.)

The earliest surviving medieval texts which describe *cursus* were not composed before the 1180s. Nevertheless, the actual use of accentual prose rhythm has a continuous history from late antiquity to the High Middle Ages, although not all writers employed it, and in some areas, such as Germany in the late eleventh century, *cur-*

*sus* seems to have fallen into temporary disfavor. (See [CF24], especially pp53–58; [CF28] pp7–13.) There was some variety of practice in the early Middle Ages, and in some parts of France in the late twelfth century a very idiosyncratic type of *cursus* was taught and apparently used by some writers. (See [CF14]; [CF24] pp35–71, 81–101; [CF53].) But during the twelfth century a process of simplification and standardization was under way in Italy and France. The method of *cursus* which prevailed was already being used by major French writers in the mid-twelfth century, and appears in papal letters by the 1180s. This so-called Roman system was also the method taught by thirteenth-century Italian professors of *dictamen*, such as Guido Faba (d. c. 1240), whose manuals circulated widely [CF5]. By the mid-thirteenth century the "Roman" *cursus* was virtually standard throughout Europe. (See [CF17]; [CF24] pp8, 69–76, 101.)

The Roman *cursus* consists of three (or four) rhythms. The final word of the cadence must consist of either three or four syllables. In the case of the preceding word what matters is not the number of syllables, but the position of the accent. There are two types of *cursus tardus,* either a trisyllabic proparoxytone (a word accented on the third syllable from the end) preceded by a word with the same stress, e.g. *insídias pónere,* or a quadrisyllabic proparoxytone preceded by a paroxytone (a word accented on the second syllable from the end), e.g. *habére commúnitas.* The *planus* consists of a trisyllabic paroxytone preceded by a word with the same stress, e.g. *serváre quaesíta,* and the *velox* is formed by a quadrisyllabic paroxytone preceded by a proparoxytone, e.g. *hóminem recepístis.* The best medieval writers tend to avoid vowel collisions, especially in *clausulae.* In cases, however, where such vowel collision does occur, it is probably safest to assume that there is hiatus and not elision. (Note some of the examples of *clausulae* given by Bene of Florence: [CF2] 1.11–16, pp26–27; see also [CF24] p32.) The Roman rules also permit *consillabicatio,* or substitution of the final word by two or three brief words containing the same total number of syllables. Hence *terrárum quas-régunt* can be treated as a *planus.* The appropriate stress distribution for the preceding word can also be created from a number of smaller units. For example, *nóvit-et impugnáre* can form a *velox.* (For some good medieval and modern discussions, see [CF2] 1.20, pp25–27, 309–10; [CF3]; [CF5] pp347–48; [CF8]; [CF14–15]; [CF17]; [CF24] pp28–32; [CF46].)

A number of modern studies and reference works employ a different method of describing *cursus.* Those who employ this method take no account of the length of the final word, but classify the cadences solely in terms of the number of syllables between the last two accents and after the last accent. For example, a *planus,* such as *ópus perégit,* may be described as two unaccented syllables between the last two accents, and one syllable after the last accent. (See [CF21] pp716–18, [CF28] pp39–54, [CF39] pp5–19, [CF40], [CF50] pp126–28.) If we view *cursus* in this fashion, nothing prevents us from classifying a form like *víneam nóstram* as a *planus,* or *vestrárum largitióne* as a *velox,* or even, if we assume a secondary accent, treating certain long words, like *tránsgrediántur,* as acceptable *clausulae* in themselves. In fact, some of these forms, as well as a rhythm called the *trispondaicus* (*ésse valebámus*), seem to have been favored by certain writers in the earlier medieval period. Hence the methodology just outlined may be a valid way of describing *cursus* as practiced in late antiquity or the early Middle Ages. (See [CF24] pp35–59.) But it has serious shortcomings if applied to the *cursus* of the later Middle Ages, since by this time the syllabic length of the last word was certainly considered important. The *dictamen* professors of this period clearly inform us that the final word of the cadence should consist of three or four syllables, or the equivalent through *consillabicatio.* (See, for example, [CF2] 1.20, pp25–27; [CF5] pp347–48.) Moreover, the actual practice of later medieval writers accords with the precepts of the teachers, since anomalous forms like those just described, as well as the *trispondaicus,* fell out of favor during the course of the twelfth century. (See especially [CF24] pp74, 104.)

## Examples

(a) From Bernard Silvester, *Cosmographia,* ed. P. Dronke (1978): *Microcosmus* 9.5–6, p139.

Erat rivus, oriundis ex alto cursibus in plana precipitans, non ut tumultus violentos incuteret, verum auribus amico *múrmure blandirétur.* Blandus auditu, blandior *fúerat visióne.* Etheree liquidum puritatis excedens, tanquam corporalitate deposita, ad purum fere *transíerat eleméntum.* Is quidem giris, amfractibus suos hactenus differebat effectus,
5   ut humoris materiam graminibus *sufficeret univérsis.* Totam loci continenciam utrobique silva lateraliter circumplectens, geminato commodo et temperabat solibus et communes *arcébat ingréssus.* Claudentes intra terminos agebat calor ethereus in humecto, ut ibi flores varii, ibi odoramenta, ibi seges aromatum *crésceret vel invísa.* Eo igitur in loco Physim residere super aspiciunt, Theorice et Practice individuo filiarum *consórtio coheréntem.*
10   Studiosa rerum, in seposito et tranquillo ubi nichil *offénderet, mansitábat.* Naturarum omnium origines, proprietates, potencias, effectus, postremo universam omnemque Aristotilis cathegoriam, materiam *cogitatiónis effécerat.* Sumptis a suprema divinitate principiis, per genera, per species, per individua, naturam, et quicquid eo nomine continetur, indeflexo *vestígio sequebátur.*

(b) From Peter of Celle, *Epistolae,* 1.25 (to Peter the Venerable), *PL* 202:431.

Haec, inquam, lego, et non inconsolabiliter inertiam meam lugeo? Ubi namque oves curae meae? Ubi *cáprae non stériles?* Qui enim a pueritia sua in claustris regulariter eruditi sunt, et tunicam vitae atque conversationis suae immaculatam servaverunt, oves Domini sunt. Qui de saeculo fetorem luxuriae fugientes, poenitentiae habitum sumunt, caprae
5   Domini nihilominus sunt. Sed ubi Jacob, ubi abbas tam sedulus exhortator, tam fervidus redargutor, tam cautus provisor, tam benevolus persuasor, tam contra rabiem luporum potens, tam contra morborum pestilentiam sapiens, tam ad aeris intemperiem patiens, tam ad latronum insidias prudens, tam fidelis in commisso, tam vigil in evitando damno, tam perseverans in *incépto servítio?* Damna Domini mei video, sed quomodo resarciam,
10   ignoro. Esset quidem justa recompensatio, si numero numerum aequarem, si pretium par pari pretio restituerem. Nunc vero cum non sit mihi nisi una anima, si perierint per culpam meam tres aut quatuor, quid faciam? Anne triplicatam vel quadruplicatam *poénam persólvam?*

(c) From Gasparino Barzizza, *Oratio habita in funere Jacobi de Turre Foroliviensis ad doctores utriusque universitatis,* in *Gasparini Barzizii Bergomatis et Guiniforti filii opera,* ed. J.A. Furietti (Rome 1723, r1969), p26 (the punctuation and capitalization in the following excerpt have been modified slightly).

Quid autem commentarios ejus in Aphorismos Hippocratis, quid sententias in primum Avicennae, quid denique suas illas in librum Tegni illustres ac praeclarissimas quaestiones commemorabo? Quae omnia vos omnes homines sapientissimi soletis divina *ópera dícere.* Nonne his ipsis ingenii sui, quod ille divinissimum habebat, operibus per-

5   fecit, ut si adesse nobis volumus, nunquam eo careamus? Reliquit quidem nobis, quod
    optimum in se habebat, animum suum, velut quamdam ejus imaginem in his, quod dixi,
    libris sculptam atque inclusam; quos quoties nostro studio, nostraque meditatione
    tractabimus, toties illum apud nos esse ac nobiscum *lóqui putábimus.* Nec est, quod
    quisquam nostrum eum sine liberis decessisse judicet. Reliquit enim ea, quae nuper dixi,
10  pulcherrima ingenii sui opera, quae is tanquam immortales filios ex se ipso genuit sem-
    piterna suae gloriae ac sui *nóminis monuménta.* Quare funus hujus Patris nostri mea sen-
    tentia ita a nobis instituendum censeo, ut omnes honores, qui homini conferri possunt,
    cumulatissime in hunc virum conferantur. Neque praetereatur ullum genus pompae
    quod ullo tempore in funere summorum hominum servatum fuit. Memoriam vero ejus,
15  quam apud nos decet esse perpetuam, si grati esse volumus, nunquam ex animis nostris
    dimittemus.

Although none of the three excerpts quoted here is long enough to constitute a statistically reliable sample, they should suffice to make us suspect that Bernard Silvester (d. c. 1160) used *cursus,* while Peter of Celle (d. 1183) and Gasparino Barzizza (d. 1431) did not. Such a suspicion would be confirmed by more extensive analysis. Bernard Silvester may be classified among the trend-setters for *cursus* usage in the mid-twelfth century. (See [CF24] pp75, 113.) Peter of Celle, however, seems to have been indifferent to *cursus* ([CF24] p75), though he obviously had a taste for the devices of parallelism such as anaphora, isocolon, and end rhyme. Barzizza, despite his occasional use of *suus* as the equivalent of *eius* in the medieval fashion (see line 2), adopts a rather classicizing style. He was one of the early Italian humanists, a group of writers who consciously rejected many Medieval Latin traditions, including accentual *cursus.* (See [CF28] pp152–60, [CF50].)

In our example from Bernard Silvester, we note that every sentence is terminated by one of the standard cadences of the Roman *cursus,* and study of a much larger sample shows that about 96 percent of Bernard's endings fit the prescribed patterns. (See [CF24] pp75, 113.) Few authors, except perhaps those employed in the papal chancery, made such a pedantic use of *cursus.* The example from Peter of Celle represents another extreme. Only three out of ten sentence endings correspond to the Roman cadences. The figure is similar (three out of nine) in our passage from Barzizza.

An investigator will encounter more difficulty when a writer's usage falls between these two extremes. Obviously we suspect a writer employed *cursus* if the standard forms occur very often in his or her work. But how often is *very* often? To consider the other end of the scale, the standard *cursus* patterns will sometimes occur at random even in the work of a writer who makes no attempt at rhythm. If this is so, how low a frequency of their occurrence can be considered insignificant? Recent investigators have employed statistical methods in the study of prose rhythm to determine when the frequency of endings in a given text suggests that the author deliberately used rhythm. In spite of the fact that all of the statistical methodologies have drawbacks, this approach has produced much more reliable results than earlier studies; it not only has helped to elucidate various phases and trends in the use of *cursus,* but also has cast new light on questions of authorship and cultural background. (See, for example, [CF24] pp61–62, 73–74; [CF25].)

In the examples quoted, only the cadences which fall at the ends of sentences have been marked, since sentence endings provide the least ambiguous criterion for the statistical evaluation of an author's use of *cursus.* It is true that *dictamen* manuals recommend *cursus* not only at the periods, but also at minor pauses, and there can be no doubt that medieval writers tended to use rhythm at breaks in sentences as well as sentence endings. (See [CF24] pp70–71.) It is, however, hazardous to use commas or semicolons in modern editions of medieval texts as a basis for a statistical enumeration of *cursus* rhythms simply because the punctuation within sentences more often reflects modern rather than medieval practice [CF42], and can frequently be a matter of subjective editorial judgment.

Nevertheless, having made this proviso, we can observe that standard rhythms of the Roman *cursus* occur at minor pauses marked by commas in all three of our examples, though these seem to be more sporadic in Peter of Celle and Barzizza than in the passage from Bernard Silvester. Without attempting an exact enumeration, we note that the *tardus* and *planus* occur frequently at commas in Bernard's text, e.g. *violéntos incúteret* (1–2), *blándus audítu* (2), *puritátis excédens* (3), *corporalitáte depósita* (3), *differébat efféctus* (4). At the sentence endings, however, there is only one *planus* (*arcébat ingréssus,* 7), and one *tardus* (*cogitatiónis effécerat,* 12). This preference for the *velox* at the end of the sentence is more or less the normal pattern encountered in texts of the High Middle Ages. (See [CF24] pp69–71, 79.)

## Select Bibliography

### Primary Works

Bede, *Historia ecclesiastica gentis Anglorum,* ed. B. Colgrave and R.A.B. Mynors (1969): the editors' introduction includes a brief assessment of Bede's style [CF1].

Bene of Florence, *Candelabrum,* ed. G.C. Alessio (1983): an early thirteenth-century *dictamen* manual, with an exhaustive commentary by the editor that includes parallels from many unpublished texts [CF2].

F. di Capua, *Fonti ed esempi per lo studio dello 'stilus curiae romanae' medioevale* (1941): a collection of medieval texts pertaining to *cursus* [CF3].

E. Faral, *AP:* some of the the texts published in this collection have appeared in more recent editions, but Faral's introduction is still an essential work on medieval stylistic theories [CF4].

Guido Faba, *Summa dictaminis,* ed. A. Gaudenzi, in *Il propugnatore* 23, n.s., 3 (1890), 1:287–338, 2:345–93: this important thirteenth-century *dictamen* textbook includes a very lucid discussion of the Roman *cursus*. A new critical edition of this *summa* is a desideratum [CF5].

*The Hisperica famina: I. The A-Text. A New Critical Edition with English Translation and Philological Commentary* (1974); *Hisperica famina: II. Related Poems. A Critical Edition with English Translation and Philological Commentary* (1987): both vols. ed. and tr. M.W. Herren [CF6].

John of Garland, *Parisiana poetria,* ed. and tr. T. Lawler (1974): both the text and the editor's comments provide information on medieval theories of style [CF7].

C. Thurot, *Extraits de divers manuscrits latins pour servir à l'histoire des doctrines grammaticales au moyen-âge* (1869, r1964) 480–85: a collection of medieval texts that give precepts on *cursus* [CF8].

## Bibliography

*MEL:* includes sections devoted to "stilistica e tecniche letterarie" and "versificazione e prosa ritmica" [CF9].

## Studies

E. Auerbach, *Literatursprache und Publikum in der lateinischen Spätantike und im Mittelalter* (1958): a fundamental work, especially on the theoretical basis of Medieval Latin style; tr. R. Manheim: *Literary Language & Its Public in Late Latin Antiquity and in the Middle Ages* (1965, r1993) [CF10].

M. Bonnet, *Le latin de Grégoire de Tours* (1890, r1968): despite its age, this is still a very useful study [CF11].

F. di Capua, "Lo stile della curia romana e il 'cursus' nelle epistole di Pier della Vigna e nei documenti della cancelleria Sveva," in *GIF* 2 (1949) 97–116 [CF12].

E.R. Curtius, *Europäische Literatur und lateinisches Mittelalter,* 7th ed. (1969): supplies much valuable information on trends, tastes, topoi, and other matters which will be of interest to students of Latin prose styles; tr. W.R. Trask: *European Literature and the Latin Middle Ages* (1953, r1990 with new epilogue) [CF13].

A. Dalzell, "The *Forma dictandi* attributed to Albert of Morra and Related Texts," in *MS* 39 (1977) 440–65: includes a good discussion of the Roman and French *cursus* [CF14].

N. Denholm-Young, "The *Cursus* in England," in *Oxford Essays in Medieval History Presented to Herbert Edward Salter,* ed. F.M. Powicke (1934) 68–103; repr. in *Collected Papers of N. Denholm-Young* (1969) 42–73 [CF15].

S. Eklund, "The Use and Abuse of Cursus in Textual Criticism," in *ALMA* 43 (1984) 27–56 [CF16].

C.B. Faulhaber, "The *Summa dictaminis* of Guido Faba," in *Medieval Eloquence: Studies in the Theory and Practice of Medieval Rhetoric,* ed. J.J. Murphy (1978) 85–111 [CF17].

J. Fontaine, "Théorie et pratique du style chez Isidore de Séville," in *VC* 14 (1960) 65–101 [CF18].

H.J.E. Goelzer, *Le latin de saint Avit, évêque de Vienne (450?–526?)* (1909): like the study by Bonnet ([CF11]), this is still an important work for anyone interested in the latinity of the early medieval period [CF19].

H. Hagendahl, *La prose métrique d'Arnobe: Contributions à la connaissance de la prose littéraire de l'empire* (1937) [CF20].

J.B. Hofmann and A. Szantyr, *Lateinische Syntax und Stilistik,* in *Handbuch der Altertumswissenschaft* 2.2.2 (1965, r1972): an essential reference work on Latin syntax and style that includes a great deal of material on late antiquity and the early Middle Ages [CF21].

M. Hubert, "Quelques aspects du latin philosophique aux XIIe et XIIIe siècles," in *REL* 27 (1949) 211–33 [CF22].

M. Hubert, "Notes de latin médiéval," in *REL* 30 (1952) 307–17 [CF23].

T. Janson, *PRML:* the best study of medieval prose rhythm published thus far. The statistical method for studying *clausulae* proposed by Janson has some disadvantages (recognized by the author himself on pp26–28), but it remains attractive for its simplicity, and because it makes fewer assumptions than any method yet devised. See the review by M. Winterbottom in *MAev* 45 (1976) 298–300;

he recognizes the value of Janson's study and presents some additional observations of his own, including a useful, if not infallible, method for gaining an initial indication of the presence of accentual rhythm in any Latin prose text [CF24].

T. Janson, "Schools of Cursus in the Twelfth Century and the Letters of Heloise and Abelard," in *Retorica e poetica tra i secoli XII e XIV: Atti del secondo convegno internazionale di studi dell'Associazione per il Medioevo e l'Umanesimo latini (AMUL) in onore e memoria di Ezio Franceschini* (3–5 October 1985), ed. C. Leonardi and E. Menestò (1988) 171–200 [CF25].

M. Lapidge, "The Hermeneutic Style in Tenth-Century Anglo-Latin Literature," in *ASE* 4 (1975) 67–111: provides information on Continental as well as English writers [CF26].

J.L. Leonhardt, *Dimensio syllabarum: Studien zur lateinischen Prosodie- und Verslehre von der Spätantike bis zur frühen Renaissance, mit einem ausführlichen Quellenverzeichnis bis zum Jahr 1600* (1989): concerned with verse doctrine and versification, but the author's observations on quantity and other matters are of interest to students of prose rhythm; includes a valuable index of primary sources [CF27].

G. Lindholm, *Studien zum mittellateinischen Prosarhythmus: Seine Entwicklung und sein Abklingen in der Briefliteratur Italiens* (1963) [CF28].

B. Löfstedt, "Some Linguistic Remarks on Hiberno-Latin," in *Studia Hibernica* 19 (1979) 161–69 [CF29].

B. Löfstedt and C.D. Lanham, "Zu den neugefundenen Salzburger Formelbüchern und Briefen," in *Eranos* 73 (1975) 69–100 [CF30].

A. Loyen, *Sidoine Apollinaire et l'esprit précieux en Gaule aux derniers jours de l'Empire* (1943) [CF31].

M. Manitius, *Geschichte der lateinischen Literatur des Mittelalters,* 3 vols. (1911–31, r1964–65): the author's remarks on style are usually limited to very general observations, but this work is still an excellent starting point for understanding any period of medieval latinity up to the end of the twelfth century [CF32].

J. Martin, "Classicism and Style in Latin Literature," in *R&R* 537–68: excellent survey of the prevalent styles in prose and poetry during the twelfth century, with very full bibliography [CF33].

A. Michel, ed., "Colloque de l'association des professeurs de langues anciennes de l'enseignement supérieur: le latin médiéval," in *Bulletin de l'Association Guillaume Budé* 4 (1981) 354–416: these discussions of different periods of medieval latinity by various specialists deal primarily with literary and cultural history, but offer useful background and supplementary information for the investigator of style. Especially welcome are the many bibliographical references pertaining to language [CF34].

C. Mohrmann, *Études sur le latin des chrétiens,* 4 vols. (1958–77): fundamental studies on the styles of patristic and medieval writers [CF35].

B. Munk-Olsen, "L'humanisme de Jean de Salisbury, un Cicéronien au 12e siècle," in *Entretiens sur la renaissance du 12e siècle,* ed. M. de Gandillac and E. Jeauneau (1968) 53–69 [CF36].

D. Norberg, *MPLM*: introductory manual which focuses on the earlier Middle Ages. The author's primary interests are romance and Latin linguistics, as well as orthography, but this survey offers some information about style [CF37].

E. Norden, *Die antike Kunstprosa vom VI. Jahrhundert v. Chr. bis in die Zeit der Renaissance,* 2 vols. (1898, r1983): the second volume of this work includes a survey of Medieval Latin prose style which is still important, even if dated in some respects [CF38].

S.M. Oberhelman, *Rhetoric and Homiletics in Fourth-Century Christian Literature: Prose Rhythm, Oratorical Style, and Preaching in the Works of Ambrose, Jerome, and Augustine* (1991): the author employs a sophisticated statistical method to study rhythm in late antique authors. The work includes an extensive bibliography [CF39].

S.M. Oberhelman and R.G. Hall, "A New Statistical Analysis of Accentual Prose Rhythms in Imperial Latin Authors," in *CPh* 79 (1984) 114–30: see also the bibliography in [CF39] for some other important studies of *cursus* and *cursus mixtus* by these authors, and by S. M. Oberhelman alone [CF40].

E. Paratore, "Alcuni caratteri dello stile della cancelleria federiciana," in *VII Centenario della morte di Federico II, imperatore e re di Sicilia (10–18 dicembre 1950): Atti del convegno internazionale di studi federiciani* (1952) 283–314; repr. in *Antico e nuovo*, Aretusa: Collezione di letteratura 22 (1965) 117–63 [CF41].

M.B. Parkes, *Pause and Effect: An Introduction to the History of Punctuation in the West* (1992): a pioneering study of a subject which is of considerable interest to students of style and rhythm; includes a great deal of information pertinent to the Latin Middle Ages [CF42].

K. Polheim, *Die lateinische Reimprosa* (1925, r1963) [CF43].

F. Quadlbauer, *Die antike Theorie der genera dicendi im lateinischen Mittelalter* (1962): study of medieval theorists' understanding of the different levels of style [CF44].

F. Quadlbauer, "Zur Theorie der Komposition in der mittelalterlichen Rhetorik und Poetik," in *Rhetoric Revalued*, ed. B. Vickers (1982) 115–31: on the distinction between *ordo naturalis* and *ordo artificialis* in the works of medieval theorists [CF45].

P. Rajna, "Per il 'cursus' medievale e per Dante," in *Studi di filologia italiana* 3 (1932) 7–86 [CF46].

H.M. Schaller, "Die Kanzlei Kaiser Friedrichs II: Ihr Personal und ihr Sprachstil"; pt2: "Der Sprachstil der Kanzlei," in *Archiv für Diplomatik* 4 (1958) 264–327: a fundamental study of chancery style in general, and that of Frederick's chancery in particular [CF47].

J. Schneider, *Die Vita Heinrici IV. und Sallust: Studien zu Stil und Imitatio in der mittellateinischen Prosa* (1965) [CF48].

J. Smit, *Studies on the Language and Style of Columba the Younger (Columbanus)* (1971) [CF49].

T.O. Tunberg, "A Study of *Clausulae* in Selected Works by Lorenzo Valla," in *HL* 41 (1992) 104–33: all evidence indicates that the Renaissance humanists rejected the accentual *cursus* of the Middle Ages. At least one of them, as suggested by this statistical study, may have gone even further and attempted to employ metrical *clausulae* similar to those favored in ancient Latin prose [CF50].

T.O. Tunberg, "What Is Boncompagno's 'Newest Rhetoric'?" in *Traditio* 42 (1986) 299–334: although this article is primarily concerned with the rhetorical theories of Boncompagno da Signa (d. c. 1240), it also discusses material pertaining to medieval theories of style and composition [CF51].

M. Winterbottom, "Aldhelm's Prose Style and Its Origins," in *ASE* 6 (1977) 39–76 [CF52].

R. Witt, "On Bene of Florence's Conception of the French and Roman *Cursus*," in *Rhetorica* 3 (1985) 77–98 [CF53].

BY MICHAEL W. HERREN

## Parameters

"Latin and the vernacular languages" is a large and diverse topic without many signposts. It deals with the mutual relationships between Latin and the fully formed vernacular languages of Europe and thus is not identical to the problem of the development of the Romance languages from Vulgar Latin. In the first place, the latter topic focuses on the question of natural linguistic evolution, whereas this topic deals with phenomena that occur, to a large extent, in a learned environment. Second, the evolution of the Romance languages is, by definition, restricted to a single language group, whereas our topic embraces all of the major European vernacular groups: Romance, Germanic, Celtic, Slavic, and Demotic Greek. In this essay the imposed chronological limits are the end of antiquity to the end of the Middle Ages, that is, roughly A.D. 500 to 1500. These dates establish the limits of the Medieval Latin literary period, beginning with the general collapse of antique literary standards and ending with their reestablishment in the early part of the Italian Renaissance.

## Historical Orientation

(a) **Written Languages.** Latin was *the* literary language of Europe, with the exception of southeastern Europe (modern Bulgaria, Greece, and parts of Yugoslavia) and those parts of southern Italy where Greek prevailed. Latin literacy was preserved in monastic and other ecclesiastical schools, and later on in the universities, throughout the Middle Ages. The vast majority of legal documents, secular and religious, were written in Latin. The same applies to writings of a theological or philosophical character and works meant to supply information: encyclopedias, technical treatises and scientific works, grammars and other linguistic aids. There is also a rich and extensive literary corpus in prose and poetry. Basically, to be literate in the Middle Ages meant to be literate in Latin.

It was only gradually—and under the influence of Latin—that the written forms of the various European vernaculars emerged. If we except Gothic, whose literary development belongs to the Greek-speaking East and still within the antique period, the earliest manifestation of vernacular literacy was Old Irish. Written Irish first appears in inscriptions dating from the fifth century. Brief texts, written on stone slabs in the Latin-derived Ogham alphabet, are to be found in Ireland and Britain. Probably by the late sixth or early seventh century Irish was already being written on parchment using the Latin alphabet. Some poems, such as the *Amra Coluim-cille,* are thought to belong to this early period. By the eighth century Irish is already being employed for works normally written in Latin: grammatical treatises, such as the *Auraicept na nÉces,* and biblical commentaries, such as the *Old Irish Treatise on the Psalter.*

Old English writing also developed early. Vernacular poetry written by Aldhelm (d. 709/10) is attested but lost. Nonetheless, an extensive Latin-Old English glossary dating from the seventh century can be reconstructed from the evidence of glossaries found in the libraries of Épinal and Erfurt. Old High German followed next. Scattered remains in the form of glossaries and legal documents date from the eighth century. Under Charlemagne the study of the vernacular in its written form was encouraged. Einhard relates (*Vita Karoli* 29) that Charlemagne ordered the transcription of native German poetry and the compilation of *grammatica patrii sermonis.* The earliest attested Old High German literature consists almost entirely of translations of Latin ecclesiastical texts: the Bible, Isidore, the hymns of Ambrose. There is also a fairly extensive corpus of glosses in Old Breton beginning in the eighth century. Glossed texts include Latin grammars and commentaries, Orosius, Isidore, and Irish collections of canons.

The late development of the written forms of the various Romance languages is well known. If indeed written Latin was pronounced like Romance in the pre-Carolingian period, it is easy to understand why literate Romance speakers were tardy in developing specialized writing systems. According to a recent theory, it was only after Latin was recreated as a school language in the Carolingian period that its difference from Romance and Romance dialects would have been perceptible, and indeed it was in the ninth century when the first tentative steps towards a form of written Romance were made. The French-language text of the Oaths of Strasbourg of 842 is the oldest discovered written Romance of any kind. The earliest literary work in French is the *Sequence of St. Eulalia,* written about 880. The earliest dated written Italian occurs in some Montecassino formulae of 960–63. However, in the same century, Gunzo of Novara, writing to the monks of Reichenau, admitted to some confusion in writing his native tongue: "licet aliquando retarder usu nostrae uulgaris linguae quae latinitati vicina est" ([CG10] p144). Literary Italian does not appear until the twelfth century. Spanish exhibits a similar history, with the earliest written examples appearing as glosses to a Latin devotional book of the mid-tenth century. The earliest literary text appears to be a Mozarabic poem written in Hebrew characters and dated c. 1100.

(b) **Latin as a Spoken Language.** Latin continued as a spoken language throughout the Middle Ages. There is evidence to show that it was pronounced according to the phonetic systems of the various regions. Nonetheless, if Latin was meant to serve as an effective lingua franca, it would have been necessary for all speakers, but Romance speakers in particular, to distinguish carefully between Latin and the vernacular. For lack of specific evidence, one can only hazard a guess as to how this was done. Presumably, the schools must have taught pupils to be especially careful about the pronunciation of word endings, so that the distinction between cases and verb inflections could be understood by the hearer. The development of scholastic Latin in the twelfth century shows that Latin could be molded to become a relatively simple, yet clear and precise, vehicle of written communication. Yet this species of Latin was also the *spoken* language of the universities, including the faculties of theology, law, and medicine. The route to a career in the professions in the later Middle Ages was paved with Latin. Ultimately this meant the acquisition of a type of bilingualism in which Latin served the needs of the professions and learning, while the vernacular sufficed for most other purposes.

On another level, however, Latin enjoyed a more popular role, indeed one akin to that of the vernacular. There is limited evidence to show that Latin was used as a kind of Esperanto for commerce and for general travel needs. A little known genre of medieval literature is the travel phrase book, offering a limited set of words and "bare-bones" phrases to the traveler ("Cut my hair," "Wash my shirt," "Will you sleep with me?"). Some of these use Romance as the base language from which the foreign language is learned; but more use Latin, indicating that anyone who could read at all could understand everyday Latin expressions and that it was more practical to keep a single widely understood language as the base language for this purpose.

All of this tends to show that Latin was more akin to an acquired second language than to either a "living language" or a "dead language." The closest modern parallel would perhaps be English as it is learned worldwide today outside English-speaking countries. Pupils do not acquire it in early childhood or learn it from native speakers, but many years of education enable them to speak, hear, write, and read this language with a high degree of precision and ease. The acquired language provides not only an important tool for one's working life, but also new ways of conceptualizing. It is a source of new words, expanded meanings of words, and, for some learners, word plays and other types of wit.

The keyword of this topic is therefore *bilingualism*. It is largely a literary bilingualism that comes into play, but oral bilingualism plays a role as well. Latin, the dominant literary language, strongly influenced the grammatical framework of the vernacular languages; it provided terms and idioms that were wholly lacking in those vernaculars not derived from it. Indeed, even those languages that derived from Latin returned to the source repeatedly for vocabulary enrichment. Latin was, however, also influenced quite strongly by the vernacular. Acquired second languages are always susceptible to influences of the native substrate, particularly in areas such as phonology, vocabulary, and idiom. Latin was no exception.

## Sources and Contexts

The mutual interpenetration of Latin and the vernacular languages is evidenced in many contexts in manuscripts: in collections of alphabets, glossaries, glossed Latin texts, grammars, translations, and macaronic texts.

(a) **Alphabets.** Collections of non-Roman alphabets reflect an interest in the study of the vernacular languages; they also reflect the Roman grammarian's method of beginning with the elements of a language: letter and syllable. Along with the shapes of the letters, the reader is usually provided with the foreign names of the vernacular-alphabet letters as well as the Roman equivalents. Hebrew and Greek alphabets (which, technically, are not vernacular) were very common, but there are also manuscript examples of Runic, Ogham, Cyrillic, and Glagolitic alphabets. Occasionally, Roman alphabets with the added English letter forms were given (e.g. in B.L. MS Cotton Titus D. XVIII).

(b) **Glossaries.** The compilation of glossaries began in late antiquity with the so-called *Hermeneumata Pseudo-Dositheana* ([BB70] v3), word lists designed to help Greek speakers learn Latin. Some texts were composed of batches of words organized by class, e.g. parts of the body, vestments, armament, etc. Others were based on scholia to literary works. A third class consists of conversation manuals: groups of phrases and expressions useful for everyday life. The methods of the classical language teachers were taken over by the glossators working in the European vernaculars. However, these soon introduced the principle of alphabetization, which is already observable in the early Latin-Old English glossaries, e.g. Epinal-Erfurt (seventh century) and Corpus Christi College (eighth century).

From earliest times the vernacular was employed as a vehicle for learning Latin. In the glossing of texts a Latin word was often first explained by an "easier" Latin word, which in turn was glossed by a vernacular word. Sometimes, of course, Latin words were glossed by the vernacular only. When *glossae collectae* were transferred to glossaries, the haphazard nature of the glosses (Latin, vernacular, or both) was carried over with them. The main purpose of the vast majority of glossaries was to aid the learning of Latin. An exception is the "travel phrase book," in which Latin is the base language from which another language is learned. A good example of the latter is to be found in a demotic Greek-Latin glossary of the tenth or eleventh century which contains corruptly transliterated Greek words organized by subject matter, followed by their Latin equivalents.

(c) **Colloquies.** Colloquies or conversation manuals provide some of our very best evidence for the teaching of Latin with the aid of the vernacular. These emanate from a school environment and deal primarily with school life. The genre is primarily insular: examples can be found in Ireland, Wales, and England. A possible prototype of the colloquy is the Irish *Hisperica famina* (seventh century). These are texts written in abstruse Latin (with elements of Greek, Hebrew, and Celtic languages) dealing with the daily life of a school, and organized, at least in part, in dialogue form. More basic in their pedagogical aims are the Welsh and Old English colloquies. The *De raris fabulis*, of Welsh origin, consists of short sentences with simple vocabulary relating to daily life. Some of the keywords are glossed in Old Welsh. There are two Old English colloquies by Aelfric Bata, a pupil of Aelfric, the homilist and grammarian. The larger of these, known as the *Colloquia aucta*, contains a running Old English gloss. The colloquies seem to have been designed to impart a speaking facility in Latin to the pupils. One Welsh colloquy refers to a pledge among the students to speak only Latin among themselves. By contrast, one Old High German text ([CG17] v5:517–24), intermediate between the colloquy and the travel phrase book, was apparently designed to teach basic German. Many of the phrases are useful for everyday situations, e.g. "Gimer min ros" ("Da mihi equum meum"). Others, however, pertain to school life: "En gualiche steta colernen ger?" ("In quo loco hoc didicisti?").

(d) **Grammars.** A "grammar" usually meant a work written in Latin for the purpose of teaching Latin. The most common examples are the *Ars maior* and *Ars minor* of Donatus (fourth century) and—at a more advanced level—the *Institutiones* of Priscian (sixth century). Clearly such works would have been of limited utility for beginners, increasingly so as time went on and Latin was universally perceived as a "foreign" language. Not surprisingly, therefore, Latin grammars were frequently glossed in the vernacular; for example, the earliest Old Irish glosses to Priscian date from the seventh century. However, it was not until the time of Aelfric (c. 955–1010 or 1015) that it occurred to anyone to write a grammar in the vernacular. Aelfric was aware of the daring nature of his undertaking; he wrote in the preface: "noui namque multos me reprehensuros quod talibus studiis meum ingenium occupare uoluissem, scilicet grammaticam artem ad anglicam linguam uertendo." In the Anglo-Norman period, English writers continued the tradition of writing grammatical works in the vernacular; note the *Tretiz* of Walter of Bibbesworth (mid-thirteenth century) and the dictaminal works of Thomas Sampson (second half of the fourteenth century) in Anglo-Norman French.

Nonetheless, the hegemony of Latin continued. A major drawback was the fact that the evolving languages were, for the most part, forced into the mold of Latin grammar. This tendency had already begun in the Carolingian period with Greek. An egregious example thereof was the compilation of "grammatical word lists," in which Greek synonyms of Latin words were arbitrarily assigned Latin genders!

(e) **Translations.** See chs. HA–HD.

(f) **Mixed Language or Macaronic Texts.** Linguistic mixture is a literary feature throughout the Middle Ages, predominating in the Celtic and Germanic Latin literatures. Sometimes the mixture is based on quite rational principles, such as in the Irish *Lambeth Commentary* (early eighth century), where the language of the "author" is Irish, but quotations from the Scriptures and the Church fathers are left in Latin. Other texts of Irish provenance are not as logically organized. Some of the later lives of St. Patrick wander freely between Latin and Irish, as does the so-called Old Irish *Life of St. Brigit.* A good example from the Old English area is the poem "Aldhelm," written in Latin (with Greek admixture) and Old English. Perhaps the most famous examples of macaronic works are to be found in the *Carmina Burana* (thirteenth century), a collection of poems (secular and religious) and liturgical drama. The linguistic mixture of Latin and Middle High German takes various forms, but in one poem (no. 218) it is found in alternating lines of each stanza:

> Sicut cribratur triticum,
> also wil ih die herren tun:
>   liberales dum cribro,
> die bosen risent in daz stro.

## Linguistic Features

(a) **Phonology and Orthography.** The tendency towards local pronunciation of Latin led to a number of orthographical influences of the vernacular on Latin. In Hiberno-Latin texts, for example, one finds Latin words where *i* is written after a vowel to indicate the palatalization of the following consonant (as was the practice in Irish), e.g. *staitim = statim*. Another feature was the diphthongization of long *e* to *ia*, e.g. *iasca = esca*. In French-Latin texts "soft *c*" sometimes replaces *s* before front vowels. The same feature crops up in a Bolognese document, where *cignum* represents *signum*, not *cygnum!* Italian manuscripts of the later Middle Ages commonly show forms assimilated in the Italian manner, e.g. *ottava* for *octava;* sometimes hypercorrections appear, e.g. *optava* for *octava*.

(b) **Vocabulary and Word Formation.** The most salient point of contact between Latin and the vernaculars was vocabulary, and it must be borne in mind that influences worked in both directions. Even after the establishment of separate Romance languages Latin continued to have a tenacious hold on the formation of their vocabularies. Old French offers numerous examples of words drawn from documents of the ninth to twelfth centuries which might be described as "relatinized," i.e. the forms are much closer to Latin than to Old French. Some examples are "new" *baptisier:* Old French *batoier;* "new" *canal:* OF *chenal;* "new" *colombe:* OF *coulon;* "new" *defense:* OF *defoise*. Many of these new forms became standard in Modern French; others did not, e.g. "new" *áneme:* OF *ame;* "new" *envidie:* OF *envie*.

While the Celtic and Germanic groups have a much lower percentage of Latin-derived vocabulary than the Romance languages, the Latin element is nonetheless significant, particularly in the fields of religion and education. In Old Irish some borrowings from Latin go back to the period of the British missions (fifth and sixth centuries), revealing a stage in their phonetic development that antedates the development of a *p*-sound in Irish: *cruimther* from Latin *presbyter, caille* from Latin *pallium*.

Borrowings from Latin into the vernacular took several forms. Chief among these were word-borrowing (*Lehnwort*) and meaning-borrowing (*Lehnbedeutung*). A nice illustration of this distinction is provided in the *Auraicept na nÉces,* where Latin *consonans* is rendered by Old Irish *consain,* while Latin *vocalis* is translated by Old Irish *gutte,* based on the native Irish word *guth,* "voice." In Old English a distinction can be shown between direct borrowings from Latin such as *bisceop, apostol,* and words drawing from the native vocabulary to express concepts taken from Latin, e.g. *ealdor* to express *presbyter* and *leorningcniht* to express *discipulus*. Sometimes it was necessary to combine the two types of borrowing, as in *heahbiscop = archiepiscopus*. An early example of a meaning-borrowing is provided by Einhard, who tells us (*Vita Karoli* 29) that Old High German lacked the names for the intermediate directions of the winds ("southwest," etc.), so that Charlemagne requested that these be supplied in German.

Reverse word-borrowings, i.e. from the vernacular into Latin, were also very common. These tend to occur most often in cases having to do with local or regional conditions, e.g. features of the terrain, local political institutions, social and legal concepts, technical terms, etc. Charters and legal documents generally provide rich hunting grounds for this phenomenon. The usual method of incorporating a "barbarism" into a Latin text was to add a Latin inflection to the stem of the vernacular word, normally a noun or an adjective. In Irish texts the general tendency was to add a Latin ending of the same gender as the native word, e.g. *tigernus* from Old Irish *tigern* (masc.), "petty king." Old Norse examples formed in the same way are *hirdmannus* from Old Norse *hirdmaðr,* accusative *hirðmann* ("bodyguard"), and *copmannus* from Old Norse *kaupmaðr,* accusative *kaupmann* ("merchant"). When Norse authors writing in Latin required a word for "ski," they had only their native language to draw from, so they coined *ondrus* and the diminutive *ondriolus* from Old Norse *ondurr,* "ski." Texts emanating from later medieval England are replete with latinized English nouns, e.g. *husbandus* and derivatives, *hutta,* "smelter," (cf. Middle High German *Hütte*), *hustingum,* "husting court." Examples of latinized words drawn from the Romance languages are also to be found. In Italian, for example, one finds a number of latinized words beginning with *gu-* (reflecting an original Germanic origin), such as *gualdarius, guarda, guardator.* Sometimes the words were originally Latin, but the roots have been made to conform to Italian phonetics before being fitted out with Latin endings, e.g. *gattus* (cf. Latin *cattus*).

Meaning-borrowings from the vernacular languages into Latin also occur. In Irish-Latin works *calvus* is used in the sense of Irish *Mael,* which means both "bald" and "servant"; thus *Calvus Brigidae* renders *Maelbrighde,* "servant of Brigit." In the same vein, *amicus animae* renders Irish *anmchara,* which means "soul-friend" in the technical sense of "confessor." In Norse-Latin works the names Iceland and Greenland are rendered, respectively, by *glacialis insula* and *viridis terra.* Occasionally meaning-borrowings extend to idiom. A fairly certain example from English to Latin is *mittere pro,* "to send for." In Irish-Latin works one occasionally finds the phrase *dixit contra eum,* meaning nothing more than "he/she spoke to him," a literal rendition of Irish *asbert fris,* where the preposition *fri* means both *ad* and *contra.* Examples of similar phenomena have been adduced from most regions of Europe, including Hungary and Finland.

## Select Bibliography

There is no standard introduction to this very diverse field. Perhaps the closest to it is the essay by B. Bischoff, "The Study of Foreign Languages in the Middle Ages," in *MittStud* 2:227–45 [CG1]. Much that is useful can be found in A. Borst, *Der Turmbau von Babel: Geschichte der Meinungen über Ursprung und Vielfalt der Sprachen und Völker,* 4 vols. in 6 pts. (1957–63) [CG2]. The concept of "the Latin Middle Ages" is put forward by E.R. Curtius, *European Literature and the Latin Middle Ages,* tr. W.R. Trask (1953, r1990), chs. 1–2 [CG3]. See also P. Wolff, *Western Languages,* A.D. 100–1500, tr. F. Partridge (1971) [CG4]; R. McKitterick, *The Carolingians and the Written Word* (1989) [CG5]; and R. McKitterick, ed., *The Uses of Literacy in Early Mediaeval Europe* (1990) [CG6].

The origins of the written vernaculars are here treated by language group:

For Irish, see J. Stevenson, "The Beginnings of Literacy in Ireland," *Proceedings of the Royal Irish Academy* 89C (1989) 127–65 [CG7].

For the Romance languages, W.D. Elcock, *The Romance Languages,* rev. ed. (1975) [CG8], is still very useful, as is M. Pei, *The Story of Latin and the Romance Languages* (1976) [CG9]. Very much on topic, but still controversial, is R. Wright's *LLER* [CG10]. For recent work, see M. Banniard, *Viva Voce: Communication écrite et communication orale du IVe au IXe siècle en occident latin* (1992) [CG11], and R. Wright, ed., *Latin and the Romance Languages in the Early Middle Ages* (1991) [CG12].

On the study of alphabets the standard work is R. Derolez, *Runica Manuscripta* (1954) [CG13].

The relation of the vernacular to Latin in glossaries has been well treated, particularly for Old English: see J.D. Pheifer, *Old English Glosses in the Épinal-Erfurt Glossary* (1974) [CG14], and N. Brooks, ed., *Latin and the Vernacular Languages in Early Medieval Britain* (1982) [CG15]. The Old English glossaries are edited in various places, for which see [CG14].

For the Old Irish glosses, see W. Stokes and J. Strachan, eds., *Thesaurus Palaeohibernicus: A Collection of Old-Irish Glosses, Scholia, Prose and Verse*, 2 vols. (1901–3, r1975) [CG16].

The Old High German glosses have been edited by E. von Steinmeyer and E. Sievers, *Die althochdeutschen Glossen*, 5 vols. (1879–1922); additions by H. Mayer, *Old High German Glosses: A Supplement* (1974) [CG17].

The colloquies of Wales and England have been edited by W.H. Stevenson, *Early Scholastic Colloquies* (1929, r1989) [CG18].

For the *Hisperica famina*, see the edition and translation of M.W. Herren, 2 vols. (1974–87) [CG19].

For grammars written in the vernacular, see G. Calder, *Auraicept na nÉces: The Scholar's Primer* (1917, r1995) [CG20], and A. Ahlqvist, *The Early Irish Linguist* (1982) [CG21]. For Aelfric's grammar, see J. Zupitza, ed., *Aelfrics Grammatik und Glossar* (1880, r1966 with preface by H. Gneuss) [CG22]. Useful for the vernacular Anglo-Norman grammars is J. Hassell, "Thomas Sampson's Dictaminal Treatises and the Teaching of French in Medieval England: An Edition and Study" (Ph.D. diss., Toronto, 1991) [CG23]. For Latin as provider of the paradigmatic grammar, see A.C. Dionisotti, "Greek Grammars and Dictionaries in Carolingian Europe," in *The Sacred Nectar of the Greeks: The Study of Greek in the West in the Early Middle Ages*, ed. M.W. Herren (1988) 1–56 [CG24].

For the phonetic influences of Irish on Latin, see especially B. Löfstedt, *Der hiberno-lateinische Grammatiker Malsachanus* (1965) [CG25].

For the Latin influences on Old English vocabulary, see H. Gneuss, *Lehnbildungen und Lehnbedeutungen im Altenglischen* (1955) [CG26]. The Latin element in German is treated extensively by O. Wittstock, *Latein und Griechisch im deutschen Wortschatz: Lehn- und Fremdwörter altsprachlicher Herkunft*, 4th ed. (1988) [CG27]. For the Latin element in Irish, see J. Vendryes, "De hibernicis vocabulis quae a lingua latina originem duxerunt" (Diss., Paris, 1902) [CG28].

There is now an extensive literature on the topic of regional differences in Medieval Latin vocabulary and idiom. For an orientation, see E. Löfstedt, *LL*, ch. 3 [CG29]; also F. Blatt, "L'évolution du latin médiéval," in *ALMA* 28 (1958) 201–19 [CG30]. For Italian-Latin, see J. Hubschmid, "Zur Erforschung des mittellateinischen Wortschatzes," in *ALMA* 20 (1947–48) 255–72 [CG31]; for Spanish-Latin vocabulary, see B. Löfstedt, "Zur Lexikographie der Mittellateinischen Urkunden Spaniens," in *ALMA* 29 (1959) 5–89 [CG32]; for Scandinavian influences, see E. Vandvik, "National Admixture in Medieval Latin," in *SO* 23 (1944) 81–101 [CG33]; for word- and meaning-borrowings from Irish, see M.W. Herren, "Old Irish Lexical and Semantic Influence on Hiberno-Latin," in *Irland und Europa/Ireland and Europe*, ed. P. Ní Chatháin and M. Richter (1984) 197–209 [CG34]. The various national Medieval Latin dictionaries [CD25–41] should also be consulted.

*See also* [BB68–86].

CH   &bull;   # HUMANISTIC LATIN

## BY TERENCE O. TUNBERG

During the fourteenth and fifteenth centuries the Italian humanists developed a distinctive latinity that was more closely based on ancient models than the Latin of other late medieval writers. By the late fifteenth century, humanistic Latin was gaining ground in northern Europe, and it became the prevailing style for Latin written throughout Europe after 1500. The term "Neo-Latin" is often used as a synonym for humanistic Latin, although "Neo-Latin" in a somewhat looser sense can refer to all Latin written during the Renaissance and later times, including some categories of Latin that continued to have much more in common with medieval traditions than with the Latin written by contemporary humanists. The present essay is primarily concerned with the Latin written by humanists before 1500 but many of the features noted here apply equally well to the period after 1500. Furthermore, most of the bibliographical aids listed here cover the whole field of "Neo-Latin" and its various styles or genres in all periods up to quite recent times. (See [CH2–6].)

Many modern scholars would argue that humanistic Latin begins with the so-called prehumanists, who were active in Padua in the late thirteenth and early fourteenth centuries, the most important of whom was probably Lovato dei Lovati (c. 1240–1309). Although these authors produced a considerable amount of classicizing verse, their prose, generally speaking, differs very little from that of their contemporaries ([CH12], [CH35]). Even the prose of Petrarch (1304–74), who probably knew more about the language and style of ancient authors than any of his contemporaries, often seems to have more in common with medieval than humanistic Latin [CH22–23].

Because the humanists placed such emphasis on the emulation of ancient writers, it was perhaps inevitable that controversies would arise about which authors were worth imitating, and how far such imitation should go. Ciceronianism, the view that Cicero should be the primary or sole model for elegant prose, was prevalent in Italy by the end of the fifteenth century ([CH11], [CH15]). Yet many important fifteenth-century Italian humanists favored a more eclectic approach. Most of the eclectics would have agreed with Lorenzo Valla (1407–57), who argued that it was much better to coin a new word, or adapt a contemporary one, than to misuse an ancient term or employ a clumsy circumlocution. (See [CH24] pp382–83; [CH31] p52, nn85–86.) The great Dutch humanist Erasmus (1466?–1536) had similar views, and Ciceronianism never achieved quite the same status in northern Europe as in Italy.

Humanistic "imitation" of ancient authors could often be a highly creative process, as exemplified by Giovanni Pontano (1429?–1503), whose innovative comic prose is based on a free adaptation of the language of Plautus [CH13]. Few humanists, however, carried imitation and adaptation to such extremes as the so-called Apuleians, who salted their writings with rare expressions from early Latin or from the archaizing writers of the second century A.D., especially Apuleius [CH15].

This humanistic interest in style and imitation led to the publication of many new stylistic handbooks and lexica based on ancient writers. (See [CH1], [CH3], [CH11], [CH23–24], [CH28].) These works—very few of which, unfortunately, exist in modern critical editions—can often be invaluable for the modern student of Renaissance latinity. Of humanistic treatises on usage, the most important is probably Lorenzo Valla's monumental *Elegantiarum linguae latinae libri sex,* in which Valla took the revolutionary step of rejecting the authority of the traditional grammarians, such as Donatus and Priscian, and of attempting to base his precepts on the observed practice of the ancient authors themselves. (See [CH8] v1:3–235.) However, the humanistic conception of "ancient usage," as Valla's *Elegantiae* and other texts (e.g [CH9–10]) show, often differs considerably from what we find in modern studies of ancient latinity.

Similarly, Renaissance dictionaries and lexica, which were generally compiled under the classicizing impulse, and therefore based on Roman authors (though they also contain postclassical words), can often give us valuable information about how Renaissance readers and writers understood and used ancient Latin words or expressions. Moreover, every Neo-Latinist must keep in mind the fact that many medieval handbooks and lexica remained in use for most of the Renaissance, especially the thirteenth-century *Catholicon* of John of Genoa (d. c. 1298), which was printed many times before 1500 [CD9]. (See especially [CH24] pp400–1.)

Renaissance Latin prose is characterized by a number of words, expressions, and constructions which occur in some ancient authors, but are not typical of Classical Latin prose: for example, in the best humanistic writers *nec* is often used for *ne . . . quidem;* we encounter *absque* + ablative and *citra* + accusative as common equivalents for *sine;* we very frequently find *id genus* instead of *eius generis;* the dative of agent seems to be more frequent than in Classical Latin. (See [CH20], [CH21] p135, [CH22], [CH30], [CH31] pp34–41.) Similarly, the technical vocabulary of the humanists, especially the vocabulary pertaining to textual scholarship, includes many ancient words employed with specialized connotations. As a result, meanings which had been rare in antiquity, and are normally only found in postclassical writers, become the usual significance of such words in humanistic Latin. For example, the verbs *castigare, recognoscere,* and *repurgare* commonly refer to textual criticism, and *publicare* means "to publish" [CH25].

Partly as a result of the rise of Greek scholarship in the Renaissance, Greek words and derivatives sometimes appear in humanistic Latin. For some humanists, such as the French scholar Guillaume Budé (1468–1540), this became a real affectation. Budé not only uses many latinized Greek words, he sometimes writes whole passages in unadulterated Greek. Most humanists, however, make much more modest use of Greek, and many of the most popular latinized Greek words, such as *methodus* (method) and *scopus* (goal, purpose), had already appeared, even if rarely, in ancient Latin authors ([CH18], [CH29]).

As noted above, medieval grammars and lexica remained in use for most of the Renaissance. Thus, humanistic writers continue to employ medieval words, especially to denote contemporary institutions and functions, such as *camerarius, capitaneus, senescallus,* etc.; we sometimes find medieval adjectives like *aliqualis* or *deiformis;* ancient words are sometimes employed with medieval meanings: for example, *applicare* can denote arrival by land (not by sea), and *resultare* can mean "to result." (See, for some examples, [CH20] pp197–98, [CH24] p383, [CH31] p42, [CH34] pp164–66.) Obviously, the modern dictionaries of Medieval Latin, many of which are still in progress (see [CD22–41]), are indispensable not only for medievalists, but also for students of Renaissance Latin.

Moreover, many new words, new compounds, and old words with entirely new meanings appear in Renaissance and early modern Latin. This expanded Latin vocabulary was especially necessary for those who wrote about such subjects as printing, seafaring and navigation, warfare, and the learned disciplines, but the coining of new words is also common in Neo-Latin texts concerned with less technical matters: for instance, *aconitum Peruvianum* = tobacco, *aurora borealis* = northern lights, *commonimentum* = reminder, *gallinago* = snipe, *impressio* = printing, *pressor* = printer. Several useful word lists and vocabularies exist ([CH2], [CH17], [CH26–27]), and a lexicon of Renaissance Latin prose is now in print [CH17]. Neo-Latin lexicography, however, is still in its infancy, and the publication of truly comprehensive dictionaries of Neo-Latin is still years away.

Humanistic Latin also retains many features of medieval syntax. Fairly well attested in humanistic Latin, at least in its earlier phases, is the juxtaposed subjunctive without a subordinating conjunction, which sometimes takes the place of an accusative and infinitive or a *quod*-clause: for instance, in his *Gesta Ferdinandi regis Aragonum* (2.10.6), Valla writes: "In quo illud precipue admirabantur . . . tam modico exiguoque contentus foret" (see [CH32] p49). In the works of Olaus Magnus (d. 1557), for example, we find *quatenus* introducing final clauses (see [CH20] p188). Humanistic writers, particularly the early ones, still employ *quod/quia* with the indicative instead of the accusative and infinitive to express indirect speech; *quod* sometimes serves for *ut* in consecutive clauses. (See [CH18–19], [CH23–24], [CH31] pp41–53, [CH34] pp159–67.)

A potentially important step in the regularization of Latin grammar and usage was the completion of Lorenzo Valla's *De reciprocatione 'sui' et 'suus'*, which he finished by 1450 (see [CH8] VI:236–49). This treatise is probably the earliest systematic discussion of the reflexive pronoun and the reflexive possessive adjective. In this little work, Valla carefully distinguished the reflexive from nonreflexive third person pronouns, and in so doing formulated some of the principles regarding Latin reflexives which are still enunciated (though with different terminology) in modern grammars. We must keep in mind, however, that Valla's rules about the reflexives are limited to independent propositions with a single finite verb, and that he provides no guidelines for the use of reflexives in more complex sentences with two or more finite verbs. The influence of *De reciprocatione* on later humanistic grammars requires further study ([CH14], [CH32]).

Classicized spelling was introduced only slowly and sporadically. *Nichil* is gradually replaced by *nihil.* Familiar medieval features, such as e-cedilla (ę) for *ae*-diphthong, persist in printed books long after 1500. At no time in the age of early printing does Latin spelling become consistent: hence we often find such forms as *caeteri, charus* (= *carus*), *lachryma, omneis,* etc. Indeed, the spelling of a fifteenth-century humanist like Valla can differ radically from modern notions of classical orthography. (See [CH31] p31, n5.)

Another factor to consider is the relationship between humanistic Latin and the vernacular languages. Renaissance Latin authors occasionally incorporate vernacular words in their writings. Sometimes an accompanying phrase such as "quod vulgo dicunt" makes this explicit. In some texts vernacular expressions are mimicked in Latin for the purpose of parody. However, modern scholars are often too ready to attribute peculiarities of humanistic Latin to the influence of the author's native language. For example, if we encounter *consulere* with the dative used to mean "advise" or "counsel" in the works of a French humanist, we cannot assume without further evidence that the author has patterned his usage on the French verb *conseiller.* This meaning of *consulere* is well attested in Medieval Latin throughout Europe, and it is sanctioned by influential humanistic treatises on latinity such as Perotti's *Cornucopiae* and Valla's *Elegantiae.* (See [CH33] pp427–28.) Some parallels between the vernaculars and Latin neologisms result from the fact that Neo-Latin usage has influenced the vernacular rather than the other way around. In general, the direct influence of vernaculars on the usage and syntax of formal humanistic prose and poetry is rare and difficult to prove. (See [CH13] pp92, 98; [CH21] pp138–41; [CH24] pp388–94; [CH33].) On the other hand, the importation of vernacular elements into less formal works is more common. School commentaries, for example, frequently contain vernacular words and phrases, especially where the author wishes to explain unusual Latin expressions [CH7].

In summary, humanistic Latin represents a departure from medieval traditions in many respects. Yet, as modern scholarship increasingly shows, this break is much less fundamental than was once thought, especially in the earlier stages of humanism.

# Select Bibliography

## Bibliographical Aids

F. Buisson, *Répertoire des ouvrages pédagogiques du XVIe siècle* (1886, r1962; updated 1979): includes titles of many manuals of Latin style printed during the sixteenth century [CH1].

*Humanistica Lovaniensia: Journal of Neo-Latin Studies* [HL] (Louvain): this journal, devoted entirely to Neo-Latin, appears annually; it includes a bibliography of the year's publications in Neo-Latin studies, as well as a list of Neo-Latin words which occur in the contributions to each volume [CH2].

J. IJsewijn, *Companion to Neo-Latin Studies* (1977) 237–61: a bibliography of works published before 1977 on the language and prosody of Neo-Latin authors which will remain fundamental until the publication of pt2 of [CH4] [CH3].

J. IJsewijn, *Companion to Neo-Latin Studies: Part I. History and Diffusion of Neo-Latin Literature. Second entirely rewritten edition* (1990): indispensable guide to the history and geographical distribution of Neo-Latin [CH4].

"Neo-Latin," in *The Year's Work in Modern Language Studies:* annual bibliography (see [BA43]) [CH5].

"Neo-Latin News," in *Seventeenth Century News:* annual bibliography [CH6].

## Primary Works

V. Fera, ed., *Una ignota Expositio Suetoni del Poliziano* (1983): for editions of similar commentaries, see pp11–12 [CH7].

Lorenzo Valla, *Opera omnia,* ed. E. Garin (1962): the first volume contains a reprint of the 1540 Basel edition of Valla's *Elegantiae* [CH8]; see [CH31], pp30–4, nn2–19, where other works by Valla pertaining to usage and style are mentioned (several of which are available in recent editions).

Mario Nizzoli (1498–1566), *M. Nizolii Brixellensis observationum in M. T. Ciceronem prima (+ secunda) pars* (1535): this thesaurus of Cicero's language, a popular handbook for those who aspired to Ciceronian style, was revised and amplified many times after its first edition; its material is derived from editions of Cicero that often differ considerably from modern ones [CH9].

Niccolò Perotti, *Cornucopiae latinae linguae* (Venice 1489): this elaborate commentary on the poems of Martial, which exists in many early editions, contains a great deal of lexical and syntactic information. See also the work now in progress by J.-L. Charlet, *Nicolai Perotti Cornu Copiae seu Linguae Latinae Commentarii,* v1–2 (1989, 1991) [CH10].

E.V. Telle, ed., *L'Erasmianus sive Ciceronianus d'Étienne Dolet (1535)* (1974): Telle's commentary is an essential reference work on Ciceronianism and humanistic debates on imitation; the bibliography includes important humanistic lexica, stylistic handbooks, and treatises [CH11].

## Studies

G. Billanovich, "Il preumanesimo padovano," in *Storia della cultura veneta,* v2: *Il trecento* (1976) 19–110 [CH12].

R. Capelletto, *La "lectura Plauti" del Pontano, con edizione delle postille del cod. Vindob. lat. 3168 e osservazioni sull'"Itala recensio"* (1988): see especially pp80–98, where Pontano's notes on Plautus are discussed in relation to Pontano's own unique Latin style; see also pp9–15 for a useful bibliography, which includes other studies of Pontano's language [CH13].

J. Chomarat, "Le 'De reciprocatione sui et suus' de Lorenzo Valla," in *HGL* 283–92 [CH14].

J. D'Amico, "The Progress of Renaissance Latin Prose: The Case of Apuleianism," in *RQ* 37 (1984) 351–92: important discussion of humanist stylistic controversies [CH15].

W.S. Heckscher, *The Princeton Alciati Companion: A Glossary of Neo-Latin Words and Phrases Used by Andrea Alciati and the Emblem Book Writers of His Time, Including a Bibliography of Secondary Sources Relevant to the Study of Alciati's Emblems* (1989) [CH16].

R. Hoven, *Lexique de la prose latine de la Renaissance* (1994): see the review by T.O. Tunberg in *RQ* 48.4 (1995) [CH17].

*L'humanisme français au début de la Renaissance: Colloque international de Tours (XIVe stage). De Pétrarque à Descartes, XXIX* (1973): see especially the chapters (pp329–59) by J. IJsewijn and M.M. de la Garanderie on the Latin of French humanists and the style of Guillaume Budé [CH18].

J. IJsewijn, "Mittelalterliches Latein und Humanistenlatein," in *Die Rezeption der Antike: Zum Problem der Kontinuität zwischen Mittelalter und Renaissance,* ed. A. Buck (1981) 71–83 [CH19].

K. Isacson, "A Study of Non-Classical Features in Book XV of Olaus Magnus' *Historia de Gentibus Septentrionalibus,* 1555," in *HL* 38 (1989) 176–99: Humanism did not reach Scandinavia until about 1500, and the Swede Olaus Magnus (1490–1557) is a representative of its earlier phases [CH20].

B. Löfstedt, "Notizen eines Latinisten zum Leviathan von Thomas Hobbes," in *Arctos: Acta Philologica Fennica* 23 (1989) 133–43: see not merely for Hobbes, but also for references to other studies pertaining to the language of humanistic authors by the same scholar [CH21].

G. Martellotti, "Latinità del Petrarca," in *Studi petrarcheschi* 7 (1961) 219–30: reprinted in *Scritti petrarcheschi,* ed. M. Feo and S. Rizzo (1983) 289–301 [CH22].

S. Rizzo, "Il latino del Petrarca nelle *Familiari,*" in *The Uses of Greek and Latin: Historical Essays,* ed. A.C. Dionisotti *et al.* (1988) 41–56: Petrarch's revisions suggest an increasing tendency to follow the usage of ancient writers; on p56 Rizzo includes a useful bibliography on Petrarch's Latin; for additional studies of Petrarch's latinity, see also [CH3], p251 [CH23].

S. Rizzo, "Il latino nell'Umanesimo," in *Letteratura italiana,* ed. A. Asor Rosa, 8 vols. (1982–), v5: *Le Questioni,* pp379–408: an important synthesis of recent studies pertaining to the language of Italian humanists; see Rizzo's notes throughout for further bibliography [CH24].

S. Rizzo, *Il lessico filologico degli umanisti* (1973): a fundamental study of humanistic vocabulary pertaining to books and textual criticism [CH25].

R.J. Schoeck *et al.,* "A Step towards a Neo-Latin Lexicon: A First Word-List Drawn from *Humanistica Lovaniensia 1973–1984,*" in *HL* 39 (1990) 340–65, 40 (1991) 423–45 [CH26].

D. Shaw, "'Ars formularia': Neo-Latin Synonyms for Printing," in *The Library,* 6th ser., 11 (1989) 220–30 [CH27].

D.T. Starnes, *Renaissance Dictionaries: English-Latin and Latin-English* (1954) [CH28].

C.R. Thompson, "Some Greek and Grecized Words in Renaissance Latin," in *American Journal of Philology* 64 (1943) 333–35 [CH29].

D.F.S. Thomson, "The Latinity of Erasmus," in *Erasmus,* ed. T.A. Dorey (1970) 115–37 [CH30].

T.O. Tunberg, "The Latinity of Lorenzo Valla's *Gesta Ferdinandi regis Aragonum,*" in *HL* 37 (1988) 30–78: study of Valla's historical style; see footnotes for bibliography on Valla in particular and humanistic latinity in general; see p51, n83, for bibliography on the continuities between medieval and humanistic Latin [CH31].

T.O. Tunberg, "Further Remarks on the Language of Lorenzo Valla's *Gesta Ferdinandi* and on *De reciprocatione 'sui' et 'suus',*" in *HL* 39 (1990) 48–53 [CH32].

T.O. Tunberg, "De locutionibus nonnullis humanisticis quae pro vestigiis linguarum nationalium habentur," in *Vox latina* 26:101 (1990) 415–30: an examination of alleged vernacular influences on the Latin of several humanists with notes providing additional bibliography; the editor has corrected several misprints in this article in *Vox latina* 27:103 (1991) VIII (appendix); add to this list p416, line 1 *asservare* = *asseverare;* p418, line 10 *numerandos* = *numerandus;* p420, line 2 *se* = *sed;* and p427, n57 *Labini* = *Lambini* [CH33].

T.O. Tunberg, "The Latinity of Lorenzo Valla's Letters," in *MLJ* 26 (1991) 150–85 [CH34].
R. Witt, "Petrarch and Pre-Petrarchan Humanism: Stylistic Imitation and the Origins of Italian Humanism," in *Humanity and Divinity in Renaissance and Reformation*, ed. J.W. O'Malley *et al.* (1993) 73–100 [CH35].

*See also* [BA8], [BA62], [BC25], [BC35–36], [BC117].

## DA ● CHRISTIAN AND BIBLICAL LATIN

BY DANIEL SHEERIN

*Itaque indignandum omnibus, indolescendum est audere quosdam, et hoc studio-rum rudes, litterarum profanos, expertes artium etiam sordidarum, certum aliquid de summa rerum ac maiestate decernere.*

MINUCIUS FELIX, Octavius 5.4

*Sed ab indoctis hominibus et rudibus scripta sunt et idcirco non sunt facili auditione credenda. . . . Triuialis et sordidus sermo est. . . . Barbarismis, soloecis-mis obsitae sunt, inquit, res uestrae et uitiorum deformitate pollutae.*

ARNOBIUS, Aduersus nationes 1.58.1, 2; 59.1

*"Christus," inquit, "Jesus" [1 Tim 1:15], id est Christus Salvator. Hoc est enim latine Jesus. Nec quaerant grammatici quam sit latinum, sed Christiani quam verum. Salus enim latinum nomen est. Salvare et salvator non fuerunt haec latina antequam veniret Salvator: quando ad latinos venit, et haec latina fecit.*

AUGUSTINE, Sermo 299.6 [PL 38:1371]

The existence of differences between the Latin of Christians (in both its written and, presumptively, its spoken forms) and the Latin of their non-Christian neighbors in the Empire has been frankly acknowledged from paleo-Christian times. It is the extent, nature, sources, and significance of these differences that have been the foci of research and dispute in modern scholarship. We shall begin with an historical overview and then describe modern formulations and controversies.

The earliest Western Christian literature was Greek (Clement of Rome, the *Pastor* of Hermas, Justin, Irenaeus, Hippolytus, the *acta* of the martyrs of Lyons and Vienne, etc.). But a Latin Christian literature emerged, first as a translation literature (versions of the Greek Scriptures and other works), and soon as an original literature, though of course under heavy influence from the translations. Texts appear fairly early, not only in North Africa, long supposed to be the *Urheimat* of Christian Latin (versions of the Scriptures, the *acta* of the Scillitan martyrs and of Perpetua and Felicity, works of Tertullian, Cyprian, and others), but also in Rome (Latin versions of the Scriptures, of the letter known as 1 Clement, and of the *Pastor;* Minucius Felix, Novatian, Pope Cornelius, and others).

The kinds of awareness of a linguistic differentiation in their Latin, intended or otherwise, on the part of earlier Latin Christian communities can only be inferred from usage and occasional comments. The Latin apologists reproduce non-Christian disparagements of Christian Latin usage (see the passages from Minucius Felix and Arnobius quoted above; see also the notes of H. Le Bonniec, ed., Arnobius, *Adversus nationes,* v1 [1982] 366–73, and G.W. Clarke, tr., *The Octavius of Marcus Minucius Felix* [1974] 183–84; P. Monat, ed. and tr., Lactantius, *Divinae institutiones,* bk. 5, 2 vols., v2 [*Commentaire et index*]; *SChr* 205 [1973] 26–34). Isolated indications are also found of an embarrassment on the part of educated members of the Christian community. Lactantius considers those of his coreligionists who have received a literary education to be vulnerable to back-sliding, and Augustine warns of the special care to be taken with those "de scholis usitatissimis grammaticorum oratorumque uenientes," not just to prevent their rejecting Scripture, but also to anticipate their reaction to the presence of the uneducated in ecclesiastical ministry:

> Maxime autem isti docendi sunt scripturas audire diuinas, ne sordeat eis solidum eloquium, quia non est inflatum. . . . Nouerint etiam non esse uocem ad aures dei nisi animi affectum: ita enim non irridebunt, si aliquos antistites et ministros ecclesiae forte animaduerterint uel cum barbarismis et soloecismis deum inuocare, uel eadem uerba quae pronuntiant non intellegere perturbateque distinguere. *De catechizandis rudibus* 9.13.3, 5; *CCSL* 46:135

By the later fourth century, however, there has been a movement beyond *apologiae* for the language of Scripture or of subliterary Christian writers and speakers. Several authors provide indications, admittedly limited, of a consciousness of linguistic differentiation, whether in practice or precept, between the usage of Latin Christians and that of their non-Christian contemporaries. Chief among these is Augustine, who, when writing, for example, to Jerome, defends the use of the term *officium* in religious texts by pointing to the precedent of St. Ambrose's usage of it, and acknowledges the existence of peculiar terms for ranks in the Church (*Ep.* 82.21, 33; *CSEL* 34.2.373, 385). Similarly, in the course of preaching (*Sermo* 21.5; *CCSL* 41:280–81) Augustine contrasts the religious usage of the term *fides* with its secular usage, and in an apologetical context (*De civitate dei* 10.21; *CCSL* 47:294–95) he explains why the Church cannot call its martyrs heroes, referring to the "ecclesiastica loquendi consuetudo" and "usus ecclesiastici sermonis." He also expresses his preference for *morbo* over *passione* to translate ἐν πάθει of 1 *Th* 4:5 (see [DA48] 25.1:225), because "passio in latina lingua, maxime usu loquendi ecclesiastico, non ad uituperationem consueuit intellegi" (*De nuptiis et concupiscentia* 2.55; *CSEL* 42:312–13), and he explains the restriction of the term *fratres* to fellow Christians in the following way: "Neque enim dicimus eos fratres nostros secundum scripturas et ecclesiasticum loquendi morem" (*Enarrationes in Psalmos* 32.2.2.29; *CSEL* 38:272). We also note his remark about his own incorrect use of a term in an early work: "Nec tamen isto nomine nos uteremur, si iam satis essemus litteris ecclesiasticis eruditi" (*Retractationes* 1.32; *CCSL* 57:13). In the passage most often quoted in this connection, we find him urging the correct Christian appellations for the days of the week and remarking: "Habent [Christiani] enim linguam suam qua utantur. . . . Melius ergo de ore christiano ritus loquendi ecclesiasticus procedit" (*Enarrationes in Psalmos* 93.3; *CCSL* 39:1303).

The most frequently remarked linguistic differentiation is that between the language of the translations of Scripture and that of classical and contemporary belles lettres. Concerning their immature reactions to Scripture we have the famous remarks of both Jerome ("sermo horrebat incultus et, quia lumen caecis oculis non uidebam, non oculorum putabam culpam esse, sed solis" [*Ep.* 22.30; *CSEL* 54:189–90]) and Augustine ("sed [scriptura] uisa est mihi indigna, quam Tullianae dignitati compararem" [*Confessiones* 3.5.9; *CCSL* 27:31]). The (apparent) artlessness of Scripture, its popular, subliterary character, its foreignness and sometimes marginal latinity came, however, to be viewed as an advantage, a medium peculiarly suited to its message, a vehicle of an unexpected and peculiar eloquence.

The Latin Church developed a scholarly apparatus [DA82–90], partly derivative from Greek sources, partly original, for the study of the texts and idiom of the biblical translations, such as Jerome's onomastic works (*Liber locorum, Liber nominum*) and his biblical commentaries; Augustine's *De doctrina christiana,* his commentaries, and *Locutionum in Heptateuchum libri VII;* or a work like Eucherius of Lyons's manual, *Formulae spiritalis intelligentiae.* In this way the Church initiated a tradition of biblical textual learning of various degrees of sophistication, a resource neatly summarized in the first book of Cassiodorus's *Institutiones.*

In addition, the language of the biblical translations was held up as the appropriate literary medium both for the explication of Scripture itself and for all Christian preaching in general. Augustine comments on this in his *De doctrina christiana,* especially in bk. 4, and in *Ep.* 36.14 Jerome writes: "sint alii diserti, laudentur, ut uolunt, et inflatis buccis spumantia uerba trutinentur: mihi sufficit sic loqui, ut intellegar et ut de scripturis disputans scripturarum imiter simplicitatem" (*CSEL* 54:281). A most important consequence of this attitude and a key feature of Christian Latin was that the formal speech and writing of Latin Christians were permeated by the vocabulary, syntax, and style of the biblical translations. The acceptance, indeed the eventual valorization, of the usage of these translations meant that the many peculiarities that so differentiated them from Latin belles lettres were now not only admitted, but even sought after in Christian compositions of whatever sophistication or affectation.

An awareness in the Middle Ages of the differences between Christian idiom and that of the pagan writers is to be observed in the repeated insistence—often recalling Gregory the Great's famous dictum "indignum vehementer existimo, ut verba caelestis oraculi restringam sub regulis Donati" (*Moralia in Job,* ed. R. Gillet, VI: *Ep. ad Leandrum* 5; *SChr* 32 bis [1975] 132; see also n4, pp133–34)—upon the exemption of biblical Latin from the usual rules of grammar. But this awareness is also to be seen in the expansion of the scope of grammatical studies to include Scripture and other works of Christian literature (see L. Holtz, "La grammaire chrétienne," *CCCM* 68:L–LVIII, and materials cited there; also B. Löfstedt, *CCSL* 133D:XVII–XX), and in the continuing development, for an increasing number and variety of Christian texts, of tools of the scholarly apparatus for literary study, e.g. the *accessus,* such works as Bede's *De orthographia, De arte metrica, De schematibus et tropis,* glosses, and formal and occasional glossaries.

The Renaissance exhibited a more vigorous assertion of this linguistic differentiation in the rejection by Italian humanists and their satellites of Christian idiom for renewed, authentic, literary composition (J.F. D'Amico, *Renaissance Humanism in Papal Rome: Humanists and Churchmen on the Eve of the Reformation* [1983, r1991] 123–42, provides a sympathetic account of Roman Ciceronianism; see also, pp154–60, his account, with many astonishing examples, of Paolo Cortesi's attempt to reform theological Latin). The use of the traditional Christian vocabulary had an earlier, famous defender in Lorenzo Valla (in his *Antidotum in Facium*, 2.1.28–34, ed. M. Regoliosi [1981] 128–29), but it was Erasmus who provided the most instructive defense and description of Christian Latin idiom, quoted here almost in full. In his *Dialogus Ciceronianus* of 1528 (ed. A. Gambaro [1965] 140, 148), one of the interlocutors, Bulephorus, complains that if we limit our repertoire of Latin expressions to those found in Cicero, we will be embarrassed when we come to speak of the Christian religion. He argues:

> Nusquam apud Ciceronem legimus *Iesu Christi, Uerbi Dei, spiritus Sancti,* aut *Trinitatis* uocabulum, nec *Euangelium,* nec *euangelistam,* nec *Mosen,* nec *prophetam,* nec *Pentateuchum,* nec *Psalmos,* nec *episcopum,* nec *archiepiscopum,* nec *diaconum,* nec *hypodiaconum,* nec *acoluthum,* nec *exorcistam,* nec *ecclesiam,* nec *fidem, spem,* et *charitatem,* nec *trium personarum eandem essentiam,* nec *haeresim,* nec *symbolum,* nec *septem ecclesiae sacramenta,* nec *baptismum* aut *baptistam,* nec *confirmationem,* nec *eucharistiam,* nec *sacram unctionem,* nec *poenitentiam,* nec *sacramentalem confessionem,* nec *contritionem,* nec *absolutionem,* nec *excommunicationem,* nec *ecclesiasticam sepulturam,* nec *missam,* nec alia innumera, quibus constat omnis uita Christianorum. . . . Nulla est ars humana, cui non concedimus ius utendi suis uocabulis: licet grammaticis dicere *supinum* et *gerundium;* mathematicis, *sesquialteram* et *superbipartientem:* habent agricolae et fabri propria suarum artium uocabula: et nos coelum terrae miscemus, si nostrae religionis mysteria suis uerbis explicemus? Uoces aliquot hebraicae, complures graecanicae (quoniam e Palaestina, Asia minore et Graecia primum ad nos demanauit christiana philosophia) una cum ipsis rebus inuectae sunt, quod genus sunt, *osanna, amen, ecclesia, apostolus, episcopus, catholicus, orthodoxus, haereticus, schisma, charisma, dogma, chrisma, Christus, baptizo, paracletus, euangelium, euangelizare, euangelista, proselytus, catechumenus, exorcismus, eucharistia, symbolum, anathema;* nonnullas prisci christianae religionis antistites usurparunt, quo commodius possent de rebus tam sublimibus disserere, cuiusmodi sunt ὁμοούσιος, quod nos *consubstantialis* uertimus, *fides, gratia, mediator,* et si qua sunt alia, quae antehac vel inaudita Latinis erant, vel non in eundum sensum usurpata. Num igitur tanti nobis erit dici ciceronianum, ut de rebus, de quibus solis erat loquendum, prorsus sileamus; aut uerbis uel ab apostolis traditis, uel a maioribus repertis, et in hunc usque diem tot seculorum consensu receptis, abstinebimus, alia quaedam in illorum locum pro suo quisque arbitrio comminiscentes?

We should note, however, by way of counterbalance to Erasmus's apparent tolerance for lexical christianisms, the angry list he appended to his *Annotations on the New Testament* of graecisms, hebraisms, and other non-Latin atrocities in the Vulgate New Testament: "Soloecismi per interpretem admissi manifestarii et inexcusabiles. . . . (in A. Reeve, ed., *Erasmus, Annotations on the New Testament: Galatians to Apocalypse* [1993] 9–12).

Consciousness of differences between Christian and pagan/classical idiom, especially of the *peregrinitas* of biblical Latin, continued down through the modern period (note the title of the small manual of I. Weitenauer: *Lexicon biblicum in quo explicantur Vulgatae vocabula et phrases, quaecunque propter linguae hebraeicae graecaeque peregrinitatem injicere moram legenti possunt* [1835]). But detailed delineations of the features of Christian Latin in general and of biblical Latin in particular did not emerge until the pioneering studies of Hermann Rönsch (1868), who provided the first sophisticated philological description of biblical Latin and situated it in the larger context of the latinity of pagan, secular, and other Christian texts, and of Gustav Koffmane (1879), whose unfinished work took the first steps towards describing the formation of Christian Latin idiom.

The straighforward, unbiased philological description of the latinity of ancient Christian texts is an interesting and, with luck, uncontroversial undertaking. Only the issues of the origin, distinctiveness (or lack thereof), and sociolinguistic character of the features described have caused controversy. The principal questions seem to come down to these: Is there a linguistic entity discernible from the common language of Late Latin that one could call Christian Latin? Or are there, rather, specialized "sublanguages" within the Christian use of the common language which, now more, now less, influenced the general Christian idiom, e.g. (1) a *Biblical Latin,* in effect a translating medium (the Latin of the scriptural translations and, perhaps, of early Latin translations of nonbiblical texts); (2) a *Theological Latin,* a technical idiom developed from the biblical language for use in theological discussion and polemic; (3) an *Ecclesiastical Latin,* a technical idiom of liturgy and ecclesiastical administration; and so on? Does Christian Latin differ from the common language only when a critical mass of features from these sublanguages is present?

As we have seen, writers in the early centuries of Christianity display in various ways an awareness of a peculiarly Christian idiom, and this awareness can be observed later both in medieval grammatical works and in the controversies of the humanists of the fifteenth and sixteenth centuries, and on into the modern era. The term "Christian Latin," however, is most associated with the work of a group of scholars clustered around the Catholic University of Nijmegen in the Netherlands. The founder of this approach to the study of Christian Latin philology was Josef Schrijnen, who sketched his theories in *Uit het Leven der Oude Kerk* (1919) and presented them in greater detail in *Charakteristik des altchristlichen Latein* (1932) [DA23], the inaugural volume of the series of publications (*Latinitas Christianorum Primaeva;* see [CC24]) which has been most influential in advancing and propagating them. His theories and approach were taken up by his students, particularly Christine Mohrmann, the most prominent and prolific of them (see memorials in *SE* 32.1). Her study of St. Augustine's sermons [DA18] served to demonstrate the application of Schrijnen's theories.

Schrijnen's views were greeted by immediate criticism, and the critical evaluation of the theory of Christian Latin, as refined and modified by Mohrmann, has continued unabated. Though many have rejected the "Christian Latin" of the Nijmegen School in whole or part, the theory, with various nuances, nevertheless continues to exercise influence. At the top of Schrijnen's agenda when developing this theory was the need to go beyond the restrictive conceptions which were in turn produced and supported by such expressions as "Biblical Latin," "Patristic Latin," and "Ecclesiastical Latin." He wished to extend the scope of study to an examination of the entire Latin language of the paleo-Christian community as a *Sondersprache* or "special language," a variant of the common language that, while not a dialect, was the distinctive and distinguishing linguistic usage of a distinct group. Indeed, later refinements introduced by Mohrmann led her to prefer to characterize Christian Latin as a *Gruppensprache* or "sociolect."

The definitions of special language upon which Schrijnen's theory of Christian Latin was based insisted that lexical peculiarity or specialization was not in itself sufficient to justify application of this description, and so the proponents of Christian

Latin were careful to insist upon the presence in their *Sondersprache* of all the elements usually found in a special language. The following sketch will attempt to incorporate the basic ideas of the Nijmegen school, while also moving beyond them to include features of language not usually considered in classic presentations of "Christian Latin," as well as some of the refinements of classification formulated by Vincenzo Loi [DA16].

### Phonology, Orthography

A peculiar phonology is not required in a special language, and so uniquely Christian developments in this area are not claimed by the Nijmegen School. Augustine's endorsement of the preacher's employment of a popular, as opposed to the cultivated, pronunciation of a term, as well as his concern for the sensibilities of highly educated converts (in the passage from *De catechizandis rudibus* quoted before), would hardly support a claim of a distinctively Christian phonology, but these and other texts surely suggest the extent to which the spoken Latin of preaching and liturgy was permeated by popular pronunciation. The popular character of the pronunciations presumed by some of the spellings in translations of the Scriptures (see [DA70] pp455–70) and in Christian inscriptions ([DA33], Index XII) suggests the same permeability in the spoken and written Latin of Christian communities. These "vulgarisms" do not set Christian Latin apart from the common language, but they do differentiate it, along with other written manifestations of the Latin vernacular, from the written and spoken Latin of the traditionally educated, who might wince at *abis* (= *habes*), *nomine* (accusative sg.), *broprius, istillicidium, locumplens, zosum* (for *deorsum*), *cludere,* and so on. At the same time, the high frequency of foreign-sounding names and Greek loanwords might, depending on location, have tended to differentiate spoken Christian Latin from that of circumjacent communities.

### Morphology

Here, too, no differentiation from the morphology of the various spoken and written varieties of the common language could be claimed, except in the density of occurrence of foreign elements in the transliteration of Hebrew and Greek words in Scripture (and discussions of it), in loanwords, and in the preference for certain formations (e.g. in the far wider use of various suffixes and prefixes that were already elements in Classical Latin). Preferred formations in Christian Latin, whether absorbed from popular speech, mediated by the biblical translations (described in [DA70] pp22–304), or both, include the following:

1. nouns ending in *-tas, -tio, -io, -sio, -ium, -tor, -atus, -arius/-arium, -tura, -tus, -sus, -tia, -ela, -men, -mentum, -monium, -icum*
2. composite nouns, e.g. *magniloquium, inobaudientia*
3. adjectives ending in *-bilis, -alis, -aris, -arius, -orius, -torius, -eus, -ius, -iuus, -anus, -osus*
4. adverbs in *-ter, -tim, -secus, -e*
5. verbs in *-ficare, -zare: magnificare, sanctificare, evangelizare, scandalizare*
6. composite verbs: *benedicere, beatificare, complacere, baiulare, dulcorare, minorare, elongare*

7. verbs with prepositional prefixes: *adimplere, coadunare, pertransire, super-exaltare*

8. compound adverbs/prepositions: *abante, desuper, depost*

9. compounds with the borrowed prefixes *archi-* and *pseudo-*

10. abundant diminutives

## Vocabulary

In vocabulary is to be found the most obvious and extensive differentiation of Christian Latin from the common language. Expression of the multiplex character of Christian institutions, beliefs, practices, and experiences in Latin posed an immense challenge, one far greater than, for example, the relatively circumscribed challenge, of which Lucretius and Cicero complained, of developing an adequate Latin philosophical idiom. Early development of Christian Latin vocabulary was crystallized in the biblical translations (see [DA70] pp305–405, [DA69] pp54–64) and thence propagated and elaborated in other Christian texts. Schrijnen's analysis of Christian Latin vocabulary (an elaboration of that of Koffmane [DA15]) posits the following categories:

(a) **Direct or Immediate Christianisms.** These are terms with specifically Christian content and application, a category composed of (1) loanwords: borrowings from Greek or, through Greek, from Hebrew/Aramaic, usually fitted out with Latin endings; (2) neologisms: new Latin words coined to translate Christian ideas; (3) semantic Christianisms ("Christianismes sémasiologiques"): traditional words, both native Latin and loanwords earlier absorbed into the common language, which were given new or narrowly restricted meanings when used in specifically Christian contexts.

(b) **Indirect or Mediate Christianisms.** These are words and expressions considered to have no specifically Christian content or association, but found exclusively in Christian texts (absolute or integral indirect Christianisms) or predominantly, with only scattered occurrence in non-Christian texts (partial or relative indirect Christianisms).

Vincenzo Loi [DA16] has provided a more refined description of the components of Christian Latin vocabulary, one that takes into account many of the criticisms raised against the details of the Nijmegen theories. We offer here an abstract of Loi's categories with illustrations selected from his excellent set of examples along with some supplements:

(a) **Lexicographic Christianisms.**

1. Loanwords, i.e borrowings from the Greek or, through Greek, from Hebrew: *ecclesia, ecclesiasticus; apostolus, apostolicus; martyr; episcopus, presbyter, diaconus, hypodiaconus, clerus; laicus, catechumenus, neophytus; catholicus, orthodoxus, haeresis, haereticus, apostata, apostatare, schisma, schismaticus, anathema, anathematizare; baptisma, eucharistia, pascha; evangelium, evangelicus, evangelista, evangelizare; propheta, propheticus, pseudopropheta; diabolus* (sometimes pronounced and spelled *zabulus*), *exorcismus.* Sometimes Greek words retained their foreign declension, as

*Pentecoste, -es; Parasceve, -es.* Hebrew words imported through Greek were unde-clined (e.g. *Amen, Hosanna, Alleluia*), declined (e.g. *gehenna, -ae; Iesus, -u; mes-sia(s), -ae; sabbatum, -i*), both declined and undeclined (e.g. *pascha* and *pascha, -ae; satan* and *satanas -ae*), or partly declined (e.g. sg. *cherub,* pl. *cherubim*). Loi adds a category of loanwords not necessarily associated with Christianity that were ab-sorbed into Christian Latin idiom, largely through biblical translations, e.g.: *abyssus, acedia, anathema, angaria, arrabon, blasphemia, blasphemus, brab(v)ium, crypta, ec-stasis, eremus, grabatus, holocaustomata, machaera, melota, nomisma, phantasma, rhomphaea, sagena, scandalum, spado, teloneum, thymiaterium, zelus, zizania; ana-thematizare, catechizare, euangelizare, parabolari, scandalizare, thesaurizare, zelare.*

As Mohrmann and Loi have observed, these loanwords were retained most com-monly in use for concrete realities (institutions, persons, rituals, ritual objects, etc.), Latin substitutes eventually being preferred for more abstract concepts.

2. Lexicographic calques, i.e. terms which would correspond exactly to the Greek words and expressions used in preaching, Scripture, and theological disputation, thus: πρωτότοκος > *primogenitus,* μονόγενής > *unigenitus,* σώτηρ > *salvator,* ἀνάστασις > *resurrectio,* ἁγιασμός > *sanctificatio,* μακαρίζειν > *beatificare,* σαρκικός > *carnalis,* δοξάζειν > *clarificare/glorificare,* ὁμοούσιος > *consubstantialis,* τρίας > *trinitas.*

3. Neologisms built up on biblical terms by adding Latin suffixes: *salus > salvare, salvator, salvatio; caro > carnalis, carneus, carnaliter; spiritus > spiritalis, spiritaliter; passio > passibilis, impassibilis; sanctus > sanctificare, sanctificatio, sanctificator; figura > figuraliter, praefigurare, praefiguratio;* this process was especially productive of *nomina agentis: adnuntiatior, confessor, exterminator, inluminator, miserator, opera-tor, sanctificator,* and of *nomina actionis: adimpletio, emundatio, exterminatio, morti-ficatio, praedestinatio, vivificatio.*

Loi offers two additional, less precisely defined categories which we only men-tion here: (4) neologisms of a popular type, attested in the Old Latin versions of Scripture (but maybe not peculiar to them), built up with normal Latin suffixes, with an evident preference in this category for formations in *-ficus, -tura, -mentum, -tor,* and *-tio;* (5) neologisms attested in the Chrisitan literary tradition and built upon terms from the common language with normal Latin suffixes, with an evident pref-erence here for formations of abstracts in *-tas* and *-tio,* the *nomen agentis* in *-tor,* and adjectives in *-bilis.*

(b) **Semantic Christianisms.** As Loi observes, in the majority of cases polysemia was operative, i.e. the word retained its traditional signficance when appropriate while bearing its new Christian meaning in new contexts; but in some cases the new Christian meaning virtually eclipsed the profane meaning:

1. Very basic terms from the common language take on a special signfiance or greater profundity of meaning in peculiarly Christian contexts, e.g. *vita, mors, salus, fides, iustitia, sanctus* and *sanctitas, caro* and *spiritus, paenitentia, peccatum.*

2. Some common terms become virtual proper nouns, e.g., *dominus* = the Lord, *adversarius* = the Devil; others take on very specific meanings: *testis* = martyr, *agon* = the martyr's struggle, *corona* = the martyr's reward; *caelum/caeli* = heaven as the abode of God and the saints; *mundus* and *saeculum* take on the pejorative meaning of "the world"; *uerbum* becomes a divine epithet, as does *spiritus.*

3. Words chosen from the common language to translate biblical terms become virtual technical words applicable to theological concepts, e.g. *redemptor* and *redemptio; surgere/resurgere* associated with resurrection; *creare* and *creator* with divine creation; *humilitas,* the lowliness of human nature, as opposed to *divinitas; virtus* as divine power or manifestation thereof.

4. A number of crucial terms used to translate biblical concepts take on a meaning quite removed from that current in the common language, e.g. *sacramentum, testamentum* = God's covenant; *confiteri* = to praise; *praedicare* = to preach.

5. Words from the common language take on peculiarly Christian signficance when in combination, e.g. adjective + noun: *sancta scriptura, divinae litterae; secunda mors (Apc* 20:6, etc.) = damnation; *secunda nativitas* = baptism; *vita aeterna;* other combinations: *absolvere peccata, dimittere peccata, remissio peccatorum, acceptio personarum, mori/vivere in aeternum, opera iustitiae, signum crucis.*

## Christian Latin Syntax and Biblical Latin

Consideration of Christian Latin syntax requires that we narrow our focus to biblical Latin, for the syntactical peculiarity of Christian Latin is mainly to be found in, or is primarily traceable to, the Latin translations of Scripture. Critics of the theory of a Christian Latin *Sondersprache* have considered the weakest part of that hypothesis to be in the area of syntax, their arguments running along these lines: syntactic peculiarities of Christian Latin are only apparent, because of the tendency to compare it to the usage of the classical, school authors; there is nothing in the supposedly peculiar syntax of Christian Latin not found either in popular, colloquial Latin or in biblical Latin.

Biblical Latin is, to be sure, the type of Christian Latin that is most characteristic of it and most obviously alien to the usage of late antique *Kunstprosa.* Ideally, biblical Latin should not be set apart from, let alone opposed to, Christian Latin, for translations of Scripture were surely made for and by Latin-speaking Christian communities. Indeed, the earliest biblical translations into Latin were both formed by and formative of the speech of the Latin Christian communities, and some specimens of biblical Latin must represent our earliest surviving examples of compositions in Latin by Christians (versions of the Bible in Latin were current in both North Africa and Rome by the second half of the second century). Nor yet, again ideally, should texts of biblical Latin be studied in isolation from the Latin translations of other Christian texts (see [DA34–36]). Yet biblical Latin does enjoy an apparent unity, if only that of the biblical canon, and can be studied, at least in terms of a readily identified and restricted corpus, relatively easily and coherently.

Unfortunately, the multiplicity of biblical versions introduces considerable complication into even this artificial simplicity. In his prefatory letter ("Cogitis me") to his revision of the Latin Gospels, Jerome complained of the multiple versions of them, asking of his potential critics: "Si enim latinis exemplaribus fides est adhibenda, respondeant quibus; tot sunt paene quot codices" ([DA50] p1515); and Augustine contrasted the character of the Latin versions of the Scriptures with the Greek as follows: "Qui enim scripturas ex hebraea in graecam uerterunt, numerari possunt, latini autem interpretes nullo modo. Vt enim cuique primis fidei temporibus in manus venit codex graecus, et aliquantum facultatis sibi utriusque linguae habere uidebatur, ausus est interpretari" (*De doctrina christiana* 2.11.16; *CCSL* 32:42). The synoptic editions of the Latin Gospel texts [DA49] and the *Vetus latina* [DA48] reveal in a glance the fundamental truth of even these exaggerations.

Though the latinity of the biblical translations has often been described in varying degrees of detail and with various foci ([DA7–8], [DA68–70]), Braun [DA56] is surely correct to see a thorough, scientific study of biblical Latin as one of the great desiderata among resources needed for the study of paleo-Christian Latin. Much that has been said here about the morphology and lexicography of Christian Latin in general is applicable to biblical Latin in particular; indeed, it takes its origin from the biblical translations. Here we can only provide examples of some of the more common syntactic peculiarities of biblical Latin, not distinguishing between the more popular features of the Old Latin versions and the somewhat more restrained treatment in Jerome's translations and revisions. The oldest extant manuscript containing all of the collection of biblical translations which came to be known as the Vulgate is the *Codex Amiatinus* of 690–716, and non-Vulgate versions exerted an influence throughout the Middle Ages. Thus, the indiscriminate use of the expression "the Vulgate" to refer generally to Latin biblical texts is inappropriate.

## Some Exotic Elements in Biblical Latin Syntax

(a) **Hebraisms.** (See [DA69] pp11–27, [DA70] pp452–54.)

1. use of feminine for neuter, e.g. *Ps* 26:4 "unam petii a Domino, hanc requiram ut inhabitem" (cf. *Ps iuxta Hebraeos:* "unum petiui a Domino hoc requiram")

2. qualitative genitive, virtually adjectival, e.g. *Ps* 25:9 "viri sanguinum," *Ps* 88:11 "in brachio uirtutis," *Ps* 142:3 "mortuos saeculi," *Act* 9:15 "uas electionis"

3. use of genitive for intensification, e.g. "rex regum," "dominus dominantium," "in saecula saeculorum," "uanitatas uanitatum," "Sanctum sanctorum," "Canticum canticorum"

4. use of *ab* after positives and comparatives, e.g. *Lc* 18:14 "descendit hic iustificatus in domum suam ab illo," *Ps* 8:6 "minuisti eum paulo minus ab angelis"

5. use of *a, ex, prae,* and *super* to express comparative, e.g. *Ps* 92:3–4 "eleuabunt flumina fluctus suos a uocibus aquarum multarum," *Ps* 138:6 "mirabilis facta est scientia tua ex me," *Ps* 44:8 "unxit te . . . oleo laetitiae prae consortibus tuis," *Sap* 7:10 "super salutem et speciem dilexi illam"

6. use of *in* with accusative, meaning "as" or "for," e.g. *Gn* 1:14 "et sint in signa," *Ier* 1:18 "dedi te hodie in ciuitatem munitam," *Act* 13:47 "posui te in lumen gentibus ut sis in salutem usque ad extremum terrae"

7. use of *in* with the ablative for instrumentality, e.g. *Idc* 15:15 "inuentamque maxillam . . . arripiens interfecit in ea mille uiros," *Lc* 22:49 "Domine si percutimus in gladio"; or for causality, e.g. *Mt* 6:7 "putant enim quia in multiloquio suo exaudiantur"; or for causality-cum-instrumentality, e.g. *Dt* 8:3 "non in solo pane uiuat homo sed in omni uerbo quod egreditur ex ore Domini"

8. use of prepositional phrases in place of simple prepositions: *a facie, ante faciem, in conspectu, in ore, de manu*

9. redundant use of demonstrative pronouns, e.g. *Ps* 18:4 "non sunt loquellae neque sermones quorum non audiantur uoces eorum," *Apc* 3:12 "qui uicerit faciam illum columnam in templo Dei mei," *Mc* 1:7 "Venit fortior post me cuius non sum dignus procumbens solvere corrigiam calciamentorum eius"

10. use of *si* and *si non/nisi* in strong assertions or oaths, e.g. *Ps* 88:36 "semel iu-

raui in sancto meo si Dauid mentiar," *Am* 8:7 "iurauit Dominus in superbia Iacob si oblitus fuero usque ad finem omnia opera eorum," *Ps* 130:2: "si non humiliter sentiebam sed exaltaui animam meam"

11. adverbial use of *addere, adicere, adponere* meaning "to do in addition, to repeat, further; to go on to do," e.g. *Lc* 20:11–12 "et addidit alterum seruum mittere. . . . Et addidit tertium mittere," *Lc* 19:11 "adiciens dixit parabolam," *Ps* 76:8 "non adponet ut complacitior sit adhuc"

12. use of interrogative to express wish, e.g. *Ps* 13:7 "quis dabit ex Sion salutare Israhel dum auertit Dominus captiuitatem populi sui"

13. emphatic use in Hebrew of infinitive + finite form of verb is reproduced by use of present participle, e.g. *Lam* 1:2 "plorans plorauit," or use of verb with ablative of cognate noun, e.g. *Ex* 21:17 "morte moriatur," *Lc* 22:15 "desiderio desiderauit," though this second phenomenon may also reproduce a Hebrew cognate accusative

14. use of *facere* and *dare* to reproduce Hebrew causative verb, e.g. *Mt* 21:17 "et eum desuper sedere fecerunt," *Ps* 15:10 "nec dabis sanctum tuum videre corruptionem"

15. frequent ellipsis of forms of *esse* (common enough also in Classical Latin)

**(b) Grecisms.** (See [DA69] pp28–40, [DA70] 434–51.)

1. use of genitive of comparison, e.g. *Mc* 12:31 "maius horum aliud mandatum non est"

2. genitive absolute: in Vulgate only at *Rm* 2:15, "et inter se cogitationum accusantium aut etiam defendentium," but elsewhere in Old Latin versions

3. use of genitive after certain adjectives, e.g. *Io* 6:45 "docibiles Dei"

4. use of genitive after certain verbs: *dominari, regnare, implere*

5. use of positive instead of comparative form of the adjective with *quam*, e.g. *Mt* 18:9 "bonum tibi est unoculum in uitam intrare quam duos oculos habentem mitti in gehennam ignis"

6. unusual uses of verbs, with accusative or in passive: *benedicere, commemorari, confundi, inluminare, nocere, petere, suadere, triumphare, zelare* (see next section)

7. use of infinitive for purpose, e.g. *Mt* 2:2 "uenimus adorare," *Act* 7:43 "figuras quas fecistis adorare eas"

8. use of infinitive with *habeo*, e.g. *Lc* 12:50 "baptisma autem habeo baptizari," *Io* 16:12 "adhuc multa habeo uobis dicere"

9. use of present participle instead of infinitive, e.g. *Mt* 11:1 "cum consummasset Iesus praecipiens," *Eph* 1:16 "non cesso gratias agens"

10. use of *in* with ablative of the gerund to translate the corresponding Greek articular infinitive (infinitive preceded by preposition ἐν and definite article in the dative), e.g. *Ps* 52:7 "Ἐν τῷ ἐπιστρέψαι κύριον τὴν αἰχμαλωσίαν Σιων" > "in convertendo Dominus captiuitatem Sion," *Ps* 141:4 "ἐν τῷ ἐκλείπειν ἐξ ἐμοῦ τὸ πνεῦμά μου" > "in deficiendo ex me spiritum meum"

11. literal translation of Greek expressions, e.g. *nisi quia* < εἰ μή ὅτι, *ut quid* < ἵνα τί, *ex hoc nunc* < ἀπὸ τοῦ νῦν, *in idipsum* < ἐπὶ τὸ αὐτό

12. use of *quia* (translating ὅτι) to introduce direct quotations, e.g *Act* 2:13 "alii autem inridentes dicebant quia musto pleni sunt"

13. reproduction in Latin translation of the Greek Scriptures' abundant use of particles

14. adjectival use of *is, hic, ille, ipse* to translate the Greek definite article; use of *unus* to translate the Greek indefinite article

15. dramatically expanded use of *ecce* to translate frequent occurrence of Greek ἰδού, e.g. in *Lc* 9:38–39 "et ecce uir de turba exclamauit, dicens magister, obsecro te, respice in filium meum quia unicus est mihi, et ecce spiritus adprehendit illum et subito clamat"

16. abundant use of formulae *factum est* and *factum est autem* to translate ἐγένετο and ἐγένετο δὲ.

(c) **Vulgarisms.** (See [DA8], [DA63], [DA68–70].). We may justify inclusion of this category under the rubric "Exotic Elements" from the point of view of "corpus se-lection," i.e. the "vulgarisms" would indeed seem exotic to those, whether in the Middle Ages, Renaissance, or modern period, whose notions of latinity are narrowly formed by classical literary texts. This category is controversial to the extent that one scholar's identification of a peculiarity of the Latin biblical translations as a He-braism or Grecism will be countered by another's description of the same or an anal-ogous phenomenon as a feature of popular Latin usage. The following are only a few of the phenomena of biblical Latin found also in non-Christian popular Latin:

1. genitive of comparison

2. neglect of restrictive norms of the literary dialect, e.g. in case usage after verbs: *nocere aliquem, benedicere/maledicere aliquem, parcere in aliquem, egere aliquid, obaudire aliquem,* and in the transitive use of intransitive verbs

3. disagreement of subject and verb, e.g. *Mt* 21:8 "Plurima autem turba strauerunt uestimenta sua in uia," *Io* 7:49 "sed turba haec quae non nouit legem maledicti sunt"

4. periphrastic forms, e.g. *Mc* 1:4 "fuit Ioannes in deserto baptizans," *Lc* 5:10 "homines eris capiens"

5. use of the infinitive to express purpose, and not, as in literary Latin, only with verbs of motion or requesting

6. use of infinitive with *habeo*

7. expansion of the use of prepositions to indicate comparison, with or without comparative, e.g. *Ecl* 6:8 "quid habet amplius sapiens ab stulto," *Lc* 18:14 "descendit hic iustificatus in domum suam ab illo"

8. use of *is, hic, ille* as definite articles, of *unus* as indefinite article

9. use of the ablative of the gerund in place of the present participle, and use of object with gerund, e.g. *Lc* 10:25 "quid faciendo uitam aeternam possideam"

10. use of *quod, quia, quoniam* to introduce indirect statements with finite verbs

11. preposition + adverb combinations, e.g. *ab, ad, in,* and *pro* with *inuicem; de deorsum, de retro, ab ante, deforis*

12. confusion in the force of demonstratives

13. extensive use of ellipsis (see [DA68] pp301–5), e.g. *Ps* 67:7 "Deus qui inhabitare facit unius moris in domo," 2 *Cor* 12:5 "pro huiusmodi gloriabor"

14. anacoloutha, e.g. *Ps* 10:5 "Dominus in templo sancto suo Dominus in caelo sedes eius," 2 *Rg* 22:41 "inimicos meos dedisti mihi dorsum odientes me, et disper-dam eos," *Sir* 34:17 "Timentis Dominum beata est anima eius," *Is* 9:2 "habitantibus in regione umbrae mortis lux orta est eis"

15. redundancies for emphasis or clarity (see [DA68] pp305–6), e.g. *Prv* 31:30

"mulier timens dominum ipsa laudabitur," *Mt* 19:28 "amen dico uobis quod uos qui secuti estis me in regeneratione cum sederit Filius hominis in sede maiestatis suae, sedebitis et uos super sedes duodecim"

There can be the same sort of division of opinion (sc. Hebraism/Grecism vs. vulgarism) about the lexical contributions to Christian Latin of the biblical translations, i.e., it is not always safe to assert that it is specifically biblical Latin and not simply the strong Greek component in the popular Latin of the Empire that is the peculiar source of this or that Greek loanword. (See G. Bonfante, "La lingua latina parlata nell'età imperiale," in *Aufstieg und Niedergang der römischen Welt* 2.29.1:413–52.) This suggests the need for a renewed study of biblical Latin in particular and of Christian Latin in general in the light both of popular Latin texts and of other similarly specialized forms of Latin.

At the same time, one can view the presence of identical or analogous phenomena in the common Latin speech or in the idioms of various subgroups as at once facilitating the production of literal biblical translations and indeed easing their reception by the less formally educated in the Latin-speaking communities. Coincidence of exotic features in the translations with "vulgarisms" in Latin will have provided, of course, yet another barrier to the reception of the Latin biblical translations by the literati. But the provenance of these exotic or popular elements in the translations of the Scriptures led, as has been suggested, to their valorization and eventually welcome admission by educated Christians into the more elevated levels of spoken and written Latin.

A word or two is in order about the influence of biblical Latin on the style of other varieties of Christian Latin. The unpretentious character of biblical Latin served as a paradigm for the idiom of exegesis, and the very words of Scripture became at once the adornment and staple of Christian preaching. The parallelism and parataxis of the Psalms and other specimens of Hebrew poetry came to influence both Christian poetry and poetic prose. The repetitive, formulaic style of Old Testament narrative and the stark accounts of the Gospels had a profound influence on narrative composition. Biblical dialogue, with its interplay of pleonasm and ellipsis, of formality, formula, and colloquialism, helped to shape speech and reports of speech in Christian Latin literature.

## Conclusion

We must conclude with the ongoing question of the existence and character of "Christian Latin." The *Sondersprache/Gruppensprache* approach of the Nijmegen School has had an abundance of critics [DA24–29]. The criticism of Ferrua [DA26] is typical. He suggested that the peculiarities of Christian Latin are exaggerated by the comparison of Christian texts with the more familiar classicizing literary Latin. Christian Latin is a blend of materials from disparate sources, archaisms, neologisms, hellenisms, the languages of the bar, the curia, the military, artisans, with an abundance of elements of popular speech. These form an idiom which gives the illusion of a radical difference from "real" Latin, but the operative difference is between living, popular Latin and the literary artifact of the schools. Apart from a limited number of syntactical oddities derived from the Scriptures, Christian idiom is marked only by the presence of a large number of technical terms, but these alone are not enough to transform a language or create a subspecies of it. One could go on multiplying criticisms, quite telling ones, whether of a theoretical kind or involving matters of detail, but it is time to move past criticism of an outdated theory.

Of course, much can be and has been said in defense of the *Sondersprache/Gruppensprache* approach to Christian Latin and refinements of it. At the very least, one can say that Schrijnen, Mohrmann, and their students stimulated wonderfully the study of Christian Latin texts and provided the leading—perhaps the only—elaborate theoretical method for their study. The main quarrel seems to concern one's understanding of *Sondersprache.* Linguistics has come so very far since Schrijnen put forward his theories that recovery of the full significance of *Sondersprache* is virtually an antiquarian enterprise.

Christian Latin is no illusion. The issue is how best to describe and account for it. What is needed is a new approach or set of approaches founded upon the best in contemporary linguistic theory, one which will take full advantage of the unprecedented resource of electronic text databases; these permit a thoroughness and precision quite beyond the reach of traditional philology. A leading scholar of Christian Latin texts has recently remarked that "the question of 'Christian Latin' as *Sondersprache* is ripe for fresh and venturesome treatment" (J.J. O'Donnell, *Augustine, Confessions* [1992] 1:lxiii), and it is to be hoped that to this the scholarly community will cry, "Amen."

## Select Bibliography

### Christian Latin

#### Current Bibliography

*APh:* in "Auteurs et Textes," s.vv. *Conciliorum acta, Christiana uaria, Hymni christiani, Liturgia, Monastica;* in "Histoire littéraire," s.v. *Littérature chrétienne;*" see also *Latin et dialectes italiques, Onomastique, Epigraphie chrétienne, Religion chrétienne, Droit ecclésiastique* [DA1].
*FRANCIS: Bulletin signalétique,* 527: *Histoire et sciences des religions:* in "Index du Christianisme," s.vv. *Langage, Latin* [DA2].
*MEL:* s.vv. *Lessicografia* and *Linguistica;* note also the *Indice lessicale* at end of each volume [DA3].

#### Cumulative Bibliography

E. Malaspina, "Gli studi sulla latinità cristiana (1951–1978) I," in *Cultura e scuola* 18 (1979), no. 71:40–47; "Gli studi sulla latinità cristiana. II," in *Cultura e scuola* 18 (1979), no. 72:64–70 [DA4].
G. Sanders and M. Van Uytfanghe, *BSLC:* divided into (1) "Auteurs et textes," the longest section (pp3–131), which includes authors (authentic works and *pseudepigraphica,* with anonymous works usually entered under their titles) and genres and varieties of text (*Acta conciliorum, Biblia sacra, Epigraphica, Hagiographica, Itineraria, Iuridica, Liturgica;* (2) "Généralités," which is futher subdivided into "Langue, style, vocabulaire," "Littérature, culture, civilisation," and "Dictionnaires, glossaires, lexiques spécialisés" (this last section, covering only one page,

is the weakest section of the work); (3) an "Index des vocables latins," in the preface of which the editors refer the reader to [DA6] and to the indices in [DA19] [DA5].

H.J. Sieben, *Voces: Eine Bibliographie zu Wörtern und Begriffen aus der Patristik (1918–1978)*, Bibliographia Patristica, Supplementum 1 (1980): arranged alphabetically by Greek (pp17–225) and Latin (pp226–427) words [DA6].

## Manuals

O. García de la Fuente, *Introducción al latín bíblico y cristiano* (1990): the most recent and thorough introductory treatment, dealing with both Christian Latin (pp9–80) and biblical Latin (pp81–144); the remainder of the work is devoted to an overview of Christian Latin authors and their works; extensive bibliography (pp401–42) and very useful index of words (pp443–58); the account of Christian Latin is largely derived from that of the Nijmegen school [DA7].

A. Blaise, *Manuel du latin chrétien* (1955, r1986); tr. G.C. Roti: *A Handbook of Christian Latin: Style, Morphology, and Syntax* (1992): Blaise asserts (p12) that his intention in both his *Dictionnaire* [DA10] and his *Manuel* "n'est pas de formuler une théorie, mais de présenter des faits." This guide is dated and less complete and scientific than one would wish, but still very useful; Blaise's notes on the style and affective qualities of Christian Latin (pp17–66) deserve reading [DA8].

## Anthology

O. García de la Fuente, *Antologia del latín bíblico y cristiano* (1990) [DA9].

## Specialized Dictionaries for Christian Latin and Greek Texts

A. Blaise, *Dictionnaire latin français des auteurs chrétiens, revu spécialement pour le vocabulaire théologique par Henri Chirat* (1954, r1967?): though the list of authors reviewed (pp9–29) is quite extensive, this lexicon is neither exhaustive nor definitive; it remains, nonetheless, an indispensable tool [DA10].

G. Kittel and G. Friedrich, eds., *Theological Dictionary of the New Testament*, tr. and ed. G.W. Bromiley, 10 vols. (1964–76) [DA11].

G.W.H. Lampe, *A Patristic Greek Lexicon* (1961–68, r1991) [DA12].

A. Souter, *A Glossary of Later Latin to 600 A.D.* (1949) [DA13].

## Studies

C. Codoñer, "Latín cristiano, ¿lengua de grupo?" in *Nova Tellus* 3 (1985) 111–26 [DA14].

G. Koffmane, *Enstehung und Entwicklung des Kirchenlateins bis auf Augustinus-Hieronymus*, Geschichte des Kirchenlateins 1.1–2 (1879–1881, r1966): the projected third part, which would have carried the study down to Isidore of Seville, did not appear [DA15].

V. Loi, *Origini e caratteristiche della latinità cristiana*, Bolletino dei classici, Supplemento 1 (1978): an informed but brief refinement of the case for "Christian Latin" [DA16].

M.R.P. McGuire, "The Origin, Development, and Character of Christian Latin," in *Teaching Latin in the Modern World*, ed. id. (1960) 37–55: a sympathetic summary of the "Christian Latin" hypothesis of the Nijmegen School [DA17].

C. Mohrmann, *Die altchristliche Sondersprache in den Sermones des hl. Augustin*, Latinitas Christianorum Primaeva 3 (1932; r1965 with Nachtrag, pp257–64, and in-dex of words, pp265–73) [DA18].

C. Mohrmann, *Études sur le latin des chrétiens,* 4 vols. (1958–77): these volumes col-lect most of Mohrmann's articles on paleo-Christian and Medieval Latin; useful indices, especially those of Greek and Latin words [DA19].

J. Oroz Reta, ed., *Actas del I simposio de latin cristiano* (1990) [DA20].

L.R. Palmer, *The Latin Language* (1954, r1988), ch. 7 (pp181–205), "Special Lan-guages—Christian Latin": a dated but still valuable summary insertion of Chris-tian Latin into the larger frame of the history of the Latin language [DA21].

G. Reichenkron, *Historische Latein-Altromanische Grammatik,* pt1: *Das sogenannte Vulgärlatein und das Wesen der Romanisierung* (1965); see especially ch. 5.1 (pp86–116), "Das Latein des Christlichen Schrifttums in 3. und 4. Jahrhundert," where a number of issues concerned with Christian Latin are considered [DA22].

J. Schrijnen, *Charakteristik des altchristlichen Latein,* Latinitas Christianorum Pri-maeva 1 (1932), repr. in [DA19] 4:367–404 [DA23].

## Alternative Views of the Latin of Christians, Criticisms of the Nijmegen School, etc.

C. Becker, *Tertullians Apologeticum: Werden und Leistung* (1954) 335–45: "Exkurs I: Das Problem der altchristlichen Sondersprache" [DA24].

R. Braun, *Deus christianorum: Recherches sur le vocabulaire doctrinal de Tertullien,* 2nd ed. (1977) 10–17 [DA25].

A. Ferrua, "Latino cristiano antico," in *La civiltà cattolica* 95.1 (1944) 34–38, 237–44, 370–77 [DA26].

J. de Ghellinck, "Latin chrétien ou langue latin des chrétiens," in *Les études classiques* 8 (1939) 449–78 [DA27].

E. Löfstedt, *Syntactica: Studien und Beiträge zur historischen Syntax des Lateins,* pt2: *Syntaktisch-stilistische Gesichtspunkte und Probleme* (1933), ch. 15 (pp458–73), "Zur Entstehung der christlichen Latinität" [DA28].

E. Löfstedt, *LL,* ch. 5 (pp68–87), "The Christian Influence" [DA29].

## Language and Style

E. Auerbach, *Literary Language & Its Public in Late Latin Antiquity and in the Middle Ages,* tr. R. Manheim (1965, r1993): a "classic" usually taken more seriously than it deserves to be [DA30].

J. Fontaine, *Aspects et problèmes de la prose d'art latine au IIIe siècle: La genèse des styles latins chrétiens* (1968) [DA31].

S.M. Oberhelman, *Rhetoric and Homiletics in Fourth-Century Christian Literature: Prose Rhythm, Oratorical Style, and Preaching in the Works of Ambrose, Jerome, and Augustine* (1991) [DA32].

## Special Types of Christian Latin Texts

### 1. Inscriptions

E. Diehl, ed., *Inscriptiones latinae christianae veteres,* 2nd ed., 3 vols. (1961); J. Moreau and H.I. Marrou, eds., v4, *Supplementum* (1967, r1985): note Index VII (v3:316–420), *Religio christiana, res christianae;* Index XII (v3:478–615), *Voces, dictiones, scribendi rationes notabiles* [DA33].

*2. Translations (nonbiblical)*

M. Geerard, *Clavis patrum graecorum,* 5 vols. (1974–87): provides item-by-item citations of Latin versions of the Greek texts catalogued there [DA34].

J. Gribomont, "The Translations: Jerome, Rufinus," in *Patrology,* ed. A. Di Berardino, tr. P. Solari, v4 (1986) 195–254 [DA35].

A. Siegmund, *Die Überlieferung der griechischen christlichen Literatur in der lateinischen Kirche bis zum zwölften Jahrhundert* (1949) [DA36].

### Analogous/Parallel Phenomena in Recent Work

*La langue latine, langue de la philosophie: Actes du colloque organisé par l'Ecole française de Rome avec le concours de l'Université de Rome "La Sapienza" (Rome, 17–19 mai 1990)* (1992): note especially J. Pepin, "Attitudes d'Augustin devant le vocabulaire philosophique grec" (pp277–307) [DA37].

M.G. Mosci Sassi, *Il linguaggio gladiatorio* (1992): in this *Fachsprache* one can see a similar pattern of drawing on a variety of linguistic resources for the development of a technical vocabulary [DA38].

M. Puelma, "Die Rezeption der Fachsprache griechischer Philosophie im Lateinischen," in *Freiburger Zeitschrift für Philosophie und Theologie* 33 (1986) 45–69 [DA39].

E.L. Wheeler, *Stratagem and the Vocabulary of Military Trickery* (1988) [DA40].

## Biblical Latin

### Current Bibliography

*APh:* in "Auteurs et Textes," s.v. *Testamenta* [DA41].

*Elenchus* of *Biblica:* see appropriate entries under sections III.D5, *Versiones latinae;* III.D5.5, *Citationes apud Patres;* XVI.J6.5, *Latina* [DA42].

The bibliography, "Bulletin d'ancienne littérature chrétienne latine," later the "Bulletin de la Bible latine," has been appearing in *RB* since 1921; see especially under the rubric "Ensemble de la Bible, langue" (or "vocabulaire") [DA43]; for ease in locating these reports see the outline of the series provided by C.B. Tkacz, "The Bible in Medieval Literature: A Bibliographic Essay on Basic and New Sources," in *Religion and Literature* 19 (1987) 72–74 (app.) [DA44].

### Cumulative Bibliography

A. Vernet and A.-M. Genevois, *La Bible au moyen âge: Bibliographie* (1989) [DA45].

G. Sanders and M. Van Uytfanghe, *BSLC:* see "Biblia sacra" (pp25–37) [DA46].

### Texts

*1. Old Latin*

P. Sabatier, *Bibliorum sacrorum latinae versiones antiquae, seu Vetus italica, et caeterae quaecunque in codicibus mss. & antiquorum libris reperiri potuerunt,* 3 vols. (1743–49, r1981) [DA47].

B. Fischer *et al.,* eds., *Vetus latina: Die Reste der altlateinischen Bibel. Nach Petrus Sabatier neu gesammelt und in Verbindung mit der Heidelberger Akademie der Wissenschaften herausgegeben von der Erzabtei Beuron* (1949–): use with H.J. Frede, ed., *Kirchenschriftsteller: Aktualisierungsheft 1988* (1988) [DA48].

A. Jülicher, W. Matzkow, and K. Aland, eds., *Itala: Das Neue Testament in altlateini-scher Überlieferung,* 2nd ed., 4 vols. (1970–): Gospels only [DA49].

## 2. *Vulgate*

Stuttgart Vulgate: *Biblia sacra iuxta Vulgatam versionem,* ed. R. Gryson *et al.,* 4th rev. ed. (Stuttgart 1994): a recommended purchase for all medievalists [DA50].

Vatican Vulgate: *Biblia sacra iuxta latinam Vulgatam versionem ad codicum fidem* iussu Pii PP. XI (*et al.*) cura et studio monachorum S. Benedicti Commissionis pontificiae a Pio PP. X institutae sodalium praeside Aidano Gasquet edita (*later,* cura et studio monachorum abbatiae pontificiae sancti Hieronymi in urbe or-dinis Sancti Benedicti edita) (Rome 1926–): latest volume to appear is the *Liber duodecim prophetarum* (1987) [DA51].

## 3. *Psalters*

T. Ayuso Marazuela, ed., *El salterio,* La vetus latina hispana 5 (1962): sec. 1: Intr. and Elementos extrabiblicos (prologues, *tituli,* etc.); sec. 2: *Ps* 1–75; sec. 3: *Ps* 76–151; texts arranged in six columns—Psalterium Gallicanum, Psalterium Mozara-bicum, Psalterium Romanum, "Psalterium patristicum," Psalterium iuxta He-braeos, LXX—with apparatus criticus at foot of each column; handy, but use with caution [DA52].

R. Weber, ed., *Le Psautier romain et les autres anciens psautiers latins,* Collectanea bib-lica latina 10 (1953) [DA53].

H. de Sainte-Marie, ed., *Sancti Hieronymi Psalterium iuxta Hebraeos,* Collectanea biblica latina 11 (1954) [DA54].

## Introduction and Orientation

P.-M. Bogaert, "La Bible latine des origines au moyen âge: Aperçu historique, état des questions," in *Revue théologique de Louvain* 19 (1988) 137–59, 276–314: concluded (pp304–14) by a selective bibliography of editions of Latin Old Testament texts [DA55].

J. Fontaine and C. Pietri, eds., *Le monde latin antique et la Bible,* Bible de tous les temps 2 (1985): contains many useful essays; note especially J.-C. Fredouille, "Les lettrés chrétiens face à la Bible" (pp25–42); J. Gribomont, "Les plus anciennes traductions latines" (pp43–65); R. Braun, "L'influence de la Bible sur la langue latine" (pp129–42) [DA56].

J.K. Elliott, "The Translations of the New Testament into Latin: The Old Latin and the Vulgate," *Aufstieg und Niedergang der römischen Welt* 2.26.1:198–245 [DA57].

B. Fischer, "Das Neue Testament in lateinishcer Sprach," in *Die alten Übersetzungen des Neuen Testaments, die Kirchenväterzitate und Lektionare,* ed. K. Aland (1972) 1–92 [DA58].

R. Gameson, ed., *The Early Medieval Bible: Its Production, Decoration, and Use* (1994) [DA59].

B.M. Peebles, "Bible, IV.13. Latin Versions," in *NCE* 2:436–57: dated, but still the most useful and practical introduction to the Latin Bible [DA60].

F. Stummer, *Einführung in die lateinische Bibel* (1928) [DA61].

E. Ulrich, "Characteristics and Limitations of the Old Latin Translation of the Sep-tuagint," in *La Septuaginta en la investigacion contemporanea: V Congreso de la IOSCS,* ed. N. Fernández Marcos (1985) 67–80 [DA62].

E. Valgiglio, *Le antiche versioni latine del Nuovo Testamento: Fedeltà e aspetti grammaticali* (1985) [DA63].

## Anthologies

A. Ceresa-Gastaldo, *Il Latino delle antiche versioni bibliche* (1975): handy bibliography (pp11–18) and introductury materials, followed by series of selections given in Hebrew or Greek, with variety of Latin versions [DA64].

O. García de la Fuente, *Antologia del latín bíblico y cristiano* (see [DA9]) [DA65].

## Introductions and Manuals

A. Blaise, *Manuel du latin chrétien* (see [DA8])): abundant illustrations drawn from Latin of biblical translations [DA66].

O. García de la Fuente, *Introducción al latín bíblico y cristiano* (see [DA7]) [DA67].

F.P. Kaulen, *Sprachliches Handbuch zur biblischen Vulgata* (1904, r1973): unscientific but handy [DA68].

W.E. Plater and H.J. White, *A Grammar of the Vulgate, Being an Introduction to the Study of the Latinity of the Vulgate Bible* (1926) [DA69].

H. Rönsch, *Itala und Vulgata: Das Sprachidiom der urchristlichen Itala und der katholischen Vulgata*, 2nd ed. (1875, r1965) [DA70].

## Concordances, Indices, Dictionaries

T.A. Bergren, *A Latin-Greek Index of the Vulgate New Testament . . . with an Index of Latin Equivalencies Characteristic of "African" and "European" Old Latin Versions of the New Testament* (1991) [DA71].

M. Britt, *A Dictionary of the Psalter, Containing the Vocabulary of the Psalms, Hymns, Canticles, and Miscellaneous Prayers of the Breviary Psalter* (1928): unscientific but useful [DA72].

B. Fischer, *Novae concordantiae bibliorum sacrorum iuxta Vulgatam versionem critice editam*, 5 vols. (1977): based on 2nd ed. of Stuttgart Vulgate (see [DA50]) [DA73].

J.M. Harden, *Dictionary of the Vulgate New Testament* (1921) [DA74].

G. Kittel and G. Friedrich, eds., *Theological Dictionary of the New Testament* (see [DA11]) [DA75].

W. Lechner-Schmidt, *Wortindex der lateinisch erhaltenen Pseudepigraphen zum Alten Testament* (1990) [DA76].

G.C. Richards, *A Concise Dictionary of the Vulgate New Testament* (1934) [DA77].

## Studies of St. Jerome's Translations

A. Condamin, "Les caractères de la traduction de la Bible par saint Jérome," in *Recherches de science religieuse* 2 (1911) 425–40, 3 (1912) 105–38 [DA78].

M. Wissemann, *Schimpfworte in der Bibelübersetzung des Hieronymus* (1992) [DA79].

## Vocabulary of Exegesis and Translation

*La terminologia esegetica nell'antichità: Atti del primo seminario di antichità cristiane, Bari, 25 ottobre 1984*, Quaderni de "Vetera Christianorum" 20 (1987): see especially P. Siniscalco, "Appunti sulla terminologia esegetica di Tertulliano" (pp103–22); J. Gribomont, "La terminologie exégétique de S. Jérôme" (pp123–34); M. Marin, "*Allegoria* in Agostino" (pp135–61); and index, "Terminologia esegetica" (pp173–75) [DA80].

G.J.M. Bartelink, ed., *Hieronymus, Liber de optimo genere interpretandi (Epistula 57):*

*Ein Kommentar* (1980): excellent, extensive commentary, followed by indices of Greek and Latin words [DA81].

### Patristic Biblical Philology (a few basic texts, primary and secondary)

Augustine, *Locutionum in Heptateuchum libri VII*, ed. I. Fraipont, *CCSL* 33:381–465 [DA82]: note study of W. Süß, *Augustins Locutiones und das Problem der lateinischen Bibelsprache*, Studien zur lateinischen Bibel 1 (1932) [DA83].

Cassiodorus, *Inst.*: the first book is, in a sense, a guide to patristic biblical scholarship; note particularly ch. 15, "Sub qua cautela relegi debeat caelestis auctoritas" [DA84].

P. de Lagarde, *Onomastica sacra*, 2nd ed. (1887, r1966): contains editions of Jerome's onomastic works; this edition of the *Liber interpretationis Hebraicorum nominum* reprinted in *CCSL* 72 (1959) 57–161 [DA85].

Eucherius of Lyons, *Formulae spiritalis intelligentiae*, ed. C. Wotke, *CSEL* 31 (1894) 1–62 [DA86].

*Glossa ordinaria*: convenientaly available in *Biblia latina cum glossa ordinaria* (the *editio princeps*), ed. A. Rusch, 4 vols. (Strassburg 1480/81, r1992); with a little trouble one can identify this basic medieval tool's abundant, but often unacknowledged, indebtedness to patristic biblical scholarship [DA87].

U. Jaitner-Hahner, *Cassiodors Psalmenkommentar: Sprachliche Untersuchungen* (1973) [DA88].

A. Kamesar, *Jerome, Greek Scholarship, and the Hebrew Bible: A Study of the "Quaestiones hebraicae in Genesim"* (1993) [DA89].

G.Q.A. Meershoek, *Le latin biblique d'après saint Jérôme: Aspects linguistiques de la rencontre entre la Bible et le monde classique*, Latinitas Christianorum Primaeva 20 (1966): note indices (pp252–56) of Hebrew, Greek, and Latin words [DA90].

*See also* [BB51], [BC21], [BC23], [BC33], [BC37], [BC81], [BC105], [BC110], [BD31], [BD38], [BD48], [BD55], [BD58], [BD64], [BD71], [BD88], [BE27], [BE41].

DB     ❋     # THE LITURGY

## BY DANIEL SHEERIN

The term *liturgy* is used here to refer to medieval communal religious ritual and worship, whose form and function were determined and sanctioned by some authoritative person or persons.

The category "Liturgical Latin" is sometimes restricted to the formalized prayer texts of the liturgy, is sometimes extended to include liturgical chants and readings, and sometimes incorporates even the language of the rubrics (*rubricae,* liturgical directions and regulations, copied in red to distinguish them from the texts). This introduction takes liturgical Latin to include the Latin of all texts involved directly or indirectly in the liturgy. It is therefore concerned with both the Latin of those documents subsidiary to the liturgy, which might be called the texts of the "liturgical apparatus," and the Latin of the liturgical texts themselves, whether they were read in silence or sotto voce, spoken, declaimed, intoned, or chanted in the course of the liturgy.

## I. Texts of the Liturgical Apparatus

The texts of the liturgical apparatus include texts employed to schedule liturgical observances, such as calendrical and computistical texts; texts used to direct the rituals, e.g. *ordines* and rubrics interposed in the texts themselves; various kinds of directories; texts designed to enhance participation in liturgical observances, e.g. commentaries on texts and rituals; and sermons that elucidate liturgical documents and events. The Latin employed here comprised a technical idiom, a "language for special purposes," that is, a mixture of common words assigned a technical meaning in liturgical contexts, Greek and Hebrew borrowings, words that had undergone semantic shifts, and more recondite terms. Its lexicon includes the names of liturgical times, functionaries (and their costumes and decorations), actions, objects (substances, vessels, instruments, etc.), structures, sites (and their ornamentation), texts (and the techniques for presenting them), and books.

(a) **Liturgical Times.** (See [DB51–52].) Scheduling the liturgy involved its own language of timekeeping, not only the more recondite technical vocabulary of the *computus* (see ch. EF), but also the more widely used language of reckoning and naming the liturgical hours of the day, the days of the week and month, and the seasons and their components. This timekeeping and date-assigning language was also used in nonliturgical and even secular contexts (see [DB52] VI for a listing).

*Hours:* The more common names of the *horae canonicae,* "canonical hours," of the liturgical *horarium* (schematized presentation in [DB14] pp46–47; diagram in [DB30] p16) are *matutinae* (matins), *laudes* [sc. *matutinales*] (lauds), [*hora*] *prima* (prime), [*hora*] *tertia* (terce), [*hora*] *sexta* (sext), [*hora*] *nona* (none), *uespera/ae* (vespers), *completorium* (compline). Sundays and major feasts were observed beginning with the vespers of the previous evening; this service is called *uesperae primae,* and vespers of the day itself is called *uesperae secundae.*

*Days and Weeks:* The liturgy did more than anything else to impose the novel Hebrew week (known by the Greek loanword *hebdomada* or Latin *septimana*) on the Greco-Roman and medieval worlds. The names of the days, dating from paleo-Christian times, are *dies dominica* or *dominica* (Sunday), *feria secunda* (Monday) to *feria sexta* (Friday), and *sabbatum* (a Hebrew loanword not unknown in Classical Latin [see *OLD,* s.v. *sabbata*] but propagated mainly through the Christian Scriptures). *Feria* was adopted by inversion from the classical usage *feriae/-arum* = holiday, day of repose; numbering the days was borrowed from the practice, familiar from the New Testament, of numbering the days of the week, i.e. *prima sabbati* = first day of the week, *secunda sabbati* = the second day, and so forth (see Isidore, *Etym.* 5.30.9). From *feria* comes *ferialis/-e* (for texts in ordinary use on the days of the week when no feast occurred, e.g. *psalmi feriales* or *hymni feriales*) and *ferialiter* (to describe the routine conduct of services).

Some weeks and days have their own names, e.g. the fasting period of Lent begins within the *Hebdomada in capite ieiunii,* specifically on *Feria quarta in capite ieiunii* or *Feria quarta cinerum* (Ash Wednesday); later in Lent come *Dominica in passione* (Passion Sunday) and the *Hebdomada passionis* (or *in passione*), followed by the *Dominica in palmis* (Palm Sunday, also called *Dominica in ramis palmarum, Dominica in palma,* or *Dominica competentium*), with its ensuing *Hebdomada sancta* or *maior* (Holy Week), including *Feria V in cena domini* (Holy Thursday with its commemoration of the Last Supper), *Feria VI in parasceue* (Good Friday; *parasceue/-es,* a Greek loanword found in the Gospels, refers to the Day of Preparation before the Passover), and *Sabbatum sanctum* or *magnum.*

The most important Sundays bear peculiar names descended from Christian antiquity, e.g. *Pascha/-ae* (fem.) and *-atis* (neut.) (Easter Sunday) and *Pentecoste/-es* (the first a Hebrew, the second a Greek loanword, both mediated through Scripture), while most are named according to their relative position in the liturgical year, whether within a particular liturgical season, e.g. *Dominica quarta aduentus* (Fourth Sunday of Advent), *Dominica infra octauas ascensionis domini* (Sunday in the week following the Feast of the Ascension), or subsequent to a major feast, as in the counting of Sundays after Pentecost or after Trinity Sunday (the Sunday after Pentecost), e.g. *Dominica XIV post Trinitatem* (Fourteenth Sunday after Trinity Sunday) or *Dominica XV post Pentecosten* (the same Sunday in an alternative scheme).

Another method for designating Sundays was to use the opening word or words of the introit of the Mass (tabular listing in [DB52] VI:98–99). The names of a few are well known, e.g *Gaudete,* the Third Sunday of Advent; *Laetare,* the Fourth Sunday of Lent; *Quasi modo,* the Sunday after Easter, also called *Clausum Pascha* and *Dominica in albis* or *post albas* (from the *albae,* white baptismal garments of the neophytes). But the system works for the less well known as well, e.g. the Second Sunday in Lent,

*Dominica II in Quadragesima,* can also be called *Reminiscere* from the incipit of its introit, "Reminiscere miserationum tuarum . . ." (*Ps* 24:6, etc.), and the weekdays following can be reckoned *Feria secunda post Reminiscere,* and so on.

Many days are also designated by a keyword or words referring to the Gospel pericope or excerpt. Thus, e.g., the Sunday otherwise referred to as *Dominica XIV post Trinitatem* (or *Dominica XV post Pentecosten*) could also be called *Vidua Naim* or *Vidua in Nain* from the Gospel narrative of *Lc* 7:11–17; Friday of the Second Week of Lent could be called *Vinicolae* from *Mt* 21:33–46, Wednesday of the Fourth Week of Lent *Caecus natus* from *Io* 9:1–38, and so on. Other types of liturgical texts provide names for the days on which they are used, e.g. the days on which the so-called *antiphonae maiores* were sung (see below) may be named after the opening words of such antiphons as "O Oriens," or the First Sunday after the Octave of Epiphany (and the ensuing period) may be referred to by the opening words of the Matins responsory "Domine, ne in ira tua." Another example concerns the termination of the singing of the *Alleluia* at Vespers on the Saturday before Septuagesima Sunday (the ninth before Easter); this day might be called *Sabbatum quo* (or *die qua*) *clauditur Alleluia* in both liturgical and extraliturgical contexts.

*Feastdays:* A feastday or day for special liturgical observance is a *festum* (also *festiuitas, dies festus,* or just *dies*), as opposed to a *feria.* The word is typically encountered in the ablative after *in* and is followed by the name of the saint in the genitive, often with a qualifying epithet or indicator of the type of saint, e.g. *in festo Sancti Stephani protomartyris;* in many liturgical books *in festo* is dropped and the genitive alone used to indicate the feast, e.g. [*in festo*] *Mauri abbatis, Agnetis virginis et martyris, Marci euangelistae.*

Most feastdays of the saints are the [*dies*] *natalis* or *natale* or *natalicium,* which really means, by devout euphemism, the day of death, except in the cases of Christ, Mary, and John the Baptist, when the *natalis* or *natiuitas* bears its usual meaning. Other types of feast include the *ordinatio* of bishops, the *depositio* (death) of confessors, the *inventio* of relics or of the Cross, the *translatio* of relics. Selected events in hagiography are observed by feasts, hence *Sancti Iohannis ante Portam Latinam, Sancti Petri ad Vincula, Apparitionis beati Michaelis archangeli,* etc. Terms describing life stages identify Marian and dominical feasts, e.g. Mary's *Conceptio, Nativitas, Presentatio, Purificatio, Assumptio;* the Annunciation, variously *Annunciatio domini, Annunciatio dominica, Annunciatio Mariae, Annunciatio dominae;* Christmas, *Natiuitas domini* or *dominica,* followed by the *Circumcisio domini, Purificatio Mariae* or *Hypapante, Epiphania domini,* and so on, through the year.

Major feasts had a preparatory feastday, a vigil, the services for which might be labeled, e.g. *In uigilia apostolorum Petri et Pauli,* whereas those for the feastday itself are marked *In die apostolorum Petri et Pauli.* Major feasts were also assigned an octave, i.e. the eight-day (counting inclusively) period immediately following, e.g. *infra/per octauas apostolorum Petri et Pauli,* during which the major feast would be recalled in the services by a set of short texts called a *memoria* (suffrage) and some of the matins readings, with a more elaborate observance on the eighth (seventh) day, e.g. *in octaua apostolorum Petri et Pauli.*

The degree of solemnity of the observance and the priorities to be assigned in the case of coincident or overlapping feasts were determined by the ranking of feasts according to a variety of systems. Some calendars rank feasts according to the number of readings (*lectiones*) at matins, so in cathedral (nonmonastic) use there were feasts of *III lectionum* and *IX lectionum,* while monastic calendars offer feasts of *III lectionum* and *XII lectionum.* Monastic communities also ranked feasts according to the garb to be worn by the monks in choir, and so there were feasts *in albis* and *in cappis,* in albs and copes. Another common nomenclature for the ranking of feasts employed the categories *festum duplex* and *festum simplex,* with various subdivisions; in Sarum (Salisbury) Use, e.g., there was the following ranking of feasts: "Festum dividitur in festum duplex et in festum simplex. Festum duplex dividitur in Principale duplex, in Majus duplex, in Minus duplex, in Inferius duplex. . . . Festum simplex dividitur in Invitatorium triplex, Invitatorium duplex, Invitatorium simplex." The last set of rankings is indicated by the number of singers (three, two, one) employed to chant the *invitatorium* (*Ps* 94, with its refrain peculiar to the feast chanted at the beginning of matins). The designation *cum regimine chori* meant that the cantor was to assign *rectores chori,* varying in number and dignity with the feast, to chant and intone certain elements of the office.

Here is an example, from a rubric in the *Sarum Breviary,* of the use of some of the terms just described:

> Et nota quod si in aliquo *sabbato* a *"Domine ne in ira"* usque ad *Passionem,* vel ab *Octavis Paschae* usque ad *Adventum Domini,* vel a *secunda Dominica Adventus Domini* usque ad *festum Nativitatis,* aliquod *festum Simplex ix vel iii Lectionum* cum *regimine chori* evenerit, *Vesperae* in *sabbato* erunt de *Dominica,* et *Memoria* de *Festo; nisi* tale *festum* fuerit quod in *sexta feria* praecedenti suas *primas Vesperas* habere non poterit: et nisi *Octava Epyphaniae* vel aliae *Octavae* cum *regimine chori* in *sabbato* contigerint. [DB67]
> v2:464–65

*Months and Seasons:* The liturgical year was divided according to two parallel and sometimes conflicting systems generally known as the sanctoral cycle and the temporal cycle; those portions of liturgical books which contain the services of these cycles are sometimes called the *proprium de sanctis* and the *proprium de tempore,* or, in more modern parlance, the *sanctorale* and *temporale.* Because the Latin liturgical year was considered to begin on the First Sunday of Advent, in liturgical books the *proprium de tempore* usually begins with the first Sunday of Advent and the *proprium de sanctis* with the Feast of St. Andrew (December 30) or its vigil; another peculiarity is the location in the *proprium de tempore* of the set of feasts of saints between Christmas and Epiphany.

The sanctoral cycle is a calendrical system based on the old Roman months and their division into days enumerated by counting down to fixed points in the months (Kalends, Nones, Ides); these are *festa immobilia* and they are easily determined by consulting the *Kalendarium* prefixed to many liturgical books. While feasts of the saints predominate in the sanctoral cycle, feasts of Christ do occur in the *proprium de sanctis* as well, e.g. *Transfiguratio domini* or *Inventio sanctae Crucis.*

The temporal cycle is arranged around the two major feasts of Christmas (*Nativitas domini*) and Easter (*Pascha*). The date of Christmas was fixed on December 25, and its associated feasts and seasons can be easily determined by calculating backwards or forwards from that date (all are *festa immobilia*): the pre-Christmas season of *Aduentus domini,* a four-week period of preparation; *Nativitas domini;* and a cluster of fixed feasts which follow it and lead up to *Epiphania* (also *Theophania*) on January 6. The post-Epiphany season varies in length, for it leads into the pre-Easter season. The date of Easter is variable from year to year, for it is determined by the cycles of the moon (usually the first Sunday after the first full moon after the vernal equinox; cf. [DB53] pp15–41); so the dates of the pre- and post-Easter seasons have to be calculated on an annual basis (these are *festa mobilia*). The period before Easter is described in terms of a countdown to that feast: first comes the pre-Lenten season with its Sundays: *Dominica in Septuagesima, Dominica in Sexagesima,* and *Dominica in Quinquagesima,* and then the Lenten period of forty days (*Quadragesima*) with its subdivisions, some of which were indicated above. Feasts of the post-Easter season are reckoned by counting forward, with *Ascensio domini* and *Pentecoste* occurring, respectively, forty and fifty days after Easter (counting inclusively).

Another set of seasonal observances with its own peculiar names is the *Quatuor tempora* (= the four seasons; in English "Ember Days"), four sets of three-day (Wednesday, Friday, and Saturday) penitential periods, with fasting, abstinence, and special liturgical observances. These took their origin from the Roman agricultural year and were part of the temporal cycle: the *Quatuor tempora aduentus, Quatuor tempora quadragesimae, Quatuor temporum Pentecostes,* and *Quatuor tempora Septembris.* Thus *in feria quarta quatuor temporum Pentecostes* means on Wednesday of the post-Pentecost ember days; *Sabbato quatuor temporum aduentus* means on Saturday of the Advent ember days, and so on.

(b) **Liturgical Onomastics.** (See [DB25], [DB52].) Calendars and particularly martyrologies were rich repositories of proper names from diverse regions and eras, providing both personal names as well as an ecclesiastical toponomy. The various sorts of necrologies used in the regular prayer for the dead furnished yet another, perhaps more familiar, onomastic corpus. The liturgical directories of particular communities contain the local place names of sites in the regions, cities, and monasteries that figure in the rituals.

(c) **Technical Terms.** (See [DB54–61].)

*Ministers:* These terms include the names (1) of the seven *ordines* or ranks of the ordained clergy: porter, reader, exorcist, acolyte, subdeacon, deacon, and priest: *(h)ostiarius, lector, exorcista, accolitus* (also *acolytus*), *subdiaconus, diaconus* (also *leuita/-ae*), *presbyter* (also *sacerdos*); (2) of the episcopate: *episcopus* (also *antistes, pontifex, praesul,* etc., also with the prefix *archi-*); (3) of unordained ministers, e.g. *ceroferarius* (candle-bearer), *thuribularius* (censer-bearer, also *thurifer*), *cambucarius* (bearer of bishop's staff, the *cambuca*), *crucifer* (bearer of the processional cross); (4) of musical ministers, e.g. the *precentor/-trix* and *succentor/trix,* the *rector principalis* and *rector secundarius* of the choir, the *versicularius,* etc.; and (5) of monastic or cathedral officials, e.g. *abbas, prior, decanus, subthesaurius, capellanus episcopi, secretarius, sacrarius* or *sacrista* (sacristan). In the later Middle Ages the names of those who were to take the various parts in services were noted on a *tabula* kept by a *tabularius,* hence *intabulare,* as, e.g., in the directive "Hic cantentur tres versus usitati . . . a quodam juvene qui intabulatur diebus ferialibus ad primam lectionem."

*Gestures/Actions:* Most of these nouns and verbs for postures and gestures are appropriated or derived from ordinary vocabulary, but take on a technical meaning in liturgical context. Some examples:

1. postures and gestures for prayer/penance: *inclinatio* + (*se*) *inclinare, ceruicem flectere* (to bow); *genuflectio* + *flectere genu* or *genua* (to genuflect or kneel, as in the

command "Flectamus genua"); *prostratio* + *se prostrare, se habere prostratum* (to prostrate oneself); [*se*] *leuare*, [*se*] *erigere* (to rise, as in the commands "Leuate" and "Erigamus nos ad dominum"); *tunsio pectoris* + *pectus tundere/percutere* (to knock the breast as a sign of remorse); *eleuatio manuum* + *manus eleuare* (from *Ps* 140:2)

2. movement and rest: *processio* + *fieri/ire/redire* or *procedere* (sometimes with *processionaliter*), for liturgical procession, and *circumitio/circumire* or *circumambulatio/circumambulare*, for a particular variety of procession; *stationem facere*, to make a ritual pause (*statio*) at the appointed place (*locus stationis*) for prayer in the course of a procession

3. blessing and consecrating: *benedictio/benedicere*; *signum* [sc. *crucis*] *facere, signare, se signare, crucem facere, consignatio/consignare,* for signing with the cross; *consecratio/consecrare; dedicatio/dedicare; ordinatio/ordinare; manus/-uus impositio/manum/-us imponere*

4. blessing with water: *aspersio/aspergere*, with or without explicit mention of *aqua benedicta;* linked with the antiphon *Asperges me* (*Ps* 50:9)

5. anointing: *unctio/ungere, inunctio/iniungere*

6. breathing: *sufflatio/sufflare, exsufflatio/exsufflare*

7. handling of eucharistic elements: *eleuatio/eleuare, fractio/frangere* and *confractio* (of the eucharistic bread), *commixitio* of eucharistic bread and wine; *ablutio* of eucharistic vessels

8. censing: *incensum facere, incensatio/incensare* or *thurificatio/thurificare, aromatizare* and *thymiatizare*

9. kissing: *osculum* (also *osculatio*)/*osculari* for a variety of liturgical kisses (see [DB137] s.v. *Kuß*, pp496–97)

10. An action which derives its name from a text chanted in association with it is the *mandatum,* a term for ritual foot-washing, derived from *Io* 13:34: "Mandatum nouum do uobis ut diligatis inuicem."

*Places:* Liturgical instructions direct participants to various locations within the liturgical structure. Here Greek loanwords predominate, with an admixture of Latin technical terms: within the *ecclesia*, which might be called a *basilica* or might be an *ecclesia cathedralis* (if it contains a bishop's *cathedra*), will be a *crypta* used for certain rites, a *navis* (nave) for processions, an *ambo* or *pulpitum*, a *chorus* (the choir), the *presbiterium,* and places for vesting and preparing called *vestiarium* or *sacrarium* (sacristy); a smaller liturgical space within it, in effect a miniature church, would be called a *capella* (chapel) from the first so to be named after the cloak of St. Martin enshrined in it; outside might be a *capitulum* (chapter house), a *claustrum* (cloister), and a *cimeterium* or *cymeterium,* the place of repose of the dead.

*Furniture:* The most prominent item of furniture in a church was the main altar (variously called *altare magnum, maius, summum, authenticum, principale*). There was also a podium for reading, called *anagogium* or *lectrina* (lectern), the one on the pulpit sometimes being called the *aquila* from its shape. In the choir each singer would have a *stallum* (stall, originally a Germanic word); these were arranged in rows called *formae,* and there was a hierarchy of seating. Thus at Salisbury, e.g., there was a descent in dignity from the *gradus superior* to the *forma secunda* and *forma prima.*

*Costumes:* Names for the vestments are a mixed bag of common terms (both Latin and latinized Greek terms), whose use came eventually to be virtually restricted to liturgical garments. For illustration's sake we list only the Mass vestments of priest and bishop as given by Innocent III (1198–1216), *De sacro altaris mysterio* (or *De missarum mysteriis*) 1.10 (*PL* 217:780–81): those worn by both bishops and priests included *amictus/-us* (amice), *alba* (alb), *cingulum* (cincture), *manipulus/-i* (maniple), *stola* (stole), *planeta* or *casula* (chasuble); vestments and accoutrements peculiar to the bishop were *caligae* (stockings), *sandalia* (shoes), *succinctorium, tunica, dalmatica, mitra* (mitre), *c(h)irotecae* (gloves), *a(n)nulus* (ring), *baculus* (staff, crozier), and, perhaps, *pallium.* Vestments worn in choir or for the administration of sacraments included the *cap(p)a* (cope) and *superpelliceum* (surplice).

Only one of the many decorative variables was color, which commonly was not merely an incidental amenity of liturgical textiles, but also carried a symbolic meaning and had to be harmonized with the type of feast or observance (see [DB57], [DB60]). Liturgical directives or inventories sometimes refer to types of ornamentation such as cloth—*aresta* (silk from Arras), *imperialis* (Byzantine silk), or *examitum* (samite)—and to details of decoration—*stragultus* (striped, also *uirgulatus*), *scaccatus* (checkered), *auripictus* and *auritextus,* and so on.

*Vessels, etc.:* Names for liturgical objects display the expected mixure of technical/symbolic use of ordinary terms, neologisms, and loanwords from Greek. In the course of the Mass, for example, the wine (mixed with a bit of water) was contained in a cup called variously *calix* (chalice), *scyphus, crater, poculum, fons,* etc., while the bread (*hostia, corpus domini, corpus dominicum*) was placed on a *patena* (paten); the latter was reserved (after conscration) in a vessel called a *ciborium, pyxis, capsa, chrismale, custodia, repositorium, tabernaculum, theca, viaticum,* etc., and displayed in an *ostensorium* or *monstrantia* (monstrance). Blessed water was sprinkled with an *aspersorium.* The censer was called *thymiaterium, t(h)uribulum,* or *incensorium. Crux* may refer to a processional cross, and *vexillum* to a pendant attached to this cross or to a variety of standards carried in procession. The English pax-brede or pax-board, called *pax, pacificale, instrumentum pacis,* or *osculatorium,* was a tablet handed around to be kissed by all as a replacement for an actual exchange of kisses of peace during the Mass.

*Liturgical Texts and Modes of Delivery:* Names for types of utterances within liturgical contexts vary with the content of the speech, as, for example: *oratio,* elsewhere a generic term for speech, is here restricted to prayer; *lectio,* the reading aloud of a text from Scripture or tradition; *absolutio* gives vocal formality to the remission of sins; an *admonitio* might be given at the beginning of a synod or council; an *allocutio* or *exhortatio* or *praefatio* is a ritual address preliminary to the conferral of a sacrament or sacramental; a *denuntiatio* gives notice of the inception of a period of fasting or of an approaching liturgical event. *Maledictio* and *anathematizatio* are parts of the ritual of *excommunicatio,* exclusion from the ecclesiastical community; the Latin *adiuratio* and the Greek loanword *exorcismus* are terms for the rite for reclaiming the Church's possessed or obsessed members.

Another quasi-technical vocabulary clusters around efforts to indicate or mandate the ways in which liturgical texts were to be read or chanted. Here are just a few examples (see the excellent index of the Exeter *Ordinale* [*HBS* 79:243], s.v. "Saying and singing, manner of"): silent recitation is described as *secrete, in secreto, privatim, sub silencio, tacite;* audible recitation moves up through *lenta voce, submissiore voce, submissius, submisse, voce submissa,* and *submisse quasi murmurando,* to *mediocri voce* and *modesta voce, modesta voce quasi legendo,* and on to *altius, exaltando vocem, elevando vocem, elevata voce, clamose,* and *excelsa et clamorosa voce.*

A more recondite element of this vocabulary of direction  is the words used to describe embellishments of texts executed musically (*cantatorie*), e.g. *alleluiatice* (with an *alleluia*), *pneumatizare* (to sing the *pneumata*, "neums"), and, more bizarre, *triumphare* (to sing thrice). Rules are provided for the singing of Psalms (*psalmodiare*) with due attention to the divisions of the Psalm verses (*metra*) and the pauses (*pausae*) they indicate. The vocabulary of the liturgical recitative used for intoned declamation of readings includes its monotone *tenor* or *tuba*, with various *positurae* or *pausationes*, flexions used to give variety to the intonation of the text and meaning to its presentation, along with the words for the punctuation marks used to point it. (On psalmody see, e.g., the chapter "De Disciplina Psallendi," in the customary of St. Mary's, York [*HBS* 73:2–4]; on punctuation and liturgical texts see [DB42–44].)

*Lights and Bells:* Technical language governing the observance of liturgical feasts extends even to provision of lights (types of candles and lamps, their mountings, etc.) and bells (names of bells, proper and common, types of ringing, etc.); see, e.g., the directions for the illumination of Exeter Cathedral (*HBS* 38:539–45) and St. Augustine's Abbey, Canterbury (*HBS* 28:268–90), and for bell-ringing at Exeter (*HBS* 38:535–39) and St. Augustine's (*HBS* 28:291–318).

*Books:* See no. IV below.

(d) **Elucidation and Symbolism.** (See [DB134–138].) Commentaries on liturgical texts employ the language of analysis and interpretation current in the eras in which they were composed, commonly taking over the hermeneutic language and method of scriptural commentary and the technical terms for representing and symbolizing, e.g. *figurare, praeferre imaginem, personam/uicem gerere;* for recalling, e.g. *commemorare, repraesentare;* for signifying or meaning, e.g. *demonstrare, designare, innuere, insinuare, respicere ad, signare, significare.* From Isidore (d. 636) on there is great interest in the origin of liturgical practices, precedents, and names, and we therefore find expressions like *sumere exordium/exemplum*, and *idcirco nuncupatur quia*. There are interesting ways of indicating hidden meanings, e.g. *a mysterio non uacat, diuinis plena sunt sacramentis,* and the whole lexicon of biblical exegesis can be brought into play, for liturgical events too can be interpreted *historice, anagogice, allegorice,* and *tropologice.*

## II. Rites of the Liturgy

We must limit our discussion here to the so-called Roman liturgy in the Middle Ages. "Roman" and "Roman rite" are common but unfortunate terms, for they carry with them much anachronism and ecclesiological baggage. Strictly speaking, such terms should apply only to the liturgical practices of the metropolitan see of Rome as they came to be formed from local developments and by appropriation of alien elements. As it is, faute de mieux ("Romano-Germanic" and "Franco-Roman" have not won general acceptance), "Roman" may refer to the elaboration of the Roman use as it was adopted by, was imposed upon, and interacted with various national or regional traditions, and went on to dominate European liturgical practice throughout the Middle Ages. Much that will be said here is, however, applicable to the liturgies of various regions (the so-called Gallican, Ambrosian, Mozarabic [or Visigothic or Old Spanish], Celtic, and other rites) and to those of the religious orders (monastic communities, various types of canons, friars, etc.), whose differences from a mainstream "Roman" use vary from the slight to the dramatic.

The principal components of medieval liturgical life were the eucharistic liturgy or Mass; the liturgy of the hours or Divine Office; and "occasional services," which include everything else in a spectrum ranging from the sacraments (*sacramenta*) to the sacramentals (*sacramentalia*). While daily Mass and the Divine Office occupied the attention of religious communities, produced the greatest bulk of liturgical texts, and have received the most attention from medievalists, it was the rites of the sacraments and sacramentals which really structured people's lives. These rites attended their birth (*baptismum/baptisma* and *purificatio mulierum*) and coming of age (*confirmatio puerorum*) and their entry into married life (*sponsalia*), or into the military (*benedictio ensis noui militis, benedictio calcarium, clypei, et ensis*), or into religious life (*ordinatio* to the various ranks of the clergy, *consecratio/velatio sacrae virginis, benedictio* of monks, etc.). More somber rites comforted them in illness (*ordo ad visitandum infirmum*) and in death (*extrema unctio, commendatio animarum*), placed them in their graves (*vigiliae mortuorum, missa pro defunctis, inhumatio defuncti*), and in the meantime provided multiplex blessings for the work of their hands and their homes, settled some of their disputes (*benedictio scuti et baculi ad duellum*), protected them from spiritual and physical enemies and the forces of nature, and so on. We have space here only for a simple orientation in the structure and terminology of the Mass and the Divine Office.

(a) **The Mass.** The eucharistic liturgy, the Mass (see [DB10–20]), was called *missa* from the end of the fifth century; earlier this term tends to appear in the plural and in a combination: *missae* or *missarum sollemnia* (see [DB20] v1:169–75 and C. Mohrmann's study in [DA19] v3:351–76). *Missa* appears in conjunction with many verbs in usages that are self-explanatory—*missam* + *celebrare, facere, agere, dicere, legere, canere/cantare/decantare, spectare/audire*—and in association with adjectives or phrases which suggest the character of the Mass: the more solemn, chanted Mass is *missa alta* or *cantata*, as opposed to the *missa bassa/privata* read by a priest with perhaps only one attendant. The *Ordinale* of St. Mary's, York (*HBS* 73, 75, 84), mentions the daily *missa matutinalis*; the later, more elaborate *missa maior;* the daily *missa familiaris*, a votive Mass of the Virgin Mary offered for friends of the community; and daily masses *pro defunctis* (or *missa de requiem*) offered for deceased benefactors, friends, and relations; there is provision for a priest-monk not otherwise engaged to offer a *missa privata*. A private Mass was commonly a *missa votiva*, i.e. a mass offered for a particular intention; it is described either, like the *missa pro defunctis*, according to its intention, e.g. *missa pro pace, pro serentate aeris*, etc., or in terms of the focus of its prayers or request for intercession, e.g. *missa de Trinitate, de spiritu sancto, de sancta cruce, de angelis, de Domina* (also *de beata* or *de beata Maria virgine*), *de Sancto Laurentio* (against fire), etc. In other contexts the sacramental associations of masses are indicated, e.g. *missa nuptialis, missa exequialis*, or *missa chrismalis* (the Mass on Holy Thursday in the course of which the holy oil was consecrated). Specific masses, i.e. sets of proper texts, were identified by the first words of their introits, as in "missa de *Requiem*" or, e.g., in the following phrases from Gertrude of Helfta (d. 1301 or 1302): ". . . inter primam missam, quae erat *Rorate*," ". . .

audire vis *In medio Ecclesiae?*" ". . . an *Dominus dixit* delectaretur audire" (*Missa* 1; *SChr* 331:284).

Only the public and principal elements of the Mass as it was celebrated through most of the Middle Ages can be mentioned here. Each of the elements from the *proprium,* i.e. those peculiar to a particular feast or Mass, is marked with an asterisk; elements from the *ordinarium* are unmarked, but it should be borne in mind that various kinds of textual elaboration, troping, farsing, etc., could be employed to make these ordinary texts specific to the season, type of feast, or particular feast.

### 1. Entrance Rite

*Introitus* (or *Officium*), the remnant of a processional psalm truncated to the point of enclosing usually only a single verse between its antiphon and doxology;

*Kyrie eleison,* probably the vestige of a processional litany;

*Gloria in excelsis Deo,* an ancient prose hymn; borrowed originally from morning prayers, it is not sung/said in penitential seasons, on less solemn feasts, and in Masses for the dead;

*Oratio* (or *Collecta*), conclusion of the entrance rite; this is the proper prayer which usually makes clearest reference to the feast or season being celebrated; a single collect would be assigned to a particular feast or Mass, but collects could be multiplied as *memoriae* or for particular intentions.

### 2. The Service of the Word, readings with interposed chants

*Epistula,* so called because the majority of these readings come from the Epistles of the New Testament, though they were also excerpted from the historical, prophetic, and sapiential books of the Old Testament, and from *Acts* and the *Apocalypse.* Most Epistle pericopes were contextualized by a formulaic salutation after the source of the excerpt had been announced, e.g. "Lectio epistolae beati Pauli apostoli ad Romanos: Fratres . . ."; readings from the Epistles were occasionally also given the formulaic conclusion "in Christo Iesu Domino nostro."  Readings from narrative texts were introduced by "In diebus illis"; prophecies were introduced by "Haec dicit Dominus Deus" and sometimes concluded by "dicit Dominus omnipotens."  The norm was a single "Epistle," but on a limited number of feasts, following antique practice, multiple readings were appointed to be read.

*Graduale* with its *Versus,* vestige of a responsorial psalm; hence its earlier name *Responsorium graduale;*

*Alleluia* and *Versus,* replaced in penitential seasons by the

*Tractus,* a slightly more extended excerpt from a Psalm;

*Sequentia* (also called *Prosa*), hymnodic compositions in poetic prose or rhythmic verse; these appear from the ninth century and are the principal medieval contribution to the texts of the Mass; provided only for major feasts.

*Evangelium,* a reading from the Gospels announced with an indication of its location and source: "Initium sancti euangelii secundum N." or "Sequentia sancti euangelii . . ."; usually the reading was given a minimum context through the introductory formula "in illis diebus," "in illo tempore (+ dixit Iesus discipulis suis)."

*Credo* (also *Symbolum*), the so-called Niceno-Constantinopolitan Creed, chanted/said only on major feasts.

*3. The Offertory Service,* an offering of bread and wine, with most of the prayers recited inaudibly by the celebrant; notable elements are the following:

\*Offertorium, a chant to "cover" the offertory rites;

\*Secreta, the concluding prayer of the offertory, anciently called *Super oblata;* it usually makes explicit reference to the offertory gifts of bread and wine and came to be said inaudibly (hence *secreta*); additional secret prayers could also be recited, corresponding to the additional collects said earlier; the concluding "Per omnia saecula saeculorum" was chanted or said audibly.

*4. The Anaphora* or eucharistic prayer, including the following:

\*Praefatio, the "pre-Sanctus" prayer; because of its variability (the number of proper prefaces in use was considerably reduced in the later Middle Ages, but the preface remained a proper text), the preface came to be regarded as separate from and preliminary to the relatively fixed prayer of the Canon; the preface was always introduced by a dialogue, chanted or recited audibly, and concluded by the chant of the *Sanctus* and *Benedictus.*

*Canon,* the so-called *Canon actionis* (from *canon,* Greek loanword for "norm" or "rule," of the *actio* [= sacred activity], which, along with *agenda,* was a term for the Mass in Christian antiquity). The canon is a complex series of prayers which frame the Institution Narrative of the Eucharist. Earlier the canon was declaimed or, perhaps, intoned, but in France by at least the ninth century it had come to be recited in a voice that was inaudible to the congregation and soon this practice was universal.

*5. The Communion Service,* a service that includes preparatory rites, among them the recitation of the following:

*Pater noster* or *oratio dominica,* chanted or said aloud, followed by the prayer *Libera nos,* during the second half of which ("Da propitius pacem . . .") the *fractio* of the consecrated bread took place; at the prayer's conclusion on Sundays or major feasts a bishop would impart his tripartite

\*Benedictio;

*Pax,* the celebrant's greeting, "Pax domini sit semper uobiscum," and the congregation's reply, "Et cum spiritu tuo," with the exchange of a kiss variously stylized;

*Agnus dei,* originally chanted during the *fractio* of the eucharistic bread, but later placed here; this chant could be troped with texts particularizing it for a specific feast or occcasion;

\*Communio, the communion antiphon; vestige of an ancient Psalm-with-antiphon chanted during the reception of communion;

\*Postcommunio, also called earlier *Ad complendum;* a proper prayer concluding the communion service with, characteristically, references to hoped for nourishment and/or healing as a result of communion; additional postcommunion prayers could also be said, corresponding to the additional collects said earlier.

*6. The Dismissal,* with the formula "Ite, missa est" on days when the *Gloria* was sung; otherwise the alternative "Benedicamus domino" was used, and in Masses for the dead "Requiescant in pace."

(b) **The Divine Office.** The Liturgy of the Hours (see [DB21–24]), called the *horae* or *officium diuinum,* or, by St. Benedict, the *opus dei,* is extremely complex; only a few observations are possible here. The services of the hours have, as common features, abundant psalmody (in an arrangement called a *cursus,* which differs in monastic and cathedral use; see [DB30] p52) chanted with antiphons, hymns, scriptural readings (usually very brief), and short prayers. Some notable longer, nonpsalmodic chants sung virtually like Psalms are the prose hymn *Te deum,* chanted at matins on Sundays and greater feasts, and the *Symbolum Athanasianum* (Athanasian Creed), chanted at prime on Sundays in cathedral use. Other major nonpsalmodic texts are the biblical canticles (*cantica*), of which the more important were drawn from the Gospels and thus sometimes called *euangelia,* i.e. the *Benedictus* (Canticle of Zachariah; *Lc* 1:68–79) at lauds, the *Magnificat* (Canticle of Mary; *Lc* 1:46–55) at vespers, and the *Nunc dimittis* (Canticle of Simeon; *Lc* 2:29–32) at compline.

The hours vary in ascending order of complexity and variety from compline and the *horae minores* of prime, terce, sext, and none (see [DB30] pp75–80) to lauds, vespers, and matins, the most complex and variable of all. Matins, lauds, and vespers are assigned more proper elements (antiphons, short readings, prayers) than the other hours and are thus the foci for study of proper texts of a given feast or season. Matins, anciently the vigil service of a feast, is most specific and most interesting from a literary point of view. For the components of the various hours of the Divine Office, the reader should consult [DB14] pp73–108, referring to [DB30] pp50–80 for details; the best way to study these is to work through such editions as [DB48–49].

The Divine Office was paradigmatic, and reduced and simplified votive offices, e.g. hours of the Virgin and of the Dead, were used by monks, clergy, and literate lay people alike; these were collected into books called *Horae* (see, e.g., SurSoc 132 [*Horae Eboracenses*]).

### III. Some Features of Liturgical Texts

Oppenheim ([DB16] pV) provides an extensive, but by no means exhaustive, list of types of liturgical texts: creeds, prayers (*orationes*), *apologiae,* exorcisms, readings, canticles, antiphons, responsories, verse-response prayers, litanies, hymns, acclamations, doxologies, oaths, and vows. Most of these types are considered briefly here, under the categories "Readings," "Chants," and "Prayers."

(a) **Readings.** Readings were fixed or variable, scriptural and nonscriptural. The readings of the Mass are always scriptural; those of the Divine Office are drawn both from Scripture and from patristic and hagiographical literature. These texts were produced by a process of selection which could involve excerption, centonization, abridgement, truncation, or, e.g., in the case of the use of a homily in matins readings, wholesale incorporation, and, of course, recontextualization. When incorporated into the liturgy and circulated apart from their original contexts, these texts often take on new literary identities in their excerpted, abridged, or centonized forms. In addition, the use of these excerpts in the liturgy gave them a greater prominence and familiarity, endowed them with particular resonances through their association with specific feasts or occasions, and caused them to be the subject of more repeated, specific exegetical attention. The various types of liturgical readings provided cumulatively a scriptural-patristic-hagiographic florilegium which was, when situated in its complete liturgical setting, in large part self-interpreting and self-propagating. The very process of excerption and collocation of texts in the liturgy was an exegetical and catechetical enterprise. Literate and sensitive exposure to the liturgy over time produced a liturgical ethos which could propagate and celebrate new doctrines, saints, and feasts precisely and beautifully in the traditional liturgical media.

(b) **Chants.** (See [DB47–50], [DB92–103].) Chants fall mostly into two categories: longer texts provided with a minimally ornamented syllabic musical setting and shorter texts with melismatic settings of varying degrees of elaboration. The first category includes the Psalms, the biblical canticles, prose "hymns" like the *Te deum* and *Gloria in excelsis,* and the creed. Selection of particular Psalms or excerpts therefrom for specific liturgical contexts was often informed by and informed their exegesis. Liturgical use of the canticles caused them to be the object of exegetical monographs sometimes in association with the creeds and the Lord's Prayer.

The traditional chant texts of the Mass were scriptural with rare exceptions; in the Divine Office, some of the chants were derived from Scripture and some from the nonscriptural readings. Yet another category of office chant texts was formed by wholly new compositions variously elaborated in prose or verse, the most extensive being the sets of versified chants texts making up a so-called rhymed office (see [DB98–100]).

Both the longer and shorter ordinary chants were elaborated, interpreted, and sometimes applied to specific liturgical occasions through tropes, musicoliterary accretions which were prefixed, intercalated, or appended to the ordinary chant texts (see [DB103] for bibliography). Proper chant texts and a very limited number of readings were also troped to the same effect.

Shorter chanted texts that were either borrowed or extrapolated from Scripture or other sources were produced generally in three ways (see [DB95] pp375–77 and materials cited there):

1. by simple excerption, with, perhaps, some minimal deletions or additions;
2. by centonization, i.e. fabrication of chant texts from borrowed sentences, phrases, and words;
3. by (relatively) free composition, the next stage after centonization, using smaller biblical elements, words, formulae, themes, to produce a virtually original composition.

(c) **Prayers.** In primitive use prayers were composed ex tempore under constraints imposed by traditional structures and formulae and concerns for propriety and orthodoxy. Intensification of these concerns led, first, to the provision of model eucharistic prayers for the guidance of the naive and uneducated, and then to the sanctioning of fixed forms by ecclesiastical authorities (see [DB84], ch. 3, especially pp151–58).

The situation is further complicated at Rome by the fact that Greek, presumably the earliest liturgical language in the Western churches, continued to dominate there until it was gradually displaced by Latin in the course of the fourth century. In fact, the developed Roman eucharistic liturgy contained elements of the three sacred languages—Latin, Greek, and Hebrew—as medieval commentators such as John Beleth liked to point out: "Et nota, quod tribus linguis celebratur missa, Hebrayca,

Greca et Latina, quia titulus Christi in cruce pendentis scriptus fuit Hebraice, Grece et Latine, id est de unaquaque illarum trium aliquid ibi apponitur: De Hebrayca, que principalior est, *Alleluia, Amen, Sabaoth, Osanna. . . .* Sequitur *Kyrieleison, Christeleison,* et est Grecum. Reliqua sunt Latina" (*Summa de ecclesiasticis officiis* 35b–36a; [DB131] v41A:64–65; see also [DB125]). The displacement of Greek as the main liturgical language coincided with the appearance of the first remains of what was to become the standard, fixed Roman anaphora or *canon,* which appears entire in almost finished form in the sixth century (see [DB84] pp200–15).

Latin Christian liturgical (and paraliturgical) prayer draws its language, formulae, and styles from all the sources of Christian Latin (see ch. DA), but especially, either directly or through intermediaries, from the following sources: Hebrew prayer forms from Scripture ([DB45] nos. 132–38) and the postbiblical tradition (see [DB86], [DB45] nos. 32–51, [DB87] pp5–57); prayers and hymnodic forms found in the New Testament  and other early Christian Greek prayer forms; Latin pagan prayers (see [DB73], [DB75], [DB85]); and the language and style of the imperial court and chancery. The Latin of the prayer texts is sui generis, a peculiar and very imitable hieratic style built up upon a strict choice and collocation of words for particular effects, including propriety and dogmatic precision, allusive catechesis, compression and pleonasm, emphasis, balance and antithesis, periodicity, and rhythmical endings (see [DB117]). At the same time the impression should not be given that the language and style of liturgical prayers are all of a piece, for there are distinct stylistic differences between the texts of the local uses of the earlier Middle Ages (see [DB74] pp7–42).

There are differences, moreover, within the "Roman" use of the Middle Ages between the styles of the many genres of prayer, between prayers that were composed at different times (see [DB113] ppLXIX–LXXXI, for attempts to date the composition of various components of the *Leonine Sacramentary*), and between Roman products and prayers of non-Roman origin. Here we can only discuss briefly the three main prayer types: *oratio, praefatio,* and the *anaphora.*

*Oratio* (see [DB76–81]) is the generic term for the terse, artfully simple prayers of the Roman liturgy. These are the prayers of the Roman Mass which vary with feast, season, and intention, and have different names and characteristics according to their function. The *collecta* is not restricted to the Mass, but is found in the Divine Office and occasional rituals. These variable or "proper" prayers had to be composed anew or adapted throughout the Middle Ages as new feasts and celebrations were introduced, but a remarkable uniformity of style and content persists. The formulaic terminations of collects varied according to content, and celebrants had to know the formulae and rules for their use (see, e.g., John Beleth, *Summa de ecclesiastics officiis* 54: "De collectarum terminatione"; [DB131] v41A:92–96], and the mnemonic verses in *HBS* 22:616, "pro collectis finiendis").

The *Praefatio* is generally the longest and most elaborate of the proper prayers of the Mass. Their number seems to have been increasingly reduced in the local Roman ritual in the early Middle Ages, but Benedict of Aniane included an extensive collection in his supplement to the *Sacramentarium Hadrianum,* and prefaces proliferated throughout Europe with new compositions for local saints and new feasts, until retrenchment limited their number to nine variable prefaces and a *praefatio communis.* Moeller's *Corpus praefationum* [DB82] invites study of these extraordinary texts. Prefaces, like hymns, provided a kind of afterlife for the highly artificial ecclesiastical rhetorical genres of encomium and panegyric when preaching had largely been reduced to relatively pedestrian exegesis and paraenesis. Elements of the form of the preface—the musical tone, introductory dialogue, formulaic opening, acclamations, recounting of apposite *magnalia Dei*, etc.—were borrowed for the pseudoprefaces of some of the sacraments and sacramental rituals.

The *Canon* of the Mass is, in a sense, the chef-d'oeuvre of Latin liturgical prayer, the very best example, perhaps, of what Christine Mohrmann has termed hieratic sacral language ([DB123] p15). At the same time, we must remember that for the greater part of the period of its use this magnificent, solemn text was recited or read in silence, and that special provisions had to be made from time to time to ensure even that the clergy had a rudimentary understanding of it (see especially [DB135], [DB138]). This introduces the great sociolinguistic issue attending Latin liturgical texts: they were, in ways and degrees varying according to time and place, inaccessible or incomprehensible to the vast majority of the people in whose ritual lives they figured so prominently. This is especially true of the prayer texts. Texts derived from Scripture may have been accessible to the less educated when and where Latin was a vernacular language, but we must wonder to what degree, even when Latin dominated, the highly stylized prayers were understood by the uneducated or even those of limited education. These texts seem to have been composed by and for a clerical, ritual elite, to satisfy their tastes and requirements, the wider community being satisfied by the sound alone of the prayers being recited or intoned and by the fact that the prayers had the sanction of society's ritual specialists. We are confronted by the phenomenon, viewed as remarkable only, perhaps, in recent years, that the vast majority of the women and men who passed through this world in the Middle Ages were served by a system of liturgical texts which they could not understand, however varied, instructive, apposite, and moving these texts may have been to those who could (see the study of only one small aspect of the problem of comprehensibility in [DB126]).

## IV. Books Containing the Liturgical Texts

This survey must be restricted to major types only (see [DB25–41]).

**(a) The Mass.** The missal (*missale*) is now the most commonly mentioned Mass book of the Middle Ages, but it is a rather late development. In the early Middle Ages several manuscripts were required for the celebration of Mass according to the multiplicity of liturgical roles in it (see schematic presentation of this in [DB31] pp42–43).

1. *Prayers:* The manuscript containing texts reserved for the priest was called variously *liber/libellus/codex sacramentorum* or *sacramentarium;* it contained, typically in various arrangements, a *kalendarium*, the *canon*, perhaps an *ordo missae* containing prayers supplementary to the canon always recited by the celebrating priest, a *proprium de tempore* and *proprium de sanctis*, with a *commune* (Mass prayers not proper to a particular feast but usable on any feast of a given category for which proper prayers were not provided), and, by way of supplement, a collection of miscellaneous rituals and a *benedictionale* containing blessings for specific feasts and special occasions.

2. *Readings:* The Old Testament and epistle readings were earlier identified by a

document called *capitulare lectionum,* which would identify the liturgical occasion and the pericope by indicating its location in Scripture and its incipit and explicit. Later the texts of the pericopes were collected and arranged into a volume variously called a *comes, liber comitis,* or *epistolarium.* The earlier source for the Gospel pericopes was a manuscript of the four Gospels in their entirety, preceded or followed by a *capitulare evangeliorum* that listed the Gospel pericopes for particular feasts—in effect a biblical manuscript with a liturgical supplement; later the pericopes were excerpted and placed in order in a properly liturgical manuscript called *liber evangeliorum* (though that could mean a complete Gospel text as well) and later *evangelistarium* and *textus* (sc. *evangelii*). Codices containing readings from both the Old and New Testaments and the Gospels might be called *comes, liber lectionium, lectionarius/m,* etc. (for an overview of this confused nomenclature see [DB18] pp318–19).

3. *Chants:* The essential chanted texts of the proper of the Mass were contained in a manuscript called variously *antiphonarius, antiphonale, graduale;* the accretions, tropes and sequences, were to be found in manuscripts called *troparium, prosarium, sequentiarius/m.* More specialized musical manuscripts included, for example, the *kyriale,* with the chants of the ordinary of the Mass, and the *cantatorium,* which contained only the solo chants between the readings.

4. *Ensemble:* Through evolutionary processes from the ninth through the eleventh century materials from the more specialized manuscripts were in various ways added to the *sacramentarium,* leading to the appearance of the *missale* (in liturgical scholarship, the *missale plenum*), the Mass manuscript of the later Middle Ages, which contained, feast-by-feast, an integrated arrangement of all the texts of the Mass along with musical notation in varying amounts. Development of this type of book was encouraged both by the emergence of the private Mass, in which the priest effectively took upon himself the roles of all the other ministers, and by the requirement (appearing in the eleventh century) that the celebrant priest or bishop recite all the texts of the Mass even when, at a more elaborate celebration, they were being chanted or read by others.

(b) **The Divine Office.** Like the *missale* for the Mass, the breviary (*breviarium,* a very generic term for a compendium which took on a technical meaning in liturgical contexts) is now the most commonly mentioned type of manuscript for the Divine Office, but it too is a later development. Earlier, as in the case of the Mass, contents of office manuscripts were more specific to the nature of the text or the role of the intended user.

1. *Psalms, Canticles, Hymns:* The liturgical or choir psalter (*psalterium feriale* or *psalterium per ferias*) is not a mere copy of the Book of Psalms, but contains the psalms divided and marked according to the liturgical hours of the week with their ferial antiphons (i.e. antiphons based on the Psalm text, sung when no proper antiphons superseded them) and, in varying arrangements, the minor texts of the hours; at the end of the manuscript will be found the larger nonpsalmodic texts, like the canticles, the *Te Deum* and *Quicumque uult* (the Athanasian Creed), and sometimes a complete hymnal (*liber hymnorum, hymnarius/m*).

2. *Antiphons and Responsories, etc.:* These were contained in a musical manuscript called *antiphonarius* or *antiphonale.*

3. *Readings:* Nonbiblical materials for the readings at matins might be located in

a *homiliarium* containing usually patristic homilies and exegetical texts and in a *passionarius/passionale* containing hagiographic texts; these liturgical books are sometimes unique or valuable witnesses to the texts they contain and sometimes part of an indirect tradition, with abridged and/or simplified versions of the texts.

4. *Prayers:* Prayers employed by the one presiding at the celebration of the Office were gathered in a book called variously *collectarium/s, collectaneum,* or *orationarius,* but also called *capitularium* because this codex often contained the *capitula* (short biblical passages read at certain of the hours), as well as texts for miscellaneous occasional rituals.

5. *Ensemble:* A paradigm for the ensemble of texts and music of the Divine Office which came to be called a *breviarium* seems to have been the preparation of *libelli* containing the complete office for the feast of a particular saint. The breviary itself is found first in a more primitive type which simply incorporated the more specialized books one after the other in a single collection. But the classic *breviarium,* which appears in the eleventh and twelfth centuries, is, like the missal, a collection, arrangement, and new integration of most of the texts required for particular feasts, along with varying amounts of musical notation; it is thus both a compendium of liturgical materials and a directory for their use.

Some other common types of liturgical books are the *martyrologium* (also spelled *martilogium*), which contained the martyrology readings for ritual proclamation at the assembly called *capitulum* (see, e.g., the directions for this in the *Ordinale* of St. Mary's, York [*HBS* 73:74–78]); the *rituale,* a collection of occasional services; the *manuale,* a similar collection for parish priests with the addition of an *ordinarium missae* and other basic texts; the *benedictionale* (see [DB72]), a collection of blessings for the bishop's use at the eucharist and of other blessings as well; and the *processionale* (see [DB92]), a collection of texts and rubrics for processions on Sundays and the greater feasts.

## Select Bibliography

### Bibliographies

#### Current

M. Johnson, "Bibliographical Resources for Liturgics in the Periodic Literature: A Guide for Students," in *Studia Liturgica* 22 (1992) 237–44: excellent survey of current bibliographies, of which those more important to Western medievalists are listed below [DB1].

*APh:* in "Auteurs et Textes," s.v. *Liturgia* [DB2].

*Archiv für Liturgiewissenschaft:* each number contains a "Literaturberichte," some more general and appearing regularly, e.g. "Der Gottesdienst der Kirche: Texte, Quellen, Studien," and "Liturgie in Arbeitsinstrumentarien und Sammelwerken;" some more focused and occasional, e.g. "Gottesdienst der Kirche im iberischen Raum" [DB3].

*Ephemerides Theologicae Lovanienses:* in "Elenchus bibliographicus," s.v. *Historia Liturgiae, Aetas mediaevalis et scolastica* [DB4].

*FRANCIS: Bulletin signalétique,* 527: *Histoire et sciences des religions:* in "Index du Christianisme," s.v. *Liturgie* and more specialized subcategories [DB5].

*IMB:* s.v. *Liturgy* [DB6].

*MEL:* s.v. *Liturgia* [DB7].

*Plainsong & Medieval Music:* "Liturgical Chant Bibliography" [DB8].

*Revue d'histoire ecclésiastique:* in *Bibliographie* II.3.C, "Sources littéraires" (see section headed "Écrits canoniques; règles monastiques; écrits liturgiques"); III.3.C, "Histoire de la liturgie et du culte" [DB9].

## Cumulative

M. Johnson, *Bibliographia liturgica/Bibliographie der Nachschlagewerke für Liturgie-wissenschaft/Reference Bibliography for Liturgics* (1992): limited (112pp) but splendidly organized basic bibliography [DB10].

R.W. Pfaff, *Medieval Latin Liturgy: A Select Bibliography* (1982) [DB11].

B. Thompson, *A Bibliography of Christian Worship,* ATLA Bibliography Series 25 (1989); very thorough, considering its scope; useful for medievalists [DB12].

## Introductory Studies

### Manuals, Overviews

L. Eisenhofer, *Grundriss der katholischen Liturgik,* 6th ed., rev. J. Lechner (1953); tr. A.J. and E.F. Peeler, ed. H.E. Winstone (1961) [DB13].

J. Harper, *The Forms and Orders of Western Liturgy from the Tenth to the Eighteenth Century* (1991): very "user-friendly" but perforce lacking in detail [DB14].

D. Hiley, *Western Plainchant: A Handbook* (1993, r1995): focuses on music, but with excellent overviews of rites [DB15].

P. Oppenheim, *Tractatus de textibus liturgicis* (1945): dated and not well documented, but the only work that provides an overview of liturgical texts of all sorts [DB16].

M. Righetti, *Manuale di storia liturgica,* 4 vols.: v1 (intro.) in 3rd ed. (1964); v2–4 (Liturgical Year, Divine Office; Eucharist; Sacraments and Sacramentals) in 2nd ed. (1950–56): dated but indispensable [DB17].

C. Vogel, *Medieval Liturgy: An Introduction to the Sources,* tr. and rev. W.G. Storey and N.K. Rasmussen (1986): substantial updating of previous edition [DB18].

### Eucharistic Liturgy (the Mass)

R. Cabié, *The Eucharist,* tr. M.J. O'Connell, The Church at Prayer, new ed., v2 (1986) [DB19].

J.A. Jungmann, *Missarum sollemnia: Eine genetische Erklärung der römischen Messe,* 5th ed. (1962): 2nd ed. (1949) tr. F.A. Brunner: *The Mass of the Roman Rite: Its Origins and Development,* 2 vols. (1951–55, r1986) [DB20].

### Liturgy of the Hours (the Divine Office)

S.E. Roper, *Medieval English Benedictine Liturgy: Studies in the Formation, Structure, and Content of the Monastic Votive Office, c. 950–1540* (1993) [DB21].

P. Salmon, *L'office divin au moyen âge: Histoire de la formation du bréviaire du IXe au XVIe siècle* (1967) [DB22].

R. Taft, *The Liturgy of the Hours in East and West: The Origins of the Divine Office and Its Meaning for Today,* 2nd ed. (1993): focuses on Christian antiquity and the early Middle Ages [DB23].

J.B.L. Tolhurst, *The Monastic Breviary of Hyde Abbey, Winchester*, v6, HBS 80 (1942): this volume of the edition (6 vols., 1932–42) is entitled *Introduction to the English Monastic Breviaries* [DB24].

## Liturgical Manuscripts and Their Study

### Nomenclature, etc.

The following deal not only with the nomenclature of liturgical books and their contents, but also with the structures of the rites and with the latinity of the texts they contain; [DB18] also belongs in this list, though its utility is generally restricted to the early Middle Ages; [DB26–27], [DB29], [DB37–38] deal with multiple types of manuscripts, the other items being more specialized, as their titles indicate.

J. Dubois, *Les martyrologes du moyen âge latin*, TSMAO 26 (1978) and updating (1985) [DB25].

A. Corrêa, ed., *The Durham Collectar*, HBS 107 (1992): with extensive introduction to the early medieval *collectaneum* [DB26].

V. Fiala and W. Irtenkauf, "Versuch einer liturgischen Nomenklatur," in *Zur Katalogisierung mittelalterlicher und neuerer Handschriften*, ed. C. Köttelwesch, Zeitschrift für Bibliothekswesen und Bibliographie, Sonderheft 1 (1963) 105–37: manual for cataloguing liturgical books; an attempt to impose a system where sometimes there is little [DB27].

K. Gamber, *Codices liturgici latini antiquiores*, Spicilegii Friburgensis Subsidia 1, 2 vols. and supp., 2nd ed. (1968–88) [DB28].

R. Grégoire, *Homéliaires liturgiques médiévaux: Analyse de manuscrits*, Biblioteca degli "Studi Medievali" 12 (1980) [DB29].

A. Hughes, *Medieval Manuscripts for Mass and Office: A Guide to Their Organization and Terminology* (1982, r1995): contains much that is introductory to the liturgy in general; disappointing from the point of view of terminology, as English technical terms predominate [DB30].

M. Huglo, *Les livres de chant liturgique*, TSMAO 52 (1988) [DB31].

V. Leroquais, *Les bréviaires manuscrits des bibliothèques publiques de France*, 5 vols., atlas, and pls. (1934) [DB32]; id., *Les livres d'heures manuscrits de la Bibliothèque nationale*, 2 vols. and pls. (1927), with supp. (1943) [DB33]; id., *Les pontificaux manuscrits des bibliothèques publiques de France*, 3 vols. and pls. (1937) [DB34]; id., *Les psautiers manuscrits latins des bibliothèques publiques de France*, 2 vols. and pls. (1940–41) [DB35]; id., *Les sacramentaires et les missels manuscrits des bibliothèques publiques de France*, 3 vols. and pls. (1924) [DB36].

A.-G. Martimort, *Les lectures liturgiques et leurs livres*, TSMAO 64 (1992) [DB37].

A.-G. Martimort, *Les "Ordines", les ordinaires et les cérémoniaux*, TSMAO 56 (1991): note also pp46–47, "La langue des *Ordines Romani*" [DB38].

H.P. Neuheuser, *Internationale Bibliographie "Liturgische Bücher": Eine Auswahl kunsthistorischer und liturgiewissenschaftlicher Literatur zu liturgischen Handschriften und Drucken* (1991): covers period 1900–1987; includes references to standard works from the nineteenth century [DB39].

E. Palazzo, *Histoire des livres liturgiques: Le moyen âge des origines au XIIIe siècle* (1993) [DB40].

G. Philippart, *Les légendiers et autres manuscrits hagiographiques*, TSMAO 24–25 (1977) and updating (1985) [DB41].

### Punctuation in Liturgical Manuscripts

This is a topic of interest for the study of liturgical manuscripts and texts and their articulation, and, because of the exemplary role of liturgical manuscripts, of punctuation in other types of codices.

A.-V. Gilles, "La ponctuation dans les manuscrits liturgiques au moyen âge," in *Grafia e interpunzione del latino nel medioevo: Seminario internazionale, Roma, 27–29 settembre 1984,* ed. A. Maierù (1987) 113–33 [DB42].

M. Hubert, "Corpus stigmatologicum minus," in *ALMA* 37 (1969–70) 5–171; *id.,* "Corpus stigmatologicum minus: *Index,*" in *ALMA* 39 (1974) 55–80: on the vocabulary of text divisions, punctuation [DB43].

M.B. Parkes, *Pause and Effect: An Introduction to the History of Punctuation in the West* (1992): see especially pp35–40, 76–80, and pls. 16–19 [DB44].

### Collections of Texts

E. Lodi, *Enchiridion euchologicum fontium liturgicorum* (1979): collects significant texts from and about rituals from (a) pagan, Jewish, and primitive Christian sources, (b) from patristic literature, and (c) from Latin liturgical documents of the various medieval uses in chronological arrangement through the sixteenth century; includes materials from Eastern liturgical sources (pp1251–1527) accompanied by Latin translations; concludes with indices of *initia,* persons and places, and topics; see companion volume: *Enchiridion euchologicum fontium liturgicorum: Clavis methodologica cum commentariis selectis* (1979) [DB45].

E. Martène, *De antiquis ecclesiae ritibus libri,* 2nd ed. in 4 vols. (Antwerp 1736–38, r1967–69): use with A.-G. Martimort, *La documentation liturgique de dom Edmond Martène: Étude codicologique* (1978) [DB46].

### Some Text/Music Editions

Strictly speaking, liturgical texts should not be studied in isolation from their musical settings. More and more editions of texts and music are appearing; the following are presented as examples:

W. Arlt, *Ein Festoffizium des Mittelalters aus Beauvais in seiner liturgischen und musikalischen Bedeutung,* 2 vols. (1970) [DB47].

O.T. Edwards, *Matins, Lauds and Vespers for St David's Day: The Medieval Office of the Welsh Patron Saint in National Library of Wales MS 20541 E* (1990) [DB48].

D.R. Lamothe and C.G. Constantine, *Matins at Cluny for the Feast of Saint Peter's Chains, After the manuscript Paris, Bibl. nat. lat. 12601 (around 1075)* (1986) [DB49].

C.D. Roederer, *Festive Troped Masses from the Eleventh Century: Christmas and Easter in the Aquitaine* (1989) [DB50].

### Liturgical Times (See also the introductory treatments in [DB14] and [DB29].)

I.H. Dalmais, P. Jounel, and A.-G. Martimort, *The Liturgy and Time,* tr. M.J. O'Connell, The Church at Prayer, new ed., v4 (1986) [DB51].

H. Grotefend, *Zeitrechnung des deutschen Mittelalters und der Neuzeit,* 2 vols. (1891–98, r1984): v1: *Glossar und Tafeln;* v2.1: *Kalender der Diöcesen Deutschlands, der Schweiz und Skandinaviens;* v2.2: *Ordenskalendar, Heiligen-Verzeichnis, Nachträge zum Glossar:* dated, restricted source materials, but still useful; replacement needed [DB52].

R.R. Newton, *Medieval Chronicles and the Rotation of the Earth* (1972): see ch. 2, "The Easter Problem" [DB53].

## Liturgical Technical Terms

J. Braun, *Der christliche Altar in seiner geschichtlichen Entwicklung,* 2 vols. (1924): index of terms in both vernacular and Latin and Greek in v2:671–85 [DB54].

J. Braun, *Das christliche Altargerät in seinem Sein und in seiner Entwicklung* (1932): index on pp695–704 [DB55].

J. Braun, *Die liturgische Gewandung im Occident und Orient nach Ursprung und Entwicklung, Verwendung und Symbolik* (1907): index on pp793–97 [DB56].

W.H. St. John Hope and E.G.C.F. Atchley, *English Liturgical Colours* (1918): see especially app. IV, "The Latin Texts of the English Colour Sequences" (pp207–30), and index and glossary (pp251–73) [DB57].

O. Lehmann-Brockhaus, *Lateinische Schriftquellen zur Kunst in England, Wales und Schottland, vom Jahre 901 bis zum Jahre 1307,* 5 vols. (1955–60): v1–3 contain excerpted passages with serial numbers; v4 contains an index of sources, places, and persons; v5:1–456 contains an extensive index of things by their Latin names [DB58].

O. Lehmann-Brockhaus, *Schriftquellen zur Kunstgeschichte des 11. und 12. Jahrhunderts für Deutschland, Lothringen und Italien,* 2 vols. (1938, r1971): the Register (v2) includes places and persons, but note especially pp223–343, "Register der technischen Ausdrücke und Sachregister" [DB59].

C. Meier and R. Suntrup, "Zum Lexikon der Farbenbedeutungen im Mittelalter. Einführung zu Gegenstand und Methoden sowie Probeartikel aus dem Farbenbereich 'Rot,'" in *FMS* 21 (1987) 390–478 [DB60].

J. von Schlosser, *Schriftquellen zur Geschichte der karolingischen Kunst* (1872, r1974): pp470–82 contain a Latin glossary of technical terms with references to the excerpts in the text [DB61].

## Some Incipitaria of Texts (by type of liturgical book)

Most printed editions and facsimiles of liturgical texts and manuscripts (e.g. the volumes of *Paléographie musicale* [1889–] [DB62] and *Corpus consuetudinum monasticarum* [1963–] [DB63]) contain incipitaria; the following are merely a few of the more extensive collections of incipits:

### Sacramentary/Missal

J. Deshusses and B. Darragon, *Concordances et tableaux pour l'étude des grands sacramentaires,* 3 vols. (1982–83): covers L (= Leonine Sacramentary), V (= Old Gelasian), H (= Hadrianum), P (= Paduanum), G (= Sacramentary of Gellone), S (= Gelasianum of St. Gall), Sp (= Supplement to the Gregorian); v1 is an incipitarium; v2 has synoptic tables [DB64].

J. Wickham Legg, ed., *Missale ad usum ecclesie Westmonasteriensis,* 3 vols., *HBS* 1, 5, 12 (1891, 1893, 1897): contains extensive collations with other British and Continental missals, all covered in the index of *initia* in v3:1637–1729 [DB65].

R. Lippe, ed., *Missale Romanum, Mediolani, 1474,* 2 vols., *HBS* 17, 33 (1899, 1907): contains both an edition of the first printing of the *Missale Romanum* and a collation with other editions printed before 1570; H.A. Wilson provided indices of *initia* (v2:388–458) and of subjects (v2:459–467) [DB66].

### Breviary

F. Procter and C. Wordsworth, eds., *Breviarium ad usum insignis ecclesiae Sarum,* 3 vols. (1879–86, r1970): see index in v3:lxii–cxv [DB67]; there is no corresponding abundant index to a monastic breviary, but many volumes of *Corpus consuetudinum monasticarum* [DB68] have extensive incipitaria.

### Pontifical

M. Andrieu, ed., *Le Pontifical romain au moyen-âge,* 4 vols. (1938–41): "Table alphabétique des *initia*" in v4:9–98 [DB69].

C. Vogel and R. Elze, eds., *Le Pontifical romano-germanique du dixième siècle,* 3 vols. (1963–72): *initia formularum, orationum et precum* in v3:91–146 [DB70].

### Benedictional

A. Franz, *Die kirchlichen Benediktionen im Mittelalter,* 2 vols. (1909, r1960): *initia* of prayers, v2:658–75; indices of places and persons, v2:676–700; of things, v2:701–64 [DB71].

E. Moeller, ed., *Corpus benedictionum pontificalium,* 4 vols., *CCSL* 162, 162A–C (1971–79): no *incipitarium,* but a complete *index verborum* in 162B–C [DB72].

## On Liturgical Texts (by type)

### Prayers, General

R. Liver, *Die Nachwirkung der antiken Sakralsprache im christlichen Gebet des lateinischen und italienischen Mittelalters* (1979): note index of Greek and Latin words on pp411–20; focuses on poetic texts, but both the data and method are of use for other liturgical texts [DB73].

G. Manz, *Ausdrucksformen der lateinischen Liturgiesprache bis ins elfte Jahrhundert* (1941): comparative collection of liturgical formulae from multiple regional traditions, Roman, Irish, Gallican, Ambrosian, Visigothic, from sacramentaries as well as pontificals and benedictionals [DB74].

E. Norden, *Agnostos Theos: Untersuchungen zur Formengeschichte religiöser Rede* (1913, r1974): see especially pt2, "Untersuchungen zur Stilgeschichte der Gebets- und Prädikationsformeln," pp143–276 [DB75].

### Orationes

P. Bruylants, *Les oraisons du missel romain: Texte et histoire,* 2 vols. (1952) [DB76].

M.P. Ellebracht, *Remarks on the Vocabulary of the Ancient Orations in the Missale Romanum,* Latinitas Christianorum Primaeva 18 (1963): index of Latin words, pp215–18 [DB77].

M. Righetti, *Manuale di storia liturgica* (see [DB17]), v1:246–57, especially 252–57, "La tecnica delle Orationes" [DB78], and dated but useful materials cited there, such as H. Rheinfelder, "Zum Stil der lateinischen Orationen," in *Jahrbuch für Liturgiewissenschaft* 11 (1931) 20–34: an application of E. Norden's approaches to the *orationes,* many of them of ancient and medieval origin, of the contemporary *Missale Romanum* [DB79]; P. Salmon, "Les protocoles des oraisons du missel romain," in *EL* 45 (1931) 140–47: provides a typology of *orationes* based on their opening words [DB80].

G.G. Willis, "The Variable Prayers of the Roman Mass," in *id.*, *Further Essays in Early Roman Liturgy* (1968) 89–131 [DB81].

## Praefationes

E. Moeller, ed., *Corpus praefationum, CCSL* 161, 161A–D (1980–81): v161 contains an introduction to the corpus (note especially secondary bibliography on ppCXC–CXCIV); v161A–D are alternating volumes of text and notes [DB82].

A.M. Triacca, "La strutturazione eucologica dei Prefazi," in *EL* 86 (1972) 233–79 [DB83].

## Anaphora

A. Bouley, *From Freedom to Formula: The Evolution of the Eucharistic Prayer from Oral Improvisation to Written Texts* (1981) [DB84].

L. Eizenhöfer, *Canon missae Romanae*, 2 vols. (1954–66): v1: *Traditio textus;* v2: *Textus propinqui* [DB85].

C. Giraudo, *La struttura letteraria della preghiera eucaristica: Saggio sulla genesi letteraria di una forma: Toda veterotesamentaria, Beraka giudaica, Anafora cristiana* (1981) [DB86].

A. Hänggi and I. Pahl, eds., *Prex eucharistica: Textus e variis liturgiis antiquioribus selecti* (1968): anaphoral prayers from the Latin traditions—Roman, Ambrosian, Gallican, Celtic, and Spanish—on pp423–513 [DB87].

## Benedictiones

A. Franz, *Die kirchlichen Benediktionen* (see [DB71]) [DB88].

E. Moeller, ed., *Corpus benedictionum pontificalium* (see [DB72]): see v162B:VII–LXXI, "La bénédiction épiscopale: Perspectives de recherche" [DB89].

## Canticles

M. Korhammer, *Die monastischen Cantica im Mittelalter und ihre altenglishcen Interlinearversionen* (1976): see especially pt1: *Die Tradition der monastischen Cantica* (English summary on pp397–402) [DB90].

J. Mearns, *The Canticles of the Christian Church . . .* (1914) [DB91].

## Antiphons/Responsories

T. Bailey, *The Processions of Sarum and the Western Church* (1971): on processional antiphons and responsories [DB92].

H. Barré, "Antiennes et répons de la Vierge," in *Marianum* 29 (1967) 153–254: incipitarium, pp246–50; "Vocabulaire marial," pp251–54 [DB93].

R. Favreau, *Les inscriptions médiévales, TSMAO* 35 (1979) and updating (1985): "Epigraphie et liturgie," pp81–87 [DB94].

U. Franca, *Le antifone bibliche dopo Pentecoste* (1977) [DB95].

R.-J. Hesbert, *Antiphonale missarum sextuplex* (1935, r1967): tabular arrangement of texts of six early (eighth–ninth century) antiphoners; general index of *initia* on pp225–30 [DB96].

R.-J. Hesbert, *Corpus antiphonalium officii*, 6 vols. (1963–79): v1–2, comparative tables of disposition of antiphons of the Divine Office in six sources through the liturgical year, by *initia* only; v3, texts of invitatories and antiphons arranged alphabetically, with some notes; v4, texts of responsories and verses arranged alphabetically; also hymns and *varii* by *initia* only; incipitaria at end of volumes; preface to v3 discusses syntax, text/melody transmission, and verse antiphons; preface to v4 discusses responsories and their varieties, with a list of verse responsories on ppxi–xii [DB97].

A. Hughes, "Late Medieval Rhymed Offices," in *JPMMS* 8 (1985) 31–49 [DB98].

A. Hughes, "British Rhymed Offices: A Catalogue and Commentary," in *Music in the Medieval English Liturgy: Plainsong & Mediaeval Music Society Centennial Essays,* ed. S. Rankin and D. Hiley (1993) 239–84 [DB99].

R. Jonsson, *Historia: Études sur la genèse des offices versifiés* (1968) [DB100].

P. Pietschmann, "Die nicht dem Psalter entnommenen Messgesangstücke auf ihre Textgestalt undersucht," in *Jahrbuch für Liturgiewissenschaft* 12 (1932) 87–144, with incipitarium (pp142–44) [101].

R. Steiner, "Matins Responsories and Cycles of Illustrations of Saints' Lives," in *Diakonia: Studies in Honor of Robert T. Meyer,* ed. T. Halton and J.P. Williman (1986) 317–32 [DB102].

## Tropes

A. Dennery, *Le chant postgrégorien: Tropes, séquences et prosules* (1989), with extensive annotated bibliography (pp179–96) [DB103].

## Repertories of Literary Sources of Liturgical Texts

C. Marbach, *Carmina scripturarum, scilicet antiphonas et responsoria ex sacro scripturae fonte in libros liturgicos sanctae Ecclesiae Romanae derivata* (1907, r1963): arranged by books of Scripture in biblical order; index of liturgical texts by *initia* on pp554–90; nonbiblical material covered in app., pp539–48, with index on pp591–95 [DB104].

J. Pascher, *Das liturgische Jahr* (1963): though concerned with the modern Latin liturgy, this volume is, when relevant, a handy compendium for the medievalist, especially for the identification of the sources of liturgical texts, with biblical index on pp732–48 and *initia* of Latin texts on pp748–65 [DB105].

## Philological and Literary Studies, Lexica, etc.

A. Blaise, *Le vocabulaire latin des principaux thèmes liturgiques* (1966): index on pp23–112; discussion arranged by topics on pp117–632, with index on pp633–39 [DB106].

M. Britt, *A Dictionary of the Psalter, Containing the Vocabulary of the Psalms, Hymns, Canticles, and Miscellaneous Prayers of the Breviary Psalter* (1928): unscientific, and based on modern practice, but sometimes handy [DB107].

W. Diamond, *Dictionary of Liturgical Latin* (1961): not a scientific work [DB108].

M.C. Díaz y Díaz, "El latin de la liturgia hispánica," in *Estudios sobre la liturgia mozarabe,* ed. J.F. Rivera Recio (1965) 55–87 [DB109].

M.C. Díaz y Díaz, "Literary Aspects of the Visigothic Liturgy," in *Visigothic Spain: New Approaches,* ed. E. James (1980) 61–76 [DB110].

P.-M. Gy, "Le vocabulaire liturgique latin au moyen âge," in *LLM* 295–301 [DB111].

E. Kasch, *Das liturgische Vokabular der frühen lateinischen Mönchsregeln* (1974): organized by activities and topics, with complete index of words on pp391–403 [DB112].

L.C. Mohlberg *et al.*, eds., *Sacramentarium Veronense* (1956): "Die sprachlichen Eigentümlichkeiten des Textes," ppXL–LIII; orthography, ppXL–XLVI; scribal errors, ppXLVI–XLIX; grammar, ppLXIX–LII; bibliography on prose rhythm, ppLII–LIII [DB113].

G. Sanders and M. Van Uytfanghe, *BSLC:* see s.v. *Liturgica*, pp91–99 [DB114].

D. Sheerin, "*In media Latinitate,*" in *Helios* 14.2 (1987) 51–67 [DB115]: see especially pp60–63, and the response of R. Hexter: "*Latinitas* in the Middle Ages: Horizons and Perspectives," *ibid.*, pp69–92, especially 80–83 [DB116].

F. Stummer, "Vom Satzrhythmus in der Bibel und in der Liturgie der lateinischen Christenheit," in *Archiv für Liturgiewissenschaft* 3 (1954) 233–83 [DB117].

## Greek Elements

C.M. Atkinson, "Zur Entstehung und Überlieferung der 'Missa greca,'" in *Archiv für Musikwissenschaft* 39 (1982) 113–45 [DB118].

E. Wellesz, *Eastern Elements in Western Chant: Studies in the Early History of Ecclesiastical Music* (1947, r1967) [DB119].

## Linguistic Studies

P. De Clerck, "Le langage liturgique: sa nécessité et ses traits spécifiques," in *Questions liturgiques* 73 (1992) 15–35 [DB120], and G. Lukken, "Liturgy and Language: An Approach from Semiotics," *ibid.*, pp36–52 [DB121]: examples (with bibliographical footnotes) of the contemporary theoretical study of liturgical language.

W. Dürig, "Die Erforschung der lateinisch-christlichen Sakralsprache: Ein Bericht über den gegenwärtigen Stand der liturgietheologischen Philologie," in *Liturgisches Jahrbuch* 1 (1951) 32–47 [DB122].

C. Mohrmann, *Liturgical Latin, Its Origins and Character: Three Lectures* (1957): introductory [DB123]; see also N.D. Mitchell, "Christine Mohrmann (1903–1988): The Science of Liturgical Language," in *Liturgy Digest* 1.2 (1994) 4–43 [DB124].

I.M. Resnick, "*Lingua Dei, lingua hominis:* Sacred Language and Medieval Texts," in *Viator* 21 (1990) 51–74 [DB125].

D. Sheerin, "*Sonus* and *Verba:* Varieties of Meaning in the Liturgical Proclamation of the Gospel in the Middle Ages," in *Ad litteram: Authoritative Texts and Their Medieval Readers,* ed. M.D. Jordan and K. Emery, Jr. (1992) 29–69 [DB126].

## Some Indices Verborum

Collected editions of liturgical texts are sometimes equipped with *indices verborum* (e.g. *CCSL* 162B:114–69, 162C [DB72]), as are editions of individual liturgical manuscripts (e.g. *CCSL* 159, 159A–C [*Liber sacramentorum Gellonensis*, etc.]); note, too, that many volumes of the *Corpus consuetudinum monasticarum* [DB127] contain excellent *indices rerum;* the following are some more extensive indices:

Amalarius, *Opera liturgica omnia,* ed. J.M. Hanssens, 3 vols. (1948–50): v3:371–438, 439–80, contain an *index verborum philologicus* and an *index rerum liturgicus* [DB128].

M. Andrieu, ed., *Le Pontifical romain au moyen-âge* (see [DB69]): v4:99–440 is an exhaustive Latin index of names and things [DB129].

J. Deshusses and B. Darragon, *Concordances et tableaux pour l'étude des grands sacramentaires* (see [DB64]): v3.1–4 is a complete verbal concordance [DB130].

John Beleth, *Summa de ecclesiasticis officiis*, ed. H. Douteil, *CCCM* 41–41A (1976): v41A:378–90, 391–433 contains an *index formularum seu initiorum* and an *index personarum et rerum* [DB131].

A. Pflieger, *Liturgicae orationis concordantia verbalia*, pt1: *Missale Romanum* (1964) [DB132].

C. Vogel and R. Elze, eds., *Le Pontifical romano-germanique du dixième siècle* (see [DB70]): v3:149–228 contains an *index personarum, rerum et vocabulorum notabilium* [DB133].

## Liturgical Commentaries (Overviews)

A. Haeussling, "Messe (Expositiones missae)," in *DSAM* 10:1083–90 [DB134].

A. Franz, *Die Messe im deutschen Mittelalter* (1902, r1963) [DB135].

M.M. Schaefer, "Latin Mass Commentaries from the Ninth through Twelfth Centuries: Chronology and Theology," in *Fountain of Life: In Memory of Niels K. Rasmussen, O.P.*, ed. G. Austin (1991) 35–49 [DB136].

R. Suntrup, *Die Bedeutung der liturgischen Gebärden und Bewegungen in lateinischen und deutschen Auslegungen des 9. bis 13. Jahrhunderts* (1978) [DB137].

A. Wilmart, "Expositio missae," in *DACL* 5.1:1014–27 [DB138].

*See also* [BC55], [BC92], [BD93], [BD101], [BD108].

DC · ECCLESIASTICAL AND
UNIVERSITY ADMINISTRATION

BY NORMAN ZACOUR

## Introduction

The clerical classes of the Middle Ages used two special forms of Latin, each with recognizable and well developed features: the Latin of theology and philosophy—the language, that is, of the scholastics (see ch. DH)—and the so-called *stilus curie romane*, the language in which the Church spoke to the world. It is the latter that concerns us here. From the eleventh century on, it spread outward from the papal court hand in hand with the growth of papal authority. It was a self-conscious form of expression reflecting a culture in which the study of grammar and rhetoric was fundamental. Its most striking characteristic was a solemnity of expression achieved in large part by an elaborate and complex use of dependent clauses and an increasingly popular rhythmic word order, the so-called *cursus* ([DC4]; see ch. CF). Its rhetoric was shaped by the sermons and treatises of Church fathers and an epistolary tradition inherited from the early correspondence between churches.

Indeed, it was in the form of letters that most administrative acts of churchmen were cast, whether at the local, diocesan level, or at the papal court itself. "For most writers in the Middle Ages a letter was any work which fitted the epistolary situation, was furnished with a salutation and subscription, and paid at least lip-service to the requirements of the *modus epistolaris* . . ." ([DC1] p25). This well describes the administrative instruments of the medieval Church dealing not only with promotions and appointments but also with graces and privileges of all kinds. They served as diplomas or charters, preserved by the recipient as evidence of the possession of some right.

Most of these texts, when written by pope or prelate, reveal a conscious effort to achieve a language appropriate to spiritual authority. The tone was always one of solemnity, stooping neither to informality nor to novelty. Like other spiritual expressions—in liturgy, in prayer, in the adornments of the altar—the correspondence of Church leaders served a purpose far beyond its immediate function.

## The Letter

Given the solemnity of such acts, there was no departure from the common forms of the letter-writing art (see chs. GM and GO). What the *dictatores* (teachers of *dictamen,* letter-writing) called the *salutatio* and the *exordium* continued to serve their traditional purposes. The *narratio* and *petitio,* forming the body of the letter, usually led to some mandatory instruction, the assignment of some task, the appointment to some office, advice, encouragement, or reproof. Depending on the subject, the *conclusio* might threaten with censure those who opposed the author's intention. Otherwise, the letter ended abruptly with the dating clause.

Medieval chanceries took great pains with the *salutatio.* This recorded at the outset the standing—rank, title, or other attributes—of the addressee. By establishing the relative dignity of writer and recipient it determined the language of the text to follow: a fitting tone of generosity, approval, condescension, command, respect, apology, as the case may be. The *dictatores* gave much attention to these matters [DC3], recommending lists of suitable adverbs to go with each verb, all of which they drew from the actual correspondence of prelates. The greater charged the lesser with verbs such as *mandamus, demandamus, precipimus, iniungimus, iubemus, imperamus,* and appropriate adverbs: *districte, firmiter, instanter, incessanter, districtius, arcius, districtissime, instantissime, constanter, indubitanter, peremptorie.* There were many ways, equally formulaic, to address one of high rank, whether prince or prelate: *nobilitatem tuam rogamus, fraternitati tue firmiter precipiendo mandamus, serenitatem tuam rogamus et monemus attente quatenus,* and so forth.

When the roles were reversed, and the lesser addressed the greater, the list of adverbs changed: *rogo devote, suppliciter, humiliter, reverenter, affectuosissime; dignemini misericorditer, pie benigne, sancte, iuste, misericordissime, piissime, benignissime, sanctissime, iustissime,* etc., with appeals to all parts of the body: *dignetur vestra benignitas honoranda misericordissime viscera pietatis, pectus consilii, manus beneficii, aures mansuetudinis, oculos misericordie, labia iusticie aperire, auxilii brachia porrigere, faciem roseam demonstrare* ([DC30] pt1:185–96).

Popes always referred to themselves in the plural, while addressing others, whatever their rank, in the singular: *in nostra presentia, tua magnificentia.* Bishops addressed, and were addressed by, their inferiors in similar fashion. In addition, there was always a strong tendency to address or refer to a person, even oneself, by some attribute or quality (*mea simplicitas, sanctitas vestra*).

For the scribes of the papal chancery the question of relative rank posed no problem. All recipients of the pope's letters were in some sense his subordinates. They inscribed his name first, followed by his stylized attribute, *servus servorum Dei,* and then the name of the recipient (in the dative) followed by his or her rank, title, or other attributes. The salutation was a brief formula: *salutem et apostolicam benedictionem.* Addresses to non-Christian princes might call for elaborate departures from the norm: *Eugenius episcopus servus servorum Sarracenorum regi (vel soldano), salutem vobis non inpendimus, non quia vestram salutem non desideramus, set quia veram salutem Jesum Christum pro salute humani generis crucifixum non creditis, et quoniam christiani nominis professores iniuriis afficere non cessatis.* For those who, though Christians, had earned the pope's disapproval, there was often an infinitive construction with a sting in the tail: . . . *recedere a malo et facere bonum,* or *de spiritu ob-*

*stinacionis ad spiritum obediencie se transferre,* or the still more terse *spiritum consilii sanioris* ([DC30] v2:731–32, [DC26] p2).

The conclusion of the letter was equally formulaic. Where the letter was a mandate, it carried a warning, variously worded, which ultimately became standardized:

> Nulli ergo omnino hominum liceat hanc paginam nostre confirmationis [inhibitionis, concessionis, protectionis, etc.] infringere vel ei ausu temerario contraire. Si quis autem attemptare presumpserit, indignationem omnipotentis Dei et beatorum Petri et Pauli apostolorum eius se noverit incursurum.

In the copy registered in the papal chancery, from which modern printed texts are often derived, this was abbreviated as *Nulli etc. Si quis etc.* Often the letter ended abruptly with the dating clause alone: *Datum Romae per manum Joannis sanctae Romanae Ecclesiae diaconi cardinalis xvi Kalend. Martii, indictione viii, incarnationis Dominicae anno mc, pontificatus autem domini Paschalis ii papae i.* Again, modern editions usually reflect the abbreviation of the registered copy, e.g., *Dat. Romae xvi Kalend. martii an. i.*

As for the other parts of a papal letter, the most important for our purposes is the *exordium.* It often emphasized the pope's supreme responsibility for the care of the universal Church, and therefore his authority to deal with the matter at hand. Concerned with general principles rather than constrained by the particular circumstances of a subject, it invited stylistic richness. It is here, from the twelfth century on, that we find the most impressive examples of chancery latinity. It sought its effect in a careful assembly of parallel structures, of verbal and syntactical contrasts, combined with a vocabulary broad enough to avoid monotony. It consciously departed from the common style favored by many where the main clause introduced a succession of subordinates (. . . and . . . and . . . and) like the following:

> si non satisfactione congrua emendaverit,
> potestatis honorisque sui dignitate careat,
> ream*que* se divino judicio existere de perpetrata
>     iniquitate cognoscat,
> *et* a sacratissimo corpore et sanguine Dei et Domini
>     Redemptoris nostri Jesu Christi aliena fiat,
> *atque* in extremo examine districtae ultioni subjaceat;
>
>> *PL* 163:499, no. 16

or again:

> Nullus legat Parisius de artibus citra vicesimum primum
>     etatis sue annum,
>     et quod sex annis audierit de artibus ad minus . . .
>     et quod protestetur se lecturum duobus annis ad minus . . .
>     et quod non sit respersus aliqua infamia,
>     et quod . . . examinetur . . .
>     et quod legant libros Aristotelis de dialectica. . . .
>
>> [DC10] v1:78, no. 20

On the other hand, a later sample of the more elaborate *exordium,* when laid out schematically, reveals some of the attributes of the *stilus curie romane* in full dress:

```
Si   Deus        incircumscriptibilis et immensus
     qui               nec aliquo includitur loco
                       nec a quoquam excluditur
     set existens      intra omnia non inclusus
                       extra omnia non exclusus
                  sua maiestate replet et circuit universa
     nichilominus
                  angelorum ministeria
                     miro ordine
                     miraque provisione        dispensat
                  alios aliis ineffabili providentia preponendo
multo magis nos
     qui               simul in diversis locis corporaliter
                          esse non possumus
                          necesse habemus dispensare
                  nostrorum ministeria subditorum
                  et potestatem nobis a Deo concessam
                       ibi exercere per alios
                       ubi esse personaliter non valemus.
                          [DC29] VI:157, no. 228
```

The hierarchy of angels is mirrored by the hierarchy of the Church, a reflection reinforced by internal parallels adopted especially for rhetorical effect. Isocola, i.e. successive phrases or clauses of equal members ("the bigger they are, the harder they fall"), end rhymes, and the *cursus* are prominent.

This high style, especially the interweaving of dependent clauses, echoed throughout the learned world, even when the subject was the mundane business of regulating booksellers in Paris:

> Quoniam ager ille fructus uberes afferre noscitur, cui cura coloni caucius undique providetur, ne nos dominico laborantes in agro ad fructum centenum virtutibus et scientia Domino disponente querendum utrunque molestari vel impediri contingat, ab illis maxime qui circa Parisiense studium propter questum in operibus mercennariis et ministerio quod impendunt malo more versantur, ordinamus statuendo et statuimus ordinando ut stacionarii, qui vulgo librarii appellantur . . . [etc.]. [DC10] VI:532–33, no. 462

## Provisions

Of all the administrative acts of the medieval Church, those that soon took the most time and energy had to do with the recruitment of clerics, their training, ordination, and appointment to office. This emphasis led to a refinement of the processes surrounding such appointments: the way in which one applied or was put forward for office, the examination of candidates, the form of appointment, and the arbitration of conflicting claims to office.

The word *beneficium,* a generic term for any kind of beneficent act, had acquired a specialized meaning in the early Middle Ages by its frequent application to the income, tenancy, or office granted by a prince or lord to some servant or follower. The Church came to use it to mean much the same thing, any kind of Church office. The income that went with it was usually called *prebenda.* One ordinarily applied to one's own bishop, especially if one hoped for a parish church, and did so usually with the support of a patron, a lord who possessed the right of advowson (*advocatio,* the right to "present" a candidate to the church in question). With the growth of papal authority over many such appointments, however, petitioners increasingly addressed their *supplicationes* to the bishop of Rome, especially for canonries.

By the fourteenth century the Roman Church was inundated with petitions: from cardinals on behalf of their *familia,* members of their numerous households; from kings and queens, princes and nobles on behalf of their households or clients; from bishops on behalf of their diocesan clergy; from university masters on behalf of their graduating students; and directly from poor clerics who, having no such important patron, still hoped for some small preferment with enough of an income to support life. If the office sought was already occupied but was thought soon to become vacant, the supplicant asked for an *expectatio.* This established a claim on the benefice upon the transfer or death of the present incumbent. The final act of appointment was called a *provisio* or *collatio.* Both words appear in verbal form in the customary appointing clause: *cum omnibus juribus et pertinenciis suis apostolica auctoritate contulimus et de illis duximus providendum.*

## Formulas and Formularies

The business of the distribution of benefices, church offices, and graces of every kind grew enormously in the thirteenth and especially the fourteenth century, compelling the adoption of standard forms. This saved time, reduced the possibility of error, and made for a uniformity that helped to limit fraud. Although form letters had been collected for centuries, a notable opportunity to bring them up to date occurred during the papal vacancy of 1268–71, a period of almost three years when there was no pope and the administrative activity of the papal court ground to a halt. As a result, the chancery had little to do but select, organize, and copy letters, whether petitions or the papal responses to petitions, to serve as new models for the future ([DC33] pp381, 437).

The letters so preserved were in turn full of formulaic expressions. The language of petitions almost always begins in much the same way: *Supplicat Sanctitati Vestre . . . quatenus dignemini providere, Supplicatur Sanctitas Vestra, Dignetur Sanctitas Vestra.* When seeking office, petitioners had to be careful to distinguish between a *gratia in forma speciali,* which required a fee but brought a good income, and a *gratia in forma pauperum,* which was free but had a limited income; to specify that the benefice asked for might be *cum cura vel sine cura,* to allow for the possibility that it might or might not carry spiritual responsibilities; to ask that the provision be written *cum omnibus aliis non obstantibus et clausulis oportunis,* referring to the various "non obstante" clauses to be inserted in the letter of provision itemizing all the conditions, such as the possession of other benefices, that might otherwise nullify the grant but were now to be explicitly allowed: *non obstante quod canonicatum et prebendam ecclesie S Petri Ariensis . . . obtinet.*

The letter of provision or grace which the court issued in response to a petition also had its formulaic expressions. These included conditions or qualifications of some pertinence to the legal standing of the text. The pope frequently acted from a fullness of authority which then had to be made explicit in the letter of appointment (*plenitudo potestatis quam non ab homine obtinet sed a Deo*). When he acted on the advice of his cardinals, this too became a matter of record (*de consilio fratrum nos-*

*trorum*). Formulas are valuable historically because, far from being vacant expressions made from routine, they accurately reflect the status and qualifications of the recipient: noble birth was bound to be mentioned (*illis apostolice provisionis dexteram libenter extendimus quibus nobilitas generis et alia virtutum dona multipliciter suffragantur*); a sufficient education was always recognized (*dum litterarum scientiam, morum elegantiam, vite honestatem . . . diligenter attendimus*); past and present service was gratefully acknowledged (*obsequiorum tuorum gratitudo laudabilis que nobis et apostolice sedi hactenus impendisti*). Though repetitious, formulas were never empty.

## Internal Communications

Communications within the papal or episcopal court were usually different in style and manner from letters sent abroad, but even here the formal rules of rhetoric can often be observed [DC7–8]. On the whole, however, the latinity of internal administrative texts is of little distinction, to judge from the evidence we have of the everyday working language of the papal court. Here is a cardinal, scribbling a quick note to the vice-chancellor about getting the pope to give him a benefice that had fallen free that very day:

> Reverendissime domine mi. Statim significatum est michi per quemdam amicum meum quod electus Constantiensis hodie promotus tenet optimam ecclesiam sive plebanatum vocatam de Veina, si dominus noster vellet michi providere, faceret opus pietatis. [DC25] intro., pxvii

There are many examples of this kind of unstructured, conversational language in the *consilia* of cardinals, which they wrote after being consulted on matters of political importance. Those that we have from the fourteenth century show little evidence of composition. They are wooden in style, limited in vocabulary, with a syntax betraying a Romance vernacular lurking just beneath the surface (e.g., *propter quod dico quod michi videtur quod non debeat fieri pro nunc passagium istud*) ([DC6] v2:294, no. 1696). On the other hand, financial committees staffed by well educated bureaucrats reported their business in a language that was unadorned but clearly "learned" in structure and syntax:

> Considerato quod illi qui assequebantur gratias super beneficiis ecclesiasticis, antequam possent suas apostolicas litteras habere, habebant se cum apostolica camera super annalibus concordare et inibi obligare . . . [etc.]. [DC7] p43, no. 85

The same can be said about the administrative Latin of the *studium generale,* the medieval university. University statutes dealt mostly with the fraternal aspect of organization: terms of membership, conduct of funerals, settlement of disputes, protection of members, and appropriate vestments for formal occasions. Most of these statutes were drawn up by notaries. As befits documents of legal standing, their language is plain, devoid of solecisms, free of rhetorical flourishes, only harboring an occasional aphorism: *qui preponendum postponit et postponendum preponit, iniuste agit et iniuriam irrogat preponendo* ([DC13] statute 4, p140).

## Vocabulary

Still, university rules dealing with occupations and officials have left a number of terms peculiar to university life, much as the administration of ecclesiastical provisions created its own technical language: institutions such as *universitas* and *facultas;* offices such as *chancellor, rector,* and *consiliarii;* internal divisions like the *nationes* in Paris, the *ultramontani* and *citramontani* in Bologna; the *stationarius, librarius,* or *pergamenarius,* not an official of the university but a local merchant who rented out approved texts from which students could make copies for their own use. It was imperative to ensure the accuracy of the *peciae,* as the various parts of these manuscripts were called. This soon produced the *peciarius,* whose job it was to inspect the work of the bookstall keepers. A student was entered on the *matricula* or roll of a *magister,* who was also called *regens* in some universities; after much study, attending lectures, and debating in *responsiones* in imitation of the *disputationes* of his elders, he became a *baccalarius.* Finally came the *inceptio,* and with it the *licentia legendi,* which allowed him in turn to begin teaching as a master.

Aside from the many terms of specialized activities, the general vocabulary of administrative texts in church and university presents little difficulty. There is a noticeable preference for compound forms of verbs, to be sure, not merely because of their intensity, but also because they lent greater flexibility to the writing of rhythmic prose, the *cursus.* There were many words whose classical meanings were obliterated by the special uses the Church put them to, e.g., *auditor, basilica, camera, paganus, pastor, sedes,* etc. There were also many words and phrases pertinent to Christian faith, liturgy, hierarchy, and Church structure (*evangelium, hymnus, episcopus, dioecesis*), most of them of Greek origin drawn from the Vulgate and the Church fathers. Many are familiar from their use in modern languages. Neologisms were generally avoided, but the subject might call for a popular vocabulary descriptive of contemporary objects or functions. This is especially the case in arrangements having to do with the Crusades—*barbotta* (a type of boat), *trabuccettum* (a type of catapult), *biscoctum* (ship's victuals)—or with churches or offices that emerged in the Middle Ages (*titulus, diaconia, camerarius, cardinalis, consistorium*). Much the same applies to financial matters. Leaving aside the large variety of confusing coinages (see ch. FL), there were several terms peculiar to the payment of fees when one received a papal provision: common services (*servitia communia*), a tenth part of the assessed income of a new office; petty services (*servitia minuta*), fixed gratuities to members of the papal staff and cardinals' households; or the tax of a proportion of the first year's income (*annate, fructus primi anni*).

From time to time one runs across an unusual word drawn from early Christian literature, e.g. *incircumscriptibilis,* marking a struggle to describe the nature of a divinity beyond description, or *inscrutabilis eterni consilii altitudo.* The occasional petitioner might describe himself, as one English bishop did, with a local neologism, *sequitor* (suitor), instead of the more usual *orator* to denote a petitioner to the Holy See. Commonplaces include the specialized use of *huiusmodi* to mean a simple "this"; *de cetero* = "henceforth"; *juxta* = "according to" (*juxta taxationem decime*). *Exsistere* (*existere*) frequently served as an auxiliary verb (*deliberatum extitit quod . . .* ). To "judaize" (*judaizare*) might in fact apply to Christians who attended or participated in Jewish religious observances. On the whole, however, the vocabulary of communications dealing with events, conditions, descriptions, requests, offices, duties, and the like, is relatively straightforward.

## Figures

The metaphors, on the other hand, may try one's ear for echoes not only of the Bible but also of the *Glossa ordinaria,* the standard collection of biblical interpretations in which medieval churchmen steeped themselves:

> Cum sit nostra sollicitudo continua, diversa mundi climata speculari et vineam domini Sabaoth vallare aggeribus sepibusque munire, ne fructus eius exterminet serpens aut reptile venenatum, subito a remotis oculorum vertentes aciem ad propinqua, Ieremie ollam conspeximus accensam in patrimonio Iesu Christi, cui universe terre malleus, qui semper circa conflatorium commoratur, ab aquilonis facie incendia ministrabat. [DC31] V1:87, no. 122

All this, leaning heavily on Jeremiah (1:13–14, 50:22–23), to describe a local conflict among communes in central Italy nominally subject to papal authority: a devastation (*olla accensa* = the boiling cauldron in which, according to one view, all sinners will be consumed) afflicting the papal territories of Italy, the so-called patrimony (*in patrimonio Iesu Christi*), brought about by the devil (*universe terre malleus* = hammer of the universe), who is always to be found at the center of any conflagration (*semper circa conflatorium*), and who has brought down fire from the north (*ab aquilonis facie* = the north wind that chills the ardor of faith).

Many metaphors are commonplace. *Navicula Petri,* i.e. the Church of Rome, not only pictured the fisherman's skiff on the Sea of Galilee but (whenever the Church of Rome was in trouble) inevitably trailed in its wake the language of storm and shipwreck. The metaphor of the mind's eye was popular, one of a class, like the bowels of mercy (*viscera misericordie*), endowing human attributes with physical features. In the following example, from an *exordium* of Alexander II in 1063, "discretion" is given eyes, "counsel" a hand:

> Ad apostolicae sedis speculam sublimati, et ad sollicitudinem et curam omnium Ecclesiarum non nostris meritis, sed divina solummodo dignatione promoti, oculos discretionis manusque consilii debemus avidius extendere, ubi piae religionis exercitia et sollicitudinis ecclesiasticae instantiam comperimus fore. *PL* 146:1284, no. 8

*Passagium generale,* at one time referring to the annual convoy of merchant ships to the eastern Mediterranean, became in the thirteenth century a metaphor for that most spirited of convoys, the Crusade. A cardinal legate on his way to settle some quarrel was certain to be called an *angelus pacis.* One writes to monks as *religiosam vitam eligentibus,* to nuns as *prudentibus virginibus;* an allusion to the deceased is almost always to *felicis recordationis N..,* who has departed *soluto debito carnis,* or *viam universe carnis ingresso.*

Some of the rhetorical techniques may seem excessively contrived; for example, the reversal of adjective and noun (*heretica pravitas*), leading to a kind of simple punning which was exceedingly common in the Middle Ages (*per circumspectionem providam et providentiam circumspectam*), not always with happy results (*ordinamus statuendo et statuimus ordinando*). Alliteration and rhymes are everywhere. Honorius III, for some time chancellor of the Church of Rome before being elected pope in 1216, had a marked taste for word play and assonance:

> Consuevit providentia sedis apostolice manum liberalitatis extendere ad devotos, ut devotiores efficiat de devotis et ad bonum devotionis alliciat indevotos. [DC31] VI:23, no. 28

Or again, taking an archbishop to task:

> . . . tu culpe culpam et contemptum contemptui superaddens, litteras nostras recipere contempsisti. . . . [DC32] VI:26, no. 32

## Syntax

Departures from classical syntax were few, but many Late Latin practices, which may have been rare in Classical Latin, grew in popularity. While the ablative absolute construction was widespread, the use of a substantive clause in an ablative absolute, unusual in Classical Latin, was very common (*dato quod . . .* ). Also rare in Classical Latin, *habere* + infinitive often served as a clause of obligation or purpose (*habebant se cum apostolica camera super annalibus concordare*). The accusative + infinitive in indirect discourse was not quite abandoned, but its place was usually taken by a clause beginning with *quod* (*voverit Deo quod . . .* ). This report of an episcopal visitation in an English parish probably reflects the vernacular—*dicunt quod Willelmus Vicarius est homo bone vite*—although the schooling of the officials making the report would occasionally assert itself: *dicunt se nichil scire.* The ablative of the gerund was commonly used as the equivalent of the present participle, presaging modern Italian and Spanish forms: *Ego Joannes Ogerii, arripiendo iter . . . ad provinciam Remensem. . . .* Clauses of purpose might still be found in the classical form of *ut* + subjunctive, but *quod* or *quatenus* + subjunctive was much more usual. The impersonal verb *contingere* was generally followed by an accusative + infinitive instead of by *ut* + subjunctive: *prout requiret onus beneficii quod eum post dispensationem huiusmodi obtinere contigerit.* Not quite so obvious is the idiomatic use of the hard worked verb *dispensare,* which placed the person receiving the dispensation in the ablative after *cum,* the fault or defect in the ablative after *super,* and the consequent privilege in a clause beginning with *quod* or *ut*:

> . . . lator presentium . . . supplicavit ut cum eo, super defectu natalium quem patitur de subdiacono genitus et soluta, quod huiusmodi non obstante defectu possit ad omnes ordines promoveri . . . sedes [apostolica] dispensare misericorditer dignaretur. [DC20] p233

In time the language of ecclesiastical administration became increasingly formulaic. A professional class came to prepare the bulk of administrative texts, each type of which had its own standard form requiring only the insertion of the particulars at hand. The language was set apart from Classical Latin as much by its style and spirit as by its syntax: free of originality or literary pretension, it was concerned only to avoid error and ambiguity.

## Select Bibliography

### General

G. Constable, *Letters and Letter-Collections, TSMAO* 17 (1976): a general introduction to the genre in the Middle Ages [DC1].

### Style

F. di Capua, *Fonti ed esempi per lo studio dello 'stilus curiae romanae' medioevale* (1941) [DC2].

G. Constable, "The Structure of Medieval Society according to the *Dictatores* of the Twelfth Century," in *Law, Church, and Society: Essays in Honor of Stephan Kuttner,* ed. K. Pennington and R. Somerville (1977) 253–67: examines salutations in the formularies of the *dictatores* [DC3].

T. Janson, *PRML:* describes the system of analysis he has used in examining Latin texts to determine the intentional use of *cursus* and its preferred forms; see [CF24] [DC4].

J. Martin, "Classicism and Style in Latin Literature," in *R&R,* pp537–68: includes extensive bibliographical notes as well as a general bibliography on Medieval Latin style [DC5].

### The Papal Chancery

A. Coulon and S. Clémencet, eds., *Lettres secrètes et curiales du pape Jean XXII (1316–1334) relatives à la France,* Bibliothèque des Écoles françaises d'Athènes et de Rome, 3rd ser., 3 vols. (1900–67): see especially v2:281ff. for a unique collection of cardinals' *consilia* [DC6].

E. von Ottenthal, *Regulae cancellariae apostolicae: Die päpstlichen Kanzleiregeln von Johannes XXII. bis Nicolaus V.* (1888, r1968) [DC7].

M. Tangl, *Die päpstlichen Kanzleiordnungen von 1200–1500* (1894, r1959): this and the previous entry provide collections of rules and regulations dealing with internal administrative practices in the papal court [DC8].

A. Theiner, *Codex diplomaticus dominii temporalis S. Sedis: Recueil de documents pour servir à l'histoire du gouvernement temporel des états du Saint-Siège: Extraits des archives du Vatican,* 3 vols. (1861–62): the letters here are complete, not abstracts, providing many examples of the epistolary style of the papal court over a long period [DC9].

### Universities

H. Denifle, ed., *Chartularium universitatis Parisiensis,* 4 vols. (1889–97, r1964) [DC10].

M. Fournier, ed., *Statuts et privilèges des universités françaises depuis leur fondation jusqu'en 1789,* 4 vols. (1890–94) [DC11].

M.B. Hackett, *The Original Statutes of Cambridge University* (1970) [DC12].

B.M. Marti, *The Spanish College at Bologna in the Fourteenth Century: Edition and Translation of its Statutes, with Introduction and Notes* (1966) [DC13].

H. Rashdall, *The Universities of Europe in the Middle Ages,* ed. F.M. Powicke and A.B. Emden, new ed., 3 vols. (1936, r1987): an old, somewhat dated history of medieval universities, still useful because of the breadth of its subject and the detail of its treatment [DC14].

## Vocabulary

L. Duchesne, ed., *Liber Pontificalis,* 2nd ed., 3 vols. (1955–57): v3, ed. C. Vogel, includes (pp191–231) an *Index praecipuorum vocabulorum latinorum,* a useful listing of the unusual or peculiarly Medieval Latin words of general significance for ecclesiastical institutions, liturgy, materials, practices, etc. [DC15].

K.H. Schäfer, *Die Ausgaben der apostolischen Kammer unter den Päpsten Urban V. und Gregor XI. (1362–1378) nebst Nachträgen und einem Glossar für alle 3 Ausgabenbänden* (1937): the glossary (pp843–74), including medicines and dyes, covers all three volumes of the *Ausgaben* edited by Schäfer; the other two vols. (1911, 1914) concern John XXII, Benedict XII, Clement VI, and Innocent VI [DC16].

O. Weijers, *Terminologie des universités au XIIIe siècle* (1987) [DC17].

O. Weijers, ed., *Vocabulaire des collèges universitaires (XIIIe-XVIe siècles): Actes du colloque, Leuven, 9–11 avril 1992, CIVICIMA* 6 (1993) [DC18].

## Episcopal Registers

T. Bonnin, ed., *Regestrum visitationum archiepiscopi Rothomagensis* (1852): this is a unique visitation record (of Odo Rigaldus), taking the form of a diary of visits and events and covering a wide range of episcopal administrative activity in the thirteenth century [DC19].

F.C. Hingeston-Randolph, ed., *The Register of John de Grandisson, Bishop of Exeter (A.D. 1327–1369),* 3 vols. (1894–99) [DC20]; id., ed., *The Register of Walter de Stapledon, Bishop of Exeter (A.D. 1307–1326)* (1892) [DC21].

G. Silano, ed., *Acts of Gubertinus de Novate, Notary of the Patriarch of Aquileia, 1328–1336: A Calendar with Selected Documents* (1990): although strictly notarial acts, they are almost all concerned with episcopal administration [DC22].

For registers of various British prelates, see D.M. Smith, *Guide to Bishops' Registers of England and Wales: A Survey from the Middle Ages to the Abolition of Episcopacy in 1646* (1981) [DC23].

## Formularies

G. Barraclough, *Public Notaries and the Papal Curia: A Calendar and a Study of a Formularium Notariorum Curie from the Early Years of the Fourteenth Century* (1934): a study of the formula as a product of the papal court, with a calendar of a notarial formula [DC24].

U. Berlière, ed., *Suppliques de Clément VI (1342–1352)* (1906): see the introduction (ppix–xxxiii) for a brief discussion of formularies of supplications in the thirteenth century [DC25].

L.E. Boyle, *A Survey of the Vatican Archives and of Its Medieval Holdings* (1972): see index, s.v. *formulae,* for archival holdings of formularies c. 1200–1500, and also bibliography on formularies [DC26].

A. Fayen, ed., *Lettres de Jean XXII (1316–1334)*, 2 vols. (1908–12): includes a formulary of letters of papal graces (benefices, expectations, dispensations, various faculties to prelates and others, permission to draw up last wills, etc.) [DC27].

H. Foerster, ed., *Liber diurnus Romanorum pontificum* (1958): a formulary in three manuscripts that originated in the ninth and tenth centuries [DC28].

C.D. Lanham, *SF:* with special attention to the development within the *salutatio* of what the author calls the independent-infinitive phrase [DC29].

L. Rockinger, *Briefsteller und Formelbücher des eilften bis vierzehnten Jahrhunderts,* 2 vols. with continuous pagination (1863–64, r1961): a collection of some eighteen treatises on *dictamen,* including the important works of Hugh of Bologna, Boncompagno of Signa, Guido Faba [DC30].

C. Rodenberg, ed., *MGH.EPP saeculi XIII e regestis pontificum Romanorum selectae,* 3 vols. (1883–94, r1982): all three volumes have introductions in which the editor has collected samples of formulas drawn from the letters he has edited [DC31].

H.E. Salter *et al.*, eds., *Formularies Which Bear on the History of Oxford, c. 1204–1420,* 2 vols. (1942): formularies dealing with internal university affairs, e.g. taking oaths, drawing and probation of wills, quittances (receipts), legacies, legal citations, various letters of absolution, testimonials [DC32].

H.M. Schaller, "Studien zur Briefsammlung des Kardinals Thomas von Capua," in *DA* 21 (1965) 371–518: Thomas of Capua, cardinal and vice-chancellor, was one of the most influential authorities on *dictamen* in the thirteenth century [DC33].

J.M. Vidal, ed., *Benoît XII: Lettres communes,* 3 vols. (1903–11): for the first year of the pontificate, the editor has given in full a sample of each type of provision or grace, which taken together serves as a kind of formulary [DC34].

*See also* [BA119].

# SECULAR ADMINISTRATION

BY BRIGITTE BEDOS-REZAK

## Introduction

Heir to Classical and Christian Latin, Medieval Latin was a living and creative language, particularly with respect to the vocabulary of secular administration. Whatever their continuity with the world of late antiquity, the institutions central to the functioning of the medieval polity were profoundly different from those of Rome, requiring terminological adaptations and innovations in Latin, which are the focus of this chapter. In the first section, identification of the sources for medieval administrative vocabulary (I.1) leads to an examination of those terms that express the processes and circumstances of administrative documentary production (I.2), and of those that designate the documents themselves and their institutional agency (I.3). The second section begins with a discussion of the cultural milieu for the linguistic formation of lay medieval administrative Latin (II.1), continues with a structural outline of the nomenclature of administrative vocabulary (II.2), and concludes with representative examples of linguistic developments (II.3). In the presentation of the nomenclature words are arranged in the following order: empire, kingdoms, and state, central administration (household and curia, and fiscal, judicial, and military officials and organization) and local administration (II.2.a); lordships: vassalic institutions, territorial units and their rulers, lordly administration (household and *curia*, finance, justice, military) (II.2.b); estate management (II.2.c); and urban administration (II.2.d). In the linguistic section separate consideration is given to Classical Latin words which were borrowed with virtually no semantic change (II.3.a), to those Classical Latin words whose meaning changed in medieval usage (II.3.b), to Medieval Latin adaptations of classical words (II.3.c), to latinized vernacular forms (II.3.d), to words of foreign and nonlocal vernacular origin (II.3.e), and to syntactical and orthographical developments (II.3.f).

In Roman times, the Latin word *administratio* carried the technical sense of government and public administration, and this meaning was retained in the Latin Christian West. Sections of the *Leges Visigothorum* denied to Jews, in the following terms, any governmental positions that would confer power over Christians: "nullus judeorum . . . ullam administrandi, inperandi, distringendi . . . potestatem super christianos exerceat" ([DD5] xii.3.17: p447). Officials in the Carolingian state were called *rem publicam administrantes,* but service to the state came to be conceived as service to the ruler, the *princeps* and *dominus,* as Hincmar of Rheims made clear in his *De ordine palatii* (882): "tales comites [rex] . . . constituere debet, qui . . . suam administrationem [i.e. regis] peragant." *Administratio,* like its cognate *minister,* came to mean the exercise of political power by high officials, performed in the name of the king and, ultimately, in their own ([DD137] ppxix–xx).

The definition of secular administration thus cannot be detached from a consideration of the nature of the medieval state. With the diffusion of regalian rights from the Carolingian period onward, the state's administrative units became political territories with their own leaders and local modes of governance. Lordly and royal administrations idiosyncratically drew from a common pool of institutions, experimented with each other's methods, and variously utilized one vocabulary to designate their administrative structures and processes.

Administrative action was not, however, consistently entrusted to the written word. Lawmaking, justice, orders, instructions, and military and fiscal procedures were partially, indeed at times only sporadically, committed to writing prior to the thirteenth century. The promulgation and enforcement of these nonetheless formal processes also entailed the spoken word, the *verbum regis,* as it was termed in Carolingian times. As a result, the administrative terminology and rhetoric of Medieval Latin retained for centuries the traces of a mental universe in which orality maintained its centrality. Up to the twelfth century lordly charters, whether of administrative or other import, were often addressed to "all those hearing these letters," "Notum sit omnibus hominibus hec audientibus quod . . ." ([DD53] p253). Classical words referring to the act of speech, such as *loquela,* acquired the extended meaning of "legal claim" in Medieval Latin. From *festuca,* literally a straw, twig, or small stick which earlier in Roman law was used symbolically in property transfers, was formed the verb *festucare,* "to ratify." The *festuca* remained a constitutive element of such transfers during the Middle Ages, but the range of its symbolic meanings and functions took on new dimensions. In Merovingian and Carolingian law courts, grasping the *festuca* signified formal and binding acceptance of the judges' decisions; and agreements made in court between parties were also formally made binding *per festucam.* The *festuca* came to be associated with the ritual of vassalage, and oral and nonverbal features of this ceremony were subsumed within the terms *festucare,* now meaning "to take possession," and *exfestucatio,* or *exfestucare,* signifying the act of breaking off homage by casting down the *festuca* ([DD104] pp246–48, 257–60).

## I. Sources, and the Production and Preservation of Administrative Documents

**I.1 Sources.** An attempt at gathering sources for a lexicon of Medieval Latin lay administrative terminology reveals that few extant texts of the early and central Middle Ages contain extended descriptions of rulers' rights, of officials' functions, or of institutions from an administrative perspective. At the beginning of all such inquiries must stand the *Etymologiae* (c. 620) of Isidore of Seville. Another text, the *Decursio* (or *Decurio*) *de gradibus,* is more difficult to appraise because its date (sixth to eighth century) is less precisely known. In his *De exordiis et incrementis quarundam in observationibus ecclesiasticis rerum,* Walafrid Strabo (c. 808–49) presents in parallel the gradations of ecclesiastical and secular hierarchies ([DD39] pp199). Hincmar's *De ordine palatii* is a treatise on government written in 882 and apparently based on an earlier work of Adalhard of Corbie (d. 826), which, if it ever existed, is no longer extant ([DD1] pp57–58, [DD73] p78). Focusing mainly on the operations of the English accounting bureau, Richard Fitz Neal, treasurer of England and bishop of London, wrote his *Dialogus de Scaccario* about 1179 [DD21]. Describing the rules of fiscal bureaucracy, Fitz Neal used a learned Latin and thus lifted mundane governmental regulation to the level of intellectual formulation. Indeed, his ideological stance extends to the very nature of English royal power, when he presents William the Conqueror as the one who decided to bring the conquered people under the rule of written law: "rex Willelmus . . . ne libera de cetero daretur erroris facultas, decreuit subiectum sibi populum iuri scripto legibusque subicere" ([DD21] p63). As the maker of written law William is aligned with classical emperors, and England enters the orbit of Roman legal culture and jurisprudence ([DD53] pp19, 25–26).

The numerous mirrors of princes, *specula regis,* which were produced from the Carolingian period through the Renaissance, discuss various aspects of secular rule while also characterizing the ideals of good government ([DD35] v8:434–36). Perhaps the best known representative of this genre is John of Salisbury's *Policraticus* (1159) [DD22], written in the same learned Latin as Fitz Neal's *Dialogus.* A criticism of King Henry II of England's government, the *Policraticus* buttresses its advice to rulers with a theoretical account of the type of state apparatus necessary to maintain order. In his *De principis instructione* (1180–83), Gerald of Wales also engaged in a criticism of the English government, comparing the Anglo-Angevin dynasty with the Capetian to the latter's advantage [DD23].

Medieval chroniclers were keen observers of contemporary politics, most interested in governmental matters, especially when, as was often the case, their patron was the king. Many chronicles contain transcriptions of important government documents and not infrequently make reference to documents preserved in royal archives, as in the *Gesta Philippi Augusti* of Rigord (d. 1206), a regnal history of Philip Augustus, king of France (d. 1223) [DD17]. Similarly, the chronicler Benedict of Peterborough combines narrative with copies of official documents in his history of Henry II of England for the years 1169 to 1192 ([DD19], [DD154] pp395–401). Several of the German chroniclers were close to the ruler's family, or belonged to his court's inner circles. Bishop Otto of Freising (c. 1114–58), for instance, formerly the Cistercian abbot of Morimund, was the grandson of Emperor Henry IV, the nephew of Emperor Henry V, the half-brother of Emperor Conrad III, and the uncle of Emperor Frederick I Barbarossa. He wrote the best account of the early Staufen period in his *Gesta Frederici,* for which he used documents from the imperial chancery [DD20]. Medieval historiographical writings are thus indispensable aids to assessing any medieval governmental operation and achievement.

The sources next to be considered are, however, more directly the product of administrative actions and institutions. Official texts prescribing specific rules of law and governance and mandating or organizing their implementation, such as *capitularia* (capitularies, see I.3), and *stabilitamenta, statuta, inhibitiones, ordinationes* (ordinances), may be expected to provide a rich lexicon of administrative terminology; such documents, however, are not uniformly available. In France, several centuries (the late ninth through the twelfth) elapsed between the promulgation of the last capitulary and that of the first royal ordinance ([DD39] p199, [DD61] p260). In England, the *Constitutio Domus Regis,* composed c. 1136 ([DD21] pp129–35), describes in detail the functions of royal household officers, some of whose domestic duties overlapped significantly with those of the royal administration (see II.2.a, *central administra-*

*tion).* Subsequent household ordinances, issued from the thirteenth century onward, document innovations in English royal domestic and public administration. In Sicily, the *Leges* or *Constitutiones Augustales,* termed *Liber Augustalis* or *Constitutions of Melfi* by modern historians, were promulgated in 1231 by Emperor Frederick II for the kingdom of Sicily, remaining this kingdom's fundamental law for five centuries. Compiled by legal experts, the three books of the constitutions discuss the origins of royal authority and spell out in some detail the administrative responsibilities of crown officials, civil and criminal procedures, and the relationship of the crown to various categories of subjects. They also provide a record of public health legislation, perhaps the first of its kind in Western Europe ([DD35] v8:268, [DD9]).

Surveys and inventories of the lands and revenues of specific estates or seigniories elucidate some aspects of domanial administration. The terminology relating to such land books varies greatly. Terms such as *polyptychum* (Greek: many-leaved tablet), *pagina, codex, liber, rotulus* refer to the external appearance of the document itself, whereas *breve, brevium, brevaria* allude to the internal organization of its contents. When the emphasis bore on landlord-tenant relations, or on the tenants' payments and obligations, the landbooks were termed *libri censuales, registra censuum, littera rectitudinum,* or *forma censualis.* Where the focus was on the landed structure of the domain, the books were called, from the eighth century onward, *libri bonorum, possessionum, terrarum, descriptio villarum, extenta terrarum, libri feodorum,* with the word *terrarium* or *terrerium* (French *terrier*) in use by the thirteenth century ([DD31] pp17–21, [DD35] v10:29–30).

*Domesday Book,* called a *descriptio* and containing a comprehensive description of England at the end of the eleventh century, was compiled from the Great Survey undertaken in 1086 by order of the Norman king, William the Conqueror (d. 1087), and completed before the king's death ([DD35] v4:237–39, [DD31] pp35, 37–38). Though there had been earlier Continental parallels during Carolingian times on a much smaller scale, when Charlemagne and his successors had sent their *missi* (official envoys) to draw up surveys of the royal estates ([DD135] p274), *Domesday* and the survey leading to its compilation are considered the greatest administrative achievements of medieval royal government. England produced another comparable inquiry when in 1279 King Edward I preceded the *quo warranto* prosecutions with a detailed survey listing the rights of the king and his feudatories ([DD53] p6, [DD142]). No such countrywide surveys exist for any other medieval European state. The details of that conducted by Emperor Frederick II in the 1220s within the (formerly Norman) kingdom of Sicily are lost ([DD53] p6).

In the twelfth century, the practice of making surveys in writing extended from royal to lordly administrations. Starting c. 1164, the count of Falkenstein commissioned a canon to record in writing his fiefs, endowments, acquisitions of people and property, and manorial rights and incomes. The resulting *Codex Falkensteinensis* is the oldest extant German survey of a secular lordship ([DD12], [DD113] pp11–13)]. In England, thirteenth-century treatises on estate management recommended the use of such surveys and the keeping of *compoti,* accounts rolls ([DD35] v12:532–34, [DD24]). Robert Grosseteste, bishop of Lincoln, is the author of the *Rules,* the first known treatise on estate management, compiled (1240–42) for the countess of Lincoln. The work contains two sets of rules, one for the management of an estate, the other for the management of a seigniorial household. Compiled in French for the countess's use, the *Rules* were based on a Latin text, the *Statuta,* which Grosseteste had written between 1235 and 1242 for his own household and estate officials [DD24]. The most famous contributions to the didactic literature of estate management, the anonymous *Seneschaucy* [DD24] and the *Husbandry* by Walter of Henley (d. c. 1290–1300) [DD24], were written in the second half of the thirteenth century, also in French, for a rising group of estate administrators who belonged to the legal profession and who, though familiar with Latin, nevertheless were used to textbooks on common law that were virtually all written in French. *Seneschaucy* and Walter's *Husbandry* were conflated in one treatise, *Fleta,* written c. 1290 in Latin [DD24–26]. The *Quoniam inter magnates* (c. 1300) and the *Forma Compoti* (c. 1300), didactic treatises on manorial accounting with the broadest circulation in early fourteenth-century England, were likewise written in Latin [DD24]. The *Forma Compoti* was compiled for use on lay estates with the lord in residence for at least part of the year. Since it was particularly common for English landlords to conduct direct agricultural exploitation through local officials (see II.2.c), manorial accounts have survived in fairly large numbers ([DD35] VI:39–40, [DD143] pp120–61).

Diplomatic sources, charters and diplomas, registers, fiscal accounts, and official records are the most valuable evidence for administrative activity and efficiency, and for the extent to which such activity was centralized. These documents will receive further consideration in the next two sections (I.2–3). Until the twelfth century the emperor and some kings were the only secular authorities in Western Europe who possessed permanently organized writing facilities to deal with the standardized preparation and dispatch of official documents. Yet not all royal and imperial charters were produced by the rulers' staffs; like seigniorial charters, they could be, and often were, prepared in monastic or episcopal *scriptoria*. During the twelfth century, state chanceries increased their control over the production of royal and imperial documents, while dukes, counts, lords, and cities began to have their own writing bureaux.

**I.2 The Vocabulary of Administrative Documentary Production.** Although the term *cancellaria*, "chancery," to designate the bureau charged with the production and validation of official documents, appeared only in the twelfth century ([DD61] p2), the office had existed for centuries. Its head bore various names, including *referendarius, notarius, protonotarius, capellanus et notarius*, before and during the Carolingian period. At this time he began to be permanently designated *cancellarius* (chancellor), or *archicancellarius*, with a few such exceptional variations as *cartigraphus, apocrisiarius, signator,* or *summus sacri palatii cancellarius* as the writing bureau separated from the chapel to form a distinct administrative unit. Initially, as early as the fifth century, the term *cancellarius* had simply indicated the official in charge of guarding the latticework barriers (*cancelli*) which separated the judges from the parties to a case. As head of the secretariat, the chancellor supervised the palace archive, and as the individual responsible for the authenticity of the documents issued by his office, he was entrusted with the custody and use of the seal: *anulus, bulla,* or *sigillum* ([DD35] VII:123–31). Because of the chancellor's very broad responsibilities in the judicial, political, and administrative spheres, the seal might alternately be placed in the care of a special keeper, *custos sigilli* or [*ille*] *qui defert sigillum*. Such a situation would also arise in late twelfth-century France when the king, taking umbrage at his officer's power, elected not to fill the office of chancellor. The chancery, then supervised by a mere *custos sigilli*, produced royal charters all inscribed with the formula *vacante cancellaria* ([DD61] pp41–42, 134–37; [DD66], at pp8–30; [DD73] pp80–85; [DD63] pp223–27; [DD65]).

Among the chancery staff, those responsible for writing the documents were the *notarius, scriptor, cartularius* (a medieval formation, like *cartularium* and *chartarium*, from the classical noun *c[h]arta*), *dictator, tabellio, amanuensis,* or the *exarator.* This last term alludes to and derives from the Classical Latin rustic image that compares to a plow (*aratrum*) the instrument that harrows and fertilizes its material (first wax and later parchment as well) ([DD64] p127).

When, during the twelfth and thirteenth centuries, lay aristocrats began to control the dispatch of documents issued in their own names, they used the services of clerical scribes who belonged to their household clergy and who were designated *capellani, clerici, scriptores, notarii,* or *cancellarii* in princely charters. *Notarii* and *scriptores* were also the names of those scribes who, by the thirteenth century, became permanently attached to urban administrations.

**I.3 Administrative Documents: Typology and Preservation.** The earliest extant documents from Western European chanceries were issued by Merovingian rulers in 625. In general, barbarian kingdoms which superseded imperial authority retained Roman documentary practices and, up to Carolingian times, the vocabulary referring to the output of royal documents retained classical structure and precision. A major distinction was maintained between the *praeceptiones regales* (royal/public documents), which were centrally produced *in palatio*, and the *cartae pagenses* (provincial/private acts), which were locally issued *in pago*. Until about the seventh century, the content of documents could be registered within the local archives, the *gesta municipalia,* so as to ensure the documents' security and executory strength. By then, however, this registration, a late Roman legacy, had become a formality with little functional value.

Merovingian and Carolingian royal charters are called *praecepta, praeceptiones, auctoritates.* The term *diploma,* which the humanists discovered and applied particularly to royal acts, was unknown in the medieval West but was a classical word of Greek origin, used in the late empire to designate a brief folded in two. Documents recording the final disposition at the end of a lawsuit were termed *placita* (judgments) after the name of the palace tribunal, the *placitum palatii,* which handled law cases ([DD66] pp68–72, [DD67], [DD69–70]). In Classical Latin, *placitum* means that which pleases, an agreement, hence a decision. In Medieval Latin, this sense was further specialized to indicate the specific agreement of parties to engage in a lawsuit and to make a joint appearance before a court of law. By extension, *placitum* came to designate a session of the law court, the court itself, the judgment of the court, and a request for judgment (thus the English term "plea"). From *placitum* further words were formed in Medieval Latin, such as *inplacitare* (to implead, to summon to appear to court) and *inplacitatio* (the summons to appear in court, the right to summon).

The communication of Merovingian and Carolingian central authorities with their local agents involved both oral and written modes. Although much of the written administrative correspondence has been lost, a sense of its nature may be uncovered from formularies. These are collections of model documents, *formulae,* which survive largely in ninth-century manuscripts even where their contents may be earlier, and which were primarily meant for the use of local administrators. Particularly important for the variety and extent of royal administrative orders is Marculf's *Formulae* [DD6]. Part of the written communications to Carolingian officials about military expeditions, assemblies, comital nominations, and estate surveys took the form of *mandata* (orders) or *monitiones* (admonitory letters), some of which still survive. Other extant Carolingian administrative and legislative decrees and instructions to state officials were divided into *capitula* (articles or sections), and for this reason such texts were known as *capitula* or *capitularia*. The term *capitulare* is first attested in this sense by the Lombard King Aistulf (757–74) and then in Charlemagne's *Capitulary of Herstal* (779). Many capitularies deal with problems of governance and sought to establish and regulate fundamental principles of state administration. With a transformed royal sphere and means of control, the capitulary tradition did not continue beyond the reign of Carloman, king of West Francia (d. 884) ([DD7], [DD66] pp62–74, [DD131], [DD135], [DD133] pp25–37, [DD72] pp1–44, [DD68]).

Carolingian local officials, the *comites* (counts), communicated with their subordinates, the *vicarii*, in writing, and were encouraged to do the same with the central government. Charlemagne had ordered that each bishop, abbot, and count was to have his own *notarius* or *cancellarius* (notary) ([DD133] pp115–20). Comital notaries could additionally produce the *cartae pagenses*, also designated by the words *carta, noticia, pagina, volumen, membrana, litterae, epistola, titulus, monumentum, chirographum, testamentum, instrumentum, memoratorium* (a medieval formation from a classical root, *memoro/-are*, "to speak, tell, remind of"). All these were used to designate a locally produced (private) charter, with reference to material (page, parchment), style (epistolary or other), writing (manuscript), or purpose (notification, testimony, memorandum).

Between the tenth and the early thirteenth century, diplomatic vocabulary tended both to blur the distinction between public and private documents and to proliferate at the expense of lexical precision. Composite terminology (*scriptum memoriale, preceptionis pagina, litterale testamentum, carta testimonialis*), diminutives (*membranula, litterulae, carticula*), and affected expressions (*tomus, thomocarta, syngraphis*) became acceptable usages. From among this extraordinary profusion, *carta* and *scriptum* emerged as the preferred terms during the eleventh and twelfth centuries, after which *litterae* stood out, replacing all other terms but *carta*. Ultimately the word *litterae* was itself often omitted and documents came to be designated as *illae, presentes,* or *patentes* [*litterae*].

By the early thirteenth century, there was a tendency toward specialization and limitation of the lexicon for administrative documentary output. At this point terms were drawn from the newly retrieved Roman legal vocabulary and from the terminology of canon law: *instrumentum publicum, instrumentum authenticum, notae, brevia* (sg. *breve*). Royal chanceries refined their nomenclature. *Privilegia* referred to the solemn diplomas which by the 1330s had been totally replaced by the diplomatic genre of the *litterae apertae, litterae patentes* (letters patent). Among these was the *mandatum* or *mandamentum,* a specific form of letter in which French rulers commanded their administrative officials to perform particular deeds by the formula "mandamus vobis expressius iniungentes quatinus . . . ," from which the letter derived its name (French *mandement*) ([DD61], [DD64] pp121–26).

The incipient administrative structure and documentary proliferation of late twelfth-century Western Europe still existed within an ambulatory court, where royal business often relied on the memory of the king's peripatetic entourage, occasionally bolstered by portable records. The records lost by the French king Philip Augustus together with his entire baggage train during the skirmish with Richard I of England at Freteval (1194) are described by the chronicler Guillaume le Breton as including *libelli computorum fisci* (tax account books) ([DD17] p197) and fiscal documents and domanial accounts: *scripta tributorum fiscique cyrographa,* including both *tributa* (payments) and *census* (rent, French *cens*). Guillaume further explains that the French royal archives came into existence as a response to this loss ([DD18] p118–20). There is no doubt that the year 1194 was crucial for the development of French royal archives, which, before that date, contained only 28 original documents for the entire preceding history of the French monarchy; after that date they held 556 original pieces for the succeeding 29 years alone ([DD154] p410).

The French Capetian attempt to collect and preserve royal records had precedents in neighboring courts. The count-kings of Barcelona had produced and collected fiscal accounts (*computa*) and a series of reports (*comemorationes,* or sg. *carta comemorationis*) of their domains since the 1150s, and letters and memoranda since 1177–78 ([DD13] v1:3–15, and passim). In Flanders, the earliest accounting record from the comital court dates from 1140; the so-called *Grote Brief* of 1187, a general financial account, testifies to a fiscal curial administration with centralized control of receipts and expenses ([DD114] p12–19). The sole document of Ottonian administration extant today is the *Indiculus Loricatorum* of 981, a set of very much abbreviated entries listing the contingents of armed and mounted warriors required to reinforce Emperor Otto II's army during the imperial campaign against Sicily ([DD170] p76). Feudal registers compiled by chanceries to facilitate the management of military resources are still extant for Norman Italy (1150, called the *catalogus baronum* in its existing form); for England (*carte baronum,* baronial charters collected and stored in 1166, copied into the *Liber niger scaccarii,* composed c. 1206 [DD14], and later inserted in the *Liber rubeus,* 1212–30 [DD15]); for Normandy (1172, the roll made of the Norman barons' written answers to the inquest was later inserted in the *Liber rubeus*); for Champagne (the *feoda Campanie,* compiled c. 1172); and for Catalonia (*Liber feudorum major,* compiled between 1194 and 1196) ([DD162] p159, [DD154] pp286–89).

For England it has been argued that the survey documents (*carte* and *breves*) used for the compilation of Domesday Book may be the first explicit evidence for a royal archive, kept *in thesauro regali* at Winchester until the mid-twelfth century, by which time it had vanished ([DD53] p33–34, 150–51, 162–63). There is greater consensus among historians that the first memoranda kept by the English crown were the London Exchequer pipe rolls extant for 1130. These mark the beginning of a royal archive; they became a continuous series during the reign of Henry II (1154–89). In the twelfth century, this type of record was referred to as the *rotulus de thesauro* and later as the *magnus rotulus pipae.* Two parchment skins were sewn together to form one long length, which, when rolled, resembled a pipe or cylinder. This seems the most likely explanation for the origin of their designation as pipes. When sewn together at the tops or heads, such pipes formed a roll ([DD35] v9:663). The pipe rolls are concerned with the accounts that the *vicecomites* (sheriffs) of the counties and other accountable officials rendered (*reddere compotum*) annually of the revenues and other charges they owed. Except in Flanders, where comparable accounting methods were used, there seem to be no similar records for other states of medieval Western Europe ([DD114] p81). The Exchequer further produced a unique record, the tally: *talea* ("stick" in Classical Latin). Tallies were wooden sticks used as receipts for payment obligations. With notches representing the various sums of money being recorded, tallies were split lengthwise through the notches into two identical halves; one was kept by the Exchequer, the other by the accountable official ([DD21] pp22–24). The permanent settlement of the Exchequer in London during the early twelfth century as the dominant royal financial organ undoubtedly crystallized this recording activity.

However, the *thesaurus* at Winchester, which had developed after the Norman Conquest into a fixed central archive for the government, was abandoned later in Henry II's reign as a permanent archival repository, and the royal archives appear to have been portable treasure chests moved between royal residences ([DD53] pp163–65). In Fitz Neal's *Dialogus de Scaccario* (c. 1180) the Master explains to the Pupil the ambiguity of the word *thesaurus,* which means both treasure (coins, silver, relics, jewels) and treasury (a place where treasure is deposited) ([DD21] pp61–62). The Master further alludes to the circulation of things, such as *Domesday Book,* the Exchequer rolls, and writs and charters, locked up in treasure chests: "plura sunt in repositoriis archis thesauri que circumferuntur" ([DD21] p62). The Latin word *archa* here means chest or strongbox containing relics, jewels, and documents, and its similarity to the terms *archia, archiva* (sg. *archium, archivum;* from the Greek *archeion,* "governmental property"), already used in ancient Rome to designate collections of important records, seems to have encouraged semantic association of the words in Latin. The connection among archives, treasure, and treasury dates back to classical Rome, which stored its public records in the treasury within the temple of Saturn and regarded as public treasures those texts deposited in the city *archiva*. As a result, throughout the Middle Ages—and to this day in France, where the nucleus of the royal archives is still called the *Trésor des chartes*—words that designated archives, treasure, and treasury were interchangeable: *c(h)artarium, c(h)artularium, archivum, scrinium*. Louis IX of France (1229–1270) built a sacristy adjoining the Sainte-Chapelle, the top floor of which housed the royal archives; these were thereafter said to be resting in the cupboards of the king, "littere reposite in almariis domini regis," or above the treasure of the Sainte-Chapelle, "archivium litterarum et privilegiorum desuper thesaurum capelle regalis Parisiensis palatii existens" ([DD11] 1:v–vi, xxiii).

By the last quarter of the twelfth century, governments expected lords and knights to submit sealed deeds of their vassalic services and obligations. Such deeds became administrative records as important to the governance of the feudal state as were the internally generated fiscal and feudal registers. Chancery archives which emerged as collections of these "feudal charters" became tools of administration ([DD162] p160, [DD161] pp282). It has been argued that the record keeping pursued from c. 1200, even more than the already familiar practice of documentary writing, was the key element in the full development and successful operation of feudal government ([DD161] pp284–85). From the thirteenth century onward lay administrations pursued an increasingly consistent archival policy. In the case of kings and princes, this included the creation of permanent repositories whose custodians were concerned with both the preservation of incoming documents, which might be copied for greater security, and the recording of outgoing documents. The copies might be made on a *rotulus* (roll) ([DD53] p136)—hence *irrotulare* and *contrarotulator,* which gave "to control" and "controller"—or in a register called primarily *liber,* although the terms *cartularium* and *registrum* were also commonly used. English chancery rolls registered documents in chronological order and were limited to out-going royal letters. French registers arranged royal charters topically and according to category and recipient and contained incoming materials as well, together with *in-quisitiones* (inquests), *compoti* (accounts), inventories, and lists ([DD154] pp412–23).

Cities maintained writing bureaus from which were issued deeds, mostly con-tracts between their citizens, that were either sealed with the seal of the town ([DD145], [DD166], [DD174]) or produced as *chirographa* (duplicate originals). These chirographs, including Jewish chirographs of loans when relevant, were kept in an *arca communi* (communal chest). As a *locus credibilis*, this archival chest imparted authenticity to the contracts kept therein ([DD165] pp37–39). Such transactions might also be transcribed to rolls for quick reference. Additionally, urban records in-cluded several copies of the *memoriale cirographum* (charter of privileges), of guild records, and of custumals summarizing municipal by-laws and customs (*consue-tudines*) that regulated justice, finance, commerce, and government ([DD165] pp39–41; [DD53] pp71, 96, 103–4).

## II. Latin

**II.1 Latin Culture and Lay Administrative Language.** Although administrative officials, particularly at the local level, included non-churchmen, most medieval ad-ministrative writing produced in Latin was generated by monks and clerics: *clerici* (> English "clerks"). The medieval identification of *clericus* with *litteratus*, i.e. a per-son who knew and was literate in Latin, and of *laicus* (layman) with *illiteratus*, i.e. a nonlatinist though not necessarily illiterate, had become virtually axiomatic by the twelfth century ([DD53] pp226–40). According to a widely accepted view, the Latin spoken and understood in the western part of the Roman Empire had become by the eighth century a dead foreign language, spoken and written only by a small learned elite. The movement of spoken Romance languages away from Latin would have re-ceived an impulse from the Carolingian efforts to restore classical rules of grammar and orthography for written Latin, which further weakened its organic connection with spoken forms. A recent analysis challenges such views, arguing that Latin, far from being a foreign or learned second language of the Carolingian Franks west of the Rhineland, was actually their primary language, possessing both spoken and more formal written forms, with intercomprehension maintained between the two. According to this view, it was not until the late ninth or early tenth century that the Romance languages emerged in Western Europe. The regions from the Rhineland eastwards were Germanic-speaking areas in the ninth century; Latin there was a clearly different language, but one that was accepted for law, religion, and writing, so that bilingualism was required of those involved in public life ([DD133] pp7–22).

Certainly from the late ninth century onward, everyone who knew Latin had learned it by reading texts, rather than acquiring it orally as a mother tongue. Me-dieval Latin continued to be spoken and, far from being a dead language, produced a number of new terms over the centuries. Yet everything spoken and written in Latin was ultimately measured against its written texts. Latin's existence depended upon these texts, and upon the study of their controlling devices, grammar and lexicogra-phy ([DD40] pp6–7). For the educated administrator with his textually based train-ing, philology and etymology were both learning and interpretive processes. Thus Richard Fitz Neal in his *Dialogus* could state, inaccurately but suggestively, that *mur-*

*drum,* "murder" (derived from the German for death), signified hidden or secret ([DD21] p52), and that *foresta* was formed from *ferarum statio,* "a haunt of wild animals" ([DD21] p60). Although modern scholars differ on the etymology of the Latin word for forest, suggesting that it derives either from Classical Latin *foris* (outside the gates, hence uncultivated land) or from the German *forst* (forest) assimilated to Latin ([DD35] 5:131), they have not retained Fitz Neal's linguistic analysis. The propriety of clerics serving as *curiales* in the retinues of princes was often disputed after the Third Lateran Council of 1179, on the ground that curial clerics executed court sentences involving the shedding of blood. In support of this interpretation, the term *curia* (whence *curiales*) was conceived as possibly deriving from *cruor,* "bloodshed": "nam et curia a cruore dicitur vel etiam a cura" ([DD146] v1:178, v2:118). Such explanations demonstrate semantic awareness, if not philological sophistication, on the part of medieval latinists, but in either case they are indicative of contemporary conceptions of administrative processes and of their implications.

Latin secular administrative documents are written renditions of medieval realities couched in the language and values of a much admired, but in its origins alien, Romano-Christian thought-world. Thus, even to speak of medieval administrative Latin is to invoke an abstraction. Such a language was learned; varied according to time, place, and cultural milieu; was sensitive to the user's level of education and his vernacular tongue; and might involve the rendering of concepts which, though devised in the vernacular, were necessarily translated for publication and dissemination. Alternatively, concepts may have been formulated in Latin by literate and learned clerics imbued with classical, biblical, and liturgical texts, who were equally skilled at applying classical and Christian nomenclature to their own contemporary realities [DD51]. By their choice of administrative terms, clerics may well be revealing their understanding, or ideological view, that a particular medieval institution is similar to, or continuous with, its alleged classical predecessor.

Classical Latin, the language of a state with a sophisticated governmental framework, offered a rich lexicon of administrative terminology which was retained by those barbarian kingdoms settled in the western part of the empire and eager to place themselves within the continuity of imperial practices and organizations. In the twelfth century, emerging nation states and state officials borrowed afresh and continued to develop from that same rich lexicon the terminology they needed to express and articulate their expanding fiscal, legal, and military bureaucracies. Yet continuous use of a term does not necessarily imply identical meaning from one period to the next, raising the issue of the relationship between the classical Roman vocabulary of statecraft and its later use and semantic evolution.

In attempting to assess the degree of change in the medieval semantic value of a Classical Latin term of administration, two considerations are relevant. First, the different mentalities at play may be revealed by examining the variations in a word's vernacular translations. *Princeps,* for instance, was translated into Old French as "leader," but into German as "old, grey, venerable" ([DD39] p205). Second, it is necessary to evaluate the cultural milieu of the writers themselves. Users of administrative vocabulary had at least two systems of reference in mind, the one provided by their own experience of, and desire to influence, surrounding realities, the other grounded in the nature of their Latin culture. The meaning of the Latin words selected by administrative writers derives in part from the texts which formed these authors' referential lexical sources and which included varying amounts of biblical, classical, and Christian elements.

A further assessment of the cultural milieu responsible for the production of administrative documents entails consideration of the three following situations, which are especially relevant for the period preceding 1200. First, royal charters prepared by ecclesiastical beneficiaries in their own *scriptoria* share lexical similarities with other historical, liturgical, or hagiographical works produced by these *scriptoria;* this points to a linguistic crucible in which was fused a common vocabulary for various discourses including that of administration. Second, medieval writers of administrative records tended to produce a variety of texts, ranging from historiography to theology and diplomatics, while they themselves moved easily between assorted institutional and cultural settings, including the judicial, financial, liturgical, scribal, or archival departments of a ruler's court, as well as those of monasteries or cathedrals ([DD53] p82, [DD138] pp158–71). A case in point is that of the monk Dudo (d. c. 1043), dean of the chapter of Saint-Quentin in the Vermandois, who had been commissioned by Richard I, duke of Normandy, to write a history of the Normans (*De moribus et actis primorum Normanniae ducum* [DD16]); this he completed during the reign of Richard II, whose chancellor he was: "Dudo capellanus Richardi Northmannorum ducis et marchionis hanc cartam composuit et scripsit"; "Dudo cancellarius scripsit and subscripsit" ([DD10] no. 13, pp86–89, at p89 [1011]; no. 18, pp100–2, at p102 [1015]). In both historical and diplomatic works Dudo consistently used idiosyncratic titles (e.g. *patricius*) and expressions to refer to the Norman chieftains and the members of their entourage ([DD10] p44, and no. 18 at p101; [DD16] p295). Third, the Latin produced during the renaissance of the eleventh and twelfth centuries was associated not so much with monks and monastic milieux as with *clerici* who, trained in cathedral schools, were profoundly influenced by classical authors. The novelty in this "new" Latin, with its expanding capacity for accommodating the growing administrative linguistic needs of kingdoms, lordships, and cities, may be less lexical than semantic and ideological, and rooted in a revitalized recourse to classical rather than biblical or Romano-Christian texts. In mideleventh-century Anjou, for instance, two *clerici* of the cathedral chapter of Angers were involved in the redaction of comital charters: Renaud, the *notarius* of the incipient comital chancery, who later became the head of the cathedral school at Angers and wrote historical works, and Berengar (d. 1088), *grammaticus* (of Tours), who served on the count of Anjou's staff and became notorious for his controversial teachings on the eucharist, which were ultimately condemned. Both clerics had been educated at the cathedral school of Chartres, a center primarily noteworthy as a school of letters; the Latin of its headmaster, Fulbert of Chartres (d. 1028), was unusually clear and precise and he was very familiar with the standard classical authors ([DD163] v1:420–22, [DD160] pp8–9). Both clerics were also responsible for drafting a charter (c. 1030) in which are summarized the donations made by the count of Anjou, Fulk Nerra, to the monastery of St. Nicholas in Angers ([DD163] v2:42, no. 36; v2:65–66, no. 77). In this charter Count Fulk is described as having cleared and leveled a piece of land given to the monastery ("cultur[am] quam extirpavi et complanavi") in a manner reminiscent of the ancient hero Cincinnatus, who, according to Livy, was ploughing his field when news reached him of his appointment as dictator at Rome. This Roman theme, further developed in later Angevin charters, was in turn taken up by the twelfth-century authors of the *Gesta consulum,* scholars at the Angevin court, who portrayed the lives and careers of the counts of Anjou with reference to Roman civilization and the works of authors such as Livy, Sallust, and Cicero. Thus Angevin counts were styled *consules,* subscribed to the idea that the *lex antiqua* (Roman law) should be sustained, performed actions for the *utilitas* of the *respublica,* conducted campaigns (*expeditiones publicae, bella publica*) that were official and legitimate and thus differentiated from *tumultus,* "local hostilities," and appointed comital agents who were called *ministeriales publici* ([DD160] pp7–16). Should this representation of the Angevin counts be dismissed as mere rhetorical anachronism on the part of twelfth-century intellectuals steeped in classical antiquity, or did the Angevin counts actually behave as rulers in a manner that encouraged and substantiated a neo-Roman image [DD160]?

To restrict an examination of the language of lay administration to administrative documents is to assume a concept of documentary classification foreign to medieval culture, especially prior to the thirteenth century. The wide variety of scribal functions performed, and of texts produced, by the medieval writers of administrative documents was coterminous with the use for medieval administrative purposes of texts that by modern standards would not fit such a function, nor even be classified as documents. When, for instance, King Edward I of England looked for evidence to support his claims in Scotland in 1291, he turned first to monastic chronicles rather than to the royal archives ([DD53] pp82–83, 101, 152–53, 162). Thus, Latin textual production and use before 1200 challenge the epistemological distinction assumed by historians between ideologically distorted literary texts and transparent documentary sources, between presumptively biased chronicle sources and official records. The Latin of lay administration is therefore less to be differentiated by textual genre than to be assessed by reference to the circumstances of its formulation and function [DD74].

### II.2 Nomenclature of Lay Administrative Vocabulary.

Lay administrative vocabulary varies from one country to another. Separate dictionaries of Medieval Latin are currently being published for most European countries ([DD36], [CD25–41]). On the other hand, within a given region, imperial, royal, and lordly administrations, though organized with differing levels of bureaucratic complexity, tend to use a common lexicon to refer to their governing structures. In estate management, the vocabulary would indeed typically be common to both lay and ecclesiastical domains. By 1300, the use of vernacular languages in administrative matters was increasingly displacing the use of Latin ([DD63] pp92–95).

It is not possible here to offer an exhaustive nomenclature sensitive to time- and place-related usages and semantics. What follows, while neither comprehensive nor uniformly applicable, deals nevertheless with the most commonly shared, or preeminent, administrative structures of the Middle Ages. For an accurate appreciation of the spatial and temporal specificities of lay administrative Latin, the reader is encouraged to consult regional and biographical monographs and national dictionaries of Medieval Latin [DD36].

### II.2.a Kingdom, Empire, State.

Medieval scribes resorted to several ambiguous terms to designate ruling power: *auctoritas, dominium, potestas* (see II.3.b), *bannum* (see II.3.d), *districtus, maiestas, mundium, imperium, possessio.* Sovereign rulers themselves were termed *reges* (*kings*; sg. *rex*), or *imperator augustus*, or *Caesar* (emperor), a title borrowed from antiquity and not the exclusive prerogative of the emperor ([DD87], [DD92]). In Anglo-Saxon England, Ethelstan, king of Wessex (d. 939), is a *basileus* in 924 and an *imperator* in 930, King Edgar I (d. 975) is *basileus et imperator omnium regnum Anglorum*, and Edward the Confessor's seal (c. 1057) bears the legend *sigillum Aedwardi Anglorum Basilei* [DD140]. In Spain, Ramiro III, king of Leon, is a *magnus basileus* (in c. 970), and Ferdinand I, king of Leon and Castile (d. 1065), is *imperator Hispaniae,* while his successor King Alfonso VI (d. 1109), who claimed sole rule over Leon, Galicia, and Portugal, assumed the title of *imperator totius Hispanie* after his conquest of Toledo in 1085. In these instances, the title *imperator* connotes the ability to rule over several *regna.*

The medieval Western empire began officially in Rome in 800 when Charlemagne, a ruler who had vastly extended his original domains and was initially titled *rex francorum et Langobardorum atque patricius romanorum* (the latter dignity connected with a protective power over the city of Rome), was crowned emperor by Pope Leo III as "a Deo coronatus magnus et pacificus imperator romanum gubernans imperium." Subsequent divisions of the Carolingian empire had reduced the imperial title to little significance by the tenth century, when in 962 Otto I, king of Germany, resumed the title on the strength of his military successes in Hungary and Italy. With Otto III (crowned 996), empire and papacy collaborated in a policy for promoting a *renovatio imperii Romanorum;* Otto III styled himself *imperator romanorum,* while the heir to the throne became the *Caesar futurus* and *spes imperii,* as in Trajan's time. From the time of Henry III (d. 1056), a German king not yet crowned emperor was titled *rex romanorum,* Roman king. The equilibrium between papal and imperial power broke down during the church-state conflict of the eleventh and twelfth centuries known as the Investiture Controversy. Frederick I Barbarossa (1122–1190) attempted to free the empire from papal control by invoking Roman law as a source of independent authority, and by championing the empire as a *sacrum romanum imperium,* "Holy Roman Empire," an autonomous divine institution in which the *dominium mundi* would include the *regnum christianum.*

The *imperium romanum* of antiquity rested on military conquest and legal fiat, with *imperium* referring simultaneously to the act and power of command, and to the territory (the empire) subject to this power. In the Middle Ages, this term connoted rule over several *regna* and ultimately the concept of universal rule, although the actual extent of such rule varied with the realities of politics. Nevertheless, the Holy Roman emperor had derived from ancient Rome the claim of rule over the entire civilized world, and from Christianity the role of God's secular deputy. Even as there was a single God in heaven, there could be only one supreme ruler on earth; as the representative of God on earth, the emperor symbolized the essential unity of *Christianitas* or "Christendom" ([DD35] v5:495–96, [DD55] pp815–28).

In contrast to the imperial claim of universal governance, the *rex* (king) ruled solely over his *regnum,* a term which, from Carolingian times onward, might also designate a territory administered by a nonroyal potentate ([DD137] pp206–21, [DD91] pp248–51]). By the twelfth century, however, *regnum* had come to mean kingdom, that is, a politically separate entity in which land and people were assumed to be one, and in which people felt themselves a community of custom and descent, with kingship both fostering loyalties and symbolizing regnal solidarity and unity ([DD58] pp256–61, 319–29]).

Prior to the thirteenth century, *status* meant the public welfare of a kingdom or city-state and was associated with the object whose condition it was qualifying, as in the expressions *status regni, status reipublicae, status civitatis, status imperii.* The usual terms for state during this period—*regnum, civitas, imperium,* and *respublica*—might refer equally to the government or to any public office or property ([DD57] pp248). *Respublica,* a Roman concept, was reintroduced into medieval texts during the reign of Emperor Louis the Pious (d. 840) and remained in use thereafter. In his *Policraticus,* John of Salisbury characterized *respublica* as a body of which the king is the head, thus equating *respublica* with the kingdom and its people. This has been considered the earliest systematic formulation of medieval secular ideology, describing a social order in which the head of a *respublica* is no longer Christ but the king. John of Salisbury's concept of *respublica,* however, did not displace the term *regnum* in political and administrative discourse. Indeed *respublica* was even successfully challenged by the notion of *corona* or *corona regni,* an expression developed during the twelfth century as an abstraction to evoke circularity and a political structure (*regnum*) at the center of which was the king ([DD58] p321, [DD54] p263–68, [DD80–81]).

The *central administration* of medieval kings and emperors might be called *palatium,* a term which also referred to the king's entourage, to a local center of royal government, and to the architectural structure sheltering the ruler. In Augustan Rome *palatium* had designated the imperial palace located on the Palatine, but in the late empire this term assumed the semantic range in use throughout the Middle Ages [DD118]. Medieval kings were mobile, as was their entourage, and hence their government, even when several administrative departments came to reside in the kingdom's capital city. In Germany, however, the rulers of the Holy Roman Empire did not have a fixed capital. They traveled constantly, and this activity determined the most carefully administered institution of the Ottonian and Salian empires, the royal *iter* or migration from *palatium* to *palatium,* and with it the system of communication with the ruler's *regna,* through which the empire received its cohesion ([DD170] p94–95).

The *familia regis* or *hospicium regis* (royal household) of most medieval courts derived its organization from a Carolingian prototype. It consisted of officers (*intimates, familiares*) and servants (*milites, ministeriales*) who attended to domestic needs (food, clothing, horses, writing, prayer, and sleep). As the functions discharged by the royal household officers entailed a delegation of authority, they came to be combined with related public duties. Thus the household operated as an organ of government, with its chief officers (*ministeriales hospitii*) becoming as well officers of the state, while the menial tasks were left to a separate class of servants ([DD35] v6:299–306, [DD141], [DD159] pp518–39, [DD158] pp48–96, [DD103] pp187–94, [DD170]). The seneschal (*senescalcus, senescallus, dapifer, maior regie domus*) was the steward; in France this head of the household was virtually a vice-king in governmental matters, whereas in England his role was minor and mainly ceremonial ([DD35] v11:159–61). After the Norman Conquest, arrangements had to be made for the government of England during the king's travel to his Continental possessions; the administrator who served as vice-regent came to be called *justiciarius,* "justiciar" ([DD35] v7:199–200). The *cancellarius* was the chancellor (see I.2), responsible for the writing, authentication, and keeping of records; he might also concurrently be the head of the *capella* (chapel) and of its staff of *capellani* and *clerici* who attended to the spiritual and clerical needs of the royal family. The office of *camerarius* (chamberlain) was in France more honorific than important and its responsibilities concerning the king's wardrobe and lodgings, as well as the *camera* (i.e. the room where the king stored his valuables and his archives), were in practice discharged by such lesser officers as the *cubicularii, camberlani,* or *cambellani.* In England, the *camera* and its attending *camerarius* developed first into the financial organ of the household and then into a second writing bureau which issued documents under its own seal, known as the *parvum sigillum* or *privatum sigillum* (privy seal) ([DD35] v3:242–43). The room adjacent to the *camera,* the *garderoba* (wardrobe), was at first a place of safe deposit for valuables before evolving into an office which ultimately superseded the *camera* in all its functions; the *garderoba* became the key household department of finance and administration as well as a sort of war office. The *buticularius* (butler) or *pincerna* (a learned Latin word meaning "cupbearer") had charge of the royal cellars ([DD35] v2:434). The *comes stabuli* or *constabularius* (constable) had military duties ([DD35] v3:543–44) and supervised the royal stables and the *marescalci* (marshals) ([DD35] v8:153–54).

In the first half of the eleventh century, a new group of men, the *ministeriales,* entered the *familia* of the German rulers ([DD35] v8:404–7). *Ministeriales* were originally servile retainers who had fulfilled military obligations and administered estates in ecclesiastical lordships. Once recruited from the servile population as warriors and household officials, these *servientes, ministri, servitores, famuli* were provided with land tenures to support the discharge of their responsibilities. By the middle of the eleventh century, however, they had formed a quasi-hereditary estate, and by the fourteenth and fifteenth centuries they had blended into the "lesser" landed nobility. In the construction of the German medieval state, whether imperial or princely, the role of this group was central. The *ministeriales regni* of the Salian Hohenstaufen rulers served them as trusted advisers and soldiers, administering both central and local governments of the empire in their manifold capacities as castellans, judges, and fiscal officials ([DD108] pp61–67).

When the king's *familia* was engaged in formal public events, during which the king took counsel or dispensed justice, it was then termed the *curia regis* (the king's court) ([DD35] v4:65). The *curia* regularly comprised the chief household officers, a group of *curiales, palatini, familiares* or *amici regis, consiliarii,* and was augmented by the occasional presence of lay and ecclesiastical magnates (*optimates*). At first the royal *curia* was a loosely organized body which helped the king to rule; with bureaucratic specialization and stability it was divided into permanent departments with defined functions. Medieval kings rendered their most important decisions with *consilium,* that is, with counsel and within a council ("judicata, arresta et sententie que de nostra curia seu nostro communi consilio processerint") ([DD156] pp129–73). The king could summon men of power to meet with him and his counselors in order to solve immediate and serious problems of government, and to seek support and money, especially during times of war. Such larger, representative, assemblies first appeared in the Iberian peninsula in the late twelfth century and were called, in Spanish, *cortes* ([DD35] v3:610–12). By the mid-thirteenth century, such an assembly of magnates and prelates was called in England *parliamentum,* and to it may be traced the origin of parliament, the English political institution and representative assembly by which was conducted the king's and the kingdom's business ([DD35] v9:422–34). In France, the meetings attended by members of the clergy, the nobility, and towns, at first called *curia, concilium, conventus, colloquium, synodus, placitum,* foreshadowed those national, consultative, representative assemblies known as the Estates General ([DD35] v10:316–28, [DD159] pp487–504). In Germany, there was no imperial representative assembly (German *Reichstag*) before the fifteenth century. Until then the emperors and kings held court (*conventus, colloquium, curia*) with lay and ecclesiastical magnates, to whom were added delegates of the imperial cities in the thirteenth century, thus forming a *generale parlamentum* ([DD35] v10:328–34).

Medieval kings considered it their duty to render justice through their *curiae,* which thus became active as courts of law. Judicial business was handled by a special group of judges (*viri prudentes* or *iurisperiti*). In thirteenth-century France, those officials involved in royal justice in Paris formed a group that became the *Parlement* of Paris (*parlamentum*), a judicial body which met regularly and heard cases from the kingdom either directly or on appeal ([DD35] v9:417–21, [DD159] pp562–76). In thirteenth-century England, three judicial organs administered justice in the name of the king. One was the circuit court of traveling judges, the *iter ad omnia placita* (general eyre) ([DD35] v7:183–86). Another court of judges, the *bancus regis* (king's bench), heard *communia placita* (common pleas) in the presence of the king (*coram rege*), following him as he traveled through his kingdom ([DD35] v7:190–95). The third court, the *communis bancus* (common bench), also known as the "court of common pleas," sat within the principal royal palace at Westminster ([DD35] v7:186–90).

The financial affairs of the king also devolved to special committees of the *curia regis,* while from the eleventh to the thirteenth century collection of royal revenues was part of local administration and performed by the *prepositus* or *vicecomes* (see below, *local administration*) ([DD35] v11:611–25, [DD159] pp335–51). Aside from the profits from their landed estates, including the *tallia* (*taille* in French, *tallage* in English)—also called *tolta, malatolta* ([DD35] v8:68) or *exactio*—; the *census* (rent); the *corrogata* (< *corrogo/-are,* "to collect, exact, requisition"), *corvea* (from Old French *corvée,* (< *corrogata*), *corvade, corveamenta* (labor services) ([DD35] v3:612–13); and *hidagium* and *carrucagium* (taxes on the hide and on plowland), medieval kings obtained such revenues as tolls (*telonaria,* sg. *telonarium*) collected by *telonarii,* income from mints generated by *monetarii,* profits from dispensing justice (*placita, forefacta, emende*) collected by the *baillivi* and *prepositi,* and sums obtained from the *auxilium* (feudal aid) that vassals owed the king under the following conditions: ransom, knighting of the king's eldest son, and marriage of his eldest daughter. Wars and especially crusades were also occasions for such *auxilia.* In England, vassals could pay a *scutagium, scuagium,* or *escuagium* (scutage, from Latin *scutum,* "shield"), a monetary compensation in lieu of providing personal military service ([DD35] v11:120–21]. In France, the commutation of military service into payment of a war subsidy (*auxilium exercitus, subsidium*) contributed to the establishment of regular taxation in the fourteenth century ([DD35] v11:576–80).

The central organization of royal financial administration entailed a distinction between the treasury and administration per se, with the treasury emerging from the *camera.* In early Capetian France, the treasurer of the Order of the Knights Templars in Paris served also as the *thesaurarius regis,* who was solely responsible for receiving, storing, and dispensing money, while the auditing of accounts and financial administration rested within the *curia regis,* as a specialized *curia in compotis* (auditing body of the royal court, the *Chambre des comptes*) ([DD114] pp41–42, 90–93). In England, the *camera* and *camerarius* (chamberlain) at first stored the royal treasure and supervised its collection and disbursement. The *thesaurus* (treasury) that had been established at Winchester, possibly before the Norman Conquest, to hold any surplus and supply the itinerant *camera* with money, began in the early twelfth century to assume administration of the royal finances. The *thesaurus* at Winchester was almost immediately superseded in this function by the *scaccarium* (Exchequer) of London, which became the principal royal financial organ in medieval England. The Exchequer had to make sure that twice yearly (at Easter and Michaelmas) financial officers discharged their obligations in full and rendered their accounts before a group of auditors, the barons (*maiores*) of the Exchequer, and to impose penalties on those who failed to do so ([DD114] pp57–60, 62–64, 68–71; [DD35] v4:530–33). Yet the Exchequer was more than a court of audit with two annual accounting sessions. Its routine as an institution concerned with royal finance throughout the year was described in detail by Richard Fitz Neal in his *Dialogus de Scaccario* [DD21].

The *familia* of post-Carolingian kings played a central role as a military force. The Carolingian military system was predicated upon the principle that all free men should participate in military expeditions, but by the tenth century kings normally went to war accompanied only by their *domestici*, the *milites regii* who received, apart from gifts and clothing, a *stipendium* (wage). By the twelfth century, fiefs in northern France and England were granted primarily for military service (see below, *vassalic institutions*), and vassals of the king owed knight service to the *exercitum* (royal host). In addition to these feudal levies, kings used *servientes equites et pedites* (mercenary soldiers). Surveys of knights' services undertaken in twelfth-century England, Normandy, Champagne, Norman Sicily, and France (see I.3) promoted systematization of the feudal military service owed to rulers. Most scholars agree that England under William the Conqueror provides the earliest evidence of *servitia debita* (military quotas) imposed on almost all *tenentes in capite* (tenants-in-chief). The practice of assigning quotas led to the transformation of such obligations into the monetary payment known as *scutagium*, with which kings might hire mercenary knights who were not limited by feudal custom to service of only 40 days per year within the kingdom ([DD35] v7:277–78).

The *local administration* of medieval kingdoms underwent major transformations from the early Middle Ages onward. In Merovingian times the *civitates* (cities with their surrounding territories), upon which the king depended for tax revenue and for some of his military manpower, were essential organs of royal administration, together with the various officials of their *curiae*—the *defensor, curator, magister militum,* and especially the *comes civitatis* (pl. *comites*) or *graphio* (pl. *graphiones*) and his subordinate officer, the *centenarius* (hundredman). A Merovingian *dux* (pl. *duces*) might be in charge of groups of *civitates,* or lead royal armies that had no clear geographic base, or participate in diplomatic missions ([DD121] pp60–61).

In Carolingian Europe, the local agents of central administration were the *comites* (counts) ([DD35] v3:658–59, [DD84]). Some controlled the *civitates,* others a *pagus* (a smaller section of these territories; French *pays*); still others were apportioned a newly formed *comitatus* (county) where Roman jurisdiction had never existed or had been eliminated. As the king's representatives within their counties, the counts were responsible for the maintenance of peace, the collection of taxes and fines, the leadership of free men liable for military service, and the administration of justice rendered in the *mallus* (public judicial assembly) composed of *scabini* (French *échevins,* German *schöffen*) or *boni homines* (legal assessors, "good men"). Subordinate agents, such as *vicarii* ("vicars") and *centenarii,* dealt with infractions at the village level. The *comites* were supervised by the *missi dominici* (imperial envoys). The emperor also relied on the help of his *vassi dominici* (king's vassals), men who had commended themselves personally to him, and who had received in exchange a *beneficium* (benefice), usually in the form of land (see II.2.b, *vassalic institutions*). As the Carolingian empire expanded, the emperor resorted to such new regional units of government as *regna* (subkingdoms), headed by a *rex* or a *prefectus* (governor), and frontier regions (*marca,* pl. *marcae*), administered by a *prefectus limitis* or *custos limitis,* later called a *marchio* (pl. *marchiones,* marquis) ([DD35] v8:133, [DD83]) or *dux* (pl. *duces,* duke) ([DD35] v4:303–4), who exercised authority over local counts ([DD137], [DD35] v5:505–8).

With the dissolution of the Carolingian empire, this network of regional administration became a structure of lordly principalities and the model for their organization (see II.2.b). The local government of post-Carolingian French kings was assumed by the *prepositus* (pl. *prepositi,* English provost, French *prévôt,* German *probst*), who, with the help of the local *maiores* (sg. *maior,* mayor, the village's elder), functioned from the larger towns of the royal domain as estate managers exercising judicial responsibilities, executing royal commands, collecting revenues, and protecting the king's regalian rights ([DD35] v10:195–97). Beginning about 1200, the *baillivus* or *baiulus* (French *bailli*) was delegated by the royal court to supervise the *prepositus.* Ultimately the *baillis* became regional officials with jurisdiction over justice, "police," and finance ([DD154] pp125–36, [DD35] v2:52–53). In England, the *baillivus* (bailiff) was an officer subordinate to the sheriff and carried out the routine tasks of administration ([DD35] v2:51–52). The *vicecomes* (sheriff, shire reeve, from the Anglo-Saxon *scírgeréfa*) had emerged after the Conquest as the sole representative of the king in the *comitatus* (county or shire, consisting of a group of hundreds; sg. *centuriata* or *hundredum*) ([DD35] v6:330–31), where, as a royally appointed official, he was in charge of defense and "police," led military levies, presided over the judicial county court, and collected the king's revenues, for which he had to account at the Exchequer. Additional governmental mechanisms and specialized officers were in turn created to supervise and review the sheriffs' government ([DD35] v11:225–26).

**II.2.b Lordships.** The lay administration of medieval people and land did not depend solely upon kings and emperors, especially after the weakening of Carolingian rule. Imperial and royal officials then began to exercise in their own names the regalian prerogatives formerly delegated to them by the central authority in order to administer the territories under their control. The system of territorial formations, government, and social relations, together with the set of rituals and institutions that came to regulate the modalities of power (and incidentally of production), is known as feudalism ([DD35] v5:52–57, [DD104]). This designation, though denounced by some as an anachronistic invention—the word "feudal" was first used in the seventeenth century—nevertheless remains a conventional if not entirely satisfactory construct [DD94–99].

The origins of *vassalic institutions,* the backbone of feudal society, go back to Merovingian times. *Gassindi, vassi,* or *vassalli* (vassals) ([DD79] pp114–22) were then retainers who entered the protection (*patronicium* or *mundiburdis,* French *maimbour*) of other men by *commendatio* (commendation, private agreement) in return for services rendered, primarily of a military nature ([DD35] v3:490–91, [DD100] pp5–9). By the time of Charlemagne's accession (768), entry into vassalage was achieved by *vassaticum, vassalaticum, hominium, hominagium, hominiaticum,* or *homagium* (homage) ([DD79] pp142–43), which involved two specific legal forms, *commendatio* achieved by *immixtio manuum* (mixing of hands), and *fides* or *sacramentum fidelitatis* (oath of fealty). The vassal owed *servitium*, service, principally military obligations ([DD100] pp26–32, [DD79] p60), and was granted in return a *beneficium* (a life-tenure of land free of rent) ([DD100] pp36–46, [DD35] v2:179–80). Neither the *commendatio* nor the *beneficium* was originally hereditary.

The Carolingian rulers (emperors and kings) promoted vassalage as an integral part of state administration in two ways. First, they increased the number of *vassi dominici* (or *regales*), whom they endowed with generous *beneficia* (see II.2.a). Second, they required that their high-ranking officials, the *comites, duces, marchiones,* become their *vassi dominici.* "Vassals of the lord," these chief officials were themselves lords to their own vassals, who were thus not immediately under the authority of the ruler.

The public office which a Carolingian count received from the ruler was termed an *honor* (honor, pl. *honores*). The landed estates attached to the office were called the *res de comitatu* or simply *comitatus* or *ministerium.* Counts, as vassals of the king, technically held these estates as *beneficia,* and thus each came to believe that he also held his *honor,* that is, the comital office itself, as a benefice. In this way the term *honor* came to designate a complex of office and land held in benefice from the king, which became heritable in the course of the ninth century ([DD79] pp33–39, ([DD100] pp52–56, [DD46] pp254–55). The fragmentation of political authority during the last years of the Frankish kingdoms extended as well down to the counties, which broke up into smaller units (see below, *territorial units and their rulers*). Lordship and vassalage had become the new form of government.

Between the tenth and thirteenth centuries, a "classical" pattern of feudalism settled in France, West Germany, parts of Italy [DD75] and Spain ([DD76], [DD176]), and England. The lord was termed *senior* (French *seigneur*) ([DD79] pp98–105), with *dominus* used more comonly from the last quarter of the tenth century onward ([DD100] pp69–70, [DD79] pp90–97). *Homo* ([DD79] pp137–43) and *vassalus* were used broadly to designate the vassal, while the terms *miles, fidelis,* and *baro* ([DD79] pp125–26, [DD156] pp152–57, [DD35] v2:111) also connoted vassals, but only within specific contexts. A vassal who had done homage to several lords, a practice tolerated in France from the late ninth century that had since spread, was required, by the mid-eleventh century, to recognize a single lord (*dominus ligius*) whom he would serve in full. The notion of "liege" (related to German *ledig,* unhampered, unengaged, free) was applied also to the vassal (who was called *homo ligius, ligius miles*), to the homage (*hominium ligium*), and to the fief (*feodum ligium*) ([DD100] pp103–5).

*Commendatio* and *homagium* continued to be central to the creation of the vassalic relationship, with the homage often accompanied by a ceremonial *osculum* (kiss) ([DD100] pp70–79, [DD104] pp242–43). The lord had power (*dominatio, dominatus, dominium, potestas*) over his vassal, from whom he expected *fidelitas* (fealty) [DD86], *auxilium,* and *consilium. Auxilium* involved primarily military mounted service (*militare servitium* or *servitium militis*), which the vassal had to provide at his lord's summons (*submonitio, commonimentum*). At first unlimited, this military service became restricted to a fixed period (often 40 days per year); it might involve participation in the *exercitus* or *hostis* (the host, a substantial military action), or in the *equitatio* or *cavalcata* (French *chevauchée*, a short expedition), supplemented by the duty of *stagium* or *custodia* (castle-guard). Military service might alternatively be discharged by a monetary payment, the *scutagium* (scutage, French *écuage*). The obligation of *auxilium* also required a vassal to contribute financial aid to his lord on occasions which became limited to four (French *aides aux quatre cas*): ransom, the knighting of an eldest son, the marriage of an eldest daughter, Crusade ([DD100] pp89–92, [DD159] pp194–201, 204–8). *Consilium* required the vassal to attend his lord's court (*curia, curtis*), which functioned as both a judicial organ and an administrative council ([DD100] pp92–93, [DD159] pp201–3).

Vassalage was a contractual relationship. The lord owed in turn loyalty, protection, and maintenance to his vassal. He could provide maintenance in two ways. When the vassal resided in his lord's court, he was called a *vassus non casatus* or *baccalarius* (bachelor, French *bachelier*) ([DD100] pp94–97). When granted a domicile (*casamentum*), the vassal was designated *vassus casatus*. By the eleventh century it became usual for a vassal to hold a fief.

Much ink has been spilled on the etymology of *feo, feus, fevum, feodum, feudum* (fief) (see II.3.d), and on its role within the political structure of medieval Western Europe ([DD35] v5:53, 57–59; [DD100] pp106–49; [DD103] pp55–63, [DD79] pp41–55). Fief is the term that came to have the same meaning as *beneficium,* which it ultimately replaced, designating the landed estate granted by a lord to his vassal so as to assure the vassal the maintenance that was his due and that enabled him to perform the services required of him. By the ceremony of investiture (*vestitura* or *investitura*) ([DD104] pp244–46), which generally followed the act of homage and the oath of fealty, the vassal received *saisina* or *tenura* (seisin) of the fief ([DD100] pp125–27). The heritability of fiefs varied with regions ([DD100] pp133–36). In order to be invested with his fief, an heir had to obtain the consent of the lord, who exacted a payment on this account called *relevium* (relief, French *relief*). The heir then had to participate in the ceremonies of homage and fealty and investiture.

Heirs to fiefs could be women. This practice, which began in southern France at the end of the ninth century, had spread in varying degrees within Western Europe by the twelfth century ([DD100] pp143–44). Women as lords, or as wives to counts, dukes, or lords, were generally titled *domine* (sg. *domina*) ([DD79] pp108–9). The female forms *ducissa* (sg.) and *comitissa* (sg.) were also used, particularly though not exclusively for women who were heiresses in their own right to ducal or comital holdings [DD147].

Fiefs, considered now as *territorial units and their rulers,* assumed sizes and carried governmental powers that differed according to time and place. The *beneficia* or *honores* of the late Carolingian chief administrators—the *comites* ([DD137], [DD84]), *marchiones* [DD83], and *duces*—became the dynastic seats from which they and their descendants exercised "the powers of the king" as virtually independent rulers. These territorial formations are called principalities by modern historians ([DD35] v5:498–504, 508–11), but *pagus, regnum, regio, patria* [DD89–90], or *comitatus* (county) in medieval sources. The ruler of a principality was a *princeps, dux, marchio,* or *comes,* in a terminology inherited from Carolingian times ([DD91] pp243–54). In the as yet inconclusive debate about the nature of the fealty owed to a king by princes, some historians have argued that the princes were the *fideles* of the king and his *vassi*, since they paid him homage, however delayed and insecure that homage was in fact ([DD103] p17). It was, in part, the enduring notion that the principalities were fiefs, and the territorial princes vassals, which helped kings and kingdoms to endure.

Many counties disintegrated into smaller units, the *castellania* (castellany, French *châtellenie*), while in others the count retained control of the region but allowed *castellani* (sg. *castellanus*) most of the rights of local government ([DD35] v3:124–25, v5:52; [DD103] pp26–28). The number of *castra* (sg. *castrum*, castle) ([DD35] v3:143–52) increased significantly during the eleventh century. Headed by a *castellanus, vicarius castri, dominus castri*, or *princeps castri*, and occupied by a garrison of *oppidani, castellani, equites castri, caballarii castri*, or *milites castri*, the fortress became an essential element of social organization catalyzing the feudal relationships among those involved in the exercise of seigniorial power ([DD103] pp63–64, [DD55] pp364–401). *Milites* (knights, sg. *miles*), once retainers ([DD79] pp129–34, [DD103] pp97–102, [DD108] passim), entered the feudovassalic bond, becoming petty nobles and gaining access to lordship and nobility ([DD35] v7:276–79), even as the magnates entered the world of knighthood, assuming the title *miles*. This title, to which during the tenth century the idea of subordination and dependence had been attached, acquired an enhanced status both from its martial connotation and from its suggestive evocation of the clerical category of *militia Dei* (warriors of God). This philological analysis has been advanced to account in part for the social elevation of the title *miles*, for the ultimate cohesion of the composite warrior group of magnates, castellans, and knights around chivalric values, and for the integration in many regions of the formerly disparate categories of knighthood and nobility ([DD110–11], [DD103] pp102–7, [DD108] pp129–32 and passim). Despite such assimilation, however, the social vocabulary retained expressions echoing the hierarchical nature of lay society ([DD105], [DD107]). Comital and ducal titles thus remained limited to the rulers of large regions who might also be titled *barones* (sg. *baro*) ([DD35] v2:111); their powerful vassals, too, were called *barones*, and *principes, proceres, primores, primates, optimates*, or *magnates*.

*Lordly administration* had its greatest scope in counties and castellanies where rulers possessed rights of government which they treated as private assets ([DD91] passim). Feudalism has in fact been defined as a system in which government became a private possession ([DD35] v5:52–53). Since many of these rights of government derived from the king, the structures and means of government resembled the king's. Dukes and counts had households and domestic officers on the model of the royal household. Any *dominus* (lord) who had vassals, judicial rights, and a substantial income also had a *curia*, and it was the scale of performance, not the particularity of actions or responsibilities (which were alike in all cases), which differentiated the *curiae* of kings, dukes, counts, and lords. Therefore most of the vocabulary of lordly administration is similar to that described previously (see II.2.a, *central and local administration*). It is, however, precisely within the sphere of administration that Continental magnates made significant innovations which kings would later imitate. The position of *prepositus*, a remunerated agent with the duty of supervising the lesser assistants of comital administration (*vicarii, famuli, forestarii, servientes, ministri*), was first instituted by counts and later adopted by the French king ([DD91] pp256–58).

Princes had registers of fiefholders before kings did (see I.3). The county of Flanders and the duchy of Normandy were the best governed provinces of twelfth-century France. In Flanders, the castles had remained in the hands of the count, thereby limiting the expansion of the local lords' power. Both Flanders and Normandy had local agents, the *baillivi*, who may well have inspired the Capetian royal *bailli* (see II.2.a, *local administration*) ([DD154] p136). A Flemish reform of 1089 maintained the *camera* (chamber) as the principal treasury where revenues were received and disbursed, but placed supervision of territorial receivers and periodic accountings in the hands of the chancellor (in his capacity as *susceptor* and *exactor*) and his assistants, the *notarii* ([DD114] pp13, 80). Toward the end of the twelfth century, the accounting session came to be named *redeningha* (French *renenghe*, Flemish *redeninge*), from the receivers of the comital domain then called *redenaars* (French *renneurs*, Latin *ratiocinatores*) ([DD114] p66). In both Flanders and Normandy, the fiscal institutions of the annual audit (*scaccarium* in Normandy, *redeningha* in Flanders) and of the accounts prepared for the auditing session (*magni rotuli* in Normandy, *Grote Brief* in Flanders) preceded similar initiatives on the part of the French royal court (see I.3) ([DD154] p147, [DD114] 90–91 and passim).

**II.2.c Estate Management.** (See [DD35] v4:511–15.) Whether kings, counts, or knights, feudal lords were almost always landlords as well (see I.1, and II.2.a, *local administration*). Carolingian estates, *villae* (sg. *villa*), *curtes* (sg. *curtis*) or *manere/manerium* (manor), had been divided into two parts. One, the *mansus indominicatus* or *casa dominicata* (reserve, demesne, home farm), was kept for direct exploitation on the lord's behalf; the other was parceled out to *hospites, villani, rustici, manentes* (peasant tenants) ([DD103] pp246–60). The standard unit of tenant landholding was first called *mansus* (from the Latin *manere*, to remain; translated in English as "hide"), later *mansellus, curtilis, censiva, hospitium, hostisia. Censarii, censuarii, censiles* (rental tenants) paid a *census* (rent) for their land and had to provide labor services in the form of week-works (*opera, corvea*) ([DD35] v3:612–13) on the demesne. From the tenth century onward, with the lease of the demesne or its reduction through division into plots, rent began to replace labor services ([DD55] pp681–728). Furthermore, by virtue of their *bannum* (power of command), *districtus*, or *potestas* (unrestricted territorial authority) ([DD103] p38, [DD35] v2:69, [DD55] pp401–22), landlords derived additional land rent from their tenants as they exercised the rights to apprehend and arrest (*vicaria, justicia*); to levy *exactiones* (taxes) such as the *taleia, talleata* ([DD35] v11:576–77), *quista*, and *tolta*; and to impose *banalités* (Medieval Latin *bannus, districtus, potestas*). *Banalités* were the various dues for the compulsory use of monopolistic utilities such as mills (*molta, farinagium*), ovens (*furnaticus, furnagium*), and winepresses (*pressoraticus, pressoragium*); payments in lieu of such obligations; and observance of the *bannum* or *bandium vini* (the lord's monopoly on the sale of wine during prescribed periods). In the early eleventh century, the collection of prerogatives and rights exercised by the lord came to be grouped under the terms *consuetudines, usagia*, or *usatica* (customs) ([DD35] v11:671–86, [DD159] pp31–351; [DD103] pp28–34, 260–64). This conflation of public duties and landed rights is seen by some historians as deriving from peasant tenure and landlordship; others suggest that it originated in peasant residence within a castle area, termed banal lordship ([DD35] v2:69, [DD55] pp401–2).

Manorial officials in charge of estate management included the reeve ([DD35] v10:280–81), the *baillivus* or *serviens* (bailiff) ([DD143] pp32–36, [DD35] v2:52), the *prepositus, decanus, maior, vicarius, villicus, minister, ministerialis* ([DD159] pp263–64). In England particularly, treatises on estate management (see I.1) enumerate the duties and functions of manorial officials with respect to supervision of labor service; levy of dues, rents, and taxes; filling of tenancies; control of estate production; and holding of court.

**II.2.d Cities.** The variety of medieval urban origins, landscapes, and experiences is reflected in the terminology for medieval urban formations: *civitas, urbs, burgus, castrum, communio, communia* ([DD56] pp153–66, [DD35] v3:493), *pagus mercatorum, portus* ([DD167], [DD58] pp156–57, [DD55] pp980–1043). Townspeople were variously designated *urbani, burgenses* (sg. *burgensis,* burgess) ([DD79] pp82–86), *cives* (sg. *civis,* citizen). The town assembly, which was the fundamental institution of early urban government, was known as the *publica concio, parlamentum,* or *arengo/arenga.* By the thirteenth century, a *consilium* or *capitulum* (council) tended to replace but not necessarily to eliminate the assembly in many towns. The urban council was staffed with aldermen (*aldermanni*) in England and Germany; *consules* (consuls) in Italy, southern France, and parts of Germany ([DD35] v3:570–71); *pares* (peers) and *jurati* (sworn men, French *jurés*) in France; *scabini* (*échevins*) in the Low Countries and northern France ([DD35] v4:378–79); *boni homines* (good men) and *probi homines* (honorable men) throughout Western Europe. Many Italian towns replaced their consuls as executive heads of the commune with a single officer, the *potestas* (Italian *podestà*) ([DD35] v9:711–12), while in England and France the *maior* (mayor, pl. *maiores*) headed the council as the chief municipal official ([DD35] v8:234–35). To varying degrees, guilds (sg. *societas, collegium, universitas, corporatio, gilda*) were integrated within the system of civic government.

Towns had law courts; they regulated trade and industry by controlling markets (*mercatus*) and prices, fixing and collecting tolls, inspecting weights and measures, enforcing work regulations to assure quality of goods; and they supported public health and public works ([DD35] v3:500–2). Much of this administrative activity is documented in vernacular languages which urban literate practice used extensively. In France, the oldest surviving document in Old French is a chirograph of 1204 from the Flemish city of Douai ([DD165] p41).

**II.3 Philological Developments.** European lexicographers are currently engaged in replacing, by country, the *Glossarium ad scriptores mediae et infimae latinitatis,* published in 1678 by Charles Du Fresne, Sieur Du Cange, and supplemented and corrected by others in the eighteenth, nineteenth, and twentieth centuries (see [CD15–16]). This endeavor has thus far produced several national dictionaries of Medieval Latin, most still incomplete, but has also inspired a flurry of debates on lexicographic methodology (see the essays assembled in *LLM,* pp455–89). In his *Epistolae morales* (3.253), Seneca complained that the teacher of literature was now less a philosopher than a philologist or grammarian ([DD42] p236). Having been subsequently and widely attacked as "deadening pedantry" throughout Western culture, philology now presents two faces. On the one hand, it continues its traditional focus on individual lexical and grammatical elements and produces dictionaries which, though indispensable, are more enabling than interpretive ([DD43] pp417, 419–20). On the other hand, a "new philology" is being advocated, one that upon this traditional foundation seeks to analyze the organization of discourse and the interaction of language with the social and cultural circumstances of its production and operation [DD44].

Lexicographers, medieval or modern, differ among themselves about the etymology of certain Medieval Latin words. The controversial origin of *foresta* (see II.1) is a relatively simple case when compared with the wide-ranging speculations surrounding the origins of the word *feodum* (see II.3.d) ([DD79] pp41–55). These instances illustrate the range of conjectural possibilities affecting the origin, development, and meaning of medieval words. Similarly, the philological derivations discussed below are presented for their illustrative value rather than as examples for which undisputed linguistic certitude may be claimed.

**II.3.a Unchanged Borrowings.** In considering words borrowed unchanged from Classical Latin, an analysis of the term *mandatum,* for example, seems to indicate that it retained its classical meaning. In the vocabulary of ancient Rome's public law, *mandatum* designated an imperial directive to administrative agents, a denotation that was retained throughout the Middle Ages with the same technical specificity of an order of the ruling administration to its own agents ([DD37] pp 156–58). The medieval term *fiscus* also preserved from classical times onward its sense of public revenues, whether imperial, royal, or seigniorial ([DD91] pp254, 281). *Calumnia,* too, often preserved in the Middle Ages its classical sense of false claim, though it also acquired additional meanings, such as a wrongful deed of violence, or a fine. Similarly, *consuetudo* retained its classical meaning of custom and customary right, though it also acquired in the tenth century the extended meaning of duties, as the notion of customary right came increasingly to pertain, in parallel with the development of the seigniory, to taxes owed to and levied by the lord. When, however, medieval scribes wrote *costuma* (French *coutume*) instead of Classical Latin *consuetudo,* they were latinizing the vernacular word *costume* (itself derived from *consuetudo*). *Drictum* presents a similar case (see II.3.c).

Medieval Latin words that retained their classical meanings remained in use continuously from the late Roman empire through the Merovingian period and thereafter.

**II.3.b Extensions or Changes of Meaning.** The persistence of classical senses did not, however, preclude an extension or change of meaning for such terms. *Auctoritas* in classical Rome had been attached to the senate and then to the emperor. Mediated by the canonical tradition, through the decretal of Pope Gelasius I (492–496), the word came to qualify papal authority in contrast to the *potestas* of secular princes. By the fifth century, the inherent content of the term had been weakened, so that *auctoritas* could refer to an order, advice, agreement, testimony, or reliable author ([DD39] pp203–4, [DD82]). Later, in the eleventh century, *auctoritas* recaptured some of its ancient Roman denotation, alluding to the government of lay magnates (*principes*) over the totality of their principalities, including the lordships therein. This was in contrast to the administrative power (*potestas*) exercised by each of these same magnates as *dominus* over his *dominium* (demesne), those lands and castles of his principality that, neither rented nor enfeoffed, he retained and governed directly. *Dominium,* ownership or property rights in Classical Latin, still conveyed this sense in Medieval Latin, although the classical legal concept of property had itself undergone complex mutations in the medieval West. *Potestas,* though also still imbued with its primary classical meaning of "power," came in Medieval Latin to designate the "real" element over which administrative power was to be exercised, that is, the district of a public officer in Carolingian times and the lordship that emerged after the collapse of Carolingian rule.

Even where words lost their original classical meanings a semantic connection might still be perceived. *Rotulus,* a (small) wheel in Classical Latin, came to mean in the eighth-century papal chancery a papyrus or parchment roll. It was not until the twelfth century that *rotulus* in England came into vogue as the normative word to designate records in roll format, and the word seems specifically to have been brought into this general use by the publication of Fitz Neal's *Dialogus de Scaccario* ([DD53] p136). *Quietus,* "quiet, at rest," in Classical Latin, gave way to the medieval form *quit(t)us* and to the following meanings: (of a dispute) closed, (of ownership) uncontested, (of a claim) renounced, and enfranchised. Bellum, "war" in Classical Latin, could also denote trial by battle, although the classical biform *duellum* came to be preferred in this judicial sense.

**II.3.c Adaptations.** The creativity of medieval administrative Latin was not restricted to semantics. Latin neologisms were generated from Classical and Late Latin either directly or through vernacular words derived from Latin, or from non-Latin vernacular roots (see II.3.d). Many latinate formations, in addition to such Late Latin developments as *exactare* (< *exactio:* tax, tribute), "to collect," belong to the Carolingian period (eighth century), e.g. *camerarius* (< *camera*), "household officer, keeper of the dressing room, treasurer, chamberlain," and to the twelfth century, when a new influx of latinate formations deal (1) with lordly rights: *fugacio* (< *fugare,* "to cause to flee, to drive away" in Classical Latin, "to hunt" in Medieval Latin), hunting right; (2) with law: *assisa* (< *assidere:* to sit, to sit as a judge), a session, a session of the king's court, a royal edict; (3) with tax: *carrucagium* (< *carruca:* a "wheeled plow" in Medieval Latin, a "traveling-carriage" in Classical Latin; < *carrus,* a Classical Latin form of Gallic origin meaning "cart, wagon"), a tax based on the *carrucate*; *scutagium* (< *scutum:* shield), commutation of the knight service into a payment of money; *tallia* (< *talea:* a cutting, rod, stick), a lordly tax, tallage; and (4) with management: *mandamentum* (< *mandatum:* mandate, imperial order), injunction, public coercive power, district subject to public power; *terrarium* (< *terra:* earth), book of land; *baiulus* or *baillivus:* bailiff. *Baiulus,* "porter, carrier" in Classical Latin, "letter-carrier, bearer at a funeral, preceptor, tutor" in Late Latin, and "royal or princely officer" (bailiff) in Medieval Latin, is a classical form with extended and changed meanings. The Medieval Latin word *baillivus* was created from the vernacular Old French *bailli(f)* (? < *baiulivus*). *Drictum* (law, right, title) is a vernacular formation from such Old French constructs as *\*drect, dreit,* and *droit,* themselves derived from Classical Latin *directum* (straight line) ([DD46] p256). Like *costuma* (see II.3.a), *baillivus* and *drictum* are Latin re-creations from vernacular forms that themselves derived from classical words.

A complex linguistic process underlies the formation of the word *registrum* (register). In Classical Latin *regestum,* meaning "(soil) thrown back or up," was formed from *regero* (to carry, throw back, make a collection of). In Late Latin the neuter substantive *regesta* (genitive *regestorum*) signified "list, catalogue, register." Into the Medieval Latin form *regestum*, meaning, among others things, a roll kept by an imperial government, an *r* was interpolated (> *regestrum*) by analogy with other Latin substantives (e.g. *magistrum*). The imperial connotation of the meaning may have come from an imaginative association with *rex, regis* (king) and *regere* (to rule, to regulate).

**II.3.d Latinized Vernacular Forms.** The pressures of vernacular languages and of new forms of society for which Latin vocabulary was, or was perceived to be, deficient contributed to the expansion of Medieval Latin terminology by word formations using Germanic roots and organizational concepts. These developed on the continent primarily during the Merovingian and Carolingian periods: *bannus* (< *bann*: proclamation commanding or forbidding, under threat or penalty), an order issued by a public authority, a king's higher jurisdiction, the district of a judicial officer invested with delegated ruling power, or an unrestricted territorial authority; *mallus* (< *mall*: meeting, meeting place), judicial assembly, regular shiremoot; *marchio* (< *mark*: boundary), margrave, marquis; *namium* (< *nehmen*: to take), goods seized; *scabinus* (< *scefenn*: assistant to a judge), a landholder of some local importance, officially appointed to serve as judgment-finder in courts of law. *Fevum* (< Frankish *\*fehu*: property, wealth), from which developed *feodum* (fief), has been the subject of other etymological theories which have not achieved consensus. Two such hypotheses involve Classical Latin roots, *foedus* (agreement, treaty, alliance) or *fiscus* (public revenues); an alternate Germanic origin, based upon *faw* (few) + *ôd* (scant or imperfect possession) ([DD79] p41, [DD100] pp108–9), has been suggested.

In medieval England from the Anglo-Norman period onward a substantial proportion of administrative terms consisted of latinized English words, perhaps reflecting lesser influence from Rome and from the Latin Renaissance of the eleventh and twelfth centuries, and testifying to the administrative and linguistic dynamism of the preceding Anglo-Saxon culture, the only culture of its time to have left a significant legacy of texts in the vernacular. *Danegeldum*, a tax, was directly latinized from Anglo-Saxon *denegeld*, and so were *lottum*, share of taxation (from *lot*: share); *soc(n)a*, a privilege granted by the king, or the area within which that franchise was exercised (from *soken*: right of local jurisdiction) ([DD35] v10:601–2); *scira*, shire (from *scira*: official charge); and *hundredum*, the hundred (from *hundred*). Both *scira* and *hundredum* also have Medieval Latin equivalents derived from classical words, *comitatus* and *centenarius*. *Lestagium*, a tax exacted on a ship's lading, entered Medieval Latin from Old English *last*, a load weight, and from the Latin form came the French *lestage*, weight to balance a ship. The Medieval Latin word *firma*, a farmed office or other source of revenue, was formed from Anglo-Saxon *feorm* (meal, payment in kind), but its semantic development was also influenced by such Classical Latin words as *firmus* and *firmare*.

The interaction between vernacular languages and Latin forms therefore took place at three levels: (1) vernacular words were made to behave like Latin words (and assigned to declensions and conjugations); (2) the sense of such latinized words might be influenced by homologous Classical Latin terms; (3) Medieval Latin words were formed from classical roots as synonyms for the latinized vernacular forms ([DD46] pp255–61). Clerics seem to have resisted the introduction of the vernacular into the Latin of administrative texts, preferring, for instance, the term *beneficium* to the Germanic *feodum* (see previous discussion) to designate a fief well into the twelfth century ([DD38] pp180–88, [DD46] pp257–58). For reasons that include the archaizing attitudes of court clerics, the administrative sophistication of classical Rome, and the resilience and flexibility of Latin as revived by the Carolingian and twelfth-century Renaissances, the vocabulary of medieval administration consists chiefly of a Classical Latin, or Latin-derived, terminology. A notable feature of administrative Medieval Latin is the semantic extension of this lexicon, from the abstract to the concrete, as exemplified by words like *potestas, mandamentum, bannus, so(c)na,* which at first referred to expressions of authority but came later to denote the land over which such authority was exercised.

**II.3.e Words of Foreign and Non-local Vernacular Origin.** The number of words that entered Medieval Latin from languages other than local vernaculars is relatively small. From the Arabic came, for instance, the name of a medieval Spanish coin, the *morabetinus,* "morabetin, maravedi" ([DD13] p430; index, s.v. *mor(a)betinus-i*). From Persian *shah,* "king," was formed the Medieval Latin word *scaccum,* "game of chess," the board of which was also used for counting money and hence gave the word *scaccarium,* the source of the word Exchequer ([DD21] pp6–7). The Greek title *basileus* was simply transcribed in Latin letters and used to designate some Western rulers (see II.2.a). The Greek word *telôn-,* tax, gave Medieval Latin *teloneum,* a toll on goods during transport and sale. The words *vassus* and *vassalus* were formed from Celtic to designate a vassal, that is, a free man who commended himself to a lord ([DD79] pp115–19).

**II.3.f Syntactical and Orthographical Developments.** With respect to syntactical and orthographical tendencies, the Medieval Latin of lay administration shares the peculiarities of the language in general throughout the postclassical period. Those features of syntax and spelling which characterize Medieval Latin are outlined in chapters CC and CB. They should be carefully distinguished from the casual and/or ignorant use of the language, which could produce errors of grammar, concord, and spelling found also in Latin administrative texts. In royal chanceries, senior clerks checked documents for accuracy with respect to form (*ratio*), script (*littera*), wording (*dictio*), and orthography (*silliba*) ([DD53] pp101–2). Still, linguistic divergences and blunders were not uncommon and reflect the training and education received by individual scribes ([DD60] pp434–64).

The characteristics and innovations specific to the Medieval Latin of secular administration reveal the extent of its ability to forge, from classical antecedents and an interplay with contemporary vernaculars, a specialized medium with a particular vocabulary by which to articulate the means and meaning of the evolving lay administrative operations of the Middle Ages.

## Select Bibliography

Lexical studies that focus on the vocabulary of lay medieval administration are here complemented by a select series of specific articles and monographs, each of which presents an analysis of medieval socioadministrative processes, contains a rich lexicon of Latin terms and a discussion of their historical and philological significance, and appends bibliographical references concerning particular institutions of secular administration. These latter, together with the general bibliographical guides cited at the beginning of this bibliography, may be consulted for additional relevant citations. The guides are followed by a select list of printed primary sources, and of entries and titles from the *TSMAO* and *DMA*. Next are works on philology, Medieval Latin, and diplomatics. Finally come essays addressing specific terms and issues of vocabulary, and several general studies listed institutionally and geographically.

A comprehensive array of sources for the Latin of lay administration, and of monographs dealing with secular government, may be found in R.C. Van Caenegem and F.L. Ganshof, *GSMH* [**DD1**]; E.B. Graves, *A Bibliography of English History to 1485* (1975) [**DD2**]; L.J. Paetow, *A Guide to the Study of Medieval History*, rev. ed. (1931, r1980 with errata and addendum) [**DD3**]; W. Baumgart, *Bücherverzeichnis zur deutschen Geschichte: Hilfsmittel, Handbücher, Quellen*, 7th ed. (1988) [**DD4**].

The *Monumenta Germaniae Historica* contain editions of early Germanic law codes, including the *Leges Visigothorum*, ed. K. Zeumer, *MGH.Leges nationum Germanicarum* (1902, r1973) [**DD5**], and of Frankish administrative texts: *Marculfi formulae*, ed. K. Zeumer, *MGH.Formulae Merowingici et Karolini aevi* (1882–86, r1963) 32–112 [**DD6**]; *Capitularia regum Francorum*, ed. A. Boretius and V. Krause, *MGH.Capitularia regum Francorum*, 2 vols. (1883–97, r1984) [**DD7**]. A collection of imperial documents has been edited by J.L.A. Huillard-Bréholles, *Historia diplomatica Friderici Secundi . . .*, 6 vols. in 12 (1852–61, r1963–66) [**DD8**]; this includes (v4.1:1–178) the *Liber Augustalis*, of which there is an English translation by J.M. Powell (1971) [**DD9**]. Royal and lordly charters are found in *Recueil des actes des ducs de Normandie de 911 à 1066*, ed. M. Fauroux (1961) [**DD10**]; *Layettes du Trésor des chartes*, ed. A. Teulet *et al.*, 5 vols. (1863–1909, r1977) [**DD11**]. An interesting example of a lordly survey of fiefs and manorial rights is the *Codex Falkensteinensis: Die Rechtsaufzeichnungen der Grafen von Falkenstein*, ed. E. Noichl, Quellen und Erörterungen zur bayerischen Geschichte, n.s., 29 (1978) [**DD12**]. The fiscal accounts and related documents of Catalonia are available in a splendid edition, preceded by an analytical introductory volume, by T.N. Bisson: *Fiscal Accounts of Catalonia under the Early Count-Kings (1151–1213)*, 2 vols. (1984) [**DD13**]. Handbooks of charters, feudal surveys, and other information pertinent to the English Exchequer and compiled in the first part of the thirteenth century are the *Liber niger Scaccarii*, ed. T. Hearne, 2nd ed., 2 vols. (Oxford 1771) [**DD14**], and *The Red Book of the Exchequer*, ed. H. Hall, 3 vols., *RSer* 99 (1896) [**DD15**]. Chronicles documenting lay administration include Dudo of St. Quentin, *De moribus et actis primorum Normanniae ducum*, ed. J. Lair (1865) [**DD16**]; Guillaume Le Breton, *Gesta Philippi Augusti*, in *Oeuvres de Rigord et de Guillaume le Breton, historiens de Philippe-Auguste*, ed. H.-F. Delaborde, v1 (1882) 168–333 [**DD17**], and *id.*, *Philippidos, ibid.*, v2 (1885) [**DD18**]; Benedict of Peterborough, *Gesta regis Henrici secundi*, ed. W. Stubbs, 2 vols., *RSer* 49 (1867) [**DD19**]; Otto of Freising (and

Rahewin), *Gesta Frederici*, ed. F.-J. Schmale, 2nd ed. (1974); tr. C.C. Mierow (1953, r1966) [**DD20**]. Treatises dealing with the theory and practice of medieval politics and governance include Richard Fitz Neal (or Fitz Nigel), *Dialogus de Scaccario: The Course of the Exchequer*, and *Constitutio Domus Regis: The Establishment of the Royal Household*, ed. and tr. C. Johnson, with corrections by F.E.L. Carter and D.E. Greenway (1983) [**DD21**]; John of Salisbury, *Poli.* [**DD22**]; Gerald of Wales, *De principis instructione liber*, ed. G.F. Warner, *RSer* 21.8 (1891) [**DD23**]. Famous English treatises on estate management are superbly introduced and edited by D. Oschinsky, *Walter of Henley and Other Treatises on Estate Management and Accounting* (1971) [**DD24**], and are also available in H.G. Richardson and G.O. Sayles, eds. and trs., *Fleta*, v2, *SelSoc* 72 (1955) [**DD25**]; tr. F.H. Cripps-Day, *The Manor Farm* (1931) [**DD26**].

Good discussions of the nature, form, and content of various administrative documents, and of the relevant literature, are to be found in various volumes of the series *Typologie des sources du moyen âge occidental* [*TSMAO*], whose general *Introduction* (1972), by editor in chief L. Genicot, describes the thematic and conceptual framework of the project [**DD27**]; the *Table des fascicules— Table of Fascicles— Register der Faszikel 1–50* (1992), also by L. Genicot, provides in French, English, and German a thematic and typological index of the sources discussed in the first 50 fascicles [**DD28**]. Among the volumes of most immediate interest are M.-A. Arnould, *Les relevés de feux*, *TSMAO* 18 (1976) and updating (1985) [**DD29**]; G. Despy, *Les tarifs de tonlieux*, *TSMAO* 19 (1976) [**DD30**]; R. Fossier, *Polyptiques et censiers*, *TSMAO* 28 (1978) [**DD31**]; L. Génicot, *Les actes publics*, *TSMAO* 3 (1972) and updating (1985) [**DD32**]; M. Pastoureau, *Les sceaux*, *TSMAO* 36 (1981) [**DD33**]; G. Van Dievoet, *Les coutumiers, les styles, les formulaires et les "artes notariae,"* *TSMAO* 48 (1986) [**DD34**].

Many entries in the *Dictionary of the Middle Ages* [*DMA*] provide useful introductions to, and recent bibliographies for, secular administrative matters. On *political theory*, see "Germany: Idea of Empire." On *administrative documents and sources for the vocabulary of lay administration*, see "Domesday Book"; "Melfi, Constitutions of"; "Mirror of Princes"; "Pipe Rolls"; "Polyptych (2)"; "Seals and Sigillography, Western European"; "Walter of Henley (ca. 1240-ca. 1290)." On *administrative officials* see "Bailli"; "Bailiff"; "Baro"; "Butler"; "Castellan"; "Chamberlain"; "Constable of the Realm"; "Consuls, Consulate"; "Echevin"; "Justices of Common Pleas"; "Justices of the King's Bench"; "Justices, Itinerant (in eyre)"; "Justiciar"; "Margrave, Marquis"; "Marshal"; "Mayor"; "Ministerials"; "Podesta"; "Provost"; "Reeve": "Seneschal"; "Sheriff." On *administrative territories*, see "Benefice, lay"; "Castles and Fortifications"; "Castrum"; "Commune"; "County"; "Duchy"; "Fief"; "Forests, European"; "Germany: Principalities"; "Germany: Stem Duchies"; "Hundred (land division)"; "Tenure of Land, Western European." On *administrative institutions and processes*, see "Accounting"; "Ban, Banalité"; "Cortes"; "Commendatio"; "Corvée"; "Curia, Lay"; "Estate Management"; "Exchequer"; "Feudalism"; "Household, Chamber, and Wardrobe"; "Knights and Knight Service"; "Maltote"; "Parlement of Paris"; "Parliament"; "Representative Assemblies, French"; "Representative Assemblies, German"; "Sac and Soc"; "Scutage"; "Taille, Tallage"; "Taxation, English"; "Taxation, French" [**DD35**].

An assessment of lexicographical studies in Medieval Latin is available in A.-M. Bautier, "La lexicographie du latin médiéval: Bilan international des travaux," in *LLM* 433–53 [**DD36**]. This survey includes bibliographies of lexica, glossaries, and card catalogues available and in preparation for each European country and for specific topics; it also makes clear that the Latin of medieval secular administration has so far been the object of only marginal attention. Many other essays in the volume are also relevant to the study of Medieval Latin; those specifically addressing secular administration include O. Guillot, "Le droit romain classique et la lexicographie des termes du latin médiéval impliquant délégation du pouvoir," pp153–66 [DD37]; J.-M. Poly, "Vocabulaire 'féodo-vassalique' et aires de culture durant le haut moyen âge," pp167–90 [DD38]; and J. Schneider, "Lexicographie du latin médiéval et vocabulaire des institutions," pp197–213 [DD39].

The goals and theories of the "new philology" are debated in W.J. Ong, "Orality, Literacy, and Medieval Textualization," in *New Literary History* 16 (1984–85) 1–12 [DD40]; *The Past and Future of Medieval Studies,* ed. J. Van Engen (1994) [DD41], especially L. Patterson, "The Return to Philology," pp231–34 [DD42], and J. Van Engen, "An Afterword on Medieval Studies, or the Future of Abelard and Heloise," pp401–31 [DD43]; S.G. Nichols, ed., "The New Philology," in *Speculum* 65 (1990) 1–108 [DD44].

A useful introduction to Medieval Latin as a language is that of D. Norberg, *MPLM* [DD45]. The Medieval Latin of lay administration is discussed by J.F. Niermeyer, "Remarques sur la formation du vocabulaire institutionnel médiolatin," in *ALMA* 28 (1958) 253–61 [DD46], and Schneider ([DD39]) [DD47]. Records and the modalities of their production are the only elements of lay medieval administration that to date include studies of their Latin usages: R. Falkowski, "Studien zur Sprache der Merowingerdiplome," in *Archiv für Diplomatik* 17 (1971) 1–125 [DD48]; W.-D. Lange, *Philologische Studien zur Latinität west-hispanischer Privaturkunden des 9.–12. Jahrhunderts* (1966) [DD49]; H.M. Martin, "A Brief Study of the Latinity of the *Diplomata* Issued by the Merovingian Kings," in *Speculum* 2 (1927) 258–67 and 4 (1929) 315–16 [DD50]; J. Monfrin, "Le latin médiéval et la langue des chartes," in *Vivarium* 8 (1970) 81–98 [DD51]; J. Vielliard, *Le latin des diplômes royaux et chartes privées de l'époque mérovingienne* (1927) [DD52]. The specifics of the style, morphology, syntax, and semantics of the Latin used for lay administration are more usually only incidentally broached in general works dealing with medieval administration, as, for example, in M.T. Clanchy, *From Memory to Written Record: England, 1066–1307,* 2nd ed. (1993) [DD53], or with medieval theories and practices of social organization, as in G. Duby, *The Three Orders: Feudal Society Imagined* (1980) [DD54]; R. Fossier, *Enfance de l'Europe, Xe–XIIe siècle: Aspects économiques et sociaux,* 2nd ed., 2 vols. (1989) [DD55]; P. Michaud-Quantin, *Universitas: Expressions du mouvement communautaire dans le moyen-âge latin* (1970) [DD56]; G. Post, *Studies in Medieval Legal Thought: Public Law and the State, 1100–1322* (1964) [DD57]; S. Reynolds, *Kingdoms and Communities in Western Europe, 900–1300* (1984) [DD58].

Manuals of diplomatics touch on latinity and contain bibliographies of diplomatic editions which also discuss the Latin of the edited documents within their introductions: H. Bresslau, *Handbuch der Urkundenlehre für Deutschland und Italien,* 2nd ed., 2 vols. (1912–31, r1958) and *index* (1960) [DD59]; A. Giry, *Manuel de diplomatique,* 2nd ed. (1925) [DD60]; G. Tessier, *Diplomatique royale française* (1962) [DD61]. A good bibliography of diplomatics and diplomatic sources has been assembled by L.E. Boyle, "Diplomatics," in *MSI* 82–113 [DD62]. The most recent survey of diplomatics and diplomatic literature is by O. Guyotjeannin *et al., Diplomatique médiévale,* L'atelier du médiéviste 2 (1993) [DD63]. On the Latin vocabulary of medieval diplomatics, see O. Guyotjeannin, "Le vocabulaire de la diplomatique en latin médiéval," in *CIVICIMA* 2:120–34 [DD64]. Essays on medieval chanceries include

"Kanzlei, Kanzler," in *LM* 5:910–25, with good bibliography [**DD65**], and R.-H. Bautier, "La chancellerie et les actes royaux dans les royaumes carolingiens," in *BECh* 142 (1984) 5–80 [**DD66**]. Studies of specific categories of documents exist for *placita*, of which the most recent is by W. Bergmann, "Untersuchungen zu den Gerichtsurkunden der Merowingerzeit," in *Archiv für Diplomatik* 22 (1976) 1–186 [**DD67**], and for capitularies: H. Mordek, "Karolingische Kapitularien," in *id.*, ed., *Überlieferung und Geltung normativer Texte des frühen und hohen Mittelalters* (1986) 25–50 [**DD68**]. *Placita* are further discussed in I. Wood, "Disputes in Late Fifth- and Sixth-Century Gaul," pp7–22 [**DD69**], and P. Fouracre, "'Placita' and the Settlement of Disputes in Later Merovingian Francia," pp23–43 [**DD70**], both in *The Settlement of Disputes in Early Medieval Europe*, ed. W. Davies and P. Fouracre (1986, r1992) [**DD71**]; and capitularies in R. McKitterick, *The Frankish Church and the Carolingian Reforms, 789–895* (1977) [**DD72**], and *eadem*, *The Frankish Kingdoms under the Carolingians, 751–987* (1983) [**DD73**]. For a discussion of charter production in eleventh- and twelfth-century northern France, see B. Bedos-Rezak, "Diplomatic Sources and Medieval Documentary Practices: An Essay in Interpretive Methodology," in [**DD41**] 313–43 [**DD74**].

Most studies of the Latin of medieval lay administration tend to be lexical, addressing issues of terminology: A.L. Budriesi Prombetti, "Prime ricerche sul vocabulario feudale italiano," in *Rendiconti* 62 (1973–74) 277–401 [**DD75**]; E. Rodón Binué, *El lenguaje técnico del feudalismo en el siglo XI en Cataluña: Contribución al estudio del latín medieval* (1957) [**DD76**]; J. Devisse, "Essai sur l'histoire d'une expression qui a fait fortune: *consilium* et *auxilium* au IXe siècle," in *MA* 74 (1968) 179–205 [**DD77**]; O. Guyotjeannin, "Le vocabulaire de la diplomatique en latin médiéval" ([**DD64**]) [**DD78**]; K.J. Hollyman, *Le développement du vocabulaire féodal en France pendant le haut moyen âge: Etude sémantique* (1957) [**DD79**]; I. Sassier, "L'utilisation du concept de 'res publica' en France du Nord aux Xe, XIe et XIIe siècles," in *Droits savants et pratiques françaises du pouvoir: XIe–XVe siècles*, ed. J. Krynen and A. Rigaudière (1992) 79–97 [**DD80**]; L. Genicot, "Sur la survivance de la notion d'Etat dans l'Europe du Nord au haut moyen âge: L'emploi de *publicus* dans les sources belges antérieures à l'an mil," in *Institutionen, Kultur und Gesellschaft im Mittelalter: Festschrift für Josef Fleckenstein zu seinem 65. Geburtstag*, ed. L. Fenske *et al.* (1984) 147–64 [**DD81**]; W. Hessler, "*Auctoritas* im deutschen Mittellatein: Eine Zwischenbilanz im mittellateinischen Wörterbuch," in *AKG* 47 (1965) 255–65 [**DD82**]. Many issues of *ALMA* contain notes on specific terms from the vocabulary of medieval lay administration, e.g. J. Dhondt, "Le titre de marquis à l'époque carolingienne," in v19 (1948) 407–17 [**DD83**]; W. Hessler, "Comes - 'Begleiter/Graf.' Marginalien zu dem Artikel im Mittellateinischen Wörterbuch," in v39 (1974) 121–53 [**DD84**]; C.-E. Perrin, "Sur les sens du mot 'centenna' dans les chartes lorraines du moyen âge," in v5 (1929–30) 167–98 [**DD85**]; O. Weijers, "Some Notes on 'Fides' and Related Words in Medieval Latin," in v40 (1975–76) 77–102 [**DD86**].

Further lexical insights are available in studies analyzing the modalities of lay medieval administration. On titles of royal and princely rulers, see *Intitulatio*, ed. H. Wolfram, 3 vols. (1967–88) [**DD87**].

On territorial units, see *Polity and Place: Regionalism in Medieval France*, ed. B. Bedos-Rezak, in *Historical Reflections/Reflexions historiques* 19 (1993) 152–278 [**DD88**]; this includes J.D. Adams, "The *Regnum Francie* of Suger of Saint-Denis: An Expansive Ile-de-France," pp167–88 [**DD89**], and B. Bedos-Rezak, "French Medieval Regions: A Concept in History," pp152–66 [**DD90**]; see also K.-F. Werner, "Kingdom and Principality in Twelfth-Century France," in *The Medieval Nobility: Studies on the Ruling Classes of France and Germany from the Sixth to the Twelfth Century*, ed. and tr. T. Reuter (1978) 243–290 [**DD91**]; H. Wolfram, "The Shaping of the Early Medieval Kingdom," in *Viator* 1 (1970) 1–19 [**DD92**], and *id.*, "The Shaping of the Early Medieval Principality as a Type of Non-Royal Rulership," in *Viator* 2 (1971) 33–51 [**DD93**].

On feudalism, see E.A.R. Brown, "The Tyranny of a Construct: Feudalism and Historians of Medieval Europe," in *American Historical Review* 79 (1974) 1063–88 [**DD94**]; Duby ([**DD54**]) [**DD95**]. In *Feudalism: Comparative Studies*, ed. E. Leach *et al.* (1985) [**DD96**], the following essays are of particular interest: E. Leach, "Talking About Talking About Feudalism," pp6–24 [**DD97**]; S.N. Mukherjee, "The Idea of Feudalism, from the Philosophes to Karl Marx," pp25–39 [**DD98**]; J.O. Ward, "Feudalism: Interpretive Category or Framework of Life in the Medieval West," pp40–67 [**DD99**]. See also F.L. Ganshof, *Feudalism*, 3rd English ed. (1964) [**DD100**]; Hollyman ([**DD79**]) [**DD101**]; Poly ([**DD38**]) [**DD102**]; J.-P. Poly and E. Bournazel, *The Feudal Transformation, 900–1200* (1990) [**DD103**]; J. Le Goff, "The Symbolic Ritual of Vassalage," in *Time, Work & Culture in the Middle Ages* (1980) 237–87, 354–67 [**DD104**].

On chivalry and nobility, see B. Bedos-Rezak, "The Social Implications of the Art of Chivalry: The Sigillographic Evidence (France 1050–1250)," pp1–31 (essay 8) [**DD105**], in *eadem, Form and Order in Medieval France: Studies in Social and Quantitative Sigillography* (1993) [**DD106**]; B. Bedos-Rezak, "Medieval Seals and the Structure of Chivalric Society," in *The Study of Chivalry: Resources and Approaches*, ed. H. Chickering and T.H. Seiler (1988) 313–72 [**DD107**]; J. Bumke, *The Concept of Knighthood in the Middle Ages* (1982) [**DD108**]; Duby ([**DD54**]) [**DD109**]; G. Duby, "The Origins of Knighthood," pp158–70 [**DD110**], and "The Transformation of the Aristocracy," pp178–85 [**DD111**], both in *id., The Chivalrous Society* (1977) [**DD112**]; J.B. Freed, *The Counts of Falkenstein: Noble Self-Consciousness in Twelfth-Century Germany, TAPhS* 74.6 (1984) [**DD113**].

On fiscal administration, see B. Lyon and A.E. Verhulst, *Medieval Finance: A Comparison of Financial Institutions in Northwestern Europe* (1967) [**DD114**].

On seigniorial administration and banal lordship, see G. Duby, *The Early Growth of the European Economy: Warriors and Peasants from the Seventh to the Twelfth Century* (1974, r1978) [**DD115**], and *id., Rural Economy and Country Life in the Medieval West* (1968, r1976) [**DD116**].

For the Merovingian kingdoms, see Falkowski ([**DD48**]) [**DD117**]; J. Barbier, "Le système palatial franc: genèse et fonctionnement dans le Nord-Ouest du *regnum*," in *BECh* 148 (1990) 245–99 [**DD118**]; Martin ([**DD50**]) [**DD119**]; Vielliard ([**DD52**]) [**DD120**]; I. Wood, *The Merovingian Kingdoms, 450–751* (1994) [**DD121**]. The most recent studies of *placita* are by Bautier ([**DD66**]) [**DD122**] and by Bergmann ([**DD67**]) [**DD123**]. For a historical analysis of the *placita*'s interactions with Frankish law, administration, and society, see Wood ([**DD69**]) [**DD124**] and Fouracre ([**DD70**]) [**DD125**].

For Carolingian Europe and the Frankish kingdoms, see Bautier ([**DD66**]) [**DD126**], Dhondt ([**DD83**]) [**DD127**], and Mordek ([**DD68**]) [**DD128**]. For a detailed survey of Carolingian history, see McKitterick ([**DD72**]) [**DD129**] and *eadem* ([**DD73**]) [**DD130**]. Carolingian literacy and its administrative implications are discussed in F.L. Ganshof, "The Use of the Written Word in Carolingian Administration," in *id., The Carolingians and the Frankish Monarchy: Studies in Carolingian History* (1971) 125–42

[DD131]; J. Nelson, "Dispute Settlement in Carolingian West Francia," in [DD71] pp45–64 [DD132]; R. McKitterick, *The Carolingians and the Written Word* (1989) [DD133]; R. McKitterick, ed., *The Uses of Literacy in Early Mediaeval Europe* (1990) [DD134], in which the following article addresses more particularly lay administration and its terminology: J. Nelson, "Literacy in Carolingian Government," pp258–96 [DD135]; Davies and Fouracre ([DD71]) [DD136]; K.F. Werner, "Introduction" and "Missus—Marchio—Comes: Entre l'administration centrale et l'administration locale de l'empire carolingien," in *Histoire comparée de l'administration (IVe–XVIIIe siècles): Actes du XIVe colloque historique franco-allemand, Tours, 27 mars–1er avril 1977*, ed. W. Paravicini and K.-F. Werner (1980) IX-XXIV and 191–239 [DD137]: this volume also contains several other articles on various aspects of medieval European administration and administrative terminology.

For England, see C.R. Cheney, *Hubert Walter* (1967) [DD138]; Clanchy ([DD53]) [DD139]. On royal government, see B. Bedos-Rezak, "King Enthroned, a New Theme in Anglo-Saxon Royal Iconography: The Seal of Edward the Confessor and Its Political Implications," in [DD105] 53–88 (essay 4) [DD140]; T.F. Tout, *Chapters in the Administrative History of Mediaeval England: The Wardrobe, the Chamber and the Small Seals*, 6 vols. (1920–33, r1967) [DD141]; D.W. Sutherland, *Quo Warranto Proceedings in the Reign of Edward I, 1278–1294* (1963) [DD142]. On estate management, see N. Denholm-Young, *Seignorial Administration in England* (1937, r1964) [DD143], and Oschinsky ([DD24]) [DD144]. On cities, see G. Pedrick, *Borough Seals of the Gothic Period* (1904) [DD145].

For France, see J.W. Baldwin, *Masters, Princes and Merchants: The Social Views of Peter the Chanter & His Circle*, 2 vols. (1970), in which are presented Parisian twelfth- and thirteenth-century theologians' understandings of the administrative structures of lay society [DD146]; B. Bedos-Rezak, "Medieval Women in French Sigillographic Sources," in [DD105] 2–36 (essay 10) [DD147]; L. Borrelli de Serres, *Recherches sur divers services publics du XIIIe au XVIIe siècle*, 3 vols. (1895–1909, r1974) [DD148]; Hollyman ([DD79]) [DD149]; Sassier ([DD80]) [DD150]. The studies assembled in [DD88] [DD151] address the issue of territorial vocabulary, particularly those by Adams ([DD89]) [DD152] and Bedos-Rezak ([DD90]) [DD153]. On royal government, see J.W. Baldwin, *The Government of Philip Augustus: Foundations of French Royal Power in the Middle Ages* (1986) [DD154]; B. Bedos-Rezak, "Ritual in the Royal Chancery: Text, Image, and the Representation of Kingship in Medieval French Diplomas (700–1200)," in *European Monarchy: Its Evolution and Practice from Roman Antiquity to Modern Times*, ed. H. Duchhardt *et al.* (1992) 28–40 [DD155]; E. Bournazel, *Le gouvernement capétien au XIIe siècle, 1108–1180: Structures sociales et mutations institutionnelles* (1975) [DD156]; J.-F. Lamarignier, *Le gouvernement royal aux premiers temps capétiens, 987–1108* (1965) [DD157]; F. Lot and R. Fawtier, *Histoire des institutions françaises au moyen âge*, v2: *Les institutions royales* (1958) [DD158]; A. Luchaire, *Manuel des institutions françaises: Période des capétiens directs* (1892, r1979) [DD159]. On lordly administration, see B. Bachrach, "Neo-Roman vs. Feudal: The Heuristic Value of a Construct for the Reign of Fulk Nerra, Count of the Angevins (987–1040)," in *Cithara* 30 (1990) 3–30; Bachrach concludes, in opposition to R.W. Southern's earlier opinion, that the counts of Anjou learned from and utilized the Roman past and that their government can be classified as neo-Roman rather than feudal [DD160]. See also J.F. Benton, "Written Records and the Development of Systematic Feudal Relations," in *id.*, *Culture, Power and Personality in Medieval France*, ed. T.N. Bisson (1991) 275–90 [DD161]; T. Evergates, "The Chancery Archives of the Count of Champagne: Codicology and History of the Cartulary Registers," in *Viator* 16 (1985) 159–79 [DD162]; O. Guillot, *Le comte d'Anjou et son entourage au XIe siècle,* 2 vols. (1972) [DD163]; K.-F. Werner ([DD91]) [DD164]. On cities, see B. Bedos-Rezak, "Civic Liturgies and Urban Records in Northern France, 1100–1400," in *City and Spectacle in Medieval Europe,* ed. B.A. Hanawalt and K.L. Reyerson (1994) 34–55 [DD165]; B. Bedos, *Corpus des sceaux français du moyen âge:* VI: *Les sceaux des villes* (1980) [DD166]; B. Bedos-Rezak, "Towns and Seals: Representation and Signification in Medieval France," in [DD106] 35–48 (essay 12) [DD167]. For Germany, see H. Fuhrmann, *Germany in the High Middle Ages, c. 1050–1200* (1986) [DD168]; *Mediaeval Germany, 911–1250: Essays by German Historians,* tr. G. Barraclough, 2 vols. (1938, r1979) [DD169]. On imperial government see K.J. Leyser, "Ottonian Government," in *id., Medieval Germany and Its Neighbours, 900–1250* (1982) 69–101 [DD170]. On chivalry and nobility, see J.B. Freed ([DD113]) [DD171]; B. Arnold, *Count and Bishop in Medieval Germany: A Study of Regional Power, 1100–1350* (1992) [DD172]; and *id., Princes and Territories in Medieval Germany* (1991) [DD173]. On cities, see T. Diederich, "Zum Quellenwert und Bedeutungsgehalt mittelalterlicher Städtesiegel," in *Archiv für Diplomatik* 23 (1977) 269–85 [DD174].

For Italy, see A.L. Budriesi Prombetti ([DD75]) [DD175].

For Spain, see H. Grassotti, *Las instituciones feudo-vassaláticas en León y Castilla,* 2 vols. (1969) [DD176]; Lange ([DD49]) [DD177]; Rodón Binué ([DD76]) [DD178].

*See also* [BB25], [BB39–40], [BB43], [BD43].

# DE ❖ CHARTERS, DEEDS, AND DIPLOMATICS

## BY RICHARD SHARPE

The study of charters has been known as "diplomatic" or "diplomatics" since Dom Jean Mabillon mapped out the principles in his treatise *De re diplomatica* (Paris 1681) [DE9], so called from the *diploma*, a Classical Latin term for a particular form of document, but used in Neo-Latin to refer to a wide range of charters and deeds. It is a name that demands definition, and definitions have changed over the centuries. An international committee on the subject recently defined it as "the discipline that studies the transmission, form, and production of written acts. Its aim is to examine such acts critically, to determine their authenticity, to appraise their textual quality, to extricate from formulaic language all those elements of their contents that may be exploited by the historian, to date them, and finally to edit them" [DE8].

The written acts concerned are those, usually though not necessarily of a legal or administrative character, that are composed in accordance with particular forms on which their validity depends—diplomas, charters, acts, treaties, contracts of all sorts, judicial records, rolls, cartularies, registers, and so on. The level of criticism that can be applied to any class of document depends on the degree of formality exhibited by representatives of the class; and one of the first principles of diplomatics is to establish a classification of documents based on forms. All documents issuing from the same authority in the same period and serving the same function tend to conform to a pattern; a comparison of specimens allows us to identify that pattern. It is then possible, on the one hand, to compare this "form" with those used by the same authority for other purposes, or those used for the same purpose at a different time, or indeed those used by a different authority. On this basis historians may understand the changing uses of the written word in government, administration, or law. On the other hand, the recognition of an established form provides a test for the authenticity of any individual specimen: a document purporting to be a grant of land by an Anglo-Saxon king but showing a form alien to such documents is most likely to be a forgery. The use of documents especially as evidence for rights over property gave ample reason for forgery throughout the Middle Ages; it was common to forge documents to bolster title to one's own existing property or established rights, and in such cases no material fraud was implied. Some forgeries are obvious to the eye, others only to someone trained in the techniques of diplomatics, and still others so exact in their replication of the appropriate forms that external evidence is needed if forgery is to be detected.

Paleography, the study of the handwriting of the past in order to determine when a manuscript or document was written, and, in the absence of other evidence, where, was refined in the context of diplomatic studies. There are obviously differences in the approach to studying a document preserved in its original form or as a later copy. Aspects of an original document that are external to the text include the size and character of the sheet on which the document is written, the layout and style of handwriting (in some cases the scribe may be identifiable), and the details of the authentication. This last may include the impression of a seal and the method of sealing, the marks or signatures of witnesses, and the formalities by which officials have completed the document for issuing. Some originals also preserve other details such as notes (*minutae*) made on the parchment at the time of the transaction and before the text was written, important as an insight into the business behind the document, or notes (usually on the dorse) that indicate the archival history of the document. All such details will most likely be lost in a copy. On the other hand, copies may be made at almost any point: an early copy on a single sheet may possess the appearance of an original, other single-sheet copies are recognizable as transcripts, and many documents are now preserved only through later copies made for archival purposes either by the beneficiary (for example, in a cartulary) or by the issuing authority (as in official registers or rolls). While the opportunities are different, the techniques of diplomatics can be applied in all cases.

In Western Europe during the Middle Ages the number of different forms employed was enormous, and no handbook can effectively describe the characteristic features of all of them. Some classes of document observe a strict formality, others are very loosely constructed. Some are in elaborate, even bombastic Latin, others are very simple and concise. It is impossible, therefore, to treat the language or style of charters and deeds as a unity. Nonetheless, there are common features in the manner in which such documents were constructed, and there is a historical explanation for this. The diplomatic tradition in Latin grew from two sources in the legal practice of the later Roman Empire [DE11]. One branch was derived from deeds that took the basic form of a letter, beginning with a greeting and ending with a farewell. This form proved remarkably flexible and underlies the great majority of diplomatic documents. The other branch descended from the record of public transactions, beginning with the names of those present, and the date and place at which the matter was transacted; and this form remains visible in the records of courts or synods for centuries after the end of the empire.

We may begin by illustrating how documents of the same class conform to a single form. The archives of the abbey of Hersfeld have preserved six original charters of Charles the Great (Charlemagne, Karl der Grosse), all issued between the years 775 and 782 [DE12–13]. Here (with all its Late Latin solecisms) is the text of one of them (no. 103):

| | |
|---|---|
| *Superscription* | + Carolus gratia Dei rex Francorum et Langobardorum nec non et patritius Romanorum. |
| *Preamble* | Quicquid enim ad locis sanctorum uenerabilium congruenter ab amore Dei concedimus uel confirmamus, hoc nobis ad laudem uel stabilitatem regni nostri et procerum nostrorum in Dei nomine pertinere confidimus. |

| | |
|---|---|
| *Disposition* | Idcirco donamus ad monasterio Haerulfesfelt, qui est constructus in honore beatorum Sanctorum Symonis et Tathei, ubi uir uenerabilis Lollo episcopus rector preesse uidetur, donatumque in perpetuum esse uolemus, hoc est illa decima de terraturio et silua ex fisco nostro qui uocatur Milinga super fluuium Uuisera partibus orientalis; similiter donamus ad ipso sancto loco alia decima ex alio fisco nostro qui uocatur Dannistath in pago Altgauui. |
| *Injunction* | Quicquid de territuriis et siluis in decimis ad ipsos fiscos superius nominatos aspicere uidetur, ad iam fato monasterio donauimus uel ad die presente tradedimus atque in omnibusindultum esse uolemus, ea uero ratione ut abhac die ipsa casa Dei uel uenerabilis uir Lollo episcopus et successoris sui ipsa decima de territoriis et siluis ex iam dictis fiscis nostris habeant teneant atque possedeant uel quicquid exinde facere elegerint pro oportunitate ecclesie ipsius uel stipendia monachorum ibidem consistentium liberam perfruantur arbitrii, quatenus delectit ipsa congregatione pro nos et uxore nostra etiam et prolis Domini misericordia attentius exorari. |
| *Sealing clause* | Et ut hec auctoritas firmior habeatur uel per tempora melius conseruetur, manu propria subter firmauimus et de anulo nostro sigillare iussimus. |
| *Signature* | + Signum (KAROLVS) Caroli gloriosissimi regis |
| *Recognition* | + Rado aduicem Hitherii scripsi et SS. (*Tironian notes:* Rado recognoui et subscripsi) |
| *Dating clause* | Datum III nonas Agustas anno VII regni nostri; actum Dura pallatio publico; |
| *Apprecation* | Feliciter. |

I have divided the document into sections to show its formal construction, adding at the left conventional terms for its elements. Documents, like this one, based on the letter, have three main components, the initial protocol, the text or "tenor," and the final protocol or eschatocol. The initial protocol may include an invocation (*inuocatio*), superscription (*intitulatio*), address (*inscriptio*), and words of greeting (*salutatio*). The text must include a clause stating the essential content of the act, the disposition (*dispositio*), which is generally introduced with some words of notification (*notificatio*). This may be preceded by a sententious preamble (*arenga*) and an exposition of the background to or circumstances of the act (*narratio, expositio*). Various final clauses may follow the disposition, but the injunction requiring the fulfillment of the act (*iniunctio*) is widespread. It may take the form of a prohibition against breaching the terms of the act (*prohibitio*), and a penalty real or spiritual (*sanctio*) may be imposed. A sealing clause (*corroboratio*) is a common conclusion to the text, introducing the authentication, the major element of the final protocol. This may comprise verbal elements such as signatures (*subscriptiones*), confirmation of the correctness of the document (*recognitio*), or a list of witnesses (*testes*). Other elements of the authentication are pictorial: the signatories' marks (*signa*), the royal monogram, or the papal *rota,* while the impression of a seal provides a tangible authentication. The final protocol will also usually include a dating clause (*datum*), stating when and where the act was completed, and perhaps a word of farewell (*ualedictio*) or a concluding prayer (*apprecatio*). These terms facilitate the analysis, comparison, and discussion of the formal construction of documents.

In the charter quoted the element of letter is small; the name of the author begins the document, but there are no address and no word of greeting, nor is there any valediction. The superscription identifies the author, using the royal style: Charles was always styled "king of the Franks and Romans" in this period, and many but not all of his charters add *patricius Romanorum*. He sometimes also included the words *uir inluster*, a late antique style preserved by the Merovingians, which Charles had used at the beginning of his reign before becoming king of the Lombards. Some of Charles's royal charters also included an address; thus the earliest of the Hersfeld charters, in which Charles confirms the foundation and takes it under his protection, begins with the solemn address: "Carolus gratia Dei rex Francorum et Langobardorum uir inluster omnibus episcopis abbatibus ducibus comitibus nostris Franciae Langobardiae" (no. 89). Another has the simple general address: "Carolus gratia Dei rex Francorum et Langobardorum ac patricius Romanorum omnibus fidelibus nostris tam presentibus quam et futuris" (no. 121). The document quoted represents the most common style, but variations were permitted.

The preamble was highly conventional. In most of the surviving documents the king granted property or privileges to churches, and most of these have a preamble reflecting on the benefits of generosity to the Church. The preamble here may be compared with others in this series: "Quicquid enim locis uenerabilibus ob amore Domini et oportunitate seruorum Dei beniuola deliberatione concedimus, hoc nobis ad aeternam beatitudinem uel remedium animae nostrae pertinere confidimus" (no. 104); "Quicquid enim locis uenerabilibus ob amore Domini et oportunitate seruorum Dei beniuola deliberatione concedimus, hoc nobis ad mercedis augmentum uel stabilitatem regni nostri in Dei nomine pertinere confidimus" (no. 121); "Quicquid enim locis uenerabilibus ob amorem Domini et oportunitate seruorum Dei beniuola deliberatione concedimus, hoc nobis procul dubio ad aeternam beatitudinem pertineri confidimus" (no. 144). This is a formula, appropriate to the character of the act, used with similar small variations in many of Charles's royal charters. Acts of a different character might have a different preamble, some similarly formulaic, reflecting, for example, on the benefits of clemency. A quite different form of preamble was used in the first charter of immunity (no. 89), where, instead of pious sentiments, we have a "narration," describing the foundation and other circumstances in which the act is issued.

The main part or "tenor" of the document, dealing with particulars, is inevitably less formulaic, though there will often be marked similarities between the wording of different documents. The disposition states precisely what benefit the king grants, the injunction commonly defines in some way the terms of the grant. The verb in the disposition is always indicative and usually a verb of giving or granting; the injunction expresses not a fact but the king's will, with a verb of command followed by a clause in the subjunctive. While dispositions vary greatly in wording, injunctions often bear a family resemblance to one another, recombining favored phrases in a varied style.

The close of the document is as formal as the opening. A corroboration or sealing clause secures the transaction and introduces the authentication. The king has signed the document by forming a monogram of the letters of his name, KAROLVS. Around this the scribe has added the formula of the royal signature, followed by his own recognition, indicating that the document has been read through and verified before it is subscribed. The formula *scripsi et subscripsi* was stylized, the last word being written simply as lines of double *Ss* in a domed shape, known in French as a *ruche* (from Latin *rusca,* "beehive"); inside the *ruche* and to the right of it, the scribe has added, in a form of shorthand known as Tironian notes, a further statement of recognition. To the right of this, the king's seal is fixed to the face of the document. Finally, there is a dating clause, stating the time when the document was completed and issued (*datum*) to the beneficiary and the place where the act was transacted (*actum*). The word *date* in the modern usage derives from this formula, and documents may be known as *acta,* "acts," or *facta,* "deeds," from the use of these words in the dating clause.

It is a straightforward and worthwhile exercise to compare the full texts of these six charters for Hersfeld, but it is important also to observe that the same construction and the same formulae are found in many others of Charles's royal charters. The consistent style of drafting and the official character of the authentication, by the king's chancellor or his deputy, show that these documents were produced by a staff of officials working for and with the king. It is no less instructive to compare these documents issued by Charles as king with those issued after the imperial coronation at Christmas 800. I have chosen an example (no. 203, from Prüm) with a preamble similar to those we have already examined:

| | |
|---|---|
| *Invocation* | + In nomine Patris et Filii et Spiritus Sancti. |
| *Superscription* | Karolus serenissimus augustus a Deo coronatus magnus pacificus imperator Romanum gubernans imperium, qui et per misericordiam Dei rex Francorum et Langobardorum. |
| *Preamble* | Quicquid igitur locis uenerabilibus ob amorem Domini nostri Iesu Christi cedimus uel condonamus, hoc nobis procul dubio ad mercedis augmentum seu stabilitatem imperii nostri pertinere confidimus. |
| *Notification* | Igitur notum sit omnibus fidelibus nostris presentibus et futuris |
| *Disposition* | qualiter donamus ad monasterium sancti Saluatoris. . . . |
| *Injunction* | Propterea praesentem auctoritatem nostram fieri iussimus, per quam specialiter decernimus et iubemus ut. . . . |
| *Sealing clause* | Et ut haec auctoritas firmior habeatur et diuturnis temporibus melius conseruetur, manus nostrae signaculis subter eam roborare decreuimus et de anulo nostro sigillare iussimus. |
| *Signature* | Signum (KAROLVS) Karoli serenissimi imperatoris |
| *Recognition* | Amalbertus adinuicem Ercambaldi scripsi |
| *Dating clause* | Data XIII kal. febr. anno VI Christo propitio imperii nostri et XXXVIII regni nostri in Frantia et XXXIII in Italia, indictione XIIII; actum Teodeneuilla palatio nostro; |
| *Apprecation* | In Dei nomine. Feliciter. Amen. |

The regnal style has been replaced with an imperial style, appropriate to Charles's new dignity. The superscription is now preceded, not only by the sign of the cross, but also by a verbal invocation, emphasizing the solemnity of the act. The royal style last appears in an act of March 801 (no. 196), and the new imperial style is first seen in May 801 (no. 197), both acts being subscribed by Genesius as deputy to the chancellor Erchenbald. Not one of Charles's authentic royal acts has an invocation. It is evident, therefore, that an act of Charles as king that begins in this way must be treated with suspicion. In later copies, it is possible that the copyist, familiar with imperial charters, added an invocation (no. 158) or even replaced the royal style with the imperial style (no. 175). Nonetheless most such examples must be regarded as not authentic documents issued by Charlemagne. The other verbal changes in the new style are minor. "King" has been replaced by "emperor" throughout; the dating clause has become more elaborate, now including the Roman imperial indiction; and so has the apprecation or concluding prayer.

There is also a conspicuous change in the linguistic character of the text. Charles's charters of the 770s and 780s are full of linguistic solecisms, characteristic of Late Latin; these include orthographic variations, such as the use of *e* for *i* (*confidemus* for the present tense, not the future), and an indifference to the grammatical use of cases (*ad ipso sancto loco* for *ipsi sancto loco*). The charters of the 790s and especially those from 801 onwards are grammatically correct. It is well known that Charles summoned Alcuin from York to Aachen to reform the palace school and the royal chapel. The charters were written by Alcuin's first pupils, and there is a sense in which a study of the corpus of these documents reveals precisely the transition from Late Latin, the written form of Latin speech, to Medieval Latin, reformed to the biblical standard that Alcuin had learned in Northumbria, unimpaired by the influence of the spoken language.

We have here compared several of Charles's royal charters from the late eighth century, and then compared these with one of his imperial charters from the beginning of the ninth century. By this means the characteristics of the form are established and their development understood. That done, the historian may safely consider the explicit import of the documents whether from the point of view of the ruler or the beneficiary. The diplomatic detail in itself serves as important evidence for how the ruler governed and what sort of bureaucracy was available to him. It is also possible to take a long-term view of the diplomatic: these Carolingian charters have their place in a recognizable diplomatic tradition that stretches back to the Merovingians and has left a legacy in the diplomatic styles of the Capetian kings of France and the Ottonian and later emperors. Within the context of understanding that tradition, deliberate changes of style or form may be identified and explained.

Turning away from the charters of the Carolingian rulers, we can make comparisons at several levels. The *ruche* in these documents was carefully drawn and provided a matrix for the subscribing official to add particulars in Tironian shorthand. By the second half of the ninth century it had lost this logic and become simply an adjunct, at times almost a pictorial adjunct, to the subscription. In this sense it was imitated outside the chancery, and one finds examples of documents subscribed by various witnesses, each adding an ill-drawn *ruche* to his subscription. In this way a formal element spreads outwards and downwards from the documents of the ruler, marking the influence of a particular diplomatic tradition.

There were other rulers whose documents belonged to a quite different tradition. For example, the diplomatic tradition of the charters issued by Anglo-Saxon kings has a continuity and coherence from the seventh century to the eleventh; developments within that form can be discerned and related to the circumstances that gave rise to them, for it was a tradition no less dynamic than Frankish royal diplomatic. Although both traditions have elements in common, reflecting the wider unity of the post-Roman tradition in the West, there are so many differences in the style of writing, formal construction, means of authentication, and so on, that the separateness of the two traditions is unmistakable. The differences between them reveal differences in the structure of government in the two realms. Both traditions stand in stark contrast to another strong diplomatic tradition, that of the papacy, which at this date still used papyrus rather than parchment as the material for its documents. Although there were some subtle cross-currents between the traditions—for example, dating by the Roman imperial indiction was preserved in the West by the papacy and spread from there to Anglo-Saxon kings and the Carolingian imperial chancery—the differences were obvious at a glance. Documents issued by popes carried lead seals in the Byzantine tradition attached by cords of hemp or silk; Frankish kings and emperors sealed their charters with a cake of warm wax placed over a cross-shaped cut on the face of the documents, into which the royal seal was impressed; and Anglo-Saxon kings did not seal their diplomas at all. By the beginning of the tenth century Anglo-Saxon kings used seals, though we do not find them attached to documents until the eleventh century. Then, for the first time in Europe, we see a double-sided wax seal impressed on a tongue of parchment made by cutting partway across the document itself. The documents on which the seal was used were not the traditional diplomas but concise, vernacular writs, carrying instructions from the king to his courts in the shires. This new form, and the new method of sealing, influenced the diplomatic traditions of France, Germany, and Scandinavia through the late eleventh and twelfth centuries. What fostered that influence was the recognition that, as government came to use the written word to a greater extent than in the previous century or more, the writ served a useful executive and administrative purpose that the solemn charter or diploma did not.

The same chancery might produce a range of documents that can be classified into a hierarchy of forms. So, for example, by the beginning of the thirteenth century an English king could issue charters, letters patent, letters close, and a variety of administrative and judicial writs. Each class of document had its own regular forms suited to the business for which it was used. These are evident in the protocol as much as in the tenor of the documents. They have in common the same royal style; for most of Henry III's reign this is "H. Dei gratia Rex Anglie, Dominus Hybernie, Dux Normannie at Aquitannie, Comes Andegauie. . . ." The address then reflects the different weight and purpose of the different forms. A charter was addressed ". . . archiepiscopis episcopis abbatibus prioribus comitibus baronibus iusticiis uicecomitibus prepositis ministris et omnibus balliuis suis Salutem," a formulation that had developed by stages over the previous hundred years. It conveyed a grant or privilege of importance, was attested by several witnesses at court, and included the words *data per manum* . . . in the dating clause. Letters patent were used for lesser privileges but were still addressed "to whom it may concern": ". . . omnibus ad quos presentes littere peruenerint salutem." These two styles of general address have antecedents in the Continental tradition going back to the charters of Charles the Great already cited (nos. 89, 121). Letters patent were sealed before folding and tying, so that the seal did not need to be broken before the letters could be unfolded and read, and there is a specific sealing clause to this effect: "In cuius rei testimonium has litteras nostras patentes fieri fecimus." For these lesser acts the king is his own witness, *Teste me ipso.* Letters close and writs were addressed to specific officials or individuals, usually conveying instructions, with the king as witness, and they were sealed "close" after folding. The development of these separate forms, in response to differing needs and in accordance with a perceived difference in the dignity of different acts, can be traced through the twelfth century and onwards. The fees charged by the chancery to the beneficiary differed according to the form of document issued. Each form increasingly developed fixed conventions. For many purposes writs in standard form were issued, sometimes in great numbers, and in these cases the enrollment did not need to copy the document but could refer, for example, to letters *de simplici protectione,* identifying a familiar fixed form. The levels in the hierarchy of forms increased in the later Middle Ages, as the bureaucracy grew and became more complex. Different forms of royal acts might be authorized under the king's sign manual, his signet, his privy seal, the seal of the Exchequer, the duplicate seal used for judicial writs, and the great seal itself. The history of administration as a key aspect of government is written in the forms of documents by which it was carried on.

The range of diplomatic documents, however, extends far beyond the diverse products of papal, imperial, or royal chanceries. Royal acts, whether solemn charters or instructions to officials, carry public authority. When the king grants an estate to the Church or to a subject, the act is different from a mere conveyance of property; the grant may carry with it privileges exempting the property from certain royal rights, whether of taxation or jurisdiction. It was normal practice for a subject to seek to reconfirm such privileges by royal charter, even when they had already been held for many years. Through the late eleventh and twelfth centuries, the king was asked to confirm rights every time they passed to an heir; when there was a new king, he required that those holding privileges have them confirmed, charging a fine for the confirmation. Grants by nobles might be made in a form close to that of royal grants, but nobles did not have the power to convey rights that were the royal prerogative. Where a great man did give land to the Church or to one of his men, the grant was often confirmed by the sovereign. So, the majority of William the Bastard's acts as duke of Normandy before 1066 were in fact grants made by his chief men, which the duke confirmed by his subscription. An ordinary conveyance, on the other hand, carries no such implications of privilege. It needs only to make clear who conveys what to whom on what terms and that the person conveying the property could legally do so. A private deed is a legal document, and in most cases these were carefully drafted according to recognized norms. There is no chancery involved here, so that the norms are not determined within a bureaucratic framework. Different forms might be equally acceptable, and the forms were learned as part of a legal training. In the early Middle Ages those forms tended to be looser than they were at a later date, and there existed formularies to serve as a guide to the usual forms. Through much of Europe in the later Middle Ages that training was confirmed by a formal authorization to practice as a notary, though in medieval England most private deeds were drawn up by unofficial clerks.

The contrast between public and private diplomatic is a real one with practical implications, but there are gray areas. Royal charters were not always drawn up by chancery officials but sometimes by an unofficial clerk, perhaps acting for the beneficiary, and in such a case the document might deviate from the correct form. The act is still a public act but its diplomatic criticism might have to be tempered by private considerations. A great noble, on the other hand, may participate in private actions but use a documentary form that imitates a public one. Sometimes the boundary can be indeterminate, for example, in charters issued by Prince John as count of Mortain that have the same form as those of his brother, King Richard I.

The acts of corporate bodies, such as religious houses or boroughs, are in these terms private.

The language of different forms of documents depends very much on the aspirations of the authority issuing them or the skills of the clerks drafting them. In the early tenth century Anglo-Saxon royal diplomas developed an elaborate style, which was seen as enhancing the solemnity of the document. What often seems to be verbiage was nevertheless governed by formulae, and we can trace wordy, pious, and conventional formulae through the preambles of many diplomas of the period. Similarly, ecclesiastical acts in the twelfth century have pious preambles, known as *arengae,* and the same preamble might be used in more than one document, or phrases might be recombined with greater or lesser variation, as we saw in the charters of Charles the Great.

The papal chancery laid down very strict rules for the drafting of the pope's letters that extended far beyond questions of forms suited to different purposes. The use of the rhythmic cursus, for example, was adhered to in all papal acts for two hundred years (see ch. CF). Popes addressed fellow bishops as *frater* but all others, kings, princes, or subjects, as *filius,* and the pope never used the honorific plural of any individual other than himself. Pope Innocent III sets these principles out in a letter of 1200 to a bishop who had been deceived by false letters purporting to come from the pope:

> Nos uero literas que tibi sub nostro nomine presentate fuerunt diligentius intuentes in eis tam in continentia quam in dictamine manifeste deprehendimus falsitatem. Ac in hoc fuimus non modicum admirati, quia tu tales literas a nobis credideras emanasse, quum presertim scire debeas apostolicam sedem consuetudinem in suis literis hanc tenere, ut uniuersos patriarchas, archiepiscopos, et episcopos "fratres," ceteros autem, siue reges sint siue principes uel alios homines cuiuscunque ordinis "filios" in nostris literis appellemus. Et quum uni tantum persone nostre litere diriguntur, nunquam ei loquimur in plurali, ut "uos" siue "uester" et his similia in ipsis literis apponamus. In falsis autem literis tibi presentatis in salutatione "dilectus in Christo filius" uocabaris, quum in omnibus literis quas aliquando tibi transmisimus te uidere potueris a nobis "fratrem uenerabilem" appellatum. [DF41] v2:820

Rules of this kind, though they might serve as a check on authenticity, were not primarily designed for that purpose. Consistency of style and form was something to which chanceries have generally aspired, since it enabled subjects to recognize an official document and it inspired the respect due to the authority embodied in such public acts. The achievement of consistency is a sign of a well-regulated writing office, but that consistency could easily open the door to imitation. Other aspects of the document were the guarantees of authenticity, and in another letter Innocent III sets out how to test the authenticity of an apparently genuine papal letter.

The identification of forgeries is one of the aims of diplomatic criticism, though individual cases of forgery in the Middle Ages may have as much historical interest as authentic documents. Another aim is to understand the legal and administrative significance implicit in diplomatic forms. The wider aim, however, is always to place on a sound footing the historical use of charters, deeds, and other documentary sources.

# Select Bibliography

## General Handbooks

There are handbooks that set out the principles of diplomatic criticism ("general diplomatics") and describe the features of documents produced by particular authorities ("special diplomatics"). Still the most authoritative is H. Bresslau, *Handbuch der Urkundenlehre für Deutschland und Italien,* 2nd ed., 2 vols. (1912–31, r1958; index 1960); though centered on documents from Germany and Italy, it is of general use [DE1]. A. Giry's *Manuel de diplomatique* (1894, r1972), is most informative on documents from France [DE2]. Both books are very long and take a broad view of the subject, including long sections on chronology and other topics. More narrowly focused on the criticism of documents is A. de Boüard, *Manuel de diplomatique française et pontificale,* 2 vols. and pls. (1929–52); this is certainly more approachable, at least in the first volume, and the albums of plates provide valuable illustrations [DE3]. A good modern introduction to the discipline is provided by O. Guyotjeannin *et al., Diplomatique médiévale,* L'atelier du médiéviste 2 (1993), which is built around some 43 examples with diplomatic commentary [DE4]. There are no comparable books in English. Concise introductions to the methods of the discipline in other languages include L. Santifaller, *Urkundenforschung: Methoden, Ziele, Ergebnisse* (1937, r1967) [DE5], and A. Pratesi, *Genesi e forme del documento medievale,* 2nd ed. (1987) [DE6]. There is an introductory essay with bibliography by L.E. Boyle, "Diplomatics," in *MSI* 82–113 [DE7]. A formal introduction with definitions of terms has been produced by an international committee, *Diplomatica et sigillographica: Travaux préliminaires de la Commission internationale de diplomatique et de la Commission internationale de sigillographie pour une normalisation internationale des éditions de documents et un vocabulaire international de la diplomatique et de la sigillographie,* Folia Caesaraugustana 1 (1984); new ed.: M. Cárcel Ortí, *Vocabulaire international de la diplomatique* (1994) [DE8].

The origins of diplomatic criticism as a tool for historians lie in the late seventeenth century, and it is instructive to consult the classic founding work by Jean Mabillon (1632–1707), *De re diplomatica libri VI* (Paris 1681) [DE9]. For a survey of the history of the subject with bibliographical references see C. Samaran, "Diplomatique," in *L'histoire et ses méthodes,* Encyclopédie de la Pléiade 11 (1961) 633–76 [DE10].

## Examples in the Introductory Essay

Examples from late antiquity will be found in K. Brandi, *Urkunden und Akten für rechtsgeschichtliche und diplomatische Vorlesungen und Übungen,* 3rd ed. (1932). His example no. 6 is a short letter of protection from the fourth century; no. 7 is the record of a synod presided over by Pope Hilarus in 469; no. 8 illustrates how a charter of King Odovacer (489) granting land to Pierius was read in the public court at Ravenna and entered on the papyrus roll with other municipal acts [DE11].

Excellent facsimiles of the documents from Hersfeld are available in *Chartae Latinae antiquiores: Facsimile Edition of the Latin Charters Prior to the Ninth Century,* ed. A. Bruckner, R. Marichal, *et al.* (1954–) v12:533–38. Each facsimile is accompanied by a "diplomatic" transcript, that is one showing the exact lineation, lettering, abbreviations, and punctuation of the original [DE12]. Edited texts will be found in *MGH.Die Urkunden der Karolinger*, v1: *Die Urkunden Pippins, Karlmanns und Karls des Grossen*, ed. E. Mühlbacher *et al.* (1906, r1979), nos. 89–90 (January 775), 103 (August 775), 104 (October 775), 121 (March 779), and 144 (July 782) [DE13].

# DF ❖ CANON LAW

BY JOHN GILCHRIST (†)

## Introduction

The history of the ecclesiastical canons or rules governing the lives of members of the Western Church in the Middle Ages falls into two distinct periods [DF3–4]. The first, ending in the mid-twelfth century, covers the formation of the law and the gathering of its ancient sources into collections. The language of the law could thus vary with the Latin of the original texts: there was neither a science of canon law nor a distinct canonistic lexicon [DF54]. Yet the canon law, with its emphasis on ancient authorities, preserved much of the rhetoric of late antiquity. Even the fabricators of spurious texts often cast them in the same antique mold.

The second period began when the earlier material was collected at Bologna c. 1140 by Gratian in the *Decretum* or *Concordia discordantium canonum* [DF41]. From this time onward, the language of the law divided into two branches: the first branch—the creation of new general law through conciliar canons and papal rescripts or decretals—built upon the ancient rhetorical forms; the second—the teaching and practice of canon law based upon the *Decretum* of Gratian—developed a *decretist* science with a distinctive Latin style. The more intensive study of the law led to the issue of hundreds of papal decretal letters, which were authoritative answers to canonical questions that were posed. Towards the end of the twelfth century the lawyers began to collect and codify the papal decisions in the decretal letters. Various compilations were made, culminating in the *Decretales*, organized in five books and promulgated by Pope Gregory IX in 1234. A spate of creative *decretalist* commentary accompanied this process, giving the finishing touches to the latinity of the law [DF57].

## The Pre-Gratian Period

The material sources of the law—the Scriptures, conciliar canons, papal letters, patristic and other ecclesiastical excerpts, as well as texts from the penitentials and various fragments whose origins are to be found in the liturgy, hagiography, or civil law—were written at different times, in different places, and for very different purposes. Their latinity can thus vary from one source to another: for example, many early conciliar texts were translations of canons of councils held in the eastern half of the empire, with the result that the Latin of the law came to incorporate such obvious Greek loanwords as *abbas, abbatissa, baptisma, canon, clerus, coenobium, diaconus, ecclesia, episcopus, metropolita, monachus, presbyter*. With the passing of time few canonists knew the material sources directly, and the majority came to rely on compilations, of which over 150 are known in this period. Some compilations survive in only one or two manuscripts, but others, such as the *Dionysiana* (c. 510) [DF29], *Hispana* (c. 633) [DF30], *Hibernensis* (c. 700) [DF31], *Dionysio-Hadriana* (c. 774) [DF32], *Pseudo-Isidorian Decretals* (c. 847–52) [DF33], *Decretum* of Burchard of Worms (c. 1015) [DF34–36], and *Panormia* (c. 1094) [DF37] of Ivo of Chartres, circulated widely and greatly influenced the law of the Western Church [DF3].

The collections as such had no legislative force. The authority of an individual text was based solely on its origin, an ecumenical or regional council, a particular pope, or a father of the Church. Even Gratian's *Decretum* remained a private production. It was not until the thirteenth century that official collections with universal application appeared.

A canonical collection is obviously not the literary work of one author and perforce has no unity of style, but this does not mean that the compiler could not leave an imprint on the text in several ways. For example, a preface required direct authorial intervention, as did the addition of short headings or rubrics to introduce individual books, titles, or chapters. The sequence and manner of treatment—the author often altered the sources to make them fit some juristic mold—also made an impression on the text. These interventions vary from one collection to another, and the problem is complicated by the degree of borrowing and scribal error in the copying of texts. It is possible, however, to discover linguistic idiosyncrasies that distinguish one collection from another.

Regional variations also affected the language of the collections. Latin was not the mother tongue of the compilers, but those who worked on Italian or Spanish collections obviously knew their classical grammar [DF10]. It was otherwise in Gaul, during the Merovingian period, when there was a substantial shift in Latin grammar and syntax. The *Collectio Vetus Gallica* [*VG*], of which the primitive version was compiled between 585 and 626/27, consisting mainly of conciliar canons and drawing heavily upon the *Dionysiana*, provides a good example of these changes [DE38]. The *VG* employs the unique expression *HIRA* (also *HERA, HYRA, ERA, HR*), e.g. *CANON CARTAGINENSIS HIRA XXIII*, instead of the standard *CAPITULUM*. The grammar and orthography exhibit all the confusions of Late Latin: e.g. *Incipit capitulacio excarpsum de canonis* or *De hoc, que offeruntur ad altario vel que ad domum sacerdotis et de oblatione*. Among vowels we find *e* instead of *i*: *cives testes* (nominative sg.); *i* where *e* is expected, in *illi*, for example; *o* and *e* for *u* and *i*: *poneretur* (*puniretur*); among consonants we find *c* instead of *g*: *evacari*; *g* instead of *c*: *vagans*; *t* omitted at the end of a word: *venire<t>*. In syntax *ut* often appears with the indicative (*ita conati sunt . . . ut . . . captivarunt*) or with an infinitive (*Decernimus ut . . . oblatio . . . offerre*). The nominative instead of the accusative is used with the infinitive (*Sepe dilectio tua . . . convenisse non dubium est*). There is confusion between the active and passive voices: *Ut festivitates praeclaras . . . non teneantur*. Cases are used loosely: *Si servum . . . fuerit ordinatus*. Prepositions do not govern their usual cases: *ab eadem mansionem, ad clero, apud episcopis, cum litteras, sine epistolam*. Words acquire special meanings: *De his, qui baptizati gentiliter* (= after the manner of heathens) *convixerunt, velamen* (= protection). Despite this flexibility, the author of the *VG* treated his texts conservatively.

The great improvement in the quality of Latin in the Carolingian era is reflected in canonical writings. The *Dionysio-Hadriana* compilation (c. 774) has sound grammar and syntax. A useful indication of the canonist's command of this "reformed" language can be found in the many forgeries produced between 750 and 855. Among them was the notorious *Donation of Constantine*, whose genuineness was rarely questioned until the fifteenth century [DF52]. The confidence of a forger in his Latin is particularly evident in the *Pseudo-Isidorian Decretals,* produced in the archdiocese of Rheims between c. 847 and 852. About one third of this work consists of forged papal letters whose purported dates range from 88 to 314. Thousands of canonistic fragments are skillfully linked together, and it was not until the seventeenth century that *Pseudo-Isidore* was definitively shown to be a confection of the ninth century [DF3].

Although somewhat tedious in form, *Pseudo-Isidore* generally follows classical rules of declensions and conjugations. A distinctive feature of this forgery is a predilection for official-sounding adverbs ending in *-iter,* even where a simpler form existed, e.g. *pleniter, veraciter, praesentialiter, irrecuperabiliter.* The authors also replace demonstrative adjectives (*ille, iste*) with *praedictus,* thus capturing earlier official usage as found, for example, in the letters of Gregory the Great [DF69–70].

The *Collection in Seventy-Four Titles* [*74T*] (c. 1075–76) is an excellent example of the way in which a compiler shaped the text of the sources. Demonstrating the sound grammatical knowledge common to collections of this period, the *74T* was an influential but relatively simple compilation containing 315 *capitula;* the majority (some 252 *capitula,* genuine as well as forged) were drawn from the *Pseudo-Isidorian Decretals.* Several sources provided the remaining *capitula,* especially the letters of Gregory the Great (15 *capitula* directly, 25 indirectly) [DF39]. Despite the variety of sources, the *74T* is not a linguistic hotchpotch. The anonymous author made the texts fit an appropriate juristic mold by way of excision, addition (e.g., *neque deinceps fieri permittimus sed omnino interdicentes prohibemus* supplied at the end of a statement, introduced by *legitur,* that no lay person had ever been given the right to dispose of ecclesiastical offices), or substitution of terms (*statuerunt* became *statuimus, decreuerunt* became *decreuimus*). Eliminating geographical specification from the inscriptions extended the text's legislative force, e.g. *Dilectissimis fratribus per Italiae provintias sanctis constitutis episcopis Sother papa* became simply *Sother papa omnibus episcopis.* Texts were shifted from *oratio obliqua* to *oratio recta: Primum quidem scias paganos . . . non posse* became *Pagani . . . non possunt.*

The author of the *74T* was probably influenced by the style of early papal letters, especially those of Gregory I (590–604), the most widely cited pope in the pre-Gratian era, which used the language of the imperial chancery [DF67]. The popes were fond of imperial verbs of commanding, granting, and advising when addressing their subordinates: *constituimus, decrevimus, decernimus, statuimus, iubemus, patitur.* Simple devices in the sources also strengthened the peremptory tone, such as the use of solemn phrases (*omni mora omnique excusatione submota* instead of *sine excusatione*); auxiliary verbs preceding the infinitive (*potest rata haberi*); subject following the verb (*uidetur inscitia*); double construction (*ualde iniquum sit et absurdum*); unusual word order for emphasis (*rectum tenet in eligendo sacerdote iudicium*); use of contractions (*copularit* for *copulaverit*); a preference for adverbs of various kinds ending in *-ter* (*providenter scienterque*), and for nouns with ablatives in *-one, -ore, -ate* (*electione, corpore, auctoritate*) or with genitives in *-onis, -oris, -atis. Capi-*

*tula* 33–38 of the *74T*, a legislative cluster from the *Codex Theodosianus* via Hincmar of Rheims (d. 882), are replete with the same imperial verbs of command (*volumus, decernimus, precipimus, firmamus*). Reducing a canonistic text to its imperative or dispositive part gave prominence to such venerable phrases as *apostolica ecclesia, apostolica sedes, apostolica auctoritate, apostolico iudicio,* used frequently of Roman or papal authority.

The *74T* illustrates the ways in which some words in the material sources had taken on new or restricted meanings. Profane terms became religious by adding adjectives such as *ecclesiasticus* (*ecclesiasticus ordo*). *Ecclesia* in the variety of material sources of *74T* has several meanings depending on the context, i.e. the divine institution (*ecclesia Christi*), the hierocratic Church ruled by a pastor or priest (*ad ecclesiam suam non prius reuertatur*), the community institution (*nemo in publico examinare presumat nisi in ecclesia*), or simply the community itself (*Si quis aduersus pastores uel ecclesias eorum commotus fuerit*). Common classical words were shifted into a Christian context: *antiquus hostis:* the devil; *baratrum:* hell; *ciuitas:* episcopal see; *communicare:* to take communion; *conuersatio* (of clergy): manner of living, way of life; *deuotio:* piety; *fides:* the faith; *gentiles:* heathens or pagans; *leuita:* deacon; *ordinari:* to be ordained to ecclesiastical office; *paganus:* unbeliever; *sacerdos:* bishop or priest.

Even where canonical collections use standard ecclesiastical terms, there are pitfalls, because, over time, these could change their meaning. *Sacer ordo* initially excluded the subdiaconate; by the 1070s it was beginning to include it, although doubts remained until 1207. *Reus* (accused *or* guilty) created difficulties well into the post-Gratian period [DF63]. Seemingly straightforward texts can be ambiguous: until recently, historians misunderstood *Dictatus papae*, ch. 17, of Pope Gregory VII (1075): *Quod nullum capitulum nullusque liber canonicus habeatur absque illius auctoritate.* "Canonicus" here refers not to canon law but to the canon of Scripture, fixed by papal teaching authority [DF64].

From the fourth to the eleventh century, the language of canon law remained rooted in the rhetoric of the trivium. There was no canonistic science *ex professo,* and the latinity was therefore basically that which characterized the public statements of the Church as a whole. But around 1090 came signs that this was about to change. Although earlier canonists such as Isidore of Seville (d. 636), Hincmar of Rheims (d. 882), Abbo of Fleury (d. 1004), and Burchard of Worms (d. 1025) were aware of the problem of conflicting canons, no firm solutions were proposed until the Gregorian era [DF66]. Bernold of Constance (d. 1100), Ivo of Chartres (d. 1115), Alger of Liège (d. c. 1131), and Peter Abelard (d. 1142) devised rules to reconcile apparently contradictory texts through interpretation ([DF56], essay 1). Canonists became increasingly conscious of the role of language and hermeneutics. The ground had been prepared for Gratian.

## The Post-Gratian Period

It is necessary first to offer some explanation of the system of canonical references used in this period. Authors used a shorthand form for references, introducing them by "ut" and identifying the pertinent text by its incipit or opening word(s). The medieval student or lawyer recognized these incipits and so could easily separate the reference from the commentary text that followed. The modern student is unlikely to have that intimate knowledge of the text and so may initially experience difficulty knowing where a legal reference ends. Here are some examples of the system of reference from Gratian onward together with their modern equivalents.

Gratian's *Decretum* consists of three parts (*Distinctiones, Causae,* and the treatise *De consecratione*). In the first part, each of the 101 distinctions contains a number of *capitula.* In a typical medieval reference, the distinction is referred to by number, but the chapter only by an opening word or two; for example, "ut d. xxxi Ante triennium" refers to distinction 31, *capitulum* (or chapter) 1 (which begins with the words "Ante triennium"). This is Gratian D. 31 c. 1 in the modern style (see [DF41]).

The second part of the *Decretum* consists of 36 *causae,* each divided into a number of *questiones,* each of these in turn containing a number of *capitula.* The medieval style cited the number of the *causa* and of the *questio* and the opening word(s) of the particular *capitulum;* thus "ut xvj. q. i. Multis" refers to *causa* 16, *questio* 1, *capitulum* 51 (beginning with "Multis"). This is Gratian C. 16 q. 1 c. 51 in the modern style. Similarly "ut i. q. iii. Non solum" refers to Gratian C. 1 q. 3 c. 11.

Within *Causa* 33, the third *questio,* dealing with penance, is expanded to such an extent that it amounts to a self-contained treatise divided into seven distinctions. Medieval lawyers referred to it in the same way as to the first part of the *Decretum,* by its distinctions, but with the addition of *de pen.,* for example, "ut *de pen.* dist. 5. falsas," meaning distinction 5, cap. 6, of *Causa* 33, *questio* 3. This refers to Gratian D. 5 de pen. c. 6 in the modern style. The third part of the *Decretum,* entitled *De consecratione,* is cited by the five distinctions into which it is divided. A typical reference is "ut *de con.* dist. 4. eos" (= D. 4 de con. c. 118), again with the chapter cited by its opening word "eos."

Finally, there are many citations of the comments (*dicta*) that Gratian himself made on his collection. A medieval reference to a *dictum* of Gratian is indicated by the sign §, for example, "xxxvii. di. § hinc etiam," referring to distinction 37, into the midst of which Gratian had inserted a comment beginning "Hinc etiam." Modern scholars note with more precision than their predecessors the location of a comment, using d. (*dictum*) and a. (*ante*) or p. (*post*) and c. (*capitulum*), together with a specific chapter number, e.g. D. 37 d.p.c. 7. It should be added that the Friedberg edition of Gratian [DF41] has an index of incipits of all the *capitula,* making the medieval references for the most part easy to identify.

The next series of references requiring some explanation are citations of *capitula* in the five compilations (*quinque compilationes antiquae*). These consist chiefly of conciliar and papal legislation after Gratian. The first of these, with the descriptive title *Breviarium extravagantium* (later known as the *Compilatio prima*), was the work of Bernard of Pavia (1191–92). This and later compilations are arranged according to subject matter into five books, each divided into titles, subdivided into *capitula.* They were called *capitula extravagantes* ("wandering around" outside the *Decretum*). The medieval canonist produced an abbreviated style of reference, citing the number of the compilation, followed by the title and initial words of the canon; thus "ut extra iii. de uita et honest. cleric. Cum ab omni" = the third compilation, title (*De vita et honestate clericorum*), *capitulum* (*Cum ab omni*). The modern style is 3 *Comp.* 3.1.1, where the second "3" denotes the book, followed by the number of the title and the number of the *capitulum.* In time these compilations were codified into the *Decretales* (1234) of Gregory IX (with the same division into five books, with titles and *capitula*). It became known as the (*Liber*) *extra* [DF41] because it constituted a collection outside or added to Gratian; hence the medieval reference "extra," represented as "X" in modern use. Thus "ut extra de eta. et qual. ord. c. Cum sit ars" = the *Decretals* of Gregory IX, title (*De aetate et qualitate et ordine praeficiendorum*), *capitulum* (*Quum sit ars*) or, in modern citation, X 1.14.14 (the first number identifies the book).

Subsequent compilations of papal decretals are identified as follows: that of Boniface VIII (1298) was seen as a sixth book added to the five books making up the *Decretals* of Gregory IX, hence the title *Liber sextus* (= the *Sext*, abbreviated as "in VI°"); it too was divided into five books, with titles and *capitula*. The *Constitutiones* of Pope Clement V, hence *Clementinae* (1317), followed the same model ("in Clem.") and is sometimes referred to as *Liber septimus* (but not in citations). The *Extravagantes* of John XXII (*Extravag. Joann. XXII*), a collection of 20 decretals of this pope from 1317 to 1320, were later arranged under 14 titles (each usually with only one *capitulum*). Citation is by title and *capitulum*. The *Extravagantes Communes* (*Extravag. comm.*), a second collection of 74 decretals largely from the period 1261 to 1342, is referred to by book, title, and *capitulum*.

The other area of medieval canonical reference requiring some care is the notation of texts from Roman or civil law (see ch. DG for further discussion). Note, for example, the following references to the *Corpus iuris civilis*: "ut ff. de uariis et extraord. cognit. l. i. § Est quidem," and "ut ff. de decur. Generaliter § penult." The first example is to Justinian's *Digest* or *Pandects* (abbreviated as "ff."), short title (*De variis et extraordinariis cognitionibus* = book 50, title 13), law one ("l. i."), and paragraph (§) by name (*Est quidem* = no. 5). The modern style (using [DF46]) is Dig. 50.13.1.5. The second example also refers to the *Digest* ("ff."), short title (*De decurionibus et filiis eorum* = book 50, title 2), the incipit (*Generaliter*) of law three, and a reference to the penultimate paragraph (= no. 2). The modern style is Dig. 50.2.3.2. A final example is "legitur C. de veteri iure enucleando l. i. ultra medium, ibi, 'in tali prato spinosum,'" whereby the reader is directed to a quotation ("in tali prato spinosum") from the second half ("ultra medium") of the first law ("l. i.") in the *Codex* (= "C."), [book 1; not given], short title (*De veteri iure enucleando* = title 17). The modern style is Cod. 1.17.1.9.

Through the *Decretum* Gratian almost single-handedly created a new canonical jurisprudence [DF4] to stand alongside the public statements of the Church, which continued to employ ancient rhetorical forms in the Latin of papal decretal letters and conciliar canons. The solemn language of papal replies—the *stilus curie romane* [DF68]—to matters brought to its attention is a constant reminder that the pope's business was God's business. The revived study of Roman law had an impact upon the style of the papal rescript: on occasion, the borrowing was heavy; for example, the decretal of Pope Lucius III (1181–85) concerning illegal church construction (= X 5.32.1 *Intelleximus*) relies heavily on a *lex* of the Roman jurist Ulpian (= Dig. 39.1.20. Praetor) [DF60].

Gratian's own Latin in the *dicta* of the *Decretum* reflects the rhetorical tradition of the trivium. The style, grammar, and syntax are clear. The eminent canonist Huguccio (d. 1210), who produced the single most important *summa* on the *Decretum* (after 1188), criticized Gratian for arguing "tantum secundum superficiem littere" [DF9]. Had Gratian missed accidentally or deliberately the protest of Gregory I: *Indignum uehementer existimo, ut uerba celestis oraculi restringam sub regulis Donati?* A canonist soon added that text to the *Decretum* as a *palea* at D. 38 c. 13. The word *palea* (prefixed to some texts in Gratian, probably by his students, to designate them as additions) is itself of uncertain derivation. One opinion is that it was derived from the Latin word for "straw" to distinguish these additional texts from the "wheat" of the master, that is, Gratian's own work.

The language of general councils shows great care to achieve solemn legislative force: the *conclusiones* of Lateran I (1123) are each worded differently; thus canon 1: *careat dignitate,* 2: *recipi procul dubio prohibemus,* 3: *absque recuperationis spe deponatur . . . ,* etc. Canon 9, entitled *Coniunctiones consanguineorum,* provides a striking example of how the clear symmetry of construction brings out the harmony between divine and secular laws. The syntax conveys the measured tone of the spiritual judge: *Nos itaque, patres nostros sequentes, infamia eos notamus et infames esse censemus.* The general terminology used for decisions illustrates the fluctuation of language: the first eight councils had used *expositio fidei, canones, symbolum, definitio, terminus;* Lateran I–III use *canones;* Lateran IV and Lyons I–II use *constitutiones;* Vienne, Constance, Basle-Ferrara-Florence-Rome use *decreta* ([DF54], [DF51]).

Gratian's revolutionary achievement lay in the manner in which he organized the ancient texts dialectically, first on one side of a question, then on the other, adding his own commentary by way of solution. With the *Decretum* as their basic manual, and influenced by the example of Roman legal studies at Bologna, the professors of law, the decretists, struggled to give contemporary meaning to the ancient texts. To this end they produced numerous commentaries (*glossae, summae, apparatus*) as well as abridgments, indices, and rearrangements of the *Decretum,* thus giving rise to a Latin quite different from that of the trivium. Canon law came to be taught *ex professo.* Outside the classroom this new jurisprudence triumphed in ecclesiastical courts all the way to Rome.

Two factors shaped the contribution of the decretists to the language of ecclesiastical law: first, the rediscovery of Roman law, and, second, the early form of the gloss upon the text (interlinear or marginal) [DF8]. Although Gratian himself rejected the connection between canon and Roman law, the rebirth of Roman legal vocabulary [DF58] enabled the decretists to replace the somewhat fantastic definitions from the *Etymologiae* of Isidore of Seville (d. 636) with the juristic terminology of the Roman lawyers [DF59]. The precise treatment of "law" in the *Summa* (1157–59) of Rufinus—*Lex autem rogatur aut abrogatur aut surrogatur aut obrogatur aut derogatur* ([DF47] 14); "a law is enacted, repealed, superseded, or modified"—goes beyond Gratian, who was himself dependent on Isidore of Seville, back to a distant Roman origin ([DF55] essay 3). In time, canonists saw the advantages of studying both kinds of law. The author of the anonymous gloss known as *Animal est substantia* (1206–10) used Roman vocabulary and was careful in his definitions [DF59].

The second factor—the practice of glossing the *Decretum* by inserting definitions of words between lines or in the margin of the text—led to that cramped, abbreviated, and somewhat arid language of more developed commentaries. As one glossator succeeded another, the glosses of predecessors were identified by a siglum such as *R., r., Ru.* for *Rufinus; H., Hu., Hug., U.,* or *Ug.* for *Huguccio.* References to the *Decretum* were also abbreviated: *gl[osa] ad c[apitulum] 5, d[istinctio] 1, v[erbum] lex* (*lex* is the word being glossed). Here is a typical gloss from the *glossa ordinaria* (the standard commentary) of "Ioan.," i.e. Johannes Teutonicus (1216), on the *Decretum,* somewhat revised by "Bart.," i.e. Bartholomew of Brescia (1245):

[*gl. ord.* ad d. 10 c. 1 v. *divisiones*]: *Divisiones.* Arguitur quod episcopus invito plebano non potest dividere parochiam eius; nec Papa invito episcopo dividere episcopatum, ut xvj. q. i. multis. Quod enim est unum, dividi non potest, ut xxiiij. q. i. loquitur et capitulo schisma. *Ioan.* Sed credo quod Papa hoc possit facere ex causa, et etiam episcopus, ut in ea. decre. sicut unire. *Bart.*

The word here being glossed (*divisiones*) comes from Gratian's excerpt from a letter of Pope Innocent I (401–17), who refused to accept the partition of an ecclesiastical province by the emperor and so would not allow the appointment of two metropolitans. Apparently someone with much imagination would try to use texts culled from *Causae* 16 and 24 to suggest that because higher authority could not arbitrarily divide parishes and dioceses, this applied to bishops and pope. Johannes Teutonicus, who would have none of it, finally cited the *Digest* in support.

In interpreting decretist texts it is risky to assume that similar terms have similar meanings for different authors. For example, *ius positivum* and *ius naturale* seem straightforward enough, but they are minefields ([DF56] essay 3). Rufinus defined *ius naturale* as "a natural force implanted by nature in each creature to do good and avoid evil," whereas Simon of Bisignano (1177/79) made it "a superior part of the soul, that is, reason itself." Not surprisingly, Huguccio urged the reader to proceed with caution ([DF55] essay 3). Rufinus and Stephen of Tournai, contemporary twelfth-century canonists at Bologna, used many identical terms "to make quite divergent or even thoroughly contrary statements" [DF62]. Thus, Rufinus treated *infamia* as the penance to be done after absolution; Stephen took it to be the criminal record, which, to be expunged, required a specific papal juridical act.

The term *praeceptum* had a very mixed history. Its classical meaning was a general order or prescription. In late antiquity it came to designate enacted legislation, imperial and later papal. It was used as such in a spurious letter attributed to Pope Gregory IV (827–44) (*Divinis praeceptis et apostolicis saluberrimis incitamur monitis*), which passed into Gratian (cf. C. 2 q. 6 c. 11; D. 12 c. 2; D. 19 c. 5), but by this time the term had lost its special legislative significance and reverted to the general meaning of the classical Roman law—with one major difference: it now had an obligatory force ([DF55] essay 4). The *Summa "Elegantius in iure divino" seu Coloniensis* of c. 1169 defined *preceptum* as something that "non impune resistes" ([DF49] pt1, 71).

Many words had multiple meanings or took on new meanings in combination with another noun. *Bigamia, bigamus* covered both the state of being twice married (the first spouse having died) and having two "wives." *Viaticum* referred to traveling expenses or the last rites. *Illusio noctis* (nocturnal emission) was but distantly rooted in *illusio* (mockery, irony, illusion). The decretists could also be evasive; for example, in a text calling for the clergy to live a common life, they found embarrassing the literal meaning of the sentence cited by Gratian—*In omnibus* [things held in common by friends] *autem sunt sine dubio et coniuges*—attributed to "a certain most wise Greek" (Plato?) and cited in C. 12 q. 1 c. 2. So they glossed it by saying that it meant to hold in respect or love and did not refer to any use of sex ([DF56] essay 11).

In the final decades of the twelfth century, the need to gather together texts wandering outside (*extravagantes*) the *Decretum*, especially authoritative papal decretal decisions made after 1140, created a new set of experts in the law schools, the decretalists. As we have already noted, their work culminated in the *Decretales* or *Liber extra* compiled under the direction of Raymond of Peñafort (d. 1275) and promulgated by Pope Gregory IX (1234). The decretalists could alter papal rescripts almost beyond recognition, abbreviating the *salutatio,* omitting the *exordium* and *conclusio,* and reducing the body to bare bones before it passed into one of the collections. Adverbs such as *item, amplius,* or *preterea* marked new argument or omission of text. Friedberg's edition supplies the missing parts, making it much easier for us to make some sense of the gutted text. The medieval lawyer or judge was not so lucky: Pope Honorius III's letter *Ex parte* has 22 lines of text, of which only the ones reprinted here were excerpted for the *Decretals* (X 2.22.11):

> Ex parte carissimae in Christo filiae B. quondam Anglorum reginae fuit propositum . . . quia rescriptum apostolicum pro eo quod in hac dictione "spoliarunt," haec figura "o" deerat, asseritur vitiosum. . . . Mandamus, quatenus hoc non obstante in negotio ipso . . . ratione praevia procedatis. [DF41]

All the formality and solemnity of the *stilus curie Romane* are abandoned in selecting only what the decretalist thought significant.

The intense round of canonistic activity set in motion by the decretalists (*glossae, summae, reportationes, notabilia, margaritae, distinctiones,* as well as *summae* on specific legal forms, e.g. "de ordine iudiciario") produced its own shorthand. The common formula "ne sede vacante aliquid innovetur" (X 3.9) might appear simply as "ne. se. va." The disposition of a case, *Fraternitati tue per apostolica scripta mandamus,* might be written "f.t.p.a.s.m." Individual titles in the *Liber extra* were often abbreviated, e.g. X 5.9 *De apostatis et reiterantibus baptisma* might become simply "aposta." In the *Liber extra* itself, the expression "Et infra" indicates that Raymond of Peñafort has omitted some part(s) of the original decretal. Decretalists also used initials: *Go., Gof.* = Godfrey of Trani (d. 1245); *Ho.* = Hostiensis, i.e. Henry, cardinal bishop of Ostia (d. 1271).

Within the period from 1140 to 1254, the lawyers, starting from scratch, had shown remarkable innovative skills. Roman law provided the decretists of the twelfth century with a lexicon of terms which they applied to defining the Church in the world as a theological reality; in the next century the decretalists applied the same resources to making the secular world conform to a juridical reality. Canonistic usage brought about linguistic changes. One must examine, for example, the law of synods, benefices, matrimony, penitential discipline, etc., in order to grasp fully innovations in words, meanings, and constructions; *accusare:* to inform against; *beneficium:* church office, benefice; *capitulum:* chapter [of canons]; *contrahere* (*contractus*): to marry (marriage); *decretista/decretalista:* lawyer; *dominium* (in marriage): either spouse's right over the other; *iuspatronatus:* law of ecclesiastical patronage; *officium:* exercise of jurisdiction; *prebenda:* income from a church benefice, prebend; *religio:* monastic life; *religiosus:* member of a religious order; *residentia:* residence (of a canon); *socius:* curate. Nouns ending in -*alitas* and adjectives in -*alis* were favored. Terms of an earlier era took on their modern usage, e.g. *parrochia* ("episcopal see" in the ninth century) became "parish."

The canonists' work hinged on definition [DF53]. A chapter headed *De verborum significatione,* adopted from Roman law (Dig. 50.16), appeared in the first compilation of decretals, the *Breviarium extravagantium* (1191–92) of Bernard of Pavia (= 1 *Comp.* 5.36), and in the definitive collections of Gregory IX (= 5.40) and Boniface VIII (= 5.12). Although the number of texts quoted is much fewer than in the *Digest,* it is still a very useful compendium. For example, Innocent III (X 5.40.20) defines *censura ecclesiastica* as *non solum interdicti, sed suspensionis et excommunicationis s-ententia.* St. Hilary (d. 366) is cited (X 5.40.6) to the effect that words should be understood according to the intention of the legislator (*non sermoni res sed rei est sermo subiectus*). Even so, canonists did not always feel constrained to maintain the original meaning of words. Thus, the term *electio* (strictly used only of the proper canonical election of a bishop) was applied by attraction to an alternative form of "election"known as the *postulatio.* Where a preferred candidate lacked the proper qualifications for election, the electors sent a direct "request" (*postulatio*) to Rome for approval, thus bypassing the need to seek confirmation from the metropolitan.

The Latin style of the canonists is dull and repetitive in comparison with that of the scholastic philosophers and theologians [DF54]. A commentator who becomes lost in repetition, supplying one solution after another merely by inserting *vel* [DF57], has difficulty holding the attention of the modern reader. But the commentators held sway in the courts, and students of medieval law may well find that the outcome of a case did indeed hinge on whether an "or" excluded the alternative or offered a choice between two alternatives. Perhaps the arid language served, unwittingly, another purpose: the lawyers faced a constant struggle to incorporate papal claims to primacy into the canonistic system without sacrificing equitable jurisprudence. Differences in the language of the canon law of the schools and of the courts from that of the public pronouncements of the Church allowed the canon law to retain some measure of independence from the papal office.

## Select Bibliography

### Bibliography

Publications from 1970 are listed annually in the *Bulletin of Medieval Canon Law* 1– (1971–) [DF1]; early annual bibliographies in *Traditio* 11 (1955) to 26 (1970) [DF2].

### History

Summaries by R. Reynolds, "Law, Canon: to Gratian" [DF3], and S. Chodorow, "Law, Canon: after Gratian" [DF4], both in *DMA* 7:395–413, 413–18.
J.A. Clarence Smith, *Medieval Law Teachers and Writers, Civilian and Canonist* (1975) [DF5].
P. Fournier and G. Le Bras, *Histoire des collections canoniques en Occident depuis les fausses décrétales jusqu'au Décret de Gratien,* 2 vols. (1931–32, r1972) [DF6].
G. Fransen, *Les collections canoniques,* TSMAO 10 (1973) [DF7], and *id., Les décrétales et les collections de décrétales,* TSMAO 2 (1972) [DF8], each with a *mise à jour* (1985).
C. Leonardi, "La vita e l'opera di Uguccione da Pisa Decretista," in *Studia Gratiana* 4 (1956–57) 37–120 [DF9].
O. Pontal, *Les statuts synodaux,* TSMAO 11 (1975) [DF10].
C. Van de Wiel, *History of Canon Law* (1991): very useful bibliographies, including a listing (p27) of periodicals and series [DF11].
In preparation is an international collaborative work, *History of Medieval Canon*

*Law,* ed. W. Hartmann and K. Pennington, to be published by The Catholic University of America Press, Washington, DC [DF12].

## Standard Reference Aids

*Dictionnaire de droit canonique,* 7 vols. (1935–65) [DF13].

M. Fornasari, *Initia canonum a primaevis collectionibus usque ad Decretum Gratiani: Repertorio . . . ,* v1: A–G (1972) [DF14].

R. Köstler, *Wörterbuch zum Codex juris canonici* (1927–29) [DF15].

S. Kuttner, *Repertorium der Kanonistik (1140–1234): Prodromus corporis glossarum I* (1937, r1981) [DF16]; id., *Index titulorum decretalium ex collectionibus tam privatis quam publicis conscriptus* (1977) [DF17].

A. Lauer, *Index verborum Codicis iuris canonici* (1941) [DF18].

F. Maassen, *Geschichte der Quellen und der Literatur des canonischen Rechts im Abendlande bis zum Ausgange des Mittelalters* (1870, r1956) [DF19].

J. Ochoa Sanz, *Index verborum ac locutionum Codicis iuris canonici,* 2nd ed. (1984): concordance of the new code of 1983 [DF20].

P. Palazzini, ed., *Dictionarium morale et canonicum,* 4 vols. (1962–68) [DF21].

W.M. Plöchl, *Geschichte des Kirchenrechts,* 5 vols., (1960–70; 2nd ed. for v1–3) [DF22].

A. Van Hove, *Prolegomena ad Codicem iuris canonici,* 2nd ed. (1945, r1959) [DF23].

J.F. von Schulte, *Die Geschichte der Quellen und Literatur des canonischen Rechts von Gratian bis auf die Gegenwart,* 3 vols. (1875–80, r1956) [DF24].

## Guides to Legal Citations

S. Kuttner, "Notes on the Presentation of Text and Apparatus in Editing Works of the Decretists and Decretalists," in *Traditio* 15 (1959) 452–64 [DF25].

W.H. Bryson, *Dictionary of Sigla and Abbreviations to and in Law Books before 1607* (1975) [DF26]: see especially pt. I.A.3–16 ("Citations in the Later Middle Ages," by H. Kantorowicz, tr. W.H. Bryson) [DF27], and pt. I.B.17–21 ("The Manner of Citing the Sources by *Partes, Leges, Capitula, etc.*," by R. Feenstra and G. Rossi, tr. W.H. Bryson) [DF28].

## Primary Works

N.B.: Modern editions of legal sources often comment on the latinity of the texts.

*Die Canonessammlung des Dionysius Exiguus in der ersten Redaktion* [= *Collectio Dionysiana* I], ed. A. Strewe (1931) [DF29].

G. Martinez Diez, *La collección canónica Hispana* (1966–) [DF30].

*Collectio Hibernensis,* ed. H. Wasserschleben, *Die irishe Kanonensammlung* (1885) [DF31].

*Collectio Dionysio-Hadriana,* in *PL* 67:135–346 [DF32].

*Decretales Pseudo-Isidorianae et capitula Angilramni,* ed. P. Hinschius (1863, r1963) [DF33].

Burchard of Worms, *Decretum,* in *PL* 140:537–1058 [DF34]; see R. Kaiser and M. Kerner, *LM* 2:950–51 (bibliography) [DF35]. The first 33 chs. of bk. 19 of Burchard's *Decretum* have been edited by H.J. Schmitz in *Die Bussbücher und das kanonische Bussverfahren nach handschriftlichen Quellen dargestellt* (1883, r1958) 403–67 [DF36].

Ivo of Chartres, *Panormia*, in *PL* 161:1037–1344 [**DF37**].

H. Mordek, *Kirchenrecht und Reform im Frankenreich. Die Collectio Vetus Gallica, die älteste systematische Kanonessammlung des fränkischen Gallien: Studien und Edition* (1975) [**DF38**].

*Diuersorum patrum sententie sive Collectio in LXXIV titulos digesta*, ed. J.T. Gilchrist, *MIC*, ser. B.1 (1973); translated with intro. by the editor in *The Collection in Seventy-Four Titles: A Canon Law Manual of the Gregorian Reform* (1980) [**DF39**].

*Dictatus papae*, ed. E. Caspar, in *Das Register Gregors VII, MGH.Epistolae selectae* 2.1 (1920, r1990) 201–8 [**DF40**].

The *Decretum* of Gratian, the *Decretales* (*Liber extra*) of Gregory IX, the *Liber sextus* of Boniface VIII, the *Constitutiones* of Clement V, the *Extravagantes* of John XXII, and the *Extravagantes Communes* are printed in the *Corpus iuris canonici*, 2 vols., ed. E. Friedberg (1879–81, r1922–28 and 1955–59) [**DF41**]. There is a useful index in *Index Analytico-Alphabeticus ad primam partem Corporis Iuris Canonici (Decretum Gratiani) secundum editionem Aemilii Friedberg* and *Index . . . ad secundam partem . . .*, assembled by F. Germovnik (1978–80) [**DF42**]. See also T. Reuter and G. Silagi, *Wortkonkordanz zum Decretum Gratiani, MGH.Hilfsmittel* 10, 5 vols. (1990) [**DF43**].

*Quinque compilationes antiquae*, ed. E. Friedberg (1882, r1958) [**DF44**].

*Extravagantes Joannis XXII*, ed. J. Tarrant, *MIC*, ser. B.6 (1983) [**DF45**].

*Corpus iuris civilis*, ed. T. Mommsen, P. Krüger, R. Schöll, and W. Kroll, 3 vols. (1872–77, 1895; 1915–28; many reprintings, including 1954); see [**DG2**] [**DF46**].

Rufinus, *Summa decretorum* (1157–59), ed H. Singer (1902, r1963) [**DF47**].

Stephen of Tournai, *Summa decreti*, ed. J.F. von Schulte (1891, r1965) [**DF48**].

*Summa "Elegantius in iure divino" seu Coloniensis*, ed. G. Fransen and S. Kuttner, 3 vols. *MIC*, ser. A.1 (1969–78, 1986) [**DF49**].

*Decrees of the Ecumenical Councils*, ed. N.P. Tanner, 2 vols. (1990): this is a corrected photographic reproduction, with English translations provided by 29 members of the Society of Jesus, of the Latin text of the *Conciliorum Oecumenicorum Decreta*, ed. G. Alberigo *et al.*, 3rd ed. (1973) [**DF50**]. See also M. Mollat, P. Tombeur, *et al.*, *Conciles oecuméniques médiévaux: Concordance, index, listes de fréquence, tables comparatives* (1974–): v1, *Les conciles Latran I à Latran IV* (1974); v2, *Les conciles Lyon I et Lyon II* (1974); v3, *Le concile de Vienne* (1978) [**DF51**].

For a humanist view of a major canonistic forgery, see Lorenzo Valla, *The Profession of the Religious and the Principal Arguments from The Falsely-Believed and Forged Donation of Constantine*, ed. and tr. O.Z. Pugliese (1985) [**DF52**].

## Latinity

E. Seckel, *Beiträge zur Geschichte beider Rechte im Mittelalter*, v1: *Zur Geschichte der populären Literatur des römisch-canonischen Rechts* (1898) [**DF53**].

Unknown words not found in *TLL*, *Lewis-Short*, *Souter*, and *Du Cange* (see chs. CD and BB) should be sought in *Blaise* (some canonists down to Gratian are incorporated), *Niermeyer* (for citations from the period between 550 and 1150, though less valuable for law), or the other major Medieval Latin lexicographical works [**CD24–41**]. For Roman legal terms see the bibliography of ch. DG. The tables and indices in *PL*, *MGH*, *CSEL*, *CCSL*, and *CCCM*, as well as other tools listed in ch. BE, can help to identify rare words.

A. Springhetti, *Latinitas fontium iuris canonici*, Pontificium Institutum Altioris Latinitatis, Bibliotheca "Veterum Sapientia," ser. A: Textus-Documenta-Commentaria, v7 (1968) [DF54], is useful mainly for the pre-Gratian era. Otherwise there is no developed body of literature on the language of canon law. The collected articles of J. Gaudemet, *La formation du droit canonique médiéval* (1980) [DF55], and of S. Kuttner, *The History of Ideas and Doctrines of Canon Law in the Middle Ages* (1980) [DF56], are valuable.

G. Fransen, "La lexicographie du droit canonique médiéval (1140–1400)," in *LLM* 191–96 [DF57].

P. Timbal and J. Metman, "La lexicographie du latin médiéval et le vocabulaire juridique," in *LLM* 147–52 [DF58].

For the influence of Roman law see E.C.C. Coppens, "L'interprétation analogique des termes de droit romain en droit canonique médiéval," in *CIVICIMA* 1:54–64 [DF59]; P. Legendre, "Le droit romain, modèle et langage. De la signification de l'"Utrumque Ius"," in *Études Le Bras* 2 (1965) 913–30 [DF60].

On university instruction see D.M. Owen, *The Medieval Canon Law: Teaching, Literature, and Transmission* (1990) [DF61].

Among studies of specific canonical terms, good examples are R.G.G. Knox, "The Problem of Academic Language in Rufinus and Stephan," in *Proceedings of the Sixth International Congress of Medieval Canon Law, MIC*, ser. C.7, ed. S. Kuttner and K. Pennington (1985) 109–23 [DF62]; R.M. Fraher, "'Ut nullus describatur reus prius quam convincatur': Presumption of Innocence in Medieval Canon Law?," in *Proceedings* [DF62] 493–506 [DF63]; S. Kuttner, "Liber canonicus: A Note on the 'Dictatus Pape' c. 17," in *Studi Gregoriani* 2 (1947) 387–401 (= [DF56] essay 2) [DF64]; T. Lenherr, "Der Begriff 'executio' in der Summa Decretorum des Huguccio," in *Archiv für katholisches Kirchenrecht* 150 (1981) 5–44, 361–420 [DF65]. J.-M. Salgado, "La méthode d'interprétation du droit en usage chez les canonistes. Des origines à Urbain II," in *Revue de l'Université d'Ottawa. Section spéciale* 21 (1951) 201–13 and 22 (1952) 23–35, deals with the general history of interpretation [DF66].

On the impact of the imperial administration upon ecclesiastical chancery style, see G. Viden, *The Roman Chancery Tradition: Studies in the Language of Codex Theodosianus and Cassiodorus' Variae* (1984) [DF67]; T. Janson, *PRML* [DF68].

Monographs on individual authors, for example, B. Dunn, *The Style of the Letters of St. Gregory the Great* (1931) [DF69], and D. Norberg, *Critical and Exegetical Notes on the Letters of St. Gregory the Great* (1982) [DF70], demonstrate the classical foundations of the Latin style.

*See also* [BA80].

# DG ❖ ROMAN AND SECULAR LAW

## BY KENNETH PENNINGTON

The language of medieval legal Latin creates significant problems for the modern reader. Law is a technical subject with a specialized vocabulary defining practices, procedures, and terms that can no longer be translated into modern languages. The institutions that put law into practice have often completely disappeared, and when we read legal texts we may have little understanding of commonplaces that the writers of the texts took for granted. Although the syntax of legal Latin is not especially difficult or different from that of other branches of learning, the concepts, terminology, and formulae can be formidable barriers for the reader. This chapter will concentrate on the special problems that confront readers of texts from the field of medieval Roman and secular law.

Ancient Roman law is the bedrock upon which medieval law was built. It influenced and shaped the legal compilations of the early Middle Ages, and with its resurrection in the late eleventh century, it furnished the core of academic law that was taught at the universities. Learned jurists carried its doctrines to the far reaches of Europe. Consequently, a student of medieval legal Latin who wishes to read legal texts must have some understanding of Roman legal vocabulary as interpreted by medieval jurists.

The resurrection of Roman law at the end of the eleventh century was a unique event in legal history that changed the future of European law. Shadowy figures with unusual names like Pepo and Irnerius began to teach the law of the ancient Romans at Bologna. The law they taught was late imperial law that had been compiled by the Emperor Justinian I (d. 565) in the sixth century. His codification, the *Corpus iuris civilis,* yielded the material for teaching Roman law in the eleventh century. Its doctrines provided medieval jurists with sophisticated models for contracts, rules of procedure, family law, testaments, and a strong monarchical constitutional system. Six hundred years after his death, Justinian's name became synonymous with legislator and codifier.

Legal historians have differed as to whether jurists at Pavia or at Bologna initiated the revival of Roman law. Research over the past 20 years has demonstrated conclusively that those in Bologna recovered the key text of Roman law, the *Digest,* in stages during the late eleventh and early twelfth centuries. These Bolognese jurists were the first to recognize the importance of the *Digest,* and, like their humanist successors in the fifteenth century, they must have searched for manuscript copies of it.

Wolfgang Müller's recent essay on the recovery of the *Digest* sums up the stages of this development [DG71].

With canon law, Roman law formed the medieval common law, the *ius commune* of Western Europe. To separate the two legal systems is artificial and even misleading. Both were taught in law schools throughout Christendom, students studied both as part of their legal education, and an understanding of medieval jurisprudence depends upon a knowledge of both systems. The vocabulary and structures of Roman and canon law shaped academic and secular law. Although we shall concentrate on Roman and secular law in this chapter, the reader should bear in mind that these two legal systems are just a part of the *ius commune,* and the terminology and concepts that we shall examine are not exclusively their own.

The first tasks for those wishing to explore the medieval *ius commune* are to learn the structure of the classical and medieval corpus of Roman law and to master the forms of citation used by medieval jurists. Justinian's codification consisted of four parts: the *Institutiones* ("Institutes"), an introduction to Roman law originally written for first-year law students; the *Codex* ("Codex," "Code"), containing imperial legislation from the second to the sixth century; the *Digesta* (*Digesta, -orum;* "Digest[s]") or *Pandectae* ("Pandects"), a compilation of excerpts from the writings of the Roman jurists; and, finally, the *Novellae* ("Novels"), a compilation of Justinian's own legislation.

The *Digest* was of fundamental importance for understanding the intricacies of Roman law. The excerpts from the Roman jurisconsults defined terms, discussed theoretical difficulties, cited court cases, and made the mass of legislation found in the *Codex* understandable and therefore usable. Without the *Digest* Roman law would have had little influence upon European legal systems of the Middle Ages.

The medieval *Digest* and *Codex,* like Justinian's codification, are divided into books; the books are then subdivided into titles, and each title contains subchapters of excerpts from the Roman jurisconsults (*Digest*) or laws (*Codex*). However, the format of the medieval *Corpus iuris civilis,* known as the *Littera Bononiensis,* was quite different from Justinian's codification. Since the *Digest* was not recovered in one piece, the early teachers of law, called glossators because they "glossed" their texts, divided the *Digest* into three sections: *Digestum vetus,* corresponding to the text from book one, title one, law one, to book 24, title two (in modern citation Dig. 1.1.1 to Dig. 24.2); [*Digestum*] *Infortiatum,* Dig. 24.3 to 38.17; and *Digestum novum,* Dig. 39.1 to 50.17. The *Codex* was separated into two parts, books 1 to 9 and books 10 to 12. The other important difference between the medieval and classical texts was that the *Novellae* were ordered very differently from Justinian's arrangement. The various titles were placed in nine *collationes* and the entire work was called the *Authenticum.*

The medieval and early modern jurists cited the *Digest* with the sign "ff." We do not know why they used this abbreviation. They followed this sign with an abbreviated title—sometimes radically abbreviated—e.g. "de sep. vi." (= *de sepulchro violato*); next in the reference came either the abbreviation for *lex* ("l.") together with a Roman numeral or the Latin incipit of the law, e.g. "l. iii." or "l. Praetor ait" (= Dig. 47.12.3), or just the incipit by itself. A few examples of medieval references to the *Digest* followed by the modern citations illustrate the jurists' method:

> ut ff. de legat. iii. l. i. § Si filius
>     = Dig. 32.1.103(102).2

> ut ff. de testamen. mil. l. In fraudem § finali
> = Dig. 29.1.15(16).6
> ut ff. de regul. iuris Cum principalis
> = Dig. 50.17.178(139)

The sign (§) is followed by a reference to a specific paragraph within the law. The numbers in parentheses indicate the divergence of the medieval *Digest* from the classical text. The medieval vulgate version of the *Digest* and the *Codex* distributed their titles within books and their chapters within titles slightly differently from the classical text. Consequently, both the classical and the medieval arrangements should be given when referring to a text. In the examples above and below, the numbers in parentheses refer to the medieval position of a title or a *lex*.

The *Codex* was cited as "C." and references to it followed the form used for the *Digest*. But since the text of the medieval *Codex* was enriched by selections from the *Novellae* that the jurists placed under appropriate titles, two forms are found for references to the *Codex*:

> ut C. de sacrosan. eccl. l. prima
> = Cod. 1.2(5).1
> ut C. de legibus l. Digna vox
> = Cod. 1.14(17).4
> ut C. de iud. authen. Ad hec
> = post Cod. 3.1.5 (ex Nov. 60.2)

The last reference indicates to the reader that under the title "De iudiciis" the jurists inserted (after the fifth law) an excerpt from the *Novellae* of Justinian with the incipit "Ad hec."

References to the *Institutiones* and the *Authenticum* (the medieval arrangement of the *Novellae*) were signaled by "inst." and "auth.," respectively. Usually the jurists referred to the *Authenticum* by citing the title and the *collatio* in which a law was found:

> ut inst. de act. § i.
> = Instit. 4.6.1
> ut in auth. de eccles. tit. § Si quis in sua, coll. ix.
> = Auth. 9.6.(Nov. 131).8

To help a reader look up a particular text, the modern reference should always include the number of the *Novellae* to which the *Authenticum* corresponds. The medieval *Authenticum* has not been printed since the early seventeenth century, and a particular text is usually most easily consulted in the standard edition of Justinian's *Corpus iuris civilis* [DG2].

The most convenient way to verify references to the entire *Corpus iuris civilis* is to use the index published by Nicolini and d'Amico [DG5]. Ochoa and Diez also published an index to the *Corpus* [DG6], but unlike Nicolini and d'Amico they did not always note the differences between the medieval vulgate text and Justinian's codification.

Although there is not a complete concordance, there are a number of reference books that help one find material in the *Corpus iuris civilis*. To locate particular words or concepts in the *Digest*, the *Vocabularium iurisprudentiae Romanae* is of great value

[DG7]. Similar works provide the same information for the *Codex* [DG8] and the *Institutiones* [DG10]. There is also a complete concordance of the *Novellae* [DG9]. A convenient dictionary of the most important terms used in Roman law is Emil Seckel's revised edition of Hermann Heumann's *Handlexikon zu den Quellen des römischen Rechts* [DG11]. Adolf Berger's *Dictionary of Roman Law* [DG12] is useful for defining terms but does not give references to where one may find the pertinent texts. There is not, unfortunately, a comprehensive dictionary of Medieval Latin legal terminology, but the *Handwörterbuch zur deutschen Rechtsgeschichte* is a valuable reference tool for the most important medieval legal terms [DG37].

Armed with a foundation in Roman law, the reader of Medieval Latin legal texts can turn to secular law. In the early Middle Ages the Germanic kingdoms compiled books of the customary laws of the folk. The early Germanic kings established two separate legal systems for their Roman and German subjects. In its most primitive form, Germanic law was personal and transcended territorial boundaries. Roman law, like modern legal systems, was territorial. By the end of the seventh century, European law no longer recognized a distinction between Romans and Germans, and separate legal systems emerged in the kingdoms of Europe (see [DG74]).

Germanic law was forged and tempered by Roman law, a process of assimilation that began very early. The first compilations of law made by the Germanic tribes that overran the Western provinces of the Roman Empire drew heavily upon Roman law, which influenced the shape and contents of these compilations of customary law. The vocabulary and doctrines of Roman law can be found in almost every compilation of Germanic law. The codes also contain many Germanic terms that have been latinized and are very difficult to translate. The editions of these codes in the *Monumenta Germaniae Historica* often provide helpful notes and glossaries. As has been indicated in the bibliography, several translators of Germanic codes into English have also compiled glossaries.

During the sixth and seventh centuries, the Visigoths, Ostrogoths, Burgundians, Franks, Frisians, Saxons, Lombards, and other tribes committed their unwritten law to written codes. Although the rulers who commanded that these compilations be made were not legislating in the modern sense of the word, they were not bereft of any sense of lawmaking. A decision of the royal Burgundian court incorporated into the Burgundian code stipulated that "its judgment should have the authority of perpetual law":

> Quotiens huiusmodi causae consurgunt, de quibus nihil praecedentium legum statuta iusserunt, ita ambiguitatem rei oportet absolvi, ut emissum iudicium perpetuae legis robur accipiat, et specialis causa generalem teneat aequitatem. [DG42], 1.2.1, p85

The idea that a judgment of a court could set a precedent was a concept of Roman law, and, not surprisingly, this section of the Burgundian code is replete with "Romanisms": *legum statuta, iudicium,* and *perpetuae legis robor.* Although the text cited might, at first glance, seem to articulate a theory of legislation, such an interpretation would be seriously misleading. The author of the text has incorporated Roman legal terminology with little understanding of technical concepts. *Legum statuta* is a tautology that no Roman lawyer would have committed. An *emissum iudicium,* in this case the "rendered opinion of the court," might attain the "authority of perpetual law," but a classical Roman lawyer would have formulated his language and thought very differently. A Roman jurist would not have created new law from a court decision but from an imperial rescript (a response to a legal question) or from an imperial constitution.

Carolingian monarchs were much more active promulgating laws that in some ways approximated modern legislation. Charlemagne (747–814) brought political and legal unity to his realm, and in his biography Einhard (d. 840) wrote that the king wanted to reform Frankish law and mandated that the laws of all nations under his jurisdiction should be written down. Charlemagne issued a large number of administrative and legislative commands, which, because they were divided into chapters (*capitula*), are called "capitularies." These documents regulated secular and ecclesiastical affairs in his kingdom and were enforced by royal envoys (*missi dominici*). The Capitulary of Herstal (779) contained a series of executive orders that mixed ecclesiastical and secular concerns. Charlemagne ordered bishops to be subject to their metropolitans and priests to their bishops, but, within the same capitulary, he regulated the penalties for murderers, robbers, and perjurers. In chapter nine of this capitulary the king ordered his vassals to render justice and threatened to deprive them of their offices if they did not:

> Ut latrones de infra immunitatem illi (= illius) iudicis ad comitum placita praesententur; et qui hoc non fecerit, beneficium et honorem perdat. Similiter et vassus noster, si hoc non adimpleverit, beneficium et honorem perdat; et qui beneficium non habuerit, bannum solvat. [DG51] v1.20.9, p48

The Capitulary of Herstal contains a number of terms that would become part of feudal law: *beneficium, placitum, vassus,* and *bannum.* Yet this terminology would mean something quite different in the twelfth century, and the reader should not assume that the meanings of words did not change between the eighth and twelfth centuries. *Placitum* means a plea or pleading in later law; it is foreign to Roman law. In the text above, *placita* should not be translated as "pleas," but as "the determination" (of the counts). In later law *beneficium* could mean a gift or a fief (*feudum* is another word for fief). Here, however, it means office. *Vassus* is "vassal" in feudal law, but in the Carolingian period a *vassus* is someone dependent upon a lord, without the contractual implications of the feudal *vassus.* Charlemagne's capitulary illustrates the difficulties of translating early medieval documents using classical or later medieval legal definitions.

The Italian communes compiled or promulgated their own statutes beginning in the twelfth century. These texts and their language were shaped by the law of the *ius commune* and local Italian practice. The northern Italian city-states were the most precocious. Piacenza published its first statutes in 1135, Genoa in 1143, Pisa in 1162. The most prosperous and important city on the Lombard plain, Milan, issued its first known statute in 1170, with a compilation of Milanese laws, the *Liber consuetudinum Mediolani,* following in 1216. The statutes of the city-states often present a patchwork of terminology taken from the *ius commune* and local customary law. A passage from the statutes of Milan regulating trials by battle (*pugna*) exemplifies this colorful mixture:

> In aliis ergo casibus fit pugna, veluti in furto sicut dictum est. In schacho similiter. De incendio quoque et guasto fit pugna, veluti si blavam in agris quis guastasse vel vites

taliasse vel arbores scorticasse dicatur et damnum fuerit solidorum sex vel plurium. [DG55] p96

*Pugna* was completely unknown to Roman law. Roman jurists distinguished between *furtum* and *rapina* (theft and theft with violence). Here the jurists who drafted this passage incorporated *furtum* into the text, but substituted an Italianism, *schachum,* for *rapina. Guastum* is an Italian spelling of *vastum. Damnum* is a technical term for the loss or expenditure incurred by a plaintiff in a legal case.

The great English treatise on law of the thirteenth century that is commonly attributed to Bracton presents a different challenge to the reader. Although Bracton's treatise is replete with allusions to the *ius commune,* his king was quite different from the "prince" of the learned law. Anyone who interprets Bracton by assuming that he adhered to the principles of Roman law to which he referred will be misled. Although Bracton knew Roman and canon law, the doctrines of kingship in those legal systems did not shape his constitutional thought. He applied the *ius commune* to English jurisprudence like a thin veneer that never transforms its conception of a monarch "bound by the law":

> Temperet . . . potentiam suam per legem quae frenum est potentiae, quod secundum leges vivat, quod hoc sanxit lex humana quod leges suum ligent latorem, et alibi in eadem, digna vox maiestate regnantis est legibus, scilicet alligatum se principem profiteri. Item nihil tam proprium est imperii quam legibus vivere, et maius imperio est legibus submittere principatum, et merito debet retribuere legi quod lex tribuit ei, facit enim lex quod ipse sit rex. [DG39] v2:305–6

In this passage Bracton refers to one of the most influential texts of Roman law and a key problem of interpretation for the *ius commune,* i.e. *Digna vox* (Cod. 1.14[17].4). *Digna vox* admonished the prince to respect the law, and medieval jurists spilled much ink interpreting this constitution. Only a few jurists of the *ius commune,* however, would have concluded that the "law makes the king." Bracton uses the terminology of the *ius commune* and even quotes the wording of *Digna vox,* but he understands law very differently from most contemporary academic jurists. "Law makes the king" is a concept that violated a central tenet of contemporary jurisprudential thought. The jurists had recently evolved a doctrine of sovereignty that affirmed the opposite: "The king's will is the source of all law." The terms in this passage—*lator, imperium, maiestas,* and *principatum*—are taken from the *ius commune,* and they describe a conception of monarchical authority that Bracton did not endorse. His *imperium* and *principatum* are not the powers of the "prince" as found in the *Corpus iuris civilis.* Bracton's English king exercised limited, circumscribed power; the *ius commune* could not accurately define his authority.

English, French, Italian, and other secular legal systems were not academic disciplines during the Middle Ages, and we therefore have very few commentaries like Bracton's on them.

The most significant accomplishment of the *ius commune* in the Middle Ages was the intense literary activity of the jurists. From the twelfth to the fifteenth century they explored every nook and cranny of Justinian's *Corpus iuris civilis,* producing a massive legacy of juristic writings. They interpreted Roman law by writing glosses (comments on individual words or phrases), commentaries and *summae* (extended analyses of law books, titles, or laws), questions (disputations on legal points held as academic exercises), and *consilia* (briefs written for actual cases). Students of juristic Latin must constantly bear in mind that, when the jurists wrote their glosses and related works, they not only cited the texts of law but also expected the reader to consider the glosses and commentaries of other jurists on the same texts ([DG74] pp340–46). A passage on the constitution *Digna vox* by Guido of Suzzara (fl. 1260–92) demonstrates how the jurists wove their thought around the texts of Roman law and the commentaries of others:

> Nota quod si imperator facit pacem cum aliqua ciuitate seu cum aliquo comite uel barone, et ineat aliqua pacta, teneretur ea obseruare, nec potest uenire contra uel ea infringere, ut hic et qui testa. fac. pos. l. Si quis (Cod. 6.22.6) et de testa. l. Ex imperfecto (Cod. 6.23.3). Item nec pacta facta per suos antecessores potest infringere, ut infra de testa. milit. l. Que a patre (Cod. 2.51.7) et de rebus alien. uel non alien. l. Venditrici (Cod. 4.51.3). Nec obstat quod dicitur quod par in parem non habet imperium, ut ff. de iniur. Nec magistratibus (Dig. 47.10.32) et ad Trebell. Ille a quo § Tempestiuum (Dig. 36.1.13.4) quod imperator dum uiuit parem non habet, et successor suus heres habet seruare facta predecessorum ut dictum est. Guido. *Suppletiones* to Cod. 1.14[17].4 [*Digna vox*]; Paris, B.N., MS lat. 4489, fol. 33v

A careful analysis of the texts of Roman law with which Guido supported his description of princely authority would puzzle a modern reader. A reading of the constitutions from the *Codex,* i.e. *Si quis* and *Ex imperfecto testamento,* would not immediately convince a modern reader that the emperor was bound by his treaties and contracts. The connection between the two constitutions and Guido's conclusion would seem tenuous at best. However, Guido cited much more than just two imperial constitutions. He referred to a century of commentaries written on them in which the jurists had developed a doctrine that the prince was limited by his contract. The result of their work was a doctrine that denied the prince any absolute power to break contracts. Guido's allegation of the two constitutions was a shorthand reference to this body of writing. The main point is that to understand the jurisprudence of the *ius commune* one must not read the jurists out of context.

When Guido referred to one of the basic principles of medieval theories of sovereignty in the second part of his gloss, *par in parem non habet imperium* ("an equal cannot exercise power and jurisdiction over an equal"), he did not buttress his allegation only with the two references to the *Digest,* but also with the commentaries on them. Again, if modern readers were to read only the texts of the *Digest* specifically cited by Guido, they would not understand how he arrived at his conclusions. *Par in parem* defined the authority of a ruler to change, promulgate, or abolish law in the jurisprudence of the *ius commune. Nec magistratibus* and *Tempestiuum* were two of the *loci classici* where the jurists discussed this doctrine of legislative sovereignty.

Beside the writings of the jurists, we also have the documents of the courts. After the twelfth century, the testimony of witnesses in legal cases was commonly recorded in writing. These records are of great value for information about legal procedure, practice, and vocabulary. An Italian court case from 1289 illustrates the shaky grammar and syntax of these documents:

> Faciollus Bonvezini testis iuratus ut supra et prelecto sibi capitulo primo dixit hic testis, "bene erat dictus Petrus sub porticu suo." Interrogatus super secundo, dixit hic testis, "bene exiverat dictus Petrus extra domum suam caussa urinandi." Interrogatus si ipse habitat in domo una cum dicto Petro, nec si ipse audivit dicere dictus Petrus, "ego vollo

ire extra domum caussa urinandi," respondit, "non audivi dicere." Interrogatus qua de caussa dixit quod ipse bene venerit extra domum caussa urinandi, respondit "quia vidi ipsum urinare et non aliter scio." [DG56] VI:292

The orthography is typical of Italian texts of this period and the syntax is characteristic of spoken Latin. The reference to *dictus Petrus* in line 6 of the passage should be to *dictum Petrum* if it is to conform to proper Latin grammar. But these texts convey a simple immediacy that more formal texts never achieve.

The technical terminology of judicial procedure can be a formidable barrier to understanding legal texts, since the language of the court can be arcane. A twelfth-century book on procedure describes basic terminology:

> Actor est, qui persequitur aliquid principaliter dicens, rem suam esse vel personam obligatam ad aliquid dandum vel faciendum. Sed et reus, si intentione adversarii fundata exceptionem opponit, ut condempnationem effugiat, actor intelligitur. Agere enim is videtur, qui exceptione utitur. Reus est, adversus quem contenditur, quia aut possidere vel debere dicatur. [DG57] V4:1.3

*Actor* is the plaintiff who brings his complaint to court. *Reus* can be, as in this case, translated as "defendant," but it can also mean someone who has been convicted of a crime. An *exceptio* is a defendant's response to an accusation of a plaintiff, which, if true, might exonerate the defendant. *Agere* has several meanings, including to assert a right in court or to pursue a legal action by means of the *ordo iudiciarius* (the technical term for the rules of court procedure).

The law did not countenance elegant variation, and the jurists consistently use the same vocabulary to define a legal situation. A plaintiff had the obligation to prove (*probare*) his case. *Convenire* was the verb used to summon a defendant before a court.

> Ad probationem actoris pertinet, si obtinere velit, ut id, quod intendit, probet. Actore enim non probante, qui convenitur, etsi nichil praestiterit, obtineat, quia rei favorabiliores sunt quam actores. [DG57] V4:1.3

The jurists formulated general legal principles in language that was not always crystal clear. In this case, the jurist wished to define the principle that "if the plaintiff does not prove his case, the defendant would be acquitted."

In describing the judicial process, ordinary words can assume technical meanings:

> Quod si ex inquisitione ipsa leves personae aliquae de homicidio ipso notentur, licet per eam contra ipsos non probetur ad plenum, ad tormenta ipsarum levium et vilium personarum postremo decernimus descendendum. [DG58] p42

A *levis persona* is not an insignificant person, but a base or infamous one. In this context *notentur* means to be blamed or implicated. *Ad plenum* is a technical expression that indicates a "full proof" (*plena probatio*). *Tormenta* are tortures. Another Roman legal expression for examination by torture is *quaestio*. Finally, *inquisitio* has none of the sinister overtones sometimes implied by the English word *inquisition;* it should be translated here as "judicial investigation" or "judicial process."

This brief survey of legal terminology can only begin to suggest the complexity of juristic Latin. An inexperienced translator of these texts must not assume that a familiar word is not also a technical term in law. Even distinguished translators of Medieval Latin legal texts can nod. One translated *auditis . . . atque perpensis criminalis negotii meritis* as "since the deserts of a criminal case which is pending . . . have been heard and considered." *Meritum* can mean "desert" in Classical Latin, but in law it means "the essential issues of the case." The phrase is formulaic and should be literally translated "the issues of the criminal case having been heard and examined . . . ." The error here is minor but it illustrates the pits into which even a legal scholar can fall.

## Select Bibliography

### General

W.H. Bryson, *Dictionary of Sigla and Abbreviations to and in Law Books before 1607* (1975); see [DF26–28] [DG1].

### Roman Law

#### (a) Sources, Guides, Histories, Manuscripts, Translations

*Corpus iuris civilis,* ed. T. Mommsen (*Digesta*), P. Krüger (*Digesta, Institutiones, Codex*), R. Schöll (*Novellae*), and W. Kroll (*Novellae*), 3 vols. (1872–77, 1895; 1915–28; many reprintings, most recently 1954): Krüger had first published his edition of the *Institutiones* in 1867; an edition of the *Digest,* prepared by Mommsen and Krüger, first appeared in 1870 [DG2]. There are facing-page English translations of the *Institutiones* by P. Birks and G. McLeod (1987) [DG3], and of the *Digesta* by a team of translators under the editorial direction of A. Watson, 4 vols. (1985) [DG4]; both have glossaries of Latin terms.

U. Nicolini and F.S. d'Amico, *Indices Corporis iuris civilis iuxta vetustiores editiones cum criticis collatas,* 3 vols. in 5 (1964–70): pt1, *index titulorum;* pt2, *index legum;* pt3, *index paragraphorum* [DG5].

J. Ochoa and A. Diez, *Indices titulorum et legum Corporis iuris civilis* (1965) [DG6].

*Vocabularium iurisprudentiae Romanae,* ed. O. Gradenwitz *et al.* (1903–) [DG7].

*Vocabularium Codicis Iustiniani,* ed. R. Mayr, 2 vols. (1923–25, r1965) [DG8].

*Legum Iustiniani imperatoris vocabularium: Novellae, pars Latina,* 10 vols. and *Indices* (1977–79); *Novellae, pars Graeca,* 7 vols. and *Indices* (1986–89): both sets ed. G.G. Archi and A.M. Bartoletti Colombo. See also A.M. Bartoletti Colombo, *Lessico delle Novellae di Giustiniano nella versione dell'Authenticum,* v1:A–D, v2:E–M (1983–86) [DG9].

*Vocabularium Institutionum Iustiniani Augusti,* ed. R. Ambrosino (1942) [DG10].

H. Heumann, *Handlexikon zu den Quellen des römischen Rechts,* ed. E. Seckel, 9th ed. (1907, r1971 [DG11].

A. Berger, *Encyclopedic Dictionary of Roman Law, TAPhS,* n.s., 43.2 (1953, r1968) [DG12].

The medieval vulgate text of the *Corpus iuris civilis* was published repeatedly from the beginning of printing in the fifteenth century to the early seventeenth. Almost all these editions also have the *Ordinary Gloss* of Accursius added in the margins. Pietro Torelli began a modern edition in the 1930s, but only a small part of the *Institutes*, with Accursius's gloss, has been published: *Accursii Florentini glossa ad Instititiones Iustiniani imperatoris* (1939) [DG13].

Theodor Mommsen, Paul Krüger, Rudolf Schöll, and Wilhelm Kroll published the modern edition of Justinian's codification with an extensive apparatus of variants in the late nineteenth century (see [DG2]). A complete facsimile edition of the *Codex Florentinus*, the earliest manuscript of the *Digest* (c. A.D. 600), has been published by A. Corbino and B. Santalucia, eds., *Justiniani Augusti Pandectarum codex florentinus*, 2 vols. (1988) [DG14].

H. Coing, ed., *Handbuch der Quellen und Literatur der neueren europäischen Privatrechtsgeschichte*, vi: *Mittelalter (1100–1500): Die gelehrten Rechte und Die Gesetzgebung* (1973): the first comprehensive survey of medieval Roman law since Savigny (see [DG22]); it lists the printed and reprinted editions of the works of all the medieval "civilians" (i.e. the authorities on the civil or Roman law) [DG15].

M. Conrat (Cohn), *Geschichte der Quellen und Literatur des römischen Rechts im früheren Mittelalter* (1891, r1963) [DG16].

G. Dolezalek, *Verzeichnis der Handschriften zum römischen Recht bis 1600*, 4 vols. (1972) [DG17], and *id.* (with L. Mayali), *Repertorium manuscriptorum veterum Codicis Iustiniani*, 2 vols. (1985) [DG18]: these volumes are an invaluable introduction to the manuscripts of Roman law.

L. Fowler-Magerl, *Ordo iudiciorum vel ordo iudiciarius* (1984): a description of the earliest Roman and canon law treatises on procedure; essential for understanding how learned law influenced the practice of law in the twelfth century [DG19].

*La Glossa di Poppi alle Istituzioni di Giustiniano*, ed. V. Crescenzi, *FSI* 114 (1990) [DG20].

*Glosse preaccursiane alle Istituzioni: Strato Azzoniano, libro primo*, ed. S. Caprioli *et al.*, *FSI* 107 (1984): the first volume of what will be a work of great importance for historians of early medieval Roman law [DG21].

F.K. von Savigny, *Geschichte des römischen Rechts im Mittelalter*, 2nd ed., 7 vols. (1834–51, r1961): Savigny is still the most complete guide to the biographies of the medieval civilians and to their works [DG22].

*Scripta anecdota glossatorum*, ed. G.B. Palmerio *et al.*, 3 vols. (1892–1913, r1962): a valuable collection of texts [DG23].

## (b) Studies

V. Colli, "Termini del diritto civile," in *CIVICIMA* 3:231–41 [DG24].

C. Donahue, Jr., "Law, Civil—*Corpus iuris*, Revival and Spread," in *DMA* 7:418–25 [DG25].

R. Feenstra, *Le droit savant au moyen âge et sa vulgarisation* (1986) [DG26].

A. Gouron, *La science du droit dans le Midi de la France au moyen âge* (1984) [DG27].

*Ius Romanum Medii Aevi* (1961–): a large-scale history of the influence of medieval Roman law on European society [DG28].

W. Kalb, *Das Juristenlatein: Versuch einer Charakteristik auf Grundlage der Digesten* (1888, r1984) [DG29]; and *id., Wegweiser in die römische Rechtssprache* (1912, r1984): the best discussion of the syntax and grammar of classical Roman law [DG30].

H. Kantorowicz and W.W. Buckland, *Studies in the Glossators of the Roman Law:*

*Newly Discovered Writings of the Twelfth Century* (1938); reissued with addenda and corrigenda by P. Weimar (1969) [DG31].

P. Koschaker, *Europa und das römische Recht* (1947, r1966) [DG32].

E.M. Meijers, *Études d'histoire du droit*, ed. R. Feenstra and H.F.W.D. Fischer, 4 vols. (1956–66) [DG33].

*Das römische Recht im Mittelalter*, ed. E.J.H. Schrage (1987) [DG34].

P. Vinogradoff, *Roman Law in Mediaeval Europe*, 2nd ed. by F. de Zulueta (1929, r1968 with new foreword by P. Stein): still one of the most readable surveys of the influence of Roman law in the Middle Ages [DG35].

## Secular Law

### (a) Sources, Guides, Histories, Translations

J. Balon, *Ius Medii Aevi* (1959–): an important series that includes detailed lexical studies and, beginning with v5, the *Grand dictionnaire de droit du moyen âge* (1972–), which is appearing in fascicles [DG36].

*Handwörterbuch zur deutschen Rechtsgeschichte*, ed. A. Erler and E. Kaufmann (1971–) [DG37].

A. Wolf, "Die Gesetzgebung der entstehenden Territorialstaaten," in *Handbuch* (see [DG15]), v1:517–800: Wolf's essay is of fundamental importance for an understanding of the creation and codification of secular law in Western Europe from c. 1100 to 1500; he lists all the printed editions for secular European codes in the national monarchies and in the Italian city-states [DG38].

Henry de Bracton (attrib.), *De legibus et consuetudinibus Angliae*, ed. G.E. Woodbine, tr. (with revisions and notes) S.E. Thorne, 4 vols. (1968–77) [DG39].

Ranulf de Glanville (d. 1190), *The Treatise on the Laws and Customs of the Realm of England Commonly Called Glanvill*, ed. and tr. G.D.G. Hall (1965, r1993) [DG40].

The sources of English legal history have been published by the Selden Society. The most recent guide to these publications is *A Centenary Guide to the Publications of the Selden Society* (1987) [DG41].

An extensive collection of early medieval legal materials can be found in the volumes of the *Monumenta Germaniae Historica [MGH]* in its various series: (a) *Leges* (in Folio), including v3: *Leges Alamannorum, Baiuwariorum, Burgundionum, Frisonum*, ed. J. Merkel, F. Bluhme, and K. von Richthofen (1863) [DG42]; v4: *Leges Langobardum*, ed. F. Bluhme and A. Boretius (1868, r1984) [DG43]; v5: *Leges Saxonum*, ed. K. and K.F. von Richthofen; *Lex Thuringorum*, ed. K.F. von Richthofen; *Lex Ribuaria*, ed. R. Sohm; *Lex Francorum Chamavorum*, ed. R. Sohm; *Lex Romana Raetica Curiensis*, ed. K. Zeumer (1875–89, r1987) [DG44]; (b) *Leges nationum Germanicarum*, including v1: *Leges Visigothorum*, ed. K. Zeumer (1902, r1973) [DG45]; v2.1: *Leges Burgundionum*, ed. L.R. von Salis (1892, r1973) [DG46]; v3.2: *Lex Ribvaria*, ed. F. Beyerle and R. Buchner (1954, r1965) [DG47]; v4.2: *Lex Salica*, ed. K.A. Eckhardt (1969) [DG48]; v5.1: *Leges Alamannorum*, ed. K.A. Eckhardt (1966, r1992) [DG49]; v5.2: *Lex Baiwariorum*, ed. E. von Schwind (1926) [DG50]; (c) *Capitularia regum Francorum*, 2 vols., ed. A. Boretius and V. Krause (1883, 1890–97; r1984) [DG51]; (d) *Constitutiones et acta publica imperatorum et regum*, ed. L. Weiland, J. Schwalm, *et al.*, 11 vols. (1893–1993, r1963–82 [of vols. 1–6.1, 8]; v6.2.2 and v7.1–2 are forthcoming) [DG52]; (e) *Fontes iuris Germanici antiqui, Nova series*, ed. K.A. Eckhardt *et al.*, 6 vols., of which v6 is forthcoming (1933–74, r1973–89 [of vols. 1, 2, 4]) [DG53]; (f)

*Fontes iuris Germanici antiqui in usum scholarum separatim editi*, ed. M. Krammer *et al.*, 14 vols. (1869–1990, r1984–89 [of vols. 8, 10]) [**DG54**].

*Liber consuetudinum Mediolani anni MCCXVI*, 2nd ed., ed. E. Besta and G.L. Barni (1949) [**DG55**].

*Albertus Gandinus und das Strafrecht der Scholastik*, ed. H. Kantorowicz, 2 vols. (1907–26) [**DG56**].

*Quellen zur Geschichte des römisch-kanonischen Processes im Mittelalter*, ed. L. Wahrmund, 5 vols. (1905–31) [**DG57**].

*Die Konstitutionen Friedrichs II. von Hohenstaufen für sein Königreich Sizilien*, ed. and tr. H. Conrad, T. von der Lieck-Buyken, and W. Wagner, *Studien und Quellen zur Welt Friedrichs II.*, v2 (1973) [**DG58**].

J.M. Powell, tr., *The Liber Augustalis; or, Constitutions of Melfi, Promulgated by the Emperor Frederick II for the Kingdom of Sicily in 1231* (1971) [**DG59**].

K.F. Drew has translated *The Burgundian Code* (1949, r1988) [**DG60**]; *The Lombard Laws* (1973), in which she provides a glossary of terms [**DG61**]; and *The Laws of the Salian Franks* (1991) [**DG62**].

T.J. Rivers provides a glossary of terms for Germanic law in *Laws of the Alamans and Bavarians* (1977) [**DG63**].

## (b) Studies

M. Bellomo, *L'Europa del diritto comune*, 5th ed. (1991); English translation (1995): a lucid and comprehensive survey of medieval secular and learned law in the Middle Ages [**DG64**].

H. Brunner, *Deutsche Rechtsgeschichte*, 2 vols., 2nd ed. (1906–28, r1961) [**DG65**].

K.F. Drew and T.J. Rivers, "Law, German: Early Germanic Codes" (Drew) and "Special Characteristics of Germanic Law" (Rivers), in *DMA* 7:468–77: lists English translations of Germanic codes in bibliography [**DG66**].

G. Giordanengo, *Le droit féodal dans les pays de droit écrit: L'exemple de la Provence et du Dauphiné, XIIe–début XIVe siècle* (1988): an excellent survey of feudal law in France [**DG67**].

O. Guillot, "Le droit romain classique et la lexicographie des termes du latin médiéval impliquant délégation de pouvoir," in *LLM* 153–66 [**DG68**].

K. Kroeschell, *Deutsche Rechtsgeschichte*, 3 vols. (1972–89) [**DG69**].

S.F.C. Milsom, *Historical Foundations of the Common Law*, 2nd ed. (1981) [**DG70**].

W.P. Müller, "The Recovery of Justinian's Digest in the Middle Ages," in *Bulletin of Medieval Canon Law* 20 (1990) 1–29 [**DG71**].

H.A. Myers, "Law, German: Post-Carolingian," in *DMA* 7:477–83 [**DG72**].

K. Pennington, "Law Codes: 1000–1500," in *DMA* 7:425–31 [**DG73**].

K. Pennington, "Medieval Law," in *MSI* 333–52: provides a brief description of the sources of early medieval law [**DG74**].

F. Pollock and F.W. Maitland, *The History of English Law Before the Time of Edward I*, 2 vols., 2nd ed. (1898); with new introduction and select bibliography by S.F.C. Milsom (1968) [**DG75**].

J.-M. Poly, "Vocabulaire 'féodo-vassalique' et aires de culture durant le haut moyen âge," in *LLM* 167–90 [**DG76**].

C. Radding, *The Origins of Medieval Jurisprudence: Pavia and Bologna, 850–1150* (1988): a work that ignores most of the secondary literature of the past 25 years and does not grapple with the textual tradition of the *Digest;* Radding's thesis that the school of Pavia was more important for the revival of Roman law than that of Bologna is untenable, and has been convincingly refuted by W.P. Müller (see [DG71]) [DG77].

K.L. Reyerson and J.B. Henneman, "Law, French: In South," in *DMA* 7:461–68 [DG78].

T.F. Ruiz, "Law, Spanish," in *DMA* 7:518–24 [DG79].

J.R. Strayer, "Law, French: In North," in *DMA* 7:457–60 [DG80].

P. Timbal and J. Metman, "La lexicographie du latin médiéval et le vocabulaire juridique," in *LLM* 147–52 [DG81].

R.C. Van Caenegem, *The Birth of the English Common Law,* 2nd ed. (1988) [DG82].

P. Weimar, "Die Handschriften des Liber feudorum und seiner Glossen," in *Rivista internazionale di diritto comune* 1 (1990) 31–98: the most important work on the development of feudal law in the last 50 years; a guide to the sources and commentaries [DG83].

*See also* [BA45], [BA104], [BA106], [BB28], [BB39–40], [BB43], [BB46], [BB63], [CD13].

DH  •  THEOLOGY AND PHILOSOPHY

BY STEPHEN F. BROWN

Philosophy in the Middle Ages generally played a subordinate role and was often cast in the figure of a servant. It was used to explain and defend the realities affirmed by Christian faith and to foster a deeper understanding of them. Theology was considered the more important study. We shall in this introduction examine some developments in the Latin terminology of both theology and philosophy, beginning, however, with the language of theology, the discipline to which was accorded the title "Queen of the Sciences" in the universities of the thirteenth century.

## The Development of Theological Language

The technical language of theology arose from many sources: sacred Scripture, the works of the Fathers of the Church, the liturgy, the declarations of councils, the writings of philosophers, and the continual creativity of the masters of theology. New theological terms were coined for different reasons: the need to defend the Church's understanding of the mysteries proclaimed in the Gospel against those who attacked or distorted the Christian message, the desire to explain evangelical teachings to educated inquirers who might be drawn to the Church, and the hope of many believers to come to a deeper understanding of their faith. These intellectual activities were seen as fulfillments of the command of 1 *Pt* 3:15: "Always be ready to satisfy anyone who demands from you an account (*ratio*) for the hope that is in you."

## The Inadaquacies of Classical Latin to Express Christian Truths

To carry out these tasks, Christian writers, both Greek and Latin, were compelled to develop a new terminology, partly by coining new words and partly by elevating old ones to higher uses. In the opening chapter of his *Protrepticus,* Clement of Alexandria (d. 211–16) employed a now famous image to illustrate this effort in the Greek world: the new song of the divine *logos* (the Word) demanded new *logoi* (expressions). In the Latin world the demand was similar. For Latin Christians even the word *logos,* found so often in the Greek Bible, but especially at the beginning of the Gospel of John, required some effort to find appropriate expression. The Roman Stoic philosophers had already translated *logos* by *ratio,* the universal and divine reason, of which human reason (*ratio*) is a spark. But in *Adversus Praxean* 5, Tertullian

(d. 220?) seemed deliberately to avoid the already existing Roman philosophical term *ratio* when searching for a corresponding Latin expression for *logos*. He chose instead the first of the two alternatives used by the Church in Africa for *logos,* namely *sermo* and *verbum.* And although Tertullian himself at a technical level might have wished to distinguish between the divine *logos* as *ratio* (immanent in God before creation) and *logos* as *sermo* (the *logos* as expressed in creation), he selected *sermo,* because the Old Latin African Bible (with its "in primordio Sermo erat apud Deum") was so familiar to African Christian communities, whereas only a few learned individuals could grasp the subtle theological distinction that Tertullian himself made between *ratio,* expressing the immanent *logos* of God, and *sermo,* expressing the *logos* of God as manifested in creation.

The pagan Romans themselves faced similar difficulty in translating the Greek word *soter.* Cicero (*Ver.* 2.2.63.154) defined it as follows: "is est nimirum 'soter,' qui salutem dedit." For *soter* he coined the term *servator,* which during the period of the empire became *conservator* in Tacitus (*Ann.* 15.71) and Pliny (*Pan.* 1) and served as one of the titles of Jupiter. This association with a pagan god caused the translators of the Old Latin Bible to avoid the use of *conservator* for *soter,* and they instead invented a new word, *salvator,* itself based on the new verb *salvare* (to save). These neologisms did not gain instant currency among all the Fathers. Tertullian, although he used *salvator,* unsuccessfully offered *salutificator* as an alternative; and Arnobius (d. c. 327) wrote of Christ as *sospitator* (a term also found infrequently, for it had likewise been a pagan title for Jupiter). By the time of Augustine (d. 430), however, *salvator* was welcomed without serious apology to Latin grammarians:

> "Christus," inquit, "Jesus," id est Christus Salvator. Hoc est enim latine Jesus. Nec quaerant grammatici quam sit latinum, sed Christiani quam verum. Salus enim latinum nomen est. Salvare et salvator non fuerunt haec latina antequam veniret Salvator: quando ad latinos venit, et haec latina fecit. *Sermo* 299.6; *PL* 38:1371

Translating the Greek *charisma,* a word with many meanings and of central importance to Christians, also required much experimentation: *donum, donatio, munus* all were tried, but in the end the choice fell on *gratia.*

Similar gropings took place as Latin translations of the Greek Bible were undertaken, or early liturgical rites developed, or apologetical treatises written. Since the Latin language was not rich in spiritual or abstract vocabulary, the Greek was at times simply transliterated, as in *anathema, angelus, apostolus, baptisma, diaconus, ecclesia, episcopus,* etc. In other cases Latin words were coined, as with *salvator, incarnatio, trinitas,* etc. In still other instances, words already existing in Latin—*sacramentum* (the soldier's oath of allegiance), *catechumenus* (originally a Greek word for a "learner," used by the Romans for an "army recruit"), and *paganus* (a soldier's contemptuous term for a "civilian")—took on new Christian meanings. Some already existing Latin terms, however, were often avoided because of their pagan associations, as we have already seen in the case of *conservator* and *sospitator.*

In a study of the linguistic changes of meaning in Tertullian's writings, St.W.J. Teeuwen examined, through verbal developments, the emergence of an entirely new Christian spiritual world [DH106]. *Pax,* for instance, during the early years of the Christian era meant for Roman Christians not so much the end of war, as it did for other Romans, but rather the cessation of persecution. But it also had another, deeper, Christian sense, the *pax* that Christ gave to his followers, that is, the peace between man and God which Christ the mediator had established. Believers were *filii pacis* and Christ himself was the *pax*. *Pax* also implied belief in Christ, a belief confirmed in baptism, which brings *pax* and enrolls its recipients in the community of the Church. Membership in the Church implied the acceptance of orthodox beliefs, so that the *litterae pacis* meant a "certificate of orthodox belief." In common worship the members of the congregation gave one another a *pax* or *osculum pacis* (kiss of peace) as a sign of their fraternity of belief and life in Christ.

More technical linguistic developments, even of *pax*, are to be found in the writings of the Fathers of the Church. Readers of *De civitate dei* 19.11–14 will find there Augustine's meditation on the Christian vision of peace. He accepted the Platonic-Stoic definition of *pax* as "the tranquillity of order," but he challenged the pagan order that placed the Stoic sage at the top of the hierarchy. For the Christian believer, God is the pinnacle of the order of reality, and until all things are reordered to God, their true apex, there can never be the tranquillity of the true order, or *pax* as the Christian conceives of it. The Fathers introduced many other similar technical clarifications into their discussions as they explained, defended, and deepened their faith.

### Key Terms: Theologia, Philosophia, and Ancilla

If not every word, then at least every technical term in theology and philosophy has its own history, and specialized terminology cannot therefore be satisfactorily translated simply be consulting a standard Latin-English dictionary. The meanings of words in these disciplines can often be both subtle and slippery, changing from author to author and even within different works by the same author. This can be illustrated by examining such central terms as *theologia* and *philosophia*, and the word most often used to express the assisting role played by philosophy in relation to theology, i.e. *ancilla*.

(a) **Theologia.** This is a very common term in many texts produced in medieval universities. It is not, however, a biblical word, and it did not easily enter the vocabulary of Christian writers. The Greek form of this word was employed by Plato in two different senses. He used it negatively or pejoratively to characterize the depictions of the gods produced by the poets whom he criticized in his *Republic*. He used it also in a positive sense to describe the philosophical study of divine things. Aristotle, on the other hand, employed the term "philosophy" (a word coined by Pythagoras) for efforts to explain the world and its events in a natural rather than poetic or mythological manner. But in his *Metaphysica* he followed Plato's lead by using the word *theological* to describe the highest and divine science, "first philosophy," and the unchanging objects that it studied.

The Roman Varro (d. 27 B.C.) inherited from the Greek tradition a more complex understanding of "theology." He wrote in fact of three types, the first being the traditional portrait of the gods sketched by the poets. The second reflected the tradition of Plato, Aristotle, and other thinkers who attempted to formulate natural explanations of the world. The third, and most influential in the lives of ordinary citizens, concerned the depiction of the gods of the city. Tertullian in his *Ad nationes* reported and rebutted this threefold depiction of the gods, wanting to have nothing to do with such a "theology."

Augustine, too, was aware of Varro's meanings for *theology*, all of which he examined in detail and rejected. He discovered other pagan writers, the Platonists, whom he considered to have come closer to the truth; they represented God as transcending the soul, and their depiction of Him as creator of the world and of human souls, and as the source of the incorporeal light that could lead men and women to human happiness, inspired Augustine to call them *Dei cognitores*, not *theologi*. His avoidance of the term *theologi* demonstrates well that it was still considered pejorative, linked as it was with the gods of the poets, philsophers, and secular rulers.

Peter Abelard (d. c. 1142) was apparently the first to use *theologia* for a compendium of specifically Christian teachings. Although it is true that none of the four surviving manuscripts of his *Theologia christiana* actually preserves this title [DH50], and that historians wonder whether any of the titles of Abelard's works with *theologia* in them is authentic, in his commentary on *Romans* Abelard referred to a *theologia*, raising a number of questions concerned with various areas of Christian teaching, and stating, "Sed harum quidem propositarum quaestionum solutiones 'Theologiae' nostrae examini reseruamus" ([DH50] VII:76). From this it would appear that at times Abelard used the term *theology* for a collection of diverse *quaestiones* connected with Christian revelation. After his death, however, *theology* seems, when used in a Christian context, to have referred specifically to the study of God, especially the triune God, whereas *beneficia* was commonly employed for discussions of Christ or the sacraments.

*Theologia* was rarely used, then, to refer to a *summa* of Christian doctrines, and it certainly did not identify a discipline that is scientific in the Aristotelian sense of "science" until the mid-thirteenth century. Before that time (and even afterwards) this term may have any of the meanings we have indicated. It could be understood in its strictly etymological sense as the study of God; it could signify, in a way that points to the special Christian view of God, the study of the Trinity; it could identify, after Aristotle's *Metaphysica* was translated into Latin, a treatise on "first philosophy." The context is the only secure guide to the precise meaning of *theologia*, and great care must be exercised in translating it. When, for example, at Oxford in the mid-1240s, the Franciscan Richard Rufus was describing the kind of explanation he was providing in his *Commentarium in Sententias Petri Lombardi,* he identified *theologia* with *divina scriptura*:

> Quod non videtur mihi necessarium, cum haec summa non sit ipsa theologia, nec aliqua pars eius. Est enim divina Scriptura in se integra, perfecta absque hac et omni alia summa. Sed sunt tales summae elucidationes aliquae aliquorum quae in illa obscure dicta sunt, propter nos utiles et adhibitae. Prologue, as in Oxford, Balliol College, MS 62, fol. 6v1

Only in the mid-thirteenth century, as a result of the growing knowledge of what Aristotle meant by "science" and the continuing debate over how the objects of Christian belief could be known, did *theologia* take on the sense of a scientific discipline concerned with all the truths of Christian faith. In his commentary on the *De trinitate* of Boethius (d. 524/6) Thomas Aquinas (d. 1274) used it in this sense, and from this period on "scientific discipline or habit" increasingly became one of the principal meanings of this complex term.

(b)**Philosophia.** Like *theologia*, the term *philosophia* was a multilayered concept in medieval texts. A neologism attributed to Pythagoras, this word served as a contrast to the *sophia* or wisdom that was beyond the reach of all mortals. Even the best of men and women could not be *sophoi* (wise); they could only be *philosophoi*, i.e. *philoi* (lovers) of *sophia* (wisdom). In the Latin world, Cicero called *philosophia* the mother of all the arts (*Tusc.* 1.64), and Seneca (*Nat.* 2.53.3) offered a division of philosophy, according to a Stoic and Platonic model, into rational philosophy (logic), natural philosophy (physics), and moral philosophy (ethics). An alternative division, that of Aristotle, was gleaned from a search of his works by Boethius and consisted of logic, theoretical philosophy (physics, mathematics, and "first philosophy" or theology), practical philosophy (ethics, politics, and economics), and poetical philosophy. The Stoic-Platonic and Aristotelian schemas were both divisions of philosophy in its strict or technical sense.

More commonly *philosophia* was taken broadly to stand for all learning and thus included among its parts the classical liberal arts (especially the *trivium*—grammar, rhetoric, and dialectic—and the *quadrivium*—arithmetic, astronomy, geometry, and music). It could also refer to the different sects of philosophy (in its strict sense) and is therefore found frequently in the plural. In his *De oratore* (3.27.107) Cicero wrote of the "exercitatio . . . propria duarum philosophiarum," i.e. the "Academics" and members of the Peripatetic school.

Unlike *theologia, philosophia* is found in the Bible, where it is used once, in *Col* 2:8—"Videte ne quis vos decipiat per philosophiam"—and has the meaning "wisdom from below or earthly wisdom" (see *Iac* 3:15). In ch. 7 of *De praescriptione haereticorum* Tertullian used *philosophy* in this sense when he attacked those who attempted to produce a mottled Christianity of Stoic, Platonic, and dialectical composition. There in a rhetorical question he sounded a warning for Christians against the limitations of purely worldly wisdom: "Quid ergo Athenis et Hierosolymis?" ("What then do Athens and Jerusalem have to do with one another?").

Other early Christian writers had pursued the study of philosophy before converting to Christianity and saw the benefits it could provide for understanding and strengthening the faith. In bk. 6 of his *Confessiones* Augustine praised Cicero's *Hortensius* as God's instrument for leading him beyond the materialist trap of Manichean philosophy. In *De doctrina christiana* he prescribed caution when studying pagan learning, but the main purpose of this work was to argue how *philosophia* (in the general sense that included the seven liberal arts and many other disciplines) could assist in the understanding of sacred Scripture. He went so far as to suggest that his Christian readers study philosophy in its more technical and strict sense, urging them to "read the Platonists" (2.40). In such exhortations he was only advocating what he and many other Greek and Latin Fathers of the Church had in fact done. Augustine contrasted *huius mundi philosophia, academica philosophia, philosophia gentium,* and *mundana philosophia* with *christiana philosophia, nostra philosophia, vera et sancta philosophia,* and *verissima philosophia* by demonstrating the difference between pagan and Christian ways of life and truth. Despite his declared opposition to pagan learning, however, in his writings he abundantly exploited the trivium and quadrivium and the writings of Cicero, Varro, and the Platonists. In *Contra Iulianum* 4 he declared, "Non sit honestior philosophia gentium quam nostra Christiana quae una est vera philosophia"; but his *De doctrina christiana* offered a complete program of Christian education employing the liberal arts and Platonist philosophy.

Through the *De artibus ac disciplinis liberalium litterarum* of Cassiodorus (d. 583) and the *Etymologiae* of Isidore of Seville (d. 636), philosophy, in the sense of the

whole of pagan knowledge as employed in Augustine's program of Christian education, was passed down to the Carolingian world. In his *De grammatica* Alcuin (d.
804) wrote of the trivium and quadrivium as the "septem philosophiae gradus" that
are necessary to lead the mind "ad culmina sanctarum Scripturarum" (*PL*
101:853–54).

Augustine's distinction between *philosophia gentium* or *mundana* and
*philosophia christiana, vera,* or *nostra* prevailed in succeeding centuries, along with
his program of studies. Though the term *philosophia* may be found without any qualification, the context will usually indicate its specific meaning, such as "worldly wisdom" or "heavenly wisdom," the second of which may also signify the dedicated pursuit of Christian wisdom within monasticism. The use of the noun *philosophus* likewise reflected this Augustinian distinction. In a sermon on the feast of St. Augustine,
Peter Comestor employed this term to describe Augustine himself, as the object of
Monica's prayer to God "ut filium de philosopho redderet catholicum" (*PL* 198:1793).
Peter also used *philosophus* as a title for Horace, a poet attached to "worldly" rather
than "heavenly" wisdom (*PL* 198:1791).

In the twelfth century, Peter Abelard, proceeding beyond the authority of the
Scriptures and the writings of the Fathers, attempted to satisfy students' requests for
reasons that would support the mysteries of faith proclaimed in the Bible. His efforts
earned him the title *philosophus,* an appellation given to him even in scriptural commentaries, such as the *Commentarius Cantabrigiensis in Epistolas Pauli* produced by
the School of Abelard ([DH40] v2:483, 535, 601).

The Augustinian "philosophy" program itself continued into and beyond the
thirteenth century, with the liberal arts and certain elements of the Stoic and Platonist philosophies that had been assimilated into it helping to direct the mind to the
heights of sacred Scripture. In the new universities, founded in the late twelfth and
early thirteenth centuries, the arts faculty served a preparatory function, providing
students with the tools for their later work in Scripture, law, or medicine. The main
element in this program that might be considered philosophy in a technical sense
could be found only in the courses in dialectic. There, the old logic (in its beginnings
made up of Latin translations of the *Isagoge* or *Introduction* of Porphyry and the
*Praedicamenta* and *Perihermenias* of Aristotle, with Boethius's commentaries) and
the new logic (*Analytica priora, Analytica posteriora, Topica,* and *Sophistici elenchi,*
translated in the twelfth century) were the core of the dialectical curriculum. After
these introductory studies, students in the faculty of theology could also indirectly
learn the philosophies of the Stoics and Platonists that had been assimilated into the
commentaries, questions, and disputations concerning dialectic and the materials
related to Scripture. *Philosophia* in the strict technical sense gradually appeared with
the translations of Aristotle's nonlogical works (such as the *Physica, De anima, Metaphysica,* and *Ethica Nicomachea*) and the Greek, Arabic, and Hebrew commentaries
on them that were translated in the late twelfth and thirteenth centuries. It was at this
stage that medieval Christendom directly encountered the challenge presented by a
"pure" philosopher to its Christian worldview. During the first half of the thirteenth
century, the public reading of Aristotle's works in courses was frequently prohibited,
but in 1255 at Paris they became part of the official curriculum. In effect, from this
time on, the faculty of arts at the University of Paris gradually became a faculty of
Aristotelian philosophy.

The subsequent condemnations of many suspect propositions in 1277 at Paris reveal how the arrival of a purely pagan view of reality could relate to a Christian view of it. A similar conflict had occurred in the patristic era among the Christians who were obliged to confront the influence of pagan education and philosophy. Augustine had, as we have seen, urged the cautious use of pagan learning as an aid to Christian understanding, and his position prevailed over that of Tertullian, who had viewed pagan philosophy as a dangerous problem. Augustine's position was that philosophy (as the study both of the liberal arts and of the teachings of the Stoics and Platonists) could assist in the study of Scripture. What, however, would happen if the "new" philosophy, that of Aristotle pure and simple, came into real competition with the scriptural view of reality, or if Aristotle's depiction of truth demanded absolute and independent status within the domain proper to its declared method and area of competence?

This was the central problem at the University of Paris from the 1260s to the 1280s. The condemnations of 1277 recorded certain unacceptable theses that claimed respect for pure philosophy or pure reason that belittled the Christian faith:

> Quod non est excellentior status, quam vacare philosophiae (no. 40). Quod sapientes mundi sunt philosophi tantum (no. 154). Quod nulla quaestio est disputabilis per rationem, quam philosophus non debeat disputare et determinare, quia rationes accipiuntur a rebus (no. 145). *Chartularium Universitatis Parisiensis*, ed. H. Denifle and E. Chatelain, vi (1889), no. 473

Here we have clear proof that *philosophia*, i.e. one particular attitude concerning Aristotelian philosophy, was viewed as a challenge to the intelligible character of Christian belief. But it is also clear that philosophical argument had gained a real hearing and was for many a respected discipline, despite the problems to which the condemations pointed. It had its limits, but it could also claim its own special area of competence.

*Philosophia*, especially in this period, had acquired very specific meanings and was sometimes criticized or even rejected, and sometimes treated with respect. Determining its meaning precisely requires close attention to the clues provided by an author and by the context in which he was writing. In relation, however, to *theologia*, the scientific study of the Scriptures, philosophy generally played the role of *ancilla* or handmaid.

(c) **Ancilla.** Philo Judaeus (d. c. 50) provided the model followed by early Christian writers when considering the relationship between human and divinely revealed knowledge. For him the liberal arts should serve philosophy, which should itself serve the revealed wisdom of Scripture. In the Greek Christian world, this concept of human wisdom as the servant of divine wisdom was adopted by Clement of Alexandria, Origen (d. 254/5), and John Damascene (d. c. 749).

In the West, Augustine, Boethius, Cassiodorus, Isidore, Bede (d. 735), and Alcuin all championed the legitimate use of pagan learning to defend and explain the Christian faith, but none employed the term *ancilla* to express this notion of service. It was used first by Peter Damian (d. 1072), in a strong admonition about the human disciplines: human learning should not pretend to offer true wisdom, but, like a handmaiden (*ancilla*), should offer her mistress, Christian wisdom, a submissive service. More postively, and without using the word *ancilla*, Hugh of St. Victor (d. 1180), Robert of Melun (d. 1167), and John of Salisbury (d. 1180) underscored the function of the humanistic disciplines as assisting Christian wisdom. But it was Peter Abelard, quoting Jerome (*Ep.* 70.2) as his authority, who used this term with specific reference to the role of the traditional liberal arts in the study of Scripture and the *quaestiones* arising from Scripture.

In a celebrated letter, *Ab Aegyptiis* (1228), *ancilla* appears again. This was sent by Gregory IX to the theologians of Paris to warn them not to put the head where the tail should be, and vice versa (cf. *Dt* 28:13–14); rather they should compel the hand-maidens (*ancillae*) to serve the queen. As the arts faculty at Paris became more and more a faculty of Aristotelian philosophy, the reversal of priorities that the pope had warned of became an even greater concern. We note this in discussions of the late thirteenth century, where a distinction is made between *ancilla* with the sense of *famulatus* ("submissive service") and *ancilla* meaning *subalternatio* ("lower in priority"). Already in England in 1253 Robert Kilwardby (d. 1279) had pointed to the tension in the two senses: "Non est hic continentia subalternationis, sed continentia principalitatis et famulatus est hic" (*In I Sent.*, q. 14); "This is not a case where one thing has merely priority over another, but rather one where one thing has a ruling function and the other a serving function." Henry of Ghent (d. 1293) stressed the difference between the two cases when he declared: "Subministratio enim et famulatus omnino aliud est a subalternatione; et est fatuum dicere quod subministratio sit aliquis modus subalternationis" (*Summa*, a. 7, q. 5); "Assistance (*subministratio*) and submissive service are related to one another in a way altogther different from that of higher and lower priority; and it is a waste of words to say that assistance is just a lower type of priority." On the other hand, John of Paris (d. 1306) insisted (*In I Sent.*, *prooem.*, q. 3) on their essential similarity, stating that *famulatus* and *subalternatio* both signify the relationship between a superior and an inferior. Henry found inadequate the claim that both words recognized the more noble status of Christian revelation; he wished to stress the role of service that he believed philosophy should play with respect to theology, a relationship conveyed by the term *famulatus* ("submissive service"). The use of *subalternatio* ("lower in priority") might well affirm the superiority of revealed truth, but this term might also come to be identified with the development of an independent type of science. For Henry, *ancilla* had become an ambivalent term, whose sense of *famulatus* required emphasis if the unity of Christian wisdom were to be preserved.

### Central Terms Concerning the Doctrines of the Trinity and the Incarnation

The two most characteristic doctrines of the Christian faith are the Trinity of Persons in God and the Incarnation of Christ. With respect to the first, the Christian faith holds that there is one God who is Father, Son, and Holy Spirit. How could this be explained without falling into modalism (the belief that there is only one divine essence and that the Father, Son, and Holy Spirit are not distinct persons or substances but only different manifestations of this one essence) or tritheism (the belief that the Father, Son, and Holy Spirit have each a distinct divine essence and thus are three distinct gods)? Christian belief concerning Christ is that He is God the Son and thus has a divine nature or essence, that He is also man and thus has a human nature or essence, and that He is nevertheless one person, substance, or subsistence.

Attempts to explain and defend these teachings required greater and greater clarity in rethinking the categories of natural things and their appropriate application to

God; they also demanded an extremely precise choice and use of key terms. In the prologue to his *Summa aurea,* written in the 1220s, William of Auxerre followed the leads of Augustine's *De trinitate* and Boethius's *Quomodo trinitas unus deus ac non tres dii,* declaring:

> Volentes autem ostendere rationibus res divinas, ex convenientibus rationibus procedemus, non ex eis que sunt <proprie> rerum naturalium. Ideo enim decepti fuerunt heretici, quia rationes proprias rerum naturalium volebant applicare rebus divinis, quasi volentes adequare naturam suo Creatori. Sic deceptus fuit Arrius. Cum enim in rebus naturalibus generaliter verum sit quod plurium plures sint naturae, ut plurium hominum plures humanitates et plurium asinorum plures asinitates, voluit Arrius applicare hanc regulam rebus divinis sic: Pater et Filius et Spiritus Sanctus sunt plures; ergo plures sunt eorum naturae; sed Pater habet deitatem et una sola est deitas; ergo Filius non habet deitatem sed aliam naturam quam sit deitas. Et ex hoc sequitur quod Filius Dei non sit Deus, sed creatura ipsa; quod ipse concessit deceptus fantastica similitudine rerum <naturalium>. Eodem modo Sabellius deceptus fuit. Cum enim verum generaliter in rebus sit quia una natura <unius> solius est; sed deitas est unica natura; ergo unius solius est; sed ipsa est Patris et Filii et Spiritus Sancti; ergo sicut Pater et Filius et Spiritus Sanctus sunt unum, ita sunt unus. Et ideo dixit Sabellius quod Pater quando vult est Pater, quando vult est Filius, quando vult est Spiritus Sanctus. Ipse ergo Sabellius personas confundit quasi de tribus faciens unam; Arrius vero separavit naturam sive substantiam personarum. [DH61] VI:18–19

The councils of Nicaea and Constantinople overcame Arius's subordinationism by declaring the unequivocal divinity of Christ. Nicaea expressed this in its claim that Christ is "of the same substance" as the Father, and Constantinople extended Nicaea's declaration of true divinity to the Third Person. But how could such beliefs be best expressed?

We note in the declarations of the councils and in William of Auxerre's statement the frequent appearance of such technical terms as *nature, substance, person.* In the Greek world, the Christian doctrine of the Trinity repudiated Arius's heresy and was expressed in St. Basil's formula *mia ousia, treis hypostaseis* (one substance, three persons). *Ousia* (substance) was part of the philosophical vocabulary of Plato and Aristotle, and it was the latter who provided, in bk. 7 of his *Metaphysica,* a detailed study of his interpretation of *ousia* in contrast to its Platonic meaning. *Hypostasis* was also used by Aristotle, but in many of his writings its meaning was not metaphysical but medical, i.e. it referred to the sediment that settles to the bottom of a liquid, as in a urine sample, and stands beneath the lighter liquid above. In legal contexts *hypostasis* could mean wealth, an adequate inheritance, or suitable means for a good life. In other contexts, however, it could express for the Stoics and for Aristotle a metaphysical sense, as in Aristotle's statement in his *Perihermenias:* "Quod non habet hypostasin (substantia) non est."

When we wish to consider how Greek words such as *ousia* and *hypostasis* were translated into Latin, we must keep in mind the declarations of Seneca and Quintillian, who observed that there was a great lack of philosophical vocabulary in the Latin language. In *Ep.* 58 to Lucilius Seneca remarked:

> Quanta verborum nobis paupertas, immo egestas sit, numquam magis quam hodierno die intellexi. Mille res inciderunt, cum forte de Platone loqueremur, quae nomina desiderarent nec haberent. . . . [Q]uomodo dicetur ousia, res necessaria, natura conti-

nens fundamentum omnium? Rogo itaque permittas mihi hoc verbo uti. Nihilominus dabo operam, ut ius a te datum parcissime exerceam; fortasse contentus ero mihi licere.

Here we note not only Seneca's comment about the dearth of Latin philosophical vocabulary but also his attempt to create a Latin equivalent for Plato's interpretation of *ousia* ("a necessary thing, a nature containing the foundation of all things"). The Latin coinage *essentia*, as the equivalent of *ousia* in Aristotle's *Categories*, was ascribed by Seneca (*Ep.* 58.6) to Cicero, but Quintillian commented that it was invented by the philosopher Plautus (*Inst.* 2.14.2, 3.6.23, 8.3.33). Apuleius would later sometimes use *essentia* and sometimes *substantia* as translations of *ousia*. Among Latin Christians, Tertullian employed *substantia* much more often than *essentia* as his equivalent of *ousia*, and he was also the first Latin Christian writer to use the word *persona* as a translation of *hypostasis*. It was under his influence that *una substantia, tres personae* was accepted, after much hesitation and even suspicion, as the Latin equivalent of Basil's formula, *mia ousia, treis hypostaseis*.

Augustine, however, replaced this traditional formula with *una essentia, tres substantiae*, declaring in *De trinitate* (5.8), "Essentiam dico quae ousia graece dicitur, quam usitatius substantiam vocamus." Why did Augustine make the change from the more customary *substantia*? He did so to avoid Marius Victorinus's explanation of Basil's original Greek formula—an explanation that tended to reduce the divine Persons to modes or forms of the divine substance. In his treatise against the Arians, who had argued that *ousia* was both untranslatable and nonscriptural, Victorinus had concluded: "Iam igitur nihil interest, utrum hypostasin divitias [= 'substance,' i.e. wealth] intellegamus an ousian, dummodo id significetur quod ipse deus est" (*Adversus Arium* 2.6). In short, for Victorinus the question whether *substantia* was equivalent to *ousia* or to *hypostasis* had lost its meaning. *Substantia* had become an ambiguous term: was it in fact the Latin for *ousia* or for *hypostasis*? The situation prompted Augustine to comment, "[N]escio quid uolunt interesse inter 'ousian' et 'hypostasin,'" and he therefore chose what he considered a more precise terminology to express St. Basil's formula. (We might also note here that *substantia*, which etymologically means "something that stands under," is a calque for *hypostasis*.)

Boethius followed Augustine's linguistic lead in his own theological writings, declaring: "Idem est . . . 'ousian' esse quod essentiam" and "Est . . . hominis quidem essentia, id est 'ousia'" (*Contra Eutychen et Nestorium* 3). It was also apparently out of deference to Augustine that in his Trinitarian work, *Quomodo trinitas unus deus ac non tres dii*, Boethius employed the word *substantia* 95 times for the Greek *hypostasis* and used *persona* once only.

Linguistic struggles and choices such as these were an essential part of patristic efforts to defend and explain Christian teachings. Because of attacks or misunderstandings, early Christian writers and translators were continually obliged to resolve issues of language and interpretation, and even to coin new words, in order to express as well as they could in human terms the realities of faith. Such mutable terms as *substantia, essentia,* and *persona* were part of the linguistic inheritance bequeathed to medieval theologians by the Fathers. Different Latin translators of the texts of councils or the works of the Greek Fathers did not always agree in their translations of key concepts. The need for theological precision led Augustine, as we have seen, to prefer *essentia* to the well-established *substantia* and *substantia* to the well-established *persona* in discussions of the Trinity. These complex patristic debates about language initiated a tradition of Trinitarian studies that influenced some medieval authors to preserve the terminology of Augustine and Boethius, and others to persist with the vocabulary of Tertullian and the earlier period.

The very method of the medieval *quaestio,* which posed different biblical, patristic, and other authorities against one another in order to raise a question that stimulates reflection and calls for resolution, forced theologians to reinterpret various conflicts among these authorities and to look beyond the words to the meanings and realities toward which the words were pointing. The same patristic author might mean exactly the same thing when he used the word *substantia* as another Father intended when choosing the word *essentia;* or he might wish, by using the term *substantia,* to convey the same meaning as intended by another's use of *persona.* Such linguisitic complexity is underscored in letter 204 of St. Anselm:

> Hac necessitate patres catholici, quando loquebantur de illis tribus [Patre, Filio, et Spiritu Sancto], elegerunt nomina quibus illos tres nominare possent pluraliter; Graeci quidem nomen substantiae, Latini vero nomen personae; sed ut omnino quod nos ibi intelligimus per personam, hoc ipsi et non aliud intelligant per substantiam. Sicut ergo nos dicimus in deo unam substantiam esse tres personas, ita illi dicunt unam personam esse tres substantias, nihil a nobis diverse intelligentes aut credentes. *Ep.* 204; [DH25] v4:96

Similar difficulties concerning *essentia, substantia, natura,* and *persona* arose in discussions of the mystery of Christ as both God and man. What terms could be found to express as adequately as possible this special union and unity of God and man that would not make Christ merely a combination of human and divine persons, or one person who only appears to have, but does not really have, a divine and a human nature?

Since in human experience, wherever we encounter a human nature we also encounter a person, it is easy to presume that there is in Christ not only a human nature but also a human person. On the other hand, whenever we encounter a person we encounter someone who has a particular nature, so in Christ there should be only one nature. Boethius, who followed Augustine very closely in the language he employed for discussions of the Trinity, adjusted his language when dealing with the unity of Christ, the God-man. Whereas he consistently used *substantia* for *hypostasis* in his Trinitarian discussions, in his *Liber de persona et duabus naturis contra Eutychen et Nestorium* he employed *persona* as its equivalent in 85 instances. In fact, his definition of *persona* as "naturae rationabilis individua substantia" (*Contra Eutychen et Nestorium* 3) became authoritative in the Middle Ages, since his theological tractates had great influence, particularly through the commentaries on them produced in the twelfth century. This definition, however, which no one could avoid considering, was problematic. If interpreted literally, its phrasing could, from a Trinitarian perspective, mask tritheism, and it is therefore no wonder that medieval theologians continually criticized Boethius's choice of words, and that Thomas Aquinas in his *Summa theologiae* (1, q. 30, a. 1) warned that *substantia* should not be understood to mean that there are three distinct essences in God. In a similar fashion, Boethius in a Christological context replaced *essentia* with *natura,* as the title of his work (*Liber de persona et duabus naturis...*) indicated. This too presented difficulties, as the criticisms of later authors brought out.

We have thus far only indicated some linguistic problems concerning the Incarnation that resulted solely from the changing meanings of such technical expressions as *essentia, natura, substantia,* and *persona.* Since almost every statement in the patristic authorities concerning the Incarnation and the Trinity contained these words, it was impossible for medieval exegetes or theologians to resolve the apparent or real conflicts among patristic authors, unless they were able to reconcile conflicting texts. The *Sic et Non* of Peter Abelard prompted medieval thinkers to attempt to resolve the conflicts and apparent inconsistencies regarding *essentia, natura, substantia, persona,* and many other central words found in traditional patristic texts.

Twelfth- and early thirteenth-century students of divine revelation, especially in the *quaestiones* that arose from the scriptural text and were gathered into *summae,* also wrestled with biblical expressions concerning the Second Person of the Trinity becoming man. The very language used in the Scriptures to describe this action was continually examined in attempts to understand it properly. The words of St. Paul— "habitu inventus ut homo" (*Phil* 2:7)—elicited in some of Abelard's students what became known as the *habitus* theory of the Incarnation. The main concern of one such student, Rolando Bandinelli (afterwards Pope Alexander III, d. 1181), in presenting this opinion was to show that the being of the divine Person did not undergo any change or receive anything new to itself upon assuming a human nature. Paul's words and Augustine's comments on them (*De diversis quaestionibus* 73.2) inspired him to coin the phrase "Deus 'habens' hominem," and from it a clothing metaphor easily developed: Christ is in His human nature in the same way that a person is in his clothing (*habitus*). This interpretation was strongly criticized by Peter Lombard in his *Sentences,* where he claimed that it denied that Christ as man was *aliquid* ("something").

To stress Christ's full humanity, Hugh of St. Victor (d. 1141) focused on the word *assumpsisti* of *Ps* 64:5 ("Beatus quem elegisti et assumpsisti . . ."), becoming one of the chief defenders of what was known as the *homo assumptus* theory of the Incarnation (*De sacramentis christianae fidei* 2.9; *PL* 176:393–99). It postulated that, at the time of the Incarnation, "a certain man was constituted by the coming together of a rational soul and human flesh." Opponents of this opinion, such as Peter Lombard, criticized it because its exaggerated emphasis on the full humanity of Christ caused them to wonder how Hugh and his followers could avoid having Christ assume a human person and not just a human nature.

Discussions of the *habitus* and *homo assumptus* theories of the Incarnation did not concern questions of orthodoxy or heterodoxy. They took place within an orthodox speculative atmosphere, where theologians were simply trying to achieve a better understanding of the mystery of the union and unity of God and man in Christ. Such discussions intensified greatly in the thirteenth-century universities as new philosophical sources reached the Latin West, opening up new avenues of interpretation and bringing new understandings to traditional language.

## The Chief Philosophical Sources of Medieval Thought

(a) **Neo-Platonic Influences.** St. Augustine spoke of the help that Christians might find in philosophers, especially the Platonists, and many scholars have pointed to the influence of Plotinus and his followers on Augustine's works. The neo-Platonic impact on Western theology, however, can also be traced to Pseudo-Dionysius the Areopagite, whose works were translated into Latin in the ninth century by John Scottus Eriugena (d. 879). Dionysius was for a long time confused with the Dionysius Areopagita converted by St. Paul (*Act* 17:34), and for this reason enjoyed special authority until the thirteenth-century discovery that he had used the writings of Proclus (d. 485) and could therefore not have been a contemporary of St. Paul. Pseudo-Dionysius's portrait of God as the *bonum diffusivum sui* ("Goodness that extends itself to all things"), however, was quite compelling in itself, gradually exerting considerable influence on medieval spiritual writings and, in different ways, on the elaboration of the doctrine of the Trinity in the works of Alexander of Hales (d. 1245) and St. Bonaventure (d. 1274).

John Damascene in his *Dialectica* and *De fide orthodoxa,* translated in the twelfth century by Burgundio (d. 1194), a judge from Pisa, was also a source of neo-Platonic vocabulary. The same might be said of a number of other authors, including Boethius and the Arabs Alfarabi (d. 950) and Avicenna (d. 1037), who flavored their commentaries on Aristotle with stong neo-Platonic condiments.

(b) **Aristotelian Influences in Logic.** The strongest philosophical influence, however, in the days of the young universities of Paris and Oxford was Aristotle. As we have already indicated, a number of his logical works had been translated by Boethius, influencing teachers and students in cathedral, monastic, and palace schools. The translations of these logical works brought to medieval dialectics a large technical vocabulary. Certain terms dealing with arguments had been coined by Cicero (*Inv.* 1.37), for whom *propositio* meant a briefly stated principle from which the whole argument in a court of law gained its force, in contrast to an *assumptio,* an additional point that was, because of its relation to the principle, pertinent to proving the case. He also termed the conclusion or brief statement of what was proved a *complexio* (literally, a "knitting together"). Cicero claimed (*Inv.* 1.61) to be following the doctrine of Aristotle and the Peripatetics, but it was an Aristotle whose *Organon* had been adapted by rhetoricians mainly for court practice. It was in fact Boethius who restored the terms *propositio, assumptio,* and *complexio* to their logical or philosophical framework, with *propositio* thus becoming the logician's "major premiss," the rhetorical *assumptio* recapturing the status of the logical "minor premiss," and *complexio* becoming the logician's "conclusion."

Latin versions of Aristotle's *Categories* were available before the translation of Boethius, as we know from a famous passage in Augustine's *Confessiones* (4.16):

> Et quid mihi proderat, quod annos natus ferme uiginti, cum in manus meas uenissent Aristotelica quaedam, quas appellant decem categorias. . . . [E]t satis aperte mihi uidebantur loquentes de substantiis, sicuti est homo, et quae in illis essent, sicuti est figura hominis, qualis sit et statura, quot pedum sit, et cognatio, cuius frater sit, aut ubi sit constitutus aut quando natus, aut stet aut sedeat, aut calciatus uel armatus sit aut aliquid faciat aut patiatur aliquid, et quaecumque in his nouem generibus, quorum exempli gratia quaedam posui, uel in ipso substantiae genere innumerabilia reperiuntur.

Boethius's commentary on the *Categories* was, however, very influential in establishing an understanding of the categories of *substantia, quantitas, ad aliquid, qualitas, facere, pati, situs* or *positio, ubi, quando,* and *habere.* These ten categories stated the ways in which a substance, such as Socrates, can be spoken about. Thus one could say that Socrates (*substantia*) was a stout (*quantitas*) teacher of Plato (*ad aliquid*), quick-witted (*qualitas*) in questioning (*facere*) and listening to answers (*pati*), who stood (*situs* or *positio*) in the marketplace (*ubi*) every day (*quando*) in his toga (*habere*). These categories became the chief means by which medieval students organized their thoughts about the realities they discussed.

Thirteenth-century logicians distingished terms that express categories (*termini categorematici*), and thus are in themselves significant, from other terms (*termini syncategorematici*) that have meaning only when they are joined to categorematic terms—words such as "every" or "only." Master Nicholas, teaching at Paris in the 1250s and 1260s, expressed this distinction by a very clear analogy:

> Ut dicit Philosophus, ea quae sunt in arte et ratione sumuntur ad proportionem et imitationem eorum quae sunt in natura. In naturalibus vero ita videmus quod sunt quaedam quae per naturam nata sunt in se aliquid agere sine alieno suffragio, alia vero sunt quae non sunt nata movere nisi mota, sicut homo a se motus et non ab alio protrahit litteras, calamus vero non a se sed ab homine motus. Similiter se habet in rebus rationis, maxime in vocibus, quod quaedam faciunt id ad quod sunt sine auxilio alterius, scilicet significant, quia omnis vox est ad significandum, quoniam, ut dicit Aristoteles, voces sunt notae earum quae sunt in anima passionum, id est significant intellectus, quia sunt signa rerum; et ita voces significant res; et tales voces dicuntur "categoreumata," id est: "significantes"; aliae sunt quae per se non significant sed in coniunctione ad alias; et tales dicuntur "sincategoreumata." [DH67] v1.2–15

Twelfth- and thirteenth-century logicians went beyond the meaning or signification of terms by themselves and began to ask what terms referred to or stood for (*supponunt*) when used in propositions. This property of a term was called its supposition (*suppositio*). In the propositions "Animal is trisyllabic" and "An animal is running across the field," the term "animal" stands for different things. In the first proposition it stands for the very word "animal"; in the second it stands for a living being of a particular class of substances. The two types of suppositions are certainly different, for a trisyllabic word could not be running across the field, nor is a living being a trisyllabic word.

In the area of reasoning or argumentation, the conditions surrounding *scientia* (Aristotle's *episteme*) attracted attention. The commentary by Robert Grosseteste (d. 1253) on Aristotle's *Analytica posteriora*, where the Philosopher treats of demonstrative reasoning, began to focus on the conditions for scientific knowledge. These issues were the prologue to the questions that would grow in importance for Christian thinkers in the thirteenth century: Can we demonstrate that God exists? Can we demonstrate that God is triune? Can we demonstrate that Christ is both God and man? In brief, what kind of argumentation is useful and valid in theology?

Logic from the twelfth century onward was developing at a rapid pace, as can be seen by examining the works of Peter Abelard; the twelfth-century *Ars Meludina* or *Introductiones Parisienses;* the thirteenth-century treatises of Peter of Spain, Roger Bacon, William of Sherwood, and Lambert of Auxerre; and the synthetic *Summa logicae* of William of Ockham in the fourteenth century. From the thirteenth century, however, logic began to take a place second in importance to the texts of a new philosophical invasion.

(b) **Aristotelian Influences in Philosophy Proper.** The translations of Aristotle's nonlogical works (*Physica, Metaphysica, De anima, Ethica, Politica,* etc.) in the twelfth and thirteenth centuries introduced into the Latin West a purely pagan philosopher—the first such serious encounter since the time of the Fathers. To complicate matters, Aristotle's works arrived with translations of the early Greek commentaries of Simplicius, Themistius, Philoponus, and Ammonius, and of the Arabic commentaries of Avicenna (d. 1037) and Averroes (d. 1198), and with the translation of *The Guide for the Perplexed* of Maimonides (d. 1204), Aristotle's great Jewish commentator. The influence of all these men on medieval Latin thinkers and on Latin philosophical and theological language is inestimable.

The language of many classroom teachers gradually became more "Aristotelianized," as they began to give new Aristotelian interpretations to words already existing in a technical vocabulary predominantly set by St. Augustine. A word like *scientia*, which, as we have noted, was the Latin equivalent of Aristotle's *episteme*, might in fact have many different Augustinian or Aristotelian meanings as various medieval authors asked "utrum theologia sit scientia." For eyes and ears accustomed to the many meanings that *scientia* conveyed in Augustine's works, it would take time for the new Aristotelian meanings of the word to be assimilated. When first posed, this question might be interpreted as asking, "Does the study of the Scriptures bring us any kind of knowledge of the realities spoken of?" Only gradually did the meanings implicit in Aristotle's *episteme* take hold and exert their effect on the interpretation of this same question, which could then be translated, "Does theology as a university discipline bring the kind of evidence required for it to be considered as providing Aristotelian demonstrations?" If understood in the first sense, the question was most often answered by "yes." Taken as conveying the second and later sense, it would most frequently elicit the answer "no." *Scientia*, it is fair to say, is a very slippery word, especially in thirteenth-century treatises.

Many new and strange words, technical expressions linked to philosophy proper, were introduced via translations of Greek, Arabic, and Hebrew terms. In the Latin translation of the *Liber de definicionibus* of Isaac Israeli (d. c. 955), for instance, appear the words *anitas* (whetherness) and *quaritas* (whyness) when inquiring whether (*an*) a thing exists or why (*quare*) something happens (DH44] p300). Many new terms, however, came into existence more naturally, as teachers in the arts and theology faculties attempted to teach with greater precision. Expressions such as *distinctio realis, distinctio formalis,* and *distinctio intentionalis* were technical inventions that explained subtle differences in the relationships among realities. The phrase *conceptus confusus* was invented by Henry of Ghent to mean a concept that some have mistakenly blended together (*con-fusus*) from two irreducible concepts (e.g. "the being of God" and "the being of creatures" have nothing common that they can share). *Esse* might be described as Aquinas had done, as "the actuality of all acts and the perfection of all perfections" (*De potentia*, q. 7, a. 2, *ad* 9). Although *esse* is usually translated as "existence," it here means this and more, namely the ultimate intrinsic metaphysical principle of perfection in any existing entity. Each teacher in the arts and theology faculties of the universities had to read carefully to determine the exact meaning of such technical terms as *esse, distinctio, identitas,* and *analogia;* these were commonly used but had different meanings for each author.

To make philosophical and theological points as precisely and directly as possible, special terms were created, including many adjectives produced by the free use of Latin suffixes (*-ivus, -alis, -orius*): *cognitivus, cognoscitivus, reparativus, subtiliativus; integralis, sermocinalis, totalis, virtualis; completorius, contradictorius, reparatorius.* New adverbs followed from adjectives in *-alis: certitudinaliter, habitualiter, improportionaliter, litteraliter, mentaliter, supernaturaliter.* The prefix *con-/com-* was similarly exploited, forming, for example, *communicabilis, condilectio, connoto, connumerabilis,* etc. Among other neologisms are, notoriously, a very large number of abstract nouns in *-itas* (e.g. *actualitas, causalitas, corporeitas, defectibilitas, interminabilitas, nihilitas, quidditas, virtuositas*), which included such formations as *heceitas,* "thisness"; *talitas,* "suchness"; and *asinitas* or *asineitas,* "donkeyness." William of Ockham criticized such abstractions as *etitas, velitas, dumitas, quandoleitas,* and *anitas,* arguing that people were often fooled by abstract philosophical and theological terms into thinking that there were realities that corresponded exactly to them. An abstract word like *dualitas* could, in Ockham's view, lead people to think that there is a "duality" that exists as a quality in each of two things that are related. Someone might, for example, think that "twinness" exists as a quality in each twin. Should we begin to think of the *etitas* of *Petrus ET Martinus,* we must be careful:

> Dicendum est quod talia nomina quae descendunt a verbis et etiam nomina descendentia ab adverbiis, coniunctionibus et praepositionibus et universaliter etiam a syncategorematibus, sive sint nomina syncategorematica sive verba sive quaecumque alia vel alterius partis orationis, non sunt introducta nisi causa brevitatis vel ornatus locutionis, et multa eorum aequivalent complexis in significando quando supponunt non pro illis a quibus descendunt, et ideo non significant aliquas alias res praeter illas a quibus descendunt, et significata eorum. *Expositio in libros Physicorum Aristotelis* 3.2; [DH62], *Opera philosophica* v4:425

The new terms, formed on nouns, pronouns, verbs, adjectives, and other parts of speech, and even on combinations of prepositions and pronouns (*per se* > *perseitas,* "perseity" [self-subsistence]), enabled their inventors to shorten their explanations or to express them in terms that would not be repetitious. Shorthand phrases such as *mutatio subita* might be used in the same way for a much longer explanation. There is no one thing that corresponds exactly to *mutatio subita;* it is a shorthand way of saying the following:

> Sed subiectum subito mutari non est aliud quam ipsum subiectum habere formam quam prius non habuit vel carere forma quam prius habuit, non tamen partialiter, ita quod non prius habet unam partem formae quam aliam nec prius caret una parte quam alia, sed totam formam simul adquirit vel totam deperdit simul, et isto posito sine omni alia re subiectum vere mutatur. Et ita mutatio non est aliqua res distincta ab omni re permanente durans tantum per instans, sicut multi imaginantur. *Ibid.*

For Ockham and many scholastics it was important in philosophy and theology to examine words carefully to determine what realities they refer to (*pro quibus supponunt*). What realities do we point to when we use words like *motus, tempus,* or *privatio,* or phrases like *mutatio subita,* or sentences like *tempus fugit?* To enhance our understanding, Ockham would have us decode noun forms, and he thus encouraged students to try to say what they meant by *mutatio subita,* or some such expression, by recasting it in longer statements that included verbs, adverbs, and conjunctions, instead of retaining the noun form, which tended to suggest that there is one reality that corresponds to it. Of course, if we were to recast these shorthand expressions every time we spoke, our discourse would become tediously long and boring. But when we want to explain reality more accurately, we often need to restate or expand upon a word or phrase to ensure that we know exactly what we are speaking about.

It is worth noting that Ockham criticized the abstract Latin forms not because they were "bad" Latin, but because they were likely to lead people astray. The expressions themselves were invented, he says, "causa brevitatis vel ornatus locutionis." He and probably all the Schoolmen believed that their inventions of new words and expressions were necessary, either to avoid long-winded explanations or to dress up their discourse.

## Conclusion

Readers of philosophical and theological texts produced in the Middle Ages, especially in university circles, will generally be struck by their technical character, subtle distinctions, and yet relative narrative simplicity. To a very great extent the Latin of the schools was a language with a particular purpose. The instructor was expected to present his materials clearly and understandably, using a classroom language allied more closely to logic than to rhetoric. Teachers and authors of technical commentaries or *summae quaestionum* did not want to bore their students, and their linguistic inventiveness must often have succeeded in capturing the attention and imagination of their audiences.

# Select Bibliography

## Tools and Guides

M. Asztalos, ed., *The Editing of Theological and Philosophical Texts from the Middle Ages: Acts of the Conference Arranged by the Department of Classical Languages, University of Stockholm, 29–31 August 1984* (1986) [DH1].

S.G. Axters, *Scholastiek Lexicon, Latijn-Nederlandsch* (1937) [DH2].

L. Baudry, *Lexique philosophique de Guillaume d'Ockham: Étude des notions fondamentales* (1958) [DH3].

B.C. Bazàn, J.F. Wippel, G. Fransen, and D. Jacquart, *Les questions disputées et les questions quodlibétiques dans les facultés de Théologie, de Droit et de Médecine,* TSMAO 44–45 (1985) [DH4].

J.-G. Bougerol, *Lexique saint Bonaventure* (1969) [DH5].

R. Busa, ed., *Index Thomisticus: Sancti Thomae Aquinatis operum omnium indices et concordantiae, in quibus verborum omnium et singulorum forme et lemmata cum suis frequentiis et contextibus variis modis referuntur quaeque,* 49 vols. (1974–80): *Sectio I:* Indices (10 vols.); *Sectio II:* Concordantia prima (23 vols.); *Sectio II:* Concordantia altera (8 vols.); *Sectio III:* Concordantia prima (6 vols.); *Sectio III:* Concordantia altera (2 vols.) [DH6]. See R. Busa, *Clavis Indicis Thomistici in Indices Distributionis, series I vol. 1–8, et in Operum St. Thomae Concordantiam Primam, Series II vol. 1–23:* in Latin and English [DH7]. A.G. Judy, "The *Index Thomisticus,* St. Thomas and I.B.M.," in *Listening* 9 (1974) 105–18, discusses the *Index*'s strengths and limits [DH8]. See also P. Guietti, "Hermeneutic of Aquinas's Text: Notes on the *Index Thomisticus,*" in *The Thomist* 57 (1993) 667–86 [DH9].

J. Croissant, *Explication de termes philosophiques grecs et latins,* 2 vols. (1977–78) [DH10].

R.J. Deferrari, M. Barry, and I. McGuiness, *A Lexicon of St. Thomas Aquinas Based on the Summa Theologica and Selected Passages of His Other Works* (1948–53): issued in fascs. [DH11].

R.J. Deferrari, *A Latin-English Dictionary of St. Thomas Aquinas Based on the Summa Theologica and Selected Passages of His Other Works* (1960): without the quotations of [DH11] [DH12].

G.R. Evans, *A Concordance to the Works of St. Anselm*, 4 vols. (1984) [DH13].

M. Fernandez Garcia, *Lexicon scholasticum philosophico-theologicum, in quo termini, definitiones, distinctiones et effata a Joanne Duns Scoto exponuntur, declarantur* (1910, r1974) [DH14].

R. Goclenius (1547–1628), *Lexicon philosophicum quo tanquam clave philosophiae fores aperiuntur* (Frankfurt 1613, r1964) [DH15].

J. Hamesse, *Thesaurus Bonaventurianus* (1972–): computer-generated vocabularies, concordances, indices, frequency word lists, and lists of Medieval Latin words [DH16].

J. Hamesse, *Thesaurus librorum sententiarum Petri Lombardi* (1991) [DH17].

R. McKeon, tr., *Selections from Medieval Philosophers*, 2 vols. (1929–30): v2 has a Latin-English glossary (pp422–506) [DH18].

J. Micraelius (1597–1658), *Lexicon philosophicum terminorum philosophis usitatorum* (Stettin 1662, r1966) [DH19].

M. Müller and A. Halder, *Philosophisches Wörterbuch* (1988): rev. ed. of *Kleines philosophisches Wörterbuch* (1971) [DH20].

R.A. Muller, *Dictionary of Latin and Greek Theological Terms Drawn Principally from Protestant Scholastic Theology* (1985) [DH21].

F.E. Peters, *Greek Philosophical Terms: A Historical Lexicon* (1967) [DH22].

L. Schutz, *Thomas-Lexikon*, 2nd ed. (1895, r1983) [DH23].


## Primary Works

Ammonius, *In Aristotelis De interpretatione commentarius*, ed. G. Verbeke (1961): Latin translation of William of Moerbeke (d. 1286) [DH24].

Anselm, *Opera omnia*, ed. F.S. Schmitt, 6 vols. (1938–61, r1968) [DH25].

*Aristoteles Latinus* (see [BG27]) (1939–) [DH26].

Arnobius the Elder, *Adversus nationes*, ed. and tr. H. Le Bonniec (1982–) [DH27].

Augustine, *Confessionum libri XIII*, ed. L. Verheijen, CCSL 27 (1981) [DH28]; *Contra Iulianum*, ed. M. Zelzer, 2 vols., CSEL 85 (1974) [DH29]; *De civitate dei*, ed. B. Dombart and A. Kalb, 2 vols., CCSL 47–48 (1955) [DH30]; *De doctrina christiana libri IV*, ed. J. Martin, CCSL 32 (1962) 1–167 [DH31]; *De trinitate libri XV*, ed. W.J. Mountain, 2 vols., CCSL 50–50A (1968) [DH32].

Averroes, *Commentaria in opera Aristotelis: Corpus commentariorum Averrois in Aristotelem*, ed. H.A. Wolfson *et al.* (1949–) [DH33]; Aristoteles, *Opera cum Averrois commentariis*, 9 vols. in 11 and 3 supps. (Venice 1562–74, r1962) [DH34].

Avicenna, *Opera* (Venice 1508, r1961) [DH35].

*Avicenna latinus*, ed. S. Van Riet (1968–); see [HC19] [DH36].

Boethius, *Opuscoli teologici*, ed. and tr. E. Rapisarda, 2nd ed. rev. (1960) [DH37]; *Theological Tractates*, ed. and tr. H.F. Stewart, E.K. Rand, and S.J. Tester, 2nd ed. (1973, r1978) [DH38].

Bonaventure, *Opera omnia*, ed. Patres Collegii a S. Bonaventura, 10 vols. (1882–1902) [DH39].

*Commentarius Cantabrigiensis in Epistolas Pauli e schola Petri Abaelardi*, ed. A.M. Landgraf, 4 vols. (1937–45) [DH40].

Gerard of Bologna, *Summa*, ed. P. de Vooght, in *Les sources de la doctrine chrétienne d'après les théologiens du XIVe siècle et du début du XVe avec le texte intégral des XII premières questions de la "Summa" inédite de Gerard de Bologna (d. 1317)* (1954) 269–483 [DH41].

Henry of Ghent, *Opera omnia*, ed. R. Macken *et al.* (1979–) [DH42]; *Summa quaestionum ordinariarum* (Paris 1520, r1953) [DH43].

Isaac Israeli, *Liber de definicionibus*, ed. J.T. Muckle, in *AHDL* 11 (1937–38) 299–340 [DH44].

John Duns Scotus, *Opera omnia*, ed. Commissio Scotistica (1950–) [DH45].

John of Paris, *Commentarium in libros Sententiarum (Reportatio)*, ed. J.-P. Müller, 2 vols. (1961–64) [DH46].

John Philoponos, *Commentum super capitulum de intellectu in libro tertio Aristotelis De anima*, ed. G. Verbeke (1966): translation of William of Moerbeke [DH47].

Marius Victorinus, *Ad Arium*, ed. P. Henry and P. Hadot, *CSEL* 83.1 (1971) 54–277 [DH48].

Nemesius of Emesa, *De natura hominis*, ed. G. Verbeke and J.R. Moncho (1975): translation of Burgundio of Pisa [DH49].

Peter Abelard, *Opera theologica*, ed. E.M. Buytaert and C.J. Mews, *CCCM* 11–13 (1969–87) [DH50]; *Dialogus inter philosophum, Iudaeum et Christianum*, ed. R. Thomas (1970) [DH51]; *Sic et Non*, ed. B.B. Boyer and R. McKeon (1976) [DH52].

Peter of Spain (Pope John XXI), *Tractatus (Summule logicales)*, ed. L.M. de Rijk (1972); tr. F.P. Dinneen (1990) [DH53].

Robert Grosseteste, *Commentarius in Posteriorum analyticorum libros*, ed. P. Rossi (1981) [DH54].

Robert Kilwardby, *Quaestiones in librum primum Sententiarum*, ed. J. Schneider (1986) [DH55].

Rolando Bandinelli, *Summa*, ed. F. Thaner (1874) [DH56].

Tertullian, *Ad nationes*, ed. J.G.P. Borleffs, *CCSL* 1 (1954) 9–75 [DH57]; *Adversus Praxean*, ed. A. Gerlo, *CCSL* 2 (1954) 1157–1205 [DH58]; *De praescriptione haereticorum*, ed. R.F. Refoulé, *CCSL* 1 (1954) 185–224 [DH59].

Thomas Aquinas, *Opera omnia*, ed. Commissio Leonina (1882–) [DH60]; see also [BE45].

William of Auxerre, *Summa aurea*, ed. J. Ribaillier, 6 vols. (1980–87) [DH61].

William of Ockham, *Opera theologica et philosophica*, ed. P. Boehner, G. Gál, S.F. Brown, *et al.* (1967–) [DH62].

## Studies

P. Batiffol, "Theologia, Theologi," in *Ephemerides theologicae Lovanienses* 5 (1928) 205–20 [DH63].

B. Baudoux, "Philosophia 'Ancilla Theologiae,'" in *Antonianum* 12 (1937) 303–5 [DH64].

J.P. Beckmann *et al.*, eds., *Sprache und Erkenntnis im Mittelalter: Akten des VI. internationalen Kongresses für mittelalterliche Philosophie der Société internationale pour l'étude de la philosophie médiévale, 29. August–3. Septembre 1977, in Bonn*, 2 vols. (1981) [DH65].

F. Blatt, "Sprachwandel im Latein des Mittelalters," in *Historische Vierteljahrschrift* 28 (1933) 22–52 [DH66].

H.A.G. Braakhuis, *De 13de eeuwse Tractaten over syncategorematische Termen*, 2 vols. (1979), v1: *Inleidende studie;* v2: *Uitgave van Nicolaas van Parijs' Sincategoreumata* [DH67].

S.F. Brown, "Key Terms in Medieval Theological Vocabulary," in *CIVICIMA* 3:82–96 [DH68].

M.-D. Chenu, "Auctor, actor, autor," in *ALMA* 3 (1927) 81–86 [DH69].

M.-D. Chenu, *Towards Understanding Saint Thomas*, trans. A.-M. Landry and D. Hughes (1964); see ch. 3 (pp100–25): "The Language and Vocabulary of Saint Thomas" [DH70].

M.-D. Chenu, *La théologie au douzième siècle* (1957, r1976): see chs. 16–17 (pp351–85): "Authentica et magistralia"; "Le vocabulaire théologique" [DH71].

M.-D. Chenu, "Notes de lexicographie philosophique médiévale," in *RSPT* 16 (1927) 435–46 [DH72].

M.-D. Chenu, "Les 'philosophes' dans la philosophie chrétienne médiévale," in *RSPT* 26 (1937) 27–40 [DH73].

M.-D. Chenu, "'Maître' Thomas est-il une 'autorité'? Note sur deux lieux théologiques au XIVe siècle," in *Revue Thomiste* 30 (1925) 187–94 [DH74].

M.-D. Chenu, "Vocabulaire biblique et vocabulaire théologique" in *Nouvelle revue théologique* 74 (1952) 1029–41 [DH75].

E.R. Curtius, "Zur Geschichte des Wortes 'Philosophie' in Mittelalter," in *Romanische Forschungen* 57 (1943) 290–309 [DH76].

M.-T. d'Alverny, "Notes sur les traductions médiévales d'Avicenne," in *AHDL* 27 (1952) 337–58 [DH77].

J. De Ghellinck, "L'entrée d'essentia, substantia, et autres mots apparentés, dans le latin médiéval," in *ALMA* 16 (1942) 77–112 [DH78].

J. De Ghellinck, "'Pagina' et 'Sacra Pagina': Histoire d'un mot et transformation de l'objet primitivement désigné," in *MAP* (1947) 23–59 [DH79].

L.-M. de Rijk, "The Origins of the Theory of the Properties of Terms," in *CHLMP* 161–73 [DH80].

L.-M. de Rijk, "Specific Tools Concerning Logical Education," in *CIVICIMA* 3:62–81 [DH81].

S. Ebbesen, "Ancient Scholastic Logic as the Source of Medieval Scholastic Logic," in *CHLMP* 101–27 [DH82].

G.R. Evans, "*Inopes verborum sunt latini:* Technical Language and Technical Terms in the Writings of St. Anselm and some Commentators of the Mid-Twelfth Century," in *AHDL* 51 (1976) 113–34 [DH83].

E. Gilson, "Les 'Philosophantes,'" in *AHDL* 27 (1952) 135–40 [DH84].

J. Hamesse, "Le vocabulaire des florilèges médiévaux," in *CIVICIMA* 3:209–30 [DH85].

J. Hamesse and M. Fattori, eds., *Rencontres de cultures dans la philosophie médiévale: Traductions et traducteurs de l'Antiquité tardive au XIVe siècle. Actes du Colloque internationale de Cassino, 15–17 juin 1989* (1990) [DH86].

R. Hissette, "Bulletin du glossaire du latin philosophique médiéval," in *BPhM* 18 (1976) 104–5 [DH87].

M. Hubert, "Notes de lexicographie Thomiste," in *ALMA* 27 (1957) 5–26, 167–87, 287–92 [DH88].

M. Hubert, "Quelques aspects du latin philosophique au XIIe et XIIIe siècles," in *REL* 27 (1949) 211–33 [DH89].

A.M. Landgraf, *Dogmengeschichte der Frühscholastik,* 4 vols. in 8 (1952–56), v1.1:20–29: "Die Sprache der früh-scholastichen Theologie" [DH90].

*La langue latine, langue de la philosophie: Actes du colloque organisé par l'École française de Rome avec le concours de l'Université de Rome "La Sapienza" (Rome, 17–19 mai 1990)* (1992) [DH91].

D. Luscombe, "Philosophy and Philosophers in the Schools of the Twelfth Century," in *CIVICIMA* 5:73–85 [DH92].

A.M. Malingrey, *Philosophia: Étude d'un groupe de mots dans la littérature grecque, des présocratiques au IVe siècle après J.C.* (1961) [DH93].

H. Merle, "Le Glossaire du latin philosophique médiévale," in *ALMA* 42 (1979–80) 142–47: description of the glossary (in the form of card indexes) initiated by R. Bayer in 1946, expanded by P. Michaud-Quantin until his death in 1972, and located at the Centre de Recherche et de Confrontation sur la Pensée Médiévale of the University of Paris [DH94].

P. Michaud-Quantin and M. Lemoine, *Études sur le vocabulaire philosophique du moyen âge* (1971) [DH95].

P. Michaud-Quantin and M. Lemoine, "Pour le dossier des 'philosophantes,'" in *AHDL* 35 (1968) 17–22 [DH96].

J. Laporta, "Pour trouver le sens exact des terms *appetitus naturalis, desiderium naturale, amor naturalis, etc.* chez Thomas d'Aquin," in *AHDL* 48 (1973) 37–95 [DH97].

C. Mohrmann, "Le latin commun et le latin des chrétiens" in *VC* 1 (1947) 1–12 [DH98].

C. Mohrmann, "Les origines de la latinité chrétienne à Rome," in *VC* 3 (1949) 67–106, 163–83 [DH99].

C. Mohrmann, "Les emprunts grecs dans la latinité chrétienne," in *VC* 4 (1950) 193–211 [DH100].

C. Mohrmann, "Linguistic Problems in the Early Christian Church," in *VC* 11 (1957) 11–36 [DH101].

M. Nédoncelle, "Les variations de Boèce sur la personne," in *Revue des sciences religieuses* 29 (1955) 201–38 [DH102].

G. Nuchelmans, "The Semantics of Propositions," in *CHLMP* 197–210 [DH103].

M. Smalbrugge, "Sur l'emploi et l'origine du terme '*essentia*' chez Augustin," in *Augustiniana* 39 (1989) 436–45 [DH104].

G. Schrimpf, "'*Philosophi*'—'*philosophantes*': Zum Selbstverständnis der vor- und frühscholastischen Denker," in *SM,* 3rd ser., 23 (1982) 697–727 [DH105].

St.W.J. Teeuwen, *Sprachlicher Bedeutungswandel bei Tertullian: Ein Beitrag zum Studium der christlichen Sondersprache* (1926) [DH106].

G. Verbeke, "Lexicographie du latin médiéval et philosophie médiévale," in *LLM* 261–87 [DH107].

J.F. Wippel, "Essence and Existence," in *CHLMP* 385–410 [DH108].

*See also* [BA61], [BA141], [BB51], [BC53], [BC57], [BC65], [BC71], [BC82], [BC84], [BC94], [BC99], [BC100], [BC104], [BC112], [BD32–33], [BD52], [BD62], [BD67], [BD74], [BD76], [BD80], [BD83], [BD99], [BD117–19].

D I    ❧    # GRAMMAR

## BY VIVIEN A. LAW

The language of medieval grammarians looks at first sight strikingly similar to our own traditional grammatical terminology. Caution is needed, however, for some familiar terms bore a different meaning, e.g. *littera, etymologia,* and *grammatica* itself; some have no modern counterpart, e.g. *figura* and *qualitas;* and a number of well-known modern terms are Renaissance innovations without any medieval counterpart, e.g. "root," "stem," "suffix," "dative of interest."

The study of grammar from late antiquity to the end of the Middle Ages may be divided into four phases, each with its own characteristic terminology.

1. Late antiquity extends roughly from 200 to 600, and the grammarians active during this period are often known as the Late Latin grammarians. Among the more important of them are Donatus (c. 350), the author of what was to become the standard beginners' grammar of Latin throughout the Middle Ages, the *Ars minor,* and of a longer work, the *Ars maior;* Priscian (c. 500), the author of the lengthiest and most respected reference grammar of Latin, a work later prescribed for study in the arts course of the medieval universities, the *Institutiones grammaticae,* as well as of several shorter works; Charisius, a contemporary of Donatus, whose grammar is in part similarly structured but on a larger scale than Donatus's; Eutyches (sixth century), the author of a work on the verb; and Isidore of Seville (d. 636), whose *Etymologiae* is a massive encyclopedia that sums up the learning of antiquity for medieval readers.

2. The early Middle Ages (600–800) was characterized by the need to study Latin as a foreign language in order to carry on the life of the Church. Grammarians such as Tatwine (d. 734) and Boniface (d. 754), as well as many anonymous writers, composed elementary grammars that set out the forms of Latin in a manner appropriate to nonnative speakers. A couple of generations earlier, however, the enigmatic Virgilius Maro Grammaticus had composed a work that, although ostensibly a grammar, belongs rather in the tradition of medieval wisdom literature, but nonetheless includes some interesting insights into language.

3. In the central Middle Ages (800–1100) the writing of commentaries, initially upon the grammars of Donatus, but later on several other ancient grammars, was the chief priority. Among the more important are the works of Murethach (c. 840) and Remigius of Auxerre (c. 900). At a more elementary level, the parsing grammar

(e.g. *Magnus quid est*) was a new genre that permitted students to apply their grammatical knowledge to the analysis of a series of representative words.

4. The later Middle Ages (1100–1400) is the age of the founding of the universities and the assimilation of Aristotelian doctrine (in Latin translation). Intensive study of Priscian, as we see from Petrus Helias's commentary (c. 1150), and of Aristotle led to the development of an approach to language that was heavily colored by dialectic, namely speculative grammar, the main proponents of which were the *Modistae* (e.g. Thomas of Erfurt, c. 1300). Many other grammarians worked relatively untouched by this fashion, however, preferring to focus more upon lexicography and etymology, like Alexander Neckam (d. 1217), John of Garland (d. after 1272), and John of Genoa (also known as Ioannes Balbus), author of the *Catholicon* (1286), or upon grammar in a more conventional sense, like Alexander of Villa Dei (*Doctrinale*, 1199), Eberhard Bethune (*Grecismus*, c. 1200), and Ludolf of Luckowe (*Flores grammaticae*, mid-thirteenth century).

In spite of the many innovations in grammatical thought and pedagogy reflected in the surviving literature, the intensive study of Donatus and Priscian that continued throughout the Middle Ages ensured that a large amount of grammatical terminology remained constant. The area subject to the greatest change was syntax, a branch of grammar that had been underdeveloped in antiquity.

Medieval grammatical terminology has received very little scholarly attention, except for that of the speculative movement of the thirteenth century and its immediate forerunners. For this reason this survey will concentrate largely upon the period up to 1100. References to the copious literature on the terminology of the later period will be found in the bibliography.

## Grammar

(*Ars*) *grammatica* was variously defined, depending upon the late antique model. The most comprehensive list of its parts was given by Isidore of Seville (d. 636) and was often cited, but in practice it rarely provided the structure for works on grammar. More often it was Donatus's *Ars maior* (c. 350) that was taken as the model. Its three books were constituted as follows: (I) *vox, littera, syllaba, pedes, toni, positurae;* (II) *partes orationis, nomen, pronomen, verbum, adverbium, participium, praepositio, coniunctio, interiectio;* (III) *barbarismus, soloecismus, cetera vitia, metaplasmus, schemata, tropi.* Thus, the first book deals with units below the level of the word; the second with the word classes; and the third with stylistic features, many of them involving collocations of words. In the later Middle Ages this structure was replaced by a fourfold division: *ortographia, prosodia, ethimologia, diasintastica* ("syntax").

## The Minimal Units

The discipline of phonetics did not appear until the early modern period. During the earlier Middle Ages such remarks as are to be found on this subject occur under the heading *de littera,* and in the later Middle Ages in discussions of *ortographia.*

*Vox* denoted both the voice and the sound it produces: any verbal utterance, articulate or inarticulate. Often, *vox* denotes "word" as a formal unit, either phonetic or morphological. The minimal unit of a *vox articulata,* an "articulate word," was the *littera.* This term should be treated with circumspection, for it by no means always corresponds directly to the modern "letter." The *littera* was a more complex entity with the properties of *nomen* ("name"), *figura* ("shape, written form"), and *potestas* ("sound value"). Thus, it corresponds to both our "letter" and our "speech sound," and upon occasion even to "phoneme." Less commonly it was used in opposition to *elementum* ("element, unit, sound") as the equivalent of "letter."

The next largest unit, *syllaba* ("syllable"), could be *brevis* ("short"), *longa* ("long"), or *communis* ("common"); the corresponding verbs are *corripi* (*correptio*) and *produci* (*productio*), denoting the shortening or lengthening of a vowel or syllable.

Other topics treated in the first book of the *Ars maior* and many medieval grammars are *pedes* ("metrical feet"), sometimes expanded into a treatise on metrics; *toni* or *accentus* ("accents"); and *positurae* or *distinctiones* ("punctuation marks"). In the later Middle Ages these subjects were placed in a separate section, that dealing with *prosodia.*

### Word, Meaning, and Form

Medieval scholars had at their disposal a more nuanced selection of terms corresponding to the English "word" than modern writers have. "Word" as an entity having both form and meaning is *dictio,* a term that is very widely used in grammatical literature throughout the period. A word as a phonic entity or word form, without regard to its meaning, is *vox.* When meaning alone was at issue, without regard to form, *verbum* was used. This term occurs relatively rarely in this sense in grammars, however, partly in order to avoid confusion with the technical sense of *verbum* ("verb"), and partly because words-as-form (*voces*) are the center of attention. (The idiosyncratic seventh-century writer Virgilius Maro Grammaticus reserves *verbum* for "word" as a semantic unit and introduces the neologism *fonum* for "word-as-form.") A word as it functions in a sentence along with other words is a *pars orationis* or simply *pars* or *oratio.* Late medieval syntacticians used *constructibile* for "word" as a syntactic unit. *Loquella* and *casus* are also found with the meaning of "word" in one context: in discussions of prepositions that either may stand before an independent word in the appropriate oblique case form (*casus*), e.g. *ad villam,* or may join with another word (*loquella*) to form a compound word, e.g. *advena.*

Terminology for larger units was less precise, *oratio,* for example, covering anything from "word" to "sentence" to "text." Although the terms *sententia* and *clausula* were in use in the rhetorical tradition, they did not have a technical sense in grammar. Virgilius Maro Grammaticus, alone among medieval grammarians, created precise terminology to cover two aspects of the sentence: *sententia* for "sentence" as a semantic unit, *testimonium* and *quassum* for "sentence" as a formal unit. During the twelfth century *subiectum* and *predicatum* were taken over from logic to denote "subject" and "predicate" with associated elements; *suppositum* and *appositum* replaced them by the end of the century, but were later restricted to the subject and (verb) predicate alone, without such additional elements as modifying adjectives, direct objects, and the like.

The fundamental distinction between meaning and form was encoded with care in the terminology. *Significatio,* preferred by most grammarians of late antiquity, gave way in the early Middle Ages to *sensus* and *intellectus* (possibly because *signifi-*

*catio* also had the technical sense "voice" with reference to verbs). "Form" was rendered by *sonus,* or in the central Middle Ages by *superficies* or *litteratura.*

## The Parts of Speech

In the early and central Middle Ages words were studied in grammars under the heading *de partibus orationis* ("the parts of speech"). Later *ethimologia,* which corresponds roughly to our "morphology," was pressed into service. At no time during the Middle Ages did *etymologia* have our sense of "the historical study of word forms"; medieval etymology was usually pursued on a synchronic rather than a diachronic basis, and its aim was to find the true *meaning* of words by revealing connections with other similar-sounding words.

Words as they functioned in sentences, the *partes orationis,* were discussed class by class in bk. 2 of Donatus's *Ars maior.* The parts of speech were listed in what became a standard sequence: *nomen, pronomen, verbum, adverbium, participium, praepositio, coniunctio, interiectio.* A few writers in the later Middle Ages followed Priscian, who adopted an order closer to that favored by the Greeks: *nomen, verbum, participium, pronomen, praepositio, adverbium, interiectio, coniunctio.* The adjective was regarded as a type of common noun, as its name reflects—*nomen adiectivum* or *nomen epitheton*—although increasingly in the later Middle Ages *adiectivum* came to stand on its own, often contrasted with *(nomen) substantivum.* Similarly, the article, *articulus,* was generally treated as a type of pronoun, *pronomen articulare.*

The features or properties (*accidentia*) of the parts of speech were said to "affect" or "happen to" them (*accidere*), an expression that has to be paraphrased in translation. For the most part the properties are familiar from our own traditional grammar, but some terms require comment. Particularly problematic are those whose literal meaning is ill defined: *qualitas* ("quality"), *species* ("appearance, form"), *genus* ("kind, type"), *figura* ("shape, appearance"), *forma* ("shape, form"). In the context of nouns, *qualitas* denotes the proper/common (*proprium/appellativum*) distinction. The *qualitas* of pronouns was their faculty of designating definite persons (*qualitas finita*) or not (*qualitas infinita,* e.g. *quis*), or an intermediate state (*minus quam finita,* e.g. *ipse iste*). In the context of verbs, on the other hand, it could refer to the finite/infinite distinction (Charisius [DI3]), or more commonly functioned as a cover term for *modi* ("moods") and *formae* (see below).

*Species* could denote the types of proper or common nouns (Donatus, Priscian); Priscian also uses it as the equivalent of the Greek *eîdos,* the property of being nonderived, a base form (*principalis, primitiva, primae positionis,* later *primae impositionis*), or derived (*derivativa*).

*Genus* was widely used in two senses. Of nouns, it meant "gender." In addition to the three genders recognized today, ancient and medieval grammarians identified the *commune duorum generum,* i.e. nouns like *sacerdos* ("priest[ess]") that may take either a masculine or a feminine modifier depending on the referent; the *commune trium generum,* i.e. adjectives; and the *epicenon/promiscuum,* i.e. nouns such as *aquila* ("eagle") that are of one grammatical gender regardless of the sex of the referent. When used of verbs *genus* meant "voice." The term *significatio* was sometimes used in this sense as well. The voices recognized included *activum, passivum, neutrum* ("intransitive"), *commune* (i.e. verbs passive in form with both active and passive meaning, e.g. *scrutor, criminor*), *deponens* ("deponent"), and, according to some early writers, *impersonale* (e.g. *itur, taedet*). Some grammarians added *neutropassivum* ("semideponent," e.g. *audeo, gaudeo*).

*Figura* denotes the property of being simple (*simplex*) or compound (*composita*). Compounds might be made up of words that retain their original form ("free forms"), or that might have lost their original independent form ("bound forms"), or of a combination: *ex integro et corrupto* ("from a free form and a bound form").

Although *forma* occurs fairly frequently in grammatical literature in a nontechnical sense, when used of verbs it usually denoted the four aspects expressed by means of derivational suffixes: *perfecta*, e.g. *lego; meditativa*, e.g. *lecturio; frequentativa*, e.g. *lectito;* and *inchoativa*, e.g. *calesco.*

## Morphology

Contrary to general belief, late antique and medieval grammarians found it difficult to think analytically about word form, and this is reflected not only in the confusion between inflectional and derivational morphology, but also in the lack of terms such as "root," "stem," "morpheme," "affix," "prefix," "suffix." These notions entered the Western grammatical tradition from the Semitic tradition at the Renaissance. Medieval grammarians worked with the complete word form, the *vox,* and recognised that it was prone to change its ending (*terminatio*, rarely *finalitas* [Eutyches] or *clausula* [central Middle Ages]). This ending was not thought of as a morpheme, the exponent of plurality or person or whatever it might be, but simply as the final letter or syllable of the word: *nouissima/ultima* (later *extrema*) *littera* or *syllaba*, or *littera/syllaba terminalis.* As is apparent from manuscripts, the segmentation was often extremely inconsistent. Ways of saying that a word "ends in" a particular letter or syllable were enormously diverse: *desinit in i litteram, in i litteram terminatur, per i litteram exit* were popular throughout the Middle Ages, but alongside them *i littera finitur, cadit in i litteram, mittit in i litteram, per i litteram effertur, per i litteram profert, (genetiuum) in i litteram facit* are found. Even the unexpected *primus ordo qui genetiuo casu ae regit* occurs in the eighth century (Boniface [DI7]). When an attempt was made to describe a morphological process, rather than simply to set out the results in paradigm form, a letter or syllable was said to be added (*adiecta, apposita, accepta, adsumpta, addita*) or dropped (*remota, sublata, abiecta, abstracta*). Less frequently one is instructed to "change" (*convertere, commutare*) one letter/syllable into another.

A *pars orationis* might be either inflecting (*declinabilis*) or uninflecting (*indeclinabilis*). To describe inflection the verbs *declinari, inclinari,* and *(in)flecti* were used of both nouns and verbs: the English distinction between "declining (nouns)" and "conjugating (verbs)" has no medieval equivalent. Similarly, it was possible to speak of *declinationes* (or *ordines*) *nominum* or *verborum*, although the term *coniugatio* gradually gained currency in the context of verb inflection. The five declensions were recognized (on the basis of the genitive singular rather than the ablative), and the cases (*casus*, in late antiquity occasionally *gradus*) were listed in a conventional order that was not modified until the nineteenth century: *nominativus, genetivus, dativus, accusativus, vocativus, ablativus.* A few writers refer to the *septimus casus*, the ablative without a preposition. In verbs there was considerable uncertainty in the early period as to whether three conjugations (subdividing the third into the *tertia correpta*, e.g. *legere*, and *tertia producta*, e.g. *audire*) or four should be identified. Five tenses were recognized: *presens* (rarely *instans*), *preteritum inperfectum, preteritum perfectum, preteritum plusquamperfectum,* and *futurum.* (The modern future perfect was labeled the *coniunctivum futurum.*) The *modi* ("moods") included the *indicativus, imperativus, optativus* (corresponding to our subjunctive forms preceded by *utinam*), *coniunc(ta)tivus* ("subjunctive," corresponding to our subjunctive preceded by *cum*), *infinitivus,* and *inpersonalis.* The gerundive, e.g. *amandus,* was identified as a future participle passive.

## Syntax

Syntax—*constructio* to Priscian, *diasintastica* and the like in the later Middle Ages—was given very little attention, apart from the famous discussion in bks. 17 and 18 of Priscian's *Institutiones grammaticae,* until the eleventh century. There was, however, a well developed repertoire of terms to denote a verb or a preposition "taking" or "governing" a case, i.e. *servire* + dative, *adiungi* + dative, *trahere* + accusative, in the early Middle Ages. By the twelfth century *sociari, iungi,* and *construi cum* were in common use, but a different metaphor was gaining currency: *exigere* (Petrus Helias [DI18]) and *regere* (found almost universally in late medieval texts). The two chief branches of late medieval syntax were *regimen,* the study of constructions in which one word "governs" another, obliging it to be in a particular case; and *congruitas* ("agreement, grammaticality"). *Regimen* takes place by virtue of a feature such as transitivity (*ex vi transitionis*) or the copulative function of the verb "to be" (*ex vi copule*). A *constructio,* made up of syntactic units, *constructibilia,* was described in terms of the relation between *dependens* ("dependent element") and *terminans* ("the element terminating the dependency"); for example, in *Socrates legit, legit* is *dependens, Socrates* is *terminans,* whereas in *Socrates albus, albus* is *dependens* and *Socrates* is *terminans.*

## Conclusion

Grammars of the later Middle Ages pose special problems for the translator. For one thing, verse was a popular medium for technical literature such as grammars, as we can see in the widely read works by Alexander Neckam (*Corrogationes Promethei*), John of Garland (*Compendium grammatice, Clavis compendii*), Alexander of Villa Dei (*Doctrinale*), Eberhard Bethune (*Graecismus*), Ludolf of Luckowe (*Flores grammaticae*), and many others; however, because metrical exigencies occasionally compelled authors to press a relatively uncommon term into service in place of a metrically inappropriate one, e.g. *rectus* for *nominatiuus,* these works do not necessarily reflect accurately the preferred terminology of their age.

The rise of Aristotelianism and the ensuing exploration of a new approach to grammar, speculative grammar, were responsible for an influx of terms borrowed from the language of dialectic, discussed in ch. DH of this volume. This is particularly (but not exclusively) apparent in the writings of the *modistae,* a small group of scholars active during the thirteenth century, most of them based at the University of Paris, who attempted to trace a systematic relationship among reality, thought, and words via the *modi significandi* ("modes of signifying"), grammatical properties that directly reflected the *modi intelligendi* ("modes of understanding") of the mind, which were in their turn a reflection of the *modi essendi* ("modes of being") or properties of real-world entities. To take an example, the noun signified by means of the *modus entis,* the "mode of being," and the *modus determinatae apprehensionis,* the "mode of fixed reference," whereas the pronoun, which also signified through the *modus entis,* was distinguished from the noun by signifying by means of the *modus indeterminatae apprehensionis,* because a pronoun such as "that" may signify anything from a stone to a shoelace, unlike a noun.

## Select Bibliography

### Primary Works

Virtually all the grammars of late antiquity are available in H. Keil, ed., *Grammatici Latini,* 8 vols. (1855–80; r1961, 1981); computerized concordance (1990; see [BB44]) [DI1]; Priscian's *Institutiones grammaticae* are in vols. 2 and 3:1–377 [DI2]. Keil's edition of Charisius's grammar (v1:1–296) has been superseded by that by C. Barwick, *Flavii Sosipatri Charisii Artis grammaticae libri V* (1964) [DI3]; Keil's edition of Donatus's two grammars (v4:353–402) has been superseded by L. Holtz, *Donat et la tradition de l'enseignement grammatical: Étude sur l'Ars Donati et sa diffusion (IVe–IXe siècle) et édition critique* (1981) [DI4].

For Isidore's *Etymologiae* see *Etym.* among the bibliographic abbreviations at the beginning of this volume [DI5].

Unfortunately, no collection like Keil's *Grammatici Latini* exists for grammars of the Middle Ages, although a number of grammars have appeared in *CCSL* and *CCCM,* most notably, in *CCSL:* the grammars of Tatwine (v133), ed. M. De Marco (1968) 1–93 [DI6], and of Boniface (v133B), ed. G.J. Gebauer and B. Löfstedt (1980) [DI7], and the *Ars Ambrosiana: Commentum anonymum in Donati partes maiores* (v133C), ed. B. Löfstedt (1982) [DI8]; and in *CCCM:* Smaragdus, *Liber in partibus Donati* (v68), ed. B. Löfstedt, L. Holtz, and A. Kibre (1986) [DI9]. A number of Continental Irish works have been published in the collection *Grammatici hibernici Carolini aevi, CCCM* 40–40D (1977–82): v40 (Murethach [Muridac], *In Donati artem maiorem,* ed. L. Holtz) [DI10]; v40A (*Ars Lauershamensis: expositio in Donatum maiorem,* ed. B. Löfstedt) [DI11]; v40B (Sedulius Scottus, *In Donati artem maiorem,* ed. B. Löfstedt) [DI12]; v40C (Sedulius Scottus, *In Donati artem minorem, In Priscianum, In Eutychem,* ed. B. Löfstedt) [DI13]; v40D ("Donatus Ortigraphus," *Ars grammatica,* ed. J. Chittenden) [DI14].

For the rest, we are thrown back upon editions published elsewhere. Texts mentioned in the introductory essay include the following:

Alexander of Villa Dei, *Doctrinale,* ed. D. Reichling (1893, r1974) [DI15].
Eberhard Bethune, *Graecismus,* ed. J. Wrobel (1887) [DI16].
John of Genoa (Ioannes Balbus), *Catholicon* (Mainz 1460, r1971) [DI17].
Petrus Helias, *Summa super Priscianum,* ed. L. Reilly (1993) [DI18].
Thomas of Erfurt, *Novi modi significandi,* ed. G.L. Bursill-Hall (1972) [DI19].
Virgilius Maro Grammaticus, *Epitomae* and *Epistolae,* ed. G. Polara (1979) [DI20].

## Studies

With the exception of the earlier parts of Thurot's great anthology [DI31], there has been almost no work devoted to earlier medieval grammatical terminology (unless we include some now inaccessible nineteenth-century studies on the grammars of late antiquity). Rosier's glossary [DI30] provides an invaluable tool for anyone reading grammars of the later periods, and to some extent for the earlier parts of the Middle Ages as well. Accounts of speculative grammar such as those of Covington [DI21] and Rosier [DI29] include a good deal on the language of that movement.

M.A. Covington, *Syntactic Theory in the High Middle Ages: Modistic Models of Sentence Structure* (1984) [DI21].

K.M. Fredborg, "Speculative Grammar," in *A History of Twelfth-Century Western Philosophy*, ed. P. Dronke (1988) 177–95 [DI22].

S. Heinimann, "Zur Geschichte der grammatischen Terminologie im Mittelalter," in *ZRPh* 79 (1963) 23–37 [DI23].

C.H. Kneepkens, "Absolutio: A Note on the History of a Grammatical Concept," in *HGL* 155–69 [DI24].

C.H. Kneepkens, "'Suppositio' and 'supponere' in Twelfth-Century Grammar," in *Gilbert de Poitiers et ses contemporains: aux origines de la Logica modernorum*, ed. J. Jolivet and A. de Libera (1987) 325–52 [DI25].

C.H. Kneepkens, "Transitivity, Intransitivity and Related Concepts in 12th century Grammar: An Explorative Study," in *De ortu grammaticae: Studies in Medieval Grammar and Linguistic Theory in Memory of Jan Pinborg*, ed. G.L. Bursill-Hall *et al.* (1990) 161–89 [DI26].

A. Luhtala, "On the Concept of Transitivity in Greek and Latin Grammars," in *Papers on Grammar* 3, ed. G. Calboli (1990) 19–56 [DI27].

R. Pfister, "Zur Geschichte der Begriffe von Subjekt und Praedikat," in *Münchener Studien zur Sprachwissenschaft* 35 (1976) 105–19 [DI28].

I. Rosier, *La grammaire spéculative des modistes* (1983) [DI29].

I. Rosier, "La terminologie linguistique latine médiévale", in *Histoire des idées linguistiques*, v2: *Le développement de la grammaire occidentale*, ed. S. Auroux (1992) 590–97 [DI30].

C. Thurot, *Extraits de divers manuscrits latins pour servir à l'histoire des doctrines grammaticales au moyen-âge* (1869, r1964) [DI31].

*See also* [BA133], [BA143], [BC30–31].

BY NANCY PHILLIPS

Medieval musical terminology in Latin was extensive and highly technical, but two important studies make this terminology more accessible. The *Handwörterbuch der musikalischen Terminologie* offers scholarly essays on a limited number of terms [DJ1]; the recently initiated *Lexicon Musicum Latinum Medii Aevi* will include a complete vocabulary of musical terminology through the fifteenth century, as well as textual contexts for each term [DJ2]. Other specialized studies can also be useful [DJ3–15].

The earliest layer of Latin musical terminology is borrowed directly from Greek writings on music. Additional terminology is drawn during the Carolingian period from medieval Greek sources, and beginning in the thirteenth century, from other vernacular sources, including Arabic. In all these periods, terms were also borrowed from other disciplines, especially arithmetic, grammar, and rhetoric.

The following sections describe the three developmental stages of the Latin music vocabulary used in medieval theoretical treatises on music [DJ16–19]. For liturgical terminology see ch. DB.

## I.

The late Latin writers who were to be most influential in the development of a Latin musical vocabulary were Censorinus (*De die natali* 10), Augustine (*De musica*), Martianus Capella (*De nuptiis Philologiae et Mercurii*), Calcidius (commentary on the *Timaeus* of Plato), Macrobius (commentary on Cicero's *Somnium Scipionis*), Cassiodorus (*Institutiones*), Isidore of Seville (*Etymologiae*), and especially Boethius (*De arithmetica* and *De musica*). These and other writings, described in [DJ22], usually repeat information found in the Greek sources, with no attention to contemporary Latin practice. Among other topics, they consider the measurement of musical space, i.e. the intervals (the space between two notes, a fourth, a fifth, etc.), consonances (those intervals that bear simple proportional relationships), and the combination of intervals into "systems," e.g. the Greater and Lesser Perfect System. These concepts were demonstrated on the monochord, an instrument that illustrated, visually and aurally, the fundamental mathematical/acoustical laws of consonance (harmonics) by dividing a single string (monochord) into sections bearing proportional relationships to one another.

Transliterations of Greek words found in Latin writings include *diatessaron* (the interval of a fourth), *diapente* (a fifth), *diapason* (the octave, an eighth), and so on. Translations from Greek to Latin, e.g. in the numerical proportions for the intervals and consonances drawn from arithmetical terminology, produced *multiplex* from *pollaplasios* and *superparticularis* from *epimorios*. The Latin vocabulary of the Greater and Lesser Perfect System also used many transliterations, e.g. for the names of the system's individual pitches (*proslambanomenos, lichanos, mese,* etc.) and for other aspects of its structure (*tetrachord, diezeugmenon*). Some terms were accompanied by their Latin equivalents, e.g. *diezeugmenon, id est disiunctio.* Similarly, one finds *monochordon* (monochord) and *monochordos* (of one string), with *chorda* by extension signifying a musical pitch, a "note."

Sometimes transliterations and translations of the same term are found. Thus Greek *symphonia* (a consonance) appears in Latin as both *symphonia* and *consonantia;* Greek *diaphonia,* the antithesis of *symphonia,* becomes both *diaphonia* and *dissonantia;* and *chorde* becomes *c(h)orda* and *nervus.* There is a wide variety of terms to express the concept of a single sound: in addition to *chorda* and *nervus,* Latin writers also use *vox, tonus, sonus, phthongus, nota,* and *notula,* with *notula* sometimes, but not consistently, signifying the notational sign for a single pitch.

The uncertainty in Latin texts about such fundamental musical concepts as *modus, tropus, harmonia, systema, diastema,* and *phthongus* reflects the inconsistency found in Greek treatises [DJ21]. However, some terminological confusion in Latin reflects interdisciplinary borrowing. Such terms as *comma, colon, periodus, arsis, thesis, levatio,* and *positio* are among those borrowed from the verbal arts (grammar, rhetoric, metrics). The grammatical term *comma* sometimes refers in music to a self-standing portion of a melodic line; it is the musical equivalent of a section or division of a *periodus* and corresponds loosely to a clause (Latin *incisum*) within a sentence. But *comma* can also identify a very small (spatial) interval, a second musical meaning derived from mathematics and therefore unconnected with the grammatical or rhetorical *comma.*

## II.

The first truly original Latin musical treatises appear north of the Alps during the Carolingian Renaissance. Unlike their predecessors, these writings most often focus on aspects of their contemporary musical practice. They draw their terminology, with occasional modifications and misunderstandings, from three kinds of sources, to be described individually below: (a) late Latin sources, (b) a medieval Greek tradition of unknown origin, and (c) a wide range of nonmusical texts. The Latin musical vocabulary that evolved from these sources during the ninth century was the foundation for all later writings on music, with relatively few additions or modifications until the end of the twelfth century, when new musical ideas required the terminological enlargement outlined in section III.

**Late Latin Sources.** The profound influence of Boethius's *De musica,* the most respected of late Latin musical treatises during the period from the ninth century to the twelfth, is evident in every major ninth-century treatise on music. The oldest extant manuscripts of Boethius's *De musica* also date from the ninth century, many with glosses that demonstrate the Carolingian desire to learn the late Latin musical vocabulary ([DJ20], [DJ23]). Other early writings on music were more selectively exploited [DJ24–25].

The most important Carolingian borrowings from these late Latin treatises pertain to the classification of pitch relationships. The terms for consonance and dissonance appear in transliterated and/or translated forms (*symphonia, diaphonia, consonantia, dissonantia*). Some terms, however, acquired new meanings, e.g. *diaphonia* provided a name for an important new musical genre, in which a melody was sung by two or more voices simultaneously, but at different pitch levels and with occasional variants. This genre was also called *organum,* a term that in earlier texts had referred to any musical instrument or perhaps the organ itself, as in Boethius (*De musica* 1.34). In some Carolingian texts, the instrument known today as the organ is described as *fistulae* (pipes), although Hucbald of St. Amand (d. 930) calls it *hydraulis* (water organ) despite its air bladders. In later writings the plural form *organa* is found for the instrument, with the singular, *organum,* reserved for the musical genre. Other terms related to *organum*—*organizo, organizatio,* and *organalis*—also begin to appear. The relationship between the names of the instrument and the genre is logical enough, for the organ can perform two or more melodic lines simultaneously. Similarly, the terms *organistrum* and *symphonia* were later used to identify the hurdy-gurdy, an instrument capable of sounding different pitches simultaneously.

**The Medieval Greek Tradition.** A number of medieval Greek terms, which appear during the late eighth or ninth centuries, are associated with lists of the chants of the Mass that are classified into eight groups by *tonus.* In this context *tonus* identifies a melodic formula or other melodic structure that was differently understood by each writer, or—more likely—was poorly understood by all. These lists of chants, often simply called *toni,* were in later centuries assembled under a variety of titles, e.g. *tonale, tonarium,* and *libellus tonarius,* and are today termed tonaries [DJ26–27]. In the ninth century several musical theorists—inspired by Boethius's *De musica* 4.15—also began to apply the late Latin terms *modus* and *tropus* to these eight tones. Although the terms *modus* and *tropus* were frequently (but inconsistently) used in the later theoretical treatises, *tonus* remained the term of choice in ecclesiastical practice. These categories are identified as modes in modern theoretical writings.

The eight tones or modes were *protus autentus, protus plagalis, deuterus autentus, deuterus plagalis, tritus autentus, tritus plagalis, tetrardus autentus,* and *tetrardus plagalis.* The Carolingian explanation of these names is sometimes found in little tracts preceding or following the tonaries. These tracts provide no discussion of the musical content of the *toni,* but emphasize that they are to be understood in four groups of two, with the two tones (modes) of each pair ending on the same pitch, the *finalis.* There are thus eight tones, but only four finals, and the second tone of each pair is in some way subordinate to the first. The four Greek ordinal numbers (*protus,* etc.) are accompanied by a qualifier, either *autentus* or *plagalis* (oblique, lateral, subordinate); all of these terms were subject to considerable orthographical variation.

The essence of each *tonus* is communicated in some way by a brief melody called a *neuma,* which is sung to syllables of uncertain origin and meaning, such as *noannoeane, noeane, noeagis.* Aurelian of Réôme (c. 840–50) calls them *litterae, litteraturae,* or *syllabae.* A somewhat similar musical terminology is found in later Byzantine musical sources (*ananeanes, aneanes,* etc.), but its function there is not identical. The origin of these syllables could perhaps be traced to the common ancestor of both Byzantine and Carolingian practices, i.e. Palestine, or to early Rome and Gaul when Greek was, until the mid-fourth century, still the liturgical language.

There are some terminological modifications: the tetrachords of the classical Greek Greater Perfect System are often reorganized so that one tetrachord contains all four finals (*protus, deuterus, tritus,* and *tetrardus*); the other tetrachords are then described by a variety of new terms: *grave, superius, acutum,* etc. In one unfortunate eleventh-century modification of the terminology, the names of the *modi* (or *tropi, toni*) found in Boethius's *De musica* (*Dorius, Phrygius, Lydius,* and *Mixolydius*) replaced *protus, deuterus, tritus,* and *tetrardus* in some theoretical treatises.

**Non-musical Texts.** The third principal source of Carolingian musical terminology is found in a variety of treatises on topics other than music, particularly grammar, rhetoric, and arithmetic. The vocabulary of some treatises also reveals the influence of logic and dialectic and of Neoplatonism.

Because the chant, the focus of the musical treatises, is closely related to the sacred text it supports and projects, and because its structure is derived from, and subordinate to, the textual structure, extensive use is made of the specialized language of grammar and rhetoric to define musical phrase structures [DJ31]. In addition to such classical terms as *colon* and *comma,* one finds *particula, membrum, incisum, distinctio,* and *periodus; arsis* and *thesis* (which aid in the definition of phrase length as well as metrical forms) often appear in their Latin forms, *(e)levatio* and *positio, levandum* and *deponendum.* From the language of rhetoric there are borrowings such as *protrahere, contrahere, productus, correptus,* and *protensio* to describe the manner in which a musical line is projected, just as these terms had once been applied to public speaking. In music theory the terms *morosus* and *morositas* (and related forms) are frequently used to describe a deliberate, sober manner of vocal delivery, particularly in the performance of *organum.*

The term *musica* is not often used directly with the chant; *cantus* (*cantio, cantilena, canticum*) is more common, and both *dicere* and *cantare* are found for sacred singing. An error in singing is described in such terms as *vitium, barbarismus, soloecismus, absonus,* all common to the verbal arts.

The influence of grammar and rhetoric cannot be overstated [DJ31] and may be further exemplified in the following ways: the lowest note in the notation represented by Boethius (4.4) is a *tau iacens,* a letter *T* lying on its side (⊢). This symbol also appears as a basic notational sign in Hucbald's *Musica* and in *Musica enchiriadis* and *Scolica enchiriadis,* but it is identified as a *dasian* (*daseia*), a Greek aspiration sign described by Latin grammarians (see Donatus, *Ars maior* 1.5); it was therefore a more familiar term to Carolingian readers than *tau iacens.* Similarly, the *Enchiriadis* treatises were created as a pair, one as an exposition for the mature student modeled on the *De musica* of Boethius, the other as a simple dialogue inspired partly by the *De musica* of Augustine [DJ28–29]. The concept of a *pair* of treatises in expository and dialogue styles was, however, in imitation of the twin *Ars maior* and *Ars minor* of Donatus.

From arithmetic the Carolingians borrowed terms pertaining to the study of proportions as the basis of consonance. Much of this terminology is drawn from Boethius's *De arithmetica* and from Cassiodorus and Isidore, but other sources were also exploited, the result being some occasional terminological confusion. In addition to *sesqu(i)alter*, the terms *sescuplus, sescuplaris, sescuplex, sesquiplex,* and *sesquiplus* were used to identify the proportion 3:2. This terminological confusion began in the late Latin treatises and was greatly intensified during the Carolingian era ([DJ29] pp373–74).

Similarly, the terminology for the proportion of the octave (2:1) was sometimes confused with the terminology for the proportion of the second (9:8). Now, the interval of the octave covers a musical space of eight pitches, whereas that of the second is composed of two adjacent pitches; however, the proportional name for the second (9:8) contains some form of the word *eight,* either the transliterated Greek *epogdoos,* with a variety of spellings, or the Latin *sesquioctava.* The root meaning of "eight" in both proportional names for 9:8 became confused with the eight pitches separating the two pitches of an octave. (The prefix *sesqui-,* when joined to ordinal numerals, denoted not a quantity multiplied by one and a half, but a number consisting of a unit and a fraction more as designated by the numeral.) The common name for the octave *interval* (not its proportion) is the transliterated Greek *diapason,* but the author of the *Musica enchiriadis* resurrected the name *diplasion* (*dysplasium,* etc.) for this interval. Used by Censorinus and other late Latin authors, but not by Boethius, it was unfamiliar and became the source of many errors. The common name for the interval of a second was *tonus,* but this word had a variety of other meanings to be summarized later.

To Carolingian logical and dialectical studies we may probably trace the musical terms *differentia* and *diffinitio* (or *definitio*), which appear during the ninth century in connection with categories of psalm tones or modes. In the tonaries each tone/mode has at least one characteristic psalm tone, a simple melodic formula also called a *tonus* or, less often, a *tenor,* to which psalm verses are sung. Each psalm tone in turn has several possible endings, and each of these is identified as a *differentia* or *diffinitio.* Like the term *modus,* which was a fundamental concept in both music and logic, these two terms could be used for specific subcategories in both fields.

Terminology characteristic of Christian Neoplatonism and partly inspired by the early writings of Augustine, Boethius's *De consolatione,* and Macrobius's *Commentarii in Somnium Scipionis,* is found in many musical treatises. In the ninth century, Calcidius's commentary and the writings of John Scottus Eriugena greatly influenced the *Enchiriadis* treatises, giving rise to such musical terms as *ordo, ornare, resolutio, socialis, coadunatio,* and *organicum melos* [DJ28–30]; this terminology was in turn carried over into many later treatises.

**Literary Style.** The major musical treatises of an expository nature often reflected the style of Boethius's *De musica,* with such connectives as *hactenus, nunc, etiam, sciendum quoque est,* and *deinde.* Other treatises took the form of dialogues or letters. More and more short tracts begin to appear, devoted to a single topic and characterized, particularly in their incipits, by the formulaic language typical of treatises on arithmetic, pharmacy and medicine, computus, and so forth. Common incipits include "Si simplex," "Qui vult," "Si vis scire" [DJ32–36]. These musical tracts most often focused on the measurements of pipes and the monochord and its division, while ranging in form from simple introductions for the novice to learned dissertations requiring an understanding of complicated arithmetical calculations. Many of these treatises were prepared for reading aloud to a group of students, that is, *per cola et commata,* a style described today as "Kunstprosa" [DJ37–38].

**Modus, Tropus, Tonus.** These terms, often used as synonyms, had a variety of meanings. Although *modus* usually referred to one of the eight church melodic modes, the anonymous early tenth-century treatise *Commemoratio brevis* identified the *differentia/definitio* of a psalm tone as a *modus*. In the eleventh century, Guido of Arezzo (*Micrologus* 4.1) and John of Afflighem (*Musica* 8.2) used the term *modus* for an interval (the spatial distance between two pitches). Two additional meanings for *modus* will appear in the thirteenth century (see section III).

*Tonus* similarly had a variety of meanings: as a single pitch (*sonus, vox*); as the spatial distance between two adjacent pitches (*intervallum, spatium, modus*); as the Boethian equivalent of a mode or trope; and as a brief melody (or melodic category) to which psalm verses or parts of the liturgy were sung. One also finds *toni*, from *tonoi*, as (pitch) accents.

In ninth-century discussions of the Church tones, *tropus, tonus,* and *modus* were used by Hucbald as equivalents, but his contemporary, the author of *Musica enchiriadis*, describes (8.1) the equation of *tonus* and *modus* as incorrect. Moreover, in the conclusion of *Scolica enchiriadis*, *tropus* is used to mean a sequence of pitches, but not necessarily a mode or tone. In the eleventh century, Guido and John both use *tropus* as if it were a synonym for *modus*, although John prefers *tonus* for this concept and Guido favors *modus*. Hermannus Contractus, following Boethius, identifies *tropus* as a species of octaves. Yet another usage of *tropus* is discussed in the following section.

**Tropus, Sequentia, Historia.** Beginning in the ninth and tenth centuries the term *tropus* is also applied to certain textual or melodic additions to the chant. Most often these additions, which precede and/or are interpolated into authentic "Gregorian" chants, are found in connection with feast days and expand and ornament the basic biblical texts [DJ39]. The origin of this particular use of *tropus*, which is not found in late Latin musical treatises, is unclear; rhetoric may be the source of its musical usage. It should also be noted that use of the term *Gregorian* to describe chant is probably erroneous, since the chant so named is generally believed to have evolved in the Carolingian empire during the eighth and ninth centuries, and not in Rome during the lifetime of Gregory the Great (d. 604).

Additions to the final portion of the Alleluia of the Mass were identified by their position, i.e. as *sequentia*, and they are perhaps older as a musical genre than tropes [DJ40–41]. The *sequentia* had a variety of forms and share with tropes a latinity that is not always grammatically flawless.

Another textual genre was the *historia*, a term for the office texts based on the *vitae* of saints [DJ42].

**Notational Terminology.** There were two basic kinds of musical notations from the ninth century through the eleventh. Chant notations first appeared in the ninth century, developing concurrently with, but independently of, the treatises on music. Found chiefly in chant sources, they did not indicate precise pitch, but only the general direction of the melodic line; they should not be confused with the notations created by the theorists to indicate precise pitch. Chant notations are *today* called "neumatic notations" and the individual signs "neumes," although the term *neuma*, as indicated above, had a different meaning until the eleventh century. A single sign of either notational system was often identified generically as a *nota* or *notula;* an individual neumatic sign was also sometimes called a *figura* and a theoretical sign a *character* (*karakter*) or *signum*.

A neume could represent from one to three or more sounds. Neumes thus have a variety of forms, to which no names were attached during the ninth and tenth centuries. During the eleventh century charts of the neume forms appear, with names often suggesting their shapes: *virga* (little stick), *punctum* (point), *apostropha* (grammatical or prosodic sign taught in some treatises on the verbal arts), *podatus* (foot), *clivis* or *clinis* (descent), *cephalicus* (head), *ancus* (bent arm), *scandicus* (rising), *torculus* (handle of a wine press), and so on. The reasons behind the selection of other names, e.g. *epiphonus* and *quilisma,* is not clear. Both the tables of neume forms and the names assigned to their individual shapes appear to have had a didactic purpose, to recall to a student the morphology of a given sign ([DJ5] s.vv., [DJ43–44]).

## III.

In the late twelfth and thirteenth centuries a new genre of polyphony appeared in Paris; it was attributed to two singer-composers, Léonin (d. c. 1201) and Pérotin (d. c. 1225). This corpus of music, its composers, and several descriptive treatises are identified collectively today as the school of Notre-Dame. Its theorists used Carolingian terminology to describe liturgical polyphonic compositions with two, three, or four voice parts (*organum duplum, organum triplum,* and *organum quadruplum*).

The most interesting additions to this theoretical terminology are two freely spelled Arabic terms, *elmuahim* and *elmuarifa,* found in a treatise by an unknown thirteenth-century English author known as Anonymous IV [DJ45]. It has been demonstrated that these terms are indirect borrowings from an Arabic translation of Euclid's *Elements* (1, definition 22). Anonymous IV uses the terms as they are found in a Latin translation of the Arabic version by another Englishman, Adelard of Bath (d. 1142) [DJ46]. The terms describe the geometric shape of two symbols in the musical notation of the Notre-Dame school.

The rhythm implicit in the notation was based on the precise measurements that had previously been applied to pitch relationships (height), but now these measurements were to be applied to the movement of music in time, i.e. the proportional *temporal* relationship of successively sounding pitches. These series of long and short notes (*longa, longae* and *brevis, breves* used as nouns) were organized into longer patterns (*ordo, ordines*) by the use of six rhythmic modes named from Latin metrics: *trocheus, iambus, dactylus, anapestus, molossus, tribrachus.* The word *modus* thus takes on yet another meaning, for in contemporary treatises it is often used without qualification to indicate these rhythmic modes [DJ47–50].

Specific terminology for a variety of musical genres and compositional procedures also appears during this period, the most frequent of which are *clausula, copula, motetus, conductus, hoquetus, lauda.* In secular music, Latin names are found for several dance or song forms, such as *ductia, estampeta, rondellus.* The free interchange of Latin with Italian and French terms is especially evident in secular genres: *rondeau, rondellus, ouvertum* [*sic*] and *clausulum, virelai* and *vireletus, braccia, crotta, bourdon, quodlibet,* and so on. The term *clausula,* borrowed from grammar, identified a textless portion of an *organum,* a term increasingly limited to the earliest polyphony of the Notre-Dame school. When words were added to a *clausula,* the composition was called a *motetus. Copula,* also borrowed from the verbal arts or logic, was a transitional or concluding section of a composition. The *conductus* was originally a form of processional. *Laudae* were Italian devotional hymns. The *hoquetus* (Old French *ho[c]quet*) was a rapid alternation of sound between two or more different voices, with the musical effect resembling a hocket or hiccup.

During the thirteenth and fourteenth centuries compositional practice rapidly developed into a musical style that was precisely measured rhythmically, based on the forms of the notational symbols (*figurae*), and without the necessity of the rhythmic modes. The terms *cantus planus* and *cantus mensurabilis* (also *musica plana* and *musica mensurabilis*) were often used to distinguish between unmeasured monophony and the rhythmically measured polyphony. In the theoretical writings of the fourteenth century the term *ars vetus* (later *ars antiqua*) is contrasted with *ars nova* to distinguish the earlier Notre-Dame school from the more highly developed rhythmic practice of the fourteenth century.

The new rhythmic procedures were transmitted by a notation that had evolved from that of the school of Notre-Dame, but with much greater precision in the notation of the temporal relationships. Special signs for measured silence (a rest: *pausa, pausatio*) were created to specify exactly how long a singer should wait between notes. The breve was divided into smaller and smaller temporal units: *semibrevis, minima, semiminima*. Just as the long could be the equivalent of two or three breves, so the breve could be equal to two or three semibreves, the semibreve could be divided into two or three minims, and so on. The term *modus* was now used to indicate the manner of division of a *longa*, and thus a *longa* that was to be divided into three breves was in the major mode, and in the minor mode when divided into two breves. Just as *modus* now identified the proportional relationship between breve and long (two or three to one), so the relationship between breve and semibreve was *tempus* (also a new meaning for this term), and that between semibreve and minim was *prolatio*. *Prolatio* ([DJ1] s.v.) was also used for a special sign placed at the beginning of a composition to indicate all proportional relationships, not merely the relationship between semibreve and minim.

**Musical Instruments.** A wide variety of musical instruments were in use throughout Europe at least from the ninth century, but they are rarely mentioned in treatises until the later Middle Ages. Much of our knowledge of them has been obtained from their unreliable representations in illuminated manuscripts and in the capitals of columns in churches [DJ51]. Each kind of instrument had many variants in both form and name. The ancestor of the violin or fiddle, for example, is certainly to be found among these medieval instruments: *vidula, fides, fidicula, fidices,* and *rebec*. *Rebec* is the Middle French name for an instrument of three strings that was probably derived ultimately from an Arabic instrument called a *rabāb* [DJ52–53]. The lute also had an Arabic origin (*al‹ūd*).

## Select Bibliography

### Terminology

*Handwörterbuch der musikalischen Terminologie,* ed. H.H. Eggebrecht, 4 vols. to date (1972–84): includes many terms discussed in this chapter [DJ1].

*Lexicon Musicum Latinum Medii Aevi/ Wörterbuch der lateinischen Musikterminologie des Mittelalters bis zum Ausgang des 15. Jahrhunderts/ Dictionary of Medieval Latin Musical Terminology to the End of the 15th Century* [*LmL*], ed. M. Bernhard (1992–): appearing in fascs. (fasc. 1 has been published to date); described and illustrated by the editor, "Die Erforschung der lateinischen Musikterminologie," in *Musik in Bayern* 20 (1980) 63–77. See also M. Bernhard, "The *Lexicon Musicum Latinum* of the Bavarian Academy of Sciences," in *JPMMS* 13 (1990) 79–82 [DJ2].

*Thesaurus Musicarum Latinarum* [*TML*]: *A Comprehensive Database of Latin Music Theory of the Middle Ages and the Renaissance* [*TML*]: an evolving project (1990–), directed by T.J. Mathiesen (Department of Musicology, School of Music, Indiana University), that will produce a full-text database of relevant texts, published and unpublished, and thereby permit users to trace occurrences of terms, phrases, or passages [DJ3].

*NGDMM* [DJ4].

*NHDM* [DJ5].

*Rieimann Musik Lexikon,* ed. W. Gurlitt *et al.*, 5 vols., 12th ed. (1959–67 and 1972–75) [DJ6].

M. Appel, *Terminologie in den mittelalterlichen Musiktrakteten: Ein Beitrag zur musikalischen Elementarlehre des Mittelalters* (1935): with alphabetical listing on pp102–8 [DJ7].

M. Bernhard, *Wortkonkordanz zu Anicius Manlius Severinus Boethius, De institutione musica, VMK* 4 (1979) [DJ8].

W. Frobenius, "Methoden und Hilfsmittel mittelalterlicher Musiktheorie und ihr Vokabular," in *CIVICIMA* 3:121–36 [DJ9].

H.P. Gysin, *Studien zum Vokabular der Musiktheorie im Mittelalter: Eine linguistische Analyse* (1958) [DJ10].

M. Huglo, "Bibliographie des éditions et études relatives à la théorie musicale du moyen âge (1972–1987)," in *AM* 60 (1988) 269–70 ("Études sur le vocabulaire de la théorie musicale médiévale") [DJ11].

M. Huglo, "La lexicographie du latin médiéval et l'histoire de la musique," in *LLM* 391–99 [DJ12].

Johannes Tinctoris (d. 1511), *Terminorum musicae diffinitorium* (c. 1475): first true dictionary of musical terminology, ed. and tr. C. Parrish (1963, r1978), with bibliographical essay by J.B. Coover; the French edition, ed. A. Machabey (1951), has a useful introduction and commentary [DJ13].

R.P. Maddox, "Terminology in the Early Medieval Music Treatises (ca. 400–1100 A.D.): A Study of Changes in Musical Thought as Evidenced by the Use of Selected Basic Terms" (Ph.D. diss., University of California, Los Angeles, 1987) [DJ14].

E.L. Waeltner and M. Bernhard, *Wortindex zu den echten Schriften Guidos von Arezzo, VMK* 2 (1976) [DJ15].

## Treatises

For a comprehensive bibliography of musical treatises, with editions and studies, see A. Gallo, "Philological Works on Musical Treatises of the Middle Ages," in *AM* 44 (1972) 78–101 [DJ16]; and M. Huglo ([DJ11]) pp229–72 [DJ17].

The manuscripts preserving theoretical texts (published and unpublished) are described in *Répertoire international des sources musicales: The Theory of Music* [*RISM*], B.III [DJ18].

See also the bibliography assembled by Y. Chartier, "Musical Treatises," in *DMA* 8:636–49 [DJ19].

## Late Latin Theory

Boethius, *De institutione musica,* tr. C.M. Bower (1989) [DJ20].

I. Henderson, "Ancient Greek Music," in *Ancient and Oriental Music,* ed. E. Wellesz, *NOHM* 1 (1957, r1975) 336–403: includes descriptions (pp340–63) of some inconsistently used terminology (*genus, harmonia, modus, species, systema, tonos, tropos,* etc.) [DJ21].

G. Wille, *Musica Romana* (1967): ch. 12 includes the Late Latin sources of music theory that were most influential throughout the Middle Ages [DJ22].

## Carolingian and Later Developments

M. Bernhard, "Glosses on Boethius' *De institutione musica,*" in *MTIS* 136–49 [DJ23].

M. Bernhard, "Überlieferung und Fortleben der antiken lateinischen Musiktheorie in Mittelalter," in *Rezeption des antiken Fachs im Mittelalter, Geschichte der Musiktheorie* 3, ed. F. Zaminer (1990) 7–35 [DJ24].

N. Phillips, "Classical and Late Latin Sources for Ninth-Century Treatises on Music," in *MTIS* 100–35 [DJ25].

W. Lipphardt, *Der Karolingische Tonar von Metz* (1965) 12–13, 62–63 [DJ26].

M. Huglo, *Les tonaires: Inventaire, analyse, comparaison* (1971) 25–32, 46–65, 477–80 [DJ27].

*Musica et Scolica enchiriadis una cum aliquibus tractatulis adiunctis,* ed. H. Schmid, in *VMK* 3 (1981); *Musica enchiriadis* and *Scolica enchiriadis,* tr. R. Erickson (1995) [DJ28]: on the terminology in these treatises see N. Phillips, "*Musica* and *Scolica enchiriadis:* The Literary, Theoretical, and Musical Sources" (Ph.D. diss., New York University, 1984) [DJ29].

E.L. Waeltner, *Organicum melos: Zur Musikanschauung des Iohannes Scottus (Eriugena), VMK* 1 (1977) [DJ30].

M. Bielitz, *Musik und Grammatik* (1977) [DJ31].

L. Thorndike and P. Kibre, *A Catalogue of Incipits of Mediaeval Scientific Writings in Latin,* rev. and augmented ed. (1963); see also [EA14]: lists most musical treatises [DJ32]; should be supplemented by M. Bernhard, *Clavis Gerberti: Eine Revision von Martin Gerberts Scriptores ecclesiastici de musica sacra potissimum* (St. Blasien 1784), pt1, in *VMK* 7 (1989) [DJ33].

C. Vivell, *Initia tractatuum musices ex codicibus editorum* (1912): provides incipits of each major subdivision of a given text [DJ34].

The pipe divisions have been edited and studied by K.-J. Sachs, *Mensura fistu-*

*larum: Die Mensurierung der Orgelpfeifen im Mittelalter,* 2 vols. (1970–80), with *Incipitregister* and *Terminologisches Register* in v1:148–59 [**DJ35**].

For the monochord divisions, see M. Markovits, *Das Tonsystem der abendländischen Musik im frühen Mittelalter* (1977): incipits and tables on pp113–16 [**DJ36**].

Concerning "Kunstprosa," see J. Smits van Waesberghe, "Die Anwendung der *ars rhetorica* in den musiktheoretischen Traktaten des Mittelalters und der Renaissance," in *Dia-pason/De omnibus: Ausgewählte Aufsätze von Joseph Smits van Waesberghe, Festgabe zu seinem 75. Geburtstag,* ed. C.J. Maas and M.U. Schouten-Glass (1976) 71–90; a more detailed version of this article, with examples, is "Studien über das Lesen (pronuntiare), das Zitieren und über die Herausgabe lateinischer musiktheoretischer Traktate (9.–16. Jahrhundert)," published in *Archiv für Musikwissenschaft* 28 (1971) 155–200, 271–87, and 29 (1972) 64–86 [**DJ37**]. See also Smits van Waesberghe's editions for the series *Divitiae musicae artis,* particularly *Bernonis Augiensis abbatis de arte musica disputationes traditae,* 2 vols. (1978–79), pt. A (*Bernonis Augiensis De mensurando monochordo* [= *Divitiae musicae artis,* series A.6a]), pp38–40; and the edition of the monochord division in "Kunstprosastil," beginning at p42 [**DJ38**].

*Corpus Troporum,* ed. R. Jonsson (alias Jacobsson) *et al.* (1975–): ongoing series of editions of the tropes, often correcting the Latin found in the manuscripts; a close reading of the notes is necessary for an analysis of the latinity of the original authors and scribes [**DJ39**].

For the sequences of Notker Balbulus (d. 912) see W. von den Steinen, *Notker der Dichter und seine geistige Welt,* 2 vols. (1948) [**DJ40**]; for southern French sequences, see L. Elfving, *Étude lexicographique sur les séquences limousines* (1962) [**DJ41**].

R. Jonsson, *Historia: Études sur la genèse des offices versifiés* (1968) [**DJ42**].

M. Huglo, "Les noms des neumes," in *Études grégoriennes* 1 (1954) 53–67 [**DJ43**].

C. Floros, *Einführung in die Neumenkunde* (1980) 130–37 ("Der Namen der lateinischen Neumen") [**DJ44**].

F. Reckow, *Der Musiktraktat des Anonymus 4,* 2 vols. (1967), v1:41, lines 6, 14 (Arabic loanwords) [**DJ45**].

C. Burnett, "The Use of Geometrical Terms in Medieval Music: *elmuahim* and *elmuarifa* and the Anonymous IV," in *SAr* 70 (1986) 198–205 [**DJ46**].

N. Phillips and M. Huglo, "Le *De musica* de saint Augustin et l'organisation de la durée musicale du IXe au XIIe siècles," in *RecAug* 20 (1985) 117–31 [**DJ47**]. For this notation see J. Knapp, "Modes, rhythmic," in *NHDM* 502–3 [**DJ48**].

J. Yudkin, "The Influence of Aristotle on French University Music Texts," in *MTIS* 173–89 [**DJ49**].

M. Huglo, "The Study of Ancient Sources of Music Theory in the Medieval Universities," tr. F.C. Lochner, in *MTIS* 150–72 [**DJ50**].

For illustrations of musical instruments, see J. Smits van Waesberghe, *Musikerziehung* (1969) [**DJ51**]. See also W.L. Monical, "Rebec" and "Violin," in *NHDM* 681–82, 917–22 [**DJ52**], with illustrations (p921) of the medieval fiddle, hurdy-gurdy, and rebec. Especially useful is S. Marcuse, *Musical Instruments: A Comprehensive Dictionary,* 2nd ed. (1975) [**DJ53**].

*See also* [BA70], [BA74], [BA144], [BC109], [BD104], [BE29].

# DK ❖ COMMERCE

## BY JOHN H. PRYOR

The many types of Latin sources for medieval economic life include the statutes and archives of guilds and municipal authorities, chronicles, private and public charters, and the cartularies of both courts and notaries. There are also private letters, informal holograph records, and merchants' manuals, although from the thirteenth century most of these sources are in vernacular languages. The range of materials surviving from the various countries and regions of medieval Europe defies comprehensive analysis in such a brief introduction. The discussion of commercial or "business" Latin here is based on notarial charters and cartularies from the Mediterranean world, where the notariate was well established and widely dispersed, and where it was normal to engage notaries to record most business contracts of any value.

Medieval public notaries (*tabelliones, notarii publici*), as opposed to private notaries or scribes in chanceries, were licensed by political authorities (popes, emperors, kings, feudal lords, or municipal officials) to issue charters (*carte*) or instruments (*instrumenta*) that had public authority when adduced in court as proof of contract. Their growing importance from the mid-twelfth century paralleled the revival and flourishing of Roman law. Notaries recorded contracts in writing to provide permanent records of their details and of the names of witnesses, among whom they themselves were numbered.

Notarial method varied considerably from place to place and time to time. Usually, however, brief notes (*abbreviature, note*) of the essential details of contracts were redacted either on loose sheets or in cartularies. Even in this abbreviated form, notarial documents were legally valid as proof of contract, and many clients therefore never bothered to obtain for themselves copies of the full, formal versions of the documents. For this reason, the cartularies themselves had value, both during the lives of notaries and after their deaths; and this is what explains the survival of so many of them. If clients did want full versions of documents, complete with the requisite legal formulae, these could be obtained for a price. In some places and at some times, *carte* or *instrumenta* were drawn up directly from the notes; in other places or at other times, extended versions known as "extents" (*extensa*) or protocols (*protocolla*) were drafted by notaries in different cartularies before the *instrumenta publica* were copied onto *carte* and delivered to the clients, completed by the notaries' eschatocols (subscription clauses), and validated by their personal signs (*signa*).

Dozens of notarial cartularies and hundreds of charters and private papers, only a part of which has been published, survive from the period before the end of the thirteenth century, especially in Barcelona, Genoa, Marseilles, Pisa, and Venice. From the fourteenth and fifteenth centuries the volume of material that has survived, both from these and from many other places, expands exponentially, and very little of this has been printed.

The style, syntax, grammar, and orthography of notarial records varied greatly over time, from place to place, and according to the type of text. Generally speaking, the quality of the Latin deteriorates both with the distance of a text's provenance from the centers of the Latin world, and also with the degree of informality of the type of document. The latinity of notarial records from such places as Trogir in Dalmatia (see [DK13]), or Khilia, the Genoese colony at the mouth of the Danube (see [DK11] v2, [DK39]), can be very poor, whereas that of a Genoese notary such as Bartolomeo de Fornari (thirteenth century) is very good indeed (see [DK20]). On the one hand, the best of the notarial formularists, such as Salatiele of Bologna [DK37], can stand beside trained civil and canon lawyers in their grasp of Latin vocabulary and grammar; on the other hand, court records (see [DK23]) and private documents are usually simplistic in their grammar and restricted in vocabulary.

Trained for the most part in an apprenticeship system, even though there were schools for notaries at Bologna and elsewhere, most notaries were little influenced by the stylistic ideals expressed in manuals on the *ars notarie*. They wrote a Latin that is graceless and frequently incorrect grammatically, but fairly simple to read, at least superficially. They and their clients were primarily concerned with precision in specification of the details of contracts: times, places, participants, third parties, witnesses, commodities, weights, measures, values, obligations under the law of particular contracts, waivers of the rights of certain classes of people in Roman law, and so on. Such precision often required repetition and respecification. Confusion arising from repeated references to the same persons, places, and things was reduced by the regular use of modifiers (*dictus, predictus, iamdictus, suprascriptus,* etc.), a device that also served to relate clearly all the parts of a document.

The constructions of notarial Latin are limited, as is the vocabulary, except for the technical terms for commodities, monies, etc. Standard formulae, drawn mostly from Roman law, are repeated almost verbatim in document after document. Once one becomes familiar with the formulae, the highly abbreviated script of unpublished texts becomes easier to read, although the deciphering of unfamiliar proper nouns (of places, names, commodities, monies, weights, measures, etc.) remains difficult. The orthography, like that of most archival or documentary Latin, often reflects the influence of the vernaculars: *t*, for example, appears for *c*, *n* for *m*, *b* for *u/v*, and vice versa; double *s* and *t* are found where single letters are expected. Orthographic variation can sometimes make tracing a word in such Medieval Latin dictionaries as *Du Cange* and *Niermeyer* very difficult.

The Latin vocabulary can be problematic because nouns may have variant forms, e.g. *capetanea, caput,* and *capitale* (all of which can mean "capital"), and may change gender from time to time and place to place under the influence of the vernaculars. They also mutated into forms different from those of Classical or Late Latin, e.g. *stancia* (a contract, understanding) from *instantia* (constancy, earnestness), or acquired new meanings, e.g. *gravamen* (impost, fee, charge), originally "trouble" or "inconvenience." New nouns were formed tropologically from verbs, e.g. *habere/abere* (goods, capital, investment) from *habere* (to have), *coperta* (blanket, cover) from *cooperire* (to cover), *vectuarius* (muleteer, transporter) from *vehere* (to carry), and *accomandatio* or *comanda* (partnership of labor and capital) from *commendare* (to entrust, commend). They were also formed from verbal associations, e.g. *compagnia* (partnership) from *cum pane* (with/sharing bread). Verbs could often acquire new meanings, e.g. *iactare* (to invest) from the idea of throwing in; and *abundare* (to invest surplus capital) from the idea of overflowing.

Much Latin business vocabulary was also completely new, developed under the influence of Arabic, Greek, or the vernacular languages. For example, we find *taxegium* (a commercial voyage), from Greek ταξείδιον; *hentica/entica* (capital, investment) from Greek ἐνθήκη; *fundicus* (warehouse or overseas "factory"/"colony") from Greek πανδοκεῖον via Arabic *funduq; avaria* (customs duty) from Arabic ʿawār; *maona/mahona* (joint stock company for an overseas enterprise) from Arabic *maʿuna; dogana/doana* (customs duty) from Arabic *dīwān; magasinus* (storehouse) from Arabic *makhzan; sensale* (broker) from Arabic *simsār;* and *galega* (auction) from Arabic *halaqa.* From the Romance vernaculars we note *campsor* (money changer) from Italian *campsore,* and *scare* (quays or booms) from Provençal *scaro.* Hundreds of other examples could be added. It is therefore frequently necessary to turn to Greek, Arabic, or vernacular dictionaries rather than to Latin ones for the vocabulary of medieval business Latin.

Notarial style, touched on above, can be difficult to comprehend until one masters and remembers the formulae. Whole contracts are frequently written as single sentences, with multiple subordinate clauses hanging from the initiating main clause. Punctuation added by modern editors is usually nothing more than an attempt to break up the texts to facilitate comprehension, but one result of this practice is that whole sentences in modern editions can appear to be grammatically incorrect, to have, for example, no subject or main verb. Participial clauses and ablatives absolute weighed down with dependent statements are common and are frequently strung together in sequence. So also are gerund/gerundive constructions. Verb forms are frequently assembled parenthetically or in apposition, giving the appearance of verbosity for its own sake; for example, procurators might be appointed *ad petendum exigendum et recipiendum,* or debtors might acknowledge the payment of creditors in the following way: *solvistis et dedistis et tradidistis.* Nouns, too, can seem to proliferate unnecessarily in apposition or parenthesis; for example, a contract may be referred to as *placitum nostraque stancia,* or agents called *certi missi actores et procuratores.*

The appearance of redundancy or amplification is, however, usually deceptive. In very few instances did notaries actually use unnecessary language. In most cases the different words chosen have shades of meaning with legal significance. Medievalists must always remember that most commercial and financial records were in fact legal documents designed to protect the rights and interests of creditors and to define the obligations of debtors. Notaries had no motive to be unduly verbose, as they were paid fees for their services according to the type of document concerned, not according to its length. When they used strings of apparently appositional terms, they usually had good reason for doing so. Here are two examples:

1. Creditors might give authority to their procurators *ad agendum opponendum transigendum paciscendum* on their behalf. *Agere* here means to prosecute a case on

behalf of another; *opponere* means to defend a suit against the claims of a plaintiff by counterclaims that would nullify his claims of obligation on the part of the defendant; *transigere* means to resolve differences out of court or to reach a composition or mutual settlement (*transactio*); *pacisci* means to reach an extrajudicial agreement (*pactum*) with another party that would override a legal obligation. A *transactio* was one form of *pactum,* but the latter had wider purview and, unlike a *transactio,* could be made even when a dispute had already been judged in court. All of these terms had precise and complementary meanings, and if the procurators chose to take action at law on behalf of their principals, they needed to be able to show the court that they had been given the authority to take the course of action they had chosen.

2. Agreement might be reached between the owners of merchandise and muleteers for carriage of their goods to another place for a fee (*precium seu loquerium*) of so much per load. *Precium* was "a price," but technically it applied only to contracts of purchase and sale (*emptio venditio*). A notary might use it loosely but then qualify it with *loquerium,* which was the rent paid for hire of services or property under contracts of lease and hire (*locatio conductio*). In this case the contract was really one of hire of services (*locatio conductio operarum*). *Loquerium* was the appropriate term for a muleteer's fee.

Notaries really did know the law in most cases and were aware of the importance of what they wrote. For example, in the cartulary (1248) of Giraud Amalric of Marseilles (see [DK40] p117), the notary recorded a contract of *commenda* consisting of capital of four quintals (hundredweights) and 37 pounds of ginger given by an investor in Marseilles to a traveling partner going to the fairs of Bar-sur-Aube. Having recorded the essentials, Giraud began to add the usual renunciation clause under which a debtor waived his rights to the *exceptio non numerate pecunie* of Roman law, whereby a defendant could counter a plaintiff's claim of obligation on his part by a counterclaim that even though he had acknowledged obligation, the money for which he had assumed the obligation had never in fact been paid to him. The notary began to write, *Renuncians inde exceptioni non numerate et non,* but he then remembered that *numeratus* referred in law solely to the payment, or counting out, of money, and could not refer to goods. In this case, since the capital was in goods not money, the clause as he had begun it would have been legally ineffective. He therefore cancelled the words *numerate et non* and finished the clause with *tradite michi comande. Traditus* meant in law the effective delivery of a thing from one person to another, and the renunciation clause was thus altered and tailored to fit the circumstances of the contract and to create a legally binding obligation. Cancellations found in the manuscripts of contracts frequently tell a whole story in themselves. Scholars using Medieval Latin business records need always to be mindful of the extremely precise nature of the vocabulary with which they are working.

Similar difficulties concerning the precise, technical meaning of the vocabulary are to be encountered at every turn. Using *Lewis-Short* to read and interpret medieval business documents can be very misleading. For example, a witness might be *interrogatus si est locatus vel rogatus, vel inimicus sive amicus pro hoc testimonio.* This should be translated very specifically as "asked whether he is hired [paid for his services] or summonsed [not paid], or hostile or friendly, in so far as his testimony is concerned." Here *locatus* refers to the contract of hire of services (*locatio conductio operarum*) and *rogatus* to the act of formally requesting in law that a person be a witness and apprising him of the details of the act to which he is to witness. Similarly, *accipere,* in the context of a contract where something has been transferred from one person to another, meant more than "to receive." It referred to the formal act of transfer of *possessio* of a thing, by which the recipient acquired not only physical possession of it but also specified legal rights to treat it in certain ways as his own property, even though he had not acquired the ownership (*dominium*) of it. The use of this verb implied a legal consequence: the transfer created an obligation on the part of the recipient that was the object of the contract.

Another example is *mecum portare,* which, in the context of a traveling partner undertaking to bring merchandise or money with him on a voyage, had a hidden meaning. There was an obligation on the part of the traveling partner in a *commenda* contract to retain the capital in his physical possession. He could not dispose of it to a third party unless express permission to do so had been granted in the contract. This is the significance of the word *mecum.*

Even the apparently simple word *dare,* in the context of any transfer of rights or possession, meant more than simply "to give." It referred to alienation of physical possession of a thing or money with transfer of rights of either ownership (*dominium*) or possession (*possessio*). *Reddere* had the same significance as *dare* concerning the transfer of rights of ownership or possession, as is stated in the *Digest* (50.16.94): "The word *reddendi,* although it has the meaning of 'giving back,' acquires also by itself the meaning of 'giving.'" When *debere* was added to *dare* or *reddere,* or indeed to any other verb signifying an obligation to do something (e.g. *portare, dividere, iactare, recipere*), it had the consequence of creating not a moral obligation but a legal one that could be grounds for an action in court. Even the apparently innocuous *promittere* used so often in contracts had a meaning at law. In Justinian's codifiction of Roman law, *promissio* replaced earlier forms that created obligation through the formal, oral contract of *stipulatio.* A *promissio* in a formal, notarized medieval business contract gave grounds for legal action.

At all turns the language of medieval business records is permeated with technical legal terminology whose meaning either created or extinguished obligations actionable at law under various forms. The nuances of the Latin language used in business transactions are frequently overlooked by medievalists, largely because they are not aware of their precise import; the result is that researchers often fail to appreciate the real meaning of contracts. The omission of a standard word from a regular formula, for example, is invariably significant. Notaries were professionals sensitive to the special requirements made of language by the world of business; they did not omit, without good reason, words that might affect the rights and obligations of their clients. A solid foundation in the Roman and canon law of contract and delict should precede any attempt to draw economic conclusions from the Latin documents of medieval commerce.

## Select Bibliography

### Works of Reference

There is no comprehensive dictionary of medieval business Latin. Of the standard Medieval Latin dictionaries, *Niermeyer* is particularly useful, as that lexicon includes the vocabulary of large numbers of documentary sources. Because of the polyglot nature of much business vocabulary, and because the Latin of notarial cartularies and other records commonly included latinizations of vernacular terms, it may be necessary to have recourse to a wide range of lexicographical works in various languages.

A.-M. Bautier, "Contribution à un vocabulaire économique du Midi de la France," in *ALMA* 25 (1955) 5–28, 26 (1956) 5–74, 27 (1957) 241–86, 28 (1958) 119–60, 29 (1959) 173–217, 30 (1960) 177–232 [DK1].

A. Berger, *Encyclopedic Dictionary of Roman Law, TAPhS,* n.s., 43.2 (1953, r1968) [DK2].

F. Edler, *Glossary of Mediaeval Terms of Business: Italian Series, 1200–1600* (1934, r1970) [DK3].

M. Gual Camarena, *Vocabulario del comercio medieval: Colección de aranceles aduaneros de la Corona de Aragón (siglos XIII y XIV)* (1968) [DK4].

G.B. Pellegrini, "L'elemento arabo nelle lingue neolatine con particolare riguardo all'Italia," in *L'Occidente e l'Islam nell'alto medioevo,* Settimane di studio del Centro italiano di studi sull'alto medioevo 12, 2 vols. (1965) v2:697–790 [DK5].

J.A. Sesma Muñoz, *Lexico del comercio medieval en Aragon (siglo XV)* (1982) [DK6].

### Texts, Studies, and Translations (very selective)

M. Amelotti and G. Costamagna, *Alle origini del notariato italiano,* Studi storici sul notariato italiano 2 (1975) [DK7]: a publication of the Consiglio nazionale del notariato, which also publishes the series *Fonti e strumenti per la storia del notariato italiano,* including, for example, v1: *Il notariato a Perugia: Mostra documentaria e iconografica per il XVI congresso nazionale del notariato* (1967), with catalogue by R. Abbondanza (1973) [DK8]; and v5: *Rolandini Passagerii contractus,* ed. R. Ferrara (1983) [DK9].

G. Astuti, ed., *Rendiconti mercantili inediti del cartolare di Giovanni Scriba* (1933): the only known surviving Latin accounts for a series of commercial voyages [DK10].

M. Balard, ed., *Gênes et l'outre-mer,* v1: *Les actes de Caffa du notaire Lamberto di Sambuceto, 1289–1290* (1973), with description (ch. 2) of the various types of commercial and financial contracts; v2: *Actes de Kilia du notaire Antonio di Ponzò, 1360* (1980) [DK11].

L. Balletto, ed., *Il cartulario di Arnaldo Cumano e Giovanni di Donato (Savona, 1178–1188)* (1978) [DK12].

M. Barada, ed., *Trogirski spomenici, Dio 1: Zapisci Pisarne Općine Trogirske, Svezak 1: od 21.X.1263 do 22.V.1273* (1948) [DK13].

L.T. Belgrano, ed., *Documenti inediti riguardanti le due crociate di S. Ludovico IX, rè di Francia* (1859) [DK14].

D. Bizzarri and M. Chiaudano, eds., *Imbreviature notarili,* 2 vols. (1934–38): v1, *Liber imbreviaturarum Appulliesis notarii comunis Senarum MCCXXI–MCCXXIII;* v2, *Liber imbreviaturarum Ildibrandini notarii MCCXXVII–MCCXXIX* [DK15].

L. Blancard, ed., *Documents inédits sur le commerce de Marseille au moyen-âge,* 2 vols. (1884–85) [DK16].

G.I. Bratianu, ed., *Actes des notaires génois de Péra et de Caffa de la fin du treizième siècle (1281–1290)* (1927) [DK17].

P. Burgarella and P. Gulotta, eds., *Le imbreviature del notaio Adamo de Citella a Palermo . . . (1286–1287, 1298–1299),* 2 vols. (1981–82), with glossary [DK18]: published in the series *Imbreviature, matricole, statuti e formulari notarili medievali,* which also includes M.S. Guccione, ed., *Le imbreviature del notaio Bartolomeo de Alamanna a Palermo (1332–33)* [DK19].

E.H. Byrne, *Genoese Shipping in the Twelfth and Thirteenth Centuries* (1930, r1970), with documents (pp68–159), especially of the otherwise unedited Bartolomeo de Fornari [DK20].

C.R. Cheney, *Notaries Public in England in the Thirteenth and Fourteenth Centuries* (1972), with app. of documents (pp152–85), including some notarial instruments [DK21].

M. Chiaudano and M. Moresco, eds., *Il cartolare di Giovanni Scriba,* 2 vols. (1935) [DK22].

M. Chiaudano and R. Morozzo della Rocca, eds., *Oberto scriba de mercato (1190)* (1938) [DK23]: v1 in the series *Notai liguri dei secoli XII [e XIII],* which also includes *Il cartulario del notaio Martino: Savona, 1203–1206,* ed. D. Puncuh (1974) [DK24].

G. Cremošnik, ed., *Spisi Dubrovačke kancelarije,* 1: *Zapisi notara Tomazina de Savere, 1278–1282* (1951) [DK25].

R. Doehaerd, *Les relations commerciales entre Gênes, la Belgique et l'Outremont d'après les archives notariales génoises aux XIII et XIV siècles,* 3 vols. (1941) [DK26].

L. Lanfranchi, ed., *Famiglia Zusto,* Fonti per la storia di Venezia, Sezione 4: Archivi privati (1955): 30 documents concerning this Venetian family, 1083–1183 [DK27].

R.S. Lopez, "The Unexplored Wealth of the Notarial Archives in Pisa and Luca," in *Mélanges d'histoire du moyen-âge, dédiés à la mémoire de Louis Halphen* (1951) 417–32 [DK28].

R.S. Lopez and I.W. Raymond, *Medieval Trade in the Mediterranean World: Illustrative Documents Translated with Introductions and Notes* (1955): translations of some 200 Medieval Latin, Greek, Italian (and its dialects), Provençal, Catalan, Old French, and Arabic documents [DK29].

J.F. McGovern, "The Documentary Language of Mediaeval Business, A.D. 1150–1250," in *The Classical Journal* 67 (1972) 227–39 [DK30]: a usefully annotated examination of the latinity of Italian notarial prose, based upon documents executed by the Genoese notary Giovanni di Guiberto (fl. 1200–1211), ed. M.W. Hall-Cole *et al.,* 2 vols. (1939–40) [DK31].

J.M. Madurell Marimón and A. García Sanz, eds., *Comandas comerciales Barcelonesas de la baja edad media* (1973) [DK32].

G. Masi, ed., *Formularium Florentinum artis notariae, 1220–1242* (1943) [DK33].

R. Morozzo della Rocca and A. Lombardo, eds., *Documenti del commercio veneziano nei secoli XI–XIII,* 2 vols. (1940) [DK34].

R. Morozzo della Rocca, ed., *Benvenuto de Brixano, notaio in Candia, 1301–1302* (1950): the first vol. in the series (not numbered) *Fonti per la storia di Venezia, Sezione 3: Archivi notarili* [DK35].

J.M. Murray, "Notaries Public in Flanders in the Late Middle Ages" (Ph.D. diss., Northwestern University, 1983) [DK36].

G. Orlandelli, ed., *Salatiele: Ars notarie,* 2 vols. (1961) [DK37].

G. Orlandelli, "Genesi dell' 'ars notariae' nel secolo XIII," in *SM,* 3rd ser., 6 (1965) 329–66 [DK38].

G. Pistarino, ed., *Notai genovesi in oltremare: Atti rogati a Chilia da Antonio di Ponzò (1360–61)* (1971): v12 in the series *Collana storica di fonti e studi,* which also includes other "notai genovesi in oltremare" [DK39].

J.H. Pryor, *Business Contracts of Medieval Provence: Selected Notulae from the Cartulary of Giraud Amalric of Marseilles, 1248* (1981) [DK40].

Rolandinus de Passageriis, *Summa totius artis notariae,* 2 vols. (Venice 1574) [DK41].

N. Sarti, ed., *Gli statuti della Società dei notai di Bologna dell'anno 1336: Contributo alla storia di una corporazione cittadina* (1988) [DK42].

*See also* [BA130].

# D L  ⬤  LATIN IN EVERYDAY LIFE

BY RICHARD SHARPE

## Introduction

When, around A.D. 800, Medieval Latin came to be clearly differentiated by speakers of Romance languages from the Late Latin assemblage of various written and spoken forms, it ceased to be perceived as a language spoken for everyday purposes. Spoken Latin was hereafter used only by the most educated classes, even though it might still be used by them in casual conversation. It was still spoken by such men until the end of the Middle Ages and after, though how often and in what contexts would vary. There were probably a good many churchmen who could adequately follow a sermon or a speech delivered in Latin but who could not have carried on a conversation. In the universities of the later Middle Ages it was naturally the language used in lectures and debates, but its use as the language for chatter between students at mealtimes had to be artificially maintained by rules. The value of speaking and understanding spoken Latin was preserved, but as a learned tongue, most often used for formal purposes and never with the same colloquial fluency as the vernacular languages.

Even so, Latin was still used for mundane purposes, in writing. A very basic use was in charters relating to property transactions or in the written records of pleadings (*placita*) in the courts, which continued to reflect a language close to spoken Latin until the tenth century in Italy or Carolingian Spain. In much of the Carolingian empire, people belonging to the peasant class had access to such procedures; one can see this particularly clearly where the evidence is rich, as, for example, in the numerous ninth-century transactions in the cartulary of Redon. Individuals would not be using written deeds on an everyday basis, but the local priest or other literate person acting as draftsman and scribe might find himself writing deeds quite regularly, and anyone attending meetings of the local courts must have seen them and heard them read. But in these centuries Latin served no domestic function outside the highest circles of ecclesiastical culture. It was the language of the liturgy, learning, and entertainment for the learned, and for the occasional business recorded in writing. Any use of Latin to deal with everyday circumstances was in some sense out of the ordinary, and there was an effective break in the tradition, which we see reflected in the vocabulary.

## Latin in Schools

When a boy begins to learn Latin, however, it would be impractical to start him off with a theological treatise. As long as languages have been taught in schools, schoolmasters have provided for use as exercises texts that deal with objects and activities familiar to the pupils. We have such texts used by ancient Roman schoolboys learning Greek [DL7]. From England at the end of the tenth century we have short dialogues composed in Latin with an interlinear gloss in Anglo-Saxon. The *Colloquy* of Abbot Aelfric presents us with a series of conversations between the learner and men in different trades—plowman, shepherd, oxherd, hunter, fisherman, fowler, chapman, cobbler, salter, baker, and cook:

"Tu, sutor, quid operaris nobis utilitatis?"

"Est quidem ars mea utilis ualde uobis et necessaria."

"Quomodo?"

"Ego emo cutes et pelles, et preparo eas arte mea, et facio ex eis calciamenta diuersi generis, subtalares et ficones, caligas et utres, frenos et falera, flascones et casidilia, calcaria et chamos, peras et marsupia; et nemo uestrum uult hiemare sine arte mea." [DL8]

The syntax is simple, and the student is introduced to the Latin vocabulary for familiar subjects, in this case a range of articles made of leather. This approach was developed by Abbot Aelfric's pupil, Aelfric Bata, who augmented his master's colloquies and composed his own, a work that can be both amusing and distasteful.

The growth in the number and influence of schools in the late eleventh and early twelfth centuries went hand in hand with an extension in the use of the written word and fostered an increase in the number of people able to use Latin for almost any purpose. There survive three popular schoolbooks, written to teach vocabulary and covering as many everyday subjects as the master could fit into a short narrative. All three were composed by Englishmen who taught at Paris, though their books were hardly intended for students in the higher schools there. Adam of Balsham's *De utensilibus* is the earliest, dating from before 1150, and this was soon followed in about 1180 by Alexander Neckam's *De nominibus utensilium* [DL10]. Their titles' reference to *utensilia*, "useful subjects," suggests that the pupils would be expected to use the vocabulary dealing with daily needs. The third of these treatises, composed about 1220 by John of Garland, has a simple story line, in which John sets out to tour the different stalls and shops near his school in Paris. Schoolmen might know the Latin words to enable them to go into the market and discuss any of the commodities on sale, their means of production or manufacture, and their uses; but, however "useful" in school, this was hardly a practical skill, since the traders did not speak Latin. Their learning to use Latin for everyday things was still largely for an out-of-the-ordinary purpose.

This shows to some extent in the character of the Latin. Take, for example, John of Garland's listing of the necessities for women's work in §65 of his *Dictionarius*. The first items are identified by classical words—*forcipes*, "tongs"; *acus*, "needle"; *fusus*, "spindle"; and *colus*, "distaff." The classical word *theca* is here applied in the limited sense, "thimble," Old French *dayel*, and Classical Latin *metaxa*, "raw silk," is used (in the variant spelling *mataxa*) in a quite different, medieval sense, "comb, hackle (for flax)," OF *serence*. Similarly *uertebrum*, "spinning whorl," is not a classical usage, though it is perhaps derived from CL *uertebra,* understood by this date as from the verb *verto, -ere.* Again Late Latin *girgillus,* "windlass," is here used in a new sense to designate a reel of yarn. Of the other words in John's list, however, only Medieval Latin *lixiua/lexiua,* "lye," has any currency at all. The rest of them may even have been coined by John, or at the least belonged only to a restricted school context: their only subsequent use is in later medieval vocabularies, copied from one another and going back to John's *Dictionarius.* It is evident that only a limited range of words had been handed down since the days when Latin was a normal spoken language; to describe a wider range of implements John and his fellow schoolmasters had to resort to invention. So *feritorium* from CL *ferio, -ire,* "I strike," is something used for beating, whether in the preparation of linen from flax or in the laundry; the glosses on John's text and in the later glossaries explain it as "battledore" or "washing-beetle." Seeing that this approach to extending the vocabulary found no users, we may see it as a linguistic dead end. The vitality of the language lay elsewhere.

In the late Middle Ages every elementary schoolmaster used both glossaries and short passages as aids to teaching Latin. They were known as *uulgaria* because they used scenes from everyday life in their linguistic examples and exercises, and several, scarcely known today, were printed and reprinted many times before about 1520 [DL12]. One such work that remained unprinted was written in the 1490s by a master at the Magdalen Grammar School in Oxford (which still exists). The longest section of the book provides several hundred short passages in English, with model Latin translations, which form an intimate picture of the schoolboy's life [DL11]. A mother looks at her son's buttocks to see whether he has been beaten at school, a young man dances with a fair lady so slim "that a man might have clipped her in two hands," a student running in fright from shadows in the street slips in the mud, and there is a fireside conversation on a windy night about the perils of traders at sea. The style of Latin offered in these books is better than we see in many medieval texts, and there is an enthusiasm for the language that we might think of as humanistic:

> Iff ye knew, Childe, what conseitts wer in latyn tonge, what fettes, what knakkes, truly your stomake wolde be choraggyde with a new desir or affeccyon to lurne. Trust ye me, all langage well nygh is but rude beside latyne tonge. In this is property, in this is shyfte, in this all swetness. / Si scires, o puer, quantas habet facecias latina oratio, quid leporis, quos sales, exuscitareris [*MS* exustitarentur] nimirum cum uobis nouo discendi affectu. Barbarus (mihi crede) est sermo fere omnis preter latinum; hic copia, hic eligancia, in hoc suauitas omnis. British Library, MS Arundel 249, fol. 11v

What these books reveal is that, however artificial was the preservation of Latin for learned or clerical uses, the language so used was not regarded as a dead language. Children learned to hear and speak as well as to read and write Latin, and even those who would go no further than secondary school and a desk job as a Latin clerk learned the language with vigor and vitality. These books, still essentially medieval, were in time superseded by more tasteful works of the best humanist Latin such as the *Colloquies* of Erasmus (who himself visited the Magdalen School in 1498–99). William Horman's *Vulgaria* [DL13], written for his pupils at Eton and printed in 1519, tries to avoid the common medieval words, seeking always for classical usage or words with a classical rather than medieval flavor. He even provides (fols. 306v–315r) lists of words to avoid, sometimes adding preferable forms; the medieval writer wishing to say "herald" or "marshal" had the obvious words *heraldus* and *marescallus,* here proscribed in favor of less readily intelligible classicism: "heraldus pro ca-duceatore," "marescallus pro ethnarca uel prefecto" (fol. 314r). In the letters of Br. Robert Joseph, schoolmaster at Evesham Abbey about 1530, we see a young teacher enjoying personal correspondence with his fellows, aspiring with as much enthusi-asm to write more Classical Latin [DL14]. The medieval tradition was coming to an end, the character of the Latin would change; it would lose its easy fluency and here-after would be used in ever more restricted circles.

## Glimpses of Everyday Life in Literary Texts

Every user of Latin in the Middle Ages probably learned the language through such exercises. Even though the greater part of the literature was not concerned with matters of everyday life, writers could always include these subjects in their books. Yet there is a necessary distinction between the treatment of everyday topics through the medium of Latin and the actual use of Latin in an everyday context. Scenes from daily life—in the home, in the fields, or in the street—may be found in texts of all types. If our object were to gather the evidence for the circumstances in which ordi-nary people lived, we might find the material scattered throughout the literature. There have been attempts to bring such material together, and the evidence of the written word can be supplemented by pictorial illustrations, by the evidence of sur-viving artifacts, and by archaeological information [DL91]. But, to take an example, William FitzStephen's account of the public cookshop in London deals with a very basic subject, not the usual material for medieval literature, but the treatment is lit-erary:

> Preterea est in Londonia supra ripam fluminis inter uina in nauibus et cellis uinariis ue-nalia publica coquina. Ibi quotidie pro tempore est inuenire cibaria, fercula, assa, pista, frixa, elixa, pisces, pisculos, carnes grossiores pauperibus, delicatiores diuitibus, uena-tionum, auium, auicularum. Si subito ueniant ad aliquem ciuium amici fatigati ex itinere, nec libeat ieiuniis expectare ut noui cibi emantur et coquantur, "dent famuli manibus lymphas, panesque canistris" [Virgil, *Aen.* 1.702]; interim ad ripam curritur, ibi presto sunt omnia desiderabilia. Quantalibet militum uel peregrinorum infinitas intrans urbem, qualibet diei uel noctis hora, uel ab urbe exitura, ne uel hi nimium ieiunent uel alii impransi exeant, illuc, si placet, diuertunt et se pro modo suo singuli reficiunt. Qui se curare uolunt molliter, accipenserem [cf. Horace, *Sat.* 2.2.47], uel Afram auem uel attagenam Ionicum [cf. Horace, *Epod.* 2.53] non querant, appositis que ibi inueniuntur deliciis. Hec equidem publica coquina est et ciuitati plurimum expediens et ad ciuili-tatem pertinens. Hinc est quod legitur in Gorgia Platonis iuxta medicinam esse cocorum officium, simulacrum et adulationem quarte particule ciuilitatis. [DL19]

This, or his fuller description of the sports of the Londoners, important though they are as glimpses of London life in the late twelfth century, has nothing to do with the everyday use of Latin.

The genre of literature that best takes us into the circumstances of ordinary life in the tenth, eleventh, and twelfth centuries is probably the lives of saints. For ex-ample, in this passage from the *Miracles of St. Frideswide,* composed by Philip, prior of St. Frideswide's priory in Oxford in the late twelfth century, we see the detail of how a crippled boy padded his crutches to reduce the soreness they caused under his arms:

> Baculis duobus sub utraque ascella collocatis, gressus impotentes dirigere compelle-
> batur. . . . Adeo autem itineris et laboris immensitate fatigatus erat quod sub utraque as-
> cella in carne tenera concauitas quedam ostendebatur quam baculorum effecerant sum-
> mitates, licet eorum duritia pannorum mollitie quoad poterat relegaretur. [DL20]

Later in the Middle Ages, such texts often take on a less literary but no less revealing character. Collections of depositions, testifying to miracles, provide an excellent source; their purpose was to record what was said in answer to questions, so they take us directly into circumstances where Latin was used in a simple manner to put the spoken word into writing. The testimonies for the canonization of St. Osmund, for example, include statements taken from 46 witnesses between January and May 1424. They testify to some very easy "miracles," such as a pain in the leg that went away through the intervention of the saint; others involve a greater element of the mirac-ulous, though in many cases normal processes may be thought to have produced the desired result. Here is a scene we may all have at some time witnessed:

> . . . et dicit ulterius iste iuratus requisitus quod decem annis elapsis in uillata de Bymer-
> ton [*Bemerton, Wiltshire*] homines uicini sui ludentes ad pilam cum baculis magnis in-
> ter se discordarunt in ludo huiusmodi, et iste deponens ueniens iuxta eos et audiens eos
> discordantes et quasi ad pugnandum paratos immiscuit se inter eos ad cedandam dis-
> cordiam et pugnam impediendam, et subito unus eorum cum baculo grandi ipsum in
> dextra parte capitis sui percussit. [DL21] p72

The sentences are simple, a series of statements connected by *et;* indirect speech is introduced by *quod,* purpose is expressed very simply by the gerundive (*ad cedan-dam discordiam,* "to calm [*sedare*] the quarrel"), and there is no ornament at all; the single adjective, *grandis,* is used only to make clear that this is a game played with big sticks and not little ones. Exactly what the game was we cannot be sure [DL82].

## Interaction of Literary and Record Sources

In the *vitae* of saints from the later Middle Ages one not infrequently encoun-ters accidents, such as a child's falling into a well and drowning; the hagiographical purpose is fulfilled by the intervention of the saint to restore the child to life, but the setting may be depicted with a richness of everyday detail. Those who compiled the testimonies for St. Osmund's canonization not only interviewed contemporary wit-nesses, but also copied out records made almost two centuries earlier. These too were based on interviews with sworn witnesses. Among them, we find six statements that refer to the same event, the miraculous survival of a child in these circumstances. The first witness is Jocastra, who was interviewed in 1230:

> Iocastra mulier iurata dicit quod quadam die dominica ante festum beati Petri ad Vin-
> cula anno pontificis Gregorii pape noni secundo [*30 July 1228*], duobus annis elapsis, cum
> transitum fecisset per quemdam fontem in atrio Walteri West apud Sarum, uidit quam-
> dam puellam [*sic*] paruam lapsam in fontem et submersam, ita quod minimam pueri
> [*sic*] particulam apparentem uidebat. [DL21] p42

She called the child's nanny (*nutrix*), who pulled him (hereafter always referred to as a boy) "stupidum et frigidum" from the water, and they cuddled him from mid-afternoon until night. The nanny and the child's father invoked St. Osmund, making a candle for his shrine as tall as the boy; and in the morning, when they took the boy to the cathedral and laid him on the shrine, he recovered. Other witnesses included Edith, the nanny, who, having pulled the boy out, tested whether he was still alive: "cum ipsa probare uellet, aperuit os eius et posuit digitos suos usque ad guttur et sensit ibi continuam frigiditatem sicut sentire solet in mortuis." She and the father, Walter West, "(cum) calefacerent eum ad ignem et postea calidis indumentis inuoluerent," to no effect. Before dawn they made the candle, and at this stage the child was seen to stir; he was taken to the shrine, where he awoke. The father's story is the same, told in slightly different words: "Credentes eum excitare per calorem, calefecerunt eum ad ignem et postea cooperuerunt pannis pluribus et coopertum tenuerunt." Ivetta West, the boy's mother, and two men who were in the house when the child was brought in, Lambert the priest and Robert Albin, confirm the account. The actions of the nanny and the father were probably the vital factors in the child's survival, though the bystanders had thought him dead. This could be a story from a local newspaper, so directly does it take us into a special day in the life of that family; commonsense actions of any age sit alongside those rooted in the thought world of the Middle Ages.

In another story, told in more elaborate prose among the miracles of King Henry VI, we hear of an incident in a deep well at Brighton during the 1480s. Two ducks had fallen into the well, and, for fear that their decaying bodies should contaminate the water, a man had himself lowered down the well:

> Erat autem illic situla quedam noua, que et nouo similiter fune dependens, sicuti fons ipse, usui seruabatur communi. In hac itaque situla positus homo, sensim rotantibus illis hauritorium, descendere cepit in puteum. Porro puteus admodum altus erat, cuius profunditas ultra octoginta pedes mensure usualis extenditur. Nam preter id quod aqua ad quatuor saltem ulnarum mensuram abundabat in imo, duodecim plane a summo usque ad laticem ulnos habuerat. Sed ista quid refero? Denique mox ut intrare cepisset pendulus in puteum essetque adhuc uix parum sub margine, repente laxato nodulo, profundiora laci ipsius expeciit, in nullo prorsus se iuuare iam preualens. Quod cernens sacerdos, ilico arrepto manu funiculo, saltu impetuoso quidem et inconsiderato nimis se dedit in puteum (erat quippe cor eius, eo quod hominem ipse uocauerat, terrore nimio perturbatum), cepitque ille similiter uersato a circumstantibus hauritorio paulatim descendere. At uero, mira fortuna, cum iam pene peruenisset ad socium, eciam corda ipsa qua pendens deorsum ferebatur, de ligno ubi fixa fuerat subito dilapsa, decidit cum eo in puteum. [DL22]

The two men in the well were miraculously saved from drowning while the crowd above organized their hauling out on ropes. We find the same sort of stories—but without the happy ending—in the records of the medieval coroner, among whose duties was to hold an inquest into any unusual death:

> Contigit apud Goldingtone [*Goldington, Bedfordshire*] die ueneris prox' post festum Assumpcionis beate Marie anno l° primo [*19 August 1267*] quod Alicia filia Henrici Wigein de Goudingtone fere duorum annorum exiuit de curia dicti Henrici et iuit in grenam ad quendam fontem et cecidit in dicto fonte et submersit per infortunium. Et Angnes mater eius primo inuenit eam. [DL23] p7

Or another story from the same source, in which a 12-year-old boy died by misadventure while bathing (presumably swimming for pleasure) in a pond:

Contigit in uilla de Wildene [*Wilden, Bedfordshire*] die mercuri prox' ante festum Apostolorum Philippi et Iacobi post horam uespertinam anno lᵒ tercio [*24 April 1269*] quod
Iohannes filius Willelmi le Wytee de Wildene etate xij annorum custodiuit agnos Willelmi le Wyte patris sui in gardino quod quondam erat Thome Tirel de Wildene. Et hora
predicta idem Iohannes deposuit uestes suas et intrauit in quadam aqua in dicto gardino
ad balniandum se et submersit se per infortunium. Adam le Sauser primo inuenit, et inuenit plegios Simonem Sprott et Nicholaum Albric de Wildene. [DL23] p12

The coroner's roll was copied in plain Latin by a clerk, and hundreds of these rolls
have been preserved from medieval England, from which we learn that children really did fall into wells and drown.

But, we may ask, what was the medieval well like? It was on the village green at
Goldington, and at Brighton in the previous story it had a bucket on a rope, which
was passed over a wooden axle, with a handle for the users to turn. Surviving examples and pictures in manuscripts will illustrate the question, and so will our schoolbooks: Adam of Balsham points out, "in angulo erat girgillus et funis cum situla, et
utres in puteum dimittebantur." Wells with such a windlass are variously described
as (*fons, puteus*) *hauribilis* or *tractabilis* or *tracticius,* representing English "draw
well," or (*fons*) *pendens,* "hanging well." The axle (*fusillus*) might be fitted with iron
rings (*circuli*) where it turned, and over the top a roof resting on posts formed the
well house (*domus putei*). And in archives, I have even found a record of someone
paid to go down a well to recover the bucket (*hauritorium*), which was lost when the
rope broke: "in stipendio j hominis querentis per iiij uices hauritorium in fondo
fontis ibidem qui ceciderat in eodem per fraccionem funis eiusdem, ij s." [DL27]. This
was entered as a charge in the annual accounts prepared by the bailiff who managed
the estate.

Legal records and accounts, such as I have drawn on here, are the two richest
sources for seeing ordinary life reflected in Latin texts written by participants in the
activities they deal with. The manner of their writing differentiates them from other
forms of text, even from some other classes of document. A literary text could be
roughed out and revised at leisure before the fair copy was made; a deed likewise
could be drafted and checked for correctness before being copied out carefully. But
most of the documents that best serve our purpose—the statements of juries or witnesses, inventories of stock or furnishings, rolls of account, and such like—were for
the most part written on the spot with no time to spare for niceties of expression or
even handwriting. The clerk composed as he wrote, without reflection and in most
cases without revision. Even the format of these workaday documents is different
from that of literary texts: almost all the archival material cited in this chapter was
written on individual membranes of parchment that may in some cases have been
made up into rolls. In cases where enrollment involved recopying the original loose
membranes, this did not lead to stylistic revision, though there may have been
changes of detail [DL25]. Such documents were rarely copied into books.

In turning to this category of sources, however, we must first recognize a serious
limitation. Until the twelfth century it was extremely unusual to put into writing particulars relating to housing or food or clothing or the management of a household.
Even the legal records of the early Middle Ages mostly deal with questions of ownership of property, not the incidents of life. Examples of accounts from the late
twelfth century are rare, tending to be of a durable character, such as surveys or cus-

tumals. Annual accounts of estate management begin to survive in the thirteenth century. Domestic accounts are known from the thirteenth century, but the number that survive is much less and the greater part of those that do survive is later in date. From the thirteenth, fourteenth, and fifteenth centuries, however, we have an incomparably rich collection in England of records that provide a firsthand and often very detailed insight into the way people lived.

### The Latin of Record Clerks

The language of such texts is markedly different from that of more literary texts. The use of the written word, and therefore of Latin, was expanding after centuries of more restricted usage, and this was a new challenge. The Carolingian land surveys of the ninth century and Domesday Book in late eleventh-century England—rare early examples of this sort of writing—demanded a vocabulary for all manner of tenures or tenants or livestock or rents that had to be precise and intelligible. Searching for clever substitutes from classical usage, as one might in writing a literary text, would not meet the need, nor would contrived words such as those in John of Garland, and so Latin vocabulary was widened by borrowing from the vernacular to meet the occasion. Words such as *bordarius,* "smallholder" (from Old French *bordier*), or *hundretum,* "hundred court" (from Old English *hundred*), are rooted in the aims of making the Domesday Book and immediately conveyed an exact meaning to the contemporary reader. This is the starting point of a new closeness in the relationship between the Latin word hoard and that of the surrounding vernacular languages, French and English. This source of vocabulary was increasingly used. Tenures and rents needed a specialized vocabulary for legal reasons. For a different reason, the same precision was needed in other areas. Household management, the keeping of horses, farming, shopping, playing sports or games, or dancing—all these have their specialist vocabulary as much as any craft or trade or science. Even for everyday objects, language is sufficiently specialized for some words to be very rare. So, though we may speak of the "prongs" of a fork and be understood, the correct English word is "tines." Even native speakers of English would very likely not know, when lacing a pair of shoes, that the metal or plastic tab fitted to each end of the lace, so that it passes easily through the eyelets, is itself called an "aglet." Words of this sort in many cases did not survive the break in the tradition of spoken Latin: shoemakers had neither spoken nor written Latin for at least four hundred years when such words came to be needed again in Latin. Some might be known from ancient texts, though (as we have seen with John of Garland) in such cases they were often used in modified senses. The Latin clerks of the later Middle Ages, needing words of this kind, used a vocabulary that was a rich mixture of Latin words and words latinized from common speech, both French and English. Words as specific as *aglet* will only be needed in very specialized texts, and these texts can be difficult to understand.

Accounts dealing with the management of agricultural estates offer many instances of the word *gropa,* something fitted to carts or ploughs. With only a few examples in front of him, H.T. Riley derived the word from OE *gripan,* "to lay hold of"; others associated it with OF *grap,* "hook," though neither made sense of the word [DL28–29]. The *Oxford English Dictionary* suggests that it was a sort of nail, on the strength of a fifteenth-century mention of "50 grope and clout nails." The editors knew what a "clout" was (or more precisely a "wain-clout"; cf. Middle English *clut,*

Medieval Latin *clutum*), but they failed to apply the same sense to "grope." Now, between the *Middle English Dictionary* and the *Dictionary of Medieval Latin from British Sources* enough examples have been collected to show that ME *grope* means an iron plate nailed to the inner part of a wooden wheel for added strength. Modern readers are as much cut off from the wheel- or cartwright's craft as thirteenth-century clerks were from the language of ancient Roman craftsmen. To bridge that gap we rely on dictionaries to have drawn together sufficient evidence to arrive at a correct interpretation.

Sometimes this is not a question of language. There is no doubt that Classical Latin *horologium* in the Middle Ages meant "clock," but many examples do not provide enough information to know the sort of mechanism in a particular case. At Bury St. Edmunds, for example, we learn that it was a water clock only because, when fire broke out in the church, the brothers ran, "quidam ad puteum, quidam ad horologium," for water [DL30]. (To understand how a clock worked we should need to look to a technical authority such as Richard of Wallingford.) Sometimes the difficulty lies in the remoteness of the craft. Few of us know much about how sea water was processed into salt blocks. Although we may recognize that ML *hoga*, "hill, mound" (from ME *hough*), was used in a specialized context as "salt-mound," the account rolls in which we find this usage are likely to be full of words that we can barely understand without experience of the techniques employed. Sometimes there are difficulties on all fronts. The *Dictionary of Medieval Latin from British Sources* quotes two examples of *hiltra*, one from the audited accounts of the manors of the bishop of Winchester in 1272, the other from an original deed, also from Hampshire, dated 1322; it is obviously a word formed from the vernacular, for the examples do not make clear its Latin inflexion, but its English equivalent, presumably a word in the local dialect, is not recorded. We can only guess at the meaning from the two examples: apparently something like a fish trap that could be fitted in a millrace, perhaps the kind of trap more generally known in Middle English as *gorce* and in Latin as *gurges*.

Records, then, can provide us with little episodes that reveal how people lived, and they can also show us the details usually lacking in ordinary narrative texts. They take us very close to the day-to-day realities of medieval life, the physical objects, how they were used, kept, and valued.

The coroner's clerk in Bedfordshire recorded that, when William Moring struck Richard of Eltisley on the shoulder, on 27 December 1265, the stick he used was made of willow (*cum quodam baculo de salice*); and he also recorded that the stick with which Henry Carpenter struck his brother on the head on 31 December 1266 was made of crabtree (*cum uno baculo de pomerio siluestri*). And we learn the characteristics of a particular sort of axe, when Aubrey of Hockwold complained that Walter Smod "percussit Walterum filium suum [i.e. Aubrey's son] cum hachia que uocatur sparht, unde manubrium fuit de corulo et hachia de ferro et acera" ([DL23] p17); with which compare "cum una achia a pik' de ferro et acera et unde manubrium fuit de coudra" (p32). The sparth was a large, long-handled axe, as we discover from another source about an assault in Dublin in 1294, committed with "una hachia que uocatur sparth, cuius capud fuit de ferro et calibe de longitudine decem pollicum et latitudine sex pollicum, et cuius hachie telum de fraxino longitudinis sex pedum et grossitudinis ['*girth*'] quatuor pollicum" [DL31]. The pike, on the other hand, might be a spike on the end of a handle, or more likely a pickaxe.

It was common practice to use a relative clause such as "que uocatur sparth" where the vernacular word conveyed precisely what kind of axe and Latin did not. Even a literary author might do this; so, for example, Ranulf Higden refers to "usum securium, qui Anglice sparth dicitur" ("the use of axes of the kind called in English *sparth*") [DL32]. This practice can be found as early as the eighth century: it is a touchstone of the status of Latin as a second language throughout the Middle Ages. In the late Middle Ages the vernacular word might be marked instead with the article *le* or *lez,* used with English words as often as with French ones: "pro araiacione et le scowrynge diuersorum armorum." By the fourteenth and fifteenth centuries clerks were less self-conscious about using the vernacular word without such verbal quotation marks. At worst English can take over from Latin almost completely: "item in xvij Sept' delivered ad clockemaker apud loge de Wynsor' xl s." [DL33].

I mentioned the concern to record what was valued. This notion is an important one here, because the major reason for writing about such details is not the love of description; it is generally the practical need to account for what is bought, sold, or repaired; to inventory the possessions one values or wishes to pass on to one's heirs. So the coroner's clerk was precise in identifying the weapons because, as instruments that had caused a person's death, they became "deodands," their value was paid to the crown, and that money was used for pious purposes. The rolls habitually mention the value of weapons or other instruments involved in an incident, as in this sorry tale:

> Contigit in uilla de Etone [*Eaton, Bedfordshire*] . . . in bracina domine Iuliane de Bello Campo die Iouis prox' post festum sancti Michaelis anno l°iiij° [*2 October 1270*] circa horam nonam quod Amicia Belamy filia Roberti Belamy et Isabella Bonchevaler portauerunt inter se unam cuuam plenam de gruto et debent reuersare grutum in quodam plumbo bulliente, ita quod Amicia Belamy titubauit cum pedibus et cecidit in dicto plumbo bulliente et cuua super eam. Dicta Sibilia Bonchevaler statim saltauit ad eam et abstraxit eam a dicto plumbo et clamauit, et famuli domus uenerunt et inuenerunt eam scaturizatam fere ad mortem. [DL23] p14–15

Amice had the rites of the Church and died next day. The vessels involved in her death became deodands; the objects themselves remained in the village, but their value had to be paid in the county court: "Plumbum apreciatur xij d., et cuua apreciatur ij d., tinellus apreciatur ad obolum, et liberantur uille de Etone." The coroner's roll here brings life and death to the vessels mentioned in many inventories that list the contents of brew houses, as quoted under *cuua* in the Medieval Latin Dictionary. The *plumbum* was a large vat, orginally made of lead, and probably supported on brickwork; such a vessel could be heated by a fire underneath. The Latin equates with ME *led,* used in precisely this sense, and occasionally more precisely, ME *breuingled.* The remarkable will of John Brompton, a very wealthy merchant of Beverley in Yorkshire who died in 1444, mentions among the vessels for brewing "j brewynglede, j leke lede, ij worteledes" [DL34]. The word *cuua,* "kettle, cauldron," common in Latin, was derived from OF *cuve* < Latin *cupa;* ME *cuve,* also from the French, is found, though rarely; the common English word for the object was simply "vat," but as often the vernacular provided greater precision, as we see, for example, in a will of 1341: "unam cuuam que uocatur maskefat [ME *mash fat*] et duas paruas cuuas que uocantur gylefatts [ME *gile fat*]." *Cuua* has sometimes been mistakenly printed *cuna* [DL35]. The kettle contained *grutum,* ME *grout,* "grout, coarse meal used in brewing," a Latin word taken from English. Finally, the piece of wood, passed through the handle of the kettle and held at either end by the women, is referred to as *tinellus,* from Anglo-Norman *tinel.* For all of these words, a well-schooled writer might have found classical words that would have conveyed the sense, though without the exactness of these medieval usages. None of these words was latinized for the occasion; all are recorded in other sources and formed part of the clerk's working vocabulary. He was not disturbed by their mixture of Latin, Old French, and English derivations.

The record style evolved almost imperceptibly between the late ninth and the late twelfth century, though during this period examples are relatively rare. From the late twelfth and especially the mid-thirteenth century there was a dramatic extension in the use of writing to record current business. This style of Latin was perfectly adapted to meet this need. Its strengths were that it was easy to learn, because of its simplicity of construction and its close dependence on the vernacular for vocabulary; it was infinitely flexible in allowing precise reference to all sorts of everyday objects for which literary Latin, using more classical words, could provide no comparable precision or clarity; and it could be composed with little pause for thought as an immediate *recorda,* "memorandum," of simple facts, even by someone whose educational qualifications were modest. The style was practiced by countless record clerks throughout England during the thirteenth to fifteenth centuries and did not entirely disappear until the late seventeenth century.

## The Keeping of Records

This workaday Latin coexisted with the more sophisticated literary styles and with the unadorned academic prose of the Schoolmen. The different styles were used for different purposes at all levels of society. In the royal household the officials who drafted the king's letters to foreign rulers did so in an elaborate style; those who recorded the income and expenditure of the Wardrobe, the main financial department of the household, used a simple record style. The same duality existed in the households of bishops and other prelates and in the universities, so that everyday Latin crosses social boundaries. It is important, however, to remember that the use of writing and the preservation of what was written did not cross boundaries to the same extent.

Getting the best out of record texts depends on knowing what kinds of archives were kept and what they deal with. Not everyone would write down his day-to-day dealings; those who did would not necessarily retain them; and those records that were kept cannot be guaranteed to have survived. Accounts and memoranda would cease to be of use in a short time and were less likely to be preserved than the muniments that secured property. With the exception of charters and deeds, therefore, and a few surveys, very little indeed survives from England before 1200. The archives of private individuals are always a rarity, because there was no route for their survival. The most widely available insight into the domestic property of private individuals is their wills, which were preserved by the bishops in whose courts they were proved. Corporations have a greater reason to keep records—so that the work of officials can be open to scrutiny—and a much better chance of handing them on from generation to generation. Some English towns, for example, have preserved long runs of records [DL36–37]. The larger monasteries had well-organized bureaucracies, with each obedientiary having his own staff; from some we have only muniments, but others—notably Durham, Norwich, and Worcester, three of the Benedictine cathedral chapters, as well as Westminster Abbey—have kept massive collections of internal accounts [DL46–47], from which a remarkable picture of the domestic life of the monks may be obtained [DL48]. These churches, and others such as Canterbury, Bury St. Edmunds, and Winchester, have also preserved their external accounts, dealing with the management of their estates. They provide a rich quarry for information on agriculture and, sporadically, for other activities, including forestry, charcoal burning, and in the case of Durham the working of coal.

The departments of central government were from the thirteenth century onwards very much concerned to receive and retain administrative records [DL16]. These extend far beyond the records produced in the central departments of the Exchequer and the Chancery. The proceedings in the royal courts were kept from the late twelfth century, but the records of assizes and eyres in the shires as well as the rolls kept by county coroners were also returned to the center for preservation. The building and management of castles, the equipping of armies, the building of ships, and countless other activities were paid for by the Treasury, and accounts would have to be rendered. (When such things were paid for directly through the king's household departments, the Wardrobe and the Chamber, accounts were not rendered in the same way.) The expenditure of the royal household itself is documented. For information on goldsmiths' work or the finest textiles, the records relating to the king's *iocalia,* "jewels," may be contrasted with inventories of church plate and vestments [DL49–54]. Just as abbeys derived their income from estates, a great many estates were held and managed by the Crown—for a longer or shorter period—and records of the bailiffs' income and expenditure had to be passed on to the center. Here, from time to time, it would be necessary to build or renovate barns, windmills, watermills, flood defenses, and so on, with the result that the accounts relating to these capital investments provide insights into both their construction and the relevant technical language. Capital expenditure was likely to be well recorded, with the result that building is probably the best documented of all medieval crafts [DL55–57].

Essentially unofficial or even private documents sometimes found their way into the public records. When a manor passed into the king's hands, the rolls of the local manor court could end up in the archives of the king's financial officials. Petitions presented to the king would be filed along with the official documents that they gave rise to. But such petitions could originate with clerks of limited experience or ability. One example, now surviving among the files of Inquisitions Miscellaneous, a subject class created by modern archivists, is a complaint about the corruption of local government in Oxford in 1253; no experienced clerk in the city would take the risk of drafting such a document, and its poor Latin shows that it was drafted by someone with less to lose by so doing. Another subject class among the public records is the files of Ancient Correspondence. Thousands of original letters are preserved here; some of them are official letters, composed in a formal style, while others are at least cultivated letters, written according to literary conventions. But others are simple business letters [DL58]. One valuable group of letters are those written in the 1220s by Simon of Senliz, land agent to Ralph Nevill, bishop of Chichester (d. 1244). These combine elements of the conventional epistolary style with some very direct and simple Latin, and they deal with everyday aspects of running a large estate. In one such letter, too badly damaged to quote, Simon reports that he has not sufficient seed for planting oats as intended at Totehall; that the vicar of Mundham has been found to have two wives, one of them living in Chichester, and has also been using letters from the pope that Simon believes to be forged; and, finally, he asks the bishop to send a man with six hunting dogs to kill the foxes that have been causing damage at Aldingbourne. He had earlier requested dogs for this purpose: "Cum sex canibus aptis ad uulpes capiendos in parco uestro de Aldingeburn, si placet, pensare uelitis, quoniam sidus capiendi illos iam preterit" ([DL59] p278).

The same variety applies to the archives of churches and universities. I have mentioned those Benedictine abbeys whose archives survived the Dissolution, providing week-by-week information on the purchase of food, drink, fuel, lamps or candles, and other household needs, annual profit and loss accounts on the management of estates, and masses of other details. Monastic archives might also include accounts of the income from keeping a saint's shrine and the expenses incurred [DL60], or copies of the prior's letters [DL61], or the precentor's expenses on the repair of service books [DL62]. Diocesan archives are to a great extent different in character, concerned largely with the provision of a parochial ministry but also including wills and cases from ecclesiastical courts [DL63]. Some great churches have kept long-term accounts of expenditure on the fabric of the building, and from the late Middle Ages there survive some annual accounts of churchwardens and even a few examples of presentments drawn up by churchwardens detailing the condition of the church at the time of a visitation [DL64]. At Oxford we might contrast the archives of Merton College, with valuable runs of accounts from estates belonging to the college [DL65], and Canterbury College (funded by Canterbury Cathedral priory and absorbed by Christ Church after the Dissolution), whose archives are primarily concerned with domestic matters, what property was kept in the college, and how its money was spent [DL66].

Almost all the records were made by junior officials or servants acting under supervision. The record clerks of late medieval England, scribbling away in their workaday language, touched on almost every aspect of life, but their coverage is not continuous. Considering the crafts and trades treated in more detail elsewhere in this volume, there is rich evidence in the records of late medieval England on aspects of every topic treated—the difficulty lies in finding it. You will see this illustrated in the quotations given in the *Dictionary of Medieval Latin,* and I have included by way of example references to some words that may be consulted there [DL2].

I have described building as "probably the best documented" of medieval crafts: building, of course, is not the same as architecture (ch. FB), but for information on how work on a building was organized, where the materials came from, how many were employed, and what they were paid, then rolls of account are the principal sources. There exist accounts for vernacular building (1 *caminus, cheuero, daubare,* 1 *furca* 3) as well as for larger buildings that should inform our approach to architecture. In these latter the attention to details (*fumerellum, houellus*) is noteworthy. For most technologies there will be valuable evidence in local accounts. The crafts of wheelwright, cartwright, and plowwright figure very largely in agricultural accounts (*axare, carretta, carruca* 2, *felga*), as does the vital craft of the blacksmith, not only in the shoeing of horses but in the making and maintenance of all manner of iron implements (*ferramentum, ferrum*); in the use of iron to strengthen wood (*clutum, gropa*); in door furniture, locks, and keys (*clauis, haspa*); and in turning mechanisms (*fusillus, gojo*) such as the draw-well. From some of the Durham accounts we learn that iron axles were greased with animal fat: **1357** "in iij petris et dim. feodi coquine et sepi emptis pro carectis et ferr' molend' ungend' iij s. vj d." ([DL6] p560) (*feodum* 13). Some information on weights and measures (ch. FD) comes from mnemonic verses, but all practical knowledge is based on their use in record contexts, where one often needs to review numerous examples to find the few that provide definitions and make clear the local variations (*ferthendella, fotmellum*). The use of weapons of war (ch. FE) will not appear in the records, but their manufacture or purchase and their mundane maintenance (*freiare, furbare*) will be largely documented, for example in the orders issued and accounts kept by the king's household. Local types of ships (ch. FF), such as *cobellus, cogga, doggera,* and *farcosta,* are principally known from records, while a detailed sense of how a warship was built can be got from ship-building accounts [DL69]. The handling of goods at docks (*caiagium, caium, carcare, discarcare*) is well illustrated, for example, in the port accounts of harbor towns. Inland waterways were also important for the passage of goods (*bargia, 1 canella* 1a), and so were ferries (*2 feria*) for crossing rivers and estuaries. Accounts will often reveal how much it cost to transport commodities, especially valuable ones such as wine, from one place to another (*carriagium, 1 carriare*). The need to maintain roads and bridges is tellingly reflected in the files of Ancient Indictments, which graphically describe the results of inadequate maintenance [DL72].

The farming of land (ch. FG) was the primary source of income for most medieval families and communities, and certainly for the crown and the abbeys and other institutions that have preserved their local bailiffs' records. Custumals reveal how many people worked land for themselves and their lord and on what terms, while accounts show every aspect of land management, including not only the obvious ones, such as sowing, reaping, sheafing, threshing, or haymaking, but also necessary arrangements for the scaring of crows (*frues*) from newly sown land or the controlled folding (*falda, faldagium*) of livestock to manure (*fimare*) the land. Animals were kept for meat, milk, wool, skins, eggs, and other produce; horses and oxen were both draft animals and beasts of burden (*auerus, bos, carrettiuus, carrucarius*); geese (*anser, auca, aucula*) were much more important in medieval husbandry than in modern. And livestock had to be driven (*ducere, minare*) on hoof, trotter, or foot to market. Woodland was managed intensively in the Middle Ages, growing a small number of timber trees per acre and coppicing (*copero, copicia*) the rest for other uses, including wood for gates and hurdles. Although pigs were regularly pastured in woods in the autumn (*pannagium*), young coppices needed to be protected from grazing animals, especially deer, and the records show the attention given to proper hedging (*fossa* 3, *haia*). Charcoal (*carbo*) for fuel was also a woodland product. "Forest," of course, was land set aside for hunting and was not necessarily wooded. And there were periods when scrubland was brought under cultivation (*essartum, 2 friscus*). In some places peat (*blesta, turbaria*) was also cut for fuel. Nor should we forget the importance of both river fishing (*gordus, gurges*) and fish-farming (*uiuarium*), and the keeping of dovecotes (*columbar*), bees, and other adjuncts to agricultural life.

It is perhaps less obvious that manuscript production and illumination (ch. FH) figure in record sources, but details of payments are found in precentor's accounts and elsewhere [DL62], and in some places the craftsmen and their workshops are identifiable in deeds and rentals (*illuminator*). The decorative arts (ch. FI) and the finest textiles (ch. FJ) are amply illustrated in accounts dealing with the decoration of high-status buildings or the commissioning of ornaments and, especially, in inventories of plate or hangings or vestments, all valuable goods [DL49–54]. At the recreational level, we know a little about the embroidery frames used by the queen and her ladies (2 *framea*). And there are countless references to the making of cloth, from washing and spinning to weaving, fulling (*fullo*), and dyeing, and, eventually, to its parceling (1 *fardellus*) and sale. We should not overlook the extensive use of skins, as leather, fleece, or fur (*furrare, grisus* 2), which had to be processed in their different ways. And at the bottom end of the textiles market, there were fripperies, reused clothes (*feliparius*).

Mining (ch. FK) is a subject for which the records provide less technical detail than one might wish but more social and economic information. The most common ways in which mines (*fossa, mina, puteus*)—generally for coal, iron, and lead—appear in records are where they are mentioned as property or where income and expenditure are accounted for. There were also circumstances in which mines might figure in litigation, as in the complaints in 1256 about the danger to travelers because of the number of pits along the road west from Newcastle (*fossa* 10). The skills of smelting and foundry were put to special use in the remelting and refining of silver for coinage (*blancus, cambitor, casura, funtare*), a subject carefully documented in the records of the Exchequer, which also appears in the accounts of those whose money was recoined (ch. FL). Detail about mills and milling (ch. FM) is again more often social or economic than technical, but sometimes in accounts for repairs, sometimes in records of accidents, one sees into the mechanism (*bracchium* 10g). Until the twelfth century, mills were powered by water, and the associated management of water had its uses in agriculture and in fish farming (*lada, stagnum*). Windmills and, in some coastal sites, tide mills used other sources of power. And, though we primarily associate mills with the grinding of corn, mill power was commonly used in fulling (*fullarius, fulleraticus, fullericius*), and by the end of the Middle Ages to power hammers in the blacksmith's forge (*ferrarius* 1h).

## Daily Living in Latin Records

Daily living, especially in the ordinary home, is one of the most elusive subjects, so much so that the historical interest of life in the home or the work place may be better served by the glimpses of information to be found in the general literature, where narrative details and the narrator's own voice are themselves important. The records, nonetheless, can certainly provide a wealth of data about the material environment in which people lived, and some records—the coroners' rolls quoted above are an example—allow keyhole insights into real moments in the lives of ordinary people. Any account of daily living must take proper account of this record evidence, but that involves first thinking through the question of what aspects of life may be seen in different classes of records.

The milestones of birth, marriage, and death can all be glimpsed in the records, but in different ways. Births as such were not recorded, but when a tenant of Crown property died, an inquest was held by the county escheator to determine what lands were held and by what services, whether there was an heir of full age, and so on. If the heir was a minor, he and his lands remained in wardship until he was proved by inquest to have reached the age of twenty-one. The files of Inquisitions *post mortem* include many "proofs of age," in which jurors come together to swear by what reason they know the heir to have reached maturity. These often include reminiscences of the baptism of the heir. So, in 1407, it was attested that Maurice Bruyn was born in 1385 and was therefore of age; John Payn, who was at the baptism, saw Henry Somer driving a cart with a pipe of red wine past the churchyard to the manor, rejoicing and delighting in the birth of the heir in such excitement that he neglected the cart, which tipped over, and the wine was lost ([DL73] p116). In 1411 one juror for the proof of age of William de Botreaux swore that two old men, William Stedeman and Nicholas atte Boure, were sitting on chairs in the church during the baptism; they fell asleep and were left there when the clerk of the church locked the door (p361). Countless such events, memorable in themselves but very often with no firm evidence of the year, appear in these inquisitions. At William's baptism the old men missed out on a party, for other jurors swore to having brought silver cups and red wine for the bystanders to drink at the church after the baptism. Baptisms are family occasions, and we find in the same records reference to settlements by grandparents on their children when the first grandson is baptized (p114). Marriages might be arranged; so in 1409 jurors remembering the baptism of Thomas Lovell in 1388 included one who contracted to marry a woman of Ramsbury, went to the church, saw the chaplain write the time of the baptism in a book, and asked him to publish the banns for his wedding (p284). On the same day, said another juror, the chaplain came to his house to write out a will for his wife, and he knows the date from that will. In the same files, where the deceased left a widow, the assignment to her of a portion of the property and income as dower would be recorded. Joan, widow of Sir Thomas Hungerford (d. 1397), held property as dower both from him and from her first husband, as well as having property of her own and property held jointly with Sir Thomas; when she died in 1412, the income of her son, Walter Hungerford, more than doubled (pp344–45).

From the files of Inquisitions *post mortem* it would be possible to assemble a substantive outline of ordinary human interaction at this level of society—mostly gentry, though their property might be quite modest. To fill in the outline with the details is more difficult: it is hardly ever possible, for example, to see such a family eating a meal together, because there was no reason to put that in the record.

Details of domestic life are most readily seen in the great households that alone documented their day-to-day expenses. The accounts kept in the royal household are sufficient during some years to allow us a very full picture of the accoutrements of court life, while other sources provide a mass of information on what happened around the king and queen. Large households, with many servants, who had to be held to account, also kept such records. I have mentioned the nearly comprehensive records from certain monasteries, which include the income and expenditure on food, drink, clothing, entertainment, and household maintenance. Similar records have in some instances been preserved from secular households [DL74]. These household accounts, whether of general expenses or specifically of food, can make dreary reading because they are so repetitive; yet among the daily entries for regular purchases, there will be occasional glimpses of something else. Week-by-week accounts survive for keeping Henry III's cousin, Eleanor of Brittany, a prisoner in Bristol Castle; most of the expenditure was on food and the keeping of horses, but among two weeks' routine entries we find that on 24 September the lady was bled (at a cost of 1 d.), and less than a week later she had a bath (cost 2½ d.).

Ordinary households, where servants were under direct supervision, had little reason to record their daily activities. The few surviving accounts of household activities not from the households of nobility, bishops, or abbots, are from the houses of substantial gentry. The most readily available picture of simpler households is from wills, which will sometimes show what furniture or clothes or even small utensils a person owned. Again, however, wills were more often made by those who had assets to bequeath than by people of lower class, and more townspeople made wills than country people. In most cases a will does not provide a full inventory but only identifies items going to other than the principal heir, and even where there is a full inventory, it is static. These are limitations within which we must work.

A particularly clear view of the domestic side of a gentry household can be got from the annual account presented by Thomas Clerk, clerk of the household of Robert Waterton of Methley, Yorkshire, who was living in fine style in 1416–17 ([DL74] pp504–22). The roll was drawn up at Michaelmas, at the end of the year of account, from memoranda made in the course of the year. Among the headings used we have sales of corn, livestock, poultry, fish, tallow and lard, fruit, wax, wine, spices, and hides, giving receipts amounting to £385. The expenses, taken from the *liber dietarum,* "day book," include purchases of pigs, hens, geese, small birds (among them curlew, plovers, godwits), partridge, salt fish, red herring, white herring, eels (counted by the eightendeal [*egtendalum*] or the stick [*stica anguillarum*]), salmon, oil, fruit, salt, wax, wine, spices, beer, onions, and fuel (coal and charcoal). Other expenses include payments to those who brought presents for the lord "ut patet per quoddam papirum longum inde factum," the cost of paper for the clerk's memoranda, arsenic "pro distruccione ratonum," additional help in the kitchen at busy times during the year, the turning of wooden cups from the lord's wood, yarn for candle wicks and wages for the woman making candles, various jugs and vessels, carriage of several loads of wine from Hull and from London, carriage of salt fish and dried fish from Boston, payments for the repair of leather bottles, payment to a goldsmith for the repair of a silver charger, two days' wages for a baker from Doncaster making paindemaine for a special occasion, payments to the cooper for repairing barrels, purchase of wafer-irons, carriage for salmon, expenses for two men and one horse driving geese from Snaith to Methley, yarn for the repair of nets, four stone of torch wick, payment to the fowler, a barrel of soap and its carriage from Hull, and so on. The total of expenses was over £387, but since there was still more than £40 worth of wine in hand, the net expense (*in claro*) was a little over £340. There then follows an account of what was consumed from store or from the produce of the lord's manors. The headings here are wheat, barley for malting, oats, peas (mostly for fattening pigs but also for potage), cattle, hides, pigs, ham, sheep, fleeces, calves, piglets, swans (eight from the previous account, twelve bred on the lord's manors, and seventeen received as presents), capons, hens, pullets, geese, roe-deer and partridges (mostly received as presents), pheasants, woodcock, herons, doves, other little birds, duck, rabbits, eggs, red and white herring, salt fish, dried fish, eels, sturgeon, salmon, porpoise, lampreys, tallow, candles, flock (wool-waste used in greasing carts), lard, oil, fruit, wax, wine, spices, beer, garlic and onions, and fuel. Arranged in this way as an annual account, the purpose of the record was financial; if we possessed the *liber dietarum* here, we should have been able to follow the fluctuations in consumption according to whether the lord was in residence or not, special occasions, and the opportunities of the season. Some very full accounts in this form have survived from other households and several have been published [DL74].

Much of the produce consumed was clearly local, some was regularly bought in.

The swans and roe-deer, received as *exennia*, "presents," were perhaps gifts from King Henry V, whom Robert Waterton served in various capacities. Some aspects of the spice trade only appear in accounts of this kind; for example, "gingerbread," that is, ginger preserved in syrup, a widely known but expensive commodity, was imported packed in dried gourds (*gurda*), as we see from the royal accounts for its purchase.

Inventories and accounts focus on things, whether furniture, clothes, utensils, or consumables, but they show little of the activity of living. Earlier we caught a glimpse into the brewhouse of a gentry home in a coroner's roll, but it is only by such chances that we may hope to see, for example, into the work of the kitchen or dairy. Some subjects, among them cleaning, laundry, and personal hygiene, will make almost no impression on the record, though barbers (*barbator, barbitonsor, tonsor*) were tradesmen who had to be regulated—and there were quacks too who would sell cures for baldness, as for example in 1288 ([DL79] p36).

The most local level of court records to be preserved are the rolls of manor and honor courts, which sometimes survive in long runs, documenting many aspects of communal life over the centuries [DL75–77]. Like other legal records these show what happened in the community, but, unlike coroners' rolls or the records of higher courts, they are not restricted to exceptional events.

To take an example, we may look at a roll from the court of the abbot of Ramsey. This now comprises five membranes of various dates, starting in 1278; when the abbey surrendered to Henry VIII, its archives passed into the king's Court of Augmentations, where many rolls were preserved; they have now been removed to form a modern subject class of local court records [DL78]. The abbot's court met on different dates on the various manors belonging to the abbey. So, at Hemingford on 17 November 1278 we find offenses against the rights of the abbey as lord of the manor recorded. Among somewhat routine matters about brewing or other restrictions on trade, we learn that the vicar of St. Ives had lopped two willows on the abbot's land and so was fined; but his crop of peas had been ruined by the villeins' cattle, for which he was compensated. A week later the court sat at Elton, where four villeins were in trouble for failing to perform boon-work in reaping or carrying for the lord at harvest time: one was fined heavily, "quia impediuit dictam precariam precipiendo quod omnes irent ad domum ante horam . . . et quia alias male messuit suos *beenes* [boon-works] super culturam domini" (p91). Elias Carpenter had unlawfully planted trees on a boundary strip (*bunda*), Maggie Carter had borne a child to Richard Male outside wedlock for which both were fined, and Agnes had raised the hue (*leuauit uthesium*) against Thomas "qui uoluit habere copulam cum eadem" (p92). Thomas did not appear, and his pledge, John Bovebrook, was fined for not making him answer this charge of attempted rape. Michael Reeve was berated in the churchyard on the last Sunday of October by three people named, for all sorts of offenses against the lord, but he charged them with slander and the jurors took his side. Another membrane, now sewn as part of this roll, deals with the view of frankpledge at Gedding, 28 November 1290. Here a woman had offended by marrying the villein of another lord, who might thus have acquired the tenure of her plot:

> dicunt quod Sarra le Monck' tenuit unum cotagium de domino abbate ad quod cepit uirum de homagio domini Reginaldi de Gray; ideo dictum cotagium fuit captum in manu domini per prepositum de Gydding' qui super hostium domus eiusdem cotagii

pendidit j seruram, et dicta Sarra uenit et fregit seruram cum j lapide, et fecit hamsok';
ideo in misericordia. p98

There was a petty theft:

Et dicunt quod Alicia uxor Iohannis Bert malo modo cepit j lintheamen pendens super
hayam Willelmi filii Rogeri, et inde fecit eidem ["for herself"] unam camisiam; ideo in
misericordia vj d. p98

Here we have a momentary glimpse of the laundry hanging to dry on a neighbor's
hedge. Another of the cases heard concerned Richard Dyer, a married man, convicted of adultery in the Church court "ubi perdidit catalla domini." His conviction
led to the loss of his chattels, but, since he was a villein, these in law belonged to his
lord. The lord therefore had a strong interest in curbing immorality among his
villeins, as appears in another case in the next century from the same manor:

Et dicunt quod Iohannes le Mononk adhuc continuat luxuriam cum Sarra le Hewen ux-
ore Simonis le Hewen, et communiter sequitur diuersa capitula ubi multociens perdit
catalla domini in adulterio cum predicta Sarra, prout sepius temporibus retroactis pre-
sentabatur, nec uult castigari. Ideo in compedibus. Et postea fecit finem pro dimidia
marca per plegium Iohannis le Lach [and others]. Et omnes predicti plegii manuceperunt
dictum Iohannem quod, si aliquo tempore de cetero conuictus fuit in adulterio cum pre-
fata Sarra, ipsum reducant et in compedibus reponant donec aliud de domino seu eius
seneschallo habuerint in precepto. p98

Life for ordinary people was very much the subject of regulation, whether in the
country or in town. Towns were for the most part controlled by the commune or corporation, comprising the free traders in the various craft and trade gilds. Local councils today have often inherited the records of these bodies. From some towns the variety of records is considerable, including gild regulations about shops and trades,
court records that tell of abuses or disturbances, coroners' rolls that focus on moments of tragedy, memoranda of proceedings in the corporation of the town, and
much else. In London the assize of nuisance dealt specially with offenses of bad
neighbors, whose gutters dripped or whose dunghill seeped onto someone else's
property [DL45]. Markets and fairs needed to be very closely regulated, and there are
some surviving examples of court rolls from courts with special jurisdiction at such
assemblies [DL79]. These for the most part are concerned with trading practices, but
they also deal with disputes over goods or payment and with disturbances at the time
of the fair.

   Because of the role of craft and trade gilds in the production of religious plays,
the history of the theater in medieval England is well documented in those towns that
have retained a major collection of municipal records [DL80]. But it is rare for any
leisure activity to be documented in this way. Probably the best recorded recreation
is hunting, on which the royal household spent a great deal of money, employing a
large staff in the specialist tasks of rearing and keeping hunting dogs and hawks; the
management of game reserves was itself a major undertaking, and royal forests were
under a special legal jurisdiction. The issuing of orders, accounting for expenditure,
and forest administration all generated records. But ordinarily how people amused
themselves was not the subject of record unless something went wrong, so that crime
or accident brought the context into the legal record. As with other aspects of life

leisure is better recorded for the highest ranks of society. So, for example, in the household of Edmund, earl of March, we learn that on 10 November 1413 the children were given a costly treat: "Item in x die Nov' apud Kenyngton' pro unum ludum in aquam pro puerris ix s. Item in x die Nov' apud Kenyngton' liberatur pro uno ludo puerorum in camera ix s. ix d." ([DL74] p595). And two weeks later, on 26 November, the 23-year-old earl had his treat: "Item pro potacione cum muliere apud Lesun in xxvi die Nov' iij s. iiij d." (p596; the woman sounds like a society call-girl who charges a large sum for a bottle of champagne but nothing for her personal services). The earl also liked gambling: on 24 November "perdebat apud Lesun apud *devaunt* viij s. iiij d.," and again on 1 December "perdebat apud Stondun ad tabellas de *schort game* xx s. iij s. iiij d. [*sic*]" (p596). Popular amusements will sometimes feature in literary sources, and I have mentioned FitzStephen's account of the sports of the Londoners [DL19]. One interest that does bring games into records, however, is the government's concern that archery should be cultivated for military reasons. So, in 1363, a writ addressed to the sheriffs of each county encouraged archery for sport, requiring "quod quilibet . . . in corpore potens diebus festiuis cum uacauerit arcubus et sagittis uel pilettis aut boltis in iocis suis utatur, artemque sagittandi discat et exerceat" [DL81]. The men, who had been amusing themselves "ad iactus lapidum, lignorum, et ferri, et quidam ad pilam manualem, pediuam, et bacularem, et ad cambucam et gallorum pugnam," are prohibited from so doing [DL82]. References of this kind are not detailed enough to enable us to interpret how the different games were played, and the same is true for those games played at tables with dice or other pieces. Only chess has an established medieval literature [DL83]. The different patterns of dancing are even more obscure (*carolare*), though an example in the abbot of Ramsey's court rolls from the fair at St. Ives in 1312 suggests it might be rather boisterously done: the merchants complained about nine named men who "uenerunt et carolauerunt ad terrorem ferie et ad graue dampnum mercatorum" [DL79]. Again, in 1325 it was *skirmesours*, "merry-andrews," who were the source of trouble (p107). And fairs encouraged other entertainments: in 1287 sixteen women were fined as harlots on the same day (p24), and some men were fined year after year for letting houses to be used by harlots for the duration of the fair (pp74–75, 83–84)

## Conclusion

Records such as those we have been using here, couched in a simple, fluid, but usually precise Latin, open up for historians a great range of different approaches to the medieval past.

Sometimes the different types of source will mesh to provide an unexpected richness: the bare record in the pleas of the Crown for Gloucestershire in 1221 of the conviction of Thomas of Eldersfield for an assault on George of Northway, and of Thomas's blinding and castration as punishment, is in itself unexceptional [DL84]. In several local abbeys, however, chroniclers recorded that Thomas was miraculously healed at St. Wulfstan's shrine in Worcester. When we turn to the *Miracles of St. Wulfstan* [DL85], compiled in the 1240s, we read the full tale of Thomas's frequent adultery with the widow of Robert of Northway, his sense of guilt and consequent rejection of her, and how she turned to George for her comfort; George picked a fight with Thomas, Thomas struck him, and George charged him with assault; Thomas was defeated in the ordeal, convicted, and mutilated, and we see small boys throwing and catching his eyeballs and testicles in sport; but a good widow of Worcester had pity on him, treated his wounds, and nursed him; and in due course he was taken to St. Wulfstan's shrine, where he was miraculously restored. After this Thomas was presented to the bishop, who inspected his person to confirm the miracle. As with the story of St. Osmund and the child in the well, the natural and the supernatural mingle: the commonplace emotions of sexual desire, shame and guilt, rejection, and jealousy lead us into the judicial violence of the criminal law at this date. The legal record confirms the judgment; but the happy ending that became a news story in the surrounding area challenges our understanding of the Middle Ages [DL86].

Even without this unusual richness, ordinary records, however barren they might seem at first reading, can be used collectively and systematically to provide an avenue to the real lives of people in different social or economic contexts. Social historians have quarried the archives of medieval England, drawing generalizations from a thorough reading of many records as much as vivid illustrations from individual sources. Economic historians, though helped by the occasional vignette, can draw a picture with different detail from sources with no narrative content. For example, the annual records of produce, stock, and investment on an agricultural estate, year by year over a long period, will provide a view of estate management quite different from that to be had from a story about an unscrupulous bailiff's wicked dealings with his neighbors. Demographic historians make a different use of archival sources, searching for texts that provide data, for example, on the age at marriage or death of large numbers of people. Inquisitions *post mortem* or proofs of age were records made for financial reasons, but they can provide individually and cumulatively key information on milestones in the life cycle of the ordinary person.

Whatever interests the reader brings to the texts, three aspects of preparation are essential. One must think carefully about the sorts of evidence that will best provide the information needed. One must be prepared for the linguistic demands of the texts. And one must read widely enough around the center of interest to form a true sense of where the evidence is discontinuous and where information may safely be taken from one class of evidence to complement the shortcomings of another.

## Select Bibliography

### The Language of the Records

Familiarity with the everyday Latin written by the record clerks must be gained by experience of reading documents, and there are no studies that provide worthwhile guidance either on the language of the clerks or on their methods of work. There are, however, works to help the reader through the documents. Old but still helpful is C.T. Martin, *The Record Interpreter,* 2nd ed. (1910, r1976), which provides a key to abbreviations used in the records, a glossary, and a guide to names [DL1]. Two dictionaries are indispensable: the *Dictionary of Medieval Latin from British Sources,* ed. R.E. Latham, D.R. Howlett, *et al.* (1975–), is a near-comprehensive historical dictionary, drawing extensively on record sources [DL2]. Until it is completed, the reader needs also to use R.E. Latham's *Revised Medieval Latin Word-List from British and Irish Sources* (1965, r1980 with supp., r1989) [DL3]. Alongside these it is often necessary to draw on the complementary information in the *Middle English Dictionary,* ed. H. Kurath, S.M. Kuhn, and R.E. Lewis (1952–) [DL4], and the *Anglo-Norman Dictionary,* ed. W. Rothwell, L.W. Stone, *et al.* (1977–92) [DL5].

Some collections of texts have been edited with glossaries. A particularly useful work of this type is *Extracts from the Account Rolls of the Abbey of Durham,* ed. J.T. Fowler, 3 vols., *SurSoc* 99, 100, 103 (1898–1901), with (in v3) lists of subjects (pp870–86) and glossary (pp889–989) [DL6].

The texts designed to help schoolboys learn the vocabulary for everyday things supply an accessible approach even today. Such works were composed in Greek and Latin for Roman schools; see, for example, the schoolboy's description of getting out of bed, washing, and dressing for school in *Hermeneumata Stephani,* printed among the *Hermeneumata Pseudo-Dosithiana* in *Corpus glossariorum latinorum,* ed. G. Goetz, 7 vols. (1888–1923), v3:376–79, 379–81 [DL7]. An example of such a text from England at the beginning of the tenth century is quoted above: *Aelfric's Colloquy,* ed. G.N. Garmonsway, 2nd ed. (1947, r1965) 34–35 [DL8]. This and other texts will also be found in *Early Scholastic Colloquies,* ed. W.H. Stevenson (1929, r1989) [DL9]. The works of Adam of Balsham, Alexander Neckam, and John of Garland are all printed in T. Hunt, *TLLTCE* [DL10]; cf. [CD11]. The late fifteenth-century Magdalen schoolbook is now London, B.L., MS Arundel 249; most of its Latin text has not been printed, but the English passages, thematically arranged, can be read in W. Nelson, *A Fifteenth Century School Book* (1956) [DL11]. Two schoolbooks were particularly popular in England in the early sixteenth century. The *Vulgaria* of John Stanbridge is known in some eighteen editions printed in England between 1508 and about 1530 (STC 23194–23198.7; see [BA38]); Robert Whittinton's *Vulgaria* survives in the same number of editions from between 1520 and 1533 (STC 25569.3–25581; see [BA38]). The two works were edited together by B. White, Early English Text Society, original ser., 187 (1932) [DL12]. A similar work that tries to avoid the common vocabulary of Medieval Latin is the work of the Eton schoolmaster W. Horman, *Vulgaria* (London 1519, r1975) [DL13]. A schoolmaster who tried to practice this "improved" style was Robert Joseph, who taught in the monastic school at Evesham: *The Letter Book of Robert Joseph, Monk-Scholar of Evesham and Gloucester College, Oxford, 1530–3,* ed. H. Aveling and W.A. Pantin, Oxford Historical Society, n.s., 19 (1967) [DL14].

## Printed Records

The records of medieval England are vast, and the great majority remains unprinted. Familiarity with the types of records that exist will enable the searcher to go to specialized guides, but there is no general guide that can be cited here. Much that has been printed was published by Her Majesty's Stationery Office as official publications, and these are listed in *British National Archives,* Sectional List 24 (H.M.S.O., frequently updated until the 1980s) [DL15]. For a guide to the history and character of the different classes of the public records see *Guide to the Contents of the Public Record Office* (P.R.O.), 3 vols., rev ed. (1963–68), v1: *Legal Records, etc.* [DL16]. There is no detailed subject index to the contents of the records.

The other common avenues for the publication of records are the historical societies (such as the Camden Series [*CamSoc*] of the Royal Historical Society) and the record societies that have existed for more than a hundred years in almost every English county. These have published samples of almost every class of record from all parts of the country, and their publications are listed and well indexed by place and by class in E.L.C. Mullins, *Texts and Calendars: An Analytical Guide to Serial Publications,* Royal Historical Society Guides and Handbook 7 (1958, r1978); Mullins added a supplementary volume covering publications of the years 1957 to 1982: *Texts and Calendars II,* Royal Historical Society Guides and Handbooks 12 (1983) [DL17].

It is extremely difficult to approach the records, even those in print, without some sense of the classes most likely to deal with the subject that concerns you. If, for example, you were interested in horse breeding, the index to the P.R.O. *Guide* [DL16] would lead you to the accounts of the keepers of the king's horses and of the king's stud farms, but only as a category included in the class of Exchequer, King's Remembrancer, Accounts Various (E.101). From there you would need to follow up the reference to the descriptive list in the *Lists and Indexes,* no. 35 (1912), to discover which individual accounts relate to the *Equitium regis.* If you know the word *equitium,* the entry in the *Dictionary of Medieval Latin* [DL2] would take you to two specific accounts in E.101 and also to two references to the stud farm of the prior of Durham, as well as to other examples in literary texts. An existing publication is the best start. So, for example, on the royal forests there are secondary studies, there are selected texts in print (and indexed in Mullins [DL17]), there are classes in the P.R.O. devoted to forest administration as well as other categories within larger classes (again, indexed in the *Guide*). It is easier to start with such a topic and then narrow one's focus, for example, to the arrangements for protecting deer during the breeding season (*feonatio*).

For the last hundred years and more it has been customary for published collections of documents to include some form of subject index. These will be found in most of the official publications and in the better publications of the record societies. A good modern example will be found in W. Hassall and J. Beauroy, eds., *Lordship and Landscape in Norfolk 1250–1350: The Early Records of Holkham,* Records of Social and Economic History, n.s., 20 (1993) 649–60 [DL18]. The subjects are arranged under these headings: AGRICULTURE, general aspects, crops, labour services, fields, soil, animals; LANDSCAPE, settlement, coastline, buildings, Holkham Park; JURISDICTION, lordship, seigneurial rights, courts, land, seigneurial documents, royal jurisdiction; SOCIAL STRUCTURE, royal officers, manorial officers, knights and freeholders, customary tenants, clerks, crafts and trades, women.

### Texts from which Linguistic Examples are Cited in the Essay

William FitzStephen, *Vita Sancti Thomae, prologus,* ed. J.C. Robertson, in *Materials for the History of Thomas Becket, Archbishop of Canterbury,* 7 vols., RSer 67 (1875–85) v3:1–13 [DL19]. Philip of Oxford [Philippus Prior], *Miracula Sanctae Frideswidae,* in *AASS.October,* v8 (1853) 568–89 (at § 23, p572) [DL20]. *The Canonization of Saint Osmund,* ed. A.R. Malden, Wiltshire Record Society (1901) [DL21]. *Henrici VI Angliae regis miracula postuma,* ed. P. Grosjean (1935), III.104, p182; for the use of *hauritorium* to mean "well-tackle" rather than "bucket" in this context, compare in the same text, V.161, p293: "erat puteus satis altus tum aqua adeo plenus ut hauritorio non egeret" [DL22].

The distinct class of Coroner's Rolls (J.I. 2) comprises some 267 rolls, but other medieval coroners' rolls are found among the assize rolls (J.I. 1) (P.R.O. *Guide,* pp123–26). The first quotation from the Bedfordshire coroner's roll, 49–56 Henry III,

J.I. 2/46 mem. 2; printed (with translation) by C. Gross, *Select Cases from the Coroners' Rolls, A.D. 1265–1413*, SelSoc 9 (1896) 7 [DL23]. The second quotation from the same roll, mem. 3; *Select Cases*, p12. See also the calendar compiled by R.F. Hunnisett, *Bedfordshire Coroners' Rolls*, Bedfordshire Historical Record Society 41 (1961) [DL24]. The rolls were made by recopying the original records, but it is extremely rare for these coroners' files to survive for comparison; the one known case seems to have been accidental and is discussed by R.F. Hunnisett, "The Reliability of Inquisitions as Historical Evidence," in *The Study of Medieval Records: Essays in Honour of Kathleen Major*, ed. D.A. Bullough and R.L. Storey (1971) 206–35 [DL25]. For a general introduction, see also R.F. Hunnisett, *The Medieval Coroner* (1961, r1986) [DL26].

In the annual account presented by the bailiff who was employed to manage an estate for the Crown; *P.R.O., Ministers' Accounts* (S.C. 6), 1147/11 mem. A2 [DL27].

H.T. Riley, *Munimenta Gildhallae Londoniensis*, 3 vols. in 4, RSer 12 (1859–62) v2.2.807: "The iron hook or groove at the end of a skid, for stopping a cart. . . . From the A.S. *gripan* 'to lay hold of'" [DL28]. N.S.B. and E.C. Gras, *The Economic and Social History of an English Village (Crawley, Hampshire) A.D. 909–1928* (1930, r1969) 243, explain the verb *gropare* as "to fit with hooks" [DL29].

Jocelin of Brakelond, *Cronica de rebus gestis Samsonis abbatis monasterii Sancti Edmundi*, ed. and tr. H.E. Butler (1949) 107 [DL30].

P.R.O., *Coram Rege* Rolls, K.B. 27/138 rot. 53d; cited, with other examples, in *Select Cases in the Court of King's Bench*, ed. G.O. Sayles, 7 vols., SelSoc 55, 57, 58, 74, 76, 82, 88 (1936–71), v3:civ [DL31].

Ranulf Higden, *Polychronicon*, ed. C. Babington and J.R. Lumby, 9 vols., RSer 41 (1865–86) v1:350 [DL32].

Account of the privy purse expenses of Edmund Mortimer, earl of March (1413–14), ed. C.M. Woolgar, *Household Accounts from Medieval England*, Records of Social and Economic History, n.s., 17–18 (1992–93), 592–603 (at p593) [DL33].

John Brompton's will provides a detailed inventory of his possessions, printed in *Testamenta Eboracensia*, ed. J. and J. Raine *et al.*, 6 vols., SurSoc 4, 30, 45, 53, 79, 106 (1836–1902), v2:96–105 (at p100) [DL34]. It is an unusually complete view of the household possessions of a rich provincial merchant.

As, for example, in *The Fabric Rolls of York Minster*, ed. J. Raine, SurSoc 35 (1859) 218 (four times) [DL35]. Errors of this kind were hard to avoid in the days before the existence even of Latham's *Revised Medieval Latin Word-List* [DL3]. For a similar example, the word *uertiuellus*, "the band or rider of a hinge" (the part fitted to the gate itself, as distinct from the hook or pintle [Latin *gumphus*], fixed to the post), has often been printed as *uertinellus*.

## Examples from Different Types of Archives

For examples of municipal archives in print one can look at *Records of the Borough of Nottingham*, ed. W.H. Stevenson *et al.*, 9 vols. (1882–1956) [DL36]; *Bridgewater Borough Archives*, ed. T.B. Dilks *et al.*, 5 vols., Somerset Record Society 48, 53, 58, 60, 70 (1933–71) [DL37]. Among the published records from the medieval archives of York are *The Register of the Guild of Corpus Christi in the City of York*, ed. R.H. Scaife, SurSoc 57 (1872) [DL38]; *Register of the Freemen of the City of York*, ed. F. Collins, v1 (1272–1558), SurSoc 96 (1897) [DL39]; *York Memorandum Book* (A/Y), ed. M. Sellers, SurSoc 120, 125 (1912–15) [DL40]; *The York Mercers and Merchant Adventurers*, ed. M.

Sellers, *SurSoc* 129 (1918) [DL41]; *York Memorandum Book* (B/Y), ed. J.W. Percy, *SurSoc* 186 (1973) [DL42]; *York City Chamberlains' Account Rolls, 1396–1500,* ed. R.B. Dobson, *SurSoc* 192 (1980) [DL43]; *York Civic Records,* ed. A. Raine, Yorkshire Archaeological Society, Record Series 98, 103, 106 (1939–42) [DL44]. Pleas originating in disputes between neighbors about walls, gutters, windows, privies, paving, or obstructions in the street are illustrated in *London Assize of Nuisance, 1301–1431: A Calendar,* ed. H.M. Chew and W. Kellaway, London Record Society 10 (1973) [DL45].

For most of the well-preserved monastic archives there is no published catalogue. For Bury, however, see R.M. Thomson, *The Archives of the Abbey of Bury St Edmunds,* Suffolk Records Society 21 (1980) [DL46]; and for Norwich, H.W. Saunders, *An Introduction to the Obedientiary & Manor Rolls of Norwich Cathedral Priory* (1930) [DL47]. For a rich study of the human realities of monastic life, founded largely on the records of Westminster Abbey, see B.F. Harvey, *Living and Dying in England, 1100–1540: The Monastic Experience* (1993) [DL48].

Printed wardrobe accounts include *Liber quotidianus contrarotulatoris garderobae* (London 1787), for the year 1299–1300 [DL49]; *Records of the Wardrobe and Household,* ed. B.F. and C.R. Byerly, v1: *1285–1286* (1977), v2: *1286–1289* (1986) [DL50]; *The Wardrobe Book of William de Norwell, 12 July 1338 to 27 May 1340,* ed. M. Lyon *et al.* (1983) [DL51]; *The Court and Household of Eleanor of Castile in 1290,* ed. J.C. Parsons (1977) [DL52]. The rich plate and textiles mentioned in these may be compared with those, for example, in the inventories from St. Paul's Cathedral, London, ed. W. Sparrow Simpson in *Archaeologia* 50 (1887) 464–500 (1245), 500–18 (1402), and 518–24 (1445) [DL53]; or *Inventories of Christchurch Canterbury,* ed. J. Wickham Legg and W.H. St. John Hope (1902) [DL54].

L.F. Salzman, *Building in England down to 1540: A Documentary History* (1952, r1992), remains an outstanding book. Notwithstanding the richness of surviving building accounts, a great deal of our understanding of medieval building must still be founded on study of the tens of thousands of medieval buildings, from modest houses to castles and cathedrals, that are still standing in England [DL55]. For the Crown's building activities, see *Building Accounts of King Henry III,* ed. H.M. Colvin (1971) [DL56], and v1–2 of his study (with R.A. Brown and A.J. Taylor), *The History of the King's Works,* 6 vols. (1963–82) [DL57].

*Ancient Correspondence* (S.C. 2), comprises some 62 guard books, in which the original letters are now bound [DL58]. The letters summarized are printed by W.W. Shirley, *Royal and Other Historical Letters Illustrative of the Reign of Henry III,* 2 vols., *RSer* 27 (1862–66) v1:271, 276–78 [DL59].

Examples of Feretrar's accounts can be found in *Extracts from the Account Rolls of the Abbey of Durham* (see [DL6]), v2:420–83 [DL60].

A generous selection from the monastic letter books of Christ Church, Canterbury, was printed by J.B. Sheppard, *Literae Cantuarienses,* 3 vols., *RSer* 85 (1887–89) [DL61].

A selection from the Norwich precentor's rolls is printed and discussed by N.R. Ker, "Medieval Manuscripts from Norwich Cathedral Priory," *Transactions of the Cambridge Bibliographical Society* 1 (1949–53), repr. in *id., Books, Collectors, and Libraries: Studies in the Medieval Heritage,* ed. A.G. Watson (1985) 243–72 [DL62].

The primary route into episcopal records is through the bishops' registers, on which see D.M. Smith, *Guide to Bishops' Registers of England and Wales: A Survey from the Middle Ages to the Abolition of Episcopacy in 1646,* Royal Historical Society Guides and Handbooks 11 (1981) [DL63].

*Churchwardens' Accounts of S. Edmund and S. Thomas, Sarum, 1443–1702, with Other Documents,* ed. H.J.F. Swayne, Wiltshire Record Society 1 (1896) [DL64].

*Manorial Records of Cuxham, Oxfordshire, circa 1200–1359,* ed. P.D.A. Harvey, Oxfordshire Record Society 50 (1976), are drawn from the archives of Merton College, which owned the manor of Cuxham from the 1260s [DL65].

*Canterbury College, Oxford,* ed. W.A. Pantin, Oxford Historical Society, n.s. 6–8 (1947–50), prints a wide range of accounts, inventories, and other documents [DL66]. Pantin's study of the college was published after his death: *Canterbury College Oxford,* v4, Oxford Historical Society, n.s., 30 (1985) [DL67]. Another example of a college whose accounts were essentially domestic was King's Hall in Cambridge, studied by A.B. Cobban, *The King's Hall within the University of Cambridge in the Later Middle Ages* (1969) [DL68].

The main source for references to shipbuilding and such like in medieval England is B. Sandahl, *Middle English Sea Terms,* 3 vols. to date (1951–82; see [FF17]) [DL69], which draws extensively on Latin sources. A good example of an account for the building of a warship is C. Johnson and R.J. Whitwell, "The 'Newcastle' Galley, A.D. 1294," in *Archaeologia Aeliana,* 4th ser., 2 (1926) 142–96 [DL70]. Some fifteenth-century port books from Southampton have been printed by the Southampton Record Society since 1913 [DL71], and the London Bridge Masters' accounts and rolls from 1381 in the Guildhall Record Office remain to be exploited.

Entries relating to the maintenance of roads, causeways, bridges and drains were extracted from the files of Ancient Indictments (K.B. 9) and the *Coram Rege* Rolls (K.B. 27) as *Public Works in Mediaeval Law,* ed. C.T. Flower, *SelSoc* 32, 40 (1915–23) [DL72].

*Calendar of Inquisitions post mortem,* in progress (1904–); quotations from v19, ed. J.L. Kirby (1992) [DL73].

C.M. Woolgar, ed., *Household Accounts from Medieval England* (see [DL33]) 689–726, supplies a catalogue of such accounts and prints some 28 examples [DL74].

Runs of court rolls have been printed from Wakefield in Yorkshire from 1274 to 1331, ed. W.P. Baildon *et al., Court Rolls of the Manor of Wakefield,* 5 vols., Yorkshire Archaeological Society, Record Series, 29, 36, 57, 78, 109 (1901–45) [DL75]; those from Hales in Worcestershire from 1270 to 1307, ed. J. Amphlett *et al., Court Rolls of the Manor of Hales,* 3 pts. in 2 vols., Worcestershire Historical Society (1910–33) [DL76]. The court rolls of Ramsey Abbey between 1255 and 1384 were edited by W.O. Ault, *Court Rolls of the Abbey of Ramsey and the Honor of Clare* (1928) [DL77]. These were also used by F.W. Maitland, *Select Pleas in Manorial and Other Seignorial Courts,* Sel-Soc 2 (1889) [DL78], and by C. Gross, *Select Cases Concerning the Law Merchant,* v1: *Local Courts, A.D. 1270–1638,* SelSoc 23 (1908) [DL79].

For abstracts relating to the production of plays see *Records of Early English Drama,* in progress (1979–) [DL80].

A writ (1363) encouraging archery for sport was printed by T. Rymer, *Foedera,* 20 vols. (London 1704–35), v6:417 [DL81]. J. Strutt, *The Sports and Pastimes of the People of England* (1801), illustrates the games of "bandy-ball" (which he relates to golf) and "club-ball" (which may be seen as the precursor of baseball). In Latin, the former is called *cambuca,* though it seems to me rather to be related to hockey than to golf; the latter game is distinguished from this as *pila bacularis* in the writ of 1363. J.C. Cox, in his much revised edition of Strutt's *Sports and Pastimes* (1903, r1968), p100, cites the story of the violent game at Bemerton and assumes that it is an "early form of cricket" (though without stumps, he must surely mean rounders or baseball) [DL82].

The history of chess in the Middle Ages has been studied by H.J.R. Murray, *A History of Chess* (1913, r1986?), who prints relevant passages in Latin from his sources. See also the supplementary text edited by L. Thorndike, "All the World's a Chess-Board," in *Speculum* 6 (1931) 461–65 [DL83].

*Pleas of the Crown for the County of Gloucester*, ed. F.W. Maitland (1884) [DL84], pp21–22 (no. 87), gives the entry in the assize roll. The full account can be found in *Miracula S. Wulfstani*, II.16, ed. R.R. Darlington, *The Vita Wulfstani of William of Malmesbury*, CamSoc, 3rd ser., v40 (1928) 168–75 [DL85]. The whole story has been discussed by P.R. Hyams, *Tales from the Medieval Courtroom: The Fall and Rise of Thomas of Elderfield*, California Institute of Technology, Humanities Working Paper 107 (1985) [DL86].

## Studies of Everyday Life

There are numerous publications concerned with how people lived. Modern works on the history of private life are less closely based on the record evidence than some older works that are still of interest. For example, an anthology of extracts chosen to illustrate life in medieval England is G.G. Coulton, *Social Life in Britain from the Conquest to the Reformation* (1918, r1968); the compiler used a large proportion of sources in Middle English, but all Latin sources used are translated rather than presented in the original language [DL87]. A more specialized essay is U.T. Holmes, *Daily Living in the Twelfth Century, Based on the Observations of Alexander Neckam in London and Paris* (1952) [DL88]. Both these books are essentially anecdotal. A more sophisticated approach will be found in C. Dyer, *Everyday Life in Medieval England* (1994) [DL89], or P. Contamine, *La vie quotidienne pendant la guerre de Cent ans: France et Angleterre, XIVe siècle* (1976) [DL90]. A useful work for the archaeological side of medieval technologies is *English Medieval Industries: Craftsmen, Techniques, Products*, ed. W.J. Blair and N. Ramsay (1991) [DL91]. For a more conspicuously economic approach, see C. Dyer, *Standards of Living in the Later Middle Ages: Social Change in England c. 1200–1520* (1989) [DL92]. For the earlier period there is H.-W. Goetz, *Leben im Mittelalter: vom 7. bis zum 13. Jahrhundert* (1986); tr. A. Wimmer: *Life in the Middle Ages from the Seventh to the Thirteenth Century*, ed. S. Rowan (1993) [DL93]. There is a bibliography in the popular work by J. and F. Gies, *Life in a Medieval City* (1969, r1981) [DL94].

# EA ❖ SCIENCE: INTRODUCTION

## BY FAITH WALLIS

Of all the domains of intellectual endeavor to find written expression in Latin during the Middle Ages, probably none experienced such extensive growth and significant change as science. Medieval thinkers, writers, and teachers succeeded at doing what classical antiquity had not, namely absorbing the heritage of Greek scientific thought into the Latin language. At the same time, they naturalized much of the Arabic elaboration of that Greek inheritance. This millennium-long process of absorption was by no means purely passive. Particularly after the twelfth century, Western scholars were actively engaged in digesting the materials they were acquiring through translation, and beginning to produce their own commentaries, treatises, critiques, and original researches. This section of the guide demonstrates the various ways in which the medieval sciences acquired an extensive and sophisticated Latin vocabulary, the essential foundation of creative scientific thought.

The thesaurus of scientific terminology and concepts that Roman civilization bequeathed to the medieval centuries was jejune and very uneven. Most branches of scientific learning were considered parts of philosophy, and Greek was the language of philosophy during antiquity. Romans who wished to study science usually did so in Greek-speaking centers like Alexandria; the same is true for medicine. On the threshold of the Middle Ages, Boethius (d. 524/26) recognized that political and cultural changes were making it less possible for even privileged Romans to acquire philosophic and scientific learning in the hitherto normal way. To compensate for lack of access to Greek centers of learning, he set out not only to translate Plato and Aristotle into Latin, but also to compose Latin handbooks of the mathematical sciences of arithmetic, geometry, music, and astronomy. Only the treatises on arithmetic and music were completed before his death. Alert to the same problem, Augustine (d. 430) had earlier embarked on a similar project to furnish reference manuals for preachers and exegetes, but never, it seems, progressed further than a treatise on music. In short, it was left to medieval science to assimilate into the Latin tongue much of the repertory of Greek scientific terminology and concepts. This it did by forging a Latin scientific vocabulary, much of it from scratch, and largely through translations from Greek and Arabic.

Though some of this work was accomplished in the early medieval period, particularly in medicine and medical botany, the great spurt of growth in scientific Latin came after the eleventh century, when texts from classical Greece and the Muslim world began to be turned into Latin in Spain and southern Italy. An intriguing fact about this spate of translation is that an overwhelming number of the texts concerned science and medicine; this suggests that the initial demand that sent scholars in quest of new texts was driven by scientific curiosity. Indeed, it can be claimed that Aristotelian metaphysics and ethics rode into Europe as stowaways in essentially scientific baggage: what excited the first translators were texts like al-Khwārizmī's mathematical treatises, Hippocrates's *Aphorisms,* and Ptolemy's *Almagest,* the book that Gerard of Cremona (d. 1187) originally went to Spain to locate. For a century and more, one of the major tasks of medieval scholarship was to master, sort out, and somehow naturalize a complex and sophisticated foreign scientific vocabulary, some of it Greek, some Arabic, some Greek-via-Arabic. One of the most fascinating aspects of studying Medieval Latin scientific texts is observing the ingenious ways in which translators and glossators selected or devised Latin equivalents. The authors of the individual chapters in this section describe some of these ploys in detail. The tension between literal translation—honest but sometimes opaque—and paraphrase—more comprehensible, but also more vulnerable to the translator's distortions—is well illustrated, for example, by Barnabas Hughes's discussion (ch. EB) of how mathematicians vacillated between *radix* and *latus* as translations of the Arabic *jidhr.* The literal, word-for-word style of much medieval scientific translation is frequently derided by modern historians, but as Peter Murray Jones observes (ch. EL), medieval scholars often intentionally chose literalism over paraphrase, in the interests of scientific clarity and exactitude.

This tidal wave of translations cast upon the shores of Christian Europe a rich, novel, but totally uncontrolled scientific vocabulary. The problem of competing, incompatible, and in some cases inadequate or misleading terminology was one in which medieval scientific thinkers were deeply engaged. Albertus Magnus's great project of digesting Aristotle included, as James Scanlan points out (ch. EH), a systematic effort to organize a zoological nomenclature. The result was a lexicon of animal names far more nuanced than anything conveyed by the Roman encyclopedists, and one that, incidentally, made use of the European vernaculars to coin Latin names for animals unfamiliar to the ancients, such as the aurochs. Nicole Oresme attempted to rationalize the terminology of mathematics in much the same manner.

In order to communicate scientific ideas, one needs a vocabulary that is precise and stable. As Charles Burnett demonstrates with reference to astrology (ch. EE), this process of "canonization" took a long time, but its realization was one of the most important achievements of the Middle Ages. With this new vocabulary in hand, Latin writers could begin to introduce into common use the ideas and procedures that the words conveyed, and build new discussion and research upon them. In the case of some sciences, such as astrology, this was basically a labor of synthesizing materials acquired from the past. But in other areas, the new repertory of words and ideas made possible real scientific progress: trigonometry was a science invented in the Middle Ages, but on the basis of geometrical and mathematical terms and concepts introduced into the domain of Latin during the twelfth century.

Each branch of science forged its own kind of latinity, shaped both by the internal history of texts and their transmission, and by the external history of practice and social context. The sciences had a distinctive hierarchy of prestige that also contributed to the character of scientific Latin. Classical manuals such as Martianus Capella's *De nuptiis Mercurii et Philologiae,* or encyclopedias like Isidore of Seville's

*Etymologiae,* conveyed two of these ancient schemata of the sciences to medieval readers. Philosophy, after theology the highest stage of intellectual endeavor, was divided into ethics, logic, and "physics" or natural philosophy. Alternately, philosophy could be distinguished as either practical (i.e. ethics) or theoretical; this latter comprised mathematics, natural science, and "theology" (cf. *Etym.* 2.24.3–16). In either case, one prepared for the study of philosophy by studying the liberal arts: the three verbal disciplines of grammar, rhetoric, and logic, and the four branches of mathematics: arithmetic, geometry, music, and astronomy. According to Varro (d. 27 B.C.), some applied sciences, particularly architecture and medicine, might aspire to the status of philosophy, and hence demand the same scientific propaedeutic.

Comprehensive as this typology was intended to be, it left out a number of areas that we would now categorize as science, for example, geography. Furthermore, the content of "natural philosophy" was fairly fluid. As Edith Dudley Sylla points out in the case of physics (ch. EC), and as Edward Grant indicates for astronomy (ch. ED) and James Scanlan for biology (ch. EH), the medieval definition of natural philosophy was essentially determined by the contents of the treatises of Aristotle recovered in the twelfth and thirteenth centuries. These, along with the mathematical sciences authorized by the quadrivium, became the formal subjects of medieval university teaching, with important results for the development of their latinity. Two forces helped to normalize the vocabulary of these school sciences: the dominating influence of Aristotle and the institutionalized methods of teaching and research practiced in the universities. All the university sciences were heavily impregnated with the scholastic formulae of argumentation and exposition. The same is true, as Peter Murray Jones observes (ch. EL), of medicine, whose vocabulary, though drawn from an eclectic range of Greek and Arabic sources, was refined and standardized under the pressure of Scholasticism.

In short, medieval scientific vocabulary is determined not only by the source materials on which it draws, but also by the interests of its practitioners, and in particular, the other kinds of vocabulary to which they are trying to relate scientific terminology. Conversely, if a science was not organized as a formal disciple, with the benefit of canonized texts and systematic teaching, it might fail to produce a distinctive vocabulary; this indeed was the case with cartography, as P.D.A. Harvey argues (ch. EG). R. James Long's essay on botany (ch. EI) reveals that the more popular a science was, like the "herbalist" wing of botany, the more diverse and disorganized its vocabulary was likely to be. Herbalism had no set textbooks and curricula to rein it in; on the other hand, it had a lot of active practitioners, whose interests and input acted as a centrifugal force on its terminology.

All scientific language is to an appreciable extent technical language, and hence a sort of jargon. Jargon is formed in various ways, for example by according a specialized or esoteric meaning to a word with a more commonplace primary meaning (the chapters on mathematics [EB], chronology [EF], and alchemy [EK] provide some good examples), by inventing nonce words (Scholastic philosophy does this freely, and so do the university sciences, particularly physics), or by naturalizing words from other languages. The percentage of Arabic loanwords is determined not only by the discipline involved, but also by the environment and cultural context of its practice. Astronomy and cosmology, as Edward Grant comments (ch. ED), use a terminology which is largely Latin, but with new or additional meanings. This is the case because, first, there was already an old Latin literature of astronomy, but also because astronomy was a school subject, a compulsory item on the university curriculum, and therefore had to be taught to a large and general body of students, not just an elite of technicians. Contrast to this the case of astrology, where, according to Charles Burnett (ch. EE), the number of Arabic loanwords is high. To some extent this is because there was to all intents and purposes no available native vocabulary of astrology. But it is also related to the social context of astrology. Astrology is not a descriptive and theoretical science, but a technique, and the role of jargon in technical language is to *restrict* the language to initiates, whether deliberately or accidentally. Schoolmen studying physics are philosophers; students of astrology are professionals who may in fact be making their living from their expertise. Burnett hints that the artifical Greek-based vocabulary of one astrological text, the *Proportiones competentes,* may have been intentionally difficult. In a similar vein, Michela Pereira (ch. EK) suggests that the curious metaphorical cant of alchemy may have been a code devised to veil a trade secret—or a mystical meaning.

Hitherto I have concentrated largely on vocabulary, but science exerted an influence on other aspects of Latin as well. Magical charms and incantations, as Richard Kieckhefer points out (ch. EM), have a largely conventional vocabulary, but very distinctive formulae and locutions. Astrological texts display characteristic syntactic and morphological Semitisms. The persistence of traces of the Arabic originals was doubtless encouraged by the literal translation style favored by medieval scholars, but the nature of astrology as a science also played a role in their survival: because astrology is such a conservative science, these syntactic peculiarities tend to be reproduced even in treatises composed originally in Latin.

In short, scientific Latin underwent significant mutation in the medieval centuries. Moreover, its diversification, sophistication, standardization, and above all continuous diffusion through university teaching and the production of texts were important preconditions of the so-called scientific revolution of the seventeenth century. Though the discoveries of Copernicus, Harvey, and Newton eventually discredited the content of medieval science, many of the Latin words through which they conceived and communicated their ideas were forged and made familiar in the Middle Ages.

## Select Bibliography

### Vocabulary

G. Beaujouan, "Le vocabulaire scientifique du latin médiéval," in *LLM* 345–54 [EA1].
*Documents pour l'histoire du vocabulaire scientifique* (1980–): publication of the Institut (national) de la langue française (C.N.R.S.): "Histoire du vocabulaire scientifique"; includes studies relevant to the medieval sciences, e.g. D. Jacquart, "Apport de quelques travaux récents à l'étude du vocabulaire scientifique médiéval," in v4 (1983) 7–24 [EA2].

## General Histories of Medieval Science and Medicine

A.C. Crombie, *Augustine to Galileo,* 2 vols., 2nd rev. and enlarged ed. (1961, r1979): v1, *Science in the Middle Ages, 5th to 13th Centuries;* v2, *Science in the Later Middle Ages and Early Modern Times, 13th to 17th Centuries* [EA3].

C.H. Haskins, *Studies in the History of Mediaeval Science,* 2nd ed. (1927, r1960) [EA4].

D.C. Lindberg, *The Beginnings of Western Science: The European Scientific Tradition in Philosophical, Religious and Institutional Context, 600 B.C. to A.D. 1450* (1992): a valuable and up-to-date survey [EA5].

D.C. Lindberg, ed., *SMA* [EA6].

P.O. Long, ed., *STMS* [EA7].

G. Sarton, *Introduction to the History of Science,* 3 vols. in 5 (1927–48, r1975): covers the period from ancient Greece to the end of the fourteenth century [EA8].

N.G. Siraisi, *Medieval and Early Renaissance Medicine: An Introduction to Knowledge and Practice* (1990) [EA9].

L. Thorndike, *HMES:* the subject range of this monumental, encyclopedic survey is broader than the title suggests [EA10].

J.E. Murdoch, *Album of Science: Antiquity and the Middle Ages* (1984): an overview of scientific diagrams and illustrations, most of which have textual components [EA11].

## Reference Works

*Dictionary of Scientific Biography,* 18 vols., including index (v16) and 2 supps. (v15, v17–18) (1970–1990) [EA12].

C.H. Talbot and E.A. Hammond, *The Medical Practitioners in Medieval England: A Biographical Register* (1965) [EA13].

L. Thorndike and P. Kibre, *A Catalogue of Incipits of Mediaeval Scientific Writings in Latin,* rev. and augmented ed. (1963), with addenda and corrigenda in *Speculum* 40 (1965) 116–22 and 43 (1968) 78–114; see also *Scriptorium* 19 (1965) 173–78 [EA14].

E. Wickersheimer, ed., *Dictionnaire biographique des médecins en France au moyen âge,* 3 vols. in 2 (1979): v1–2 are reprint of 1936 edition; v3, ed. G. Beaujouan, includes supp. of D. Jacquart; see also D. Jacquart, *Le milieu médical en France du XIIe au XVe siècle: en annexe, 2e supplément au "Dictionnaire" d'Ernest Wickersheimer* (1981) [EA15].

## Bibliographical Resources

*Isis:* a bibliography of current work in the history of science is published annually as a supplement to this journal; periodically, a cumulated form of these annual bibliographies is published as *Isis Cumulative Bibliography,* ed. M. Whitrow and J. Neu (1971–) [EA16].

C. Kren, *Medieval Science and Technology: A Selected, Annotated Bibliography* (1985) [EA17].

National Library of Medicine (Bethesda, MD), *Bibliography of the History of Medicine* (1965–): annual, with quinquennial cumulations [EA18].

Wellcome Institute for the History of Medicine and Related Sciences, *Subject Catalogue of the History of Medicine . . .* , 18 vols. (1980): continued by *Current Work in the History of Medicine,* appearing quarterly [EA19].

**Sources in Translation**

E. Grant, *SBMS* [EA20].

*See also* [BA58], [BD30], [BD46], [BD90].

# EB ❉ MATHEMATICS AND GEOMETRY

## BY BARNABAS HUGHES, O.F.M.

In his *Institutiones*, bk. 2, *praef.* 4, Cassiodorus (d. c. 583) defines mathematics in the following way: "[M]athematica, quae quattuor complectitur disciplinas, id est, arithmeticam, geometricam, musicam et astronomicam, . . . est scientia quae abstractam considerat quantitatem" [EB18]. Isidore of Seville (c. 560–636) in his *Etymologiae* ([EB22], bk. 3, *praef.*) uses similar language. This mathematics formed the thinking of medieval students and teachers in their exploration and contemplation of the world about them, from natural philosophy to sacred Scripture.

The student of Medieval Latin mathematics needs five tools in addition to a working knowledge of Latin. First is a good grasp of arithmetic, algebra, geometry, and trigonometry, without which much of what the medieval authors wrote will be lost to the reader. Second is an overview of medieval mathematics: Michael Mahoney's article [EB56] is strongly recommended. The next two tools are paper and pencil. Follow the text by writing out the procedures described therein and by drawing diagrams; these help considerably. The fifth is an introduction to the various kinds of specialized Latin terms one will meet. This last tool is the principal subject of this brief essay.

For the most part, the Medieval Latin vocabulary used in mathematics is a continuation of Classical Latin terminology, although one meets the variations in orthography outlined in ch. CB. Five arithmetic operations are signaled by the usual classical words—*addere, subtrahere, multiplicare, dividere,* and *quadrare*—although *producere* also appears for multiplication, as does *partire* for division. The term for a sixth operation, to halve (*mediare*), is postclassical. Classical words for geometric terminology continue to be used in the Middle Ages: *punctum, linea, circumferentia, area, angulus, arcus, circulus, quadratum,* and so on. These words may be particularized as in *recta linea* (straight line) or *costa quadrati* (side of a square).

There is a physical or natural source for certain generic number words: *digitus,* "finger," came to mean a unit, any of the numbers from one to nine; *articulus,* "knuckle," could mean a multiple of ten. A combination of the two is called *numerus compositus,* e.g. the number 12. Words for categorizing numbers arose from natural descriptions: principal numbers (*cardinales,* e.g. *duo*), ordering numbers (*ordinales,* e.g. *secundus*), grouping numbers (*disperticivi,* e.g. *bini*), adverbial numbers (*adverbiales,* e.g. *bis*), and comparing or measuring numbers (*ponderales,* e.g. *duplum*). Extensive lists of these numbers are to be found in the Paris manuscript, B.N., lat. 5565B, fol. 34v, from c. 1275.

Mathematical and geometric words were borrowed from both Greek and Arabic sources. Many Greek words became incorporated into Classical Latin vocabulary, such as *cubus, parallilos, polyedron,* and *problema,* while others did not. For example, in a theorem translated from Euclid's *Elements* (IV.4), such terms as *isogonius* (equiangular) and *omologus* (corresponding) are among 29 words in the entire work that were merely transliterated and not translated. One suspects that the translator simply did not know their Latin equivalents, because another 28 Greek terms appear both transliterated and translated, including *trigonum* and *triangulus, conus* and *columpna,* and *epipedus* and *planus.* Lists of both sets of vocabulary are in [EB17], pp14–5.

Similarly, some Arabic words were taken over directly into Latin while others were translated. In the first class is *algebra,* from the title of al-Khwārizmī's text, *Hisab al-jabr wa'l-muqābala* (c. 825). The words together signify at once the science and a series of operations ([EB42] p95). Two theorems in a Latin translation of the Arabic version of Euclid's *Elements* incorporate transliterated Arabic words with their Latin equivalents:

> (X.28) Quociens due linee potentia tantum rationales communicantes directe iunguntur, totam lineam mutam fieri necesse est qua *dulithmei,* id est *binomium,* vocatur; (X.29) Quociens mediales linee due potentia tantum communicantes superficiem rationalem continentes directe iunguntur, tota linea muta [= "irrational"] est vocaturque *dulmonsithatein al awwalein,* qualis nos *bimediale primum* dicere possumus. [EB16] pp96–97

Some Arabic words, of course, received literal translations: *res* for *shay⁾, census* for *māl,* and *cubus* for *ka'b.* Al-Khwarizmi's name in Latin, *Algorismus,* came to describe any kind of routine mathematical operation. *Sinus,* however, does not translate the Arabic word for "bosom" but that for the "curved line" to which the sine is attached ([EB45] p177).

Bridging the Greco-Arabic transmission is *radix* (root). Its immediate source is Arabic *jidhr,* which in turn translates the Greek πλευρά. Now the Greek means "the side on which something rests," as does *one* of the meanings of the Arabic word. But in the twelfth century, when Gerard of Cremona (d. 1187) was translating, he hit on *radix* as the primary meaning of the Arabic word. When Euclid's Greek geometry text was translated directly into Latin during the Renaissance, πλευρά was interpreted as *latus.*

Latin translations from Arabic sources sometimes produced verbal variations on the same statement. Consider the following three examples, each by a different translator of the same Arabic sentence:

> Robert of Chester (1144): *Tres autem radices et 4 ex numero vni coequantur substancie.* ([EB35] p35)
> Gerard of Cremona (c. 1170): *Tres radices et quattuor ex numeris equantur censui uni.* ([EB20] p236)
> William of Lunis (c. 1210): *3 radices et 4 dragme equiualent censui.* ([EB28] p56)

The shared terms are obvious; the differences significant. The constant numbers are the same, and the idea of equality runs through all the statements despite the use of three different verbs. The word *radix* (pl. *radices*) had become fixed for a time (eventually it would yield to *res*), and both the idea of "root" and the word itself would remain to modern times. The difference appears in *substancia* and *census,* Latin words for the Arabic *māl.* For all practical purposes, both words are translated into English as "square." The Arabic, however, means "money," "wealth," or "treasure," and was so translated into Latin. Some modern literal translators use "wealth," but this is awkward when a plural is needed. Hence the word "treasure" is more helpful, since its plural is easily at hand, as in "three treasures."  The third of our translations has the word *dragma,* from the Arabic word *dirham,* "coin," and reminds us that Arabic algebra found its greatest use in preparing solutions to problems involving money.

Parenthetically, two remarks are noteworthy. First, the word *census* gained currency in medieval times and *radix* yielded to *res,* which in turn became *cosa* in Italian, whence "The Arte of Cossike Nombers" of Robert Recorde in *The Whetstone of Witte* (1557). Second, the presence of concepts and procedures from Latin-Arabic sources in later Latin works often does not reveal their origin. For instance, consider the Latin of Jordanus de Nemore (fl. early thirteenth century): *Si quadratus cum additione radicis suae per datum numerum multiplicatae datum numerum fecerit, ipse etiam datus erit* ([EB27] p100). Jordanus took a proposition, presumably from one of the translations, and reworded it, thereby making it his own. There is no suggestion of money here. Furthermore, he seems to have been comfortable mixing geometry (*quadratus* and *radix*) with numbers. This is a development in mathematical exposition, whereby words are used analogically and not strictly.

Several other peculiarities, of which readers of mathematical works need to be aware, cut across medieval texts and mathematical topics. Where the letters in figures are Roman in style, they often represent the Greek alphabet. For instance, the vertices of a triangle appear as *ABG* (alpha, beta, gamma) rather than *ABC*. Further, *proportio* means "ratio" and "proportion" becomes *proportionalitas*. These words and meanings apply to any tract where ratio and proportion are discussed, as in computations, theory of numbers, and algebra. Such terms as *duplare, triplare,* and the like, can mean "the double of" or "the square of," "thrice a number" or "the cube of the number." Where the relative sizes of two unequal numbers are compared, the larger is often called *antecedens* or *dux* and the smaller is *consequens* or *comes*. Furthermore, some writers, like Nicole Oresme (d. 1382), strike out on their own in the use of common vocabulary ([EB31] pp24–68). Finally, a word of caution: do not expect any one-to-one correspondence between English and Medieval Latin mathematical vocabulary. Some words simply were not available to medieval writers, such as *coefficient*. For them, the *number* of roots (*radices*) or things (*res*) was the focus of attention; they did not consider the number as a multiplier. Other, now common, words were used in other fields. The best example is *equatio*. Astronomy and astrology had prior claim on this term, and Latin mathematics would not completely absorb it until the mid-sixteenth century in the *Artis Magnae, sive de regulis algebraicis, liber unus* (1545) of Girolamo Cardano (d. 1576).

Many of the foregoing observations come together in trigonometry, a mathematical science that was organized in the Middle Ages. Its vocabulary is geometric, with assistance from arithmetic. Regiomontanus (d. 1476) began his tract on triangles with a list of definitions borrowed mostly from those two sciences ([EB33] p30). Proper to what we call trigonometry (a word invented by Bartholomaeus Pitiscus for the title of his book *Trigonometriae sive De dimensione triangulorum libri quinque,*

1595) is the Latin word *sinus* or "sine," used to render the Arabic *jaib*. There are three kinds: *sinus totus* (whole sine), *sinus rectus* (right sine), and *sinus versus* (versed sine). The first is the length of the radius AD in the figure, the second is the half-chord BC of the half-arc BD, and the third is CD, the length of the radius that remains between the base of the right sine and the circumference of the circle ([EB33] pp31 and 33n). Our word *cosine* appeared as "the sine of the complement" of the arc and did not have its

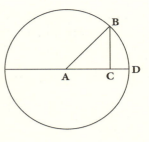

own table. "Tangent" and "cotangent" were *umbra versa* and *umbra recta,* respectively. As the Latin words suggest, the tangent was the shadow of a rod affixed to a wall and horizontal to the ground. The cotangent was the shadow cast by a rod fixed vertically in the ground. The secant and cosecant relationships were identified as hypotenuses: the first "of the shadow" and the second "of the reversed shadow." For details of these "shadow" terms, which originated with the Arabs, see [EB38] pp132–34.

It is helpful, in the absence of a comprehensive dictionary of medieval mathematical terminology, to begin one's study of mathematical tracts by perusing the *indices verborum* and glossaries that often accompany editions of the texts. The following are recommended: for *general mathematics* ([EB21] pp579–612); *algebra* ([EB27] pp205–7, [EB20] pp262–63, [EB35] pp20–21, [EB34] pp159–64, [EB28] pp84–86); *geometry* ([EB1] v1:691–708, v3.4:1521–56, v4.2:521–52; [EB31] pp453–57, [EB30] pp394–405, [EB23] pp239–56, [EB6] pp615–22).

## Select Bibliography

### Primary Works

#### (a) Collections

M. Clagett, ed. and tr., *Archimedes in the Middle Ages,* 5 vols. (1964–84) [EB1].

M. Clagett, *Studies in Medieval Physics and Mathematics* (1979): contains excerpts or complete texts in Latin of works by Euclid, Hero of Alexandria, and an unknown writer [EB2].

M. Curtze, ed., [*Various Medieval Latin Algebraic Tracts*], *Abhandlungen zur Geschichte der Mathematik* 7 (1895), *passim* [EB3].

M. Curtze, ed., *Urkunden zur Geschichte der Mathematik im Mittelalter und der Renaissance,* 2 vols. in 1 (1902, r1968): contains the *Liber embadorum* of Savasorda and the correspondence of Regiomontanus, Giovanni Bianchini, and Jacob von Speier [EB4].

J.O. Halliwell, ed., *Rara Mathematica; or, A Collection of Treatises on the Mathematics,* 2nd ed. (1841, r1977): contains the Latin texts of John of Holywood's *Tractatus de arte numerandi,* Alexander of Villa Dei's *Carmen de algorismo* (see [EB10]), and John Norfolk's *In artem progressionis summula* [EB5].

S.K. Victor, ed. and tr., *Practical Geometry in the High Middle Ages: Artis cuiuslibet consummatio and the Pratike de geometrie* (1979) [EB6].

Numerous anonymous or minor mathematical works were edited and published under the auspices of the *Zeitschrift für Mathematik und Physik,* ed. O.

Schlömilch *et al.* (1856–1917) [EB7], and the *Bullettino di bibliografia e di storia delle scienze matematiche e fisiche,* ed. B. Boncompagni (1868–87), with index in v20 (1887) 668–749 [EB8]. See also *Bibliotheca mathematica,* 3rd ser., 14 vols. (1900–15) [EB9].

**(b) Individual Authors and Texts** (very selective)

Alexander of Villa Dei, *Carmen de algorismo,* ed. R. Steele, in *The Earliest Arithmetics in English* (1922, r1988) 72–80 [EB10].

Bede, *De computo uel loquela digitorum* [= ch. 1.1 of *De temporum ratione*], ed. C.W. Jones, in *CCSL* 123B (1977) 268–73 [EB11].

Ps.-Bede, *De arithmeticis numeris,* etc., in *PL* 90:641–52 (*De arithmeticis numeris*), 677–80 (*De ratione calculi libellus*), 681–84 (*De numerorum divisione*), 685–98 (*De loquela per gestum digitorum et temporum ratione*) [EB12].

Thomas Bradwardine, *Geometria speculativa,* ed. and tr. G. Molland (1989): with commentary and index of Latin terms [EB13]; *Tractatus de proportionibus,* ed. and tr. H.L. Crosby, Jr. (1955) [EB14].

H.L.L. Busard, ed., *L'algèbre au moyen âge: Le "Liber mensurationum" d'Abû Bekr,* in *JS,* April–June 1968, 65–124 [EB15].

H.L.L. Busard, ed., *The Latin Translation of the Arabic Version of Euclid's Elements Commonly Ascribed to Gerard of Cremona* (1984) [EB16].

H.L.L. Busard, ed., *The Mediaeval Latin Translation of Euclid's Elements Made Directly from the Greek* (1987) [EB17].

Cassiodorus, *Inst.* [EB18].

M. Folkerts, ed., *Die älteste mathematische Aufgabensammlung in lateinischer Sprache: Die Alkuin zugeschriebenen Propositiones ad acuendos iuvenes,* Österreichische Ak. der Wiss., mathematisch-naturwissenschaftliche Klasse, Denkschriften 116, v6 (1978) [EB19].

"Gerard of Cremona's Translation of al-Khwārizmī's *al-Jabr*: A Critical Edition," ed. B.B. Hughes, in *MS* 48 (1986) 211–63: with Latin-English glossary [EB20].

Gerbert [of Aurillac; Pope Sylvester II, 999–1003], *Opera mathematica,* ed. N. Bubnov (1899, r1963): in addition to the certain and dubious works of Gerbert, this collection contains excerpts from Boethius, Cassiodorus, unknown abacists, and other minor writers [EB21].

Isidore of Seville, *Etym.* [EB22].

S. Ito, ed. and tr., *The Medieval Latin Translation of the Data of Euclid* (1980) [EB23].

John of Meurs, *Quadripartitum numerorum,* ed. G. L'Huillier: with glossary (1990) [EB24].

C.W. Jones, ed., *Bedae Pseudepigrapha: Scientific Writings Falsely Attributed to Bede* (1939): see especially the *Romana computatio* (pp106–8), a source of Bede's knowledge of finger reckoning [EB25].

Jordanus de Nemore, *De elementis arithmetice artis,* ed. and tr. H.L.L. Busard, 2 vols. (1991): a medieval treatise on number theory [EB26].

Jordanus de Nemore, *De numeris datis,* ed. and tr. B.B. Hughes (1981) [EB27].

W. Kaunzner, ed., *Die lateinisch Algebra in MS Lyell 52 der Bodleian Library, Oxford, früher MS Admont 612,* in Österreichische Ak. der Wiss., philosophisch-historische Klasse, Sitz., 475 (1986) 47–89 [EB28].

G. Libri, ed., "Liber augmenti et diminutionis vocatus numeratio divinationis, ex eo quod sapientes Indi posuerunt, quem Abraham compilavit et secundum librum qui Indorum dictus est composuit," in *Histoire des sciences mathématiques en*

*Italie, depuis la renaissance des lettres jusqu'à la fin du 17e siècle,* 4 vols. (1838–41, r1967): see v1:304–76 ("note XIV") [EB29].

*Nicole Oresme and the Kinematics of Circular Motion: Tractatus de commensurabilitate vel incommensurabilitate motuum celi,* ed. and tr. E. Grant (1971) [EB30].

Nicole Oresme, *De proportionibus proportionum* and *Ad pauca respicientes,* ed. and tr. E. Grant (1966) [EB31].

John Pecham, *De numeris misticis,* ed. B.B. Hughes, in *AFH* 78 (1985) 3–28, 333–83 [EB32].

Regiomontanus, *De triangulis omnimodis,* tr. B.B. Hughes (1967): includes facsimile of the 1533 edition of the Latin text, ed. Johann Schöner [EB33].

*Robert of Chester's Latin Translation of the Algebra of al-Khowarizmi,* ed. and tr. L.C. Karpinski (1915) [EB34].

*Robert of Chester's Latin Translation of al-Khwārizmī's al-Jabr: A New Critical Edition,* ed. B.B. Hughes (1989) [EB35].

S. Unguru, ed., "Witelo as a Mathematician: A Study in Thirteenth-Century Mathematics, including a Critical Edition and English Translation of the Mathematical Book of Witelo's *Perspectiva*" (Ph.D. diss., University of Wisconsin, 1970) [EB36].

## Studies, Aids, Reference Works

A. Allard, "La formation du vocabulaire latin de l'arithmétique médiévale," in *CIVICIMA* 3:137–81 [EB37].

J.L. Berggren, *Episodes in the Mathematics of Medieval Islam* (1986) [EB38].

M. Clagett and J.E. Murdoch, "Medieval Mathematics, Physics and Philosophy: A Revised Catalogue of Photographic Reproductions," in *Manuscripta* 2 (1958) 131–54, 3 (1959) 19–37 [EB39].

J.F. Daly, "Mathematics in the Codices Ottoboniani Latini," in *Manuscripta* 8 (1964) 3–17, 9 (1965) 12–29 [EB40].

J.W. Dauben, *The History of Mathematics from Antiquity to the Present: A Selective Bibliography* (1985) [EB41].

Y. Dold-Samplonius, "The Solution of Quadratic Equations According to Al-Samawʾal," in *Mathematica: Festschrift für Helmuth Gericke,* ed. M. Folkerts and K. Lindgren (1985) 95–104 [EB42].

M.G. Ennis, *The Vocabulary of the Institutiones of Cassiodorus* (1939): on pp112–31 is a dictionary of technical terms used by Cassiodorus in arithmetic, geometry, music, and astronomy [EB43].

G.R. Evans, "The Use of Technical Terms of Mathematics in the Writings of St. Anselm," *Studia Monastica* 18 (1976) 67–75 [EB44].

H. Eves, *An Introduction to the History of Mathematics,* 6th ed. (1990) [EB45].

H. Gericke, *Mathematik im Abendland von den römischen Feldmessern bis zu Descartes* (1990) [EB46].

E. Grant and J.E. Murdoch, eds., *Mathematics and Its Applications to Science and Natural Philosophy in the Middle Ages: Essays in Honor of Marshall Clagett* (1987) [EB47].

C. Hay, ed., *Mathematics from Manuscript to Print, 1300–1600* (1988) [EB48].

T.L. Heath, *The Thirteen Books of Euclid's Elements,* 3 vols., 2nd ed. rev., with additions (1926, r1956) [EB49].

B.B. Hughes, "Franciscans and Mathematics," in *AFH* 76 (1983) 98–128: the footnotes offer many selections from mathematical texts used to support philosophical and theological arguments [EB50].

A.P. Juschkewitsch, *Geschichte der Mathematik im Mittelalter* (1964) [EB51].

W.R. Knorr, *Textual Studies in Ancient and Medieval Geometry* (1989) [EB52].

G. Kousoff, "Le vocabulaire latin des mathématiques: Problèmes de recherche," in *DHVS* 2 (1981) 37–44 [EB53].

D.C. Lindberg, ed., *SMA* (1978): chapters on mathematics, optics, astronomy, and the science of weights show medieval mathematics in action [EB54].

K.O. May, *Bibliography and Research Manual of the History of Mathematics* (1973) [EB55].

M.S. Mahoney, "Mathematics," in *DMA* 8:205–22 [EB56].

# EC ❋ PHYSICS

## BY EDITH DUDLEY SYLLA

For the Middle Ages "physics" meant first of all the book of that name by Aristotle along with the commentaries on it, including that of Averroes (d. 1198) and those of the many teachers in medieval universities who used Aristotle's *Physics* as a set text. The Latin used in medieval treatises concerned with physics therefore derives in large part from translations of Aristotle's text either directly from Greek or via the earlier Arabic translations. These translations are quite frequently obscure, partly because of the difficulties of the original Greek text, which may have been composed of reports of Aristotle's rather discursive lectures, and partly because of the translators' difficulties when latinizing it: they often resorted to word for word renderings with insufficient concern for the overall meaning. Aristotle's physics, as compared, say, with some of his biological writings, is abstract and theoretical rather than concrete, so that the vocabulary of physics consists of (relatively few) theoretical terms with considerable overlap with metaphysics.

Works associated with Aristotle's *Physics* are not, however, the only medieval treatises that might be taken to fall under the rubric "physics," given a somewhat more modern definition. Works written in the twelfth century and earlier, using Plato's *Timaeus* or even medical works as sources, often described the world from what might be considered a physical point of view (and in this earlier period *physica* might mean medicine rather than physics in the modern sense). There is also the surprisingly empirical work of Peter Peregrinus of Maricourt on the magnet (1269). Moreover, throughout the Middle Ages there are works belonging to the so-called middle sciences (*scientiae mediae*)—those midway between natural philosophy and mathematics—that might well be considered part of physics. These works treat physical topics in a way subordinated to mathematics, for instance, optics (*perspectiva*), said to be subalternate (*subalternata*) to geometry, or statics (*scientia de ponderibus*). In the fourteenth century and afterwards the science of motion (*scientia de motu*) is often treated as a middle, mathematical science, and there were also the so-called physical *sophismata*, logical unravelings of perplexing-sounding propositions that appear to concern physical topics, such as the sophisma of Richard Kilvington (d. 1361): *Socrates et Plato incipient aeque velociter moveri* ("Socrates and Plato will begin to be moved equally fast").

To understand Aristotelian and medieval physics one should know that the Aristotelian and medieval universe was a cosmos consisting of (1) concentric shells (*sphaera, orbis, caelum, corpus caelestis*) of an element called ether (*aether, ether*) containing the stars and planets (including the sun and moon), and (2) a plenum, within the sphere of the moon, consisting of four elements or kinds of simple bodies—earth, water, air, and fire—along with the compounds they make up (minerals, plants, animals). In this cosmos all bodies are continuous (i.e. they are not made up of atoms or indivisibles, but are divisible into smaller and smaller finite parts without limit) and comprised of prime matter (*materia prima*) given character by substantial and accidental forms (*forma substantialis, accidens* or *forma accidentalis*). The etherial heavenly element naturally moves in circles around the center of the universe. Earth and water are heavy (*gravis*) and, as such, naturally move toward the center of the universe; air and fire are light (*levis*) and, as such, naturally move away from the center of the universe toward the sphere of the moon.

By the fourteenth century, physics as a theoretical science (*scientia demonstrativa*) was assumed to consist of the habits of mind by which the philosopher knows its ordered true propositions—habits of mind being more long-lasting and firmly established qualities than mere dispositions. Knowing the science of physics was equated with knowing in general the causes of the motions observed in the world. Whereas the subject of metaphysics was being (*ens*) in general, the subject of physics was things that move (*res movens, corpus movens*), both celestial and terrestrial. Less general than physics, the science of the heavens (*de caelo*) considered only the local motions (*motus localis*) of stars and planets (they had no other movements), whereas the science of generation and corruption (*de generatione et corruptione*) considered the means by which one sort of thing (*substantia*) turned into another, for instance, water into air. Motion (*motus*) in the Aristotelian and medieval sense thus included local motion, alteration (*alteratio*), and augmentation and diminution (*augmentatio et diminutio*). It was defined in general (in a definition much scorned by some of the founders of modern physics) as *actus entis in potentia secundum quod in potentia* ("the act of a being in potentiality insofar as it is potentiality"). Thus motion was the actualization of a potency, potentiality and act being two very important concepts for medieval physics. Substantial change, by which one thing became something else, was thought to occur instantaneously and hence, properly speaking, was a mutation (*mutatio*), taking place suddenly, rather than a motion, taking place in time. Human beings first learn about moving things from sensation and experience (*experientia, experimenta*), but they later learn the causes of motion, so that physics as a theoretical science has a deductive form in which observed motions are explained by four causes (*materialis, formalis, efficiens,* and *finalis*) based on relatively few fundamental principles; one of these, for example, was the principle *omne quod movetur ab alio movetur* ("everything that is moved is moved by something else").

By the fourteenth century also questions on Aristotle's *Physics* were often answered with the assistance of logical and grammatical distinctions (*distinctiones*) concerning the propositions in which physical knowledge was stated, so that a great deal of logical theory regarding the categories (*praedicamenta*), the supposition (*suppositio*) of terms, compounded and divided senses (*sensus compositus, sensus divisus*), and so forth, may be found in questions on the *Physics*. Here the ten Aristotelian categories are substance (*substantia*), quantity (*quantitas*), quality (*qualitas*), relation (*relatio, ad aliquid*), place (*ubi, locus*), time (*quando, tempus*), position (*positio, situs*), state (*habitus*), action (*actio*), and passion (*passio*). Supposition is the relation of terms in propositions to the things they signify or refer to, either things in the outside world, or terms, concepts, etc. If the proposition "something white can be black" were taken in the compounded sense, it would mean that a thing can be white and black at the same time; if it were taken in the divided sense it would mean that a thing that is now white can later be black. When one first knows a fact of nature (*natura*), one has knowledge *that* (*demonstratio quia*), and when one can demonstrate the effects from their causes or principles (*principia*), one has science in the strict sense or knowledge *why* (*demonstratio propter quid*). True science requires certitude (*certitudo*), but it is also possible to have only an opinion (*opinio*) about physical matters or, somewhat better, to have arguments that fall short of certitude but that are credible (*probabilis*). Such arguments could include the evidence of the senses, experience, and propositions known in themselves (*per se nota*).

Although the specialized vocabulary of medieval physics was fairly small and centered on Latin translations of words used by Aristotle, the content of the field was highly theoretical. Individual words might therefore have different connotations or nuances for those who believed in different metaphysical systems. The work of some authors reveals a relatively rich ontology, whereas the ontology of others, notably the nominalists or Ockhamists, was very sparse. For many Ockhamists, the only kinds of things that exist in the world are things in the categories of substances (*substantia*) and qualities (*qualitas*). Other words (for instance, those referring to other categories) might correspond only to mental concepts and not immediately to things in the outside world. Thus a typical question of medieval physics was whether alteration (as when a body becomes hotter) requires anything in addition to the body and the qualities it gains. This question was sometimes phrased by asking whether motion is only a form flowing (*forma fluens*), e.g. the degrees of heat gained (*qualitas quae acquiritur pars post partem*), or whether it also involves a flux (*fluxus formae*), i.e. the motion in itself as separate from the result of motion (*motus ut est passio*). Alternatively, one could ask whether in addition to the permanent things (*ens permanens*) in the universe there are also successive things (*ens successivum*).

Another issue that medieval physics took from Aristotle was whether the cosmos included only continua, or atoms or indivisibles (*atomus, indivisibilis*) as well. The majority of medieval philosophers followed Aristotle in denying the existence of indivisibles, but some asserted their existence. An indivisible of a line (whether conceptualized or truly existing) was a point (*punctum* or *signum*); an indivisible of time was an instant (*instans* or *nunc*); an indivisible of motion was called by the awkward term *motum esse* or, for instantaneous changes, *mutatum esse;* and an indivisible of quality was sometimes called a uniform degree (*gradus uniformis*). If there were indivisibles, one could ask whether, when a permanent or successive thing came into or went out of existence, it had a first instant of being (*primum instans esse*) or a last instant of nonbeing (*ultimum instans non-esse*), and so forth. For example, if a body were uniformly of the highest degree (*summum*) and began to be cooled, then it might have a last instant of being the highest (indivisible) degree (*ultimum instans esse summum*), but no first instant of being of some degree less than the maximum degree. Such questions might be asked in treatises on beginning and ceasing (*de incipit et desinit*).

Following Aristotle, medieval natural philosophers generally assumed that all three kinds of motions (i.e. local motion, alteration, and augmentation or diminution) involved a continuing subject (*subiectum*) or substance that moved from one contrary to the opposite or from a privation (*privatio*) to a form. In the natural local motions of the elements the contraries are up and down (*sursum et deorsum*) or toward the center of the earth (*mundus*) and away from it. In alteration the contraries might be hot and cold (*caliditas et frigiditas*), white and black (*albedo et nigredo*), or wet and dry (*humiditas et siccitas*). In augmentation and diminution the contraries might be large and small (*magis et minus*) or rare and dense (*raritas/subtilitas* and *densitas/spissitudo*). To cause the motion, an agent (*agens*) acted on a body that suffered the action (*passum*), the agent causing an action (*actio*) and the body on which it acted suffering a *passio*. The agent has a force (*virtus, vis, potentia*) and the body or medium (*medium*) on which it acts offers a resistance (*resistentia*) to the action, without which resistance there would not be a motion in time, but a mutation. Many thought that the action of a light source (*lux*) in causing an illumination (*illuminatio, lumen*) was instantaneous, because the medium offered no resistance. Other than the elements, the types of bodies considered in physics included drops, beams, ships, projectiles, the heavenly spheres, or animals. A mover had to be in contact with the moved thing (*tangere, esse simul/contiguus*) and could pull, push, carry (*trahere, pulsare, vehere*), or undertake some combination of these.

In addition to the bodies in the Aristotelian cosmos and their motions, the text of the *Physics* made a number of other concepts central to medieval questions on physics: the Aristotelian and medieval cosmos is full, there are no vacua (*vacuum*) within it, and it ends with an outermost sphere outside which there is nothing, not even empty space. Space (*spatium*) was a concept used in the Middle Ages when discussing Euclidean geometry or refuting the theories of the ancient atomists, but it was much less commonly used than place (*locus*) in physics. *Locus* was defined as the innermost surface of the surrounding body or medium. Since the outermost sphere of the cosmos has no other body outside it, it is not in place, unless it could be said to be in place by its parts. A body's place was also called its *ubi*, and in local motion the *ubi* might be said to change, as described by Albertus Magnus (d. 1280) in his *Physics* (5.1.8): *motus in ubi magis dicitur esse in ubi quam in loco, quia locus est immobilis; ubi autem, quod est circumscriptio mobilis a loci circumscriptione procedens, est mobile et fluens* ("motion in place [*ubi*] is said to be in *ubi* more than in *locus*, because the place [*locus*] does not move; but the *ubi*, which is the circumscription of the mobile proceding from the circumscription of place, is mobile and flowing"). Extension (*extensio*) or dimension (*dimensio*) in place only existed according to these theories where there was a body (*corpus*) with extension, and hence impenetrability was associated with extension. The modern concept of mass was lacking, although the word *massa* existed and was used to refer to bulk. What might have corresponded to mass was sometimes called quantity of matter (*quantitas materiae*), but since prime matter (*materia prima*) had no differentiating characteristics, it was difficult to imagine how one part of matter could be distinguished from another except by place. Sometimes, however, underneath the ordinary dimensions there were supposed to be *dimensiones interminatae*, where the idea was of an indeterminate or changeable extension. Time (*tempus*), in the Aristotelian system, is the measure of motion, and hence exists only when there are bodies that move and minds (*anima*) to measure their motion. For Aristotle the world has existed and the heavens have been moving with the same velocity eternally. Medieval philosophers debated whether it could be proved naturally, in accord with Christian faith, that the world is not eternal, often distinguishing God's eternity (*eternitas*) from the sort of eternity of the world (*aeviternitas, perpetuitas*) proposed by Aristotle. If before the creation of the cosmos there were no bodies and no motion, there would then also be no time as Aristotle defines it.

Physics in the Middle Ages concerned the normal course of nature and not the supernatural or what God might do miraculously. This was expressed by saying that physics concerns the *potentia Dei ordinata,* not the *potentia Dei absoluta.* Nevertheless, one could attempt to make logical distinctions by considering in imagination (*secundum imaginationem*) what might happen if God did act by his *potentia absoluta.* Thus, although in fact no vacua or voids exist within the cosmos, one might consider what could happen if God chose, by his *potentia absoluta,* to annihilate a body and thereby create a void.

Infinity (*infinitas*) was another concept treated in detail in Aristotle's *Physics,* and medieval natural philosophers therefore frequently discussed it. The cosmos was supposed to be finite, but a continuum was thought to be infinitely divisible, at least in the sense that no matter how finely it was divided, it could still be divided further. This latter "infinite" was called the potential (*in potentia*) or syncategorematic infinite, as opposed to the actual (*in actu*) or categorematic infinite.

In the later books of the *Physics* Aristotle discussed forces (*vis, potentia*), resistances (*resistentia*), and the velocities (*velocitas*) that result when forces move with resistances. All motion in the cosmos was supposed to originate with one or more intelligences (*intelligentia, substantia separata,* sometimes assumed to be angels), immaterial prime movers (*primus motor*) that move the celestial spheres, which in turn cause motion and change below the moon. Movement of a body away from its natural place was called violent (*violens*). An agent causing a violent motion experiences a reaction (*reactio*) and is subject to decrease of its power or fatigue (*fatigatio*), whereas the intelligences moving the celestial spheres experience no resistance and never tire (they are *infatigabilis*). Humans, with free will (*voluntas, liberum arbitrium*), may apply a greater or lesser power at will, unlike natural forces. Some thinkers described a type of sublunar motion that is neither natural (bringing the body closer to its natural place) nor violent (moving it farther away from its natural place), for instance the upper atmosphere dragged in a circle by the motion of the lunar sphere. This motion was said to be "neutral" (*neuter*).

It was difficult for Aristotle to explain both the acceleration of bodies in natural motion and the continuation of projectile motion, and medieval natural philosophers developed the concept of impetus (*impetus*) to solve these problems. Impetus was supposed to be a sort of quality that inhered in a body and caused its further motion. In arguing that the motion of the celestial spheres must be the fundamental eternal motion, Aristotle had reasoned that linear projectile motion could not continue indefinitely. This led to discussion as to whether there must be a *quies media* interrupting the continuity of motion when, for instance, a ball bounces off a wall—rest (*quies*) was, of course, the opposite of motion. Proceeding beyond Aristotelian physics to more mathematical approaches, fourteenth-century natural philosophers invented a number of terms to describe motions or velocities, for instance *uniformis*—motion with constant velocity, *difformis*—motion with varying velocity, *uniformiter difformis*—motion with a constant acceleration or deceleration, *difformiter difformis*—motion with an irregularly changing velocity. Authors wrote of the measurement of motion *tanquam penes effectum*—with respect to the local, qualitative, or quantitative distances traversed—and *tanquam penes causam*—with respect to the forces and resistances causing the motion. The "distance" to be traversed in motions of alteration was called a *latitudo,* and latitudes, like motions, could be uniform, uniformly difform, etc. When a quality like hotness became greater or less, it was said to intensify or decrease (*intendere et remittere*). When medieval authors asked for the measure of motion with respect to cause or effect, they used the phrase *penes quid attenditur*—on what does it depend?

If the terminology of medieval physics after the twelfth century is rather limited, general, and simple, its theories are more difficult. Although natural philosophers in the Middle Ages made a clear distinction between what was true naturally and what was true in faith, conceptual developments intended to settle theological questions often affected the sense and connotations of words used in physics. Thus "being" (*esse*) could have many differing connotations according to the author, and varying distinctions were made among things (*res*), modes (*modus*), and concepts (*conceptus, intentio animae*). The Scotistic concept of "thisness" (*haeccitas*) might be imported into physics, the unity and plurality of substantial forms might be assumed, and so forth. Since most texts in medieval physics were written in scholastic format, in which opposing opinions were proposed and attacked before the author's own opinion was given, it is important always to understand the status within the complete work of any section under review, for it may be expressing a view with which the author disagrees rather than the author's own opinion.

## Select Bibliography

### Texts, Translations

The editions of works on physics by or attributed to William of Ockham ([EC16–18]), with their useful indices of terms, provide an excellent starting point for reading the texts of medieval physics. It is also helpful to compare the editions and translations of Aquinas's works on the *Physics* ([EC12–14]), and to become familiar with the Medieval Latin translations of Aristotle's *Physics* itself, e.g. [EC3].

Albertus Magnus, *Physicorum libri,* ed. A. Borgnet, *Opera omnia,* v3 (1890) [EC1]; or, *Physica: Pars I, libri 1–4,* and *Pars II, libri 5–8,* ed. P. Hossfeld, in *Opera omnia,* v4.1–2 (1987–93): with *Index rerum et vocabulorum,* pp313–94, 663–766 [EC2].

Aristotle, *Physica: Translatio Vaticana,* ed. A. Mansion, *Aristoteles Latinus,* v7.2 (1957) [EC3].

Averröes, *Aristotelis de physico auditu libri octo cum Averrois Cordubensis variis in eosdem commentariis* in *Aristotelis opera cum Averrois commentariis,* v4 (Venice 1562, r1962) [EC4].

Benedict Hesse, *Quaestiones super octo libros "Physicorum" Aristotelis,* ed. S. Wielgus (1984) [EC5].

Boethius of Dacia, *Quaestiones super libros physicorum,* ed. G. Sajó, *Opera,* v5.2 (1974): with index verborum, pp333–62 [EC6].

Giles of Rome, *Commentaria in octo libros Phisicorum Aristotelis* (Venice 1502, r1968) [EC7].

John Buridan, *Questiones super octo Phisicorum libros Aristotelis* (Paris 1509, r1964) [EC8].

John of Jandun, *Super octo libros Aristotelis de physico auditu subtilissimae quaestiones* (Venice 1551, r1969) [EC9].

Pseudo-Marsilius of Inghen, *Questiones subtilissime . . . super octo libros Physicorum secundum nominalium viam* (Lyon 1518, r1964) [EC10].

Robert Grosseteste, *Commentarius in VIII libros Physicorum Aristotelis,* ed. R.C. Dales (1963) [EC11].

Thomas Aquinas, *Expositio in octo libros Physicorum Aristotelis,* ed. Commissio Leonina, *Opera omnia,* v2 (1884) [EC12]; or, *In octo libros De physico auditu sive Physicorum Aristotelis commentaria,* ed. A.M. Pirotta (1953) [EC13]; tr. R.J. Blackwell *et al.* (1963) [EC14].

Walter Burley, *In Physicam Aristotelis expositio et quaestiones* (Venice 1501, r1972) [EC15].

William of Ockham, *Expositio in libros Physicorum Aristotelis: Prologus et libri I–III,* ed. V. Richter and G. Leibold, *Opera Philosophica,* v4 (1985) [EC16]; *Libri IV–VIII,* ed. G. Gál *et al., Opera Philosophica,* v5 (1985) [EC17].

William of Ockham, *Brevis summa libri Physicorum, Summula philosophiae naturalis, et Quaestiones in libros Physicorum Aristotelis,* ed. S.F. Brown, *Opera Philosophica,* v6 (1984) [EC18].

For lists of questions in unedited commentaries, see A. Zimmermann, *Verzeichnis ungedruckter Kommentare Zur Metaphysik und Physik des Aristoteles aus der Zeit von etwa 1250–1350* (1971) [EC19].

For other texts, translations, and commentaries on selections from various works (including Platonic/Neoplatonic works and the middle sciences) see, for example:

M. Clagett, ed. and tr., *Archimedes in the Middle Ages,* 5 vols. (1964–84) [EC20].

M. Clagett, *The Science of Mechanics in the Middle Ages* (1959, r1961) [EC21].

M. Clagett and E.A. Moody, eds., *The Medieval Science of Weights (Scientia de Ponderibus): Treatises Ascribed to Euclid, Archimedes, Thabit ibn Qurra, Jordanus de Nemore and Blasius of Parma* (1952, r1960), with translations [EC22].

E. Grant, *SBMS:* translations only [EC23].

Texts by individual authors include the following:

Bernard Silvester, *Cosmographia,* ed. P. Dronke (1978) [EC24]; tr. W. Wetherbee (1973, r1990) [EC25]: an example of medieval physics before the impact of the Aristotelian translations.

Gerard of Brussels, *Liber de motu,* ed. M. Clagett, in *Osiris* 12 (1956) 73–175 [EC26].

John Pecham, *Perspectiva communis,* ed. and tr. D.C. Lindberg, in *John Pecham and the Science of Optics* (1970) [EC27].

Nicole Oresme, *Tractatus de configurationibus qualitatum et motuum,* in *Nicole Oresme and the Medieval Geometry of Qualities and Motions,* ed. and tr. M. Clagett (1968) [EC28].

Peter Peregrinus of Maricourt, *Epistola de magnete,* ed. G. Hellmann, in *Rara magnetica* 1269–1599 (1898); tr. S.P. Thompson (1902) [EC29].

Richard Kilvington, *Sophismata,* ed. N. and B.E. Kretzmann (1990); tr. N. and B.E. Kretzmann: *The Sophismata of Richard Kilvington: Introduction, Translation, and Commentary* (1990) [EC30].

Richard Swineshead, *Calculationes* (Venice 1520); excerpt edited by M. Hoskin and A.G. Molland, "Swineshead on Falling Bodies: An Example of Fourteenth-

Century Physics," in *British Journal for the History of Science* 3 (1966) 150–182 [EC31].

Richard of Wallingford, *Opera*, ed. and tr. J.D. North, in *Richard of Wallingford: An Edition of His Writings with Introductions, English Translation and Commentary*, 3 vols. (1976): with glossary of Latin words in v3:277–89 [EC32].

Roger Bacon, *De multiplicatione specierum*, ed. D.C. Lindberg, in *Roger Bacon's Philosophy of Nature: A Critical Edition, with English Translation, Introduction, and Notes, of "De multiplicatione specierum" and "De speculis comburentibus"* (1983) [EC33].

Thomas Bradwardine, *Tractatus de proportionibus*, ed. and tr. H.L. Crosby, Jr. (1955) [EC34].

William Heytesbury, *Regulae cum sophismatibus* (Venice 1494) [EC35].


Studies

D.C. Lindberg, *Theories of Vision from al-Kindi to Kepler* (1976, r1981) [EC36].

A. Maier, *Studien zur Naturphilosophie der Spätscholastik*, 5 vols.: v1, *Die Vorläufer Galileis im 14. Jahnhundert*, 2nd ed. rev. (1966); v2, *Zwei Grundprobleme der scholastischen Naturphilosophie: das Problem der intensiven Grösse, die Impetustheorie*, 3rd ed. rev. (1968); v3, *An der Grenze von Scholastik und Naturwissenschaft: die Struktur der materiellen Substanz, das Problem der Gravitation, die Mathematik der Formlatituden*, 2nd ed. (1952); v4, *Metaphysische Hintergründe der spätscholastischen Naturphilosophie* (1955); v5, *Zwischen Philosophie und Mechanik* (1958) [EC37].

A.G. Molland, "The Geometrical Background to the 'Merton School': An Exploration into the Application of Mathematics to Natural Philosophy in the Fourteenth Century," in *British Journal for the History of Science* 4 (1968) 108–25 [EC38].

J.E. Murdoch, "The Medieval Language of Proportions: Elements of the Interaction with Greek Foundations and the Development of New Mathematical Techniques," in *Scientific Change: Historical Studies in the Intellectual, Social and Technical Conditions for Scientific Discovery and Technical Invention, from Antiquity to the Present: Symposium on the History of Science, University of Oxford, 9–15 July 1961*, ed. A.C. Crombie (1963) 237–71 [EC39].

J.E. Murdoch and E.D. Sylla, "The Science of Motion," in *SMA* 206–64 [EC40].

E.D. Sylla, *The Oxford Calculators and the Mathematics of Motion, 1320–1350* (1991) [EC41].

E.D. Sylla, "Medieval Concepts of the Latitude of Forms: The Oxford Calculators," in *AHDL* 40 (1973) 223–83 [EC42].

W.A. Wallace, *Prelude to Galileo: Essays on Medieval and Sixteenth-Century Sources of Galileo's Thought* (1981): for those ideas transmitted from the Middle Ages [EC43].

C. Wilson, *William Heytesbury: Medieval Logic and the Rise of Mathematical Physics* (1956) [EC44].


*See also* [BC76].

ED • ASTRONOMY, COSMOLOGY,
AND COSMOGRAPHY

BY EDWARD GRANT

## Sources

Although a rudimentary, largely Platonic, Latin astronomy and cosmology existed prior to the twelfth century, it was the influx of Greco-Arabic science, especially Aristotle's *De caelo* and Ptolemy's *Almagest,* in the twelfth and thirteenth centuries that established cosmology or cosmography as a major component of natural philosophy in the Latin curriculum and introduced astronomy as a science. To this body of secular literature was added a significant mixture of Christian theological ideas drawn largely from the creation account in Genesis and expressed in the hexaemeral literature of the Church fathers.

From this intellectual inheritance, medieval scholastic authors fashioned a literature of astronomy and cosmology. In addition to primarily astronomical treatises, such as Campanus of Novara's *Theorica planetarum* [ED6] (composed c. 1261–64) and the brief, anonymous *Theorica planetarum* [ED1] (composed c. 1260–80), the major sources of cosmology were scholastic commentaries and *questiones* on Aristotle's *De caelo, Physica* (bks. 2, 5, and 8), *Metaphysica* (bk. 12), and *Meteora*; commentaries on John of Sacrobosco's treatise *De spera* [ED9] (composed c. 1220); commentaries on the *Sentences* of Peter Lombard (composed c. 1140), bk. 2, which treats of the creation; and encyclopedias such as the *De proprietatibus rerum* of Bartholomaeus Anglicus (fl. 1220–50) [ED3] and the *Speculum naturale* of Vincent of Beauvais (d. c. 1264). The terminology that emerged from these treatises was largely one of traditional terms that sometimes took on new or additional meanings.

## Astronomy

Astronomy (*astronomia*) was commonly defined as the science concerned with the dimensions and quantities in the celestial orbs and bodies, while astrology (*astrologia*) was defined as the science concerned with the celestial powers that caused changes and events in the terrestrial region. Despite differing definitions, the two terms were usually interchangeable ([ED8] 34.14–17; 35.2–5, 19–23).

Although it appeared to the naked eye that the planets were self-moved, like fish in water or birds in the air, natural philosophers denied appearances and followed

Aristotle and Ptolemy in thinking that each planet (*planeta* or *sidus*) was embedded in its own etherial sphere and carried around by it. Similarly, the stars (*stellae;* less commonly *astra*) that always remained at fixed intervals from each other were located on a single sphere. Not only was each planet assigned a single sphere, but *each motion* of the planet—daily motion, sidereal motion, motion in latitude, etc.—was also assigned its own orb. Thus although Ptolemy and Aristotle assumed that each planet was attached to a single sphere, both employed a plurality of spheres to account for the motion of each planet. By assigning one orb for each motion of a planet, both Aristotle and Ptolemy were compelled to assign multiple orbs to each planet. All told, Aristotle assigned as many as 55, while Ptolemy may have assigned as many as 41.

But there was a fundamental difference in the kinds of orbs they assigned. Aristotle's spheres were all concentric with respect to the earth, whereas Ptolemy's were basically eccentric and epicyclic. Shortly after these rival cosmologies entered Western Europe, sometime between 1160 and 1250, it became evident that Aristotle's concentric orbs could not account for observed variations in the distances of the planets and that Ptolemy's eccentrics and epicycles had been devised to cope with that problem.

Medieval natural philosophers accepted a compromise that retained both concentricity and eccentricity. It was a compromise that had already been made by Ptolemy in the latter's *Hypotheses of the Planets* and hinged on a distinction between the concept of a "total orb" (*orbis totalis*) and a "partial orb" (*orbis partialis*), to use medieval terminology. The "total orb" was a concentric orb whose center is the center of the earth, whereas a "partial orb" was an eccentric orb (sometimes called an "eccentric circle," *circulus eccentricus*), that is, an orb whose center is a geometric point lying outside the center of the world.

The concentric *orbis totalis,* the concave and convex surfaces of which have the earth's center as their center, is composed of at least three partial orbs, the middle of which, the eccentric deferent (*deferens eccentricus*), contains an epicyclic orb (*orbis epicyclus*) within which the actual planet is embedded. In this compromise "three-orb system," the concentric orbs of Aristotle were fused with the eccentric orbs of Ptolemy. In this system, two points of a planet's relationship to the earth were distinguished: the "aux" (*aux, augis*), which is the apogee of the planet or its farthest point from the earth; and the "opposite of the aux" (*oppositum augis*) or perigee, which represents the planet's least distance from the earth.

## Cosmology and Cosmography

Medieval natural philosophers followed Aristotle in dividing the world into two distinct domains: (1) a celestial region of fixed stars, planets, and orbs that was composed of a special ether or fifth element (*quinta essentia*) possessing special properties of indivisibility and unchangeability; and (2) a sublunar or terrestrial realm that commenced below the concave surface of the lunar orb and extended to the center of the earth. The four elements—earth (*terra*), water (*aqua*), air (*aer*), and fire (*ignis*)—and the bodies compounded of them were arranged in concentric spheres within this space, which, in stark contrast with the celestial region, was perceived as a region of continual change where things were always coming into being and passing away.

The Medieval Latin words that best describe what we understand by cosmos are *mundus, caelum,* and *universum,* all three of which were used interchangeably. (The Greek-derived terms *cosmos* and *cosmologia* were rarely used in the Middle Ages). The first, *mundus,* embraced heaven and earth and all that lay between. The second, *caelum,* was more limited in scope. In its narrowest signification, it could represent a single planetary sphere (as it does in the depiction of the world in the figure), but it could also signify the celestial region as a whole and was even occasionally used for subdivisions of the world that excluded only the earth. The third term, *universum,* was usually synonymous with *mundus.* Pierre d'Ailly (d. 1420) reported that *universum* could be taken as the totality of celestial bodies, but also allowed that it could embrace "the aggregate of celestial bodies, the intelligences that are applied to them, all the mixed bodies and the four elements contained under the moon" ([ED2] fol. 147v), insofar as these elements and mixed bodies are ruled or governed by the motions of the celestial bodies.

A typical representation of the medieval cosmos has been reproduced from Peter Apian's *Cosmographicus liber* (1524). What we see at first glance is a series of nested spheres or orbs. The terms *spera* and *orbis* were usually used interchangeably, although d'Ailly observed that strictly speaking "'orbicular' and 'spherical' differ because orbicular [is a figure that] ought to be contained by two surfaces, namely concave and convex; the heaven is this way. Spherical, however, ought to be contained by a single surface, namely by a convex [surface] only" ([ED2] fol. 153r). In this simplified version of the cosmos, eccentric and epicyclic orbs are omitted and the planetary orbs are represented as simple concentric orbs with the earth as center. At the center of the world lies a combination of earth and water, surrounded by a circle of air, which is, in turn, encompassed by the sphere of fire. Beyond these terrestrial elements lie the seven planetary spheres, where each planetary orb is itself a distinct *coelum* or heaven, as in *coelum Mercurii.* The eighth orb or heaven (*octavum coelum*) is the *firmamentum* of the fixed stars, which was perhaps its most popular signification. But some, such as Robert Grosseteste (d. 1253) and Giles of Rome (d. 1316), thought of *firmamentum* as a vast single orb embracing the entire celestial region from the moon to the fixed stars.

The ninth heaven was frequently called the crystalline heaven (*nonum coelum et cristallinum*) and was usually identified with the biblical waters above the firmament. For some, however, those waters were conceived as solid and hard—hence crystalline—whereas others considered them fluid. The tenth heaven (*decimum coelum*) was usually called the *primum mobile* or "first movable sphere," because it was the first orb that moved with a natural circular motion. The *primum mobile* was responsible for the daily motion of the fixed stars and planets. Finally, the outermost sphere of the world is the *coelum empyreum* or empyrean heaven, an immobile sphere that enclosed the world and was "the dwelling place of God and all the elect" (see fig.), that is, the dwelling place of God and the angels, as well as the abode of the blessed. It was a region of pure light.

A major problem was to explain the cause of motion of the celestial orbs. The ultimate mover of all orbs was the "Prime Mover" (*primus motor* or *primum movens*), none other than God, who could achieve this effect either directly or through a secondary cause. He could have assigned motion as part of the innate nature of the celestial orbs that had forms that enabled them to move; or, as some assumed, He might have impressed a force (*impetus*) into each orb, a force that was essentially in-

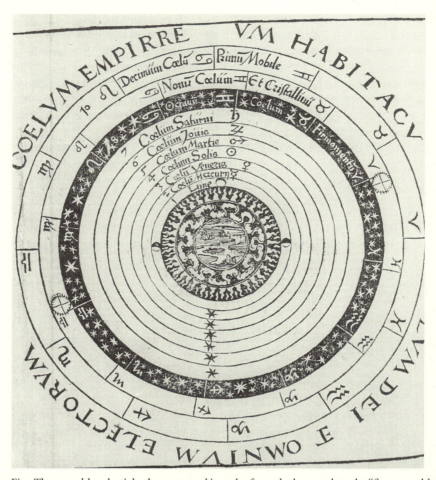

Fig.: The movable celestial spheres ranged in order from the lunar orb to the "first movable heaven" (*primum mobile*). Encompassing the whole is the immobile empyrean heaven, "dwelling place of God and all the elect." From Peter Apian, *Cosmographicus liber* (1524), col. 6. Reproduced by courtesy of the Lilly Library, Indiana University, Bloomington, Indiana.

corruptible and therefore constant, so that each orb would move with a constant speed ([ED4] fols. 120v, col. 2–121r, col. 1 [bk. 8, qu. 12]; [ED12] p536). The most popular interpretation was that God had chosen to employ an external motive power by assigning a motive intelligence (*intelligentia*) or angel (*angelus*) to each sphere. With a few major exceptions, intelligences and angels were assumed to be identical and the terms were used interchangeably. To cause the motion of the orb to which it was assigned, an intelligence exercised its will to activate a motive force (*virtus motiva* or simply *virtus*) within itself. Thus it was not an impressed force or *impetus*. The *virtus* was often described as an "executive power" or "executive force" (*potentia executiva*).

The constantly turning celestial orbs were thought to cause all manner of changes on and within the earth. Durand of St. Pourçain (d. 1334) argued further that God had even conferred on each orb a power analogous to a seed (*semen*). Although Durand believed that a seed was not itself alive, he inferred that it could produce a living thing because it was derived from a living thing. Similarly, a heaven or orb is not alive, yet God confers upon it the power to produce life, a power that Durand called *virtus generativa rerum viventium* ([ED7] fol. 157v, col. 1, par. 7 [bk. 2, dist. 15, qu. 1]).

## Select Bibliography

### Texts

There are no published glossaries of Medieval Latin astronomical and/or cosmological terms. Relevant terms do appear, however, in modern editions. These are indicated in certain studies cited below. See also [ED15–17].

Anonymous, *Theorica planetarum,* tr. O. Pedersen, in *SBMS* 452–65: this treatise is actually a compilation of definitions of technical astronomical terms. The translation was made from Copenhagen, Royal Library, MS Latin Add. 447, 2°, 49r–56r [ED1].

Pierre d'Ailly, *XIV Quaestiones,* in *Spherae tractatus Ioannis de Sacro Busto Anglici viri clariss.; Gerardi Cremonensis Theoricae planetarum veteres; Georgii Purbachii Theoricae planetarum novae; . . . Petri Cardin. de Aliaco episcopi Camaracensis 14 Quaestiones* (Venice 1531) [ED2].

Bartholomaeus Anglicus, *De proprietatibus rerum* (Frankfurt 1601, r1964): a thirteenth-century encyclopedia that includes many definitions of astronomical and cosmological terms [ED3].

John Buridan, *Questiones super octo Phisicorum libros Aristotelis diligenter recognite et revise a Magistro Johanne Dullaert de Gandavo* (Paris 1509): repr. in facsimile with the title *Kommentar zur Aristotelischen Physik* (1964) [ED4].

John Buridan, *Quaestiones super libris quattuor De caelo et mundo,* ed. E.A. Moody (1942, r1970) [ED5].

Campanus of Novara, *Theorica planetarum,* ed. and tr. F.S. Benjamin, Jr., and G.J. Toomer (1971): includes most of the relevant astronomical terminology [ED6].

Durand of St. Pourçain, *In Petri Lombardi Sententias theologicas commentariorum libri IIII* (Venice 1571) [ED7].

Robert Kilwardby, *De ortu scientiarum,* ed. A.G. Judy (1976) [ED8].

John of Sacrobosco, *"The Sphere" of Sacrobosco and Its Commentators,* ed. and tr. L. Thorndike (1949) [ED9].

G. Federici-Vescovini, ed., *Il "Lucidator dubitabilium astronomiae" di Pietro d'Abano. Opere scientifiche inedite* (1988): see the "index rerum notabilium" [ED10].

### Studies

A. Le Boeuffle, *Les noms latins d'astres et de constellations* (1977) [ED11].

M. Clagett, *The Science of Mechanics in the Middle Ages* (1959) [ED12].

E. Grant, "Cosmology," in *SMA* 265–302 [ED13].

E. Grant, *Planets, Stars, and Orbs: The Medieval Cosmos, 1200–1687* (1994) [ED14].

P. Kunitzsch, "Mittelalterliche astronomisch-astrologische Glossare mit arabischen Fachausdrücken," Bayerische Ak. der Wiss., philosophisch-historische Klasse, Sitz., Jahrgang 1977, Heft 5 (1977) [ED15].

R. Lorch, "Astronomical Terminology," in *CIVICIMA* 3:182–96 [ED16].

E. Poulle, "Le vocabulaire de l'astronomie planétaire du XIIe au XIVe siècle," in *La diffusione delle scienze islamiche nel medio evo europea* (1987) 193–212: with list of sources on pp210–12 [ED17].

N. Schneider, *Die Kosmologie des Franciscus de Marchia: Texte, Quellen und Untersuchungen zur Naturphilosophie des 14. Jahrhunderts* (1991) [ED18].

N. Steneck, *Science and Creation in the Middle Ages: Henry of Langenstein (d. 1397) on Genesis* (1976) [ED19].

*See also* [BA125].

# EE ❋ ASTROLOGY

BY CHARLES BURNETT*

## Introduction

Although the Latin terms for "astrology" (*astrologia*) and "astronomy" (*astronomia*) were often interchanged in the Middle Ages, medieval authors commonly distinguished the subject matter of the two sciences. Astronomy was the mathematical science that measured the position and the movements of the celestial bodies. Astrology was more akin to a physical science; it predicated that public and personal events on earth, as well as human characters and dispositions, were caused, influenced, or indicated (the usual term is *significata*) by the movements of the fixed stars and planets. Western astrology as we know it probably arose in Ptolemaic Egypt in the second century B.C.; it became popular in Hellenistic Greece and Rome, where it found support in Aristotelian and Stoic world systems. Claudius Ptolemaeus (second century A.D.) in his *Apotelesmatika* (also known as the *Tetrabiblos* or *Quadripartitum* from the fact that it contains four books) helped to establish astrology on a philosophical base, dealing with general astrology and nativities. Ptolemy understood that the character of a person and the course of his life could be inferred from the configuration of the heavens when that life "started" (i.e. at birth or, better, at conception). But other Greek astrologers—in particular, Dorotheus of Sidon (first century A.D.)—considered that a horoscope could be cast for the beginning of *any* activity and hence established "catarchic" astrology (from Greek *katarchein,* "to begin").

As a branch of scientific learning astrology was transmitted with Greek science to the Arabs, where it was blended with important contributions from Persian, Indian, and native Islamic sources to form the intricate science bequeathed by the Arabs to Western Europe. The transmission of astrological texts and their specialized terminology in the Latin West may, therefore, be divided into two stages, the first from classical and late antiquity into the early medieval period, the second from the time of the translations of Arabic texts.

(a) **Antiquity to the Early Medieval Period.** The names of stars and constellations were transmitted in the translations of the *Phaenomena* of Aratus (d. 240/39

*I am grateful for the help of Silke Ackermann, Luc Deitz, Danielle Jacquart, Peter Kingsley, David Pingree, Graeme Tobyn, Clare Woods, and Sylvia Wright.

B.C.), by Cicero, Germanicus Caesar, and Avienus, and in the *Astronomica* of Hyginus. Two Latin textbooks on astrology date from the classical period—Marcus Manilius's *Astronomica* (first century A.D.) and Julius Firmicus Maternus's *Mathesis* (A.D. 334–37). The existence of Manilius's work was known to Gerbert of Aurillac in 983 and at least two copies were made in the eleventh century; but then it appears to have been neglected until Poggio Bracciolini rediscovered a copy in 1417. Three copies of Firmicus's text are known from the eleventh century, and several French and English writers of the following century knew the work; but among astrologers it was replaced by the new Arabic-Latin translations. Specifically astrological doctrine can be found in several Latin works that had a wide diffusion: e.g., the *De architectura* of Vitruvius (first century B.C.; see bk. 9), the anonymous *Epitome disciplinarum* (before A.D. 19), the *Naturales Quaestiones* of Seneca (d. A.D. 65; see 2.32.6–8, 7.3.2–4.1 and 28.1), the *Pharsalia* of Lucan (d. A.D. 65), the second book of the *Naturalis historia* of Pliny the Elder (d. A.D. 79), the *De die natali* of Censorinus (A.D. 238/39), the commentary on Virgil by Servius (fourth century; e.g., *ad Aeneidem* 1.314), the partial translation of and commentary on Plato's *Timaeus* by Calcidius (late fourth century), the *De nuptiis Mercurii et Philologiae* of Martianus Capella (410–39), and, especially, the commentary on Cicero's *Somnium Scipionis* by Macrobius (c. 430; see 1.21–6). Astrological terms, from these and other, lost, sources, are quoted by early Christian writers in their criticisms of astrology, such as Augustine (d. 430; *De civitate dei* 5.1–9; *Ep.* 55), the Pseudo-Clement (see Rufinus's early fifth-century translation of his *Recognitiones*, 9.17), Gregory the Great (d. 604; *Homilia in Evangelia* 1.10), Caesarius of Arles (d. 543; *Sermones* 18, 59), Isidore of Seville (d. 636; *Etymologiae* 3.71.38–39), and Bede (*De temporum ratione* [written in 725] 3). Other early medieval works, however, use the same sources, while adopting a neutral or even approving attitude towards astrology: e.g., Pseudo-Bede's *De mundi celestis terrestrisque constitutione* (late eleventh to early twelfth century), which enthusiastically takes up the horoscopes rejected by Pseudo-Clement. Meanwhile astrology at a more popular (nonscientific) level is witnessed by several *lunaria* (i.e. predictions or recommended activities for each day of the moon; [EE48–49]), *zodiologia* (ditto, according to the sign of the zodiac the moon is in; [EE49]), *herbals* (advice on collecting herbs at astrologically appropriate times), *parapēgmata* (the correlation of the rising and setting of the fixed stars with the weather and certain seasonal activities through the civil year [EE65]), and texts such as the *Letter of Petosiris to Nechepso* and the *Sphere of Pythagoras*, which might already have existed in Latin in late antiquity [EE65].

The standard text for the definition of astrology in this first period was Isidore's *Etymologiae* (3.27), where *astronomia* as a mathematical science is distinguished from *astrologia*, which Isidore subdivides into natural (*naturalis*) and superstitious (*superstitiosa*) parts. What Isidore appears to mean by the natural part is that which observes the influences of the course of the sun (the seasons), the moon (the tides, etc.), and certain stages in the courses of the planets. The superstitious part is that practiced by astrologers (*mathematici*), who make predictions from the planets, dispose the 12 signs of the zodiac around the human body, and try to predict the births and characters of men and women from the course of the stars.

(b) **The Translation of Arabic Texts.** The period of Arabic influence begins in the late tenth or early eleventh century with the insertion of Arabic and Jewish material into a corpus of native popular astrology in the *Liber* or *Mathematica Alchandrei* and the *Proportiones competentes in astrorum industria* ([EE62], [EE95]). The bulk of Arabic astrological texts known in Europe was translated in the first half of the twelfth century by Adelard of Bath in Sicily and England and by John of Seville (Johannes Hispalensis et Limiensis), Hermann of Carinthia, Robert of Ketton, Plato of Tivoli, and Hugo of Santalla in Spain. A few more works were added in the thirteenth century by Salio of Padua in Spain; by those who produced for Alfonso X, king of Castile and León (1256–84), translations of the popular *De iudiciis astrorum* of Albohazen Hali filius Abenragel and the guide to magic, *Picatrix*, both from Arabic into Castilian and from Castilian into Latin; and by Pietro d'Abano, who translated Abraham ibn Ezra's astrological writings (originally written in Hebrew) in 1293.

Although the *Quadripartitum* of Ptolemy was respected as the ancient fount of this astrology and was translated from Arabic by Plato of Tivoli in 1138, it was the works of Arabic authors themselves that proved to be the more popular. These included Albumasar's magisterial *Great Introduction to Astrology* (translated twice); more succinct introductions by Alcabitius, Alkindi, and Albumasar himself; convenient textbooks for all the branches of astrology by Zahel; handy astrological tips attributed to Ptolemy but probably originally composed in Arabic (the *Centiloquium*); and more detailed works on specialized topics such as conjunctions and anniversary horoscopes (both by Albumasar), on general astrology and elections (Messahala), on nativities (Albubater), on interrogations (Aomar Alfraganus Tiberiadis), and on astrological weather forecasting (Alkindi and "Jafar"). By early in the second half of the twelfth century it was possible to put together a compendium from nine Arabic authorities giving a thorough introduction to astrology and a complete guide to interrogations, elections, and astrological weather forecasting (the *Liber novem iudicum*).

Before the middle of the twelfth century Latin authors were starting to write their own books on astrology, and we can trace a continuous tradition from John of Seville's *Epitome totius astrologie* (1142) and Raymond of Marseilles's *Liber iudiciorum* (1141) to Eudes of Champagne's *Libellus de efficatia artis astrologice* and Roger of Hereford's *Liber de quattuor partibus astronomie* (both late twelfth century and dependent on Raymond). The thirteenth and fourteenth centuries were the period of *summae* of astrology, some of which reached massive proportions. These included Michael Scot's *Liber introductorius* (before 1236), Guido Bonatti's *Liber astronomicus* and Leopold of Austria's *Compilacio de scientia astrorum* (both late thirteenth century), Bartholomew of Parma's *Breviloquium* (1286), and John of Ashenden's *Summa astrologiae de accidentibus mundi* (mid-fourteenth century). Meanwhile the astrological vocabulary of the translations and original Latin texts appears in works that criticize astrology: the *Dragmaticon* of William of Conches (c. 1144); the *Chronicon* of Hélinand of Froidmont (early thirteenth century), which is the source of our knowledge of Eudes of Champagne; Gerard of Feltre's *Summa de astris* (1264); Nicole Oresme's *Tractatus contra iudiciarios astronomos* (before 1364); and Pico della Mirandola's *Disputationes adversus astrologiam divinatricem* (1493–96). Astrological vocabulary and concepts were also used symbolically or allegorically, for example, in the history of Bologna included in John of Legnano's *Tractatus de bello, de represaliis et de duello* (1360).

In the mid-thirteenth century, Albertus Magnus (d. 1280) wrote his *Speculum astronomiae,* whose aim was to sort out the acceptable books on the science of the stars from those that should be rejected. He goes through each of the branches of astrology, first describing its subject matter and giving a list of the Latin works devoted to that subject, then examining the cogency and acceptability of the branch. The *Speculum astronomiae* marks the stage at which the translations from Arabic had been fully assimilated into the Latin-reading world and a common astrological vocabulary had become established. As such it provides a convenient starting point for the investigation of the terms used in astrology.

## Vocabulary and Syntax

In this section terms are usually given in the singular; when several terms exist for one concept, those already used in the first, pre-Arabic, period precede a colon, whereas those introduced in the second period follow it. An absence of a colon indicates that the terms are common to both periods; an asterisk before a colon indicates the lack of an equivalent term from the early period. Terms that became standard in thirteenth-century astrology are capitalized. The list of terms is not exhaustive.

First, it should be noted that the distinction between the terms *astronomia* and *astrologia* made by Isidore in his *Etymologiae* was by no means universally accepted. Dominicus Gundissalinus, for example, quotes Isidore's definitions but reverses the terms, and Raymond of Marseilles states that the words are interchangeable. Albertus calls both mathematical astronomy and astrology *astronomia,* but gives, as a special term for astrology, a literal translation of the Arabic designation: *scientia iudiciorum astrorum.* This phrase and its variants (*scientia iudiciaria, iudicia, ars iudicialis,* etc.) occur frequently—for example, in titles of introductions to astrology. The classical term "Chaldaica ars" and its variants die out, except in nonastrological sources.

Introductions to astrology discuss the zodiac (*circulus signorum*, ORBIS SIGNO-RUM, *signifer* [*circulus*], *zodiacus*: *circulus*), a belt or zone along the middle of which is the ecliptic (ORBIS SOLIS, *ecliptica*), the apparent path of the sun around the earth. The zodiac is divided into 12 equal parts called signs (SIGNUM: *turris, borg*), each of 30 degrees (*pars*: GRADUS). These signs are named after the constellations that were once (second century B.C.) present in them, but that, with the precession of the equinoxes (i.e. the slow west-east movement of the vernal point with respect to the fixed stars), have shifted over time, so that the fictive zodiac of the astrologers is different from the real zodiac. The signs are further divided into decans or faces (*decani*: FACIES) of 10 degrees each, into ninth parts or "navāṃśas" ( * : NOVENA, *novenarium, elnowarat* [pl.], *neuhahar*), and twelfth parts or dodecatemoria (*dodecatemorion*), all of equal length, and terms (FINIS: *terminus*), of which there is one for each of the five planets, but of varying length. The signs are classified according to the elements, the seasons, the ages of man, the sexes, and so on, but the primary astrological classification is into signs that are cardinal (*conversivum, tropicum*: MOBILE), fixed (*solidum*: *firmum*, FIXUM, *stabile*), and mutable (*biforme, duplex*: COMMUNE, *bicorpor, bipertitum*). The signs are the houses (*domicilium*, DOMUS: *hospitium*) of the planets, which are the signs' lords or rulers (*dominus*); the opposite signs are the detriments ( * : *alienatio*, DETRIMENTUM) of the planets. Moreover, a planet may be in the sign of its exaltation (*altitudo*: *regnum*, EXALTATIO) or of its fall or dejection (*deiectio, humilitas*: *descensio*, CASUS, *servitus*), which is the degree 180 degrees from the exaltation. Every fourth sign shares the same elemental character, and signs in this relationship are called a triplicity (*trigonum* : TRIPLICITAS, *trigonalitas, ternarius*).

Superimposed on the zodiacal division is the division of the ecliptic in respect to where it cuts the horizon and the meridian at the significant time. This is usually— and confusingly—called the division of houses, since the Latin writers of the second stage, following the Arabs, used the word *house* (DOMUS and *domicilium,* but also *turris*) in this context for the Greek term *topos* ( = *locus* in the first period of Latin astrological writings). The astrological chart (*genesis, genitura, thema, constellatio, figura*) is set up using these 12 places as its frame. Although there are several ways in which this division can be made (see [EE83]), the most commonly used methods take their starting point from the degree where the ecliptic cuts the horizon, i.e. the ascendant (*horoscopus, ortus* : *oriens,* ASCENDENS). From this point the 12 places are counted off in the order of ascending degrees of the zodiac, so that the beginning or cusp of the fourth place is the nadir or *IC* (IMUM CELUM : *nadair*), that of the seventh place is the setting point or descendant (*occasus* : *occidens*), and that of the tenth place is the midheaven or *MC* (MEDIUM CELUS, *medium celi, centrum mundi*). The first, fourth, seventh, and tenth places are the angular houses or cardines (*centrum* : ANGULUS, CARDO); the second, fifth, eighth, and eleventh are succedents (*anafora* : SUCCEDENS [ANGULORUM]); the third, sixth, ninth, and twelfth are cadents (*catafora* : CADENS [AB ANGULIS]). The places are associated with different aspects of the life of the individual, and hence are also named after these aspects: I life (*vita*); II possessions, money (*substantia, pecunia*); III brothers (*fratres*); IV parents (*patres*); V children (*filii*); VI illnesses (*infirmitates, morbi*); VII wife, women (*uxor, mulieres*); VIII death (*mors*); IX religion and travel (*fides, iter*); X honors (*honores*); XI hope and friends (*spes, amici*); and XII domestic and riding animals and enemies (*animalia, inimici*). On an astrological chart (see the figure, for example), the degree and sign of the ascendant and (often) of the cusps of other astrological places are indicated, and the planets with their degrees and signs are shown within the places.

The planets (STELLA, *planetes,* PLANETA) are classified according to their natural properties—masculine or feminine; benefic (*bonus, prosper, saluber, salutaris, benivolus* : FORTUNA) or malefic (*malus, malivolus, malignus* : INFORTUNA, *infortunium*); diurnal or nocturnal; hot, cold, dry, or moist; etc.—and according to their position and their relation to other planets. The points where the moon's orbit crosses the ecliptic—i.e. the north or ascending node (*draco,* CAPUT [DRACONUS]) and the south or descending node (*cauda* [*draconis*])—are also considered to function like planets. The astrological judgment is made from the planet's position in respect to another planet: these include the relations of aspect (ASPECTUS : *respectus*), when the number of signs that separate planets are considered—this may be trine (*triquetrum, tricetum,* TRIGONUM : *trigonalis, trinus*), square (*quadricetum, tetragonum,* QUADRATUM : *tetragonalis*), sextile (*exagonum* : SEXTILIS, *exagonalis*), opposition (*diametrum, adversus, contrarium* : OPPOSITIO, *oppositus*), or conjunction (*conventus,* CONIUNCTIO : *alistima*); or of application (APPLICATIO : *alitisal*), when one planet is decreasing the number of degrees between itself and another planet. Further judgments are made according to the strength of the planets, which depends on the number of dignities (\* : *dignitas, fortitudo*) they have, i.e. whether they are in houses, triplicities, decans, ninth parts, twelfth parts, or terms, of which they are lords, or in the signs of their exaltations. They may also be received (\* : *receptus*) when they are in positions in which other planets have dignities. In any as-

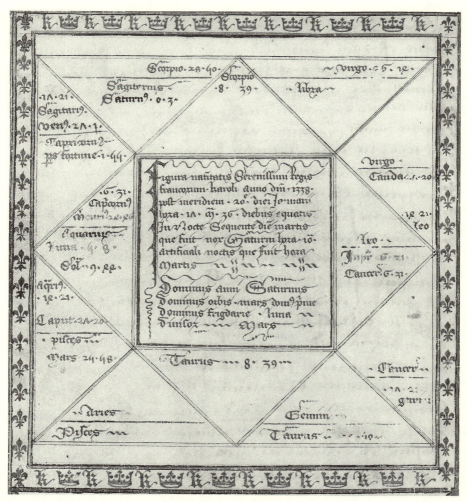

Fig.: Horoscope (*figura*) of Charles V, king of France (1364–80). The triangles indicate the 12 places, counted in a counterclockwise direction from left center. The boundaries of the zodiacal signs are indicated by horizontal lines. The degrees and minutes in the signs of the planets are given, as are those of the north and south nodes (*caput*, *cauda*), the part of fortune (*pars fortune*), and the beginning of each place. The central cartouche records Charles's "astronomical" time of birth (= Wednesday, 21 January 1338, at 5:36 a.m.) and the various lordships of the planets (including that of the "frigdaria," i.e. *firdaria*). From Oxford, St. John's College, MS 164, fol. 158v. Reproduced by kind permission of the President and Fellows of St. John Baptist College, Oxford.

trological chart the planet that has the most dignities is called the *almuten* ( * : *al-mutaz, almu[b]tez, almutes id est victor* [Arabic *al-mubtazz*], SIGNIFICATOR). Moreover, planets are in their joys (*gaudium*) when they are in specific places (e.g., the moon is in her joy in the third place).

Particularly important is a planet's relationship to the sun. If it is within 17 minutes of the sun it is "cazimi" or in the heart ( * : *zamimi, zamin*), within 8½ degrees it is burnt (*adustus*, COMBUSTUS), within 17 degrees it is under sunbeams (*sub radiis*). The moon also has decisive effects, which can be hindered by any one of 11 corruptions (*damnum* : *infortunium*, IMPEDIMENTUM). Furthermore, the degrees between planets (or other significant points) are added (usually) to the ascendant to reveal the place of the parts or lots (*sors* : PARS, *cehem*), the most commonly used being the part of fortune (*locus fortune* : PARS FORTUNE, *cehem prosperitatis, zahmazada*), which is obtained by adding the number of degrees between the sun and the moon by day (and the reverse by night) to the ascendant.

If astrologers wish to draw up a chart for the present moment they may use an astrolabe (or other timepiece) trained on the sun (by day) or on a conspicuous star (by night) and ascertain the precise time. Otherwise they may wish to draw up a chart for a predetermined time. In any case they represent the 12 places and indicate the positions, in terms of signs and degrees, of the ascendant, the planets, and the lunar nodes in these places by consulting astronomical tables. They are then ready to deal with the different branches of astrology.

The first of these, according to Albertus Magnus, is general astrology (*de revolutionibus*), which pertains to whole nations and regions. This is divided into three parts: (1) conjunctions (*coniunctiones*), by which significant events happen when planets—in particular Saturn and Jupiter—are in conjunction; (2) revolutions of the years of the world (*revolutiones annorum mundi*), in which the events of the year are predicted from the planet that is most important in the astrological chart when the sun enters the first minute of Aries—this planet being the lord of the year (*dominus anni*); (3) astrometeorology, by which the weather can be forecast. Texts on the last subject are called "about rain" (*de imbribus, de pluviis*) or "on changes of weather" (*de mutationibus temporum*) and preserve a division of the zodiac into 28 parts according to the course of the moon (these are the lunar mansions: *astra*/MANSIONES *lune*).

Next comes genethlialogy or nativities (*nativitates* : *genezia*), by which birth charts are drawn up and the course of life of the newborn child—or native (*natus*)—is predicted. One must determine the "hyleg" or "prorogator" (*dator vite* : *hileg, hylech, yleg* [Arabic *haylāj*], *dominus/significator vite*), which is a point on the ecliptic worked out by complicated means, and the planet with the most dignities in this point, which is called the lord of the house (*dominus geniture* : *alc[h]ochoden, altothoden*—Arabic *al-kadhkhudah*). The combined evidence of these two gives the length beyond which the life of the native cannot naturally extend, as well as indicating diseases and hardships in the course of the life. The events in different areas of the native's life can be discovered from looking at the situation of the planets in regard to the 12 places. Moreover, each planet as chronocrator rules over a certain number of years of the native's life; these are called the planet's "firdaria" ( * : *afraadet* [pl.], *alfardaria, alfirdariech, alfridaria,* FIRDARIA [Arabic *fardār*]). It was a common practice to cast a horoscope when the sun returned to the same degree of the zodiac where it was at the time of birth, and to compare it to the astrological chart of the birth (*radix*). This subbranch of genethlialogy is called solar returns or anniversary horoscopes (*revolutiones nativitatum*).

Albertus next deals with interrogations (*interrogationes*), in which the astrological chart of the moment when the question is posed determines the outcome of what is asked. In this case the state of mind of the inquirer—the radical intent (*intentio radicalis*)—is important. This branch of astrology is often confused (in medieval and modern sources) with "catarchic" astrology, Albertus's next division, in which the best time for beginning an activity is determined. There is no evidence that interrogational astrology was known in classical times; it seems to have been an Indian invention that achieved great popularity amongst Islamic astrologers.

The Medieval Latin term for catarchic astrology is *electiones* or *electiones horarum laudabilium*. In both interrogations and elections we find the first place assigned to the querent (*querens*) and the seventh to the thing asked about (*quesitum*), and the relationship of this chart to the birth chart (*radix*) can also be considered. Interrogational and electional chapters often occur together in works loosely entitled *iudicia*.

The last branch is that of making astrological talismans (*imagines, prestigia*), which is often accompanied by fumigation (*suffumigatio*), the invocation of angels or demons (*angeli, demones, spiritus*), and the inscription of magical signs (*characteres*).

Albertus omits medical astrology, which has a tradition of its own, involving the assignation of the different parts of the body to the different signs of the zodiac (as mentioned by Isidore) and the "openings" of the body to the planets. This was particularly relevant in bloodletting (*flebotomia*) and surgery (*cirurgia*) and in determining the days when crises occur in an illness (*dies cretici*).

Each of the two periods outlined above made its own contribution to the vocabulary and syntax of astrological Latin. In the first period many terms were transliterations of, or calques on, Greek terms. This applies even to the common term for "astrologers"—*mathematici*—which gave way to *astrologi* as the practitioners' preferred designation in the later period. Firmicus gives many Greek terms alongside Latin translations—such as *aporroicus, cenodromos, oecodespotes*, and *schema*. In the *Proportiones competentes* astrology is dressed up in highly artificial— often Greek—language: e.g., *onoma* for name, *xela* for the claws (of Scorpio, i.e. Libra), *limpha* for water, *lar* for fire, and the Greek names for the planets. The vocabulary of the first period continues to be used in literary sources throughout the Middle Ages, e.g., in the *Mathematicus* of Bernard Silvester and in John of Salisbury's *Policraticus* (see 2.19), and was favored again by Renaissance humanists wishing to use only Greek texts and translations.

The main criterion in assessing the language of the texts of the second period is the fact that these texts are to an overwhelming extent translations of Arabic texts, or derived from these translations.

The translators experimented with a variety of styles. Adelard of Bath, Hermann of Carinthia, and Robert of Ketton adopted a succinct style in which they sacrificed accuracy for latinity. Hugo of Santalla's style is florid, and he likes to vary the translation of recurring Arabic terms and constructions, for rhetorical effect, in a way that is hardly appropriate for an astrological manual. He is probably responsible for imposing a uniform florid style on all the texts in the *Liber novem iudicum,* the obscurity and inappropriateness of whose language were commented on by Robert Godefroye when he translated it (1359–62) into French for Charles V [EE90]. The literal style of translation was adopted by John of Seville, who was responsible for the largest number of translations and thus had the greatest influence on the style of later astrologers. It was perfected by Gerard of Cremona, who may have revised translations by John [EE86]. Since most of the translations were made in Spain, and some texts were transmitted via a Castilian version, the influence of the Spanish vernacular is sometimes apparent (as is pointed out by Antonius Stupa in his preface to Albohazen [EE3]), but Arabic influence is more dominant.

At the level of vocabulary, a large number of Arabic terms were retained by the translators. The following characteristics of these transliterations may be observed:

The Arabic definite article is often retained as a part of the noun that follows it ("al-"; but "el-" in translations of the circle of Adelard of Bath). Sometimes this "al-" intrudes into words that did not have such an article in Arabic, in Albumasar (for Abū Maʿshar) and Albubater (for Abū Bakr). Arabic transcriptions are usually undeclined. Sometimes, however, the Arabic sound feminine plural ("āt") is preserved; at other times the Arabic term is declined like a Latin noun. Note, for example, that for the Arabic *al-fardār(iyya)* Adelard of Bath preserves a plural form, *afraadet,* as does John of Seville (*alfirdariech*), while Hugo of Santalla transcribes the term as *al-fardaria* (*alphardaria*) and declines it fully as a first declension Latin noun. Other naturalized words are *aux/augis, telesmaticus,* and *cifra/cifre* (but also *sifre,* undeclined).

When the Arabic term is not transliterated, a Latin calque may be substituted, such as *turris* for sign of the zodiac (since *burj* in Arabic means both "tower" and "sign of the zodiac") and *differentia* for "chapter" (Arabic *faṣl* = "separation," but also "section," "chapter"). The structure of Semitic languages is particularly well suited to indicating different parts of speech and different nuances of the same concept by adding or inserting particular letters or syllables to the root expressing that concept. Occasionally this appears to be happening in the Latin translation. When, for example, Adelard writes *natura* and *connaturalis,* he is representing the relationship between Arabic *ṭabīʿa* ("nature") and *muṭabbaʿ* ("of similar nature"), and *figura* and *configuratio* represent Arabic *shakl* ("form") and *mushākala* ("similarity"). Hermann of Carinthia likes to substitute a Greek-looking word for an Arabic word, e.g., *telesmatici* for Arabic *aṣḥāb aṭ-ṭilasmāt* and *genezia* (used also by Hugo of Santalla) for nativities [EE61].

A literal translation is bound to reflect Arabic syntax, and arabisms are especially likely to occur in the context of Arabic terms. For example, *almuten* is regularly followed by *super* rather than the genitive, reflecting the Arabic construction *al-mubtazz ʿalā* ("the almuten of") ([EE77] p38). Similarly the supposed activity of the heavenly bodies over earthly things is described in Arabic as *dalla ʿalā,* which is rendered literally by John of Seville as *significat super.* (Hermann of Carinthia would use the more Latinate *ducere* with a direct object.)

A common way of expressing "every X" in Arabic is to say "every X of (*min*) the X's," which in Latin gives "in omni individuo ex individuis." *Min,* with a partitive meaning, is very common in Arabic and regularly rendered by *ex* or *de.* The usual way of expressing possession in Arabic is to write "there is a Y to X," of which an example is "fuit significatio huic signo" (= "this sign had a signification"). Finally, a sequence of sentences in paratactic structure (joined by *et* and without subordination) reflects the style of Arabic astrological texts. It must be noted, however, that paratactic structure is appropriate to the subject matter of astrology, which often can be set forth in the form of sequences of combinations of planets, of planets and signs of the zodiac, of planets in the astrological places, etc. The obfuscating effect of subordinating phrases that are paratactic in the original Arabic can be seen from the translations of Adelard of Bath and Robert of Ketton.

The subject matter also, to a great extent, determines the larger structures of Arabic works on astrology, and these too left their mark on Latin astrological texts. Each book (*tractatus, liber* [Arabic *maqāla*]) is divided into several chapters (*differentia, capitulum, porta* [Arabic *faṣl, bāb*]); the titles of all the books and their chapters are given at the beginning of the text, and the titles of all the chapters are repeated at the beginning of each book. This clear definition of the subject matter is followed in the Latin translations, thereby helping to establish the format of the scientific book in the West.

The bulk of astrological literature is derived from earlier texts. Astrological authors are cautiously innovative, and the history of Latin astrological literature after the period of translations is that of increasingly comprehensive compilations drawn from earlier works. The Latin style of the translations is therefore reflected in later, original, texts. Thus Guido Bonatti begins his *Liber astronomicus* with a Christian equivalent of the pious invocation that opens every Islamic book (and is preserved in the literal translations of John of Seville): "In nomine Dei nostri Ihesu Christi miseratoris et pii veri dei et veri hominis. . . ." Only with the humanistic movement of the late fifteenth and early sixteenth century is an attempt made to purge the old texts of their "barbaric" language, a policy expounded at greatest length by Antonius Stupa in the preface to his revision of the late thirteenth-century Latin translation of Albohazen's *Libri de iudiciis astrorum.* Stupa claimed to have "rescued" this work "from extreme barbarity and restored it to good Latin" ("de extrema barbarie vindicati ac Latinitati donati" [EE3]).

## Select Bibliography

### Primary Works

Abraham ibn Ezra, *Abrahe Avenaris Judei . . . in re iudiciali opera, ab excellentissimo philosopho Petro de Abano post accuratam castigationem in Latinum traducta* (Venice 1507) [EE1].

Albertus Magnus, *Speculum astronomiae,* ed. S. Caroti *et al.* (1977): with apparatus of variant readings and glossary (pp197–206); see [EE99] [EE2].

Albohazen Haly filii Abenragel [Abū l-Ḥasan ʿAli b. Abī r-Rijāl], *Libri de iudiciis astrorum,* ed. A. Stupa (Basel 1551) [EE3].

Albubater [Abu Bakr], *Liber genethliacus sive de nativitatibus* (Nuremberg 1540) [EE4].

Albumasar [Abū Maʿshar], *Introductorium maius in astronomiam* (Augsburg 1489): Latin translation of Hermann of Carinthia (1140), ed. J. Engel; editions of Latin translations of John of Seville, Gerard of Cremona, and Hermann of Carinthia, prepared by R. Lemay, are forthcoming from the Istituto Universitario Orientale (Naples) [EE5].

Albumasar, *Liber de magnis coniunctionibus* (Augsburg 1489, repr. Venice 1515): Latin translation of John of Seville [EE6]. For citations from this work concerning comets see *Latin Treatises on Comets Between 1238 and 1368 A.D.,* ed. L. Thorndike (1950), s.v. "Albumasar" as indexed [EE7].

Albumasar, *Flores astrologiae* (Augsburg 1488): Latin translation of John of Seville [EE8].

Albumasar, *The Abbreviation of The Introduction to Astrology, Together with the Medieval Latin Translation of Adelard of Bath,* ed. and tr. C. Burnett, K. Yamamoto, and M. Yano (1994): with English-Arabic-Latin glossary, pp152–59 [EE9].

Alcabitius [al-Qabīsī], *Ad magisterium iudiciorum astrorum isagoge, commentario Ioannis Saxonij declarata* (Paris 1521) [EE10].

Alfarabi [al-Fārābī], *Catálogo de las ciencias,* ed. A. González Palencia (1932): edition of the Arabic text and of two Medieval Latin translations [EE11]; for the section on astrology see T.-A. Druart, "Astronomie et astrologie selon Farabi," in *BPhM* 20 (1978) 43–47 [EE12].

Alkindi [al-Kindī] and Jafar Indus, *De temporum mutationibus* (Paris 1540): two important works on astrometeorology [EE13].

Bartholomew of Parma, *Breviloquium,* in Cambridge, Emmanuel College, MS 70 [EE14].

Bede, *De temporum ratione,* ed. C.W. Jones, *Bedae opera de temporibus* (1943) 175–291; repr. in *Bedae opera didascalica,* v2, *CCSL* 123A (1977) [EE15].

Pseudo-Bede, *De mundi celestis terrestrisque constitutione: A treatise on the Universe and the Soul,* ed. and tr. C. Burnett (1985): with annotated glossary [EE16].

Al-Bīrūnī, *The Book of Instruction in the Elements of the Art of Astrology,* ed. and tr. R. Ramsey Wright (1934): provides a useful guide to the kind of astrology introduced into the West [EE17].

Censorinus, *De die natali,* ed. N. Sallmann (1983): includes the *Epitoma disciplinarum* [EE18].

Cicero, *Aratea,* ed. V. Buescu (1941, r1966) [EE19].

*Epitoma disciplinarum:* see [EE18] 61–86 [EE20].

Eudes of Champagne, *Libellus de efficatia artis astrologice,* ed. M.H. Malewicz, in *Mediaevalia Philosophica Polonorum* 20 (1974) 3–95 [EE21].

Firmicus Maternus, *Mathesis* [*Matheseos libri VIII*], ed. W. Kroll, F. Skutsch, and K. Ziegler, 2 vols. (1897–1913, r1968) [EE22]; ed. P. Monat (1992–): v1 (bks. 1–2) [EE23]; tr. J.R. Bram, *Ancient Astrology: Theory and Practice* (1975) [EE24].

Guido Bonatti, *Liber astronomicus,* ed. J. Engel (Augsburg 1491) [EE25].

Hermann of Carinthia, *De essentiis,* ed. C. Burnett (1982) [EE26].

Hermes Trismegitus, *De triginta sex decanis* [= *Liber Hermetis Trismegisti*], ed. S. Feraboli, *Hermes Latinus* v4.1, *CCCM* 144 (1994) [EE27].

Hyginus, *Astronomica,* ed. A. Le Boeuffle (1983) [EE28].

John of Legnano, *Tractatus de bello, de represaliis et de duello,* ed. T.E. Holland (1917): use of astrology in an allegorical way in a history of Bologna [EE29].

John of Salisbury, *Poli.* [EE31].

John of Seville, *Epitome totius astrologiae,* ed. J. Heller (Nuremberg 1548) [EE32].

Leopold of Austria, *Compilatio de astrorum scientia* (Augsburg 1489) [EE33].

*Liber nouem judicum in judicijs astrorum* (Venice 1509) [EE34]

Marcus Manilius, *Astronomica,* ed. G.P. Goold (1985) [EE35]; also ed. and tr. G.P. Goold (1977) [EE36].

Meseallach [Messahala = Māshāᵓallāh] and Ptholemeus, *De electionibus* (Venice 1509) [EE37].

Messahala, *Libri tres . . . De reuolutione annorum mundi . . . De significatione planetarum in natiuitatibus . . . De receptione,* ed. J. Heller (Nuremberg 1549) [EE38].

Messahala, *Astrological History,* ed. and tr. E.S. Kennedy and D. Pingree (1971): Arabic text, translation, and commentary [EE39].

Nicole Oresme, *Tractatus contra astronomos,* in *Nicole Oresme and the Astrologers: A Study of His Livre de divinacions,* ed. G.W. Coopland (1952) 123–41 [EE40].

*Picatrix: The Latin Version of the Ghāyat al-Ḥakīm,* ed. D. Pingree (1986) [EE41].

Pietro d'Abano, *Lucidator dubitabilium astronomiae,* ed. G. Federici-Vescovini (1988) [EE42].

Ptolemy, *Apotelesmatica,* ed. F. Boll and E. Boer (1954) [EE43]; *Tetrabiblos,* ed. and tr.

F.E. Robbins (1940, r1980) [EE44]; *Quadripartitum* (Venice 1484): Latin translation of Plato of Tivoli [EE45].

Ptolemy, *Almagest* (Venice 1515): Latin translation of Gerard of Cremona (1175)
[EE46].

Pseudo-Ptolemy, *Centiloquium* (Venice 1484), with the *Quadripartitum* (see [EE45])
[EE47].

E. Svenburg, ed., *Die Latinska Lunaria* (1936) [EE48]; *Lunaria et zodiologia latina*
(1963) [EE49].

Thābit ibn Qurra, *Liber de imaginibus,* ed. F.J. Carmody, in *The Astronomical Works
of Thābit b. Qurra* (1960): Latin text, pp180–97 [EE50].

Zahel Ysmaelita [Sahl b. Bishr al-Isrāʾīlī], *De principiis iuditiorum astrologie Introductorium* (Frankfurt/Oder 1508) [EE51].

Zahel Ismaelita, ed. C.M. Crofts: "Kitāb al-ikҭiyārāt ʿalā l-buyūt al-iṯnai ʿašar by Sahl
ibn Bišr al-Isrāʾīlī with its Latin Translation *De electionibus*" (Ph.D. diss., Glasgow University, 1985): one of the very few modern critical editions of Medieval
Latin astrological texts [EE52].

## Studies and Reference Tools

For initial orientation see O. Pedersen, "Astrology," in *DMA* 1:604–10 [EE53]; G.
Saliba, "Astrology/Astronomy, Islamic," in *DMA* 1:616–24 [EE54]; and D. Pingree,
"Astrology," in *Dictionary of the History of Ideas,* ed. P.P. Wiener (1968, r1973),
v1:118–26 [EE55].

R. Bonnard, "Notes sur l'astrologie latine au VIe siècle," in *RBPhH* 10 (1931) 557–77
[EE56].

A. Bouché-Leclercq, *L'astrologie grecque* (1899, r1963): still unsurpassed as an introduction to classical astrology [EE57].

C. Burnett, "A Group of Arabic-Latin Translators Working in Northern Spain in the
Mid-12th Century," in *Journal of the Royal Asiatic Society,* 1977, 62–108: concerning the *Liber trium iudicum* and the *Liber novem iudicum* [EE58].

C. Burnett, "Some Comments on the Translating of Works from Arabic into Latin in
the Mid-Twelfth Century," in *Orientalische Kultur und Europäishes Mittelalter,*
ed. A. Zimmermann and I. Craemer-Ruegenberg, *MiscM* 17 (1985) 161–71 [EE59].

C. Burnett, "Arabic, Greek, and Latin Works on Astrological Magic Attributed to
Aristotle," in *Pseudo-Aristotle in the Middle Ages: The "Theology" and Other
Texts,* ed. J. Kraye *et al.* (1986) 84–96 [EE60].

C. Burnett, "Literal Translation and Intelligent Adaptation amongst the Arabic-Latin
Translators of the First Half of the Twelfth Century," in *La diffusione delle scienze
islamiche nel medio evo europeo* (1987) 9–28 [EE61].

C. Burnett, "Adelard, Ergaphalau and the Science of the Stars," in *Adelard of Bath: An
English Scientist and Arabist of the Early Twelfth Century,* ed. id. (1987) 133–45
[EE62].

C. Burnett, "A New Source for Dominicus Gundissalinus's Account of the Science of
the Stars?," in *Annals of Science* 47 (1990) 361–74 [EE63].

C. Burnett, "Al-Kindī on Judicial Astrology: 'The Forty Chapters,'" in *Arabic Sciences
and Philosophy* 3 (1993) 77–117: includes sample texts from Alkindi's *Iudicia* in the
translations by Robert Ketton and Hugo of Santalla [EE64].

C. Burnett, "An Unknown Latin Version of an Ancient *Parapēgma*: The Weather-
Forecasting Stars in the *Iudicia* of Pseudo-Ptolemy," in *Making Instruments*

*Count: Essays on Historical Scientific Instruments Presented to Gerard L'Estrange Turner*, ed. R.G.W. Anderson *et al.* (1993) 27–41 [EE65].

C. Burnett, "Michael Scot and the Transmission of Scientific Culture from Toledo to Bologna via the Court of Frederick II Hohenstaufen," in *Micrologus* 2 (1994) 101–26: on the astrological work of Scot and Bartholomew of Parma [EE66].

F.J. Carmody, *Arabic Astronomical and Astrological Sciences in Latin Translation: A Critical Bibliography* (1956): indispensable but often unreliable [EE67].

P. Curry, ed., *Astrology, Science, and Society: Historical Essays* (1987): includes J.D. North, "Medieval Concepts of Celestial Influence: A Survey," pp5–17; G. Federici-Vescovini, "Peter of Abano and Astrology," pp19–39; H.M. Carey, "Astrology at the English Court in the Later Middle Ages," pp41–56; R. Lemay, "The True Place of Astrology in Medieval Science and Philosophy: Towards a Definition," pp57–73; S. Caroti, "Nicole Oresme's Polemic against Astrology, in his *Quodlibeta*," pp75–93 [EE68].

M.-T. d'Alverny, "Astrologues et théologiens au XIIe siècle," in *Mélanges offerts à M.-D. Chenu, Bibliothèque Thomiste* 37 (1967) 31–50: on Eudes of Champagne [EE69].

M.-T. d'Alverny, "Abélard et l'astrologie," in *Pierre Abélard–Pierre le Vénérable* (1975) 611–28: discusses the astrology of Raymond of Marseilles [EE70].

M.-T. d'Alverny, "Translations and Translators," in *R&R* 421–61 [EE71].

G. Federici-Vescovini, *Astrologia e scienza: La crisi dell'aristotelismo sul cadere del Trecento e Biagio Pelacani da Parma* (1979) [EE72].

V.I.J. Flint, "The Transmission of Astrology in the Early Middle Ages," in *Viator* 21 (1990) 1–27; appears in revised form in *eadem, The Rise of Magic in Early Medieval Europe* (1991) 87–172 [EE73].

J. Fontaine, "Isidore de Séville et l'astrologie," in *REL* 31 (1953) 271–300 [EE74].

W. Hübner, *Die Eigenschaften der Tierkreiszeichen in der Antike, SAr*, Beiheft 22 (1982) [EE75].

P. Kunitzsch, "Eine bilingue arabisch-lateinische Lostafel," in *Revue d'histoire des textes* 6 (1976) 267–304 [EE76].

P. Kunitzsch, "Mittelalterliche astronomisch-astrologische Glossare mit arabischen Fachausdrücken," Bayerische Ak. der Wiss., philosophisch-historische Klasse, Sitz., Jahrgang 1977, Heft 5 (1977) [EE77].

A. Le Boeuffle, *Astronomie. Astrologie. Lexique latin* (1987): to be used with caution; see review of W. Hübner in *Gnomon* 60 (1988) 509–16 [EE78].

R. Lemay, "Origin and Success of the Kitāb Thamara of Abū Jaʿfar Aḥmad ibn Yūsuf ibn Ibrāhīm from the Tenth to the Seventeenth Century in the World of Islam and the Latin West," in *Proceedings of the First International Symposium for the History of Arab Science* (5–12 April 1976), ed. A.Y. Al-Hassan *et al.*, 2 vols. (1977–78), v2:91–107: concerning the *Centiloquium* of Pseudo-Ptolemy [EE79].

R. Lemay, *Abu Mashar and Latin Aristotelianism in the Twelfth Century: The Recovery of Aristotle's Natural Philosophy through Arabic Astrology* (1962) [EE80].

R. Lemay, "Fautes et contresens dans les traductions arabo-latines médiévales: L'*Introductorium in astronomiam* d'Abou Maʿshar de Balken," in *Revue de synthèse* 83 (1968) 101–24 [EE81].

W. Lilly, *Christian Astrology* (London 1647, r1985): Lilly includes a comprehensive annotated catalogue of printed astrological works known to him; most of these are medieval [EE82].

J.D. North, *Horoscopes and History* (1986): provides detailed instructions on how to set up an astrological chart [EE83].

J.D. North, *Stars, Minds, and Fate: Essays in Ancient and Medieval Cosmology* (1989) [EE84].

D. Pingree, ed. and tr., *The Yavanajātaka of Sphujidhvaja*, 2 vols. (1978): see v2:419–44 for biobibliographies of Arabic, Persian, Syriac, Greek, and Latin astrologers [EE85].

D. Pingree, "The Diffusion of Arabic Magic Texts in Western Europe," in *La diffusione* ([EE61]) 57–102 [EE86].

M. Préaud, *Les astrologues à la fin du moyen âge* (1984) [EE87].

B. Ribémont, ed., *Observer, lire, écrire le ciel au moyen âge: Actes du colloque d'Orléans* (22–23 April 1989) (1991): includes J.-P. Boudet, "Les astrologues et le pouvoir sous le règne de Louis XI," pp7–62; J. Fuhrman, "L'influence de l'astrologie dans les écrits médicaux du moyen âge," pp101–14; M. Lejbowicz, "Les antécedents de la distinction isidorienne: *astrologia/astronomia*," pp173–212; A. Llinares, "Le *Traité d'astrologie* de Raymond Lulle," pp213–28 [EE88].

F. Sezgin, *Geschichte des arabischen Schrifttums*, v7 (1979): an index of Latin book titles (pp474–76) and the inclusion of Latin writers in the index of authors (pp425–42) enable the reader to find the Arabic originals of many Latin astrological texts [EE89].

L.A. Shore, "A Case Study in Medieval Nonliterary Translation: Scientific Texts from Latin to French, in *Medieval Translators and Their Craft*, ed. J. Beer (1989) 297–327 [EE90].

S.J. Tester, *A History of Western Astrology* (1987, r1990) [EE91].

L. Thorndike, *HMES* [EE92].

L. Thorndike, "The Three Latin Translations of the Pseudo-Hippocratic Tract on Astrological Medicine," in *Janus* 49 (1961) 104–29 [EE93].

L. Thorndike, "The Latin Translations of Astrological Works by Messahala," in *Osiris* 12 (1956) 49–72 [EE94].

A. Van de Vyver, "Les plus anciennes traductions latines médiévales (Xe–XIe siècles) de traités d'astronomie et d'astrologie," in *Osiris* 1 (1936) 658–91 [EE95].

C. Weißer, *Studien zum mittelalterlichen Krankheitslunar: Ein Beitrag zur Geschichte laienastrologischer Fachprosa* (1981) [EE96].

L. White, Jr., "Medical Astrologers and Late Medieval Technology," in *Viator* 6 (1975) 295–308; repr. in *id.*, *Medieval Religion and Technology: Collected Essays* (1978) [EE97].

E. Wickersheimer, "Figures médico-astrologiques des IXe, Xe et XIe siècles," in *Janus* 19 (1914) 157–77 [EE98].

P. Zambelli, *The Speculum Astronomiae and Its Enigma: Astrology, Theology and Science in Albertus Magnus and His Contemporaries* (1992): with revision of edition (variant readings omitted) and commentary in [EE2], English translation, and extensive bibliography of primary and secondary sources [EE99].

# EF ❧ CHRONOLOGY AND SYSTEMS OF DATING

BY FAITH WALLIS

## Computus

The science of reckoning time and the technique of constructing calendars were known in the Middle Ages as *computus* (also spelled *compotus* or *conpotus*). Their earliest, and always most crucial, task was determining the date of Easter, a problem at once scientific, theological, and disciplinary. Computists (*computistae*) chose to solve it by devising a cycle of Easters that was both reliable and easy to teach to the clergy, who were increasingly obliged to assume local responsibility for the calendar.

The earliest literary representatives of the genre of *computus* are letters or prologues explaining or justifying rival forms of the paschal cycle, but Bede's *De temporibus* (703) and *De temporum ratione* (725) were its first comprehensive treatises. Their pedagogical and encyclopedic qualities appealed to Carolingian schoolmasters, who recast them for schoolroom use. In the eleventh century, however, evident defects in the astronomical premises upon which the official *computus* was based inaugurated a new literature of criticism and proposals for reform. Intensified by scholastic research in astronomy, this pressure to reform the calendar became an object of papal and conciliar concern in the fourteenth and fifteenth centuries. But *computus ecclesiasticus* remained an obligatory subject for clerical education and spawned textbooks in verse and prose for university audiences. Throughout the medieval period, however, the primary vehicles of *computus* were not formal treatises, but variable anthologies consisting of calendars, tables, formulae, notes, and mnemonics.

As an evolving and "popular" science, *computus* is rich in jargon. Like the computer argot of today, most of its terms are appropriations of words with more general primary meanings. The word *computus* itself, for instance, denotes mathematical reckoning of any type, and in the Middle Ages it was most commonly used of accounting, but it long retained a restricted sense of calendrical calculation or a treatise on this subject. Much of this specialized vocabulary concerns the apparatus of calendars and tables that made up *computus* manuscripts. Words like *sedes, locus,* and *terminus* had technical meanings as fixed calendar dates for computistical phenomena, e.g. *sedes concurrentium, locus epactarum*. A diagram, table, or (occasionally) a formula is a *pagina* (diminutive: *paginiola*), but a textual formula is usually an *argu-*

*mentum.* Classical meanings of calendar terms were extended: *annale* and *kalendarium,* for example, came to mean "calendar table," and *Kalendae* was not only "the first day of the month" but "a calendar date" (by the twelfth century, the word *data* was used as a synonym). The origin of much *computus* lore in Alexandria is reflected in Greek loanwords like *epacta, ogdoas, (h)endecas,* and *embolismus.* The following specialized Latin terms are also common:

*saltus lunae:* the omission or "leaping over" of one lunar day at the end of the nineteen-year paschal cycle (*cyclus decemnouennalis*) in order to bring sun and moon back into phase

*lunatio:* lunar cycle, lunation

*littera dominicalis:* in medieval calendars, recurring sequences of seven letters (A–G) run parallel to the 365 days of the year; in any given year, one of the letters, the "dominical letter," will designate Sundays (*dominica*)

*claues terminorum:* "key" numbers, one for each year of the 19-year paschal cycle, which, when added to the fixed *terminus* date for a movable feast, will give its actual date in that year

*numerus aureus:* a number representing the position of the year within the 19-year paschal cycle, used as an index for finding the dates of new moons and the *terminus a quo* of Easter; its name, "golden number," was said to be a homage to its usefulness

*Computus* texts are usually written in a plain style befitting their scientific content and instructional intention. *Argumenta* are highly formulaic ("Si uis scire. . . ."), but considerable variety and ingenuity are invested in narrating mathematical operations, with numerous synonyms for *addere* (e.g. *iungere, adiungere*), *subtrahere* (e.g. *subferre, tollere, demere*), *multiplicare* (e.g. *ducere*), etc., and in describing tables and the procedures for reading them, with a heavy concentration of words for "column," "row" (*linea, trames*), "space" (*interuallum, sedes*), etc. This makes *computus* literature an unexpectedly rich source of information about medieval modes of conveying both visual perception and abstract thought.

## Systems of Dating

Computus provided a universal framework of time-reckoning for the medieval West, but when chroniclers assigned dates to historical events, or clerks to charters, they used systems of dating that mingled local or professional custom with computistical convention. To specify the day, for example, a scribe might use the Julian calendar. Usually this was expressed in the Roman manner, i.e. counted backwards, and reckoned inclusively, from the three key days of Calends (*Kalendae, -arum*), Nones (*Nonae, -arum*), or Ides (*Idus, -uum*). A medieval innovation was the use of *II Kalendas, II Nonas,* etc. as a synonym for the classical *Pridie Kalendas, Pridie Nonas,* etc. However, after a few sporadic appearances in the early Middle Ages (the chancery of Pope Gregory I, some Anglo-Saxon royal charters), direct forward count from the first of the month became the norm in secular documents after the twelfth century, e.g., *die uicesima februarii mensis* (= 20 February). Instead of a Julian date, an author may prefer to date by the ecclesiastical calendar, selecting as the point of reference either a saint's day, a fixed or movable feast, or a Sunday within a liturgical season (see ch. DB). Often this last was identified by the opening word or words of the *introitus* used in the mass of that Sunday (e.g., the first Sunday after Easter was *dominica Quasimodo geniti*). A feast day's vigil or eve (*vigilia*), morrow (*crastinus*), or octave (*octaua*) could similarly serve as a dating reference. An author might also specify a weekday by its Roman name (*dies Solis* [Sunday], *dies Lunae* [Monday], *dies Martis* [Tuesday], *dies Mercurii* [Wednesday], *dies Iovis* [Thursday], *dies Veneris* [Friday], *dies Saturni* [Saturday]) or by its ecclesiastical numerical designation ([*feria prima*, Sunday], *feria secunda, feria tertia*, etc.). Note that *feria prima* (Sunday) is replaced by (*dies*) *dominicus* or *dominica*, and *feria septima* (Saturday) by *sabbatum* or *dies sabbati*. *Feria* (= weekday) was adopted from classical *feriae*, religious festival, holy day, holiday. *Septimana* and *hebdomada* are the medieval Latin words for "week."

To express the year, a medieval writer might use one of the prospective universal eras, most commonly the Christian era (*annus Domini, annus ab incarnatione Domini, annus gratiae*), devised by Dionysius Exiguus in A.D. 525 and popularized by Bede. A scholar might affect a "literary" era, for example, by numbering the years in the ancient style *ab urbe condita* (*A.U.C.*), after the manner of Orosius's *Historia adversos paganos*. An official might use the *indictio* or indiction year (together with *prima, secunda*, etc.) to record the number of the year within a fifteen-year cycle counted from A.D. 312, a relic of Roman taxation practice that survived in the West through notarial routine and the antiquarianism of computists. Another choice might be the use of an eponymous year, e.g., the regnal year of a king or other ruler, reckoned from the day of accession. For computistical purposes, the calendar year was the Julian year, beginning on 1 January. But at different periods and in different localities, the beginning of the year varied. For the Church, and for the West in general in the early Middle Ages, the year began at Christmas, but the practice of starting the year on the feast of the Annunciation (25 March)—whether *calculo Pisano* (counting from 25 March, 1 B.C., as the Pisans did) or *calculo Florentino* (from 25 March, A.D. 1, like the Florentines)—gained ground after the thirteenth century, except in France, where the year began at Easter. A clerk might even identify the year by its computistical markers, e.g., the "golden number" or dominical letter. Dating clauses both in annals and in diplomatic *acta* are notorious for redundancy, i.e. the date is expressed according to more than one of the chronological systems sketched here, but this helps the modern reader check the date, or at least put a doubtful date within a range of years or days.

## Select Bibliography

### Computus

#### (a) Primary Works

A small number of *computus* treatises have appeared in modern critical editions. Some of the more characteristic and influential are the following:

Alexander of Villa Dei, *Massa compoti*, ed. W.E. Van Wijk, in *Le nombre d'or: Étude de chronologie technique suivie du texte de la Massa compoti d'Alexandre de*

*Villedieu avec traduction et commentaire* (1936): scholastic textbook of *computus ecclesiasticus* in verse [EF1].

Roger Bacon, *Compotus,* ed. R. Steele, in *Compotus fratris Rogeri. Accedunt Compotus Roberti Grossecapitis Lincolniensis Episcopi [et] Massa Compoti Alexandri de Villa Dei* (1926) [EF2].

Bede, *Opera de temporibus,* ed. C.W. Jones (1943); repr. in *Bedae opera didascalica,* vols. 2–3, *CCSL* 123A–B (1977–80): the earlier edition is still valuable for its historical introduction [EF3].

Cummian, *De controversia paschali,* ed. D. Ó Cróinín and M. Walsh, in *Cummian's Letter De controversia paschali, Together with a Related Irish Computistical Tract, De ratione conputandi* (1988) [EF4].

Hrabanus Maurus, *De computo,* ed. W.M. Stevens, *CCCM* 44 (1979) 165–323 [EF5].

Nicholas of Lynn, *Kalendarium,* ed. S. Eisner, tr. G. Mac Eoin and S. Eisner (1980): a major source of Chaucer's astronomical lore [EF6].

Sigebert of Gembloux, *Liber decennalis,* ed. J. Wiesenbach, *MGH.Quellen zur Geistesgeschichte des Mittelalters* 12 (1986): an early essay in calendar criticism and reform [EF7].

### (b) Studies

To date, there is no study of the latinity of *computus,* the nearest approach being the glossaries of *computus* terms found in the handbooks of chronology listed below, and in R.T. Hampson, *Medii aevi kalendarium: or, Dates, Charters, and Customs of the Middle Ages,* 2 vols. (1841, r1978) [EF8]. Also useful in this respect are technical overviews such as Van Wijk's introduction to his edition of Alexander of Villa Dei (see [EF1]) and U.C. Merzbach, "Calendars and Reckoning of Time," in *DMA* 3:17–30 [EF9]. To a large extent, therefore, the researcher must rely on historical studies of *computus* and for orientation and bibliographic guidance may consult two recent surveys by A. Borst: "Computus: Zeit und Zahl im Mittelalter," in *DA* 44 (1988) 1–82 [EF10], and *The Ordering of Time: From the Ancient Computus to the Modern Computer,* tr. A. Winnard (1993) [EF11].

For the patristic and early medieval period, B. Krusch, *Studien zur christlich-mittelalterlichen Chronologie,* pt1: *Der 84jährige Ostercyclus* (1880), and pt2: *Die Entstehung unserer heutigen Zeitrechnung* (1938) [EF12], and A. Strobel, *Ursprung und Geschichte des frühchristlichen Osterkalendars* (1977) [EF13], furnish editions of early texts and discuss the origins of *computus* techniques and terminology. A. Cordoliani, "Contributions à la littérature du comput ecclésiastique au haut moyen âge," pt1, in *SM,* 3rd ser., 1 (1960) 107–37; pt2, in *SM,* 3rd ser., 2 (1961) 167–208 [EF14]; and "Les traités du comput au haut moyen âge (526–1003)," in *ALMA* 17 (1943) 51–72 [EF15]; and A. Van de Vyver, "Hucbald de Saint-Amand, écolâtre, et l'invention du nombre d'or," in *MAP* 61–79 [EF16], discuss developments and innovations, particularly in the formative early medieval period, which engendered new vocabulary.

### Systems of Dating

On medieval chronology and dating in general, see R. Dean Ware, "Medieval Chronology: Theory and Practice," in *MSI* 252–77 [EF17]; R.L. Poole, *Medieval Reckonings of Time* (1918) [EF18]; and A. Cordoliani, "Comput, chronologie, calendriers," in *L'histoire et ses méthodes,* ed. C. Samaran (1961) 37–51 [EF19].

In unraveling medieval dates, researchers may rely on a number of excellent handbooks, many with useful technical introductions. The basic reference tools are C.R. Cheney, *Handbook of Dates for Students of English History* (1945, r1981 with corrections and additional bibliography, r1995) [EF20], and A. Cappelli, *Cronologia, cronografia e calendario perpetuo dal principio dell'era cristiana al giorni nostri: Tavole cronologico-sincrone e quadri sinottici per verificare le date storiche*, 2nd ed. (1930); 6th updated edition (1988) [EF21].

H. Grotefend, *Zeitrechnung des deutschen Mittelalters und der Neuzeit*, 2 vols. (1891–98, r1984): contains, inter alia, a complete list of *introitus;* see also [DB52]. A convenient abridgment is *Taschenbuch der Zeitrechnung des deutschen Mittelalters und der Neuzeit*, 10th ed. (1960) [EF22].

A. Giry, *Manuel de diplomatique* (1894, r1976), although not always reliable on points of detail, remains an excellent technical overview and provides a detailed list of saints' feasts [EF23]. More specialized manuals are listed in [EF16] and [EF19].

For an instructive map showing the beginnings of the civil year in various parts of Europe in the later Middle Ages, see *Grosser historischer Weltatlas*, 3 vols., 3rd ed. (1958–84), v2: *Mittelalter*, 122a [EF24].

*See also* [BF96].

EG       # CARTOGRAPHY AND ITS
WRITTEN SOURCES

BY P.D.A. HARVEY

In the world of imperial Rome maps seem to have been widely understood and used: diagram maps and picture maps, as well as the maps drawn to consistent scale either by geographers, showing the world and its regions, or by surveyors, showing fields and buildings. After the barbarian invasions these traditions of map making were lost, and we find only vestigial traces of Roman cartography in the maps drawn in medieval Europe. Few medieval maps are earlier than the thirteenth century, and it was only in the late fifteenth that maps began to pass beyond limited or occasional use to become widespread throughout Europe in the course of the century following. Italy was the part of medieval Europe where maps were most likely to be encountered, but there were also particular, if limited, traditions of map making in England in the thirteenth century, Catalonia and Majorca in the fourteenth and fifteenth, and south Germany in the fifteenth.

Medieval maps fall into three distinct groups, and until the mid-fifteenth century there was little correlation or cross-fertilization among them. World maps and their derivatives are the most likely to have stemmed directly from Roman originals. Many were no more than simple diagrams of the continents (a "⊤" within a circle) or of climatic zones (a circle divided by horizontal bands). Others, however, provided a coastal outline, certainly of Roman origin, which through successive copying by scribes who knew nothing of geographical coordinates, consistent scale, or the actual shape of the continents, now bore little relation to reality. It was only when Jacobus Angelus, about 1406, translated the second-century Greek treatise of Claudius Ptolemy that maps of the world and its regions based directly on coordinates of classical origin became available to Latin Christendom.

The second group of maps comprises the so-called portolan charts; their name derives from the Italian *portolano*, written sailing-directions, with which, however, they seem to have no specific connection. From the late thirteenth century onwards they provided accurate scale outlines first of the Mediterranean alone, but then extended to the Atlantic coasts of Europe and (in the fifteenth century) Africa. Developed apparently to meet practical needs of navigation, they may have had a world map as their starting point, but probably achieved their impressive accuracy by a process of continuing correction through measurement of many directions and distances.

The medieval maps in the third group are those of small areas known personally to the map maker: local maps and plans showing a single building, a few fields, a town, a small region. Some of the whole of Palestine, and of individual towns and buildings there, may represent a continuing tradition from classical times, but the last known map in the style of the Roman surveyors is an ideal plan of a monastery drawn probably at Reichenau and given to the prior of St. Gall in the early ninth century, and other local maps seem to owe nothing to Roman antecedent. Few in number, they are distributed in strangely patchy concentrations: thus there are some 35 of all kinds from England but none from Wales or Scotland, 14 regional maps from the Po valley but none from southern Italy.

In the Middle Ages these various sorts of maps do not seem to have been regarded as constituting a single class of object, and there is no Medieval Latin word that means, simply, map. However, *mappa mundi,* "cloth of the world," already used of world maps by the ninth century and certainly in wide use by the thirteenth, was occasionally applied to other maps as well: it occurs in 1270 in what is almost certainly our earliest reference to a portolan chart, and in 1423 a map to be drawn of two counties in France was *figura ad modum mappemondi.* Local maps in France were more often simply *figura;* the same word occurs in England, and also *effigies* and *pictura,* and an early fifteenth-century map of Thanet calls itself *mappa Thaneti insule.* A world map by Giovanni Leardo in 1448 is entitled both *mapa mondi* and *figura mundi,* and some maps added to Ptolemy's in early printed editions of the *Geographia* are headed *tabula moderna.* Probably any word meaning picture might, on occasion, be applied to a map. *Carta* in its various forms, certainly used of a map in Italian in the late fourteenth or early fifteenth century, may have been confined to vernacular usage.

Place names are the only class of inscription found on all sorts of medieval maps; they range from the names of continents on maps of the world to names of individual fields and buildings on local plans. Except perhaps the names of the continents—Africa, Asia, Europa—we cannot say with confidence that any names derive directly from classical maps. However, the place names on the maps accompanying Ptolemy's *Geographia* are clearly linked with those in his text, though with some concessions to later usage, as *Lucotetia hodie Parisium,* and there is scope for potentially important work on their precise relationship. Other world or regional maps drew names from other treatises—75 of the 146 names on the tenth- or eleventh-century Cotton map occur in the *Cosmographia* of Orosius—and some were taken from Roman administrative records or itineraries. Thus the five places named in Britain on an eleventh-century copy of the so-called Beatus world map are given their Roman names, significantly all in the ablative, as so often in the itineraries, and though two, *Lindinio* (London) and *Lindo* (Lincoln), were important centers, the others were minor, distant places that may well have been an itinerary's terminal points: *Condeaco* (Benwell), *Moriduno* (Carmarthen), *Virigonio* (Wroxeter). Medieval itineraries were also drawn on by map makers; thus in the thirteenth century they are thought to have contributed series of names on the Ebstorf and Hereford world maps and on Matthew Paris's maps of Britain and Palestine. These names would be in contemporary form, sometimes latinized, sometimes not, like most of the other names of places that fell within Europeans' direct experience—most but not all. Thus on Matthew Paris's maps of Britain London is *London',* Lincoln *Lincolnia,* Exeter *Exon'* or *Excestria,* and Gloucester *Glovernia* or *Gloucest',* but York and the River Severn both appear in classical guise as *Eboracum* and *Sabrina,* a reflection of the map maker's learning.

There is seldom much written on portolan charts except place names, in strictly vernacular form; the Latin geographical notes on Angelo Dulcert's chart of 1339 are exceptional. Many world maps, however, offer varied information, geographical in the widest sense, on individual regions and places. This is especially marked on the large world maps drawn in the thirteenth century in northwest Europe, and later in Italy; some are virtually covered in notes and pictures that make them compendia of any facts that could be attached to particular places, historical, biblical, mythical, zo-ological, and so on. But many smaller and simpler world maps have geographical notes on or beside them, and where the map appears as an illustration in a book these notes are distinct from the book's text. Before the mid-fifteenth-century maps by Giovanni Leardo and Fra Mauro, with inscriptions in Italian, nearly all medieval world maps were written in Latin; the superbly detailed Catalan atlas of 1375 is exceptional in being in the vernacular. Even when a diagrammatic map of the continents illustrates the thirteenth-century French text of Gautier de Metz, *L'image du monde,* the map's short note on each continent and other inscriptions are all in Latin.

Much of the information on world maps comes from Pliny's *Naturalis historia,* either directly or by way of later writers, notably Isidore of Seville. Other early writings, from the third century to the seventh, that were particularly drawn on include the works of Solinus, Eusebius, and Orosius; the Latin works attributed to Aethicus; and the Latin translation of the *Physiologus.* But much later sources were also used. Thirteenth-century world maps take information from Adam of Bremen's eleventh-century account of northern Europe, the twelfth-century encyclopedia of Honorius of Autun, the miscellany *Otia imperialia* written by Gervase of Tilbury in 1211, and the popular romances of Alexander the Great. Actual accounts of travel had little immediate influence. References to the book of the travels of Marco Polo (c. 1254–1324), written in the 1290s, do not appear on any surviving map before the Catalan atlas of 1375, and the journeys of the Polos were first fully related to a world map by Fra Mauro in 1459. The Vulgate Bible too contributed less than one might expect in view of the world maps' clear spiritual import: they displayed the world as God's creation, and from behind the world on the Ebstorf map protrude the head, hands, and feet of Christ. The Bible supplied place names in the near East and—on the Hereford map—the imaginatively interpreted route of the Exodus from Egypt to Jericho, but very few more extensive notes.

In all, though, the sources used by the compilers of world and regional maps varied greatly in origin, subject matter, and language, and no simple vocabulary can be offered of often-recurring technical terms. Nor did a tradition develop of a single collection of material that would form the basis for what was placed within the outlines of any world map; map makers seem rather to have used their sources eclectically, following their individual interests or preferences. Thus the Ebstorf and Hereford maps are closely related, but, whereas the Hereford map, following Aethicus, places the *cynocephali,* the dog-headed people, in northern Europe, the Ebstorf map places them in Ethiopia, like Pliny and Solinus, while describing them in words apparently based on Isidore of Seville, who places them in India. Nor did the map makers follow their sources slavishly. Even where, exceptionally, the Hereford map names its sources, what we are offered may be an adaptation rather than a direct quotation. On two islands south of Africa it notes: *Insula Sirtinice, ubi Ethicus invenit bestiolas adi-*

*pistas aculeis plenis velud strix* and *Hic sirene abundant;* the relevant passage in Aethicus reads: *donec insolam Syrthinicem incurrit, et illic invenit bestiolas pessimas, ignotas, crydositas plenas aculeis velut istrix, et syrenarum multitudinem.* Unnamed sources would likewise be paraphrased, more or less closely. Matthew Paris, having read in the *Descriptio Kambrie* of Gerald of Wales of *gens levis et agilis, gens aspera magis quam robusta, gens armis dedita tota,* notes on south Wales on one version of his map of Britain: *Terra . . . homines agiles generans et bellicosos,* and on another: *incolas habet agiles, incultos et bellicosos.*

World maps and their regional derivatives were the work of learned scholars; local maps mostly were not. As we might thus expect, the vernacular occurs more often in the wording on local maps; its incidence is of interest and deserves more attention than it has received. However, the earliest use of the vernacular on maps is in the mid-thirteenth century by Matthew Paris, whose learning need not be doubted: the various versions of his itinerary from London to Apulia and of one of his maps of Palestine are written all or mostly in French. The earliest local map known from the Netherlands, drawn on a roll of payments in 1307 to show an area near Sluis, is in Dutch, but the next oldest, showing the boundary between two *nationes* of the University of Paris in 1357, is in Latin. Published local maps from France are in Latin to the mid-fifteenth century, then mostly in French. Of the 35 local maps (or closely associated groups of maps) known from England only five are in English, none of them earlier than the late fourteenth century, and the rest are in Latin or, in two cases, a mixture of Latin and English. Others, of course, have many place names in fully vernacular form, and these may dominate the map so that the Latin of other inscriptions is all but submerged.

Broadly speaking, Latin is found on a local map if this was the language of the map's context and use. Some or all of the regional maps from north Italy in the mid- and late fifteenth century were drawn for the government of Venice; their inscriptions are in Italian, the language of Venetian administration. On the other hand, contemporary plans of Rome are inscribed in Latin: they show the principal ancient monuments and reflect humanist interest in the classical past. The reason why Latin is the language of most of the English local maps is that until late in the fifteenth century Latin was used in England for nearly all records of public or private administration. However, maps did not invariably use the language of their immediate context. The wording on the only city plan from medieval England, of Bristol about 1480, is in Latin, although it was drawn to accompany the local chronicle by the town clerk, Robert Ricart, which was written in English.

The context of most medieval local maps was either legal or administrative or antiquarian, but their subjects were too varied to produce a recurrent technical vocabulary. The use of *hic* as the first word of an inscription is of interest. It provides, for instance, an intriguing link between the ninth-century monastic plan at St. Gall and the earliest English local map, a mid-twelfth-century plan of Canterbury Cathedral: on both it introduces what are mostly full sentences. It may well also provide a link, of great interest, between the maps drawn at Westminster Abbey and at Durham Cathedral Priory in the mid-fifteenth century. Generally the vocabulary and phrasing of the maps' inscriptions, like their language, reflect their particular context. To take two quite different English examples of the early fifteenth century, the wording on the map of Thanet is closely related to the section of Thomas of Elmham's chronicle that it illustrates, and on both versions of a map of Inclesmoor, Yorkshire, there are phrases taken from agreements made a century earlier about property rights that were still contentious. Drawing local maps in the Middle Ages was mostly an occasional expedient. There were few traditions that could create linguistic or other conventions.

## Select Bibliography

### Texts

Adam of Bremen, *Gesta Hammaburgensis ecclesiae pontificum,* ed. B. Schmeidler, *MGH.SRG* (1917, r1977); tr. F.J. Tschan: *History of the Archbishops of Hamburg-Bremen* (1959) [EG1].

Aethicus Ister, *De cosmographia,* ed. M.A.P. D'Avezac, in *Mémoires présentés par divers savants à l'Académie des inscriptions et belles-lettres,* 1st ser., 2 (1852) 455–541 [EG2]; ed. H. Wuttke (1853) [EG3].

Eusebius, *Ecclesiastica historia,* tr. Rufinus, ed. T. Mommsen, 3 vols., *Griechischen christlichen Schriftsteller,* v9.1–3 (1903–9) [EG4].

Gerald of Wales, *Opera,* ed. J.S. Brewer *et al.,* 8 vols., *RSer* 21 (1861–91); the *Descriptio Kambrie* is in v6:153–227 [EG5].

Gervase of Tilbury, *Otia imperialia,* ed. G.W. Leibniz, in Scriptores rerum Brunsvicensium 1 (Hanover 1707) 881–1004, 2 (Hanover 1710) 751–84 [EG6].

Honorius Augustodunensis, *Imago mundi,* ed. V.I.J. Flint, in *AHDL* 49 (1982) 7–153 [EG7].

Isidore of Seville, *Etym.* [EG8].

Marco Polo, *The Book of Ser Marco Polo, the Venetian, Concerning the Kingdoms and Marvels of the East,* tr. and ed. H. Yule, 2 vols., 3rd ed. (1903) [EG9]; *The Description of the World,* ed. and tr. A.C. Moule and P. Pelliot, 2 vols. (1938, r1976) [EG10].

Orosius, *Historiarum adversus paganos libri VII,* ed. and tr. M.-P. Arnaud-Lindet, 3 vols. (1990–91) [EG11].

*Physiologus latinus,* ed. F.J. Carmody (1939): *versio* B [EG12]; ed. F.J. Carmody, in *The University of California Publications in Classical Philology* 12 (1941) 95–134: *versio* Y [EG13]; tr. M.J. Curley (1979) [EG14].

Pliny the Elder, *NH* [EG15].

Solinus, *CRM* [EG16].

Thomas of Elmham, *Historia monasterii S. Augustini Cantuariensis,* ed. C. Hardwick, *RSer* 6 (1858) [EG17].

### Collections of Medieval Maps

There are few collected editions of medieval maps, and there is no clear distinction between well illustrated studies and editions with full commentary. The following, however, place particular emphasis on reproducing the maps and their texts.

R. Almagià, *Monumenta Italiae Cartographica* (1929, r1980): a collection of reproductions of Italian maps with commentary, but without a full copy of their inscriptions [EG18].

J.P. Gilson, *Four Maps of Great Britain Designed by Matthew Paris about* A.D. *1250*

(1928): reproductions with a full table of place names and other inscriptions [EG19].

K. Miller, *Mappaemundi: Die ältesten Weltkarten,* 6 vols. (1895–98): a definitive edition of the most important world maps and their derivatives, printing their inscriptions in full and identifying the source of each [EG20].

A.E. Nordenskiöld, *Facsimile-Atlas to the Early History of Cartography,* tr. J.A. Ekelöf and C.R. Markham (1889, r1973 [with new introduction by J.B. Post]): includes a full reproduction of Ptolemy's maps from the 1490 Rome edition, besides other fifteenth-century printed maps [EG21].

A.E. Nordenskiöld, *Periplus: An Essay on the Early History of Charts and Sailing-Directions,* tr. F.A. Bather (1897, r1967?): reproduces portolan charts and some other medieval maps [EG22].

R. Röhricht, "Karten und Pläne zur Palästinakunde aus dem 7. bis 16. Jahrhundert," in *Zeitschrift des Deutschen Palästina-Vereins* 14 (1891) 8–11, 87–92, 137–41, pls. 1, 3–5; 15 (1892) 34–39, 185–88, pls. 1–9; 18 (1895) 173–82, pls. 5–7: a pioneer collection of maps of Palestine and Jerusalem, reproducing their outlines with their inscriptions typeset [EG23].

R.A. Skelton and P.D.A. Harvey, eds., *Local Maps and Plans from Medieval England* (1986): reproductions with a transcription of the wording and a historical discussion of each map [EG24].

## Guides and Studies

H. Andersson, *Urbanisierte Ortschaften und lateinische Terminologie: Studien zur Geschichte des nordeuropäischen Städtewesens vor 1350* (1971) [EG25].

J.-G. Arentzen, *Imago mundi cartographica: Studien zur Bildlichkeit mittelalterlicher Welt- und Ökumenekarten unter besonderer Berücksichtigung des Zusammenwirkens von Text und Bild* (1984) [EG26].

P. Gautier Dalché, *La "Descriptio mappae mundi" de Hugues de Saint-Victor: Texte inédit, avec introduction et commentaire* (1988) [EG27].

J.G.T. Grässe, F. Benedict, and H. and S.-C. Plechl, *Orbis latinus: Lexikon lateinischer geographischer Namen des Mittelalters und der Neuzeit,* 3 vols. (1972): the latest and much enlarged edition of the standard reference work on Latin forms of place names, containing 120,000 medieval or modern names; a shorter manual in one volume (1971) includes 15,000 names [EG28]. Several other such toponymical guides are listed, by country, together with atlases and works of historical geography, in *GSMH,* ch. 4 [EG29].

J.B. Harley and D. Woodward, eds., *The History of Cartography,* v1 (1987) 283–500: supersedes all earlier studies, of which, however, it provides a substantial bibliography, and includes many illustrations [EG30].

P.D.A. Harvey, *Medieval Maps* (1991): a brief general survey with many illustrations [EG31].

G.H.T. Kimble, *Geography in the Middle Ages* (1938, r1968) [EG32].

H. Kugler and E. Michael, eds., *Ein Weltbild vor Columbus: Die Ebstorfer Weltkarte* (1991): the well-illustrated papers given at a 1988 colloquium on the Ebstorf map, greatest of medieval world maps [EG33].

M. Mulon, "Lexicographie du latin médiéval et toponymie," in *LLM* 137–44 [EG34].

R.A. Peddie, *Place Names in Imprints: An Index to the Latin and Other Forms Used on Title Pages* (1932) [EG35].

M. Pelletier, ed., *Géographie du monde au moyen âge et à la renaissance* (1989): includes important and well-illustrated articles on new discoveries on medieval world maps [EG36].

J.P. Tilmann, *An Appraisal of the Geographical Works of Albertus Magnus and His Contributions to Geographical Thought* (1971) [EG37].

A.-D. von den Brincken, *Kartographische Quellen: Welt-, See- und Regionalkarten*, *TSMAO* 51 (1988): an important account and assessment of all kinds of medieval maps, with a valuable select bibliography [EG38].

J.K. Wright, *The Geographical Lore of the Time of the Crusades* (1925, r1965 with additions): still the standard work on geographical books and thus on many of the written sources drawn on for world maps [EG39].

An important periodical in the field is *Imago mundi* (1935–), from 1975 the journal of the International Society for the History of Cartography [EG40].

*See also* [BA81], [BD100].

# EH • ZOOLOGY AND PHYSIOLOGY

BY JAMES J. SCANLAN, M.D.

Medieval notions of animals were based, directly or indirectly, on Aristotle's books about animals: *Historia animalium, De partibus animalium,* and *De generatione animalium.* Aristotle was quoted extensively by Pliny in his *Historia naturalis* and by Solinus in his *Collectanea rerum memorabilium* (90 percent of which is grounded in Pliny), and these works formed the basis for medieval studies of the character, habits, properties, and classification of animals. For the meaning of Latin zoological names naturalists depended heavily on the seventh-century *Etymologiarum sive originum libri XX* of Isidore of Seville (d. 636), especially bk. 12; this work preserved many elements of Greek and Roman culture for the scholars of Latin Europe. It was virtually the only source for the historical meaning of individual Latin names, though its etymologies were often fanciful: Isidore derived *cat* from *captura,* "capture," or *catus,* "shrewd" (12.2.38–39).

Relatively few medieval authors wrote about animals. Isidore's successors include the encyclopedists Hrabanus Maurus (in bk. 8 of his *De rerum naturis* [also known as *De universo*], written after 842), Hildegard of Bingen (*Physica,* bks. 5–8, from the mid-twelfth century), Bartholomaeus Anglicus (*De proprietatibus rerum,* c. 1225), Thomas of Cantimpré (*De natura rerum,* bks. 4–9, c. 1240), and Vincent of Beauvais (*Speculum naturale,* 1244–64); another important writer was Emperor Frederick II, who compiled an empirically based treatise on falconry, *De arte venandi cum avibus* (1248), a rich source of information about birds in general as well as about hunting with them. In addition to encyclopedic works and guides for hunters, there were the bestiaries (*bestiaria,* sg. *bestiarium*), collections of moralized tales about real, imaginary, or mythical animals (and plants and stones). These allegorical works, all derived ultimately from Late Latin versions of the anonymous *Physiologus,* circulated widely and may be said to typify medieval writing about animals before the reintroduction of Aristotle. The most important author in the history of medieval zoology was Albertus Magnus, the bulk of whose works, including the influential *De animalibus,* were written between 1250 and 1262.

Underlying all zoological and physiological beliefs of the medieval period were the biological theories of Hippocrates and Aristotle, modified by the Greek physician Galen. It was probably Hippocrates who first enunciated the theory of the four bodily humors or fluids—*sanguis,* "blood," *cholera rubea,* "red choler," *cholera nigra,* "black choler," and *phlegma,* "phlegm"—that determined by their relative proportions and combinations in the body not only general health but also certain physical qualities or temperaments: *sanguineus,* "sanguine" (moist and hot), *cholericus,* "choleric" (hot and dry), *melancholicus,* "melancholic" (dry and cold), and *phlegmaticus,* "phlegmatic" (cold and moist). Albertus Magnus described the black falcon as a choleric animal, the juvenile peregrine falcon as phlegmatic, and the cow as melancholic. Humoralism permeated Western physiology and psychology into the nineteenth century and has experienced a revival of sorts in the twentieth century with the advent of knowledge of the endocrine system. The four humors and their corresponding four qualities were also linked to the four elements or constituents of the physical universe (*aer, ignis, terra, aqua:* air, fire, earth, and water) and the four seasons, which were matched with the four stages of human life (childhood, youth, maturity, and old age). These stages were variously schematized, in a system going back to Isidore. One common version was based on sevens, and the principal stages were *infantia* (0–7), *pueritia* or *puerilitas* (8–14), *adolescentia* (15–28), *iuventus* or *virilitas* (29–49), *senilitas* or *gravitas* (50–70), *senectus* or *senium* (71+).

Latin translations, with commentaries, of Aristotle's works (initially via Arabic) began to appear in the twelfth and thirteenth centuries; biological theories increasingly reflected his influence. In Italy in the early thirteenth century the Arabic commentary of Averroës (1126–98) on Aristotle's *De anima,* which included Aristotle's complete text, was translated into Latin, probably by Michael Scot (d. c. 1235). Discussions of Aristotle's theory of cognition referred to those internal brain functions that coordinate, record, retrieve, juxtapose, and utilize the data from the five outer senses. The *sensus communis,* common sense, combines the visual image, sound, taste, smell, and feel of a tree to form the composite, integrated sensory concept of a tree; the *sensus memorativus,* memory, stores sensory data and makes them available for retrieval; the *sensus imaginativus,* imagination, combines disparate sensory data to form arcane concepts (e.g., a purple cow); and the *sensus aestimativus,* estimative sense, combines, for example, visual and auditory information to estimate the distance of an object, such as a clanging buoy. Terms such as these became commonplace in scholastic Latin and were applied to the biological constitution of animals and people.

Aristotle's hylomorphic theory, which postulated the soul (*anima*) to be the form (*forma*) of the material body (*corpus materiale*), had profound implications for all the medieval biosciences. Thus, a vegetative soul (*anima vegetativa*) animated plant life and growth in higher forms; an animal soul (*anima animalis*) gave life to animals and human beings; the human soul (*anima humana*), however, belonged only to the human body.

Like the *De anima,* Aristotle's books on animals were also translated from Arabic by Michael Scot, possibly before 1220; the translator used the ninth-century Arabic version by Ibn al-Biṭrīq. This Latin translation, extant in more than 60 thirteenth- and fourteenth-century manuscripts, was very influential, especially in Albertus Magnus's paraphrase. Albertus also exploited Michael's translation of Avicenna's Arabic commentary, *De animalibus* or *Abbreviatio de animalibus,* which the translator dedicated to Frederick II and which became a source for the emperor's *De arte venandi.* Incorporating material from other writings (including Avicenna's *Liber canonis medicinae*), as well as the results of his own observations, Albertus produced a work comprising 26 books. These contain information about anatomy, physiognomy, reproduction, embryology, etc.; the last five books discuss man and 113 quadrupeds (bk. 22), 114 birds (bk. 23), 139 marine animals (bk. 24), and 110 other as-sorted creatures (bks. 25–26).

An inchoate system of classifying animals resulted in their division into five groups based largely on their modes of locomotion. Walking animals (*gressibilia*) in-cluded humans and quadrupeds; flying animals (*volatilia*) included birds and bats; swimming animals (*natatilia*) included fishes, aquatic mammals, and shellfish; crawling animals (*serpentia*) included snakes, crocodiles, and lizards; *vermes*, a catch-all category, included worms, grubs, snails, slugs, toads, butterflies, moths, and other insects. This system, crude as it was, was in place to anticipate Linnaeus's eighteenth-century codification of animals by genera and species.

Medieval zoology gradually progressed toward a more scientific taxonomy. In Pliny's day the word *cetus* connoted any large sea animal, particularly the whale, shark, dogfish, seal, and dolphin. Albertus Magnus narrowed it to the whale and wal-rus. He referred to the female of the species as *ball(a)ena*, merely employing the fem-inine noun (ultimately from Greek), which had originally been restricted to the whale (rather than the more general *cetus*). In Classical Latin *damma* was a generic term for members of the deer family, including fallow deer, antelope, and chamois. Albertus equated *damma* with the Arabic *algazel*, the gazelle, and his description best fitted the *gazella dorcas* of Africa.

In general, the medieval biological sciences used words from Classical Latin (e.g. *canis*, "dog" and *equus*, "horse"), classical words with changed senses (e.g. *cetus*, "whale"), words from Greek via Classical Latin (e.g. *pardus*, "leopard," Greek πάρδος), words from Arabic (e.g. *algazel*, "gazelle"), and words borrowed locally from the developing vernaculars (e.g. *mula*, "chilblain," from French *mule*, "slipper, chilblain"; *erminium*, from French *ermin*, "ermine"; *ratus*, "dormouse," from Ger-man *rat*; *zubrones*, "aurochs," from Polish *zubrzyca*).

It is well known that transliteration posed a thorny problem for readers of the Latin recensions of Aristotle. A case in point is Albertus Magnus's use of Michael Scot's Latin translation of Aristotle's books on animals. As indicated above, Michael used the Arabic version rendered by Ibn al-Biṭrīq. In some instances the Arabic translator encountered animal names in the Greek for which he was unable to give Arabic equivalents. Conscientiously, rather than give a false reading, he chose to transliterate the phonetic components of the Greek names into their Arabic coun-terparts, thereby creating Arabic neologisms. Subsequently Michael Scot was forced to transliterate the Arabic names into Latin phonetic equivalents. Albertus Magnus fell heir to these sometimes garbled transliterations when he compiled his own *De animalibus*. It was not until the second half of the thirteenth century that the new translation of Aristotle by the Dominican William of Moerbeke, directly from the Greek (c. 1260), helped to alleviate the problems associated with transliteration.

Semantic extension was common. Classical Latin *ficus*, "fig," had already been extended to mean piles or hemorrhoids, because of the superficial resemblance of the anal swelling to the fruit of the fig tree; in Medieval Latin this sense was stretched to include angleberry, a skin tumor of horses with a denuded surface resembling a fig.

Finally, the use of the word *experimentum* in the Latin Aristotelian corpus should be noted. It was used to describe a close encounter with nature, a direct ex-perience, hands-on sensory contact. In the medieval period it did not mean a planned, controlled "experiment." The scientific method involving deliberate tests with reproducible results lay far in the future, but the seeds of the method were planted when Roger Bacon (b. c. 1219) and others recognized that cognition begins by contact with the real world. It was simple observation that enabled Albertus Magnus to develop a theory of contagion that preceded by five hundred years Louis Pasteur's discovery of the microorganic cause of infectious diseases. In bk. 22 of his *De animalibus,* which includes an extensive discussion of equestrian diseases and their treatment, Albertus postulated that *stranguilina,* "strangles," an acute contagious disease of horses, was contracted by intimate association with another horse similarly afflicted, and that the mode of transmission was the inhalation of the breath from the ailing horse. Similarly, he attributed *scabies,* "scabies, mange," to direct contact of healthy horses with afflicted ones, one nipping the other, or eating at a common trough, or being rubbed down with the same cloth or strigil used on an affected horse. These observations are all the more remarkable when one considers that he had no sensory extenders, such as Leeuwenhoek's microscope, to establish a connecting cause.

## Select Bibliography

### Texts and Translations

Albertus Magnus, *De animalibus libri XXVI,* ed. H. Stadler, 2 vols. (1916–20): an edition based upon the autograph manuscript in Cologne, Historisches Archiv W 258a [EH1]; English translation of bks. 22–26 by J.J. Scanlan, *Albert the Great: Man and the Beasts* (1987), with intro. and detailed index that includes Latin technical terms (pp461–516) [EH2]; edition and English translation of complete work in two volumes, by K.F. Kitchell and I.M. Resnick, has been scheduled for publication by the Johns Hopkins University Press, Baltimore [EH3]. For brief descriptions of the *De animalibus* and Albert's other works on natural science, see [EH48], app. 1, pp566–77.

Aristotle, *Historia animalium,* 3 vols., ed. and tr. A.L. Peck (v1–2) and D.M. Balme (v3) (1965–91) [EH4]; *De partibus animalium,* ed. and tr. A.L. Peck, rev. ed. (1945) [EH5]; *De generatione animalium,* ed. and tr. A.L. Peck (1943) [EH6].

Aristotle, *De animalibus: Michael Scot's Arabic-Latin Translation, Part Three, Books XV–XIX: Generation of Animals,* ed. A.M.I. Van Oppenraaij (1992); pt1 (bks. I–X: *History of Animals*), ed. A.M.I. Van Oppenraaij, and pt2 (bks. XI–XIV: *Parts of Animals*), ed. A.M.I. Van Oppenraaij and A.P. Orbán, are in preparation [EH7].

Aristotle, *Generation of Animals: The Arabic Translation Commonly Ascribed to Yahyâ ibn al-Bitriq,* ed. J. Brugman and H.J. Drossaart Lulofs (1972) [EH8].

Aristotle, *De generatione animalium: Translatio Guillelmi de Moerbeka,* ed. H.J. Drossaart Lulofs (1966) [EH9].

Averroës (Ibn Rushd), *Commentarium magnum in Aristotelis De anima libros,* tr. Michael Scot, ed. F.S. Crawford, in *Corpus Commentariorum in Aristotelem,* v6.1 (1953) [EH10].

Avicenna (Ibn Sina), *Liber canonis medicinae* (Venice 1527, r1971) [EH11]; *Liber de animalibus Avicennae super librum De animalibus Aristotelis,* tr. Michael Scot (Lyons 1515) [EH12]; *Liber de anima, seu Sextus de naturalibus,* ed. S. Van Riet, 2 vols. (1968–72), with introduction to Avicenna's psychology by G. Verbeke [EH13].

Bartholemaeus Anglicus, *De proprietatibus rerum* (Frankfurt 1601, r1964) [EH14]; bks. 3–4: *On the Properties of Soul and Body*, ed. R.J. Long, *TMLT* 9 (1979) [EH15].

Frederick II, *De arte venandi cum avibus*, ed. C.A. Willemsen (1942) [EH16]; ed. and tr. C.A. Wood and F.M. Fyfe (1943, r1955) [EH17].

Hildegard of Bingen, *Physica*, in *PL* 197:1117–1352, with table of contents at cols. 1379–84; German translation by P. Riethe: *Naturkunde: Das Buch von dem inneren Wesen der verschiedenen Naturen in der Schöpfung* (1959) [EH18].

Hrabanus Maurus, *De rerum naturis* [*De universo*], in *PL* 111:9–614, with table of contents at cols. 1617–21 [EH19].

Hugh of Fouilloy (c. 1100–72/73), *Aviarium*, ed. and tr. W.B. Clark (1992) [EH20].

Isidore of Seville, *Etym.*: bk. 12 is concerned with animals [EH21].

Pliny the Elder, *NH* [EH22].

Solinus, *CRM* [EH23].

Thomas of Cantimpré, *Liber de natura rerum*, ed. H. Boese (1973) [EH24].

G. Tilander, ed. and tr., *Dancus Rex, Guillelmus Falconarius, Gerardus Falconarius: Les plus anciens traités de fauconnerie de l'occident, publiés d'après tous les manuscrits connus* (1963) [EH25].

B.L.R. Van den Abeele, "The Latin Treatises on Falconry of the Middle Ages" (Diss., Université catholique de Louvain, 1991): study of 29 texts written from the tenth century to the fourteenth, with app. of texts of the unedited treatises (two thirds of those identified) [EH26].

Vincent of Beauvais, *Speculum maius*, 4 vols. (Douai 1624, r1964–65): the *Naturale*, in 32 bks., is one of the four parts of Vincent's encyclopedia; it treats of God, human beings, and nature [EH27].


## Studies and Lexical Aids

J.N. Adams, *The Latin Sexual Vocabulary* (1982, r1990) [EH28].

P. Aiken, "The Animal History of Albertus Magnus and Thomas of Cantimpré," in *Speculum* 22 (1947) 205–25 [EH29].

J. André, *Les noms d'oiseaux en latin* (1967) [EH30]; id., "Noms de plantes et noms d'animaux en latin," in *Latomus* 22 (1963) 649–63 [EH31]; id., *Le vocabulaire latin de l'anatomie* (1991) [EH32].

H. Balss, *Albertus Magnus als Biologe* (1947) [EH33].

J.A. Burrow, *The Ages of Man: A Study in Medieval Writing and Thought* (1986), with app. of *loci classici* (including Augustine, Isidore, and Bede) and useful bibliography [EH34].

F. Capponi, *Ornithologia latina* (1979) [EH35].

W.B. Clark and M.T. McMunn, eds., *Beasts and Birds of the Middle Ages: The Bestiary and its Legacy* (1989) [EH36].

D.M. Dunlop, "The Translations of al-Biṭrīq and Yaḥyā (Yuḥannā) b. al-Biṭrīq," in *Journal of the Royal Asiatic Society* (1959) 140–50 [EH37].

W. George and B. Yapp, *The Naming of the Beasts: Natural History in the Medieval Bestiary* (1991) [EH38].

L.A. Gozmany *et al.*, *Vocabularium nominum animalium Europae septem linguis redactum*, 2 vols. (1979): polyglot dictionary—Latin, German, English, French, Hungarian, Spanish, Russian [EH39].

R. Klibansky *et al.*, *Saturn and Melancholy: Studies in the History of Natural Philosophy, Religion, and Art* (1964) [EH40].

F. Klingender, *Animals in Art and Thought to the End of the Middle Ages,* ed. E. Antal and J. Harthan (1971) [EH41].

C. Lecouteux, *Les monstres dans la pensée médiévale européenne: Essai de présentation* (1993) [EH42].

D.C. Lindberg, *The Beginnings of Western Science: The European Scientific Tradition in Philosophical, Religious, and Institutional Context, 600 B.C. to A.D. 1450* (1992) [EH43].

F. McCulloch, *Mediaeval Latin and French Bestiaries,* rev. ed. (1962) [EH44].

E. de Saint-Denis, *Le vocabulaire des animaux marins en latin classique* (1947) [EH45].

E. Sears, *The Ages of Man: Medieval Interpretations of the Life Cycle* (1986) [EH46].

J. Stannard, "Natural History," in *SMA* 429–60: with valuable footnote references [EH47].

J.A. Weisheipl, ed., *AMS:* important collection of 21 studies in English, with valuable bibliography (pp585–616) [EH48].

*See also* [BA69].

# E1  ✳  BOTANY

## BY R. JAMES LONG

The science of plants in the Middle Ages developed according to two distinct traditions, the one theoretical, the other practical. The former, an integral part of the natural philosophy of Aristotle, was reborn in the thirteenth century as a part of the flood of texts coming across the Pyrenees passes from Spain. It was rooted in a single text, called the *De plantis* or *De vegetabilibus,* which was translated from the Arabic by the end of the first decade of the thirteenth century, and until the sixteenth century was almost universally ascribed to Aristotle. The translator of the *De plantis* was an Englishman, Alvredus Anglicus or Alfred of Sareshel (fl. c. 1210), who writes in the prologue of the difficult task of rendering into the "narrowness" (*angustias*) of the Latin tongue from the "flowing" (*fluido*) mode of Arab speech works that were originally written in Greek.

The *De plantis,* whose true author was a peripatetic named Nicolaus of Damascus (b. c. 64 B.C.), is a repetitious work, murky and insipid. Albertus Magnus (d. 1280), one of the most perspicacious commentators on the work, blamed the inferior quality of the text on the ignorance of translators, who failed to understand either the mind of Aristotle (the putative author) or the language from which they were translating.

Its defects notwithstanding, within a generation of its having been translated into Latin the *De plantis* had become a set text in university curricula and by 1254 was prescribed by the statutes of the University of Paris as an examination subject. The survival of 159 manuscript copies bears witness to its importance and influence. As an integral part of natural philosophy, the science of plants fell within the domain of the arts faculty, and soon Arts masters were writing commentaries on the work.

The mode of analysis in these commentaries was largely zoomorphic, the plant being regarded as an imperfect animal. Hence questions were raised concerning the nature of plant life, its growth, reproduction, shedding of leaves, and death. The doctrine of the four elements, moreover, and its corollary, the four qualities, were used to explain all plant processes from germination to the ripening of fruit. In terms of classification five or six "species" were generally adduced: *arbor,* "tree"; *arbustum* or *frutex,* "shrub" or "bush"; *olus* or *olus virens,* "bushy herb"; *herba,* "herb with radical leaves"; *gramina,* "grasses"; and *fungus,* "mushroom." Finer discriminations among the more common herbs and garden vegetables were achieved by the use of modifiers: for example, *maior/minor, albus/niger, masculus/femina, aes-*

*tivum/hiemale.* As applied to leaves, thick was *spissus* and narrow was *strictus,* not *angustus.*

The word *arbustum* provides a good illustration of how certain terms gradually changed meaning from the classical period to the thirteenth century. Pliny the Elder (d. A.D. 79) had used the word to denote a vineyard or plantation of trees on which vines were trained; by the time Isidore of Seville was writing in the seventh century the word had acquired the additional meaning of sapling; and in the thirteenth century it came to mean shrub, as in the modern French word *arbuste.*

The second parallel tradition, as practical as the *De plantis* tradition is theoretical, is known generically as herbalism, though no Medieval Latin name identified it. Only in the Renaissance did it acquire a name, coined in the classical style: *res herbaria.* Beginning with Theophrastus, or in a more narrow sense with Dioscorides's *De materia medica,* this empirical and, from the medieval perspective, unscientific tradition prospered uninterruptedly from the Hellenic age through the Renaissance and indeed into modern times. The *De materia medica* entered the Latin West via two channels: the *Naturalis historia* of Pliny, probably the single most influential text for medieval botany, and an alphabetized and latinized version of the Dioscorides text, called *Dioscorides alphabeticus.*

Plants themselves were usually referred to in this tradition by their medicinal use as *simplices,* "simples" or "simple drugs," as opposed to the elaborate "compound drugs." The word *simplex,* which came into currency when Galen's treatise on the subject was translated into Latin as *De simplicium medicamentorum facultatibus* or *De simplicibus,* signified any substance—vegetable, animal, or mineral—that was used as a drug in its unalloyed state, not as an ingredient in a compound. The common name for the practitioner of herbalism was *rhizotome,* the Latin transliteration of the Greek word for "root cutter." *Apotheca,* used in an edict of Frederick II in the sense of a storehouse for drugs, and *apothecarius,* "druggist," evolved from the Byzantine word for import-export depots in main harbors and road termini, thus demonstrating the close relationship between trade and drugs in the early Middle Ages.

The growth of plant terminology was haphazard at best. The majority of plant names are Latin, though many hundreds of vernacular names occur in late medieval texts. Latin transliterations of Greek and (later in the tradition) Arabic names are common: for example, *menthe,* "mint," for the Greek *minthe,* or *scilla,* "squill," for the Greek *skilla.* When, as often happened, the translator neglected to determine whether there already existed a Latin or vernacular equivalent, the confusion was compounded. During the thirteenth century, for example, there were in circulation many different words for "amber," including *ambra* (from the Arabic for ambergris), *karabe* (Arabic), *succinum* (Latin), *lugerion* (latinized Greek), *electrum* (latinized Greek), and *Bernstein* (German). In fact, as many as 15 synonyms for the same plant have been counted, and it is not unheard of that two or more words for the same herb appear *in the same recipe.*

In short, until the epoch-making work of the Swedish botanist Carolus Linnaeus in the eighteenth century, there was no generally accepted scientific name that uniquely and unambiguously denoted one species of plant. Though there were some Latin polynomials in use in the Middle Ages, most plants were known by a single-word name. These terms, whether in Latin or the vernacular, were usually philologically cognate and hence readily understandable by most educated people. The family of vegetables that we call "lettuce," for example, was termed *lactuca, lattuga,* French *laitue,* and German *Lattich;* and the exotic "sugar" was called *sachar, saccharum,* Italian *zucchero,* French *sucre,* and German *Zucker.* On the rare occasion that a folk name occurred, it would in more formal or academic texts be accompanied by the phrase *ut rustici dicunt,* "as peasants say," to warn the reader of its restricted currency.

The literary forms of plant science were several: (1) herbals or *Kräuterbücher:* lists of descriptions of plants believed to be of therapeutic value, accompanied by medical, pharmacological, and sometimes botanical data; (2) leechbooks: general medical handbooks designed to incorporate everything necessary for the practicing physician, including plant lore; (3) *receptaria,* "recipe collections," and *antidotaria,* "antidote collections": arrangements of various complaints and the recipes that correspond thereto; (4) glossaries and lexica: lists of botanical terms and their synonyms, an indispensable aid in a bilingual culture; and (5) encyclopedias: compendia of information in a variety of fields, encompassing plant lists as well.

Occasionally the two traditions, philosophical/scientific and empirical/descriptive, would converge, as for example in the great encyclopedic compilations of the thirteenth century, the *De proprietatibus rerum* of Bartholomaeus Anglicus (which alphabetically lists 194 plants), the *De natura rerum* of Thomas of Cantimpré, the *Speculum maius* of Vincent of Beauvais, and even more notably in the aforementioned *De vegetabilibus* of Albertus Magnus. The latter was, however, explicitly apologetic in introducing the herbal books (6–7) of his massive commentary: he includes his catalogue of individual plants, he says, "more to satisfy the curiosity of students than philosophy, since particulars do not fall within the competence of philosophy."

A study of library catalogues that survive from the Middle Ages confirms the bifurcation of the botanical tradition. The herbals, such as Dioscorides, parts of Galen's *Canon,* and Pliny, are virtually unknown outside monastic collections, and the Pseudo-Aristotle and the commentaries thereon are located almost exclusively in university collections. On the premise that the book that is not there is not going to be read, it is no mystery that philosophical botany, which was for the medievals the *science* of plants, remained distinct from the herbalist tradition throughout the Middle Ages.

## Select Bibliography

### Primary Works

The *De plantis* was first edited by E.H.F. Meyer (1841): *Nicolai Damasceni De plantis libri duo Aristoteli vulgo adscripti* [EII]. As was the case, however, before ease of travel and microfilming made wider access to manuscripts possible, Meyer's edition was based on only three manuscripts, and those apparently chosen on the grounds of convenience (two of the codices are at Wolfenbüttel, the third at Basel). The *Aristoteles Semitico-Latinus* Project, under the auspices of the Royal Dutch Academy of Sciences, has recently published a new edition of the Syriac, Arabic, Hebrew, and Latin versions of the *De plantis,* ed. H.J. Drossaart Lulofs and E.L.J. Poortman:

*Nicolaus Damascenus, De plantis: Five Translations* (1989) [EI2]. Though reviewers may disagree with this or that detail, this edition is clearly definitive.

Of the nine extant Latin commentaries on *De plantis*, only three have thus far been published: Alfred of Sareshel, *Super librum De vegetabilibus*, ed. R.J. Long, in *MS* 47 (1985) 125–67 [EI3]; Roger Bacon, *Quaestiones supra De plantis*, in *Opera hactenus inedita Rogeri Baconi*, ed. R. Steele and F.M. Delorme, fasc. 11 (1932) 171–252 [EI4]; and Albertus Magnus, *De vegetabilibus libri VII*, ed. E.H.F. Meyer and K. Jessen (1867) [EI5]. An edition of the Bodleian epitome by R.J. Long has been published in *Aspectus et Affectus: Essays and Editions in Grosseteste and Medieval Intellectual Life in Honor of Richard C. Dales*, ed. G. Freibergs (1993) 87–103 [EI6]. Critical editions by R.J. Long of Adam of Buckfield's commentary and by E.L.J. Poortman of Peter of Auvergne's commentary are in preparation [EI7].

For the principal sources of herbalistic botany see Dioscorides, *De materia medica libri quinque*, ed. M. Wellmann, 3 vols. (1907–14, r1958) [EI8]; Isidore of Seville, *Etym.* [EI9]; Pliny the Elder, *NH* [EI10]; and Theophrastus, *Historia plantarum*, ed. and tr. A. Hort, 2 vols. (1916) [EI11].

## Studies

E.H.F. Meyer's four-volume study entitled *Geschichte der Botanik* (1854–57, r1965) is exhaustive but dated [EI12]. Another recent study focuses on Albert's work on plants: K.M. Reeds, "Albert on the Natural Philosophy of Plant Life," in *AMS* 341–54 [EI13]. And the stages in the development of the science of plants, at Oxford in particular, are the focus of R.J. Long, "The Reception and Interpretation of the Pseudo-Aristotelian *De plantis* at Oxford in the Thirteenth Century," in *Knowledge and the Sciences in Medieval Philosophy: Proceedings of the Eighth International Congress of Medieval Philosophy (S.I.E.P.M.)*, v3, Annals of the Finnish Society for Missiology and Ecumenics 55, ed. R. Työrinoja, A.I. Lehtinen, and D. Follesdal (1990) 111–23 [EI14]. See also R.J. Long, "The Anonymous Peterhouse Master and the Natural Philosophy of Plants," in *Traditio* 46 (1991) 313–26 [EI15].

For secondary literature on herbalism and the herbalist tradition one could not do better than to begin with the impressive body of writings by Jerry Stannard, the English-speaking world's leading authority on the subject: see, for example, "Medieval Herbals and Their Development," in *Clio Medica* 9 (1974) 23–33 [EI16]; "Alimentary and Medicinal Uses of Plants," in *Medieval Gardens*, ed. E.B. MacDougall, Dumbarton Oaks Colloquium on the History of Landscape Architecture, v9 (1986) 71–91 [EI17]; "Albertus Magnus and Medieval Herbalism," in *AMS* 355–78 [EI18]; "Byzantine Botanical Lexicography," in *Episteme* 5 (1971) 168–87 [EI19]; "Greco-Roman Materia Medica in Medieval Germany," in *Bulletin of the History of Medicine* 46 (1972) 455–68 [EI20]; "Identification of the Plants Described by Albertus Magnus, *De vegetabilibus*, lib. VI," in *RPL* 2 (1979) 281–318 [EI21]; "Medicinal Plants and Folk Remedies in Pliny, *Historia Naturalis*," in *History and Philosophy of the Life Sciences* 4 (1982) 1–23 [EI22]. For a modern lexicon of botanical terms see J. André, *Lexique des termes de botanique en Latin* (1956) [EI23]. For further bibliographic entries see Jerry Stannard's entry, "Botany," in *DMA* 2:344–49 [EI24], to which may be added J. André, *Les noms de plantes dans la Rome antique* (1985) [EI25]; T. Hunt, *Plant Names of Medieval England* (1989) [EI26]; A. Dietrich, *Die Dioskurides-Erklärung des Ibn al-Baitar: Ein Beitrag zur arabischen Pflanzensynonymik des Mittelalters* (1991) [EI27]; B.

Ribémont and G. Sodigné-Costes, "Botanique médiévale: tradition, observation, imaginaire: L'exemple de l'encyclopédisme," in *Le moyen âge et la science. Approche de quelques disciplines et personnalités scientifiques médiévales: Actes du colloque, Orléans* (22–23 April 1988), ed. B. Ribémont (1991) 153–69 [EI28]; W.T. Stearn, *Botanical Latin: History, Grammar, Syntax, Terminology, and Vocabulary*, 4th ed. (1992) [EI29]; and K.M. Reeds, *Botany in Medieval and Renaissance Universities* (1991), with a recent and comprehensive bibliography (pp262–83) of the science of botany as it was taught in medieval and renaissance universities [EI30].

# EJ ❋ GEOLOGY

## BY JOHN M. RIDDLE

Information about Medieval Latin terms for rocks, minerals, and metals (our modern science of geology and the related fields of mineralogy and gemmology) can be gleaned from encyclopedias (in such sections as *de metallis* and *de lapidibus*) and from specialized works on alchemy, stones (lapidaries), medicine, and astrology. The encyclopedic tradition extends from Pliny (and the derivative Solinus), through Isidore (d. 636), to Lambert of St. Omer (d. c. 1125), Hildegard of Bingen (d. 1179), Alexander Neckam (d. 1217), Bartholomaeus Anglicus (d. after 1250), Arnold of Saxony (fl. early thirteenth century), Vincent of Beauvais (d. 1264), Thomas of Cantimpré (d. c. 1270/72), and Albertus Magnus (d. 1280). Among the ultimate sources were Aristotle (d. 322 B.C.), especially his *De coelo et mundo* and *De meteoris,* which were not available directly until the later Middle Ages, and the *De lapidibus* of Theophrastus of Eresus (quoted by Pliny). Also important were the pseudo-Aristotelian *De proprietatibus elementorum* and *Lapidarium* and early Latin versions of Dioscorides (*De materia medica*) and Damigeron (*De virtutibus lapidum*). The Arabic tradition is a primary source, including the *De congelatione et conglutinatione lapidum* (or *De mineralibus*) of Avicenna (d. 1037), the *Kitāb Sirr al-asrār* (*Secretum secretorum*), the translations of medical treatises by Constantine the African (d. c. 1087), and the works of such alchemical, medical, and astrological writers as Jābir ibn Ḥayyān (d. 815), Thābit ibn Qurra (d. 901), Qusṭa ibn Lūqā (d. c. 912), and al-Rāzī (d. 925). Some relevant texts, e.g. the *Tabula smaragdina* and the *De quindecim stellis, quindecim lapidibus, quindecim herbis, et quindecim imaginibus,* are attributed simply to "Hermes." One of the most popular lapidaries was the *De lapidibus* by Marbode of Rennes (d. 1123), written in Latin hexameters.

Minerals were thought to be a mixture of two of the four elements, earth and water, more rarely with small increments of fire and air. They were uniform (*homiomera*), in contrast to animal and vegetable substances, which were *anhomiomera,* and they were divided into three or four groups: stones (*lapides*), metals (*metalla*), and substances intermediate (*media*) between stones and metals.

Stones were thought to be born continuously because of the *virtus mineralis:* river pebbles (*terminati*) were produced by the action of water on earth, "moonshells" (*lunares*) by the effect of the moon on marine animals; stones were transformed (*transmutati*) by clouds, rain, and snow. Some stones are of animal and vegetable substances—e.g. *ambra* (hardened rosin), *gagates* (jet), *gegolitus* (olive seed), and *sadda* (barnacle shell)—so that there was debate over whether a stone had an *anima* corresponding to animal and vegetable souls.

Metals were distinguished from stones by their fusibility (*comminuabilitas*) and malleability (*ductilitas*), and all metals were believed to contain *sulphur,* called the *pater,* and quicksilver (*argentum*), the *mater.* Terms for metals and metallic ores overlapped and are not easily distinguished: iron included *ferrum, oritis, sideritis, chalybs, ematites,* and *magnes;* copper included *misum, aes, cuprum,* and *melochites.* Metals could suffer from diseases (*egritudines,* such as *antrax* and *venenum*) and changes were described in medical terms (*putrefactio, purgatio, generatio*). The influence of alchemical writers is seen in much of the vocabulary (*coagulatio, conglutio, congelatio, balbutio, dolabilitas, transparens, lac virginis, lachryma*) and in words describing mineral formation (*elixatio, transmutatio, calcinatio, inhumatio, levigatio*).

The intermediate minerals included various salts, sulfates of both copper and iron, alum, arsenic sulfides (*arsenicum*), various metallic ores called *marchasita* that were not recognized clearly as metals, and *nitrum,* which was used for different substances that include our niter and saltpeter. On the authority of Avicenna some medieval lapidaries identified a fourth class of minerals, sulphurs, but this group was placed within the category of intermediate minerals by Albert and most other authorities.

Much attention was paid to stones because of their supposed medical, magical, and prophylactic properties: *calcedonius* was worn to win lawsuits, *smaragdus* to ward off fevers, *topazius* against hemorrhoids. This attention was focused in lapidaries, which are extant in over 1,000 manuscripts and were composed all over Europe (and often translated into the vernaculars). One type of lapidary was concerned with the three closely related lists of stones in the Bible (*Ex* 28:17–20, 39:10–13; *Ez* 28:13; and *Apc* 21:19–20), to which commentators such as Bede (d. 735), in his *Explanatio Apocalypsis,* assigned allegorical or mystical meanings. Sometimes the stones were made to correlate with the signs of the zodiac. Another type of lapidary concentrated on stones with distinctive appearances (*imago, prestigiatura*), whether natural (likenesses of persons or objects formed by the irregular distribution of minerals in strata) or artificial (engraved or incised sigils, fossil molds, or impressions). The naturally formed *agathes, pantherus, hiena,* and *ophthalmus* were named for their appearance. Whether natural or artificial, the images on stones were often thought to have been impressed by celestial bodies. Lapidaries concerned with engraved images or sigils are usually found in codices associated with astrology. In contrast, the medical powers of stones are illustrated by the juxtaposition of lapidaries with herbals in codices; their effects were psychological (*lunatica, timorosa, malefica*) and physical (*infirma, suspiriosa, abortiva,* etc.).

There was no systematic nomenclature for stones, minerals, and metals, as many names were distorted in their transmission from antiquity or from Arabic texts, and many minerals did not have formal names, or changed their names, or had several different names. Modern geological and gemmological terminology is not always accurate in a medieval context, as some medieval names could identify several different minerals.

The primary sources for the medieval lexicon of stones, minerals, and metals are as follows: Classical Latin (*aurum, ferrum, carbunculus, aes ustum*) and classical metaphors (*squama aeris, flos aeris*); Greek via Classical Latin (*nitrum, arsenicum, gypsum, cadmia*); Greek directly (*andromanta, borax, calcaphanos*), especially in the terms for heating of metals (*pepansis, epsesis, optesis*) and underheating (*molynsis*). From Arabic came *ambra, kacabre, marchasita,* and *sal alkali.* On classical roots Medieval Latin produced *specularis* and on Greek roots *filacterium* and *orphanus.* Some stones were named for places: *lippares* (*liparea, lypparea*), found in the Lipari islands; *memphites* from Memphis; *medius* from Media; *lapis armenicus* from Armenia; and (Arabic-derived) *balagius* from Badakhshan. A magical gem found in the brain of a vulture was called a *quandros,* and the *alectorius* was said to come from the gizzard of a castrated cock.

## Select Bibliography

### Texts and Translations

Albertus Magnus, *De mineralibus* [*Mineralium libri quinque*], in *Opera omnia,* ed. A. Borgnet, 38 vols. (1890–99), v5:1–103; tr. D. Wyckoff (1967): expert translation with extensive commentary, Latin-English glossary, brief history of lapidaries (app. B), and useful bibliography (pp293–301) [EJ1].

Alexander Neckam, *De naturis rerum,* bks. 1–2, ed. T. Wright, in *RSer* 34 (1863) 1–354; bks. 3–5 unprinted: see bk. 2:48–98 on the earth, its minerals, plants, precious stones [EJ2].

Pseudo-Aristotle, *De proprietatibus elementorum,* in *Aristotelis opera* (Venice 1496) [EJ3].

Pseudo-Aristotle, *Lapidarium Aristotelis,* or *De lapidibus* (two versions), in V. Rose, ed., "Aristoteles *De lapidibus* und Arnoldus Saxo," in *ZDADL* 18, n.f., 6 (1875) 321–455 (with texts on pp349–82, 384–97) [EJ4]; ed. J. Ruska, *Das Steinbuch des Aristoteles* (1912) [EJ5]: important treatise because of Aristotle's prestige and popularity and the possibility that the text was based on a lost work by him.

Arnold of Saxony (Arnoldus Saxo), *De finibus rerum naturalium,* ed. E. Stange (1905–7): bk. 3, *De gemmarum virtutibus,* lists 81 stones [EJ6].

Avicenna, *De congelatione et conglutinatione lapidum,* ed. and tr. E.J. Holmyard and D.C. Mandeville (1927, r1982): a Latin paraphrase (c. 1200) by Alfred of Sareshel of three chapters of the *Shifāʾ* of Avicenna [EJ7].

Bartholomaeus Anglicus, *De proprietatibus rerum* (Frankfurt 1601, r1964), bk. 16 [EJ8].

Bede, *Explanatio Apocalypsis, PL* 93:129–206 [EJ9].

Constantine the African, *Opera,* 2 vols. (Basel 1536–39); eight of his translations were also published in the *Opera Isaac* (Lyons 1515): see especially *De gradibus liber* (Basel 1536) 342–87 [EJ10].

Damigeron, *De virtutibus lapidum,* ed. E. Abel, *Orphei Lithica* (1881, r1971) 161–95 [EJ11], and J. Evans (see [EJ30]), app. A, pp195–213 [EJ12]: two of the surviving forms of the Latin Damigeron are preceded by the spurious letter of Evax, king of the Arabs, to the emperor Tiberius concerning the use of stones.

Dioscorides, *De materia medica libri quinque,* ed. M. Wellmann, 3 vols. (1907–14, r1958); tr. J. Goodyer, *The Greek Herbal of Dioscordies,* ed. R. Gunther (1934, r1959) [EJ13]. For the Latin tradition see J.M. Riddle, "Dioscorides," in *CTC* 4:1–143, at p20ff. [EJ14].

Hermes (Trismegistus), *Tabula smaragdina,* ed. J. Ruska (1926) [EJ15]; *De quindecim stellis, quindecim lapidibus, quindecim herbis, et quindecim imaginibus,* ed. L. De-latte, *Textes latins et vieux français relatifs aux Cyranides* (1942) 235–89 [EJ16]

Hildegard of Bingen, *Physica* [*Liber simplicis medicinae*], *PL* 197:1117–1352, with table of contents at 1379–84; German translation of bk. 4, on stones, by P. Riethe: *Das Buch von den Steinen* (1979), with photographs, notes, and bibliography [EJ17].

Isidore of Seville, *Etym.*: see bk. 16, on stones and metals, drawn chiefly from Pliny [EJ18].

Lambert of St. Omer, *Liber floridus,* ed. A. Derolez (1968) [EJ19].

Marbode (Marbod) of Rennes, *De lapidibus,* ed. J.M. Riddle: *Marbode of Rennes' (1035–1123) "De Lapidibus" Considered as a Medical Treatise, with Text, Commentary and C.W. King's Translation Together with Text and Translation of Marbode's Minor Works on Stones* (1977) [EJ20].

Pliny the Elder, *NH:* see bks. 33 (precious metals), 34 (base metals), 35 (earths), 36 (stones, building materials, etc.), 37 (precious stones, gems, other stones with re-markable properties); indices of minerals: v9:419–21, v10:341–44 [EJ21].

*Secretum secretorum* (two Arabic versions): "short" version, in Latin translation (c. 1150) of John of Toledo, ed. J. Brinkmann, *Die apokryphnen Gesundheitsregeln des Aristoteles für Alexander den Grossen in der Übersetzung des Johann von Toledo* (1914) 39–46; "long" version, in Latin translation (early thirteenth century) of Philippus Tripolitanus, ed. Roger Bacon: *Opera hactenus inedita Rogeri Baconi,* ed. R. Steele and F.M. Delorme, fasc. 5 (1920) 1–175, with Steele's English trans-lation of the Arabic original (pp176–266) [EJ22].

Solinus, *CRM* [EJ23].

Theophrastus, *De lapidibus,* ed. and tr. D.E. Eichholz (1965) [EJ24].

Thomas of Cantimpré, *Liber de natura rerum,* ed. H. Boese (1973): see bks. 14–15 on precious stones and the seven metals [EJ25].

Vincent of Beauvais, *Speculum maius,* 4 vols. (Douai 1624, r1964–65): see the *Speculum naturale* (one of the four parts of the *Speculum maius*), bks. 8 (on metals) and 9 (on stones) [EJ26].

## Studies

L. Baisier, *The Lapidaire Chrétien, Its Composition, Its Influence, Its Sources* (1936, r1969) [EJ27].

E.H. Byrne, "Some Medieval Gems and Relative Values," in *Speculum* 10 (1935) 177–87 [EJ28].

A. Closs, "Die Steinbücher in kulturhistorischer Überschau," in *Graz Landesmuseum Joanneum Mineralogisches Mitteilungsblatt* 8 (1958) 1–34 [EJ29].

J. Evans, *Magical Jewels of the Middle Ages and the Renaissance, particularly in England* (1922, r1976) [EJ30].

D. Goltz, *Studien zur Geschichte der Mineralnamen in Pharmazie, Chemie und Medi-zin von den Anfängen bis Paracelsus* (1972); thorough study with background on ancient West Asian and Arabic terminology [EJ31].

R. Halleux, "Damigéron, Evax et Marbode," in *SM,* 3rd ser., 15 (1974) 327–47 [EJ32].

U.T. Holmes, "Mediaeval Gem Stones," *Speculum* 9 (1934) 195–204 [EJ33].

P. Kitson, "Lapidary Traditions in Anglo-Saxon England: Part I, The Background; the Old English Lapidary," in *ASE* 7 (1978) 9–60; and *id.,* "Lapidary Traditions in Anglo-Saxon England: Part II, Bede's *Explanatio Apocalypsis* and Related Works," in *ASE* 12 (1983) 73–123 [EJ34].

C. Meier, *Gemma spiritalis: Methode und Gebrauch der Edelsteinallegorese vom frühen Christentum bis ins 18. Jahrhundert,* Münstersche Mittelalter-Schriften 34 (Munich 1977–), 2 vols., of which only the first has appeared [EJ35].

F. de Mély, *Les lapidaires de l'antiquité et du moyen âge,* vols. 1–2, 3.1 (1896–1902) [EJ36].

J.M. Riddle, "Lithotherapy in the Middle Ages: Lapidaries Considered as Medical Texts," in *Pharmacy in History* 12 (1970) 39–50: describes the medical uses of many lapidary works, which could be consulted for psychosomatic, physical, or pathological problems [EJ37].

J.M. Riddle and J.A. Mulholland, "Albert on Stones and Minerals," in *AMS* 203–34 [EJ38].

V. Rose, "Damigeron de lapidibus," in *Hermes* 9 (1875) 471–91 [EJ39].

G.F.H. Smith, *Gemstones,* 13th ed., rev. F.C. Phillips (1962): useful for classical and biblical nomenclature [EJ40].

M. Steinschneider, "Lapidarien: Ein culturgeschichtlicher Versuch," in *Semitic Studies in Memory of Rev. Dr. Alexander-Kohut,* ed. G.A. Kohut (1897) 42–72 [EJ41].

H. Strunz, "Die Mineralogie bei Albertus Magnus," in *Acta Albertina, Regensburger Naturwissenschaften* 20.1 (1951–52) 19–39 [EJ42].

P. Studer and J. Evans, *Anglo-Norman Lapidaries* (1924, r1976) [EJ43].

L. Thorndike, *HMES* v1–2 [EJ44].

L. Thorndike, "De Lapidibus," in *Ambix* 8 (1960) 6–23 [EJ45].

L. Thorndike, "The Latin Pseudo-Aristotle and Medieval Occult Science," in *Journal of English and Germanic Philology* 21 (1922) 229–58 [EJ46].

L. Thorndike, "Traditional Medieval Tracts Concerning Engraved Astrological Images," in *MAP* 217–74 [EJ47].

K.W. Wirbelauer, *Antike Lapidarien* (1937) [EJ48].

# EK · CHEMISTRY AND ALCHEMY

## BY MICHELA PEREIRA

We cannot properly speak of "chemistry" when approaching the alchemical writings of the Middle Ages because, unlike sciences such as mathematics or astronomy, today's chemistry does not derive *directly* from any classical or medieval discipline. A medieval Latin "chemical" terminology— especially names of chemical substances, operations, tools—may be gathered by referring to chapters EJ, FI, and FK.

Alchemy reached the Latin West about the middle of the twelfth century through translations from the Arabic. Islamic alchemy had inherited the Hellenistic tradition, adding to it ideas probably derived from the Chinese Taoist search for a medicine of immortality. No Classical Latin tradition of alchemical writings existed: the language of alchemy is a product of the Middle Ages.

## Alchemical Doctrines

Alchemy is the philosophical search for material perfection by means of the manipulation of rough materials. The origin of the name (*alchemia, alkimia*) is uncertain, though the prefix *al-* is clearly the Arabic definite article. In the earliest writings (e.g. the so-called *Testament of Morienus*—sometimes identified simply as *Morienus*—the first alchemical work to be translated from Arabic in 1144), the word *alchemia* refers to the product of the operative process (*opus* or *compositio*); later it was used as the general label for the *ars* or *magisterium transmutationis*. The transmutation was produced by means of a substance called *elixir* (from Arabic *al-iksīr*), *medicina,* or *lapis philosophorum* ("lapis qui non est lapis"; not literally a stone, but an incorruptible substance resistant to fire) that changed base metals into silver or gold. An elixir that produced silver was termed *lunificus* because of the association between the moon and silver; one that produced gold was *solificus* from the association between gold and the sun. Some alchemists, however, searched for a more general agent of transformation, ascribing perfection even to human bodies. The *elixir* or *medicina* could be multiplied (*multiplicatio*), thus radiating its perfection (*proicere, proiectio*) through a potentially infinite amount of matter.

Metallurgical alchemy was grounded on a theory of metal structure deriving from Aristotle's *Meteorologica* (or *Meteora*), developed by Albertus Magnus (d. 1280) in his *De mineralibus* (c. 1254) and in the alchemical works attributed to him. The four elements (earth, water, air, fire) produced two exhalations, one hot (*sulphur*), the other cold (*mercurius*). Their composition according to different proportions formed the seven metals (also called *corpora*): *plumbum, stannum, ferrum, aes, mercurius* (*argentum vivum*), *argentum, aurum* (lead, tin, iron, copper, mercury or quicksilver, silver, gold). These corresponded to the planets—Saturn, Mars, Jupiter, Venus, Mercury, Moon, Sun—whose names were often used synonymously, as for example *luna*, "silver"; moreover, they were arranged on a "ladder" rising from the least perfect, lead (*plumbum*, also called *aurum leprosum*), to the most perfect, gold (*aurum*). Concrete operations were generally performed on mineral bodies rather than on pure metals, and during the thirteenth century reagents (*arsenicum, borax, sal* of various kinds, *atramenta, alumina*) and mineral acids (*aquae fortes* or *acutae*) are for the first time prepared and used in the *opus*. The term *opus* cannot be rendered in any modern language without a reduction of its full and proper meaning. It refers to the true conceptual core of all alchemical doctrine, indicating the close association between the imitation of natural processes and man's creative effort and concrete carftsmanship in producing the agent of transmutation.

The technological development of Western alchemy is best illustrated by the *Summa perfectionis* of Paul of Taranto, an otherwise unknown Franciscan friar who is generally known as the "Latin Geber." William Newman has shown [EK16] that this friar is the author of the famous *Summa perfectionis* as well as of another alchemical work, *Theorica et practica*. Paul assumed the name of the Arabic alchemist known in the Latin West as "Geber"—a name, by the way, under which the writings of a group of Islamic alchemists had been collected—perhaps to point to the source of his alchemical doctrines.

A more general theory of alchemy, developed by Roger Bacon (d. c. 1291), was based on the idea that it was possible to regress from elementary bodies (*elementata*) to their unitary root (*radix*), called the first matter (*materia prima*), in order to separate the four elements and then refine and unite them again, producing a more balanced mixture.

## The Alchemical *Opus*

The basic procedure of the alchemical *opus* was the dissolving of bodies into a dark mass (*putrefactio*), from which their constitutive principles were extracted or separated and eventually reunited (*coniunctio*). These principles were sulphur and mercury, or the four elements, often defined as the "body" (*corpus*, the solid part) and the "soul" or "spirit" (*anima/spiritus*, the airy part). The extraction or separation was achieved by several operations: *ablutio* (washing), *calcinatio* (drying), *ceratio* (softening to produce a waxlike consistency), *coagulatio* or *congelatio* (solidifying), *dissolutio* (dissolving), *distillatio* (distilling), *fixio* (hardening), *sublimatio* (sublimating), etc. These operations involved different degrees of fire (*ignis regimina*) and glass or pottery vessels (*alembicum, aludel, cucurbita, pelicanum*, etc.) hermetically sealed with a special clay (*lutum sapientium*) and cooked in special furnaces (*athanor, furnus philosophorum*). Each operation had to be repeated until all principles had reached a state of extreme refinement (*subtiliatio, exuberatio*), so that what was solid became airy (*volatile*) and what was airy became solid (*fixum*), uniting in an intermediate state.

The stages of the *opus* are treated differently by different authors, but all alchemical writers assumed that the colors (*colores*) revealed in its fulfillment were signs of the rightness (or wrongness) of their work. The beginning was characterized by blackness (*nigredo*); the intermediate stage by a multitude of colors (*cauda pavonis*) or by greenness (*viriditas*); the final attainment was called *albedo* (whiteness) when silver was obtained, or *rubedo* (redness) when the ultimate stage, gold, was reached (or even when silver or gold, respectively, was used as the yeast, *fermentum*, of the elixir).

When base metals were involved, the ultimate goal of alchemy was defined as *tingere* (to dye) and the transmutation agent as *tinctura* (dyeing). If human bodies (or alchemically made gems) were involved, alchemists claimed to bring them to a perfect elementary balance (*perfectum temperamentum*).

## Alchemy and Medicine

The idea of *temperamentum* linked alchemy and medicine in Roger Bacon's "experimental science" and in the *elixir* treatises of the fourteenth century attributed to Arnald of Villanova and Raymond Lull. The term *temperamentum* was used in medicine to mean the stability and bodily health produced by the even distribution of the four humors; in alchemy it indicated the perfect balance of the four elementary qualities in the agent of transmutation, the elixir, whereby incorruptibility was conferred upon every kind of body, both metallic and human.

An important development occurred when alchemical practice was joined to the tradition of the *aquae medicinales.* In a treatise (*De consideratione quintae essentiae,* 1351–52) written by John of Rupescissa, the *elixir* evolved into the idea of a *quinta essentia* (fifth essence) or *aqua vitae* (water of life), which derived from the repeated distillation (*circulatio*) of wine; it could extract (*extrahere*) medical virtues from herbs and mineral substances, especially gold. The therapeutic use of artificial gold had already been advocated by Roger Bacon, who distinguished poisonous gold extracted from ore (*aurum vulgi*) from alchemical gold, later called *aurum potabile* (potable gold). *Aqua vitae* was also given the name *aqua ardens* (burning water) to stress its paradoxical character.

## Metaphorical Language

Since the period of the first translations, alchemical language was characterized by obscurity and by the use of metaphors, often intended either to disguise truth, the knowledge of which was reserved to the initiate (*filius*), or to communicate phenomena that could not be described literally. The use of aliases by Arabic authors contributed to the obscurity of the language associated with this previously unknown science. The Latin texts are generally rich in imagery, but alchemists never developed for their *ars* a technical language (although some tried to assign to it a "scientific" value), and they neither would nor could entirely free their writings of metaphors.

It is impossible to list exhaustively the hundreds of metaphorical names, symbolic images, and paradoxes that were selected from various fields. A few examples must suffice. From biology and sexuality came the notion of the metals as father, mother, and children; the final product as *filius philosophorum;* and a wasting acid as *menstruum.* From astronomy came the use of *sol* and *luna* for gold and silver, and *coelum philosophorum* for the wine alcohol. From theology came the analogy between Christ's *opus salvationis* and the restorative effect on base metals and human bodies attributed to the *lapis philosophorum*. From the social hierarchy came the description of gold as the *rex* of metals. The volatility of quicksilver was expressed by employing the image of the *servus fugitivus* (the runaway servant), the causticity of an acid by calling it *acetum acerrimum* (the strongest vinegar) or *leo viridis* (the green lion), and the paradoxical simplicity of the *opus* by defining it as *opus mulierum, ludus puerorum* (women's work, children's play).

## Select Bibliography

### Introductions and Bibliographies

There are brief historical orientations, with bibliographies, by R. Halleux ("Alchemy") [EK1] and M.W. Dols ("Alchemy, Islamic") [EK2] in *DMA* 1:134–40 and 1:140–42.

R. Halleux, *Les textes alchimiques, TSMAO* 32 (1979) [EK3].
C. Kren, *Alchemy in Europe: A Guide to Research* (1990) [EK4].
R.P. Multhauf, *The Origins of Chemistry* (1966, r1993) [EK5].
M. Pereira, *L'oro dei filosofi: Saggio sulle idee di un alchimista del Trecento* (1992) [EK6].

### Studies of Alchemical Language

M.P. Crosland, *Historical Studies in the Language of Chemistry,* rev. ed. (1978) [EK7].
D. Goltz, *Studien zur Geschichte der Mineralnamen in Pharmazie, Chemie und Medizin von den Anfängen bis Paracelsus* (1972) [EK8].
R. Halleux, "Problèmes de lexicographie alchimiste," in *LLM* 355–65 [EK9].

### Translations from the Arabic and Early Latin Texts

Avicenna, *Liber Abuali Abincine De anima in arte alchimiae,* in *Artis chemicae principes* (Basel 1572), pp. a1–G4 [EK10].
Constantine of Pisa, *Liber secretorum alchimie,* ed. and tr. B. Obrist (1990) [EK11].
Morienus, *A Testament of Alchemy,* ed. and tr. L. Stavenhagen: *A Testament of Alchemy; being the Revelations of Morienus . . . of the Divine Secrets of the Magisterium and Accomplishment of the Alchemical Art* (1974) [EK12].
Razi [= Abū Bakr Muḥammad ibn Zakariyyā al-Rāzī], *Liber secretorum de voce Bubacaris* (MS Paris, B.N., lat. 6514, fols. 101v–112v; Arabic original in J. Ruska, "Übersetzung und Bearbeitungen von al-Razis Buch *Geheimnis der Geheimnisse,*" in *Quellen und Studien zur Geschichte der Naturwissenschaften und der Medizin* 4.3 (1935) 1–87 [EK13].

### Metallurgical Alchemy

Albertus Magnus, *De mineralibus* [*Mineralium libri quinque*], in *Opera omnia,* ed. A. Borgnet, 38 vols. (1890–99), v5:1–103; tr. D. Wyckoff (1967) [EK14].

Ps.-Albertus Magnus, *Libellus de alchemia,* in *Opera omnia* (see [EK14]), v37:545–73; tr. V. Heines (1958) [EK15].
W.R. Newman, ed. and tr., *The "Summa perfectionis" of Pseudo-Geber* (1991) [EK16].

## Theories of the Elixir

Roger Bacon, *Secretum secretorum cum glossis et notulis,* in *Opera hactenus inedita Rogeri Baconi,* ed. R. Steele and F. Delorme, fasc. 5 (1920) 1–175 [EK17]; *Opus tertium* and *Opus minus* in *Fr. Rogeri Bacon opera quaedam hactenus inedita,* ed. J.S. Brewer, in *RSer* 15 (1859) 3–310, 311–89 [EK18]; *Un fragment inédit de l'Opus Tertium,* ed. P. Duhem (1909) [EK19].
*Der Alchemistische Traktat "Von der Multiplikation" von pseudo-Thomas von Aquin: Untersuchungen und Texte,* ed. D. Goltz, J. Telle, and H.J. Vermeer (1977) [EK20].
Ps.-Arnald of Villanova, *Rosarius philosophorum,* in *BCC* v1:662–76 [EK21].
Ps.-Ramon Lull, *Testamentum,* in *BCC* v1:707–78 [EK22].

## Theories of the Fifth Essence

John of Rupescissa, *De consideratione quintae essentiae rerum omnium* (Basel 1561) [EK23].
Ps.-Ramon Lull, *De secretis naturae siue quinta essentia,* in *Raimundi Lulli De alchimia opuscula* (Nuremberg 1546) [EK24].

## Metaphorical Language

Ps.-Arnald of Villanova, *Exempla philosophorum,* in Venice, Biblioteca Nazionale Marciana, MS VI.214, fols. 164r–168v [EK25].
John Dastin, *Visio,* in *BCC* v2:324–26 [EK26].

## Paracelsian Dictionaries

Dictionaries compiled by followers of Paracelsus (1493–1541), such as M. Ruland, *Lexicon alchemiae* (Frankfurt 1612, r1964), tr. A.E. Waite (privately printed 1893; first public ed., London 1964) [EK27], or W. Johnson, *Lexicon chymicum* (London 1652), repr. in *BCC* v1:217–91 [EK28], are of limited utility, as they were intended to codify the "new meanings" given by Paracelsus to the established alchemical terminology. A.-J. Pernety, *Dictionnaire mytho-hermétique* (Paris 1758, r1972) depends largely on Renaissance alchemy [EK29].

# EL ❧ MEDICINE

BY PETER MURRAY JONES

Medicine in the Middle Ages was both science and art—a learned discipline and a means of maintaining or restoring health—despite the best efforts of tidy-minded philosophers to characterize it finally as one thing or the other. Consequently the literature of medicine displays an extraordinary variety of tone, language, and even physical appearance, from the most rigidly scholastic commentary written in a formal *textura* hand to collections of recipes scribbled on spare blanks of parchment or paper. As well as diversity we find copiousness—medical writings are the most common sort of secular prose to be met with (and there is a significant amount of medical writing in Latin verse, too). In the universities medicine was understood to include both *theorica* (philosophy of medicine and the principles of physiology and pathology) and *practica* (the study of specifics of diagnosis, prognosis, and treatment), but outside the universities the Latin literature of medical practice far outweighed more theoretical concerns. At the practical end medicine was closely allied through prognosis with physiognomy, astrology, and magic, and through therapeutics with the practices of herbalism, pharmacy, and alchemy. The point of reference of this practical literature might be the human body, but so also could be the body of an animal, for the health of livestock and draft animals was of course of vital importance to human well-being.

The Latin medical literature that survives from the sixth to the tenth centuries represents but a fragment of the corpus that had been assembled in the era of Rome and Alexandria. A mixture of pseudo-Galenic and Hippocratic texts with digests excerpted from Byzantine compilations, and overall a strong bias towards practice (especially antidotaries and herbals), are characteristic of this early period. Translation from Greek gave a distinctive literary form to this material, in which straightforward transliterations from the Greek and terms of demotic Latin stand out. Ravenna and south Italy seem to have been centers for translating Greek texts between the fifth and seventh centuries A.D.

The second half of the eleventh century marks a new era in the history of medical Latin, with the first fruits of the translations from Arabic by Constantine the African (d. c. 1087) and his contemporaries at or near Salerno. Constantine was a Benedictine of Monte Cassino, but the new translations seem to have played an important role in the creation of a secular center of medical teaching at Salerno. The new texts were often represented as being the works of Hippocrates and Galen but were in fact translations of Arabic authors, who themselves had adapted the Greek texts in accord with their own preoccupations. Thus the famous *Pantegni* is a Constantinian version of the *Kitāb al-Malikī* of Haly Abbas (Abū⁾l-Ḥasan ʿAlī ibn al-ʿAbbās al-Majūsī), who died in 994. Constantine's technique as a translator was very free, and he left out whole passages or paraphrased as he saw fit. But the effect was to introduce into the West for the first time a rudimentary corpus of Galenic medicine, including the first works of *theorica,* notably physiology and the theory of the elements, qualities, and humors.

The first original writings on medicine in Latin can be attributed to Salernitan authors, as the new Galenic medicine was assimilated. As well as the famous *Antidotarium Nicolai*—lists of ingredients for named medicaments authorized by the Salernitan teachers—which dominated pharmacy for centuries to come, a new genre of *quaestiones* or *problemata* [EL6] on medical topics was spawned there. Still more influential than these, however, was the assemblage of texts known as the *articella,* which was the cornerstone of medical education in Europe until the sixteenth century. It included the *Isagoge* of Johannitius (d. 873), an introduction to Galen's medicine written originally by Ḥunayn ibn Isḥāq al-ʿĪbādī Abū Zayd (d. 873) [EL7]; the *Aphorismata* and *Prognostica* of Hippocrates; and short works of Byzantine origin on urine and the pulse. Later the *Tegni* or *Ars parva* of Galen and his commentary on the Hippocratic *Regimen* in acute disease were added. These came to form the backbone of the medical curriculum at the universities founded from the twelfth century onwards.

New translations from the Greek supplemented the Arabic material in the twelfth century, based again in Salerno and in Sicily. Burgundio of Pisa (d. 1193) translated as many as ten of Galen's works into Latin, including bks. 7 to 14 of his chief therapeutic manual, *De methodo medendi.* The center of activity in translation from Arabic shifted from Italy to Spain, and the indefatigable Gerard of Cremona (d. 1187), based in Toledo, was responsible for the *Ad Almansorem* of Rhases (Abū Bakr Muḥammad ibn Zakariyyā al-Rāzī), the surgery of Abulcasis (Abū⁾l-Qāsim Khalaf ibn ʿAbbās al-Zahrawī), and the *Canon* of Avicenna (Abū ʿAlī al-Ḥusayn ibn ʿAbdallah Ibn Sīnā), all of which became key texts for European medicine. The new translations, from both Greek and Arabic, were much more literal than earlier efforts, proceeding more *de verbo ad verbum.* This new material provided fodder for medical scholasticism at the universities, where Galen was cross-fertilized by the new techniques of Aristotelian logic and natural philosophy. The Italian universities took the lead in academic medicine and pioneered the writing of *consilia,* purporting to be professorial medical advice in particular cases, written down in response to the request of the patient's doctor. The language of university medicine became increasingly technical, employing fine distinctions based not only on the interplay of qualities and humors within the patient's body, but also on an understanding of the outside world in terms of food, drink, drugs, environment, and way of life (the so-called nonnaturals). Quantification and measurement of these distinctions had an impact right down to the prescribing of compound remedies recommended by the doctors.

Whether within or without university walls medical literature in the Middle Ages was distinguished by the prevalence of lists of all kinds. Receptaries and antidotaries present lists of remedies organized in head-to-toe order of disease or alphabetically. The structure of individual recipes can be broken down into rubrics, indications, lists of ingredients, instructions for preparation, and application, terminating often with a statement of efficacy. The philosophical symmetry of the four elements, qualities, and humors, etc., to which might be added the refinement of measurement by degrees, encouraged scholastics to compile tables based on the sorting into kinds of everything in the sublunar world, whether natural, nonnatural, or contranatural. Medical writings tend not to be discursive, but to join rigid organization under logical hierarchies of heading with a constant use of formulae (as with *Recipe* . . .), followed by a list of ingredients that goes back to classical medicine and beyond, but that became sufficiently standardized in the Middle Ages to give rise to the modern term *recipe*. Case histories are an exception to this characterization of scholastic medical Latin, insofar as they have a narrative structure, but any tendency towards discursiveness was normally reined in strictly by didactic needs.

Medical texts are also marked of course by technical language of a number of kinds. At the most philosophical end there was debate over the exact meaning of such crucial terms as *commixtio* or *complexio* [EL26], signifying the individual's unique humoral balance that represented healthy equilibrium. In therapeutics terms like *derivatio* and *revulsio* signified the differing roles that bloodletting might play in maintaining or restoring health (by attracting blood towards or drawing it away from the member in question). The parts of the body, both seen and unseen, had necessarily to be described down to minute, even invisible, levels. Diseases were legion, and although in medieval medicine disease was seen more as a disturbance of natural equilibrium than as an entity in its own right, practical medicine had necessarily to override such philosophical subtleties by naming a huge variety of different ailments. Plants, minerals, and animals played a vital role as ingredients in recipes, and the compounding of these simples gave rise to another order of names, those referring to compound drugs. With all these different but overlapping terminologies there arose difficulties with exact translation from Greek or Arabic, so that many terms were simply transliterated, while doubts arose about what objects were denoted by terms inherited from ancient authorities. Medical dictionaries, glossaries, and quid pro quo's abounded in the Middle Ages as aids to the solution of these difficulties. The difficulties of course were of more than merely scholarly significance. The quid pro quo's, for example, gave lists of simples that could be regarded as local equivalents to those prescribed in ancient texts—a need particularly acute for practitioners living amidst a northern European flora but reading texts originating in the Mediterranean or the Middle East.

## A Note on the System of Measures Used in Medieval Pharmacology

There were actually surprising variations over space and time in the relative value of different measures of weight, and we cannot be at all sure of their modern equivalents. But the core measures were as follows:

1 libra = 12 unciae
1 uncia = 8 drachmae
1 drachma = 3 scripula
1 scripulum = 2 oboli
1 obolus = 3 siliquae

At Salerno the system was standardized on the base unit of the grain or *granum,* so that the *scripulum* or *scrupulum* was equivalent to 20 grains. At Salerno, too, the *uncia* comprised 9 *drachmae,* but this was by no means universally accepted.

## Select Bibliography

### Primary Works

A very small proportion indeed of medieval works on medicine has appeared in modern critical editions. The complete work of only one medical author of the Middle Ages (Arnald of Villanova, c. 1240–1311) is now being critically edited: *Opera medica omnia,* ed. L. Garcia-Ballester, J.A. Paniagua, and M.R. McVaugh (1975–) [EL1].

Other significant modern editions include the following:

R.J. Durling, ed., *Burgundio of Pisa's Translation of Galen's Peri Kraseon "De complexionibus,"* Galenus latinus 1 (1976) [EL2].

R. Foerster, ed., *Scriptores physiognomonici graeci et latini,* 2 vols. (1893) [EL3]

E. Howald and H.E. Sigerist, eds., *Antonii Musae De herba vettonica liber, Pseudoapulei Herbarius, Anonymi De taxone liber, Sexti Placiti Liber medicinae ex animalibus etc.,* Corpus medicorum latinorum 4 (1927) [EL4].

D. Jacquart and G. Troupeau, eds., *Le livre des axiomes médicaux (Aphorismi)* (1980): Arabic text of Yūḥannā ibn Māsawayh (Johannes Mesue) and Latin versions, with French translation and glossary [EL5].

B. Lawn, ed., *The Prose Salernitan Questions, Edited from a Bodleian Manuscript (Auct. F.3.10)* (1979): an anonymous collection of c. 1200 concerned with science and medicine [EL6].

G. Maurach, ed., "Johannitius, Isagoge ad Techne Galieni," in *SAr* 62 (1978) 148–74 [EL7].

H. Mørland, ed., *Oribasius latinus, SO,* fasc. supp. 10 (1940) [EL8].

M. Niedermann, ed., *Marcelli De medicamentis liber,* Corpus medicorum latinorum 5 (1916) [EL9].

J.L. Pagel, ed., *Die Chirurgie des Heinrich von Mondeville (Hermondaville)* (1892) [EL10].

J.L. Pagel, ed., *Die Areolae des Johannes de Sancto Amando (13. Jahrhundert)* (1893) [EL11].

J.L. Pagel, ed., *Die Concordanciae des Johannes de Sancto Amando* (1894) [EL12].

V. Rose, ed., *Egidii Corboliensis Viaticus de signis et symptomatibus aegritudinum* (1907) [EL13].

H.E. Sigerist, *Studien und Texte zur frühmittelalterlichen Rezeptliteratur,* Studien zur Geschichte der Medizin 13 (1923, r1977) [EL14].

L.E. Voigts and M.R. McVaugh, eds., *A Latin Technical Phlebotomy and Its Middle English Translation, TAPhS* 74.2 (1984) [EL15].

A valuable collection of translations is included in *SBMS* 700–808 [EL16].

## Studies

### (a) Translations and Transmission

Translations from the Greek in northern Italy are examined in G. Baader, "Early Medieval Latin Adaptations of Byzantine Medicine in Western Europe," in *Symposium on Byzantine Medicine*, ed. J. Scarborough, *DOP* 38 (1984) 251–59 [EL17]; in I. Mazzini, "Il latino medico in Italia nei secoli V et VI," in *La cultura in Italia fra tardo antico et alto medioevo: Atti del convegno tenuto a Roma* (12–16 November 1979), ed. M. Simonetti *et al.*, 2 vols. (1981) v1:433–41 [EL18]; and in D. Langslow, "The Formation of Latin Technical Vocabulary with Special Reference to Medicine," in *New Studies in Latin Linguistics*, ed. R. Coleman (1991) 187–200 [EL19].

Arabic translations are surveyed in D. Jacquart and F. Micheau, *La médecine arabe et l'occident médiéval*, Collection Islam-Occident 7 (1990) [EL20]. Still useful are H. Schipperges, *Die Assimilation der arabischen Medizin durch das lateinische Mittelalter* (1964) [EL21]; and *id.*, *Arabische Medizin im Lateinischen Mittelalter*, in Sitz. der Heidelberger Ak. der Wiss., mathematisch-naturwissenschaftliche Klasse 2 (1976) 91–274 [EL22].

Studies of the transmission of the vast range of practical medical literature in Latin are few in number, reflecting the intrinsic difficulty of the material. A good impression of this difficulty can be gained from G. Keil, "Gestaltwandel und Zersetzung Roger-Urtext und Roger-Glosse vom 12. bis ins 16. Jahrhundert," in *Der Kommentar in der Renaissance*, ed. A. Buck and O. Herding (1975) 209–24 [EL23].

### (b) The Language of Latin Medical Literature

For the early Middle Ages see G. Baader, "Lo sviluppo del linguaggio medico nell'antichità e nel primo medioevo," in *Atene e Roma*, n.s., 15 (1970) 1–19 [EL24]; and *id.*, "Zur Terminologie des Constantinus Africanus," in *Medizinhistorisches Journal* 2 (1967) 36–53 [EL25]. One key term is analyzed by D. Jacquart, "De *crasis* à *complexio*: Notes sur le vocabulaire du tempérament en latin médiéval," in *Textes médicaux latins antiques*, ed. G. Sabbah, Centre Jean Palerne, *Mémoires*, v5 (1984) [EL26]. See also R.J. Durling, "Burgundio of Pisa's Translation of Galen's ΠΕΡΙ ΤΩΝ ΠΕΠΟΝΘΟΤΩΝ ΤΟΠΩΝ: 'De interioribus,'" in *Traditio* 42 (1986) 439–42 [EL27]; D. Jacquart and G. Troupeau, "Traduction de l'arabe et vocabulaire médical latin: Quelques exemples," in *LLM* 367–76 [EL28]; D. Jacquart, "A l'aube de la renaissance médicale des XIe–XIIe siècles: L''Isagoge Johannitii' et son traducteur," in *BECh* 144 (1986) 209–40 [EL29]; and *eadem*, "L'enseignement de la médecine: Quelques termes fondamentaux," in *CIVICIMA* 3:104–20 [EL30].

### (c) Bibliographies of Western Medieval Medicine

For information concerning recently published work and editions of texts in progress, see *Society for Ancient Medicine and Pharmacy Newsletter* (1976–) [EL31], which also provides a regular supp. to H. Leitner, *Bibliography to the Ancient Medical Authors* (1973) [EL32]. The Centre Jean Palerne (Saint-Étienne) publishes *Lettres d'informations* (1982–) [EL33] and was also responsible for the *Bibliographie des textes médicaux latins: Antiquité et haut moyen âge*, compiled by G. Sabbah, P.-P. Corsetti, and K.-D. Fischer (1987) [EL34]. A useful survey of recent literature is that of N.G. Siraisi, "Some Recent Work on Western European Medical Learning, ca. 1200–ca.

1500," in *History of Universities* 2 (1982) 225–38 [EL35]. For discussion, with bibliography, of the evolution of the medical book in the Middle Ages, see P.M. Jones, "Medical Books before the Invention of Printing," in *Thornton's Medical Books, Libraries, and Collectors: A Study of Bibliography and the Book Trade in Relation to the Medical Sciences,* ed. A. Besson, 3rd rev. ed. (1990) [EL36].

*See also* [BA80], [BB54], [BC72].

EM  •  MAGIC

BY RICHARD KIECKHEFER

Medieval writings on magic are indebted to various classical sources, especially Pliny the Elder's *Naturalis historia* [EM10] (A.D. 77), which deals extensively with the practices of the Persian magi (from whom the Latin terms *magia* and [*ars*] *magica* derive). Among patristic writers, the most influential was Augustine, who articulated his conception of magic most fully in *De civitate dei*, bks. 8–10 [EM2].

Discussion of the Medieval Latin terminology of magic must take into account (1) the definitions and classifications given by encyclopedists who included magic among the branches of knowledge, (2) the technical terminology used by practitioners to explain and analyze specific magical procedures, and (3) the verbal formulae recommended as part of the practice of magic.

## Classification of the Branches of Magic

The most influential categorization of magic in medieval Europe was that of Isidore of Seville, who dealt with the subject in his *Etymologiae*, bk. 8.9 [EM6]. He says magic was initiated by the Bactrian king Zoroaste[r], expanded by Democritus, much used among the Assyrians, bestowed on people throughout the world over many centuries by *angeli mali*, and exemplified in the stories of Moses (*Ex* 7–9), Circe (*Odyssey* 10; *Aeneid* 7), and Saul (1 *Rg* 28). He says that magi are popularly known as *malefici* because of the greatness of their crimes; they disrupt the elements, disturb human minds, and kill people by charms alone, without poison. The bulk of the chapter, however, classifies the varieties of magic, and here Isidore restricts himself (except for a reference to *praestigium*, or ocular illusion) to forms of divination. Following Varro (d. 27 B.C.), he speaks of four species of divination that employ the four elements: *geomantia* (earth), *hydromantia* (water), *aeromantia* (air), and *pyromantia* (fire). He then distinguishes between divination by *ars* and divination by *furor* (i.e. ecstatic prognostication). The divinatory arts include those of the *incantatores* (who use verbal formulae), *arioli* (who pray and make sacrifices at the altars of idols), *haruspices* (who observe hours), *augures* and *auspices* (who observe the flights and calls of birds and other such signs), *pythonissae* (named for Pythius Apollo, the founder of divination). Elsewhere in the chapter Isidore mentions *necromantici* (who resuscitate and interrogate the dead), *sortilegi* (who rely on lots, and especially on the *sortes sanctorum* or inspection of sacred writings), and *salisatores* (who interpret the throbbing of bodily members). Also among the divinatory arts is that of the *astrologi* (who observe the stars), and more specifically the *genethliaci* (who observe heavenly signs at people's births and are popularly known as *mathematici*). The interpreters of the stars were first known as magi, as in the Gospel of Matthew (2:1–12), and afterward as *mathematici;* their art was allowed until the coming of Christ, but not thereafter. All these arts, he says, arise from the pestiferous association of humans and evil angels, and are thus to be shunned by Christians.

Hrabanus Maurus (d. 856) incorporates Isidore's discussion in *De magicis artibus* (*PL* 110:1097–99), and it was further adapted by Hincmar of Rheims (d. 882) and the canonists Burchard of Worms (d. 1025), Ivo of Chartres (d. 1115), and Gratian (twelfth century). John of Salisbury (d. 1180) also borrowed from Isidore's discussion in his *Policraticus,* 1.9–12 [EM7]; in further elaboration of the branches of knowledge John discusses astrology (2.19–26) and divination (2.27–28) much more fully. The *Didascalicon* (6.15) of Hugh of St. Victor (d. 1141) [EM5] again borrows from Isidore, but organizes the branches of magic into a tighter system under five heads: *mantice* includes divination by necromancy and by the four elements; *mathematica* embraces the divinatory practices of *aruspicina* (which Hugh derives alternatively from the observation of times, *horae,* or from the inspection of altars, *arae,* on which sacrifice has been offered), *auspicium,* and *horoscopica; sortilegium* is divination by lots; *maleficium* (which Hugh also uses as a generic term equivalent to *magica*) involves the use of demonic incantations, ligatures, and other procedures carried out (albeit for healing) by demons; and *praestigium* deludes the senses by demonic art.

## Technical Terminology Regarding the Practice of Magic

The most important single compendium of information is *Picatrix* [EM9], a thirteenth-century Latin translation of an Arabic work, which gives long lists of astral *imagines* and *figurae* (figures representing the planets and constellations, inscribed on metal or other material, and organized according to the purposes they serve or the heavenly bodies whose power they absorb), *petitiones* and *orationes* addressed to various planets, *virtutes* of the planets, *confectiones* made of stones and other material (to be given in food or otherwise administered), *suffumigationes* (substances to be burned to attract planetary spirits or accomplish other magical purposes), powers associated with the lunar *mansiones,* etc. Although this is a prime repository of magical terminology, its unsystematic nature makes it difficult to use as a source.

The terminology of magic is more systematically set forth in Henry Cornelius Agrippa's *De occulta philosophia* [EM1], in effect a *summa* of medieval magic, written in the early sixteenth century. This work deals with natural magic (which uses the *virtutes* in sublunary nature) in bk. 1, celestial magic (using the *virtutes* in the heavenly bodies) in bk. 2, and ceremonial magic (which appeals to various spirits) in bk. 3.

## Verbal Formulae Used in Magic

Various types of verbal formulae (*carmina,* or charms) are used in magic for healing or protection: (a) Adjurations are addressed to the disease or to its agent (the demon or elf seen as causing the illness) and are phrased as commands; the disease or its cause is commanded to depart from the patient, and the key terms are *adiuro,* *coniuro,* or even *exorcizo,* all used interchangeably for "command." (b) Blessings are addressed to the patient and are expressed as wishes (of the form "may you be healed"). (c) Prayers are addressed to God and are formulated as requests. While not inherently magical, prayers of blessing are sometimes used in healing procedures that otherwise involve magic, and it is not always possible to distinguish rigorously between the magical and religious elements. Sometimes biblical or liturgical formulae occur in Latin that in themselves are not specifically magical, but the way they are used suggests that they are thought of as having magical efficacy: the Anglo-Saxon *Lacnunga* (B.L., MS Harley 585, fols. 137r–138r) recommends writing *Io* 1:1–5, *Mt* 4:23–25, and three psalms from the *Vulgate* on a paten, then washing the writing off the paten and administering them (after other ceremonies) as a potion.

The Latin used in these formulae often deviates markedly from literary standards, suggesting that the scribes knew little Latin or were not concerned to observe these standards. One charm for childbirth, for example, contains the lines "In nomine patris Lazarus et filij veni foras et speritus scantus [*sic*], christus te uocat + christus + stonat [*sic*] + iesus predicat + christus regnat + erex + arex + rymex + christi eleyzon + eeeeeeeee +"; the standard formula "In nomine patris, et filii, et spiritus sancti" is here meshed with *Io* 11:43b, to which "Christus te uocat" is added, followed by variations on this phrase, in turn followed by nonsense words presumably based on the word *rex* (which has been suggested by the phrase "Christus regnat") [EM20].

When magic is intended to cause harm or arouse love, it is often accompanied by incantations, which usually serve to interpret the symbolic action that is performed. These incantations typically involve correlative terms explicitly comparing the symbolic action with the result intended (e.g., "Sicut hec candela extingwitur, ita omnis virtus in tali [persona] permanens penitus consumetur").

In the explicitly demonic magic of the later Middle Ages, often referred to as *nigromantia* (a Latin deformation of *necromantia* under the influence of *niger*), demons are conjured with formulae resembling the adjurations used to dispel illness. Typically these conjurations involve (a) an address to the spirits whose aid is being invoked, with or without proper names; (b) a term of command (*adiuro, coniuro, exorcizo,* or some equivalent); (c) appeal to a series of sacred persons, names, events, or objects, by whose power the spirits are to be constrained (e.g., "per natiuitatem et passionem ac resurrectionem domini nostri Iesu Christi," "per solem et lunam et omnia sidera celestia," "per omnes sanctos et sanctas dei," "per hec preciosissima ac ineffabilia nomina omnium creatoris"); and (d) specification of the service required and the manner in which it is to be performed (e.g., "quatenus vos, insolubiliter ad mei potenciam alligati, ad me sine prestolacione venire debeatis, in tali habitu vt me aliqualiter non terreatis"). [Examples given are from the Munich MS, clm. 849.] Adjurations or conjurations, whether intended for healing or for summoning demons, are formally analogous to exorcisms used in cases of possession.

# Select Bibliography

## Texts and Translations

Henricus Cornelius Agrippa, *De occulta philosophia libri tres*, ed. V. Perrone Compagni (1992) [EM1].

Augustine, *De civitate dei*, ed. B. Dombart and A. Kalb, *CCSL* 47–48 (1955); tr. H. Bettenson (1984) [EM2].

Augustine, *De divinatione daemonum liber*, ed. J. Zycha, *CSEL* 41 (1900) 597–618; tr. R.W. Brown, in *Saint Augustine: Treatises on Marriage and Other Subjects*, ed. R.J. Deferrari (1955) 421–40 [EM3].

Marsilio Ficino, *De vita libri tres*, ed. and tr. C.V. Kaske and J.R. Clark (1989) [EM4].

Hugh of St. Victor, *Didas.* [EM5].

Isidore, *Etym.* [EM6].

John of Salisbury, *Poli.* [EM7].

G. Luck, tr., *Arcana Mundi: Magic and the Occult in the Greek and Roman Worlds: A Collection of Ancient Texts* (1985) [EM8].

*Picatrix: The Latin Version of the Ghāyat al-Ḥakīm*, ed. D. Pingree (1986) [EM9].

Pliny the Elder, *NH* [EM10].

## Studies

D.E. Aune, "Magic in Early Christianity," in *Aufstieg und Niedergang der römischen Welt: Geschichte und Kultur Roms im Spiegel der neueren Forschung* 23.2, ed. H. Temporini and W. Haase (1980) 1507–57 [EM11].

W. Dürig, "Die Verwendung des sogenannten Fluchpsalms 108 (109) im Volksglauben und in der Liturgie," in *Münchener theologische Zeitschrift* 27 (1976) 71–84 [EM12].

V.I.J. Flint, *The Rise of Magic in Early Medieval Europe* (1991) [EM13].

T.R. Forbes, "Verbal Charms in British Folk Medicine," in *PAPS* 115 (1971) 293–316 [EM14].

M. Geier, "Die magische Kraft der Poesie: Zur Geschichte, Struktur und Funktion des Zauberspruchs," in *DVJSLW* 56 (1982) 359–85 [EM15].

R. Halleux and C. Opsomer, *Herbiers, bestiaires et lapidaires*, *TSMAO* (in preparation) [EM16].

I. Hampp, *Beschwörung, Segen, Gebet: Untersuchungen zum Zauberspruch aus dem Bereich der Volksheilkunde* (1961) [EM17].

D. Harmening, *Superstitio: Überlieferungs- und theoriegeschichtliche Untersuchungen zur kirchlich-theologischen Aberglaubensliteratur des Mittelalters* (1979) [EM18].

R. Kieckhefer, *Magic in the Middle Ages* (1989) [EM19].

L. Olsan, "Latin Charms of Medieval England: Verbal Healing in a Christian Oral Tradition," in *Oral Tradition* 7 (1992) 116–42 [EM20].

G.R. Owst, "*Sortilegium* in English Homiletic Literature of the Fourteenth Century," in *Studies Presented to Sir Hilary Jenkinson*, ed. J.C. Davies (1957) 272–303 [EM21].

F.C.R. Thee, *Julius Africanus and the Early Christian View of Magic* (1984) [EM22].

L. Thorndike, "Some Medieval Conceptions of Magic," in *The Monist* 25 (1915) 107–39 [EM23].

L. Thorndike, *HMES* [EM24].

P. Zambelli, "Le problème de la magie naturelle à la Renaissance," in *Magia, astrologia e religione nel Rinascimento: Convegno polacco-italiano, Varsavia, 25–27 settembre 1972* (1974) 48–79 [EM25].

*See also* [BD75].

FA   •   # TECHNOLOGY AND CRAFTS: INTRODUCTION

BY BERT HALL

The dichotomy between words and actions is especially stark where practical arts and crafts are concerned. This is true even today, and it was even more the case in the Middle Ages, when technologies were closer to actual practice and less the subject of discourse than at present. In addition, Latin's status as a learned language shaped the way it represented technical subjects. Most Latin sources are likely to have been written by men who did not know craft terms in common use and often did not care to be precise in their choice of words. Exceptions to this rule—the *Mappae clavicula,* Theophilus Presbyter, Georg Agricola—are as precious as they are rare (see chs. FI and FK). Much of our knowledge of technological Latin derives from "unintentional" sources—histories, chronicles, hagiography, commercial accounts, sermons, and much else besides.

Under these circumstances, the study of technical language never fully overcomes the stubborn primacy of brute facts. "Les langues techniques latines sont des langues réduites au lexique," says Jacques André [FA1]. Classical Latin terms remained in use in all manner of sources, of course, but they were subject to variation over time and prone to be supplemented or even supplanted by latinized vernacular terms. The apparent semantic stability created by the retention of classical vocabulary is often illusory. For example, the socially and economically momentous shift in the twelfth century from the vertical or "warp-weighted" loom to the horizontal or "treadle" loom is simply ignored in Latin documents, where all looms are *telae* (see ch. FJ). Lesser examples of something similar include *ciborium,* originally a drinking cup and then a canopy or covered area, but later also a bay in a vaulted ceiling; and *caminus,* a smelter or forge in Classical Latin, but later a domestic fireplace with a chimney (see ch. FC).

Words can change meanings radically without altering in appearance at all. A *carpentarius* in the later Middle Ages was a carpenter, whereas in the classical world he was a worker who built wooden carts, a "wainwright." (This, incidentally, explains why Jesus and Joseph are called simply *fabri* in the Vulgate.) Changes in function create the need for differentiation, and medieval writers sometimes responded by proliferating terms based on classical roots; see, for example, in ch. FG, the multiplicity of words for farm horses (*carectarius, hercarius,* etc.) or hunting dogs (*cervericius, leporarius,* etc.). There is, as always in such matters, a central paradox: context alone determines meaning, but only through words can we understand contexts.

Technological change is a rich source of neologisms in most modern languages, and this was true in the Middle Ages as well. Then vernacular artisans and workers were the source of Latin coinages by record clerks, and large numbers of new Latin words visibly betray their vernacular roots. *Staggus,* from English *stagge* ("stag deer"), represents the process at its simplest (see ch. FG). Late medieval heavy shields, designed to offer protection against crossbow shots and often requiring struts or even wheels, were called *pavesii,* presumably after the city of Pavia (see ch. FE). English plowmen measured distances in *roda,* from "rod" (see ch. FD). A Romance root, *tamis-* (also leading to West Germanic forms such as *temse*), gave rise to the Medieval Latin verb *tamisare,* "to strain through a sieve" (see ch. FI), and ultimately to the French and somewhat archaic English "tamis"/"tammy" ("sieve"). Part of the vitality of Latin throughout the Middle Ages undoubtedly consisted in its unself-conscious ability to assimilate terminology from widely scattered sources, and examples of this vigorous creativity are to be found in every chapter of this section of the guide.

Often, however, the simple assimilation of vernacular words became much more complicated. Classical Latin *palus* ("stake") begot the nautical term *palleria,* "a plank flooring below decks"—misleadingly called a "ceiling" (see ch. FF) by an elusive process that also engendered *galeria* from a latinized vernacular word for porch, *galilaea* (see ch. FC). The Latin diminutive *trabecula,* from *trabs,* "architectural beam," yielded terms meaning both an uneven-arm balance used by minters and assayers—*trabucha* (see ch. FL)—and a large, uneven-beam, counterweight catapult used in sieges—*trabuca/trabiculus/trebuchettum.*

Even more complex relationships can be found. Late Medieval Latin used *pixis* (pl. *pixides*) to mean "gun," although English sources often preferred *gonna* or *gunna* (see ch. FE), terms apparently derived from "Gunnhilda" (see *OED* [BF32]). *Pyxis* means a small box, commonly the one used for the reserved host; its transference to firearms presumably came about because many early guns had separate powder chambers (cf. German *Büchse* ["case," "box," "gun"], Dutch *busse,* and such English compounds as harque*bus,* blunder*buss*). The use of the powder chamber to refer to the whole weapon is an example of synecdoche, "the part for the whole" (cf. *rifle*). The complex etymology of technical words creates stumbling blocks for scholars and students and is a field needing further work.

The informality associated with the formation of technical vocabulary in Medieval Latin met its limits in two special circumstances. The first was the treatment of technology by learned, later scholastic, commentators. Medieval educated elites often held the useful arts in high regard, but they were nevertheless unable to articulate well the general idea of technology. The term they used most frequently, *artes mechanicae,* was a philosophical neologism of the ninth century, pluralizing an earlier singular form and in effect making it a metaphor (see ch. FB). As the term *artes mechanicae* spread, so did the tendency to see the mechanical arts as subordinate both morally and epistemologically to more abstract and theoretical subjects. The scholastic genius for classifying things into hierarchical relationships marks a break with older monastic traditions grounded in direct experience of the craftsmanship of artisans. In their place we find a more distant philosophical and theological approach rooted in the university environment.

The second circumstance that changed technical Latin was the rise of Renaissance humanism. Inevitably, humanist intellectuals looked askance at the rough-and-ready technical Latin of the Middle Ages. The German physician-scholar Georg Agricola believed strongly in the need to create a standardized and etymologically justifiable set of terms for the field he knew and loved, mining and mineralogy. From his early dialogue *Bermannus* to his late masterpiece *De re metallica*, Agricola expanded the range of Latin in these neglected fields (see ch. FK). Yet his success also marks the end of the medieval way of continuously renewing technical Latin through contact with the vernacular. Agricola's approach signifies a new, postmedieval world with different relations between language and technology—a world in which the textual sources became far richer, but also one in which the vernacular languages, not Latin, would become the major beneficiaries of new terminology for technology and crafts.

# Select Bibliography

## Vocabulary

J. André, "Sur la constitution des langues techniques en latin," in *Sciences et techniques à Rome, Études de lettres* (1986), no. 1:5–18 [FA1].

H. Blümner, *Technologie und Terminologie der Gewerbe und Künste bei Griechen und Romern*, 4 vols. (1875–87, r1979) [FA2].

J. Delmas, "La lexicographie du latin médiéval et l'histoire des techniques," in *LLM* 421–32 [FA3].

C. De Meo, *Lingue tecniche del latino*, 2nd ed. (1986) [FA4].

P. Radici Colace and M. Caccamo Caltabiano, eds., *Seminario di studi sui lessici tecnici greci e latini: Atti del I seminario . . . : Messina, 8–10 marzo 1990* (1991) [FA5].

## Bibliography

C. Kren, *Medieval Science and Technology: A Selected, Annotated Bibliography* (1985) [FA6].

## General Histories and Studies of Medieval Technology

M. Clagett, *The Science of Mechanics in the Middle Ages* (1959, r1961) [FA7].

F.M. Feldhaus, *Die Technik der Antike und des Mittelalters* (1931, r1971) 219–425 [FA8].

R.J. Forbes, *Studies in Ancient Technology*, 3rd ed., 3 vols. (1993) [FA9].

F. and J. Gies, *Cathedral, Forge and Waterwheel: Technology and Invention in the Middle Ages* (1994) [FA10].

B. Gille, "Le moyen âge en occident (Ve siècle–1350)," in *Histoire générale des techniques,* ed. M. Daumas, 5 vols. (1962–79) v1:427–597; tr. E.B. Hennessy, *A History of Technology and Invention: Progress through the Ages,* 3 vols. (1969–79) v1:422–576 [FA11].

B. Gille, "Technological Developments in Europe: 1100–1400," in *The Evolution of Science: Readings from the History of Mankind,* ed. G.S. Metraux and F. Crouzet (1963) 168–219 [FA12].

B.S. Hall and D.C. West, eds., *On Pre-Modern Technology and Science: A Volume of Studies in Honor of Lynn White, Jr.* (1976) [**FA13**].

D.R. Hill, *A History of Engineering in Classical and Medieval Times* (1984) [**FA14**].

F. Klemm, *Technik: Eine Geschichte ihrer Probleme* (1954); tr. D.W. Singer, *A History of Western Technology* (1959, r1964): see pp55–107 [**FA15**].

P.O. Long, ed., *STMS* [**FA16**].

G. Ovitt, Jr., *The Restoration of Perfection: Labor and Technology in Medieval Culture* (1987) [**FA17**].

L.F. Salzman, *English Industries of the Middle Ages*, 2nd ed. (1923) [**FA18**].

C. Singer *et al.*, eds., *HTech* [**FA19**].

A.P. Usher, *A History of Mechanical Inventions*, 2nd ed. (1954, r1988) [**FA20**].

L. White, Jr., *Medieval Technology and Social Change* (1962, r1980) [**FA21**].

L. White, Jr., *Medieval Religion and Technology: Collected Essays* (1978) [**FA22**].

*See also* [**BA68**], [**BD30**], [**BD69**].

# FB · ARTES MECHANICAE

## BY ELSPETH WHITNEY

The term *artes mechanicae* first appears in the commentary by John Scottus Eriugena (d. c. 877/79) on the *De nuptiis Philologiae et Mercurii* of Martianus Capella (fl. 410) [FB12]. In the Middle Ages the term referred less to specific technological activities than to the collective identity of those arts that made use of the physical world for human utility, pleasure, and comfort. Roughly equivalent to the modern term *technology, artes mechanicae* became from the twelfth century onwards a standard division in classifications of the arts and sciences and continued to be used in this sense into the seventeenth century. It remained far more closely tied to an intellectual or philosophical tradition than to the actual practice of technological activities. This bookish quality is reflected in the fact that treatises that consider the idea of the mechanical arts rarely provide specific terminology for technological devices, tools, or instruments. The development of a distinctively medieval term for technology, however, represents an important stage in the development of modern attitudes toward human control of the environment.

Classical categorizations of technological arts were fragmentary, imprecise, and unsystematic. The Romans used the singlar *ars mechanica* to refer to the art of machines, such as making engines of war, astronomical models, or lifting devices, but the plural form does not seem to have been used in antiquity. Nor did the classical world possess a term equivalent to the medieval *artes mechanicae*. Although a variety of labels served generally to distinguish arts directed toward the body and the physical world from those directed toward the mind (the liberal arts), these terms failed to define crafts or technological arts comprehensively as a group. The term "productive arts," for example, found in Plato and Aristotle, and recurring later in Hellenistic and Latin texts, generally meant only those arts that brought into being, or produced, a physical object. Although some technological arts, such as architecture or metalworking, clearly were counted among the productive arts, others, such as medicine and agriculture, were not. The idea of the productive arts remained current into the fifth century, but the lack of any standard Latin translation of the Greek term (*poietikai*) helped ensure the disappearance of the idea in the early Middle Ages. Similarily, the pejorative label "banausic arts," appearing in Latin as *artes sordidae, artes illiberales,* or *artes vulgares,* and often translated as "(mere) mechanical arts," was applied only to those arts that were seen by individual authors as appealing to the body in dishonorable or unworthy ways. Both Plato and Aristotle, for example, used the term *banausikos* when they wished to emphasize the baseness and inferiority of activities that, in contrast to the liberal arts, involved the body without a redeeming moral or intellectual purpose or were pursued only for the purpose of earning money. Although such arts were mainly, though not exclusively, crafts, many authors also included crafts or technological arts, especially agriculture, medicine, and architecture, in the opposing category of the liberal arts. A significant group of authors influenced by Platonism and Neoplatonism, moreover, made use of a category of "semiliberal" arts that included medicine, agriculture, navigation, gymnastics, sculpture, and painting. Mechanics and, occasionally, architecture and carpentry were also sometimes associated with mathematics as the practical side of theoretical mathematical knowledge.

The creation of a comprehensive and coherent conception of technology under the rubric *artes mechanicae* was a distinctively medieval achievement. During the early Middle Ages it became common, following Isidore of Seville (d. 636), for certain crafts, namely medicine, astrology, and "mechanics," to be associated with the quadrivium and hence with the liberal arts and philosophy [FB10–11]. The definition of mechanics seems to have gradually evolved in the hands of early medieval commentators, who had little, if any, knowledge of classical mathematics, from the classical meaning to one that simply designated handicrafts, including farming, cloth making, and stone working. Hrabanus Maurus, for example, in the ninth century, defines mechanics as follows: *Mechanica est peritia fabricae artis in metallis et in lignis et in lapidibus.* This tradition survived into the twelfth century, where it appears in the *De animae exsilio et patria* of Honorius Augustodunensis (d. c. 1156) [FB8]. Here the author describes and defines ten liberal arts, the usual quadrivium and trivium plus *physica, mechanica,* and *oeconomica,* each allegorized as a "city" or way station along the road from spiritual ignorance to wisdom. According to Honorius, mechanics, the ninth city, teaches "every work in metal, wood, and stone, in addition to painting, sculpture, and all arts which are done with the hands" (*omne opus metallorum, lignorum, marmorum, insuper picturas, sculpturas, et omnes artes, quae manibus fiunt*).

John Scottus Eriugena attempted to reconcile this tradition with the newly influential *De nuptiis Philologiae et Mercurii,* which explicitly excluded medicine and architecture from the "celestial" company of the liberal arts. He created a new category of arts, the *artes mechanicae,* explicitly defined as seven (unnamed) arts paralleling in form and function the seven liberal arts but distinguished from them by their human, rather than divine, orientation. The concept of the mechanical arts was fleshed out and given substance in the twelfth and thirteenth centuries. Decisive in this development was Hugh of St. Victor (d. 1141), whose influential treatise, the *Didascalicon* [FB9], names and describes seven mechanical arts—fabric making, armament, commerce, agriculture, hunting, medicine, and theatrics (*mechanica septem scientas continent: lanificum, armaturam, navigationem, agriculturam, venationem, medicinam, theatricam*—and outlines a comprehensive account of the mechanical arts as comprising the third major division of philosophy, after theoretical and practical knowledge. Hugh's descriptions of the individual mechanical arts are concrete and detailed but strongly emphasize handicrafts rather than practical mathematics. In general, they consist of lists of common materials, tools, and techniques but omit mention of "state-of-the-art" technology such as the stirrup, heavy plow, or windmill. Hugh's categories, moreover, are broad: *armatura* includes weapons, architecture, carpentry, and metalworking; *venatio* includes food gathering, cookery, and the selling and serving of food and drink; *theatrica* includes all entertainments and games.

Hugh's definition and list of mechanical arts were taken over by numerous authors, including Richard and Godfrey of St. Victor (d. 1173 and 1196) ([FB16, FB6]), Bonaventure (d. 1274) [FB3], Vincent of Beauvais (d. c. 1264) [FB19], Robert Kilwardby (d. 1279) [FB17], and Albertus Magnus (d. 1280) [FB1–2], as well as many lesser known figures. Many of these writers introduced variations in the names given to the individual mechanical arts or altered the list somewhat. Theater, for example, was often omitted, and magic, alchemy, or architecture substituted. The greatest variation occurred in the terminology for commerce, which was named *mercatura* in the anonymous *Ordo artium* (c. 1200) [FB13], and by Godfrey of St. Victor and Robert Kilwardby, and *negotiatoria* by Radulfus Ardens (1193–99) [FB14]. Radulfus renames several of the mechanical arts, listing them as *victuria* (nourishment, including both hunting and agriculture), *lanificaria, architectoria, suffragatoria* (supports, including beasts of burden, tools, equipment, and vehicles), *medicina, negotiatoria* (including *mutuatio* and *accommodatio*), and *patrocinia* (defenses). Kilwardby also modifies Hugh's categories, substituting *ars vestitiva* (art of garments) or *coopertiva* (coverings) for *lanificia, terraecultus* for agriculture, *cibativa* (food science) or *nutritiva* (nutrition) for hunting. Several of these alternative names also occur in Albertus Magnus. Unlike Hugh's, these later treatises generally provide little or no description of the technological content of particular mechanical arts; those that do more than simply list the arts by name are more likely to describe the moral or social effects of practicing these arts.

The Victorine tradition often merged with ideas and vocabulary borrowed from newly available Arabic writers on the arts or from newly accessible Greek texts. Albertus Magnus, for example, occasionally refers to *artes factivae* and *artes [quae] dicuntur in Greco apotelesmata,* as well as using the more common term *artes mechanicae.* These authors, strongly influenced by an Arabic philosophical tradition heavily colored with Neoplatonism and in the thirteenth century by Aristotle, typically divided the arts into corresponding theoretical and practical, or operative, branches. In the hands of such writers as Gundisalvi (fl. second half of the twelfth century) and Roger Bacon (d. c. 1291), the craft tradition of the Victorines was combined with a new emphasis on practical mathematics, harking back to the Classical Greek *ars mechanica.* Gundisalvi [FB7], for example, includes under practical mathematics the science of weights and the science of machines (*scientia de ingeniis*). The latter embraces knowledge of instruments, including those used by stone masons, engines for lifting, musical instruments, weapons, mirrors and other optical devices, and tools used in carpentry and other crafts. Practical arithmetic similarly includes the use of the abacus. Traditional crafts (*fabriles . . . sive mechanice artes*) were subsumed under the art of ruling the family. Bacon [FB4–5] develops an even more elaborate scheme, dividing practical geometry into numerous parts, including agriculture, the sciences of measurement, construction, the construction of engines/machines, and the building of weapons. Practical arithmetic includes the use of the abacus and astronomical tables, calendars, weights and measures, the measurement of distances, mathematical games, and business techniques. Gundisalvi and Bacon provide almost no specialized vocabulary for particular instruments, tools, or mechanical devices.

This lack betrays their ties to a philosophical and theological tradition rather than to the practical ambience of the monastic or artisan workshop.

## Select Bibliography

### Primary Works and Translations

Albertus Magnus, *Opera omnia,* ed. B. Geyer (1951–) [FB1]; ed. A. Borgnet, 38 vols. (1890–99) [FB2]: Albertus makes scattered remarks on the mechanical arts throughout his commentaries on Aristotle as well as occasionally elsewhere; the more important of these are in his commentaries on the *Metaphysics:* 1.1.6, 1.1.10, and 2.8 ([FB1] v16:9, 15, 100); on the *Physics:* 2.1.11 ([FB2] v3:114–15); and on the *Ethics:* 1.3.2 ([FB2] v7:32). For additional references see [FB27].

Bonaventure, *De reductione artium ad theologiam,* ed. and tr. E.T. Healy, 2nd ed. (1939) [FB3].

Roger Bacon, *Communia naturalium,* fasc. 2:5–9 [FB4], and *Communia mathematica,* fasc. 16:38–55 [FB5], both in *Opera hactenus inedita Rogeri Baconi,* ed. R. Steele and F.M. Delorme, 16 fascs. (1905–40): the introductions to these two works provide Bacon's fullest discussion of the parts of knowledge.

Godfrey of St. Victor, *Microcosmus,* ed. P. Delhaye (1951) [FB6].

Dominicus Gundissalinus [= Gundisalvi], *De divisione philosophiae,* ed. L. Baur (1903): includes an extensive introduction [FB7].

Honorius Augustodunensis, *De animae exsilio et patria,* in *PL* 172:1241–46 [FB8].

Hugh of St. Victor, *Didas.*: with useful introduction by the translator [FB9].

Isidore of Seville, *Differentiae,* in *PL* 83:9–98 [FB10]; *Liber numerorum,* in *PL* 83:179–200 [FB11].

John Scottus Eriugena, *Annotationes in Marcianum,* ed. C. E. Lutz (1939) [FB12].

*Ordo artium,* ed. L. Gompf, "Der Leipziger 'Ordo artium,'" in *MLJ* 3 (1966) 94–128 [FB13].

Radulfus Ardens, *Speculum universale,* in M. Grabmann, *Die Geschichte der scholastischen Methode,* 2 vols. (1909–11, r1957) v1:252–54: Grabmann has reproduced a diagram of Radulfus's division of the sciences and quoted the section of the work that divides the sciences into theory, ethics, logic, and mechanics [FB14].

Radulphus de Longo Campo (fl. 1216), *In Anticlaudianum Alani commentum,* ed. J. Sulowski (1972) [FB15].

Richard of St. Victor, *Liber exceptionum,* ed. J. Châtillon (1958) [FB16].

Robert Kilwardby, *De ortu scientiarum,* ed. A.G. Judy (1976) [FB17].

Theophilus, *DDA* [FB18].

Vincent of Beauvais, *Speculum doctrinale* [= pt3 of Vincent's *Speculum maius*] (Douai 1624, r1964–65) [FB19].

Pseudo-William of Conches, *Un brano inedito della "Philosophia" di Guglielmo di Conches,* ed. C. Ottaviano (1935) [FB20].

## Studies

F. Alessio, "La filosofia e le 'artes mechanicae' nel secolo XII," in *SM*, 3rd ser., 6 (1965) 71–155 [**FB21**].

G.H. Allard and S. Lusignan, eds., *Les arts mécaniques au moyen âge* (1982) [**FB22**].

*Arts libéraux et philosophie au moyen âge*, Actes du quatrième congrès international de philosophie médiévale (27 August–2 September 1967) (1969): contains several useful articles on the mechanical arts [**FB23**].

R. Jansen-Sieben, ed., *Artes mechanicae en Europe médiévale: Actes du colloque du 15 octobre 1987* (1989) [**FB24**].

G. Ovitt, Jr., "The Status of the Mechanical Arts in Medieval Classifications of Learning," in *Viator* 14 (1983) 89–105 [**FB25**].

P. Sternagel, *Die Artes Mechanicae im Mittelalter: Begriffs- and Bedeutungsgeschichte bis zum Ende des 13. Jahrhunderts* (1966) [**FB26**].

E. Whitney, *Paradise Restored: The Mechanical Arts from Antiquity through the Thirteenth Century* (1990) [**FB27**].

FC     ●     # ARCHITECTURE

## BY JOSEPH F. O'CONNOR

Architectural terminology may be found in any Medieval Latin texts that mention buildings, including official records, chronicles, lives of saints, biographies, pilgrim accounts, narrations of the translation of relics, sermons, letters, diplomatic and administrative papers; but there are no technical treatises on architecture between Vitruvius's *De architectura* and Leon Battista Alberti's *De re aedificatoria* in the fifteenth century. A basic architectural vocabulary was inherited from late antiquity. Isidore's *Etymologiae* recollect the classical orders of Vitruvius and excerpt from technical passages of Pliny the Elder's *Naturalis historia,* but Isidore explores verbal associations rather than actual architectural practice. Scriptural passages such as the building of Solomon's Temple (3 *Rg* 5:1–6:38, 2 *Par* 1:18–4:22) also influenced the way in which architecture was described, particularly among authors seeking to invest architecture with allegorical content.

Since economic and political circumstances in most of Western Europe inhibited building in the earliest centuries, there are relatively few architectural descriptions before the year 1000 (the *Liber pontificalis* is an important exception). In the eleventh century, however, building and renovation on a large scale revived and continued through the rise of the Gothic into the Renaissance. Church architecture is more prominent in our sources than secular or civic buildings, because cathedrals and abbeys (and the relics and treasures they contained) possessed great cultural and religious significance, and because the increasing scale and expense of these projects made them notable.

In the eleventh century and after, a general architectural vocabulary would have been familiar to patrons and to the educated public. Reapplied from classical use, this vocabulary could not express with great precision the morphology of nonclassical innovations in medieval architecture. Although church architecture remained a recognizable extension of the classical basilica form in its most general features, the Gothic style accelerated radical changes in building dynamics. The Latin terminology of our sources, however, lagged behind, and thus we have no terms in common use for ribbed groin vault, chevet, compound pier, or even stained glass.

Artisans and builders must have had a far more developed technical terminology than has reached us from our sources. The thirteenth-century *Dictionarius* of John of Garland (c. 1195–c. 1272) suggests that they did and that this Latin vocabulary was influenced by the vernacular. Because the architectural vocabulary available to the Medieval Latin writer was general and specialized terminology varied from place to place, the reader must exercise caution in interpreting texts. Fortunately some major texts, such as Abbot Suger's description of St. Denis (written between 1144 and 1149) or the monk Gervase's account of the building of the choir at Canterbury (completed in 1184), can be compared with the extant fabric to learn, for example, that Gervase uses the word *ciborium* to indicate a hitherto unknown feature, the quadripartite vault.

## Church Buildings

Although round and hexagonal buildings recollecting the Holy Sepulcher are not unknown in the late antique period and the Middle Ages, the rectangular Roman basilica or public building form, rather than the pagan temple, was established as the norm for Christian churches. Various elements and elaborations of the basilica form dominate the vocabulary of medieval church buildings. Above a masonry foundation (*fundamentum*) the main structural piers or columns (*pilarii, colum[p]nae*) are set, supporting the wall of the central nave (*navis, aula*) and the exterior walls (*parietes, muri*). Columns or piers set off the nave from the aisles (*alae*); the nave leads to the central apse (*absida, absis, apsida, caput ecclesiae*), typically, but not always, towards the east. Within or in front of the apse stands the altar, perhaps covered with a canopy (*ciborium*), and often an area is marked out for the choir (*chorus*) or the clergy (*cancellus, presbyterium, sanctuarium*). The basic rectangle of the basilica can be altered to a T-shape or cruciform by transepts (*cruces*). The principal altar often stood over the relics of martyrs or saints (*martyrium, confessio*) or a crypt (*cripta*). Chapels and side altars were common (*capellae, sacella; titulus* and *aditum* also indicate burial sites within the church). The columns of the nave and the transepts were joined by the architraves (*trabes*) or by arches (*arcus*), and galleries (*porticus, trifo-ria*) were added below the upper windows (*fenestrae superiores*). The ceiling (*tectum*) may be beamed (*trabeatum*), covered with ceiling panels (*laquearia*), or a vault (usually *fornix*, sometimes *testudo* or *voltura; ciborium* can mean a vaulted compartment; the principal vault over the main crossing is called the *fornix maior*). The end opposite the apse may contain a vestibule (*vestibulum*) and the facade (*frons*) may open onto a court or garden (*atrium, paradysus*), or a porch at the western end (*galilaea*). Subsidiary structures may be noted, such as a vestry (*revestiarium*), sacristy (*sacrarium*), cloister (*claustrum*), tower (*turris*). This basic vocabulary persists even when the buildings become larger, the vaulting and ambulatories (*deambulatoria*) more complex, the finish work more elaborate, and the galleries (*solaria*) and windows more numerous.

Although church buildings are the principal concern of ecclesiastical architecture, these were often located within the wider architectural contexts of abbeys and episcopal residences. Thus descriptions of cathedrals might include the episcopal palace (*domus episcopalis, palatium*), lodging for the canons (*canonica*), private chapel (*capella*), wardrobe (*vestiarium*), and other subsidiary buildings. The major abbeys encompass extensive, specialized outbuildings (*officinae*) and other features: chapter house (*capitulum*), audience hall (*auditorium*), heated room (*calefactorium*), bathing rooms (*balnea*), refectory (*refectorium*), infirmary (*infirmantium domus*), guest house (*xenodochium*), almshouse (*eleemosynarium*), kitchen (*coquina*), bakery (*pistrina*), pantry (*cellarium*), buttery (*cella vinaria*), dormitories (*dormitoria*), workshops (*ergasteria*), barns (*grangiae*), and stables (*stabula*). Some standardization in vocabulary and design resulted from communications between monasteries, such as the *Consuetudines Farfenses* (before 1049), and, later, from architectural regulations by the religious orders.

## Secular Buildings

Security was the principal concern in secular architecture. Thus the fortification of cities and noble estates was of great interest to writers, with principal attention given to towers, gates, and walls. With the rise of the medieval castle (*castellum, castrum, fortericia, domus firma* or *turrita*) and keep, and their transformation from wooden stockades into large stone and masonry ensembles, the elements of fortification and of living spaces expanded. The outer perimeter often continued the practice of Roman encampment fortification with earthworks (*vallum*) and ditch (*fossa*), and frequently the earth excavated for the ditch was piled up to form a platform or motte (*agger, mota*). The enclosing wall or curtain (*murus, ambarium*), first of wood and then of masonry, received definition from the placement of towers (*turres*). Both the wall and the towers could be surmounted by battlements (*propugnacula*) or a parapet (*antepectus, clipeus, scutum*) or projecting galleries and scaffolding to allow missiles to be hurled at assailants below (*bretescha, bretica, machicolamentum*); these often were distinguished with crenellations (*crenelli, quernelli*) and merlons or openings (*cancelli*) to accommodate ballistic devices. The walls and towers were fitted with loopholes (*tueriae*) or windows with loopholes (*arcubalistares fenestrae*) for added defense. Bastions (*torneae*) and turrets (*tornellae, turellae*) extended the surface of the walls for enlarged defensive scope. Outworks (*antemuralia*) included barbicans to fortify the main gate and other barriers such as a parapet (*obstaculum*) or a portcullis (*colacia*). The castle perimeter is thus distinguished by architectural defenses, and elements of these may also be found in abbeys and churches as well as manor houses.

Inside the gates and walls was often a community in miniature. Many castles are dominated by a rectangular or round keep or donjon (*dunjo, donjio, arx*) whose spaces were arranged in successive stories with rooms (*diversoria*) distributed off the main stairway (*gradale*) by means of winding passageways (*diverticula*). Before the introduction of the fireplace (*caminus*) and rooms heated by fireplaces (*caminatae, camerae cum camino*), a high, hearth-warmed hall (*aula, hala, triclinium*) for dining and entertainment was common. The hall often opened onto the private family quarters, frequently on an upper story (*solarium*), containing the master bedroom (*thalamus*) and built over storage areas (*cellaria*). Living quarters may be furnished with a "garderobe" or privy (*camera privata, latrina*), built in such a way that wastes were deposited outside the structure proper. Various chambers (*camerae*), dormitories (*dormitoria*), and lodgings (*mansiones, habitacula*, etc.) could accommodate guests and the household staff and were sometimes arranged along the inside perimeter of the wall. The closed environment was somewhat relieved by an interior open space or bailey (*platea, ba[i]llium*) or courtyard (*curtis*).

The morphology of the manor house shares the features of both the abbey in its orientation towards communal amenities and productive work, and of the castle in its arrangements of open and closed, public and private, spaces. As with the vocabulary of ecclesiastical foundations, the Latin terminology of secular architecture varied in time and place and was influenced by the vernacular as innovations in fortifications and living spaces evolved.

## Architects and Workmen

Care must be exercised in interpreting the term *architectus* in the sources; more often than not, it simply means a master carpenter, a master mason, or the artisan who lays the foundations (so Isidore). Sometimes it in fact means the "architect" who designs and plans the work, supervises (with the help of foremen, *magistri caementariorum, lignorum, lapidum*, etc.), and brings the plan to completion. So too *faber, artifex*, and *magister*. Skilled workers are carpenters (*carpentarii, operarii lignorum*) or masons in brick or stone (*caementarii, maciones, operarii lapidum, lat[h]omi*).

## Materials and Ornamentation

The technology of concrete was lost to the Middle Ages. Structures were composed of wood (*opus ligneum*), brick (*lateres*), or, by the eleventh century, dressed stone (*lapides quadrati* or *secti*). Surfaces may be covered with a variety of other materials: lead sheeting (*tabula plumbea*) or tiles (*tegulae*) for the roof; revetment (*crusta*) of marble or other stone, plaster (*plastrum*), and stucco (*gipsum*) for the walls. Decorative features may include carvings (*caelatura*) or gilding (*deaurata*). Mosaic art (*ars musiva*) was revived, as well as decorative pieced stone work on walls and pavements (*opus sectile, ars quadrataria*). Rare materials such as gold, silver, glass, bronze, ivory, and exotic marbles are mentioned, as well as the furnishings and treasures of the place.

# Select Bibliography

## Primary Works and Translations

Vitruvius, *De architectura*, ed. and tr. F.S. Granger, 2 vols. (1931, r1983) [FC1]; L. Cherubini, *Vitruvius Pollio: Indices nominum et verborum* (1975) [FC2]; H. Plommer, *Vitruvius and Later Roman Building Manuals* (1973): text and translation of Cetius Faventinus, *De diversis fabricis architectonicae*, with index of Latin technical terms [FC3].

Gervase of Canterbury, "Tractatus de combustione et reparatione Cantuariensis ecclesiae," in Gervase's *Chronica*, ed. W. Stubbs, *RSer* 73.1 (1879) 3–29 [FC4].

John of Garland, *Dictionarius*, ed. T. Hunt, in *TLLTCE* v1:191–203 [FC5].

E. Panofsky, ed. and tr., *Abbot Suger on the Abbey Church of St.-Denis and Its Art Treasures* (1946); 2nd ed. by G. Panofsky-Soergel (1979) [FC6].

Leon Battista Alberti (1404–72), *De re aedificatoria*, ed. and tr. G. Orlandi, with intro. and notes by P. Portoghesi (1966); tr. J. Rykwert, N. Leach, and R. Tavernor: *On the Art of Building in Ten Books* (1988) [FC7].

No medieval treatise on architecture survives. The most useful anthologies of Latin texts relating to architecture focus on France. The first, V. Mortet, *Recueil de textes relatifs à l'histoire de architecture et à la condition des architectes en France au moyen âge, XIe–XIIe siècles* (1911), contains a splendid introduction and an indispensable glossary of terms. Its sequel, V. Mortet and P. Deschamps, *Recueil de textes relatifs à l'histoire de l'architecture et à la condition des architectes en France au moyen âge, XIIe–XIIIe siècles* (1929), follows Mortet's original plan and expands the glossary [FC8]. See also D. Parsons, *Books and Buildings: Architectural Description Before and After Bede* (1988) [FC9]; H.M. Colvin, ed. and tr., *Building Accounts of King Henry III* (1971) [FC10].

For an overview of the various genres of architectural description, see J. von Schlosser, *Quellenbuch zur Kunstgeschichte des abendländischen Mittelalters* (1896, r1976) [FC11].

For the city of Rome, there is the monumental work of R. Valentini and G. Zucchetti, *Codice topografico della città di Roma*, 4 vols. (1940–53) [FC12].

Three anthologies in English translation contain a preponderance of architectural texts: C. Davis-Weyer, *Early Medieval Art 300–1150: Sources and Documents* (1971, r1986) [FC13]; T.G. Frisch, *Gothic Art 1140–c. 1450: Sources and Documents* (1971, r1987) [FC14]; and, for the Byzantine East, C.A. Mango, *The Art of the Byzantine Empire, 312–1453: Sources and Documents* (1972, r1986) [FC15].

## Studies and Guides

The secondary bibliography on medieval architecture is enormous. An introduction has been assembled by D.L. Ehresmann, *Architecture: A Bibliographic Guide to Basic Reference Works, Histories, and Handbooks* (1984) 87–132 [FC16]. See also H.M. Colvin, *English Architectural History: A Guide to Sources*, 2nd ed. rev. (1976) [FC17]; C. Cable, *Medieval Architectural Design and Structure: A Bibliography with Selected Annotations,* Vance Bibliographies (1981) [FC18]; *id., Smaller Medieval English Domestic Buildings: A Bibliography,* Vance Bibliographies (1984) [FC19].

For the morphology of classical architecture, its variations, and its incorporation in other styles, see R. Adam, *Classical Architecture: A Comprehensive Handbook to the Tradition of Classical Style* (1991) [FC20].

A more detailed, authoritative discussion is found in three volumes of the Pelican History of Art: R. Krautheimer, *Early Christian and Byzantine Architecture*, 4th ed. rev. (1986) [FC21]; K.J. Conant, *Carolingian and Romanesque Architecture, 800 to 1200*, 2nd ed. rev. (1979) [FC22]; P. Frankl, *Gothic Architecture* (1962, r1963) [FC23].

For the relation of literary sources to architectural practice, see P. Frankl, *The Gothic: Literary Sources and Interpretations through Eight Centuries* (1960) 1–234, as well as the introductions to Mortet and to Mortet/Deschamps (see [FC8]) [FC24].

For a study of actual construction from an architect's point of view, see J. Fitchen, *The Construction of Gothic Cathedrals: A Study of Medieval Vault Erection* (1961, r1981) [FC25].

Three recent works discuss the development of the medieval castle in England: M.W. Thompson, *The Rise of the Castle* (1991) [FC26], and *id., The Decline of the Castle* (1987) [FC27]; N.J.G. Pounds, *The Medieval Castle in England and Wales: A Social and Political History* (1990) [FC28]. A.J. Taylor, *Studies in Castles and Castle-Building* (1986), contains a collection of miscellaneous essays that include useful

Latin source materials: accounts, regulations, correspondence, etc. [FC29]. For the development of domestic architecture in England, see M. Wood, *The English Mediaeval House* (1965, r1983) [FC30].

For the architecture of a large monastic complex, see W. Horn and E. Born, *The Plan of St. Gall*, 3 vols. (1979) [FC31].

For more detail on the medieval mason, see the helpful articles by L.R. Shelby, particularly "The Role of the Master Mason in Medieval English Building," in *Speculum* 39 (1964) 387–403 [FC32]; "The Geometrical Knowledge of Medieval Master Masons," in *Speculum* 47 (1972) 395–421 [FC33]; "Medieval Masons' Tools: The Level and the Plumb Rule," in *TC* 2 (1961) 127–30 [FC34]; and "Medieval Masons' Tools II: Compass and Square," in *TC* 6 (1965) 236–48 [FC35].

Other useful works include the following:

E. Battisti, "Architettura ed urbanistica nelle enciclopedie medievali," in *Momenti e modelli nella storia dell'enciclopedia: Il mondo musulmano, ebraico e latino a confronto sul tema dell'organizzazione del sapere* (1985) [= *Rivista di storia della filosofia* 40] 146–58 [FC36].

D.J. Cathcart King, *Castellarium Anglicanum: An Index and Bibliography of the Castles in England, Wales and the Islands*, 2 vols. (1983) [FC37].

H.M. Colvin *et al.*, *The History of the King's Works* (1963-): v1–2 concern the Middle Ages [FC38].

J. Harvey, *The Mediaeval Architect* (1972): with appendix of texts on the architect, aesthetics and symbolism, style and fashion, contemporary description of architecture, and other topics [FC39].

J. Harvey, *English Mediaeval Architects: A Biographical Dictionary Down to 1550, Including Master Masons, Carpenters, Carvers, Building Contractors and Others Responsible for Design*, rev. ed. (1984), with listing of sources (ppxxv–xxxvii); supp. (1987) [FC40].

R. Marta, *Tecnica costruttiva romana/Roman Building Techniques* (1986) [FC41].

C.E. Norton, *Historical Studies of Church-Building in the Middle Ages: Venice, Siena, Florence* (1880, r1969 of 1902 edition): with app. of Latin documents concerned with the duomo of Siena [FC42].

N. Pevsner, "Terms of Architectural Planning in the Middle Ages," in *Journal of the Warburg and Courtauld Institutes* 5 (1942) 232–37 [FC43].

N. Pevsner, "The Term 'Architect' in the Middle Ages," in *Speculum* 17 (1942) 549–62 [FC44].

L.F. Salzman, *Building in England down to 1540: A Documentary History* (1952, r1967 with corrections and additions, reissued 1992) [FC45].

H.L. Turner, *Town Defences in England and Wales: An Architectural and Documentary Study, A.D. 900–1500* (1970) [FC46].

J. Verbruggen, "Note sur le sens des mots castrum, castellum et quelques autres expressions qui désignent des fortifications," in *RBPhH* 21 (1950) 177 [FC47].

L. Villena *et al.*, *Glossaire: Burgenfachwörterbuch des mittelalterlichen Wehrbaus*, ed. W. Meyer (1975): a multilingual (German, English, French, Spanish, and Italian) card index of medieval military architectural terms [FC48].

M. Warnke, *Bau und Überbau: Soziologie der mittelalterlichen Architektur nach den Schriftquellen* (1976) [FC49].

B. Ward-Perkins, *From Classical Antiquity to the Middle Ages: Urban Public Building in Northern and Central Italy,* A.D. *300–850* (1984): with appendices of texts [FC50].

J.A. Wight, *Brick Building in England from the Middle Ages to 1550* (1972): with section on "early brick vocabulary" and glossary of technical terms [FC51].

*See also* [BA105], [BA142].

# FD　•　WEIGHTS AND MEASURES

### BY RONALD EDWARD ZUPKO

In discussions of the terminology of metrology there was no literary continuity from the ancient to the medieval world. Medieval authors did not expand upon ancient writings on weights and measures, such as Vitruvius's *De architectura* and the works of Varro, Columella, and the Roman *agrimensores* (land surveyors), but tended merely to provide a rehash of earlier texts. Our construction of medieval systems of weights and measures is based upon such sources as acts, assizes, decrees, ordinances, regulations, and statutes; annals, chronicles, and histories; brokerage and port books; calendars; cartularies; charters; custumals; government accounts, reports, and surveys; industrial ordinances and regulations; inventories; ledgers; letters and private papers; rolls; university statutes; and wills.

The Medieval Latin terminology for weights and measures reveals a variety of linguistic creativity. The usages described in this brief introduction are drawn chiefly from medieval England, but the principles apply to all the regions of Europe that had experienced Roman occupation.

The standard of measurements of length may be primary (such as *passus,* "pace," or *palma,* "palm") or derive from an arbitrary unit, such as the three medium-sized barleycorns that made up the medieval English inch when placed end to end. A measure of area, commonly the square of the linear unit, is usually expressed in terms of square feet, square yards, or square perches. A capacity measure, i.e. the cube of the linear unit, was usually based on a vessel containing a certain mass of liquid or dry substance. In medieval England, weight, i.e. the mass of a given body, was based on the barley or wheat grain. The troy pennyweight, for instance, contained 24 barleycorns, the troy ounce 480, and the troy pound 5,760. Counting to measure quantity was mainly by 12s or 20s (12 for the dozen, 12 dozen for the gross, 20 for the score, etc.).

## Terms Derived from Classical Latin

Classical Latin words were appropriated in the Middle Ages for specific, local uses. *Caritas,* "charity," for example, could designate an allowance of food or drink provided to monks. Many Roman measuring units became part of the national system in England, though their values often changed in ways that would have surprised the Romans, who had sought to enforce a standardized system of weights and measures similar in intent to the modern metric system. *Stadium,* a unit of linear measurement equal to 625 Roman *pedes,* was in England later used for the urban and rural furlong, equal to 1/8 mile and generally containing 660 feet; *cubitus* (Classical Latin *cubitum*), the distance from the elbow to the end of the middle finger, was standardized in England at 18 inches; *milia passuum,* literally the thousand paces of the Roman mile, varied in England between 5,000 and 6,600 feet and was often reckoned by paces from 1,000 to 1,500; the *scripulum* or *scrupulus,* a Roman weight equal to 1/24 of an *uncia* or 1/288 of a *libra,* became the English scruple, an apothecary weight of 20 grains equal to 1/24 apothecary ounce; *cadus,* a large, usually earthenware jar for wine or foodstuffs, was in medieval England a "cade," a small barrel or keg for fish; similarly *uncia,* "ounce" or "inch," *pertica,* "perch." Their values would often change along with their vernacular equivalents (perch, ounce, etc.), while the Latin term remained the same.

During the Middle Ages other Classical Latin words came to designate specific measurements: *dolium,* "large storage jar," was used in England for a tun of any liquid or dry product; *arc(h)a,* "chest, box, coffer," was similarly used for capacity measures of fruit, grain, etc.; *lagena,* "bottle, flask," usually denoted a gallon vessel; *tertianus* (adjective) gave the substantive *tertiana,* a third of a tun of 252 gallons, i.e. 84 gallons; *quarta* was a quarter of a gallon; *saccum* (Classical Latin *saccus*), "bag or sack," was a measure used principally for apples, ashes, charcoal, cloves, coal, flour, and grain; *granum,* "grain" or "seed," was the building block on which all English divisions of weight were built. Other measures included the *palma,* "palm," referring to the handsbreadth (minus the thumb) and equaling three inches; *virga,* "twig" or "rod," was a yard (itself an English word meaning "rod"). *Vannus,* "winnowing instrument," led to the "fan," a wide, shallow wicker basket for chaff containing three heaped bushels.

## Medieval Latin Formations

The suffix *-ata* turned a base noun into a term of measurement: *bovata* (*bos/bovis,* "ox") referred to the amount of land worked by one ox or a team of oxen over a certain period (usually a year) and was a "bovate" or serf's holding; its exact area depended on the quality of the soil, but it was frequently reckoned at 1/2 virgate or 1/8 hide. *Virgata* (*virga,* "rod") or "virgate" was generally equal to 1/4 hide or 2 bovates, but it also varied according to the nature of the soil. A *carrucata* (from *carruca,* "cart," which in Medieval Latin came to mean "plow") was the same as a hide, originally the amount of land needed to support a peasant family for a year. *Denariata* (*denarius,* a Roman coin, penny) was a pennyworth, i.e. of land (with reference to the yearly rental) or of goods.

Many Medieval Latin terms of measurement are latinizations of vernacular words. Celtic gave CL *leuga* (ML *leuca,* English "league"); originally measuring 1,500 paces, it came to mean three miles, though other lengths, from 7,500 to 15,000 feet, were also common. Classical Latin *amphora,* "large jar" (ultimately Greek), entered Old English as *amber* and was then relatinized as *ambra;* used for grain and liquids, it varied in size, with 4 bushels being the most common. Classical Latin *decuria,* a group of ten, entered Germanic, giving rise to Anglo-Latin *dicra,* German-Latin *decora/decara,* and French-Latin *dacra* (entering English through Anglo-Norman); it was a measure of any ten items or sets of items (see *dicker* in the *OED* [BF32]). From

French or Anglo-Norman (and ultimately from Classical Latin, Germanic, or Celtic) came *barellus* (Old French *baril*), "barrel," e.g. of ale (32 gallons), beer (36 gallons), herrings (30 gallons fully packed), etc.; *bussellus* (Old French *boissel*), "bushel" (the Winchester grain bushel was of 4 pecks or 8 gallons); *galo/galona* (ML *galleta*, "bucket," perhaps ultimately Celtic), "gallon," of 4 quarts or 8 pints, the actual measure differing by product; *pinta* (OF *pinte*), "pint"; *fardellus* (OF *fardel*; Arabic *fardah*, "pack, bundle"), a measure of cloth or other items collected in bundle or bale. Common Germanic \**fat* (OE *fæt*, "vessel, vat"; Swedish *fat*) gave ML *fatta, vatta, fattum*, which was used to designate various capacity measures for grain.

During the Middle English period (c. 1150–1400) many English words, mainly of Germanic origin, were latinized: *hida*, "hide"; *bolla*, "bowl," employed in northern England and Scotland as a measure for grain and coal; *acra*, "acre" (a Germanic word, ultimately related to CL *ager*), standardized at 160 square perches of 16½ feet each or 43,560 square feet; *fotmellum*, "foot measure," a 70-pound measure of weight for lead; *lastum* (ME *last*, "load"), a cargo measure for large bulk shipments; *pecca*, "peck" (ultimate origin uncertain), used for grain and generally containing 2 gallons or 1/4 bushel; *roda* (ME *rod*, "pole"), a measure of length (generally 16½ feet) or area (40 square perches or 1/4 statute acre); *tonellus* (ME *tonne*, "barrel"), a capacity measure for wine, oil, honey, and other liquids, generally containing 252 gallons.

Other Latin words used for English measurements during the Middle Ages include *butticula*, "bottle"; *celdra*, "chalder"; *chargia/carca*, "charge"; *drachma*, "dram"; *ferlota*, "firlot"; *furlonga*, "furlong"; *hundredum*, "hundred"; *pecia*, "piece"; *pipa*, "pipe"; *poca*, "poke"; *potellus*, "pottle"; *quarterium*, "quarter"; *quintallus*, "quintal"; *sarpellarium*, "sarplar"; *sauma*, "seam"; *strica*, "strike"; *wista*, "wist"; and *weya*, "wey."

Many Medieval Latin formulations of such technical terms represent attempts to provide, for record purposes, appropriate Latin equivalents of the ordinary vernacular words that would have been used in verbal transactions: they may have had no usage outside the documents.

## Select Bibliography

### Primary Works

*Annales de Burton (A.D. 1004–1263)*, ed. H.R. Luard, in *Annales monastici*, 5 vols., RSer 36 (1864–69) v36.1:183–510: valuable for many different land measures [FD1].

*The Brokage Book of Southampton, 1443–1444*, ed. O. Coleman, 2 vols. (1960–61): thousands of entries for weights and measures with numerous variant spellings [FD2].

*The Chronicle of Battle Abbey*, ed. E. Searle (1980): a major source for agricultural measures of all kinds [FD3].

*The Durham Household Book; or, the Accounts of the Bursar of the Monastery of Durham from Pentecost 1530 to Pentecost 1534*, [ed. J. Raine], SurSoc 18 (1844): an excellent compilation of capacity and cloth measures [FD4].

*The Fabric Rolls of York Minster*, [ed. J. Raine], SurSoc 35 (1859): many documents of capacity and land measures [FD5].

*Fleta,* v2–4, ed. and tr. H.G. Richardson and G.O. Sayles, *SelSoc* 72, 89, 99 (1955–84): much documentation for weights and capacity measures [FD6].

*The Inventories and Account Rolls of the Benedictine Houses or Cells of Jarrow and Monk-Wearmouth, in the County of Durham,* [ed. J. Raine], *SurSoc* 29 (1854): extensive coverage of all divisions of weights and measures [FD7].

*The Local Port Book of Southampton for 1435–36,* ed. B. Foster (1963): this and other port books are essential for all weights and measures used in regional and inter-regional commerce [FD8].

*Munimenta Gildhallae Londoniensis: Liber Albus, Liber Custumarum, et Liber Horn,* ed. H.T. Riley, 3 vols. in 4 pts., *RSer* 12 (1859–62): the first two volumes contain most of the valuable metrological discussions [FD9].

*Select Tracts and Table Books Relating to English Weights and Measures (1100–1742),* ed. H. Hall and F.J. Nicholas, *CamSoc,* 3rd ser., v41 [= *Camden Miscellany* 15] (1929), pt5:1–68: a good selection of medieval sources exemplifying the evolution of Latin, Medieval Latin, and Latin and vernacular admixtures [FD10].

## Reference Works, Studies, and Dictionaries

A. Heit and K. Petry, *Bibliographie zur historischen Metrologie,* 2 vols. (1992–95) [FD11].

R.C. Van Caenegem and F.L. Ganshof, *GSMH;* see ch. 7, "Historical Metrology," pp372–80 [FD12].

R.E. Zupko, "Weights and Measures," in *DMA* 12:582–96 [FD13].

R.E. Zupko, *British Weights & Measures: A History from Antiquity to the Seventeenth Century* (1977): extensive bibliography; this work and [FD16–19] also contain selections of books and articles dealing with medieval linguistic issues of metrology [FD14].

R.E. Zupko, *Revolution in Measurement: Western European Weights and Measures Since the Age of Science* (1990): extensive bibliography and much coverage of all aspects of medieval metrology in the text, notes, tables, and appendices [FD15].

R.E. Zupko, *Italian Weights and Measures from the Middle Ages to the Nineteenth Century* (1981): extensive bibliography, etymologies, variant spellings, and citations; important for the Roman system and its influence on English and other Western European metrologies [FD16].

R.E. Zupko, *A Dictionary of English Weights and Measures from Anglo-Saxon Times to the Nineteenth Century* (1968): thousands of Medieval Latin citations and variant spellings, complete etymologies for all units, and extensive bibliography [FD17].

R.E. Zupko, *A Dictionary of Weights and Measures for the British Isles: The Middle Ages to the Twentieth Century* (1985): a large expansion of [FD17] to include Ireland, Wales, and Scotland [FD18].

R.E. Zupko, *French Weights and Measures before the Revolution: A Dictionary of Provincial and Local Units* (1978): extensive bibliography, etymologies, variant spellings, and citations; important for French and Latin importations in English metrology [FD19].

# FE • WEAPONS AND WARFARE

BY E. MALCOLM PARKINSON

Little has been written on the latinity of arms, armor, and warfare. Like Contamine in his comprehensive *War in the Middle Ages* [FE12], historians have tended to offer only fragmentary information on the Latin terminology of weapons and armor. Few lists of words are available: in *Du Cange* an extensive vocabulary has been assembled [FE8], and Nicolle includes Latin terms in his polyglot dictionary for the Crusade period 1050–1350 [FE9]. Along with comparatively few studies, the student of arms and armor must confront the variations in modern terminology among historians, archaeologists, ethnologists, and curators. A guide to recent terminology in the major modern European languages is the *Glossarium Armorum* [FE16], though in English the standard terminology largely follows that of Blair's classic *European Armour* [FE11].

Original written sources include military manuals and treatises. The *Epitoma rei militaris,* a manual of the fifth century by Vegetius, discusses soldiers, equipment, training, discipline, organization, strategy, and fortification [FE7]. Influential in the Middle Ages, the manual was often cited and translated. Treatises on weapons and military equipment, such as Kyeser's *Bellifortis* of the early fifteenth century, also reveal Latin usage [FE3]. One of the most enlightening manuals, Pietro Monte's *Exercitiorum atque artis militaris collectanea* of 1509, offers a breathtaking array of descriptions of weapons and components of armor with instructions on how to wield or wear them [FE4]. A Spaniard's manual for fighting men, the *Collectanea,* suffered prolonged neglect until the historian Sydney Anglo began recently to analyze it [FE10].

Chronicles and narrative accounts of warfare span the Middle Ages. The military historian and soldier of the later Roman Empire, Ammianus Marcellinus (c. 330-c. 396), writes about the battles and sieges of the mid-fourth century, referring frequently to weapons and armor and describing siege equipment [FE1]. For the Crusades, narratives are replete with military action. Odo of Deuil (d. c. 1162), for example, in his *De profectione Ludovici VII in orientem,* recounts the skirmishes and raids of the Second Crusade (1146–49), in which he served as Louis VII's chaplain [FE5].

Laws, legal documents, and inventories also help to show the development of martial Latin. The capitularies of Charlemagne are important in this regard [FE13]. And wills can identify a person's martial possessions [FE17]. Inventories can be particularly helpful in uncovering specialized vocabulary and usage. The records of the Tower of London, for example, show the language of early gunpowder weaponry and associated equipment ([FE2], [FE6]).

In the Middle Ages, warfare changed profoundly. Working vocabularies were needed to encompass not only old and new weapons and armor, but also the changing social and military standing of fighting men. The coming of mounted shock combat and the figure of the knight, for instance, entailed a shift in the meaning of *miles* from a professional soldier to a mounted warrior, the *milites* becoming a distinct social group. As Duby has shown, that shift was complete in the Mâcon region of France by 1100 [FE14]. And renewed attention to the meaning and chronology of the language of tournaments has engendered study of the twelfth-century *tornea-mentum* and its relationship to the contemporary French term *tornoi* [FE19–20].

A wide range of types of body armor is found in the Middle Ages. The Carolingian terms were the classical *lorica*, and *brunia*, a Germanic loanword; *thorax*, too, was used. Ninth-century texts also mention *bainberga*, armor for the legs, perhaps greaves or scale armor. *Manicae* or another Germanic loanword, *wanti*, referred to protection for the hands; *bauga* protected the arms. (See [FE13].)

By the eleventh century, *brunia* and *halsberga*, the hauberk, had become interchangeable, the latter a mail shirt composed of metal rings, covering the trunk, head, arms, and the legs down below the knees. Numerous variant spellings appeared, as well as the diminutive *halsbergellum*. *Lorica* too could refer to a hauberk. A short version not reaching down as far as the knees was the haubergeon, known as the *halsbergio* or *halsbergatum*.

By the late twelfth century, the hauberk was worn over a quilted garment, the gambeson or pourpoint, the *gambesio*, *gambesiata lorica*, *wambasio*, or *propunctum*. In the fourteenth century the gambeson for the infantry was called the *alcoto* or *alketo* (borrowed, in Spain, from Arabic *al-quṭūn*), which later became known as the arming doublet, the *dublet de fens*. The jack, the *jakkum defensionis*, served as a cheap version of the brigandine, the *brigandina* being an armored jacket without sleeves and consisting of overlapping metal lames attached by rivets to a cloth backing or to a combination of leather and cloth. (See [FE11], [FE16–17], [FE22].) From the thirteenth century, armor evolved rapidly, with full suits constructed for specialized purposes by the mid-fifteenth century. Monte offers a working Latin vocabulary for plate armor [FE4].

The Classical Latin words for helmet, *galea* and *cassis*, saw extensive medieval use, even when the variety of helmets kept increasing after the twelfth century. Both terms appear up to the sixteenth century—after the introduction of the barbut, bascinet, sallet, and armet—showing the limitations of a pair of classical terms to signify an increasing number of objects. *Helmus* or *elmus*, a Germanic loanword, denoted the great helm. The *bacinetum* or *cervellerium*, a small metal skull cap known today by its French name *cervellière*, fitted over or under the *coifa*, the mail hood that was part of the hauberk or attached to it. Infantry often wore the *capellus ferreus*, an iron hat with a broad brim, from the twelfth century until after the end of the medieval period. (See [FE1], [FE4], [FE11], [FE13], [FE17].)

*Arma defensibilia* included not only armor and helmets, but also shields. The Roman names, *clipeus* and *parma* for round shields, *pelta* for a crescent-shaped one, and *scutum* for a large rectangular or oval type, persisted, though there were many variations in form and material in medieval shields. The Carolingians used the word *scutum. Pelta* denoted the small, round shield of the Moslems during the Crusades. The large, rectangular *pavesium,* used from the late fourteenth century, protected archers and infantry; its name may derive from the city of Pavia in Italy. (See [FE4], [FE9], [FE13], [FE16–17], [FE22].)

The *spatha,* originally the long sword of the Roman cavalry, usually denoted a long double-edged sword. The *semispatha* was shorter. *Gladius,* originally the Roman legionnaire's weapon, also referred to a sword shorter than the *spatha,* though the words *spatha, gladius,* and the more literary *ensis* could be interchanged. *Ferrum* referred to swords in general. The *saxa* was a short sword or long dagger, as was *cultellus. Pugio* retained its Roman meaning of dagger. *Ensis duarum manuum* indicated the two-handed sword that dated from the early fourteenth century and could be six feet in length; *ensis unius manus* was a one-handed sword. *Stocchus* could refer to a late medieval thrusting sword such as the French *estoc,* anglicized as *tuck. Vagina* retained its meaning of scabbard. (See [FE4], [FE7–8], [FE12–13], [FE17], [FE22].)

One of the most difficult and confusing areas of the terminology of arms has been staff weapons. Also called pole arms or hafted weapons, these had a metal head on a long or short haft. The *francisca* and the *bipennis* were Frankish axes. The Carolingian infantry and cavalry carried the *lancea* primarily for thrusting, compared with the *hasta,* a light throwing spear of the same period [FE13]. The word *gisarma,* used frequently from the twelfth century to the fifteenth, has engendered disagreement among historians of arms. Previously taking the *gisarma* to be the bill, a hook with curved cutting edges mounted on a shaft, historians now assume that in England it meant an axe with a long handle. (See, for example, [FE17], [FE22].)

Staff weapons proliferated in the later Middle Ages, with loanwords or simple adaptations of the vernacular predominant. Among the most common of the weapons for the infantry, the *alabarda,* or halberd, sported a spike above an axe blade with a balancing fluke. The *partisana* had a long triangular head with a broad point and two lugs at the bottom. The *rhonca* was the ranseur—like the partisan, but with prongs on the sides; the *spetum,* the corseque; the *clava,* the mace with a metal head; the *aza,* the bec de faucon or pole hammer. And mounted combat at tournaments often required special lances such as the heavy *grossa lancea* or *ponderosa lancea.* (See [FE4], [FE8], [FE22].)

The word *arcus* for the self-bow and the composite bow was used throughout the medieval period, as was *sagitta* for the arrow [FE17]. Numerous terms for the crossbow derived from Classical Latin *ballista* (the ancient siege machine that the later crossbow resembled [FE1]), among which we find medieval Latin *arcubalista,* whence came OF *arbaleste,* itself the source of Medieval Latin *arbalista. Balista* itself was also appropriated for the weapon [FE3]. A bolt, or quarrel, shot from a crossbow was called a *quadrellus,* with variant spellings including *quarrellus* and *carellus,* though *sagitta* could also be used.

With the advent of gunpowder artillery in the fourteenth century, it is sometimes unclear whether references are to siege machines or guns, but gradually the ambiguity vanishes. *Artilleria* covered martial machines and missile weapons in general, its meaning being extended to include gunpowder weaponry. Thus the (Old French) *artiller* (whence Medieval Latin *artillator*) made or looked after military engines, not just guns [FE6].

In England *gonna* or *gunna* appeared in the fourteenth century ([FE2], [FE6])—a reference to the use of this term by Thomas Walsingham (d. 1422) even found its way unexpectedly into *Lewis-Short* (s.v. *canon*)!—while Italian sources used the word *canon* [FE17]. *Pixis,* the term used in the German *Bellifortis,* could apply to large and small guns alike [FE3]. Sometimes little distinction was made among sizes and types of guns except for the addition of the words large and small: *gunnes magni,* for example, are distinguished from *gunnes parui,* the latter designating smaller or hand-held weapons. *Sclopus* referred to an arquebus, which a man could hold [FE4]. *Ribaldus* (in French, *ribaudequin*) indicated a group of small cannon mounted together to be fired in salvo ([FE2], [FE6]). *Bombarda* (OF *bombarde*), usually a large cannon, had the diminutive *bombardella,* perhaps derived from the *bombus* or boom of the weapon.

## Select Bibliography

### Primary Works and Translations

Ammianus Marcellinus, *Res gestae,* ed. and tr. J.C. Rolfe, 3 vols., rev. ed. (1963–64) [FE1].
"Inventories 1353–1833," in H.L. Blackmore, *The Armouries of the Tower of London,* v1: *Ordnance* (1976) 251–389: contains selections from inventories in Latin to 1405 [FE2].
Conrad Kyeser aus Eichstatt, *Bellifortis,* ed. and tr. G. Quarg, 2 vols. (1967): facsimile edition of a treatise on war machines and weapons, composed between 1402 and 1405 [FE3].
Pietro Monte, *Exercitiorum atque artis militaris collectanea* (Milan 1509) [FE4].
Odo of Deuil, *De profectione Ludovici VII in orientem: The Journey of Louis VII to the East,* ed. and tr. V.G. Berry (1948, r1965) [FE5].
T.F. Tout, "Firearms in England in the Fourteenth Century," in *English Historical Review* 26 (1911) 666–702: extracts mainly from the accounts of the monarch's privy wardrobe at the Tower of London [FE6].
Flavius Vegetius Renatus, *Epitoma rei militaris,* ed. C. Lang (1885, r1967); tr. N.P. Milner (1993) [FE7].

### Studies

For the Latin vocabulary of arms, armor, and warfare, "Res militaris, seu vocabula ad eam pertinentia," in *Du Cange* v10 (indices), no. 27, ppCLXII–CLXVI, remains the most extensive list available [FE8], though the polyglot "Dictionary of Terms," in D. Nicolle, *Arms and Armour of the Crusading Era, 1050–1350,* 2 vols. (1988) v2:576–627, offers translations of many unusual Latin terms [FE9].

S. Anglo, "The Man Who Taught Leonardo Darts: Pietro Monte and His 'Lost' Fencing Book," in *AntJ* 69 (1989) 261–78 [FE10].
C. Blair, *European Armour, circa 1066 to circa 1700* (1958): the standard work [FE11].
P. Contamine, *War in the Middle Ages,* tr. M. Jones (1984) [FE12].
S. Coupland, "Carolingian Arms and Armour in the ninth Century," in *Viator* 21 (1990) 29–50 [FE13].
G. Duby, "Les origines de la chevalerie," in *Ordinamenti militari in Occidente nel-*

*l'alto medioevo* (1968) 739–61; repr. in G. Duby, *The Chivalrous Society,* tr. C. Postan (1977) 158–70 [FE14].

J. Flori, "Les origines de l'adoubement chevaleresque: Étude des remises d'armes et du vocabulaire qui les exprime dans les sources historiques latines jusqu'au début du XIIIe siècle," in *Traditio* 35 (1979) 209–72 [FE15].

*Glossarium armorum: Arma defensiva,* ed. O. Gamber (1972–): a proposed terminology for defensive arms, which include armor; line drawings explicate the lists of terms in ten modern European languages, with separate identification of contemporary terms, usually in the vernacular [FE16].

J. Hewitt, *Ancient Armour and Weapons in Europe: From the Iron Period of the Northern Nations to the End of the Seventeenth Century,* 2 vols. and supp. (1855–60, r1967 with preface by C. Blair): still useful for its variety of Latin quotations [FE17].

C.W. Hollister, "Knights and Knight Service," in *DMA* 7:276–79: discusses the vocabulary of the evolving concept of the knight in his relationship to the aristocracy [FE18].

U. Mölk, "Philologische Aspekte des Turniers," in *Das ritterliche Turnier im Mittelalter: Beiträge zu einer vergleichenden Formen- und Verhaltensgeschichte des Rittertums,* ed. J. Fleckenstein (1985) 163–74 [FE19].

M. Parisse, "Le tournoi en France, des origines à la fin du XIIIe siècle," in *Das ritterliche Turnier im Mittelalter* (see [FE19]) 175–211 [FE20].

N. Pétrin, "Philological Notes on the Crossbow and Related Missile Weapons," in *GRBS* 33 (1992) 265–91 [FE21].

L. Tarassuk and C. Blair, eds., *The Complete Encyclopedia of Arms & Weapons,* tr. S. Mulcahy, S. Pleasance, and H. Young (1982): by prominent specialists [FE22].

M. Troso, *Le armi in asta delle fanterie europee (1000–1500)* (1988): a comprehensive work on staff weapons with many extracts from Latin documents, mostly of Italian origin [FE23].

*See also* [BA100], [BB32], [BD43], [BD73].

# FF ❖ SHIPS AND SEAFARING

BY JOHN H. PRYOR

Information about medieval ships and shipbuilding and the related fields of navigation and maritime traffic can be found in a wide range of Latin sources, both literary and documentary. These include histories and chronicles, encyclopedias (the first part of bk. 19 of Isidore's *Etymologiae* is concerned with ships), saints' lives, pilgrimage accounts and travel literature, private letters and official correspondence, maritime law codes and municipal statutes, chancery and treasury registers, sales and leases of ships, various types of commercial notarized contracts, arsenal accounts, descriptions of Crusade projects and associated works of propaganda, and treaties between political powers. The literary sources must be used with reservation because their authors were frequently landsmen who often did not need or wish to be precise; for example, the Classical Greek/Latin ἄφλαστον/*aplustre,* the ornamented stern post of a galley, was commonly understood to mean steering oar or rudder. And it was Isidore (*Etymologiae* 19.2.7) who derived *antemna/antenna* (sailyard) from *ante amnem.*

Although there are no extant treatises on shipbuilding in Latin—even the earliest are in the Venetian dialect of Italian—the sources identified above are rich. Extant English shipbuilding accounts in both Latin and the vernacular provide technical information for about 134 ships from the period between 1294 and c. 1500 [FF72], and the registers of the chancery of the Kingdom of Sicily for the reign of Charles I of Anjou between 1269 and 1284 contain information about hundreds of war galleys (*galee*) and transport galleys (*taride*) in dozens of different squadrons [FF66]. The *De nominibus utensilium* and *De naturis rerum* of Alexander Neckam (d. 1217) record the first known Latin references to lodestones, magnetized needles (*acum super magnetem ponunt*) floating on water, the ancestor of the mariner's compass (*bussola*), but far removed from it and of very little practical use.

In the Middle Ages, as in all eras, maritime terminology was amongst the more fertile and changeable elements of language. To landsmen most watercraft may be either "ships" or "boats" and either "rowed" or "sailed." To mariners every slight variation in design, size, rigging, usage, capability, etc. produces new nouns, adjectives, and verbs for names, functions, and handling. Moreover, these terms mutate constantly and rapidly. The nomenclature for ship types, elements of construction, rigging, and handling is astonishingly varied. In addition, problems of anachronism are frequently encountered in the literary sources.

*Navis* may have been the generic term for a sailing ship, a smaller version of which was a *na(vi)cella,* but one also meets *buscia* ("bus," literally "belly"), *carraca* (late medieval carrack), *cocha/cogga* (Germanic cog), *ganganella* (meaning unknown), *hulcus/hulka* (Anglo-Saxon sailing ship), *lignum* (literally "plank"), and *vacheta/vascellum. Galea* may have been the generic name for an oar-powered ship by the high Middle Ages in the West, but one also meets *brigantinus* (small galley), *chelandium* and *tarida* (both transport galleys), *esneka* and its variants (Scandinavian dragon ship), *galeacea/galeassa* (galliass, large galley), *galeonus/galiota* (galliot, small galley), *gattus/cattus* (large galley of Muslim design), and *pamphilus* (from Byzantine πάμφυλος). Composite ship types employing both oars and sails included the *balingaria, barca, caravela, fusta,* and *sagitta/sagetia.*

The Latin terminology used in the literary sources of the early Middle Ages is fraught with imprecision. Names for ship types derived from Classical Greek through Latin, or from Byzantine Greek or Arabic, are frequently used with little or no understanding of the types of ships to which they originally referred, e.g.: *celox* (type of merchant galley), *cymba/cumba* (skiff), *hippagogus* (horse transport galley), *lembus* (type of galley), *myoparo* (fast galley), *phaselus* (small, light galley), and *scapha* (ship's boat), all from Classical Greek κέλης, κύμβη, ἱππαγωγός, λέμβος, μυοπάρων, φάσηλος, and σκάφη, respectively; *corbita* (merchant ship) from Classical Latin; *chelandium* (transport war galley), *dromo(n)* (type of war galley), and *sagena* (type of Dalmatian war galley) from Byzantine χελάνδιον, δρόμων, and σαγήνη, respectively; and *carabus* (type of war galley) and *tarida* (transport galley) from Arabic *qārib* and *ṭarrāda* via Byzantine κάραβος and ταρίτα.

Many other Latin nautical terms derived from Classical Latin and commonly used in the early Middle Ages had their origins in Classical Greek: *ancora* (anchor) from ἄνκυρα, *artemo(n)* (foresail or foremast) from ἀρτέμων, *dolo* (foresail) from δόλων, *nauclerus* (ship owner or master) from ναύκληρος, *nauta* (sailor) from ναύτης, *prora* (prow) from πρώρα, and *scalmus* (thole pin) from σκαλμός. Other Classical Latin terms in wide use in the medieval period include *antenna* (sailyard), *arbor* (mast), *carina* (keel), *clavus* (tiller), *funis* (sheet, cable, rope), *gubernator* (helmsman), *malus* (mast), *pons* (gangplank), *puppis* (stern), *remex* (oarsman), *remus* (oar), *sentina* (hold), *temo* (steering oar), and *velum* (sail).

In the western Mediterranean the ninth and subsequent centuries were a period of linguistic synthesis, when the older Greco-Roman terminology began to be influenced by the emerging vernaculars and by Arabic and Byzantine demotic Greek. As the volume of maritime traffic increased and international contacts became more frequent and sustained, particularly after the First Crusade, older terms acquired new meanings and new Latin words were formed. This could happen tropologically: for example, *cooperta* (from *cooperire,* "to cover") began to be preferred to Classical Latin *forus* and *constratum* for "deck," and *corva/corba* (from *curvare,* "to bend") replaced, via Italian *corva/corba,* the earlier Greco-Latin terms for the frames or ribs of a ship.

Maritime terminology was profoundly polyglot, as has been clearly demonstrated in the magisterial works of Augustin Jal ([FF1], [FF44]). In the Mediterranean world, words were exchanged with great frequency among Greek, Arabic (and later Turkish), Latin, and the Western vernaculars. Thus *sperone* (beak or spur of a galley) was derived from Greek περόνη, and *fersum* (sail cloth strip) from φάρσος. Similarly we find *cursus/cursarius* (privateering/corsair, pirate), Greek κοῦρσον; *tarida* (transport galley), Greek ταρίτα from Arabic *ṭarrāda; usseria* (horse transport), Arabic *ʿushārī; agumina* (cable), Greek γομένη from Arabic *jumal; amiratus* (admiral), Greek ἀμίρατος from Arabic *amīr; darsena* (arsenal, dry dock), Greek ταρσανάς, Arabic *dār al-ṣināʿ; caravana* (convoy) from Arabic *kārwān; stolum* (fleet), Greek στόλος, Arabic *usṭūl; avaria* (averaging after jettison) from Greek ἀβαρία; and *scala* (port of call) from Greek σκάλα. In many cases the exchange of terminology was so trilateral that it is impossible to trace clearly the processes of transmission.

Other Latin terms were not borrowed from either Greek or Arabic but were developed within the European vernacular languages from Latin roots. Thus, in the Statutes of Marseilles of 1253 we find *avera* (goods or merchandise), derived from *habere* via Provençal *aver; cargaria* (cargo, provisions) and *cargator* (victualler), from Late Latin *carica* and *caricare* via Provençal *cargaria* and *cargador;* and *parcionarius* (shareholder/part-owner), from *particeps* via Provençal *parsonier.*

Many Medieval Latin documents from the Mediterranean concerning ships and seafaring are characterized by wide orthographical and terminological variation. On the one hand, this variation sometimes resulted from latinizations of written or dictated originals in vernacular languages and dialects, made by notaries and chancery scribes with little or no knowledge of ships and seafaring. They were expected to latinize words with whose technical meaning and vernacular spelling (which itself varied widely) they were often unfamilar. Frequently they operated phonetically, producing widely differing Latin spellings.

On the other hand, many of the most important documents concerned with ship construction in the Mediterranean and edited by Belgrano, Champollion-Figéac, de Boislile, Du Chesne, Filangieri and the archivists of the Archivio di Stato di Napoli, and Jal survive only in postmedieval printed texts established from manuscripts now lost ([FF23], [FF27], [FF28], [FF30], [FF37], [FF43]). With the exception of Jal's transcriptions, the texts as we have them were the work of scholars who had little or no practical knowledge of seafaring and less of maritime history. They experienced considerable difficulties deciphering technical terms in manuscripts whose script was often late medieval *bastarda,* and their confusion added to the wide orthographical variation already characteristic of the manuscripts.

Vernacular terms and dialectical variants with the same meaning in the original languages may have Latin forms so bizarrely divergent as to inhibit identification of the different forms of the same word. For example, in three transcriptions of one document *vallumina* (the fall or leech of a sail) appears as *vallumina, vallina,* and *valliterna/vallunurium.* In other documents we find *balinvernia.* Similarly, *palleria* (movable floor of planks, "ceiling," in a ship's hold) appears as *palleria, palearia, pallera,* and in other documents as *palliolus.*

In many cases, documents relating to medieval maritime history have some sort of legal character and one has to beware of terms that may have a range of meanings in literary Latin but a very specific one in legal Latin. It may be necessary, for example, to intepret the verb *conducere* in the context of signing on a sailor, and therefore with specific reference to the contract of *locatio conductio operarum,* the hire of labor. *Conducti* in the same context will refer to men hired for payment in money (*precium/loquerium/merces*). Payment had to be made in money, *pecunia numerata,* for *locatio conductio operarum* to be a valid contract. The verb *convenire* may refer to the agreement (*conventio*) between a ship owner and sailor without which no contractual obligation could be created. The texts of statutes and contracts contain an array of legal nuances that may easily be overlooked by medievalists (see ch. DK).

## Select Bibliography

### Works of Reference

The classic *Glossaire nautique: Répertoire polyglotte de termes de marine anciens et modernes*, 2 vols. (1848, r1964) of Augustin Jal (1795–1873) remains the starting point, although it is showing its age [FF1]. Maritime terms from antiquity to the eighteenth century and from many countries (but comparatively little from England) are arranged in a single alphabetical sequence, with descriptions in French and innumerable citations. For medievalists the *Nouveau glossaire nautique d'Augustin Jal* (1970–) is less useful than the original since many medieval terms have been eliminated [FF2]. See C. Villain-Gandossi, "Lexicologie du vocabulaire maritime: Le Nouveau glossaire nautique," in *DHVS* 6 (1984) 9–26 [FF3].

*Du Cange* and *Niermeyer* are also useful, but their explanations are frequently imprecise or even inaccurate. Because of the polyglot nature of maritime terminology, and because so many Latin terms in texts were scribal latinizations of vernacular words, it is frequently necessary to have recourse to a wide range of lexicographical works.

Useful studies of medieval ships and seafaring, including many bearing on nautical terminology, have appeared in such journals as *The Mariner's Mirror* [MM] (London 1911–) [FF4], *International Journal of Nautical Archaeology and Underwater Exploration* (London 1972–) [FF5], and *The American Neptune* (Salem 1940–) [FF6]. The volumes of published papers delivered at the Colloques internationaux d'histoire maritime (Paris 1957–), sponsored by the Commission internationale d'histoire maritime, are also valuable; see, for example, *Le navire et l'économie maritime du moyen-âge au XVIIIe siècle, principalement en Mediterranée: Travaux du deuxième colloque* (1958) [FF7]; and *Les sources de l'histoire maritime en Europe, du moyen âge au XVIII siècle: Actes du quatrième colloque* (1962) [FF8].

Other useful reference tools include the following:

J. Amades and E. Roig, "Vocabulari de l'art de la navegació i de la pesca," in *Butlletí de dialectologia Catalana* 12 (1924) 1–116 [FF9].

A.-M. Bautier, "Contribution à un vocabulaire économique du Midi de la France," in *ALMA* 25 (1955) 5–28, 26 (1956) 5–74, 27 (1957) 241–86, 28 (1958) 119–60, 29 (1959) 173–217, 30 (1960) 177–232 [FF10].

R. Bevere, "Ordigni ed utensili per l'esercizio di arti, ed industrie, mezzi di trasporto, ed armi in uso nelle province napoletane dal XII al XVI secolo," in *Archivio storico per le province Napoletane* 12 (1897) 702–38 [FF11].

L. Fincati, *Vocabulario nautico inglese-italiano e italiano-inglese* (1877) [FF12].

H. and R. Kahane and L. Bremner, *Glossario degli antichi portolani italiani* (1968) [FF13].

H. and R. Kahane and A. Tietze, *The Lingua Franca in the Levant: Turkish Nautical Terms of Italian and Greek Origin* (1958) [FF14].

Reale Accademia d'Italia, *Dizionari di arti e mestieri*, VI: *Dizionario di marina medievale e moderne* (1937) [**FF15**].

E. de Saint-Denis, *Le vocabulaire des manoeuvres nautiques en latin* (1935) [**FF16**].

B. Sandahl, *Middle English Sea Terms: I. The Ship's Hull*, Essays and Studies on English Language and Literature 8 (1951); id., *Middle English Sea Terms: II. Masts, Spars, and Sails*, Essays and Studies on English Language and Literature 20 (1958); id., *Middle English Sea Terms: Vol. III. Standing and Running Rigging* (1982); id., *Middle English Sea Terms: Vol. IV. Cordage and Equipment* (forthcoming) [**FF17**].

## Texts and Studies

H. Ahrweiler, *Byzance et la mer: La marine de guerre, la politique et les institutions maritimes de Byzance aux VIIe–XVe siècles* (1966) [**FF18**].

H. Antoniadis-Bibicou, "Vocabulaire maritime et puissance navale en méditerranée orientale au moyen-âge d'après quelques textes grecs," in *Mediterraneo e Oceano Indiano: Atti del sesto colloquio internazionale di storia marittima* (Venice, 20–29 September 1962), ed. M. Cortelazzo (1970) 317–48 [**FF19**].

W. Ashburner, ed., *ΝΟΜΟΣ ΡΟΔΙΩΝ ΝΑΥΤΙΚΟΣ: The Rhodian Sea-Law* (1909): pt3 of the intro. (ppcxv–ccxciii) contains an extensive discussion of medieval maritime law [**FF20**].

L. Balletto, *Genova nel duecento: Uomini nel porto e uomini sul mare* (1983): with many documents [**FF21**].

R. Bastard de Péré, "Navires méditerranéens du temps de Saint Louis," in *Revue d'histoire économique et sociale* 50 (1972) 327–56 [**FF22**].

L.T. Belgrano, "Une charte de nolis de S. Louis," in *Archives de l'Orient latin* 2 (1884) 231–36 [**FF23**].

D. Burwash, *English Merchant Shipping, 1460–1540* (1947, r1969) [**FF24**].

E.H. Byrne, *Genoese Shipping in the Twelfth and Thirteenth Centuries* (1930, r1970): with edition of Latin documents (pp68–159) from Genoese notarial cartularies [**FF25**].

L. Casson, *Ships and Seamanship in the Ancient World* (1971, r1972): with glossaries of nautical terms (pp383–87) and of Greek and Latin terms (pp389–402) [**FF26**].

J.-J. Champollion-Figéac, "Traités passés en l'année 1246 entre les commissaires du roi Saint Louis et le procureur du podestat de la commune de Gênes," in id., *Documents historiques inédits*, 4 vols. (1841–48) v2:50–67 [**FF27**].

A. de Boislile, "Informationes pro passagio transmarino," in *Annuaire-bulletin de la société de l'histoire de France* 9 (1872) 248–55 [**FF28**].

G. del Giudice, *Diplomi inediti di Re Carlo I. d'Angio riguardanti cose marittime* (1871) [**FF29**].

F. du Chesne, "Contractus navigii domini regis cum Venetis factus anno domini 1268," in id., *Historiae Francorum scriptores*, 5 vols. (Paris 1636–49) v5:435–37 [**FF30**].

J.E. Dotson, "Merchant and Naval Influences on Galley Design at Venice and Genoa in the Fourteenth Century," in *New Aspects of Naval History: Selected Papers Presented at the Fourth Naval History Symposium, United States Naval Academy* (25–26 October 1979), ed. C.L. Symonds (1981) 20–32 [**FF31**].

J.E. Dotson, "Jal's Nef X and Genoese Naval Architecture in the 13th Century," in *MM* 59 (1973) 161–70 [**FF32**].

K. Djupedal, "The Innovation and Construction of the Wooden Sailing Ship, 1150–1650" (M.A. thesis, University of Oregon, 1978) [FF33].

R. Eberenz, *Schiffe an den Küsten der Pyrenäenhalbinsel: Eine kulturgeschichtliche Untersuchung zur Schiffstypologie und -terminologie in den iberoromanischen Sprachen bis 1600* (1975) [FF34].

E. Eickhoff, *Seekrieg und Seepolitik zwischen Islam und Abendland: Das Mittelmeer unter byzantinischer und arabischer Hegemonie (650–1040)* (1966) [FF35].

D. Ellmers, *Frühmittelalterliche Handelsschiffahrt in Mittel- und Nord-Europa* (1972) [FF36].

R. Filangieri *et al.*, eds., *I registri della cancelleria angioina* (1950–): see especially v12:126–29, 159–63, 175–76, 242–45; v13:242–43; v18:302–5; v21:264–66; v24:33–37 [FF37].

N. Fourquin, "Navires marseillais du moyen-âge: Les galères de Narbonne," in *Navigation et migrations en Méditerranée de la préhistoire à nos jours* (1990) 182–250 [FF38].

A. Guglielmotti, *Storia della marina pontificia nel medio evo dal 728 al 1499*, 2 vols. (1871) [FF39].

J.B. Hattendorf *et al.*, eds., *British Naval Documents 1204–1960* (1993): pt1 (1204–1485) provides translations of Latin and other texts [FF40].

J. Haywood, *Dark Age Naval Power: A Re-Assessment of Frankish and Anglo-Saxon Seafaring Activity* (1991): with glossary [FF41].

P. Heinsius, *Das Schiff der hansischen Frühzeit*, 2nd ed. (1986) [FF42].

A. Jal, "Pacta naulorum des années 1246, 1268 et 1270," in *Documents historiques inédits* (see [FF27]), v1:507–615 [FF43].

A. Jal, *Archéologie navale*, 2 vols. (1840): nine essays on ancient and medieval ships, with glossary of technical terms; now outdated in many respects but still a starting point [FF44].

C. Johnson, "London Shipbuilding, A.D. 1295," in *AntJ* 7 (1927) 424–37 [FF45].

C. Johnson and R.J. Whitwell, "The 'Newcastle' Galley," in *Archaeologia Aeliana*, 4th ser., 2 (1926) 142–96 [FF46]: for references to other inventories of large English galleys see [FF68].

K. Kretschmer, *Die italienischen Portolane des Mittelalters* (1909, r1962) [FF47].

B.M. Kreutz, "Ships, Shipping, and the Implications of Change in the Early Medieval Mediterranean," in *Viator* 7 (1976) 79–109 [FF48].

F.C. Lane, *Venetian Ships and Shipbuilders of the Renaissance* (1934, r1992) [FF49].

S. Lebecq, *Marchands et navigateurs frisons du haut moyen âge*, 2 vols. (1983): v2 is a "corpus des sources écrites . . . de la navigation et du commerce frisons" [FF50].

C. Manfroni, *Storia della marina italiana*, 3 vols. (1897–1902): still the most comprehensive naval history of the medieval Mediterranean [FF51].

S. McGrail, *Ancient Boats in N.W. Europe: The Archaeology of Water Transport to A.D. 1500* (1987) [FF52].

M. Mollat, *Le commerce maritime normand à la fin du moyen-âge: Étude d'histoire économique et sociale* (1952) [FF53].

A. Moore, "Accounts and Inventories of John Starlyng, Clerk of the King's Ships to Henry IV," in *MM* 4 (1914) 20–26, 167–73 [FF54].

L.W. Mott, "The Development of the Rudder, A.D. 100–1600: A Technological Tale" (M.A. thesis, Texas A&M University, 1991) [FF55].

B.R. Motzo, ed., *Il compasso da navigare: Opera italiana della metà del secolo XIII* (1947) [FF56].

G.G. Musso, *Navigazione e commercio genovese con il levante nei documenti del-*

*l'archivio di stato di Genova (secc. XIV–XV)* (1975): with app. of documents edited by M.S. Jacopino [FF57].

*La navigazione mediterranea nell'alto medioevo*, Settimane di studio del Centro italiano di studi sull'alto medioevo 25, 2 vols. (1978): includes M.A. Bragadin, "Le navi, loro strutture e attrezzature nell'alto medioevo" (pp389–407); M. Cortelazzo, "Terminologia marittima bizantina e italiana" (pp759–73); G.B. Pellegrini, "Terminologia marinara di origine araba in italiano e nelle lingue europee" (pp797–841) [FF58].

A.E. Nordenskiöld, *Periplus: An Essay on the Early History of Charts and Sailing-Directions*, tr. F.A. Bather (1897, r1967?) [FF59].

J.-M. Pardessus, ed., *Collection de lois maritimes antérieures au XVIIIe siècle*, 6 vols. (1828–45): a convenient single collection, but many of the editions have been superseded [FF60].

R. Pernoud, ed., *Les statuts municipaux de Marseille* (1949) [FF61].

J.H. Pryor, *Geography, Technology, and War: Studies in the Maritime History of the Mediterranean, 649–1571* (1988, r1992) [FF62].

J.H. Pryor, "Transportation of Horses by Sea during the Era of the Crusades: Eighth Century to 1285 A.D.," in *MM* 68 (1982) 9–27, 103–25 [FF63]; id., "The Naval Architecture of Crusader Transport Ships: A Reconstruction of Some Archetypes for Round-Hulled Sailing Ships," in *MM* 70 (1984), 171–219, 275–92, 363–86 [FF64]; id., "The Naval Architecture of Crusader Transport Ships and Horse Transports Revisited," in *MM* 76 (1990) 255–73 [FF65].

J.H. Pryor, "The Galleys of Charles I of Anjou King of Sicily: ca. 1269–84," in *Studies in Medieval and Renaissance History*, n.s., 14 (1993) 34–103 [FF66].

J.B. Sosson, "Un compte inédit de construction de galères à Narbonne (1318–1320)," in *Bulletin de l'Institut historique belge de Rome* 34 (1962) 57–318 [FF67].

J.T. Tinniswood, "English Galleys, 1272–1377," in *MM* 25 (1949) 276–315 [FF68].

R.W. Unger, *The Ship in the Medieval Economy, 600–1600* (1980) [FF69].

C. Villain-Gandossi, *Le navire médiéval à travers les miniatures* (1985): with "vocabulaire en français médiéval relatif aux parties du navire" (pp64–67) [FF70].

C. Villain-Gandossi, S. Busuttil, and P. Adam, eds., *Medieval Ships and the Birth of Technological Societies*, v1: *Northern Europe* (1989) [FF71]: includes I. Friel, "The Documentary Evidence for Shipbuilding in England, 1294–c. 1500" (pp139–49) [FF72]; J. Litwin, "Some Remarks Concerning Medieval Ship Construction" (pp151–73) [FF73]; B. Sandahl, "Names in English Naval Documents, 1280–1380" (pp175–92) [FF74]; U. Schnall, "Medieval Nomenclature of Logboats" (pp193–202) [FF75].

Other useful studies are mentioned by B.M. Kreutz, "Ships and Shipbuilding, Mediterranean," *DMA* 11:229–38 [FF76]; R.W. Unger, "Ships and Shipbuilding, Northern European," *DMA* 11:238–45 [FF77]; C. Verlinden, "Navigation: Western European," *DMA* 9:87–90 [FF78].

# FG • AGRICULTURE, ANIMAL HUSBANDRY, AND FORESTRY

BY JOHN LANGDON

Since they involved the major economic activities of the time, it is hardly surprising that the written sources bearing on medieval agriculture, animal husbandry, and forestry are voluminous. Heading the list of such texts are the great medieval agricultural treatises, of which the most famous written in Latin was the thirteenth-century *Opus ruralium commodorum* by the Italian lawyer Pietro de Crescenzi ([FG15], [FG27]). Often drawing heavily on classical precedents, these treatises provide a wealth of information concerning the received wisdom about agriculture in particular, although how far this reflected actual practice is sometimes debatable ([FG23], [FG26]). In addition to the treatises, a vast array of documentation has survived, from royal decrees and other government records, often seeking to regulate farming and forestry, to those documents that actually describe events "on the ground," particularly seigneurial documents such as surveys, accounts, and manorial court rolls. In short, the diversity of the records provides an impressive range of perspectives from which to study medieval farming and forestry, particularly from the thirteenth century onwards.

The interpretation of Latin in these materials is not without its difficulties. Although there is seldom much grammatical complexity, the precise meaning of a passage can be problematic, partly because of the technical nature of the subject. The major difficulty, however, lies in the terminology used to describe various objects and activities, which could change with disconcerting rapidity. Over time, Medieval Latin documents dealing with farming and forestry developed a vocabulary of bewildering variety. This consisted of (a) Classical Latin words that continued in regular use (see the discussion of crops and types of trees below); (b) Classical Latin words subject to semantic change (see, for example, the discussion of *tribulum* below); (c) Classical Latin words whose forms were changed, perhaps by the addition of a new suffix to the original base, or in more complex ways (see the discussion of *foresta* below); (d) latinized words of vernacular origin (for example, *staggus*, "stag deer," from Middle English *stagge*). The route followed by many words in Medieval Latin texts could be circuitous: for instance, the Classical Latin term *vicia*, meaning "vetch," i.e. various types of leguminous plants cultivated as fodder, became *vesce* in French; thence it entered English Latin documents during the thirteenth century as *vesca.* Furthermore, the spelling of these new words was by no means uniform: such variants of *vesca* as *vescia, vessa,* and *vecia* are also found.

Medieval scribes were aware of this linguistic fluidity and often attempted to clarify terminological imprecision by compiling short glossaries. Generally speaking, the more quickly a farming or forestry practice changed, the more complex the terminology that arose around it (see, for example, the terms for horses and hunting dogs discussed below). Moreover, the speed of technological change might not be accurately reflected in certain types of records. Agricultural treatises and custumals, for instance, tended to emphasize past practice and therefore to employ more antiquated language than, say, manorial accounts and court rolls, which described contemporary events. As a result, contemporaneous texts may use markedly different technical terminology, and this can confuse or mislead the unwary reader.

One point that is very clear about the latinity of medieval agriculture and forestry is that the difficulties to be encountered vary significantly by subject. One of the least troublesome areas is the crops grown by medieval farmers. In general, the basic grains usually retained their Classical Latin names—*frumentum* (wheat), *siligo* (rye), *hordeum/ordeum* (barley), *avena* (oats). New terminology for crops developed because of the increasing popularity of sowing a mixture of grains, e.g. *mixtilio* or *mixteolum,* English "maslin" or "mancorn" (sometimes meaning a mixture of wheat and rye, more often mixed grains of any type), or *dragetum* ("dredge," a mixture of barley and oats). Among Latin names for legumes, increasingly an important part of medieval crop regimes, we note not only *pisae* ("peas") and *fabae* ("beans") but also *vesca* or *vicia,* "vetch," already mentioned.

More problematic than the names of the grains themselves were the units used to measure them. Here a wide variety of terms, such as *bussellus, quarterium, sextarius, summa,* and *modius,* are found (see also ch. FD). Specific amounts represented could also vary considerably, especially when converted from one measurement to another. For example, one of the most common terms, *quarterium,* generally consisted of eight bushels in England but might be only three to five in parts of France, an imprecision reflected in the many medieval tracts that attempted to standardize these measurements (see [FG10]). Some of these terms of measurement were regional, such as the *truga,* "trug," a dry measure of approximately two thirds of a bushel used in northwest England. Caution must be used when applying these terms to such statistical exercises as yield measurements.

Equally problematic is the question of the plow, whose terminological evolution is more obscure than is generally recognized. The distinction between the scratch plow (or ard) and the heavier moldboard plow, crucial in the development of medieval agriculture, was thought to be represented by the Latin words *aratrum* and *carruca,* respectively, which were considered equivalent to French *araire* and *charrue.* It is plain, however, that this distinction was blurred in many areas, so that the terms *aratrum* and *carruca* were virtually interchangeable. This was particularly the case as the heavy plow began to dominate in many parts of Europe. Different terms were also often used to identify the subtypes of these "heavy" plows, whether of the wheeled, foot, or swing variety (see [FG25]), with the result that determining the distribution of medieval plow types on terminological grounds requires considerable care.

The technical terms for vehicles might also be a source of confusion, especially as horses began to play a greater role in haulage (see below). The *carecta/car(r)eta* (with many orthographical variants) was a horse-hauled, two-wheeled cart predominant in Europe by the thirteenth century, but there were also a host of other terms for vehicles (*biga, quadriga, rheda, curtena, curta,* etc.) One of the more deceptive of these is *plaustrum,* an increasingly common term from about the twelfth century onwards for a type of farming or household vehicle. Most glossaries define it simply as a four-wheeled wagon, but in England at least it was used to denote a two-wheeled, ox-hauled cart, equivalent to the later sixteenth-century "wain." Even more confusing was the term *carrus,* which for a time in the twelfth and thirteenth centuries identified both two-wheeled and four-wheeled vehicles, depending on the context [FG25].

Smaller farm implements, such as hand tools, which were less affected by change over time, tended to retain the same names. But here, too, striking semantic adjustments might occur, one of the most curious being the change in the meaning of *tribulum* from "threshing sledge" in Roman times to "fork" or "shovel" in the Middle Ages [FG20].

In the realm of animal husbandry, the versatile horse was the beast most subject to changes in terminology. As its functions changed radically during the medieval period, it attracted to itself a profusion of Latin terms, easily a dozen or more, as medieval scribes and farmers attempted to assign instantly recognizable tags to particular types of horses [FG25]. The common word *equus* itself often tended to be swamped by this expanding equine terminology, as exemplified in the following citation: *Centum equos, quorum alii erunt manni, alii vero runcini, alii summarii, alii veredarii, alii vero averii.* Horses were often named according to the agricultural task they performed—*carectarius* (cart horse), *hercarius* or *occatorius* (harrowing horse), *summarius* (pack-horse). More general terms for the farm workhorse seem to have caused confusion. One such term, which came into use for this animal during the twelfth and thirteenth centuries, was *averus,* apparently derived from *averium,* a general name for any farm animal. Because medieval writers seem soon to have become concerned that these two terms might be confused when abbreviated in documents, in England the term *averus* for workhorse quickly became *affrus,* a change that was apparently complete by the end of the thirteenth century [FG25].

The abundant permutations evident in equine terminology do not seem to have affected other domestic animals, which by and large retained their Classical Latin names (*bos* for ox, *vacca* for cow, *porcus* for pig, *ovis* for sheep, etc.). It was when the young of these species began to be grouped by age that a specialized descriptive terminology was created to identify the various stages of development before adulthood.

The latinity descriptive of forest activities also had its complexities, partly because forests were used for both economic and recreational pursuits. The term *forest* itself is interesting, deriving originally from the adverb *foris* ("outside") and referring eventually in Classical Latin to uncultivated land or bush (see *DMA* v7:353). By the medieval period the term *forestum* or *foresta* had come to represent a much wilder, more wooded landscape, very much separated from the cultivated land around villages. Although this picture of wilderness is illusory given the very managed nature of most medieval woodland, the forest as a reserve of plant, animal, and mineral resources very much outside the normal pattern of manorial and village life was maintained right throughout the medieval period.

Plant products were probably the most important resource of forests, supplying firewood, wood for building, and fodder for animals (particularly for pigs, who fed off acorns and other vegetable matter in the forests). The terminology of forest vegetation was extensive, but also fairly consistent. Oak (*quercus*) figures predominantly in forest records, particularly in northern Europe, largely because of its key importance for building and other uses, but a plethora of other woods is also mentioned in the Latin records, including alder (*alnus* or *alneta*), ash (*fraxinus*), beech (*fagus*), birch (*betula*), maple (*arabilis;* sometimes confused with "arable" land), pine (*pinus*), cypress (*cypressus*). More generally, the term *boscus* or *buscus,* of Germanic origin, is an extremely common one in medieval documents to identify variously woodland, brushwood, and timber.

Animal life, of course, thrived in the forest, which was always an important resource for the grazing of domestic livestock. But as the passion for hunting gripped medieval elites, an emphasis on reserving forests for game, especially deer and wild boar, became increasingly important. As a result, the terminology for types and age groups of deer in particular expanded markedly: *damus* (buck), *dama* (doe), *vitulus bisse* (deer calf), *hynulus* (fawn), *sorellus* (young deer in its third year?), *sorus* (deer in its fourth year), *staggus/staggardus* (stag; possibly a deer in its fifth year), etc. This was accompanied by an even greater proliferation of terms to describe the types or breeds of dogs needed to hunt this game. The following are only a sample of the descriptive terminology associated with hunting dogs during this period, which in complexity rivaled that for horses: *berselettus* (bercelet) and *brachettus* (brach), both of which hunted by smell; *cervericius* (deerhound, usually for hunting harts); *damaricius* (deerhound, usually for bucks); *haericius* (harrying or running hound); *leporarius* (greyhound; originally for hunting hares, *lepores,* as the Latin name suggests); *limarius* (lime or lyam hound; a bloodhound, usually mute); *lutericius* (otter hound); *mastinus* or *mastivus* (mastiff); *porkaricius* (boar hound); and *valtrus* (dog for chasing, possibly similar to a greyhound) [FG18].

The preceding are only a few examples of the variability that characterizes the agricultural and forestry terminology of medieval records. There are, of course, many glossaries that one may consult when pursuing the technical meaning of a particular word, ranging from *Du Cange* to more specialized lexica or word lists (see, for example, [FG7]). Studies focusing on particular aspects of agriculture and forestry will also occasionally include glossaries of technical terms (e.g. [FG18], [FG25]). But it is all too easy to be lulled into a complacent acceptance of the meanings listed in glossaries. A reader should always be sensitive to the context of a document when interpreting a particular term and ready to adopt a different interpretation under the weight of the evidence.

## Select Bibliography

### Primary Works, Translations, and Guides

S. Andrei, *Aspects du vocabulaire agricole latin* (1981): deals with Classical rather than Medieval Latin, but supplies much of the basic terminology of agricultural documents of the Middle Ages; similar to [FG3] [FG1].

W.O. Ault, *Open-Field Husbandry and the Village Community, a Study of Agrarian By-Laws in Medieval England,* TAPhS, n.s., 55.7 (1965): with appendix of Latin by-laws, taken from manorial court rolls, that regulated English agricultural activities from the thirteenth century to the sixteenth; tr. W.O. Ault, *Open-field Farming in Medieval England: A Study of Village By-Laws* (1972) [FG2].

M.G.T. Bruno, *Il lessico agricolo latino*, 2nd ed. (1969): very full list of Classical Latin farming terms; useful foundation for the vocabulary of medieval documents [FG3].

Columella, *De re rustica* and *De arboribus*, ed. and tr. H. Boyd, E.S. Forster, and E.H. Heffner, 3 vols. (1941–55): Columella (first century A.D.) was one of the best known of Roman agricultural writers; much of his work was echoed in medieval treatises, such as that of de Crescenzi (see [FG15]) [FG4].

C. De Meo, *Lingue tecniche del latino*, 2nd ed. (1986); deals with Classical rather than Medieval Latin, but ch. 1 is concerned with "la lingua dell'agricoltura" [FG5].

G. Duby, *Rural Economy and Country Life in the Medieval West* (1968); translation by C. Postan of *L'économie rurale et la vie des campagnes dans l'occident médiéval* (1962): contains, among other things, a useful set of translated documents from all the regions of Europe relating to medieval rural life [FG6].

J.L. Fisher, *A Medieval Farming Glossary of Latin and English Words, Taken Mainly from Essex Records* (1968) [FG7].

E.A. Gooder, *Latin for Local History: An Introduction*, 2nd ed. (1978): primer for students just beginning to work on medieval documents, especially from England; includes a fairly extensive listing of relevant classical and medieval terms, as well as an introduction to paleography [FG8].

B. Guérard, ed., *Polyptyque de l'abbé Irminon*, 2 vols. (1844): authoritative edition (v2) with useful introduction; English translation in [FG6] of a few entries [FG9].

H. Hall and F.J. Nicholas, eds., *Select Tracts and Table Books Relating to English Weights and Measures (1100–1742)*, CamSoc, 3rd ser., v41 [= *Camden Miscellany* 15] (1929): indispensible collection of documents relating to English measurements, including many from the medieval period [FG10].

P.D.A. Harvey, ed., *Manorial Records of Cuxham, Oxfordshire, circa 1200–1359* (1976); fine edition of the Latin documents from a single manor; excellent for giving the flavor and potential of the documents of medieval English agriculture [FG11].

S.F. Hockey, ed., *The Account-Book of Beaulieu Abbey*, CamSoc, 4th ser., v16 (1975); excellent collection of accounts covering all facets of agricultural and household activity on a large seigneurial estate [FG12].

N.R. Holt, ed., *The Pipe Roll of the Bishopric of Winchester, 1210–1211* (1964); transcription of the second of the famous series of pipe rolls (i.e., enrolled accounts) of the bishopric of Winchester [FG13].

D. Oschinsky, *Walter of Henley and Other Treatises on Estate Management and Accounting* (1971): authoritative edition in pt2 (pp261–457) of most of the medieval English agricultural treatises, the majority of which are in French; good app. (pp459–78) of various Latin documents [FG14].

Pietro de Crescenzi (1233–1320), *Opus ruralium commodorum* (completed in 1304), ed. J. Schüssler (Ausburg 1471) and published as *Liber ruralium commodorum*, available on microfiche; also ed. B. Sorio (with Italian translation by B. de Rossi, 1605): *Trattato della agricoltura di Piero de' Crescenzi* (1851–52): the most exhaustive and authoritative agricultural treatise from the medieval period [FG15].

H.G. Richardson and G.O. Sayles, eds. and trs., *Fleta*, v2–4, SelSoc 72, 89, 99 (1955–84); legal treatise written soon after 1290; bk. 2 (in v2) is particularly useful for forestry and agriculture [FG16].

D.J. Stagg, *A Calendar of New Forest Documents, 1244–1334* (1979): mostly in English translation, although a few of the original Latin documents are included in app. A (pp219–25) [FG17].

G.J. Turner, ed., *Select Pleas of the Forest*, SelSoc, v13 (1901); useful selection from various places in England; in both Latin and English translation, with excellent glossary (pp133–53) of problematic terms [FG18].

## Studies

B. Andreolli and M. Montanari, eds., *Il bosco nel medioevo* (1988) [FG19].

G. Astill and A. Grant, eds., *The Countryside of Medieval England* (1988): studies of various aspects of medieval agriculture, including much on the use of Latin documents [FG20].

R. Bechmann, *Trees and Man: The Forest in the Middle Ages* (1990): translation by K. Dunham of *Des arbres et des hommes: La forêt au moyen-âge* (1984): useful survey of the medieval forest, its products and activities, drawn largely from French sources [FG21].

R. Fossier, *Peasant Life in the Medieval West* (1988): translation by J. Vale of *Paysans d'occident (XIe–XIVe siècles)* (1984); helpful, if occasionally speculative, account of peasant life in Western Europe [FG22].

G.E. Fussell, *The Classical Tradition in West European Farming* (1972): contains a good survey of ancient and medieval agricultural treatises [FG23].

P.D.A. Harvey, *A Medieval Oxfordshire Village: Cuxham, 1240 to 1400* (1965): excellent case study of agriculture in one medieval village (see [FG11]) [FG24].

J. Langdon, *Horses, Oxen and Technological Innovation* (1986): study of the use of draft animals in medieval England, drawing on a broad range of Latin documents; with app. (pp293–97) on problems of translation [FG25].

M. Mate, "Medieval Agrarian Practices: The Determining Factors," in *Agricultural History Review* 33 (1985) 22–31: an investigation of the degree to which the advice given in agricultural treatises was actually adopted by medieval farmers [FG26].

L. Olson, "Pietro de Crescenzi: The Founder of Modern Agronomy," in *Agricultural History* 18 (1944) 35–40: short but useful introduction to de Crescenzi [FG15] [FG27].

M.M. Postan, ed., *The Cambridge Economic History of Europe*, v1: *The Agrarian Life of the Middle Ages*, 2nd ed. (1966, r1971): somewhat dated survey of medieval agriculture across Europe [FG28].

O. Rackham, *Ancient Woodland: Its History, Vegetation and Uses in England* (1980): masterful analysis of the development of woodland in southeast England, with much on the medieval period [FG29].

W. Rösener, *Peasants in the Middle Ages* (1992): translation by A. Stützer of *Bauern im Mittelalter* (1985); valuable survey of medieval peasant life with strong emphasis on agriculture, drawn mainly from German sources [FG30].

B.H. Slicher van Bath, *The Agrarian History of Western Europe, A.D. 500–1850* (1963): translation by O. Ordish of *Die agrarische Geschiedenis van West-Europa (500–1850)* (1960): somewhat out-of-date, but still useful survey [FG31].

J.Z. Titow, *English Rural Society, 1200–1350* (1969): collection, with good introduction, of translated documents concerned with medieval English rural life [FG32].

J.Z. Titow, *Winchester Yields: A Study in Medieval Agricultural Productivity* (1972): exhaustive examination of medieval crop yields, drawn from the grain sections (*exitus grangie*, "issue of the grange") of manorial account rolls [FG33].

# FH • MANUSCRIPT PRODUCTION

BY R.H. ROUSE

The word *manuscript* denotes something written by hand. It is usually assumed to mean a codex but can also mean a roll. Manuscript codices, in contrast to rolls, are composed of set numbers of papyrus, parchment, or paper bifolia (sheets folded once), which may be ruled, written upon, decorated, and possibly illustrated, and then placed one inside the other and sewn with thread to form a quire or gathering. Manuscript books can be divided into two types, those produced commercially or in the scriptorium, and those produced privately by an owner/user. The difference between the two is usually a matter of quality. Normally, the text in an owner-produced book is more accurate, while the physical quality of the production is less elegant. The process of commercial production alters with the closing of the Roman book trade in the sixth century and its replacement by the monastic scriptorium. It alters again in the late twelfth century in Italy, and at the beginning of the thirteenth century in northern Europe, with the passage of production into lay hands in the medieval city and the gradual closing of the monastic scriptoria. The process alters yet again with the revitalizing of scriptoria among houses of the *devotio moderna* in the fifteenth century and the increase in production associated with Italian humanism. Beginning in the second half of the fifteenth century, manuscript book production exists side by side with the printing press until the mid-sixteenth century; it continues on into the nineteenth century in the case of large liturgical manuscripts.

The Latin terms employed in descriptions of manuscript production refer to portions of the manuscript itself, to implements employed in the making of manuscripts, and to the people involved in the process. In most instances we know what these terms describe; in some cases we can only offer suggestions.

Manuscript books are constructed of quires or *quaterni* made of parchment (*pergamenus*) or paper (*papirus*). Each *quaternus* is composed of a number of *folia*. The bifolia, while the manuscript is unbound, are tied together by a *sc(h)edula* (*scidula*) or thin parchment tie. Each *folium* has two *paginae,* a recto and a verso. The written space of each *pagina* or double-page opening is laid out or designed with the help of a *registrum* or template(?), on the basis of which the writer makes a number of pricks or *punctae* with a *punctorium*, at the top and bottom of the page and in the outer margins, to serve as the guide marks for the *regula* or ruler with which the writer rules the written space using a lead point or *plumbum*. The text is written in ink (*incaustum*) with a quill (*penna*). The titles, chapter headings, or colophon are called *rubricae* ("rubrics") because they traditionally are written in red ink. The writer of the manuscript is the *scriptor* and its painter is the *illuminator*. In the commercial world of the thirteenth century and later, the contractor is the *librarius*, and the person who rents manuscripts in quires, termed *pecie* or pieces, is the *stationarius* or stationer because he occupies a *statio* or official position at the university. The binder or *ligator* often earns the majority of his income from some other function in the book trade, as, for example, *librarius* or *pergamenarius* (parchment seller). Most of these terms vary slightly in their orthography depending upon where they are recorded—i.e., *testus* (Italian) for *textus*—because of the influence on the Latin language of the developing regional vernaculars.

## Select Bibliography

Regarding manuscript production in general see R.H. Rouse "Manuscript Books, Production of," in *DMA* 8:100–5 [FH1]; C. de Hamel, *Scribes and Illuminators* (1992) [FH2]; id., *A History of Illuminated Manuscripts* (1986) [FH3]; *Medieval Book Production: Assessing the Evidence*, ed. L.L. Brownrigg (1990) [FH4]; J. Stiennon, *Paléographie du moyen âge*, 2nd ed. (1991) [FH5]; and B. Bischoff, *Latin Palaeography: Antiquity and the Middle Ages*, tr. D. Ó Cróinín and D. Ganz (1990) [FH6]. Bibliography regarding the historical (nonartistic) aspects of manuscript production can be found in L.E. Boyle, *Medieval Latin Palaeography: A Bibliographical Introduction* (1984) [FH7].

The vocabulary of manuscript production can be examined through W. Wattenbach, *Das Schriftwesen im Mittelalter*, 3rd ed. (1896, r1958), unsurpassed despite its age [FH8]. A successful recent attempt to survey the subject is seen in the papers in *CIVICIMA* 2 [FH9]. A systematic presentation of the codicological terminology can be found in D. Muzerelle, *Vocabulaire codicologique: Répertoire méthodique des termes français relatifs aux manuscrits* (1985) [FH10].

Illustration of aspects of the process of manuscript making is to be found in B.A. Shailor, *The Medieval Book, Illustrated from the Beinecke Rare Book & Manuscript Library* (1991) [FH11]; V. Trost, *Scriptorium: Book Production in the Middle Ages*, tr. C. Reinisch and T. Kwasman (1986) [FH12]; J.J.G. Alexander, *Medieval Illuminators and Their Methods of Work* (1992) [FH13].

For studies based on specific manuscripts and types of manuscripts see A. Cohen-Mushlin, *The Making of a Manuscript: The Worms Bible of 1148 (British Library, Harley, 2803–2804)* (1983) [FH14]; C. de Hamel, *Glossed Books of the Bible and the Origins of the Paris Booktrade* (1984) [FH15]; *La production du livre universitaire au moyen âge: exemplar et pecia: Acts du symposium tenu au Collegio San Bonaventura de Grottaferrata en mai 1983*, ed. L.J. Bataillon, B.G. Guyot, and R.H. Rouse (1988) [FH16]; J.D. Farquhar, *Creation and Imitation: The Work of a Fifteenth-Century Manuscript Illuminator* (1976) [FH17].

Regarding the physical materials, see D.V. Thompson, Jr., *The Materials and Techniques of Medieval Painting* (1956): repr. of *The Materials of Medieval Painting* (1936) [FH18]; and R. Reed, *Ancient Skins, Parchments and Leathers* (1972) [FH19].

Concerning model books see *The Göttingen Model Book: A Facsimile Edition and Translations of a Fifteenth-Century Illuminators' Manual,* ed. (with commentary) H. Lehmann-Haupt (1972, r1978) [FH20].

*See also* [BA27], [BA49], [BA134].

FI  ·  **PANEL AND WALL PAINTING,
MOSAICS, METALWORK, AND
OTHER DECORATIVE ARTS**

BY CAECILIA DAVIS-WEYER

The Latin terminology used to describe the techniques of panel and wall painting, mosaic making, metalwork, and the decorative arts has come to us from various written sources. The texts to be highlighted in this brief introduction are the recipe collection of the so-called *Mappae Clavicula* and the treatises of Heraclius and Theophilus.

The *Mappae Clavicula* (*MC*) began as a Greek collection, no longer extant. Recent research ([FI20], [FI23]) has suggested that the curious title applied originally only to the oldest part of the Greek collection [FI18], a group of late Hellenistic recipes dealing mainly with gold, gold amalgams, and chrysography. A Latin translation was available by the end of the eighth century, by which time the collection had expanded to cover a surprisingly wide spectrum of activities and to include a considerable variety of recipes for dyers, painters, mosaic and glass makers, jewelers, and military engineers. Such a collection would have been important for artists, who were called on to deliver a variety of services in times of peace and war. This broad approach, as well as the emphasis on purple, gold, and silver, suggests the varied activities of a court.

The oldest manuscript of the Latin translation of the *MC* is from Lucca, written in northern Italy ([FI10], [FI27]) towards the end of the eighth century in Latin that is rough and replete with Grecisms. Other whole or partial copies were available at Monte Cassino, Reichenau, Salzburg, and perhaps Aachen as early as the ninth century ([FI18] pp284–85). The Klosterneuburg [FI5] and Madrid [FI3] manuscripts share with the Lucca copy an Italian and Lombard cast ([FI18], [FI20] p21), whereas the manuscripts in Selestadt [FI11] and Corning ([FI9], [FI11]), which depend on the same translation, make an effort to purify the Latin ([FI18] pp284–86). The twelfth-century Corning version, probably an English manuscript, is the most comprehensive copy, but its length is to some degree the result of repetition and addition.

The *MC* continued to expand, drawing on both antique sources, such as Palladius (see *MC* 254–55, [FI18] p287), and more recent ones: the chapters on the assaying of gold-silver alloys (*MC* 194) and the ratios of weights of wax and metals for use in a foundry (*MC* 194A) were probably added in or after the ninth century ([FI18] p290); other additions belong to the late eleventh or twelfth century and are conspicuous because they use Arabic terms (*MC* 195–203; see [FI11] pp57–58), or because they concentrate in a novel way on the process of image making (*MC* I–XI; see [FI26] and [FI11] pp26–28).

Of similar interest as a source of technical language is the earliest medieval treatise, the eleventh-century *De coloribus et artibus Romanorum*, attributed to Heraclius ([FI7], [FI12], [FI26], [FI24]) and possibly written by an artist in order to educate a patron. The 21 versified chapters of the first two books of this treatise extol the patronage of the "senate" and the "kings" of Rome, but lack detail and belong only marginally to our genre. However, the 58 prose chapters of the third book, in large part a later addition, contain more detailed and practical information.

Slightly later, from the beginning of the twelfth century, is the *De diversis artibus* of Theophilus [FI15]. Theophilus was himself a goldsmith, and his treatise, like the *MC* collection, was intended for an audience of artists and craftsmen.

In addition to these treatises, the technical language and vocabulary of art are also reflected in encyclopedias [FI8], and especially in inventories ([FI13], [FI19]) and in documents recording commissions and payments ([FI6]). Some recipes occur as short entries in extraneous contexts and may contain unique information or language [FI1–2]; others are excerpts from the *MC* collection or the treatises [FI22]. In either case, the singling out of a specific set of recipes is of interest, because it implies a link with contemporary practice ([FI18] p285).

The language of the recipes and the treatises varies. The oldest manuscript of the *MC* (from Lucca) pays little or no heed to grammar, particularly case endings (e.g., *in vaso . . . suffrens ignem = in vaso . . . sufferente ignem*), and especially after prepositions (*absque plumbum = absque plumbo, ex plumbum = ex plumbo, cum aquam = cum aqua*). The second person indicative (present or future) is used frequently for the imperative: *eice et confrangis . . . prasino tingues*. The word division is, by later standards, inadequate: *tolles miram viba = tolle smiram vivam*. Spellings vary widely: *b* for *v*, as in *nobus* for *novus, musibum* for *musivum; pecula, pectalum, petalum; refricdet = refrigidet; faciam = faciem; conficantur = conficiantur* (though the latter two may be faulty inflections). A contemporary hand (L2) went over the text and corrected some of the errors, and, as mentioned above, other manuscripts of the *MC* tried to purify the Latin further. As for Heraclius, the versified portions of his treatise reveal obvious literary ambitions. The language of Theophilus is admirable, precise in the technical chapters and eloquent in the exhortatory and theological passages of the prefaces.

The technical vocabulary sometimes derives from the specialized use of a classical word, e.g. *membrana:* "flesh color," *incidere:* "to shade," *folium:* "purple or blue pigment made from plants such as turnsole"; sometimes a classical word is modified, especially in its suffix, e.g. *mediolum:* "(egg) yolk," presumably from *meditullium*. Roman authors such as Vitruvius and Pliny, when writing about art and architecture, referred frequently to Greek examples, and their vocabulary contained many Greek and latinized Greek words. Similarly, the earliest Latin version of the *MC* absorbed many Greek words, as in these names for colors: *simity, psimithin:* "lead white" (Greek *psimuthion*); *coccus, coccarin:* "crimson"; *iarin, iarim:* "green made from copper"; *ficarin, ficarim:* "brownish red"; *lulax, lulaccin, lulacin:* "indigo, blues made from woad"; and the enigmatic *pandius,* which applied to a whole series of dyes and pigments ([FI26]; [FI27] p48). A glossary, providing more familiar synonyms for some of these terms, was added by a contemporary hand at the end of the twelfth-century Corning manuscript.

Theophilus refers with admiration to the glass vessels made by Byzantine craftsmen (bk. 2.13–14), mentioning their glazes (bk. 2.16) and their golden mosaic cubes, which he calls *vitrum grecum* (bk. 2.15), and praising them especially for their colors (prologue 1). It has been suggested that he based the first of the three books of his treatise on a Byzantine painter's guide, now lost; this would explain his curious emphasis on panel painting (bk. 1.14) and the use of the rare Oriental term *menesc* for violet, found in Byzantine Greek ([FI25] p161).

Influences from the newly conquered Moslem lands around the Mediterranean introduced Arab terminology into the West during the eleventh and twelfth centuries. Such terms, mostly concerning goldsmith work, are found in later additions to the *MC* in the Corning manuscript (*MC* 195–203) and in at least one recipe in Theophilus (bk. 3.29), e.g. *almenbuz:* "silver," *atincar:* "borax," *arragaz:* "lead," *alcazir:* "tin," *natronum:* "soda." These Arabic terms (like some of the Greek words in the older parts of the *MC* collection) became unintelligible, and a second hand in the Corning manuscript supplied interlinear Latin equivalents.

Provincial and vernacular elements are also common in most of the technical texts, as in the Lucca manuscript of the *MC* (*guatum/guattum:* "woad," *anfus:* "bowl," *lixare:* "polish" (see [FI27] pp16–17, [FI18] p291). A set of glassmaker's recipes from a Frankish manuscript of the ninth century [FI1]) offers early occurrences of the French words *pot* (*pottus:* a ceramic container) and *tamiser* (*tamisare:* strain through a cloth or sieve) and of the attributive use of nouns (*eramen laminas:* "bronze plates"). References in the Corning manuscript of the *MC* (*MC* 190–91) to the plant names *gatetriu* ("goatweed") and *greninpert* (= *greninwert,* "greenwood") reveal this copy's English provenance; Theophilus's German origin is apparent in his use of the word *meizel:* "chisel" (bk. 3.72).

Not only the vocabulary, but the very purpose of technical treatises and collections underwent change during the medieval period. If one takes a broad view of the literary tradition, it is plain that there is a break between the classical and late antique texts and those produced in the central Middle Ages. When Vitruvius writes about wall painting, he offers a few moralizing remarks about the need to select appropriate subjects for representation. Otherwise he limits himself to such problems as the preparation of the walls, the composition of pigments, and their price, durability, and source (patron or contractor). The *MC* collection displays a similar reserve: most of its recipes concern the preparation of materials, media, and surfaces, but do not try to anticipate the artist's efforts or their iconographic outcome. The later medieval additions to the *MC* (*MC* IX–XI), the treatise of Theophilus, and some of the recipes in the third book of Heraclius's work (bk. 3.56–58) do just that, prescribing the proper color combinations and in some cases even the sequence of brushstrokes for painting such objects as garments, towers, trees, or rainbows. Theophilus is particularly precise in this respect. He adopts the same approach to the making of stained glass (bk. 2.20–21) and especially to metalwork, his own craft (bk. 3.26, 27, 30, 42–44, 50, 52, 53, 60, 61, 74, 78). Here he takes the reader step by step from the preparation of the implements and materials to the finished object, describing its iconography and ornamentation in detail.

Measured against this standard the technical information in the older parts of the *MC* collection appears incomplete and diffuse, although these features may suggest discretion rather than any lack of effort. The compilers and translators of this collection were probably aware that there existed other and perhaps more effective channels for the dissemination of technical information, primarily in the workshop, as most of the recipes seem to have been collected in order to supplement workshop traditions, especially in the case of requests for unusual artifacts and services. Theophilus, on the other hand, seems to have wanted to replace these craft traditions. This is apparent in his strictures against colleagues who, either to enrich themselves or perhaps to protect the professional welfare of their children, were unwilling to divulge their trade secrets (prologue 1 and 3).

Theophilus's stance may have resulted from a competition between monastic and lay artisans, or from his involvement in a particular artistic movement promoted by the Gregorian reform. The reformers favored a pictorial idiom that had originated in Italy under Byzantine influence and during the lifetime of Theophilus replaced older local workshop traditions all over Europe. The new manner was highly structured and lent itself well to verbal description. Theophilus was clearly responding to changing artistic conditions. Other artists were also aware of these changes, as is apparent from some of the twelfth-century additions to the *MC* collection and to Heraclius's treatise, which adopt an approach not unlike that of Theophilus.

Although Theophilus's *De diversis artibus* was copied throughout the thirteenth, fourteenth, and fifteenth centuries, no new technical treatises of similar scope were written. Furthermore, the later copies of the *MC*, listed by Johnson, are, with one exception, excerpts ([FI22], [FI20] pp15–16). This development suggests a new interest in artistic specialization, of which Cennini's fifteenth-century vernacular treatise on painting, *Il libro dell'arte*, may be typical [FI4].

As for monumental sculpture, it became the leading artistic medium in northern Europe during the twelfth and thirteenth centuries, but no technical treatises about statuary are known to have been written during this period. This is a remarkable absence and may indicate the extent to which the Western literature relied on Byzantine precedent.

## Select Bibliography

### Editions and Translations

B. Bischoff, ed., "Farbrezepte aus karolingischer Zeit (IX. Jahrhundert)," in *Anecdota novissima: Texte des vierten bis sechzehnten Jahrhunderts*, Quellen und Untersuchungen zur lateinischen Philologie des Mittelalters 7 (1984) 219–22: this set of recipes for making colored glass is remarkable for its independent vocabulary [FI1].

B. Bischoff, ed., "Ein Mosaikrezept (IX. Jahrhundert)," in [FI1], p223 [FI2].

J.M. Burnam, ed., *Recipes from Codex matritensis A16 (ahora 19): Palaeographical Edition from a Black-on-White Facsimile (1912)*: with glossary (pp32–47) [FI3].

Cennino d'Andrea Cennini, *Il libro dell'arte*, ed. and tr. D.V. Thompson, Jr., 2 vols. (1932–33; translation [v2] r1960) [FI4].

W. Ganzenmüller, ed., "Ein unbekanntes Bruchstück der Mappae Clavicula aus dem Anfang des 9. Jahrhunderts," in *Mitteilungen zur Geschichte der Medizin, der*

*Naturwissenschaften und der Technik* 40 (1941/42) 1–15; repr. in *id., Beiträge zur Geschichte der Technologie und der Alchemie* (1956) 336–49 [FI5].

C. Harding, "The Production of Medieval Mosaics: The Orvieto Evidence," in *DOP* 43 (1989) 73–102: contains a selection of fourteenth-century documents concerned with the making of mosaics and stained glass for Orvieto Cathedral; a bibliographical note lists older publications of similar documents [FI6].

Heraclius, *De coloribus et artibus Romanorum,* ed. and tr. A. Ilg: *Von den Farben und Künsten der Römer,* 2nd ed. (1888) [FI7].

Isidore of Seville, *Etym.*: for technical information concerning the decorative arts see especially bks. 16 (*De lapidibus et metallis*) and 19 (*De navibus, aedificiis et vestibus*) [FI8].

*Mappae Clavicula* [*MC*]: ". . . a transcript of a MS. Treatise on the preparation of Pigments, and on various processes of the Decorative Arts practised during the Middle Ages, written in the twelfth century, and entitled *Mappae Clavicula,*" ed. T. Phillips, in *Archaeologia* 32 (1847) 183–244: the only edition of the Corning manuscript of the *MC* collection [FI9]; *Compositiones ad tingenda musiva,* ed. and tr. H. Hedfors (1932): the best edition of the Lucca manuscript of the *MC* [FI10]; *Mappae Clavicula: A Little Key to the World of Medieval Techniques,* tr. C.S. Smith and J.G. Hawthorne, *TAPhS,* n.s., 64.4 (1974): an English rendering of the *MC* with reduced facsimiles of the Selestadt and Corning manuscripts and concordances of the Corning, Selestadt, Lucca, and Klosterneuburg copies; see the review of this edition by H. Silvestre in *Scriptorium* 31 (1977) 319–23 [FI11].

M.P. Merrifield, ed. and tr., *Original Treatises . . . on the Arts of Painting,* 2 vols. (1849), repr. with new introduction and glossary of technical terms by S.M. Alexander (1967): a pioneering publication of technical treatises, among them (in v1) Archerius (Iohannes Alcherius), *De coloribus diversis modis* (fifteenth century; see [FI29]); Eraclius (Heraclius), *De coloribus et artibus Romanorum* (c. 1100, with later additions; see [FI7] and [FI24]); Petrus de S. Audemaro (Peter of St. Omer), *De coloribus faciendis* (fourteenth century); this corpus of "pre-Raphaelite" treatises has a practical rather than historical focus and contains interesting technical information [FI12].

*Mittelalterliche Schatzverzeichnisse,* v1, ed. Zentralinstitut für Kunstgeschichte and B. Bischoff (1967): edition, with glossary, of early medieval treasure inventories from Germany [FI13].

H. Silvestre, ed., "Le MS Bruxellensis 10147–58," in *Académie royale des sciences, des lettres et des beaux-arts de Belgique, Commission royale d'histoire, Bulletin* 119 (1954) 95–140: edition of a thirteenth-century *compendium artis picturae* [FI14].

Theophilus, *DDA:* the best edition of the treatise is that by C.R. Dodwell [FI15].

D.V. Thompson, Jr., ed. and tr., "*Liber de coloribus illuminatorum siue pictorum* from *Sloane MS. No. 1754,*" in *Speculum* 1 (1926) 280–307, 448–50 [*addenda et corrigenda*] [FI16].

## Studies

B. Bischoff, "Die Überlieferung des Theophilus Rugerus nach den ältesten Handschriften," in *MJbK,* 3rd ser., 3/4 (1952/53) 145–49; repr. in *id., MittStud,* v2:175–82: an analysis of the earliest manuscripts of Theophilus [FI17].

B. Bischoff, "Die Überlieferung der technischen Literatur," in *Settimane di studio del centro italiano di studi sull'alto medioevo* 18 (1971) 267–96; repr. in *id., MittStud,* v3:277–97: a magisterial survey, including an attempt to reconstruct the shape of the Greek collection that survives in the Latin *MC*, and to date this collection to the pre-Constantinian period. Bischoff believed that all recipes that were obvious translations from the Greek had been part of the original *MC*. For a different view, see [FI20] and [FI22] [**FI18**].

J. Croquison, "L'iconographie chrétienne à Rome d'après le 'Liber Pontificalis,'" in *Byzantion* 34 (1964) 535–606: a survey of the entries relating to textiles and the work of goldsmiths in the early medieval parts of the *Liber pontificalis* [**FI19**].

R. Halleux and P. Meyvaert, "Les origines de la *Mappae Clavicula*," in *AHDL* 62 (1987) 7–58: an important reconstitution of the original text of the *MC*, with a new interpretation of its almost unintelligible title. The authors argue that the title *MC* referred originally to a small fraction of the Greek material in the collection [**FI20**].

P. Hills, *The Light of Early Italian Painting* (1987): with a hand list (pp146–47) of medieval technical treatises, including the vernacular treatises of the late Middle Ages [**FI21**].

R.P. Johnson, "Some Manuscripts of the *Mappae Clavicula*," in *Speculum* 10 (1935) 72–81; *id.*, "Some Continental Manuscripts of the *Mappae Clavicula*," in *Speculum* 12 (1937) 84–103 [**FI22**].

P. Meyvaert, "The Original *Mappae Clavicula* and Its Date," in *Manuscripta* 19 (1975) 79: abstract of paper in which Meyvaert argued that the original *MC* "must be dated not later than the fourth century A.D." [**FI23**].

J.C. Richards, ed., "A New Manuscript of Heraclius," in *Speculum* 15 (1940) 255–71: an edition of the earliest known form of the treatise from an eleventh-century manuscript [**FI24**].

H. Roosen-Runge, "Die Buchmalereirezepte des Theophilus," in *MJbK*, 3rd ser., 3/4 (1952/53) 159–71 [**FI25**].

H. Roosen-Runge, *Farbgebung und Technik frühmittelalterlicher Buchmalerei: Studien zu den Traktaten "Mappae Clavicula" und "Heraclius"*, 2 vols. (1967) [**FI26**].

J. Svennung, *Compositiones Lucenses: Studien zum Inhalt, zur Textkritik und Sprache* (1941): an indispensable companion to [FI10] [**FI27**].

D.V. Thompson, *The Materials and Techniques of Medieval Painting* (1956): reprint of *The Materials of Medieval Painting* (1936) [**FI28**].

B.S. Tosatti Soldano, "Le 'Tabula de vocabulis sinonimis et equivocis colorum': ms. lat. 6741 della Bibliothèque Nationale di Parigi in relazione a Giovanni Alcherio. Ipotesi su un protagonista della trasmissione delle fonti di tecniche pittoriche tra Milano e Parigi ai primi del Quattrocento, con qualche nota bibliografica sulla trattatistica tecnico-artistica medievale," in *Acme* 36.2 (1983) 129–87 [**FI29**].

S. Waetzold, "Systematisches Verzeichnis der Farbnamen," in *MJbK*, 3rd ser., 3/4 (1952/53) 6–14 [**FI30**].

D. Winfield, "Byzantine Wallpainting Methods," in *DOP* 22 (1968) 63–139: this study succeeds in analyzing Byzantine wall paintings in the light of such Western texts as Theophilus and Peter of St. Omer, highlighting the pervasive influence of Byzantine techniques as well as the indebtedness of the Western technical literature to Byzantine sources [**FI31**].

*See also* [BD61], [BD72], [BE36].

F J   &bull;   # TEXTILES

## BY JOHN H. MUNRO

Textile manufacturing is a very ancient industry, and it was certainly the predominant industry of medieval Europe. In west European languages the word *textile* is derived from Classical Latin *textilis,* based on the verb form for the central process in almost all such manufacturing: *texere,* to weave. In medieval European society, the most important textile, for both industrial production and apparel, was the woolen cloth: *pannus lanae* (usually just *pannus,* but also *drapa*). Although medieval Europe produced a very wide variety of these cloths, the true woolen owed its definitive form, especially as those luxury fabrics woven from very fine, short-fibered wools, to several technological innovations during the eleventh and twelfth centuries in the weaving and finishing processes.

Unfortunately there are no known contemporary Latin treatises that describe these revolutionary changes; and much of our evidence about medieval cloth industries is to be found in vernacular texts. In the Low Countries (including Artois), Europe's predominant cloth-producing region before c. 1320, the major centers were francophone; and most of their documents were composed in Old French (highly evolved). Some Latin, along with French, was used by the purely Flemish-language towns; but, after the anti-French urban revolts of 1302–18, when the textile guilds gained some share of power in their town governments (and when their urban industries gained ascendancy over the francophone towns), almost all their guild and other official records concerning cloth production were thereafter drafted in Flemish (i.e. Middle Dutch). One of the very best sources for textile terminology is the *Livre des mestiers,* composed at Bruges c. 1369, in both Flemish and French (but regrettably not Latin).

The chief sources for textile terminology in Medieval Latin must therefore be found elsewhere, in guild, civic, commercial, and even some literary records from cloth towns in England, France, and Italy, even though, paradoxically, some of these developed much later than the Flemish-Artesian urban industries. For the traditional cloth-making processes, many or most of the Medieval Latin terms are the same as, or directly derived from, those of Classical Latin. Some terms, however, especially those related to the technological innovations and changes in the nature of the medieval woolen, were adapted from current vernacular languages; and it will be self-evident that some of them are structurally rather more Italian, French, or English than Latin.

A proper understanding of the textile terms in Medieval Latin thus requires a brief survey of those historical changes in both industrial technology and the fabrics themselves. During the earlier Middle Ages, before those innovations, the predominant textile in Western Europe seems to have been much more typically worsted than woolen; and the term *worsted*, if and when differentiated from *pannus*, though chiefly in later documents, is variously rendered as *sagum, saium, saia, saya, assaia, essaia, essaia de Worsted(e)*. The true worsted was a relatively light but strong fabric that was woven with tightly twisted, generally longer-stapled yarns (*filum, filetum, filacia lana; lana ad filandum*) for both the warp (*stamen*, occasionally *tela*) and weft (*trama*), in a highly distinctive weave, typically in a lozenge or diamond twill. There also evolved a third, bastard variety of cloth, with a long-stapled worsted warp and a short-stapled woolen weft, sometimes also called *saia*, but more frequently *sargium, sargium de Worsted, pannus de Worstede vocatus sargium*, and thus simply "serge" in both French and English.

In this earlier era, cloths were woven on a vertical or upright loom (*tela*) that dates from distant antiquity: the "warp-weighted" loom, in which the warp yarns, weighted with stones, pottery, marble, or bone, were hung from the top bar (*liciatorium*) of a framework that rested against vertical posts or a wall, while a movable lower bar, the "shed rod," separated the warps to allow the passage of the transverse weft yarns to produce the weave. Subsequently, this traditional loom was displaced, though gradually at first, by a revolutionary new loom, first described in a Hebrew commentary on the Babylonian Talmud by Rabbi Solomon ben Isaac (Rashi of Troyes, c. 1040–1105): the horizontal, foot-powered treadle loom, which permitted the creation of an entirely new, much finer and heavier cloth—the true woolen. With far-reaching social consequences, it also converted the weaver's occupation, which had been overwhelmingly female in early medieval Europe (*textrix, tessitrix*, employed in a Carolingian *gynaecium*), into one that ultimately became almost universally male (*textor, tessitor, telarius*), especially as the new loom developed into the much more mechanically complex and far bigger broadloom, normally requiring two male weavers. No hint of this momentous innovation can be found in Latin documents, however, for the same Latin term *tela* is used for both looms, old and new; for the woven webs; and sometimes also, as noted above, for the loom-warps themselves.

The construction of the fully evolved new loom permitted a much longer and wider cloth (what indeed is called broadcloth; *tela lata, pannus latus*), about three yards wide, to be more finely, densely, and evenly woven, with proportionately much more weft than warp. Placed on one end of this boxlike loom was a rotating warp-beam (*liciatorium*—from *licium*, "end of the web"), ratcheted by a lever, on which hundreds of woolen warps, each about 30 yards long, were tightly wound. The warps were then individually fed through a multitude of looped leather cords called heddles or healds (*lamina, licium; tenia*), then through the "reed" (*harundo*) or "wool comb" (*pecten*, discussed below), and finally wound tautly onto the rotating cloth beam (*trochlea circumvolubilis*), similarly ratcheted, at the other end of the box loom. The heddles themselves were suspended from a series of wooden or iron rods (*verga, virga*), or "harnesses" (the late twelfth-century author Alexander Neckam uses the terms *strepa, scansile*, "stirrup"), each of which was attached to a cord that ran through a pulley, fixed on top of the loom (*capudium*), to its own treadle (*pedalis*) underneath the front of the loom, where the weaver sat. By depressing a treadle (the left treadle to raise the right harness, and vice versa), the weaver "opened a shed" to separate groups of warps through which he passed the wooden boatlike shuttle (*navicula*) containing the woolen weft-yarn, wound on a spool or bobbin (*spola; panus,* "spooled yarn"), along a grooved wooden channel, the "laysword," to his assistant weaver on the other side. Attached to this laysword was a heavy wooden frame, the "batten," containing the removable and appropriately named wool comb (*pecten*) or reed (*harundo*); two narrow, leather-encased, horizontal, wooden laths (*cidula, scindula*), the width of the cloth, served as the upper and lower frame for hundreds of thin wire teeth (*cavilla*), which held the warps firmly and evenly in place. After the insertion of the weft through each "shed" of warps, the two weavers pulled this laysword with batten and wool comb (reed) to the front of the loom in order to beat the weft into the fell of the woven cloth. As each section was woven, it was wound onto the cloth beam by the ratcheted lever. A standard cloth, 30 yards long (before any shrinkage), took the two weavers about two weeks to produce.

Unlike worsteds, the now woven woolen cloth (*textum*) was far too weak and fragile when removed from the loom, subject to damaging tears; and it would become a true woolen only after being subjected to the final manufacturing stage known as fulling (*fullatio, fullonia, fullatura*). The art of fulling had been well known in Roman times (as *fullonica*); but the task of the Roman and early medieval fuller (*fullo*) seems to have been little more than scouring and cleansing the cloth of the greases, warp-sizing, and dirt it had acquired from the manufacturing processes. In later medieval fulling, such scouring and degreasing, using "fuller's earth" (*terra fullonis*, with hydrous aluminum silicates), was only the first stage of what had become a far more complex process. Its more crucial objectives were to felt and compress the cloth, up to half its surface area or more, by forcing the short, scaly, and serrated fibers of true woolen yarns to interlock, intermesh, and then shrink. Those objectives were achieved by water, chemicals, heat, and pressure from incessant pounding, as two male fullers trod and stomped upon the woven cloth in large wooden or stoneware vats, filled with warm water, fuller's earth (often illegally adulterated with urine), and soap, for three but sometimes even five days.

That enormously wearisome and time-consuming process was reduced to just several hours by one of the most important mechanical innovations in the history of textiles: the water-powered fulling-mill (*molendinum ad fullandum, molendinum fullonum* or *fullonis*), in which a rotating waterwheel alternately raised and then dropped two very large, extremely heavy, wooden hammers to pound the cloth many times a minute. Also dating from the eleventh century, this was in fact the only cloth-manufacturing process to be mechanically powered before the modern Industrial Revolution. It did not, however, eliminate traditional foot fulling, which long continued to be used in the production of the very highest grade luxury woolens, at least by those draperies that believed that mechanical fulling impaired the woolen's texture or "handle" and luxury quality.

Thus shrunken and felted, by either process, the fulled woolen cloth was now very strong and durable—indeed virtually indestructible—and very heavy (per square yard) because of its densely packed structure, heavier than most modern-day woolen overcoats; its weave pattern had also been almost totally obscured by felting, and its "handle" had become very soft. But the fuller had not yet completed his task, nor was the cloth yet "finished." The still-wet fulled cloth was then hung on a tentering-frame (*licie, litie*; cf. Old French *lices*, but Italian *tiratoio*) to dry; and the tenterer (*tirator*) carefully but tautly stretched the wet cloth by its four borders (*lista, listeria;* cf. English "list") with "tenterhooks" to remove all the creases and wrinkles from fulling and to ensure uniformity in width and length throughout the cloth; in some Medieval Latin texts produced in England, *brochire* is the verb for these actions. The fuller then proceeded to "raise the nap" on the still wet cloth, i.e. to raise all the loose fibers, to remove any entanglements, and to correct any faults, especially in perfecting the felted appearance. His instrument was a small wooden rectangular frame box, with a long handle, containing a packed collection of teasels or cards, i.e. a prickly thistle plant with the Classical Latin name *carduus,* and modern scientific name *Dipsacus fullonum.*

This instrument also played a crucial role in the hands of the cloth finishers: the teaseller (*cardinarius, cardator*) and the shearer (*tonsor, tonditor*), who, after fixing the now dry cloth to a flat sloping table (*tabula tonsuris*), alternately and successively subjected it to raising and shearing (*tonsura*) so as to nap (*cardare*) and then to clip or shear off (*tondere*) all the protruding fibers. The result was not only the total obliteration of any remaining trace of weave but a texture that closely rivaled that of any silken fabrics. Pure worsted textiles rarely underwent any of these fulling or finishing processes, but the semiworsted serges, because of their greased woolen wefts, with some felting properties, did undergo a cursory fulling, napping, and shearing.

The finished cloth, even those with already dyed wools, was then delivered to the dyers (*tinctor, teintarius, teinturarius,* but in Classical Latin also *infector*), whose two major groups were determined by the basic ingredients for dyeing (*tinctura, tincturatio*): in blue (*blavus, blavium, blaveum, blodius, blodium, bluetem, blavetum*) with woad (*waida, waidum, waisdia, gaida, gualda, gualdum*), and in red (*ruber, rubeus*) with madder (*rubia, rubia major*). Both woad and madder were vegetable dyes, which, though by no means cheap, could not compare in cost with the most extravagantly expensive dyestuff of the Middle Ages, the scarlet-producing insect substance now called *kermes* (from the Arabic *qirmiz,* a "worm"), but better known throughout the medieval European world as *granum* (*tinctio in grano,* "in grain"), from its granular substance, the eggs of Mediterranean shield lice of the *Coccidae* family. That dyestuff was responsible not only for the glorious red color but also for the enormously high price of medieval Europe's most famous luxury woolen, the *scarlet* (*scarlata, scarlatum, scarletum, scarletus, escarlata*).

Late medieval dyers, like their fellow shearers and cloth finishers, were highly paid professionals, the aristocrats of textile artisans, whose clients were more often cloth merchants (*mercatores*)—wholesalers, brokers, and exporters—than drapers (*draperii*). The drapers themselves were really more mercantile than industrial entrepreneurs, whose essential roles were to supply the prepared wools, other raw materials, and credit, and to sell the manufactured, fulled cloths to the cloth finishers, brokers, or merchants, while delegating to the weavers (weaver-drapers) the task of organizing the actual manufacturing processes and hiring the other artisans, including the fullers. In most medieval European urban draperies, the dyers, shearers, weavers, and fullers were usually organized into professional craft guilds or *artes,* while cloth merchants and drapers often had their own mercantile guilds; rarely, however, did other woolen textile artisans enjoy such guild protection.

No discussion of medieval cloth making could be complete, however, without mention of the important innovations that affected the preliminary, preweaving processes, i.e. wool combing (*pectere*), carding (*cardare*), and spinning (*nere, filatio*) to produce the warp and weft yarns for weaving. From ancient times, all forms of wool—fine or coarse, short- or long-stapled, for woolen or worsted yarns—had been prepared by combing with a pair of heated, long, fine-toothed, iron combs (*pecten*, i.e. with the same name as the loom instrument) to disentangle the fibers, separating the long-fibered "tops" from the short "noils." From about the twelfth century, however, some European draperies (*draperia*) began utilizing metal "cards" (*carduus*, more commonly *carda*, or *garda*; cf. Old French *garder*), which they evidently borrowed from the cotton industries of Muslim Spain and Sicily, to disentangle the short-stapled, curly-fibered wools with the best felting properties. Also used in pairs, they were hand-held, rectangular, leather-covered blocks with hundreds of protruding hooked wires. That this metal instrument bears precisely the same name as the fuller's and finisher's teasel is indeed perplexing, but may be explained by its initial or early use in napping fulled cloths. Metal cards were quickly banished from such finishing functions, however, because their fine wires, so much less resilient than the teasel plant's prickles, were too damaging to the cloth. Similar suspicions may explain why, in late medieval Western Europe, cards were so strongly resisted in preparing the wools, even though they were so clearly labor-saving; and some Italian and French draperies preferred an alternative carding process using a tautly strung gut-string bow, with which the *battitor ad arcum* beat short-fibered wools to disentangle and cleanse them (by its vibrations).

Very closely associated with carding, evidently emanating from the same Muslim sources, was the almost simultaneous introduction of the spinning wheel (*rota*), a hand-powered wheel with a continuous looped driving band that rapidly rotated a spindle (*fusus*) to draft (draw, *trahere*) and twist the prepared wool fibers into yarn (thus *lanam trahere* or *ducere*, "to spin"). This, quite simply, was a mechanization of the very ancient and universal method of hand spinning. From the mass or "roving" of combed wool placed on the cleft of the distaff (*colus* or *conuclus*), a Y-forked stick, the traditional hand spinster (*filatrix*) drew out and attached some fibers to the tip of the spindle (also *fusus*), a short tapered rod; she then inserted its bottom pointed end through the center of a weighted disk (*verticillus*) or whorl of wood, bone, or stone, and dropped this device—commonly called the "rock" (*rocca, roka, rochea*)—to the ground. As it descended, this whorl produced a very rapid continuous rotation in the spindle that simultaneously drafted and twisted the wool fibers into yarn, which was then wound onto the spindle's other end.

In the spinning wheel, the spindle was grooved and mounted horizontally between two uprights to serve as a pulley for the wheel's driving band; but otherwise the wheel spinster (*filatrix ad rotam*) spun her yarn in essentially the same fashion, drawing the roving, which became principally carded wools, away from the spindle tip with one hand as her other hand spun the wheel. The wheel vastly increased spinning productivity, but exacted a high cost in quality, at least in the medieval era: the yarns so spun were too often weak, uneven, knotty, and too easily broken to serve as warps on the loom. Consequently, most later medieval woolen draperies, after grudgingly accepting the wheel, would permit its use, along with the associated carded wools, only for weft yarns, while strictly requiring both combing and hand spinning (i.e. the "rock") for producing warp yarns, at least for luxury-quality woolens.

Thus, although all of the technological innovations in textile production discussed here—metal cards, the spinning wheel, the horizontal loom, and the fulling mill—greatly increased industrial productivity, only the broadloom radically improved the quality of woolens. Later medieval foot fulling, however, had become so much more complex than Roman fulling that, even without any mechanical changes, it should also be counted as part of the innovations that resulted in the creation of the true woolen as medieval Europe's most important textile.

Unfortunately, limitations of space do not permit a comparable discussion of the Medieval Latin terminology for the other, lesser, but still significant branches of textile manufacturing, two of them also dating from distant antiquity. The most famous was, of course, the industry that produced a wide variety of silks (*serica* in Classical Latin, but more often *sericum, cericum* in Medieval Latin), the world's costliest fabrics, whose predominant medieval forms were damasks (*sericum de Damasco*), velvets (*sericum villosum*), satins (*satinum, sathana*), and brocades (*broccatus,* from Spanish *brocado*), often in embroidered form (*brouderia, brauderia, brodatura*). The silk industry supposedly originated in China c. 2700 B.C., and by the Roman era, silk weaving had spread to Syria and Egypt. Sericulture itself, however, in producing raw silk (*sericum crudum*) by cultivation of *Bombyx mori* moths that fed on mulberry leaves, was a late Roman introduction initiated at Constantinople in Justinian's reign (c. 560, according to his chronicler Procopius). The Arabic conquests then transmitted both sericulture and silk manufacturing westward, especially to Spain, where production of scarlet-dyed *siglatun* (partly responsible for the Medieval Latin term *scarlata*) became world-renowned by the ninth century. By the early thirteenth century silk manufacturing, employing *sereatrices* or *cericatores,* had been introduced into Italy via Muslim Sicily. Thanks to their invention and development of water-powered silk-throwing factories (whose throwsters were known in Italian as *filatore di seta, filatoiaio*), first recorded at Bologna in 1272, the Italians quickly gained supremacy throughout Europe in the silk trades. This they retained for almost four centuries, encountering their first significant competition only when the French established a silk industry at Tours in 1470.

An even more ancient (possibly dating to 7000 B.C.) and certainly far more widespread textile industry, of much more humble origins, was the manufacture of linens (*linea*), woven from retted flax fibers (*linum usitatissimum*). The major medieval European industrial centers, producing for international markets, were in northeastern France (especially at Rheims), the Rhineland, the Low Countries, and to a lesser extent Italy. Italy, however, became much more prominent by developing a closely related industry, one of Egyptian origin, which was again introduced via Muslim Sicily during the later eleventh or twelfth century. This was the manufacture of *fustians* (*fustaneum, fustanea, fustannum, fustianum,* probably derived from the Arabic *al-Fusṭāṭ,* an industrial district of Cairo), woven with a warp of linen-flax and a weft of cotton (*coto, cotona, cotonus, cutunus,* from the Arabic *al-quṭūn*). By the fourteenth century, this industry had spread into South Germany (Augsburg, Ulm, and Nuremberg), which became the leading European producer of these relatively cheap and light textiles during the fifteenth and sixteenth centuries, exporting them even to cotton-producing regions of Asia. Entries in the bibliography of this essay and of appropriate articles in the *DMA* provide further information about these textiles and their Medieval Latin nomenclature.

# Bibliography

## Documentary and Other Primary Sources

Alexander Neckam (1157–1217), *De nominibus utensilium*, ed. T. Hunt, in *TLLTCE* 1:184–85 [FJ1].

A.M.E. Agnoletti, ed., *Statuto dell'arte della lana di Firenze (1317–1319)* (1940–48) [FJ2].

Francesco Balducci Pegolotti (fourteenth century), *La practica della mercatura*, ed. A. Evans (1936) [FJ3].

G. Barbieri, ed., "Documenti inediti sull'arte dei fustagneri a Milano," in *Archivio storico lombardo*, 3rd ser., 17 (1902) [FJ4].

F.B. Bickley, ed., *The Little Red Book of Bristol*, 2 vols. (1900): with important Latin texts on Bristol's medieval cloth industry [FJ5].

O. Delepierre and J.F. Willems, eds., *Collection des keuren ou statuts de tous les métiers de Bruges* (1842) [FJ6].

N. De Pauw, ed., *Ypre jeghen Poperinghe angaende den verbonden: Gedingstukken der XIVe eeuw nopens het laken* (1899) [FJ7].

G.-B. Depping, ed., *Réglemens sur les arts et métiers de Paris, rédigés au XIIIe siècle et connus sous le nom du Livre des Métiers d'Étienne Boileau* (1837): see pp113–52, 392–404 for textiles (chiefly in French) [FJ8].

R. Doehaerd, ed., *Les relations commerciales entre Gênes, la Belgique et l'Outremont d'après les archives notariales génoises aux XIII et XIV siècles*, 3 vols. (1941): with Latin documents on textile commerce [FJ9].

M. Dubois, ed., "Textes et fragments relatifs à la draperie de Tournai au moyen âge," in *Revue du Nord* 32 (1950) 145–65, 219–35 [FJ10].

F. Edler, *Glossary of Mediaeval Terms of Business: Italian Series, 1200–1600* (1934, r1970): with numerous Italian texts that employ textile terms often close to Latin [FJ11].

G.C. Fagniez, ed., *Documents relatifs à l'histoire de l'industrie et du commerce en France*, 2 vols. (1898–1900, r1974) [FJ12].

G. Espinas, ed., *Documents relatifs à la draperie de Valenciennes au moyen âge* (1931) [FJ13].

G. Espinas and H. Pirenne, eds., *Recueil de documents relatifs à l'histoire de l'industrie drapière en Flandre*, pt1: *Des origines à l'époque bourguignonne*, 4 vols. (1906–24) [FJ14].

S.F. Hockey, ed., *The Account-Book of Beaulieu Abbey*, CamSoc, 4th ser., 16 (1975): see documents 52–53 (pp214–24), "Tabula lanarie cum vestiario" [FJ15].

H. Joosen, ed., "Recueil de documents relatifs à l'histoire de l'industrie drapière à Malines, des origines à 1384," in *Bulletin de la Commission Royale d'Histoire* 99 (1935) 365–569 [FJ16].

L. Liagre-De Sturler, ed., *Les relations commerciales entre Gênes, la Belgique et l'Outremont, d'après les archives notariales génoises (1320–1400)*, 2 vols. (1969): with Latin documents on textile commerce [FJ17].

F. Melis, ed., *Documenti per la storia economica dei secoli XIII–XVI*, Istituto internazionale di storia economica F. Datini, *Documenti*, v1 (1972) [FJ18].

H.V. Michelant, ed., *Le livre des mestiers: Dialogues français-flamands composés au XIVe siècle par un maître d'école de la ville de Broges* (1875) [FJ19].

K.G. Ponting, ed., *Leonardo da Vinci: Drawings of Textile Machines* (1979) [FJ20].

N.W. Posthumus, ed., *Bronnen tot de geschiedenis van de Leidsche textielnijverheid*, vi: *333–1480* (1910) [FJ21].

G. Rebora, ed., *Un manuale di tintoria del quattrocento* (1970) [FJ22].

H.T. Riley, ed., *Munimenta Gildhallae Londoniensis; Liber Albus, Liber Custumarum, et Liber Horn*, 3 vols. in 4 pts., *RSer* 12 (1859–62): with extensive Latin documentation on the English cloth industry [FJ23].

J.M. Roland de la Platière, *L'art du fabricant d'étoffes en laines rases et sèches, unies et croisées* (1780): perhaps the best extant treatise on European textile manufacturing with relevance for the medieval era [FJ24].

Gioanventura Rosetti (fl. 1530–48), *The Plictho: Instructions in the Art of the Dyers Which Teaches the Dyeing of Woolen Cloths, Linens, Cottons, and Silk by the Great as Well as by the Common*, tr. S.M. Edelstein and H.C. Borghetty (1969): with documents [FJ25].

C. Santoro, ed., *La matricola dei mercanti di lana sottile di Milano* (1940) [FJ26].

F. Sartini, ed., *Statuti dell'arte dei rigattieri e linaioli di Firenze (1296–1340)* (1940) [FJ27].

T. Smith, L.T. Smith, and L. Brentano, eds., *English Gilds*, Early English Text Society, 2nd ed. (1892) [FJ28].

## Studies

A.R. Bridbury, *Medieval English Clothmaking: An Economic Survey* (1982) [FJ29].

H. Businská, "Terminologie textilní vyroby v období vrcholného stredovéku," in *Listy filologické* 96.2 (1973) 74–76: with German summary [FJ30].

E.M. Carus-Wilson, "An Industrial Revolution of the Thirteenth Century," in *EHR*, 1st ser., 11 (1941) 39–60; repr. in *id.*, *Medieval Merchant Venturers: Collected Studies* (1954, r1967) 183–210 [FJ31].

E.M. Carus-Wilson, "Haberget: A Medieval Textile Conundrum," in *Medieval Archeology* 13 (1969) 148–66 [FJ32].

E.M. Carus-Wilson, "The Woollen Industry," in *The Cambridge Economic History of Europe*, v2: *Trade and Industry in the Middle Ages*, 2nd ed., ed. M.M. Postan and E. Miller (1987) 613–90 [FJ33].

A. Clementi, *L'arte della lana in una città del Regno di Napoli (sec. XIV–XVI)* (1979): with Latin and Italian documentation [FJ34].

Comité des travaux historiques et scientifiques, *Recherches sur l'économie de la France médiévale: Les vois fluviales, la draperie: Actes du 112e congrès national des sociétés savants, Lyon 1987* (1989) [FJ35].

F. Consitt, *The London Weavers' Company*, v1: *From the Twelfth Century to the Close of the Sixteenth Century* (1933): with some documentation [FJ36].

E. Coornaert, *Un centre industriel d'autrefois: La draperie-sayetterie d'Hondschoote (XIVe–XVIIIe siècles)* (1930): with extensive documentary appendices [FJ37].

A. Doren, *Studien aus der Florentiner Wirtschaftsgeschichte*, v1: *Die Florentiner Wollentuchindustrie vom 14. bis zum 16. Jahrhundert* (1901, r1969): see especially "Trattato dell'Arte della Lana" (fifteenth century), pp484–93 [FJ38].

J.F. Drinkwater, "The Wool Textile Industry of Gallia Belgica and the Secundinii of Igel: Questions and Hypotheses," in *TH* 13 (1982) 111–28 [FJ39].

W. Endrei, *L'évolution des techniques du filage et du tissage du moyen âge à la révolution industrielle*, tr. J. Takacs and J. Pilisi (1968) [FJ40].

W. English, "A Study of the Driving Mechanisms in the Early Circular Throwing Machines," in *TH* 2 (1971) 65–75: on the silk industry [**FJ41**].

G. Espinas, *La draperie dans la Flandre française au moyen âge*, 2 vols. (1923): with many documentary appendices [**FJ42**].

G. Gandi, *Le arti maggiori e minori in Firenze*, 2 vols. (1929, r1971): "L'Arte della Lana," pp119–42; "L'Arte di Por Santa Maria o della Seta," pp143–64; "L'Arte dei Linaioli e Rigattieri," pp225–30; includes some documentation [**FJ43**].

A. Geijer, *A History of Textile Art: A Selective Account* (1979, r1982) [**FJ44**].

V.A. Harding, "Some Documentary Sources for the Import and Distribution of Foreign Textiles in Late Medieval England," in *TH* 18 (1987) 205–18 [**FJ45**].

N.B. Harte and K.G. Ponting, eds., *Cloth and Clothing in Medieval Europe: Essays in Memory of Professor E.M. Carus-Wilson* (1983). See especially the following studies: J.H. Munro, "The Medieval Scarlet and the Economics of Sartorial Splendour," pp13–70; A. Geijer, "The Textile Finds from Birka," pp80–99; R. Van Uytven, "Cloth in Medieval Literature of Western Europe," pp151–83; H. Hoshino, "The Rise of the Florentine Woollen Industry in the Fourteenth Century," pp184–204; H. Kellenbenz, "The Fustian Industry of the Ulm Region in the Fifteenth and Early Sixteenth Centuries," pp259–76; V. Gervers, "Medieval Garments in the Mediterranean World," pp279–315 [**FJ46**].

A.E. Haynes, "Twill Weaving on the Warp Weighted Loom: Some Technical Considerations," in *TH* 6 (1975) 156–64 [**FJ47**].

H. Heaton, *The Yorkshire Woollen and Worsted Industries from the Earliest Times up to the Industrial Revolution*, 2nd ed. (1966) [**FJ48**].

M. Hoffmann, *The Warp-Weighted Loom: Studies in the History and Technology of an Ancient Implement* (1964, r1974) [**FJ49**].

M. Höfler, *Untersuchungen zur Tuch- und Stoffbenennung in der französischen Urkundensprache: Vom Ortsnamen zum Appellativum* (1967) [**FJ50**].

H. Hoshino, *L'arte della lana in Firenze nel basso medioevo: Il commercio della lana e il mercato dei panni fiorentini nei secoli XIII–XV* (1980) [**FJ51**].

K. Lacey, "The Production of 'Narrow Ware' by Silkwomen in Fourteenth and Fifteenth Century England," in *TH* 18 (1987) 187–204 [**FJ52**].

H. Laurent, *Un grand commerce d'exportation au moyen âge: La draperie des Pays-Bas en France et dans les pays méditerranéens (XIIe–XVe siècle)* (1935) [**FJ53**].

T.H. Lloyd, "Some Costs of Cloth Manufacturing in Thirteenth-Century England," in *TH* 1 (1970) 332–36: with some Latin citations [**FJ54**].

R.S. Lopez, "Silk Industry in the Byzantine Empire," in *Speculum* 20 (1945) 1–42 [**FJ55**].

P. Malanima, "The First European Textile Machine," in *TH* 17 (1986) 115–28 [**FJ56**].

M.F. Mazzaoui, *The Italian Cotton Industry in the Later Middle Ages, 1100–1600* (1981) [**FJ57**].

F. Melis, "L'industria laniera," in *id., Aspetti della vita economica medievale (Studi nell'archivio Datini di Prato)* (1962) 455–729: with extensive documentation [**FJ58**].

L. Monnas, "Silk Cloths Purchased for the Great Wardrobe of the Kings of England, 1325–1462," in *TH* 20 (1989) 283–307 [**FJ59**].

J. Munro, "Linen," in *DMA* 7:584–86; "Silk," in *DMA* 11:293–96; "Textile Technology" and "Textile Workers," in *DMA* 11:693–715 [**FJ60**].

J. Munro, "Wool-Price Schedules and the Qualities of English Wools in the Later Middle Ages, c. 1270–1499," in *TH* 9 (1978) 118–69: with references to some Latin texts in the notes [**FJ61**].

J. Munro, *Textiles, Towns and Trade: Essays in the Economic History of Late-Medieval England and the Low Countries* (1994) [FJ62].

A. Muthesius, "From Seed to Samite: Aspects of Byzantine Silk Production," in *TH* 20 (1989) 135–49: a very important recent study [FJ63].

A. Nahlik, "Les techniques de l'industrie textile en Europe orientale, du Xe au XVe siècle, à travers les vestiges de tissus," in *Annales* 26 (1971) 1279–90 [FJ64].

N. Oikonomidès, "Silk Trade and Production in Byzantium from the Sixth to the Ninth Century: The Seals of Kommerkiarioi," in *DOP* 40 (1986) 33–53 [FJ65].

C. Ouin-Lacroix, *Histoire des anciennes corporations d'arts et métiers et des confréries religieuses de la capitale de la Normandie* (1850) 90–147, 616–22 ("Statuts des drapiers-drapants, tisseurs, fouleurs, lanneurs, tondeurs de draps" of 1424) [FJ66].

R. Patterson, "Spinning and Weaving," in *HTech* 2:191–200 ("Fibres and Their Preparation") [FJ67].

F. Piponnier, *Costume et vie sociale: La cour d'Anjou XIVe–XVe siècle* (1970) [FJ68].

G. de Poerck, *La draperie médiévale en Flandre et en Artois: Technique et terminologie*, 3 vols. (1951) [FJ69].

K.G. Ponting, "Sculptures and Paintings of Textile Processes at Leiden," in *TH* 5 (1974) 128–51 [FJ70].

E. Rossini and M.F. Mazzaoui, "Società e tecnica nel medioevo: La produzione dei panni di lana a Verona nei secoli XIII–XIV–XV," in *Atti e memorie della Accademia di Agricoltura, Scienze, e Lettere di Verona* (1969–70), 6th ser., 21 (1971) 571–624 [FJ71].

A. Sapori, *Una compagnia di Calimala ai primi del trecento* (1932): with very extensive Latin and Italian documentation on textiles, northern and Italian [FJ72].

M. Spallanzani, ed., *Produzione, commercio, e consumo dei panni di lana (nei secoli XII–XVIII)* (1976): an important collection of articles on textiles, chiefly medieval [FJ73].

K. Staniland, "The Great Wardrobe Accounts as a Source for Historians of Fourteenth-Century Clothing and Textiles," in *TH* 20 (1989) 275–81 [FJ74].

W. von Stromer, *Die Gründung der Baumwollindustrie in Mitteleuropa: Wirtschaftspolitik im Spätmittelalter* (1978): the fullest and best study of the later medieval German cotton-fustian industry [FJ75].

P. Váczy, *La transformation de la technique et de l'organisation de l'industrie textile en Flandre aux XIe–XIIIe siècles* (1960) [FJ76].

H. Van der Wee, "Structural Changes and Specialization in the Industry of the Southern Netherlands, 1100–1600," in *EHR*, 2nd ser., 28 (1975) 203–21 [FJ77].

R. Van Uytven, "The Fulling Mill: Dynamic of the Revolution in Industrial Attitudes," in *Acta historiae neerlandica* 5 (1971) 1–14 [FJ78].

R. Van Uytven, "Technique, productivité et production au moyen âge: Le cas de la draperie urbaine aux Pays-bas," in *Produttività e tecnologie nei secoli XII–XVII*, ed. S. Mariotti (1981) 283–94 [FJ79].

P. Walton, "Textiles," in *English Medieval Industries: Craftsmen, Techniques, Products*, ed. J. Blair and N. Ramsay (1991) 319–54 [FJ80].

J.-B. Weckerlin, *Le drap "escarlate" au moyen âge: Essai sur l'étymologie et la signification du mot écarlate et notes techniques sur la fabrication de ce drap de laine au moyen âge* (1905) [FJ81].

J.P. Wild, *Textile Manufacture in the Northern Roman Provinces* (1970) [FJ82].

K. Zangger, *Contribution à la terminologie des tissus en ancien français attestés dans les textes français, provençaux, italiens, espagnols, allemands et latins* (1945) [FJ83].

See also other articles published in the journal *Textile History* [*TH*] (Newton Abbot, Devon, England, 1968–) [FJ84].

# FK • MINING AND ORE PROCESSING

BY PAMELA O. LONG

The mining and processing of ores—especially iron, copper, tin, lead, silver, and gold—were widespread in medieval Europe and involved primarily local operations. The most important mining areas, especially after the mining revival of the eleventh and twelfth centuries, included tin mines in Cornwall and Devon and lead mines in the Mendips in England; copper, tin, and silver mines in the Spanish Meseta; lead-zinc mines in the Ardennes in France; silver and lead mines (with some copper) in the Harz mountains in central Germany; copper mines in Mansfeld in the eastern (lower) Harz and in Sweden; silver mines in Saxony, Bohemia, Kutnà Hora, and Slovakia; and silver-lead, mercury, and gold mines in the eastern Alps and the Balkans. Iron mining was widely distributed throughout Western Europe; coal mining became significant in the medieval period only in the thirteenth century in the Lowlands, England, and northern Italy. (See [FK2–3], [FK8–12], [FK25–26], [FK29], [FK33], [FK36], and [FK39]).

Ore processing took place near the mine. Until the thirteenth century, most ores were obtained by quarrying or digging caves that extended only a few feet below the surface. Shaft mining became important in the thirteenth century in Central Europe, where it was utilized to obtain silver-bearing ores. Water drainage became a problem as depth increased. After the ore was brought to the surface, it was broken, washed, and crushed. Smelting (a heating process in which the ore reacts with the fuel) was carried out nearby in a hearth or furnace. Furnaces and forges, often equipped with bellows, were also utilized, especially in iron ore processing. In the extraction of silver from argentiferous lead ore, the ore was washed, broken and crushed, then smelted. Argentiferous lead was then oxidized in a cupelling hearth to remove the lead or litharge. The silver was refined further in another heating process ([FK4–5] and [FK9–13]). Mining declined from the mid-fourteenth until the mid-fifteenth century, at which time a central European mine boom began. This led to new forms of organization, new technologies, and the development of a mining literature ([FK9], [FK37]). For Latin terminology, the most important of the new writings were the treatises of Georg Agricola [FK14–17].

Although there is little evidence of continuous mining between the ancient and medieval eras, the basic Latin terminology of mining and ore processing was established in antiquity and can be found in a number of ancient treatises. Since the Romans took over Hellenistic mines and adopted much Greek terminology, Greek as well as Latin writings are relevant to the development of Latin terminology. The most significant writings from classical antiquity include the *Meteorologica*, bk. 4 (by Aristotle? or perhaps Straton); the *De lapidibus* of Theophrastus; Pliny the Elder's *Naturalis historia* [FK19], the most important Classical Latin source; and the third-century collections of Greek craft recipes known as the Leiden and Stockholm papyri [FK21]. Other ancient writers such as Strabo (*Geography*, 3.2.8–10) and Polybius (*Histories*, 34.9.8–11) occasionally discuss mining. Dioscorides's treatment of minerals in his *De materia medica* became an important source of terminology for Georg Agricola's *Bermannus* in the sixteenth century ([FK14], [FK31]).

The medieval period did not produce treatises on mining or ore processing, although some craft recipes and other kinds of writings contain evidence for these topics. These texts include lapidaries (see [FK18] and ch. EJ); the *Mappae clavicula* [FK22–23], a compilation of craft recipes dating from the ninth century, which Halleux and Meyvaert have shown to be related to Greek alchemical writings, including the Leiden and Stockholm papyri [FK32]; the *De diversis artibus* (c. 1126) of Theophilus [FK24]; and the writings of Albertus Magnus (d. 1280) on mineralogy [FK18]. Other important written evidence includes archival sources such as accounts, cartularies, notarial records, mining regulations, and laws ([FK2], [FK8], [FK20], [FK25–27], [FK35], [FK38–39], [FK42]). Yet most of what we know about medieval mining comes from archaeology rather than texts. Medieval mining consisted of local operations performed by people who would not necessarily have been literate and did not know Latin. Vergani has shown that the immigration of German miners into northern Italy and the Veneto in the twelfth and thirteenth centuries and thereafter influenced the development of technical vocabulary in Italy. This largely concerned vernacular transmission, although Latin was influenced as well. For example, the term *werkus* (*werchus, vercus, guercus, guelcus*), signifying miner and/or metalworker, comes from the German *werck* ([FK42] p59).

Medieval Latin was an impoverished language as far as the technical vocabulary of mining and ore processing was concerned. This general dearth of specialized terminology caused the humanist and physician Georg Agricola (1494–1555) to coin many new terms in the sixteenth century. His treatises are fundamental to a study of the Latin terminology of mining and ore processing. Agricola was particularly concerned with the development of technical vocabulary, and his *De re metallica* [FK16–17], with its detailed descriptions, labeled illustrations, and Latin glossary, is an essential source for the student of Latin mining vocabulary. Agricola lived, however, at a time of great change in mining and processing technology. The medievalist must be careful to determine whether he is describing a traditional process or a new one.

Medieval Latin vocabulary concerning mining and ore processing encompasses geological features such as veins, the mine and the miner, ores and other substances, tools and machines, and ore processing. This terminology cannot be understood without some knowledge of the processes being described and of the medieval conceptual framework of geology and geological substances. Existing Latin sources were usually not written by or for working miners and ore processors, and they therefore often do not contain sufficient detail to instruct practitioners or to inform modern historians about exactly how something was done. Careful knowledge of traditional mining and ore processing techniques makes the technical vocabulary more accessible, but familiarity with ancient terminology is also essential.

## Veins and Stringers

One of the meanings of *vena* in Classical Latin is "a vein of metal or ore." Agricola elaborated upon this by coining terms descriptively: *vena profunda* = fissure vein; *vena dilatata* = bedded deposit; *vena cumulata* = stockwork or impregnation; *fibra* (in Classical Latin, a section or segment of anything divided by fissures) = stringer; *canales* = fissures in the rock; *commissurae saxorum* = seams or joints; *interventum* = space between two veins; *origo* and *finis* = beginning and end of a vein from a horizontal point of view, left to right; *caput* and *cauda* = head and tail or top and bottom of a vein from a vertical point of view. (See [FK17] pp43–76.)

## The Mine, Ore Extraction, and the Miner

French cartularies call an iron mine *ferraria, mineria ferri,* or *minerium ferri;* its excavation is termed *fossa mine, foviculum,* or *terra fodienda;* the ore is *ferrum* and *mina ferri.* Verbs used for extraction were *trahere, extrahere miniam, fodire,* and *effodere* ([FK35] p19). A Venetian privilege of 1442 gives someone the right to mine— *fodere sive foderi facere* ([FK38] p349). (In Classical Latin *fodio, fodere* is a mixed conjugation verb with passive infinitive *fodi.* Note the change to the fourth conjugation [*fodire*] in the French example, and to the second [passive *foderi*] in the Venetian example.) Menant cites Lombard documents referring to extractions made from a gallery, *foramen* or *medallum* ([FK39] p783). Miners, ore processors, and those who bought and sold the products of mining were usually different people. In a letter of 1198 (the first extant document of the stannaries), William de Wrotham, first royal warden of the tin mines of Devon and Cornwall, distinguished the diggers, *foditores;* the buyers of black tin (i.e. tin ore that has been dressed and crushed but not smelted), *nigri stagni emptores;* smelters, *de stagno primi fusores;* and merchants of smelted tin, *de stagno primae funturae mercatores* ([FK36] p235, [FK33] p51).

## Substances

An introduction to the complex subject of the nomenclature of substances is available in the works listed in the bibliography, as well as in ch. EJ. This nomenclature reflected the classification scheme being used. Albertus ([FK18], [FK40]) divided substances into metals (*metalla, materia metallorum*), stones (*lapides*), and intermediates (*quae media [sunt] inter naturas lapidum et metallorum*). Agricola [FK15] separated "simple minerals" into earths (*terrae*), solidified juices (*succi*), stones (*lapides*), metals (*metalla*), and mixed minerals (*mixta*). The studies of Robert Halleux [FK30–31] are the best guides to the changing meanings of the term *metallum* in Greek and in Classical and Medieval Latin.

Before Agricola, ores and alloys were often not distinguished in terminology from purer metals. There were, for example, two Classical Latin terms for copper, *aes* and *cyprum* (from the island of Cyprus, the location of famous copper mines). In antiquity, *aes* usually meant bronze, a copper-tin alloy, but many old bronzes contain lead, and the Romans also used this term for brass, a copper-zinc alloy. *Aes Corinthium* was thought to be an alloy of copper, gold, and silver. The Classical Latin world *orichalcum* (or *aurichalcum*) meant "mountain copper," a metal resembling gold, or it could mean brass or a similar alloy. In medieval writings, *aes* and *cyprum* (or *cuprum*) were often used interchangeably to indicate copper and a variety of its alloys. However, for a metal that is clearly copper (*quod alii "ciprum" vocant*), some recipes (e.g. nos. 6 and 7) in the *Mappae clavicula* [FK22–23] use the term *batracium metallicum,* the adjective deriving ultimately from the Greek word for "frog" and referring here to the metal's green color. In recipes 117 and 124 of the same collection, the term *caucucecaumenum* appears; this is a Latin transliteration of the Greek *chalkos kekaumenos* (roasted copper) and refers to a copper oxide. (See [FK23] pp44–45, nn68, 73.) In recipes 3.66–67, Theophilus uses *aes* as brass not freed from lead and *auricalcum* as brass purified from lead that will be gilded. He uses the term *aeramentum* for copper and any of its alloys in his instructions concerning bell founding (3.85). (See [FK24], [FK41] pp320–21). Agricola developed a number of more specific terms for copper compounds. (See [FK18] pp221–23; [FK22–23]; [FK41] pp320–21; [FK17] p109; and [FK19] v2:25–39, 159–71.)

### Furnaces, Forges, Tools, and Machines

Recipe 119 of the *Mappae clavicula* uses *calidum* for a furnace, the usual word being the Classical Latin *fornax*. French cartularies refer to the forge as *fabrica* and *forgia*. There is also *furnellum* for a furnace ([FK35] p20). A thirteenth-century document concerned with silver mining in Trent mentions the *rotae . . . cum uno furno,* referring to the use of water wheels to operate the bellows of a smeltering furnace ([FK26] p753, [FK20] p19). Some documents distinguish between a *furnum,* a furnace that produces iron, *ferrum crudum,* and a *fucina* that produces steel (*ferrum coctum*) ([FK39] p784). Agricola [FK16], especially in bk. 6, vastly expanded the terminology for tools and machines and included many labeled illustrations. For example, the first to fourth iron implements (*ferramentum primum, ferramentum secundum,* etc.), the wedge (*cuneus*), the iron block (*lamina*), and iron plate (*bractea*) are illustrated, as are various types of crowbars, picks, shovels, buckets, carts, and lifting machines for ore and water removal. Processing apparatus discussed by Agricola includes the assay furnace (*fornacula*), blast furnace (*prima fornax*), cupellation furnace (*secunda fornax*), crucible (*catillus triangularis*), and muffle (*tegula*). (See [FK17] p150–51, n2, and pp219–22, n1.) In bk. 8, he also described machines for crushing and washing ore [FK16].

### Ore Processing

"Roasting" in modern terminology is *mittere in ignem* in Medieval Latin. An ore that is smelted is "cooked," *coquitur.* French documents describe iron ore processing as *facere ferrum,* as in the expression *ad ferrum faciendum.* Also used are *coquere ferrum* and *sufflare* ([FK35] p20). Braunstein cites thirteenth-century documents that refer to *fabrice* (works near the mine for processing ore and metals) that are further defined by the stage of production: *de minis* refers to the reduction of the ore in the furnace and *de massis* to hammering the product into bricks or bars, while *de patellis* refers to making the final products such as pans ([FK26] p753). Ore smelting and separation are treated in detail by Agricola ([FK16], bks. 9–11), who for these and other topics developed a far more extensive descriptive Latin vocabulary than had previously been available.

# Select Bibliography

## Bibliography

P.M. Molloy, *The History of Metal Mining and Metallurgy: An Annotated Bibliography* (1986) [FK1].

## General Guides

P. Benoit and P. Braunstein, eds., *Mines, carrières, et métallurgie dans la France médiévale: Actes du colloque de Paris, 19, 20, 21 juin 1980* (1983): many articles in this collection discuss Latin archival sources in France relevant to mining and ore processing [FK2].

K. Blaschke and G. Heilfurth, "Bergbau," in *LM* 1:1946–51 [FK3].

C.N. Bromehead, "Mining and Quarrying to the Seventeenth Century," in *HTech* 2:1–40 [FK4].

R.J. Forbes, "Metallurgy," in *HTech* 2:41–80 [FK5].

R.J. Forbes, *Metallurgy in Antiquity: A Notebook for Archaeologists and Technologists* (1950) [FK6].

J.F. Healy, *Mining and Metallurgy in the Greek and Roman World* (1978) [FK7].

W. Kroker and E. Westermann, eds., *Montanwirtschaft Mitteleuropas vom 12. bis 17. Jahrhundert: Stand, Wege und Aufgaben der Forschung*, Der Anschnitt, Beiheft 2 (1984): an outstanding collection of specialized studies [FK8].

J.U. Nef, "Mining and Metallurgy in Medieval Civilisation," in *The Cambridge Economic History of Europe*, v2: *Trade and Industry in the Middle Ages*, 2nd ed., ed. M.M. Postan and E. Miller (1987) 691–761, 933–40: remains one of the best short summaries of medieval and late medieval mining [FK9].

N.J.G. Pounds, "Mining," in *DMA* 8:397–404 [FK10].

R. Sprandel, *Das Eisengewerbe im Mittelalter* (1968): the standard study of medieval iron mining and ore processing [FK11].

L. Suhling, *Aufschliessen, Gewinnen und Fördern: Geschichte des Bergbaus* (1983): covers antiquity to the modern period but with much material on medieval and late medieval mining and ore processing [FK12].

R.F. Tylecote, *The Early History of Metallurgy in Europe* (1987): the best general treatment of the technology of early metallurgy [FK13].

## Primary Works and Translations

Georg Agricola, *Bermannus sive de re metallica*, ed. and tr. R. Halleux and A. Yans (1990): an edition with French translation, bibliography, and useful index of Latin words; first published in 1530, this work is a dialogue in which the interlocutors discuss regional ores and those mentioned in ancient writings [FK14].

Georg Agricola, *De natura fossilium libri X* (Basel 1546); tr. M.C. and J.A. Bandy, The Geological Society of America Special Paper 63 (1955), with Latin mineral index (pp225–32): this treatise on mineralogy includes a classification of minerals and theories of origin [FK15].

Georg Agricola, *De re metallica libri XII* (Basel 1556, r1967): the most important early source for mining and ore processing, this work contains an extensive Latin-

German glossary [FK16]; tr. H.C. Hoover and L.H. Hoover (1912, r1950): the result of collaboration between a mining engineer and a latinist, with notes containing many Latin-English glossaries derived from the glossary in the Latin text [FK17].

Albertus Magnus, *De mineralibus* [*Mineralium libri quinque*], in *Opera omnia*, ed. A. Borgnet, 38 vols. (1890–99), v5:1–103; tr. D. Wyckoff (1967): the notes and translation by a geologist and latinist provide an expert commentary; a Latin-English glossary of minerals and rocks and a list of ancient and medieval lapidaries are included [FK18].

K.C. Bailey, ed. and tr., *The Elder Pliny's Chapters on Chemical Subjects,* 2 vols. (1929–32): the best edition for these topics, with numerous notes concerning terminology [FK19].

D. Hägermann and K.-H. Ludwig, *Europäisches Montanwesen im Hochmittelalter: Das Trienter Bergrecht, 1185–1214* (1986): the Latin text of the mining law of Trent, with German translation, extensive commentary, and Latin-German glossary [FK20].

R. Halleux, ed., *Les alchimistes grecs*, v1: *Papyrus de Leyde. Papyrus de Stockholm. Fragments de recettes* (1981) [FK21].

*Mappae clavicula*, ed. T. Phillips, in *Archaeologia* 32 (1847) 183–244: a collection of technical recipes, including some about ore processing [FK22]; *Mappae Clavicula: A Little Key to the World of Medieval Techniques,* tr. C.S. Smith and J.G. Hawthorne, in *TAPhS*, n.s., 64.4 (1974): the translation is accompanied by notes that provide a useful commentary on technical terminology [FK23]. See also [FI9–11].

Theophilus, *DDA:* standard edition of the most important medieval treatise on the technical arts, with some ore processing recipes; the English translation has valuable notes concerning techniques and terminology [FK24].

## Studies

P. Braunstein, "Les entreprises minières en Vénétie au XVe siècle," in *Mélanges d'archéologie et d'histoire de l'École française de Rome 77* (1965) 529–607: by a leading scholar of medieval French and Italian mining; appendices list archival documents and reproduce some Latin examples [FK25].

P. Braunstein, "Les forges champenoises de la comtesse de Flandre (1372–1404)," in *Annales* 42 (1987) 747–67 [FK26].

P. Braunstein, "Le travail minier au moyen âge d'après les sources réglementaires," in *Le travail au moyen âge: Une approche interdisciplinaire: Actes du colloque international de Louvain-la-Neuve, 21–23 mai 1987,* ed. J. Hamesse and C. Muraille-Samaran (1990) 329–38: a good introduction to the sources for medieval European mining laws and regulations [FK27].

N.F. George, "Albertus and Chemical Technology in a Time of Transition," in *AMS* 235–61 [FK28].

J.W. Gough, *The Mines of Mendip*, rev. ed. (1967) [FK29].

R. Halleux, *Le problème des métaux dans la science antique* (1974–) [FK30].

R. Halleux, "Le *Bermannus* de Georg Agricola et la réinterprétation du vocabulaire minéralogique," in *DHVS* 4 (1983) 81–95 [FK31].

R. Halleux and P. Meyvaert, "Les origines de la *Mappae Clavicula*," in *AHDL* 62 (1987) 7–58 [FK32].

J. Hatcher, *English Tin Production and Trade before 1550* (1973) [FK33].

J.F. Healy, "Pliny on Mineralogy and Metals," in *Science in the Early Roman Empire: Pliny the Elder, His Sources and Influence,* ed. R. French and F. Greenaway (1986) 111–46 [FK34].

S. Lauzanne, "L'apport des cartulaires à l'histoire des mines, des carrières et de la métallurgie dans la France du Nord-Est," in [FK2], pp17–30: includes discussion of Latin documents and vocabulary [FK35].

G.R. Lewis, *The Stannaries: A Study of the Medieval Tin Miners of Cornwall and Devon* (1908, r1965): although this study is outdated in certain respects, its appendices provide transcriptions of Latin documents, including charters and a letter (1198) written by the royal warden, William de Wrotham, concerning the tin mines and their workers [FK36].

P.O. Long, "The Openness of Knowledge: An Ideal and Its Context in 16th Century Writings on Mining and Metallurgy," in *TC* 32 (1991) 318–55: includes bibliography for medieval mining and metallurgy [FK37].

G. Mandich, "Privilegi minerari e agricoli a Venezia nel sec. XV," in *Rivista di diritto industriale* 7.1 (1958) 327–58: includes transcriptions of Latin documents [FK38].

F. Menant, "Pour une histoire médiévale de l'entreprise minière en Lombardie," in *Annales* 42 (1987) 779–96: includes bibliography of relevant archival documents [FK39].

J.M. Riddle and J.A. Mulholland, "Albert on Stones and Minerals," in *AMS* 203–34 [FK40].

D.V. Thompson, "Theophilus Presbyter: Words and Meaning in Technical Translation," in *Speculum* 42 (1967) 313–39: an astute discussion of technical vocabulary [FK41].

R. Vergani, "Lessico minerario e metallurgico dell'Italia Nord-Orientale," in *Quaderni storici* 40 (1979) 54–79 [FK42].

D. Wyckoff, "Albertus Magnus on Ore Deposits," in *Isis* 49 (1958) 109–22 [FK43].

FL     ❖     # MINTING AND MONEY

BY ALAN M. STAHL

Though a universal aspect of medieval life, coinage as such received little attention from medieval authors. The *De moneta* of Nicholas Oresme [FL10], a fourteenth-century French scholastic theologian and royal adviser, is virtually the only contemporary treatise on the subject; it is concerned almost entirely with the political and fiscal aspects of minting. Information on minting techniques, the chronology and value of coin issues, and the use of coins in the economy is scattered through a wide variety of sources, of which the anthology of Jesse [FL9] reproduces a wide selection.

The law codes of the various Germanic peoples and the Carolingian capitularies are the main written sources for information on early medieval coinage. For the central Middle Ages, grants of minting rights, coinage decrees, and charters give much specific information on regional issues and their relative values. Chronicles sometimes recount coinage changes, but these accounts are often incomplete or inaccurate. Mint contracts from the later Middle Ages are an important source for the coinage process, as are guild regulations and the manuals of mint officials. Coinage treaties between minting authorities, tax and tithe records, and account books provide valuable information on the circulation of coinage.

The minting process and monetary exchange were chiefly in the hands of craftsmen and merchants, whose discourse on these subjects was in the vernacular. As Latin sources relating to these activities often involved translation by scribes and notaries, these texts frequently contain vocabulary that is derived from vernacular forms and shows regional variation. The vocabulary of minting and coin exchange presented here is drawn heavily from Italian sources, where texts documenting these activities are most detailed and were recorded in Latin through the late Middle Ages.

## Minting

For most of the Middle Ages, the mint was called simply the *moneta* in Latin, although two other words for mint—*bulganus* and *zecha*—are found in Italy in the thirteenth century. The term *moneta* had several other uses; it could refer to a coin in general or low-denomination coinage in distinction to gold coinage. A minting privilege was also called a *moneta*, as was a tax exacted in many places to compensate a ruler for forgoing a coinage debasement.

Metals usually arrived at the mint in the form of an ingot (*virga*), sometimes stamped (*bullata, sigillata*) with a mark indicating its origin. Rather than being used in their pure form, gold was often alloyed with silver for coinage and silver with copper. The alloy (*lex*) of gold was expressed in terms of the carat (commonly *caratum*, from Arabic *qīrāt*). As today, 24 carats represented pure gold; a coin of two thirds gold and one third silver in its alloy would be said to have 16 carats of gold. In a similar way, pure silver was often expressed as having 12 *denarii* of silver; each *denarius* was further divided into 24 *grana*. This system varied widely: in England the fineness of silver was expressed in terms of 12 *unciae* (ounces) each of 20 *denarii* (pennyweights), and in Germany pure silver was said to be 16 lots (*lotones*) fine. Certain standard alloys were recognized in international trade, such as the English sterling silver (*argentum esterlingum*, 92.5 percent fine), the German "lötiges Silber" (*marca usualis*, 93.75 percent fine), and the French "argent-le-roi" (*argentum regis*, 95.8 percent fine).

The alloy of gold could be determined reasonably well with a touchstone (*tocha*); the sample was rubbed against the dark stone and the color of the resulting streak was compared to a set of 24 (or 48) needles whose fineness was graduated from pure silver to pure gold. The touchstone was inadequate to determine the fineness of a silver alloy. Silver was usually subjected to an assay (*exagium, sagium, essaium*) by cupellation; the sample was melted with lead in a special vessel, the *cupella*. The pure silver drew up into a bud, while the copper joined the lead in the runoff (*callus*); the ratio of the weight of the remaining silver to that of the sample put in the vessel revealed the fineness of the original alloy.

The basic unit of weight in medieval Europe was the ounce, or *uncia*, derived from the ancient Roman unit of that name; its value varied from place to place. The ounce was divided and subdivided into units that were variously called *denarii, oboli, carata*, and *grana*. Ounces were grouped together to form a local pound, *libra*, usually from 12 to 18 ounces, and a local mark (variously *marcum, marcus*, and *marca*), usually comprising 8 ounces. Weights of most commodities were usually expressed in pounds, but the mark was the weight commonly used for gold and silver. Bullion was weighed with scales (*balanciae*) using the local mother weights (*matrices*) as standards; individual coins could be weighed with a trip balance, or *trabucha*.

A mint was usually under the direction of a master, *magister* or *massarius*, who might be a state functionary or a private entrepreneur operating under a lease or farm (*affictus*). Most mints also had a warden, an individual charged with the day-to-day operations of the mint and with monitoring the transactions of the master; these officials were given such names as *custos, gastaldus*, and *sententiator*.

Within the mint, coin metal was melted (*coctus*) by the *infunditor*, then cast (*projectus*) and hammered into sheets (*quarelli*). These were then cut into blanks or flans (*flavones*) by the *operarii* or *laborantes*. The weight of the blanks would then be checked by the *emendatores* to make sure they were within the prescribed tolerance (*remedium*); if they were overweight, they could be clipped down (*tonsi*). A *faber* forged dies (*cunia, ferri*), which were then engraved by the *intaliator*, either manually or with the use of punches (*punzones*), before being hardened. One die, the *pilla*, was fixed in the anvil and a second die, the *torsellus*, was held in the hand of the *monetarius* and struck with a hammer. The process of striking was variously referred to by the verbs *coniare, cudere*, and *percutere*.

## Coins and Money

Four words for "coin" commonly appear in Medieval Latin sources: *moneta*, *denarius*, *nummus*, and *pecunia*. *Moneta* was often used for coinage in general or a particular coinage system, while *denarius* could also refer to a particular denomination. *Nummus* generally referred to a physical object, and *pecunia* had a general connotation of wealth. In practice, the terms were often interchangeable or subject to regional usages.

Medieval coins were generally based on either gold (*aurum*, abbreviated *AV* often in ligature) or silver (*argentum*, *AR*); when only one coin of a metal was in regular circulation, it might be referred to simply as an *aureus* or *argenteus*. Coins that were mainly silver were referred to as white coinage (*moneta alba*); those with a preponderance of copper (*aes, cuprum, ramum*) were called black (*nigra*) or, more properly, billon (*billio*). Silver-based coinages were frequently debased (*vitiati*); such a change in standard (*mutatio*) could be effected either by lowering the weight of each coin or by increasing the proportion of copper to silver in the alloy.

Most medieval coinages were local in production and circulation, and specific coins were often called by the name of the issuing authority or mint town, or by a characteristic aspect of their appearance. Throughout the Middle Ages, however, some coin names arose that were used generically to refer to a denomination. In the sixth and seventh centuries, the dominant coins were the gold *solidus* and its third, the *tremissis* or *triens* (*thrymsa* in England), both derived from late Roman issues. In the course of the eighth century, silver coinage became dominant in most of Europe, usually under the name of another ancient Roman coin, the *denarius*. A gold Islamic or Byzantine coin was usually called a *mancus* in early Medieval Latin sources; later *bisancius* could refer to either. *Miliarensis* was sometimes used for an Islamic or Byzantine silver coin or a European imitation of one.

Charlemagne (c. 742–814) regularized the standards of the *denarius* in his kingdom and then empire, and this term was also applied to the English coin called in vernacular the penny. The *denarius* and the occasional half-penny (called an *obolus* or *medalia*) were the only coins regularly issued by Latin European mints from about A.D. 800 to 1200. Certain issues of pennies had an importance beyond their immediate area of circulation. The term sterling, *esterlingus*, of disputed origin, was applied to the penny of England and its many imitations, especially those of the Low Countries. Among French royal coinages, the distinction between the denier parisis, *denarius parisiensis*, and the somewhat weaker denier tournois, *denarius turonensis*, was to last into the modern period; the tournois became the model and designation for medieval pennies of other regions, including Italy and Greece. Among French seigneurial pennies, the denier provinois, *denarius proveniensis*, of the counts of Troyes and Champagne, became the basis for the denaro provisino of Rome, originally intended for use at the Champagne fairs. The denier melgorien, *denarius melgoriensis*, issued by the counts of Melgueil and then the bishops of Maguelonne, financed the commercial activity of Montpellier and became the basic coinage for southern France and adjacent areas of Spain and Italy. The pennies of le Puy were of such low fineness that pougeois, *pugensis*, became the generic term for one-quarter of a penny. The *denarii imperiales* were those issued by the imperial mints of northern Italy in the twelfth century at a standard considerably above that of local communal coinages.

The thirteenth century saw the introduction of various larger silver coins throughout most of Europe under the name *grossus* (groat in English, grosso in Italian, gros in French, Groschen in German); concurrently the old *denarii* began to be termed *parvi*. Outside purely local contexts, the term *grossus* usually bore a modifier such as *turonensis* (gros tournois) or *pragensis* (Prager Groschen). A few were not geographical: the *grossus ambrosinus* (ambrosino) was that of Milan; the *aquilinus* (aquilino) of Verona, Trent, and Tyrol; the *carlinus* (carlino) and *gigliatus* (gigliato) of Naples.

The gold *augustalis* of Frederick II (1194–1250) minted in Messina and Brindisi in 1231 was of limited circulation and duration, but the florin (*florenus*) introduced by Florence in 1252 became the linguistic as well as the metallic standard for many of the gold issues that followed. Among other gold coins were the ducat (*ducatus*) of Venice (a term earlier used for a silver coin of Sicily), the dobla (*dupla*) of Castile, the *philippus* of the Low Countries, the besant (*bisancius*) of the Latins in the Crusader states, the noble (*nobilis*) and angel (*angelus*) of England, and a number of French coins including the écu (*scutum*), the ange d'or (*angelus*), and the franc (*francus*).

As well as standardizing the circulating coinage, Charlemagne promulgated an accounting system in which 12 *denarii* were counted as a *solidus* and 20 *solidi* were counted as a *libra*, a system that survived in England as pence, shillings, and pounds until 1971. In the central Middle Ages, *solidus* and *libra* were just terms for counting, like "dozen" and "score"; only the *denarius* existed as an actual coin. Regional systems were also sometimes used for counting; in England 160 pennies were often counted as a *marca*, while the mark of Lübeck comprised 192 pennies. Other accounting systems flourished beyond the old Carolingian frontiers, including the *morabetinus* (maravedi) of account in Castile; the *uncia* of 30 *tari*, each of which had 20 *grana*, in Sicily; and the *iperperum* of Latin Greece (derived from the Byzantine hyperperon). The introduction of large silver coins often created dual systems of account: a *libra grossorum* (240 groat coins) and *libra parvorum* (240 pennies), whose relative value varied with that of the coins on which they were based. Accounting systems sometimes became even more complicated, as in the *libra grossorum ad aurum* of Venice, whose value was based on that of the gold ducat but expressed in terms of a traditional relationship of the ducat to the silver grosso.

## Select Bibliography

For the terminology of Medieval Latin numismatics three dictionaries are most helpful (though *Du Cange* is still indispensable): A.R. Frey, *A Dictionary of Numismatic Names* (1917, r1973): with glossary of terms in several languages added by M.M. Salton [FL1]; E. Martinori, *La moneta: Vocabolario generale* (1915) [FL2]; and F. von Schrötter, ed., *Wörterbuch der Münzkunde* (1930, r1970) [FL3].

The terminology and procedures of medieval minting are discussed in several articles in *Later Medieval Mints: Organisation, Administration and Techniques*, ed. N.J. Mayhew and P. Spufford, Oxford Symposium on Coinage and Monetary History 8, British Archaeological Reports, International Series 389 (1988) [FL4].

A treatise that explains and illustrates terminology is A. Luschin von Ebengreuth, *Allgemeine Münzkunde und Geldgeschichte des Mittelalters und der neueren*

*Zeit,* 2nd ed., Handbuch der mittelalterlichen und neueren Geschichte, ed. G. von Below and F. Meinecke, Abt. 4 (1926, r1969) [FL5].

For interpreting the Latin legends on coins themselves, see W. Rentzmann, *Numismatisches Legenden-Lexicon des Mittelalters und der Neuzeit,* 3 vols. in 1 (1865–78, r1969) [FL6]; F.W.A. Schlickeysen, *Erklärung der Abkürzungen auf Münzen der neueren Zeit, des Mittelalters und des Altertums, sowie auf Denkmünzen und münzartigen Zeichen,* 3rd ed., rev. R. Pallmann (1896, r1961) [FL7]; and A. Wenzel, *Auflösungen lateinischer Legenden auf Münzen und Medaillen* (1974) [FL8].

A useful, if not always totally reliable, collection of texts related to minting is W. Jesse, *Quellenbuch zur Münz- und Geldgeschichte des Mittelalters,* 2nd ed. (1924, r1983) [FL9]. The text of the major medieval treatise on coinage, as well as a few other texts, is published and translated in C. Johnson, *The De Moneta of Nicholas Oresme and English Mint Documents* (1956) [FL10].

Useful bibliographies of medieval coinage in general can be found in E. Clain-Stefanelli, *Numismatic Bibliography* (1985) [FL11], and P. Grierson, *Bibliographie numismatique,* 2nd ed. (1979) [FL12], with a topical treatment in Grierson's "Numismatics," in *MSI* 114–61 [FL13].

A valuable history of medieval money is P. Spufford, *Money and its Use in Medieval Europe* (1988) [FL14]; E. Fournial, *Histoire monétaire de l'occident médiéval* (1970), focuses primarily on France [FL15].

A concise illustrated history of medieval coinage is P. Grierson, *The Coins of Medieval Europe* (1991) [FL16]; a more detailed survey is A. Engel and R. Serrure, *Traité de numismatique du moyen âge,* 3 vols. (1891–1905) [FL17]. These should eventually be superseded by *Medieval European Coinage,* of which only v1 has appeared to date: P. Grierson and M. Blackburn, *The Early Middle Ages (5th–10th Centuries)* (1986) [FL18].

For the relative values of various coins, and summaries of the main commercial coinages, see P. Spufford, *Handbook of Medieval Exchange,* Royal Historical Society Guides and Handbooks 13 (1986) [FL19].

The most complete and accurate reference for the weights used as the basis of various medieval coinages is still A. Martini, *Manuale di metrologia* (1883, r1976) [FL20].

*See also* [BA107].

FM    •    # MILLS AND MILLING

BY JOHN MUENDEL

## Grain Mills

In Europe the earliest known name for a grain mill run by water was the Greek derivative *hydraleta*. The latinized form (*hydraletes, -ae*) appears in Vitruvius (*De architectura* 10.5.2). Generic terms such as *fabrica* were also used, but *molinum, mola aquaria,* and *farinarium, -a, -us,* became more popular. In the early ninth century, the chancellery of Louis the Pious chose *molendinum* to designate a water mill, and this became the standard term throughout Europe. In most cases, the terminology for the internal parts of these machines can only be determined for those areas of Europe where manorial accounts and notarial registers of the following centuries have been fully explored. At present, the documentation of medieval England and Italy has produced the most information relating to Latin designations for those components whose names are still not entirely known.

From the late twelfth century, the vernacular came to be used in preference to Latin to describe milling apparatus. The time of this change cannot be precisely determined, but the mixture of languages will be apparent from the technical descriptions that follow. In the notarial documents, where Latin usually predominated, the customary *molendinum* as well as Latin words with direct derivatives in Romance tongues continued to be used, but the parts of mills appear more and more frequently in vernacular forms. By the fifteenth century, the notebooks of Mariano Taccola of Siena provide excellent examples of this transformation, while occasionally presenting unusual Latin terms for the components of his frequently imaginative hydraulic machines.

The simplest grain mill was the hand mill (*mola versatilis, mola a manu, molendinum de brachiis*), which the operator turned by means of one or two handles attached to an upper concave stone rotating upon a convex stone. Vitruvius describes a grain mill run by a vertical waterwheel (*rota*) that communicated power to an upper millstone through two toothed gears (*tympani dentati*) set at right angles to one another. One gear was fixed into the waterwheel's axle so that its teeth (*dentes*) would interlock with those of the other gear stationed horizontally on the separate drive shaft. Vanes or paddles (*pinnae*) turned the wheel, while grain descended from a hopper (*infundibulum*) into the eye of the upper millstone so that it could be ground upon the grooved surface of the bedstone.

Vitruvius's mill, placed directly into the water so that its waterwheel received

497

power from below, is called an undershot mill. An overshot mill has its motive force falling on top of the wheel, usually into enclosed receptacles, so that the weight of the water acts as a propellant rather than mere impulsion. The term *molendinum coisellarium* is later used for a Norman overshot mill, and *molendinum orbicum* for a Florentine undershot mill, but these mills are not usually distinguished elsewhere by specific Latin terminology. In the documents, a waterwheel with paddles (*palae*) rather than compartments (*capixecti* in Taccola, *De ingeneis*) normally indicates an undershot type, as does a delivery system with a canal (*canalis*) of brick or stone. With mills of a few runs or gearing systems, the presence of a dam (*exclusa, sclusa*) and millpond (*stagnum, piscina, vivaria*) to direct and store waterpower will usually identify the overshot type of mill as long as it possesses the vertical waterwheel identified by the key word *rota*.

Both types are found in operation during the late empire and the early Middle Ages. The overshot variety, easily adapted to rural streams and small tributaries, survived in northern Europe throughout the medieval period, but the undershot wheel appears to have been much less common until the twelfth century. In Tuscany and, presumably, the rest of Italy north of the heel and toe, both types had simply disappeared until they were reintroduced at this time by way of France. An intermediate type, known as a breast wheel because its paddles were struck near the level of the axle, apparently operated in England during the late eleventh century and may have been common in France by the late thirteenth. At Turin, the development of an introductory flue (*caminacius*) for feeding a breast wheel could have begun in the late fourteenth century, if not before.

When the Goths cut off Rome's water supply, the Byzantine general Belisarius (d. 565) concocted a makeshift floating mill, a type that soon became prevalent on the navigable rivers of Europe. To obtain the most efficient movement from the slowly moving waters of the river, the wheel of a medieval floating mill (*molendinum navale, in navibus, ad navem*) was usually broad and set between one large boat that carried gears and millstones and a much smaller one that held the end of the axle. Moored close to shore to accommodate the delivery of grain, the whole complex could be pulled to its port (*portus*) if a barge had to pass.

Another early type, the suspension mill (*molendinum pendens, molendinum penzolum*), first appears in documents of the twelfth century. Lodged on stakes stationed in the firmest part of the riverbed, the waterwheel and gearing mechanism were located underneath the millhouse on a movable frame that was raised and lowered by hoists and held in place by jacks in accordance with the height of the water. During the fourteenth century, the waterwheel of this type of grain mill in and near Florence had at least four spokes (*razzi*). The pivots or gudgeons (*caviglozi de ferro*) of the waterwheel's axle (*stelus*) turned upon supporting blocks (*capitagni*) at each end. Surrounding the axle and the circular plates (*rotellae*) of the lantern wheel were iron bands (*cerchielli de ferro*) to give them greater strength. A crossbar or rynd (*nottola*) was attached to the top of the secondary drive shaft (usually *fusolus*) and fitted into the upper millstone so that it could turn upon the bedstone. The stones themselves were enclosed in a wooden casing (*palmentum*) and the grain fell into the eye of the upper millstone from a hopper (*tremoggia*) attached to two crossbeams (*trastones ad latus*). The millhouse (*solarium*) was placed above the paddles (*supra palas*) of the wheel. This mill apparently had two sluice gates (*cataractae*), each manipulated by a crook (*uncinocchius*). But since the frame within which the waterwheel was set had to be raised or lowered to the various levels of the river, the millhouse must have had openings for tackle. At this time in Florence, the millhouses of landed undershot grain mills, which had to adjust their wheels to the elevation of the water, possessed one opening as well as a windlass (*verricello*) with two handles or sticks (*girigami*) to turn it.

Another variety of grain mill had its waterwheel turning on a horizontal rather than a vertical plane. This wheel (*roticinus, ritrecine, rodezno*) had paddles radiating from its vertical axle (*palus ferri*), and when water, descending from a millpond via an inclined chute (*canalis*), fell upon these enclosed blades, it acted like a primitive turbine as its pivot (*puntaruolus*) turned on a bearing (*ralla*) and communicated power directly to the upper millstone. This type, originating perhaps as early as the second century B.C., may have been the progenitor of the upright shaft mill (*arubah*) that, along with its variety of forms, became dominant throughout the Mediterranean. By the second half of the fourteenth century, certain parts of the countryside of Florence had witnessed a symbiosis of the principal mechanisms of the supposedly earlier horizontal mill and the overshot type. Although the gear wheels may have been interchangeable, one plausible arrangement for the parts of the new system was this: affixed to the vertical axle of the horizontal waterwheel was a lantern gear that interacted with a horizontal crown wheel (*rubecchium*) that on its opposite side communicated with another lantern gear whose independent axle sent power to the upper millstone.

An equally dramatic development was the appearance of the vertical windmill (*molendinum ad ventum*) during the last quarter of the twelfth century on both shores of the North Sea and English Channel. Four sailyards were set upon the end of a horizontal axle that turned to provide energy through a Vitruvian gearing system to the upper millstone located below on a crown tree affixed across the central part of the fundamental framework. Because the sails had to face into the wind, the whole structure, known as a buck, was balanced by means of the crown tree on the circular bearing of a large upright post (*standardus*), so that the edifice could be rotated by a tailpole that extended out from the back of the building. The post of this vertical or "post" mill was stabilized by using either reinforced pits or submerged posts provided with horizontal cross-trees (*crosbondes, crostres*) and supportive quarter bars.

## Other Industrial Mills

Mills were designed for purposes other than the grinding of grain. Some had antecedents in the ancient world; some incorporated practical, labor-saving modifications of older devices; and some included totally new mechanisms such as toggle joints and cranks and connecting rods. A water mill used in the fulling of woolen cloth (*molendinum fullonarium, paratorium, draperium, vualcarium*), the pounding of iron blooms (*molendinum ad ferrum, fabrica ad aquam*), and the beating of rags for paper (*molendinum ad papirum*), hemp for cordage (*molendinum batatorium*), or malt for beer (*molendinum brasarium, molendinum ad grudum*) used a trip-hammer mechanism that featured a lug or cam, which, projecting from the horizontal axle of a rotating vertical waterwheel, activated strikers (*pilae, mazzi, maglii*) set horizontally or vertically. A sawmill for cutting logs (*molendinum de planchia, molendinum resseguae, sega ad aquam*) could also utilize lugs to depress a toggle joint attached to the lower end of a vertically mounted blade that moved upwards through the action of a spring pole, but a more common device for this sort of mill was the crank and connecting rod, the former being fastened directly to the end of the revolving horizontal axle. For breaking the tough outer skin of the olive or crushing the leaves of woad for the production of a dark-blue dye, an edge-runner mill (*infrantorium ad infrangendum olivas, infrantorium ad infrangendum guadum*) was set in motion. Although waterpower could drive this machine equipped with one or two broad stones turning perpendicularly within a sturdy basin, horses and humans normally propelled the horizontal axle that went through its stones and vertical drive shaft. Throughout the Middle Ages, horsepower, particularly when it was used to grind grain (*molendinum equinum, cabellarium, ad siccum*), remained a viable alternative to waterpower. In northern France, the water-powered trip hammer was employed in a mill for mashing woad (*molendinum pastellerium*), a method further indicating the variety of mechanisms that could be used in medieval Europe even to obtain one product.

## Select Bibliography

### Primary Works

#### (a) Unpublished Documents

Archivio di Stato di Firenze, Notarile antecosimiano, A435, fol. 11v (11 December 1317) [FM1], and R145, fol. 129r (6 March 1300) [FM2]: these entries lack full detail, but nonetheless present basic information regarding both types of *infrantorii*.

Archivio di Stato di Firenze, Notarile antecosimiano, R348, fols. 333r–v (27 May 1325): contains a tabulation of the essential parts of a fulling mill [FM3].

#### (b) Editions

J. Muendel, "The 'French' Mill in Medieval Tuscany," in *JMH* 10 (1984) 215–47, at 241–43: includes complete appraisals of a suspension mill with two runs (Archivio di Stato di Firenze, Notarile antecosimiano, P566), two landed undershot mills, and another suspension mill located near Florence; also contains illustrations of different types of water mills taken from the notebooks of Mariano Taccola (1419–33), Francesco di Giorgio Martini (1489), and Agostino Ramelli (1588) [FM4].

J. Muendel, "The Horizontal Mills of Medieval Pistoia," in *TC* 15 (1974) 194–225, at 215–16 and 224, n105: provides assessments of a horizontal mill and a *fabrica ad aquam* [FM5].

F.D. Prager and G. Scaglia, *Mariano Taccola and His Book De ingeneis* (1972): contains an edition and translation of this treatise composed between 1419 and 1433 [FM6].

Vitruvius, *De architectura*, ed. F.S. Granger, 2 vols. (1931, r1983): includes (v2:304, 306) his description of a water mill for grinding grain [FM7].

## Dictionaries and Glossaries

*Du Cange:* see *faricellus–farinum* and *mola–mollegium* [FM8].

L. Durand-Vaugaron, "Technologie et terminologie du moulin à eau en Bretagne," *Annales de Bretagne* 76.2/3 (1969) 285–353: clearly distinguishes (pp306–10) the *molendinum coisellarium* as a water mill with an overshot wheel [FM9].

H.G. Gengler, *Deutsche Stadtrechts-Alterthümer* (1882) 225–56: provides what amounts to a glossary of Latin and German terms relating to the mills of medieval Germany [FM10].

A. Jespersen and E.G. Loeber, "Terminologia molinologiae," in *Transactions of the Second International Symposium on Molinology* (1971) 195–210: introduces a means for developing a dictionary of molinology [FM11].

*Novum glossarium* ([CD24]): see *mola–mollendinum* [FM12].

## Studies

P. Aebischer, "Les denominations du 'moulin' dans les chartes italiennes du moyen âge," in *ALMA* 7 (1932) 49–109 [FM13].

M.-A. Arnould, "Les moulins en Hainaut au moyen âge," in *Produttività e tecnologie nei secoli XII–XVII: Atti della "terza Settimana di Studio" dell'Istituto internazionale di storia economica "F. Datini"* (23–29 April 1971), ed. S. Mariotti (1981) 183–99: covers Hainaut as well as its neighbors in northern France [FM14].

A.-M. Bautier, "Les plus anciennes mentions de moulins hydrauliques industriels et de moulins à vent," in *Bulletin philologique et historique (jusqu'à 1610) du comité des travaux historiques et scientifiques* 2 (1960) 567–626 [FM15].

B.B. Blaine, "The Application of Water-Power to Industry during the Middle Ages" (Ph.D. diss., University of California, Los Angeles, 1966): furnishes useful information on the derivation of molinological terms, including (p73, n139) the possible origins of the word *cam* from the Latin *camba* [FM16].

G. Bracco, ed., *Acque, ruote e mulini a Torino,* 2 vols. (1988): Latin/Italian terminology for the parts of mills and evidence for the development of the breast wheel are found in the contributions of G. Alliaud, M.T. Bonardi, R. Comba, A. Dal Verme, and V. Marchis [FM17].

A. Chédeville, *Chartres et ses campagnes (XIe–XIIIe siècles)* (1973): makes a clear terminological distinction between the *farinarii* of the Carolingian period and the *molendina* that appear after 950 (pp194–55) [FM18].

M. Dembińska, *Przetwórstwo zbożowe w Polsce średniowiecznej (X–XIV wiek)* (1973): distinguishes, through a close examination of Latin texts, the variety of mills that became prevalent in Poland during the thirteenth and fourteenth centuries; includes summary in French (pp261–67) [FM19].

A.G. Drachmann, *Ancient Oil Mills and Presses* (1932): provides an excellent textual analysis of the subject, which, through archaeological remains, extends into the Middle Ages [FM20].

B. Gille, "Le moulin à eau: Une révolution technique médiévale," in *Techniques et civilisations* 3 (1951) 1–8: believes that a breast wheel is depicted in a sketch drawn in the *Veil Rentier* of Jehan de Pamele-Audenarde (c. 1275) [FM21].

R. Holt, *The Mills of Medieval England* (1988): presents a thorough analysis of the archival materials relating to English mills run by water, wind, and horses [FM22].

W. Horn, "Water Power and the Plan of St. Gall," in *JMH* 1.3 (1975) 219–57: suggests, through interpretation of Latin texts, that the water-driven trip hammer (*pila*) was an integral part of the Benedictine monastic economy during the seventh century [FM23].

A. Lanconelli and R.L. De Palma, *Terra, acque e lavoro nella Viterbo medievale* (1992): excellent Latin transcriptions (pp63–71) that mention the parts of the hydraulic grain mills of Viterbo between 1336 and 1365 [FM24].

J. Langdon, "The Birth and Demise of a Medieval Windmill," in *History of Technology* 14 (1992) 54–76: provides a case history of a post mill at Turweston in Buckinghamshire, England, during the early fourteenth century; in a valuable app. detailing the costs of constructing the mill in 1302–3, items such as the tailpole (*tayltre*) and the beam in which runs the secondary drive shaft (*fusillus*) are estimated [FM25].

J. Muendel, "The Internal Functions of a 14th-Century Florentine Flour Factory," in *TC* 32 (1991) 498–520 [FM26].

J. Muendel, "Medieval Urban Renewal: The Communal Mills of the City of Florence, 1351–1382," in *Journal of Urban History* 17 (1991) 363–89: presents a history of the urban mills of medieval Florence and includes texts dealing with floating mills and their relationship to *portus* [FM27].

J. Muendel, "The Mountain Men of the Casentino during the Late Middle Ages," in *STMS* 29–70: includes a comparison between an Italian term used for a crank (*manfaro*) in a sawmill and the Latin expression for the same device (*manubreus ferreus*) in a grindstone [FM28].

J.P. Oleson, *Greek and Roman Mechanical Water-Lifting Devices: The History of a Technology* (1984): supplies full texts and analyses relating to the hydraulic wheels and pumps of antiquity [FM29].

A. Sáenz de Santa Maria, *Molinos hidráulicos en el valle alto del Ebro (s. IX–VX)* (1985) [FM30].

Ö. Wikander, "Mill-Channels, Weirs and Ponds: The Environment of Ancient Water-Mills," in *Opuscula Romana* 15 (1985) 149–54: offers the solutions devised for the proper delivery of water to landed undershot and overshot wheels with excellent documentary evidence as late as the eleventh century [FM31].

# PART THREE

# G-H · VARIETIES OF MEDIEVAL LATIN LITERATURE

## GA · TOWARDS A HISTORY OF MEDIEVAL LATIN LITERATURE

BY JAN M. ZIOLKOWSKI

Imagine that you could assemble an exhaustive library, either parchment, paper, or digitized, of all medieval literature. If you took *Beowulf* and the rest of Old English verse and prose; if you collected the *Song of Roland* and other chansons de geste, the oeuvre of Chrétien de Troyes and all other romances, and every other surviving Old French work; if you generated a complete corpus of Old Norse sagas; if you had at your disposal Dante and each line of Italian poetry and prose from the Middle Ages; and if you amassed the same material written in every other mother tongue of medieval Western Europe—in sum, if you mustered before you every single word that has come down to the present day in a medieval vernacular language—what you would possess would occupy little space in proportion to what was composed in Latin during the same period and is extant. Yet the abundance of Medieval Latin in comparison with the medieval vernacular literatures remains generally unappreciated, because most handbooks and surveys of medieval literature (and, even sadder to say, most teachers of medieval literature) deal with Medieval Latin either not at all or only marginally. Apart from a few notable exceptions from around the turn of the twentieth century, guides to literatures such as Old English and Old High German have begun only very recently to incorporate Medieval Latin to any meaningful degree.

Medieval Latin literature deserves wonderment not only for its sheer quantity but also for its unusual and attractive qualities. Despite a slow-dying prejudice that during the postclassical period the classical language degenerated into a kind of "kitchen Latin," little of Medieval Latin language deserves to be caricatured as degraded in this way. Medieval Latin was not just a hard-won language of instruction, frequently correct (though not by rigidly Classical Latin standards), occasionally elegant, and sometimes even beautiful. Nor was it solely or even primarily the language of monks. Rather, it functioned as a medium of communication in many environments. It served as a language of record keeping, religion, and entertainment not only among monks, clerics, and students but also among courtiers (royal, noble, papal, and episcopal), diplomats, travelers, and merchants. Its literature covered a broad spectrum that ranged, in both content and style, from the most conservatively classicizing to the most freely innovating, from the most pious to the most irreverent.

In one sense, this literature is connected intimately with all other Western European literatures of the Middle Ages and Renaissance. Latin and its literature provided a means—a lingua franca, if the oxymoron and anachronism may be permitted!— that enabled the Christianized peoples of Western Europe to transcend the localism of many different languages and dialects, and to form a true "European Community" *avant la lettre*. They contributed so substantially to the cultures and subcultures of Europe that Medieval Latin has been termed "the mother-tongue of western civilization" ([GA62] p62, [GA53] p104, [GA64] pp51 and 64 n2). Indeed, Latin and the texts written in it played a leading role in endowing all the vernacular literatures with a common store of vocabulary, rhetoric, images, and much more that persists even to this day. Medieval literature in Latin enhanced the unity of later European vernacular literatures—especially but not exclusively later Romance literatures—because Latin masters and students disseminated compositional techniques and materials throughout Western Europe. The literatures of medieval Europe could not have been literatures in the etymological sense of the word—could not have been written—without the presence of clerics and clerical culture; and this clericization was by definition a latinization, since to be latinate, literate, and clerical were closely related states. As a consequence, when the medieval writers of Western Europe referred to their shared culture, they could resort to the restricted linguistico-cultural universalism of the phrase *tota latinitas* rather than to the geographical designation *Europa* ([GA64] p51, [GA58] pp69–72). Although from today's global and multicultural perspective Europe forms only one of many regions and cultures on earth, to those authors the world meant mainly the *orbis latinus*. Thus it is important to be sensitive to the complex, and sometimes fruitful, diglossia that prevailed in many locales. Particularly in the twelfth century, the learned language of Latin coexisted not merely peaceably but even prosperously with the spoken languages.

In another sense, Medieval Latin literature stands alone because of features that differentiate it from all other European languages of the Middle Ages. Whereas the vernaculars were living tongues that took centuries to become fully literary, Latin was not entirely live—even though it was anything but dead. How should this unusual second language be described? The literary corpus written in Latin has had the dubious distinction of being likened to a corpse, the hair and nails of which continue to grow after death ([GA66] p44, [GA59] p51 n5). Other similes equate it with flowers that have been transplanted from their native habitat but that nonetheless continue to bloom, or with a caged animal that has been trained to perform stunts but sometimes shows flashes of its former feral vitality ([GA61] p64, [GA59] p51 n5, [GA70] p30 n26). It has also been characterized as "one of those timeless elemental spirits, perhaps gnomes under the earth or even a female water spirit which in secret commerce with a chosen man obtains real, living children" ([GA67] p57, quoted in [GA70] p30 n25). For all their vividness, such comparisons cast only faint light on the unique temper of Medieval Latin language and literature.

The best way to conceive of Latin in the Middle Ages may be as a *father tongue*. This description conveys Latin's special quality as a language spoken by no one as a mother tongue. Furthermore, it hints at the status of Latin as a mainly male language, since most of the people who had the opportunity to learn Latin were boys and men (more likely to be figurative Fathers in the Church than flesh-and-blood *patresfamilias*) who occupied posts within a strongly patriarchal system. This is not to say that Medieval Latin was restricted solely to reading and writing, since the Latin used in churches, courts, schools, and universities was oral as well as written, and the language was still unquestionably entitled to be considered a tongue (*lingua*) because of the frequency with which it was spoken. For example, the Latin Quarter in Paris earned its name because within this precinct Latin acted as the main channel of both oral and written communication.

Then again, the best way to appreciate the special circumstances of Latin in the Middle Ages may be to cease compartmentalizing languages binarily into the dead, such as ancient Greek and Latin, and the living, such as Modern English and Spanish. Many linguistic milieus are distinguished by a different arrangement, one that is commonly termed *cultural diglossia* [GA71]. Although analogies could be drawn to various phases in the history of Greek, Hebrew, or Sanskrit, probably the closest parallel in the present-day world to the situation of Latin in medieval Europe is found in Islamic countries. For instance, in many areas of northern Africa and Asia Minor daily life goes on in a spoken form of Arabic that coexists with an ancient scriptural version of the language that remains essential in religion, diplomacy, law, education, and other types of formal communication. Like Latin in the Middle Ages, Classical Arabic is a scriptural language that must be learned for the fulfillment of religious observances. In this language treaties are written and textbooks produced. Thus colloquial Arabic is a living but not fully literary language, whereas Classical Arabic is literary but not entirely living. Furthermore, between the two extremes of the most illiterate or unlearned colloquial and the most literate and learned Classical Arabic exist myriad hybrids—types of Classical Arabic that accommodate colloquial words and constructions, as well as forms of the colloquial that are peppered with classicizing features.

Latin was what could be styled a "prestige language." Picked up by no one from the cradle in household conversation, facility in Latin was a skill that was prized and admired because the language had to be mastered in schools—which is to say, in grammar schools. As a result, exposure to Latin grammar and all that it entailed, such as the authority of its texts and the technology of its books, was held in such reverence that *grammatica* took on almost magical allure to lay people. In Old French the noun *gramaire* came to designate an astrologer, a magician, and even a magic book. The mystique of the Latin word *grammatica* and of the learning that it connotes abides with us in the Scottish English derivative *glamour*.

During most of the Middle Ages, to be literate and to have acquired elementary Latin were one and the same thing. As a consequence, the literate throughout Europe (then known by the Latin word *litterati* rather than its Italian derivative, *literati*) had in common the insights and experiences of a five- to ten-year rite de passage—a grammar-school education that emphasized the close reading of set texts. From their schooling these *litterati* shared many of the same textbooks, had suffered many of the same brutal teaching techniques, and commanded the basic principles and terminology of Latin grammar. It became natural for intellectuals to employ Latin grammatical terms in metaphors, even when expressing activities as far afield from grammar as sex, and for theologians to explain the deep truths of the Christian faith on the basis of Latin grammar and its structure. The person who knew only his own language, his own idiom, was an *idiota*—an idiot ([GA71] p198).

Revered for the antiquity and authority of its literary tradition, Latin became the language of the masters—and not only the schoolmasters—in contrast to the language of the masses, the *vulgar* tongue. It constituted a code of rules that had to be learned through conscious study, rote learning, and parsing over a long period, whereas the vernacular could be absorbed without formal rules from imitation of household speech. From the vantage point of the educated, the mother tongues were subordinate to Latin in the social hierarchy, as the etymologies of the words *vernacular* (from the Latin *verna*, "a native slave") and *vulgar* (from *vulgus*, "common people") convey. Even when Dante composed sections of a treatise on the advantages of what he called the "illustrious vernacular," he elected the learned language as the vehicle in which to express his views. There is no equivalent apologia for Latin, no *De latina eloquentia* by Dante or anyone else, for the simple reason that it was not needed. The benefits of Latin remained undisputed. But like celebrities in our day, Latin had to embrace not only the advantages but also the disadvantages of its special stature and notoriety; for better or worse, it lived somewhat in isolation from everyday life.

But what exactly does the formulation *Medieval Latin literature* signify? Although defining basic and oft-used terms is usually difficult and can easily swell into a never-ending task, the project of moving towards a history of Medieval Latin literature requires at least cursory clarification of what the words *Medieval, Latin,* and *literature* are understood to mean, both individually and in combination.

The middle member of the triad *Medieval Latin literature* presents no major obstacles; for even though many readers who judge all Latin by Classical Latin norms will find shortcomings and anomalous features in Medieval Latin texts, few will question that most of these texts are indeed lexically, morphologically, and syntactically Latin rather than, say, German, Irish, or Polish. Medieval Latin texts may incorporate Greek and Hebrew words and syntax, they may attribute Christian meanings to words that were used in Classical Latin in other senses, they may juxtapose words from Old Latin and Classical Latin, and they may merge stylistic features acceptable in classical verse with those in prose; but only rarely are Medieval Latin texts recorded in an orthography or literary style that prevents them from being identified almost instantly as forms of Latin and not as dialects of even closely related tongues such as French, Occitanian, Italian, or Spanish.

Yet coming to grips with the nature and extent of Medieval Latin presupposes recognition not only of what is Latin but also—and here our problems begin in earnest—of what is medieval. However straightforward it may be to decry popular prejudices that associate what is medieval with whatever is felt to be barbaric (most notably, poor hygiene, brutal torture, rank injustice, and blind superstition), it proves to be far more complex to devise a hard-and-fast periodization of a phenomenon, or rather of phenomena, such as Medieval Latin. In the absence of decisive linguistic developments such as the replacement of simple verb tenses by compound ones or the loss of nominal, pronominal, and adjectival cases, we do not encounter the sorts of markers within texts that help us to distinguish one language from another. We have no single litmus test for discerning whether a text is written in Classical or Medieval Latin. In other words, the progression from Classical to Medieval Latin is not even so clear-cut linguistically as is that from Old to Middle English, Middle to Modern English, Old High to Middle High German, or Middle High to Modern High German. Classical Latin did not end abruptly in a given year, decade, or century, and Medieval Latin begin in the next. The one shaded into the other and, although in the Middle Ages much new vocabulary and some new syntactical features were transferred into Latin from Greek, Hebrew, and the vernacular languages, the transition from Classical to Medieval Latin resulted at least as much from cultural as from linguistic transformation. Yet however they are described, and whatever caused them, the changes run very deep and real.

For the purposes of this volume Medieval Latin is defined broadly, to facilitate tracing the trajectory of literature in genres written between 200 and 1500—encompassing at one boundary the entire period of latinity conventionally designated Late Latin and at the other end the initial part of the period known sometimes as Neo-Latin. Here a few words must be said about the standard periodization of Latin, since it can bewilder newcomers to the field, and since chronologies designed to capture the linguistic circumstances of a given language do not always suit the developmental stages of the literature written in it.

The Latin that has been taken for centuries as the touchstone against which to test all expressions of the language is Classical Latin (also known as "Golden Latin"), which is to say, the poetry and prose of the Augustan age, from 88 B.C. to A.D. 14 (sometimes designated as the "Golden Age"). Latin of the period before about 100 B.C. became bracketed as Old or Archaic Latin. Latin of the succeeding phase, from about A.D. 15, earned the tag Silver Latin, which yielded in its turn, from about 150, to Late Latin. Complicating this stratification of Latin is the acceptance that in all of these periods a deep cleft in grammar and diction sundered the formal Latin of most written records from the informal Latin of speech, among both cultured and uncultured classes. When this spoken Latin, the so-called Vulgar Latin, ceased to be Latin and when the Romance languages commenced are questions that have stirred fierce dispute.

For a long time Late Latin was defined as having existed from some time after A.D. 150 until the end of the sixth century. Rome fell in the fifth century—but did Latin topple at the same time? Recently Romance historical linguists have hotly debated the theory that the spoken languages in regions that would later become Romance-speaking (*romana lingua*) did not diverge decisively from Latin (*latina lingua*) until around 800, when Charlemagne imposed linguistic reforms. According to this new outlook, many pre-Carolingian Latin texts, when read aloud, would have remained comprehensible even to illiterate listeners whose spoken dialect was a grade of Latin or Proto-Romance [GA68–69]. Thereafter, thanks to Charlemagne, a normative *written* Latin language and style prevailed that diverged ever more from the local spoken dialects in what has come to be known as Romania. This achievement of Charlemagne's may be regarded either negatively, as having ensured that Latin and the spoken languages would go their separate ways, or positively, as having secured the internationalization of Latin by establishing it as a standard and stable language.

Of course, the situation differed markedly in regions where the native tongues were as remote from Latin as are Celtic or Germanic languages. The Irish and Anglo-Saxons had special needs when learning Latin, and they took with them their own blend of Latin, their characteristic pronunciation, and their distinctive techniques for learning the language as they traveled about on the Continent. Here Charlemagne unquestionably deserves credit, since his efforts to bring together the best and the brightest of Europe effectively guaranteed that the Latin of his reform efforts would be manufactured and exported by the finest latinists of his day: from Italy such figures as Paulinus of Aquileia (d. 802) and Peter of Pisa, from England Alcuin of York (d. 804), and from Spain Theodulf of Orléans (d. 821).

Whatever periodization of Late Latin and Medieval Latin we adopt, we must be

alert to local variations; for when the Middle Ages and Medieval Latin began and
ended varies from region to region. According to the schema that nineteenth-century
historical linguistics imposed wherever possible, languages are subsumed under the
headings Old, Middle, and Modern (corresponding to the *Alt-, Mittel-,* and *Neu-* of
the German terminology that set the standard). This template fails to respond to the
peculiarities of Latin, a language that has been used continuously for two and a half
millennia in stunningly diverse circumstances. Seen from a postclassical vantage,
Old Latin, Classical Latin, Silver Latin, and Late Latin all occupied bands in one
swath of a continuum—the swath in which the language was still unquestionably living. Since the awakenings of Italian humanism in about 1300 A.D., Renaissance writers claimed to have revived the aesthetics of the Classical section of this phase, and
hence in English their Latin has come to be called Neo-Latin. (By an unfortunate coincidence, in various other languages the same adjective denotes the Romance languages.) If Neo-Latin is accepted as corresponding roughly to the modern form of a
spoken language, then the millennium or so that intervened between Classical Latin
and Neo-Latin could be called Middle Latin—and in German it has commonly been
designated *Mittellatein* or *Mittellateinisch* since Jacob Grimm used the term in 1838
([GA56] pviii, [GA70] p24 n2), in Italian regularly *Mediolatino,* and in French increasingly *Médiolatin;* but this term cannot be applied to the unique situation of
Latin without awkwardnesses, not the least of which is the illogicality of having
Middle Latin *follow* rather than precede Late Latin. In English the ungainlinesses of
the designation *Middle Latin* have been circumvented happily by the use of the term
*Medieval Latin,* although the tendency until recently to employ the adjective in the
lowercase—medieval Latin—has obscured the separate identity of the literature and
culture preserved in this stage of the language.

The Latin Middle Ages as they are here conceived extend from the earliest of
many dates that have been selected to fix the beginning of Medieval Latin to the latest that have demarcated its end. A few examples will demonstrate the periodizations
that have been formulated in previous literary histories. In one influential anatomy
of Medieval Latin literary history that was intended for the consumption of Romance
philologists, Gustav Gröber envisaged the literature as spanning a period from the
middle of the sixth century through the middle of the fourteenth. In the three-
volume *Geschichte der lateinischen Literatur des Mittelalters* that remains a standard
reference work, Max Manitius took as his two termini the middle of the sixth century and the close of the twelfth. In *A History of Later Latin Literature* F.A. Wright
and T.A. Sinclair surveyed the somewhat longer sweep from the middle of the fourth
century through 1321, at which point they located the origins of Renaissance Latin.
In four volumes on the Latin literature of the Middle Ages J. De Ghellinck took as his
purview the epoch from around 500 to the end of the twelfth century. F.J.E. Raby's
*History of Secular Latin Poetry in the Middle Ages* begins in the fourth century and
concludes in the twelfth, apart from occasional forays into the thirteenth. The most
ambitious of one-person undertakings is Franz Brunhölzl's *Geschichte der lateinischen Literatur des Mittelalters,* still in progress, which is designed to comprehend the
entire period from the sixth century through the fifteenth.

Authors who have ventured briefer surveys of Medieval Latin language and literature have taken a more panoramic view of the chronology. Maurice Hélin and
Karl Langosch defined Medieval Latin as a language that lived for an entire millennium, from 500 to 1500. In so doing they shared the motivation of those anthologists

to whom the impressive symmetry of a thousand years has proven irresistible as a principle of organization: F.E. Harrison chose for his readers the thousand years from 374 to 1374, while K.P. Harrington implied a dating from 476 to c. 1476. Hélin's motive for choosing 500 as his point of departure was the practical desire to start where most reference works on Classical Latin literature stopped short. Langosch—who in circumscribing Medieval Latin between 500 and 1500 adhered to the policy of the influential *MGH*, which is both a publication series and the research institute that publishes it—was quick to concede that features of Medieval Latin can be discerned both earlier and later than these dates ([GA19] pp8–9). Both Hélin and Langosch emphasized especially that early Christian Latin belongs more properly with Medieval Latin than with Classical Latin—an opinion implicitly shared by the editor of the standard Latin-English dictionary for scholars, the *OLD*; for he not only set out to cover Latin only through A.D. 200 but even deliberately *excluded* Christian Latin from consideration! A similar predisposition to equate Christian Latin with Medieval Latin underlies the decision of F.J.E. Raby to take into account all early texts in his *History of Christian Latin Poetry*, which runs from the third through the fifteenth century.

Just as Medieval Latin has too often been considered in isolation from Late Latin, many histories are arranged so as to taper off at 1200 or so, paying little or no heed to the subsequent period. This schematization highlights the twelfth century as culminating a train of renascences that leads in turn to the true Renaissance. According to this construction, Latin literature from the sixth through the late eighth century is transitional—caught between late antiquity and the Middle Ages. The ninth century, when Charlemagne and his successors oversaw a renewal that consolidated Europe culturally (as well as politically), deserves to be labeled a renaissance, namely, the Carolingian Renaissance. The tenth and early eleventh century witness the undoing of the Carolingian Renaissance—a time somewhat similar to the upheaval that preceded Charlemagne, although Germany and northern Italy participate in a cultural revival that has been called the Ottonian Renaissance. But the real renaissance of the Latin Middle Ages is the so-called twelfth-century Renaissance, which extends from the late eleventh through the early thirteenth century. An unspoken assumption behind chronological frameworks that have the Latin Middle Ages rise to a crescendo in the twelfth century and then suddenly trail off in a diminuendo may be that the phase between 1200 and whatever year is taken as the onset of the Renaissance and Neo-Latin (it scarcely matters whether one chooses a cutoff date of 1300, 1321, or 1374) is to be shunned. Because Scholasticism provoked the wrath of the humanists, the Middle Ages have often been tarred with the same brush: they have been perceived as being not only ante- but even unwittingly anti-Renaissance. Overemphasis upon renascences or renaissances creates the misimpression that the Middle Ages were no more than an alternation between barbarism and classicizing renewals that gradually paved the way for the one true renewal, the Renaissance.

Even if an agreement can be reached on the meaning of Medieval Latin, a further obstacle looms; and indeed *literature* may pose the thorniest intractabilities of the three elements in the formulation *Medieval Latin Literature*. Various earlier attempts to produce histories of Medieval Latin literature have been indiscriminate in their understanding of literature, since they have assumed that anything written—whether historical, didactic, moral-theological, belletristic, or other—qualifies as literature. Because of the sheer quantity of extant Medieval Latin texts, such all-inclusiveness is impracticable. *Literature* is not simply a collective noun denoting all texts. At the risk of seeming pedantic, the concept literature must be sharpened, but without allowing the definition to become overly restrictive or rigid.

The realities of present-day presuppositions about literature must be weighed carefully against the realities of the Medieval Latin texts that survive, for critics in the nineteenth and twentieth centuries, especially in the New World, have been strongly inclined to equate literature with belles lettres in general and love lyric in particular, even though such texts represent only a fraction of extant Medieval Latin writings. Even when taking a broader outlook, Anglo-American critics have been predisposed until recently to define literature as encompassing little beyond prose fiction, drama, and most poetry. Such a framework would have seemed bizarre to many in the Middle Ages. In this guide literature is understood to include not only poetry, and not only what could be regarded as "imaginative" or "creative" writing such as fables, but also some other genres that could be designated as practical or informative. In the case of proverbs, rhetoric, sermons, and *pastoralia,* we run across forms that played major roles in shaping verbal expression in the Latin Middle Ages. If we turn to encyclopedias and translations, we find types of writing that conveyed the information and knowledge underlying many other genres.

Biography, hagiography, and travel literature, which might be judged more meaningfully to fall within the realm of historical sources, have been included, because the distinction between fiction and nonfiction that has been drawn so readily in modern libraries and curricula did not hold the same importance in the Middle Ages. These genres are narrative. At the same time other sorts of historiography, such as annals and chronicles, have not been accorded separate subsections. Many literary critics and somewhat fewer historians have recently shown a penchant for treating historiographic texts—regardless of their value as historical sources—as rhetorical or literary constructions, just as they have demonstrated an equally strong proclivity for explicating literary texts as the products of historically determined ideologies. Although both tendencies can be justified in many individual instances, it is neither feasible nor desirable to accept all medieval texts written in Latin as literature. In addition, it is worth bearing in mind that the inclusion of a given genre in this guide to Medieval Latin literature does not presume that the texts in that genre were understood to be fictitious when they were written and read in the Middle Ages.

Apart from the complicated—and sometimes arbitrary—divide between history and literature, we must somehow stake out a boundary or even an array of boundaries between the vast zone of theology and religion on the one hand and that of literature on the other, but without falling into the old trap of drawing a rigid line between religious and secular in domains where such a delineation reflects present-day rather than medieval thinking. Thus the following essays could pay heed to Alan of Lille (d. 1202/3) for his poems and his art of preaching but not for his theology, or to Thomas Aquinas (d. 1274) for his poems but not for his *Summa theologica.*

It would be disingenuous not to admit that the desire for circumscribing the term *literature* arises in part from the daunting expanse of the corpus that must be charted and characterized. To this point the chronological spread of Medieval Latin has been stressed, but its geographical diffusion also calls for attention. What should be appreciated as not just the language or the literature of Medieval Latin but the very culture of Medieval Latin permeated wherever the Western Church exerted its influence. It is a wonderful paradox that the dismemberment of the Roman Empire did not see the collapse of the imperial language. Although the spoken dialects of Latin in what had been the Latin half of the Roman Empire gradually went their own ways under the pressure of linguistic changes caused—or accelerated—by the barbarian invasions of the fifth and sixth centuries, the written language of Latin that had seemed poised to break apart during the Merovingian era was revitalized and unified under Charlemagne and his successors. This renewal was facilitated by the reedition of the main Latin texts to which students and scholars were exposed, so that their knowledge of correct vocabulary, morphology, and orthography was reinforced rather than subverted. In other words, the Carolingian *renovatio* was fostered through a normalization of texts and teaching; and the norm was a form of Latin as it had been promulgated in Classical and Late Latin texts, such as Virgil's *Aeneid,* the *Distichs of Cato,* the fables of Avianus and "Romulus," and the Vulgate Bible as revised under the direction of Theodulf, Alcuin, and their successors. This Carolingian norm of Latin constituted the basis of most later Medieval Latin.

Latin was the vehicle for the study not only of grammar (the art of speaking and writing correctly) but also of rhetoric (the art of persuasion) and logic (the art of distinguishing truth and falsehood). Although the equilibrium among these three disciplines shifted constantly throughout the Middle Ages, all three verbal arts remained linked with each other in a triad known as the trivium. The trivium was fundamental to the formation of an educated person. Though these three arts of discourse were associated with elementary education, they had not yet come to be demeaned as *trivial,* and studying them for years was never deemed a trivial pursuit. Indeed, they demanded much more of the time and effort lavished upon education than did the quadrivium of arithmetic, geometry, astronomy, and music to which the trivium was purportedly propaedeutic. All seven of the liberal arts were purveyed through Latin textbooks and teaching, as was theology, the branch of knowledge toward which they were supposed to be preliminary.

In the Middle Ages Latin suffused throughout Western Christendom—Latin Christendom—not merely Romania (by which is meant particularly present-day Italy, France, parts of Belgium, Spain, Portugal, and Rumania), not merely continental Germanic regions (particularly Germany, Austria, Denmark, Netherlands, and parts of Belgium), but also the Scandinavian peninsula and islands west of continental Europe that were inhabited by, among others, Germanic and Celtic peoples (such as England, Wales, and Scotland; Ireland; and Iceland). Even this list is incomplete, since into the Latin orbit eventually gravitated Slavic and Baltic Catholic regions to the east and south (such as Poland, Bohemia, and the Dalmatian coast), areas settled by speakers of non-Indo-European languages who came under the sway of Latin Christendom (e.g. Hungary, Finland, and Estonia), and territories in Spain and Italy wrested from Muslims and Greek Orthodox. Finally, Latin would not have been unknown in the Crusader settlements in the eastern Mediterranean ([GA19] pp8–9).

Of course, to superimpose today's national boundaries upon the Middle Ages would be anachronistic under the best of circumstances, but it is especially so when the topic under observation is Medieval Latin. The national literatures of Europe have tended to grow up around urban centers: for instance, London and Paris occupy special places in English and French literature, respectively. But Medieval Latin must be visualized differently. It can be viewed as having come into its own through decentralization, after Rome and the western sector of its empire fragmented. Alternatively, it can be understood as having remained centered upon Rome, but upon Rome as the seat of a church rather than as the capital city of an empire. In either case, it must not be confused with *national* languages or literatures as we know them. Whether we conceive of Medieval Latin as postnational (coming into its own after the fall of the Roman Empire), prenational (holding sway before the nations of early modern Europe emerged), international, or supranational, we must not misconstrue it as a national language and literature, for it was nothing of the sort.

However we choose to regard the geography and ethnography of Medieval Latin, we must always recall that the language served numerous audiences throughout Western Europe, primarily in modest-sized communities such as monasteries, cathedrals, episcopal and archiepiscopal courts, or noble and imperial courts, but sometimes in larger assemblies such as the papal curia or universities, and sometimes in such modest and isolated locales as the cells of hermits or anchorites and the schoolrooms of small towns.

The profusion of literature from this chronologically and geographically extensive language and culture is overwhelming. Contemplate a few of the main corpora of published texts: the ambitious series *Patrologia Latina* [*PL*] published by J.-P. Migne totals 222 volumes and covers theological and other writings from the second century to about 1216; the *Monumenta Germaniae Historica* [*MGH*] comprises hundreds of works, many of them literary or theological, and many of them Germanic rather than, strictly speaking, German; the *Corpus Scriptorum Ecclesiasticorum Latinorum* [*CSEL*] amounts to about 90 volumes; the *Series Latina* [*CCSL*] and its *Continuatio Mediaevalis* [*CCCM*] of the *Corpus Christianorum* contain more than 250; and the *Analecta Hymnica* [*AH*] of Guido Maria Dreves and Clemens Blume reached 55. Heaving even a single tome of the *Acta Sanctorum* [*AASS*] from the shelf is a weighty moment, but eyeing the run of hagiographical texts as it now stands—even though it has not yet reached completion after 350 years of collective toil by the Bollandists—is still more daunting. Even the guides to such corpora, the so-called handbooks, are sometimes herniatingly heavy and numerous: representative are the six volumes of Ulysse Chevalier's *Repertorium Hymnologicum* (and Clemens Blume's *Repertorium repertorii,* which offers a guide to Chevalier's guide!); Dieter Schaller and Ewald Könsgen's incipitarium, *Initia carminum latinorum saeculo undecimo antiquiorum;* and Friedrich Stegmüller's 11-volume *Repertorium biblicum.*

In addition to works that made the transition from medieval script to modern print, attention must be paid to what has remained only in manuscript until the present. Through reports in the newspapers and other media the general public has become familiar with finds of documents such as the Dead Sea Scrolls, and perhaps has even come to recognize the length of time that experts require as they seek to digest the meanings of such troves and to disseminate their insights. Yet most people remain unaware of the multifarious fields—alongside Medieval Latin studies could be set countless other small specializations that depend upon documents carved into stone, clay tablets, papyrus, parchment, paper, and dozens of other materials—where many texts survive in time-worn and partially illegible media that cannot even be adequately catalogued, let alone understood, except by specialists. Nor is the world outside universities and other research communities alone in its incomprehension of the challenges inherent in working with old manuscripts. Many people have no notion of what editing a manuscript entails, in contradistinction to editing a collection of essays or a novel. The activities differ so much as to warrant the introduction of separate verbs. Even professors who are not personally acquainted with the editorial process sometimes need to be alerted to the great distance, not to mention the bloodshot eyes and overtaxed minds, that lies between the discovery or identification of an unedited document and the eventual publication of a serviceable edition. Finally, few people are aware of the heated controversies that swirl around the enterprise of editing—controversies that take us to the very heart of philosophical questions about how we can be true to the past while mediating it to the present.

Though it would be foolhardy to hazard any estimate, no one who has delved extensively into Medieval Latin literature will deny that the number of critically edited texts pales beside the multitude of works that has either not been edited according to scholarly principles or never been edited at all. And although rapid strides are being made these days, partly as a result of the increasing availability of digitized incipitaria, the tally of unidentified texts still in manuscript remains high, especially for the period after 1200. Finally, it must also be mentioned that, however much literature is still extant—whether identified or not—much that is known to have existed in the Middle Ages has disappeared. A little of what has perished can be reconstructed if only sketchily on the basis of what has survived, some is known at least by title or other vague references, some will be recognized and recovered in due course, but much has vanished altogether forever.

The extent of the literary remains has caused would-be literary historians many perplexities. The sheer bulk of works and pages to be perused would outstrip the capacities of even a sizable *équipe* of dedicated scholars; and how are the texts to be interpreted, so as to make them meaningful and attractive to the largest possible audience without oversimplifying or misrepresenting them? At this juncture arises the question of determining priorities. If Medieval Latin literature forces us to engage in a kind of triage, the first step has been the tacit establishment of the literary canon or canons that will merit study and discussion. This process has necessarily entailed the equally tacit construction of an anticanon of texts that will not be accorded the same hallowed status—the same canonization.

Where should Medieval Latin be placed in the curriculum, which texts should be read, and how should they be read? Especially since the Romantic era, the national literary histories of many individual European countries have benefited from the energies of innumerable researchers and from the support not only of universities and academies but also of governments, banks, and other institutions committed to fostering awareness of local heritages and of the relationship of present-day European cultures to earlier ones. When the study of national literary history reached the Middle Ages, it concentrated upon medieval forms of the national vernacular language in question. Latin was sometimes welcomed because of the light it shed on a given vernacular literature or on the history of a given locale. For this reason, the menu of texts to be read and studied in Germany, France, Italy, and England varied greatly. The diversity of choices appears plainly in the ways in which series of texts (such as the *Rolls Series* [*RSer*] in England or the *MGH* in Germany) were formulated, since they were launched deliberately as national or ethnic enterprises. The same motivations underpin the national or ethnic Latin dictionaries, which have progressed far more rapidly than have the corresponding attempts to produce pan-European dictionaries of Medieval Latin. The realization of a pan-European dictionary has been impeded not only by the unmanageable scope of such a project but also by the difficulty of organizing and funding a team directed to a goal that over-steps modern-day frontiers.

Such choices have of course affected the contours of Medieval Latin in lexica and handbooks of literary history, since such reference works are usually devoted to specific national languages or regions of Europe. Often Medieval Latin has been quarantined to a subsection within manuals devoted to a vernacular literature, such as Old High German or Old English, or to the history of a specific geographic-ethnic region ([GA40], [GA43], [GA44], [GA51]). Sometimes it has been treated on its own but refracted through the optic of a single geographic region ([GA9], [GA14], [GA49]). Few and far between have been general literary histories of medieval Europe into which Medieval Latin has been closely integrated (e.g. [GA8]).

Because Medieval Latin literature has often been apprehended through the filter of vernacular literatures, many of the most intensely studied texts are those that have been regarded as Latin reworkings of poems or stories that had circulated originally in vernacular languages. Also seen through especially favorable lenses have been those Latin texts that are known to have influenced vernacular literature. Many of these texts would provoke enlightening interpretations if analyzed using the methods of folkloristics; some would be clarified if studied according to the theory of oral composition ([GA101], [GA103]). Regrettably, medieval latinists have been as resistant to experimentation with such methods and theories as folklorists have been to exploration of evidence that has received the consummately literary dress that is almost ubiquitous in Medieval Latin texts.

For instance, the ninth- or tenth-century heroic epic *Waltharius* is rightfully esteemed as precious because, although composed in Latin, it belongs to a very small class of early Germanic epic lays or epics such as *Beowulf*. Furthermore, it provides us with our fullest evidence in any language of the hero Walter of Aquitaine, whose legend is otherwise familiar only from snippets in medieval Germanic languages such as Old English and Middle High German. Or, to take another famous example, the *Gesta Danorum* of Saxo Grammaticus (fl. 1185–1205), which has earned increasing respect for its own literary attainments, first drew notice because it helped to illuminate otherwise dark corners of Scandinavian history and literature; it offers Latin versions of poems and sagas attested in Old Norse—and the earliest treatment of the Hamlet story.

The stuff of romance was recorded at length in writing first in Latin and only later in the vernaculars. Because many basic materials of Arthurian romance were made known and accessible through Geoffrey of Monmouth's mid-twelfth-century prose text, his *Historia regum Britanniae* is commonly assigned in courses on medieval romance. The spirit of romance is also evident in many ways in the late eleventh-century *Ruodlieb*, but because its hero does not belong to the Arthurian cycle it has yet to receive its due of attention outside the remote circuit of Medieval Latin studies. All of these texts have attracted notice in part because of their utility in mapping the transmigration of tales and legends that earned niches in later vernacular literature.

The eleventh-century *Ecbasis captivi* and twelfth-century *Ysengrimus* (often ascribed to one Nivard of Ghent) have been granted special stature because of the belief that they afford glimpses of animal trickster stories about the fox that circulated in the vernacular languages but have been lost. The *Ysengrimus* has the additional distinctions not only of having anticipated but even of having influenced the Old

French fox stories. It should not be forgotten that Renard the Fox, the character whose popularity supplanted from French the usual word for fox (*goupil*) and replaced it with his own name (*renart*), is attested in Latin securely before his début in French literature. Both the *Ecbasis captivi* and *Ysengrimus* are remarkable poems in their own right, the *Ecbasis captivi* for the intricacy of its quotation from earlier Latin literature, the *Ysengrimus* for the complexity of its structure and the polish of its verse and rhetoric.

Animal trickster stories were not the only folktales to be absorbed into Latin; the eleventh and twelfth centuries witnessed a heightened willingness to give written form to stories that circulated orally. For instance, the eleventh-century *Unibos* gives us our earliest version of a tale that became most famous in written literature in the fairy tales of Hans Christian Andersen as "Little Claus and Big Claus"; and the roughly contemporary *Fecunda ratis* of Egbert of Liège contains a short story that records a kernel of what developed later into "Little Red Riding Hood." Whereas the eleventh-century authors seem to have tapped only hesitantly into oral folktales that were familiar to them from local storytelling, twelfth-century and later authors sometimes turned with enthusiasm to tales that arrived from the East; one possible latinization of such Oriental material would be the *Asinarius,* an anonymous version of a fairy tale that the Brothers Grimm later incorporated into their collection of *Kinder- und Hausmärchen,* and another would be John of Alta Silva's *Dolopathos,* a very early European adaptation of the frame-tale narrative structure that we associate first and foremost with Scheherazade (Shahrazad) and the *Thousand and One Nights.*

Although sifting Medieval Latin literature to uncover evidence of sources in folktales or parallels to vernacular literature helps to understand one subset of texts, a larger group of Medieval Latin texts will be illuminated by attending to their relationship to the words and acts in which Christianity expressed itself in the Middle Ages. Here we must bear in mind that although none of the Bible was composed originally in Latin, in Western Christendom Latin acquired the unchallenged status of a scriptural language. It was enshrined alongside Hebrew and Greek as one of the *tres linguae sacrae* ("three sacred languages"). The Bible itself was an imposing work, not only spiritually but also physically: without the thin "Bible paper" that is now available, it was copied most often in a multivolume format. Small wonder that the word *bibliotheca,* which usually meant a library, could be used without qualification to signify the Bible.

The commitment to the Bible and the concept of the three sacred languages encouraged occasional exegetes to what is now termed "Christian Hebraism," which is to say, they consulted Jewish experts on the Torah or even studied Hebrew themselves. Long after Jerome undertook systematic study of Semitic languages so as to piece together a more reliable Latin version of the Bible than had existed before him, Christian exegetes sought to solve imbroglios in biblical interpretation through exploration of the Hebrew language and Jewish scholarly resources. To take one exceptional group of Christians who went beyond the customary lip service to the ideal of the three sacred languages, late twelfth-century scholars at the school of St. Victor in Paris seem to have engaged in serious study of Hebrew language and texts.

Despite its preeminence the Bible was only one of the pillars upon which medieval Christian culture rested. Much that is characteristic of Medieval Latin derives from the wedding of Latin literary culture with Christianity, which found verbal expression not only in the various forms of the Latin Bible and the exegetic writings that burgeoned around them but also in canon law, saints' lives, liturgy, hymns, tropes, and sequences, sermons, and computus. In large part it is the infusion of scriptural and ecclesiastic elements into the language and culture that distances Medieval Latin from both Classical Latin and Neo-Latin.

Sometimes the liturgy was directly responsible for literary developments. For instance, the signal achievement of extant tenth- and early eleventh-century Latin lyric poetry (to judge from the surviving body of poems) was the gradual coordination of the musical and the verbal in melodies and texts that embellished the liturgy. In the succeeding period this matching of text and melody ascends to unprecedented heights. The sequences of Adam of St. Victor (d. c. 1180) have received nearly universal praise for qualities that offer evidence of the interpenetration of Christian genres. Besides a formal perfection in their wedding of words and music, the sequences have an intricate content that draws upon the mystical theology of Adam's fellow Victorine monks, Hugh (d. 1141) and Richard (d. 1173).

The effects of Christianity reached far beyond overtly Christian art forms. For example, it would be foolish to approach Medieval Latin love lyric without paying heed to the language, atmosphere, and dramatic situation of the *Song of Songs*. The marvelous eleventh-century collection of religious and secular poetry that goes by the title of *Cambridge Songs* anticipates later collections such as the *Carmina burana* in blending Ovidian features with the *Song of Songs* in the presentation of love. This blending stands out most spectacularly in the so-called *Inuitatio amicae* (incipit "Iam, dulcis amica"), which eight centuries later evoked beautiful resonances from Baudelaire in the "Invitation au voyage."

Interesting and even enlightening lists could be drawn up of Latin texts that stand in a special relation to a particular personage in the Bible. To single out only one of untold possible examples, the prophet Jonah not only elicited masterpieces of exegesis such as Jerome's *Commentary on Jonah* but also played a leading role in Letaldus of Micy's short narrative on a man swallowed by a whale and the Archpoet's "confessional" lyric with the incipit "Fama tuba dante." In short, the conception of Christian Latin poetry is a valid and even ineluctable route by which to approach much Medieval Latin literature, so long as it does not force us into anachronistic dichotomies between "Christian" and "secular" that would not have occurred to people in the Middle Ages. Although the Church had its share of hermits, on the whole even its unworldliest institutions had ties to the outside world; and in turn the outside world was bound to be touched by the rituals and songs of the Church, which must have seemed impressively elaborate and sophisticated to common folk who had no resources or traditions for such entertainment. From a practical point of view, the participation of the Christian Church in the maintenance of Latin culture during the Middle Ages must not be understated: the Church alone afforded the institutional continuity that enabled Latin texts, classical as well as medieval, to survive to our day.

If one criterion for making a selection from Medieval Latin literature is relevance to vernacular literature and another is indebtedness to Christian literature, a third—and even older—touchstone is its proximity to classical literature. In large measure thanks to the resilience of the Latin language and its literary culture, the Romanization of Europe continued long after the Romans themselves had ceased to be. Because of the influence that Roman literature exercised upon Medieval Latin literary culture, it is possible to identify those Medieval Latin texts that served as vehicles for the transmission and reception of classical texts and style.

In appraising the classical tradition and its influence in the Latin Middle Ages we must bear in mind that medieval readers encountered in their curricula and had at their disposal in their libraries a different and somewhat more restricted range of classical texts than we do today. Very little Greek literature had been translated into Latin before knowledge of Greek declined precipitously in late antiquity in the West. Some compositions in Classical Latin that have secured canonical status since the Renaissance were barely known or even altogether unknown in the Middle Ages. To name just three prominent examples, such was the fate endured by the lyric poetry of Catullus, the *Satyricon* of Petronius, and the *Golden Ass* of Apuleius. Other works that enjoy a relatively low standing in our day, such as the fables of Avianus, the distichs of Cato, or the *Ilias latina,* were read almost everywhere as one stage in a pupil's initial training in Latin. To single out a further divergence from our own experience, Terence was a favorite, whereas Plautus endured near total disregard. Lucan and Statius were regarded more positively than they have been until recent times.

Other classical works had a wide readership in one part of the Middle Ages and not in another: relevant examples of this circumstance would be Cicero, many of whose writings became steadily better known and sought out from the tenth century, and Lucretius, whose reception followed the diametrically opposite trajectory. Even their profile of individual authors differed strongly from ours: for most of the Middle Ages Horace was extolled primarily as an ethicist who wrote *Satires* ("Orazio satiro" as Dante called him) rather than as the lyric poet who left the *Odes* and *Epodes.* Ovid, although sometimes repudiated, was often redeemed as a closet moralist whose poetry hid ethical verities behind allegorical veils that moralizing interpretation lifted in the so-called *Ovidius moralizatus;* a little less frequently he was co-opted as a role model by medieval poets who had been exiled or who had suffered other political mishaps. In some eyes Virgil became a precocious Christian, in others a cross between a sage and a shaman.

Although many Classical Latin texts prompted imitations and adaptations, none was more influential than Virgil's *Aeneid.* The Troy story exercised a seemingly irresistible magnetism upon the educated classes and nobility of Western Europe, who often sought—as had the Romans—to attach their lineage, however fantastically and tenuously, to that of the Trojans. The *Aeneid* lived: all of it was studied and explicated, important scenes were reproduced in many forms of art, and especially emotional episodes were set to music and performed. This fascination for the Troy story never loomed larger than in the twelfth century, when Joseph of Exeter wrote his *De bello Troiano*—and when the Old French *romans d'antiquité,* such as the *Eneas,* gained prominence. Another cycle of stories revolved around Alexander the Great. The foremost Medieval Latin contribution to the cycle was an epic by Walter of Châtillon, the *Alexandreis.* Once again, equivalent interest can be traced in the vernacular, where we find the *Roman d'Alexandre.*

Special attention to such clusters of Medieval Latin texts is appropriate, so long as it does not lead to the reductive outlook that Medieval Latin literature was nothing more than the projection of Classical and Late Latin literature into the Middle Ages. At issue is the separate identity of Latin in the Middle Ages—whether it should be bracketed as merely the medieval reflex of Classical Latin language and literature or whether it should be accorded full standing as Medieval Latin. Each of the two views—and the attendant antinomy between continuity and discontinuity—has been clearly enunciated in handbooks: contrast the statement "The Latin of the Middle Ages is the continuation of the scholarly and literary Latin of the late empire" ([GA23] p14) with the declaration "Medieval Latin literature is not merely the continuation of Latin literature beyond antiquity" ([GA17] p5). How are we to reconcile such apparently unreconcilable convictions?

Long periods in the history of European literature, and of European literary history, can be presented as quests to recover—or fabricate—roots in the Greco-Roman past. In the Renaissance this search for classical roots led to the defamation of the Middle Ages as an era of decadence and of Medieval Latin language as a degeneration from the ideal—the impure Latin of the Middle Ages was contrasted to the pure Latin of the Augustan age, which the Renaissance imagined itself able to reinstate if only it repudiated the monkish decay of the Middle Ages. Thus in the Renaissance Medieval Latin literature was gradually stricken from the syllabi of schools and universities and stripped from the shelves of the Latin-educated elite, and the grammar and rhetoric that had functioned as the norm for centuries were slowly but surely supplanted by new ones.

Even today Medieval Latin language and literature still suffer from the aftermath of the prejudices that led to their banishment during the Renaissance. Disappointingly, many professors of vernacular literatures find a convenient rationale for not studying Latin—and for not having their students do so—by overstating the divides between Latin and vernacular, religious and secular, and learned and popular. Furthermore, students and scholars of Medieval Latin language and literature remain afflicted by a schizophrenia: sometimes they focus their studies upon the light the literature sheds on vernacular languages and literatures, sometimes upon the materials and insights it proffers to those engrossed mainly in the classical tradition. Much valuable work has accumulated on the role of Medieval Latin in delivering the classical "deposit" to future debtors, or account managers, such as ourselves. Alongside individual studies of "the classical tradition," "the classical heritage," and "classical scholarship," there have been team projects to graph the transmission of classical texts from antiquity to the present day and to chart the glosses, commentaries, paraphrases, translations, epitomes, and florilegia that have grown up around those same texts. Finally, a similar impulse motivated E.R. Curtius not only to coin the expression *Latin Middle Ages* but also (and what is even more important) to write what has become the most enduring study of premodern literature and intellectual culture published in the twentieth century: *European Literature and the Latin Middle Ages* [GA75].

One way to avoid the anachronism and partiality of drawing up a canon on the basis of vernacular-Latin or classical-medieval relations would be to establish one reflecting medieval rather than modern tastes. For instance, various canons could be created by consulting prescriptive booklists and tracking the most frequently copied medieval texts—the "best-sellers," as it were. The flaw in such an approach is that it would lead to the selection of the most-used school texts, such as the so-called *Libri catoniani* or *Auctores octo morales*. Texts in these class books in the early Middle Ages include Arator, Juvencus, Prosper, Prudentius, Sedulius, Boethius, Avianus, Maximian, and Theodulus. If we seek out comparable best-selling textbooks in the later Middle Ages, we meet such varied texts as the twelfth-century romantic comedy *Pamphilus*—a short work so often copied by itself as a brochure-like manuscript that it left its mark in the word *pamphlet*—and Walter of Châtillon's magnificent hexameter epic *Alexandreis*. Yet, despite the excellence of the last two texts, compilations of this sort have never coincided fully with the best or most outstanding compositions of any given age.

All of the possible canons—the national-ethnic ones (which are closely related to the vernacular), the classicizing ones, and the medievalizing ones—make sense so long as we acknowledge that every list can be only selective; and even if we fused the contents of all the canons, the total would fail to comprehend all the works that have won the affection and admiration of many modern readers. Here it pays to save a place, not for sheer randomness, but for what might be called informed connoisseurship—an acknowledgment that, by virtue of having been written at the wrong time or distributed inadequately, a true work of art may not have had the great success or influence it otherwise deserved until many long years after its creation ([GA49] pp4–5). To make this case in very different terms, it is paramount not to let the virtues of a comparative approach—comparing a Medieval Latin work with Judeo-Christian literature, Classical literature, vernacular literature, or any of the infinite possible interpenetrations of the three—blind us to the artistry of the Medieval Latin work in its own right. Both approaches have their virtues.

To study the incorporation of elements from one text within another has long held the fascination of readers, regardless of whether they have envisioned the process as "sources and influences" (as English describes the much-maligned and misunderstood undertaking of *Quellenforschung*), quotation, citation, allusion, reference, adaptation, imitation or "intertextuality." But attention to this incorporation will never answer all the questions that a text can raise, since even within so profoundly textual a culture as the Latin Middle Ages texts were not spawned by other texts but by authors; and many forces conspire to create a work of art. Therefore we need to ponder what is known of the authors and of their contexts, namely, the coteries and historical circumstances in which they operated. Looking at the situation from a different vantage point, and using the language currently in vogue in poststructuralist literary theory, we ought to understand the text in terms of the different codes and discourses operative within it.

Some genres of Medieval Latin literature have rightly been appraised as patchworks of earlier texts; to name but two (besides centos) we could instance the anthology and the *florilegium*. Yet much exists that is more alive than any quilt stitched out of previous literature could be. We would err grievously if we convinced ourselves that signs of true life and energy in Medieval Latin were all lifted from somewhere else—as if Medieval Latin authors were Dr. Frankensteins, suturing together their corpus from the spoils of a literary graverobbing. To employ a happier metaphor drawn from twentieth-century literary theory, Medieval Latin texts allow us to hear many of the *voices* that resonated among the literate in the Middle Ages: among many others in the polyphony we would have to mention the local or folkloric, the learned or classicizing, and the doctrinal or Christianizing.

The commonplace in our century of the literary masterpiece that becomes famous only after the author's death, when it is uncovered in a dusty old trunk, can occasionally prove true of medieval works. Such is the case with the anonymous eleventh-century *Ruodlieb*, which survived into the print era only fragmentarily, for the most part in strips recovered from the bindings of other medieval manuscripts. Many Medieval Latin poems await only the right social climate, an able translator and interpreter, and an affordable medium of publication if they are to earn again, or finally, the attention to which their merits entitle them.

Perhaps the most formidable stumbling block that Medieval Latin literature in general and Medieval Latin poetry in particular must overcome before they receive openminded evaluation is the raw prejudice that many people, even very educated and intelligent people, have against texts not written in a vernacular. When the composer Richard Wagner, in the essay "Jews and Music," advanced the claim that people cannot write true poetry in a language not their own, he revealed an assumption that would be regarded rightly as anti-Semitic when applied to European Jewish writers in many earlier eras but that would not raise eyebrows when made of post-classical Latin writers. If Petrarch is remembered for his sonnets and not for his *Africa,* and Dante for the *Commedia* and not for his Latin eclogues, one explanation could be that their writings in the medieval father tongue are cut off—or are now felt to be cut off—from the intense access to language and emotion that is automatic in the mother tongue. And if the plight of Latin compositions by Petrarch and Dante is acute, imagine the misfortune of Medieval Latin masterpieces by authors who have no standing as vernacular poets. What chance do these Medieval Latin *magna opera* have of ever being apotheosized into the pantheon of *Weltliteratur*—or, to state the case less grandiosely, into Penguin Classics?

In at least one fundamental sense composing a guide to a literature as extensive as Medieval Latin and aspiring to take into account canons (whether medieval or modern) are mismatched activities: a guide can be sensibly divided so as to proceed genre by genre, but canons are not always structured with such literary-critical self-consciousness. Indeed, medieval taxonomies of literature often seem as odd and quaint to today's readers as do the bestiaries that class bees among the birds. To cite two examples of such classificatory systems as they are enunciated in the medieval introductions to canonical texts (*accessus ad auctores*)—Ovid's *On the Art of Love* was subsumed under ethics, Horace's *The Art of Poetry* under ethics or logic!

Although genre theory is seldom as precise or as relevant to actual literature as literary theorists would claim (even in times when literary studies attain the heights of rarefied sophistication they have reached in postmodern Europe and America), assembling some basic information about genres from medieval sources can offer insights into medieval attitudes toward literature. Most pertinent is to realize that the relatively taut correspondence between meter and content that held true in the classical period loosened appreciably in the Middle Ages. For example, narratives that we would pigeonhole as epics are to be found not only in dactylic hexameters but also in rhythmic meters and even in elegiac distichs. As for sources of information, we must remember that because the conceptions of genre that underlay medieval literature are not often articulated in the texts, we must look elsewhere—especially in works on grammar and rhetoric—for guidance.

Few general discussions of genre are retrievable from the early Middle Ages. One of the exceptions is Isidore of Seville (d. 636), who divides literature into prose and poetry and subdivides poetry into lyric, tragedy, comedy, and theological poetry [GA88]. These subdivisions of poetry can be detected not by specific formal features but by the varying intentions of their authors. In addition Isidore indicates that poetry can be classified according to the voices in which it is delivered: thus there are poems in which only the poet speaks, in which both the poet and characters speak, and in which only the characters speak ([GA75] pp440–41).

Toward the end of the eleventh century Bernard of Utrecht sets forth a much fuller generic system, encompassing bucolic, comic, tragic, satiric, lyric, apologetic, panegyric, epithium, epithalamium, threnody, epitaph, epode, quotidian, calendar, annual, secular or chronicle, festival, elegiac, heroic, fable (Aesopic and Libistic), historia, and argument. John of Garland (d. c. 1272) elaborates a similar grid of narrative and poetic genres. His system includes three types of narrative: fable, history, and argument. Poetry is either dramatic, narrative, or mixed. Historical poetry comprises epithalamium, epicedium, epitaph, apotheosis, bucolic, georgic, lyric, epode, hymn, invective, satire, and elegiac.

These different generic systems belong, in turn, to a comprehensive framework of human knowledge and wisdom. Writing in the twelfth century, Hugh of St. Victor in his *Didascalicon* (3.4) draws a major distinction between the arts—which pertain to philosophy—and the appendages of the arts—which are exophilosophical. In the second category he subsumes most forms of poetry (tragedies, comedies, satires, heroic verse, lyric, iambics, didactic poetry), not to mention fables, histories, and the writings of would-be philosophers who were his contemporaries! Although the genre schemata of vernacular poetry have been studied somewhat ([GA85], [GA87]), those of Medieval Latin poetry require further scrutiny and could yield promising results.

Alongside genre theory, medieval writers on the verbal arts, especially those who produced handbooks of rhetoric and poetics for educational purposes, devised many treatments of style. Most of these expositions cling to ancient rhetoric in subscribing to a tripartite conception of style: humble, middle, and grand. But after Augustine's *De doctrina christiana* radical transformation of the three styles to satisfy new religious or social expectations became the norm. For instance, John of Garland espoused the doctrine that each of these three styles corresponded to one of three social strata, and that each of them found an ideal expression in a work of Virgil. In his *rota Vergilii* ("Virgil's wheel")—designed for true rote learning!—he diagrammed three levels of style, with each of which he paired a specific character, name, animal, instrument, setting, and tree: the *Bucolics* were composed in the lowest style for herdsmen, the *Georgics* in the middle style for husbandmen, and the *Aeneid* in the high style for important men. Furthermore, even the radically transformed tripartite schema no longer sufficed for theoreticians writing in the late twelfth and early thirteenth centuries. Both a redactor of Geoffrey of Vinsauf's *Documentum* and John of Garland in his *Parisiana poetria* identified four styles of accentual prose rhythm: Gregorian, Tullian, Hilarian, and Isidorian.

Most evident to many readers today are styles attested in early medieval poetry but not touched upon in later medieval manuals of rhetoric or poetics. Particular attention has been focused on the so-called "Hisperic" style found in texts written by Irish-Latin authors and other Latin writers who were impressed by them, and by the hermeneutic or glossematic style that is especially salient in tenth-century writings from both England and the Continent.

Although the dynamics that motivate authors may include conscious or unconscious consideration of genre and style, the forces that move writers also include the readings they and their audiences share and the reactions they and their audiences experience to those readings. Investigation of the readings need not sink to mechanical source seeking and is in fact a sine qua non if we aspire to situate authors and their audiences in the context of their times and aesthetics and not simply in terms of our responses to them. Whether we set our sights upon detecting references, allusions, quotations, or "intertexts," we shall find an extraordinary density and sophistication in Medieval Latin literature—as in Latin literature across the ages. If we wish to understand the ways in which Medieval Latin authors were inspired and conditioned by their readings, we must seek to isolate those readings and to be sensitive to the modes in which people were trained to interpret them.

One major reality to bear in mind is the centrality of both authoritative authors (*auctores*) and their authoritative written statements (*auctoritates*) in medieval intellectual life, which is to say, in Medieval Latin culture. Whether we choose to speak in old-fashioned terms of "imitation and emulation" or more modishly of "the anxiety of influence," we must confront the reality that Medieval Latin authors had to cope with the impressive burden of their literary past. If those of us who read and write in modern English, French, German, or Spanish feel daunted by the five hundred or so years of our literary traditions, imagine what a Latin author would have felt in A.D. 1300, under the weight of a millennium and a half of great texts!

Yet Medieval Latin writers did not writhe in constant insecurity at the literary tradition behind them, and they did not behave as if they had been beaten into a slavish subservience to the ancient past. On the contrary, despite their reverence toward antiquity, they felt entitled to a measure of superiority thanks to their Christian culture. The twelfth century left the image of "dwarfs standing on the shoulders of giants," which merges an unmistakably medieval reverence for the past with an equally distinctive recognition of the present's superiorities over that past: however limited intellectuals found their own aptitudes in comparison with those of their intellectual and cultural forebears, they cherished a conviction that nonetheless their perspectives surpassed those of their predecessors. Just as later Dante would draft Virgil into service as his guide but would make clear that his pagan predecessor could accompany him only so far in his heavenward journey, so Hildebert of Lavardin (d. 1133) could lament the demise of pagan Rome in one elegy while in the next he could rejoice over the flourishing of the same city as the capital of Christianity. This force of pride in Rome's special Christian status stands out in many medieval lyric songs.

Another memorable instance of the self-confidence that the Middle Ages manifested toward the pagan past is the criticism that one great twelfth-century poet levels against two rivals who wrote epics, respectively, on the Trojan War and Alexander the Great. The critic is Alan of Lille, his targets Joseph of Exeter and Walter of Châtillon, and his criticism that his rivals resemble Ennius and Maevius, respectively. Alan's disapproval turns explicitly against the literary styles of his two rivals but perhaps implicitly against the classical subject matter of their poems, even though he opts to criticize them by associating them with ancient poets whose names were bywords for poetasters in the twelfth century.

During the first five hundred years or so of the new faith Christian writers often manifested an incontestable ambivalence about Latin—about the literary adequacy of the Latin Scriptures as gauged by classical standards, about the levels of style and rhetoric to be employed in their own Latin writing and speaking. Above all, early Christians in Western Europe faced a troubling predicament: to understand Scripture they had to learn Latin satisfactorily, but to acquire this language they had to devote themselves to the close study and imitation of pagan authors in pagan schools. Ultimately these Christians had to strike a precarious balance, by Christianizing pagan literature while simultaneously fostering an authentically Christian Latin literature. Just as Roman audiences had been quick to embrace Latin authors whose writings could replace those of Greeks, so Christian audiences revealed themselves as responsive to Christian Latin authors whose writings could supplant, rival, or complement those of pagan Latins.

One striking technique of early Christian Latin authors was to design centos— to pluck lines and phrases from pagan poets such as Virgil and to rearrange them so as to express a new meaning—especially to paraphrase a section of the Scriptures in epic language. If the usual species of literary composition can be metaphorized as a "woven thing"—and this metaphor inheres in the very word *text*—then these unusual poems live up to the original meaning of the Greek word from which their name derives, since they are "patchwork cloaks." Perhaps the most successful of the early centoists was a fourth-century woman named Proba, whose idiosyncratic retelling of salvation history was copied widely even after it was listed—or blacklisted—among apocrypha in an influential decree that was attributed to Pope Gelasius I.

Even when Bible poets did not comply with the rigorous procedures of the centoists by recasting the message of the Scriptures in hexameters, they still hewed closely to the policy of the rhetorical tradition and the pagan epic poets. In the early Middle Ages three of these Bible poets—Sedulius, Juvencus, and Arator—were absorbed enthusiastically into the curricula of the schools.

Another prestigious approach of early Christians to the classical literary tradition was to glean pagan literature for its moral insights. Upholding a tradition that had long been associated with Platonism, pupils and students were trained to decode ethical and religious messages latent in texts. This procedure of allegorization found expression both in Jerome, who envisaged pagan learning as a female slave (*Dt* 21.11–12) whose service could benefit Christianity only after her nails had been pared and her locks trimmed, and in Augustine, who saw it as the gold of the Egyptians that the Israelites had plundered before escaping (*Ex* 3.22 and 12.35–36). Interpreters took an active role when they engaged with texts, and their work was aptly likened to shelling the nut to reach the meat, winnowing the grain to separate the fruit from the chaff, and drawing away the veil that protected the beauty of the truth.

In most of the Middle Ages genuine discomfort toward ancient literature was a matter of the remote past—one could say that it had become *ancient history*! Indeed, medieval authors did not perceive themselves to be postclassical rather than classical: both the designation *postclassical* and the distinction that it embodies are modern, not medieval. Accordingly, we must beware of reducing Medieval Latin literature to any single model, whether it be postclassical Latin in the Middle Ages, European literature in the Latin Middle Ages, or Latin literature in the European Middle Ages. Each of these models, each of these formulations, has its share of truth, but (like so many truths) each is only partial.

The self-confidence of Medieval Latin writers as they measured themselves against the ancient past left a trace verbally in words that were medieval neologisms, *modernus* and *modernitas*. (It reveals much about the cultural legacy of the Middle Ages, and about our reluctance to profess it, that when we define ourselves as modern or postmodern in contradistinction to the premodern or modern—and the medieval is often represented popularly as the exact opposite of what we moderns or postmoderns hope ourselves to be—we resort unwittingly to a term coined in the Middle Ages.) *Modernity* in the medieval sense was the epoch in which they lived, as distinguished from antiquity. The *modern* was the new, the present—the modern. A *modern* was a contemporary, as opposed to an ancient.

But it is surely erroneous to refer to Medieval Latin writers collectively, seeing that their personalities and places in society were very diverse—and so were the audiences they reached. Although Medieval Latin writers belonged to an elite, it was an elite of surprising breadth. To begin with the issue of gender, Medieval Latin writers were predominantly men, but it would be a foolish mistake to surmise that they were all male. Indeed, despite the misogyny and misogamy that are widespread if not endemic in Medieval Latin literature, the ranks of Medieval Latin writers included such remarkable women as Egeria, the fourth-century traveler to the Holy Land; Hrotsvitha of Gandersheim, tenth-century playwright, hagiographer, and epic poet; Heloise (d. 1163/4), letter writer and lifelong lover of unfortunate Abelard; and Hildegard of Bingen (d. 1179), mystic poet and cosmological writer. Thus Medieval Latin contains much that could suit the ends of women's studies and feminist literary criticism, both in important texts by women and in texts that bear the impress of a pervasively patriarchal stage in Western culture. Finally, Medieval Latin literature offers extensive information about relations between men in all-male communities and about male friendship. It is probably the Latin Middle Ages that holds the key to many aspects of prevailing Western attitudes toward homosexuality. For all of these reasons, Medieval Latin literature should not be overlooked in studies of gender and sexuality.

As for social class, the authors of Medieval Latin texts could be monks and later friars, canons or clerics of other ranks connected with courts both episcopal and noble, students, or professional entertainers. Furthermore, an author sometimes progressed through several of these different social classes in the course of a lifetime. A son of a knight could become a student, a student could become a cleric in the service of a bishop or king, and a cleric could elect later in life to don monastic habit. Thus Peter Abelard (d. c. 1142) was born into a knightly family; lived for two decades as a student, cleric, and teacher; and became a monk for the remainder of his life.

And who patronized Latin literature in the Middle Ages? We can gain a sense of this from the dedications found in medieval manuscripts, although we must take care to be certain that patron and dedicatee are one and the same. Dedications may sometimes have emanated not from the author but from a scribe who happened at a later date to dedicate a *copy* of the text to the person who commissioned the transcription. From indisputably authorial dedications we can infer that most often authors directed their texts to close friends; abbots and abbesses; bishops, chancellors, and archchancellors; and members of noble and royal families.

What gains could have accrued to those who composed Medieval Latin texts? Obviously authors did not write potboilers as nineteenth- or twentieth-century writers have done: without publication in the print-era sense of the word they had no prospect of royalties or other such income to be received from the purveyors or readers of their work. Sometimes the only profits that authors sought were purely spiritual, and recognition of this fact helps us to understand why so many Medieval Latin texts, especially from the centuries when literacy was the virtually exclusive domain of monks, are anonymous: to advertise one's authorship of a text would have been vainglorious. But not all Medieval Latin authors were modest monks. No doubt authors often devoted their writings to particular patrons in the hope of thereby securing particular benefits (or benefices!). An author who was not a monk in a well-endowed community or who was not a cleric with a good prebend might require the very basics of life, such as food, shelter, and clothing, which a wealthy patron could offer.

Although the ninth-century Sedulius Scottus is undoubtedly striving for comic effect as he recounts the joy of the Irish coterie at Liège in receiving gifts of mutton from Bishop Hartgar, at the same time he is probably adverting to a real necessity, and a heartfelt gratitude, that his countrymen felt. He is also likely to be in earnest when he expresses his need for sheepskin as a writing material, since parchment was costly. Although Hugh Primas (d. c. 1160) is unquestionably planting himself in a tradition that reaches back to antiquity when he jokes about his desperation for a winter coat, he too is likely to be telling the truth about a painful gap in his wardrobe; why should he have differed from many vernacular poets, some of whom were indeed remunerated with garments?

Apart from such specific items as food, writing materials, and clothing, Latin writers could and did seek other benefits from those to whom they addressed their compositions. To ensure for themselves secure lives, they could hint at their suitability for preferment in the Church. If they were monks or if they had their sights set on loftier matters than their own material well-being, they could aim at securing the favorable disposition of a patron toward their institution or toward a particular cause. At the very least, the backing of a highly placed patron could facilitate the copying and dissemination of their work.

To have support in the circulation of a text was no negligible consideration in an age when publication was a time-consuming ordeal of copying and recopying by hand upon parchment or vellum, which, no matter how soft and supple, are still leather—a durable but resistant substance. The entire project of composition and publication was labor-intensive. The person who composed the text generated a rough draft by writing it upon wax tablets or scraps of inferior parchment, or by dictating it to a scribe or scribes who did so. After reviewing the draft, the scribe or scribes wrote a clean copy. This stage often involved the labors of several copyists, with the ruling of the folios, writing of the text, rubricating, and other such tasks being distributed among the members of a small squadron. Until the twelfth century such teams were housed mainly in the scriptoria of monasteries, but later an organized commercial book trade came into being in cities such as Paris.

The nature of manuscript production, in which the ideal of the exact copy is unattainable and irrelevant, heightened the individuality and intimacy of the reception that texts received. Apart from those transmitted orally, texts reached their audiences through reading, but reading would not have resembled reading as most of us know it today, regardless of whether we consult printed books or computer monitors. As has been implied, reading took place not from volumes that offered identical texts and looked the same, but from manuscripts that presented texts with different abbreviations, different slips of the pen, different alterations (what the most rigid or purist textual criticism would label corruptions or emendations) on the part of scribes or readers, and that differed also in the color and quality of the writing surface and ink, and in the page format. Each exemplar of a text was unique. Perhaps more important, the reading took place at a pace far more leisurely (or painstaking) than most of our reading. In our culture most reading involves scanning, skimming, and jumping from one text to another. Our eyes flit over far more words in a week than the eyes of a medieval reader could have surveyed, or would have wanted to survey, in a month or even a year. Medieval readers had to contend with the difficulties of not having adequate lighting or spectacles and of having to decipher scripts that were never as uniform as movable type and lacked consistent punctuation. Yet it is not a given that medieval readers would have judged all these conditions to be detrimental. After all, they belonged to a culture in which slow reading was prized—in which readers were supposed to read and reread texts until they had internalized them to the point of being able to regurgitate them or, to use the medieval term, ruminate upon them. Although this kind of perusal was intended to result in a nearly verbatim recall of the texts, it was anything but mindless or soulless. On the contrary, it was meant to allow readers to appropriate the texts—to make them their own and retain them within their memories and hearts.

Silent and solitary reading was relatively rare and noteworthy. In most cases, when individuals read texts by themselves, they seem to have pronounced them aloud, at least at the level of a whisper. More often reading took place when a text was recited to a group. Such was the case when a master read a *lesson* (a word that derives ultimately from the Latin *lectio*) to his pupils or gave a *lecture* to his students, or when a lector read a passage to a refectory of monks or a preacher to a congregation.

Whether reading alone or listening as part of a group, the person who engaged with a Latin text was often supposed to derive from it a spiritual boon. Although this frequent imposition of a need to extract an ethical or Christian meaning may seem constrictive to many people now, it took place within an interpretive system that permitted almost unbounded flexibility—with the major proviso that interpreters must endeavor to find the true meaning of the authors who wrote the texts. In his *Confessions* (12.18.27) Augustine gave clear and definitive utterance to this theory and to the multiple interpretations of the same passage that it allowed. This Augustinian strategy of reading became routine in the Middle Ages. In the monasteries it complemented the meditative reading that went by the name of *ruminatio*—reading that aimed at the physical and spiritual incorporation (the metaphor of cud-chewing embedded etymologically in *ruminatio* has a real significance). Both inside and outside the monasteries, interpreters manifested a deep appreciation for the related notions that ambiguity can be a source of richness, that there is seldom a single right interpretation, and that the meanings of a text are achieved as much through the interpretive efforts of the audience as through the expressive efforts of the author. In many respects the stances of these readers toward their texts anticipated aspects of literary theory as it has been elaborated over the past half century, from the New Critics with their esteem for ambiguity and sensitivity to it, through the contestation of authorial control and meaning on the part of deconstructionists, to the emphasis of reception theorists upon the contributions and perspectives of audiences in the making of meaning. Even the recent welling of interest in semiotics can be construed as a resurgence of a medieval predilection, since Scholasticism took sign theory to heights of refinement and subtlety that exercised an influence on literature long before Umberto Eco—semiotician and medievalist—dreamed of *The Name of the Rose: plus ça change.* . . .

The cozy proximity of author, reader, and audience that Medieval Latin literature often assumes differs acutely from the typical experience of these same participants in communicative acts today, and created intimacies that are impossible to replicate at the remove of many centuries. Texts take for granted a common knowledge—of books that the entire audience has read, of experiences that they all have shared, and of people and topical events that they all know—and make allusions and inside jokes that sometimes elude us. In this sense Medieval Latin literature relies upon textual communities in a way far removed from the experience of the average European or American today. Accordingly, we must not allow the formidable equipment that technology has put at our disposal to lull us into the mistaken belief that all past cultures were unsophisticated in comparison with our own. If we had a humbler outlook, we would have to concede that in the Latin Middle Ages the readers and writers—true technicians of the written word—attained a much closer engagement with the texts they read and wrote than most of their peers today are able to do.

Although those of us who live and work in the industrialized and postindustrialized world at the turn of the second millennium in the Christian era may spend more of our waking hours reading than many monks or clerics in the Middle Ages were able to do, it is no hollow coincidence that the phenomenon of bricolage is so much studied and commented upon these days. Our reading is forced to have a random, magpie quality: from peering at the numbers on the digital alarm clock and skimming cereal boxes and newspapers; through glancing at billboards and posters as we drive to work; to evaluating term papers, admissions recommendations, and job applications; to sifting mail, both paper and electronic; and occasionally even to reading our beloved Latin texts—in the course of all these activities we are often browsing rather than digesting as medieval readers would have done. In contrast, in the diglossia of Western Europe in the Middle Ages, Latin (far more than is the case today with any fully living language) was learned through sustained contact with a limited array of texts. The readers and writers of the Middle Ages—and the listeners and speakers or singers—were supreme craftsmen of the word, and at most times and in most locales the supreme word was Latin. Although many of us profess to be fascinated by rhetoric, they were schooled in it from an early age; and although many of us devote boundless hours and energies to visual activities, they pieced together figure poems and pattern poems, not to mention acrostics and telestichs, with a tenacity that is now hard to conceive. Their virtuosity makes the texts of the Middle Ages an incomparable laboratory in which to explore our ideas about the changes that occur in cultures—and in the intellect and spirit of individuals—when transitions in literacy and in the organization of knowledge occur. Needless to say, the results of running tests in such a fanciful laboratory will have relevance to people today, mutatis mutandis.

Medieval Latin displayed intense vitality and originality in form as well as in content. As regards verse forms, Medieval Latin poets not only exploited almost the entire repertoire of quantitative meters known from Classical Latin literature, but also devised innumerable new rhyme schemes for those meters, especially the dactylic hexameters and pentameters; they wrought many permutations upon the internally rhymed dactylic hexameter, often known as the leonine hexameter. Nor did their innovation restrict itself to quantitative meters, since they also engineered a seemingly endless range of accentual patterns. In addition, these poets reinvented the relationship of text and melody in both secular and religious song. In terms of genre they supplemented the options available from Roman poets by introducing new ones such as religious drama and personification allegory. Writers of prose were equally industrious and inventive, developing rhymed and accentual patterns that won favor in the twelfth-century Renaissance ([GA19] pp25–26).

The richness of Medieval Latin literature in both form and content cries out for a corresponding wealth of knowledge and approaches. The starting point must be what is often labeled *philology*. Philology entails an understanding of how the texts that we read have been constituted and how we may need to correct them. Such a discernment is urgent when we are dealing with compositions from an epoch in which the exact copy was unknown and perhaps unwanted, when the concepts of originality and copyright as we encounter them today had not been devised. But philology does not stop with textual criticism. Rather, it goes on to demand a knowledge of grammar and vocabulary, so that we can seize the literal meanings of the texts word by word, phrase by phrase, and sentence by sentence; for we must never forget that, no matter how elusive a firm grasp of words may be in everyday communication in our own spoken languages, the problems of making out meaning multiply as we recede from today into the diction of the past. Finally, philology is not just a matter of editions, dictionaries, and verbatim translation. Instead, it should prompt us to seek methods for interpreting and commenting upon the texts.

Which methods we employ will depend upon the nature of the given text and our understandings of it. When confronted with an anonymous lyric about whose author and audiences nothing can be surmised with any certainty, we may begin with a formalistic approach (whether New Critical or deconstructionist) that focuses upon the inner workings of the text. In other cases we may conclude that setting a text in the context of its author's biography or historical circumstances helps us to make sense of the text—or, then again, we may find such contextualization altogether useless. In other instances we may find that other methods are helpful, whether Freudian analysis of psychological undercurrents, Jungian analysis of mythological archetypes, Marxist analysis of the socioeconomic background, feminist criticism of the role of gender in the author's writing and in our reading, or any other of the interpretive tools that have become commonplace through the recent predilection for critical theory in literary and cultural studies.

What has just been described is a philologically grounded eclecticism. Such an outlook presupposes that interpreting medieval texts requires us to discover for ourselves a place between the present and the past where we can gain a perspective, perhaps even a panorama, both of the past encoded in our texts and of the present in which we live. To stay in this spot is tiring, since it requires us to see and understand the currents of our own times without allowing them to sweep us away so thoroughly that we lose interest in the past as an entity in its own right. In the end we win in breadth of perspective, since we gain a vista of both the past and the present. Ideally we learn to be true, insofar as we are able, to the past and the present alike. On the one hand we find out that we cannot look at the past entirely through the eyes of the present, for by doing so we remake the past in our own images. On the other hand we see that the past is not fully meaningful unless it can be grasped in human terms by people today.

To write the literary history of any literature whatsoever may be a foredoomed project. Whatever the case may be with literary history as an overall pursuit, a history of Medieval Latin literature is certainly not possible now—and perhaps not desirable ever—if it is conceived of as a repertory of all prose and poetry compositions, with biographies of all their authors and other germane factual information. But a history can indicate in a fashion at once honest, intelligent, and stimulating the range of a literature that abounds in treasures. Such a history is only the more inspirational if it does not conceal from readers that some of these riches remain to be retrieved and proclaimed. Much of Medieval Latin literature languishes, either poorly edited or altogether unedited, and still more has been edited but has not yet been interpreted even rudimentarily. Finally, only a smattering of the literature has been translated into modern languages so as to make it accessible to those for whom even Shakespeare's "small Latin and no Greek" is an unattained ideal. If ever a rich lode of literature existed that awaited finders and appraisers, it is Medieval Latin.

The field of Medieval Latin literary studies is at an excitingly paradoxical point in its cultivation. Although much basic groundwork remains to be done, the field also has an urgent need of synthesizers who can bring together what has already been achieved. Additionally, the field requires judicious popularizing to ensure that future workers are enticed into it and that a larger public gains an awareness of it. Only through a combination of such monographic, synthetic, and popularizing work will Medieval Latin win the niche that it merits in the shelves or bytes of *Weltliteratur* or, since that mythical assemblage will probably never materialize, then at least in the paperback ranks of Western literature.

## Select Bibliography

### Histories and Primers of Medieval Latin Literature

L. Alfonsi, *La letteratura latina medievale* (1972) [GA1].

C. Beeson, *A Primer of Medieval Latin: An Anthology of Prose and Poetry* (1925, r1986) [GA2].

R.L. Benson *et al.*, *R&R* [GA3].

R.R. Bezzola, *Les origines et la formation de la littérature courtoise en occident (500–1200)*, 3 vols. in 5, Bibliothèque de l'École des hautes études: Sciences historiques et philologiques 286, 313, 319–20 (1944–63) [GA4].

F. Brunhölzl, *Geschichte der lateinischen Literatur des Mittelalters*, 2 vols. in a projected ser. of 4 (1975–); tr. H. Rochais: *Histoire de la littérature latine du moyen âge* (1990–): provides in an updated form a coverage similar to that found in [GA21] [GA5].

G. Cavallo, C. Leonardi, E. Menestò, *et al.*, eds., *Lo spazio letterario del medioevo*, 2 vols. in a projected ser. of 5 (1992–) [GA6].

P. Dronke, *Women Writers of the Middle Ages: A Critical Study of Texts from Perpetua (d. 203) to Marguerite Porete (d. 1310)* (1984) [GA7].

A. Ebert, *Allgemeine Geschichte der Literatur des Mittelalters im Abendlande bis zum Beginn des XI. Jahrhunderts*, 3 vols. (1880–89, r1971) [GA8].

F. Ermini, *Storia della letteratura latina medievale dalle origini alla fine del secolo VII*, Centro italiano di studi sull'alto medioevo 2 (1960) [GA9].

J.P. Foucher, *La littérature latine du moyen âge* (1963) [GA10].

E. Franceschini, *Lineamenti di una storia letteraria del medio evo latino* (1944) [GA11].

J. de Ghellinck, *L'essor de la littérature latine au XIIe siècle*, 2 vols., 2nd ed. (1955) [GA12].

J. de Ghellinck, *La littérature latine au moyen âge*, 2 vols. (1939, r1969 in one vol.) [GA13].

G. Gröber, *Übersicht über die lateinische Litteratur von der Mitte des VI. Jahrhunderts bis zur Mitte des XIV. Jahrhunderts* (1902, r1974): despite its age, this book covers a broad span chronologically and, for that reason, has not yet been entirely superseded [GA14].

K.P. Harrington, *Mediaeval Latin* (1925, r1975) [GA15].

F.E. Harrison, *Millennium: A Latin Reader, 374–1374* (1968) [GA16].

M. Hélin, *A History of Medieval Latin Literature*, tr. J.C. Snow (1949): a concise sketch [GA17].

M.L.W. Laistner, *Thought and Letters in Western Europe*, A.D. 500 to 900, 2d ed. (1957) [GA18].

K. Langosch, *Lateinisches Mittelalter: Einleitung in Sprache und Literatur*, 2nd ed. (1975, r1983) [GA19].

C. Leonardi and G. Orlandi, eds., *Aspetti della letteratura latina nel secolo XIII*, Quaderni del Centro per il collegamento degli studi medievali e umanistici nell'Università di Perugia 15 (1986) [GA20].

M. Manitius, *Geschichte der lateinischen Literatur des Mittelalters*, 3 vols. (1911–31, r1964–65): these volumes remain indispensable, although their value will decline if Brunhölzl [GA5] completes his project [GA21].

F. Nichols, "Latin Literature," in *The Present State of Scholarship in Fourteenth-Century Literature*, ed. T.D. Cooke (1982) 195–257 [GA22].

D. Norberg, *MPLM* [GA23].

V. Paladini and M. De Marco, *Lingua e letteratura mediolatina*, 2nd ed. (1980) [GA24].

G. Polara, *Letteratura latina tardoantica e altomedievale* (1987) [GA25].

K. Sidwell, *Reading Medieval Latin* (1995) [GA26].

K. Strecker, *Introduction to Medieval Latin*, tr. R.B. Palmer (1957, r1968): a concise sketch [GA27].

F.A. Wright and T.A. Sinclair, *A History of Later Latin Literature from the Middle of the Fourth to the End of the Seventeenth Century* (1931, r1969) [GA28].

## Histories of Medieval Latin Poetry

P. Dronke, *PIMA* [GA29].

P. Godman, *Poetry of the Carolingian Renaissance* (1985): contains a succinct introduction to a well-chosen selection of Latin texts with English translations on the facing pages [GA30].

M. Manitius, *Geschichte der christlich-lateinischen Poesie bis zur Mitte des 8. Jahrhunderts* (1891) [GA31].

F.J.E. Raby, *CLP* [GA32].

F.J.E. Raby, *SLP*: although this ends with the twelfth century, the author includes the *Carmina Burana* in his consideration of Medieval Latin lyric poetry [GA33].

J. Szövérffy, *Weltliche Dichtungen des lateinischen Mittelalters: Ein Handbuch*, 1 vol. in an incomplete ser. (1970). The same author has produced an updated, English version of this undertaking: *Secular Latin Lyrics and Minor Poetic Forms of the Middle Ages: A Historical Survey and Literary Repertory from the Tenth to the Late Fifteenth Century*, 3 vols. (1992–94) [GA34].

## Histories of Literature in Specific Regions

F. Bertini, *Autori latini in Africa sotto la dominazione vandalica* (1974) [GA35].

F. Bertini, *Letteratura latina medievale in Italia (secoli V–XIII)* (1988) [GA36].

S. Bodelón, *Literatura latina de la edad media en España* (1989) [GA37].

W.F. Bolton, *A History of Anglo-Latin Literature, 597–1066* (1967): 1 vol. (A.D. 597–740) in an incomplete ser. [GA38].

H. de Boor, *Die deutsche Literatur von Karl dem Grossen bis zum Beginn der höfischen Dichtung, 770–1170*, 9th ed. (1979): V1 of *Geschichte der deutschen Literatur von den Anfängen bis zur Gegenwart* [GA39].

J.K. Bostock, *A Handbook on Old High German Literature*, 2nd ed., rev. K.C. King and D.R. McLintock (1976) [GA40].

M. Carrara, "Gli scrittori latini," in *Verona e il suo territorio* (1960–), V2:351–420 [GA41].

G. Ehrismann, *Geschichte der deutschen Literatur bis zum Ausgang des Mittelalters*, 2 vols. (1918–35) [GA42].

A. Gransden, *Historical Writing in England*, 2 vols.; V1: *c. 550 to c. 1307* (1974); V2: *c. 1307 to the Early Sixteenth Century* (1982) [GA43].

S. Greenfield and D.G. Calder, *A New Critical History of Old English Literature* (1986): with a survey of the Anglo-Latin background by M. Lapidge [GA44].

M.W. Herren, ed., *Insular Latin Studies: Papers on Latin Texts and Manuscripts of the British Isles, 550–1066* (1981) [GA45].

R. Kögel, *Geschichte der deutschen Litteratur bis zum Ausgange des Mittelalters*, 2 vols. (1894–97): old handbooks of this sort are frequently still useful [GA46].

K. Langosch, *Die deutsche Literatur des lateinischen Mittelalters in ihrer geschichtlichen Entwicklung* (1964) [GA47].

M. Lapidge, *Anglo-Latin Literature, 900–1066* (1993) [GA48].

A.G. Rigg, *A History of Anglo-Latin Literature, 1066–1422* (1992) [GA49].

W. Wattenbach and W. Levison, *Deutschlands Geschichtsquellen im Mittelalter: Vorzeit und Karolinger*, 6 vols. (1952–90) [GA50].

W. Wattenbach and R. Holtzmann, *Deutschlands Geschichtsquellen im Mittelalter: Die Zeit der Sachsen und Salier*, ed. F.-J. Schmale, 3 vols. (1967–71) [GA51].

## The Nature of Medieval Latin Language and Philology

E. Auerbach, "Philology and *Weltliteratur*," tr. M. and E. Said, in *Centennial Review* 13 (1969) 1–17; original German version, "Philologie der Weltliteratur," in *Weltliteratur: Festgabe für Fritz Strich zum 70. Geburtstag* (1952) 39–50 [GA52].

L. Bieler, "Das Mittellatein als Sprachproblem," in *Lexis* 2 (1949) 98–104 [GA53].

J. Clark, "Teaching Medieval Latin," in *Classical Journal* 75 (1979–80) 44–50 [GA54].

*La Filologia medievale e umanistica greca e latina nel secolo XX: Atti del congresso internazionale, Roma, Consiglio nazionale delle ricerche, Università La Sapienza, 11–15 dicembre 1989*, 2 vols. (1993) [GA55].

J. Grimm and A. Schmeller, eds., *Lateinische Gedichte des X. und XI. Jahrhunderts* (1838, r1967) [GA56].

S. Hellmann, "Das Problem der mittellateinischen Philologie," in *Historische Vierteljahrschrift* 29 (1935) 625–80 [GA57].

R. Hexter, "*Latinitas* in the Middle Ages: Horizons and Perspectives," in *Helios* 14.2 (1987) 69–92 [GA58].

C.D. Lanham, "The Bastard at the Family Reunion: Classics and Medieval Latin," in *Classical Journal* 70.3 (1974–75) 46–59 [GA59]; *eadem*, "More on Teaching Medieval Latin," in *Classical Journal* 75 (1979–80) 335–39 [GA60].

P. Lehmann, "Aufgaben und Anregungen der lateinischen Philologie des Mittelalters" (1918), repr. in *id., Erforschung des Mittelalters*, V1 (1941, r1959) 1–46 [GA61].

E. Löfstedt, *LL* (1959) [GA62].

A. Önnerfors, ed., *MP* (see [CC18]) [GA63].

D. Sheerin, "*In media latinitate,*" in *Helios* 14.2 (1987) 51–67 [GA64].

W. Stach, "Mittellateinische Philologie und Geschichtswissenschaft," in *Historische Vierteljahrschrift* 26 (1931) 1–12 [GA65].

L. Traube, *Einleitung in die lateinische Philologie des Mittelalters* (1911); repr. in *id., Vorlesungen und Abhandlungen,* ed. P. Lehmann, v2 (1911, r1965) [GA66].

K. Vossler, *Geist und Kultur in der Sprache* (1925); tr. O. Oeser (1932, r1977) [GA67].

R. Wright, *LLER* [GA68].

R. Wright, "Review Article: Michel Banniard, *Viva voce: Communication écrite et communication orale du IVe au IX siècle en occident latin,*" in *JMLat* 3 (1993) 78–94 [GA69].

E.H. Zeydel, "The Medieval Latin Literature of Germany as German Literature," in *PMLA* 80 (1965) 24–30 [GA70].

J.M. Ziolkowski, "Cultural Diglossia and the Nature of Medieval Latin Literature," in *The Ballad and Oral Literature,* ed. J. Harris, Harvard English Studies 17 (1991) 193–213 [GA71].

## Classical Tradition and Classicism

E. Auerbach, *Literary Language and Its Public in Late Latin Antiquity and in the Middle Ages,* tr. R. Manheim (1965, r1993) [GA72]: although less known than Auerbach's *Mimesis: The Representation of Reality in Western Literature,* tr. W.R. Trask (1953, r1974) [GA73], this book is more relevant to Medieval Latin studies because it offers a detailed exposition of his interpretive technique and close analyses of several Medieval Latin passages.

R.R. Bolgar, *The Classical Heritage and Its Beneficiaries* (1954, r1977) [GA74].

E.R. Curtius, *European Literature and the Latin Middle Ages,* tr. W.R. Trask (1953, r1990); originally published in German as *Europäische Literatur und lateinisches Mittelalter* (1948): an attempt to prove that the European vernacular literatures possess a certain unity, thanks to the commonplaces of rhetoric and poetic that were transmitted from classical antiquity through Medieval Latin culture [GA75].

H. Hagendahl, *Latin Fathers and the Classics: A Study on the Apologists, Jerome, and Other Christian Writers* (1958) [GA76].

R.J. Hexter, *Ovid and Medieval Schooling: Studies in Medieval School Commentaries on Ovid's "Ars Amatoria," "Epistulae ex Ponto," and "Epistulae Heroidum,"* *MBMRF* 38 (1986) [GA77].

G. Highet, *The Classical Tradition: Greek and Roman Influences on Western Literature* (1949, r1985) [GA78].

H. Hunger *et al., Geschichte der Textüberlieferung der antiken und mittelalterlichen Literatur,* 2 vols. (1961–64) [GA79].

P.O. Kristeller, F.E. Cranz, *et al.,* eds., *CTC* [GA80].

J. Martin, "Classicism and Style in Latin Literature," in *R&R* 537–68 [GA81].

R. Pfeiffer, *History of Classical Scholarship,* v1: *From the Beginnings to the End of the Hellenistic Age;* v2: *From 1300–1850* (1968–76) [GA82].

L.D. Reynolds and N.G. Wilson, *Scribes and Scholars: A Guide to the Transmission of Greek & Latin Literature,* 3rd ed. (1991) [GA83].

J.E. Sandys, *A History of Classical Scholarship*, VI: *From the Sixth Century* B.C. *to the End of the Middle Ages*, 2nd ed. (1906, r1967) [GA84].

## Genre Classification and Theory

P. Bec, "Le problème des genres chez les premiers troubadours," in *Cahiers de civilisation médiévale* 25 (1982) 31–47 [GA85].

M. Camargo, "The Varieties of Prose *Dictamen* as Defined by the *Dictatores*," in *Vichiana*, 3rd ser., 1 (1990) 61–73: very clear and useful consideration of generic divisions presented in medieval rhetorical sources, with initial overview of previous work on medieval genre theory [GA86].

H.R. Jauss, "Theory of Genres and Medieval Literature," in *id.*, *Toward an Aesthetic of Reception*, tr. T. Bahti (1982) 76–109 [GA87].

U. Kindermann, "Gattungssysteme im Mittelalter," in *Kontinuität und Transformation der Antike im Mittelalter: Veröffentlichung der Kongreßakten zum Freiburger Symposion des Mediävistenverbandes*, ed. W. Erzgräber (1989) 303–13 [GA88].

## Literary Theory and Criticism in the Middle Ages

H. Brinkmann, *Mittelalterliche Hermeneutik* (1980) [GA89].

W. Haug, *Literaturtheorie im deutschen Mittelalter von den Anfängen bis zum Ende des 13. Jahrhunderts* (1985) [GA90].

A.J. Minnis, *Medieval Theory of Authorship: Scholastic Literary Attitudes in the Later Middle Ages* (1984, r1988) [GA91].

A.J. Minnis and A.B. Scott, eds., *Medieval Literary Theory and Criticism c. 1100–c. 1375: The Commentary Tradition*, rev. ed. (1991) [GA92].

## Memory

M. Carruthers, *The Book of Memory: A Study of Memory in Medieval Culture* (1990, r1992) [GA93].

M.T. Clanchy, *From Memory to Written Record: England 1066–1307*, 2nd ed. (1993) [GA94].

J. Coleman, *Ancient and Medieval Memories: Studies in the Reconstruction of the Past* (1992) [GA95].

H. Hajdu, *Das mnemotechnische Schrifttum des Mittelalters* (1936, r1967) [GA96].

B. Roy and P. Zumthor, eds., *Jeux de mémoire: Aspects de la mnémotechnie médiévale* (1985): includes P. Riché, "Le rôle de la mémoire dans l'enseignement médiéval," pp133–48 [GA97].

## Orality, Literacy, and Textuality

J. Balogh, "'Voces Paginarum': Beiträge zur Geschichte des lauten Lesens und Schreibens," in *Philologus* 82 (1926) 84–109, 202–40 [GA98].

H.J. Chaytor, *From Script to Print: An Introduction to Medieval Vernacular Literature* (1945, r1976) [GA99].

E.P. Goldschmidt, *Medieval Texts and Their First Appearance in Print* (1943, r1969) [GA100].

W.J. Ong, *Orality and Literacy: The Technologizing of the Word* (1982, r1991) [GA101].

B. Stock, *The Implications of Literacy: Written Language and Models of Interpretation in the Eleventh and Twelfth Centuries* (1983) [GA102].

L. Treitler, "Oral, Written, and Literate Process in the Transmission of Medieval Music," in *Speculum* 56 (1981) 471–91 [GA103].

L. Treitler, "The 'Unwritten' and 'Written Transmission' of Medieval Chant and the Start-Up of Musical Notation," in *Journal of Musicology* 10 (1992) 131–91 [GA104].

## Patronage

J. Bumke, ed. *Literarisches Mäzenatentum: Ausgewählte Forschungen zur Rolle des Gönners und Auftraggebers in der mittelalterlichen Literatur,* Wege der Forschung 598 (1982) [GA105].

J. Bumke, *Mäzene im Mittelalter: Die Gönner und Auftraggeber der höfischen Literatur in Deutschland, 1150–1300* (1979) [GA106].

W.F. Schirmer and U. Broich, *Studien zum literarischen Patronat im England des 12. Jahrhunderts* (1962) [GA107].

*See also* [BA113], [BA154].

# GB • THE LATIN LITERATURE OF LATE ANTIQUITY

BY MICHAEL ROBERTS

In the literary history of the late Roman Empire the last years of the third century, roughly from the accession of Diocletian in A.D. 284, mark a critical moment of transition. Little Latin literature survives from earlier in the century—the only substantial figures are the Christian writers of North Africa, Tertullian (d. c. 220) and Cyprian (d. 258). In particular, poetry is almost entirely absent. Thereafter, a continuous development extends until roughly the late sixth century, with a final flourishing of literary culture in Visigothic Spain extending into the seventh century. The period shows a common literary culture and taste, formed primarily by the grammatical and rhetorical education that all who aspired to intellectual interests shared. Christian and pagan alike, if they were from the educated classes, participated in these common attitudes and aesthetic preferences. Though Christian sermons and hymns were less exclusive in their intended audiences, most poetry (the main high literary form of the late Empire, and the one on which this section will concentrate), including Christian hymnody, reflects in some way the prevailing literary canons of the period. (The chief exceptions are the metrically irregular didactic poems of Commodian, of uncertain date [third or fifth century], and Augustine's accentual *Psalmus contra partem Donati*.)

This period is named in modern scholarship "late antiquity." The first late antique poet, Nemesianus (fl. late third century), is the writer of four eclogues, modeled on Virgil and Calpurnius Siculus, and a now only partially preserved didactic poem, the *Cynegetica*, which dates to 283–84. Nemesianus is a typical Late Latin poet in turning to Virgil and the poetry of the first century A.D. for models, and in his taste, especially in the eclogues, for variation, small-scale composition, and virtuoso descriptive passages. The *De concubitu Martis et Veneris* of Reposianus and the genre pieces of Tiberianus (fl. early fourth century), to whom the *Pervigilium Veneris* should probably now be attributed, share the poetic values of Nemesianus, but the masterpiece of this style of composition in late antiquity, though generically elusive, is the *Mosella* of Ausonius (written in the early 370s). It is a substantial poem (of over 480 lines) on the Moselle River, put together from largely self-contained compositional elements in a way that in defying classical criteria of unity exemplifies the alternative aesthetic of *variatio* that characterizes much Late Latin literature. The *De ave phoenice* (early fourth century), probably by Lactantius (d. 325), a poem that allows but does not demand a Christian interpretation, is an early example of the same attitude to poetic composition. Worked-up descriptive passages are characteristic of Late Latin poetry as a whole; in the Christian tradition descriptions of paradise lend themselves especially to this treatment. The description of Prudentius (d. c. 405) of the Temple of the Soul in the *Psychomachia* (lines 826–87) is a particularly well-known example of the same aesthetic, as it may be applied to portraying works of art and architecture.

The taste for description in late antiquity is an illustration of the influence of epideictic literary forms (i.e. those appropriate to speeches of praise and blame and to the oratory of display) on the literature of the period. Description (*ecphrasis*) was one of the preliminary exercises in composition (*progymnasmata*) practiced by students of rhetoric; the panegyric (*laus*) was another such rhetorical form especially suited to the society and culture of late antiquity, a society that put a premium on ceremony, the maintenance and communication of hierarchy, and the use of language as a medium of display. Eleven speeches from late antiquity, all but one imperial panegyrics, are preserved in the collection of *Panegyrici Latini;* Ambrose (d. 397), too, turned his hand to the related form of imperial funerary oration, while Paulinus of Nola (d. 431) composed a panegyric, now lost, on Theodosius, and in the early sixth century Ennodius a panegyric of Theoderic. It was Claudian, following Greek tradition, who at the end of the fourth century wrote the first Latin verse panegyrics (as well as invectives) of late antiquity, setting a precedent that was to be followed in the fifth century by the Spanish-born Merobaudes and by the Gaul Sidonius Apollinaris, and in the sixth by the African poets, writing in the Eastern court, Priscian (on the emperor Anastasius) and Corippus (the *Iohannis* and *In laudem Iustini* augusti minoris). Claudian was a professional poet and much of his poetry serves the political interests of his patron, Stilicho. His political poems blur the line between panegyric and historical epic: they combine epic compositional elements, especially extensive narrative passages not always subordinated to the topical structure of panegyric, with the partisan point of view of the speech of praise. In Christian poetry pagan rhetorical traditions of hymn and panegyric and biblical and liturgical traditions of giving praise to God, ultimately derived from the Psalms, reach a new synthesis, in which biblical traditions are dominant, in the *De laudibus dei* of the African poet Dracontius (fl. late fifth century).

The first substantial poem of unambiguously Christian content in classical meters is the New Testament biblical epic of the Spanish priest Juvencus, the *Evangeliorum libri quattuor* (329/30). Constantine's conversion (A.D. 312) and the new situation of the Church in the Roman Empire provided the preconditions for Juvencus's work: a Christian poet could now expect to find readers from the educated classes for whom the Gospel narrative would be lent special attraction by being clothed in the idiom of Virgilian epic. At the same time, Lactantius, in his *Divinae institutiones,* had provided theoretical legitimization for the employment of rhetorical and poetic stylistic elaboration (*ornatus*) in the interest of the Christian message. Juvencus's example, however, did not find immediate imitators. With the exception of Proba's Virgilian cento (normally dated to around the 360s), which took as its subject the early chapters of Genesis and the Gospels and was to be severely criticized by Jerome on theological grounds, it was not until the last decade of the century that Christian poets again turned their hand to extended compositions in dactylic meters, while the

writing of biblical epic, if an ambiguous reference in Gennadius's notice on Prudentius is disregarded, was suspended till the fifth century.

By comparison, Latin hymnody enjoyed more rapid acceptance. Three hymns
of Hilary of Poitiers, traditionally dated to the 360s, survive, though all are incomplete. Responding to liturgical and catechetical needs and employing an idiom derived from the Bible and pagan poetry in a variety of classical meters, the hymns
show a sometimes uncomfortable blend of doctrinal and poetic aspirations. With
Ambrose, however, two decades or so later theology and aesthetics coincide in the
first classics of Western Christian hymnody. The poems for the hours of daily prayer,
the chief Christian festivals, and the martyrs combine lexical and stylistic virtuosity
with regularity of structure and uniformity of meter—each is made up of eight four-
line stanzas of iambic dimeters. Originally intended for church song in Milan, Ambrose's hymns enjoyed immediate success and exerted a widespread and long-lasting
influence on Christian Latin lyric and hymnody.

Christian Latin poetry came of age under the emperor Theodosius and his sons,
in the decades immediately preceding and following the turn of the fourth century.
Circumstances were then very different from those of the period of Constantine. The
number of Christians among the Roman aristocracy and educated classes was ever
increasing. The resources of exegesis were opening up new approaches to Christian
texts and experience; the sacred geography of the West was being transformed by the
growth of the cult of the martyrs; new forms of asceticism, the beginnings of monasticism, took root in the West in response to the increasing worldliness of the Church.
Both Paulinus of Nola and Prudentius, the two major poets of the period (along with
the secular poet Claudian), were *conversi,* men of standing who retired from public
careers to devote themselves to lives of asceticism in country retreats. For both poetry was an expression of devotion.

Paulinus was a pupil of Ausonius who retired to Nola in Campania and the service of St. Felix. Despite the words of his verse epistles to his former tutor, which talk
of renouncing secular learning, Paulinus retained a taste for poetic *variatio* and a
moderate mannerism, though in the service of Christian edification. His poems
include Christian counterparts for epideictic poetic genres, *laudes, propemptikon*
(speech of farewell to a departing traveler), *epithalamium,* and *consolatio.* The *natalicia* that make up the bulk of his poetic corpus, poems for recitation on Felix's saint's
day, combine panegyric elements and the epideictic language of ceremony with the
specifically Christian conceptual world of the cult of the saints. His employment of
dactylic meters for hagiographical subject matter, especially in the poems relating the
saint's life, death, and posthumous miracles, anticipates the later hagiographical
epics on the life of St. Martin by Paulinus of Périgueux (late fifth century) and Venantius Fortunatus (574–76).

Paulinus makes extensive use of the resources of Christian allegory in his poetry.
It is his contemporary Prudentius, however, who fully integrates traditional poetic
idiom and the multiple levels of Christian exegesis into an original body of poetry.
Unlike the works of Paulinus, most of Prudentius's poems can be described as liter-
arily ambitious equivalents of specifically Christian genres: apologetic (the *Libri contra Symmachum*), antiheretical and dogmatic treatises (the *Apotheosis* and *Hamarti-
genia*), and Ambrosian hymnody (the *Cathemerinon* and *Peristephanon*—the latter
showing also the influence of martyr passions and in some poems the epigrams of
Pope Damasus). In his lyric in particular Prudentius, by combining the figurative

language of Latin poetry with the multiple interpretive strata of Christian allegoresis, finds an idiom for the spiritualization of time, place, nature, and experience that is a distinctive mark of the late antique Christian imagination. Alone of his poems Prudentius's *Psychomachia* derives from a classical poetic genre, the epic battle narrative. In personifying the Virtues and Vices Prudentius can call on a long tradition of personifications of abstractions in Latin epic, represented in his own time by the poetry of Claudian, as well as on Christian homiletic, though to make the abstractions the main agents of the plot is a new development. At the same time, the multiple interpretive levels of the poem depend on the hermeneutic codes of contemporary exegesis. Prudentius's innovative combination of epic narrative and personification allegory was destined for great influence. The poem is often transmitted apart from his other works in medieval manuscripts. In late antiquity the account by Avitus (d. c. 518) of the exodus from Egypt in the fifth book of his Old Testament biblical epic, the *De spiritalis historiae gestis* (last decade of the fifth century), shows its influence. It too is recast as a battle narrative and can be read as a kind of *psychomachia,* but the primary narrative remains at the historical level of a conflict between Egyptians and Israelites.

By the end of the fourth century Christian and Roman were inseparably interconnected in the mental world of the educated classes. Despite occasional protests against pagan literature—most famously Jerome's dream (*Ep.* 22.30)—literary production was inconceivable apart from classical categories of rhetoric and poetics. The poetic koine of late antiquity incorporated contextually neutralized phrases from the classical poets, especially Virgil. By the late fourth century allusions that evoke a classical context frequently serve to contrast Christian and pagan concepts or to give a Christian reinterpretation of a classical text, while at the same time recognizing a basic continuity with the world of pre-Christian Rome. Mythical references are rare in poetry of Christian content except as a contrast to Christian belief. Claudian's unfinished *De raptu Proserpinae* is the last Latin mythical epic of antiquity. In Dracontius's *Romulea* and *Orestis tragoedia* myth is reduced to ideologically neutral epyllia; the traditional mythical references of epithalamia are much diminished and become formal surface decoration. Despite Augustine's criticisms in the fourth book of the *De doctrina christiana,* late antique mannerism, the delight in the formal play of language and in coloristic abundance and variation, continues to be well represented in the poetry of the period, after Ausonius especially by Sidonius, Dracontius, and Venantius Fortunatus. In general, poetry of Christan content tends to make more inhibited use of this style. (Dracontius's *De laudibus dei* is an exception.) In biblical epic it is more at home in the Old Testament tradition—the *Heptateuchos,* a pseudonymous work transmitted under the name of Cyprian, the *Alethia* of Claudius Marius Victorius (both early fifth century), and Avitus's *De spiritalis historiae gestis*—with their greater narrative and descriptive content, than in the New Testament poems of Juvencus, Sedulius (the *Carmen Paschale,* second quarter of the fifth century), and Arator (the *Historia apostolica,* A.D. 544). In hagiographic epic Paulinus of Périgueux is closer to Sedulian restraint; Fortunatus, also in a poem on St. Martin, deploys all the stylistic mannerisms of the Ausonian and Sidonian tradition.

With the barbarian invasions of the fifth century and the consequent breakup of Roman imperial administration, poetry too becomes more regionalized. In Gaul, which bore the first brunt of the invasions, a number of poems written by *conversi* or those close to ascetic circles respond to contemporary sufferings by renouncing material and worldly concerns and seeking consolation in spiritual values. The most important are the *Carmen de providentia dei,* probably the work of Prosper of Aquitaine (c. 390–after 455), a poem of Christian didactic defending divine providence; the *Commonitorium* of Orientius, normally identified with Orientius, bishop of Auch (fl. first half of fifth century), a poem of moral exhortation; and the *Eucharisticos* of Paulinus of Pella (d. c. 460), which takes the form of a verse autobiography and shows the influence of Augustine's *Confessions.* Rutilius Namatianus's *De reditu suo* (A.D. 417) makes a striking contrast to this group of poems. The work, which breaks off in the second book, is composed as a *hodoeporikon* describing the poet's journey from Rome to his native Gaul. Written in the context of the barbarian invasions, it gives the perspective of a Gallo-Roman aristocrat and patriot, and an outspoken critic of asceticism.

The fifth century is a period of substantial poetic output in Gaul, with, in addition to the poetry of the barbarian invasions, the biblical epics of Claudius Marius Victorius and Avitus (and probably also the *Heptateuchos*), the hagiographical epic of Paulinus of Périgueux, and the panegyrics, epideictic genre poetry, verse epistles, and epigrams of Sidonius Apollinaris. In the second half of the century the poetry of Dracontius and the epigrams of the *Codex Salmasianus* mark a revival of literary activity in Vandal North Africa. So long as the grammatical and rhetorical curriculum of the ancient school system survived, so too did the continuing tradition of late antique poetry. With the exception of Visigothic Spain, of which Eugenius of Toledo (bishop 646–57) is the only significant poet, that system survived longest in Italy. The last major poets of late antiquity all were educated or composed most of their poetry in north Italy, in and around the city of Ravenna. Ennodius, the author of epigrams, verse epistles, and hagiographic/epideictic poetry, as well as a large corpus of prose works, was Gallic born but spent most of his productive life in that milieu, and became bishop of Pavia. Arator, the author of the biblical epic *Historia apostolica,* was educated in Ravenna, though his poem was written and recited in Rome and is dedicated to Pope Vigilius. Finally, Venantius Fortunatus, the "last poet of antiquity and the first of the Middle Ages," migrated from northern Italy to Gaul and brought the literary talents acquired in his homeland to the service of secular and ecclesiastical patrons in the Frankish kingdoms.

Fortunatus, as a Christian poet writing occasional poetry for Church and court, was especially congenial to Carolingian literary circles. He transmitted to that period the late antique tradition of small-scale poetry: epigrams, figure poetry—first and most fully represented in late antiquity by the collection of the Constantinian poet Optatianus Porfyrius (fl. early fourth century)—and the epideictic poetic genres. His hymns *Vexilla regis* and *Pange lingua,* more successful than those of his predecessor Ennodius, were destined for use in the liturgy, where they communicate something of the spirit of late antique mannerism. A second major influence on Anglo-Latin and Carolingian poetry was the New Testament biblical epic. The combination of abbreviated narrative pericopes with spiritualizing commentary developed by Sedulius and Arator was very much to the taste of succeeding centuries. Sedulius's decision to follow his *Carmen paschale* with a prose version of the same work (the *Opus paschale*) also left its mark. It inaugurated a new literary form, the double work (*opus geminatum*), that found imitators in the *De virginitate* of Aldhelm (d. 709/10), the *Vita S. Cuthberti* of Bede (d. 735), and the *Vita S. Willibrordi* of Alcuin (d. 804). Finally, the tendency to see prose and verse as complementary rather than discrete means of expression encouraged experiments with prosimetric forms, most importantly in the *De nuptiis Philologiae et Mercurii libri novem* (fifth century) of Martianus Capella and in Boethius's *Consolatio philosophiae* (mid-520s).

## Select Bibliography

### Primary Works

Most of the poets of late antiquity were edited late in the nineteenth or early in the twentieth century in the *CSEL, MGH* (*Auctores antiquissimi* [= *AA*]) or, occasionally, the Teubner series. Since then new editions have appeared of some poets, though without always entirely superseding the earlier editions.

Aldhelm, *Opera*, ed. R. Ehwald, *MGH.AA* 15 (1913–19, r1984) [**GB1**].

Ambrose, *De obitu Valentiniani* and *De obitu Theodosii*, ed. O. Faller, *CSEL* 73 (1955) [**GB2**].

Ambrose, *Hymni*, in *Hymni Latini antiquissimi LXXV, Psalmi III*, ed. W. Bulst (1956) [**GB3**]; ed. J. Fontaine *et al.* (1992) [**GB4**].

Arator, *De actibus apostolorum* [*Historia apostolica*], ed. A.P. McKinlay, *CSEL* 72 (1951) [**GB5**].

Augustine, *De doctrina christiana libri quattuor*, ed. W.M. Green, *CSEL* 80 (1963) [**GB6**].

Augustine, *Psalmus contra partem Donati*, ed. C. Lambot, "Texte complété et amendé du 'Psalmus contra partem Donati,' de saint Augustin," in *RB* 47 (1935) 312–30 [**GB7**].

Ausonius, *Opuscula*, ed. R.P.H. Green (1991) [**GB8**]; ed. S. Prete (1978) [**GB9**].

Avitus, *Opera*, ed. R. Peiper, *MGH.AA* 6.2 (1883) [**GB10**].

Bede, *Bedas metrische Vita Sancti Cuthberti*, ed. W. Jaager (1935) [**GB11**].

Boethius, *Philosophiae consolatio*, ed. L. Bieler, 2nd ed., *CC* 94 (1984) [**GB12**].

Claudian, *Carmina*, ed. J.B. Hall (1985) [**GB13**].

Claudian, *Oeuvres*, ed. J.-L. Charlet (1991) [**GB14**].

Claudius Marius Victorius, *Alethia*, ed. P.F. Hovingh, *CCSL* 128 (1960) [**GB15**]; ed. C. Schenkl, *CSEL* 16 (1888) [**GB16**].

*Codex Salmasianus*, ed. D.R. Shackleton Bailey, *Anthologia Latina* 1.1 (1982) [**GB17**].

Commodian, *Carmina*, ed. J. Martin, *CCSL* 128 (1960) [**GB18**].

Corippus, *Iohannis*, ed. J. Diggle and F.R.D. Goodyear (1970) [**GB19**].

Corippus, *In laudem Iustini augusti minoris*, ed. A. Cameron (1976) [**GB20**]; ed. S. Antès (1981) [**GB21**].

Cyprianus Gallus, *Heptateuchos*, ed. R. Peiper, *CSEL* 23 (1891) [**GB22**].

Damasus, *Epigrammata*, ed. A. Ferrua (1942); a new edition of the epigrams is expected, ed. J.-L. Charlet, P.A. Février, and J. Guyon [**GB23**].

Dracontius, *Carmina*, ed. F. Vollmer, *MGH.AA* 14 (1905) [**GB24**]; ed. C. Moussy and C. Camus (1985–) [**GB25**].

Dracontius, *Romulea*, ed. J.M. Diaz de Bustamente: *Dracontio y sus carmina profana: Estudio biográfico, introducción y edición crítica* (1978) [**GB26**].

Ennodius, *Opera*, ed. F. Vogel, *MGH.AA* 7 (1885) [**GB27**]; ed. W. von Hartel, *CSEL* 6 (1872) [**GB28**].

Eugenius of Toledo, *Carmina et epistulae*, ed. F. Vollmer, *MGH.AA* 14 (1905) [GB29].

Fortunatus, *Opera*, ed. F. Leo, *MGH.AA* 4.1–2 (1881–85) [GB30].

Gennadius, *Liber de viris illustribus*, ed. E.C. Richardson, *Texte und Untersuchungen zur Geschichte der altchristlichen Literatur* 14.1 (1896) 57–97 [GB31].

Hilary, *Hymni*, in *Hymni Latini Antiquissimi LXXV* (see [GB3]) 31–35 [GB32].

Jerome, *Epistulae*, ed. J. Labourt, 8 vols. (1949–63) [GB33].

Juvencus, *Evangeliorum libri quattuor*, ed. J. Huemer, *CSEL* 24 (1891) [GB34].

Lactantius, *Opera*, ed. S. Brandt and G. Laubmann, *CSEL* 19 and 27 (1890–97) [GB35].

Martianus Capella, *De nuptiis Philologiae et Mercurii*, ed. J. Willis (1983) [GB36].

Merobaudes, *Reliquiae*, ed. F. Vollmer, *MGH.AA* 14 (1905) [GB37].

Nemesianus, *Oeuvres*, ed. P. Volpilhac (1975) [GB38].

Optatianus Porfyrius, *Carmina*, ed. G. Polara, 2 vols. (1973) [GB39].

Orientius, *Carmina*, ed. R. Ellis, *CSEL* 16 (1888) [GB40].

Orientius, *Commonitorium et carmina Orientio tributa*, ed. C.A. Rapisarda (1958) [GB41].

*Panegyrici Latini*, ed. R.A.B. Mynors (1964) [GB42].

Paulinus of Nola, *Opera*, ed. W. von Hartel, *CSEL* 29–30 (1894) [GB43].

Paulinus of Pella, *Eucharisticos*, ed. C. Moussy, *SChr* 209 (1974) [GB44].

Paulinus of Périgueux, *Vita Sancti Martini*, ed. M. Petschenig, *CSEL* 16 (1888) [GB45].

*Pervigilium Veneris*, ed. A. Cameron, in *La poesia tardoantica* (see [GB57]) 209–34 [GB46].

Priscian, *De laude Anastasii imperatoris*, ed. E. Baehrens, *Poetae latini minores* 5 (1883) 264–74 [GB47].

Proba, *Cento Vergilianus*, ed. C. Schenkl, *CSEL* 16 (1888) [GB48].

Prosper of Aquitaine, *Carmen de providentia dei*, ed. M. Marcovich (1989) [GB49].

Prudentius, *Carmina*, ed. J. Bergman, *CSEL* 61 (1926) [GB50]; ed. M.P. Cunningham, *CCSL* 126 (1961) [GB51].

Prudentius, *Oeuvres*, ed. M. Lavarenne, 4 vols., 2nd ed. (1955–63) [GB52].

Rutilius Namatianus, *De reditu suo sive iter Gallicum*, ed. E. Doblhofer, 2 vols. (1972–77) [GB53].

Sedulius, *Opera*, ed. J. Huemer, *CSEL* 10 (1885) [GB54].

Sidonius Apollinaris, *Opera*, ed. A. Loyen, 3 vols. (1960–70) [GB55].

## Studies

### (a) General Treatments

There are three collections of papers that are especially important and provide a useful introduction to the study of Late Latin poetry:

*Christianisme et formes littéraires de l'antiquité tardive en occident*, Entretiens sur l'antiquité classique 23 (1977): for Late Latin poetry the most important contributions are by P.G. Van der Nat (on the importance of Lactantius for early Christian literature; pp191–225), R. Herzog (on the issue of continuity between pagan and Christian literary genres; pp373–411), and J. Fontaine (a fundamental study of the common aesthetic presuppositions of late fourth-century literature, whatever the subject matter of a text or the confessional status of the author; pp425–72) [GB56].

*La poesia tardoantica: Tra retorica, teologia e politica: Atti del V corso della Scuola superiore di archeologia e civiltà medievali* (6–12 December 1981) (1984): important for rhetoric and epideictic literary forms in late antiquity; also contains a major study by A. Cameron on the date and authorship of the *Pervigilium Veneris* [GB57].

*Philologus* 132 (1988): a volume dedicated to Late Latin literature, especially poetry; it contains literary historical studies by S. Döpp (pp19–52) and H. Hofmann (on the panegyrical epic of late antiquity; pp101–59), articles on aesthetic trends and the question of genre by J.-L. Charlet (pp74–85) and J. Fontaine (pp53–73), and among many other studies of individual authors and problems a contribution by F. Stella (pp258–74) on the genre of Dracontius's *De laudibus dei* [GB58].

In addition, the following books, monographs, and articles provide an overview of Late Latin literature, or of some aspect or genre of that literature:

G. Bernt, *Das lateinische Epigramm im Übergang von der Spätantike zum frühen Mittelalter* (1968) [GB59].

P. Courcelle, *Histoire littéraire des grandes invasions germaniques,* 3rd ed. (1964) [GB60].

P. Courcelle, *Late Latin Writers and Their Greek Sources,* tr. H.E. Wedeck (1969) [GB61].

S. D'Elia, *Letteratura latina cristiana* (1982) [GB62].

J. Fontaine, *Études sur la poésie latine tardive d'Ausone à Prudence* (1980): a collection of articles by one of the leading scholars of Late Latin literature. The first two articles, on the interference of genres in late antiquity and a reprint of Fontaine's article in [GB56], are especially important. The volume also contains a study of the style of early Christian hymnody (Hilary and Ambrose) and its relation to the classical poetic tradition (= *REL* 52 [1974] 318–55) [GB63].

J. Fontaine, *Naissance de la poésie dans l'occident chrétien: Esquisse d'une histoire de la poésie latine chrétienne du IIIe au VIe siècle* (1981) [GB64].

H. Hagendahl, *Von Tertullian zu Cassiodor: Die profane literarische Tradition in dem lateinischen christlichen Schrifttum* (1983) [GB65].

R. Herzog, *Die Bibelepik der lateinischen Spätantike: Formgeschichte einer erbaulichen Gattung,* v1 (1975) [GB66].

R. Herzog *et al.,* eds., *Restauration und Erneuerung: Die lateinische Literatur von 284 bis 374 n. Chr.* (1989), Handbuch der lateinischen Literatur der Antike, Bd. 5 [GB67].

W. Kirsch, *Die lateinische Versepik des 4. Jahrhunderts* (1989) [GB68].

P. Klopsch, *Einführung in die Dichtungslehren des lateinischen Mittelalters* (1980) [GB69].

S.G. MacCormack, *Art and Ceremony in Late Antiquity* (1981) [GB70].

H.I. Marrou, *Saint Augustin et la fin de la culture antique,* 4th ed. (1958) [GB71].

P. Riché, *Education and Culture in the Barbarian West from the Sixth through the Eighth Century,* tr. J.J. Contreni (1976) [GB72].

M. Roberts, *Biblical Epic and Rhetorical Paraphrase in Late Antiquity* (1985) [GB73].

M. Roberts, *The Jeweled Style: Poetry and Poetics in Late Antiquity* (1989) [GB74].

K. Thraede, "Epos," in *RLAC* 5:983–1042 [GB75].

K. Thraede, "Untersuchungen zum Ursprung und zur Geschichte der christlichen Poesie I–III," in *JBAC* 4 (1961) 108–27, 5 (1962) 125–57, and 6 (1963) 101–11 [GB76].

C. Witke, *Numen litterarum: The Old and the New in Latin Poetry from Constantine to Gregory the Great* (1971) [GB77].

## (b) Specific Authors and Problems

D.F. Bright, *The Miniature Epic in Vandal Africa* (1987) [GB78].

A. Cameron, *Claudian: Poetry and Propaganda at the Court of Honorius* (1970) [GB79].

J.-L. Charlet, *La création poétique dans le Cathemerinon de Prudence* (1982) [GB80].

J.-L. Charlet, *L'influence d'Ausone sur la poésie de Prudence* (1980) [GB81].

P.-A. Deproost, *L'apôtre Pierre dans une épopée du VIe siècle: L'Historia apostolica d'Arator* (1990) [GB82].

S. Döpp, *Zeitgeschichte in Dichtungen Claudians* (1980) [GB83].

P. Fabre, *Essai sur la chronologie de l'oeuvre de saint Paulin de Nole* (1948) [GB84].

J. Fontaine, "Christentum ist auch Antike: Einige Überlegungen zu Bildung und Literatur in der lateinischen Spätantike," in *JBAC* 25 (1982) 5–21 [GB85].

J. Fontaine, "Ennodius," in *RLAC* 5:398–421 [GB86].

J. Fontaine, "Die westgotische lateinische Literatur: Probleme und Perspectiven," in *A&A* 12 (1966) 64–87 [GB87].

M. Fuhrmann, "Die lateinische Literatur der Spätantike: Ein literarhistorischer Beitrag zum Kontinuitätsproblem," in *A&A* 13 (1967) 56–79 [GB88].

J.W. George, *Venantius Fortunatus: A Latin Poet in Merovingian Gaul* (1992) [GB89].

C. Gnilka, *Chresis: Die Methode der Kirchenväter im Umgang mit der antiken Kultur*, 2 vols. (1984–93) [GB90].

C. Gnilka, "Interpretation frühchristlicher Literatur Dargestellt am Beispiel des Prudentius," in *Impulse für die lateinische Lektüre: Von Terenz bis Thomas Morus*, ed. H. Krefeld (1979) 138–80 [GB91].

C. Gnilka, *Studien zur Psychomachie des Prudentius* (1963) [GB92].

I. Gualandri, *Furtiva Lectio: Studi su Sidonio Apollinare* (1979) [GB93].

H. Hagendahl, *Augustine and the Latin Classics*, 2 vols. (1967) [GB94].

H. Hagendahl, *Latin Fathers and the Classics: A Study on the Apologists, Jerome, and Other Christian Writers* (1958) [GB95].

R. Herzog, *Die allegorische Dichtkunst des Prudentius* (1966) [GB96].

R. Herzog, "Exegese—Erbauung—Delectatio: Beiträge zu einer christlichen Poetik der Spätantike," in *Formen und Funktionen der Allegorie: Symposion Wolfenbüttel 1978*, ed. W. Haug (1979) 52–69 [GB97].

H. Junod-Ammerbauer, "Le poète chrétien selon Paulin de Nole: L'adaptation des thèmes classiques dans les Natalicia," in *REAug* 21 (1975) 13–54 [GB98].

H. Junod-Ammerbauer, "Les constructions de Nole et l'esthétique de saint Paulin," in *REAug* 24 (1978) 22–57 [GB99].

U. Keudel, *Poetische Vorläufer und Vorbilder in Claudians De consulatu Stilichonis: Imitationskommentar* (1970) [GB100].

I. Lana, *Due capitoli Prudenziani: La biografia, la cronologia delle opere, la poetica* (1962) [GB101].

A. Loyen, *Sidoine Apollinaire et l'esprit précieux en Gaule aux derniers jours de l'empire* (1943) [GB102].

S.G. MacCormack, "Latin Prose Panegyrics: Tradition and Discontinuity in the Later Roman Empire," in *REAug* 22 (1976) 29–77 [GB103].

M. Malamud, *A Poetics of Transformation: Prudentius and Classical Mythology* (1989) [GB104].

W. Meyer, *Der Gelegenheitsdichter Venantius Fortunatus* (1901) [GB105].

G. O'Daly, *The Poetry of Boethius* (1991) [GB106].

A.-M. Palmer, *Prudentius on the Martyrs* (1989) [GB107].

J.-M. Poinsotte, *Juvencus et Israël: La représentation des Juifs dans le premier poème latin chrétien* (1979) [GB108].

M. Roberts, "Rhetoric and Poetic Imitation in Avitus' Account of the Crossing of the Red Sea (*De spiritalis historiae gestis* 5.371–702)," in *Traditio* 39 (1983) 29–80 [GB109].

M. Roberts, "The Use of Myth in Latin Epithalamia from Statius to Venantius Fortunatus," in *Transactions of the American Philological Association* 119 (1989) 321–48 [GB110].

M. Roberts, *Poetry and the Cult of the Martyrs: The Liber Peristephanon of Prudentius* (1993) [GB111].

I. Rodriguez-Herrera, *Poeta Christianus: Prudentius' Auffassung vom Wesen und von der Ausgabe des christlichen Dichters* (1936) [GB112].

C.P.E. Springer, *The Gospel as Epic in Late Antiquity: The "Paschale Carmen" of Sedulius* (1988) [GB113].

K. Thraede, *Studien zu Sprache und Stil des Prudentius* (1965) [GB114].

M.M. Van Assendelft, *Sol Ecce Surgit Igneus: A Commentary on the Morning and Evening Hymns of Prudentius (Cathemerinon 1, 2, 5 and 6)* (1976) [GB115].

*See also* [BB50], [BC21], [BC37], [BD41], [BD58], [BD71].

# GC • EPIC

BY JAN M. ZIOLKOWSKI

Epics are generally defined as long narrative poems, in a grand style, that celebrate heroic deeds. The heroes, who have intimate relationships with divine beings, perform feats in battles or travels. Often they found or save nations or races. Conventions of classical epic include invocations, epithets, formulae, extended speeches and similes, descriptions of warriors and battles, vast settings, narrative structures that throw audiences in medias res, and catalogues of combatants, nations, and ships. In Classical Latin the heroic line is the dactylic hexameter; in Medieval Latin the hexameter continued to be preferred, although distichs and even rhythmic meters were also employed.

The preeminent Classical Latin epic was the *Aeneid* of Virgil (70–19 B.C.), which became a standard school text soon after the poet's death. Other long classical poems on epic themes in heroic hexameters were the *Metamorphoses* of Ovid (43 B.C.–A.D. 17), the unfinished *Bellum civile* of Lucan (c. A.D. 39–65), the *Thebaid* and incomplete *Achilleid* of Statius (c. A.D. 45–96), and the unfinished *De raptu Proserpinae* of Claudian (d. c. 404).

Christians had to reach difficult decisions about Virgil and other pre-Christian epic poets. They could not dispense with the educational system erected around these authors, but at the same time they could not accept pagan writings without achieving an accommodation. They could keep Virgil's oeuvre, but for its style rather than content. They could cite his "Messianic" fourth eclogue and other data to confirm that Virgil had been covertly or unwittingly Christian. Whether or not they believed in a Christian Virgil, they could interpret the *Aeneid* as conveying philosophical or even religious truth: for instance, they could explain that the literal account of Aeneas's wanderings disguised an allegory of the Christian soul. Such allegoresis enabled Christians to justify retaining pagan poets in the curriculum.

To complement or even replace the *Aeneid* poets could write hexameter poems in Virgilian style but on Christian topics. Isidore of Seville (d. 636) pointed out (*Etymologiae* 1.39.9–13) the epic quality of songs about the deeds of Moses and others, but already earlier writers had begun to view biblical events as heroic and to paraphrase in hexameter narratives many parts of the Bible, especially of the New Testament. One work from late antiquity, Proba's *Cento Virgilianus* (c. 360), offered an exposition of salvation history from a Christian point of view in lines and half-lines garnered almost entirely from Virgil.

Bible epics of the fourth through sixth centuries, by such poets as Juvencus (*Evangeliorum libri IV*, 329/30), Caelius Sedulius (*Carmen paschale*, c. 450), Avitus (*De spiritalis historiae gestis*, c. 500), and Arator (*De actibus apostolorum*, 544), became enshrined in the schoolrooms of the Latin Middle Ages. Such epic-length biblical narratives were not attempted again in Latin verse until the twelfth century, when Hildebert of Lavardin (d. 1133) produced several recastings of Bible books, Matthew of Vendôme (fl. second half of the twelfth century) versified the Book of Tobit, and Peter Riga (d. 1209) composed *Aurora*, a highly successful commentary on allegorical and moral dimensions of episodes in the historical books.

Another innovation of Christian antiquity was the allegorical epic, narrating actions of personified abstractions. The first poem based almost entirely upon such personification was the *Psychomachia* of Prudentius (d. after 404); truly epic in martial theme and hexametric form, it describes a battle between virtues and vices for the human soul. Twelfth-century allegorical epics, such as the *Anticlaudianus* (1181–84) of Alan of Lille and the *Architrenius* (completed 1184–85) of John of Hauville, devote little space to martial activity but retain travels of epic scope. Most of the *Anticlaudianus* tracks Lady Nature and her fellow abstractions as they construct a new man and secure for him a soul from heaven. John's "archmourner" guides the reader on a quest for Lady Nature, with stops at the palace of Venus, the house of Gluttony, the schools of Paris, the mountain of Ambition, the hill of Presumption, and Ultima Thule.

Into the haze between Bible epic and personification allegory falls the extraordinary work of a poet known by the Greek pseudonym Eupolemius (c. 1100). In two books of hexameters, it translates the cosmic myth of the contention between God and Satan over humanity into an epic that takes full advantage of epic accoutrements. Although the poet does not diverge grossly from major events of salvation history such as the fall, Babylonian captivity, and arrival of the Messiah, he takes care not to adhere slavishly to the Bible. He coins names from Greek elements for half of his characters; and although he assigns biblical names to the rest, he declares that they and their namesakes are not identical.

If the central figures of epics are heroes closely related to divine beings, then saints—those distinguished imitators of Christ—were candidates for leading roles in hagiographic epics. In the fifth century, Paulinus of Périgueux (d. 472) wrote a six-book hexameter account of the life and miracles of St. Martin that rested largely upon the biography by Sulpicius Severus (d. c. 420). In turn Venantius Fortunatus (second half of sixth century) based his four-book *De virtutibus sancti Martini* on both Paulinus and Sulpicius.

The lives, deaths, and miracles of saints could be presented variously. Some hagiographic narratives contain motifs found in romances, such as extraordinary births, prophetic dreams, tests of chastity, and mortifications of the flesh for the sake of a higher love. Such motifs appear in the prose *Vita sancti Alexii* (probably tenth century). Often the lives encompass sections reminiscent of heroic epics. For example, the Latin prose life of Guthlac (c. 730–40) attributed to Felix portrays a young man who progresses from living as an actual warrior to fighting as a soldier of God against demonic temptations. The *Navigatio sancti Brendani abbatis* (probably tenth century) follows a saint as he sails with companions from one marvelous island to another.

Another class of historical poems that related deeds of holy men was the *vitae* of abbots and bishops. Two typical examples, both in leonines, would be an anonymous life of Archbishop Albero of Trier (1131–56) and Anselm of Mainz's celebration (1141–42) of the attainments of Archbishop Adalbert II.

Through most of the Middle Ages Latin was the preferred language for recording important events, such as military campaigns, in the lives of emperors, kings, and dukes. A Latin poem in the epic manner of Virgil not only demonstrated the heights of culture attained by a given court but also guaranteed that the achievements of the person or place celebrated could be transmitted to people elsewhere and to later generations. These historical poems offer broad perspectives on literary culture during the transitional periods between the classicizing Latin epics of late antiquity and the Old French chansons de geste of the eleventh and later centuries.

The epoch of Charlemagne and his inheritors was rich in hexameter compositions that employed epic language and conventions. This wealth is evident in *Karolus Magnus et Leo Papa,* also called "The Paderborn Epic" (c. 799). In describing the building of Aachen the anonymous poet draws language from the construction of Carthage in the *Aeneid;* in portraying a hunt, from descriptions of combats in Virgil's poem and other ancient epics. An anonymous poet, conventionally designated Poeta Saxo, wrote a poem (c. 888) about Charlemagne, *De gestis Caroli Magni.* Each of its five books treats a decade in the ruler's life, from 771 on. Beyond the reign of Charlemagne is a poem (c. 827) honoring Louis the Pious by Ermoldus Nigellus (d. after 835); now entitled *In honorem Hludowici,* it was called *Elegiacum carmen* by Ermoldus and includes accounts of wars in Spain and Brittany.

Few historical epics are extant from the later ninth and tenth centuries. From the end of the ninth century comes the *Bella Parisiacae urbis* by Abbo of St. Germain-des-Prés (d. after 921). Two books are concerned mainly with the unsuccessful siege of Paris by the Danes in 885–86; the third proffers moral precepts to the clergy. After Abbo, the next important historical epic is the *Gesta Berengarii* (915–24) by an anonymous Italian, which relates the martial accomplishments of the emperor Berengar (crowned in 915). Intended to demonstrate Berengar's legitimacy, it achieves its own validity within epic tradition through classical allusions, similes, and descriptions of single combats. The *Gesta Ottonis* of Hrotsvitha of Gandersheim (c. 935–1001/3) recounts the deeds of Otto the Great until his coronation as emperor.

In the late eleventh and twelfth centuries historical epics abound in Western Europe, as poets gratify the desires of nobles to memorialize their ancestors. Sometime after the Battle of Hastings, a poet—perhaps Bishop Guy of Amiens (1058–75)—wrote the *Carmen de Hastingae proelio* in elegiacs indebted to Ovid and early medieval epic poets. In the winter of 1075–76 an unknown poet composed *Carmen de bello saxonico,* a panegyric on Henry IV's triumphs in suppressing the Saxon revolt (1073–75). Toward the end of the century William of Apulia commemorated the accomplishments in Italy of the Norman Robert Guiscard (d. 1085) in the five-book *Gesta Roberti Wiscardi.* Gunther of Pairis (d. c. 1208) wrote two historical poems, one (the fragmentary *Solimarius*) versifying Robert of Reims's account of the First Crusade and the other (entitled *Ligurinus*) books 2–4 of the *Gesta Friderici* by Otto of Freising and Rahewin.

Italy was particularly productive of epics to honor deeds performed in its lands or by its peoples. Late in the first quarter of the twelfth century Henry of Pisa wrote an early Crusade epic, the eight-part *Liber Maiorichinus* that recounts the campaign of the Pisans against the Arabs of Majorca in 1114–15. At approximately the same time, the anonymous poet of *De bello urbis Comensis* gave a long account of the war between Milan and Como (autumn 1118–27). Within a few decades (c. 1120–30) Moses of Bergamo described the topography and history of his native city in *Pergaminus*. Between 1162 and 1166 the anonymous poet of the *Carmen de gestis Frederici I imperatoris in Lombardia* celebrated the deeds of the emperor in northern Italy (1152–60). In the *Liber ad honorem Augusti* (also known as *De rebus Siculis carmen*) Peter of Eboli (d. c. 1221) praised Emperor Henry VI and recorded events after the death of William the Good of Sicily (1189). A peculiar historical epic is the *Draco Normannicus* (c. 1169) by Stephen of Rouen, a monk of Bec. Although essentially a history of the house of Anjou and a panegyric of Henry II, the three-book poem in distichs also includes legends about the legendary Arthur and Merlin.

The line between history and story, fact and legend, truth and fiction, was never more blurred than in the Middle Ages. Although Medieval Latin historians were often conditioned stylistically by their knowledge of the classics, for information they often relied upon local oral traditions. Despite opposition from Church authorities, native poetic traditions did not disappear. Indeed, these traditions were widely cultivated. In the eighth century Alcuin rebukes the monks of Lindisfarne for listening to songs of the hero Ingeld when instead they should consider Christ. In the ninth century (c. 833) Einhard informs us (*Vita Karoli* 29) that Charlemagne caused "age-old narrative poems" to be collected. In the eleventh century (1057–64) Meinhard of Bamberg complains of his bishop's predilection for stories of Attila and Dietrich of Bern.

What impact did native songs and traditions have upon Medieval Latin literature? Prose works, such as the *Historia Langobardorum* of Paul the Deacon (c. 720–99) and the anonymous *De obsessione Dunelmi* (late eleventh century), sometimes drew heavily upon oral traditions of the Germanic peoples whose history they relate. On rare occasions authors strove to replicate in Latin not only the content but even the style of native epics; such is the case with the translation of the Old English *Brunanburh* by Henry of Huntingdon (d. 1155).

A spectacular and complex transposition of native Germanic heroic legends is the *Waltharius,* which relates the destiny of Walter of Aquitaine: his sojourn as a hostage at Attila's court, escape with Hildegund and the Huns' treasure, and battle with Gunther's men and his friend Hagen. Apart from it and the Old English *Beowulf* (dated variously from the late eighth through the early eleventh century), no other early Germanic epic survives in toto; apart from it and the Old High German *Hildebrandslied* (dated variously from the eighth century through 840) no major native heroic poem is extant from Germany and its environs from before the twelfth century. (The *Waltharius* itself has been dated variously in the ninth and tenth centuries.) The poem covers a little of the same ground as the fragmentary Old English *Waldere,* but the two poems diverge substantially in characterization, style, and narrative sequence.

Not only Germanic native traditions conditioned Medieval Latin writers. Within the Latin prose of the Hague Fragment (c. 980–1030) lies embedded a hexameter poem that culminates in a fight led by Charlemagne and four heroes from the William Cycle of chansons de geste. Whereas the Hague Fragment antedates the Old French poems with which it is related, the *Carmen de prodicione Guenonis* (c. 1200) was plainly influenced by the *Chanson de Roland* (c. 1100).

Celtic legends of Arthur entered Latin most enduringly in Geoffrey of Monmouth's prose *Historia regum Britanniae* (completed c. 1138). Other Arthurian material appears in the possibly twelfth-century prose *De ortu Waluuanii* and *Historia Meriadoci;* the only verse epic is Geoffrey's extraordinary *Vita Merlini* (after 1148), which exercised little or no effect on later authors.

An arresting antecedent of vernacular romances is the anonymous *Ruodlieb* (eleventh century), extant in 20 fragments of leonine hexameters. It tells of a young nobleman who goes into exile with a wise king and experiences adventures on his way home. Remarkable for incorporating folk motifs within a portrayal of knighthood, the poem comes tantalizingly close to romances composed a century later.

The first generation of Old French romances dealt with the "matter of Rome"—classical myths, histories, stories, and legends. Similar adaptations were attempted in Latin, especially in the twelfth century. The adventures of Alexander the Great had been recorded in Quintus Curtius Rufus's prose *Historiae Alexandri Magni Macedonis* (mid-first century A.D.). Apart from episodes in an incomplete ninth-century abecedary, the most significant Latin reshaping of the Alexander story is Walter of Châtillon's hexameter *Alexandreis* (c. 1182). This poem swiftly won a niche in the schools from which it was not soon dislodged.

The only Latin romance from antiquity, the prose *Historia Apollonii regis Tyri* (fifth or sixth century), inspired no imitators in Latin, apart from a partial reworking in leonines (tenth century). In contrast, the story of Troy attracted repeated attention, thanks to the grandeur of Virgil and the ambition of rulers to validate their dynasties by claiming Trojan genealogy. Poets knew not only Virgil but also the prose accounts of the purported eyewitnesses Dares and Dictys and the verse *Ilias latina* sometimes ascribed to Baebius Italicus; the last-mentioned offered poets in the West their closest approach to Homer. The first book of the *Ilias latina* was recast in leonines in the twelfth century. Dares, who as a Trojan appealed more to Western allegiances, was versified (c. 1150) by an anonymous poet. Simon Capra Aurea (Chèvre d'Or) drew upon Dares and Virgil to create *Ylias,* the most extensive version of which is 994 verses. The two most important epic retellings of the Trojan War relied principally upon Dares: the *Frigii Daretis Yliados libri sex* (c. 1185) in hexameters by Joseph of Exeter (d. ca. 1210) and the *Troilus* in distichs by Albert of Stade (d. 1265).

Space permits only fleeting mention of epyllia, narrative poems that elaborate single episodes from the heroic past and resemble epics in theme, tone, and descriptive technique. A representative epyllion on a historical topic is the *Rhythmus pisanus* (291 rhythmic verses in 72 tetrastichic strophes), on the victory of 1087 over African pirates; an epyllion on a folktale is Letald of Micy's *De quodam piscatore quem ballena absorbuit* (second half of the tenth century). A related genre is mock epic, which burlesques epic by treating a trivial topic in epic style. Amusing representatives are the *Altercatio nani et leporis* and the *De Lombardo et lumaca.*

More important than epyllia and mock epics are epics themselves. The overview presented here should suffice to rebut the opinion expressed in a standard history of medieval literature that "[t]he Latin epic of the Middle Ages is not significant in the history of literature." Medieval Latin epics are important for the evidence they provide of lost or poorly documented traditions in both Germanic and Romance, but especially for the artistic excellence attained by many of them, and for the strong influence they exerted on such later vernacular poets as Dante and Chaucer.

## Select Bibliography

### Primary Works

Abbo of St. Germain-des-Prés, *Bella Parisiacae urbis*, ed. P. von Winterfeld, in *MGH.Poetae* 4.1 (1899, r1978) 77–122 [GC1]; bks. 1–2, ed. and tr. H. Waquet, *CHFMA* 20 (1942, r1964) [GC2]; bk. 1, ed. and tr. A. Pauels (1984) [GC3].

Alan of Lille, *Anticlaudianus*, ed. R. Bossuat, Textes philosophiques du moyen âge 1 (1955); tr. J.J. Sheridan (1973) [GC4].

Albert of Stade, *Troilus*, ed. T. Merzdorf (1875) [GC5].

*Altercatio nani et leporis*, ed. E. Dümmler, "Lateinische Gedichte des neunten bis elften Jahrhunderts," in *Neues Archiv der Gesellschaft für ältere deutsche Geschichtskunde* 10 (1885) 333–57: text, pp354–55; tr. J.M. Ziolkowski, *TA*, app. 32, pp303–4 [GC6].

Anonymous poem (*Gesta metrica*) on life of Archbishop Albero of Trier, ed. G. Waitz, in *MGH.Scriptores* (in Folio) 8 (1848, r1992) 236–43 [GC7].

Anselm of Mainz, verse life of Archbishop Adalbert II (*Vita Adelberti II Moguntini*), ed. P. Jaffé, *Bibliotheca rerum Germanicarum* 3 (1866, r1964) 568–603 [GC8].

*Carmen de bello saxonico*, ed. O. Holder-Egger, *MGH.SRG* 17 (1889, r1978) [GC9]; ed. and tr. F.-J. Schmale, *Quellen zur Geschichte Kaiser Heinrichs IV*, Ausgewählte Quellen zur deutschen Geschichte des Mittelalters 12, 3rd ed. (1974) 144–89 [GC10].

*Carmen de gestis Frederici I. imperatoris in Lombardia*, ed. I. Schmale-Ott, *MGH.SRG* 62 (1965) [GC11].

*Carmen de prodicione Guenonis*, ed. G. Paris, "Le Carmen de prodicione Guenonis et la légende de Roncevaux," in *Romania* 11 (1882) 465–518 [GC12].

*De bello urbis Comensis liber Cumanus*, ed. L.A. Muratori, in *Rerum Italicarum Scriptores* 5 (Milan 1724) 413–58 [GC13].

*De Lombardo et lumaca*, ed. and tr. M. Bonacina, in *Commedie latine del XII e XIII secolo*, Pubblicazioni dell'Istituto di filologia classica e medievale dell'Università di Genova 79.4 (1983) 95–135: text, pp124–33; tr. J.M. Ziolkowski, *TA*, app. 22, pp292–93 [GC14].

*De obsessione Dunelmi*, in *Symeonis monachi opera omnia*, ed. T. Arnold, *RSer* 75.1 (1882) 215–20 [GC15].

*De ortu Waluuanii nepotis Arturi*, ed. and tr. M.L. Day (1984) [GC16].

Ermoldus Nigellus, *In honorem Hludowici*, ed. E. Dümmler, in *MGH.Poetae* 2 (1884, r1978) 4–79 [GC17]; ed. and tr. E. Faral, *CHFMA* 14 (1932, r1964) [GC18].

Eupolemius, *Das Bibelgedicht*, ed. K. Manitius, *MGH.Quellen zur Geistesgeschichte der Mittelalters* 9 (1973); tr. J.M. Ziolkowski, "The Eupolemius," in *JMLat* 1 (1991) 1–45 [GC19].

Fulco, *Historia gestorum viae nostri temporis Jerosolymitanae*, ed. Académie royale des Inscriptions et Belles-Lettres, in *RHC.Historiens occidentaux* 5.2 (1895) 697–720 [GC20].

Geoffrey of Monmouth, *Historia regum Britanniae*, 5 vols. (1985–91): v1 is an edition by N. Wright, of Bern, Burgerbibliothek, MS 568; v2 is Wright's edition of "the first variant version"; v5 is an edition and translation by Wright of the *Gesta regum Britannie*; v3–4, by J.C. Crick, are a catalogue of manuscripts and a study of the *Historia*'s medieval dissemination and reception [GC21]; id., *Vita Merlini*, ed. and tr. B. Clarke (1973) [GC22].

*Gesta Apollonii*, ed. E. Dümmler, in *MGH.Poetae* 2 (1884, r1964) 484–506 [GC23].

*Gesta Berengarii imperatoris,* ed. P. von Winterfeld, in *MGH.Poetae* 4.1 (1899, r1978) 355–401 [GC24].

Gunther of Pairis, *Ligurinus,* ed. E. Assmann, *MGH.SRG* 63 (1987) 151–495 [GC25]; fragments of *Solimarius, ibid.,* 501–12 [GC26].

Gilo, *Ad historiam gestorum viae nostri temporis Jerosolymitanae,* ed. Académie royale des Inscriptions et Belles-Lettres, in *RHC.Historiens occidentaux* 5.2 (1895) 727–800 [GC27].

Guy of Amiens, *Carmen de Hastingae proelio,* ed. and tr. C. Morton and H. Muntz (1972) [GC28].

*Hague Fragment,* ed. and tr. H. Suchier, *Les Narbonnais: Chanson de geste,* Société des anciens textes français, 2 vols. (1898, r1965) 41.2:167–92 [GC29].

Henry of Pisa, *Liber Maiorichinus* (less accurately known as *Liber Maiolichinus de gestis Pisanorum illustribus*), ed. C. Calisse, *FSI,* Scrittori, secolo XII, v29 (1904) [GC30].

Hildebert of Lavardin, *De ordine mundi,* in *PL* 171:1223–34 [GC31]; and *id., In libros Regum,* in *PL* 171:1239–64 [GC32].

*Historia Meriadoci, regis Cambrie,* ed. and tr. M.L. Day (1988) [GC33].

Hrotsvitha of Gandersheim, *Gesta Ottonis,* ed. H. Homeyer, *Hrotsvithae opera* (1970) 406–38 [GC34].

*Ilias latina* (bk. 1 in leonine hexameters), ed. W. Meyer, "Eine gereimte Umarbeitung der Ilias latina," in *NKGWG* (1907) 235–45 [GC35].

John of Hauville, *Architrenius,* ed. P.G. Schmidt (1974) [GC36]; see also [GE18].

Joseph of Exeter, fragment of *Antiocheis* and *Frigii Daretis Yliados libri sex,* ed. L. Gompf, *Joseph Iscanus: Werke und Briefe,* in Mittellateinische Studien und Texte 4 (1970) 77–212; tr. G. Roberts: *Joseph of Exeter: The Iliad of Dares Phrygius* (1970); tr. A.K. Bate: *Joseph of Exeter: Trojan War I–III* (1986) [GC37].

*Karolus Magnus et Leo Papa: Ein paderborner Epos vom Jahre 799,* ed. and tr. F. Brunhölzl, Studien und Quellen zur westfälischen Geschichte 8 (1966) 60–97 [GC38].

Letald of Micy, *De quodam piscatore quem ballena absorbuit,* ed. P. Pascal, "The Poem of Letaldus: A New Edition," in *Hrotsvit of Gandersheim: Rara Avis in Saxonia?,* ed. K.M. Wilson (1987) 211–28: text, pp218–23) [GC39].

Matthew of Vendôme, *In Tobiam paraphrasis metrica,* ed. F. Munari, *Mathei Vindocinensis opera* 2 (1982) 159–255 [GC40].

Moses of Bergamo, *Pergaminus,* ed. G. Cresmachi, *Mosè del Brolo e la cultura a Bergamo nei secoli XI–XII,* Collezione storica Bergamasca 3 (1945) 201–28 [GC41].

*Navigatio sancti Brendani abbatis,* ed. C. Selmer (1959, r1989); tr. J.J. O'Meara (1976) [GC42].

Paul the Deacon, *Historia Langobardorum,* ed. G. Waitz, *MGH.SRG* 48 (1878, r1978); tr. W.D. Foulke (1907, r1974) [GC43].

Peter of Eboli, *De rebus Siculis carmen,* ed. E. Rota, in *Rerum Italicarum Scriptores,* ed. L.A. Muratori, rev. G. Carducci and V. Fiorini, n.s., 31.1 (1904) [GC44]; *id., Liber ad honorem Augusti,* ed. G.B. Siragusa, *FSI,* Scrittori, secolo XII, v39 (1906) [GC45].

Peter Riga, *Aurora,* ed. P.E. Beichner, 2 vols. (1965) [GC46].

Poeta Saxo, *De gestis Caroli Magni imperatoris,* ed. P. von Winterfeld, in *MGH.Poetae* 4.1 (1899, r1978) 7–71; tr. M.E. McKinney (1956) [GC47].

*Rhythmus pisanus,* ed. E. du Méril, *Poésies populaires latines du moyen âge* (1847, r1969) 239–51 [GC48]; ed. G. Scalia, "Il carme pisano sull'impresa contro i Saraceni del 1087," in *Studi di filologia romanza offerti a Silvio Pellegrini* (1971) 565–627: text, pp597–627 [GC49].

*Ruodlieb,* ed. B.K. Vollmann (1974-) [GC50]; ed. and tr. C.W. Grocock (1985) [GC51]; ed. and tr. D.M. Kratz (1984) 74–199 [GC52].

Simon Chèvre d'Or (Capra Aurea), *Ylias,* ed. A. Boutemy, "La Geste d'Enée par Simon Chèvre d'Or," in *MA* 52 (1946) 243–56 [GC53]; "La version parisienne du poème de Simon Chèvre d'Or sur la guerre de Troie (Ms. lat. 8430)," in *Scriptorium* 1 (1946–47) 267–88 [GC54]; and "Quatre poèmes nouveaux de Simon Chèvre d'Or," in *RMAL* 3 (1947) 141–52 [GC55].

Stephen of Rouen, *Draco Normannicus,* ed. R. Howlett, in *Chronicles of the Reigns of Stephen, Henry II., and Richard I., RSer* 82.2 (1885) 585–781 [GC56].

Walter of Châtillon, *Alexandreis,* ed. M.L. Colker, Thesaurus mundi 17 (1978); tr. R.T. Pritchard (1986) [GC57].

*Waltharius,* ed. K. Strecker, in *MGH.Poetae* 6.1 (1951, r1978) 1–85: text, pp24–83 [GC58]; ed. K. Strecker, tr. P. Vossen (1947, r1987) [GC59]; ed. and tr. D.M. Kratz (1984) 2–71 (with [GC52]) [GC60].

William of Apulia, *Gesta Roberti Wiscardi,* ed. R. Wilmans, in *MGH.Scriptores* (in Folio) 9 (1851, r1983) 241–98 [GC61]; ed. and tr. M. Mathieu, *La Geste de Robert Guiscard,* Istituto siciliano di studi bizantini e neoellenici, Testi e monumenti, Testi 4 (1961) [GC62].

## Studies

E. Archibald, *Apollonius of Tyre: Medieval and Renaissance Themes and Variations* (1991) [GC63].

G. Cary, *The Medieval Alexander,* ed. D.J.A. Ross (1956, r1987) [GC64].

G. Chiri, *La poesia epico-storica latina dell'Italia medioevale,* Istituto di filologia romanza della R. Università di Roma: Studi e testi (1939) [GC65].

A. Ebenbauer, *Carmen historicum: Untersuchungen zur historischen Dichtung im karolingischen Europe,* v1 (1978) [GC66].

G. Gröber, *Übersicht über die lateinische Litteratur von der Mitte des VI. Jahrhunderts bis zur Mitte des XIV. Jahrhunderts* (1902, r1974) [GC67].

W. Haug and B.K. Vollmann, *Frühe deutsche Literatur und lateinische Literatur in Deutschland, 800–1150,* Bibliothek des Mittelalters 1 (1991) [GC68].

D. Kartschoke, *Bibeldichtung: Studien zur Geschichte der epischen Bibelparaphrase von Juvencus bis Otfrid von Weißenburg* (1975) [GC69].

K. Langosch, *"Waltharius": Die Dichtung und die Forschung,* Erträge der Forschung 21 (1973) [GC70].

B. Naumann, *Dichter und Publikum in deutscher und lateinischer Bibelepik des frühen 12. Jahrhunderts: Untersuchungen zu frühmittelhochdeutschen und mittellateinischen Dichtungen über die kleineren Bücher des Alten Testaments,* Erlanger Beiträge zur Sprach- und Kunstwissenschaft 30 (1968) [GC71].

E.E. Ploss, ed., *Waltharius und Walthersage: Eine Dokumentation der Forschung* (1969) [GC72].

F.J.E. Raby, *SLP,* passim [GC73].

M. Roberts, *Biblical Epic and Rhetorical Paraphrase in Late Antiquity* (1985) [GC74].

D. Schaller, "La poesia epica," in *Lo spazio letterario del medioevo,* ed. G. Cavallo, C. Leonardi, and E. Menestò, pt1.2 (1993) 9–42 [GC75].

D. Schaller, "Vergil und die Wiederentdeckung des Epos im frühen Mittelalter," in *Medioevo e Rinascimento: Annuario del Dipartimento di studi sul Medioevo e il Rinascimento dell'Università di Firenze* 1 (1987) 75–100 [GC76].

D. Schaller, "Das mittelalterliche Epos im Gattungssystem," in *Kontinuität und Transformation der Antike im Mittelalter,* ed. W. Erzgräber (1989) 355–71 [GC77].

C.P.E. Springer, *The Gospel as Epic in Late Antiquity: The "Paschale Carmen" of Sedulius* (1988) [GC78].

M. Tyssens, "L'épopée latine," in *L'épopée,* ed. R. Boyer *et al., TSMAO* 49 (1988) 37–52 [GC79].

B.K. Vollmann, *Ruodlieb,* Erträge der Forschung 283 (1993) [GC80].

*See also* [BB31], [BB62].

# GD • BEAST EPIC AND FABLE

## BY JILL MANN

The tradition of Medieval Latin beast fable largely derives from the classical poets Phaedrus (first century A.D.), whose work is purportedly based on Aesop (sixth century B.C.), and Avianus (? fourth/fifth century A.D.). The fables of Avianus, written in elegiac couplets, were copied and read as a school text throughout the Middle Ages, but the Phaedran fables, at some undetermined date, were recast into prose, possibly because their verse form (iambic senarii) was deemed too difficult for the young scholars who were given beast fables as reading material in the early stages of learning Latin. Three slightly different recensions of this prose version survive, one in a manuscript of the late ninth century (providing a terminus ad quem for the adaptation). They are known under the generic title *Romulus vulgaris,* after a new preface which (falsely) represented the work as having been translated from Greek into Latin by a fictitious "Romulus" for "his son Tiberinus." The prose collection copied by Adémar of Chabannes (c. 988–1034), a monk of Saint-Cybard in Angoulême, is a similar reworking of Phaedran material which has close contacts with the Romulan tradition.

The interest in copying and rewriting Latin fables in this early period may well have been stimulated by the renewed educational activity at the imperial courts from the time of Charlemagne onwards. Certainly the educational function of fables is clearly evident in their later history. They bulk large, for example, in the *Fecunda ratis* of Egbert of Liège (composed between 1010 and 1026), a miscellany of proverbs and short anecdotes designed to provide edifying and entertaining matter for his young pupils to memorize. Although Egbert's fables show strong links with the Romulan tradition, they can also treat the traditional material with a surprising freedom, exemplifying the way in which these narratives were constantly refashioned and reworked throughout the medieval period. Several variant versions of the *Romulus* can be identified, among them the eleventh-century *Romulus Nilantii* (named after its eighteenth-century editor, Frédéric Nilant); it was this collection that served as the source for the first 40 fables in the French collection of Marie de France (twelfth century). The rest of Marie's hundred-odd fables are drawn from a wider variety of sources, including beast epic and Eastern tales; later still this rich miscellany was turned into Latin, to become the collection dubbed by modern scholars "LBG" (since the three most important manuscripts are preserved in London, Brussels, and Göttingen). Finally, in the late twelfth or early thirteenth century the Romulan material was recast into elegiac verse; it was this elegiac *Romulus* (whose author was known as the Anonymus Neveleti, after the seventeenth-century editor Isaac Nevelet, until Léopold Hervieux identified him, unconvincingly, as an otherwise unknown "Gualterus Anglicus") that quickly outstripped all the others in popularity. Its advantage over its competitors was that it provided moral wisdom and a model for verse composition at one and the same time. Over 100 manuscripts survive, many of them bearing the marks of their educational function in the form of glosses and other annotations. To the average educated person of the thirteenth to fifteenth centuries, "Aesop" would have meant the elegiac *Romulus*. This does not mean that the flow of adaptations dried up. Alexander Neckam (d. 1217), for example, produced a "Novus Aesopus" and the beginnings of a "Novus Avianus," although in general reworkings of Avianus were less numerous than those of Phaedrus.

The Latin *Physiologus,* which formed the core of the medieval bestiary, was also used as a school text, as medieval *accessus ad auctores* testify. Medieval bestiaries, however, generated a human meaning from animals in a quite different way from the beast fable. The narrative of fable is frankly fictitious, whereas the bestiarist at least pretends to deal with the real behavior of animals. The *moralitas* of beast fables has the pragmatic, down-to-earth, unsystematic character of proverb; it teaches worldly wisdom, not Christian doctrine. The bestiarists, in contrast, "read" natural animal behavior for moral or religious meanings on the assumption that creation bears the imprint of its Creator.

Different from both fable and bestiary is the beast epic, which made its appearance relatively late, in the eleventh and twelfth centuries. Its beginnings can be seen in the eleventh-century *Ecbasis captivi,* the story of a runaway calf which falls into the clutches of a wolf and is rescued by a posse of other animals under the leadership of the fox. The wolf recalls, in an "inner fable," how the fox cunningly brought about the death of his (the wolf's) ancestor by persuading the sick lion that he would be cured if wrapped in a wolf's skin. A century later, the hatred between the fox and the wolf became the leitmotiv of the *Ysengrimus* (1148–49); here for the first time they bear their familiar names of Reinardus and Ysengrimus. The narrative begins with an account of the single occasion on which the wolf outwits the fox; in the rest of the work, this supposedly terrifying predator is constantly tricked, humiliated, and physically battered and tortured, until he is finally devoured alive by 66 pigs. The *Ysengrimus* is among the most witty and inventive productions of the Latin Middle Ages, and its powerful influence on the later vernacular Reynard cycles is now generally acknowledged, although the relatively small number of surviving manuscripts suggests that it was not itself widely read. Less influential on the vernacular, but more popular in its own right, was the *Speculum stultorum* of Nigel of Longchamp (also known as Wireker or Whiteacre), a monk of Christ Church, Canterbury. This lively narrative, which rivals the *Ysengrimus* in wit and originality, was written, according to its editors, around 1180; its "hero" is a donkey, Burnellus, who hankers after a longer tail, and whose futile quest leads him on many comic adventures.

The epic is distinguished from the fable not only by its length, but also by the fact that the *moralitas* is absorbed into the narrative. Neither beast fable nor bestiary applies morality *directly* to animals; their behavior is judged "natural" or "unnatural," "wise" (in a self-interested sense) or "foolish," rather than "good" or "bad." It is the *moralitas* that translates these judgments into ethical terms more suitable for humans. In contrast, the animals in beast epic offer a stream of moral commentary on each other and on the world at large. Yet paradoxically the epic is thus *less* moral than fable or bestiary, for its moralizing proclaims itself as comic both by its inapplicability to animals and by its absurd excess. Another distinguishing feature of epic is its satiric aspect. In the *Ecbasis,* the wolf is a monk intent on breaking the rule against meat eating; the whole of the *Ysengrimus* is a satiric attack on the hybrid figure of the abbot-bishop, who is represented by the wolf; the *Speculum stultorum* ridicules the monastic orders and is accompanied by a prose epistle in which Nigel explains it as a critique of monastic ambition and those who parade a superficial learning.

Some of the narrative material used in these epics comes from beast fable; other stories have earlier analogues in short animal poems whose primary aims, like the epic's, seem to have been comic/satiric rather than moral. Two of these shorter pieces—Alcuin's *De gallo* and the "sick lion" poem ("Aegrum fama fuit") found in a St. Gall manuscript containing poems by Paul the Deacon—are products of the Carolingian court and strengthen the view that beast literature was familiar in this milieu—familiar enough to become the vehicle for jokes and topical satire. Other poems that can be counted among the ancestors of the later medieval tradition of beast literature include a comic one about a priest and a wolf found in the eleventh-century *Cambridge Songs* collection, and another poem (*De lupo*), of the turn of the century, in which the wolf appears as a monk. The poem *Gallus et Vulpes,* probably written in the eleventh century, differs from these in having a much stronger moral/didactic element.

One final strand in the rich tradition of medieval beast literature is the Eastern animal tale. Stories from the Oriental tale collection, which in its passage from one language to another was variously entitled the *Pañchatantra, Kalila and Dimna,* or *The Fables of Bidpai,* first reached the Latin West, as far as we know, in the collection of a certain Baldo (ineptly named the "Novus Aesopus"). Around 1270, the Hebrew version of *Kalila and Dimna* was translated into Latin by John of Capua under the title *Directorium vitae humanae.* The lack of separation between animal narrative and human moral marks off this narrative from the Aesopic fable, while its lack of comedy differentiates it from the epic.

In the thirteenth century, beast fable underwent changes in its form, and the boundaries between fable and other forms of beast literature began to be blurred. In the fable collection that the cleric Odo of Cheriton compiled in the early thirteenth century for use in preaching, the *moralitas* is often no longer a single maxim; it has swollen into detailed allegorization of the kind familiar from the bestiaries. In the *De naturis rerum* of Alexander Neckam, beast fable rubs shoulders with bestiary lore and classical legend, all of them being treated as material for moral edification.

The moralizing impulse also predominates in the *Speculum sapientiae* (? thirteenth/fourteenth century), a collection of narratives in which the animals give moral accounts of their own actions without provoking any of the comic response that would greet this procedure in the beast epic. The *Dialogus creaturarum* of Nicholas Pergamenus (mid-fourteenth century) similarly "ventriloquizes" moral reflections through animal speakers in a manner that has more in common with bestiary than with fable. As for the comic irreverence of beast epic, it had long ago migrated to the vernaculars.

# Select Bibliography

## Primary Works

### (a) Beast Fable

The three recensions of the *Romulus vulgaris* have been edited by G. Thiele, *Der lateinische Äsop des Romulus und die Prosa-Fassungen des Phädrus* (1910): Thiele's dating of the work to between 350 and 500 rests on extremely flimsy arguments and should be discounted; his claim that the source of the *Romulus* was a hypothesized "Latin Aesop" is equally unfounded [GD1].

Ademar's collection has been edited by F. Bertini, *Il monaco Ademaro e la sua raccolta di favole fedriane* (1975) [GD2]; ed. rev. and expanded by Bertini and P. Gatti, *Ademaro di Chabannes: Favole*, Favolisti latini medievali 3 (1988) [GD3]. The ed. by G. Thiele, *Der illustrierte lateinische Äsop in der Handschrift des Ademar: Codex Vossianus lat. oct. 15, fol. 195–205* (1905), includes pls. of the illustrations with which Ademar's manuscript is liberally embellished [GD4]. The textually garbled nature of several of the fables in Ademar's collection makes it more likely that he was its scribe than its author, despite Bertini's arguments to the contrary.

Egbert of Liège, *Fecunda ratis,* has been edited by E. Voigt (1889) [GD5].

The largest edition of medieval beast fables is that of L. Hervieux, *Les fabulistes latins depuis le siècle d'Auguste jusqu'à la fin du moyen âge,* 2nd ed., 5 vols. (1893–99). Its contents are as follows: v1, Introductory survey; v2, Reworkings of Phaedrus, including the *Romulus vulgaris, Romulus Nilantii,* and other *Romulus* collections; "Gualterus Anglicus" (= elegiac *Romulus*); "Romuli Anglici Cunctis Exortae Fabulae" (= "LBG"); v3, Reworkings of Avianus; v4, Odo of Cheriton and his derivatives; v5, Reworkings of *Kalila and Dimna* [GD6]. Hervieux's work was reviewed in *JS* (1884) 670–86 (G. Paris), (1885) 37–51 (G. Paris), (1896) 111–23 (B. Hauréau), (1898) 158–73 (L. Delisle), (1899) 207–26 (G. Paris) [GD7]. The fables of Odo of Cheriton have been translated by J.C. Jacobs (1959) [GD8].

There is still no modern critical edition of the elegiac *Romulus;* it has been printed (according to manuscripts where the Latin text accompanies a French version) by W. Forster, *Lyoner Yzopet* (1882) 96–137 [GD9]; by J. Bastin, *Recueil général des Isopets,* Société des anciens textes français, 2 vols. (1929–30) [GD10]; and by K. McKenzie and W.A. Oldfather, *Ysopet–Avionnet: The Latin and French Texts* (1919, r1967) [GD11].

Alexander Neckam's *Novus Aesopus* has been edited by G. Garbugino as v2 (1987) in the series Favolisti latini medievali (1984–) [GD12]; his *Novus Avianus* is in [GD6], v3 [GD13].

### (b) The Bestiary

The textual history of the many different versions of the bestiary is extremely complicated; for surveys and lists of editions see F. McCulloch, *Medieval Latin and French Bestiaries,* rev. ed. (1962) [GD14]; N. Henkel, *Studien zum Physiologus im Mittelalter* (1976) [GD15]; and W.B. Clark and M.T. McMunn ([GD35]) [GD16]. There is an English translation by T.H. White (1954) [GD17].

### (c) Beast Epic

The standard edition of the *Ecbasis captivi* is that by K. Strecker, *MGH.SRG* 24 (1935, r1992) [GD18]; it is also edited in the Teubner series by W. Trillitzsch ([1964]) [GD19]. The translation in the parallel-text edition by E.H. Zeydel (1964) contains many inaccuracies [GD20].

*Ysengrimus*, ed. E. Voigt (1884, r1974) [GD21]; ed. J. Mann: *Ysengrimus: Text with Translation, Commentary and Introduction* (1987) [GD22].

Nigel de Longchamps, *Speculum stultorum*, ed. J.H. Mozley and R.R. Raymo (1960); tr. G.W. Regenos: *The Book of Daun Burnel the Ass* (1959). Nigel's prefatory epistle has been separately edited by J.H. Mozley, "The *Epistola ad Willelmum* of Nigel Longchamps," in *MAev* 39 (1970) 13–20 [GD23].

### (d) Short Animal Poems

"Aegrum fama fuit," ed. K. Neff, *Die Gedichte des Paulus Diaconus: Kritische und Erklärende Ausgabe* (1908) 191–96 [GD24]; ed. E. Dümmler, in *MGH.Poetae* 1 (1881, r1978) 62–64 [GD25].

Alcuin, *De gallo*, ed. E. Dümmler, in *MGH.Poetae* 1 (1881, r1978) 262 [GD26].

*De presbitero et lupo*, no. 35 in *Carmina Cantabrigiensia*, ed. K. Strecker (1926, r1966) 88–90 [GD27].

*De lupo*, in *Kleinere lateinische Denkmäler der Thiersage*, ed. E. Voigt (1878) 58–62 (followed by two further reworkings, pp62–68) [GD28].

*Gallus et Vulpes*, ed. L. Herrman, in *Scriptorium* 1 (1946–47) 260–66 [GD29].

### (e) Oriental Tales

John of Capua, *Directorium vitae humanae*, ed. F. Geissler (1960) [GD30].

Baldo, *Novus Aesopus*, in *Beiträge zur lateinischen Erzählungsliteratur des Mittelalters*, ed. A. Hilka, Abhandlungen der Gesellschaft der Wiss. zu Göttingen, phil-.hist. Klasse, n.s., 21.3 (1928) [GD31].

### (f) Hybrid Forms

Alexander Neckam, *De naturis rerum*, bks. 1–2, ed. T. Wright, in *RSer* 34 (1863) 1–354 [GD32].

The *Speculum sapientiae* and *Dialogus creaturarum* have been edited by J.G.T. Grässe under the misleading title *Die beiden ältesten lateinischen Fabelbücher des Mittelalters* (1880, r1965) [GD33].

### Studies

H. de Boor, "Über Fabel and Bîspel," in *Sitz. der Bayerischen Ak. der Wiss., phil.-hist. Klasse* (1966) 3–40: seminal analysis of the differences between fable and bestiary [GD34].

W.B. Clark and M.T. McMunn, *Beasts and Birds of the Middle Ages: The Bestiary and Its Legacy* (1989) [GD35].

G. Dicke and K. Grubmüller, *Die Fabeln des Mittelalters und der frühen Neuzeit: Ein Katalog der deutschen Versionen und ihrer lateinischen Entsprechungen* (1987): an index of beast fables, arranged alphabetically by animal, covering French, Spanish, and English material as well as Latin and German [GD36].

K. Doderer, *Fabeln: Formen, Figuren, Lehren* (1970, 1977) [GD37].

K. Grubmüller, *Meister Esopus: Untersuchungen zur Geschichte und Funktion der Fabel im Mittelalter* (1977): chs. 2 and 3 give an extended history of the development of Medieval Latin beast fable [**GD38**].

H.R. Jauss, *Untersuchungen zur mittelalterlichen Tierdichtung,* Beihefte zur *ZRPh* 100 (1959): a fundamentally important study, covering both fable and epic [**GD39**].

F.P. Knapp, *Das lateinische Tierepos,* Erträge der Forschung 121 (1979): covers the *Ecbasis captivi* and the *Ysengrimus,* with a very brief app. on the *Speculum stultorum* [**GD40**].

J. Mann, "The *Speculum Stultorum* and the *Nun's Priest's Tale,*" in *Chaucer Review* 9 (1974–75) 262–82 [**GD41**]; *eadem,* "La favolistica latina," in *Aspetti della letteratura latina nel secolo XIII: Atti del primo convegno internazionale di studi dell'Associazione per il Medioevo et l'Umanesimo Latini (AMUL), Perugia, 3–5 ottobre 1983,* ed. C. Leonardi and G. Orlandi (1986) 193–219 [**GD42**]; see also Mann's introduction to *Ysengrimus* in [GD22] [**GD43**].

D. Sternberger, *Figuren der Fabel: Essays* (1950): contains two important essays on fable [**GD44**].

J.M. Ziolkowski, *TA:* provides English translations of [GD24], [GD26], [GD28], and [GD29] [**GD45**].

GE  *  SATIRE

BY A.G. RIGG

Although some medieval writers, such as Walter Map (d. c. 1208), conform to the ancient Roman sense of *satira* as "mélange," satire is normally understood—then and
now—as the literature of criticism. The writer invites the audience, directly or indirectly, to share his mockery of or distaste for something specific or general; there is
also an expectation of humor. The direct approach identifies the object of satire; the
indirect way employs allegory or exemplificatory story. Specific objects include persons, events, institutions, and nations or groups of people. General satire is directed
at human failings, such as ambition or greed. Broader targets include women, doctors, lawyers, peasants, and bureaucracy. Most satires move between the general and
the particular, exemplifying avarice, for instance, by the greed of lawyers, or placing
criticism of monks within a context of gluttony. It is often difficult to know whether
a general lament on the times has a specific object in mind; for example, writings on
the death of Archbishop Thomas Becket (1170) include what appears to be general
satire on bishops, but in fact this arises specifically from the participation of some
English bishops in the coronation of Henry II's eldest son. Real people disappear beneath literary stereotypes, partly because satirists categorize in black and white,
partly because religious thinking saw human behavior in terms of the shared faults
that arose from the Fall.

Further, Christian satire is sometimes tempered by charity: Juvenal's *saeva in-
dignatio* was usually reserved for abstract sins rather than individuals. In Latin, the
difficulty of separating stereotype from individual is compounded by literary tradition. Much Medieval Latin satire is derived from classical models (Horace and Juvenal); the biting epigrams of Martial were transformed into literary exercises. On the
other hand, a classical source does not necessarily mean that a satire had no "real"
object, and it was possible, for example, for specific courtiers to be satirized under
names taken from Roman comedy.

Satire employs both verse (hexameters, elegiacs, and the new rhythmical meters,
especially Goliardics and rhythmical asclepiads) and prose (anecdotes, sermons, historical literature, and parodies). As satire achieves its effect by contrasting the ideal
or normal with the aberrant, parody is one of its most effective forms: the element
of surprise and contrast mirrors the gap between the ideal and reality. Thus, a biblical parody, such as the popular *Gospel According to the Silver Mark*, sets up the expectation of the Christian Gospels against the venality of the papal curia. Parody also

has the advantage of providing the opportunity for the essential element of humor. A comic poem describing a drunken scene in an abbey ("Quondam fuit factus festus") is written in deliberately ungrammatical Latin. Irony is common: there is a whole literary genre of the "Devil's Letter," in which Satan writes to the Church congratulating it on its good work on his behalf. Sustained sarcasm is rare, but Walter Map, picking on the claim of the Cistercians to be the Hebrews who plundered the treasures of the Egyptians, adopts their vocabulary entirely and calls the Cistercians "Hebrews" and the rest of humanity "Egyptians," just as some political parties (Whigs and Tories) adopted the names used for them by their opponents. Personification allegory—in which abstractions are given the characteristics of real people— is a common vehicle for general satire: the starting point is the portrayal by Prudentius (d. c. 405) of the sins in the *Psychomachia*. In a long satire on the conflict between the pope and the emperor, *Visio Petri de statu mundi* (1280), the French poet Petrus Presbyter utilized the theme of the Devil's daughters, the seven deadly sins. A century later John Gower (d. 1408) in the *Vox clamantis* described the activities of Fraud and Usury, daughters of Avarice, who ply their trade among the merchants and bankers of England. Some allegories are on a large scale: the *De planctu naturae* of Alan of Lille (d. 1202/3) satirizes sodomy; the *Architrenius* of John of Hauville (d. 1200) is a nine-book epic quest by the "Archmourner," who seeks out Nature to present his complaint about human misery. Another satirical mode is the beast fable: the whole Aesopic tradition uses stock types among animals, such as the fox and the wolf, to satirize human failings.

Even if we exclude those works to which satirical or parodic intent has been imputed only by modern critics, the field of satire is too vast for more than a general sketch. Here we first provide brief descriptions of a few of the most important satirists, followed by a broad account of the variety of satiric objects. One of the earliest was the eleventh-century German poet Sextus Amarcius, who wrote four books of satires on general topics in a classical style. Walter of Châtillon (c. 1135–1202/3), sometime courtier of Henry II of England, is one of the most brilliant; his greatest work was his epic, *Alexandreis,* but his satirical poems were also popular in his own time. He employs rhythmical stanzas of various kinds, especially the Goliardic *cum auctoritate,* fusing biblical and classical allusions in a dazzling fashion. He writes particularly about ecclesiastical abuses, but like many others he was also enraged by the murder of Becket. Another courtier of Henry II was Walter Map, archdeacon of Oxford, whose *De nugis curialium* is probably the best prose satire of the Middle Ages. This extraordinary mélange (*satira* in the old sense) includes anecdotes, history (and pseudohistory), ghost stories, romances, tales about the Welsh, and much satire, particularly against all the new religious orders (especially the Cistercians, whom he hated, but also the Templars, who, he said, deliberately prolonged the wars against the Saracens to maintain their fighting role). His *Epistola Valerii,* now absorbed into the *De nugis,* enjoyed immense popularity. It is a brilliantly constructed piece of antifeminism, drawn mainly from classical sources. Another anecdotist of anti-Cistercian feelings was the historian Gerald of Wales (1146–1223), who gave a wider circulation to many of Walter Map's tales. Not all the satirists were secular: Nigel Whiteacre (d. c. 1200; formerly known as Wireker, sometimes called Nigel of Longchamps) was a Benedictine monk of Canterbury. His verse satire, the *Speculum stultorum,* is the story of an ass who wanted a longer tail; he traveled all over Europe, suffering various misfortunes, and tried to get a degree at Paris (but came away still knowing no more than "hee-haw" and the first syllable of the name Paris).

Most short satirical poems (of which there are thousands) are anonymous. Many were gathered around the pseudonyms Primas, Golias, and Archpoet. Some of the Primas poems can be attributed to one known poet, Hugh (Primas) of Orléans (c. 1095–c. 1160), who wrote both Latin and macaronic (Latin-French) verse, and is famous for his brilliant rhymes and extempore wit. Most of his satires are personal and against specific targets. Another such poet has been identified as the "Archpoet of Cologne." Only one of his poems achieved wide circulation, the *Confessio Goliae,* which is satire against himself and contains one of the most famous lines in Medieval Latin, "Meum est propositum in taberna mori." The name "Golias" is attached to many of the poems of this type, and there is another pseudonymous satirical writer known as "Eraclius." No better representative of personal satire can be found than the Englishman Michael of Cornwall, whose thirteenth-century verse contest with Henry of Avranches exhibits some of the most flamboyant Latin rhymes ever written.

The satirists just listed are those most likely to appeal to modern tastes, but medieval bibliographers would probably have selected some who exhibited more moral fervor, particularly John of Hauville (mentioned above) and Bernard of Cluny (long known as Bernard of Morlas or Morval [c. 1091–1153]). The latter wrote *De contemptu mundi,* three long books on the sorry state of the world in *dactylici tripertiti* ("Hora novissima, tempora pessima sunt, vigilemus"). Others include Godfrey of Winchester (d. 1107), who wrote epigrams in the manner of Martial; Hildebert of Lavardin (d. 1133), the author chiefly of saints' lives and biblical epigrams, but also of satires, including a popular antifeminist one; Serlo of Bayeux (d. 1113/22), whose approach was strongly antimonastic, and Sextus Amarcius.

The objects of Medieval Latin satire ranged from the general to the specific. The most general are those texts that describe humanity's postlapsarian sinful state. Some, such as the *De miseria humanae conditionis* of Innocent III (d. 1216), with its account of our loathsome birth and pathetic old age, approximate more to penitential literature than satire. Others, like the *Architrenius* and *De contemptu mundi,* survey the gamut of human folly. Somewhat more specific is estates satire, in which the faults of the major classes of society are criticized, the usual order being princes, ecclesiastics, knights, merchants, and peasants. A fairly short one was written by the Yorkshire poet Hugh Sottovagina (d. 1139); far longer is John Gower's fourteenth-century *Vox clamantis* (which takes its name from John the Baptist, the "voice of one crying" in the wilderness). Another general target was the seven deadly sins, sometimes all together (and often in one of the traditional orders, such as SIIAAGL: *Superbia, Ira, Invidia, Avaritia, Accidia, Gula, Luxuria*), sometimes individually. One form of Pride was ambition, and the ambitious courtier is a common satiric object, often associated with the vice of flattery. John of Salisbury (d. 1180), John of Hauville (d. 1200), and Walter of Wimborne (thirteenth century) have much to say about flattery, and their portraits go back ultimately to the character of Gnato in Terence's *Eunuch.* For Envy the poets drew heavily on Ovid's account of Aglauros. Avarice was an easy and common target; often, as in Walter of Wimborne, the gathering of material goods is offset by warnings of impending death. Sloth likewise is an entertaining topic, and usually makes use of the lazy slave Birria, a stock figure from comedy who will not wake up in the morning. It is often said that the majority of all jokes concern food or sex, and Medieval Latin satirists run true to this pattern: the gluttonous and lecherous monk or abbot is a common figure, and there are several versions of a Glutton's or Drinker's Mass.

Various groups in society provided somewhat more specific targets but were equally prone to stereotyping. Several critics of monks (Walter Map, Gerald of Wales, even the Benedictine Nigel Whiteacre) have already been mentioned, as has Serlo of Bayeux, one of the earliest. During the twelfth century, satirists turned their attention to the proliferation of new orders, some formed for specific purposes, like the Templars, others simply (at least initially) stricter. In the thirteenth century there appeared a great number of mendicant orders, whose members did not live enclosed lives but were active in preaching (and begging). They were harshly criticized, and in 1274 all such orders were suppressed except the Franciscans, Dominicans, Carmelites, and Augustinians. Even these, however, remained the object of fierce criticism, both from monks and from the secular clergy. In Paris in the 1250s, William of St. Amour had seen the friars as predecessors of Antichrist, and satirists followed his lead into the late fourteenth century. In Oxford, for example, there was a flurry of pro- and antifraternal satire. Throughout the later Middle Ages, ecclesiastical bureaucracy, from Rome downwards, was constantly satirized, usually because of the amount of lobbying and bribery necessary to ensure that appeals were heard. The *Gospel According to the Silver Mark* gives a typical picture of the unsuccessful appellant to the curia. Indeed, any kind of court—papal, episcopal, or royal—was seen as a nest of ambitious, avaricious sycophants and produced much satire from Peter of Blois (d. 1211) and many others. At the other end of the scale, peasants were also mocked, as in the *Peasants' Catechism*.

All satire, whether justified or not, is essentially a literary activity, written as much for the pleasure of writing, however perverse, as for any intention to reform. This is most evident in antifeminist and antimatrimonial satire, which has its roots in antiquity (Theophrastus and Juvenal). The tradition was given a vigorous push in the early Middle Ages by Jerome's (serious) treatise *Adversus Jovinianum,* but it quickly became a literary topos, in Hildebert, Walter Map (*Epistola Valerii*), the very popular *De coniuge non ducenda,* and Matheolus's *Lamentationes.* Almost every satirist turned his pen to the topic (John of Salisbury, Lawrence of Durham, Peter of Blois).

There is also satire of particular nationalities or even smaller geographical groups. In 1281–83 Nicholas de Bibera (Biberach, in southwest Germany) wrote an immense poem on the personalities of his day, together with an account of the city of Erfurt and its taverns. The county of Norfolk was particularly mocked for the greed and stupidity of its people (the usual fate of those who live in isolated communities). Another specific type of satire concerned politics, but we must also remember that even general satire (such as that directed against monks and friars) may often have been stimulated by a particular set of circumstances. Among English events that provoked literary satire were the murder of Becket in 1170; the inglorious career of William of Longchamps in the 1190s; the conflicts between Emperor Frederick II and the pope; the Wars of the Barons, between Henry III and Simon de Montfort; the downfall of Piers Gaveston, the favorite of Edward II; the Hundred Years' War between England and France, which produced both anti-French and anti-Scots literature; the Peasants' Revolt of 1381; the Lollard movement; and the disastrous reign of Richard II.

From the eleventh to the fourteenth century, satirical and comic literature—at least as far as we can tell from published material—flourished mainly in northern France, and especially in England. The anticlericalism of the fourteenth century (evident among the English Lollards) spread to Bohemia, and many satirical texts of English origin circulated widely in Eastern Europe during the fifteenth century. Eventually the satirical corpus formed a nucleus for the Protestant propaganda that emanated from Switzerland and Germany in the sixteenth century.

## Select Bibliography

### Primary Works

#### (a) Collections

*Devil's Letters:* there are several editions of these, as in W. Wattenbach, "Über erfundene Briefe in Handschriften des Mittelalters, besonders Teufelsbriefe," in *Sitz. der königlich preussischen Ak. der Wiss. zu Berlin* (1891) pt1:91–123 [GE1].

O.A. Dobiache-Rojdestvensky, *Les poésies des Goliards groupées et traduites avec le texte latin en regard* (1931): edition of the principal lyrics, with study of the Golias tradition [GE2].

P. Lehmann, *PM:* 24 parodic texts are printed in the app., including the *Gospel According to the Silver Mark, Glutton's Mass, Drinker's Mass, Peasants' Catechism,* and political satires [GE3].

*Libelli de lite imperatorum et pontificum,* ed. E. Dümmler *et al., MGH,* 3 vols. (1891–97): contains many political satires, mainly twelfth-century [GE4].

Matthias Flacius Illyricus (1520–75), *Varia doctorum piorumque virorum de corrupto ecclesiae statu poemata* (Basel 1557): this anticlerical collection was a primary source for the "Golias" tradition [GE5].

G.F. Whicher, *The Goliard Poets: Medieval Latin Songs and Satires with Verse Translations* (1949, r1979) [GE6].

T. Wright, ed. and tr., *The Political Songs of England, from the Reign of John to that of Edward II, CamSoc* 6 (1839) [GE7].

T. Wright, ed., *The Latin Poems Commonly Attributed to Walter Mapes, CamSoc* 16 (1841) [GE8].

T. Wright, ed., *Political Poems and Songs Relating to English History, Composed during the Period from the Accession of Edw. III to that of Ric. III,* 2 vols., *RSer* 14 (1859–61): extends, in fact, to 1399 [GE9].

T. Wright, ed., *The Anglo-Latin Satirical Poets and Epigrammatists of the Twelfth Century,* 2 vols., *RSer* 59 (1872): most of these editions have been superseded, except (of the satires) Serlo of Bayeux, Hugh Sottovagina, and other antimonastic poems [GE10].

N.B.: All texts edited by Wright should be read with caution, as they were produced in great haste.

#### (b) Individual Authors and Texts (very selective)

Alan of Lille, *De planctu naturae,* ed. N.M. Häring, in *SM,* 3rd ser., 19 (1978) 797–879 [GE11].

*Die Gedichte des Archipoeta,* ed. H. Watenphul and H. Krefeld (1958) [GE12].

Bernard of Morval, *De contemptu mundi*, ed. H.C. Hoskier (1929) [GE13].

*Gawain on Marriage: The Textual Tradition of the "De coniuge non ducenda,"* ed. A.G. Rigg (1986): with translation [GE14].

Gerald of Wales, *Opera*, ed. J.S. Brewer *et al.*, 8 vols., *RSer* 21 (1861–91), especially the *Speculum ecclesiae*, v4:3–354 [GE15].

Hugh Primas: see *OPHP* [GE16].

John of Hauville, *Architrenius*, ed. P.G. Schmidt (1974) [GE17]; tr. and ed. W. Wetherbee (1994) [GE18].

John Gower, *The Complete Works*, ed. G.C. Macauley, v4: *The Latin Works* (1902) [GE19].

Matheolus, *Lamentationes*, ed. A.-G. Van Hamel, in *Bibliothèque de l'École des hautes études* 95–96 (1892–1905) [GE20].

"Eine mittellateinische Dichterfehde: *Versus Michaelis Cornubiensis* [Michael of Cornwall] *contra Henricum Abrincensem* [Henry of Avranches]," ed. A. Hilka, in *Mittelalterliche Handschriften: paläographische, kunsthistorische, literarische und bibliotheksgeschichtliche Untersuchungen: Festgabe zum 60. Geburtstage von Hermann Degering*, ed. A. Börner and J. Kirchner (1926, r1973) 123–54 [GE21].

*Nicolai de Bibera occulti Erfordensis carmen satiricum*, ed. T. Fischer, in *Erfurter Denkmäler* (1870) [GE22].

Nigel de Longchamps, *Speculum stultorum*, ed. J.H. Mozley and R.R. Raymo (1960) [GE23].

Petrus Presbyter, *Carmina*, ed. M. Rener (1988) [GE24].

"*Quondam fuit factus festus*: Ein Gedicht in Spottlatein," ed. W. Meyer, in *NKGWG* (1908) 406–29 [GE25].

Sextus Amarcius, *Sermones*, ed. K. Manitius, *MGH.Quellen zur Geistesgeschichte des Mittelalters* 6 (1969, r1989) [GE26].

*Moralisch-satirische Gedichte Walters von Châtillon*, ed. K. Strecker (1929) [GE27].

Walter Map, *De nugis curialium: Courtiers' Trifles*, ed. and tr. M.R. James, rev. C.N.L. Brooke and R.A.B. Mynors (1983) [GE28].

*The Poems of Walter of Wimborne*, ed. A.G. Rigg (1978) [GE29].


## Studies

U. Kindermann, *Satyra: Die Theorie der Satire im Mittellateinischen: Vorstudie zu einer Gattungsgeschichte* (1978): thorough survey of medieval theory and practice [GE30].

B. Konneker, *Satire im 16. Jahrhundert: Epoche, Werke, Wirkung* (1991) [GE31].

P. Lehmann, *PM*: the most thorough study, with texts (see [GE3]) [GE32].

J. Mann, *Chaucer and Medieval Estates Satire: The Literature of Social Classes and the General Prologue to the Canterbury Tales* (1973): draws on Medieval Latin satire [GE33].

J. Mann, "Satiric Subject and Satiric Object in Goliardic Literature," in *MLJ* 15 (1980) 63–86: an analysis of how satire actually works [GE34].

R.E. Pepin, *Literature of Satire in the Twelfth Century: A Neglected Mediaeval Genre* (1988): a survey of extracts from four satirists—Bernard of Cluny, Hugh (Primas), Walter of Châtillon, and Nigel of Canterbury [GE35].

F.J.E. Raby, *SLP*, v2, especially chs. 10, 11, 13 [GE36].

A.G. Rigg, "Golias and Other Pseudonyms," in *SM*, 3rd ser., 18 (1977) 65–109: studies the attributions to Archpoet, Golias, Primas, and "Walter," with a discussion of what can properly be called "Goliardic" [GE37].

A.G. Rigg, "Eraclius Archipoeta: Bekynton Anthology Nos. 14, 15, 20, 27," in *MAev* 53 (1984) 1–9: argues that "Eraclius" is a pseudonym akin to "Golias" in these poems [GE38].

P.R. Szittya, *The Antifraternal Tradition in Medieval Literature* (1986) [GE39].

H. Walther, "Scherz und Ernst in der Völker- und Stämme-Charakteristik mittellateinischer Verse," in *AKG* 41 (1959) 163–301: survey of Latin poems on national characteristics, with index [GE40].

C. Witke, *Latin Satire: The Structure of Persuasion* (1970): with chs. on Theodulf of Orléans, Hugh Primas, and Walter of Châtillon [GE41].

M. Wolterbeek, "*Ridicula nugae satyrae:* Comic Narratives of the Tenth, Eleventh, and Early Twelfth Centuries" (Ph.D. diss., University of California, Berkeley, 1984) [GE42].

J.A. Yunck, *The Lineage of Lady Meed: The Development of Mediaeval Venality Satire* (1963) [GE43].

GF • PROVERBS AND EPIGRAMS

BY A.G. RIGG

## Proverbs

A proverb is a general truth, or perceived truth, expressed concisely in a memorable form; sometimes it is expressed as a command. Proverbs are as old as literature—possibly older, as they are the commonplaces of generalizing discourse, requiring little thought or analysis. They may form the very fabric of conversation and can be alluded to by only part of the whole proverb (as when we refer to "shutting the stable door" or "crying wolf"). An anonymous poet of 1315, rejoicing in the death of Edward II's hated favorite, Piers Gaveston, wrote: "Flexis ramis arbor alta ruit in proverbia" (alluding to "The highest tree has the greatest fall"). Henry of Avranches invented a whole story about St. Francis's being set upon by robbers as he walked on his way singing a merry song, simply to refute Juvenal's famous line, "Cantabit vacuus coram latrone viator" (*Satires* 10.22).

Proverbs achieve memorability through their packaging. This may be numerical, as in the biblical "Tria sunt nimis difficilia mihi, / et quattuor penitus ignoro: / viam aquilae in caelo, / viam colubri super petram, / viam navis in medio mari, / et viam viri in adolescentia" (*Prv* 30:18–19); they may be based on nature, as in Serlo's "Cum locus igne caret, iam fumus non ibi paret" ([GF16] 62.1), or simply on a striking image, as in Cato's "Fronte capillata, post haec occasio calva" ([GF6] 2.26), on the need to seize opportunity when it occurs. In Medieval Latin the most common metrical form for proverbs is the leonine hexameter; it is possible that many of them are exercises in versification of vernacular (or other well known) proverbs. For example, the biblical "Qui parcit virgae, odit filium suum" ("Spare the rod, spoil the child," *Prv* 13:24) is rendered into a couplet of *elegi cruciferi*:

> Natum virga docet et moribus instruit; ergo
>    Qui parcit tergo, non iuvat, imo nocet.
> [GF17] p102

There are many sources for Medieval Latin proverbs. A great number were supplied by the Bible (especially the sapiential books, *Proverbs, Wisdom, Ecclesiasticus,* etc.) and by classical literature (Seneca for prose, and Horace, Ovid, and Juvenal for verse). Animal fables were a staple of elementary education, and tags from them became common fare ("at mihi, qui quondam, semper asellus eris"; Avianus 5.18). Surprisingly (or perhaps not so surprisingly) rich sources for general maxims were the law ("vim vi repellas iure quovis gentium"; [GF3] v5:33384b) and the fathers of the Church ("Non dimittitur peccatum, nisi restituatur ablatum"; [GF3] v3:17503). By far the greatest number, however, have no known literary source; where a Latin proverb coincides with a popular vernacular one, it is probably fairly safe to assume that the source is the irrecoverable "popular wisdom" of "the folk." Weather lore ("Red sky at night, shepherd's delight," with many Latin analogues) is a good example of the latter.

The impulse to organize proverbial wisdom into collections is almost as old as the proverbs themselves. The biblical *Proverbs, Wisdom,* and *Ecclesiasticus* are themselves proverb collections. The habit extends to the Renaissance (Erasmus's *Adages*) and to modern times (La Rochefoucauld [d. 1680], Victorian copybook headings, and some modern engagement books and calendars). The earliest Medieval Latin literary collection is the *Distichs of Cato* [GF6–7]. This was one of the most common elements in the basic Latin curriculum, and its proverbs turn up everywhere in medieval literature. There can hardly be a discussion of dreams that does not include the tag "Somnia ne cures" (*Distichs* 2.31); an excuse for frivolity could be found in "Interpone tuis interdum gaudia curis" (*Distichs* 3.6).

There would be little point in listing collections of proverbs: they vary in shape and size according to the energy of the compilers and are known to modern scholars only if they have been published (see [GF1]). Two such collections can be used as paradigms. Serlo of Wilton (d. 1181), known for his grammatical verses and entertaining lyrics, assembled a collection of alternative Latin translations of French proverbs [GF16]. This was relatively popular and circulated with grammatical poems; it was also amplified by later scribes and compilers. The English proverb "Need makes an old wife trot" appears in Serlo as

> *Busuinne fait veille trotter.*
> Ut cito se portet vetule pes, cogit oportet.
> Fert indefesse vetulam currendo necesse.
> [GF16] p120

The same proverb is used appositely by Henry of Avranches when recording St. Birinus's cure of an old blind woman and her haste to reach the saint ("articulus compellit anum trottare"). Serlo's motive was, in the widest possible sense, literary. William de Montibus (d. 1213), however, an indefatigable organizer and compiler, may have been aiming at a preaching manual when he made an enormous collection of proverbs, both prose and verse, from biblical, patristic, and classical sources [GF10].

To recognize and identify a proverb requires either prior knowledge or a sense that something in a statement is off-key. For example, the phrase "to plough sand" (of futile endeavor) should send one in search of *litus arare* (which can be found in *Lewis-Short*). Readers who wish to determine whether or not a proverb was already circulating in the classical period would do well to consult first the work of August Otto, *Die Sprichwörter und sprichwörtlichen Redensarten der Römer* [GF2], and then Reinhard Häussler's supplement [GF2]. In addition to the usual array of concordances (to the Bible, the fathers, classical authors), medievalists also have the monumental index compiled by Hans Walther and Paul Gerhard Schmidt, *Proverbia sententiaeque latinitatis medii aevi,* with an *index verborum* [GF3]; this has nearly 35,000 entries, and its list of sources shows the range of published collections as well as of manuscripts utilized by Walther (though this only scratches the surface). W.A. Pantin printed only a few proverbs from a manuscript in the John Rylands Library, Manchester, noting that the whole collection contained over 1500 proverbs [GF17]. Another useful aid is the Whitings' *Proverbs, Sentences* [GF4]; although this, like *The Oxford Dictionary of English Proverbs* [GF5], contains only English proverbs, it frequently can give a lead to an earlier Latin source.

Proverbs (along with riddles, epigrams, word games, and the like) are often scribbled into blank spaces in manuscripts; for an example, see the few printed in the present writer's account of the Oxford manuscript, Bodley 851 [GF18].

## Epigrams

*Epigram* (now divorced from its earlier sense of "inscription") usually refers to a short saying with a pithy message; sometimes it is a kind of protoproverb that may, if successful, enter the wider and more anonymous field of proverbial sayings. Epigrams, at least in the literary sense, are usually contrived and artificial, and are given a specific context (for example, by supplying a name for the addressee). The best classical writer in this genre is Martial, whose epigrams were imitated in the amorphous *Anthologia Latina* [GF19], which was greatly amplified in the Middle Ages. An imitator of the genre was Godfrey of Winchester (d. 1107) [GF9], though his tone and morals were considerably less pungent and more wholesome than Martial's. Many of Hugh Primas's witty poems, at least the short ones, could be described as epigrams, e.g. his lament on a threadbare cloak (itself a literary genre):

> Pontificum spuma, fex cleri, sordida struma,
> Qui dedit in bruma michi mantellum sine pluma!
>   [GF14] p30

Epigrams are often satirical and sometimes personal (though the personal tone may be an artificial device). Those commenting on historical and topical events are common in chronicles and may often be the work of the author of the chronicle himself.

## Select Bibliography

### Guides

W. Mieder, *International Proverb Scholarship: An Annotated Bibliography* (1982); *id.,* *International Proverb Scholarship: An Annotated Bibliography: Supplement (1800–1991)* (1990–93): the numbered entries in these 3 vols. have been arranged alphabetically by modern author/editor; there are indices of *names* ("mentioned in the titles of the bibliographical entries and in the annotations"); *subjects* (see under "Latin" for works concerned with Medieval Latin proverbs, e.g. 61, 203, 334, 349, 706 [weather proverbs], 857, 862, 1184, 1452, 1598, 1691, 1700, 1742, 1790, 1802, 2007, 2164, 2529, 2699, 2875, 2983 [national and ethnic stereotypes], 3006); and *individual proverbs.* Nos. 1691 and 1700, by F. Seiler, examine several Medieval Latin proverb collections, e.g. the *Fecunda ratis* (tenth century), *Proverbia*

*Henrici* (eleventh century), *Florilegium Vindobonense* (thirteenth century), *Proverbia Rustici* (thirteenth century), *Florilegium Gottingense* (fourteenth century) [GF1].

A. Otto, *Die Sprichwörter und sprichwörtlichen Redensarten der Römer* (1890, r1965); R. Häussler, *Nachträge zu A. Otto, Sprichwörter und sprichwörtlichen Redensarten der Römer* (1968) [GF2].

H. Walther, *Proverbia sententiaeque latinitatis medii aevi/Lateinische Sprichwörter und Sentenzen des Mittelalters in alphabetischer Anordnung,* 5 vols. (1963–67); v6: *Register der Namen, Sachen und Wörter zu Teil 1–5* (1969); three additional volumes (7 [A–G], 8 [H–O], 9 [P–Z]; 1982–86) edited by P.G. Schmidt, *Proverbia sententiaeque latinitatis medii ac recentis aevi, nova series/Lateinische Sprichwörter und Sentenzen des Mittelalters und der frühen Neuzeit in alphabetischer Anordnung:* Walther-Schmidt is the indispensable reference work, based on published proverbs, manuscript catalogues, and some manuscripts [GF3].

B.J. Whiting and H.W. Whiting, *Proverbs, Sentences, and Proverbial Phrases from English Writings, Mainly before 1500* (1968) [GF4].

F.P. Wilson, *The Oxford Dictionary of English Proverbs,* 3rd ed. (1970) [GF5].

## Texts and Studies (very selective)

M. Boas, ed., *Disticha Catonis* (1952) [GF6]: this edition differs significantly from that of J.W. Duff and A.M. Duff in *Minor Latin Poets* (1934) 585–639 [GF7].

G. Bernt, *Das lateinische Epigramm im Übergang von der Spätantike zum frühen Mittelalter* (1968) [GF8].

H. Gerhard, ed., *Der "Liber proverbiorum" des Godefrid von Winchester* (1974) [GF9].

J. Goering, *William de Montibus (c. 1140–1213): The Schools and the Literature of Pastoral Care* (1992): includes an edition (pp339–48) of William's *Prouerbia et alia uerba edificatoria* [GF10].

L.B. Hessler, "The Latin Epigram of the Middle English Period," in *PMLA* 38 (1923) 712–28: a rather quaint survey [GF11].

S.M. Horrall, "Latin and Middle English Proverbs in a Manuscript at St. George's Chapel, Windsor Castle," in *MS* 45 (1983) 343–84 [GF12].

W. Maaz, *Lateinische Epigrammatik im höhen Mittelalter: Literarhistorische Untersuchungen zur Martial Rezeption* (1992) [GF13].

C.J. McDonough, *OPHP* [GF14].

J.I. McEnerney, "Proverbs in Hrotsvitha," in *MLJ* 21 (1986) 106–13 [GF15].

J. Öberg, ed., *Serlon de Wilton: Poèmes latins* (1965) [GF16].

W.A. Pantin, "A Medieval Collection of Latin and English Proverbs and Riddles from the Rylands Latin MS 394," in *Bulletin of the John Rylands Library* 14 (1930) 81–114: a selection [GF17].

A.G. Rigg, "Medieval Latin Poetic Anthologies (II)," in *MS* 40 (1978) 387–407 [GF18].

D.R. Shackelton Bailey, ed., *Anthologia Latina* (1982) [GF19].

S. Singer, *Sprichwörter des Mittelalters,* 3 vols. (1944–47) [GF20].

F. Suard and C. Buridant, *Richesse du proverbe,* 2 vols., v1: *Le proverbe au moyen âge,* v2: *Typologie et fonctions* (1984): the focus here is chiefly on vernacular materials, but see A.-M. Bautier, "Peuples, provinces et villes dans la littérature proverbiale latine du moyen âge," pp1–22 [GF21].

Taylor, B., "Medieval Proverb Collections: The West European Tradition," in *Journal of the Warburg and Courtauld Institutes* 55 (1992) 19–35 [GF22].

J. Werner and P. Flury, *Lateinische Sprichwörter und Sinnsprüche des Mittelalters aus Handschriften gesammelt,* 2nd ed. (1966): a collection (arranged alphabetically) based on 21 manuscripts [GF23].

A. Wilmart, "Les épigrammes liées d'Hughes Primat et d'Hildebert," in *RB* 47 (1935) 175–80 [GF24].

T. Wright, ed., *The Anglo-Latin Satirical Poets and Epigrammatists of the Twelfth Century,* 2 vols., *RSer* 59 (1872) [GF25].

GG   &#42;   DRAMA

BY STEPHEN K. WRIGHT

With few exceptions, the Latin drama of the Middle Ages was chanted music-drama intended not for popular entertainment but as an act of worship. Because the so-called liturgical drama originated in and continued to be closely associated with Christian ritual, the study of these texts is necessarily interdisciplinary in nature. The reader of Medieval Latin drama must thus be equipped not only with the standard tools of the paleographer, philologist, and literary historian, but also with skills from such disparate fields as musicology, iconography, liturgical studies, theology, and church history. Since the bibliography on the topic is as vast as it is diverse, the article that follows can give only an abbreviated overview. The indispensable *Forschungsberichte* by Flanigan [GG34–35] and Hughes [GG38] must serve as guides to further reading.

From as early as the fourth century, Christian moralists had condemned the pagan spectacles that entertained the populace of the late Roman Empire. The work of the preachers was completed by invading Germanic tribes, whose hostility to theatrical and gladiatorial performances eventually resulted in their abolition. The ensuing theatrical hiatus was not absolute. Wandering minstrels, acrobats, jugglers, and mimes continued to ply their craft. The comedies of Plautus and Terence were preserved (although it was mistakenly supposed that Roman playwrights had recited their texts while players silently mimed the action), and scholars such as Isidore of Seville, Gerald of Wales, and John of Salisbury accurately described the Roman stage. Moreover, games, dances, and other mimetic enactments associated with the seasonal rites of pre-Christian communities continued to be practiced throughout the period in question. Nevertheless, it is fair to say that theater as an organized social and literary institution ceased to exist in Western Europe between the sixth and tenth centuries.

No area of Latin drama studies has produced such lively and continuing controversy as the question of how to explain the reemergence of dramatic activity in the late tenth century. Stumpfl [GG60], Cargill [GG24], and Hunningher [GG39] emphasize the ludic customs of native Germanic peoples, but their arguments have failed to win wide acceptance. Dunn [GG31] suggests that the recitation of saint's lives in the Gallican liturgy, the performance practices of the Roman mime, and the traditions of Spanish sacred dance may have combined to lay a foundation for later drama. Similarly, Flanigan [GG36] concludes that the appearance of Easter dialogues in monastic worship is linked to the imposition of the austere Roman rite in areas where the more elaborate Gallican liturgy had formerly prevailed; the expressive power of the older form of worship may have reasserted itself in the guise of liturgical drama. Finally, one should mention Hardison's thesis [GG37] that drama originated in the Vigil Mass of Easter, an opinion that has been seriously challenged on musicological grounds by Smoldon ([GG54], [GG56]).

Most attempts to explain the reemergence of drama, however, focus on the innovative troping movement of the Carolingian period. (A trope is simply a brief literary and musical composition added as an embellishment to the regular service.) In particular, the troped introit to the Mass of Easter Sunday, a short dialogue to be chanted antiphonally by a single cantor and a group of respondents, seems to be closely linked to the earliest quasi-dramatic ceremonies. The oldest surviving *Quem quaeritis* trope, a three-line dialogue between the three Marys and the angel at the empty tomb, comes from the abbey of St. Martial at Limoges and dates from before 936: "Quem queritis in sepulchro, o Christicole? / Jhesum Nazarenum crucifixum, o caelicole. / Non est hic, surrexit sicut predixerat; ite nuntiate, quia surrexit. Alleluia" [GG13]. In the late tenth century the *Quem quaeritis* was apparently moved from its original position at the beginning of the Mass to the end of Easter matins, where it was interpolated between the third responsory and the final *Te Deum.* Freed from the surrounding processional antiphons of the Mass, the brief exchange between the angel and the women could be expanded by the addition of newly composed material. As the culmination to a sequence of quasi-mimetic Holy Week ceremonies (the adoration, deposition, and elevation of the cross), the Winchester *Regularis concordia* (c. 965–75) [GG15] preserves the earliest *Visitatio sepulchri,* an extension of the *Quem quaeritis* dialogue whose rubrics provide detailed instructions for the requisite vestments, properties, and acting styles. Although this reenactment of the events of Easter morning is explicitly conceived of as *officium* rather than *ludus,* the deliberate use of costume, props, gestures, and vocal modulations as elements of impersonation is unmistakably dramatic in nature.

Hardison's enormously influential work [GG37] overturned the long-standing theory of the history of early drama that had been erected upon the monumental scholarship of Chambers [GG25] and Young [GG17]. According to this once-canonical scheme, simple versions of the visit to the sepulcher gave rise to successively more complex texts in an orderly evolutionary development that culminated in plays of substantial length and intricacy. Hardison exposed the untenable Darwinian presuppositions of this view and demonstrated that in many cases more elaborate versions actually predate simpler ones. Although it is no longer possible to regard the three types of *Visitatio sepulchri* identified by Chambers and Young as stages in a chronological sequence, scholars continue to use their terminology as a convenient way to categorize the texts. Thus, Stage I plays are those that restrict the dialogue to the three Marys and the angel. Stage II plays include the scene in which the apostles Peter and John race to the tomb and then display the empty shroud as visual proof of the resurrection (cf. *Io* 20:1–10). Stage III plays depict the so-called *Hortulanus* scene in which Mary Magdalene mistakes the risen Christ for a gardener (cf. *Io* 20:11–18). Other characters might include Pilate and the Jewish elders, the soldiers sent to guard the tomb, and the spice seller from whom the women purchase their ointments. Lipphardt's magisterial compilation of all the extant Easter ceremonies [GG13], which unfortunately perpetuates the misconception of music-drama as a purely literary form, contains more than one thousand texts, arranged according to "stage" and manuscript provenance. De Boor [GG27], Dolan [GG28], and Bjork [GG21] have made important preliminary attempts to elucidate the tangled textual history of the *Visitatio sepulchri* in its various forms from the tenth to the sixteenth centuries (when the practice was suppressed by the Council of Trent). Michael Norton's current effort to compile a computerized database of Easter ceremonies holds forth the promise of a comprehensive textual history based on both musical and verbal evidence.

The earliest Christmas dramas are apparently indebted to the *Visitatio sepulchri*. An eleventh-century troped introit for the third Mass of Christmas from Limoges consists of a dialogue between the shepherds and a witness at the manger: "Quem queritis in presepe, pastores, dicite? / Salvatorem Xpistum Dominum, infantem pannis involutum secundum sermonem angelicum. / Adest hic parvulus cum Maria matre sua" [GG11]. Various types of Christmas ceremonies proliferated in the eleventh and twelfth centuries. Again, it is impossible to trace a clear evolutionary line from simple to more ambitious texts. Only a few unprepossessing examples of the *Officium pastorum* (the shepherds at the manger) have come down to us, perhaps because Christmas morning was so replete with preexisting services as to provide little scope for further dramatic elaboration. By way of contrast, the *Officium stellae* (the Adoration of the Magi) for the Feast of the Epiphany (6 January) exhibits far greater variety and more ornate staging. In addition to the royal procession and offering of gifts, many plays of this type include a mechanical star to guide the kings, scenes at Herod's court, the angelic warning, and the Flight into Egypt. Similarly, Holy Innocents' Day (28 December) gave rise to plays depicting the Slaughter of the Innocents (*Ordo Rachelis*), an event that could also be incorporated into the *Officium stellae*. A fourth kind of Christmas performance was the *Ordo prophetarum*, a series of monologues based on a pseudo-Augustinian sermon in which Hebrew and Gentile prophets (including Balaam and his ass, Virgil, and the Erythraean Sibyl), attempt to convince the Jews of Christ's divinity.

The famous thirteenth-century *Carmina Burana* manuscript ([GG4], [GG12]), long associated with the monastery of Benediktbeuern but now thought to have been produced in South Tirol [GG57], preserves a *Ludus de nativitate* that, as the title implies, was performed independently of the liturgy. A work of rare poetic, musical, and theatrical power, it opens with a procession of the prophets and goes on to encompass a debate between St. Augustine and Archisynagogus, the Annunciation, the Salutation of Elizabeth, the birth of Jesus, the arrival of the Magi and the shepherds, and the Massacre of the Innocents. The play ends with an unprecedented *coup de théâtre*: "Postea Herodes corrodatur a vermibus et excedens de sede sua mortuus accipiatur a diabolis multum congaudentibus." It has been argued that the unique *Ludus de rege Aegypti*, which follows the *Ludus de nativitate* in the manuscript and was long considered to be an independent text, may actually have once been part of the Christmas play [GG40].

The twelfth and thirteenth centuries also provide a handful of large-scale Passion plays that draw upon the hymns, antiphons, and lections of the Church but were produced apart from any particular liturgical setting. The rarity of such works may be attributable to the fact that since the Mass itself offered a daily repetition of Christ's sacrifice, there was little need to reenact it as drama. The earliest example is a fragmentary play of the betrayal and crucifixion from Montecassino [GG59] that was perhaps less influenced by ritual practice than by a reading of the Gospels in light of the new affective, christocentric piety embodied by Anselm and Bernard of Clairvaux. The *Carmina Burana* manuscript ([GG4], [GG12]) preserves two specimens of the genre. The longer *Ludus de passione* is a sophisticated and deeply moving synthesis of preexisting chants [GG20] that encompasses the preaching and ministry of Christ, the entry into Jerusalem, the raising of Lazarus, the agony in the garden, and the betrayal, trial, and Crucifixion. Especially noteworthy are the highly emotional portrayals of the sinful life and eventual conversion of Mary Magdalene and the lament of the Virgin at the cross, both of which introduce vernacular lyrics into the Latin music-drama.

Dramatizations of Old Testament episodes were rare [GG17]. In addition to fragmentary plays of Jacob and Esau (Austria, twelfth century) and Joseph and his brothers (Laon, thirteenth century), there also exist two remarkable music-dramas based on the life of Daniel. The first of these is a poetic tour de force by Hilarius, a former student of Abelard's from whose pen we also have plays about the Raising of Lazarus and St. Nicholas. Even more spectacular is the *Ludus Danielis* performed during Christmas festivities by students at the cathedral school of Beauvais ([GG1], [GG32]). The play reenacts Belshazzar's feast and Daniel's interpretation of the mysterious writing on the wall, the triumph of Darius, and the deliverance of the prophet from the lion's den. A bare synopsis fails to do justice to the visual and musical splendor of a play that includes no fewer than eight majestic processions, singers accompanied by instruments, characters cloaked in regal robes, the display of sumptuous vessels, and general revelry and dancing ("Eius et curia / resonat laetitia, / adsunt et tripudia").

In addition to representations of biblical episodes, the corpus of twelfth-century liturgical drama also includes plays on four events from the life of St. Nicholas for performance on his feast day (6 December) [GG17]. Given the saint's role as patron of children and scholars and the inherent appeal of miracles and adventures, it is not surprising that several versions of the Nicholas legends survive. The *Tres filiae* (Hildesheim and Fleury) recalls how the saint rescues the daughters of a poor man from a life of prostitution by tossing bags of gold through their window. In the *Tres clerici* (Hildesheim, Fleury, and Einsiedeln), Nicholas resurrects three wandering students who have been murdered by a larcenous innkeeper. In the *Iconia sancti Nicolai* (Hilarius and Fleury), a miser castigates, threatens, and (in Hilarius's version) actually flogs an icon of the saint when it fails to ward off thieves, but he is converted to Christianity when Nicholas forces the robbers to return the stolen treasure. The *Filius Getronis* (Fleury) depicts the abduction of a boy by the soldiers of a heathen king; the parents' devotion to the cult of Nicholas causes the saint to intrude upon a pagan banquet, seize the boy, and return him to his home.

The abbess Hildegard of Bingen (1098–1179), a prolific theologian, hagiographer, scientist, visionary, and poet, composed the enigmatic *Ordo virtutum* ([GG5], [GG9]), a unique musical *psychomachia* of incomparable beauty in which 17 personified virtues liberate an endangered soul from the devil. Long regarded as an unperformable precursor of the vernacular morality play [GG46], Hildegard's idiosyncratic work has recently been reinterpreted in the context of her convent's ceremony for the consecration of virgins ([GG30], [GG53]).

An even greater anomaly is the *Ludus de Antichristo* from the Bavarian monastery of Tegernsee [GG16]. The play, which dates from c. 1160, synthesizes apocalyptic imagery from biblical and exegetical sources, the legend of the Last Roman Emperor, allegorical figures, and allusions to contemporary events in order to create a unique piece of theatrical propaganda on behalf of the nationalistic, antipapal politics of Frederick I Barbarossa. This vision of imperial conquest and eschatological terror was performed by a large cast in an open playing area surrounded by eight raised structures with thrones (*sedes*) for the various nations of the world.

Finally, one must mention the attempts of medieval educators and intellectuals to imitate Roman comedies. In the tenth century, the canoness Hrotsvitha of Gandersheim (c. 935–c. 975) composed six dialogues extolling female chastity and martyrdom (*Gallicanus, Dulcitius, Calimachus, Abraham, Pafnutius, Sapientia*) to replace the scandalous erotic works of Terence in the convent curriculum [GG14]. It is not known whether her carefully crafted poems were meant to be performed as dramas ([GG22], [GG62]), declaimed and perhaps mimed, or simply studied as stylistic models, but most scholars favor the last-mentioned view [GG44]. Similar problems face students of the so-called elegiac comedies, a group of witty, erudite poems composed mainly in the schools of the Loire valley in the late twelfth century ([GG2], [GG6]). These pieces are written in elegiac couplets and are sometimes indebted to ancient comedy. Since the dialogues contain narrative interpolations and other nondramatic elements, it is likely that they too were intended for private study rather than public performance ([GG19], [GG47], [GG50], [GG61]). Even if one accepts the possibility that some of these compositions may have been used for semidramatic classroom recitation, there is scant evidence to connect them with a putative twelfth-century tradition of secular Latin theater ([GG18], [GG42], [GG51–52]). Several of the *comediae* (e.g. the *Geta* of Vital of Blois [fl. 1150–60] and the anonymous *Pamphilus*) were widely disseminated through school curricula and the florilegia and thus influenced late medieval vernacular authors such as Boccaccio, Deschamps, Chaucer, Gower, Juan Ruiz, and Fernando de Rojas.

## Select Bibliography

### Primary Sources

W. Arlt, ed., *Ein Festoffizium des Mittelalters aus Beauvais in seiner liturgischen und musikalischen Bedeutung,* 2 vols. (1970) [GG1].

F. Bertini, ed., *Commedie latine del XII e XIII secolo,* 5 vols. (1976–86) [GG2].

D. Bevington, ed., *Medieval Drama* (1975) [GG3].

B. Bischoff, ed., *Carmina Burana: Facsimile Reproduction of the Manuscript Clm 4660 and 4660a,* Publications of Mediaeval Musical Manuscripts 9 (1967) [GG4].

M. Böckeler and P. Barth, eds., *Der heiligen Hildegard von Bingen Reigen der Tugenden: Ordo virtutum* (1927) [GG5].

G. Cohen, ed., *La "Comédie" latine en France au XIIe siècle,* 2 vols. (1931) [GG6].

F. Collins, Jr., ed., *Medieval Church Music-Dramas: A Repertory of Complete Plays* (1976) [GG7].

C.E.H. de Coussemaker, ed., *Drames liturgiques du moyen âge* (1860, r1964) [GG8].

P. Dronke, ed., "The Text of the *Ordo Virtutum*," in *PIMA* 180–92 [GG9].

P. Dronke, ed. and tr., *Nine Medieval Latin Plays* (1994): includes *Sponsus, Officium stelle, Tres filie, Tres clerici, Verses pascales de tres Maries, Versus de pelegrino, Danielis ludus, Ordo virtutum,* and *Ludus de passione* [**GG10**].

P. Evans, ed., *The Early Trope Repertory of Saint Martial de Limoges* (1970) [**GG11**].

A. Hilka, O. Schumann, and B. Bischoff, eds., *Carmina Burana:* v1.3, *Die Trink- und Spielerlieder—Die geistlichen Dramen* (1970) [**GG12**].

W. Lipphardt, ed., *Lateinische Osterfeiern und Osterspiele,* 9 vols., Ausgaben deutscher Literatur des XV. bis XVIII. Jahrhunderts: Reihe Drama 5 (1975–90) [**GG13**].

K. Strecker, ed., *Hrotsvithae opera,* 2nd ed. (1930) [**GG14**].

T. Symons, ed., *The Monastic Agreement of the Monks and Nuns of the English Nation [Regularis Concordia]* (1953) [**GG15**].

G. Vollmann-Profe, ed., *Ludus de Antichristo,* 2 vols., Litterae 82 (1981) [**GG16**].

K. Young, ed., *The Drama of the Medieval Church,* 2 vols. (1933, r1962) [**GG17**].

## Studies

A.K. Bate, "Twelfth-Century Latin Comedies and the Theatre," in *Papers of the Liverpool Latin Seminar, Second Volume, 1979,* ed. F. Cairns, ARCA: Classical and Medieval Texts, Papers and Monographs 3 (1979) 249–62 [**GG18**].

D. Bigongiari, "Were There Theaters in the Twelfth and Thirteenth Centuries?" in *RomRev* 37 (1946) 201–24 [**GG19**].

T. Binkley, "The Greater Passion Play from *Carmina Burana:* An Introduction," in *Alte Musik: Praxis und Reflexion,* ed. P. Reidemeister and V. Gutmann (1983) 144–57 [**GG20**].

D. Bjork, "On the Dissemination of *Quem quaeritis* and the *Visitatio sepulchri* and the Chronology of Their Early Sources," in *CD* 14 (1980) 46–69 [**GG21**].

M. Butler, *Hrotsvitha: The Theatricality of Her Plays* (1960) [**GG22**].

T.P. Campbell and C. Davidson, eds., *The Fleury Playbook: Essays and Studies,* Early Drama, Art, and Music Monograph Series 7 (1985) [**GG23**].

O. Cargill, *Drama and Liturgy* (1930) [**GG24**].

E.K. Chambers, *The Mediaeval Stage,* 2 vols. (1903, r1963) [**GG25**].

F. Collins, Jr., *The Production of Medieval Church Music-Drama* (1972) [**GG26**].

H. de Boor, *Die Textgeschichte der lateinischen Osterfeiern,* Hermaea: Germanistische Forschungen, n.s., 22 (1967) [**GG27**].

D. Dolan, *Le drame liturgique de Pâques en Normandie et en Angleterre au moyen-âge,* Publications de l'Université de Poitiers: Lettres et sciences humaines 16 (1975) [**GG28**].

R.B. Donovan, *The Liturgical Drama in Medieval Spain* (1958) [**GG29**].

P. Dronke, "Hildegard of Bingen as Poetess and Dramatist," in *PIMA* 150–92 [**GG30**].

E.C. Dunn, *The Gallican Saint's Life and the Late Roman Dramatic Tradition* (1989) [**GG31**].

M. Fassler, "The Feast of Fools and *Ludus Danielis:* Popular Tradition in a Medieval Cathedral Play," in *Plainsong in the Age of Polyphony,* ed. T.F. Kelly (1992) 65–99 [**GG32**].

C. Flanigan, "The Liturgical Context of the *Quem Queritis* Trope," in *CD* 8 (1974) 45–62 [**GG33**].

C. Flanigan, "The Liturgical Drama and Its Tradition: A Review of Scholarship 1965–1975," in *Research Opportunities in Renaissance Drama* 18 (1975) 81–102, 19 (1976) 109–36 [**GG34**].

C. Flanigan, "Medieval Latin Music-Drama," in *The Theatre of Medieval Europe: New Research in Early Drama*, ed. E. Simon (1991) 21–41 [GG35].

C. Flanigan, "The Roman Rite and the Origins of the Liturgical Drama," in *University of Toronto Quarterly* 43 (1974) 263–84 [GG36].

O.B. Hardison, Jr., *Christian Rite and Christian Drama in the Middle Ages: Essays in the Origin and Early History of Modern Drama* (1965, r1983) [GG37].

A. Hughes, "Liturgical Drama: Falling Between the Disciplines," in *The Theatre of Medieval Europe* (see [GG35]) 42–62 [GG38].

B. Hunningher, *The Origin of the Theater* (1955, r1978) [GG39].

H. Linke, "Der Schluss des mittellateinischen Weihnachtsspiels aus Benediktbeuern," in *Zeitschrift für deutsche Philologie* 94 (1975) 1–22 [GG40].

W. Lipphardt, "Liturgische Dramen," in *MGG* 8:1010–51 [GG41].

R.S. Loomis and G. Cohen, "Were There Theatres in the Twelfth and Thirteenth Centuries?" in *Speculum* 20 (1945) 92–98 [GG42].

T.J. McGee, "The Liturgical Placements of the *Quem quaeritis* Dialogue," in *Journal of the American Musicological Society* 29 (1976) 1–29 [GG43].

B. Nagel, *Hrotsvit von Gandersheim* (1965) [GG44].

M. Norton, "Of 'Stages' and 'Types' in *Visitatione Sepulchri*," in *CD* 21 (1987) 34–61, 127–44 [GG45].

R. Potter, "The *Ordo Virtutum*: Ancestor of the English Moralities?," in *CD* 20 (1986) 201–10 [GG46].

F.J.E. Raby, "The 'Comoedia' or Versified Tale," in *SLP* 2:54–69 [GG47].

S. Rankin, "Liturgical Drama," in *NOHM* 2:310–56 [GG48].

S. Rankin, *The Music of the Medieval Liturgical Drama in France and England*, 2 vols. (1989) [GG49].

S. Rizzo, "Due note sulla commedia elegiaca medievale," in *GIF* 31 (1979) 97–103 [GG50].

B. Roy, "Arnulf of Orléans and the Latin 'Comedy,'" in *Speculum* 49 (1974) 258–66 [GG51].

P.G. Schmidt, "The Vision of Thurkill," in *Journal of the Warburg and Courtauld Institutes* 41 (1978) 50–64 [GG52].

P. Sheingorn, "The Virtues of Hildegard's *Ordo Virtutum*," in *The "Ordo Virtutum" of Hildegard of Bingen: Critical Studies*, ed. A.E. Davidson (1992) 43–62 [GG53].

W. Smoldon, "The Melodies of the Medieval Church Dramas and Their Significance," in *Medieval English Drama: Essays Critical and Contextual*, ed. J. Taylor and A.H. Nelson (1972) 64–80 [GG54].

W. Smoldon, *The Music of the Medieval Church Dramas*, ed. C. Bourgeault (1980) [GG55].

W. Smoldon, "The Origins of the *Quem Quaeritis* Trope and the Easter Sepulchre Music-Dramas, as Demonstrated by Their Musical Settings," in *The Medieval Drama*, ed. S. Sticca (1972) 121–54 [GG56].

G. Steer, "'Carmina Burana' in Südtirol: Zur Herkunft des clm 4660," in *ZDADL* 112 (1983) 1–37 [GG57].

T. Stemmler, *Liturgische Feiern und geistliche Spiele: Studien zu Erscheinungsformen des Dramatischen im Mittelalter*, Buchreihe der Anglia, Zeitschrift für englische Philologie 15 (1970) [GG58].

S. Sticca, *The Latin Passion Play: Its Origins and Development* (1970) [GG59].

R. Stumpfl, *Kultspiele der Germanen als Ursprung des mittelalterlichen Dramas* (1936) [GG60].

I. Thomson, "Latin 'Elegiac Comedy' of the Twelfth Century," in *Versions of Medieval Comedy*, ed. P. Ruggiers (1977, r1987) 51–66 [GG61].

E.H. Zeydel, "Were Hrotsvitha's Dramas Performed During Her Lifetime?" in *Speculum* 20 (1945) 443–56 [GG62].

*See also* [BA47–48], [BD34].

GH · EXEMPLA

BY NIGEL F. PALMER

The use of the word *exemplum* as a literary term is fraught with ambiguity and inconsistency. The most important distinction to make is between "exemplum" as a functional term in rhetorical theory, where it designates a proof by analogy (and more particularly a historically true analogy), and "exemplum" as the conventional term for a particular medieval text type. In the first sense—and here the term is applicable to ancient and medieval literature equally—the exemplum offers an authoritative historical precedent that will command belief and persuade the audience or reader. The rhetorical exemplum, as employed by a medieval author such as John of Salisbury (d. 1180), typically quotes the deeds of well-known historical figures (such as Brutus or Saul) that are reported in authoritative literary sources (such as Virgil or the Bible). The definition in the influential *Rhetorica ad Herennium* stresses the naming of the doer or author: *Exemplum est alicuius facti aut dicti praeteriti cum certi auctoris nomine proposito* (4.49.62). The concept of the exemplum includes both the event itself and literary reports of the event; it embraces historical figures, facts, customs, apothegmata, and other nonnarrative forms; also abbreviated forms and allusions (such as *alter Achilles*). Rhetorical exempla in this sense do not simply have an illustrative function (*exornatio*); they may also be employed as facts to be interpreted and accorded a particular place within an argument, or as an aid to the solution of problems.

The work that stands at the beginning of the classical and medieval tradition of theoretical statements concerning the rhetorical exemplum is Aristotle's *Rhetoric*. Later discussions are to be found, for example, in the *Rhetorica ad Herennium* (4.49.62), Cicero's *De inventione* (1.30), Quintilian (5.11.1ff.), Gervase of Melkley, and Engelbert of Admont. Aristotle's analysis of the forms of oratorical argument (*Rhetorica* 2.20.1393a–1394a) can be schematized in the figure below:

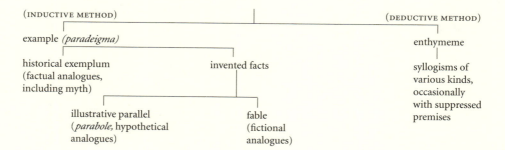

(INDUCTIVE METHOD)          (DEDUCTIVE METHOD)

example *(paradeigma)*          enthymeme

historical exemplum    invented facts        syllogisms of
(factual analogues,                       various kinds,
including myth)                           occasionally
                                            with suppressed

illustrative parallel      fable            premises
(*parabole,* hypothetical    (fictional
analogues)             analogues)

Aristotle's account combines functional definitions, such as *paradeigma/exemplum* in the broader sense, with more narrowly defined categories, such as the historical exemplum and fable, which refer to specific instances of a class. Both the examples cited for *exemplum* in the strict sense include narrations of events, but the definition concentrates on their logical status as res gestae, not on such literary aspects as their narrative character, and it thus embraces the whole range of forms that are found in rhetorical practice. An important definition of the exemplum from late antiquity is that of Isidore: *Inter exemplum et similitudinem hoc interest, quod exemplum historia est, similitudo approbatio* (*Differentiae* 191; *PL* 83:1329). This definition might seem to narrow down the term to narrative examples, but the main stress is on the logical status of historical veracity. The distinction between the logical status of the functionally defined rhetorical exemplum and the literary character of the exemplum as a text type is not always easy to maintain.

The term *exemplum* has been widely used in medieval studies, not always with adequate definition, to refer to one particular text type, namely short narratives with a spiritual message of the kind that was widely used in sermons in the later Middle Ages. The standard definition is as follows: "un récit bref donné comme véridique et destiné à être inséré dans un discours (en général un sermon) pour convaincre un auditoire par une leçon salutaire" (a brief narrative, claiming to be true, and intended for insertion into a discourse [in general a sermon] for the purpose of convincing an audience through a salutary lesson) ([GH6] pp37–38). In their own context such homiletic exempla (as they are best called) fulfill a literary function very similar to that of the rhetorical exempla, but it should be noted that the term is at once narrower and broader. The most recent definitions of the exemplum as a text type limit it, at least implicitly, to narrative texts. Welter [GH1] and Schenda [GH5], however, attempted to preserve the full range of forms that a functional definition permits: "Das Exemplum ist ein unterhaltsam vorgetragenes Lehrstück, das die Sittlichkeit fördern will" (An exemplum is an amusingly recounted piece of instruction aimed at the promotion of morality) ([GH5] p81). Many homiletic exempla are indistinguishable in their literary form from rhetorical exempla, but it is also true that many would have to be classified, in Aristotelian terms, as illustrative parallels or fables. The strategies used to underline the veracity of the events adduced vary considerably. Some homiletic exempla make use of the authoritative source (*Refert Augustinus de ciuitate Dei . . .*) or famous names (*Quaedam matrona rogauit abbatem Arsenium . . .*) in the manner of the rhetorical exemplum; others refer to the testimony of the experience of the writer/preacher (*Audiui de quodam . . .*), whereas others simply present the story of a nameless type character as a fact to be noted (*Item nota de sacerdote qui . . .*). The affinity of exempla and enthymematic argument is apparent from the frequency with which the lesson emerges from words spoken by the characters, often using the kind of language characteristic of deductive reasoning. The feature that the homiletic exemplum is a discrete entity embedded in a broader literary context (or, in the case of collections, designed to be so employed) is shared with the tradition of the rhetorical exemplum.

The direction of the exemplum towards a particular spiritual (or moral/pragmatic) lesson arises from its rhetorical function in the homiletic context and distinguishes it from other narrative forms such as the novella or anecdote. At the same time it must be recognized that all such stories will contain matter that goes beyond the requirements of the immediate homiletic context: for example, the tale of Emeranciana and Arsenius in the *Tabula exemplorum secundum ordinem alphabeti* ([GH3] no. 356) raises questions over and above the undesirability of contact with women, such as the function of memory and the holy man's moral duty towards a woman of such exceptional piety. There is therefore a tension between the narrative as such, as a literary entity, and the exemplary function assigned to it. The lesson may be implicit and unstated, or the narrative part of the exemplum may be followed by a second section in which the lesson is made explicit. In the latter case a distinction is to be made between exempla where the lesson is briefly summed up at the end, for example, in the form of an *epimythion*, and those cases where a point-by-point allegorical interpretation is provided (as in the *Gesta Romanorum*). In such cases the *allegoresis* is an integral part of the exemplum and can often be seen to have determined the selection of details in the narrative.

The characteristic context of the homiletic exemplum is the sermon. Guibert of Nogent (d. c. 1125) recommends the use of *simplices historias et veterum gesta* as a form of *exornatio* in sermons (*PL* 156:25). Authors of sermon collections whose use of exempla has attracted attention include Abelard (d. 1142), Honorius Augustodunensis (d. c. 1156); Jacques de Vitry, Can. Aug. (d. 1240); Hélinand of Froidmont, O. Cist. (d. after 1229); Caesarius of Heisterbach, O. Cist. (d. c. 1240); Odo of Cheriton (d. c. 1246); Gilbert of Tournai, O.F.M. (fl. 1240–84); "Greculus" (c. 1300); Peregrinus of Opole (fl. 1303–33); Vincent Ferrier (d. 1419); "Meffreth" (fl. 1443–47); Johannes Grütsch, O.F.M. (fl. 1424–68); Gottschalk Hollen, O.E.S.A. (c. 1411–81); Olivier Maillard (c. 1430–1502). Such typical sermon exempla as the extracts from Jacques de Vitry and Odo of Cheriton printed by Welter ([GH1] pp457–75) function in context as *paradeigmata* in the broader Aristotelian sense (although only a few could be defined as historical exempla) and are situated in the context of an enthymematic argument; functionally they are comparable to the historical exempla employed, for example, by John of Salisbury. Collections of sermons such as those listed above served not only as models for preaching, but also as repertoria of exempla. The exempla from the *Sermones vulgares* of Jacques de Vitry are also transmitted as an exempla collection without the sermon context. Exempla are found in Bible commentaries, such as those of Stephen Langton (d. 1228) and Robert Holcot, O.P. (d. 1349); in many forms of historiographical literature (for example, in the works of Godfrey of Viterbo [d. c. 1192/1200]; Hélinand of Froidmont; Vincent of Beauvais, O.P. [d. c. 1264]; and Martinus Polonus, O.P. [fl. 1261–78]); and in religious treatises. Here, too, they may be functionalized in context, but these works were also used as repertories of extractable exempla.

Most studies of exempla have concentrated on the exempla collections, which themselves constitute a distinctive medieval text type. Collections of exempla were useful treasure houses of tales that could be extracted for use in preaching and religious instruction. However, when the exemplum is seen in the context of a collection, the unidirectional thrust towards a particular lesson is counteracted by the wealth of diverse (and potentially contradictory) doctrine contained in the whole. This polarity, which is always possible but only rarely demonstrably intended, asserts itself as a principle in collections with a narrative framework. This is the case, for example, in the *Historia septem sapientum,* where the tales are set within an outer story and arranged in contradictory pairs, and in the *Pañcatantra* translation of John of Capua. Such works implicitly question the idea that an exemplum can form a compelling basis for a particular course of action: and so the literary form turns, play-fully, against itself.

Valerius Maximus, the *Vitaspatrum*, and the *Dialogues* of Gregory the Great are the precursors of important branches of the medieval exemplum tradition, repre-sented by the *Libellus de moribus hominum et officiis nobilium ac popularium super ludo scachorum* of Jacobus de Cessolis (fl. 1288–1322), with its classicizing exempla; the *Vitae fratrum ordinis praedicatorum* of Gerard of Frachet, O.P. (d. 1271); and the *De miraculis libri duo* of Peter the Venerable (after 1135; *PL* 189:851–954). In the twelfth and early thirteenth centuries a tradition of monastic exempla, particularly favored by Cistercians, became established, in which miracle stories, apparitions, and Mari-ological narratives prevailed. The authors of these collections include Herbert of Clairvaux (de Torrès, datable c. 1178), Engelhard of Langheim (fl. 1140–1200/10), Conrad of Eberbach (fl. 1210–21), and Caesarius of Heisterbach (*Dialogus miraculo-rum*, 1219–23; *Libri miraculorum*, 1225–26), whose exempla often drew on recent events from local history.

The major homiletic collection of the thirteenth century is the *Tractatus de di-versis materiis predicabilibus* of Stephen of Bourbon (c. 1250–61), which contains nu-merous *dicta, similitudines,* and almost 3,000 exempla. This work was followed by derivatives, the *Liber de abundancia exemplorum* or *De dono timoris* of Humbert of Romans (c. 1263–77), and the *Promptuarium exemplorum* of Martinus Polonus (c. 1261–71). Whereas these collections are arranged systematically, others have an al-phabetical arrangement, notably the *Liber exemplorum* in Durham Cathedral Li-brary (c. 1275–79), the *Tabula exemplorum secundum ordinem alphabeti* (c. 1277), the *Speculum laicorum* (c. 1279–92), the widespread *Alphabetum narrationum* of Arnold of Liège (c. 1297–1308), and the *Scala celi* of Johannes Gobius (c. 1323–30).

A distinctive group of late medieval collections is formed by those where the ex-empla are "moralized," that is, interpreted allegorically point by point. The technique was used by earlier writers (for example, in the sermons of Jacques de Vitry), but in a number of collections from the later thirteenth century onwards it determines the literary form. The most important of these works are the *Libellus . . . super ludo sca-chorum* of Jacobus de Cessolis, the *Moralitates* of Robert Holcot (before 1342), and, most famous of all the exempla collections, the *Gesta Romanorum* (before 1342).

## Select Bibliography

### Guides and Studies

For the standard history of the homiletic exemplum see J.-T. Welter, *L'exemplum dans la littérature religieuse et didactique du moyen âge* (1927, r1973) [GH1].

The most valuable handbooks are those of J.A. Herbert, *Catalogue of Romances in the Department of Manuscripts in the British Museum,* v3 (1910, r1962), which lists the contents of exempla collections in the British Library together with biographical and bibliographical references [GH2]; and F.C. Tubach, *Index exemplorum: A Hand-book of Medieval Religious Tales* (1969), indexing a large number of exempla collec-tions by subject [GH3]. Some help in using Tubach is provided by J. Berlioz and M.A.

Polo de Beaulieu, *Les exempla médiévaux: Introduction à la recherche, suivie des tables critiques de l'Index exemplorum de Frederic C. Tubach* (1992) [GH4].

For the state of research in the field see R. Schenda, "Stand und Aufgaben der Exemplaforschung," in *Fabula* 10 (1969) 69–85 [GH5]; C. Bremond, J. Le Goff, and J.-C. Schmitt, *L'"exemplum"*, TSMAO 40 (1982) [GH6]; and above all two collections of essays: *Rhétorique et histoire: L'exemplum et le modèle de comportement dans le discours antique et médiévale*, [ed. J. Berlioz and J.-M. David], in *Mélanges de l'École française de Rome: Moyen âge, temps modernes* 92 (1980) 1–179 [GH7]; *Exempel und Exempelsammlungen*, ed. W. Haug and B. Wachinger (1991), which includes the most important recent theoretical statements concerning the definition and function of the exemplum and a *Forschungsbericht* on French research, 1968–88, by J. Berlioz [GH8].

On the rhetorical exemplum and the bridge between antiquity and the Middle Ages see above all P. von Moos, *Geschichte als Topik: Das rhetorische Exemplum von der Antike zur Neuzeit und die "historiae" im "Policraticus" Johanns von Salisbury* (1988) [GH9]; id., "The Use of Exempla in the *Policraticus* of John of Salisbury," in *The World of John of Salisbury*, ed. M. Wilks (1984) 207–61 [GH10].

Further useful studies that demonstrate the direction of recent scholarship are those of C. Delcorno, *Exemplum e letteratura tra Medioevo e Rinascimento* (1989) [GH11]; B.P. McGuire, "The Cistercians and the Rise of the Exemplum in Early Thirteenth Century France: A Reevaluation of *Paris BN MS lat. 15912*," in *Classica et Mediaevalia* 34 (1983) 211–67 [GH12]; A. Strubel, "Exemple, fable, parabole: Le récit bref figuré au moyen âge," in *MA* 94 (1988) 341–61 [GH13]; J. Berlioz, "*Exempla*: A Discussion and a Case Study, I: *Exempla* as a Source for the History of Women," tr. S. Michelman, in *Medieval Women and the Sources of Medieval History*, ed. J.T. Rosenthal (1990) 37–50 [GH14]; B. Weiske, *Gesta Romanorum*, VI: *Untersuchungen zu Konzeption und Überlieferung* (1992) [GH15]; L. Scanlon, *Narrative, Authority, and Power: The Medieval Exemplum and the Chaucerian Tradition* (1994) [GH16].

For current bibliography see the subsection on exempla under the heading "Generi letterari" in *MEL* [GH17].

## Texts

### (a) Modern Editions

Many of the important medieval exempla collections are still unpublished. Extracts from the work of Stephen of Bourbon are published by A. Lecoy de La Marche, *Anecdotes historiques, légendes et apologues, tirés du recueil inédit d'Étienne de Bourbon . . .* (1877); a modern edition, of which three parts have been prepared as doctoral theses at the École nationale des chartes (Paris) by J. Berlioz (1977), D. Ogilvie-David (1978), and J.-L. Eichenlaub (1984), is not yet in print [GH18].

For the unpublished, but widely copied *Alphabetum narrationum* of Arnold of Liège, see P. Toldo, "Dall'Alphabetum narrationum," in *Archiv für das Studium der neueren Sprachen* 117 (1906) 68–85, 287–303; 118 (1907) 69–81, 329–51; 119 (1908) 86–100, 351–71 [GH19].

Modern editions include the following:

Caesarius of Heisterbach, *Dialogus miraculorum,* ed. J. Strange, 2 vols. and index

(1851–57, r1966) [GH20]; *Die Wundergeschichten des Caesarius von Heisterbach*, ed. A. Hilka, vols. 1, 3 (1933, 1937) [GH21].

*Gesta Romanorum*, ed. H. Oesterley (1872, r1980): based on a printed edition of c. 1472 (nos. 1–150) with an app. of additional exempla from manuscripts of the *Gesta* and other works [GH22]; *Die Gesta Romanorum nach der Innsbrucker Handschrift vom Jahre 1342 und vier Münchener Handschriften*, ed. W. Dick (1890, r1970): follows the best manuscript but omits the moralizations [GH23].

Henmannus Bononiensis, *Viaticum narrationum*, ed. A. Hilka, Abhandlungen der Gesellschaft der Wiss. zu Göttingen, phil.-hist. Klasse, 3. Folge, no. 16 (1935) [GH24].

*Historia septem sapientum I*, ed. A. Hilka (1912) [GH25]; *Historia septem sapientum. II. Johannis de Alta Silva Dolopathos, sive De rege et septem sapientibus*, ed. A. Hilka (1913) [GH26].

*Hugo von Trimbergs lateinische Werke*, ed. E. Seemann, VI: *Das Solsequium* (1914) [GH27].

Gerard of Frachet, *Vitae fratrum ordinis praedicatorum*, ed. B.M. Reichert (1896) [GH28].

Jacobus de Cessolis, *Libellus de moribus hominum et officiis nobilium ac popularium super ludo scachorum*, ed. M.A. Burt (Ph.D. diss., University of Texas, 1957) [GH29].

*The Exempla or Illustrative Stories from the Sermones* vulgares *of Jacques de Vitry*, ed. T.F. Crane (1890, r1971) [GH30].

*Beispiele der alten Weisen des Johann von Capua: Übersetzung der hebräischen Bearbeitung des indischen Pañcatantra ins Lateinische*, ed. F. Geissler (1960): John of Capua's *Directorium vitae humanae*, with German translation [GH31].

Jordan of Saxony, *Liber Vitasfratrum*, ed. R. Arbesmann and W. Hümpfner (1943) [GH32].

*Liber exemplorum ad usum praedicantium saeculo XIII compositus a quodam fratre minore Anglico de provincia Hiberniae*, ed. A.G. Little (1908, r1966) [GH33].

*Die Disciplina clericalis des Petrus Alfonsi (das älteste Novellenbuch des Mittelalters) nach allen bekannten Handschriften*, ed. A. Hilka and W. Söderhjelm (1911) [GH34].

*Le Speculum laicorum: Édition d'une collection d'exempla, composée en Angleterre à la fin du XIIIe siècle*, ed. J.-T. Welter (1914) [GH35].

## (b) Early Printings

Early printed editions remain fundamental to the study of exempla and include the following:

Pseudo-Albertus Magnus [= Humbert of Romans], *Liber de abundantia exemplorum* (Ulm 1478/81) [GH36].

[Jacobus van Gruitrode], *Lauacrum conscientie omnium sacerdotum* (Augsburg 1489) [GH37].

Johannes Bromyard, *Summa predicantium* (Basel, not after 1484; Paris 1518) [GH38].

[Johannes Gallensis], *Summa collationum* [*sive Communiloquium*] (Cologne 1472) [GH39].

Johannes [Gobius] junior, *Scala celi* (Lübeck 1476) [GH40].

[Johannes Herolt], *Promptuarium discipuli* (Cologne, c. 1474) [GH41].

Johannes Nider, *Liber formicarii* (Cologne, before 1473) [GH42].

Martinus [Polonus], *Promptuarium exemplorum,* in *id., Sermones de tempore et de sanctis* (Strasbourg 1484), fols. 234r–254v [GH43].

Robert Holcot, *Moralitates,* in *id., In Librum Sapientiae Regis Salomonis Praelectiones ccxiii* (Basel 1586) 708–50 [GH44].

*Speculum exemplorum ex diuersis libris in vnum laboriose collectum* ([Deventer] 1481); repr., with app., as *Magnum speculum exemplorum* (Douai 1603) [GH45].

[Thomas of Cantimpré], *Bonum vniuersale de proprietatibus apum* (Cologne, c. 1473) [GH46].

### (c) Important Sources of the Medieval Exempla Collections

*Valerii Maximi Factorum et dictorum memorabilium libri novem,* ed. K. Kempf (1888, r1982) [GH47].

*Vitaspatrum,* ed. H. Rosweyde (Antwerp 1615; repr. *PL* 73–74) [GH48].

J.G. Freire, *A versão latina por Pascásio de Dume* [Paschasius of Dumium] *dos Apophthegmata Patrum,* 2 vols. (1971) [GH49].

Jacobus de Voragine, *Legenda aurea,* ed. J.G.T. Grässe, 3rd ed. (1890, r1969) [GH50].

# GI • LYRIC

BY CHRISTOPHER J. MCDONOUGH

In English the meaning of the term *lyric* is not precise, and it is currently used to describe any short poem. For the Greeks lyric was the form of poetry sung to the accompaniment of the lyre and composed for a specific social occasion. In subsequent Hellenistic and Roman literature, lyric was freed from the constraints of place, occasion, and performance and was built around a set of literary conventions comparable to those in other genres. Thus although originally written for musical accompaniment, the lyric came to be written as if to be sung, and the lyric mode or attitude in English retains links with the language of song. Latin secular lyric developed a musical aspect that was closely related to the growth of music in the liturgy, but it cannot be identified exclusively with poetry that was meant to be sung.

Among the characteristics of modern lyric verse is an attempt to create through a voice expressing itself emotionally in the first person the imitation of personal experience. Medieval Latin lyric, however, relied heavily on the rhetorical tradition that derived from antiquity, and from it the poet fashioned its many commonplaces into new syntheses to express feelings and ideas. The voice of the medieval lyric is preponderantly male, but examples of Latin love lyrics related in the female voice have survived, although they were probably written by men.

Although the lyric covered a wide range of topics, in Medieval Latin lyric the erotic experience in all its aspects is the theme most frequently addressed. But its range extended to include the matter of Troy, poems on the nature and power of music, songs of farewell, pastoral description, praise of kings and God, laments for the dead, meditations on friendship, humorous and political satire, episodes from classical mythology, descriptions of human beauty, and themes of poverty, begging, drinking, eating, and gambling. Lyrics were rarely written as a reaction to specific historical events, but the category of lyric was comprehensive enough to include such compositions, as shown by a political poem of Peter of Blois (d. 1211) protesting against the imprisonment of Richard Lionheart by Leopold of Austria.

It is difficult to associate the various types of Latin lyric with any particular form. For grammarians of late antiquity and medieval scholars interested in the classification of literary genres, like Honorius Augustodunensis (d. c. 1156) and, later, Alexander Neckam (d. 1217) and John of Garland (fl. c. 1240), Horace remained the exemplar for lyric poetry, but in practice his influence on the Latin lyric of the Middle Ages was not great. For the language and culture that nourished the poet from the eighth century on was Christian, and it reverberated with a distinctive imagery, typology, and terminology. Latin, acquired as a second language through the schools according to written classical models, incorporated the idiom of Christian cultural life and enriched the possibilities of expressing new insights in new ways. In the cloister schools the Roman literary achievement was transmitted by close exegesis of whole texts and excerpts from them, but, equally important, the cleric or monk who wrote in Latin was also thoroughly familiar with the Latin of the Bible, the liturgy, the breviary, and the Church fathers. From this rich amalgam of classical and Christian Latin, of the quotidian and the poetic, the medieval lyric poet created new meanings and forms.

The enrichment of the Latin language was not accompanied, however, by a detailed knowledge of the classical lyric meters. Despite the renewed interest in Horace in the late ninth century by Heiric of Auxerre and the commentaries that explicated Horatian meters, the *De consolatione philosophiae* of Boethius and Martianus Capella's *De nuptiis Philologiae et Mercurii*, written alternately in prose and verse, were more influential in the dissemination of the lyric meters among medieval scholar-poets. But stronger forces were at work that prevented the renaissance of the classical lyric forms. Rhyme had emerged in late antique Christian poetry and exercised its fascination upon the composition of both accentual and quantitative verse, and by the tenth and eleventh centuries simple rhyme schemes built around a strong syllabic base had brought to the Latin lyric a new formal art, which may be exemplified in the rhythmical poetry of Gottschalk of Orbais (d. 869). During the same period the lyrical themes of lamentation and love continued to be composed in quantitative dactylic verse, in elegiac distichs in particular. Together with the hexameter, they both incorporated over time various combinations of rhyme to ornament the verse.

To these two formal principles for writing Latin lyric was added that of the sequence. Motivated originally by a desire to enrich liturgical singing, the sequence first appeared in the late ninth century as a musical expansion of the liturgy and was to provide an important impetus to the musical development of the secular Latin lyric. In the divine service the *Alleluia* was intoned by the choir leader and the choir repeated it with a long vocalization of the concluding -*a*. Then the precentor performed the *versus,* usually taken from a psalm, until finally the choir repeated the *Alleluia* with the *iubilus* (the melisma to which the last syllable of the word *Alleluia* was set) in an expanded form. This richly ornamented sequence of sounds was called a *sequentia,* an extension of the *Alleluia.*

Before the middle of the ninth century words began to be furnished for the sequence, which was termed *sequentia cum prosa* or *prosa ad sequentiam,* usually abbreviated to *prosa,* or *versus ad sequentiam.* From the late eleventh century this musical extension of the *Alleluia* was adapted to love lyrics and other secular songs. In this new verse technique, which was gradually transferred from the realm of music to poetry, strophe and antistrophe were so constructed that they corresponded to each other in the number of syllables and, therefore, in melody. In the well-known *Swan sequence,* which portrays a swan struggling in flight over the sea, this responsorial aspect is mediated by the -*a* rhyme that runs throughout the poem. The formal possibilities of this type of poetry were later skillfully exploited in the *Liber hymnorum* of Notker Balbulus of St. Gall (d. 912). Particularly influential was his Whitsuntide sequence with its linguistic and conceptual correspondences, its parallelism between man the microcosm and the macrocosm, and the pairing of the Old and New Testaments. Secular poets were quick to develop the sequence form to express profane concerns.

The recorded evidence for the knowledge of the Latin lyrical tradition is fragmentary, but written records attest the existence of love lyrics in the early tenth century. Peter Dronke has observed that the historical importance of the *Cambridge Songs*, the oldest collection of Latin songs, lies in the breadth and diversity of its lyrical repertoire. Among these 49 poems assembled in the middle of the eleventh century are to be found the story of the "snow-child," lyrical praise of the nightingale's voice, and six love poems. A request to the beloved for love (a type of poem classified as an *invitatio*), heavily influenced by the language and imagery of the *Song of Songs*, forms the subject of *Iam, dulcis amica, uenito* (no. 27 in this collection). In another (no. 40: *Leuis exsurgit zephirus*) a young woman gives voice to a lament, while in a third (no. 48: *O admirabile Veneris idolum*) the narrator hymns the praises of a person, who may be male or female. One of the obstacles that endangered the survival of the love lyric is apparent in the same miscellany. Three pieces survive only in fragments, the consequence, presumably, of their subject matter: a dialogue on love (no. 28), the lament or *planctus* of a woman (no. 49), and another (no. 39), whose contents have been so successfully effaced that no reconstruction of the theme is possible. Many subjects, such as that of sexual love, may have been offensive in a clerical milieu.

Other novel forms of the Latin love lyric from the same period include the *alba*, a dawn song of lament at the departure of a lover, and the *pastorela* or *pastourelle*, which usually depicted a dialogue between a young woman and a suitor of superior social rank and offered great scope for erotic fantasy and satirical treatment. Although the Latin lyric was probably being written at the same time as the vernacular, the latter was not considered worthy of being recorded by educated clerics until the emergence of a chivalric and courtly lay culture at the start of the eleventh century produced an audience for them.

Although the *Cambridge Songs* provide important evidence that new poetic forms were being developed alongside continued attention to lyrics and lyric moments in Classical Latin poetry, poets since the time of Venantius Fortunatus (d. c. 600) had continued to write on lyrical subjects in the form and idiom of the classical rhetorical tradition, with its conventional language, themes, and tropes. Poetry of friendship, much favored by Venantius and the Carolingian poets, often took the form of poetic letters to women of high rank. In them it is difficult to detect personal emotions, whether in the lyrical oeuvre of Walafrid Strabo (d. 849) or in the later work of Marbod of Rennes (d. 1123), Baudri of Bourgueil (d. 1130), or Hildebert of Lavardin (d. 1133). The importance of the three French poets lies in their humanism and the notable place given to women in their lyrical writings.

Yet signs of power and originality can be found in the Latin lyric of the eleventh century. A dramatic *planctus* for the Trojan warrior Hector, written in rhyming couplets and followed with a sung refrain, shows imagination and intensity of feeling. In choosing to concentrate emotion on Hector's meeting with his wife and his confrontation with Achilles, the poet isolated from his prosaic historical source two moments of great power, and in the treatment of the mythography he exercised a freedom of invention that recurs in the Trojan lyrical poetry of the next century, in, for example, the lament of Dido (*Carmina Burana* 100).

The Latin lyric of the twelfth and thirteenth centuries was closely connected with the emergence of new social and intellectual movements. Two themes are dominant: the depiction of the life of the wandering cleric and the criticism of the officials and institutions of the Church, specifically monks, prelates, the Roman curia, and the pope.

Many of the poems in the well-known *Carmina Burana* deal with love, gambling, drinking, and begging. That these Latin poems were composed and performed by itinerant scholars is not in doubt. No longer was education restricted to the cloister and cathedral schools. The twelfth century saw the appearance of the renowned intellectual, who, although he may have been initially attached to an institution, later came to command the loyalty of pupils who had often traveled great distances to study with the master. However, since no single center of learning could excel in all disciplines, scholars were forced to travel from city to city in search of a comprehensive education.

The social reality of the twelfth century was such that poets who were unbeneficed or lacked the support of a monastery needed the patronage of a highly placed ecclesiastical or secular lord. The outlines of this precarious existence are sketched in the poems of Hugh Primas (d. c. 1160), which dwell on the material insecurity of the educated cleric. For such people the wheel of Fortune could turn quickly. A poet dependent on the favor of a prelate might soon find himself outside the protection of a social institution. In his best known narrative lyric Primas constructs a pitiable picture of his disastrous condition as a homeless person on the open road. Other verses pillory a bishop for an ungenerous gift and deplore an attempt by an episcopal candidate in Beauvais to buy ecclesiastical office. With verse of this type the threshold of political invective was reached, a genre that was to open new vistas for the Latin lyric of the twelfth and thirteenth centuries, with its criticism of the venality and corruption of the Church.

Of the Archpoet little is known except that his origins lay north of the Alps. Between 1162 and 1164 he was attached to the retinue of Rainald of Dassel (d. 1167), the chancellor of Frederick I Barbarossa (d. 1190), and his surviving nine poems give glimpses of his poetic service to his patron while traveling in Italy, in Vienne in Burgundy, and in Cologne. Forced to live by his wits, he, like Hugh Primas, presents himself in his poems as a beggar, whether requesting money from Rainald or asking pardon for his many grievous sins. His second poem, the so-called *Jonah Confession,* has been highly praised for its brilliant rhyme and the cleverness with which the story of Jonah is shaped to fit the Archpoet's own needs.

The concept of lyric now embraced the literary forms of invectives, debate poems, lamentations over the state of the world, poetic letters, and rhymed prayers. A broadly educated class of clerics found much to criticize in their society. The unrestricted power of the pope as legislator and judge over the entire Church that developed in the twelfth century resulted in an endless procession of delegations to Rome to seek rulings on legal questions and appeals against judgments that had already been handed down. The referral of juridical matters to the curia often took months and entailed great expense. Not surprisingly, the favor of curial officials and judges was courted through gifts, and the decisions of this body were often greeted with bitter cynicism and astringent criticism.

A great number of these productions remain anonymous, but many lyrics are attributed in their manuscripts to authors who are known to have belonged to the upper clergy, or who had lived at the courts of the powerful, or who were influential teachers. Walter of Châtillon (d. 1202/3) moved from place to place, first studying in Paris and Reims before teaching at Laon. After service in the court of Henry II of England, he returned to teach at Châtillon, where he achieved great renown as a poet. A student of jurisprudence, a diplomat, and a poet, this talented cleric used the occasion of the election of two popes in 1159 to meditate on the simony and divisions in the Church, using images and allusions drawn from the Bible and the classical world, and placing himself in the tradition of the great Roman satirists.

Peter of Blois (d. 1211), archdeacon of Bath, had been a student in Paris and Bologna. The author of a number of satires, he may also have written some of the most distinctive love lyrics of the twelfth century, known from the manuscript that has preserved them as the Arundel lyrics. Many are introduced by the topos of the spring landscape, which marks an idealized time and setting for the burgeoning of thoughts on love that follows. The poems not only fuse the author's literary and philosophical learning and his knowledge of Virgil, Ovid, Martianus Capella, and Bernard Silvestris's *Cosmographia* into forms of dazzling technical virtuosity, but also reflect on subject matter of contemporary philosophical interest, such as the relationship of human love to the love that was thought to bind the cosmos. Some are cast in the form of lyrical debates that depict internal emotional conflict.

The outstanding lyricist of the thirteenth century was Philip the Chancellor, born in Paris sometime after 1160. After studying theology he was appointed archdeacon of Noyon, and after 1218 he became chancellor in the Church of Paris. To him the chronicler Salimbene attributed nine songs, eight of which were set to music by Philip's music teacher, Henry of Pisa. The formal range of this poet's lyrical compositions was unusually large; it included motets, *conductus,* classical sequences, *lais lyriques,* and *descorts.* Four of his poems are attacks against Rome and the corruption of the clergy.

After Philip the lyric continued to show technical ability, but no poet succeeded in creating the novel reformulations of the familiar *topoi* that would have allowed the secular Latin love lyric to live on. In Spain and Italy there is little evidence of Latin lyric. Among the factors that may have contributed to its decline are those isolated by Dronke. The cultivation of music in northern France in the thirteenth century saw great progress in polyphony, which may have resulted in poets being assigned a role subordinate to that of musicians. Further, by 1230 the vernacular lyric in Provence and northern France had a tradition confident enough to compete successfully with the learned Latin one. Finally, lyrical creativity by the end of the century had passed over to the mendicant orders, including the followers of St. Francis, such as John Pecham (d. 1292), who wrote so ardently about divine, not human, love.

## Select Bibliography

### Primary Works and Translations

#### (a) Collections

G. Bernt, *Carmina Burana* (1992) [GI1].
G.M. Dreves, *Analecta hymnica medii aevi,* v21 (1895, r1961) [GI2].

P. Godman, *Poetry of the Carolingian Renaissance* (1985): with English translations [**GI3**].

A. Hilka, O. Schumann, and B. Bischoff, *Carmina Burana* (1930-): Band I: *Texte*. Band I.1: Die moralisch-satirischen Dichtungen; Band I.2: Die Liebeslieder; Band I.3: Die Trink- und Spielerlieder; Band II: *Kommentar*. Band II.1: Einleitung (Die Handschriften der Carmina Burana). Die moralisch-satirischen Dichtungen [**GI4**].

K. Langosch, *Lyrische Anthologie des lateinischen Mittelalters* (1968) [**GI5**].

F.J.E. Raby, *The Oxford Book of Medieval Latin Verse* (1959) [**GI6**].

B. Stock, *Medieval Latin Lyrics* (1971) [**GI7**].

K. Strecker, *Carmina Cantabrigiensia, MGH.SRG* 40 (1926, r1955) [**GI8**].

H. Waddell, *Mediaeval Latin Lyrics*, 4th ed. (1933) [**GI9**].

H. Waddell, *More Latin Lyrics, from Virgil to Milton* (1976) [**GI10**].

P.G. Walsh, *Love Lyrics from the Carmina Burana* (1993): with translation and commentary [**GI11**].

H. Watenphul and H. Krefeld, *Die Gedichte des Archipoeta* (1958) [**GI12**].

J.J. Wilhelm, *Lyrics of the Middle Ages: An Anthology* (1990) [**GI13**].

J.M. Ziolkowski, *Carmina Cantabrigiensia* (1994): with translation [**GI14**].

### (b) Individual Authors and Texts

K. Hilbert, *Baldricus Burgulianus: Carmina* (1979) [**GI15**].

C.J. McDonough, *OPHP* [**GI16**].

W. Meyer, *Die Oxforder Gedichte des Primas (des Magisters Hugo von Orleans)*, *NKGWG* (1907, r1970) v1:75–111; v2:113–75, 231–34 [**GI17**].

W. Meyer, *Die Arundel-Sammlung mittellateinischer Lieder*, Abhandlungen der königlichen Gesellschaft der Wiss. zu Göttingen, phil.-hist. Klasse, n.s., 11.2 (1908, r1970) [**GI18**].

K. Strecker, *Die Gedichte Walters von Chatillon*, v1: *Die Lieder der Handschrift 351 von St. Omer* (1925) [**GI19**].

K. Strecker, *Moralisch-satirische Gedichte Walters von Châtillon* (1929) [**GI20**].

### Studies

P.S. Allen, *The Romanesque Lyric: Studies in Its Background and Development from Petronius to the Cambridge Songs, 50–1050* (1928, r1969): contains in ch. 12 an appreciative sketch of the Carolingian lyric [**GI21**] .

P.S. Allen, *Medieval Latin Lyrics* (1931): discusses the origins of German and Latin lyric and proposes a theory of continuity for the genre [**GI22**].

H. Bergner, ed., *Lyrik des Mittelalters*, 2 vols. (1983): includes a section (v1:19–196) by P. Klopsch, "Die mittellateinische Lyrik," which provides an historical overview of the development of the Latin lyric, punctuated with detailed exegeses of poems from Walafrid Strabo to the Archpoet [**GI23**].

A. Betten, "Lateinische Bettellyrik: Literarische Topik oder Ausdruck existentieller Not?" in *MLJ* 11 (1976) 143–50 [**GI24**].

P. Bourgain, "Les chansonniers lyriques latins," in *Lyrique romane médiévale: La tradition des chansonniers* (1989) 61–84 [**GI25**].

P. Bourgain, *Poésie lyrique latine du moyen âge* (1989): contains a survey of the technical, cultural, and historical characteristics of rhythmic Latin poetry from Augustine to the *Carmina Burana* [**GI26**].

H. Brinkmann, *Geschichte der lateinischen Liebesdichtung im Mittelalter* (1925) [G127].

H. Brinkmann, "Anfänge lateinischer Liebesdichtung im Mittelalter," in *Neophilologus* 9 (1924) 49–60 [G128].

F. Brittain, *The Medieval Latin and Romance Lyric to A.D. 1300*, 2nd ed. (1951, r1969): a survey of the main features of lyric and a discussion of the origin and development of lyrics in several languages, with selected lyrics presented in chronological order [G129].

P. Dronke, *Medieval Latin and the Rise of European Love-Lyric,* 2 vols., 2nd ed. (1968): traces the development of the courtly love lyric and the influence of Latin learning on it, before comparing the Latin traditions of love poetry to courtly themes in medieval vernaculars. The second volume contains 150 Latin texts with translations and brief notes [G130].

P. Dronke, *PIMA:* ch. 4 (pp114–49) is devoted to Abelard's *planctus* [G131].

P. Dronke, "Poetic Meaning in the *Carmina Burana,*" in *MLJ* 10 (1974–75) 116–37 [G132].

P. Dronke, "Peter of Blois and Poetry at the Court of Henry II," in *MS* 38 (1976) 185–235 [G133].

P. Dronke, *The Medieval Lyric,* 3rd ed. (1996): a literary introduction to aspects of medieval lyric, with emphasis on interpretation and critical reading of particular texts, that includes a selective and personal approach to poems written from 850 to 1300 [G134].

P. Dronke, "Dido's Lament: From Medieval Latin Lyric to Chaucer," in *Kontinuität und Wandel: Lateinische Poesie von Naevius bis Baudelaire. Franco Munari zum 65. Geburtstag,* ed. U.J. Stache, W. Maaz, and F. Wagner (1986) 364–90 [G135].

P. Dronke, "La lirica d'amore in latino nel secolo XIII," in *Aspetti della letteratura latina nel secolo XIII: Atti del primo convegno internazionale di studi dell'Associazione per il Medioevo et l'Umanesimo Latini (AMUL), Perugia, 3–5 ottobre 1983,* ed. C. Leonardi and G. Orlandi (1986) 29–56 [G136].

P. Dronke, "Hector in Eleventh-Century Latin Lyrics," in *Scire litteras: Forschungen zum mittelalterlichen Geistesleben,* ed. S. Krämer and M. Bernhard (1988) 137–48 [G137].

P. Dronke, "The Lyrical Compositions of Philip the Chancellor," in *SM,* 3rd ser., 28 (1987) 563–92 [G138].

T. Frings, "Ein mittellateinisches Frauenlied zwischen volkstümlicher Lyrik und Ovid," in *Beiträge zur romanischen Philologie* 7 (1968) 311–18 [G139].

P. Godman and O. Murray, eds., *Latin Poetry and the Classical Tradition: Essays in Medieval and Renaissance Literature* (1990) [G140].

R. Herde, "Das Hohelied in der lateinischen Literatur des Mittelalters bis zum 12. Jahrhundert," in *SM,* 3rd ser., 8 (1967) 957–1073 [G141].

W.T.H. Jackson, "Interpretation of *Carmina Burana* 62, 'Dum Diane vitrea,'" in *id.,* ed., *The Interpretation of Medieval Lyric Poetry* (1980) 44–60 [G142].

W.R. Johnson, *The Idea of Lyric: Lyric Modes in Ancient and Modern Poetry* (1982) [G143].

P. Klopsch, *EMV* [G144].

P. Klopsch, *Einführung in die Dichtungslehren des lateinischen Mittelalters* (1980) [G145].

T. Latzke, "Die *Carmina erotica* der Ripollsammlung," in *MLJ* 10 (1974–75) 138–201 [G146].

P. Lehmann, *PM* [G147].

W. Offermans, *Die Wirkung Ovids auf die literarische Sprache der lateinischen Liebesdichtung des 11. und 12. Jahrhunderts,* Beiheft zum Mittellateinischen Jahrbuch 3 (1970) [**GI48**].

F.J.E. Raby, *SLP* v1: ch. 5.3, "The Ninth Century" (pp221–47); ch. 6.5, "The 'Cambridge Songs'" (pp291–306); v2: ch. 13, "The Latin Lyrics (I)" (pp171–235); ch. 14, "The Latin Lyrics (II)" (pp236–348) [**GI49**].

A.G. Rigg, "Golias and Other Pseudonyms," in *SM,* 3rd ser., 18 (1977) 65–109 [**GI50**].

D.W. Robertson, Jr., "Two Poems from the *Carmina Burana,*" in *id., Essays in Medieval Culture* (1980) 131–50: comments on *Dum Diane vitrea* and *Si linguis angelicis* [**GI51**].

O. Sayce, *Plurilingualism in the Carmina Burana: A Study of the Linguistic and Literary Influences on the Codex* (1992) [**GI52**].

D. Schaller, "Bemerkungen zum Schlussband der kritischen Edition der 'Carmina Burana,'" in *MLJ* 10 (1974–75) 106–15 [**GI53**].

O. Schumann, "Eine mittelalterliche Klage der Dido," in *Liber Floridus: Mittellateinische Studien Paul Lehmann . . . gewidmet,* ed. B. Bischoff and S. Brechter (1950) 319–28 [**GI54**].

H. Schüppert, *Kirchenkritik in der lateinischen Lyrik des 12. und 13. Jahrhunderts* (1972) [**GI55**].

A.H. Schotter, "Woman's Song in Medieval Latin," in *Vox Feminae: Studies in Medieval Woman's Song,* ed. J.F. Plummer (1981) 19–33: discusses Latin love lyrics presented by a female voice [**GI56**].

W. von den Steinen, *Menschen im Mittelalter: Gesammelte Forschungen, Betrachtungen, Bilder,* ed. P. von Moos (1967): with articles on *Exiit diluculo* (pp246–48) and *Invitatio amicae* (pp150–56) and on Abelard as a lyric poet (pp215–30) [**GI57**].

J. Szövérffy, *Weltliche Dichtungen des lateinischen Mittelalters: Ein Handbuch,* v1: *Von den Anfängen bis zum Ende der Karolingerzeit* (1970) [**GI58**].

J. Szövérffy, *Secular Latin Lyrics and Minor Poetic Forms of the Middle Ages: A Historical Survey and Literary Repertory from the Tenth to the Late Fifteenth Century* (1992–): an ongoing series [**GI59**].

P. Tordeur, "Réflexions sur la rime," in *Latomus* 51 (1992) 315–28 [**GI60**].

D.A. Traill, "Notes on '*Dum Diane vitrea*' (CB 62) and '*A globo veteri*' (CB 67)," in *MLJ* 23 (1988) 143–51 [**GI61**].

B.K. Vollmann, "Liebe als Krankheit in der weltlichen Lyrik des lateinischen Mittelalters," in *Liebe als Krankheit. 3. Kolloquium der Forschungsstelle für europäische Lyrik des Mittelalters,* ed. T. Stemmler (1990) 105–25 [**GI62**].

H. Waddell, *The Wandering Scholars,* 7th ed. (1934, r1989) [**GI63**].

P. Wareman, "Les débuts du lyrisme profane au moyen âge latin," in *Neophilologus* 42 (1958) 89–107 [**GI64**].

W. Wetherbee, *Platonism and Poetry in the Twelfth Century* (1972) 126–51: documents the influence of philosophy on twelfth-century Latin lyric poetry [**GI65**].

W. Wetherbee, "Dum Diane vitrea," in *Medievalia et Humanistica,* n.s., 7 (1976) 54–55 [**GI66**].

F.J. Worstbrock, "Zu Gedichten Walthers von Châtillon und seiner 'Schule,'" in *ZDADL* 101 (1972) 200–8 [**GI67**].

*See also* [GJ13].

# GJ   •   HYMNS

### BY DANIEL SHEERIN

## Introduction

Definitions of the term *hymn* vary considerably in extension. Patristic and medieval usage of *hymnus* is so flexible as to be applied to almost any chanted liturgical text (see [GJ31] p178, [GJ53] pp993–94). Modern definitions vary from the musicologists' restriction of "hymn" to specific types of chant in the Liturgy of the Hours, e.g., "a strophic poem in praise of God set to fairly simple music in the Divine Office" ([GJ54] p838), to the concept of hymnody current in liturgical studies that embraces all liturgical poetry, to an understanding of "hymn" that seems to include virtually any religious poem shorter than an epic (see, e.g., [GJ2] p30).

This broad view governed the choice of materials for inclusion in the largest collection of medieval Latin hymnodic texts, the *Analecta hymnica medii aevi* ([GJ15]; there are a breakdown of contents of the *AH* in [GJ19] pp2917–18, a generic index in [GJ10] v2:9–56, and a bibliography by genre in [GJ2] pp12–18). The following outline of medieval hymnodic types is based on a schema provided by G.M. Dreves ([GJ16] v1:VIII–IX).

I. *Liturgical poetry*
- A. Poetry of the Liturgy of the Hours (breviary)
  1. Hymns
  2. Versified antiphons and responsories, rhymed offices
  3. Tropes
  4. Biblical canticles, prose hymns, creeds
- B. Poetry of the eucharistic liturgy (and of other rituals)
  1. Chants in poetic prose, biblical and nonbiblical
  2. Versified antiphons
  3. Tropes
  4. Sequences
  5. Hymns of occasional liturgies, especially processional hymns

II. *Nonliturgical poetry*
- A. Hymnlike spiritual poems, songs (*conductus, motet, cantio, planctus,* etc.); longer meditations and prayers in verse for devotional use
- B. Versified prayers for devotional observance of the canonical hours

C. Glossing-poems (versified gloss-cum-paraphrase of well-known hymns, antiphons, prayers)

D. Rhymed psalters (versified prayers in 150 stanzas in imitation of the Psalter)

E. *Rosaria* of 50–51 stanzas, *abecedaria* of 23 stanzas, and other, especially Marian, confections: *gaudia, salutationes,* etc.

This perhaps overextended concept of hymnody, with its jumble of genres, entails a literary corpus as vast as the *AH* it produced. Because of restrictions of space and the need for a generic focus, hymns will be understood here generally as chanted liturgical poetry in extended, stanzaic compositions.

## The Legacy of Christian Antiquity

Much that is often supposed to be "medieval" in Latin hymnody is, in fact, part of the hymnodic legacy from Christian antiquity, and a fresh and comprehensive study of early Latin hymnody is a desideratum. The remains of hymnody from the fourth and fifth centuries suggest experimentation across a spectrum of poetic forms for a variety of occasions and venues and for audiences that varied considerably in level of sophistication.

The North African rhythmical *abcedaria* (the fragmentary *Psalmus responsorius,* Augustine's *Psalmus contra partem Donati,* composed in 393 or 394, and a later imitation of it, the *abecedarium* of Fulgentius [d. 533] against the Vandal Arians) are examples of popular works derived from the biblical-liturgical tradition, works unconsciously or purposely indifferent to the learned literary tradition. But the emergent Christian hymnody also interacted with the learned Latin poetic tradition, imitating and adapting elements of it, intermixing them with the biblical-liturgical tradition, and emulating pagan religious verse as well as elements of the broader pagan poetic tradition, to produce more sophisticated compositions for both public chanting and/or private reading. Paulinus of Nola (d. 431) assimilated hymnodic texts from the Scriptures to the learned tradition in his hexameter psalm paraphrases (*CSEL* v31:18–23). Traditional quantitative verse patterns were adapted for liturgical hymnody by Hilary of Poitiers (d. c. 367) and Ambrose (d. 397), but their hymns show an effort to maintain isosyllabic lines, presumably as an aid in the choral chanting of the texts to fixed melodies. The poems of Prudentius (d. 405) in his *Liber cathemerinon* (for the hours and feasts of the Christian year) and *Peristephanon* (on the martyrs) are polymetric and usually of considerable length; they seem to have been intended for devotional reading by a literary elite, as do the three *hymni* of Marius Victorinus (d. after 363), which are rhythmical adaptations of the philosophical hymn (e.g. Cleanthes's *Hymn to Zeus;* cf. hymns of Gregory the Theologian, Synesios of Cyrene) to Christian doctrinal polemic and devotion.

Towards the end of antiquity, some hymnographers, e.g. Ennodius (d. 521), Sedulius (early fifth century), and Fortunatus (d. c. 610), continued earlier patterns of composition of hymns in quantitative verse. Innovation took the form of the cultivation of rhyme (at first of monosyllabic end-rhyme or assonance; see [GJ49] p38f.) and of rhythmical verse. Models available from earlier experiments in this style found some favor (Marius Victorinus, the *psalmi*), but for most works these seem to have been passed over in favor of rhythmical imitations of quantitative verse structures. In these, syllable quantity is ignored, and the organizational principle is the distribution of stress accents, not as a substitute for the verse *ictus* of the quantitative models, but in imitation of the pattern of word accents produced when the quantitative verse was read as prose, as Dag Norberg has shown (e.g. [GJ51] pp25–41).

Christian antiquity provided the medieval liturgy with a large and influential part of its hymnodic repertory. Ancient hymns were incorporated whole or reworked (e.g. Prudentius's long poems, which were variously divided, abridged, or centonized; see [GJ15], v27:37–39, v50:23–46; [GJ17] pp115–48; [GJ14] pp54–67) to adapt them to specific liturgical requirements, and provided authoritative precedents and models for subsequent hymnodic composition, particularly in these respects:

**1. Uses of Hymns.** Hymns were composed for use in association with the daily hours of prayer as lyrics of communal meditation and prayer and for the feasts and rituals of the developing temporal and sanctoral cycles of the liturgical year as highly compressed poetic panegyrics with narrative, encomiastic, and hortatory elements.

**2. Hymnodic Genres.** Texts were produced both for public, liturgical use, e.g. shorter pieces like Ambrose's (hence the generic term *ambrosiani*), and for private, devotional practices mimetic of the liturgy, e.g. longer lyrics like those of Prudentius. Extended discursive compositions, some with refrains, like the rythmical *psalmi*, were composed to supplement the biblical Psalms and canticles and as an interactive alternative to homilies.

**3. Verse Forms.** Early hymns employ quantitative meters with a preference for isosyllabic lines (especially iambic dimeter and trochaic septenarius), rhythmic imitations of quantitive verse, rhythmic innovations (e.g. Augustine's *Psalmus*), and rhythmic prose. Their stanzaic structures include the ambrosian stanza of four lines of iambic dimeter, the three-line stanza of trochaic septenarius, the elegiac distich, and even the more complex lyric stanzas. The rhythmical *psalmi* appropriated from their psalmodic models the use of acrostic, stanza, and refrain.

**4. Hymnodic Diction.** This involved (a) the canonization of a poetic euchology, i.e. the definitive development of the language and formulae of praise and petition in hymnodic meters and stanzas; (b) the development of language and techniques for highly compressed narrative and dialogue suitable to a lyric medium in hymnody that reproduced biblical and martyrological narratives; (c) the development of a lyric medium for dogmatic exposition; (d) the development of patterns of concise allusion to Scripture and other ecclesiastical texts; (e) experimentation with verse paraphrase of biblical and other texts (paraphrases of the psalms and canticles and creeds continued to be composed, e.g. by Bede [d. 735] and Florus of Lyons [d. c. 860], but were not adopted for liturgical use, with some exceptions, e.g. the setting by Walafrid Strabo [d. 849] of the canticle *Benedicite* (see [GJ15] v50:169–70); (f) early establishment of hymnody as a high literary medium for an affective and, ultimately, actual alignment of hymnody with the learned poetic tradition, more popular compositions notwithstanding.

For all this, it must be noted that application of the categories "literary" and "popular," "devotional" and "pastoral" to Latin hymnody should be essayed only after more extended consideration and definition than are possible here.

## Genres of Chanted Liturgical Poetry

**1. Hymns of the Liturgy of the Hours (Breviary Hymns).** The earliest clearly documented liturgical use for the new hymns was in connection with the pattern of prayer traditionally called the Divine Office, but in more recent liturgical scholarship the Liturgy of the Hours. Following antique precedent, hymns were appointed for these canonical hours: ferial (daily) hymns that were eventually to vary for the more important hours according to days of the week and divisions of the year; and festal hymns, either hymns specific to a feast or generic hymns drawn from a *commune* (a collection of liturgical texts that could potentially be used for any feast of a particular type, e.g. *In natali unius virginis et martyris.*

Repertories peculiar to regions and religious communties developed early (see [GJ2] ch. 4: "Diffusion of Hymnody," and bibliography on pp19–24), and even after the widespread adoption of a more or less standard hymnal, variants, substitutes, and supplements continued (note causes for the expansion of the hymnodic repertory listed in [GJ27] pp121–22); new hymnodic varieties and new uses for hymns, which interacted with the traditional repertory, were developed as well.

Helmut Gneuss has reoriented our understanding of the collections of office hymns in general use in the Middle Ages. He has identified an Old Hymnal (*AHy*) containing around 15 hymns, all of them in the quantitative or rhythmic ambrosian stanza (see analytic table in [GJ52] p11). This collection came into existence perhaps as early as the fifth century and continued in widespread use until the eighth and ninth centuries. A collection that Gneuss calls the "Frankish Hymnal" supplemented this repertory (see conspectus of these early hymnals in [GJ33] pp24–25). Both of these were displaced by the New Hymnal (*NHy*), which came into existence in the ninth century. Earlier manuscripts of the *NHy* contain 35–50 hymns; the convenient edition of the *NHy* from the Bosworth Psalter (second half of the tenth century, [GJ38]) contains over 100 pieces. The ambrosian stanza continues to dominate in the *NHy*, but other meters are represented as well (see [GJ38] pp 10–12). This *NHy* provided the basic hymnodic repertory of the Liturgy of the Hours for most of Europe through the Middle Ages and beyond, being displaced only by hymnal reforms (e.g., the Cistercian Hymnal, Peter Abelard's compositions, and Brigittine hymns). The hymnal became, like other liturgical texts, a subject for study, and Latin and vernacular glosses, paraphrases, commentaries, and translations were produced.

**2. Hymns of the Eucharistic Liturgy.** The hymnodic genre associated with the eucharistic liturgy, called the sequence or prose (*sequentia* or *prosa*; usage varies in the Middle Ages and in modern scholarly literature), belongs to the Liturgy of the Word, where it was chanted between the Alleluia and the Gospel. Discussions of the genesis of the sequence have been many and obsessive (see comments in [GJ24] p82). A spectrum of musical and literary influences, sacred and secular, Greek, Latin and vernacular, has been suggested as contributory to the development of the new genre of the liturgical sequence and its secular counterpart; some of these suggestions seem quite plausible; even more of them cannot be categorically excluded. Derivation of the sequence solely from the *sequentia*, a substitute melody attached to the conclusion of the second Alleluia of the Mass, does not adequately account for the multiplex phenomenon that is the early sequence.

The genesis of the sequence remains a *non liquet*, but it is safe to say that this literary-musical phenomenon appears in a remarkably well-developed form in the first half of the ninth century, finding its first great identified artist in Notker of St. Gall, whose collection of sequences, entitled *Liber hymnorum* (in Huglo's view, [GJ18] p123, the first sequentiary), was assembled between 880 and 884. Codices containing the collected texts and melodies were called variously *sequentiarium* or *prosarium* (see [GJ46]); such an assemblage combined with collected tropes in a *troparium* is sometimes called in English a troper-proser (see, e.g., [GJ47]). Later, sequence texts were included in the *graduale* and *missale*.

Sequence texts are syllabic settings to newly composed or, very often, preexisting melodies; the melodies can be found on their own, transcribed as a melismatic pattern of notes, or copied *syllabatim* over the sequence text (see [GJ42] p142, pls. 1–2); reference to these melodies is managed through mnemonic titles (see [GJ46] ppXXV–XXVI). The simplest form of the sequence is the "a-parallel" sequence, a straightforward text underlay for the musical *sequentia*. The "classic" form of the early sequence is the "parallel" sequence, which is characterized by parallel isosyllabic lines of text set to the same melodic units in a variety of configurations, with, perhaps, nonparallel elements as introduction and/or coda, or within the piece, e.g. A BB CC DD EE FF, or A BB C DD EE F. The most extended type is the "double cursus" sequence, wherein a pattern of paired stanzas is repeated and concluded by a coda.

The Latin term *prosa* is often invoked in support of the characterization of sequence texts as prose, or, more ambitiously, *Kunstprosa*, given the isocolon (equal syllabic length of successive *cola*) and occasional parison (parallel syntactic structure in successive *cola*) and homoeoteleuton of the parallel stanzas. This involves, perhaps, a misleadingly narrow formalism. Greek liturgical poetry, once considered prose until the musical basis for the colometry and isosyllabism of the texts was realized, provides a crucial aid in our understanding of the verse form of the early sequence.

Sequences of the transitional type (eleventh century) show a further parallel with the Greek pattern by taking accent into account as well, and one can observe a growing tendency to add homotony (identical pattern of stresses) to the isosyllabism (identical number of syllables) of the parallel lines, and to go beyond homotony to regular rhythmical patterns.

The additional ornament of rhyme was added, first ad libitum, and then as a required feature, and regular rhythm and real rhymes became generic characteristics of the type of sequence referred to as late, new, regular, or rhyming sequence. This type emerged in the late eleventh century, though sequences of the earlier types continued to be composed. The rhyming sequence has been viewed by many as the supreme or, at least, the characteristic achievement of medieval Latin hymnody. The formal aspects of the rhymed sequence were adopted for secular lyric and for nonliturgical, devotional compositions, some of which proved so popular that they were taken over for liturgical use (e.g. the *Stabat mater* and the *Dies irae*).

**3. Hymns of the Occasional Liturgies; Processional Hymns.** These poems, sometimes called *versus*, by synecdoche for their *versus* or refrains, were chanted to accompany processions or to "cover" a liturgical action. They were collected not in the hymnal but in the *graduale*, in a book peculiar to the rite (*rituale, pontificale*), or in a *processionale*. Their chief, though not ubiquitous, characteristic is the chanting between stanzas of a refrain, a distinct verse or the repetition of an initial or thematic stanza or part thereof. The most popular meters are elegiac distichs and three-line stanzas of trochaic septenarii. Many famous processionals are reworkings, often involving considerable reductions, of late antique or early medieval works, e.g. Prudentius's *Cathemerinon* 5 and 9 ([GJ15] v50:30–32, 25–37), Fortunatus's *Pange lingua* and *Salve festa dies* ([GJ15] v50:71–73, 76–84), Theodulf of Orleans' *Gloria, laus, et honor* ([GJ15] v50:160–63). The relatively little studied *rythmi*, a meditational/devotional genre in the later Middle Ages, may have begun as processionals. Of the earlier *rythmi* (collected by Strecker in *MGH.Poetae* 4.2; emendations by Norberg in [GJ50]), a number are long, stanzaic, sometimes abecedarian poems with refrains for communal response, like the African *psalmi*. In this category also belong the versifications of litanies sung during processions or other liturgical activities (see, e.g., [GJ15] v50:242–43, 246–47, 253–55).

## Conclusion: Intertextuality, Transfers, Transformations

The corpus of hymns (liturgical, paraliturgical, devotional, etc.) is part of the immense intertextual network of the medieval liturgy. Whether indirectly, through this network, or directly, through their authors' education, reading, and ambitions, hymns are in varying degrees derivative from, and/or connected to, contemporary and ancient Christian literature, the pagan literatures of classical antiquity, and the Semitic literature of the Scriptures, as well as to the apparatus and techniques employed for their study.

Hymns enjoyed a canonical standing as part of the liturgy. This status, along with their conciseness and familiarity, caused them to be frequently quoted, authoritative texts in all religious discourse, but especially in hymnody itself. Intertextualities within the office hymns are evident in imitations and revivals of traditional verse forms, and in the repetition, incorporation, or adaptation into new compositions of images, phrases, lines, and whole stanzas from earlier hymns (whether significantly, as quotations, or for convenience's sake, as formulae). Another aspect of intertextuality in the larger hymnodic corpus can be seen, e.g., in the allusions to hymns in sequence texts or in the common motifs of hymns and versified antiphons.

Transfers from other genres abound, for the hymns incorporated elements of liturgical prayer, panegyric, biblical and hagiographic narrative, exegesis, apologetic, and protreptic, and served as substitutes for, or alternatives to, some of these genres.

Transformations of literary form are also found in hymnody: texts received as prose were paraphrased in verse; inherited longer poems were divided, centonized, or rearranged; verse hymns were paraphrased and glossed in prose in the commentary tradition, and paraphrased with gloss and amplification in verse as well.

Hymns were the most widespread and best known poetic forms, for they were encountered cyclically through the course of every day, week, season, lifetime, and were the most readily available texts for literary reflection and study. Hymns explained and compressed the larger corpus of liturgical works and were also a conduit for influences, often unrealized, of literatures that lay well outside the liturgy. Hymns played a definitive role in shaping the poetic taste and imagination of those who sang and studied them, offering readily imitated paradigms of literary creation and recreation.

# Select Bibliography

## Bibliographies

### (a) Cumulative

J. Szövérffy, *Repertorium hymnologicum novum* (1983–): v1.1 contains an unwieldy, alphabetically arranged *Hauptbibliographie* of editions and important secondary literature to 1983; the second volume of the first section is to contain a supplementary bibliography [GJ1]. See also [GJ12].

J. Szövérffy, *Latin Hymns, TSMAO* 55 (1989) 11–28: analytic bibliography [GJ2].

### (b) Current

*APh:* in section "Auteurs et textes" see under individual authors and s.vv. "Hymni christiani," "Liturgica," "Monastica," "Christiana varia" [GJ3].

*FRANCIS: Bulletin signalétique, 527: Histoire et sciences des religions:* in "Index du christianisme" see s.vv. "Hymnaire," "Hymne," "Hymnographie," "Hymnologie" [GJ4].

*IMB:* see s.v. "Hymns" in index [GJ5].

*MEL:* see under "Autori e Testi" for specific authors and also under "Poesia," "Liturgia," "Sequentiae" [GJ6].

*Répertoire international de littérature musicale: Abstracts of Music Literature,* sec. 93 ("Music in Liturgy and Ritual: Catholic"): in index see under "Hymn," "Hymnals," "Hymnology" [GJ7].

## Repertoria

U. Chevalier, *Repertorium hymnologicum: Catalogue des chants, hymnes, proses, séquences, tropes en usage dans l'église latine depuis les origines jusqu'à nos jours,* 6 vols. (1892–1919): two sets of *incipitaria* in v1–2 (A–K, L–Z), v3 (A–Z), v4 (A–Z), with addenda and corrigenda in v5 and indices in v6 (note especially index 1: Festorum, sanctorum; index 2: Auctorum, editorum; index 3: Librorum liturgicorum [by locations]) [GJ8]. Guide and massive corrections in C. Blume, *Repertorium repertorii: Kritischer Wegweiser durch U. Chevalier's Repertorium hymnologicum,* Hymnologische Beiträge 2 (1901, r1971), which contains a guide to [GJ8] and its contents, with vast alphabetical list of false, garbled, or misleading initia [GJ9].

M. Lütolf *et al., Analecta hymnica medii aevi: Register,* 2 vols. in 3 (1978): assembled to accompany [GJ15]; v1.1 (A–J) and v1.2 (K–Z) are an *incipitarium* with a serial number assigned to each hymn; v2 contains indices of hymns by type, liturgical function, and author, referring, by number, to the hymns listed in v1.1 and v1.2 [GJ10].

D. Schaller, E. Könsgen, and J. Tagliabue, *Initia carminum Latinorum saeculo undecimo antiquiorum: Bibliographisches Repertorium für die lateinische Dichtung der Antike und des früheren Mittelalters* (1977) [GJ11].

J. Szövérffy, *Repertorium hymnologicum novum* (1983–) (see [GJ1]): only one volume of the announced eight has so far appeared of this computer-generated replacement for [GJ8], which, it is said, will remedy the defects of [GJ10] and expand coverage to a far more extensive corpus of materials published more recently in more scientific editions; v1 contains an introductory essay and the preliminaries to the new *Repertorium,* sigla, and an extensive bibliography; a listing of the contents of the volumes yet to appear is given on p5 [GJ12].

H. Walther, *Initia carminum ac versuum medii aevi posterioris latinorum/ Alphabetisches Verzeichnis der Versanfänge mittellateinischer Dichtungen,* 2nd ed. (1969); see *Nachträge* in *MLJ* from v7 (1972) onward [GJ13].

## Collections and Anthologies

W. Bulst, ed., *Hymni Latini antiquissimi LXXV, Psalmi III* (1956): critical edition (apparatus, pp182–99) of principal monuments of earlier Latin hymnody; collection of *testimonia* about early hymnody on pp161–71 [GJ14].

C. Blume and G.M. Dreves, eds., *Analecta hymnica medii aevi,* 55 vols. (1886–1922, r1961): the vast size of this collection guarantees its limited reliability (conspectus of collection in [GJ19] 2917–18). See [GJ19] 2918–19 for H. Leclercq's indications of what is required for a really scientific edition of hymnodic texts [GJ15].

G.M. Dreves, *Ein Jahrtausend lateinischer Hymnendichtung: Ein Blütenlese aus den Analecta Hymnica,* ed. C. Blume, 2 vols. (1909): useful indices in v2:470–513 [GJ16].

A.S. Walpole, *Early Latin Hymns, with Introduction and Notes* (1922, r1966): note the "Grammatical Notes" (pp402–9) and "Index of Words" (pp411–45) [GJ17].

## Studies: Literary History, Criticism

### (a) General Studies

M. Huglo, in *Les livres de chant liturgique, TSMAO* 52 (1988) 27–28 [GJ18].

H. Leclercq, in *DACL* 6.2:2901–28 [GJ19].

J. Szövérffy, in *NCE* 7:287–95 [GJ20], and in *DMA* 6:379–85 [GJ21].

N.B.: Major encyclopedias have entries both on hymnological topics and on individual hymns; see, e.g., the index of "Hymnen und Hymnologica" in *Lexikon für Theologie und Kirche, Register,* pp412–13 [GJ22].

F. Brunhölzl, *Geschichte der lateinischen Literatur des Mittelalters,* 2 vols. to date (1975, 1992): note *initia* of poems in indices, v1:586 and v2:658–61 [GJ23].

P.S. Diehl, *The Medieval European Religious Lyric: An Ars Poetica* (1985) [GJ24].

F.J.E. Raby, *CLP* [GJ25].

J. Szövérffy, *Die Annalen der lateinischen Hymnendichtung: Ein Handbuch,* 2 vols. (1964–65): indices in each volume (*initia,* names, things); addenda in v1; supplementary material to v1 with *Nachträge* at the end of v2 [GJ26]; summary and update in *id., A Concise History of Medieval Latin Hymnody: Religious Lyrics between Antiquity and Humanism* (1985) [GJ27].

### (b) Developmental Period

A. Di Berardino, ed., *Patrology,* v4: *The Golden Age of Latin Patristic Literature: From the Council of Nicea to the Council of Chalcedon,* tr. P. Solari (1986): pp52–54 (Hilary); 72–73 (Marius Victorinus); 177–79 (Ambrose); 193–94 (*Te deum*); 285–86, 293–95 (Prudentius); 340–41 (*Psalmus responsorius*); 383 (Augustine) [GJ28].

J. Fontaine *et al., Ambroise de Milan: Hymnes* (1992): detailed intro. followed by texts/translations (with commentary) of the 14 hymns considered authentic; extensive indices and concordance [GJ29].

A. Franz, *Tageslauf und Heilsgeschichte: Untersuchungen zum literarischen Text und liturgischen Kontext der Tagzeitenhymnen des Ambrosius von Mailand* (1994) [GJ30].

M. Lattke, *Hymnus: Materialien zu einer Geschichte der antiken Hymnologie* (1991) [GJ31].

J. McKinnon, *Music in Early Christian Literature* (1987): collection of texts, translated with introductions and comments; thorough "Index of musical and liturgical terms and concepts" [GJ32].

## Hymnals

H. Gneuss, *Hymnar und Hymnen im englischen Mittelalter* (1968) 3–83 [GJ33].

H. Gneuss, "Latin Hymns in Medieval England: Future Research," in *Chaucer and Middle English Studies in Honour of Rossell Hope Robbins,* ed. B. Rowland (1974) 407–24 [GJ34].

M. Huglo, in *Les livres de chant liturgique* (see [GJ18] above) 108–10 [GJ35].

J. Mearns, *Early Latin Hymnaries: An Index of Hymns in Hymnaries before 1100, with an Appendix from Later Sources* (1913): dated, but indispensable [GJ36].

C. Waddell, *The Twelfth-Century Cistercian Hymnal,* 2 vols. (1984) [GJ37].

G.R. Wieland, ed., *The Canterbury Hymnal, Edited from British Library MS. Additional 37517, TMLT* 12 (1982) [GJ38].

## Medieval Commentaries on the Hymnal

H. Gneuss, *Hymnar und Hymnen* (see [GJ33]), pp194–206 [GJ39].

J.M. Beers, ed., *A Commentary on the Cistercian Hymnal/Explanatio super hymnos quibus utitur ordo Cisterciensis: A Critical Edition of Troyes Bib. Mun. MS. 658, HBS* 102 (1982) [GJ40].

## Sequences

L. Brunner, "Sequence (Prosa)," in *DMA* 11:162–66 [GJ41].

R.L. Crocker and J. Caldwell, "Sequence," in *NGDMM* 17:141–56 [GJ42].

R.L. Crocker, "Prosa," in *NGDMM* 15:308 [GJ43], and *id.,* "Sequentia," in *NGDMM* 17:156 [GJ44].

M.E. Fassler, "Sequence, Late," in *DMA* 11:166–67 [GJ45].

N. de Goede, *The Utrecht Prosarium,* Monumenta musica neerlandica 6 (1965) [GJ46].

R.-J. Hesbert, ed., *Le tropaire-prosaire de Dublin: Manuscrit Add. 710 de l'Université de Cambridge (vers 1300),* Monumenta musicae sacrae 4 (1966) [GJ47].

N. Van Deusen, "Research Report: The Medieval Latin Sequence: A Complete Catalogue of the Sources and Editions of the Texts and Melodies," in *JPMMS* 5 (1982) 56–60: select analytic bibliography [GJ48].

## Metrics

D. Norberg, *Introduction à l'étude de la versification latine médiévale* (1958) [GJ49].

D. Norberg, *La poésie latine rhythmique du haut moyen âge* (1954) [GJ50].

D. Norberg, *Les vers latins iambiques et trochaïques au moyen âge et les répliques rythmiques* (1988) [GJ51].

P. Klopsch, *EMV* [GJ52].

## Music

B. Stäblein, "Der lateinische Hymnus," in *MGG* 6:993–1018 [GJ53].

R. Steiner, "Hymn, §II: Monophonic Latin," in *NGDMM* 8:838–41 [GJ54].

R.L. Crocker, "The Sequence," in *Gattungen der Musik in Einzeldarstellungen: Gedenkschrift Leo Schrade*, ed. W. Arlt *et al.* (1973–) v1:269–322 [GJ55].

R.L. Crocker, "Strophic Hymns" (pp232–43), "Sequence and Prose" (pp256–64), "Text and Melody in the Later Sequence" (pp288–93), in *NOHM* 2 [GJ56].

D. Hiley, *Western Plainchant: A Handbook* (1993, r1995): note especially in this fine volume "Hymns" (pp140–48), "Sequences" (pp172–95), "Latin Liturgical Songs" (pp238–50) [GJ57].

B. Stäblein, ed., *Hymnen*, v1: *Die mittelalterlichen Hymnenmelodien des Abendlandes*, Monumenta monodica medii aevi 1 (1956) [GJ58].

J. Stevens, *Words and Music in the Middle Ages: Song, Narrative, Dance, and Drama, 1050–1350* (1986), ch. 2.1: The medieval hymn (pp52–55); ch. 3: The sequence (pp80–109) [GJ59].

## Later Developments

A. Moss, "The Counter-Reformation Latin Hymn," in *Acta Conventus Neo-Latini Sanctandreani,* ed. I.D. McFarlane (1986) 371–78 [GJ60].

A. Moss, "Latin Liturgical Hymns and their Early Printing History," in *HL* 36 (1987) 112–37 [GJ61].

J. Szövérffy, "Zur Frage von Funktionstypen mittellateinischer Lyrik: Paraliturgische Hymnenformen und Pia Dictamina im späteren Mittelalter," in *Lyrik des ausgehenden 14. und des 15. Jahrhunderts,* ed. F.V. Spechtler (1984) 249–308 [GJ62].

*See also* [BC42].

# GK ◦ BIOGRAPHY

BY WALTER BERSCHIN
(translated from German by SIEGFRIED A. SCHULZ)

## The Concept of Biography

*Biography* means representation of life; it is an expression that became current only through a series of translations of Plutarch (1683) associated with John Dryden. The ancient Greek word for biography is *bios;* the Latin term is *vita.* Other Latin words for biography, not as frequently used, include *passio, gesta, legenda,* and in some cases also *historia, translatio, miracula.* Biography is not a branch of historiography, a distinction expressed quite clearly by Plutarch: "I do not write history, I sketch pictures of life" (*Alexander,* ch. 1). Many untenable propositions of the nineteenth century regarding medieval biography can be attributed to the misapplication of historiographical criteria to the biographies of the Middle Ages. The twentieth century runs the risk of dismissing too many medieval biographies as "hagiographies." Only as late as the eighteenth century did the concept of "hagiography" acquire the meaning assigned to it now by modern scholarship. In the Middle Ages the overlap shared by biography and hagiography was greater than is today commonly assumed. In this guide, however, the two are treated as distinct if related categories, reflecting the modern tendency to treat them separately despite their considerable overlap. Together chapters GK and GL (*Hagiography*) seek to provide an introduction to the full range of biographical writing in the Middle Ages.

## The Period and Extent of Biographical Production

Histories of medieval literature commence with Boethius, Cassiodorus, or various other authors around the year 500, but this cannot be called a significant turning point in the history of biography. A rather pronounced cleavage is instead evident in the third century A.D., and the biographies produced in this and the subsequent century served as basic models until the reception of Plutarch in early Humanism. As for numbers, only a rough estimate of extant Latin biographies can be given: there may be about ten thousand such texts from the period c. 200–1500 A.D., inclusive of "hagiographies."

## The Martyr Acts of the Third and Fourth Centuries

In the dark third century A.D., so barren in literary output, the Christians who spoke Latin also began to write in that language (they had previously written in Greek or not at all). They produced something like minutes of the legal proceedings that were concerned with interrogating Christians during the persecutions, a kind of biography that has been called "pamphlet literature" ("Flugblatterzählung") ([GK19] p179). The most beautiful of these texts is the *Passio SS. Perpetuae et Felicitatis;* the most surprising is the *Passio S. Acacii martyris.* From the point of view of literary history, the written records associated with the martyred bishop Cyprian of Carthage (d. 258) are illuminating. First we have the *Acta Cypriani* (*Passio Cypriani*) written in the plain style characteristic of a court record, and then, as early as A.D. 260, there is the *Vita S. Cypriani,* composed by the deacon Pontius of Carthage. It was Pontius who brought to martyr biographies a concern for rhetoric and who wrote what was in fact a Christian panegyric. He was the first to portray the life of a bishop in Latin.

## Fourth-Century Biographies of Monks: St. Jerome

After the early martyrs came the monks. To Christian authors and readers of biographies in late antiquity, the lives of ascetics were in the beginning of greater interest than those of bishops. Augustine (*Confessiones* 8.6) was greatly impressed by the *vita* of the monk Antony (d. 356), which has become a classic of Christian biography not only because Antony was an important personality, but also because Athanasius of Alexandria (d. 373), the author of the *vita,* was a distinguished Greek writer and Evagrius (d. 392) an ideal translator of the text into Latin.

The early fame of the *Vita B. Antonii* prompted Jerome to write three lives, the *Vita S. Pauli primi eremitae* (376), the *Vita S. Hilarionis,* and the *Vita Malchi monachi captivi* (both c. 390), each of which in its own way competed with the *vita* of Antony. The *Life* of Malchus is the most illuminating as far as the modern history of the genre of medieval biography is concerned, because it made it plain that the hero of a Christian biography need not be a saint, and that birth and death, though the beginning and end of human existence, did not have to be part of a *vita.* Other decisive events in a person's life were, for Jerome, sufficient material for a biography, as was the case in his very exciting *Vita Malchi.*

In the Middle Ages many of Jerome's letters were also considered to be biographies, and at least ten of them (23, 24, 38, 39, 60, 77, 79, 108, 127, 130) may indeed be called biographical letters. Two others could also be mentioned in this context: no. 46, with its invitation to pilgrimage, and no. 66, with features of family biography. A final contribution was his transplantation of a type of biographical writing from classical literature to a Christian milieu. Jerome's *De viris illustribus* was a history of literature by means of short biographies, and his catalogue of authors, published in 393, listed 135 Christian writers, starting with Peter and ending with himself! In this work he superseded all his classical precursors.

## Lives of Bishops in the Fourth and Fifth Centuries

Martin of Tours (d. 397) was first a monk, then a bishop, and, in the eyes of his contemporaries, an outsider. His biography, composed in his lifetime (c. 397), was the work of Sulpicius Severus (d. c. 420), one of the most resourceful stylists of his time. So great was the success of this biography that Sulpicius was able to append two sequels, the *Epistulae* and the *Dialogi*. This life of the miracle worker Martin was to become the most successful Latin biography of late antiquity and the Middle Ages.

Biographies of bishops now began to flourish. A life of Ambrose of Milan (d. 397) was composed in 422 by his confidant, Paulinus of Milan, who had been urged by Augustine to take on this work of piety. In its very first sentence we find the oldest authoritative listing of works of Christian biography:

> Hortaris, venerabilis pater Augustine, ut sicut beati viri Athanasius episcopus et Hieronymus presbyter stilo prosecuti sunt vitas sanctorum Pauli et Antonii in eremo positorum, sicut etiam Martini venerabilis episcopi Turonensis ecclesiae Severus servus dei luculento sermone contexuit, sic etiam ego beati Ambrosii episcopi Mediolanensis ecclesiae meo prosequar stilo.

Augustine in his autobiographical *Confessiones* (387) had furnished the prototype for autobiography that prevailed until the eighteenth century. The psychological autobiography was a new literary genre, and it has been called the product of the Roman interest in the individual and in personal experience ([GK1] v2:1057). A biography of Augustine was produced c. 435, some five years after his death, by the North African bishop Possidius. While Paulinus's *Vita S. Ambrosii* was the kind of work that was disparaged in the nineteenth century as a typical "valet's biography" ("Kammerdienerbiographie"), i.e. full of admiration and replete with anecdotes, Possidius's *Vita S. Augustini* is a superior work, excelling in, among other things, its description of Augustine's everyday habits, a literary feature that Georg Luck believes may be attributed to the influence of Suetonius ([GK15] p240). But the biographer's many denials, i.e. statements about what Augustine did not do, remind us of another model, the *Vita Attici* of Cornelius Nepos.

## Serial Biographies of the Sixth Century

Biographies in a series were by no means an invention of the sixth century A.D. Plutarch and Suetonius had produced such serial works, and in fact the majority of the biographies of Greco-Roman antiquity, as we know them, were parts of series. In the Christian world, the individual biography prevailed in the beginning, but in Jerome's *De viris illustribus* (393) we have, early on, a prominent representative of a biographical series. Gennadius, a priest from Marseilles, continued it a century later (c. 470–95).

Around 530 there appeared in Rome the serial biographies of the popes that, with some interruptions, continued throughout the Middle Ages. These were collected in the *Liber pontificalis,* the "book of the popes." The most conspicuous feature of the early medieval *Liber pontificalis* is the fact that saintliness is not a criterion: the authors of these biographies, who are probably to be found in the papal vestry, were much more interested in the foundations established by the popes than in whether an individual pope was or was not a saint.

Venantius Fortunatus (d. c. 600) was known for his ability to convert any subject into a notable *vita*. All such works are biographies of bishops, except the *Vita S. Radegundis,* which describes the life of Radegund (518–87), Thuringian princess, Frankish queen, and founder of the nunnery of the Holy Cross at Poitiers. Her life was filled with extraordinary events: while a prisoner of war, the Thuringian king's young daughter gathers the children together at St. Quentin in northern France, washes their heads and hands, assembles a wooden crucifix, and marches her small flock to church in a sixth-century kindergarten scene; she endures as long as possible the marriage forced upon her; she compels a bishop to invest her with a nun's veil; in Poitiers she builds for herself a mighty fortress of a convent, through whose fiery curtain of penance and prayer no vile Merovingian can ever again pass, not even her own husband. The most peculiar part of her biography is that her death is not reported. Only within the framework of a *miraculum post mortem* is there a glance back at this event (ch. 38). The saint is just as present beyond the threshold of death as she is on this side of it. It was in exactly the same way that Goethe simply avoided, as too unpleasant, any mention of death in his biography of Winckelmann (1805).

At the end of the sixth century, Gregory of Tours (d. c. 594) and Pope Gregory the Great (d. 604) composed many short biographical notices. The latter's *Dialogi*, written in 593/4, preserve the life of the priest and monk Benedict (in bk. 2) and notices of the lives of 49 other saints.

## Merovingian Biographies

Following the biographical model developed by Venantius Fortunatus, the Merovingian era (481–751) produced a great number of bishops' *vitae*. Whoever was then a bishop of noble origin and observed certain ground rules could almost certainly be assured of a biography after his demise. Biography in fact became in the seventh century the leading literary genre amongst the Merovingians. But the most eminent *vita* of this epoch is that of a monk, the *Vita S. Columbani* of Jonas of Bobbio, completed c. 642. In its very first chapter we again encounter a canon of Christian biographical writings as follows: Athanasius/Evagrius, *Vita B. Antonii;* Jerome, *Vita S. Pauli* and *Vita S. Hilarionis;* Sulpicius Severus, *Vita S. Martini* and *Dialogi;* Venantius Fortunatus, *Vita S. Hilarii;* Paulinus, *Vita S. Ambrosii;* Possidius, *Vita S. Augustini.*

In the first book of his *vita* Jonas describes the life of the Irish monk Columbanus, who died in 615 at Bobbio; in the second he recounts the lives of some of Columbanus's students, just as St. Luke had described Jesus's life in his Gospel and the lives of several disciples in the *Acts of the Apostles*. Jonas's *vita* thus deals with a group of individuals and can be read as the history of a religious movement in the seventh century.

## Italy and Spain in the Early Middle Ages

Italian biographical writing in the early Middle Ages was under the spell of Gregory the Great's *Dialogi*, with the curious exception of Rome, where until 870 papal *vitae* continued to be written after the model of the *Liber pontificalis*. At times a papal biographer succeeded in imbuing this biographical model with astounding life. The first pope in whose *vita* were incorporated elements of a saint's life was Paschal I (817–24). The first time the tradition of official papal biography came to a halt was in 870, and soon afterwards (873–76) John the Deacon of Rome wrote an impressive biography of Gregory the Great, the model pope who eclipsed all the others.

Serial biographies of bishops were also produced in Aquileia, Ravenna, and

Naples under the inspiration of the *Liber pontificalis*. An Italian specialty was the translation into Latin, first at Rome by Anastasius Bibliothecarius (d. c. 880), and then at Naples by a large number of translators active between 875 and 960, of Greek biographies and hagiographies.

The first "golden age" of Spain in the seventh century influenced biographical writing in a positive way, producing the *Vita S. Aemiliani* by Braulio of Saragossa (d. 651) and the *Historia Wambae regis* by Julian of Toledo (d. 690), the two most prominent works among a good number of noteworthy biographies. Spain's leading role at this time may also be inferred from the fact that only in Spain was the tradition of writing histories of Christian literature continued, in the form of abridged biographies *de viris illustribus*, which were produced by Isidore of Seville (d. 636), Ildefonsus of Toledo (d. 667), Julian of Toledo (d. 690), and Felix of Toledo (d. c. 700).

The Moorish conquest in 711 was a disaster for Latin culture in Spain, but with Eulogius of Córdoba (d. 859), Paulus Albarus of Córdoba (d. c. 860), and the "Mozarabic" martyrs there arose a Latin island in the *mare magnum* of Arabic Spain. The *Vita B. Eulogii* of Paulus Albarus is one of the most appealing medieval biographies to stress the theme of friendship.

### Ireland and England in the Early Middle Ages

Five biographies from Ireland, written in the second half of the seventh century, have survived: Cogitosus, *Vita (II) S. Brigidae*; Ultan (?), *Vita (I) S. Brigidae*; Múirchu, *Vita S. Patricii*; Tírechán, *Vita S. Patricii*; Adamnan, *Vita S. Columbae*.

Medieval latinists love to dwell on this period of European cultural history, because the Irish were the first European people to begin to speak and write Latin without ever having been part of the Roman Empire and without ever having been compelled to use this language by force of arms. The five Hiberno-Latin biographies named above are filled with fascinating scenes of great appeal to modern readers, e.g. the Druid's divination about the yet unborn Brigit (*Vita I*), the encounter of white Ethne and red Fedelm with Patrick at the fountain Clebach (Tírechán, *Vita S. Patricii*), and Columba's farewell to his white horse (*Vita S. Columbae*).

The most significant Hiberno-Latin biography from the following three centuries was the *Navigatio S. Brendani*, a bestseller of "travel biography." Unique in biographical literature, it is extant in many manuscripts and contains a wealth of narrative detail.

The heirs to the Irish were the Anglo-Saxons, who published the following important biographies during the first half of the eighth century: the Anonymous of Whitby, *Liber beati et laudabilis viri Gregorii papae*; the Anonymous of Lindisfarne, *Vita (I) S. Cuthberti*; the Anonymous of Jarrow, *Vita S. Ceolfridi*; Bede, *Vita S. Felicis, Vita S. Cuthberti metrica, Vita (II) S. Cuthberti, Historia abbatum*; Stephanus (Eddius), *Vita S. Wilfridi*; Cuthbert of Jarrow, *De obitu Baedae*; Felix, *Vita S. Guthlaci*. Both prose and metrical versions of Bede's life of Cuthbert have become classics of biography.

As was the case in Ireland, the first great period of Latin biographical writing lasted only half a century in England, followed as late as 893 by Asser's *De rebus gestis Aelfredi*, an important and influential Anglo-Latin biography. In the tenth century biographical writing enjoyed a second heyday in England, while also acquiring a kind of affectation. For example, Frithegod of Canterbury's *Breviloquium vitae B. Wilfredi*

(c. 950) and the *Vita S. Dunstani* (c. 1000) were both written, as Michael Lapidge has observed, in a "hermeneutic" style finally abandoned at the time of the Norman Conquest in 1066 ([GK13] p103).

## Carolingian Biographies (750–920)

Anglo-Latin biographical writing moved with the English missionaries to the Continent around the middle of the eighth century. Willibald of Mainz's *Liber S. Bonifatii* (c. 760) and the nun Hugeburc's dual biographies, written between 767 and 785, of the brothers Willibald of Eichstätt and Wynnebald, are stylistically more English than their Continental counterparts. On the whole, particularly in the areas of culture and education, the Anglo-Saxons played an important role during the first 50 years of Carolingian rule. The first biography that may be called "Carolingian" in terms of style and purpose was the *Vita S. Willibrordi*, written by Alcuin in 796 for Beornrad of Sens. The hero of this work, its author, and the bishop who had commissioned it were Anglo-Saxons, but Alcuin has succeeded at shaping it in such a way that the Carolingian mayors of the palace become the focus of the work. The subject matter of the *vita* is in this way Carolingian, and so is its style: the extravagant peculiarities of the English tradition have given way to a grammatically normalized latinity.

Carolingian classicism in biographical literature began in the year 800 with Alcuin's preface to the *Vita (II) S. Richarii,* dedicated to Charlemagne. It contains a program for a stylistic transformation of Merovingian biography, something that in fact became a strong element in Carolingian cultural affairs. Around 830, Einhard wrote the *Vita Karoli,* modeled after the *De vita Caesarum* of Suetonius. Just as others had made use of biblical formulae to portray plausibly their heroes' Christian virtues, so Einhard selected locutions from Suetonius to give to Charlemagne (768–814) the veneer of classical antiquity. In this kind of imperial biography Einhard could not have had, and did not wish to have, any successor; he never gave away the secret of his recipe—the Suetonian conceit or model—and biographies of rulers were therefore compelled to develop along other lines. Thegan's *Vita Hludowici imperatoris* (c. 837), written during the lifetime of Louis the Pious (814–40), was composed *more annalium,* as the literary critic Walafrid Strabo correctly observed; and a second life of this emperor (*Vita Hludowici imperatoris*), composed immediately after his death by "Astronomus," has a strong historiographical focus and is a type of biography best described as *gesta* (for this type see [GK10] pp38–45).

Within the rich panorama of biographies from the central Carolingian era (800–870), the "official" biography deserves special mention. In Fulda, founded by Boniface in 744, every one of the first five abbots received a *vita: Vita S. Sturmi* (744–79), by Eigil, c. 795; *Vita Baugulfi* (779–802), by Bruno Candidus, after 802; *Vita Ratgarii* (802–17), after 817; *Vita Eigilis* (818–22), by Bruno Candidus, c. 840; *Vita Hrabani* [*Miracula sanctorum in Fuldenses ecclesias translatorum*] (822–41/2; Hrabanus died in 856), by Rudolf, 842–47.

The first, fourth, and fifth of these *vitae* are extant; the first may perhaps be characterized as a "saint's life" or hagiography. The fact that even the third abbot, Ratgar, dismissed in 817, received a *vita* indicates the importance attached to official biographies.

The most reflective and artful biographical product of Carolingian classicism, apart from Einhard's work, was the double biography, by Paschasius Radbertus of Corbie (d. c. 860), of the abbots Adalhard (d. 826) and Wala of Corbie (d. 836), both of whom belonged to the Carolingian clan and to the pious branch of it that was under Italian influence. The earlier biography is entitled *Vita S. Adalhardi* and the later one *Epitaphium Arsenii* or *Vita (S.) Walae.*

Carolingian classicism ended c. 870, followed until 920 by a late mannerist phase when impressive works were produced that eclipsed all previous ones. Heiric of Auxerre composed c. 875 the *Vita S. Germani,* the most significant metrical biography of the Carolingian era; c. 878 Hincmar of Reims completed an extensive revision of an older *vita* (*Vita S. Remigii*); Notker I of St. Gall wrote (884–87) his *Gesta Karoli,* paraphrasing and surpassing Einhard's biography, at least in terms of imagination and variation. The Carolingian impulse also crossed the boundaries of the realm, providing the stimuli necessary for the writing of the *Vita S. Gregorii* of John the Deacon in Rome and Asser's *De rebus gestis Aelfredi* in England.

## The Tenth and Eleventh Centuries: Ottonian Biography

For more than a generation—from 920 to 960—there was in the Latin West almost no literary life, a crisis attributable to many causes, certainly external ones (the Normans, Saracens, and Hungarians, who paralyzed the West), but perhaps also internal. In this dark period, however, the new forces of Cluny (the "world power") and the German *imperium* began to take shape.

Already Odo, the second abbot of the reformed monastery of Cluny (910–1790), was a biographer, writing, 916–42, the life of a saintly count, the *Vita S. Geraldi,* with a layman as its hero. Although this was not entirely an innovation in medieval biographical writing—the Merovingian *Passio S. Ragneberti* (St. Rambert) is an account of a layman without ecclesiastical rank—it was still unusual. Odo himself found a biographer in his friend Johannes Italus, whose *vita* begins the famous series of biographies of the abbots of Cluny. The most important of these are as follows: *Vita (I) S. Odonis* (927–42), by Johannes Italus, soon after 942; *Vita (I) S. Maioli* (954–94), by Syrus, c. 1000; *Vita (I) S. Odilonis* (994–1049), by Jotsald of Cluny, 1051–53; *Vita (I) S. Hugonis* (1049–1109), by Gilo, 1120–22; *Vita (I) Petri Venerabilis* (1122–56), by Rudolf of Cluny, c. 1160.

In Central Europe there arose, c. 960, a powerful literary movement, which apparently resulted from the ascent of Otto I (936–73) and his successors; its productions may be called "Ottonian literature." Biography played an important role in this movement, becoming in fact the leading literary genre in the tenth century, just as it had previously in the seventh. Essential works of Ottonian biography are the following:

[Ekkehard I of St. Gall], *Vita (I) S. Wiboradae,* c. 960–70
Hrotsvitha of Gandersheim, *Gesta Ottonis,* before 968
Ruotger of Cologne, *Vita domni Brunonis,* c. 968–69
Gumpold of Mantua, *Passio (I) S. Vencezlavi,* 968–73
Johannes of St. Arnulf, *Vita domni Iohannis Gorziensis,* c. 974
*Vita (I) Macthildis reginae,* c. 974
Gerhard of Augsburg, *Vita (I) S. Uodalrici,* 982–93
Purchart of Reichenau, *Gesta Witigowonis,* 995–1000

Odilo of Cluny, *Epitaphium domne Adalheide auguste,* c. 1000
Johannes Canaparius, *Passio (I) S. Adalberti,* c. 1000
*Vita (II) gloriosae reginae Mahthildis,* 1002–6
Bruno of Querfurt, *Passio (II) S. Adalberti,* c. 1004
Bruno of Querfurt, *Vita quinque fratrum,* c. 1004
Adalbold of Utrecht, *Vita Heinrici [II] imperatoris,* c. 1012
Thangmar of Hildeshein, *Vita Bernwardi,* c. 1020
*Vita Burchardi Wormatiensis,* c. 1025–30
Wipo, *Gesta Chuonradi imperatoris,* 1039/40–46
Lantbert of Deutz, *Vita (I) S. Heriberti,* c. 1050

Biography proved again that it could set the pace for literature, and it was in fact by means of *vitae* that Poland and Bohemia, and Hungary soon after, gained access to the *orbis latinus.*

What Ottonian biographies had in common was their closeness to historical writing, and that is what threatened their survival; almost all of them were reworked to make them fit into the customary mold of biography/hagiography, which admitted historiographical materials and methods only to a very limited degree.

## The Investiture Controversy and the Twelfth Century

During the Investiture Controversy (1076–1122) Central Europe's loss of power and influence extended also to the field of literature. Literary production did, however, increase and more and more biographies were written, but the status of the *vita* within the panorama of literature was reduced. Pope Gregory VII (1073–85), Peter Damian's "holy Satan," was described by Wido of Ferrara in bk. 1 of the *De scismate Hildebrandi* (1086), a polemical treatise in biographical form; it was only after a long interval (c. 1128) that Paul of Bernried, a German partisan of the pope, could describe him in a biography as a saint. We also have the *Vita Heinrici IV imperatoris* (c. 1107), a biography of Gregory's antagonist, Henry IV (1056–1106), in which the influence of Sallust's style is evident.

It was characteristic of the growth of biographical writing in the twelfth century that no fewer than seven biographies appeared as a consequence of the canonization of abbot Hugh of Cluny in 1120. Such a figure was, however, soon surpassed by the biographical efforts associated with Bernard of Clairvaux (d. 1153) and Thomas Becket of Canterbury (d. 1170). Bernard, who in the words of de Ghellinck was "le guide écouté de la chrétienté durant 35 ans" ([GK8] p394), had a coterie of loyal biographers like a modern politician's, who immediately noted down his every miracle. Becket's murder in the cathedral caused one author after another to come forward, from John of Salisbury, the twelfth-century humanist, to T.S. Eliot. In *passiones* people had read and heard a great deal about the martyrs of the early Church; now there was once again a genuine martyr, and this caused a sensation.

There were now Latin biographies everywhere as the world that could read and write this language again increased in size to include Denmark, Iceland, Sweden, Norway, and even Finland and a large part of the Baltic coast. It was in Ireland that once again a characteristic biographical literature appeared, in the *Vitae sanctorum Hiberniae,* which stands out because of its great number of animal miracles. In England, as Grundmann has observed, "almost every king since William the Conqueror was accorded a special description of his *gesta* that was progressively more realistic and detailed" ([GK10] p43). France in the twelfth century produced biographical works of particular interest to the modern reader: the *Vita Ludovici Grossi regis* by Suger of St. Denis (d. 1151) and the autobiographies of Guibert of Nogent (*De vita sua*) and Abelard (*Historia calamitatum*). In Germany biographical writing modeled on the *De viris illustribus* was revived by Sigebert of Gembloux, Honorius Augustodunensis, and the "Anonymous Mellicensis," and this type of biography has continued to be written from that time until our own.

## The Thirteenth Century

The most important biographies of the thirteenth century were those of St. Francis (c. 1182–1226), of which there are several versions. Thomas of Celano (d. c. 1260) even introduced some of the saint's "modern" character traits, mentioning, for example, that his attitude in youth was thought by some to be arrogant. These aspects of his personality were smoothed over in the official biography by Bonaventure (d. 1274), third general of the Franciscans, who introduced instead a "theological" interpretation of the life of the founder of the Minorite order: Francis was the *angelus sexti sigilli,* the angel whose appearance had been described in the *Apocalypse* in the account of the opening of the sixth seal.

Generally speaking, the thirteenth century was for Latin a critical period; it was, in the words of G. Toffanin (*Storia dell'umanesimo,* v1 [1952]), "il secolo senza Roma." Though an international language, Latin lost one field of literature after another in the face of the awakening of national idioms, a development that may also be observed in biographical writing. Jean de Joinville (d. 1317) wrote his *Histoire de saint Louis* in Old French; biographies of the German mystics of the later Middle Ages were usually composed in Middle High German, and it was a singular event when Gertrude of Helfta (d. 130l or 1302) wrote her spiritual autobiography, the *Legatus divinae pietatis,* in flawless Latin and when another (anonymous) nun of the same community supplied an introductory Latin *vita.*

## The Fourteenth Century and Beginning of the *Aetas Plutarchiana*

In the fourteenth century one can observe a greater interest in classical antiquity, something that may partially reflect certain twelfth-century preoccupations. The English writer Walter Burley (d. c. 1344) provided a biographical example of this in his *De vita et moribus philosophorum,* which focused exclusively on the philosophers of ancient Greece and Rome. Burley here made use of the biographical history of philosophy by Diogenes Laertius, to which he had access through a Latin version (now lost) prepared by a twelfth-century Sicilian school of translators.

Decisive literary innovations during this period originated in Italy. With Petrarch (1304–74) an Italian movement became influential and once again secured a leading and lasting role for Latin. Petrarch's biographical contribution is his *De viris illustribus, vitae* only of ancient Romans, with special prominence given to Scipio Africanus; Boccaccio (1313–75) actually contrasted the *viri illustres* with a book *De claris mulieribus.* Petrarch's biographical model paved the way for an important humanist innovation, the history of art in the form of biographies of artists, but the master of this particular genre, Giorgio Vasari, wrote in Italian (1550).

For Petrarch the preeminent classical biographer was Suetonius, author of the *De vita Caesarum,* and he owned three copies of this work. Soon after Petrarch's death, the *bioi paralleloi* of Plutarch began to appear in the West, and c. 1384–88 Juan Fernández de Heredia, grand master of the Order of the Knights of St. John, prevailed upon a Dominican missionary bishop in Avignon to translate into Latin 39 of Plutarch's 48 biographies. But Plutarch did not enjoy immediate success. It was in fact only in 1440, when Giannozzo Manetti published his compelling *Vita Socratis et Senecae,* parallel Latin biographies fashioned after Plutarch, that the triumphal march of the "Bible of Heroes" (as R.W. Emerson called Plutarch's *Lives*) commenced, arousing irresistible enthusiasm for the heroic individual as late as the nineteenth century. Nevertheless, the archetypal biographical models of late antiquity and the Middle Ages continued to be influential for some time to come.

The biographical cycle was completed by Roper's *Lyfe of Sir Thomas More* (c. 1556), written in English and described in 1935 by R.W. Chambers, More's modern biographer, as "one of the most perfect little biographies in the [English] language." It had certain novelties—its hero was a layman, a victim for reasons of state, a martyr for reasons of conscience—but also some features that were very old. Before More mounted the scaffold, it was reported that "of that little money that was lefte him did he send one Angell of gold to his executioner," to reward the man for sending him to eternal bliss. Bishop Cyprian of Carthage had done exactly the same thing in A.D. 258, an *ultimum factum* that had made this bishop famous. Thus the last act in Thomas More's life begins with a literary *imitatio,* for it is almost certain that he actually did what was reported. *Imitatio* is acted out as a real event, and a literary topos becomes a topos in real life. As Leo Spitzer has remarked ("Erhellung des 'Polyeucte' durch das Alexiuslied," in *Archivum Romanicum* 16 [1933] 484), it is when motivated by *imitatio* that all mankind is uplifted ("Die ganze Menschheit wird an der Kette der imitatio auf der Himmelsleiter emporgerissen").

In conclusion we would suggest that biography is a literary form that in its own special way possesses an anthropological dimension. There can be no doubt that the epic, lyric, drama, and perhaps even the modern novel, the leading literary genre of our time, are more ambitious fields of literature, more demanding technically, and more intensely reflective. But biography has a direct link with anthropology and thus with philosophy. Our interest in biography is, to a certain degree, a search for a philosophy of life.


## Select Bibliography

See also the bibliography of ch. GL, which supplements the one that follows.

### Primary Works

References to editions of the works cited in this survey are to be found in [GK2] 1:325–37, 2:307–17, 3:431–53.

## Studies

M. von Albrecht, *Geschichte der römischen Literatur*, 2 vols. (1992) [GK1].

W. Berschin, *Biographie und Epochenstil im lateinischen Mittelalter*, 3 vols. (1986–91) [GK2].

W. Berschin, "Sueton und Plutarch im 14. Jahrhundert," in *Biographie und Autobiographie in der Renaissance*, ed. A. Buck (1983) 35–43 [GK3].

W. Berschin, ed., *Biographie zwischen Renaissance und Barock: Zwölf Studien* (1993) [GK4].

R. Bossard, *Über die Entwicklung der Personendarstellung in der mittelalterlichen Geschichtsschreibung* (1944) [GK5].

P. Cox, *Biography in Late Antiquity: A Quest for the Holy Man* (1983) [GK6].

T.A. Dorey, ed., *Latin Biography* (1967): includes chapters on Suetonius and his influence, William of Poitiers' *Gesta Guillelmi*, William of Malmesbury, and the *Lives* of St. Francis of Assisi [GK7].

J. de Ghellinck, *L'essor de la littérature latine au XIIe siècle*, 2 vols., 2nd ed. (1955) [GK8].

A. Gransden, *Historical Writing in England*, 2 vols. (1974–82): see v1, chs. 4, 5, 7, 14; and v2, ch. 7 [GK9].

H. Grundmann, *Geschichtsschreibung im Mittelalter* (1965) [GK10].

J. IJsewijn, "Die humanistische Biographie," in *Biographie und Autobiographie* (see [GK3]), pp1–19 [GK11].

P. Kirn, *Das Bild des Menschen in der Geschichtsschreibung von Polybios bis Ranke* (1955) [GK12].

M. Lapidge, "The Hermeneutic Style in Tenth-Century Anglo-Latin Literature," in *ASE* 4 (1975) 67–111 [GK13].

F. Leo, *Die griechisch-römische Biographie nach ihrer literarischen Form* (1901, r1965) [GK14].

G. Luck, "Die Form der suetonische Biographie und die frühen Heiligenviten," in *Mullus: Festschrift Theodor Klauser*, ed. A. Stuiber and A. Hermann (1964) 230–41 [GK15].

G. Misch, *Geschichte der Autobiographie*: (a) *Das Altertum* (1907), 3rd ed., 2 pts. (1949–50); tr. E.W. Dickes with the author's collaboration: *A History of Autobiography in Antiquity*, 2 vols. (1950–51); (b) *Das Mittelalter*, 2 vols. (1955–59); 2nd ed., 3 vols., each in 2 pts. (1959–70) [GK16].

A. Momigliano, *The Development of Greek Biography: Four Lectures* (1971) [GK17].

R. Morse, "Medieval Biography: History as a Branch of Literature," in *The Modern Language Review* 80.1/2 (1985) 257–68 [GK18].

R. Reitzenstein, "Bemerkungen zur Märtyrerliteratur," in *NKGWG* (1919) 177–279 [GK19].

J. Romein, *Die Biographie* (1948) [GK20].

R.J. Schoeck, "Neo-Latin Resources for Biography: A Preliminary View," in *Acta Conventus Neo-Latini Torontonensis*, ed. A. Dalzell, C. Fantazzi, and R.J. Schoeck (1991) 101–10 [GK21].

D.A. Stauffer, *English Biography before 1700* (1930, r1964) [GK22].

*See also* [BA127].

BY DAVID TOWNSEND

A number of the world's religions have produced bodies of sacred biography that represent the lives of believers as a lived expression of the tradition's perceived spiritual truths. The Buddhist, Sufi Muslim, and Jewish traditions have all produced hagiographical literatures. Occasional examples of rapprochement are found, as in the tale of Barlaam and Josaphat, which Christianizes the life of the Buddha, or the echoes of dominant Christian culture in the richly developed body of Jewish martyrology in eleventh- through thirteenth-century Germany. In general, however, these various traditions developed apart from one another, as one might well expect of mutually antagonistic systems of belief.

## Features of the Genre: An Overview

Elements of Christian Latin hagiography correspond to aspects of secular biography; the latter in turn is often frequently influenced by hagiographical convention. Hagiographical narrative can, however, be distinguished as a body of texts sharing, from the fifth through the fifteenth centuries and throughout Western Europe, characteristic conventions of style and content. The sense of sameness and repetition quickly impresses itself on the modern student, and consequently the approach of *Toposforschung* has itself amounted to a commonplace of hagiographical scholarship for several generations. Latin hagiography began with nonliterary records that often seem accurately to reflect spoken usage in the late Roman Empire. As hagiography developed greater literary self-consciousness, authors came to cultivate a straightforward and widely accessible latinity as the appropriate style for texts ostensibly aimed at edification and spiritual instruction. Saints' lives often appeal to eyewitness accounts mediated by a reliable and unbroken chain of oral witnesses. The reduction of the events to literary form occasions the author's protestations of his or her inadequacy to the task—the so-called "humility topos." The texts affect a language of heroic combat transposed to the level of spiritual struggle, beginning with the accounts of martyrs as *milites Christi*, and continuing later with martial images of ascetics and missionaries.

Individual characterization is largely suppressed. Descriptions of the saint may feature conventional catalogues borrowed whole or in part from other texts. Episodic construction often emphasizes discrete anecdotes at the expense of any substantial narrative development. Texts typically but not invariably include a sequence of infancy episodes, a description of the saint's person and qualities, an account of his or her career with a heavy emphasis on miracle stories, a death narrative, and a series of posthumous miracles. In the case of martyrs, the *passio* remains an alternative to the writing of a full-scale *vita*. Collections of posthumous *miracula* often come to constitute a separate book within the *vita*, or to be composed as independent works. Narratives of *translatio*, the ceremonial removal of a saint's relics to a new site, comprise another subcategory of hagiography, marked by its own conventions.

It is important to bear in mind the variety of purposes for which *vitae* were written. Although some were intended originally for individual reading, the development of liturgical cults necessitated a series of lections for the office of the saint's feast. Some texts were thus composed with ritual usage in mind; some were abridged or otherwise adapted for such purposes. As the canonization process became increasingly formalized in the eleventh and twelfth centuries, many texts came to be written with an eye to their subject's promotion to official status. The surviving manuscripts witness to a rich diversity of intended uses and receptions. *Vitae* sometimes appear in manuscripts of mixed content, sometimes in *libelli* devoted to a dossier of materials related to a given saint's veneration, and sometimes in increasingly comprehensive legendaries and passionals, collections of lives clearly intended for paraliturgical usage and organized according to the sequence of feasts in the liturgical year.

## A Chronological Survey

The Christian Latin tradition begins with the early Church's impulse to record the acts of believers killed during the intermittent persecutions of their religion before its state establishment. These *acta martyrum* often narrate the trials and sufferings of ordinary women and men in straightforward and relatively sober language. They sometimes include official transcripts of trials. We also find instances of the martyrs' own prison memoirs, as in the remarkable account of the last days of the young matron Perpetua, her pregnant slave Felicitas, and their companions, who were executed at Carthage on 7 March 202. The text as we have it was long erroneously attributed to Tertullian. It incorporates Perpetua's own account of her imprisonment, recording her solicitude for her nursing infant, her father's pressures on her to recant, and the visions she experienced. A narrative by her companion Saturus follows her memoir. The text's detailed presentation, expressed vividly in Perpetua's own voice, invites a richly layered and nuanced reading. Its language captures a "subliterary" latinity presumably in touch with actual North African usage at the turn of the third century. While such accounts may well be conditioned by the narrative expectations of the communities that gave rise to them, they impart an impression of spontaneous language directly in touch with the circumstances and attitudes of their time.

As Christianity's changing political status made martyrdom less likely, steadfast public profession of the faith could no longer of itself mark out a protagonist as extraordinary. New criteria of sanctity came to justify the writing of a biography, and lives of ascetics and hermits, and soon of ecclesiastics, took their place beside martyrial records as models of Christian heroism. The early life of the third-century desert hermit Anthony of Egypt, commonly attributed to Athanasius of Alexandria, was translated from the original Greek into Latin by Evagrius of Pontus (345–99). In this version it became one of the most influential models for the subsequent development of saints' lives in the West. Similarly influential were the hagiographical romances of St. Jerome, such as the life of Malchus, a monk who departs from his community. Enslaved by nomads and forced into cohabitation with a female slave, he enters into a pact with her to remain chaste. They escape despite extraordinary danger, and he survives to narrate his story in his eremitical old age.

In these texts of the patristic period one of the ongoing stylistic preoccupations of Latin hagiography emerges. The anxiety of such rhetorically accomplished figures as Jerome and Augustine over the cultural status of biblical language profoundly shaped expectations of diction in saints' lives as well. Straightforward, rhetorically simple *sermo humilis* became fixed as the genre's stylistic norm, linked as the texts ostensibly were to the instruction and edification of the wide body of Christian believers. Authors' prefaces often explicitly renounce classical elegance of style, yet these introductions are frequently couched in more highly wrought language than the main body of their respective works. Alongside this abnegation of high style, the writer commonly protests his or her inadequacy to the task of composition. A patron's request, or the sheer necessity of not allowing the subject to be forgotten, often offers the mitigating excuse for the work's existence despite these authorial misgivings. Such a rhetorical strategy figures in the preface by Sulpicius Severus to his fifth-century life of Martin of Tours, which enjoyed perhaps an even wider influence as a model than the texts of Evagrius and Jerome.

The collapse of the Western Empire and the relations of Church and state in the barbarian kingdoms introduced new subject matter into the genre. Particularly noteworthy in this respect are lives of royal saints among the Merovingian Franks. These texts both reflect and propagate ideals of sanctity among the powerful, at the same time appropriating spiritual authority to the existing political order. Two lives of Radegund represent the state of texts around the turn of the seventh century, though these lives may perhaps be read more for their reflection of Radegund's vehement detachment from the status quo than for their positive engagement with it. Radegund, a Thuringian princess married to King Clothair, fled her marriage and went on to found a monastery dedicated to the Holy Cross at Poitiers. There she became friend and patron of Venantius Fortunatus, the poet of the hymn *Vexilla regis* and the author as well of a lengthy verse retelling of Severus's *Vita Sancti Martini*. Fortunatus also composed a life of Radegund in prose, shortly after her death in 586. A second text was written not much later, but after 600, by the nun Baudonivia, who draws on the prefaces of other prose saints' lives by Fortunatus in the prologue of her own text. She declares her intention not to supplant the earlier biography, but to supplement it with material that Fortunatus had omitted.

At the same time, the relation of hagiographical Latin to vulgar speech becomes increasingly problematic, as the gap between Latin and the emerging Romance languages widens. The Merovingian lives include texts of seriously erratic latinity. This may reflect a deteriorating knowledge of Latin; but it may also suggest the accommodation of the written language to a spoken idiom not yet perceived as a separate tongue. One might thus see the texts' increasingly nonclassical grammar as continuing the traditional hagiographical employment of a language ostensibly accessible to the common reader or hearer.

The more standard grammar of lives written around or after the middle of the eighth century already anticipates the reform of Latin usage generally associated with the program of Charlemagne and his English scholar Alcuin (d. 804). With the Carolingian period comes an irrevocable split between Latin as a language of ecclesiastical high culture and a vulgar language that ceases in essence to be recognized as a variety of the same tongue. This does not, as one might have expected, result in the immediate transfer of hagiographical activity into the continental vernaculars. Saints' lives continue to be written almost exclusively in Latin. (By the eleventh century the texts show something of the predilection for artificial and recondite ornamentation characteristic of the period's literary production in general. We see this development exemplified in the original material added by Drogo of Bergues to his life of Oswald, a text in substance simply rearranged from material in Bede's *Historia ecclesiastica*.) In the Carolingian period one also finds continued the amalgamation of saintly and secular values observed in some Merovingian texts: this trend coincides with the administrative centralization of both Church and state by Charlemagne and his successors. Alcuin wrote a double life of Willibrord in parallel prose and verse versions, comprising, respectively, bks. I and II of a single work. It commemorates the career of the early Anglo-Saxon missionary to the Frisians. At the same time it glorifies the future virtues and victories of the descendants of Pippin and his son Charles Martel.

Developments in eighth-century England reflect the different linguistic context of insular literature. There was no question of close resonance between Latin and the vernacular, as on the Continent, so that the language of saints' lives from the beginning can only be called "common" with respect to the makeup of a nearly exclusively ecclesiastical subculture. England was in fact prolific of literature at a period when Merovingian letters had reached stagnation. Among the earliest saints' lives from England are the first *vita* of Gregory the Great and an anonymous life of St. Cuthbert. The first half of the eighth century also saw the production of Bede's *Historia ecclesiastica;* of his lives in prose and verse of St. Cuthbert, upon which Alcuin subsequently drew as models for his double life of Willibrord; of Felix of Croyland's remarkable *vita* of the East Anglian hermit Guthlac, with its debt to the Evagrian life of Anthony; and of Stephanus of Ripon's biography of the ecclesiastical politician Wilfrid.

A single author's production of twinned prose and verse versions of the same narrative poses one of the more interesting problems of early medieval literary history. Before the examples by Bede and Alcuin had come Aldhelm's compendium of short narratives, *De virginitate,* which itself builds on the Continental tradition of Sedulius's *Carmen paschale* and *Opus paschale.* Such *opera geminata* usually make some brief prefatory statement of the rationale for the narrative's duplication. In the case of Alcuin's work, the dedication informs the reader that Alcuin intends the prose for public reading to the community, whereas the verse is to be an object of instruction and private study. The issue of how the parts of such texts relate to one another, however, is elided by the briefest of metaphors, and room remains for speculation on the experience of reading these works: the reader's consciousness can grasp only a part of the narrative at any given point, so that each half of the work depends in some sense upon the other for supplementation.

Any consideration of stylistics in the *opera geminata* must take into account the more general narratological problems of verse hagiography. Early medieval verse lives often announce their choice of form rather apologetically: the adoption of hexameter verse, with its indisputably literary pretensions, runs counter to the declared instructional and devotional aims of hagiography and to the preference for simple, widely accessible language. On the other hand, the texts sometimes defend versification as offering a treatment of the material more worthy of divine glory. But permutations of such standard topoi cannot always be seen as wholly ingenuous, and to grasp the motivations of verse hagiographers it may be necessary to read behind their declared intentions for less explicit but historically more specific agendas.

At least partly under the pressure of Viking raids, English literary production halted almost entirely for the middle fifty years of the ninth century. Hagiographical writing in the tenth century, under the aegis of the so-called Benedictine revival, included the earliest substantial body of vernacular lives in Europe, the narrative homilies of Aelfric of Eynsham (c. 955–1020). Latin *vitae*, in general, exhibited a variety of stylistic excesses, although the bizarre latinity of many writers was in evidence chiefly in prologues, where generic expectations allowed for more rhetorical display. Elaborately contorted syntax and abstruse conceits may be found in the Latin works of Byrhtferth of Ramsey, for example his lives of Sts. Ecgwin and Oswald of York, as in the prologue of the life of Dunstan by a writer known only as "B." The neologisms of such writers vastly proliferate in Frithegod's verse *Breviloquium* based on Stephanus's life of Wilfrid. The simple, straightforward narrative of Aelfric in his Latin life of Aethelwold is exceptional for his generation and reflects the same concerns for accessible instruction embodied in his vast program of vernacular preaching materials. The English reform drew much impetus from contemporary Continental sources, and this is reflected in literary exchanges as well. Abbo of Fleury (d. 1004), a Continental churchman of considerable importance, dedicated his life of King Edmund to Archbishop Dunstan, whom he met during his two-year stay as a teacher at Ramsey. Its style is relatively restrained, although not without intricacy.

Hagiographical writing in England trails off once again through the eleventh century, only to revive with the production of numerous texts in the generation after the Norman Conquest. These later texts are associated in particular with the names of Goscelin and Osbern. Goscelin was himself a Fleming who seems to have gone to England during the reign of Edward the Confessor, and who traveled extensively from monastery to monastery until his eventual settlement in the late 1080s at St. Augustine's, Canterbury. The early manuscripts present his lives of Canterbury saints as a single cycle commemorating figures honored in a great translation ceremony of 1091. Osbern, a native English monk of the neighboring cathedral of Christ Church, composed a life of Dunstan intended to supplant the earlier production of "B"; a second book recording the posthumous miracles of Dunstan; a life of Archibishop Aelfheah, slain by the Danes in 1012 and subsequently venerated as a martyr; and an account of the latter saint's translation from London to Canterbury under Cnut. (The attribution of martyrdom to Aelfheah, slain essentially for refusing to arrange his own ransom, illustrates the ongoing adaptation of older narrative structures to new political circumstances. The best-known example of this process will be the extensive hagiography of another archbishop of Canterbury, Thomas Becket.) Lives by a number of other identified authors also derive from the period just after the Norman invasion, along with various anonymous texts such as a life of Birinus, the seventh-century apostle of Wessex, written in the diocese of Winchester. About a generation after Osbern, his fellow monk of Christ Church, Eadmer, wrote a number of lives, of which the best known is the biography of Eadmer's friend and master Archbishop Anselm.

The sudden post-Conquest proliferation of the *vitae* of early English saints does not reflect a single simple political and social context. The backgrounds of the various texts must be understood on the specific terms of the readerships for which they were produced. The defense of native cults against the antagonism of the new Norman hierarchy has often been cited as an explanation for the writing of *vitae* to bolster traditions that were now threatened without adequate literary support; but circumstances vis-à-vis the newcomers varied markedly from house to house and from region to region. What can in any case be observed is that the various texts are marked by a diversity of perspective within the implied audience, suggesting the need to bridge a cultural gap between English and Norman elements in the community. At the same time, these works in general employ a much more restrained and simplified style than those produced at the end of the tenth century. The anonymous life of Birinus, for example, affects a style whose easy aural accessiblity calls to mind homiletic rhetoric. At the same time, its deployment of standard commonplaces sometimes emphasizes themes that would have had politically charged currency in the period before the Norman and English elements in monastic communities synthesized completely.

Latin lives of Celtic saints through the twelfth century present interesting variations from the mainstream. Sanctity of place sometimes overshadows the importance of relics as a guarantee of continuity with the saint's earthly life: the saint's bodily remains often figure less prominently in accounts of posthumous miracles than in, for example, the Frankish materials. The balance here seems more to favor oral aspects of transmission, perhaps of ultimately non-Christian origin, as opposed to literate and more specifically Christian narrative models. The earliest life of the Welsh saint Cadog, written by Lifris at the end of the eleventh century, includes richly circumstantial detail suggestive of a long oral or even folkloric orientation. The account of Cadog's foundation of a monastery includes a cure of blindness. This episode is marked by strong biblical echoes, but it incorporates as well much that recalls secular Celtic narrative. The revelation of the monastery's appropriate site by a large, brilliant white boar on the one hand echoes Virgil's *Aeneid;* but on the other it recalls as well the animals of the otherworld that appear, for example, in the *Mabinogion.* The presence of such motifs in English lives of the West Country, in the traditions of Glastonbury, for example, reflects exchanges between the Welsh and English-Roman traditions.

The rise of the schools and their increasing intellectual leadership at the expense of traditional monastic orders affected hagiography as well as other major genres. Simultaneously, the widening variety of lay piety and its encouragement (and containment) by the mendicant orders meant that literary conventions had to accommodate a new diversity of personal stories. As social pluralism in an increasingly urban culture was countered by more extensive phenomena of social repression, hagiography also upon occasion became a tool of propaganda against marginalized groups. Such deployments of the genre include the legends of child "martyrs" like William of Norwich and Little St. Hugh of Lincoln (not to be confused with the remarkable Bishop Hugh I of Lincoln), whose *vitae* were an effective means of exacerbating anti-Jewish sentiment. The life of William written by Thomas of Monmouth shortly after the boy's death in the mid-twelfth century is one of the earliest literary documents of the charge of ritual murder of Christian children by Jews. Such "blood libel" legends found their way into English literature in the tale of Chaucer's prioress.

We can observe characteristic features of more respectable thirteenth-century *vitae* in the body of verse lives written by the prolific poet Henry of Avranches. Henry dedicated his magnum opus, a version of the life of Francis of Assisi based on Thomas of Celano's first prose life of the saint, to Pope Gregory IX in the early 1230s. The Conventualist wing of the order eventually suppressed Henry's prose model as too open to Spiritualist interpretation. Henry's text celebrates the great early exponent of the new spirituality of everyday life. At the same time, it displays a considerable wealth of classical literary reference. One notes as well passages that deploy recognizably scholastic vocabulary, sometimes to digress on theological matters, sometimes to explain miracles in terms of the new Aristotelian categories. Henry's versification of his prose sources shows none of the anxiety over literary pretentions of earlier verse texts. His prologues characteristically assume the legitimacy of a classicizing and even epic treatment of his subjects; verbal and formal references evoke the most popular of Medieval Latin epics, the *Alexandreis* of Walter of Châtillon.

The spirituality of the laity is also reflected in the lives of women who renounce the social expectations of their stations to live according to a personal spiritual discipline outside the established orders. The life of the Belgian *inclusa* Juetta of Huy by her confessor Hugh of Floreffe presents the story of a young mother who resists familial pressure to marry again after her husband's death. She devotes herself for a time to the care of lepers and is subsequently enclosed. From her cell she makes provision for her three sons; she attracts the attention of a number of followers, to whom she dispenses spiritual advice.

At the same time that lives of recent saints reflect new conditions, the scholastic impulse towards the making of compendia and the practical homiletic needs of preachers contribute to the compilation of large collections of brief *vitae*. These are variously arranged according to the liturgical calendar or some other principle. Among the best known is the *Legenda aurea* of the Dominican James of Voragine (d. 1298), printed in an English version by William Caxton. Its short texts deal mostly with biblical and early saints, incorporating into their legends a variety of fantastic and sometimes charming detail. The *vita* of Martha treats of her postbiblical arrival with Mary and Lazarus in Provence, to which she brings the Gospel. Down the Rhône from Avignon she defeats a man-eating monster, the Tarasque, by displaying the cross and sprinkling the creature with holy water. At the end of her life, she receives a vision of her sister awaiting her in heaven, tells her followers of her coming death, and gives very specific directions for the circumstances surrounding her passage from the world. Other collections focus on saints less universally commemorated. The *Sanctilogium* of John of Tynemouth, with its legends of a great variety of saints of largely English veneration, was compiled in the fourteenth century. Later arranged alphabetically instead of by death date, it was revised by John Capgrave and printed in 1516 with a new title, *Nova legenda Angliae*.

## Modern Scholarship

The study of hagiography has crossed disciplines in complex and productive ways. The research of the Bollandists into the historical authenticity of cults has included the editing of a vast array of texts and the assembly of much hagiological material pertinent to the *vitae*. At the same time, many saints' lives have been investigated in large measure for their bearing on political and social history. Historians have carefully sifted hagiographical materials for their reliability and have honed a sharp awareness of the texts' highly conventional nature. The texts have also provided evidence for intellectual history and reconstructions of contemporary *mentalités*. Both historians and literary scholars have examined the relation between oral and literate modes in the texts. The influence of Latin *vitae* on vernacular versions of the legends has long been a focus of attention for studies based in other medieval languages, as in the case of the relations between Felix of Croyland's life of Guthlac and the Old English poems on the saint in the Exeter Book. Literary studies of hagiography have relatively recently broadened from primarily philological considerations to include a variety of structuralist and poststructuralist approaches. Literary considerations of the Latin texts have often suffered in the presence of sometimes limiting prejudices in favor of the vernaculars. Although some recent work has perpetuated such dismissals of the Latin sources, one also sees in fresh methodologies the opportunity to facilitate more appreciative interpretations.

## Select Bibliography

An indispensable tool for the identification of extant texts associated with the cult of a given saint is the Bollandists' *Bibliotheca hagiographica latina antiquae et mediae aetatis* (hereafter *BHL*), 2 vols. (1898–1901, r1949) and 2 supps. (1911, 1986), which lists surviving *vitae*, as well as miracle collections and accounts of translations, alphabetically by saint [GL1]. On the work of the Bollandists, a small group of Jesuits in Antwerp, Belgium, who were organized by Jean Bolland in the seventeenth century to study and publish the lives of the saints, see D. Knowles, "The Bollandists," in his *Great Historical Enterprises* (1963) 1–32. This work includes accounts of the early history and development not only of the Bollandists' *Acta sanctorum* [*AASS*], but also of the *Monumenta Germaniae Historica* [*MGH*] (pp65–97) and the *Rolls Series* [*RSer*] (pp101–38) [GL2].

On hagiographical manuscripts and their arrangements, see G. Philippart, *Les légendiers latins et autres manuscrits hagiographiques*, TSMAO 24–25 (1977), with a *mise à jour* (1985) [GL3].

A useful dictionary of saints and their cults can be found in the *Bibliotheca sanctorum*, 12 vols. and index (1961–70) [GL4]. Less scholarly and up-to-date but available in English is A. Butler, *Lives of the Saints*, ed., rev., and supplemented by H. Thurstan and D. Attwater, 4 vols. (1956) [GL5]. D. Attwater, *The Penguin Dictionary of Saints*, 2nd ed., rev. and updated by C.R. John (1983), provides brief, ready reference in a single volume [GL6].

Major collections of primary texts are the *PL*, the *AASS*, the *RSer*, and the *MGH* (see [GL2]). Texts in the first two series are sometimes less than satisfactorily edited, and for close scholarly work all four should be used with caution. The *MGH*'s selection and arrangement of material reflect the very specific priorities of nineteenth-century German scholarship, with results that readers with a different focus can sometimes find frustrating. Many texts have appeared in *Analecta Bollandiana* [*AB*], which also includes much important secondary scholarship and an annual *Bulletin des publications hagiographiques* [GL7].

The works cited as examples in the introductory essay above are listed here, in the order of the account, with reference numbers from the *BHL*. The passion of Perpetua and her companions (*BHL* 6633) has been edited by C.I.M.I. Van Beek, *Passio Sanctarum Perpetuae et Felicitatis* (1936) [GL8]. Evagrius's Latin translation of the life of Anthony (*BHL* 609) is found in *PL* 73:115–94 [GL9]; Jerome's life of Malchus (*BHL* 5190) in *PL* 23:55–62 [GL10], and in C.C. Mierow, ed. and tr., *Sancti Eusebii Hieronymi Vita Malchi Monachi Captivi*, in *Classical Essays Presented to James A. Kliest, S.J.*, ed. R.E. Arnold (1946) 31–60 [GL11]; Sulpicius Severus's life of Martin of Tours (*BHL* 5610) in J. Fontaine, ed. and tr., *Vie de Saint Martin*, 3 vols., *SChr* 133–35 (1967–69), v1:248–317 [GL12]; the lives of Radegund by Fortunatus (*BHL* 7048) and Baudonivia (*BHL* 7049) in *MGH.AA* 4.2:38–49 [GL13] and *MGH.SRM* 2:358–95 [GL14], respectively; Drogo of Bergues's life of Oswald (*BHL* 6362) in *AASS.August*, 2:94–103 [GL15].

The anonymous life of Gregory the Great (*BHL* 3637), Felix's life of Guthlac (*BHL* 3723), the anonymous life of Cuthbert (*BHL* 2019) and Bede's prose life (*BHL* 2021), and Stephanus of Ripon's life of Wilfrid (*BHL* 8889) have all been edited by B. Colgrave, *The Earliest Life of Gregory the Great, by an anonymous Monk of Whitby* (1968) [GL16]; *Felix's Life of Saint Guthlac* (1956) [GL17]; *Two Lives of Saint Cuthbert: A Life by an Anonymous Monk of Lindisfarne and Bede's Prose Life* (1940) [GL18]; and *The Life of Bishop Wilfrid by Eddius Stephanus* (1927) [GL19]; all 4 vols. were reprinted by Cambridge University Press in 1985.

Bede's verse life of Cuthbert (*BHL* 2020) has been edited by W. Jaager, *Bedas metrische Vita Sancti Cuthberti* (1935) [GL20].

For Byrhtferth of Ramsey's life of Ecgwin (*BHL* 2432), see T. Wright, ed., *Vitae quorundam Anglo-Saxonum* (1854) 349–96 [GL21]; for his life of Oswald of Worcester (*BHL* 6374): *RSer* 71.1:399–475 [GL22]; for Bede's life of Dunstan (*BHL* 2342): *RSer* 63:3–52 [GL23]; for Frithegod's versification of Eddius (*BHL* 8891): A. Campbell, ed., *Frithegodi monachi breviloquium vitae beati Wilfridi* (1950) [GL24], as well as *RSer* 71.1:105–59 [GL25]; for Abbo of Fleury's life of Edmund (*BHL* 2392): M. Winterbottom, ed., *Three Lives of English Saints*, *TMLT* 1 (1972) 65–87 [GL26].

Goscelin of Canterbury's extensive work can be represented by his *Historia maior*, miracles, and translation of St. Augustine of Canterbury in *AASS.May*, 6:372–440 [GL27].

Osbern's life of Dunstan, miracles of Dunstan, life of Aelfheah, and translation of Aelfheah (*BHL* 2344, 2345, 2518, and 2519) are in *RSer* 63:69–128 [GL28]; *ibid.*, 63:129–61 [GL29]; *AASS.April*, 2:628–40 [GL30]; and *PL* 149:387–94 [GL31], respectively; and the prose life of Birinus (*BHL* 1361) in D. Townsend, ed., "An Eleventh-Century Life of Birinus of Wessex," in *AB* 107 (1989) 129–59 [GL32].

Lifris's life of Cadog (*BHL* 1491) is found in A.W. Wade-Evans, ed., *Vitae sanctorum Britanniae et genealogiae* (1944) 24–141 [GL33]; Thomas of Monmouth's life of William of Norwich (*BHL* 8926) in A. Jessopp and M.R. James, eds., *The Life and Miracles of St. William of Norwich* (1896) [GL34]; Henry of Avranches's versified life of Francis (*BHL* 3101) in *Analecta Franciscana* 10 (1926–41) 405–521 [GL35]; Hugh of Floreffe's life of Juetta of Huy (*BHL* 4620) in *AASS.January*, 2:145–69 [GL36].

For two later medieval legendaries, see J.G.T. Grässe, ed., *Jacobi a Voragine Le-*

*genda aurea vulgo Historia lombardica dicta,* 3rd ed. (1890, r1969) [GL37]; and C. Horstmann, ed., *Nova legenda Anglie,* 2 vols. (1901) [GL38].

The work of the Bollandists is an essential background to an understanding of the development of modern hagiographical studies (see [GL2]). Useful explanations by the Bollandists of their views and procedures, along with accounts of the genre, are found in H. Delahaye, *The Legends of the Saints* (1907, r1961) [GL39]; and R. Aigrain, *L'hagiographie: Ses sources, ses méthodes, son histoire* (1953) [GL40]. Other guides to the genre include R. Grégoire, *Manuale di agiologia* (1987) [GL41], and, most recently, J. Dubois and J.-L. Lemaître, *Sources et méthodes de l'hagiographie médiévale* (1993) [GL42].

T.J. Heffernan provides a more recent general survey in *Sacred Biography: Saints and Their Biographers in the Middle Ages* (1988) [GL43].

W. Berschin gives a comprehensive survey of extant texts in his important work, *Biographie und Epochenstil im lateinischen Mittelalter,* 3 vols. (1986–91) [GL44].

Two useful collections of conference proceedings on a variety of subjects in the field are (a) *L'agiografia latina nei secoli IV–VII: XII Incontro di studiosi dell'antichità cristiana* (5–7 May 1983), with the majority of papers reprinted in the first two fascicles of *Augustinianum* 24 (1984) [GL45]; and (b) *Hagiographie. Cultures et sociétés, IVe–XIIe siècles: Actes du colloque organisé à Nanterre et à Paris* (2–5 May 1979) (1981) [GL46].

Studies of hagiographical writing in specific historical milieux are exemplified by F. Graus, *Volk, Herrscher und Heiliger im Reich der Merowinger* (1965) [GL47]; and more recently by J.M.H. Smith, "Oral and Written: Saints, Miracles, and Relics in Brittany, c. 850–1250," in *Speculum* 65 (1990) 309–43 [GL48] (the latter more historical than textual in focus); T. Head, *Hagiography and the Cult of Saints: The Diocese of Orléans, 800–1200* (1990) [GL49]; and R. Sharpe, *Medieval Irish Saints' Lives: An Introduction to Vitae sanctorum Hiberniae* (1991) [GL50].

The texts' persuasive agendas and manipulations of stylistic expectation are considered, for example, by A. Kleinberg, "Proving Sanctity: Selection and Authentication of Saints in the Later Middle Ages," in *Viator* 20 (1989) 183–206 [GL51]; and by D. Townsend, "Anglo-Latin Hagiography and the Norman Transition," in *Exemplaria* 3 (1991) 385–433 [GL52].

On *opera geminata,* see G.R. Wieland, "*Geminus stylus:* Studies in Anglo-Latin Hagiography," in M.W. Herren, ed., *Insular Latin Studies: Papers on Latin Texts and Manuscripts of the British Isles, 550–1066* (1981) 113–33 [GL53].

A structuralist approach to the lives of the desert Fathers can be found in A.G. Elliott, *Roads to Paradise: Reading the Lives of the Early Saints* (1987) [GL54].

For the interplay of oral and literate expectations in the genre, see, in addition to Smith ([GL48]), E.B. Vitz, "Vie, legende, littérature: Traditions orales et écrites dans les histoires des saints," in *Poétique* 72 (1987) 387–402 [GL55]; and "From the Oral to the Written in Medieval and Renaissance Saints' Lives," in R. Blumenfeld-Kosinski and T. Szell, eds., *Images of Sainthood in Medieval Europe* (1991) 97–114 [GL56].

The relation of Latin texts to derived vernacular versions includes a vast bibliography most easily traced through the tools of the respective national literatures. For a treatment of a specific problem in Old English studies, with some consideration of deconstructionist possibilities, see C. Chase, "Source Study as a Trick with

Mirrors: Annihilation of Meaning in the Old English 'Mary of Egypt,'" in P.E. Szarmach, ed., *Sources of Anglo-Saxon Culture* (1986) 23–33 [GL57].

All these works provide some further secondary bibliography, as does *AB*'s "Bulletin" [GL58]. See as well the bibliographies in S. Boesch Gajano, ed., *Agiografia altomedioevale* (1976) [GL59]; S. Wilson, ed., *Saints and Their Cults: Studies in Religious Sociology, Folklore, and History* (1983) [GL60]; T. Baumeister, *Heiligenverehrung* I," in *RLAC* 14:96–150 [GL61]; and M. Van Uytfanghe, "Heiligungverehrung II," *ibid.*, 150–83 [GL62].

*See also* [BA94], [BA110], [BC47], [BC79], [BD27], [BD29], [BD44], [BD91], [BD95], [BD113], [BD122].

BY JAMES J. MURPHY

Rhetoric studies the uses of purposeful language, preparing a speaker or writer for the creation of future discourse. Writers in ancient Greece, especially Aristotle, laid out sets of principles that would enable a speaker to perform effectively in public situations. By approximately 100 B.C. Hellenistic teachers had codified these principles into an elaborate system that the Romans inherited and transmitted to the Middle Ages.

Two Roman works had special influence on medieval rhetoric: the *De inventione* (c. 87 B.C.) of Marcus Tullius Cicero, and the anonymous *Rhetorica ad Herennium* (c. 80 B.C.), universally ascribed to Cicero during the Middle Ages; the *De inventione* is typically called Cicero's *Rhetorica vetus*, while the *Ad Herennium* is called his *Rhetorica nova*. The six other rhetorical works of Cicero were virtually unknown until the rediscovery of *De oratore* and the others by humanists in the early fifteenth century, though his *Topica* had some medieval circulation through commentaries. Another major Roman work, the *Institutio oratoria* (A.D. 96), of Quintilian shares the same rhetorical system but had little direct influence on medieval rhetorical theory; however, the Roman educational process based on *imitatio* and *progymnasmata* (which Quintilian describes) did survive largely intact throughout the Middle Ages—not because of his book but because of the continuity of teaching methods deeply embedded in European culture through centuries of Roman domination.

The standard Roman rhetorical doctrine is laid out succinctly at the beginning of the *Rhetorica ad Herennium:*

> Oratoris officium est de iis rebus posse dicere quae res ad usum civilem moribus et legibus constitutae sunt, cum adsensione auditorum quoad eius fieri poterit. Tria genera sunt causarum quae recipere debet orator: demonstrativum, deliberativum, iudicale. Demonstrativum est quod tribuitur in alicuius certae personae laudem vel vituperationem. Deliberativum est in consultatione, quod habet in se suasionem et dissuasionem. Iudicale est quod positum est in controversia, et quod habet accusationem aut petitionem cum defensione. [GM34] 1.2

The author then names five parts of the art of rhetoric: *Inventio,* or the discovery of matter; *Dispositio,* or the ordering of parts in an oration; *Elocutio,* or the putting of words to the matter invented and arranged; *Memoria,* or the retention in the mind of things, words, and their order; and *Pronuntiatio,* or delivery through voice, gesture, and facial expression.

Under Arrangement (*Dispositio*) Roman doctrine states that there are six standard parts of the oration itself: *Exordium,* or introduction, rendering the audience attentive, docile, and well-disposed; *Narratio,* or account of the background in a case; *Divisio,* or statement of issues involved and the plan to cover them; *Confirmatio,* or proof of one's own case; *Refutatio* (*Confutatio*), or disproof of an opponent's case; and *Peroratio* (*Conclusio*), or recapitulation with an appeal to emotion.

The Roman tradition includes detailed methods for employing Topics (*Loci*) and Status (*Constitutio causae*) in invention, and for using Figures (*Exornationes*) under the rubric of Style (*Elocutio*). As a matter of fact the *Rhetorica ad Herennium* is the first known treatise to spell out the 64 Figures of Speech (including ten *Tropi*) and Figures of Thought that were to become canonical in the West; book IV containing the figures was frequently circulated in the Middle Ages as a separate publication.

The Romans, then, bequeathed to the Middle Ages a complete system of rhetoric designed primarily for the public speaker. No significantly different Latin rhetorical works appeared between the time of Quintilian and A.D. 1000, with the possible exception of the *De doctrina christiana* of St. Augustine (completed in A.D. 426); even this work, while seeing a new Christian use for the art, accepts the basic Roman concepts of rhetoric. The major encyclopedists (Martianus Capella [fl. after 410], Isidore of Seville [d. 636], and Cassiodorus [d. c. 583]) transmit the basic Roman doctrine with only minor variations, placing rhetoric second in the now common listing of the "Seven Liberal Arts."

Rhetoric in the High Middle Ages—say, the period from 1000 to about 1400— has four cognate tracks. The first of these is the treatment of ancient rhetorical texts, especially those of Cicero; the second is the *ars dictaminis,* the art of applying Ciceronian doctrines to letter writing; the third is the *ars poetriae,* the art of applying rhetoric to the composition of both verse and prose; the fourth is the *ars praedicandi,* or art of preaching, the most eclectic of the rhetorical arts. Each produced large numbers of Latin texts, many of which remain unedited.

**1. Medieval Treatment of Ancient Rhetorical Texts.** Formal commentaries on rhetorical treatises were common in late antiquity. The commentary of Marius Victorinus (fl. mid-fourth century) on Cicero's *De inventione* was cited frequently up to A.D. 1400 and then became a major source for humanist rhetoric as part of a renewed interest in Ciceronian style. Boethius (d. 524/6) wrote a commentary, *In topica Ciceronis,* in addition to his more famous *De topicis differentiis* (*Topica Boetii*), whose fourth book became an important university text from the thirteenth century onwards.

Medieval commentaries on ancient rhetoric are typically commentaries on Cicero—his *De inventione* and *Topica* and the pseudo-Ciceronian *Rhetorica ad Herennium.* Quintilian's *Institutio oratoria* was known only in fragments, and Cicero's other rhetorical works were extremely rare. The best modern guide to medieval commentaries on Cicero's rhetoric is by John Ward, who has published two extensive studies of the numerous works written between the twelfth and the sixteenth centuries [GM45–46]. Major authors are Menegaldus (twelfth century), Thierry of Chartres (fl. second half of the twelfth century), Bartolinus (fourteenth century), and Guarino da Verona (d. 1460), though numerous others are known. Ward has identified more than 500 separate items, ranging from simple glosses to full-scale commentaries that quote each line and then add comments. Typically there is great concern for definition. Thierry of Chartres's introduction outlines his concerns:

> Circa artem rhetoricam decem consideranda sunt: quid sit genus ipsius artis, quid ipsa ars sit, quae eius materia, quod officium, quis finis, quae partes, quae species, quod instrumentum, quis artifex, quare rhetorica vocetur. [GM40] p49

In general the commentaries deal with rhetoric as theory, remaining at an abstract level even at the end of the Middle Ages when humanist writers enter the field. (The practical or applied rhetoric of the Middle Ages lay in the genres of the *ars dictaminis, ars poetriae,* or *ars praedicandi,* whereas the *ars arengandi* [art of pleading] of authors like Jacques de Dinant [mid- to late thirteenth century] comes from a reworking of ideas from the *Rhetorica ad Herennium* rather than from any advances gleaned from the commentative movement.) Nevertheless the practice of commentation—usually a sign of school use of a text—continued throughout the medieval period and was to become an important tool of humanist study at the end of the Middle Ages.

Aristotle's one work on rhetoric had a curious medieval history. His *Rhetorica* was translated into Latin three times during the Middle Ages, the most popular version being that of William of Moerbeke (c. 1280). It survives in 97 manuscripts, but was used as a moral treatise rather than a rhetorical one. Giles of Rome wrote a full commentary about 1316, using the Moerbeke text.

The study of ancient rhetoric continued throughout the Middle Ages, then, as a field separate from the three applied rhetorical arts that drew upon that theory.

**2. Ars Dictaminis.** Roman/Ciceronian rhetoric was applied most directly when the principles of oration parts were appropriated to produce a standardized format for writing formal letters. Ancient rhetorical theory was intended to apply to all forms of language use, and the Roman educational system used writing as well as speaking to prepare young men for any conceivable language situation—to provide them, as Quintilian says, with *copia rerum ac verborum* (*Inst.* 10.1.5). The aim was *facilitas,* the capacity to improvise language in any situation. An educated Roman could then with equal ease prepare an oration, compose a history, or write a letter (*epistola*) to a friend.

The exigencies of postbarbarian Europe made this *facilitas* less and less possible. One interim solution to widespread illiteracy in written Latin was the development of *formulae* that in effect offered preset communications—form letters, contracts, indulgences, and the like—to which proper names could be added as needed; the seventh-century *Marculfi formulae,* for example, presented 109 formulas, 57 dealing with royal acts and 52 with private acts.

Although William Patt [GM44] and Carol Lanham [GM43] have argued that a stylized format for letters began to emerge in Europe prior to A.D. 1000, the first theoretical statement about what came to be called "the approved format" appeared in the writings of Alberic of Monte Cassino about A.D. 1087. His *Dictaminum radii* and *Breviarium de dictamine* laid the groundwork for the application of rhetoric to writing; he addresses himself to a *lector* rather than a hearer and devotes considerable space to the *salutatio* of a writing (rather than an *exordium*), based on such considerations as "the person to whom and the person from whom it is sent."

After Alberic the *ars dictaminis* developed rapidly in Bologna. The major early works were the *Praecepta dictaminum* (1111–18) of Adalbert of Samaria, the *Rationes dictandi prosaice* (1119–24) of Hugh of Bologna, and the anonymous *Rationes dictandi* (1135) and *Praecepta prosaici dictaminis secundum Tullium* (1138–52). Some of these were accompanied by sets of model letters (*dictamina*)—a feature to become common in the genre. Separate collections of model letters also appeared, one of the most famous being the *Aurea gemma* (1119) of Henricus Francigena, written at Pavia.

Bolognese writers dominated the early stages of the *ars dictaminis*, and even in the following century the satirical *La bataille des VII arts* of Henri d'Andeli cites "The Lombard Lady Rhetoric" (*Li Lombart dame Rectorique*). Eventually other Italian cities like Florence had teaching centers with such writers as Bene of Florence, and by the fourteenth century the *ars dictaminis* had become a core subject in Italian schools. As Paul Kristeller [GM42] and Ronald Witt [GM48] have pointed out, this language-based curriculum was to become a launching place for Italian humanism.

The typical manual uses the term *dictamen* to denote all writing, with letters (*epistolae*) treated as prose rather than rhythmical or metrical productions.

More than 300 separate dictaminal manuals have survived, of which fewer than a dozen have been edited. Only one has been translated into English. They are highly standardized, following what the Anonymous of Bologna calls "the approved format" of a five-part letter based on the Roman/Ciceronian plan for a six-part oration. A tabular comparison shows the relation of the two plans:

| CICERONIAN PARTS | BOLOGNESE FORMAT |
| --- | --- |
| *Exordium* | *Salutatio*, or greeting to addressee |
| | *Captatio benevolentiae*, or introduction |
| *Narratio* | *Narratio*, or narration of circumstances leading to a petition |
| *Divisio* | [omitted in format] |
| *Confirmatio* | *Petitio*, or presentation of request |
| *Refutatio* | [omitted in format] |
| *Peroratio* | *Conclusio*, or final part |

What the medieval *ars dictaminis* does, then, is to divide the three functions of the Roman *exordium* into two segments by using the letter's *salutatio* to gain the addressee's "attention" and the *captatio benevolentiae* to serve the other two functions of making the audience "docile and well-disposed." Far and away the largest section of any manual is the one dealing with the *salutatio*, for here is treated the language used to identify the complex feudal relations between equals, superiors, and inferiors. Typically this section will occupy up to 60 percent of a manual, with extensive examples; Hugh of Bologna's *Rationes dictandi prosaice*, for example, treats 16 types of salutations. These carefully wrought distinctions provide an interesting index to relationships in a feudal society.

Naturally there are some differences in emphasis, and many writers point out ways of varying the format to suit different occasions. Moreover, French dictaminal authors tend to include grammatical concerns and even literary examples not used by their Italian colleagues. Some writers, both French and Italian, suggested using *proverbia* at the conclusion of the *captatio benevolentiae,* apparently to enhance the writer's reputation for learning.

The rigidity of the five-part letter format, combined with the homogeneity of model letters, resulted in the rise of a separate *ars notaria* by the end of the twelfth century. This art was concerned with the physical rather than the rhetorical form of documents like letters and contracts; some major authors were Rainerius of Perugia (fl. 1220) and Rolandinus Passagerius (d. 1300), and there was a guild of notaries at Bologna by 1304. In a sense the rise of the *ars notaria* was due to some failures of the dictaminal movement.

Finally, two other characteristics of the *ars dictaminis* may be noted. The first is that many treatises include a discussion of the *rhythmical cursus* (see ch. CF); John of Gaeta (onetime pupil of Alberic of Monte Cassino), who later became Pope Gelasius II (1118–19), is often cited as a major influence in introducing the *cursus* into the papal chancery and thus associating it with formal letter writing throughout Europe. A second characteristic is a paleographical one: since the *artes* are usually written by professional letter writers for other professional letter writers, the manuscript hands are heavily abbreviated and often hurried, making them one of the most difficult kinds of scripts for the modern reader.

3. **Ars Versificandi et Prosandi.** The third medieval form of rhetoric was firmly fixed in the curriculum of the schools, an integral part of the teaching of grammar and indebted both to ancient rhetorical doctrines and to the pedagogical processes of *imitatio* and *progymnasmata* (*praeexercitamenta*) inherited from Roman education. All the writers in this genre were schoolmasters.

Unlike the *ars dictaminis,* which rapidly acquired a standard format and a common vocabulary, the works in this genre are identified more by shared sources and objectives than by similarities of title or organization. All profess to lay down principles and procedures for writing, and most argue that they deal with both verse and prose. Insofar as the authors discuss future composition, just as ancient rhetoric dealt with future speaking, they have often been termed "rhetoricians" by modern critics. The authors are northern European, mostly French. Their works are preceptive rather than analytical, giving practical advice to the would-be writer.

Six major works of this type appeared from A.D. 1170 to a little before 1280. The earliest was the *Ars versificatoria* (c. 1175) of Matthew of Vendôme, followed about 1200 by the most popular of the treatises, the hexameter *Poetria nova* of Geoffrey of Vinsauf; he was also the author of the prose work *Documentum de modo et arte dictandi et versificandi,* which survives in two versions, one longer (and presumably later) than the other. Gervase of Melkley published his *Ars versificaria* about 1215. The most ambitious was John of Garland's *De arte prosayca, metrica, et rithmica* (after 1220), which purported to lay down precepts for all types of composition. The final text, by Evrard of Bremen, is the *Laborintus* (before 1280), which paints a gloomy picture of the labor demanded of the teacher. All except the "long" *Documentum* have been published in modern editions, and there are translations available of all but this text and that of Eberhard.

Geoffrey of Vinsauf's *Poetria nova* has received the greatest scholarly attention, partly because it survives in 200 manuscripts (some with commentaries) and partly because it is the most "rhetorical" of the group. It is divided into seven sections paralleling the five Roman "parts of rhetoric"— Invention, Arrangement, Style, Memory, and Delivery. Geoffrey begins by stressing the need for planning and concludes with remarks on the value of oral delivery of the completed poem. His frequent use of verse examples undoubtedly helped make the book a useful teaching tool for other masters. For example, in a literary tour de force, Geoffrey presents a coherent poem that consists of his own examples for the 64 tropes and figures from the *Rhetorica ad Herennium,* used in the order in which these figures appear in that text.

John of Garland's *De arte prosayca, metrica, et rithmica* is also divided into seven sections: invention (including advice from both Horace and Cicero), methods of selecting material, arrangement and ornamenting of material (by use of tropes and figures), the parts of a letter and the vices to be avoided in letter writing, amplification and abbreviation of material, examples of letters, and examples of metrical and rythmical compositions (e.g. liturgical hymns). Although he does not succeed in his grand plan to identify a metagenre underlying all writing, his work is an interesting example of a grammarian's seeking to go beyond the mere rules inherited from Donatus and Priscian. He is, like Vinsauf and the others, looking to future composition.

The works of Gervase of Melkley, Evrard of Bremen, and Matthew of Vendôme are clearly in the same tradition but are less sharply organized. In terms of new treatises the movement fades out in the latter half of the thirteenth century, but this may have been due to the preemptive success of Vinsauf's *Poetria nova* as a teaching tool. All the evidence indicates that methods of elementary language instruction remained substantially unchanged in Europe throughout the Middle Ages and indeed received a conceptual boost in the fifteenth century with the rediscovery of Quintilian's *Institutio oratoria* by Poggio Bracciolini. The centuries-long popularity of Vinsauf's work is a further indication of this continuity in educational methods.

**4. Ars Praedicandi.** The Christian Church took nearly twelve centuries to develop a rhetorical form unique to its preaching mission. From its earliest days the Church based a significant part of its liturgy, or worship service, on a practice inherited from Judaism—that is, the oral, public reading of Scripture followed by commentary on the text that was read. Moreover, Jesus Christ had given the Church an evangelizing ("apostolic") mission of spreading his message to all humanity (see *Mt* 28:19–20); this was confirmed in the Nicene Creed, which defined the Church as "one, holy, catholic, and apostolic."

Under these circumstances it might have been expected that some peculiarly Christian form of rhetoric would have been developed at an early stage in the Church's development. This did not occur. Instead, the basic Roman tradition of rhetoric seems to have been regarded as sufficient, and indeed the only major work on preaching theory before A.D. 1200 (Augustine's *De doctrina christiana,* completed in A.D. 426) does little more than argue for the value of Cicero's rhetoric in preaching.

This situation changed shortly after 1200, probably as a result of studies in French schools about the relations among grammar, dialectic, and rhetoric during the so-called renaissance of the twelfth century. There is a hint of the change in Alan of Lille's *De arte praedicandi* (1198) and Alexander of Ashby's *De modo praedicandi* (c. 1205), but the landmark treatise establishing the new genre was the *Summa de arte praedicandi* of Thomas Chobham ("Thomas of Salisbury"), written sometime between 1210 and 1221.

Chobham's work is divided into two sections: the longer first section treats the *materia* of preaching—vices and virtues, the seven deadly sins, and the like—and the second discusses what Thomas calls "those things necessary to be considered in artistic preaching." Chobham first distinguishes preaching from secular oratory, from drama, from fictional poetry, and from dialectical exposition. He then lays out a theoretical structure that was to become the core of more than 300 *artes praedicandi* over the next five centuries; these treatises are so uniform in doctrine that they can truly be said to belong to a separate genre. The three key elements are (1) oral reading of a "theme" (*thema*) or scriptural excerpt; (2) division (*divisio*) of the theme, typically into three, or sets of threes; (3) amplification (*amplificatio, prosecutio, dilatatio, confirmatio*) of each of the parts resulting from the division(s).

This represents a radical departure from Roman rhetorical principles. The purpose is no longer persuasion through a calculated sequence of linear argumentative steps. Rather, the *ars praedicandi* lays out a pyramid whose base is a potentially infinite number of items, each of which is to be supported individually ("amplified") in a wide variety of ways. No progression of ideas is intended; each divided part is offered as a separate micro-idea relating to the *thema*.

As a practical matter the actual sermon structure came to have six (sometimes seven) parts to deal with the exigencies of preaching within the liturgical setting: (1) opening prayer; (2) introduction of the theme (*antethema, prothema*); (3) *thema*; (4) *divisio*, or statement of parts (*membra*) to be discussed; (5) *subdivisio* or division of divisions; (6) *amplificatio membrorum*; and (7) final prayer. The basic structure nevertheless remains Theme, Division, Amplification.

One virtue of this method is that it solves a preaching problem identified as early as the lifetime of Gregory the Great (540–604)—that is, that any audience/congregation is composed of people with greatly varying backgrounds, knowledge, and intellectual capabilities. The thematic sermon enables the preacher to employ an equally wide range of "modes" of support, thus speaking within a few minutes to a great variety of minds and souls even if only one or two *membra* actually affect a given person in the congregation. To accomplish this, of course, the preacher needs to know—or know how to find—varied means of amplification.

A considerable apparatus grew up around the *ars praedicandi* to fill this need: alphabetical concordances to Scripture to locate parallel passages, collections of sermon outlines as well as sermon copies, collections of *distinctiones*, anthologies of scriptural passages grouped by subject, and the like. Richard of Thetford (fl. c. 1245) composed a widely circulated treatise dealing solely with modes of amplification; his *Ars dilatandi sermones* proposes eight modes: (1) employing a locution in place of a name, as in defining, describing, interpreting, or any other kind of exposition; (2) dividing; (3) reasoning, including syllogism, induction, example, or enthymeme; (4) using concordant authorities; (5) etymology; (6) proposing metaphors and showing their aptness for instruction; (7) the "four senses of interpretation" (historical or literal, allegorical, tropological, and anagogical); and (8) cause and effect. When Robert of Basevorn composed his *Forma praedicandi* at Oxford in 1322, he was able to list these as "the eight main species" of amplification, before proceeding to treat another 25 of his own; one indication of the complexity of his discussion is that he lists the 64 tropes and figures of the *Rhetorica ad Herennium* as merely one of three subdivisions under "coloration."

Another mode of amplification, the narrative *exemplum* (see ch. GH), also led to the creation of collections whose impact on medieval culture is still to be assessed completely. A famous one was that of Jacques de Vitry (c. 1160/70–1240), which added moral interpretations to each tale to assist the preacher in making a point. Franciscan preachers were especially known for their use of *exempla*.

The medieval *ars praedicandi* thus presented both a new approach to the preaching needs of the Church and a new theoretical answer to the general problem of varied audiences. Its insatiable demand for means of amplification produced large numbers of ancillary treatises that undoubtedly had an effect on literature in all languages, including Latin.

The great majority of the *artes praedicandi* remain unedited, and very few have been translated (e.g. Robert of Basevorn and Henry of Hesse [d. 1397]).

## Select Bibliography

### Histories and Bibliographies

*MEL* [GM1].

J.J. Murphy, *RMA:* this general survey is also available in Spanish and Italian editions [GM2].

J.J. Murphy, ed., *Medieval Rhetoric: A Select Bibliography,* 2nd ed. (1989) [GM3].

E.J. Polak, *Medieval and Renaissance Letter Treatises and Form Letters: A Census of Manuscripts Found in Eastern Europe and the former U.S.S.R.* (1993); id., *Medieval . . . Letter Treatises . . . Found in Part of Western Europe, Japan, and the United States of America* (1994) [GM4].

F.J. Worstbrock, M. Klaes, and J. Lütten, *Repertorium der artes dictandi des Mittelalters,* pt1: *Von den Anfängen bis um 1200* (1992) [GM5].

For short summaries see J.J. Murphy, "Western Rhetoric," in *DMA* v10:351–64 [GM6]; and J.J. Murphy and M. Camargo, "The Middle Ages," in *The Present State of Scholarship in Historical and Contemporary Rhetoric,* ed. W.B. Horner, rev. ed. (1990) 45–83 [GM7].

### Primary Works, Including Translations

#### (a) Collections

M. Camargo, *Medieval Rhetorics of Prose Composition: Five English Artes dictandi and Their Tradition* (1995): the writers are "Peter of Blois," John of Briggis, Thomas Merke, Thomas Sampson, and the anonymous author of *Regina sedens Rhetorica* [GM8].

T.-M. Charland, ed., *Artes praedicandi: Contribution à l'histoire de la rhétorique au moyen âge* (1936) [GM9].

E. Faral, *AP* [GM10]: see also [GM21], [GM22], and [GM33].

C. Halm, ed., *Rhetores latini minores* (1863, r1964) [GM11].

J.J. Murphy, ed., *Three Medieval Rhetorical Arts* (1971): includes translations of typical texts from each of the three medieval rhetorical genres, i.e. Anonymous of Bologna, *The Principles of Letter-Writing* (*Rationes dictandi*) [see GM19]; Geoffrey of Vinsauf, *The New Poetics* (*Poetria nova*) [see GM22]; and Robert of Basevorn, *The Form of Preaching* (*Forma praedicandi*) [see GM39] [GM12].

L. Rockinger, ed., *Briefsteller und Formelbücher des eilften bis vierzehnten Jahrhunderts*, 2 vols. with continuous pagination (1863–64, r1961) [GM13]: see also [GM16], [GM19], and [GM28].

## (b) Individual Authors and Texts (very selective)

Adalbert of Samaria, *Praecepta dictaminum*, ed. F.-J. Schmale, in *MGH.Quellen zur Geistesgeschichte des Mittelalters* 3 (1961) [GM14].

Alan of Lille, *Summa de arte praedicatoria*, in *PL* 210:109–98; tr. G.R. Evans (1981) [GM15].

Alberic of Monte Cassino, *Breviarium de dictamine*, ed. L. Rockinger (see [GM13] 29–46) [GM16].

Alberic of Monte Cassino, *Dictaminum radii* [*Flores rhetorici*], ed. M. Inguanez and H.M. Willard, in *MiscC* 14 (1938) [GM17].

Anonymous, *Praecepta prosaici dictaminis secundum Tullium*, ed. F.-J. Schmale (1950) [GM18].

Anonymous of Bologna, *Rationes dictandi* (*Principles of Letter-Writing*), ed. L. Rockinger (see [GM13] 9–28); tr. J.J. Murphy (see [GM12] 5–25) [GM19].

Bene of Florence, *Candelabrum*, ed. G.C. Alessio (1983) [GM20].

Evrard of Bremen, *Laborintus*, ed. E. Faral (see [GM10] 336–77); tr. E. Carlson (M.A. thesis, Cornell University, 1930) [GM21].

Geoffrey of Vinsauf, *Poetria nova*, ed. E. Faral (see [GM10] 194–262); tr. M. Nims (1967); tr. E. Gallo (1971); tr. J.B. Kopp (see [GM12] pp29–108) [GM22].

Geoffrey of Vinsauf, *Documentum de modo et arte dictandi et versificandi*, ed. E. Faral (see [GM10] 263–320); tr. R.P. Parr, *Instruction in the Method and Art of Speaking and Versifying* (1968) [GM23].

Gervase of Melkley, *Ars poetica*, ed. H.-J. Gräbener, Forschungen zur romanischen Philologie 17 (1965); tr. C. Giles (Ph.D diss., Rutgers University, 1973) [GM24].

Giles of Rome (Aegidius Romanus), *Commentaria in Rhetoricam Aristotelis*, ed. by A. Achillinus (Venice 1515, r1968): includes William of Moerbeke's translation of the *Rhetorica* with Giles's commentary [GM25].

Henry d'Andeli, *The Battle of the Seven Arts, a French Poem by Henri d'Andeli* . . . (pt1 of *Two Medieval Satires on the University of Paris*), ed. and tr. L.J. Paetow, in *Memoirs of the University of California*, v4.1 (1914, r1927) [GM26].

Henry of Hesse (Henry of Langenstein), *De arte praedicandi*, ed. H. Caplan, in *PMLA* 48 (1933) 340–61 [GM27].

Hugh of Bologna, *Rationes dictandi prosaice*, ed. L. Rockinger (see [GM13] 53–94 [GM28].

Jacques de Dinant, *Ars arengandi*, ed. A. Wilmart, in *Analecta reginensia* (1933) 113–51 [GM29].

Jacques de Vitry, ed. T.F. Crane, in *The Exempla or Illustrative Stories from the Sermones vulgares of Jacques de Vitry* (1890, r1971) [GM30].

John of Garland, *De arte prosayca, metrica, et rithmica*, ed. and tr. T. Lawler, in *Parisiana Poetria of John of Garland* (1974) [GM31].

*Marculfi formulae*, ed. K. Zeumer, in *MGH.Formulae Merowingici et Karolini aevi* (1882–86, r1963) 32–106 [GM32].

Matthew of Vendôme, *Ars versificatoria*, ed. E. Faral (see [GM10] pp106–93); tr. A. Galyon (1980); tr. R.P. Parr (1981) [GM33].

[Pseudo-Cicero], *Rhetorica ad Herennium,* ed. and tr. H. Caplan (1954) [GM34].

Quintilian, *Institutio oratoria,* ed. and tr. H.E. Butler, 4 vols. (1953) [GM35].

Rainerius of Perugia, *Ars notariae,* ed. L. Wahrmund, *Quellen zur Geschichte des römisch-kanonischen Processes im Mittelalter* 3.2 (1917) [GM36].

Ranulph Higden, *Ars componendi sermones,* ed. M. Jennings (1991) [GM37].

Richard of Thetford, *Ars dilatandi sermones,* published as pt3 of Bonaventure, *Ars concionandi,* in *Opera omnia* (1882–1902) 9:16–21; tr. H. Hazel (Ph.D. diss., Washington State University, 1972) [GM38].

Robert of Basevorn, *Forma praedicandi,* ed. T.-M. Charland [GM9]; tr. L. Krul (see [GM12] 109–215) [GM39].

Thierry of Chartres, ed. K.M. Fredborg, in *The Latin Rhetorical Commentaries by Thierry of Chartres* (1988) [GM40].

Thomas de Chobham (Thomas of Salisbury), *SAP* [GM41].

## Studies

P.O. Kristeller, "Philosophy and Rhetoric from Antiquity to the Renaissance," in *id., Renaissance Thought and Its Sources,* ed. M. Mooney (1979), pt5 [GM42].

C.D. Lanham, *SF* [GM43].

W.D. Patt, "The Early 'Ars dictaminis' as Response to a Changing Society," in *Viator* 9 (1978) 133–35 [GM44].

J.O. Ward, "From Antiquity to the Renaissance: Glosses and Commentaries on Cicero's *Rhetorica,*" in *Medieval Eloquence: Studies in the Theory and Practice of Medieval Rhetoric,* ed. J.J. Murphy (1978) 25–67 [GM45].

J.O. Ward, "Renaissance Commentators on Ciceronian Rhetoric," in *Renaissance Eloquence: Studies in the Theory and Practice of Renaissance Rhetoric,* ed. J.J. Murphy (1983) 126–73 [GM46].

J.O. Ward, "Rhetoric and the Art of Dictamen," in *CIVICIMA* 3:20–61: this includes seven pages of tables of rhetorical nomenclature from Cicero, Aristotle, and medieval commentators; the text discusses commentaries and education as well as *dictamen* [GM47].

R. Witt, "Medieval 'Ars dictaminis' and the Beginnings of Humanism: A New Construction of the Problem," in *RQ* 35 (1982) 1–35 [GM48].

*See also* [BA85], [BA87], [BA113], [BA140].

# GN • HISTORIOGRAPHY

BY ROGER RAY

In the Middle Ages the word *historia* was applied to parts or all of the Bible, the first or grammatical sense of the biblical text, a section of the Divine Office, versified offices, statements made in court, proceedings of secular and ecclesiastical councils, and several genres discussed elsewhere in this volume (epic, secular biography, florilegia, encyclopedias, and hagiography), besides the books to be considered here. The following pages will be limited to Latin prose narratives that claim or seem to treat real events of primarily nonsaintly experience over some stretch of time. Often they display somewhere, as if to identify their genre, one or more terms like *chronicon, annales, historia,* or *gesta*. One should recognize, however, that in the Middle Ages far more than these books was taken to be history. Indeed when the typical medieval *historicus* or *historiographus* went to work, he was likely to write not chronicles but saints' lives, the most numerous and beloved form of newly written *historia*. In the medieval period "historiography" was a vast field of literature, but here we will keep strictly to those books that since the nineteenth century have been discussed together because from them we have taken the main lines of our medieval history.

These works include accounts of the barbarian peoples, a steady stream of more or less literary or laconic chronicles and annals, many monastic local and regional chronicles, royal and episcopal histories, Crusade chronicles, a few world chronicles, and a small deposit of urban histories. With but rare exceptions they were written by churchmen, mainly monks, many of them anonymous. The cloister was the great institutional sponsor of historical writing and reading. At the heart of its daily liturgical piety was a highly charged *historia,* the story of salvation; it conferred meaning on all of history and sanctioned the writing of new books about the past, even works that attempted to carry forward the *series temporum* from the creation or Christ onwards. The monastic school, refectory, and cult, especially the *lectio divina,* provided the most typical context for the reading of history, and the abbey libraries were the main repositories of historical works, including pagan titles. Monks were recruited from the free lay and clerical classes, the habitual subject matter of their new histories. Monastic hospitality and other incidents of landholding often provided windows on the world, but only seldom were monastic historians permitted to travel in the interests of a writing project. Bound by irrevocable vows to the cloister, they usually had no choice but to gather materials from other works, and so compilation and rewriting are much more characteristic of medieval historiography than of its ancient precursor. Monasteries had the patronage and resources to support the production of new books, which could be extremely expensive. At any rate, few monks wrote the history of anything but the saints, although in sheer numbers they nonetheless outstripped by far the secular clergy and laymen who practiced the art. Some secular clergy, like Gregory of Tours (d. 594) and John of Salisbury (d. 1180), created remarkable books of history, but throughout the Middle Ages the burden of historiography was borne by the regulars. Thus the great expanse of this literature reflects the religious and communal interests of the abbeys, and for this reason, too, medieval chroniclers seem a world apart from Greco-Roman historians.

If one turns to the question of genre, however, a powerful ancient legacy appears. Medieval historians continued to use classical terms like *annales, chronicon,* and *historia* as if they were the language of genre, but research has shown that in the Latin historiographical tradition the discussion of these and other apparently basic generic words was inconsistent, sometimes contradictory or even confused, and in any case rare. It is more helpful to look not at the few who tried to define them in theory but at the many who used them in practice. There one sees that among even the most learned of historians they were virtually interchangeable, all synonyms referring generally to narratives of real events over time. In the locus classicus of Hellenistic historiographical theory Cicero says (*Orat.* 2.35ff.) that historical writing has no separate rules of its own. It takes its foundational precepts from rhetoric, especially the theory of invention (*inventio*). These were indeed the only available principles for the credible representation of the past, and the Middle Ages created no alternative to them. First among them was that the historian, like the forensic orator, takes *veritas* to be his special subject matter. This truth is only vaguely analogous to our modern notion of historiographical objectivity. Ancient and medieval historians never tired of saying that they would write the truth without flattery or malice, but this left them free to roam in the broad region that separates these extremes of attitude. *Veritas* meant real events, as opposed to events that sprang from sheer imagination. As Isidore of Seville (d. 636) taught (*Etym.* 1.44.5), the historian narrates *res verae,* whereas other narrators, like the fabulist, have other subject matters. Yet classical and medieval historians took for granted that *veritas* embraced both the real and the verisimilar, and that the final judge of these was not the historian himself but the anticipated audience. If in the narrative the readers saw *veritas,* it made no difference whether the material rested on real events or just on plausible grounds. In medieval culture the Bible inculcated a vision of reality that intermingled divine and human agendas and denied to historians a strictly secular measure of all things. In the historian's notion of what happens *in veritate,* the vertical dimension of God's relationship with men and women competed with the horizontal plane of human interactions. The wonders of saints were as real as the more prosaic doings of ordinary folk. In fact some writers complained that in their age there were too few saintly marvels, as if other forms of *veritas* were second-rate. The feats of the saints were the favorite form of *res verae,* but the checkered deeds of other people were the usual stuff of what we here call medieval historiography.

If *veritas* was the distinctive subject matter of history, the goal of the genre was to affect the reader. Thus, as in forensic oratory, the recounting of real events served some persuasive end. The historian wrote to convince his reader that his praise or blame of featured people imparted instruction about the proper conduct of life. History was written primarily to teach by example, and historians began with rhetorical goals and then told their stories to reach them. Among medieval historians rhetorical prose varies widely from simple paratactical language, in which the usual conjunction is *and,* to complex hypotactical narrative, in which subordinate clauses develop causal and temporal relationships between choices and events. There was more of the former than the latter. To hear Cicero tell it, the same was true in antiquity. Once he complains (*Orat.* 2.54) that among historians there are too many mere narrators (*tantummodo narratores*) and too few *exornatores rerum,* writers who adorn events to some social benefit. In the twelfth century Gervase, a monk of Christ Church Canterbury, lamented the opposite, that many historians commit the sin of literary pride, while not enough stick to a humble language more friendly to moral truth. The former he calls *historici;* the latter, *cronici* (*Cronica, RSer* 73, v1:87–88). He was right to say that the Middle Ages certainly had its share of *historici,* persons who tried to write in the high tradition of rhetorical historiography. Yet he certainly meant to affirm that the *chronici* also wrote to teach by example. He was speaking out of the piety of the Christian *sermo humilis.* The Latin Church fathers, mainly Augustine (d. 430), taught the Middle Ages that the Gospels had turned the ancient theory of style levels (*genera dicendi:* simple, moderate, sublime) on its head. The Evangelists were said to have related sublime truth not in the high style but in lowly words reserved usually for the reporting of (say) business matters. This was a doctrine with a great future in medieval cloisters. Even the plainest of the anonymous monastic annalists thought that their bare-bones narratives of disasters, bloodshed, or mere oddities would suggest to the reader at least the mystery and power of divine providence. Gervase and many others believed that through simple words moral messages and theological intimations were supposed to shine. Thus theology charged rhetorical historiography with new potential: now the *tantummodo narratores* were outfitted to teach in ways that would have been incomprehensible to Cicero. Yet, to Gervase's grief, many monastic historians belonged among the medieval *exornatores rerum. Veritas* often came decked out in artful words more pagan than Christian in origin. At any rate, no medieval historian wrote simply to record events. In the rhetorical tradition all wrote to influence in some way the thought and behavior of their audience. *Veritas* was therefore unequally yoked to rhetorical purpose, and in the development of it one was likely to write more or less, perhaps even something other, than what real life itself would seem to warrant.

On rhetorical terms, moreover, any res gestae could be retold variously to suit changing rhetorical purposes. In medieval culture the great example of this rhetorical retelling was of course the four Gospels. The biblical commentators taught that the Gospels were the same because all alike reflected one *veritas,* but different because each Evangelist had his own didactic intention. It was accordingly taken for granted that other narrators might disagree in details while recounting to differing ends the same actual events. Several famous medieval developments were retold in varying forms and particulars, but the most telling and striking case of this rewriting is the Norman Conquest of England. It was narrated again and again for decades, and several times by authors who worked from previous written acounts. For example, Orderic Vitalis (d. c. 1142) wrote his version from the earlier (1070s) narrative of William of Poitiers (d. c. 1087/1101), and even while largely copying his source verbatim reinflected the story to give it a very new tone and message. William was no longer an epic hero but a flawed and sometimes frustrated sovereign. The astonishing artistic *historia,* the Bayeux Tapestry, may also have rested on William of Poitiers's account, but here again the point of the story is brand new. Meanwhile, no one seems to have complained that the various versions of the Conquest were in disagreement about the facts. The prevailing assumption was that historians were authorized by genre to reinvent *veritas* in light of worthy new applications. The example of the Gospels would have made it heresy to think anything else. Rhetorical inventional premises were imbedded deeply in medieval culture.

They gave historians a method of gathering the materials of narrative. It was not similar to our method of critical inquiry and empirical validation. It was a method of finding. One was supposed to look to what the classical rhetors called inartificial and artificial stockpiles. Inartificial contents came from various *données*. Mainstays among them were oral testimony and previously written narratives, but there were also letters, wills, charters, and other documents. These were not always, or even very often, extensive. Indeed it has often been said that the medieval historian worked typically with a dearth of information. Yet many works are full and detailed. What made at least part of the difference was artificial contents, narrative materials that sprang from imagination controlled by the rule of versimilitude. Once one had gathered the *données*, one was expected to amplify them by looking about in thought for things that adhered credibly to them and gave point and appeal. These were often found by contemplating the usual conditions of human experience, what the rhetors and grammarians called *circumstantiae*: who, what, where, when, why, how, wherewithal. To elaborate these one needed only to stay within the limits of what the anticipated audience was prepared to believe about real events, *veritas*. So long as invented details were credible and served one's rhetorical purpose, nothing else mattered. Among the narrators of the Norman Conquest Harold Godwinson's famous oath to Duke William is said to have occurred at no less than three different places, but this did not become problematical to readers until the nineteenth century. If the place was suitable to the action and otherwise plausible, medieval readers would have raised no question unless they had independent knowledge of the truth.

In medieval culture the liturgical year imparted enormous interest in the calendar, and the triumph in medieval historiography of the *annus Domini* was a major contribution to the history of historical writing. Yet dates were never much of a weapon in the arsenal of rhetorical historiography. Whether the time was right was more important by far than what the time actually was. Thus dates easily gave way to temporal references like "after this," even in the *Historia ecclesiastica* of Bede (d. 735), who wrote the standard medieval textbook on reckoning time. A favorite form of rhetorical amplification was direct discourse, and here again verisimilitude ruled. There was no search for transcripts or notes. All that was needed were words that the audience would recognize as likely to have been said by such a person on such an occasion. Within these limits the stereotyping of kings, princes, and other sorts of history makers was widely practiced in both classical and medieval historiography. In all, artificial contents were ready to hand, and in antiquity and the Middle Ages they freed the historian from the strictures of scarce information and permitted him to make his case in a full field of verisimilar narrative.

It might seem that the classical and Christian resources of medieval historiography jostled uneasily alongside each other. Once one comes to terms, however, with the basically rhetorical nature of this literature, it becomes clear that the classical subsumed the biblical. For medieval historians the Bible was a vast *locus communis*, an immense storehouse of contents for winning discourse about human affairs. Monastic authors, from the unremitting practice of the daily *horarium*, often knew by heart long stretches of the Bible, especially the Gospels and the Psalms. Biblical material was therefore on the tip of the tongue, and it suffused monastic historiography. It was used typically to capture the goodwill of the reader by appealing to *ethos,* the character of the historian. It was more frequently employed to evoke *pathos,* the emotions of the reader, in the face of either saintliness and miracles or sin, judgment, and retribution. The exegetes, especially Jerome and Augustine, helped the historians to see that the Bible suggests not only the meaning of history (redemption) but also its orderly structure. The six days of creation in *Genesis,* ch. 1, were thought to contain figuratively the six ages of the world, five from Adam to Christ, the sixth from Christ to the present and beyond to the end of time. The exegetes also taught that corresponding to these ages of the world were six ages of mankind, from infancy to senility. Few were inclined to write about the decrepitude of man, but all wrote as if they were filling out some part or all of the history of the sixth and final age of the world. Some, most notably Otto of Freising (d. 1158), tried to provide an account of the whole from creation onwards.

Yet the Bible and its exegetes fired the inventional imagination with far more than macrocosmic visions. They provided other themes that might guide the finding and shaping of narrative contents. For example, Bede saw in the early church at Jerusalem a figure of the new church in England. Thus, like the *Acts of the Apostles,* his *Historia ecclesiastica* presents a young church born of the feats of great evangelists, wracked at first by a dispute over customs, saved from schism by a pivotal church council, and then blessed by miracles in a show of divine favor toward a new Christian people destined to preach the Gospel even beyond the seas. Not many other historians, however, were skilled enough to develop themes of this sort. The general run used biblical contents mainly to bring judgment on human conduct. Cicero tells us (*Orat.* 2.62–64) that the historian should always say what he admires and rejects in human affairs. In medieval culture this rhetorical principle was practiced on a biblical standard. The Bible presented a wide array of historical players, from kings to shepherds, who acted out paradigmatic and cautionary *exempla* that were brought to bear on their medieval counterparts.

Some historians turned to classical historiography to find narrative contents. The first to do so aggressively was Charlemagne's biographer Einhard (d. 840), who in the context of a revival of the Latin verbal arts took from Suetonius elements that helped him to present the Frankish emperor in the tradition of the caesars. Others after Einhard—Widukind of Corvei (d. c. 973), Dudo of St. Quentin (d. c. 1043), William of Poitiers (d. c. 1087/1101), William of Malmesbury (d. 1143), among others—found contents in classical historians, mainly Sallust. The most frequently cited Roman author was Virgil, whose *Aeneid* was read in the Middle Ages as history. This culling of the ancients rested on the rhetorical assumption that human behavior is repetitive, so that what the caesars did in Rome and elsewhere tells one what rulers are likely to do in other times and places. A few medieval writers, like William of Poitiers, liked to use classical material in order to claim that the princes of their world outstripped the Roman emperors. William argued, for example, that as an invader of England William the Conqueror put Julius Caesar in the shade. Several authors took contents from classical texts to show that European peoples sprang originally from Troy. The continuity of the Roman Empire was another myth that lived on among medieval historians. The knowledge of classical historiography was, however, generally poor in the Middle Ages; some Greco-Roman authors, like Tacitus, were only names, and there were no Greek historical texts in Latin translation besides the Christian works of Eusebius of Caesarea. The great link between ancient and medieval historiography was the set of inventional assumptions of Greco-Roman rhetoric that empowered the writing of history in both worlds. These were not extrapolated from classical narratives, but were taught continuously in the schools, better by the ninth century, best in the eleventh and twelfth.

Medieval historians applied their rhetorical tools to a wide variety of subject matters. The earliest of them gave to the Germanic peoples a Latin history that both provided an alternative to an illiterate social memory and told the story of their past in the language of the Roman Church. The first was Jordanes (d. c. 554), who in his *De origine actibusque Getarum* was primarily concerned with Constantinople but nonetheless recounted the known history of the Goths, especially the Ostrogoths. A string of other writers, from Gregory of Tours (d. 594/5) to Widukind of Corvei (d. c. 973), trained their attention on the world of Germanic tribes from which Europe sprang. Among them conversion to Christianity was perforce a central theme. By far the most successful of these works was Bede's *Historia ecclesiastica gentis Anglorum,* completed not long before his death in 735. Written from largely regional and mainly oral information, the finished edifice of this work is full of rhetorical art. A preface that reminds one of Livy, an ethnographical essay that calls to mind Tacitus, a Latin style that smacks often of Cicero, and an inventional imagination that rivals any of these make the *Historia* a great triumph of medieval historiography. It was popular: more than 150 manuscript copies survive, most of them full copies, and an extraordinary number of them were written in the twelfth century, when fine rhetorical prose was newly admired. In the Renaissance it was one of the first books to roll off the printing press, another evidence of its stature in the tradition of Latin literature. Its prestige was due partly to Bede's reputation as one of the fathers of the Church, partly to his fame as a writer of textbooks and biblical commentaries, but mainly to its synthesis of saintly *mirabilia* and other material worthy of memory. In the *Historia* Bede explored a rich *veritas,* a divine and human reality that was the envy of later historians, especially in the twelfth-century revival of Latin letters.

Bede also wrote two historical works arranged by the year, the second of which, the *Chronicon de sex aetatibus mundi,* ranked with the chronicle of Eusebius of Caesarea (as translated and continued to the 370s by Jerome) as an exemplar to a busy future literature that from year to year ranged over long expanses of time in brief reports. Bede's *Chronicon* is a milestone in the history of Latin and Western historiography, since it is the first historical work to use the Christian era (A.D.), a scheme created in the sixth century by a Roman monk named Dionysius Exiguus. It would grow like a mustard seed, perhaps mainly because Bede also used it in the often-copied *Historia.* In this work Bede gave one date counting back from Christ, but in the Middle Ages dating events B.C. would have no chance because of the canonical authority of the Eusebian chronology, which counted forward from the creation. Chronicles are scarcely separable from works that in the ninth century would be called *annales.* The difference is that chronicles clearly descend from Eusebius, whereas *annales* appeared in the Carolingian revival of Roman studies. Annals may have owed something to the seventh-century Easter tables on which short historical notes were made. That the term *annales* first appeared in the context of Carolingian Romanism suggests that they owed something to the classical annalistic tradition.

The first annals dealt only with the Carolingian world. The most famous of them, the *Annales regni Francorum,* starts in 741 and continues into the eighth century. Annals are usually anonymous, monastic, and sometimes difficult to localize, since they were sent around for additions to be made at various places. They provide a virtually continuous account of European affairs from the eighth century to the end of the Middle Ages and beyond. Seldom do they have any literary merit, though all were staked to the rhetorical premise that the visible things of humanity reflect the invisible things of God.

The keeping of chronicles and annals seems to have led to the writing of monastic local and regional history, works designed to review the story, possessions, and privileges of great and small abbeys. The first in this field was Bede's *Historia abbatum,* which gave an account of the leadership and resources of the double Northumbrian abbey of Wearmouth-Jarrow. The heyday of the monastic local histories was, however, the twelfth century, a litigious age in which it was prudent to have more than a cartulary to protect one's interests. The massive *Historia ecclesiastica* of Orderic Vitalis (d. 1142) began in this tradition; his original charge was to produce an account of the abbots and landholdings of the Norman abbey of St. Évroul. A more typical example is the *Chronica majora* of Hugh of Poitiers (d. 1167), which considers the Abbey of Vézelay in the middle decades of the twelfth century. From Bede's *Historia abbatum* onwards the monastic local histories were a fair field for rhetorical exposition, since their subject matter was good and sometimes bad abbots, more or less pious benefactors, and the world of war and peace in their region.

In general the twelfth century was the great age of medieval historiography, partly because there were fascinating questions and developments, partly because some of the best writers of the time tried their hand at it. The single most frequently chronicled happening was the Crusade. The First Crusade was recounted repeatedly, once by a layman who wrote in Latin. This successful adventure was just the topic for the paratactical style, since it was confidently thought to be a triumph of God not mankind. The more tangled record of the next three Crusades attested mainly to the frailties of men, and so powerful writers like John of Salisbury (d. 1180) and William of Tyre (d. 1186) unleashed the powers of *hypotaxis* to explain a largely human field of developments. The twelfth century was also a fine time to narrate political history. The *Gesta Frederici* of Otto of Freising (d. 1158) is an especially brilliant example of the rhetorical representation of an extraordinary king in his early years. Good books of Latin history were even written about troubled monarchs, like King Stephen of England. Ecclesiastical politics was the subject of writers like Orderic Vitalis and John of Salisbury. The one wrote intently about papal reform and the conflict between the Cluniacs and the Cistercians; the other narrated a few years of papal history. In the twelfth century the tradition of chronicles and annals flourished in the writing of world chronicles, especially the *Chronicon sive historia de duabus civitatibus* of Otto of Freising (d. 1158). He joined diverse ideas—Augustinian, Orosian, canonistic, monastic, eschatological—to frame a sweeping synthesis reaching back to the creation. Some would say, however, that a similarly elevated vision informs the *Chronica majora* of Matthew Paris (d. 1259), whose work at St. Albans marks the end of the great tradition of medieval historiography.

Though Latin historiography continued to be written till the end of the Middle Ages, it competed ever more poorly for the best writers. The institutional bulwark of Latin historiography, the Benedictine monasteries, lost social prestige and gave ground to the mendicant orders, among which theological treatises, not historical narratives, were the preferred genre. Now the center of Latin culture was the university, and it was not friendly to historiography. In the fourteenth and fifteenth centuries vernacular writers took charge of the budding new field of urban history and even contributed to the medieval chronicle tradition. By then many monks were writing history in the vernacular, but Latin historiography would have a last hurrah in the Renaissance.

## Select Bibliography

### Bibliography

R. Ray, "Historiography, Western European," in *DMA* 6:258–65: general article and bibliography that cites other bibliographies of both texts and studies [GN1].

### Texts (very selective)

*Annales regni Francorum inde ab a. 741. usque ad a. 829*, ed. G.H. Pertz and F. Kurze, *MGH.SRG* 6 (1895, r1950) [GN2].

Bede, *Historia ecclesiastica*, ed. and tr. B. Colgrave and R.A.B. Mynors (1969, r1991 with corrections): makes use of the "Leningrad Bede," a manuscript copied while Bede was still alive or soon thereafter [GN3].

Bede, *Historia abbatum*, ed. C. Plummer, in *Venerabilis Bedae opera historica*, 2 vols. (1896), v1:364–87 [GN4].

Bede, *Chronicon de sex aetatibus mundi* [*Chronica maiora*], ed. T. Mommsen, *MGH.AA* 13 (1898, r1981) 223–354; printed with the earlier *Chronicon* [*Chronica minora*] [GN5].

Dudo of St. Quentin, *De moribus et actis primorum Normanniae ducum*, ed. J. Lair (1865): Vikings/Normans walk and talk like Romans [GN6].

Einhard, *Vita Karoli Magni*, ed. O. Holder-Egger, *MGH.SRG* 25 (1911, r1965) [GN7].

Gervase of Canterbury, *Chronica*, ed. W. Stubbs, in *The Historical Works of Gervase of Canterbury*, 2 vols., *RSer* 73 (1879–80), v1: see pp87–88 for Gervase's comments on *historici et cronici* [GN8].

*Gesta Stephani*, ed. and tr. K.R. Potter, 2nd ed. (1976): the editor argues that the work was written by Robert of Lewes, bishop of Bath, and uses a newly found manuscript to fill out the last four years of Stephen's reign [GN9].

Gregory of Tours, *Libri historiarum X*, ed. B. Krusch and W. Levison, *MGH.SRM* 1.1 (1937–51, r1992): biblical visions of recent Frankish history [GN10].

Hugh of Poitiers, *Historia Vizeliacensis*, ed. R.B.C. Huygens, in *Monumenta Vizeliacensia: Textes relatifs à l'histoire de l'abbaye de Vézelay*, *CCCM* 42 (1976): tr. J. Scott and J.O. Ward, *The Vezelay Chronicle* (1992): excellent example of a monastic local history [GN11].

John of Salisbury, *Historia Pontificalis*, ed. and tr. M. Chibnall (1956, r1986): thrives on the theory of rhetorical probability [GN12].

Jordanes, *De origine actibusque Getarum*, ed. T. Mommsen, *MGH.AA* 5.1 (1882, r1982): Gothic history with an eye on Constantinople [GN13].

Lampert of Hersfeld, *Annales*, ed. O. Holder-Egger, *MGH.SRG* 38 (1894, r1984):

reaches back to creation; imitates Livy in the account of recent times (c. 1040–77), years in which the Investiture Controversy was brewing [GN14].

Orderic Vitalis, *Historia ecclesiastica*, ed. M. Chibnall (1968–80), 6 vols: the longest, most ramifying, and perhaps most interesting book of history written in the Middle Ages [GN15].

Otto of Freising (with Rahewin), *Gesta Friderici I imperatoris*, ed. G. Waitz and B. von Simson, *MGH.SRG* 46 (1912, r1978) [GN16].

Otto of Freising, *Chronica sive historia de duabus civitatibus*, ed. A. Hofmeister, *MGH.SRG* 45 (1912, r1984): brooding, rich universal chronicle [GN17].

Sigebert of Gembloux, *Chronographia*, ed. L.C. Bethmann, *MGH.Scriptores* (in Folio) 6 (1844, r1980) 268–374: spare but typical monastic chronicle of the central Middle Ages [GN18].

Widukind, *Res gestae Saxonicae*, ed. A. Bauer and R. Rau, *Quellen zur Geschichte der Sächsischen Kaiserzeit: Widukinds Sachsengeschichte*, 2nd ed. (1971): best edition of this work by Widukind of Corvei, who ranks perhaps only below Bede as a historian of a Germanic people [GN19].

William of Poitiers, *Gesta Guillelmi*, ed. R. Foreville, *CHFMA* 23 (1952): an early and especially effusive narrative of the Norman Conquest down to 1071, where the text breaks off [GN20].

William of Malmesbury, *De gesta regum Anglorum*, ed. W. Stubbs, 2 vols., *RSer* 90 (1887–89): Bede's successor as the historian of his people; William was one of the most learned men of the twelfth-century Renaissance [GN21].

William of Tyre, *Chronicon*, ed. R.B.C. Huygens *et al.*, *CCCM* 63A (1986): zenith of the Crusade chronicle [GN22].

**Studies** (primarily to supplement those listed in [GN1])

E. Auerbach, *Literary Language and Its Public in Late Latin Antiquity and in the Middle Ages*, tr. R. Manheim (1965, r1993): treats *parataxis* and the medieval *sermo humilis* in authors like Gregory of Tours [GN23].

H. Beumann, "Topos und Gedankengefüge bei Einhard," in *AKG* 33 (1951) 337–50; repr. in *id.*, *Ideengeschichtliche Studien zu Einhard und anderen Geschichtsschreibern des früheren Mittelalters* (1962, r1969) 1–14: pioneering study of the rhetoric of medieval historiography [GN24].

H. Beumann, *Wissenschaft vom Mittelalter: Ausgewählte Aufsätze* (1972): various essays of interest to the historical and philological study of medieval historiography [GN25].

H. Beumann, *Widukind von Korvei: Untersuchungen zur Geschichtsschreibung und Ideengeschichte des 10. Jahrhunderts* (1950): sets new standards for the study of historical authors [GN26].

E. Breisach, ed., *Classical Rhetoric & Medieval Historiography* (1985): includes N.F. Partner, "The New Cornificius: Medieval History and the Artifice of Words," pp5–59; R. Ray, "Rhetorical Scepticism and Verisimilar Narrative in John of Salisbury's *Historia Pontificalis*," pp61–102; J.O. Ward, "Some Principles of Rhetorical Historiography in the Twelfth Century," pp103–65 [GN27].

E. Breisach, *Historiography: Ancient, Medieval, & Modern* (1983): contains (pp77–152) the best general treatment in English of medieval historiography; good bibliography [GN28].

A.-D. von den Brincken, *Studien zur lateinischen Weltchronistik bis in das Zeit-*

*alter Ottos von Freising* (1957): most important study of the world chronicle [GN29].

M. Chibnall, *The World of Orderic Vitalis* (1984) [GN30].

J. Coleman, *Ancient and Medieval Memories: Studies in the Reconstruction of the Past* (1992): places historiography in the larger context of remembering in the Middle Ages; good bibliography [GN31].

B. Croke, "The Origins of the Christian World Chronicle," in *History and Historians in Late Antiquity,* ed. B. Croke and A.M. Emmet (1983) 116–31 [GN32].

S. Fleischman, "On the Representation of History and Fiction in the Middle Ages," in *History and Theory* 22 (1983) 278–310 [GN33].

V.I.J. Flint, "The *Historia regum Britanniae* of Geoffrey of Monmouth: Parody and Its Purpose. A Suggestion," in *Speculum* 54 (1979) 447–68: discusses the rhetoric of a work that floated between history and fiction [GN34].

W. Goffart, *The Narrators of Barbarian History* (A.D. *550–800): Jordanes, Gregory of Tours, Bede, and Paul the Deacon* (1988): uses an exemplary combination of historical and literary methods; excellent bibliography [GN35].

H. Grundmann, *Geschichtsschreibung im Mittelalter: Gattungen—Epochen—Eigenart,* 3rd ed. (1978): excellent short summary of the whole subject; heavily influential on subsequent discussions of genre and genres [GN36].

B. Guenée, *Histoire et culture historique dans l'Occident médiéval* (1980): situates historiography in social and cultural milieux [GN37].

B. Guenée, "Histoires, annales, chroniques: Essai sur les genres historiques au moyen âge," in *Annales* 28 (1973) 997–1016 [GN38].

R.W. Hanning, *The Vision of History in Early Britain: From Gildas to Geoffrey of Monmouth* (1966): a pivotal book for the study of medieval historiography in the English-speaking world; uses literary methods and perspectivistic approach [GN39].

C.J. Holdsworth and T.P. Wiseman, eds., *The Inheritance of Historiography, 350–900* (1986): ten essays, ranging from Athanasius to Asser, written by Averil Cameron, Robert Markus, James Campbell, and others [GN40].

U. Knefelkamp, ed., *Weltbild und Realität: Einführung in die mittelalterliche Geschichtsschreibung* (1992) [GN41].

K.F. Morrison, *History as a Visual Art in the Twelfth-Century Renaissance* (1990): argues learnedly that historiography was basically a visual not a verbal art; sets history beside art and theater, suggesting that it was to be "seen," not read [GN42].

R. Morse, *Truth and Convention in the Middle Ages: Rhetoric, Representation, and Reality* (1991): probes the foundations of medieval narrative literature, mainly historiography and biography [GN43].

G. Musca, *Il Venerabile Beda, storico dell'alto medioevo* (1973): the only book devoted entirely to Bede's historiography; relates the *Historia ecclesiastica* to his other works [GN44].

N.F. Partner, *Serious Entertainments: The Writing of History in Twelfth-Century England* (1977): clever interdisciplinary reading of three authors—Henry of Huntingdon, William of Newburgh, and Richard of Devizes [GN45].

R. Ray, "Bede and Cicero," in *ASE* 16 (1987) 1–15: argues that Bede's narrative skill sprang partly from his reading of Cicero's *De inventione* [GN46].

R. Ray, "The Triumph of Greco-Roman Rhetorical Assumptions in Pre-Carolingian Historiography," in [GN40] 67–84: contends that early medieval historiography was a continuation of that of Greco-Roman antiquity [GN47].

G.M. Spiegel, *Romancing the Past: The Rise of Vernacular Prose Historiography in Thirteenth-Century France* (1993) [GN48].

B. Stock, *The Implications of Literacy: Written Language and Models of Interpretation in the Eleventh and Twelfth Centuries* (1983): resourceful passages on medieval historiography in a revival of literature and literacy [GN49].

R.M. Thomson, *William of Malmesbury* (1987): intellectual inventory of a twelfth-century polymath for whom history was primarily a Roman art [GN50].

J.M. Wallace-Hadrill, *Bede's Ecclesiastical History of the English People: A Historical Commentary* (1988): a masterful commentary written to stand alongside that produced by C. Plummer almost a hundred years ago [GN51].

J.O. Ward, "Classical Rhetoric and the Writing of History in Medieval and Renaissance Culture," in *European History and Its Historians,* ed. F. McGregor and N. Wright (1977) 1–10: a ground-breaking essay [GN52].

T.P. Wiseman, *Clio's Cosmetics: Three Studies in Greco-Roman Literature* (1979) 3–53: fundamental for anyone interested in rhetorical historiography [GN53].

*See also* [BA16], [BA114], [BA115], [BA127], [BA139], [BB45], [BC32], [BC85].

GO ❋ EPISTOLOGRAPHY

BY JULIAN HASELDINE

In the Middle Ages the letter was far more than simply a vehicle for the transmission of information, and often it was only an adjunct to that process. It could be a political proclamation, a treatise, a bond of patronage or friendship, an administrative document, a gift, and a work of art in its own right. In all its forms it was more or less a public document, intended for a wider audience than the recipient alone. It could be almost anything except a private exchange of confidential information.

During the medieval period the most influential classical models of letter collections were those of Cicero and Seneca. There was also a strong patristic tradition of epistolography, which included Augustine, Ambrose, Jerome, and Gregory the Great, and the letters in the New Testament provided exemplars of letter writing at its most public and authoritative for the Christian world.

The main function of a letter was to represent the speaker who was absent and to convey the spoken word over distance. Throughout the Middle Ages the medium was conceived of as the *sermo absentium,* and the exchange of letters as a form of conversation. The earliest Western letters, in ancient Greece, were mnemonic notes that enabled messengers to recite, to illiterate recipients, words dictated by illiterate senders. In the Middle Ages letters were still written primarily to be read aloud, and the physical process of writing, if not the ability to read, remained the preserve of specialists.

Both medieval and modern commentators have attempted to categorize the immense variety of topics and forms of the medieval letter, but beyond St. Ambrose's statement that "the epistolary genre was devised in order that someone may speak to us when we are absent," it is hard to produce a restrictive definition of the form, content, or even function of letters. So long as it contained a salutation, a letter did not even have to be sent to its nominal recipient.

During the twelfth century the *ars dictamimis* (or *dictamen*) was widely developed. This art, or science, of letter writing sought to define types of letter and to establish rules for their form and composition. The letter theoretically comprised five parts: salutation, exordium, narration, petition, and conclusion. The most strictly defined part was the salutation, where the names of recipient and sender had to appear in order of seniority; thus a cleric writing to a bishop would put his recipient's name before his own. By the eleventh century the practice of addressing recipients, particularly those senior in rank, with the polite plural (*vos*) was widespread. There was also an increasing tendency for writers to refer to themselves as *nos*. The purpose of the exordium was to set an appropriate tone for the letter and to win the recipient's sympathy for its argument or petition. Often based on a suitable biblical quotation or moral paradigm, the exordium was commonly known as the *captatio benevolentiae*. In addition, there were considered to be discrete categories of letters, each with its appropriate form. These included letters of exhortation, consolation, petition, and admonition.

Few of the great original writers of letters obeyed these rules slavishly, but the *ars dictaminis* produced formularies that made the use of letters more accessible, increasing their importance as administrative documents and in routine communication, while also possibly contributing to the ossification of the genre as a literary idiom in the thirteenth century. Constable divides letters into real and fictional, depending on whether or not they were sent to the named recipient, but demonstrates the impossibility of applying any stricter rules to a very flexible genre [GO1].

The second concern of *dictamen* was the *cursus,* the rules governing prose rhythm (see ch. CF). The medieval *cursus* was based primarily on accent rather than meter, and was particularly important for letters as they were intended to be read aloud. A highly wrought rhetorical style, which can appear verbose to modern tastes and unduly preoccupied with puns and word play, also characterizes much of medieval letter writing. A modern translator of St. Bernard (d. 1153) complained that "it would be quite impossible for [Bernard] to speak of patient zeal without promptly mentioning zealous patience" ([GO33] pxv).

The letter itself was rarely a complete, self-contained document including all the information necessary to its purpose and must be considered in its relation to the spoken word. Not only was the letter written to be read aloud, with an audience as well as readers in mind, but often it contained only reflections on the general moral principles relating to a particular case or issue, the precise details of which, especially if of a delicate or sensitive nature, might be entrusted to the memory of the messenger. The surviving text may therefore be only one part of a complete verbal and written message.

The production and delivery of a letter were neither casual nor convenient processes. Generally letters were dictated to a scribe, who would, if necessary, translate them into Latin and then transcribe the text from wax tablet to parchment. The parchment was folded and addressed on the outside. Whereas bishops and abbots of large houses might be able to dispatch messengers whenever they wished, many senders were obliged to wait for a suitable carrier traveling in the right direction. Authentication could be by some autograph mark, but was usually by seal. Letters could be sealed closed, but were more often sealed open, the seal then remaining intact as a permanent record of the letter's validity. Confidentiality was achieved by entrusting specific details or delicate matters to the memory of the bearer. Letters were valued in themselves and were occasionally requested of a writer as a gift.

As important as an understanding of the functions of medieval letter writing is an understanding of the aims and purposes of letter collecting. A letter collection might be regarded as an integral part of the literary output of a learned author, intended to stand as a work of art for posterity. Many letters were written with this in mind, and thoroughly revised and edited before final transcription, either by the authors or by their pupils or monks. The process of selection tended to remove letters concerned with mundane or routine business and to favor those dealing with theological or spiritual themes, as in St. Anselm's collection, or with significant political issues, as in the case of the Becket correspondence. Other letters were collected in formularies and were therefore chosen to exemplify the best epistolary approaches to a variety of different topics, ranging from consolation to requests for financial support. For many authors we have not a randomly accumulated archive, but a consciously and carefully planned work of art. It is essential for the modern reader to investigate how and why a medieval letter has survived: Is it part of a carefully prepared collection, a register, or an archive? If so, was the collection assembled by the sender or the recipient? Or did the letter survive merely by chance? The reader should also determine whether the principles governing a letter's selection were those of style or content.

From its earliest stages, letter writing was associated with the pursuit of *amicitia,* a concept based on the classical tradition of disinterested friendship practiced among the virtuous for the public good. It was a formal and public ideal, with its own distinct intellectual tradition, far removed from the modern notion of emotional ties between intimates. Cicero's treatise *De amicitia* was for the Middle Ages the most important authority on the classical concept of friendship, and medieval writers adapted this tradition to their own religious ideology, treating friendship as an extension or manifestation of divine grace rather than of natural virtue. The letter of friendship could stand as a token of affection, of political allegiance, or of shared ideals. It could be directed to strangers and to whole communities. Thus St. Bernard could write to a monk: "Although you are not known to us personally, although you are far away in the flesh, yet you are a friend, and friendship makes you known to us now and here with us" (*Ep.* 103; [GO33] v7:259).

This sentiment was no mere literary embellishment. Friendship was requested formally, was granted carefully, and carried obligations akin at times to those of formal allegiance. The circles of friends cultivated by the great medieval letter writers are evidence not only of bonds of affection, but also of clear patterns of social ties and political allegiances among the literate élites of the Western Church.

From late antiquity and the early Middle Ages few letters survive, but as signs of the continuity of the tradition of epistolography between the fourth century and the Carolingian revival we have the letters of such writers as St. Patrick (d. c. 461?), Columbanus (d. 615), and Aldhelm (d. 709/10). The recurring requests for prayers and exchanges of gifts and books in the correspondence of St. Boniface (d. 754), as well as the declarations of friendship, are themes characteristic of letter writing throughout the Middle Ages. The varying standards of latinity to be found in the letters to Boniface illustrate that letter writing was not an activity restricted to the most highly trained latinists, but was practiced more widely, even if it is the work of the finest stylists that has typically stood the best chance of survival.

In the eighth century the art of letter writing was developed, like many other cultural pursuits of the Carolingian Renaissance, among the scholars and theologians of Charlemagne's court. Alcuin of York (d. 804) used his letters to promote the ideal of Christian kingship and to encourage the revival of learning. He sent letters of advice and admonition to English kings and bishops, most famously on the occasion of the sack of Lindisfarne, which he interpreted as divine vengeance for the moral laxity of the kingdom. His letters to Charlemagne reflect the full range of concerns of the Carolingian Renaissance, educational, theological, and political. The shared jokes and use of classical and biblical nicknames that characterize his letters to friends and pupils illustrate the development of a self-consciously literary and erudite culture. The letters of Lupus of Ferrières (d. 862) are well known chiefly as evidence of the author's activities as an enthusiastic collector and collator of texts.

Sustained interest in writing and collecting letters is apparent again at the end of the tenth century in the correspondence of Gerbert of Aurillac (Pope Sylvester II, c. 945–1003). His collection contains the characteristic mix of public business, expressions of friendship, and requests for prayers and exchanges of books that typifies the concerns of the learned and influential who wrote letters.

It is with Pope Gregory VII (c. 1020–85) that the letter emerges as a powerful political weapon. He used letters as he used legates, as extensions of his personal power and tools to influence local politics. He appealed to people to rise against their bishops, demanded the loyalty of bishops to the see of St. Peter, and released vassals from their obligations to the emperor. Here the force of the letter depended upon its public nature. As a tool of politics, however, letters were not the preserve of the papacy, and those of the Emperor Henry IV (1056–1106) record the arguments on the other side of what was the first war of propaganda in the medieval West. In the twelfth century Bernard of Clairvaux bombarded kings and popes with his letters, and his collection is in part a testimony to his powerful influence on the events of the day.

The popes of course had always used letters to call attention to their authority within Christendom (see ch. DC). The papal curia kept registers of such letters from the late fourth or early fifth century, although no complete registers survive in their original form from before the pontificate of Innocent III (1198–1216). This practice was for centuries the only continuation of the Roman tradition of registering documents in a public archive for consultation and reference. The letters concerned a variety of issues from matters of routine ecclesiastical administration and judgments to advice to kings or missionaries and clarifications of points of law and theology. The papal chancery was famed for its mastery of *cursus* and diplomatic style (the *stilus curie romane*), and its practices had considerable influence subsequently on the role of letters as records and in administration.

The twelfth century was the greatest period of medieval letter writing. A wider range of writers than ever before was active in a variety of contexts and included bishops, monks, nuns, clerks, and scholars at work in episcopal households, in religious communities, in the new schools, and even on Crusade. A greater diversity of epistolary themes and the development of more personal styles may be said to characterize the period.

St. Anselm (d. 1109) saw the cultivation of spiritual friendship through letter writing as an integral part of his theological and religious activities. Many of his letters read like prayers and have the introspective quality of meditations, not unlike those of the enigmatic abbess Hildegard of Bingen (d. 1179). Before the scholastic movement confined theological discussions to rigidly structured and encyclopedic texts, the letter was considered a perfectly acceptable medium for serious theological debate and spiritual teaching.

Abelard (d. c. 1142) and Heloise (d. 1164) are famous for providing us with the first "love letters" of the Western literary tradition—although they proclaim the supremacy of the monastic ideal—and with a prolonged modern debate on their authenticity. Whether or not they represent a genuine mutual exchange, these were still public letters. Their elaborate and formal diction and semitechnical vocabulary, and their reference to classical and biblical moral precepts, make them sound austere at times, when measured against the expressions of intimacy and romantic sensibilities usually associated with love letters.

John of Salisbury (d. 1180) is often portrayed as the epitome of the erudite man of affairs, combining a wide knowledge of the literary classics with an active life and reflecting both in his profuse writings. He was a clerk educated at Paris, who spent his life in the service of bishops. He traveled widely. His letters give us a detailed picture of the concerns and activities of Archbishops Theobald (d. 1161) and Thomas Becket (d. 1170) of Canterbury and valuable insights into the politics of the day, while also recording a vivid account of the murder of Becket. At the same time, his letters to friends reveal the sophistication and wit of a writer able to draw on an impressive array of classical authors and to indulge in flights of allusive, imaginative humor.

Letters could be addressed to whole communities as readily as to individuals, without any appreciable change in tone, content, or style. The so-called *Golden Letter* of William of St. Thierry (d. 1147/8) exemplifies many of the possibilities of the medieval letter. It is addressed to the Carthusian community of Mont-Dieu in the Ardennes and professes to be a letter of guidance for young monks, but in fact it is a treatise whose real aims are twofold. It provides a defense of the Carthusians as a religious order while also describing the experience of spiritual meditation in ways that indicate that the "letter" could not have been intended for novices. It thus combines a political aim with a profoundly personal expression of spirituality, both of which are accommodated within the flexible medium of the letter.

The eleventh and twelfth centuries also saw the flourishing of episcopal letter collections, including those of Fulbert of Chartres (d. 1028), Lanfranc of Bec (d. 1089), Arnulf of Lisieux (d. 1184), and Gilbert Foliot of Hereford and London (d. 1187). These collections provide a wealth of concrete details about kingdoms and churches and offer insights into the preoccupations of influential members of the Church. Lanfranc's collection even includes the proceedings of two councils.

The leaders of the two greatest monastic movements of the twelfth century, Peter the Venerable (d. 1156) and Bernard of Clairvaux (d. 1153), both left substantial collections of letters. Compared to papal and episcopal letters, those of these writers reveal a far greater freedom of style and expression. It was in fact in the monastic milieu that the letter as a work of literary value, as well as of spiritual and political significance, was fully developed. With Peter of Celle (d. 1183) we have a writer who, although highly influential in the world, has left us a letter collection devoted to the cultivation of a pious and learned circle of friends, and to the pursuit of *amicitia* in one of its purest, most disinterested forms.

Alongside the great collections of medieval letters there exists a profusion of smaller collections, formularies, and registers; these are frequently anonymous; survive only in one, or very few, manuscripts; are largely unavailable in modern critical editions; and represent the wider world of letter writing outside the scriptoria of leaders and scholars. Monastic letter books, serving as formularies and as repositories for the work of one or more authors, exist in great numbers. Other collections take the form of private registers, such as that of Master David of London [GO38].

Devotional, exhortational, and satirical literature all appeared in epistolary form throughout the Middle Ages, often in the form of the fictitious letter. This included epistles from Christ and from Heaven, as well as the fictitious correspondence between such figures as St. Paul and Seneca, and also the popular Devil's letters, wherein the Church is thanked for its good work on Satan's behalf and novel religious orders are attacked. The epistolary genre was also broad enough to include a strong tradition of verse epistles, with such classical antecedents as Ovid's *Heroides,* and represented in the Middle Ages by writers like Baudri of Bourgueil (d. 1130).

By the end of the twelfth century the *ars dictaminis* was growing more elaborate and influential. Peter of Blois (d. 1211) was the last great figure among the twelfth-century letter writers, combining a command of *dictamen* and *cursus* with a stylistic flare soon to disappear from epistolography. Denounced by modern scholars for flagrant plagiarism, Peter wrote letters that were famous in his lifetime, and for the following four centuries, as supreme examples of epistolographical style. His range of interests embraced theology, church politics, and the pursuit of *amicitia.* After Peter the standardized correspondence of the formulary becomes the norm.

Humanist writers such as Petrarch (d. 1374) and Erasmus (d. 1536) revived the art of Latin letters and an interest in *dictamen* and *cursus.* Petrarch compiled a collection in conscious imitation of Cicero, composing letters with a wide public in mind and including fictitious pieces addressed to Cicero, Seneca, and Virgil. Most of these appear in his *Epistolae familiares,* but among his other letter collections is the *Liber sine nomine,* a small collection that was in fact a scathing indictment of the Avignon papacy. This was intended for posthumous publication, and the identities of recipients were deliberately concealed to prevent compromising their author or his friends.

Fictitious letters to classical figures and uncirculated letters written for posterity take us as far as possible from the notion of a letter as a convenient vehicle for the exchange of greetings or essential information. A new style of vernacular epistolography was already making its appearance, in the form of the private, personal letters of the fourteenth and fifteenth centuries, such as those of the Stonor (1290–1483), Paston (1440–86), or Cely (1472–88) collections. Here the modern reader will observe that the letter has taken on a form and function at once more familiar and recognizable than those that characterized the epistolography of the humanists and their predecessors.

## Select Bibliography

### Guides and Tools

A good general introduction to the subject, with extensive bibliography, is G. Constable, *Letters and Letter-Collections, TSMAO* 17 (1976) [GO1].

Guides to sources include R. Schieffer and H.M. Schaller, "Briefe und Briefsammlungen als Editionsaufgabe," in *Mittelalterliche Textüberlieferungen und ihre kritische Aufarbeitung* (1976) 60–70 [GO2]; W.A. Pantin, "English Monastic Letter Books, in *Historical Essays in Honour of James Tait,* ed. J.G. Edwards, V.H. Galbraith, and E.F. Jacob (1933) 201–22 [GO3]; J.M. Bak *et al., Medieval Narrative Sources: A Chronological Guide (with a List of Major Letter Collections)* (1987) [GO4]; and L. Santifaller, *Neuere Editionen mittelalterliche Königs- und Papsturkunden: Eine Übersicht* (1958) [GO5]. See also E.J. Polak, *Medieval and Renaissance Letter Treatises and Form Letters: A Census of Manuscripts Found in Eastern Europe and the Former U.S.S.R.*

(1993), and *id., Medieval...Letter Treatises...Found in Part of Western Europe, Japan, and the United States of America* (1994) [GO6].

On the *ars dictaminis* see J.J. Murphy, *Medieval Rhetoric: A Select Bibliography*, 2nd ed. (1989) [GO7].

## Primary Works

### (a) Collections

Many Frankish and German collections are edited in the *MGH*, including those of *Boniface* and *Lullus*, ed. M. Tangl, *MGH.EPP selectae* 1 (1916, r1989) [GO8]; *Alcuin*, ed. E. Dümmler, *MGH.EPP* 4 (1895, r1978) [GO9]; *Lupus of Ferrières*, ed. E. Dümmler, *MGH.EPP* 6 (1902–25, r1978) [GO10]; *Gerbert of Aurillac*, ed. F. Weigle, *MGH.Die Briefe der deutschen Kaiserzeit* 2 (1966, r1988) [GO11]; *Pope Gregory VII*, ed. E. Caspar, *MGH.EPP selectae* 2 (1920–23, r1990) [GO12]; and *Emperor Henry IV*, ed. C. Erdmann, *MGH.Deutsches Mittelalter* 1 (1937, r1978) [GO13].

The papal collections can be approached through P. Jaffé *et al.*, eds., *Regesta pontificum Romanorum ab condita ecclesia ad annum post Christum natum MCXCVIII*, 2 vols. (1885–88, r1956) [GO14], and A. Potthast, *Regesta pontificum Romanorum inde ab a. post Christum natum MCXCVIII ad a. MCCCIV*, 2 vols. (1874–75, r1957) [GO15]; see also [BC93]. Many have been published in *PL* and *MGH* (e.g. [GO11–12]), and the index volumes of these series should therefore be consulted.

The *PL* also contains many other letter collections, including those of Abelard and Heloise (*PL* 178:113–378) [GO16], Peter of Celle (*PL* 202:405–636) [GO17], Peter of Blois (*PL* 207:1–560) [GO18], and many others that have been reedited subsequently elsewhere (see below).

### (b) Individual Authors and Texts (very selective)

*Early Middle Ages*

Patrick, *Writings and Muirchu's Life,* ed. and tr. A.B.E. Hood (1978) [GO19].
Columbanus, *Opera,* ed. G.S.M. Walker, *Scriptores Latini Hiberniae* 2 (1957) [GO20].
Aldhelm, *Opera* (see [GB1]); *The Prose Works,* tr. M. Lapidge and M.W. Herren (1979) [GO21].
Boniface: see [GO8].

*Carolingian Period*

Alcuin: see [GO9].
Lupus of Ferrières: see [GO10].

*Central Middle Ages*

A great deal of work has been done on the eleventh- and twelfth-century material. The following is a small sample of the best known and most important works, in the order in which the authors appear in the introductory essay.

Gerbert of Aurillac: see [GO11].
Gregory VII: see [GO12] and *The Epistolae Vagantes of Pope Gregory VII,* ed. and tr. H.E.J. Cowdrey (1972) [GO22].

John of Salisbury, *Letters*, ed. and tr. W.J. Millor, H.E. Butler, and C.N.L. Brooke, 2 vols. (1955–79) [GO23].

Anselm, *Opera omnia*, ed. F.S. Schmitt, 6 vols. (1938–61, r1968): see v3–5 [GO24].

Abelard and Heloise: see [GO16]; *Historia calamitatum* and letters 1–7, ed. J.T. Muckle and T.P. McLaughlin, in *MS* 12 (1950) 163–213, 15 (1953) 47–94, 17 (1955) 240–81, 18 (1956) 241–92 [GO25]; *Historia calamitatum*, with app. of letters, ed. J. Monfrin, 2nd ed. (1962); tr. B. Radice (1974, r1985) [GO26].

William of St. Thierry, *Epistola ad fratres de Monte Dei*, ed. and tr. J. Déchanet, *SChr* 223 (1975) [GO27].

Fulbert of Chartres, *Letters and Poems*, ed. and tr. F. Behrends (1976) [GO28].

Lanfranc, archbishop of Canterbury, *Letters*, ed. and tr. H. Clover and M.T. Gibson (1979) [GO29].

Arnulf of Lisieux, *Letters*, ed. F. Barlow, *CamSoc*, 3rd ser., v61 (1939) [GO30].

Gilbert Foliot, *Letters and Charters*, ed. Z.N. Brooke, A. Morey, and C.N.L. Brooke (1967) [GO31].

Peter the Venerable, *Letters*, ed. G. Constable, 2 vols. (1967): with valuable comments on medieval letter collections in v2:1–12 [GO32].

Bernard, *Opera*, ed. J. Leclercq *et al.*, 8 vols. (1957–77): the letters are in v7–8; tr. B.S. James: *The Letters of St. Bernard of Clairvaux* (1953, r1980) [GO33].

Peter of Celle: see [GO17]; a new edition of Peter's correspondence, with English translation, is being prepared by Julian Haseldine for publication in the series, Oxford Medieval Texts [GO34].

Peter of Blois: see [GO18] and *The Later Letters of Peter of Blois*, ed. E. Revell (1993) [GO35].

*Minor Letter Collections, etc.*

P. Chaplais, "The Letter from Bishop Wealdhere of London to Archbishop Brihtwold of Canterbury: The Earliest Original 'Letter Close' Extant in the West," in *Medieval Scribes, Manuscripts & Libraries: Essays Presented to N.R. Ker*, ed. M.B. Parkes and A.G. Watson (1978) 3–23 [GO36].

M.L. Colker, ed., "Epistolae ad amicum and Three Poems," in *Analecta Dublinensia: Three Medieval Latin Texts in the Library of Trinity College Dublin* (1975) pt2: a good introduction to the nature of a literary collection of 30 letters, extant in only two manuscripts, by an unknown author [GO37].

Z.N. Brooke, "The Register of Master David of London, and the Part He Played in the Becket Crisis," in *Essays in History Presented to Reginald Lane Poole*, ed. H.W.C. Davis (1927) 227–45 [GO38].

On fictional correspondence, including that of St. Paul and Seneca, see J.K. Elliott, *The Apocryphal New Testament: A Collection of Apocryphal Christian Literature in an English Translation* (1993) 537–88 [GO39].

*The Humanists*

Francesco Petrarca, *Epistole*, ed. U. Dotti (1978) [GO40]; N.P. Zacour, *Petrarch's Book without a Name: A Translation of the Liber sine nomine*: with useful introduction (1973) [GO41].

Desiderius Erasmus, *Opus epistolarum*, ed. P.S. Allen, H.M. Allen, and H.W. Garrod, 12 vols. (1906–58, r1992) [GO42].

## Studies

References to many studies are listed in [GO1]. Among the most useful are C. Erdmann, *Studien zur Briefliteratur Deutschlands im elften Jahrhundert* (1938) [GO43], and J. Leclercq, "Le genre épistolaire au moyen âge," in *RMAL* 2 (1946) 63–70 [GO44]. See also:

K. Cherewatuk and U. Wiethaus, eds., *Dear Sister: Medieval Women and the Epistolary Genre* (1993) [GO45].

P. Cugusi, *Evoluzione e forme dell'epistolografia latina nella tarda repubblica e nei primi due secoli dell'imperio, con cenni sull'epistolografia preciceroniana* (1983) [GO46].

A. Duggan, *Thomas Becket: A Textual History of His Letters* (1980): a good example of a scholarly study of a letter collection with a complex manuscript tradition [GO47].

C.D. Lanham, *SF* [GO48].

A. Morey and C.N.L. Brooke, *Gilbert Foliot and His Letters* (1965) [GO49].

N. Valois, *De arte scribendi epistolas apud Gallicos medii aevi scriptores rhetoresve* (1880, r1964) [GO50].

On the *ars dictaminis* and *cursus,* see J.J. Murphy, *RMA* [GO51].

On the papal chancery and the *stilus curie Romane,* see *Selected Letters of Pope Innocent III Concerning England (1198–1216),* ed. and tr. C.R. Cheney and W.H. Semple (1953) xvi–xxiv [GO52].

On friendship see B.P. McGuire, *Friendship & Community: The Monastic Experience, 350–1250* (1988): an extensive survey of the sources with comprehensive bibliography [GO53]. Studies of particular cases include J. McLoughlin, "*Amicitia* in Practice: John of Salisbury (*circa* 1120–1180) and His Circle," in *England in the Twelfth Century: Proceedings of the 1988 Harlaxton Symposium,* ed. D. Williams (1990) 165–81 [GO54], and I.S. Robinson, "The Friendship Network of Gregory VII," in *History* 63 (1978) 1–22 [GO55].

On humanist epistolography, see *La correspondance d'Erasme et l'épistolographie humaniste: Colloque international* (November 1983) (1985) [GO56].

GP    ❖    SERMONS

BY BEVERLY MAYNE KIENZLE
AND DAVID L. D'AVRAY

## A. Sermons before 1200

(BEVERLY MAYNE KIENZLE)

### Definition and Terminology

The sermon was and is a central part of Christian worship. It can be defined as a religious discourse delivered to an audience by a preacher who gives instruction on questions of faith and morals. Although the sermon is at root an oral genre, it served not only for preaching but also for private or public reading, such as the private study or communal refectory reading prescribed in the *Rule* of St. Benedict (d. 540). The Carolingian exegete Hrabanus Maurus (d. 856) describes his collection of sermons as being intended for preaching and reading: "hoc opusculum ad legendum vel ad praedicandum" (*PL* 110:10). Isaac of Stella, a Cistercian abbot of the mid-twelfth century, explains how the monastic sermon is related to reading when he defines it as a necessary spiritual exercise that is a type of reading: "Tria sunt, lectio, meditatio et oratio. Lectione vel sermone, qui et ipse quaedam lectio est, loquitur tibi Deus" (*Sermo* 1.14.7). The sermon written to be read is also near in form to other genres such as letters or exegetical treatises that at times imitate oral form. In fact, sermons were frequently exchanged like letters.

To designate the sermon genre, the term *sermo* predominates in Christian Latin from the fourth century onwards. However, various synonyms also appear, such as *tractatus* and *homilia*. Carolingian compilers used *sermo, omelia,* and *tractatus,* with *sermo* employed most often. By the twelfth century, *sermo* is clearly the preferred term, although *homilia*, transmitted through collections, remained in use for readings in the Divine Office.

### Form

Frequently *homilia* and *sermo* serve to indicate different forms: the homily gives a sequential exegesis of an entire pericope; the sermon develops a theme from certain elements of the lection. The form of the homily with its progressive structure is known primarily from the works of Gregory the Great (d. 604) and Bede (d. 735). Together their homilies constitute more than one third of the sermons or homilies included in the homiliary of Paul the Deacon (d. c. 799), the compilation commissioned by Charlemagne for use at the night office. The sequential structure is also apparent in the homiliary Hrabanus Maurus composed for Haistulf, archbishop of Mainz (813–26). Homily 20, for example, explains the Lord's Prayer phrase by phrase from beginning to end (*PL* 110:39–42). Within the monastery the sermon form came to predominate by the twelfth century. Like the homily, the monastic sermon has as its point of departure a biblical or liturgical lection. The preacher or author selects key words from the lection and uses them to develop a motif or theme. With the growth of the schools in the twelfth century, sermon structure became more complex and moved toward the formalization that characterizes the university preaching of the thirteenth century.

## Style

Generally before 1200, the style of sermons, like that of other Christian Latin literature, draws on the language and imagery of the Bible and of earlier preachers, particulary Augustine (d. 430). The complexity of the style varies in accordance with the audience for which the sermon is intended and the extent of revision made to the text. A sermon designed for catechetical public preaching employs much simpler syntax and style than a sermon aimed at a select monastic audience or a text that has undergone numerous revisions before its eventual publication. Methods of developing the sermon also vary among authors. One or more senses of Scripture may be employed; *exempla* from the Bible, the lives of the saints, or the lives of contemporaries may be used. Word associations lead preachers to adduce additional texts and scriptural or patristic authorities. Some preachers draw on classical literature and occasionally on the bestiaries. On the whole, authors are fond of rhetorical figures that involve parallelism, antithesis, and repetition of sounds. Highly figurative language was intended to enhance the emotive level of the sermon and doubtless to capture the audience's attention. The care exhibited by Bernard of Clairvaux (d. 1153) for language and style elucidates the attention brought to a text by a sermon author who was also a great writer.

## Content

Although there is great variety in the content of sermons before 1200, a broad distinction can be drawn between catechetical public preaching and monastic preaching. Catechetical sermons reflect the Church's missionary efforts and expound fundamental tenets of belief or texts such as the Creed or the Lord's Prayer. Carolingian legislation stressed the didactic function of preaching and the need to expound correct doctrine. These sermons may also provide instructions for observing liturgical feasts and for cultivating certain virtues while avoiding their corresponding vices.

Monastic sermons deal primarily with topics relevant to monastic life: prayer, meditation, compliance with monastic discipline, and issues in the life of the monastery. Through the sermon, the monk's observance of the Rule is related to his spiritual progress. Preaching calls him to contemplation that leads to the purification of heart and life that is necessary for meriting a reward in heaven. Some monastic sermons are exegetical series but retain the goals of the monastic life as their point of reference. Occasionally life in the world is examined by the preacher and at times monks were engaged to preach outside the monastery and to address specific issues or causes, such as the Crusades.

Written examples of the preaching done by nuns and abbesses in their monasteries are uncommon. Baudonivia's *Acta Radegundis* (early seventh century) contains two accounts of the message Radegund gave her nuns about keeping the discipline of religious life (*AASS.August*, 3:77, 81). The twelfth-century abbess and visionary Hildegard of Bingen preached publicly, and the text of some of those public sermons has been preserved, recast in letter form (e.g. *PL* 197:244–53, 254–58; *CCCM* 91:34–44; see [GP77]). Sixty of her gospel homilies, *Expositiones evangeliorum*, have also come down to us, probably as they were taken down by her nuns (see [GP21]). Double monasteries may also provide more information about women's involvement in preaching. At Admont, a Benedictine double monastery in Austria, there is clear evidence that learned nuns recorded the sermons of the abbot, Irimbert (1172–77), which he included in his commentaries on *Kings* and *Judges* just as they were copied down by the nuns (see [GP24] p319). Furthermore, on feast days when the abbot was unable to be present, nuns whose learning and knowledge of Scripture Irimbert had praised were appointed to preach (see [GP23] p456 and [GP63]).

## Representative Authors

So intent on his sermons was Caesarius (d. 542), bishop of Arles, that his friends reported that he could be heard preaching in his sleep. Caesarius was a frequent source for Carolingian sermon authors, and more than 230 of his sermons have survived.

Gregory the Great, pope from 590 to 604, established patterns for liturgical preaching and exegetical commentary in sermon form with his *Homiliae XL in evangelia, Homiliae in Ezechielem,* and *Moralia in Job.* His *Homiliae in evangelia* were used for the major feasts of the year in Paul the Deacon's homiliary. Carolingian legislation required priests to be familiar with Gregory's *Regulae pastoralis liber,* which set norms for the life and work of the preacher.

Bede (d. 735), monk of Wearmouth-Jarrow, was an admirer and continuer of Gregory. Among his numerous works are two collections of homilies that are principally exegetical commentaries.

Hrabanus Maurus (d. 856) was the author of two sermon collections, the *Homiliae de festis praecipuis, item de virtutibus,* prepared for Archbishop Haistulf, and the *Homiliae in evangelia et epistolas,* composed at the emperor Lothar's request.

The many twelfth-century monastic sermon authors whose works have been edited include the Benedictines Julian of Vézelay (d. 1160/65), Peter the Venerable (d. 1156), and Peter of Celle (d. 1183); and the Cistercians Bernard of Clairvaux (d. 1153), Guerric of Igny (d. 1157), Aelred of Rievaulx (d. 1178), Gilbert of Hoyland (d. 1172), Isaac of Stella (d. c. 1169), John of Ford (d. c. 1214), and Hélinand of Froidmont (d. 1237).

The works of Bernard of Clairvaux comprise the most extensive and influential collection of twelfth-century monastic sermons. Among them are found compositions dealing with many themes and representing varying degrees of revision from the simple *Sententiae* to the polished *Sermones super Cantica Canticorum.* In addition to these two collections, there are the sermons *in laudibus virginis matris,* those *ad clericos de conversione,* the *Sermones per annum,* and the *Sermones de diversis.*

## B. Sermons after 1200

(DAVID L. D'AVRAY)

The history of Latin sermons from the early thirteenth century to the end of the medieval period is dominated by the friars, though monks (notably Cistercians) and secular university clerics (above all at Paris) continued to play a significant role. The bulk of the surviving sermons by friars were models that would be turned by the preacher from Latin into the vernacular if the congregation were predominantly lay. The manuscripts containing these models are archaeological survivals of a system of mass communication directed principally at the laity. Other sermons survive because they were noted down, as the preacher spoke, by a listener (this is called *reportatio*). Even if the sermon were delivered in English or French or some other vernacular, it would be quite normal to "report" it in Latin. Even "reported" sermons could be and perhaps usually were models, in the sense that they might be designed to help with subsequent preaching; however, the term *model sermon* will be restricted here to sermons diffused (as preaching aids) in multiple copies. Both "reported" and model sermons reach us sometimes in an abridged and sometimes in an unshortened form. Each sort has its interest for the medieval Latinist. The abridged ones lay bare the skeleton of the sermon's structure—in most cases a distinctive structure that was a thirteenth-century innovation, though its origins can be traced back earlier; the fuller ones give the flavor of the Latin spoken at universities and in mendicant convents—an unpretentious but vivid language capable of an impact much harder to achieve in a more humanistic Latin.

The structure so evident in the abridged sermons consists of divisions and subdivisions, which are normally derived (proximately or ultimately) from a scriptural text. Often the division is derived from a single word (which might be taken from or suggested by the scriptural text), in which case they are more properly called "distinctions" (to simplify slightly a complicated story). It was usual to "confirm," by another scriptural text, each of the sections thus created. This structure was normal by the middle to later thirteenth century. It encouraged a particular kind of rhymed prose. A fourteenth-century treatise by Geraldus de Piscario tries to provide a bizarre form of technical assistance and shows us how seriously the need for rhymed divisions could be taken. One of the chapters of his treatise is full of word lists like the following:

> *Inexpressibilis:* malorum punitio, miseria, calamitas,
>     incendium, luctus, dolor, jactura
> *Optabilis:* Dei dilectio, divina gratia, proximi caritas,
>     Christi amplexus, Dei subsidium, divinus amor, rectitudo; eadem
>     *optanda*
> *Odibilis:* culpe transgressio, superbia, iniquitas,
>     defectus, excidium, severitas, mors; eadem *odienda.*
>     [GP57] p185

To make sense of this list, one has to read it vertically, as it were, rather than horizontally:

| (A) | (1) | (2) | (3) |
|---|---|---|---|
| Inexpressi*bilis* | malorum punit*io* | miser*ia* | calami*tas*... |
| Opta*bilis* | Dei dilect*io* | divina grat*ia* | proximi cari*tas*... |
| Odi*bilis* | culpe transgress*io* | superb*ia* | iniqui*tas*... |

If we separate the adjectives ending in -*bilis,* and join each to the substantive that immediately follows it, we get a rhymed partition that could be used in a sermon:

> Inexpressi*bilis* punit*io*
> Opta*bilis* dilect*io*
> Odi*bilis* transgress*io*

The same principle works equally efficiently if we join each -*bilis* word to the substantive next to it but one, as follows:

> Inexpressi*bilis* miser*ia*
> Opta*bilis* divina grat*ia*
> Odi*bilis* superb*ia*

There are further refinements that may be ignored here. The point is that rhymed divisions or distinctions were so much a part of sermon style that a special sort of mini-dictionary could be invented to make the process easier.

A structural principle closely related to that of distinctions was the long comparison or similitude, a technique analyzed by Bataillon [GP48]. Similitudes can also illustrate a particular point in a sermon, rather than serving to hold together parts of the structure. This sort of similitude functions in much the same way as an *exemplum.*

In medieval manuscripts the word *exemplum* has a rather general meaning (not unlike the English "example"), but modern scholars often confine its meaning to short illustrative narratives. *Exempla* in this narrower sense are among the most immediately likable forms of Medieval Latin literature. They are closely associated with the preaching of the friars, but in fact any preacher might use them. A good example of an *exemplum,* drawn from the sermons of Ranulphe de la Houblonnière (thirteenth century) ([GP42] v2:114–15), concerns a poor cleric at the University of Paris who loved a married lady. He takes degree after degree—the story gives a good idea of an academic *cursus honorum*—under the impression, which she encourages, that the next one will do the trick. The ending need not be revealed here. Another thirteenth-century *exemplum,* by the French Dominican Pierre de Remiremont, is too good not to quote:

> There was a certain poor man in the Holy Land; he had a son and he was old, and his son said: "Father, you cannot leave me many temporal goods; would you teach me something of your wisdom?" His father said: "Willingly." His father had a donkey. He told his son to lead the donkey with them when he [*sic*] went into town. He said to his son: "Get on it." Certain people met him and said: "That peasant is stupid: he loves his son more than himself." He said to his son: "Get down;" and he himself then got on. Other people met them who said: "That peasant is harsh and cruel, he has no [mercy] on that small lad (*non habet* [*pietatem?*] *de isto iuuene paruo*); the peasant has long and strong legs, he gets

on the horse and lets that young boy go on foot." "Listen, son," said the father, "get up with me." And other people met him who said that: "He is very cruel, that peasant: he has no pity on the dumb animal; both ride it; at least one ought to go on foot." The father said: "Let us both get down." And other people met [them] who said: "That peasant is stupid: he loves his animal more than himself and his son; at least one ought to mount." The father said: "The only thing left is for us to carry the donkey: there's nothing we can do without people talking. This I say to you, therefore, that (*Hoc dico tibi pro tanto quia*) when you do good actions, you should pay no attention to what people say, but you should always do the right thing, since, if you should want to pay attention to what people say, you will never do good actions." [GP48] p198

*Exempla* have traditionally been used by historians as a source of social detail. More recently, they have been analyzed in formalist or structuralist terms and explored as an interesting borderland between academic and popular culture [GP52]. Despite, or (as we have suggested) to some extent even because of, the distance that lies between their kind of Latin and classical good taste, they can have considerable aesthetic value, which, as with biblical parables, cannot be easily separated from their religious function.

We have noted that *exempla,* as a genre, cannot be sharply separated from comparisons or similitudes. Another form with which they rub shoulders is scriptural exegesis. A good example is from a sermon designed to serve as a model for a funeral or memorial service and written in the first half of the fourteenth century by Nicolaus de Asculo, O.P. Here he uses the Old Testament story of Mardocheus the Jew, who suffered tribulation and faced hanging because of the enmity of the king's minister Aman, but was then raised to high honor by the king. Mardocheus is the dead man, the gallows are sin, and Christ is the king. (The Latin text translated here is in a Munich MS [clm. 2981, fol. 16vb].)

> This was beautifully prefigured in Hester, ch. 5 [and 6] in connection with Mardocheus. When he was covered in such tribulation that Aman [*MS* Naaman], that accursed man, had a very high beam prepared in order to hang him, at that point King Assuerus ordered that he be brought to him, and he made recompense to him for the good turn he had done him when he had made known the men who were out to kill him: Assuerus placed him on the king's own horse (cf. *Est* 6:8) and had him proclaimed throughout the whole city. Thus will the man be honored whom the king wishes to honor. By Mardocheus I understand [the just man, and, especially,] this man, whom Aman, who is called "the side of the Gentiles," that is, this world, in which the rich are suffocated, [according to the words of St. Paul, 1 *Tim* 6:9] *those who want to become rich fall into the nets of the devil*— this man he wanted at that time to suffocate on a most high beam, that is, he wanted to lead him to the gallows of sin. . . . (etc.)

This kind of use of Old Testament stories is very typical of Nicolaus de Asculo, who has an especial predilection for Genesis stories in which Joseph figures. Aficionados of medieval sermons come to recognize traits that help to characterize particular preachers, as this one does Nicolaus. Such tendencies are usually not exclusive to the preacher in question, but serve to individuate him nonetheless.

Authorial individuality is probably not, however, the first thing that strikes the average reader of Latin sermons of this period. Indeed, the concept of *topoi,* as developed by E.R. Curtius to include all sorts of formulaic images, motifs, and clusters of ideas, is one of the handiest tools for analyzing their content. An example of such a topos is the idea that marriage is (metaphorically) a religious order. One preacher who uses it is the thirteenth-century Dominican Henry of Provins (in a sermon of 15 January 1273):

> You see that our order and the Franciscan order began not long ago; and similarly the other orders began after the Incarnation: but this order [i.e., marriage] began from the origins of the world. Furthermore, a certain mortal man from Spain created our order, and a certain man from Lombardy the Franciscan Order; but God himself made this order, and not as an innovation, but from the origin of the world. [GP51] p514

The same basic idea that marriage is like a religious order appears in various other sermons, but it would probably be pointless to try to work out a family tree of the relations among the instances that have so far been noticed, because we are almost certainly dealing with a commonplace that was widely known and used. This does not make it uninteresting. On the contrary, such *topoi* are doubly interesting, first because their diffusion makes them, as it were, part of the mentality of their time; and second because a good preacher could impart a personal touch to them that could make them effective even from a purely literary point of view, as Peter Dronke has shown with reference to medieval poetry.

Most of the foregoing analysis applies to the vast majority of Latin sermons between about the middle of the thirteenth century and the end of the Middle Ages. Few major changes within that span of time have so far been noted by historians. One significant development that did occur has been misunderstood and antedated, probably because of unsatisfactory terminology and too much reliance on the *artes praedicandi* (technical treatises on how to compose sermons). The change in question is the slow penetration of preaching by the scholastic method. It may be that historians have failed to emphasize this development because they have tended to describe *all* preaching that systematically employed divisions and authorities as "scholastic," leaving themselves short of an adjective to describe the introduction of explicit logical argument, *quaestiones*, and quotations from unambiguously scholastic theological works. The use of logical terminology by *artes praedicandi* to analyze preaching techniques that may themselves have developed without any significant help from formal logic may well have contributed to this confusion.

The invention of printing did not so much replace as reinforce the medieval system of mass communication through preaching. In the thirteenth and fourteenth centuries model sermon collections were diffused in very large numbers of manuscripts. This was in effect a form of publication. Printing was doubtless cheaper and more efficient, but not essentially different. Thus the history of preaching in this period cuts across the antithesis between manuscripts and printing, as well as the antithesis between oral and written culture.

## Select Bibliography

### Texts

Many medieval sermons remain unedited. For work in progress one should consult the *Medieval Sermon Studies Newsletter* (1977–; now *Medieval Sermon Studies*), ed. V. O'Mara, published twice yearly for the International Medieval Sermon Studies Society under the auspices of the Centre for Medieval Studies, Leeds [GP1]. For the later period, J.B. Schneyer, *Repertorium der lateinischen Sermones des Mittelalters für die Zeit von 1150–1350*, 11 vols. (1969–90), is especially valuable; it has transformed the study of medieval sermons transmitted in Latin and is a starting point for original investigations in the field [GP2].

### (a) Sermons before 1200 (very selective)

Aelred of Rievaulx, *Sermones* I–XLVI, ed. G. Raciti, *CCCM* 2A (1989) [GP3]; *Opera homiletica*, ed. G. Raciti, A. Hoste, and C.H. Talbot, *CCCM* 2 (1991) [GP4].

Bede, *Homeliarum evangelii libri II*, ed. D. Hurst, *CCSL* 122 (1955) [GP5].

Bernard of Clairvaux, *Opera*, ed. J. Leclercq, C.H. Talbot, and H. Rochais, v1–2, 4–6 (1957–72) [GP6].

Caesarius of Arles, *Sermones*, ed. G. Morin, *CCSL* 103–4 (1953) [GP7]; ed. and tr. M.-J. Delage, *SChr* 175, 243, 330 (1971–86): with excellent introductions by the editor [GP8]. For a listing of additional sermons see W.E. Klingshirn, *Caesarius of Arles: The Making of a Christian Community in Late Antique Gaul* (1994) 288 [GP9].

Gilbert of Hoyland, *Sermones in Canticum Salomonis*, in *PL* 184:9–252 [GP10].

Gregory the Great, *Homiliae XL in evangelia*, in *PL* 76:1075–1312 [GP11]; tr. D. Hurst (1990), with very valuable notes and references to Bede [GP12]; *Homiliae in Hiezechihelem prophetam*, ed. M. Adriaen, *CCSL* 142 (1971) [GP13]; *Moralia in Job*, ed. M. Adriaen, *CCSL* 143, 143A–B (1979–85) [GP14]; *Regulae pastoralis liber*, in *PL* 77:13–128 [GP15].

Guerric of Igny, *Sermones*, ed. J. Morson and H. Costello, tr. P. Deseille, *SChr* 166, 202 (1970, 1973) [GP16].

Hélinand of Froidmont, *Sermones*, in *PL* 212:481–720 [GP17]; additional sermons published by B.M. Kienzle, "Cistercian Preaching against the Cathars: Hélinand's Unedited Sermon for Rogation, B.N. MS. Lat 14591," in *Cîteaux* 39 (1988) 297–314 [GP18]; and "Mary Speaks against Heresy: An Unedited Sermon of Hélinand for the Purification, Paris B.N. ms. lat. 14591," in *SE* 32 (1991) 291–308 [GP19].

Hildegard of Bingen, *Epistolae*, in *PL* 197:244–58; see also [GT20] v91:34–44 [GP20]; *Expositiones evangeliorum*, ed. J.-B. Pitra, in *Analecta S. Hildegardis*, in *Analecta sacra*, v8 (1882) 245–327 [GP21].

Hrabanus Maurus, *Homiliae de festis praecipuis, item de virtutibus* and *Homiliae in evangelia et epistolas*, in *PL* 110:9–134, 135–468 [GP22]; consult H. Barré [GP49].

Irimbert of Admont, *De incendio monasterii sui, ac de vita et moribus virginum sanctimonialium Parthenonis Admuntensis narratio, excerpta ex inedito ejusdem Commentario in libros Regum ad capitulum XIV, versus 7, libri IV*, ed. B. Pez, *Bibliotheca ascetica antiquo-nova*, v7 (Ratisbon 1725) [GP23]; see also J.W. Braun, "Irimbert von Admont," in *FMS* 7 (1973) 266–323 [GP24].

Isaac of Stella, *Sermones*, ed. and tr. A. Hoste *et al.*, *SChr* 130, 207, and 339 (1967, 1974, 1987) [GP25].

John of Ford, *Super extremam partem Cantici Canticorum sermones CXX*, ed. E. Mikkers and H. Costello, *CCCM* 17–18 (1970) [GP26].

Julian of Vézelay, *Sermones*, ed. and tr. D. Vorreux, *SChr* 192–93 (1972) [GP27].

Peter of Celle, *Sermones*, in *PL* 202:637–926 [GP28]; additional sermons published by G. de Martel, "Recherches sur les manuscrits des sermons de Pierre de Celle," in

*Scriptorium* 33 (1979) 3–16 [GP29]; and E. del Basso, "I Sermones di Pietro di Celle," in *Atti dell'Accademia pontaniana* 17 (1968) 97–154 [GP30].

Peter the Venerable, *Sermones*, in *PL* 189:953–1006 [GP31]; three sermons have also been edited by G. Constable, "Petri Venerabilis Sermones Tres," in *RB* 64 (1954) 224–72 [GP32].

## (b) Sermons after 1200 (very selective)

Anthony of Padua (Antonius Patavinus), *Sermones dominicales et festivi*, ed. B. Costa et al., 3 vols. (1979) [GP33].

N. Bériou and F.-O. Touati, *Voluntate dei leprosus: Les lépreuz entre conversion et exclusion aux XIIème et XIIIème siècles* (1991) [GP34].

Bonaventure, *Sermones*, ed. J.-G. Bougerol: *Sermones dominicales* (1977) [GP35]; *Sermons de tempore: Reportations du manuscrit Milan, Ambrosienne A 11 sup.* (1990) [GP36]; *Sermons de diversis*, 2 vols. (1993) [GP37].

C. Casagrande, *Prediche alle donne del secolo XIII: Testi di Umberto da Romans, Gilberto da Tournai, Stefano di Borbone* (1978) [GP38].

Giacomo della Marca (Jacobus de Marchia), *Sermones dominicales*, ed. R. Lioi, 3 vols. (1978) [GP39].

John de la Rochelle, *Sermones*, ed. K.F. Lynch: *Eleven Marian Sermons* (1961) [GP40].

Ranulph Higden, *Ars componendi sermones*, ed. M. Jennings (1991) [GP41].

Ranulphe de la Houblonnière, *Sermones*, ed. N. Bériou: *La prédication de Ranulphe de la Houblonnière: Sermons aux clercs et aux simples gens à Paris au XIIIe siècle*, 2 vols. (1987) [GP42].

Thomas Brinton, *Sermones*, ed. M.A. Devlin, 2 vols., *CamSoc*, 3rd ser., 85–86 (1954) [GP43].

Thomas de Chobham, *SAP* [GP44].

William Herebert, *Sermones*, ed. S.R. Reimer: *The Works of William Herebert, O.F.M.* (1987) [GP45].

Stephen Langton, *Sermones*, ed. P.B. Roberts: *Selected Sermons of Stephen Langton* (1980) [GP46].

## Studies

T.L. Amos, E.A. Green, B.M. Kienzle, eds., *De Ore Domini: Preacher and Word in the Middle Ages* (1989); this includes T.L. Amos, "Preaching and the Sermon in the Carolingian World," pp41–60 [GP47].

L.J. Bataillon, "*Similitudines* et *exempla* dans les sermons du XIIIe siècle," in *The Bible in the Medieval World: Essays in Memory of Beryl Smalley*, ed. K. Walsh and D. Wood (1985) 191–205; repr. in his *La prédication au XIIIe siècle en France et Italie: Études et documents* (1993), essay 10 [GP48].

H. Barré, *Les homéliaires carolingiens de l'école d'Auxerre: Authenticité, inventaire, tableaux comparatifs, initia* (1962) [GP49].

N. Bériou, "La prédication au béguinage de Paris pendant l'année liturgique 1272–1273," in *RecAug* 13 (1978) 105–229 [GP50].

N. Bériou and D.L. d'Avray, "Henry of Provins, O.P.'s Comparison of the Dominican and Franciscan Orders with the 'Order' of Matrimony," in *AFP* 49 (1979) 513–17 [GP51].

C. Bremond, J. Le Goff, and J.-C. Schmitt, *L'"exemplum"*, *TSMAO* 40 (1982) [GP52].

P. Cole, *The Preaching of the Crusades to the Holy Land, 1095–1270* (1991) [GP53].

T.-M. Charland, *Artes Praedicandi: Contribution à l'histoire de la rhétorique au moyen âge* (1936) [GP54].

R. Cruel, *Geschichte der deutschen Predigt im Mittelalter* (1879, r1970) [GP55].

D.L. d'Avray, *The Preaching of the Friars: Sermons Diffused from Paris before 1300* (1985) [GP56].

D.L. d'Avray, "The Wordlists in the 'Ars faciendi sermones' of Geraldus de Piscario," in *Franciscan Studies* 38 (1978) 184–93 [GP57].

C. Delcorno, *La predicazione nell'età communale* (1974) [GP58].

C. Delcorno, "Rassegna di studi sulla predicazione medievale e umanistica (1970–1980)," in *Lettere Italiane* 33 (1981) 235–76 [GP59].

A. Franz, *Drei deutsche Minoritenprediger aus dem XIII. und XIV. Jahrhundert* (1907) [GP60].

C. Garda, "Du nouveau sur Isaac de l'Étoile," in *Cîteaux* 37 (1986) 8–22 [GP61].

R. Grégoire, *Les homéliaires du moyen âge: Inventaire et analyse des manuscrits* (1966) [GP62].

B.M. Kienzle, "The Typology of the Medieval Sermon and Its Development in the Middle Ages: Report on Work in Progress," in *De l'homélie au sermon: Histoire de la prédication médiévale*, ed. J. Hamesse and X. Hermand (1993) 1–19 [GP63].

F. Landmann, *Das Predigtwesen in Westfalen in der letzten Zeit des Mittelalters* (1900) [GP64].

M.-M. Lebreton, "Les sermons de Julien, moine de Vézelay," in *StA* 37 (1955) 118–37 [GP65].

J. Leclercq, "Etudes sur S. Bernard et le texte de ses écrits," *Analecta Sacri Ordinis Cisterciensis* 9 (Rome 1953) [GP66].

J. Leclercq, "Prédicateurs bénédictins au XIe et XIIe siècles," in *Revue Mabillon* 33 (1943) 48–73 [GP67].

J. Leclercq, "Sur le caractère littéraire des sermons de S. Bernard," in *SM*, 3rd ser., 7 (1966) 701–44 [GP68].

J. Leclercq, *The Love of Learning and the Desire for God: A Study of Monastic Culture*, tr. C. Misrahi, 3rd ed. (1982, r1988) [GP69].

J. Leclercq, "The Making of a Masterpiece," tr. K. Waters, in *Bernard of Clairvaux on the Song of Songs IV*, tr. I. Edmonds (1980) ix–xxv [GP70].

J. Longère, *La prédication médiévale* (1983) [GP71].

J. Longère, "Le vocabulaire de la prédication," in *LLM* 303–20 [GP72].

H. Martin, *Le métier de prédicateur en France septentrionale à la fin du moyen âge, 1350–1520* (1988) [GP73].

J.M. McManamon, *Funeral Oratory and the Cultural Ideals of Italian Humanism* (1989) [GP74].

C. Mohrmann, "Praedicare—tractare—sermo," in *eadem, Études sur le latin des chrétiens* 2 (1961) 63–72 [GP75].

J.J. Murphy, *RMA:* see ch. 6 (pp269–355) on the *Ars Praedicandi* [GP76].

B. Newman, *Sister of Wisdom: St. Hildegard's Theology of the Feminine* (1987) [GP77].

J.W. O'Malley, *Praise and Blame in Renaissance Rome: Rhetoric, Doctrine, and Reform in the Sacred Orators of the Papal Court, c. 1450–1521* (1979) [GP78].

G.R. Owst, *Literature and Pulpit in Medieval England: A Neglected Chapter in the History of English Letters & of the English People*, 2nd rev. ed. (1961) [GP79].

P.B. Roberts, *Thomas Becket in the Medieval Latin Preaching Tradition: An Inventory of Sermons about St. Thomas Becket c. 1170-c. 1400* (1992) [GP80].

R.H. and M.A. Rouse, *PFS* [GP81].

R. Rusconi, *Predicazione e vita religiosa nella società italiana da Carlo Magno alla Controriforma* (1981) [GP82].

J.B. Schneyer, *Geschichte der katholischen Predigt* (1969) [GP83].

C.L. Smetana, "Paul the Deacon's Patristic Anthology," in *The Old English Homily and Its Backgrounds,* ed. P.E. Szarmach and B.F. Huppé (1978) 75–97 [GP84].

A. Squire, "The Literary Evidence for the Preaching of Aelred of Rievaulx," in *Cîteaux* 11 (1960) 165–79, 245–51 [GP85].

Z. Zafarana, *Da Gregorio VII a Bernardino da Siena: Saggi di storia medievale,* ed. O. Capitani *et al.* (1987): essays on "la predicazione francescana" and "predicazione francescana ai laici" [GP86].

*See also* [BA85], [BC26], [BC89], [BC97], [BC119].

# PASTORALIA: THE POPULAR LITERATURE OF THE CARE OF SOULS

BY JOSEPH GOERING

When the Fourth Lateran Council of 1215 declared that the guidance of souls (*regimen animarum*) was the art of arts, it implied that the pastoral care of souls was a skill or "art" that could be taught and learned in the schools. In the years that followed, a distinctive type of didactic literature emerged to educate pastors and to prepare them to teach their people by word (in preaching and in administering the sacraments) and by example (in living an exemplary life).

This literature of pastoral care drew on a long tradition of Christian writings, from the Pauline and Apostolic letters of the New Testament through the texts of learned bishops and monks like Augustine of Hippo (d. 430), Gregory the Great (d. 604), Hrabanus Maurus (d. 856), and Honorius Augustodunensis (d. c. 1156). By the thirteenth century, however, pastoral texts were being written and copied in profusion. Not just bishops and learned monks, but every priest charged with the care of souls was expected to learn the techniques of pastoral care. The didactic literature (*pastoralia*) that emerged at this time summarized the older teachings on soul care and introduced new methods and new materials to make accessible to every priest written instruction in the art of arts, the pastoral care of souls.

As a literary genre, *pastoralia* is somewhat amorphous. It includes short treatises and poems of only a few hundred lines as well as massive *summae* of more than 500 pages. Its content ranges widely to include discussions of the seven deadly sins, the techniques of hearing confessions, the art of preaching, and the disciplinary teachings of canon law and of Church councils. What these texts all have in common is a desire to convey in writing (and sometimes in pictures) the basic knowledge and skills necessary for exercising the pastoral care of souls in the parishes of Latin Christendom. Thousands of such texts were composed between 1200 and the end of the Middle Ages; what follows is a survey of the distinctive style, forms, and content of *pastoralia*.

## Style of Pastoralia

The Latin style of pastoral texts is usually simple and straightforward. It is designed for priests (and eventually the laity) who have had little formal education and for those who have learned their Latin primarily by speaking it in the schools. Ornate styles and complex periodic sentences are eschewed in favor of the language of ordinary speech. As a general rule, the higher the status of the author and of the intended recipients, the more complex the style: thus the decrees of ecumenical councils are more ornate than those composed by archbishops and bishops, and treatises written for diocesan officials are more stylized than those directed to simple priests.

A second characteristic of pastoral texts is the use of new techniques for presenting information. Alphabetical organization, for example, is often used to structure texts (see John Bromyard's *Summa praedicantium* [GQ22]) and to make them into useful tools for the preacher and teacher. Even more common is the *distinctio*. *Distinctiones* are lists of related materials, sometimes set out in schematic form on the page and sometimes written in continuous prose. They allow the reader to take in at a glance the essential elements of an argument, the diverse meanings of a word, or the key points of a doctrine. An example is the schematic presentation, illustrated in the figure, of the virtue of courage by Robert Grosseteste (d. 1253) in his *Templum Dei* ([GQ16] II.3; p31).

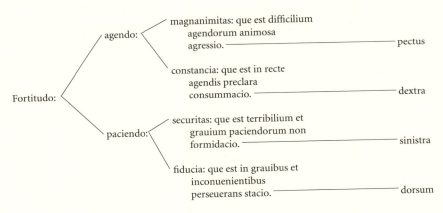

What such distinctions lack in literary elegance they make up in efficient and practical presentation of materials.

A third stylistic element common to many pastoral texts is the frequent use of didactic verses to introduce, summarize, or emphasize particular teachings (see William de Montibus, *Peniteas cito peccator* [GQ13]; Aag of Denmark, *Rotulus pugillaris* [GQ21]). These verses make no pretensions to great poetry, but they are ubiquitous in the pastoral literature. They were highly prized as a means of conveying complex information concisely and memorably.

## Forms of Pastoralia

An adequate classification of the various forms of *pastoralia* is difficult. Medieval authors and scribes used many terms to describe the pastoral works they composed and copied: *compendium, distinctiones, libellus/liber, manuale, speculum, summa,* and *tractatus* are some of the more common designations. These terms were used rather loosely, however, and the same work might be called *summa, distinctiones,* and *manuale,* in various manuscript copies.

Beneath this welter of contemporary terminology it is possible to identify three broad categories of pastoral works, each with its own distinctive forms and models. The three categories—preaching, confession, and ecclesiastical discipline—correspond to the three most popular and most innovative areas of Church life in the thirteenth and subsequent centuries. Not every pastoral work, of course, fits easily into one or the other of these categories, and some works include aspects of all three. A brief discussion of each will reveal the diversity of forms that constitute the genre of pastoral literature.

1. *Preaching.* In the first 12 centuries of the Christian Church, preaching was primarily the preserve of bishops and learned monks. With the gradual extension of this office to the parish priest and the introduction of new religious orders (the regular canons and the mendicant friars) that emphasized popular preaching, guides to the preaching office flourished. Many of these were modeled on Gregory the Great's *Regula pastoralis* [GQ7], which enjoyed a renewed popularity in the twelfth and thirteenth centuries. Collections of sermons for the temporal cycle (Advent to Pentecost) and the sanctoral cycle (feasts of the saints) proliferated. Guides to the "art of preaching," based on classical rhetorical doctrines and on medieval practice, supplemented the more informal method of learning to preach by imitating actual preachers. Material for sermons was collected in a vast array of reference aids, encyclopedias, and handbooks. Lives of the saints, histories, proverbs, exempla and similitudes (brief stories or descriptions to illustrate a point), and treatises on the vices and virtues all provided the preacher with ready access to the material he needed for his sermons.

2. *Confession.* Closely linked with preaching from the thirteenth century on, confession was one of the most popular religious activities of the later Middle Ages. When the Fourth Lateran Council required that all Christians confess at least once a year to their proper (or parish) priest, it was giving authoritative form to an already popular exercise. Many types of pastoral literature designed to train simple priests to be skilled confessors grew up in the years following this council. These include general works (*summae de penitentia, summae confessorum*) as well as more specific treatises on "how to hear confessions," "how to examine one's conscience," and "how to impose fitting penances."

Penitents, both clerical and lay, were taught to feel remorse for their sins (*contritio*), to confess fully (*confessio*), and to make amends (*satisfactio*) for sins through interior and exterior penances. Many types of pastoral literature served as instructional aids. Since penitents were taught to examine their lives in light of the seven deadly sins, the Ten Commandments, and the articles of faith, treatises on these subjects proliferated. Moreover, as the skilled confessor would need to know the latest teachings of the canonists and theologians in order to give moral advice and direction through confession, treatises on usury, simony, vows, sacraments, excommunication, and a multitude of other matters were composed to meet their needs. Finally, works describing the spiritual economy of heaven, hell, and purgatory, along with the joys of the blessed and the pains of the damned, helped to encourage the penitent in contrition, confession, and satisfaction for sins.

3. *Ecclesiastical Discipline.* The twelfth-century reforms of the Church gave com-

mon currency to the notion that all priests should teach not only with words, by preaching and hearing confessions, but also by example, in their lives and offices. Canonists and theologians clarified the general norms for clerical and Christian behavior; these were embodied in the legislation of general Church councils and specified in local councils and synods throughout Christendom. From the earliest years of the thirteenth century we have collections of statutes and constitutions that illustrate the type of instruction being given to clerics and, by extension, to the laity.

In the chapter beginning *Cum sit ars artium regimen animarum* (ch. 27), the Fourth Lateran Council (1215) required that every priest be diligently instructed in the proper celebration of the Divine Office and the Church's sacraments. Elements of such instruction can be found in various synodal documents, in treatises on the seven sacraments, in commentaries on the fourth book of Peter Lombard's *Sententiae* and on the sections *De penitentia* and *De consecratione* of Gratian's *Decretum*, and in numerous other texts emerging from the schools of canon law and theology.

## Content of Pastoralia

As the preceding discussion makes clear, the literature of pastoral care was wide-ranging and diverse; it might take the form of a guide to preaching, a confessional handbook, synodal instructions, or a "mirror for priests." Whatever the form, however, a general consensus about the proper and sufficient content of pastoral instruction emerged during the thirteenth century. Authors selected a number of topics from the mass of pastoral and religious themes available to them and developed these as the foundation for "catechetical" instruction. One of the most famous presentations of these themes is the chapter "De informatione simplicium sacerdotum" of the Council of Lambeth in England (1281).

Somewhat fuller lists of topics were circulating from the early years of the thirteenth century. The list of pastoral themes in the unpublished *Summa "Qui bene presunt"* of Richard of Wetheringsett (d. 1232) will serve to illustrate the general content of pastoral instruction in the thirteenth and succeeding centuries.

Richard identified the topics that belong most basically to Christian instruction. He urged that priests should understand all of them thoroughly, and then preach them frequently and in simple terms to the people:

1. *The Creeds* (*Apostles', Nicene*, and the *Quicunque vult* of the liturgy) and the *Articles of Faith* (*articuli fidei*). The *Articles of Faith* are an invention of the twelfth century; usually twelve or fourteen in number, they summarize and elaborate the basic doctrines of the creeds. Most lists of the "articles" emphasize the life of Christ, and Richard of Wetheringsett suggests that three articles—the Nativity, the Passion, and the Second Coming of Christ—should receive special attention.

2. *The Lord's Prayer*. Every Christian was expected to learn and repeat this prayer frequently. For instruction, it was divided into seven petitions (*sanctificetur nomen tuum, adveniat regnum tuum*, etc.), and the meaning and importance of each were explained.

3. *God's Gifts*. Both natural gifts (creation and sustenance) and supernatural gifts (especially the seven gifts of the Holy Spirit) were emphasized.

4. *Virtues*. Most frequently these were divided into the four "cardinal" or "polit-

ical" virtues (prudence, justice, fortitude, and temperance) and the three "theologi-cal" or "gratuitous" virtues (faith, hope, and charity).

5. *Vices.* More systems of cataloguing and discussing the vices were known to the Middle Ages than can be conveniently summarized. Every preacher and every con-fessor would have encountered a number of these. But the most enduring format was that of the seven deadly (*mortalia*) or chief (*capitalia*) sins: Pride, Envy, Wrath, Sloth, Avarice, Gluttony, and Lust.

6. *Sacraments.* When Hugh of St. Victor wrote his *De sacramentis christianae fidei* in the twelfth century, he could list thousands of major and minor sacraments (signs of holy things), from Baptism and the Eucharist to the sign of the cross and holy oils. By the thirteenth century, pastoral instruction had come to focus on the seven ma-jor sacraments of the Church: Baptism, Confirmation, Eucharist, Penance, Holy Or-ders, Marriage, and Extreme Unction.

7. *The Ten Commandments and the Two Evangelical Precepts.* The Ten Com-mandments of the Old Testament and the Two Precepts (love of God and neighbor) of the New become especially prominent in the *pastoralia* of the thirteenth and sub-sequent centuries. Confessors began to use the commandments as a means of in-quiring about sins, and preachers ensured that their audiences knew the command-ments and the precepts well.

8. *Works of Mercy.* The seven corporal works of mercy (feed the hungry, give drink to the thirsty, clothe the naked, harbor the stranger, visit the sick, care for those in prison, bury the dead; cf. *Mt* 25:35ff.) also became a commonplace element in con-fession and preaching. Penitents were taught to search their consciences for "sins of omission" in neglecting the works of mercy, and preachers urged the life-giving ben-efits of performing them. They were soon accompanied by the seven spiritual works of mercy (convert the sinner, instruct the ignorant, counsel the unsure, comfort the sorrowful, bear wrongs patiently, forgive injuries, pray for the living and the dead) in pastoral instruction.

9. *The Rewards of the Just and the Pains of the Wicked.* Sermons on heaven and hell became commonplace. The joys of heaven, if preached effectively, could draw sinners to contrition, confession, and amendment of life; fear of the pains of hell could have the same effect. The pains of purgatory, where the wicked suffered who had repented but had failed to make full satisfaction for sin, also became an impor-tant topic in pastoral literature.

10. *The Errors of the People.* Preachers, teachers, and confessors at all levels of the ecclesiastical hierarchy learned to identify ideas and practices that were dangerous to the spiritual health of the people. They were taught to recognize in themselves and in others various types of popular superstition, heresy, negligence, and malpractice, and to extirpate them.

11 and 12. *The Things to be Avoided (vitanda) and to be Done (agenda).* These are general categories of moral analysis: one should avoid evil and do good. Because the opportunities for sinning and for doing good varied according to one's status and calling in life, pastoral writers often specified the particular temptations and oppor-tunities of different segments of the population (peasants, merchants, nobles, wid-ows, clerics, etc.).

Few of these topics are new in the thirteenth century and some are as old as the Judeo-Christian tradition, but the consensus about the proper content of pastoral instruction, first achieved in the thirteenth century, continued to shape religious consciousness for centuries thereafter. Chaucer's parson and the Canterbury pilgrims are steeped in this tradition, and the *Exercitia spiritualia* (c. 1535) of St. Ignatius ring the changes on these pastoral commonplaces.

## Select Bibliography

### Texts

#### (a) Early Examples

Augustine, *De catechizandis rudibus,* in *PL* 40:309–48 [GQ1]; ed. I.B. Bauer, in *CCSL* 46 (1969) 115–78 [GQ2].

Augustine, *Enchiridion ad Laurentium de fide, spe et caritate,* in *PL* 40:231–90 [GQ3]; ed. E. Evans, in *CCSL* 46 (1969) 21–114 [GQ4].

Augustine, *De doctrina christiana libri quattuor,* in *PL* 34:15–122 [GQ5]; ed. W.M. Green, *CSEL* 80 (1963) [GQ6].

Gregory the Great, *Regulae pastoralis liber,* in *PL* 77:13–128 [GQ7].

Gregory the Great, *Moralia in Job,* in *PL* 75:509–1162, 76:1–782 [GQ8]; ed. M. Adriaen, *CCSL* 143, 143A–B (1979–85) [GQ9].

Jonas of Orleans, *De institutione laicali,* in *PL* 106:122–278 [GQ10].

Hrabanus Maurus, *De clericorum institutione,* in *PL* 107:293–420 [GQ11].

Honorius Augustodunensis, *Speculum ecclesiae,* in *PL* 172:807–1108 [GQ12].

#### (b) Representative Texts (thirteenth century and after, in chronological order):

William de Montibus, "Peniteas cito peccator," in *PL* 207:1153–56: a short didactic poem on penance, written about 1200 and used throughout Europe for elementary religious education [GQ13]. For a recent edition see [GQ31] pp107–38.

Thomas de Chobham, *Summa confessorum,* ed. F. Broomfield (1968): much more than a penitential handbook; written about 1216, it is one of the fullest and most interesting pastoral *summae* produced in the Middle Ages [GQ14].

Thomas de Chobham, *SAP:* a work, by the author of [GQ13], on the art and content of preaching [GQ15].

Robert Grosseteste, *Templum Dei,* ed. J. Goering and F.A.C. Mantello, *TMLT* 14 (1984): a brief and accessible summary (largely in schematic form) of what a priest needs to know about the pastoral care of souls; written between 1220 and 1230 [GQ16].

Raymund of Peñafort, *Summa . . . De poenitentia, et matrimonio* (Rome 1603, r1967) [GQ17]; a more recent edition is that of J. Ochoa and L. Diez (1976) [GQ18]: an early and very influential application of canon law to the problems of pastoral care; written c. 1225 and revised c. 1234.

William Peraldus, *Summa vitiorum* (1236) and *Summa virtutum* (1248/49): no modern edition, but many early printings, e.g. Lyons 1668 [GQ19].

*Councils & Synods, with Other Documents Relating to the English Church,* v2, ed. F.M. Powicke and C.R. Cheney, 2 pts. (1964): an exemplary edition, with background and notes, of the diocesan, provincial, and legatine legislation issued in England between A.D. 1205 and 1313. Also included are editions of several pastoral manuals that were written to supplement the statutes of the dioceses of Coventry and Exeter [GQ20].

Aag of Denmark, *Rotulus pugillaris,* ed. A. Walz, in *Classica et Mediaevalia* 16 (1955) 136–94: a representative pastoral *summa* written by the Dominican provincial master of Dacia (Scandinavia) in the second half of the thirteenth century [GQ21].

John Bromyard, *Summa predicantium* (c. 1348): no modern edition, but several early printings, e.g. Paris 1518 [GQ22].

Geoffrey Chaucer, "The Parson's Prologue and Tale," in *The Riverside Chaucer,* ed. L.D. Benson, 3rd ed. (1987) 287–327: the Parson's "Tale" is an excellent example of the use to which medieval *pastoralia* were put [GQ23]. It derives from the Latin literature of pastoral care, and one of Chaucer's sources for this tale has been published by S. Wenzel, *Summa virtutum de remediis anime* (1984) [GQ24].

## Studies

M.W. Bloomfield, *The Seven Deadly Sins* (1952): now superseded by [BA118] [GQ25].

M.W. Bloomfield *et al.*, *Incipits of Latin Works on the Virtues and Vices, 1100–1500 A.D., Including a Selection of Incipits of Works on the Pater Noster* (1979) [GQ26].

L.E. Boyle, "The Fourth Lateran Council and Manuals of Popular Theology," in *The Popular Literature of Medieval England,* ed. T.J. Heffernan (1985) 30–43 [GQ27].

L.E. Boyle, "The Inter-Conciliar Period 1179–1215 and the Beginnings of Pastoral Manuals," in *Miscellanea Rolando Bandinelli, Papa Alessandro III,* ed. F. Liotta (1986) 45–56 [GQ28].

L.E. Boyle, *Pastoral Care, Clerical Education and Canon Law, 1200–1400* (1981) [GQ29].

L.E. Boyle, "Summae confessorum," in *Les genres littéraires dans les sources théologiques et philosophiques médiévales: Définition, critique et exploitation: Actes du Colloque international de Louvain-la-Neuve (25–27 May 1981)* (1982) 227–37 [GQ30].

J. Goering, *William de Montibus (c. 1140–1213): The Schools and the Literature of Pastoral Care* (1992): full bibliography, pp614–31 [GQ31].

P. Michaud-Quantin, "A propos des premières *Summae confessorum*," in *Recherches de théologie ancienne et médiévale* 26 (1959) 264–306 [GQ32].

P. Michaud-Quantin, "Les méthodes de la pastorale du XIIIe au XVe siècle," in *MiscM* 7 (1970) 76–91 [GQ33].

P. Michaud-Quantin, *Sommes de casuistique et manuels de confession au moyen âge (XII–XVI siècles)* (1962) [GQ34].

W.A. Pantin, *The English Church in the Fourteenth Century* (1955, r1980) [GQ35].

R.H. Rouse and M.A. Rouse, *PFS* [GQ36].

R.H. Rouse and M.A. Rouse, "*Statim invenire:* Schools, Preachers, and New Attitudes to the Page," in *R&R* 201–25 [GQ37].

S. Wenzel, *The Sin of Sloth: Acedia in Medieval Thought and Literature* (1967) [GQ38].

S. Wenzel, "Vices, Virtues, and Popular Preaching," in *Medieval and Renaissance Studies* 6 (1976) 28–54 [GQ39].

*See also* [BA85], [BA89], [BA131].

# DEBATES AND DIALOGUES

BY PETER BINKLEY

Defined broadly, a dialogue is any literary treatment of a conversation between two or more persons. For the Latin Middle Ages the form generally raised the expectation of a confrontation of persons or allegorical figures representing strongly opposed points of view, often before a judge. This confrontational aspect of the dialogue is indicated by the terms used to describe the works: *altercatio, conflictus, processus, lis,* and so on.

The genre of the dialogue in medieval Europe had its roots in the classical dialogue as practiced in Greek by Plato, and in Latin by Cicero. Alongside these philosophical dialogues ran the pastoral dialogue or eclogue, in which shepherds are represented competing in song; for the Latin West the most influential model was Virgil. In late antiquity the philosophical dialogue was accompanied by didactic magisterial dialogues such as the grammar text of Donatus, in which a *magister* answers the questions of a *discipulus,* and school exercises on themes from history, mythology, and the courtroom.

The classical philosophical dialogue developed in late antiquity into defenses of Christian doctrine against pagan philosophy, Judaism, and Christian heresies. St. Jerome, for example, wrote dialogues between orthodox Christians and Luciferian and Pelagian heretics. The most influential instance of the philosophic dialogue for the Latin Middle Ages was the *De consolatione philosophiae* (c. 520) of Boethius. It is in the form of Menippean satire (in which prose sections alternate with poems). St. Augustine (d. 430) provided models for philosophical dialogue in his early works (the Cassiciacum dialogues) and for the magisterial dialogue in *De magistro* and *De musica.* Hagiography also made use of the dialogue format, as is demonstrated by two dialogues on St. Martin of Tours by Sulpicius Severus (d. c. 420), and later by the *Dialogi* of Gregory the Great (d. 604), which recount the miracles of various saints of Italy. The *Song of Songs* was a model for spiritual dialogues. All of these forms were often imitated in the Middle Ages.

After the flourishing of Christian dialogues, the genre declined until the revival of interest in classical models in the Carolingian period. Poets imitated the eclogue form. This period presents a crucial transition in the development of the later medieval altercation. Whereas the writers of classical eclogue presented contestants competing in song, with nothing in particular of substance to argue, the Carolingian poets began to make the contestants representative in their persons of opposed points of view or states of life. By far the most influential debate from this period was the semiallegorical *Theoduli Ecloga* (probably mid-ninth century) [GR13], in which a pagan shepherd Pseustis (Falsehood) matches stories from mythology against the biblical incidents recounted by a Christian shepherdess Alithia (Truth). It became one of the standard introductory Latin texts in later medieval schools. The *Debate of Spring and Winter* (*Conflictus Veris et Hiemis*) attributed to Alcuin (d. 804) has the allegorical figures of Spring and Winter appear at a gathering of shepherds and argue their merits. At the same time, the revival of education led to new magisterial dialogues. The best known is Alcuin's dialogue on rhetoric (*Dialogus de rhetorica et virtutibus*) [GR9], purportedly with Charlemagne himself as Alcuin's interlocutor. The new need to teach Latin as a second language prompted the use of "colloquies" in the classroom. These are model conversations set in the schoolroom or elsewhere, which the students could read out and construe; many survive from Insular sources [GR16].

The revival of education in the eleventh and twelfth centuries in the monasteries and increasingly in cathedral schools and beyond was accompanied by renewed interest in literary dialogues. Poetic dialogues on stereotyped themes proliferated: Spring vs. Winter, Water vs. Wine, Wine vs. Beer, and many more. The largest thematic group is the dialogue between body and soul, in which the soul visits the body after death to complain of the suffering it undergoes in hell because of the physical temptations to which it yielded in life. The foremost example is the *Visio Philiberti* [GR17], composed in Goliardic stanzas; it survives in well over 100 manuscripts and was translated into most vernaculars. In debates among the Daughters of God Justice, Mercy, Peace, and Truth contend over humanity's fate: Justice argues for damnation, while Mercy urges salvation.

Estates satires were also common, particularly the debate between Clerk and Knight over the value of their respective professions. Since no disinterested male judge can be found, the participants sometimes defer to the judgment of ladies; and indeed the substance of the debate is sometimes over their success as lovers. In a remarkable twelfth-century poem, *The Love-Council of Remiremont* [GR11], nuns debate the value of clerks and knights as lovers; those who favor clerks carry the day, and anathemas are pronounced against their opponents. The Goliardic corpus includes love dialogues of considerable charm, as well as compositions cruder in style and content.

Theologians and philosophers employed the dialogue to explore complex ideas. Our best investigation of the thought of Gilbert of Poitiers (d. c. 1154) is a dialogue between the Cistercian Everard of Ypres and a learned Greek named Ratius [GR6]. Although the setting is realistic and the story includes humorous incidents extraneous to the discussion, the allegorical tinge of Everard's interlocutor is indicated by his signature to a letter to Everard: "Ratius tuus, immo ratio tua." Aelred of Rievaulx's *De spiritali amicitia* (c. 1160) [GR1] likewise treats a philosophical topic in a realistic style.

The dialogues between Christians and Jews were resumed and became very widespread. For example, Gilbert Crispin, abbot of Westminster (1085–1117), produced a dialogue between himself and a Jew, based (he says) on an actual conversation. It is remarkable for the respectful tone on both sides, and for the depth of the Jewish scholar's knowledge of Christian texts. Crispin also wrote a dialogue between a Christian and a pagan philosopher. Peter Abelard combined these forms in his *Dialogus inter philosophum, Iudaeum et Christianum* [GR14].

Political dialogues were produced, for example, out of the tensions of the Investiture controversy. The topos of the clerk and knight debate was easily extended to embrace the conflicting claims to authority of pope and emperor, as in the *Certamen papae et regis* [GR10] written by Hugo Metellus early in the twelfth century. *Papa* and *Rex* discuss first the specific right of investiture, then more generally the basis of their authority; finally, at the king's suggestion, they agree to submit their cause to the judgment of *sapientes*. Dialogues between nations are also common, especially between Englishmen and Frenchmen during the period of the Hundred Years War.

The essential intellectual characteristic of the emerging universities was the scholastic method, exemplified by the *Sic et Non* of Peter Abelard (d. c. 1142). In the disciplines of philosophy, theology, and law and the arts of the trivium and quadrivium, scholars sought to bring the tremendous intellectual patrimony of the Christian West under control by exposing the contradictions among authoritative texts and resolving them: sometimes by proving the exclusive truth of one position, but more often by finding a share of truth on both sides. The academic exercise of the *disputatio* joined the classroom model dialogue. All of these characteristics had a strong influence on debate poetry: stylistic dexterity tended to be displaced by dialectical ingenuity, with an emphasis on logic.

After the mid-fourteenth century, Italian humanists reacted against the scholastic dialogue. Boccaccio (d. 1375) expressed scorn for all eclogues written between Virgil's day and his own. Petrarch (d. 1374) revived the Ciceronian dialogue, characterised by freedom of rhetoric, and contributed to the development of the quattrocento dialogue. The influence of these Italian humanist compositions was felt beyond Italy in the sixteenth century, notably by Erasmus (d. 1536).

## Select Bibliography

### Texts

Aelred of Rievaulx, *De spiritali amicitia*, ed. A. Hoste, *CCCM* 1:279–350 (1971) [GR1].

A. Boutemy, "Pulicis et musce iurgia: Une oeuvre retrouvée de Guillaume de Blois," in *Latomus* 6 (1947) 133–46 [GR2].

E. Braunholtz, "Die Streitgedichte Peters von Blois und Roberts von Beaufeu über den Wert des Weines und Bieres," in *ZRPh* 47 (1927) 30–38 [GR3].

L.W. Daly and W. Suchier, eds., *Altercatio Hadriani Augusti et Epicteti philosophi* (1939) [GR4].

R.P.H. Green, ed., *Seven Versions of Carolingian Pastoral* (1980) [GR5].

N.M. Häring, "A Latin Dialogue on the Doctrine of Gilbert of Poitiers," in *MS* 15 (1953) 243–89: the *Dialogus Ratii et Everardi* [GR6].

M. Haupt, "Hermanni contracti conflictus ovis et lini," in *ZDADL* 11 (1859) 215–38 [GR7].

A. Hilka, ed., "Eine Mittellateinische Dichterfehde: *Versus Michaelis Cornubiensis* [Michael of Cornwall] *contra Henricum Abrincensem* [Henry of Avranches]," in *Mittelalterliche Handschriften: paläographische, kunsthistorische, literarische und bibliotheksgeschichtliche Untersuchungen: Festgabe zum 60. Geburtstag von Hermann Degering*, ed. A. Bömer and J. Kirchner (1926, r1973) 123–54 [GR8].

W.S. Howell, ed. and tr., *The Rhetoric of Alcuin & Charlemagne* (1941, r1965) [GR9].

"Hugonis Metelli opuscula," ed. H. Boehmer, in *MGH.Libelli de lite imperatorum et pontificum* 3 (1897) 711–19 [GR10].

W. Meyer, ed, "Das Liebesconcil in Remiremont," in *NKGWG* (1914) 1–19 [GR11].

H. Omont, "Satire de Garnier de Rouen contre le poète Moriuht (Xe–XIe siècle)," in *Annuaire-Bulletin de la Société de l'histoire de France* 31 (1894) 193–210 [GR12].

J. Osternacher, ed., *Theoduli Ecloga* (1902) [GR13].

Peter Abelard, *Dialogus inter philosophum, Iudaeum et Christianum*, ed. R. Thomas (1970) [GR14].

P.G. Schmidt, "'Causa Aiacis et Ulixis I–II': Zwei ovidianische Streitgedichte des Mittelalters," in *MLJ* 1 (1964) 100–32 [GR15].

W.H. Stevenson, ed., *Early Scholastic Colloquies* (1929, r1989) [GR16].

*Visio Philiberti* [*Dialogus inter corpus et animam*], in *The Latin Poems Commonly Attributed to Walter Mapes*, ed. T. Wright, *CamSoc* 16 (1841) 95–106 [GR17].

## Studies

T. Batiouchkof, "Le débat de l'âme et du corps," in *Romania* 20 (1891) 1–55, 513–78: still the most thorough survey [GR18].

B. Blumenkranz, *Les auteurs chrétiens latins du moyen âge sur les juifs et le judaisme*, Études Juives 4 (1963) [GR19].

B. Blumenkranz, "La *Disputatio Judei cum Christiano* de Gilbert Crispin, abbé de Westminster," in *RMAL* 4 (1948) 237–52 [GR20].

M.-A. Bossy, "Medieval Debates of Body and Soul," in *Comparative Literature* 28 (1976) 144–63 [GR21].

C. Burnett, "Peter Abelard 'Soliloquium,'" in *SM*, 3rd ser., 25 (1984) 857–94: with edition and translation [GR22].

A. Cantin, "Sur quelques aspects des disputes publiques au XIe siècle latin," in *Études de civilisation médiévale, IXe–XIIe siècles: Mélanges offerts à Edmond-René Labande* (1974?) 89–104 [GR23].

H. Cooper, *Pastoral: Mediaeval into Renaissance* (1977) [GR24].

E. Faral, "Les débats du clerc et du chevalier dans la littérature des XIIe et XIIIe siècles," in *id.*, *Recherches sur les sources latines des contes et romans courtois du moyen âge* (1913, r1983) 191–303 [GR25].

D. Goldin, "Monologo, dialogo e 'disputatio' nella 'commedia elegiaca,'" in *Il dialogo: Scambi e passaggi della parola*, ed. G. Ferroni (1985) 72–86 [GR26].

R.S. Haller, "The *Altercatio Phylidis et Florae* as an Ovidian Satire," in *MS* 30 (1968) 119–33 [GR27].

J.H. Hanford, "Classical Eclogue and Mediaeval Debate," in *RomRev* 2 (1911), 16–31; 129–43 [GR28].

N.M. Häring, "The Cistercian Everard of Ypres and His Appraisal of the Conflict between St. Bernard and Gilbert of Poitiers," in *MS* 17 (1955) 143–72 [GR29].

B.N. Hedberg, "The *Bucolics* and the Medieval Poetical Debate," in *TAPhS* 75 (1944) 47–67 [GR30].

M. Hoffmann, *Der Dialog bei den christlichen Schriftstellern der ersten vier Jahrhunderte*, Texte und Untersuchungen zur Geschichte der altchristlichen Literatur 96 (1966) [GR31].

S. Lerer, *Boethius and Dialogue: Literary Method in The Consolation of Philosophy* (1985) [GR32].

D. Marsh, *The Quattrocento Dialogue: Classical Tradition and Humanist Innovation* (1980) [GR33].

F.J.E. Raby, "The Poetical Debate," in *SLP* 2:282–308 [GR34].

E. Reiss, "Conflict and Its Resolution in Medieval Dialogues," in *Arts libéraux et philosophie au moyen âge*, Actes du quatrième congrès international de philosophie médiévale (27 August–2 September 1967) (1969) 863–72 [GR35].

E.C. Ronquist, "Learning and Teaching in Twelfth-Century Dialogues," in *RPL* 13 (1990) 239–56 [GR36].

P.L. Schmidt, "Zur Typologie und Literarisierung des frühchristlichen lateinischen Dialogs," in *Christianisme et formes littéraires de l'antiquité tardive en occident*, Entretiens sur l'antiquité classique 23 (1977) 101–90: see [GB56] [GR37].

W.S. Seiferth, *Synagoge und Kirche im Mittelalter* (1964); English translation (1970) [GR38].

J. Suchomski, *"Delectatio" und "Utilitas": Ein Beitrag zum Verständnis mittelalterlicher komischer Literatur* (1975) [GR39].

H. Traver, "The Four Daughters of God: A Mirror of Changing Doctrine," in *PMLA* 40 (1925) 44–92 [GR40].

P. von Moos, "Literatur- und bildungsgeschichtliche Aspekte der Dialogform im lateinischen Mittelalter: Der 'Dialogus Ratii' des Eberhard von Ypern zwischen theologischer 'disputatio' und Scholaren-Kömodie," in *Tradition und Wertung: Festschrift für Franz Brunhölzl zum 65. Geburtstag*, ed. G. Bernt et al. (1989) 165–209 [GR41].

B.R. Voss, *Der Dialog in der frühchristlichen Literatur*, Studia et testimonia antiqua 9 (1970) [GR42].

H. Walther, *Das Streitgedicht in der lateinischen Literatur des Mittelalters*, ed. P.G. Schmidt, Quellen und Untersuchungen zur lateinischen Philologie des Mittelalters 5.2, 2nd ed. (1984): the fundamental study of the genre; the *Nachträge* supplied by Schmidt provide a bibliographical overview of published works since 1920 [GR43].

J.M. Ziolkowski, *TA* [GR44].

# TRAVEL LITERATURE

BY JEAN RICHARD

(translated from French by GEORGE E. GINGRAS)

Those medieval travelers who have left accounts of their journeys were either ambassadors sent to foreign princes or persons who had had unusual adventures in little-known countries where they had gone, sometimes as merchants, more often as missionaries, and especially as pilgrims who visited sanctuaries whose cult they wished to encourage. As a result, their narratives belong to different literary genres: either to diverse types of historical or autobiographical writing, or to the reports associated with the accomplishment of missions of one kind or another, or indeed to an even better defined type, the pilgrimage narrative.

Travel literature also includes works intended for future travelers, guidebooks if you will. Early on, there was a need to inform pilgrims en route to the Holy Land as to which sites they should visit. Information was drawn from the *Itineraria* of late antiquity, which enumerated both the way stations and the distances between them, as well as from the writings of St. Jerome (d. 420). Particular attention was paid to his *Ep.* 108 on Paula's pilgrimage as well as to any other texts containing scriptural references to the places to be venerated, along with a suggested etymology for each one. It is this sort of data that is found in the *De situ terrae sanctae* of Theodosius (c. 518), in Bede (d. 735), and in Peter the Deacon (d. after 1153)—the librarian of Monte Cassino who in 1137 wrote a *De locis sanctis*—as well as in other treatises of the eleventh and twelfth centuries, notably that of the shadowy Eugesippus. Other authors sought their information in the recollections of pilgrims whom they questioned on their return home in the fashion of Adamnan of Iona, who, sometime between 679 and 704, interrogated the Gallic bishop Arculf, to obtain from him news of what he had seen on his pilgrimage, including sketches of the Holy Sepulcher.

The most famous of the pilgrimage guidebooks is the *Descriptio terrae sanctae*, written in 1137 by a cleric of the Holy Land, Rorgo Fretellus of Nazareth, for Henry Sdyck, bishop of Prague, and reworked (in 1148?) for a Spanish count, perhaps Rodrigo of Traba. Equally famous are the "Descriptions of the Holy Land" by two German pilgrims, Theoderic of Würzburg (fl. 1172) and Burchard of Mount Sion (c. 1283), both of whom included recollections of their own travels. Other "descriptions" of the same genre, often deeply indebted to Burchard, were written in the fourteenth and fifteenth centuries. One such text, which dates from 1463, concludes with an expression of hope for the recovery of the Holy Land by the Christians, a motif that places the work within the purview of treatises variously entitled *De recuperatione terrae sanctae*, although the text in question is very definitely a pilgrims' guidebook.

The masterpiece of this type of literature does not, however, deal with the Holy Land. Rather it is "the pilgrim's guide to St. James of Compostella," as Jeanne Vielliard has called it [GS17], and it makes up bk. 5 of the *Liber sancti Jacobi.* It dates from the years 1139–79 and informs pilgrims of the roads to take, the chances of finding fresh supplies, the quality of the water, the precautions to be taken against illness, the level of hospitality to be expected, and the anticipated expenses. Listed are the sanctuaries to be visited en route, along with information on the saints venerated at each. The basilica of St. James is described in detail, just as a guidebook for modern tourists might do. For visits to Rome there exist other such guides, albeit less detailed ones, of which the first in date is a purely descriptive text from the late twelfth century, the anonymous *Mirabilia Romae.*

The transition from guidebook to pilgrimage narrative is hardly perceptible, as the intention of the narrator of a pilgrimage is shared by the author of a *tractatus de terra sancta.* Theoderic stated that he had described the places where Christ had lived both from his own recollections and from what he had learned from the accounts of others, "so as to satisfy the yearnings of those who could not themselves visit them," in other words as a pilgrimage in spirit ([GS10] p9). John of Würzburg, who wrote at approximately the same time, told the friend for whom he intended his narrative that it could either serve him as a guidebook, should he himself undertake a pilgrimage, or assist him in his meditations, if he did not travel to the Holy Land. But the author of such a narrative tends to structure his account around his own experiences. He presents the places that he describes in the same order in which he visited them, he puts himself in the picture, he highlights his impressions and feelings. An Anthony de Reboldis (d. 1331) or an Anselm Adorno (d. 1471), for example, described the emotions experienced on spending a night at the Holy Sepulcher.

The oldest of these narratives, that of Egeria, was written between 381 and 384; that of the Pilgrim of Piacenza around 570; and Bernard the Monk's in 870. Leaving aside the Crusader narratives, which are also to a degree *itineraria,* we have, starting in 1102, the report of the journey of the English monk Saewulf, and after him a number of accounts from visitors to the Hold Land in the time of the Latin States: the Icelandic abbot Nicholas of Munkathvera (Nicholas Saemundarson); John of Würzburg in 1172; Wilbrand of Oldenburg and Thietmar at the beginning of the thirteenth century; and Ricold of Monte Croce (d. 1320) at the end of the century. After the fall of the Latin States, pilgrimages ceased for a time, only to begin anew around 1330, and accounts thereof grew steadily in number: Anthony de Reboldis of Cremona, the Irishman Simon Semeonis, Humbert of Dijon, William of Boldensele, Ludolf of Sudheim (Suchem), James of Verona, Nicholas of Martoni. More and more these accounts went beyond a simple description of the holy places to encompass the journey as a whole. This was true as well of the Latin accounts of the fifteenth century by Felix Fabri (Schmidt) of Ulm, Anselm Adorno, and Bernard of Breydenbach. Indeed, the latter's *Peregrinationes* represented a veritable compilation, illustrated with engravings. All of these narratives, from the thirteenth century on, allowed considerable space for notations of an ethnographic nature. Both the customs of the Muslims and the rites of Near Eastern Christians were on occasion the object of very detailed descriptions.

In this way the pilgrimage narrative gradually came to resemble other forms of travel writing, especially the accounts of ambassadors sent to the Mongols either to reach an understanding with them or to invite them to accept the Christian faith. These envoys were expected, of course, to bring back information about this unknown people, whose aggressive intentions were feared. John of Plano Carpini (d. 1252) was careful to clarify both their way of fighting and their customs, and William of Rubruck (Guillelmus de Rubruquis, fl. thirteenth century) received instructions from St. Louis to collect for him as much information as possible. Finally, the missionaries who sought to interest European readers in their efforts at proselytizing also contributed substantially to a detailed description of the peoples of the East.

All authors of such accounts behaved like explorers eager to share their discoveries. This was already true of the merchant Ohthere, who had informed King Alfred of what he had seen in the northern reaches of Scandinavia. Gerald of Wales, after a preaching circuit in Wales, devoted a section of his *Itinerarium Kambriae* to describing the geography of the country. The envoys to the Mongols also did the work of geographers, and it is possible to see in William of Rubruck the first ethnologist.

Their great concern was to make known what are popularly called the "wonders of the world"—whether these were unknown animals, natural phenomena, human behavior, monuments, or simply the incubators for hatching eggs in the Nile Valley. Jordan Cathala of Séverac (fl. mid-fourteenth century), who spent years evangelizing the peoples of India, outdid ancient authors when he drew up his listing of the wonders of that land. He also took note of the extraordinary things he had seen elsewhere and his book is entitled *Mirabilia descripta*. In any case it would be a mistake to accuse these travelers of credulity. If Odoric of Pordenone (1286–1331) readily accepted fabulous data, others strove to verify the claims of ancient authors and to rectify geographical errors. What made, however, for the success of their narratives was the fact that their own curiosity was matched by that of readers eager to know more of the world.

These writers were also inclined to round out their personal discoveries with information drawn from other sources. Felix Fabri tells us that he is writing for his conventual brothers at Ulm, who asked him to inform them about foreign countries, and he filled in his travel notes by incorporating whole chapters about lands he had not visited. William of Boldensele and Ludolf of Sudheim did likewise. The travel narrative form was the one that seemed most suitable for a "description of the world."

It should also not be forgotten that certain travelers were especially enthusiastic to recount their adventures. This is particularly true of knights who had gone in search of adventure and who wished to valorize their chevalric experiences, as did, for example, Jörg von Ehingen in his *Itinerarium* (1454).

Even mystical experience could find expression in travel narrative form. Such is the case with the narratives of St. Patrick's visit to purgatory, the most ancient of which is that of Oengus O'Brien (*Visio Oenii*, c. 1200), but a number of them were composed in the fourteenth century as well [GS31]. Irish hagiography preserved narratives of travels in quest of the other world, the most famous of which, the *Navigatio Sancti Brendani*, combined elements from actual Atlantic voyages with imaginary data.

The pilgrimage narrative had a rather well-defined form. The descriptive portion could sometimes overshadow, however, the pilgrim's account of the journey, which, from the thirteenth century on, constituted the major part of the text. Compilers of travel narratives could adopt more varied models; John of Marignola (fl.

1338–53) even interspersed recollections of his journey to China and India through-out the text of his Bohemian chronicle. Travelers often took notes day by day and wrote out a fair copy after their return, filling in lacunae from their readings, a prac-tice that accounts for the frequent borrowings.

Sometimes travelers had recourse to comparisons with what was familiar to their readers, in order to allow them to gauge the width of a river or the size of a city. Since their vocabulary itself had to express realities that were alien to their readers, these travel writers would borrow words from the local languages or give to the Latin words a different meaning from what was commonly understood. They rendered place names by phonetical equivalents that are often only approximations. As for the names of persons, they are sometimes unrecognizable. The interpretation of these texts calls, therefore, for a commentary and identifications that require the inter-vention of historians, ethnologists, and other specialists.

In summary, as early as the Middle Ages travel literature enjoyed great success, evidence of which is to be found both in the number of surviving manuscripts of cer-tain texts and in their frequent translation into the vernacular. These translations have markedly increased in our day, and both the Palestine Pilgrims' Text Society and the Hakluyt Society have produced excellent examples that often include indispens-able commentaries.

## Select Bibliography

### Primary Works

#### (a) Collections

S. De Sandoli, ed., *Itinera Hierosolymitana crucesignatorum (saec. XII–XIII)*, 4 vols. (1978–84): includes Saewulf, *Certa relatio de situ Jerusalem*, v2:1–32; Rorgo Fretel-lus, *Liber locorum sanctorum terrae Jerusalem*, v2:119–52; Peter the Deacon, *De locis sanctis*, v2:171–206; Nicholas of Munkathvera (Nicholas Saemundarson), *Iter ad loca sancta*, v2:207–24; John of Würzburg, *Descriptio terrae sanctae*, v2:225–95; Wilbrand of Oldenburg, *Itinerarium terrae sanctae*, v3:195–50; Thiet-mar (Magister Thetmarus), *Iter ad terram sanctam*, v3:251–96; Burchard of Mount Sion, *Descriptio terrae sanctae*, v4:119–220; Ricold of Monte Croce, *Liber peregrinationis*, v4:255–332 [GS1].

G. Golubovich, *Biblioteca bio-bibliografica della Terra Santa e dell'Oriente frances-cano*, 5 vols. (1906–27) [GS2]

*Itineraria et alia geographica*, 2 vols., CCSL 175–76 (1965): v175 includes the *Itinerari-um* of Egeria, ed. E. Franceschini and R. Weber, pp37–90; Peter the Deacon, *Liber de locis sanctis*, ed. R. Weber, pp93–103; Theodosius, *De situ Terrae Sanctae*, ed. P. Geyer, pp115–25; the *Itinerarium* of Pseudo-Antoninus Placentinus (the Pil-grim of Piacenza), ed. P. Geyer, pp129–53, 157–74 (*recensio altera*); Adamnan, *De locis sanctis*, ed. L. Bieler, pp183–234, and Bede, *De locis sanctis*, ed. I. Fraipont, pp251–80. Vol. 176, of indices, includes an "index nominum" (*Itineraria Hierosolymitana*), an "index nominum et rerum" (*Itineraria Romana* and *Geographica*), and an "index verborum et locutionum." Bibliographies: v175:IX–XIII, 31–34 (*Itinerarium Egeriae*), 107; v176:851–52 [GS3].

J.C.M. Laurent, ed., *Peregrinatores medii aevi quatuor*, 2nd ed. (1873): includes Burchard of Mount Sion, *Descriptio terrae sanctae*, pp1–100; Ricold of Monte Croce, *Liber peregrinationis*, pp101–41; Odoric of Pordenone, pp142–53; and Wilbrand of Oldenburg, *Itinerarium terrae sanctae*, pp154–91 [GS4].

*Recueil de voyages et de mémoires, publié par la Société de Géographie*, v4 (1839): includes Jordan Cathala of Séverac, *Mirabilia descripta*, ed. C.-É. Coquebert de Montbret, pp37–64; William of Rubruck, *Itinerarium*, ed. F. Michel and T. Wright, pp213–396; John of Plano Carpini, *Historia Mongalorum*, ed. M.A.P. d'Avezac, 603–733; Bernard the Monk (Bernard the Wise), *Itinerarium*, ed. F. Michel, pp785–94; Saewulf, *Relatio de peregrinatione ad Hierosolymam et Terram Sanctam*, ed. M.A.P. d'Avezac, pp833–54 [GS5].

*Revue de l'Orient latin*, 12 vols. (Paris 1893–1911): includes Louis of Rochechouart (1461), v1:168–274; James of Verona, v3:155–302; Nicholas of Martoni, v3:516–669; Franciscan Anonymous (1463), v12:1–67 [GS6].

A. Van den Wyngaert, *Itinera et relationes Fratrum Minorum saeculi XIII et XIV*, Sinica Franciscana 1 (1929): includes John of Plano Carpini, William of Rubruck, John of Montecorvino, Odoric of Pordenone, Paschal of Vitoria, John of Marignola [GS7].

## (b) Individual Authors and Texts (very selective)

P.C. Boeren, ed., *Rorgo Fretellus de Nazareth et sa Description de la Terre Sainte: Histoire et édition du texte* (1980) [GS8].

J.S. Brewer *et al.*, eds., *Girardi Cambrensis opera*, 8 vols., RSer 21 (1861–91): see v6:3–152 for the *Itinerarium Kambriae* [GS9].

M.L. and W. Bulst, eds., Theodericus, *Libellus de locis sanctis* (1976) [GS10].

M. Esposito, ed. and tr., *Itinerarium Symonis Semeonis ab Hybernia ad Terram Sanctam* (1960) [GS11].

C.D. Hassler, ed., *Fratris Felicis Fabri Evagatorium in Terrae Sanctae, Arabiae et Egypti peregrinationem*, 3 vols., Bibliothek des literarischen Vereins in Stuttgart 2–4 (1843–49) [GS12].

H. Jordan, ed., *Mirabilia urbis Romae*, in *Topographie der Stadt Rom im Altertum* 2 (1871) 607–43 [GS13].

G.A. Neuman, ed., Ludolf of Sudheim, *Descriptio terrae sanctae*, in *Archives de l'Orient latin* 2 (1884) 305–77 [GS14].

R. Pernoud, ed., *Un guide du pèlerin en Terre Sainte au XVe siècle* (1940) [GS15].

C. Selmer, ed., *Navigatio Sancti Brendani abbatis* (1959, r1989); tr. J.J. O'Meara [GS16].

J. Vielliard, ed. and tr., *Le guide du pèlerin de Saint-Jacques de Compostelle* (1938, r1984) [GS17].

H. Yule, ed. and tr., *Cathay and the Way Thither: Being a Collection of Medieval Notices of China* (1866); new ed. rev. H. Cordier, 4 vols., Hakluyt Society, 2nd ser., vols. 33, 37, 38, and 41 (1913–16, r1966–72): includes, in v33, an edition and translation of Odoric of Pordenone [GS18].

For additional information about texts and editions see [GS22]; C.R. Beazley, *The Dawn of Modern Geography*, 3 vols. (1897–1906, r1949), v1:525–30, v3:552–56 [GS19]; and J.K. Wright, *The Geographical Lore of the Time of the Crusades* (1925, r1965 with additions) 503–43 (where English translations are also listed) [GS20].

## Bibliographies and Studies

M.B. Campbell, *The Witness and the Other World: Exotic European Travel Writings, 400–1600* (1988): bibliography (pp267–78) includes references to English translations of Adamnan, Burchard of Mount Sion, Egeria, Felix Fabri, Odoric of Pordenone, William of Rubruck, etc. [GS21].

L.K. Davidson and M. Dunn-Wood, *Pilgrimage in the Middle Ages: A Research Guide* (1993) [GS22].

M. Dunn and L.K. Davidson, *The Pilgrimage to Santiago de Compostella: A Comprehensive, Annotated Bibliography* (1994) [GS23].

X. von Ertzdorff and D. Neukirch, eds., *Reisen und Reiseliteratur im Mittelalter und in der frühen Neuzeit* (1992) [GS24].

M. Haren and Y. de Pontfarcy, eds., *The Medieval Pilgrimage to St. Patrick's Purgatory, Lough Derg, and the European Tradition* [GS25].

R. Henning, *Terrae incognitae: Eine Zusammenstellung und kritische Bewertung der wichtigsten vorcolumbischen Entdeckungsreisen an Hand der darüber vorliegenden Originalberichte*, 2nd ed., 4 vols. (1944–56): v2–4 concern the medieval period, with useful bibliography at the end of v4 [GS26].

E.D. Hunt, *Holy Land Pilgrimage in the Later Roman Empire*, A.D. 312–460 (1982) [GS27].

A.P. Newton, ed., *Travel and Travellers of the Middle Ages* (1926, r1949) [GS28].

N. Ohler, *The Medieval Traveller*, tr. C. Hiller (1989) [GS29].

J. Richard, *Les récits de voyages et de pèlerinages*, TSMAO 38 (1981) and updating (1985) [GS30].

J. Richard, "Un comte d'Auxerre en Irlande au XIVème siècle: Louis d'Auxerre au Purgatoire de Saint Patrice," in *Bulletin de la Société des sciences historiques et naturelles de l'Yonne* 123 (1991) 47–59 [GS31].

H. Rohrbacher, "Bernhard von Breydenbach und sein Werk 'Peregrinatio in Terram Sanctam' (1486)," in *Philobiblon: Eine Vierteljahrsschrift für Buch- und Graphiksammler* 33 (1989) 89–113 [GS32].

R. Röhricht, *Bibliotheca geographica Palaestinae: Chronologisches Verzeichniss der auf die Geographie des Heiligen Landes bezüglichen Literatur von 333 bis 1878* (1890, r1963 with additions by D. Amiran) [GS33].

J.-P. Roux, *Les explorateurs au moyen âge* (1985): bibliography, pp319–25 [GS34].

B.N. Sargent-Baur, ed., *Journeys toward God: Pilgrimages and Crusade* (1992): includes J.G. Davies, "Pilgrimage and Crusade Literature" (pp1–30) [GS35].

J. Sumption, *Pilgrimage: An Image of Mediaeval Religion* (1975) [GS36].

*Wallfahrt und Alltag in Mittelalter und früher Neuzeit: Internationales Round-Table-Gesprach, Krems an der Donau, 8. Oktober 1990* (1992) [GS37].

S.D. Westrem, ed., *Discovering New Worlds: Essays on Medieval Exploration and Imagination* (1991) [GS38].

J. Wilkinson, *Jerusalem Pilgrims before the Crusades* (1977) [GS39].

J. Wilkinson *et al.*, eds., *Jerusalem Pilgrimage, 1099–1185* (1988) [GS40].

P. Wunderli, ed., *Reisen in reale und mythische Ferne: Reiseliteratur in Mittelalter und Renaissance* (1993) [GS41].

*See also* [BC117].

GT  •  VISION LITERATURE

BY PETER DINZELBACHER
(translated from German by SIEGFRIED A. SCHULZ)

We speak of a vision when a person experiences being transferred by an exterior force from his or her natural environment into another place, when he or she visually perceives this place or its contents, when this transfer occurs in a state of ecstasy or during sleep, and when, as a result, things previously hidden are revealed. In most cases this revelation is effected through the voice of a creature beheld in the vision, or through a disembodied voice, or by immediate, "infused" intellectual cognition. Often people in a state of ecstasy are taken to be dead by those in attendance, or their state is described as apparent death. The visionaries themselves feel this experience as a separation of soul and body, the soul moving through terrestrial and extraterrestrial expanses before reentering the body. Thanatology, a new branch of medical psychology, has in very recent times recorded a great number of such experiences of people who appeared to be dead [GT55].

While records of visions have rarely come down to us from Greek antiquity (Plato, *Republic* 614b–621d), and none whatsoever from Roman times, they constituted a frequent topic of Jewish apocryphal literature in the form of apocalypses. The *Visio S. Pauli,* a Latin version of the Apostle Paul's (fictitious) otherworld journey originally written in Greek, was destined to circulate widely, especially in Western monasteries. This vision, as well as those found in bk. 4 of the *Dialogi* of Gregory the Great, served as prototypes, and later visionaries who had read them experienced anew elements of these authoritative texts in their own states of ecstasy. One therefore often finds in these later visions parallel motifs that have their origin partially in literary *imitatio.* The term *vision literature* pertains for the most part to those kinds of texts that are autobiographical reports of experiences, or to biographies based on the protagonists' own statements (most visions are not recorded by the visionaries themselves, but are dictated to amanuenses). There are also isolated examples of falsified texts compiled for political purposes and of purely fictional works of a pious and didactic nature. Fictitious visions and dreams are not uncommon both in Latin (e.g. Walter of Châtillon, *Dum contemplor animo*) and in the vernacular (e.g. Rutebeuf, *La voie de paradis*).

The Middle Ages were the heyday of vision literature, and the *Visio Baronti* (678/9) may be considered its earliest independent text. In 824 the vision of the dying Benedictine, Wetti, which describes above all the punishments of the hereafter, was recorded in the monastery of Reichenau by Heito of Basel and soon versified (in hexameters) by Walafrid Strabo (d. 849). In some saints' lives, too, visions have an important role to play, e.g. in Rimbert's life of St. Ansgar of Bremen (d. 865). An early forerunner of collections containing various visions, either one's own or those of others, is the *Liber visionum* of the Benedictine Otloh of St. Emmeram (before 1070). Numerous historical works also preserve reports of visions, including those by Gregory of Tours (d. 594/5), Bede (d. 735), and the Cistercian Hélinand of Froidmont (d. after 1229). But the best known medieval vision of the hereafter, extant in some 200 manuscripts, is the *Visio Tnugdali*, recorded in elegant Latin in 1149 at Regensburg by an Irish monk named Marcus. It was printed early; was translated into all the vernaculars, including Old Norse and Old Russian; and was quoted even by Martin Luther (d. 1546). It describes the visions of the Irish knight Tundal, employing a wealth of bizarre, sadistic motifs typical of the genre, e.g. the bridge of nails, six inches wide, under which towering, fire-spewing monsters lie in wait for their victims; the winged beast that digests the souls of monks and nuns and discharges them, transformed, upon a lake of ice, where they are impregnated by snakes that tear them apart from within; the Prince of Darkness fettered to a grill, and so on. Another example, almost unique in the tradition, is the journey through purgatory of the Holstein peasant Gottschalk (1189), as described independently by two anonymous clerics. Here one can recognize clearly the fusion of elements of Germanic mythology with Christian concepts.

With respect to structure, visions of the hereafter usually begin with the circumstances leading to the visionary's rapture; descriptions of the visions themselves follow, and the accounts conclude with a report of the soul's return into its body. Occasionally the visionary's further fate is also alluded to: Wetti dies; Alberic of Settefrati enters a monastery; and Tundal repents of his sins and marches as a crusader to the Holy Land.

Until the High Middle Ages, medieval visionary literature consisted mainly of visions of the hereafter. This type reached its apex in the twelfth century (and in an abbreviated form was included in later collections of sermon *exempla*). At the same time there arose experiential mysticism and with it books of revelations consisting entirely or partially of visions. There is also, slowly, a change in authorship: until the High Middle Ages primarily the visions of monks were recorded, but now many lay people contribute to the genre. And it is women who plainly dominate the visionary literature of mysticism.

The works of the Benedictine nun Hildegard of Bingen (1098–1179), such as her *Scivias, Liber vitae meritorum,* and *Liber divinorum operum,* remain somewhat apart in the history of visionary literature, not only because of their wide-ranging and carefully assembled contents, but also because of the nonecstatic character of their inspiration. They are allegorical interpretations of images drawn from salvation history, ethics, and the secrets of nature. The three books of visions of the Benedictine nun Elizabeth of Schönau (d. 1164) are the beginning of the type of revelations experienced by mystically gifted women, which, in Catholicism, extends to modern times. Visions inspired by liturgical feasts reveal the celestial as well as the underworld to a saintly woman, who is accompanied by her angel; these visions take her to the Lord's Passion in Jerusalem, lead her up God's symbolic mountain, and so forth. Such visions as recorded in the books of revelations of Gertrude the Great (d. 1301 or 1302) and Mechthild of Hackeborn (d. 1299) in the monastery of Helfta center around the encounter with Christ as loving spouse. Similar were the experiences of many south German Dominican nuns of the thirteenth century to the fifteenth, whose lives of grace have come down to us, first in Latin and later in German, in monastic chronicles or collections of *vitae*. The visions of a number of women, e.g. of Angela of Foligno (d. 1309), a Franciscan tertiary from Italy; of Lukardis of Ober-weimar (d. 1309), a Cistercian nun from Saxony; and of Agnes Blannbekin (d. 1315), an Austrian Beguine, were recorded in much greater detail; all of these were passed down by their confessors in mixtures of vision reports and biographical data. The revelations of St. Bridget of Sweden (d. 1373) were the most widely circulated Latin examples of this kind of text from the period towards the end of the Middle Ages. Her revelations were, however, more auditory in character than visual.

Most of the later books of revelations, e.g. those of the Dominican tertiary Catherine of Siena (d. 1380), Julian of Norwich (d. 1416/23), and Margery Kempe (d. after 1439), were written in the various vernaculars, although one also continues to find such Latin accounts as the record of the visions of Alan de la Roche, O.P. (d. 1475), and the *Compendium revelationum* of Girolamo Savonarola, O.P. (d. 1498). It was a consequence of differing educational opportunities that men preferred to use Latin and women used the vernacular.

The literature of visions of the hereafter became, in the late Middle Ages, the basis for an entire branch of allegorical poetry: the dream journey to another world, whether Christian or secular. The *Commedia* of Dante (d. 1321), the masterpiece of medieval literature, belongs to this category, but other eminent poets have also made use of the genre: Raoul de Houdenc, Guillaume de Lorris, Rutebeuf, Guillaume de Deguileville, Boccaccio, Chaucer, Gower, Lydgate, Santillana, Dunbar, and many others; John Bunyan (1628–88) is a more recent successor. Reports of mystical visions by both male and female mystics have continued until the present day, as a (vernacular) genre within Catholicism; modern examples are those of Gemma Galgani (d. 1903) and Therese Neumann of Konnersreuth (d. 1962).

## Select Bibliography

### Primary Works

#### (a) Anthologies

M.P. Ciccarese, *Visioni dell'aldilà in Occidente* (1987): deals only with late antiquity and the early Middle Ages; Italian translations [GT1].

P. Dinzelbacher, *Mittelalterliche Visionsliteratur: Eine Anthologie* (1989): covers the whole period and both Latin and vernacular texts; with German translations [GT2].

#### (b) Translations

O. Delepierre, *L'enfer décrit par ceux qui l'ont vu*, Miscellanies of the Philobiblon Society 8.5 and 9.10 (1863, 1866) [GT3]

E. Gardiner, *Medieval Visions of Heaven and Hell: A Sourcebook* (1993) [GT4].

J. Marchand, *L'autre monde au moyen âge: Voyages et visions* (1940) [GT5].

E.A. Petroff, *Medieval Women's Visionary Literature* (1986) [GT6].

(c) **Individual Authors and Texts** (very selective)

*Visio Alberici*, ed. M. Inguanez, in *MiscC* 11 (1932) 81–103 [GT7].

*La vie de la bienheureuse Alpais de Cudot*, ed. M. Blanchon (1893) [GT8].

*Visio Baronti monachi Longoretensis*, ed. W. Levison, in *MGH.SRM* 5 (1910, r1979) 368–94 [GT9].

Birgitta of Sweden, *Revelationes caelestes* (1680); *Liber I*, ed. C.-G. Undhagen (1977); *IV*, ed. H. Aili (1992); *V* and *VII*, ed. B. Bergh (1971, 1967); *Revelaciones extravagantes*, ed. L. Hollman (1956) [GT10].

*Visio monachi* [Edmund of Eynsham], ed. H.E. Salter, in *The Eynsham Cartulary*, v2 (1908) 257–371 [GT11].

*Die Visionen der hl. Elisabeth [von Schönau] und die Schriften der Äbte Ekbert und Emecho von Schönau*, ed. F.W.E. Roth, 2nd ed. (1886) [GT12].

*Visiones Flothildae*, ed. P. Lauer, in his *Le règne de Louis IV d'Outre-mer* (1900) 315–19 [GT13].

*Le visioni de S. Fursa*, ed. M.P. Ciccarese, in *Romanobarbarica* 8 (1984/85) 231–303 [GT14].

*Visiones Georgii*, ed. L.L. Hammerich (1930) [GT15].

Gertrude of Helfta, *Legatus divinae pietatis*, ed. P. Doyère, J.-M. Clément, the nuns of Wisques, and B. de Vregille, 4 vols., *SChr* 139, 143, 255, 331 (1968–86) [GT16].

*Godeschalcus und Visio Godeschalci*, ed. E. Assmann, Quellen und Forschungen zur Geschichte Schleswig-Holsteins 74 (1979) [GT17].

Hildegard of Bingen, *Opera*, *PL* 197 [GT18]; *Scivias*, ed. A. Führkötter, *CCCM* 43–43A (1978) [GT19]; *Epistolarium*, pts1–2, ed. L. Van Acker, *CCCM* 91–91A (1991–93) [GT20].

*Vita venerabilis Lukardis*, ed. J. De Backer, in *AB* 18 (1899) 305–67 [GT21].

Mechthild of Hackeborn, *Liber specialis gratiae*, ed. Monachi Solesmenses, *Revelationes Gertrudianae ac Mechthildianae*, v2 (1877) [GT22].

Otloh of St. Emmeram, *Liber visionum*, ed. P.G. Schmidt, *MGH.Quellen zur Geistesgeschichte des Mittelalters* 13 (1989) [GT23].

*Visio cuiusdam paupulae mulieris*, ed. H. Houben, in *Zeitschrift für Geschichte des Oberrheins* 124 (1976) 31–42 [GT24].

Peter of Cornwall, *The Visions of Ailsi and His Sons*, ed. R. Easting and R. Sharpe, in *Mediaevistik* 1 (1988) 207–62 [GT25].

*Vision de Robert, abbé de Mozat*, ed. R. Rigodon, in *Bulletin historique et scientifique de l'Auvergne* 70 (1950) 22–55 [GT26].

*Le "Livre des révélations" de Marie Robine (d. 1399)*, ed. M. Tobin, in *Mélanges de l'École française de Rome: Moyen âge, temps modernes* 98 (1986) 229–64 [GT27].

*Visio Thurkilli*, ed. P.G. Schmidt (1978) [GT28].

Robert d'Uzès, *Liber visionum*, ed. J. Bignami-Odier, in *AFP* 25 (1955) 258–310 [GT29].

*Visio Tnugdali, lateinisch und altdeutsch*, ed. A. Wagner (1882, r1989) [GT30].

*Visio Wettini*, ed. E. Dümmler, in *MGH.Poetae* 2 (1884, r1964) 267–75 [GT31]; ed. and tr. D.A. Traill (1974) [GT32].

## Studies

J. Amat, *Songes et visions: L'au-delà dans la littérature latine tardive* (1985) [GT33].

E.J. Becker, "A Contribution to the Comparative Study of the Medieval Visions of Heaven and Hell, with Special Reference to the Middle-English Versions" (Ph.D. diss., Johns Hopkins University, 1897) [GT34].

E. Benz, *Die Vision: Erfahrungsformen und Bilderwelt* (1969): fundamental analysis of the phenomenon in Christianity through the ages [GT35].

C. Carozzi, *Le voyage de l'âme dans l'au-delà, d'après la littérature latine (Ve–XIIIe siècle)* (1994) [GT36].

P. Dinzelbacher, "'*verba hec tam mistica ex ore tam ydiote glebonis*': Selbstaussagen des Volkes über seinen Glauben unter besonderer Berücksichtigung der Offenbarungsliteratur und der Vision Gottschalks," in *Volksreligion im hohen und späten Mittelalter,* ed. P. Dinzelbacher and D.R. Bauer (1990) 57–99: shows the importance of the genre for the study of medieval popular religion [GT37].

P. Dinzelbacher, "La littérature des révélations au moyen âge: Un document historique," in *Revue historique* 275 (1986) 289–305 [GT38].

P. Dinzelbacher, *An der Schwelle zum Jenseits: Sterbevisionen im interkulturellen Vergleich* (1989): compares medieval and modern visions and apparitions [GT39].

P. Dinzelbacher, *Vision und Visionsliteratur im Mittelalter* (1981): the only full study of medieval visions [GT40].

P. Dinzelbacher, "Jenseitsvisionen-Jenseitsreisen," in *Epische Stoffe des Mittelalters,* ed. V. Mertens and U. Müller (1984) 61–80: stresses the epic structure of the genre [GT41].

P. Dinzelbacher, "Zur Interpretation erlebnismystischer Texte des Mittelalters," in *id.,* *Mittelalterliche Frauenmystik* (1993) 304–31: emphasizes that most mystical visions are the result of real psychic experiences and are not didactic fiction [GT42].

P. Dinzelbacher, "*Revelationes*", TSMAO 57 (1991): the most up-to-date analysis of the genre, with full bibliography and list of editions [GT43].

P. Dinzelbacher, "Visionary Literature," in *Medieval Scandinavia: An Encyclopedia,* ed. P. Pulsiano *et al.* (1993) 706–7 [GT44].

P. Dinzelbacher, "Nova visionaria et eschatologica," in *Mediaevistik* 6 (1993) 45–84: critical overview of nearly all studies of medieval visions published between 1980 and 1994; the best guide to the secondary literature [GT45].

E. Dünninger, "Politische und geschichtliche Elemente in mittelalterlichen Jenseitsvisionen bis zum Ende des 13. Jahrhunderts" (Doctoral diss., Bayerische Julius-Maximilians-Universität, Würzburg, 1962) [GT46].

T.C. Gardner, "The Theater of Hell: A Critical Study of Some Twelfth Century Latin Eschatological Visions" (Ph.D. diss., University of California, Berkeley, 1976): an examination of their function for the reader [GT47].

A. Gurevich, *Medieval Popular Culture: Problems of Belief and Perception,* tr. J.M. Bak and P.A. Hollingsworth (1988) [GT48].

M. Himmelfarb, *Tours of Hell: An Apocalyptic Form in Jewish and Christian Literature* (1983): an account of an important source for medieval visionaries' conceptions of the other world [GT49].

C.J. Holdsworth, "Visions and Visionaries in the Middle Ages," in *History* 48/163 (1963) 141–53 [GT50].

H.J. Kamphausen, *Traum und Vision in der lateinischen Poesie der Karolingerzeit,* Lateinische Sprache und Literatur des Mittelalters 4 (1975) [GT51].

J. Le Goff, *The Birth of Purgatory,* tr. A. Goldhammer (1984) [GT52].

K.L. Lynch, *The High Medieval Dream Vision: Poetry, Philosophy, and Literary Form* (1988) [GT53].

M. Moe, *Samlede skrifter,* v3 (1927) 248–359: history of visions of the other world and their influence in Scandinavia [GT54].

R.A. Moody, Jr., *Life after Life: The Investigation of a Phenomenon—Survival of Bodily Death* (1975) [**GT55**].

A. Morgan, *Dante and the Medieval Other World* (1990): the most recent of many comparisons between the *Divina Commedia* and Latin visions [**GT56**].

F.X. Newman, "*Somnium:* Medieval Theories of Dreaming and the Form of Vision Poetry" (Ph.D. diss., Princeton University, 1963) [**GT57**].

N.F. Palmer, "*Visio Tnugdali*": *The German and Dutch Translations and Their Circulation in the Later Middle Ages* (1982): an exemplary study of the manuscript tradition of one of the most widely read medieval visions [**GT58**].

H.R. Patch, *The Other World, According to Descriptions in Medieval Literature* (1950, r1970) [**GT59**].

H. Röckelein, *Otloh, Gottschalk, Tnugdal: Individuelle und kollektive Visionsmuster des Hochmittelalters* (1987): a psychological approach [**GT60**].

C. Rowland, *The Open Heaven: A Study of Apocalyptic in Judaism and Early Christianity* (1982): cf. [**GT49**] [**GT61**].

A. Rüegg, *Die Jenseitsvorstellungen vor Dante und die übrigen literarischen Voraussetzungen der "Divina Commedia"*, 2 vols. (1945): retellings of the earlier visions of the other world [**GT62**].

St. J.D. Seymour, *Irish Visions of the Other-World: A Contribution to the Study of Mediaeval Visions* (1930, r1970) [**GT63**].

D. Strömbäck, "Visionsdiktning," in *Kulturhistorisk leksikon for nordisk middelalder* 20 (1976) 171–86 [**GT64**].

R.E.V. Stuip and C. Vellekoop, eds., *Visioenen*, Utrechtse bijdragen tot de medievistiek 6 (1986) [**GT65**].

S. Tanz and E. Werner, *Spätmittelalterliche Laienmentalitäten im Spiegel von Visionen, Offenbarungen und Prophezeiungen* (1993) [**GT66**].

C. Zaleski, *Otherworld Journeys: Accounts of Near-Death Experience in Medieval and Modern Times* (1987): a good comparative study [**GT67**].

# GU • DEVOTIONAL AND MYSTICAL LITERATURE

## BY THOMAS H. BESTUL

The devotional and mystical literature of the Latin Middle Ages is both extensive and varied, and as a consequence difficult to categorize and define. In a broad sense, medieval Christian devotional literature includes those works intended to bring the reader closer to God by preparing him or her for private prayer, meditation, and contemplation. It is useful to divide such works into two categories. In one category belong the prose treatises explaining the nature and theory of contemplation or showing how the life of contemplation is to be conducted; this is a category related to, and frequently overlapping, that of the general manual of spiritual guidance. In another, more amorphous category belong texts that describe, often in emotional language, some aspect of the human encounter with the divine, or dwell upon aspects of the deity, including the earthly life of Christ. Such works may be in the form of personal monologues and are often best considered as extended prayers or meditations. Very often these texts depend upon emotional appeals, as explained in the classic formulation from the prologue to the *Orationes sive meditationes* of Anselm of Canterbury (d. 1109): the prayers and meditations were set forth "ad excitandam legentis mentem ad dei amorem vel timorem, seu ad suimet discussionem" (to excite the mind to the love or fear of God, or for examination of the self). When the works purport to record the direct personal experience of the writer with the divine, we may describe them as mystical, although the term is difficult to define precisely. Such mystical experiences were often received in the form of visions; the literature resulting from those visions is treated in ch. GT of this volume. Much Medieval Latin verse seems primarily devotional in intent—for example, the great Cistercian poem "Jesu dulcis memoria," the "Philomena" of John Pecham (d. 1292), and the poetry of John of Howden (fl. mid-thirteenth century)—but prose is the dominant form.

From the patristic and early medieval period, we can identify few works that are primarily devotional in purpose. The *Confessiones* of Augustine (d. 430) describe in intimate and moving language his striving to attain a vision of God, and that work, together with his *Soliloquia* and the final prayer in the *De trinitate,* were profoundly influential in the development of devotional literature in the Middle Ages. The laments of the sinful soul found in the *Synonyma* of Isidore of Seville (d. 636) were similarly important. The teaching of the Eastern Fathers on contemplation was absorbed by Gregory the Great (d. 604) and passed on to the Middle Ages, particularly

694

in the *Homilia in Ezechielem,* which contains the classic definition of the distinction between the active and the contemplative life, and much valuable counsel of lasting influence. Such treatises as the *Diadema monachorum* of Smaragdus (d. c. 830) transmitted the teaching of Gregory, adapting it to a specifically monastic context.

From about the middle of the eighth century onward are found collections of private prayers that seem to have been intended for devotional use. The earliest examples are from Anglo-Saxon England and reveal Irish influence: one of the oldest and largest of such prayerbooks is the *Book of Cerne.* In the Carolingian age, anthologies of prayers proliferated; they were often placed at the end of Psalters, reflecting the central position of the Psalms in the devotional life of the time. Although the primary audience for most devotional texts from the early Middle Ages was clerical, chiefly monastic, there is some attention paid to the promotion of lay piety in the Carolingian age, for example, in such works as the *De psalmorum usu* of Alcuin (d. 804) and the *Liber manualis* written by the countess Dhuoda (fl. 840) for her son.

The middle of the eleventh century marks a turning point in the development of devotional literature. From this time forward to the close of the Middle Ages devotional texts are found in great abundance, and in the twelfth century begins a steady stream of mystical and visionary literature that reaches a full tide in the fourteenth. The reasons for these developments are many. In general there was new concern for interior psychology and personality, which was reflected in a spirituality marked by increased attention to both the theory and the practice of contemplation and the cultivation of the inner life. An affective piety resulted that emphasized meditation on the humanity of Jesus and the events of his earthly life. At the same time, social and economic conditions accompanied by reforms in religious orders allowed for increased opportunities for private reading and reflection, opportunities that also extended increasingly to the laity, including women, especially of the aristocratic class. These developments led to a demand for greater numbers of manuscripts and texts of all kinds, including devotional and contemplative writings.

Peter Damian (d. 1072) and John of Fécamp (d. 1078) were among the first eleventh-century writers to reflect the new spirit of the age. The latter left a treatise, the *Confessio theologica,* praising the delights of contemplation and stressing the importance of devotional reading within a culture that was in the midst of an accelerating transition from orality to literacy. From the late eleventh century is an anonymous body of meditations attributed to various authors (most plausibly to John of Fécamp), but most commonly known to the Middle Ages as the *Meditationes* of Augustine. Written in a strongly affective style in the form of an intimate self-examination and personal confession directed to the three Persons of the Trinity, they were continuously influential to the close of the Middle Ages. Even more important are the *Orationes sive meditationes* of Anselm of Canterbury (d. 1109), a collection of 19 prayers and three meditations, which are remarkable for their subjectivity, emotional intensity, and depth of introspection.

In the twelfth century these developments are further advanced in the writing of the Cistercian monks, particularly Bernard of Clairvaux (d. 1153). Bernard's *Sermones super Cantica Canticorum* were important in giving eloquent expression to an affective piety rooted in love for Christ in his human form, and in holding out hope that through repentance and prayer individuals might restore within themselves the divine image tarnished by sin. Bernard had many followers among the Cistercians of the following generations, among whom we may mention Aelred of Rievaulx (d.

1167), Gilbert of Hoyland (d. 1172), Guerric of Igny (d. 1157), and Isaac of Stella (d. c. 1169). Aelred's treatise *De Iesu puero duodenni* (*On Jesus at the Age of Twelve*) is a notable expression of the new feelings of tender devotion to the events of Christ's earthly life. It espouses a method of meditation making use of visual imaginings to evoke the events of the life of Christ, a method that would attain full development among the Franciscans of the following century.

William of St. Thierry (d. 1148) knew St. Bernard and became a Cistercian later in life; he left a significant body of work on contemplation and a collection of meditations whose major theme is longing for the sight of God. The *De contemplando deo* is a sophisticated treatise on the spiritual progress of the soul toward God, which fully expresses the twelfth-century preoccupation with interiority and the psychology of the soul. The treatise stresses the importance of the Trinity as a source of love and reveals the influence of Gregory the Great, John Scotus Eriugena, and Neoplatonism as transmitted by Augustine.

This approach to contemplation, which succeeds in being both analytical and mystical at the same time, is further developed by a group of French Augustinian canons known as the Victorines, including Hugh of St. Victor (d. c. 1141), but especially Richard of St. Victor (d. 1173). Richard's influential treatises, *Benjamin minor* and *Benjamin major,* define varieties of contemplation, offer analyses of the affections and the faculty of the imagination, and emphasize love as the energizing force behind the soul's journey to God through a series of stages leading from the contemplation of the visible to the invisible. Similar ideas in a more practical form are expressed in the *Scala claustralium* of the Carthusian monk Guigo II (d. c. 1188), which describes the soul's journey to God through ascending stages of reading, meditation, prayer, and contemplation. Finally, the twelfth century saw the emergence of a vision literature with strong mystical overtones that was often written or dictated by women. Hildegard of Bingen (d. 1179) and Elizabeth of Schönau (d. 1164) are the outstanding examples.

In the thirteenth century the institution of the new orders of friars, especially the Franciscans and the Dominicans, and the revitalized spirituality that at first ensued led to continuing interest in devotional literature and works on contemplation. The piety of the Franciscans became the hallmark of the age and was characterized by an intensification of many elements present in the Cistercian tradition established by St. Bernard, among which were a strongly affective bias with an emphasis on love; an intense devotion to the humanity of Christ, especially his Passion; and, increasingly as the century progressed, devotion to the Virgin Mary.

The greatest spiritual writer among the Franciscans of this century, and among the greatest of the entire Middle Ages, was Bonaventure (d. 1274), who left a remarkable body of work on mysticism and contemplation that inspired many later generations of devotional writers. Among his works are the *Itinerarium mentis in Deum,* describing how the mind is elevated to a vision of God through love, and the *De triplici via* (or *Incendium amoris*), which outlines the purgative, illuminative, and unitive ways of attaining God through the interior exercises of meditation, prayer, and contemplation, a formulation that would be especially influential even beyond the Middle Ages. There are also two noteworthy devotional works on the Passion of Christ, both organized around elaborate allegories, the *Lignum vitae* and the *Vitis mystica.* These latter place intense focus on the details of the suffering endured by Christ in the Passion, employing a graphic, emotional style that is characteristic of the Franciscan devotional writing of the time and would have many imitators. Throughout his devotional works Bonaventure, in common with his Cistercian predecessors of the twelfth century, is especially concerned with the restoration in man and woman of the divine image.

Of the many devotional works inspired by the Franciscan piety given its classic expression by Bonaventure we may mention the spiritual writings of the Franciscan tertiary Angela of Foligno (d. 1309), and two extremely popular examples written in Franciscan circles at the end of the thirteenth century or at the beginning of the fourteenth, the *Stimulus amoris* of James of Milan and the *Meditationes vitae Christi* by an unknown Franciscan, perhaps John de Caulibus. The *Meditationes* was the more popular of the two; it became one of the most widely read works of the later Middle Ages. It is a work that makes a strong appeal to the emotions of the reader by presenting highly detailed visual scenes and images from the life of Christ, often making additions to the Gospel account through imaginative elaborations, a technique that was common in medieval devotional retellings of Christ's life from the thirteenth century onward. The same tradition is continued in the *Vita Christi* of the Carthusian Ludolf of Saxony (d. 1377), an enormous devotional biography of Christ that was especially influential in the fifteenth century.

Other important thirteenth-century devotional works include the *Meditationes* of the English Cistercian Stephen of Sawley (d. 1252), which contain a systematic spiritual exercise based upon visual images drawn from the life of the Virgin Mary. The *Speculum ecclesiae* of Edmund Rich (d. 1240), archbishop of Canterbury, is properly speaking a work of spiritual guidance, but it includes a systematic meditative exercise based on devotion to Christ's humanity. Dating from about the middle of the century is a series of anonymous meditations, usually falsely attributed to Bernard, which had enormous popularity throughout Western Europe until the close of the Middle Ages. These meditations, beginning "Multi multa sciunt," stress the importance of self-knowledge, self-examination, and penance and were a staple item of late medieval devotional anthologies. We may also mention here another work falsely attributed to Bernard, the very popular lament of the Virgin by Ogier of Locedio (d. 1214) beginning "Quis dabit capiti meo aquam," a text that in its graphically detailed account of the sufferings of Mary and Christ fully expresses the intense devotion to the Passion that developed in the thirteenth century, and inspired many similar Marian laments.

In the thirteenth century we find for the first time a significant body of devotional works written in the vernacular as well as in Latin, and from this time forward it is impossible to consider Latin developments in isolation from the steady growth of a rich devotional and mystical literature in the vernacular languages; indeed, by the fifteenth century, most devotional works were written in the vernaculars, being translated into Latin mainly on occasions when an international audience was sought or envisioned for them.

Some of the chief authors of the thirteenth century who used the vernacular in devotional writing were women. Notable are the visionaries Hadewijch of Brabant (fl. 1320–40), who wrote in Flemish, and Mechthild of Magdeburg (d. 1282/94), who wrote in Low German and was one of a group of women mystics associated with the German monastery of Helfta in the later years of the century. Of these Helfta nuns, Gertrude the Great (d. 1301/2) composed in Latin prose a series of meditations and prayers of extraordinary power and density, written in an evocative, imagistic style.

Gertrude's meditations are notable for their manifestation of what is known as *Brautmystik*, or the use of bridal imagery derived from the *Song of Songs* to describe the union of the soul with Christ, often in erotic and emotionally charged language. The imagery and language of *Brautmystik* were common characteristics of the German mysticism of the thirteenth and fourteenth centuries, especially among women.

The audience for the works described here was quite certainly primarily clerical, although the growth of the vernacular suggests a steadily increasing lay readership. The literary products resulting from the loose associations of devout laity known as the Beguines and the Beghards that developed in the thirteenth century were relatively few and mainly in the vernacular. An important type of devotional text that emerges in its definitive form in this century and that in addition to a clerical audience found a relatively wide lay readership, particularly in aristocratic circles, was the *Book of Hours*. This was a collection of prayers, hymns, litanies, canticles, Psalms, and biblical readings organized according to the canonical hours of monasticism and intended as an aid to private devotion. These books, often sumptuously produced and richly decorated, were a mainstay of medieval devotional practice until the end of the Middle Ages. Less formal in structure, and perhaps more widely diffused across the social spectrum, were the numerous highly eclectic devotional anthologies made up of prayers, meditations, hymns, litanies, and the like, which were compiled in abundance from about 1100 onward.

The fourteenth century was a great age of mysticism, particularly in the Rhineland and the Low Countries. The writers on mysticism of this period wrote largely in the vernacular: the leading figures were Meister Eckhart (d. 1327/8), who developed a form of mysticism known as *Wesenmystik*, or mysticism of the essence; John Tauler (d. 1361); Henry Suso (d. 1366); and John Ruysbroec (d. 1381). Mysticism also flourished in England. Richard Rolle (d. 1349) wrote several devotional and mystical works in Latin, including the popular *Incendium amoris*, as well as in English; other English mystics include Walter Hilton (d. 1396), the anonymous author of the vernacular treatise *The Cloud of Unknowing*, and from the following century the female visionaries Julian of Norwich (d. 1416–23) and Margery Kempe (d. after 1439), who should be associated with their earlier Continental counterparts Bridget of Sweden (d. 1373) and Catherine of Siena (d. 1380).

The Franciscan devotional tradition with its emphasis on devotion to the Passion of Christ continued strong in the fourteenth and fifteenth centuries, and the number of treatises and meditations on the Passion continued to grow. A devotion to the instruments of the Passion (the *arma Christi*) came into being and achieved wide popularity. At the same time, Latin devotional writing in the older, monastic tradition was also produced, for example, the *Meditationes* of John Whiterig, known as the Monk of Farne (d. 1371), and the compendium entitled *Stimulus peccatoris* of William of Rimington (d. c. 1385). A group of relatively brief prayers known as the *Fifteen Oes* (*Quindecem orationes*), apparently written toward the end of the century and often falsely attributed to Bridget of Sweden, was to become one of the most popular devotional texts of the later Middle Ages in both Latin and the vernacular. On a more intellectual and philosophical level, Jean Gerson (d. 1429) wrote a treatise on contemplation, *De mystica theologia tractatus primus speculativus*.

The greatest development in the spirituality of the closing centuries of the Middle Ages was the devotional movement that came to be known as the *Devotio moderna*. The proponents of this movement, which originated and enjoyed its greatest strength in the Low Countries, did not strive for mystical union with the deity, nor were they concerned with speculation on the nature of the mystical experience; rather they emphasized a simple devotion, grounded in love, to Christ in his human form. From the first, the movement was notable for the involvement of the laity, and it may be regarded as one sign of the dramatic growth of lay piety, especially among the increasingly literate merchant middle class. Most writers of the movement used the vernacular, but its chief monument is the *De imitatione Christi*, written in Latin by Thomas à Kempis (d. 1471). The themes of the book are affective devotion to Christ's humanity and the cultivation of the inner life. It became one of the most widely read of all devotional works, its influence extending well beyond the Middle Ages even into our own time.

## Select Bibliography

### Primary Works

Aelred of Rievaulx, *Opera omnia*, v1: *Opera ascetica*, ed. A. Hoste and C.H. Talbot, *CCCM* 1 (1971) [GU1].

Anselm, *Opera omnia*, ed. F.S. Schmitt, 6 vols. (1938–61, r1968) [GU2].

Bernard, *Opera*, ed. J. Leclercq *et al.*, 8 vols. (1957–77) [GU3].

Pseudo-Bernard, *Meditationes piissimae de cognitione humanae conditionis*, in *PL* 184:485–508 [GU4].

T.H. Bestul, ed., *A Durham Book of Devotions Edited from London, Society of Antiquaries, MS. 7, TMLT* 18 (1987): a representative twelfth-century anthology, including a text of the *Meditationes* of Pseudo-Augustine [GU5].

Bonaventure, *Opera omnia*, ed. Patres Collegii a S. Bonaventura, 10 vols. (1882–1902): the mystical and ascetic works are in v8 [GU6]; *Opera omnia*, ed. A.C. Peltier, 15 vols. (1864–71): see v12 for the *Meditationes vitae Christi* [GU7].

Dhuoda, *Liber manualis*, ed. and tr. P. Riché, *SChr* 225 (1975); tr. C. Neel (1991), with lengthy introduction [GU8].

Edmund Rich, *Speculum religiosorum* and *Speculum ecclesie*, ed. H.P. Forshaw (1973) [GU9].

Gertrude of Helfta, *Exercitium pro recuperanda innocentia baptismali* and *Legatus memorialis abundantiae divinae pietatis*, ed. and tr. J. Hourlier and A. Schmitt (v1), P. Doyère (v2–3), J.-M. Clément, the nuns of Wisques, and B. de Vregille (v4–5); 5 vols., *SChr* 127, 139, 143, 255, 331 (1967–86) [GU10].

Guigo II [Guigues II le Chartreux], *Scala claustralium* and *Meditationes*, ed. and tr. E. Colledge and J. Walsh, *SChr* 163 (1970) [GU11].

James of Milan, *Stimulus amoris*, ed. Patres Collegii a S. Bonaventura, 2nd ed. (1949) [GU12].

Jean Gerson, *Selections from A Deo exivit, Contra curiositatem studentium and De mystica theologia speculativa*, ed. and tr. S.E. Ozment (1969) [GU13].

John Whiterig, "The Meditations of the Monk of Farne," ed. H. Farmer, in *StA* 41 (1957) 141–245; *The Monk of Farne: The Meditations of a Fourteenth Century Monk*, ed. H. Farmer, tr. a Benedictine of Stanbrook (1961) [GU14].

A.B. Kuypers, ed., *The Prayer Book of Aedeluald the Bishop Commonly Called The Book of Cerne* (1902) [GU15].

J. Leclercq and J.-P. Bonnes, eds., *Un maître de la vie spirituelle au XIe siècle: Jean de Fécamp* (1946): a study with editions of the devotional works [GU16].

Richard of St. Victor, *Benjamin minor* and *Benjamin major*, in *PL* 196:1–63, 64–202 [GU17].

Richard Rolle, *Incendium amoris*, ed. M. Deanesly (1915) [GU18].

Smaragdus, *Diadema monachorum*, in *PL* 102:593–690 [GU19].

Stephen of Sawley, *Meditationes*, ed. A. Wilmart, in *Auteurs spirituels* (see [GU42]) 317–60 [GU20].

Thomas à Kempis, *Opera omnia*, ed. M.J. Pohl, 7 vols. (1902–19) [GU21].

William Rimington, *Stimulus peccatoris*, ed. R. O'Brien, in *Cîteaux: Commentarii Cistercienses* 16 (1965) 278–304 [GU22].

William of St. Thierry, *De contemplando deo* and *Oratio domni Willelmi*, ed. and tr. J. Hourlier, *SChr* 61 (1959) [GU23].

A. Wilmart, ed., "Le *Jubilus* sur le nom de Jésus dit de Saint Bernard," in *EL* 57 (1943) 3–283; A Wilmart, ed., *Le "Jubilus" dit de Saint Bernard: Étude avec textes* (1944) [GU24].

A. Wilmart, ed., *Precum libelli quattuor aevi Karolini* (1940) [GU25].

## Studies and Bibliographies

J.A.W. Bennett, *Poetry of the Passion: Studies in Twelve Centuries of English Verse* (1982): useful analysis of the "meditative movement" in medieval devotion [GU26].

T.H. Bestul, "Devotional Writing in England between Anselm and Richard Rolle," in *Mysticism: Medieval & Modern*, ed. V. Lagorio (1986) 12–28 [GU27].

L. Bouyer, J. Leclercq, and F. Vandenbroucke, *The Spirituality of the Middle Ages*, tr. the Benedictines of Holme Eden Abbey (1968, r1982): a comprehensive and indispensable guide with valuable bibliography in the notes [GU28].

E.C. Butler, *Western Mysticism: The Teaching of Augustine, Gregory and Bernard on Contemplation and the Contemplative Life*, 3rd ed. (1967) [GU29].

C.W. Bynum, *Jesus as Mother: Studies in the Spirituality of the High Middle Ages* (1982): with important chapter on Gertrude and the Helfta mystics [GU30].

O. Davies, *God Within: The Mystical Tradition of Northern Europe* (1988) [GU31].

J.V. Fleming, *An Introduction to the Franciscan Literature of the Middle Ages* (1977) [GU32].

R. Kieckhefer, *Unquiet Souls: Fourteenth-Century Saints and Their Religious Milieu* (1984): includes chapter on devotion to the Passion [GU33].

D. Knowles, *The English Mystical Tradition* (1961, r1965) [GU34].

V.M. Lagorio and R. Bradley, *The 14th-Century English Mystics: A Comprehensive Annotated Bibliography* (1981): includes entries on the Latin forerunners [GU35].

J. Leclercq, *The Love of Learning and the Desire for God: A Study of Monastic Culture*, tr. C. Misrahi (1960, r1982): essential for its understanding of monastic devotional literature [GU36].

G.J. Lewis, F. Willaert, and M.-J. Govers, *Bibliographie zur deutschen Frauenmystik des Mittelalters*, Bibliographien zur deutschen Literatur des Mittelalters 10 (1989) [GU37].

R.W. Southern, *Saint Anselm: A Portrait in a Landscape* (1990): important description of the Anselmian transformation of earlier devotional traditions [GU38].

S. Sticca, *The Planctus Mariae in the Dramatic Tradition of the Middle Ages,* tr. J.R. Berrigan (1988): strong on the Latin tradition [GU39].

P.E. Szarmach, ed., *An Introduction to the Medieval Mystics of Europe* (1984): collection of 14 essays with good bibliographies [GU40].

A. Vauchez, *La spiritualité du moyen âge occidental, VIIIe–XIIe siècles,* (1975): treats popular piety and lay movements [GU41].

A. Wilmart, *Auteurs spirituels et textes dévots du moyen âge latin: Études d'histoire littéraire* (1932, r1971): fundamental articles, with valuable indices [GU42].

R. Woolf, *The English Religious Lyric in the Middle Ages* (1968): valuable treatment of the devotional milieu of the High Middle Ages [GU43].

See also the articles on individual writers and on general topics such as "Contemplation" in *DSAM*. The introductions to the translations in the *Cistercian Fathers Series* (Kalamazoo, MI, 1970–) [GU44], the *Classics of Western Spirituality* (Mahwah, NJ, 1978?–) [GU45], and *Sources chrétiennes* [*SChr*] (Paris 1941–) [GU46] are often useful.

*See also* [BA149], [BB38], [BB49], [BD42], [BD125].

# GV · ENCYCLOPEDIAS

## BY GREGORY G. GUZMAN

Today the term *encyclopedia* generally refers to a multivolume collection of all available branches of knowledge, or to a comprehensive treatment of a particular subject, usually arranged in alphabetical order for easy use and prepared by scholars under the direction of an editorial staff. The word *encyclopedia*, however, is much older than is the practice of summarizing knowledge and scholarship in single collections. The term itself is of Greek origin: pseudo-Greek *enkyklopaideia*, for *enkyklios paideia*, was latinized as *encyclopaedia*. Initially it referred to a circle of knowledge (or encircling knowledge) and thus to a complete system of learning—to what is now called a liberal arts education.

Although most medieval compilations contain what are now accepted as errors of fact and interpretation, they are very important benchmarks in the cultural and intellectual history of the Middle Ages, as they record, reflect, and illustrate the most advanced information and knowledge attained and valued by Western society. Since most medieval encyclopedias were written by Christian clerics for a profoundly religious society, they had a primarily theological and spiritual purpose—to teach morality and salvation. Thus most were aids to preaching and teaching the tenets of Christianity.

Whereas the Greeks initiated the practice of classifying and summarizing all branches of knowledge, a Roman, Pliny the Elder (A.D. 23–79), is usually given credit for producing the first true Western encyclopedia in A.D. 77. His *Naturalis historia* is the earliest extant compilation that conforms most closely to the modern conception of an encyclopedia. This large uncritical anthology (he mixes fact with fiction and fable, and solid science with legend and old wives' tales) consists of 37 books and approximately 2,500 chapters; needless to say, it was not designed for continuous reading. Pliny was a practical Roman administrator accustomed to viewing everything in terms of divisions and subdivisions, i.e. as elements in a rationally organized pattern or plan. His primary emphasis was on secular subjects and concerns and on practical matters; all topics, including religion, were covered in an impartial and objective manner. This compilation was very popular and a highly regarded authority in the Middle Ages, but it was Gaius Iulius Solinus's third-century *Collectanea rerum memorabilium* (which was almost completely derived from Pliny) that provided the format used with confidence by many medieval compilers.

With the decline and fall of Rome, the Western Church was eager to provide the foundation for a thoroughly Christian organization and interpretation of knowledge. As Augustine (d. 430) contributed the theological base and Jerome (d. 419) supplied the historical and biographical foundation for future medieval encyclopedias, it is Cassiodorus (d. c. 583) who is commonly credited with producing the first collection of knowledge that bridged the gap between the classical and Christian perspectives in his *Institutiones divinarum et humanarum lectionum* (c. 562). This Roman aristocrat and statesman compiled his encyclopedia, arranged in 36 chapters, after he had retired in 551 to his monastery of Vivarium; his work was designed to provide a summary of learning for the simple and uneducated brothers in his community. Although concerned with preserving classical knowledge, Cassiodorus was more interested in making it serve Christian revelation. He drew a clear line between the sacred and the profane, starting in the first book of the *Institutiones* with things divine (God and Scripture) and, in his second and much shorter book, dealing with things human (a comprehensive discussion of the seven liberal arts). The latter were presented as useful studies for understanding and interpreting the Bible.

Isidore of Seville (d. 636) is usually considered to have compiled the first truly Christian encyclopedia, and his *Etymologiarum seu originum libri XX*, edited and corrected by Bishop Braulio of Saragossa, became one of the central texts of the Middle Ages and the model for later medieval encyclopedias. Some 1,000 manuscripts are extant. Isidore was interested in the origins of everything—of languages, institutions, customs, and skills, as well as words. The contents of this encyclopedia were organized as follows: bks. 1–3 (the liberal arts), 4 (medicine), 5 (jurisprudence, time, a world chronicle), 6 (the Bible), 7 (the heavenly hierarchy), 8 (the Church and heresies), 9 (people, language, statecraft), 10 (an etymological dictionary in alphabetical order), 11 (man), 12 (zoology), 13 (heaven, the atmosphere, seas and oceans), 14 (geography), 15 (cities and towns, buildings), 16 (geology, weights and measures), 17 (agriculture and horticulture), 18 (warfare, public games), 19 (ships, houses, costume), 20 (food, tools, furniture) ([GV19] p34).

The *De rerum naturis* of Hrabanus Maurus (d. 856) is basically a rearrangement (with omissions) of Isidore's text; the nature of its relationship with the *Etymologiae* has been studied by E. Heyse [GV23]. Hrabanus's compilation (22 books in 325 chapters) is more "medieval" than Isidore's: in addition to adopting a hexaemeral scheme, Hrabanus placed the theological section first, starting, that is, with God and the angels, and he suppressed any discussion of the liberal arts as irrelevant to the study of Scripture. His practice was to quote Isidore and then to supply figural explanations.

A few twelfth-century compilations introduced slight modifications and/or innovations that foreshadowed the thirteenth-century explosion of medieval encyclopedic writing. The *Imago mundi* of Honorius Augustodunensis (d. c. 1156) was divided into three books (1, the creation and the physical world; 2, time; 3, human history, arranged in the order of the six world ages, with special attention to German history) and drew on a wider range of authorities than any of its predecessors; it is sometimes considered the bridge between Hrabanus and Vincent of Beauvais. Lambert of Saint-Omer's popular *Liber floridus* (compiled c. 1112 through 1121) is an eccentric miscellany with no discernible structure. It touches randomly on an enormous range of topics from history, geography, and cosmology to plants, magic, and marvels and has an unusual predilection for metaphysical discussions. Hugh of Saint Victor's *Didascalicon* (c. 1130), a survey of learning in six books with a preface and appendices, introduced a classification of knowledge with 21 divisions (including the *artes mechanicae*) and provided guidance as to authors and methods of study appropriate for monastic education. The *Hortus deliciarum* of Herrad, abbess of Hohenburg (d. 1195), contains nothing new, but she deserves mention as the first European woman to compile an encyclopedia. Her work, compiled for the nuns in her charge, was illustrated with hundreds of miniatures. The last major twelfth-century encyclopedia deserving of comment here is Alexander Neckam's *De naturis rerum* (c. 1195), a carefully structured commentary on *Ecclesiastes* that examines, with information drawn fron classical, patristic, and medieval sources, the composition of the material world.

The compilation of later medieval encyclopedias was influenced by the new sources and information made available by translations from Greek, Hebrew, and Arabic during the twelfth century. Scholasticism also introduced new schemes of classifying and organizing material. There was greater stress on individual parts and advances in format like paragraph marks, chapter titles, marginal rubrication, and tables of contents. Since many of these new and more readily available epitomes were intended to help the mendicant preachers prepare sermons, it is not surprising that the major thirteenth-century encyclopedias were assembled by Franciscan and Dominican friars.

Two such compilations, which were more comprehensive than the work of Albertus Magnus (d. 1280) on the natural sciences, deserve further mention here. The Franciscan Bartholomaeus Anglicus wrote *De proprietatibus rerum* (c. 1225), and the Dominican Thomas of Cantimpré compiled *De natura rerum* (c. 1240). Of the two collections, that of Bartholomaeus (in 19 books) was more popular; it was in fact the most widely read and quoted late medieval encyclopedia, largely because of its superior organization (the compiler introduced the use of alphabetical order within each book whenever possible and practical) and its extensive excerpts from Aristotle and Arabic scholars. It was also better informed and more authoritative and complete than those of his predecessors and his contemporary Thomas, whose work, extant in three versions of 19, 20, and 18 books, was especially valued by preachers for its *exemplum* material.

By common consensus, however, the *Speculum maius* of Vincent of Beauvais, O.P. (c. 1190–1264), represents the zenith of medieval encyclopedic achievement. This compendium or *summa* mirrored the culture and thought of the scholastic age, as it contained a complete overview of all available classical and Christian knowledge. Vincent was industrious and learned, but essentially a compiler; his purpose was to illustrate the progress and triumph of the Church in human history, to strengthen Christian belief, and to make all previous information permanently and practically accessible to his fellow clerics. The *Speculum* is therefore a composite of quotations and excerpts from earlier pagan and Christian authors, all carefully collected, classified, and arranged into a single unified whole. One of its unique merits is that it is a valuable source for numerous fragments from many documents that have since been lost.

The first part of the *Speculum maius* was completed in 1244; some of the latter parts were written under the patronage of King Louis IX of France (1214–70), who supplied some copyists for the longer extracts. All parts were subject to revision and expansion until several years before Vincent's death in 1264. Initially the *Speculum* consisted of only two parts, the *Naturale* and *Historiale,* but reorganization and additional material resulted in a third part, the *Doctrinale.* Early in the thirteenth century an anonymous author added a fourth part, the *Morale,* drawn chiefly from the writings of Aquinas. The *Naturale* (32 books) deals with God, man, and nature according to the six days of creation. The *Doctrinale* (17 books) was originally scheduled to be part of the *Naturale,* but its growing size and the demand for copies of specific parts led Vincent to produce a separate section for the liberal arts and sciences and education. This part presents the theoretical and practical arts and sciences in accord with the model of classification introduced by Hugh of Saint Victor. The *Historiale* (31 books) includes a summary of the first two parts and is a universal chronicle of human history from creation until 1254. Although it stresses the early Christian centuries, its detailed coverage of the second quarter of the thirteenth century is especially accurate and useful.

Vincent's organization and orchestration of different sources reveal a logical and rational mind. Borrowing freely from over 400 classical and medieval authorities, the *Speculum maius* is the first universal encyclopedia on a grand scale; it dwarfed and superseded the earlier compilations of Isidore and Hrabanus and, with over 3 million words in 80 books and almost 10,000 chapters, went significantly beyond a traditional encyclopedic collection. Though its size and bulk prevented it from circulating as readily as did the short popular encyclopedia of Bartholomaeus Anglicus, Vincent's compilation became the indispensable book of reference for the late Middle Ages, unrivaled in magnitude and comprehensiveness. It was the last major work of its kind; later encyclopedists began to write for wider audiences than the narrow and limited world of religious communities of monks and friars and, like Brunetto Latini (d. 1295) in his *Li livres dou trésor,* to use the vernacular.

## Select Bibliography

### Primary Works

Alexander Neckam, *De naturis rerum,* bks. 1–2, ed. T. Wright, in *RSer* 34 (1863) 1–354; bks. 3–5 unprinted [GV1].

Bartholomaeus Anglicus, *De proprietatibus rerum* (Frankfurt 1601, r1964); bks. 3–4, ed. R.J. Long, *TMLT* 9 (1979); bk. 19, ed. J.G. Lidaka (Ph.D. diss., Northern Illinois University, 1987) [GV2].

Cassiodorus, *Inst.* [GV3].

Herrad of Hohenburg [Herrad of Landsberg], *Hortus deliciarum,* ed. R. Green *et al.,* 2 vols., Studies of the Warburg Institute 36 (1979) [GV4].

Honorius Augustodunensis, *Imago mundi,* ed. V.I.J. Flint, in *AHDL* 49 (1982) 7–153 [GV5].

Hrabranus Maurus, *De rerum naturis,* in *PL* 111:9–614 [GV6].

Hugh of St. Victor, *Didas.* [GV7].

Isidore, *Etym.* [GV8].

Lambert of St. Omer, *Liber floridus,* ed A. Derolez (1968) [GV9].

Thomas of Cantimpré, *Liber de natura rerum,* ed. H. Boese (1973) [GV10].

Of the encyclopedia of Vincent of Beauvais no modern critical edition exists, and one must use the last readily available edition of this text: *Speculum maius,* 4 vols. (Douai 1624, r1964–65) [GV11].

Modern editions of parts of Vincent's *Speculum* have been prepared by (a) A.-D. von den Brincken, "Geschichtsbetrachtung bei Vincenz von Beauvais: Die *Apologia actoris* zum *Speculum Maius*," in *DA* 34 (1978) 410–99 [**GV12**]; (b) S. Lusignan, *Préface au "Speculum maius" de Vincent de Beauvais: Réfraction et diffraction* (1979) [**GV13**]: these two items are concerned with the Latin texts of Vincent's evolving preface and/or introduction; (c) G.G. Guzman, "Vincent of Beauvais' *Epistola actoris ad regem Ludovicum:* A Critical Analysis and a Critical Edition," in [**GV33**] 57–85: a critical edition of Vincent's letter of dedication to King Louis IX [**GV14**].

## Studies (very selective)

The entries in the *DMA* are strongly recommended as a starting point for the study of the major medieval encyclopedists. See also T. Lawler, "Encyclopedias and Dictionaries, Western Europe," in *DMA* 4:447–50 [**GV15**], and the annotated bibliographies assembled by M.W. Twomey, "Medieval Encyclopedias," in R.E. Kaske, A. Groos, and M.W. Twomey, *Medieval Christian Literary Imagery* (1988), app., pp182–215 [**GV16**].

M.T. Beonio-Brocchieri Fumagalli, *Le enciclopedie dell'occidente medioevale* (1981) [**GV17**].

*Cahiers d'histoire mondiale* 9 (1966): this special issue, entitled "Encyclopédies et civilisations," contains six essays on medieval encyclopedists, including separate studies of Isidore (pp519–38), Hugh of St. Victor (pp539–52), and Vincent of Beauvais (pp571–79). These essays have been reprinted separately by M. de Gandillac *et al.* as *La pensée encyclopédique au moyen âge* (1966) [**GV18**].

R. Collison, *Encyclopaedias: Their History Throughout the Ages,* 2nd ed. (1966): provides a general overview of medieval encyclopedias as part of a general coverage of the growth of encyclopedias from 3500 B.C. to the present [**GV19**].

M. Curschmann, "Text-Bilder-Strukturen: Der "Hortus deliciarum" und die frühmittelhochdeutsche Geistlichendichtung," in *DVJSLW* 55 (1981) 379–418 [**GV20**].

A. Derolez, ed., *Liber floridus Colloquium: Papers Read at the International Meeting Held in the University Library, Ghent, on 3–5 September 1967* (1973) [**GV21**].

J. Fontaine, *Isidore de Séville et la culture classique dans l'Espagne wisigothique,* 2nd ed., 3 vols. (1983) [**GV22**].

E. Heyse, *Hrabanus Maurus' Enzyklopädie, "De rerum naturis": Untersuchungen zu den Quellen und zur Methode der Kompilation,* MBMRF 4 (1969) [**GV23**].

P. Lehmann, "Cassiodorstudien," in his *Erforschung des Mittelalters,* 5 vols. (1959–62), v2:38–108: reprinted articles from *Philologus* 71–74 (1912–18) [**GV24**].

J.J. O'Donnell, *Cassiodorus* (1979) 202–22 [**GV25**].

T. Plassmann, "Bartholomaeus Anglicus," in *AFH* 12 (1919) 68–109 [**GV26**].

W. Schipper, "Rabanus Maurus, *De Rerum Naturis:* A Provisional Check List of Manuscripts," in *Manuscripta* 33 (1989) 109–18 [**GV27**].

G.E. Se Boyar, "Bartholomaeus Anglicus and His Encyclopedia," in *Journal of English and Germanic Philology* 19 (1920) 168–89 [**GV28**].

E. Voigt, "Bartholomaeus Anglicus, *De proprietatibus rerum*," in *Englische Studien* 41 (1910) 337–59 [**GV29**].

G.F. Wedge, "Alexander Neckham's *De naturis rerum:* A Study, together with Representative Passages in Translation" (Ph.D. diss, University of Minnesota, 1967) [**GV30**].

In addition to G.G. Guzman's bibliographical listing for Vincent of Beauvais in *DMA* 12:453–55 [GV31], the following works should be noted:

M.-C. Duchenne, G.G. Guzman, and J. B. Voorbij, "Une liste des manuscrits du *Speculum historiale* de Vincent de Beauvais," in *Scriptorium* 41 (1987) 286–94 [GV32].

M. Paulmier-Foucart, S. Lusignan, and A. Nadeau, eds., *Vincent de Beauvais: Intentions et réceptions d'une oeuvre encyclopédique au moyen-âge* (1990): 21 studies by the most active scholars currently engaged in research on Vincent and his numerous writings, especially his encyclopedia [GV33].

M. Paulmier-Foucart and S. Lusignan, "Vincent de Beauvais et l'histoire du *Speculum maius*," in *JS* (1990) 97–124: an excellent, up-to-date overview of the man and his work [GV34].

J. Schneider, "Vincent de Beauvais: Orientation bibliographique," in *Spicae* 1 (1978) 7–29: *Spicae* is published by the Atelier Vincent de Beauvais, established in 1974 at the Centre de recherches et d'applications linguistiques, Université de Nancy II, France [GV35].

M.C. Seymour *et al.*, *Bartholomaeus Anglicus and His Encyclopedia* (1992) [GV36].

J.B. Voorbij, "The *Speculum historiale:* Some Aspects of Its Genesis and Manuscript Tradition" in *Vincent of Beauvais and Alexander the Great*, ed. W.J. Aerts, E.R. Smits, and J.B. Voorbij (1986) 11–55 [GV37].

J.B. Voorbij, *Het 'Speculum historiale' van Vincent van Beauvais: Een studie van zijn ontstaansgeschiedenis* (1991) [GV38].

For recent and ongoing developments in the field of Vincent studies, see the *Vincent of Beauvais Newsletter* (Peoria, IL 1976–), ed. G.G. Guzman [GV39].

BY A.G. RIGG

Although both words mean "gathering of flowers," *anthologia* is usually restricted to a collection of complete items (normally poems), and *florilegium* to a collection of excerpts. The word *excerpt* is itself a metaphor from plucking flowers. Both anthologies and florilegia are valuable sources for literary history, not only as the vehicles of textual transmission of known and unknown material, but as indices to the tastes of the compilers. They were often the shortcuts by which writers learned the literature of the past, and they are now recognized as major sources for our understanding of medieval culture.

## Florilegia

The simplest kind of florilegium consists of self-evident extracts. Collections of legal *concilia* (assemblies of legal precedents and decisions) or of scientific and medical prescriptions served an obvious function. Extracts from philosophers or satirists formed moral collections, such as the *Oxoniense* (Oxford, Bodleian Library, MS Bodley 633). Some florilegia were simply of memorable "purple passages," which may have served as rhetorical models. Sometimes extracts have been clearly abstracted from a context but have been adjusted textually (by altering names, for example), so that they stand alone as proverbial utterances. Presumably each florilegium was originally the selection of an individual, but many took on a textual life of their own, copied from each other but subject to accretion and subtraction according to the scribe's choice. In this way an identifiable work was created, such as the *Florilegium Gallicum* and the *Florilegium Angelicum,* which probably originated in the literary center of Orléans. Both of these are found in many manuscripts, though the texts vary considerably around a core of several hundred excerpts.

Florilegia could also serve other functions, especially preaching: the extracts were organized under topic headings and alphabetically arranged. A good example is the *Manipulus florum* of Thomas of Ireland.

Then, as now, authors would simply reorganize the work of others: judicious selection (*compilatio*) and arrangement (*ordinatio*) produced what appeared to be entirely new works, such as William of Malmesbury's *Polyhistor.* In a culture that lacked concepts such as "plagiarism" or "originality," this way of writing a book would be not only not reprehensible but positively desirable, as it responded to the needs of a new generation.

## Anthologies

Poetic anthologies developed in various ways. Some have the poems of a single author as their core; some began as song books; some have themes; some exemplify rhetorical figures; many simply exhibit variety. All these types could merge or separate, and it is dangerous to infer common authorship of poems merely because of their proximity in an anthology.

The oldest anthology with a medieval circulation, the *Anthologia Latina* in the *Codex Salmasianus* (Paris, B.N., MS lat. 10318), was compiled, apparently in the sixth century, solely for its variety. It contains short poems, mainly of an epigrammatic character, by Late Latin authors such as Ausonius (d. c. 395). Many of its elements reappear frequently in later medieval anthologies, and there were many imitations.

The short poems of individual authors—such as Baudri of Bourgueil, Robert Partes, Matthew of Rievaulx—occasionally survive in single collections. Such authorial groupings often form the central core of other anthologies, though it is often difficult to disentangle them. A major group of anthologies contains the short poems of Hildebert of Le Mans (d. 1133) and Marbod of Rennes (d. 1123), mixed in with others; the most important example of the Hildebert-Marbod type is the "Saint-Gatien." Hildebert and Marbod also wrote verse saints' lives, which in turn attracted other verse lives into the anthologies. Their poems often merge with those of Peter Riga (d. 1209), who was himself the author of a large collection of short poems, the *Floridus Aspectus.* Works by Hildebert, Marbod, and Peter Riga continue to appear together as late as the fifteenth century. The satires of Walter of Châtillon (d. 1202/3) also form a significant block in some anthologies and attract other satires into the collections.

The contrast between anthology and florilegium is well exemplified by two manuscripts of Alexander Neckam (d. 1217). The Paris manuscript, B.N., lat. 11867, contains a large group of his short poems, constituting a block within the anthology, whereas Cambridge, University Library, MS Gg.6.42, is a florilegium from all his works, both prose and verse.

Many anthologies betray an origin in musical performance. The eleventh-century *Cambridge Songs,* based on a German collection, contain lyrics, political poems, fables, short extracts, etc. Some indicate the tune to which they were to be sung (e.g. "Modus Liebinc"), others are marked with neumes, and the satirist Sextus Amarcius (fl. eleventh century) actually describes the repertoire of a minstrel that corresponds in part to the collection. The *Later Cambridge Songs* are laid out for musical notation. In other manuscripts the lyric meters may suggest that they were to be—or had been—sung, such as the *Arundel Lyrics* and the *Carmina Burana* (see below).

Of the thematic anthologies the most common are the moral-penitential and the rhetorical. A classic example of the former is the *Florilegium morale Oxoniense;* among the latter are the *Hunterian,* in which long treatises on poetics (by Geoffrey of Vinsauf and others) are interspersed with illustrative poems. Some collections, such as Cambridge, University Library, MS Gg.5.35, were designed for teaching. This large eleventh-century manuscript from Canterbury contains full-length early

Christian poems, laid out with ample space for glosses and arranged in three books of ascending levels of difficulty; at the end are the *Cambridge Songs* mentioned above.

The most famous anthology of all is the *Carmina Burana,* named for the monastery of Benediktbeuern in Bavaria. This contains about 250 satires, love lyrics, and drinking songs, as well as some drama. It owes its modern fame to the musical setting by Carl Orff (1895–1982). Other collections, however, deserve equal attention for their variety. Oxford, Bodleian Library, MS Rawlinson G.109, has a core of northern French–Latin poetry of the mid-twelfth century, including twenty-three poems by Hugh Primas, some by Hildebert and contemporary poets, some by Simon Chèvre d'Or, and many anonymous poems, both satirical and erotic. Perhaps the best anthology of all is the *Bekynton*—Oxford, Bodleian Library, MS Bodley Add. A.44—originally compiled about 1200. This contains both prose (some serious, some satirical) and verse, including a complete epic, several long verse works, and over seventy-five shorter poems: there are love lyrics, satires, moral and religious poems, and comic verse. The *Bekynton* alone would make a good text for a course on Medieval Latin.

Anthologies, like florilegia, developed their own textual tradition. Sometimes the resemblances among them simply reflect the shared tastes of the compilers and thus of their age: twelfth-century anthologies differ considerably from fifteenth-century ones. In other cases there is a textual link. Three fourteenth- and fifteenth-century collections—Oxford, Bodleian Library, MS Bodley 851, and London, B.L., Cotton MSS Titus A.XX and Vespasian E.XII—are closely related textually in one particular item, and must share a common exemplar. They probably circulated originally in Oxford, where students may have passed copies of interesting poems among each other. There are also diachronic links: the Titus A.XX anthology shares a large block of poems with Rawlinson G.109 (mentioned above) and is closely linked textually to the fifteenth-century manuscript, Oxford, Bodleian Library, Rawlinson B.214, compiled in the fifteenth century by John Wilde of Waltham Priory. Another vertical link is between the twelfth-century manuscript, Oxford, Bodleian Library, Bodley 603, and the fourteenth-century manuscript, Oxford, Bodleian Library, Digby 166, which probably derives ultimately from Oxford. The latter, like many such collections, was compiled from booklets, which in this case bear their original prices of two or three shillings each.

Anthologies provide a window into the Middle Ages, not just for their contents and the tastes of their compilers, but for the ways in which they were gathered together, from old and new sources and from social interaction in universities and monasteries.

## Select Bibliography

### Florilegia

See first M.A. Rouse, "Florilegia," in *DMA* 5:109–10 [GW1], and J. Hamesse, "Le vocabulaire des florilèges médiévaux," in *CIVICIMA* 3:209–30 [GW2].

It is not possible here to do more than hint at the range of florilegia of nonliterary material, such as legal *concilia,* medical recipes, etc. For theology and philosophy see H. Rochais, "Florilèges latins" [GW3], and P. Delhaye, "Florilèges médiévaux d'éthique" [GW4], both in *DSAM* 5:435–75 ("Florilèges latins"). Perhaps the best example of a moral one is the *Florilegium morale Oxoniense* (Oxford, Bodleian Library, MS Bodley 633), in *Analecta mediaevalia Namurcensia* 5–6 (1955–56): *Prima pars: Flores philosophorum*, ed. P. Delhaye (entirely prose); *Secunda pars: Flores auctorum*, ed. C.H. Talbot (mixed prose and verse) [GW5]. An example of a collection of "scientific" recipes is the *Mappae Clavicula* (see [FI9–11]) [GW6].

Two major classical florilegia are the *Gallicum* and the *Angelicum*: see A. Gagnér, *Florilegium Gallicum* (1936), textual study with extracts [GW7]; J. Hamacher, *Florilegium Gallicum: Prolegomena und Edition der Exzerpte von Petron bis Cicero, De Oratore* (1975) [GW8]; R. Burton, *Classical Poets in the "Florilegium Gallicum"* (1983) [GW9]; R.H. and M.A. Rouse, "The *Florilegium Angelicum*: Its Origin, Content and Influence," in *Medieval Learning and Literature: Essays Presented to Richard William Hunt*, ed. J.J.G. Alexander and M.T. Gibson (1976) 66–114 [GW10]; R.H. Rouse, "*Florilegia* and Latin Classical Authors in Twelfth- and Thirteenth-Century Orléans," in *Viator* 10 (1979) 131–60 [GW11]. For an illustration of the importance of florilegia for literary history, see A.A. Goddu and R.H. Rouse, "Gerald of Wales and the *Florilegium Angelicum*," in *Speculum* 52 (1977) 488–521 [GW12]. For the contents of such florilegia, see also E.M. Sanford, "The Use of Classical Authors in the *libri manuales*," in *TAPhS* 55 (1924) 190–247 [GW13], and the series of articles by B.L. Ullman on Tibullus, *Laus Pisonis*, Petronius, and Valerius Flaccus in florilegia, in *CPh* 23 (1928) 128–74, 24 (1929) 109–32, 25 (1930) 11–21, 26 (1931) 21–30, 27 (1932) 1–42 [GW14]; also *id.*, "Virgil in Certain Medieval Florilegia," in *SM*, n.s., 5 (1932) 59–66 [GW15].

Excerpts from moral writings were utilized for preaching. For an introduction to the whole subject, see R.H. and M.A. Rouse, *PFS*, with extensive bibliography [GW16].

Medieval works that may be described as compilations are almost limitless. For a study of the process (based on manuscripts), see M.B. Parkes, "The Influence of the Concepts of *Ordinatio* and *Compilatio* on the Development of the Book," in *Medieval Learning* (see [GW10]) 115–41 [GW17]. A few striking examples of such compilations are *Das Moralium dogma philosophorum des Guillaume de Conches*, ed. J. Holmberg (1929), a treatise on ethics with many verse quotations [GW18]; William of Malmesbury, *Polyhistor*, ed. H.T. Ouellette (1982), a concatenation of stories and information in prose [GW19]. Many "encyclopedias" (see ch. GV) are essentially florilegia, such as Vincent of Beauvais's *Speculum maius*, in three parts (*naturale, historiale,* and *doctrinale,* to which was later added *morale*), completed by c. 1260; an early printed edition (Douai 1624) has been reprinted (1964–65) [GW20].

## Anthologies

See first A.G. Rigg, "Anthologies," in *DMA* 1:317–20 [GW21].

The oldest anthology of late Latin poetry is the *Codex Salmasianus* (Paris, B.N., MS lat. 10318): see *Anthologia Latina*, 1: *Carmina in codicibus scripta*, ed. D.R. Shackleton Bailey, fasc. 1: *Libri Salmasiani aliorumque carmina* (1982) [GW22].

The importance of the study of anthologies of medieval verse is stressed by A. Boutemy, "A propos d'anthologies poétiques au XIIe siècle," in *RBPhH* 19 (1940) 229–33 [GW23].

For a list of 25 published accounts of medieval verse collections, see A.G. Rigg,

"Medieval Latin Poetic Anthologies (I)," in *MS* 39 (1977) 281–330 [GW24]. This list (on pp282–84) provides bibliographies for Cambridge, University Library, MS Gg.5.35 (of which the last part contains the *Cambridge Songs: Carmina Cantabrigiensia*); Cambridge, University Library, MS Ff.1.17 (*Later Cambridge Songs*); Munich, Bayerische Staatsbibliothek, clm. 4660 (*Carmina Burana*); Paris, Bibliothèque de l'Arsenal, MS 1136 (*Floridus Aspectus*); Oxford, Bodleian Library, MS Add. A.44 (*Bekynton*); Glasgow, University Library, Hunterian Museum, MS V.8.14 (*Hunterian*); Tours, Bibliothèque municipale, MS 890 ("*Saint-Gatien*"). This article ([GW24]) also provides descriptions of London, B.L., Cotton MS Titus A.XX, and Oxford, Bodleian Library, MS Rawlinson B.214. Subsequent articles (II-IV) in the same series by the same author—*MS* 40 (1978), 387–407; *MS* 41 (1979), 468–505; *MS* 43 (1981), 472–97—describe (in II) Oxford, Bodleian Library, MS Bodley 851; (in III) Oxford, Bodleian Library, MS Digby 166; Oxford, Bodleian Library, MS Bodley 603; and London, B.L., Cotton MS Vespasian E.XII; and (in IV) Oxford, Bodleian Library, MS Rawlinson G.109 [GW25].

See also *OPHP* [GW26] and JM.. Ziolkowski, "A Bouquet of Wisdom and Invective: Houghton MS Lat. 300," in *Harvard Library Bulletin*, n.s., 1 (1990) 20–48 [GW27].

# HA • MEDIEVAL TRANSLATIONS: LATIN AND HEBREW

BY CHARLES H. MANEKIN

Knowledge of Latin was not common among the Jews in the Middle Ages, nor was Hebrew well known to most Christians. Jews in Islamic countries wrote in Arabic and Hebrew, the former for science, philosophy, and everyday discourse, the latter for liturgy, religious commentaries, and poetry. In Christian countries Jews wrote almost entirely in Hebrew, and they conducted their relations with the outside world in the vernacular. The Latin works that were translated into Hebrew never achieved the status of the Arabic classics, nor did the Hebrew works translated into Latin. Still, as time went by, Jewish thinkers in medieval Europe became increasingly influenced by the writings of their Christian neighbors, either in Latin or in translation. This process began in Italy in the thirteenth century and in Spain and Provence shortly thereafter.

Most of the translations into and from Latin were in philosophy, medicine, astronomy, and other sciences. They were either commissioned by patrons or resulted simply from the translator's desire to benefit his circle of readers. A few specifically Christian works were translated into Hebrew, some by Jewish apostates for conversionary purposes, others by Jews engaged in disputations and polemics.

## Translations From Hebrew into Latin

During the thirteenth and fourteenth centuries the great works of science and philosophy were translated from Arabic to Hebrew, partly because of the new climate of learning in the West, but mostly because of developments within the Jewish world itself, such as the spread of the teachings of Moses Maimonides (d. 1204) and the immigration of prominent families from Moslem Spain to southern France and Italy. Arabic writings were also translated into Latin, often with the aid of Jewish intermediaries working side by side with Christian scholars. Few works written in Hebrew were translated into Latin. With the reigning intellectual winds blowing from the Islamic world, most European Jews and Christians lived in cultural isolation from each other. There were exceptions: Maimonides's *Guide of the Perplexed,* originally written in Judeo-Arabic, was translated into Latin anonymously from a Hebrew translation; the work had a profound influence on Albertus Magnus (d. 1280) and Thomas Aquinas (d. 1274). But, on the whole, Jews and Christians were busy assimilating the glories of the classical tradition that had been preserved in Arabic science and philosophy.

Some early translators were apostates, like John of Capua (d. 1278), who translated the Hebrew version of the popular Indian book of fables, *Kalila and Dimna* (c. 1260), and Armengaud Blasius (d. 1314), who produced one of several Latin versions of a work on the quadrant by Jacob ben Ma'hir ibn Tibbon (d. 1307). Armengaud worked directly with Jacob ben Ma'hir at Montpellier. Among the Hebrew works translated into Latin during the fourteenth century is the anonymous *Book of Education*, a work on the 613 precepts of the Torah.

Not until the fifteenth and sixteenth centuries do we find a burst of activity in translation from Hebrew to Latin. Italian Jewish scholars had always been well versed in Hebrew and Latin, and among them Elijah ben Moses Delmedigo (d. 1497), Abraham de Balmes (d. 1523), Abraham Farissol (d. 1525), and Jacob Mantino (d. 1549) translated vast amounts of material at the request of their Christian friends and patrons. Delmedigo was commissioned to translate several treatises of Averroës from Hebrew by his student, Pico della Mirandola (d. 1494), the Renaissance humanist. These translations superseded the thirteenth-century translations from Arabic into Latin, and they engendered a renewed interest in Averroës, especially in Padua. They were later printed with the translations of Balmes, Mantino, Paul of Burgos (d. 1435), Vital Nissus, and Giovanni Burana in the standard Juntine edition of *Opera omnia Aristotelis et Averrois* (1550–52 and 1573–76).

This Juntine edition of Averroës is the crowning achievement of the medieval Jewish translators of Hebrew. Although it appeared in the sixteenth century, most of the translations were completed in the previous century, and the texts translated were the medieval Hebrew translations. The new translations were criticized by the German scholar Bartholomew Keckerman (d. 1609) for the "crass and tenacious barbarisms" of their Latin style, but the translators themselves aimed for *veritas* rather than *eloquentia,* to use the words of Abraham de Balmes. The hebraicized Latin of the translations has proved to be quite close to the Arabic text of the originals, some of which were recovered in the last century. Other Moslem authors translated from Hebrew into Latin during this period include Ibn Haytham (d. 1039), Ibn Bājja (d. 1139), al-Ghazālī (d. 1111), al-Biṭrūjī (fl. c. 1190), and Avicenna (Ibn Sīnā, d. 1037); Greek authors include Themistius and Galen.

Pico della Mirandola was interested in cabala, which he took to be an ancient science, and he commissioned his teacher, the orientalist Flavius Mithridates, to translate cabalistic works into Latin. Mithridates also translated the commentary on the *Song of Songs* of Levi ben Gershom (Gersonides, d. 1344) and a treatise on bodily resurrection by Maimonides. Other Christian cabalists included Giles of Viterbo (d. 1532), who translated such classics as the *Zohar,* the *Ginnat Egoz,* and the *Book of Raziel.*

## Translations From Latin into Hebrew

The earliest Hebrew translations of Latin works appeared as sections of Hebrew works without attribution, or with vague references to "the Gentile sages," etc. Thus, in Hillel of Verona's *Book of the Rewards of the Soul* (1291) one finds fragments from the Latin Avicenna and Averroës woven with passages of Domingo Gundisalvo (Gundissalinus) and Thomas Aquinas in a less than coherent whole. Over a century earlier Jacob ben Reuben had translated sections of the *Disputatio Iudaei et Christiani* of Gilbert Crispin (d. 1117), abbot of Westminster, for his *Wars of the Lord* (1170), a manual for polemics. By the first quarter of the fourteenth century, however, translations of Gundisalvo, Giles of Rome, Albertus Magnus, Alexander of Alessandri (d. 1314), Angelo of Camerino (late thirteenth century), and Thomas Aquinas flowed from the pen of the philosopher Judah Romano, who also translated Averroës into Hebrew from the Latin! This is not as unusual as it appears; throughout the thirteenth and fourteenth centuries one finds Hebrew translations from the Latin of original Arabic material, especially in science and medicine. In the fifteenth century the Iberian peninsula became a major center of translation activity, thanks to the labors of Elijah Habillo, Abraham Shalom (d. 1492), Meir Alguadez (d. 1410), and Azaria ben Joseph, who rendered works by Aristotle, Boethius, Albertus Magnus, Aquinas, Ockham (d. 1347/49), and Marsilius of Inghen (d. 1396).

In the Jewish communities of Provence the situation was different. The few philosophical texts translated from the Latin did not have the immediate impact that they did in Italy, and none became standard. Some books were translated several times in different locales as the need arose; the *Tractatus* of Peter of Spain (d. 1277), a standard textbook on logic, merited no fewer than four separate versions in Provence, Spain, and Crete. Quite a few medical works were translated in Provence, such as the *Regimen sanitatis* of Arnald of Villanova (d. 1311) and the *Introductorium in practicam* of Bernard Albert (d. 1358?). How much Latin was known by the Provençal Jewish intellectuals is a matter of scholarly dispute. Some of Gersonides's scientific writings were translated into Latin by his Christian assistant, Phillip of Alexander, perhaps at the behest of Pope Clement VI (1342–52). By the mid-fifteenth century the physician and philosopher Mordecai Nathan (d. c. 1470) was citing the Latin original of the *Tractatus* in his Hebrew commentary on Averroës's *Logic*. Nathan (or his brother Isaac) also completed the first Hebrew concordance of the Bible between 1437 and 1448 as a tool for Jewish polemical debates with Christians. A Latin translation appeared in Rome in 1621.

Nathan's case is not atypical; Jewish authors did not necessarily learn of scholastic doctrines from Hebrew translations. Unlike Christian scholars, whose knowledge of Arab and Jewish culture derived almost entirely from the Latin, Jews could rely on several sources: the original text, direct translations, and discussion with Christian savants in the vernacular. That there were relatively few translations from Latin is a reflection of the conservatism of the Jewish thinkers, who were deeply rooted in the Arabic philosophical tradition. When scholastic teachings made inroads in Hebrew science and philosophy, they added to, rather than replaced, this older tradition.

### Christian Hebraism in the Middle Ages

Medieval Christians' main interest in Hebrew centered on the Bible, its text and interpretation. Although most readers relied on the "Vulgate," St. Jerome's Latin translation based partly on the Hebrew text, there were exceptions. In the twelfth century Bible scholars such as Nicholas of Manjacoria and Stephen Harding of Cîteaux attempted to determine a more precise meaning of the Scriptures by appealing to *Hebraica veritas*. It is difficult to determine how much Hebrew they knew and how much they consulted Jewish rabbis for their information, but they clearly possessed a rudimentary knowledge. There are also indications that Abbot Sigo of

Saint-Florent (d. 1070) as well as Peter Abelard (d. 1142) knew Hebrew, and the latter commended the study of this language to Heloise and the nuns of the Paraclete
in his correspondence (the authenticity of which is disputed). During the late twelfth
and thirteenth centuries a small number of Christian Hebraists arose, prominent
among whom were Robert Grosseteste (d. 1253), bishop of Lincoln, and his student,
Roger Bacon (d. 1291). Instead of the Vulgate Grosseteste often preferred a literal
Latin translation of the Bible made directly from the Hebrew; Bacon, who compiled
Greek and Hebrew grammars, did much to promote the study of Hebrew. His stated
motives were twofold: (a) to learn the arguments of the Jews in order to convert them
(*Opus majus,* 3.13); and (b) to have a deeper understanding of the language in which
God had revealed wisdom to his creatures (*Opus tertium,* 10 and 14). Like many other
medieval scholars Bacon believed that the roots of all wisdom and science were to be
found in the Bible, properly interpreted. A more literal approach to Scripture was
adopted by Nicholas of Lyra (d. 1340), whose famous commentary borrowed heavily from medieval Jewish sources. And Beryl Smalley has demonstrated convincingly
the influence of Hebrew and of medieval Jewish exegesis on the College of Saint-
Victor in the twelfth and thirteenth centuries. It is true that Hebrew might have appealed to a Medieval Latin scholar's "emotions, philosophy, and . . . sense of history,"
to use Smalley's phrase [HA19], but the great period of Christian Hebraism would
not come until the end of the Renaissance and the Reformation.

## Select Bibliography

### Primary Sources

Among the few Latin-Hebrew translations that have been edited are Judah Romano's translation of Aquinas's *De ente et essentia,* ed. G. Sermoneta (1978) [HA1];
and Hillel of Verona's *Sefer Tagmulei ha-Nefesh* (Book of the Rewards of the Soul),
ed. G. Sermoneta (1981), which includes passages from scholastic authors [HA2].

Both Hebrew and Latin versions of Gersonides's astrological prediction are
found in B.R. Goldstein and D. Pingree, *Levi ben Gerson's Prognosticon for the Conjunction of 1345, TAPhS* 80.6 (1990) [HA3].

Several of the Hebrew-Latin translations of Averroës have been edited in the series, *Corpus commentariorum Averrois in Aristotelem* (1931–) [HA4]; for a listing see
D. Urvoy, *Ibn Rushd (Averroes)* (1991) 142–44 [HA5].

### Studies

M. Steinschneider's monumental *Die hebräischen Übersetzungen des Mittelalters
und die Juden als Dolmetscher* (1893, r1956) remains, after a century, the standard
work on the subject [HA6]. Abbreviated versions of Steinschneider's list of transla-
tions are contained in A.S. Halkin, "Translations and Translators (Medieval)," in the
*Encyclopedia Judaica* (1971–72) 15:1318–29 [HA7], and I. Broyde, "Translations," in *The
Jewish Encyclopedia* (1906) 12:219–29 [HA8]. (Halkin's list is arranged generically;
Broyde's, chronologically.) See also C. Sirat, *A History of Jewish Philosophy in the
Middle Ages* (1985, r1990) [HA9].

For sketches of Judah Romano and Abraham Farissol see G. Sermoneta, "Jehuda ben Moseh ben Daniel Romano, traducteur de Saint Thomas," in *Hommage à Georges Vajda: Études d'histoire et de pensée juives,* ed. G. Nahon and C. Touati (1980) 231–62 [HA10], and D.B. Ruderman, *The World of a Renaissance Jew: The Life and Thought of Abraham ben Mordecai Farissol* (1981) [HA11].

On the Renaissance translations of Averroës see H.A. Wolfson, "The Twice-Revealed Averroes," in *Inquiries into Medieval Philosophy: A Collection in Honor of Francis P. Clarke,* ed. J.F. Ross (1971); repr. in *Studies in the History of Philosophy and Religion,* 2 vols., ed. I. Twersky and G.H. William (1973–77) v1:371–401 [HA12]; see also F.E. Cranz, "The Editions of the Latin Aristotle Accompanied by the Commentaries of Averroes," in *Philosophy and Humanism: Renaissance Essays in Honor of Paul Oskar Kristeller,* ed. E.P. Mahoney (1976) 116–28 [HA13], and C.B. Schmitt, *The Aristotelian Tradition and Renaissance Universities* (1984) [HA14].

For the early Latin Bible translations see B. Kedar-Kopfstein, "The Latin Translations," in *Mikra: Text, Translation, Reading, and Interpretation of the Hebrew Bible in Ancient Judaism and Early Christianity,* ed. M.J. Mulder (1990) 299–338 [HA15]. See also A. Kamesar, *Jerome, Greek Scholarship, and the Hebrew Bible: A Study of the "Quaestiones hebraicae in Genesim"* (1993) [HA16].

On Christian Hebraism in the Middle Ages see I.M. Resnick, "*Lingua Dei, Lingua Hominis:* Sacred Language and Medieval Texts," in *Viator* 21 (1990) 51–74 [HA17], and A. Grabois, "The *Hebraica Veritas* and Jewish-Christian Intellectual Relations in the Twelfth Century," in *Speculum* 50 (1975) 613–34 [HA18]. See also B. Smalley, *The Study of the Bible in the Middle Ages,* 3rd ed. (1983) 112–95 [HA19]. For the main (postmedieval) period of Christian Hebraism see the comprehensive entry by R. Loewe, "Christian Hebraism," in the *Encyclopedia Judaica* ([HA7] 8:9–71), which lists every known translator and translation [HA20].

BY BERNICE M. KACZYNSKI

The Greek and Latin languages existed side by side in the classical world of the Mediterranean, and the boundary between them was porous. The Romans, who knew themselves to be dependent upon Greek culture, were the first to advance a theory and practice of translation. Cicero recognized two styles of translation: the "free" and the "literal," one for literature, the other for law and business (*Opt. Gen.* 14). The translator of a literary text sought to express sense for sense; he went about his work as an *orator*. The translator of a nonliterary text, on the other hand, expressed word for word; he simply acted as *interpres* or, as Horace dismissively put it, *fidus interpres* (*Ars* 133–34).

The classical formulae were transmitted to the Middle Ages by St. Jerome (d. 419/20), who adhered to them in practice in much of his own work, but who made an exception for Scripture. In the translation of Scripture, "ubi et verborum ordo mysterium est," Jerome advocated a strict literalism (*Ep.* 57, *De optimo genere interpretandi* 5). With this emphasis, then, the old dichotomy between literary and nonliterary translation broke down. Jerome's approach to Scripture conferred new prestige on word-for-word translation, and thereafter most scholars would favor it. In the ninth century, when John Scottus Eriugena (d. c. 877–79) translated the *De caelesti hierarchia* of Pseudo-Dionysius, he remarked in the preface that his literal style of translation might seem to some to earn him the scorn of Horace. But, he said, it was his free choice: he wished to be an *interpres* and not an *expositor* of the text. Not until the Renaissance would scholars—at least those working from Greek to Latin— again see themselves primarily as *oratores*. Medieval translation was, as a rule, literal translation.

The scholars of the Middle Ages turned in the first instance to a series of bilingual texts they had inherited from the educational systems of late antiquity. The *Ars grammatica* of Dositheus (late fourth century), for example, comprised an outline of Latin grammar together with a Greek translation. It was used in the East for teaching Latin; in the West for studying Greek. Bilingual schoolbooks known as *Hermeneumata*, containing vocabulary lists and texts for reading practice, also served for instruction in both languages. But while the late antique world had contained many populations fluent in both Greek and Latin, the medieval world did not.

From the fifth or sixth century onwards, people with a knowledge of Greek were scarce in the West, as were people in the East with a knowledge of Latin.

Therefore translations made in late antiquity remained in use for many centuries. Particularly important, in the sphere of Greek to Latin, were Jerome's translations of Scripture and Rufinus's of Origen and other Church fathers, Boethius's translations of Aristotle, and the translations of exegetical, philosophical, and scientific works commissioned by Cassiodorus at Vivarium.

New translation from Greek to Latin in medieval Europe seems to have been conducted in an episodic fashion. In the eighth and ninth centuries, Carolingian scholars made much of the late antique material; certainly they had access to more texts than survive today. They studied Jerome's translations of Scripture and prepared bilingual editions in order to compare the texts. John Scottus Eriugena, an Irishman at the West Frankish court of Charles the Bald, translated the works of Pseudo-Dionysius into Latin, as well as some works of Maximus Confessor and Gregory of Nyssa. Anastasius Bibliothecarius (c. 815–79), librarian at the papal court in Rome, criticized John's literal renderings and provided his own translations of Greek hagiographical, historical, and theological works.

The pace of translation from Greek to Latin quickened in the twelfth and thirteenth centuries. Burgundio of Pisa (d. 1193), who had spent some years in Constantinople as an interpreter, gave new versions of works by John of Damascus, John Chrysostom, Pseudo-Basil, and Nemesius of Emesa, as well as medical texts by Hippocrates and Galen. Indeed, the range of materials available in the West broadened considerably. Translators in Norman Sicily turned their attention to Greek technical writings. North of the Alps, in the universities, scholars became interested in philosophical and scientific works, especially those of Aristotle. In England, Robert Grosseteste (d. 1253) produced an annotated edition of Aristotle's *Nicomachean Ethics*. The Fleming William of Moerbeke (d. c. 1286) was extremely prolific, translating a variety of medical and mathematical treatises and—perhaps at the request of Thomas Aquinas (1224–74)—a series of works by Aristotle and his commentators.

In 1397 Coluccio Salutati invited the Byzantine diplomat Manuel Chrysoloras (d. 1415) to teach Greek in Florence. Chrysoloras and his pupils, among them Leonardo Bruni (d. 1444), turned to the task of translation with optimism and assurance. The Italian humanists produced translations in large numbers. Some were of familiar works, but many were new, particularly in the realms of philosophy, poetry, oratory, and historiography. The nature of the enterprise changed as well. The translators of the fifteenth century rejected the word-for-word style of translation. They saw themselves instead as working in the classical tradition of Cicero's *oratores*, whose task it was to fashion literary works in elegant Latin. Their translations were not, however, always better than the earlier ones, and they sometimes relied upon them without acknowledgment. Humanist translations could be very free, and modern mistrust of this approach is reflected in the Italian expression "Traduttore—traditore!"

Scholars today are just beginning to explore the history of translation from Latin to Greek. Throughout the Middle Ages speakers of Greek insisted upon their cultural superiority to Latins. The amount of translated material appears to have been relatively slight.

Latin was the language of administration in the early Eastern Empire, and it was probably known best there in the fourth century. To the deposit of bilingual schoolbooks, Greek translators added juxtalinear versions of Cicero and Virgil. These translations were word for word; their purpose was utilitarian. A more free and literary approach is found in a polished verse translation of Virgil's *Fourth Eclogue*, appended to Eusebius's *Life of Constantine*.

The thirteenth and fourteenth centuries saw a renewed interest in translation. Maximus Planudes (d. 1305) was an exceptional figure, for he knew and understood a range of Latin literature. He translated works by Augustine, Boethius, and Macrobius. He put Ovid's *Heroides, Metamorphoses*, and amatory verse into very plain Greek prose, and when he encountered words like *amor, Venus*, and *cultissima femina*, he sought discreet equivalents. In the next century, Byzantine theologians learned to know scholasticism through the work of Demetrius Kydones (d. 1398), a scholar who had spent time in Italy. Of lasting importance were his translations of the *Summa contra gentiles* and *Summa theologica* of Thomas Aquinas.

## Select Bibliography

On the theory and practice of translation, see S. Brock, "Aspects of Translation Technique in Antiquity," in *GRBS* 20 (1979) 69–87 [**HB1**]; R. Copeland, "The Fortunes of 'non verbum pro verbo': or, Why Jerome Is Not a Ciceronian," in *The Medieval Translator: The Theory and Practice of Translation in the Middle Ages*, ed. R. Ellis (1989) 15–35 [**HB2**]; P. Chiesa, "*Ad verbum o ad sensum?* Modelli e coscienza metodologica della traduzione tra tarda antichità e alto medioevo," in *Medioevo e Rinascimento* 1 (1987) 1–51 [**HB3**]; and J. Schneider, "*Graecizare, latinizare* und verwandte Verben im mittelalterlichen Latein," in *Griechenland, Byzanz, Europa*, ed. J. Herrmann, H. Köpstein, and R. Müller (1985) 142–52 [**HB4**]. For a discussion of medieval attitudes towards foreign languages in general, see A. Borst, *Der Turmbau von Babel: Geschichte der Meinungen über Ursprung und Vielfalt der Sprachen und Völker*, 4 vols. in 6 pts. (1957–63) [**HB5**].

For an introduction to the bilingual texts of late antiquity, see H.I. Marrou, *Histoire de l'éducation dans l'antiquité*, 6th ed. (1965) 374–88, 590–96; 3rd ed. tr. G. Lamb: *A History of Education in Antiquity* (1956, r1982) [**HB6**]. The *Ars grammatica* of Dositheus is edited by H. Keil in *Grammatici latini* 7:363–436 (1880, r1981) [**HB7**]. Some *Hermeneumata* are edited by J. Kramer, *Glossaria bilinguia in papyris et membranis reperta* (1983) [**HB8**], and by G. Goetz, *Corpus glossariorum latinorum* 3 (1892, r1965) [**HB9**]. See also A.C. Dionisotti, "From Ausonius' Schooldays? A Schoolbook and Its Relatives," in *Journal of Roman Studies* 72 (1982) 83–125 [**HB10**].

Scholars approaching the subject of medieval translation from Greek to Latin are well served by W. Berschin, *Greek Letters and the Latin Middle Ages: From Jerome to Nicholas of Cusa*, rev. and expanded edition, tr. J. Frakes (1988), with comprehensive bibliography [**HB11**]. B. Bischoff, "Das griechische Element in der abendländischen Bildung des Mittelalters," in *MittStud* 2:246–75, remains a classic statement of the theme [**HB12**]. For lists of available texts, see J.T. Muckle, "Greek Works Translated Directly into Latin before 1350," in *MS* 4 (1942) 33–42, 5 (1943) 102–14 [**HB13**]; and P.O. Kristeller, F.E. Cranz, *et al.*, eds., *CTC* [**HB14**]. To become familiar with some recent trends in scholarship, see the essays in G. Contamine, ed., *Traduction et traducteurs au moyen âge: Actes du colloque international du C.N.R.S.* (Paris, 26–28 May 1986) (1989) [**HB15**].

Much specialized work has been published on translation from Greek to Latin in particular historical periods. On late antique Hellenism, see P. Courcelle, *Late Latin Writers and Their Greek Sources*, tr. H.E. Wedeck (1969) [HB16]. On Christian literature, see A. Siegmund, *Die Überlieferung der griechischen christlichen Literatur in der lateinischen Kirche bis zum zwölften Jahrhundert* (1949) [HB17]. To locate translations of individual Christian authors, consult the entries in J. Quasten, *Patrology*, 4 vols. (1950–86) [HB18].

On the transmission of Greek texts in early medieval Europe, see B. Kaczynski, *Greek in the Carolingian Age: The St. Gall Manuscripts* (1988) [HB19]. On texts and translations in early medieval England, see B. Kaczynski, "Greek Texts," in *Sources of Anglo-Saxon Literary Culture*, ed. F.M. Biggs, T.D. Hill, and P.E. Szarmach (forthcoming) [HB20]. The working habits of Carolingian translators may be studied by looking at facsimile editions of their manuscripts, e.g. *Psalterium graeco-latinum: Codex Basiliensis A.VII.3*, with intro. by L. Bieler, Umbrae codicum occidentalium 5 (1960) [HB21]. The methods of two ninth-century scholars are analyzed by E. Jeauneau: "Jean Scot Érigène et le grec," in *ALMA* 41 (1979) 5–50 [HB22], and "Pour le dossier d'Israël Scot," in *AHDL* 52 (1985) 7–71; repr. in *id.*, *Études érigéniennes* (1987) 639–706 [HB23].

The accelerated pace of translation activity in the twelfth and thirteenth centuries is well documented. For a discussion of some individual translators, see P. Classen, *Burgundio von Pisa: Richter, Gesandter, Übersetzer* (1974) [HB24], and A.C. Dionisotti, "On the Greek Studies of Robert Grosseteste," in *The Uses of Greek and Latin: Historical Essays*, ed. A.C. Dionisotti *et al.* (1988) 19–39 [HB25]. For translations of Aristotle, see B. Schneider, *Die mittelalterlichen griechisch-lateinischen Übersetzungen der aristotelischen Rhetorik* (1971) [HB26]. Many medieval translations of Greek philosophical works have been edited, e.g. Proclus: *Commentaire sur le Parménide de Platon. Traduction de Guillaume de Moerbeke*, 2 vols. ed. C. Steel (1982–85) [HB27].

On the fifteenth-century scholars, see K.M. Setton, "The Byzantine Background to the Italian Renaissance," in *PAPS* 100 (1956) 1–76; repr. in *id.*, *Europe and the Levant in the Middle Ages and the Renaissance* (1974) [HB28]; D.J. Geanakoplos, *Greek Scholars in Venice: Studies in the Dissemination of Greek Learning from Byzantium to Western Europe* (1962, r1973) [HB29]; and A. Grafton and L. Jardine, *From Humanism to the Humanities: Education and the Liberal Arts in Fifteenth- and Sixteenth-Century Europe* (1986) 99–121 [HB30]. See also A. Sottili, "Humanistische Neuverwendung mittelalterlicher Übersetzungen," in *Die Rezeption der Antike: Zum Problem der Kontinuität zwischen Mittelalter und Renaissance*, ed. A. Buck (1981) 165–85 [HB31].

The bibliography on translation from Latin to Greek is sparse. Much work remains to be done, especially in the identification and edition of texts. For overviews, see H. and R. Kahane, "The Western Impact on Byzantium: The Linguistic Evidence," in *DOP* 36 (1982) 127–53 [HB32], and A. Lumpe, "Abendland und Byzanz: Literatur. Abendländisches in Byzanz," in *Reallexikon der Byzantinistik*, ed. P. Wirth (1970), v1.4:304–45 [HB33].

To learn about Latin in Constantinople, see B. Hemmerdinger, "Les lettres latines à Constantinople jusqu'à Justinien," in *Byzantinische Forschungen* 1 (1966) 174–78 [HB34]; G. Dagron, "Aux origines de la civilisation byzantine: Langue de culture et langue d'état," in *Revue historique* 241 (1969) 23–56 [HB35]; and B. Baldwin,

"Latin in Byzantium," in *From Late Antiquity to Early Byzantium*, ed. V. Vavrinek (1985) 237–41 [HB36].

On Christian translation, see E. Schwartz, "Zweisprachigkeit in den Konzilsakten," in *Philologus* 88 (1933) 245–53 [HB37], and E. Dekkers, "Les traductions grecques des écrits patristiques latins," in *SE* 5 (1953) 193–233 [HB38].

On literary translation in the early period, see E.A. Fisher, "Greek Translations of Latin Literature in the Fourth Century A.D.," in *Yale Classical Studies* 27 (1982) 173–215, an exemplary study [HB39]. See also V. Reichmann, *Römische Literatur in griechischer Übersetzung* (1943) [HB40], and, on a specialized point, B. Baldwin: "Vergilius Graecus," in *American Journal of Philology* 97 (1976) 361–68 [HB41], and "Vergil in Byzantium," in *A&A* 28 (1982) 81–93 [HB42].

For the translators of the later period, see N.G. Wilson, *Scholars of Byzantium* (1983) [HB43]. On Maximus Planudes, see C. Wendel, "Planudes," in *Paulys Realencyclopädie der classischen Altertumswissenschaft*, v20.2:2202–53 [HB44], and E.A. Fisher, *Planudes' Greek Translation of Ovid's "Metamorphoses"* (1990) [HB45].

# HC • MEDIEVAL TRANSLATIONS: LATIN AND ARABIC

## BY DEBORAH L. BLACK

Most of the translations from Arabic into Latin were made between the middle of the twelfth and the middle of the thirteenth century, although there were some earlier sporadic efforts. The majority of works translated were in the areas of science, medicine, and philosophy, and translations from Arabic played an integral part in the recovery of Greek learning. However, not all translations were of scientific and philosophical works. Some texts, including the *Qurʾān* itself, were translated in order to serve the goals of religious apologetics.

## Historical Overview of the Translation Activity

The early translations from Arabic made in the eleventh century were motivated by a practical interest in medical and scientific works. The most significant medical translations were the effort of Constantine the African (d. 1087), and they were part of the movement to recover the Galenic tradition in medicine. The height of Arabic-Latin translation activity, however, occurred in the mid-twelfth century and was generally the effort of scholars working in Spain. Although Sicily was a center for translation as well, and many Sicilian translators could have worked with Arabic texts, they generally chose to do so only when Greek originals were not available. In Spain itself, the translators from Arabic were sometimes local men who knew Arabic, the vernacular, and perhaps Latin; but there were also a number of learned foreign scholars from other European centers who traveled to Spain for the express purpose of studying Arabic authors.

Despite the focus on scientific and philosophical works in this period, translations made for apologetic purposes can also be traced to twelfth-century Spain. Many, although not all, of these efforts were carried out under the sponsorship of Peter the Venerable (c. 1092–1156). Two important translators of scientific works, Robert of Ketton and Hermann of Carinthia (fl. 1138–43), participated in the enterprise, as did otherwise unknown translators who may have been solicited to help Robert and Hermann. Along with the *Qurʾān*, a number of accounts of the prophet Muhammad's life, and some Islamic theological writings, were translated into Latin.

Works of scientific interest, covering subjects such as astronomy, optics, mathematics, and alchemy, were amongst the most important products of translation in twelfth-century Spain. The principal translators of scientific texts were Adelard of Bath (d. 1142/46), Robert of Ketton, Hermann of Carinthia, and John of Seville (d. 1157). Some of the more important works translated (sometimes more than once) were al-Khwārizmī's algebraic tables, Euclid's *Elements* (via Arabic translations), Abū Ma‹shar's *Introductorium maius* (1140), an influential astronomical text, and Ptolemy's *Planisphere.*

Scientific texts preoccupied most of the translators of the first half of the twelfth century. In the next generation, however, the work of translators centered in Toledo was directed to philosophical texts. Most important amongst the texts translated at this time was the philosophical encyclopedia of Avicenna (Ibn Sīnā, d. 1037), the *Shifā›* (Healing). The Latin version of the work, which is almost complete, was the joint effort of Domingo Gundisalvo (Dominicus Gundissalinus) and various collaborators, the most important of whom was a certain "Avendauth" (Abraham Ibn Dawud, d. 1180). Works by al-Fārābī (d. 950), al-Kindī (d. 870), al-Ghazālī (d. 1111), and the Jewish philosopher Ibn Gabirol (Avicebron, d. c. 1058 or 1070) were also translated at this time: the most important texts were Farabi's *Iḥṣa› al-‹ulūm* (*De scientiis*), short treatises by Farabi and Kindi entitled *De intellectu,* and Avicebron's *Fons vitae.* In addition to Gundissalinus, Gerard of Cremona (d. 1187) stands out as an important translator of Arabic treatises in this period, and of a number of Aristotelian texts via Arabic intermediaries.

The final phase of translation from Arabic takes us into the early thirteenth century, when the philosophical commentaries of Averroës (Ibn Rushd, d. 1198) were translated by Michael Scot during the period between 1220 to 1235. Since the *Long Commentaries* of Averroës reproduce the entire text of Aristotle, these translations also introduced new versions of the Aristotelian corpus into the Latin West. In addition to the translations of Michael Scot, a very influential translation of Averroës's *Middle Commentary* on Aristotle's *Poetics* was made by Hermannus Alemannus in 1256. Hermannus also made translations from the Arabic version of Aristotle's *Rhetoric,* along with related Arabic commentaries on the text. Hermannus's translation of Averroës's commentary on the *Poetics* was the only version of this Aristotelian text available in Latin until William of Moerbeke translated the work directly from the Greek in 1272. It was also important for another reason: through Hermannus's renditions of the Arabic poetry cited by Averroës to illustrate his points, the Latin West was given a rare glimpse at the Arabic literary tradition.

## Methods and Character of the Translations

Although the methods and characteristics of the translations done from Arabic into Latin vary over the course of the translation movement and with the different subject matters of the translated works, some generalizations can be made regarding the linguistic skills of the translators, their styles of translation, and their handling of the disparities between the Arabic and Latin languages.

Medieval translators in all fields were generally quite conscious of their methodological principles and goals, and many translations contain prefaces in which the authors explicitly describe and defend the procedures they have followed. Still, many of the translators did face difficulties in their efforts, which they attempted to remedy in various ways. In some cases, they resorted to general paraphrases of texts whose literal meaning posed difficulties. This method could also be applied within otherwise literal translations to deal with difficult passages, unknown technical terms, or differences between Latin and Arabic syntax.

One obvious solution to the difficulties posed to translators by the Arabic language was collaboration, a widespread practice during the twelfth and thirteenth centuries. Such collaboration was necessary not only to ensure the accurate understanding of the Arabic, but also to aid Arabic and Jewish scholars in rendering texts correctly into Latin. Of course, not all translators required collaborators: those of Mozarabic origin often had sufficient skills in both languages to render Arabic into Latin accurately, if not elegantly. Perhaps the most famous account of collaboration is that recounted in the prologue of Avicenna's *De anima*. In this passage, Dominicus Gundissalinus and "Avendauth" explain how they have translated Avicenna's text from Arabic into Latin, with "Avendauth" rendering the original word for word into the vernacular (*singula verba vulgariter proferente*), and Gundissalinus translating it in the same manner into Latin (*singula in latinum convertente*). This account has produced a somewhat caricatured view of the entire translation movement and must be interpreted cautiously. Although it is generally the case that translations involving collaboration tend to be literal and inelegant, the procedure described here does not necessarily indicate either ignorance of Arabic on the part of the Latin member of the team or ignorance of Latin on the part of his Arabic or Jewish collaborator. The use of the vernacular and the general need for collaboration probably indicate that both translators had some knowledge of Latin and Arabic, but that neither felt sufficiently secure with both the original and the target language to undertake the translation on his own. As to the use of a word-for-word technique of translation, this was generally the favored method in all translations of technical scientific and philosophical material, and it was followed by most translators from Greek as well as by those teams of translators working from Arabic by way of the vernacular.

Although the quality of the translations made from Arabic is uneven, by and large those executed at the height of the translation movement, including the ones involving collaboration, are sufficiently accurate to give the Latin reader a sound understanding of the content of often difficult Arabic texts. Some of the errors that do occur are the inevitable result of the differences between the structures of the Arabic and Latin languages, and of the relative paucity of terms for concepts in one language for which the other language has a much richer lexicon. An example of the problems caused by structural dissimilarities between Latin and Arabic occurs in philosophical translations of the adverbial phrases *ʿalā al-qaṣd al-awwal* and *ʿalā al-qaṣd al-thānī*, as *prima intentione* and *secunda intentione*, respectively. Since Arabic does not have a standard means for deriving adverbs, prepositional phrases often serve an adverbial function: in this example, the Arabic phrases, in everyday parlance, mean "primarily" and "secondarily." But in the technical terminology of Arabic philosophy, first and second intentions are used to differentiate first-order concepts ("first intentions," e.g. the concepts "human being" and "horse") from the second-order concepts studied in logic ("second intentions," e.g. the concepts "genus" and "species"). Studies of Arabic-Latin logical translations have shown that translators often mistook the nontechnical adverbial use of these phrases for technical uses, sometimes producing confusing results (see [HC26]).

Philosophical translations also provide numerous examples of the difficulties posed by dissimilarities in the vocabularies of Latin and Arabic. Jean Jolivet has noted, for example, that in the translation of Avicenna's *Metaphysics* the Latin word *esse* is used to render as many as 34 different Arabic terms for "being" and "becoming" and related concepts (see [HC14] pp118–19). Conversely, the use of two different terms, *intellectus* and *intelligentia*, to translate the single Arabic term ʿaql, "intellect," led Latin audiences to discover an unintended technical distinction between human and angelic intellects in some Arabic philosophical texts (see [HC27]). Other apparent infelicities in the Latin versions of Arabic texts stem from the inevitable coinage of technical terms in scientific and philosophical Arabic—itself the result of the Greek basis of Arabic philosophy and science—that foster neologisms in the Latin translations. One of the most pervasive and well-known of these neologisms is the term *quidditas*, used in the Latin versions of Avicenna's *Metaphysics* to translate the Arabic *māhiyya*, meaning the "whatness" or essence of a thing. Here the translator simply constructed an abstract Latin noun from the relative pronoun *quid*, "what," just as the Arabic philosophical tradition had constructed an abstract noun from the Arabic relative particle *mā*, also meaning "what."

Although there are clear examples of misunderstandings of original Arabic texts that stem from poor or mistaken translations, as some of the preceding examples show, these have often been overemphasized by modern scholars. Such exaggeration has been engendered in part by the skepticism that tales of collaboration such as Gundissalinus's inevitably produce. But recent and more detailed studies of particular translations in relation to their Arabic originals, where these are extant, have served to remedy the myth that the work of Arabic-Latin translators in the Middle Ages was on the whole unreliable and uncritical.


## Select Bibliography


The most reliable overview of translations from Arabic is found in M.-T. d'Alverny, "Translations and Translators," in *R&R* 421–61 [HC1]; it supersedes and corrects earlier general accounts and contains an annotated bibliography. Some of the best studies of the techniques of translation are contained in the introductions to critical editions, especially those in which the editor is familiar with the original Arabic text. It is not possible to provide a comprehensive list of all such editions in all disciplines here; some of the best examples, however, are S. Van Riet's editions in the *Avicenna Latinus* series ([HC19]). See also M.-T. d'Alverny, "Motives and Circumstances, Methods and Techniques of Translation from Arabic to Latin," in *Invited Papers: Colloquium on the Transmission and Reception of Knowledge, Dumbarton Oaks, Washington, D.C., 5–7 May 1977*, 2 vols. (1977), v1:155–73 [HC2].

For scientific translations, see C.H. Haskins, *Studies in the History of Mediaeval Science*, 2nd ed. (1927, r1960) [HC3]. A number of articles by C.F.S. Burnett should also be consulted: "Scientific Speculations," in *A History of Twelfth-Century Western Philosophy*, ed. P. Dronke (1988) 151–76 [HC4]; "A Group of Arabic-Latin Translators Working in Northern Spain in the Mid–12th Century," in *Journal of the Royal Asiatic Society* (1977) 62–108 [HC5]; "Arabic into Latin in Twelfth-Century Spain: The Works of Hermann of Carinthia," in *MLJ* 13 (1978) 100–34 [HC6]; "Some Comments on the Translating of Works from Arabic into Latin in the Mid-Twelfth Century," in *MiscM* 17 (1985) 161–71 [HC7]. See also ch. EE in this guide.

For medical works, see the chapter by D. Jacquart, "Aristotelian Thought in

Salerno," in [HC4] 407–28 [HC8], and "A l'aube de la renaissance médicale des XIe–XIIe siècles: L'Isagoge Johannitii' et son traducteur," in *BECh* 144 (1986) 209–40 [HC9]; see also D. Jacquart and G. Troupeau, "Traduction de l'arabe et vocabulaire médical latin: Quelques exemples," in *LLM* 367–76 [HC10]. See also ch. EL in this guide.

For the translation of texts for apologetic purposes, valuable background is provided in J. Kritzeck, *Peter the Venerable and Islam* (1964) [HC11]. M.-T. d'Alverny has studied the translations of the *Qurʾān* in "Deux traductions latines du Coran au moyen âge," in *AHDL* 16 (1948) 69–131 [HC12]; see also her study, with G. Vajda, of the translation of theological works, "Marc de Tolède, traducteur d'Ibn Tûmart," in *Al-Andalus* 16 (1951) 99–140, 259–307; 17 (1952) 1–56 [HC13].

On philosophical translations, see J. Jolivet, "The Arabic Inheritance," in [HC4], pp113–48 [HC14]; M.-T. d'Alverny, "Notes sur les traductions médiévales des oeuvres arabes d'Avicenne," in *AHDL* 19 (1952) 337–58 [HC15]; "Avicenna latinus, I–XI," in *AHDL* 28–37, 39 (1961–70, 1972) [HC16]; "Les traductions d'Avicenne (Moyen Age et Renaissance)," in *Avicenna nella storia della cultura medioevale* (1957) 71–87 [HC17]; S. Van Riet, "Influence de l'arabe sur la terminologie philosophique latine médiévale," in *Actas del V Congreso internacional de filosofia medieval* 1 (1979) 137–44 [HC18]. Van Riet's editions of the Latin versions of Avicenna are invaluable for information regarding the methods and vocabulary of philosophical translations and contain complete Arabic-Latin, Latin-Arabic indices. See *Avicenna Latinus*, ed. S. Van Riet (1968–): *Liber de anima, seu Sextus de naturalibus*, 2 vols. (1968–72); *Liber de philosophia prima, sive, Scientia divina*, 2 vols. (1977–80); *Liber de tertius naturalium, De generatione et corruptione* (1987) [HC19]. Arabic-Latin versions of Aristotelian works are included in the editions of the *Aristoteles Latinus* series (see [BG27]) [HC20]. A number of Averroës's works have been edited in their Latin versions in the series *Corpus commentariorum Averrois in Aristotelem*, published by the Mediaeval Academy of America (1931–) [HC21], but few of these include any explicit references to the Arabic originals (where they exist), and the editors of some volumes did not themselves read Arabic. For information about the Latin versions of Averroës, see H.A. Wolfson, "Revised Plan for the Publication of a *Corpus Commentariorum Averrois in Aristotelem*," in *Speculum* 38 (1963) 88–104 [HC22]. The translations of Aristotle and his Greek and Arabic commentators from both Greek and Arabic sources are discussed by B.G. Dod, "Aristoteles Latinus," in *CHLMP* 45–79 [HC23].

For discussions of the literary elements in Hermannus Alemannus's translations of Arabic *Rhetoric* and *Poetics* commentaries, see W. Boggess, "Hermannus Alemannus' Latin Anthology of Arabic Poetry," in *Journal of the American Oriental Society* 88 (1968) 657–70 [HC24], and "Hermannus Alemannus's Rhetorical Translations," in *Viator* 2 (1971) 227–50 [HC25]. On the philosophical translations relating to first and second intentions, see K. Gyekye, "The Terms 'Prima Intentio' and 'Secunda Intentio' in Arabic Logic," in *Speculum* 46 (1971) 32–38 [HC26]; on the intellect-intelligence distinction, see J. Jolivet, "Intellect et intelligence: Note sur la tradition arabo-latine des 12e et 13e siècles," in *Mélanges offerts à Henry Corbin*, ed. S.H. Nasr (1977) 681–702 [HC27].

*See also* [BB67] v7.

## HD ⁕ MEDIEVAL TRANSLATIONS: LATIN AND THE VERNACULAR LANGUAGES

BY JEANETTE M.A. BEER

It is difficult to determine the moment at which the sum total of differences between *parabolare romanice* and *parler romanz* constituted vernacular Romance languages, distinctive, self-contained, and self-aware. When did a separate non-Romance Medieval Latin begin? Certainly, with the appearance of those new Romance systems came a need for Latin-vernacular translation. Indirect evidence of that need was seen in the eighth century when the Church made various attempts to legislate for the use of "the rustic tongues" in preaching and instruction. These ecclesiastical directives indicated the existence of distinctive languages that the preaching clergy needed to use in order to be understood by a lay congregation. Another landmark date was that of the "Strasbourg Oaths." In A.D. 842 Carolingian scribes converted the Latin formulae for a *sacramentum firmitatis* and a *sacramentum fidelitatis* into sets of vernacular oaths for the use of Louis the German, Charles the Bald, and their respective armies. Those particular pieces of Latin-vernacular translation were preserved for propagandist purposes by Charles's court historian. They demonstrate that by the ninth century a vernacular "German" (*teudisca* [*lingua*]) and a vernacular "French" (*romana lingua*) existed, and that those languages were actually employed at Strasbourg to ensure the comprehension of all there present. Unfortunately, such pieces of early translation are rare because much of the translating from Latin to the vernacular took place in contexts of impermanence: the preparation of letters and their reading upon delivery; the preparation of legal/administrative documents; ambassadorial expeditions and interpreting; and other bilingual activities where the comprehension of all parties was required.

Various types of circumstance have preserved those rare examples of Latin-vernacular translation that have come down to us. The "Strasbourg Oaths" mentioned above were embedded in the Latin history *De dissensionibus filiorum Ludovici Pii*, III.5, of Nithard (d. 844/45). Other translations survived even more serendipitously. The "Valenciennes Fragment," a sentence-by-sentence translation from the Vulgate Book of Jonah and from St. Jerome's commentary *In Ionam*, was used to bind an unrelated manuscript (the *Annales* of Flodoard [d. 966]). Had the unpretentious Jonah sermon not been valued for the parchment on which it was written, its bilingual jottings (produced, no doubt, in response to the Church's insistence upon vernacular preaching!) would certainly have perished. The paucity of the survivals should not obscure the fact, however, that Latin-vernacular translation was practiced constantly from the earliest centuries onward in all European countries. It ensured comprehension in important matters such as religious instruction and devotion; registration of births, deaths, marriages, property transfers, successions, and legal transactions; letterwriting; and diplomacy. The most crucial feature of such pragmatic translation was its extreme literality—it was important not to misrepresent even the slightest detail in contexts of authority.

Another pragmatic form of Latin-vernacular translation was the explanatory gloss. Single words, phrases, or even sentences were inserted in the margins or between the lines of the source text as an aid to understanding. The *Abrogans*, an early Latin-Latin dictionary of Lombardic origin (c. 764–84), was glossed with Old High Bavarian. Its name derives from the first word in the list of Latin synonyms. Some extant fragments of the *Lex Salica* and other legal texts from the sixth century onward show Old High German glossing and, sometimes, translations of complete sections. Scriptural and devotional material was frequently glossed. The eighth-century Lindisfarne Gospels have interlinear Anglo-Saxon additions to explain difficult words or phrases, as do many medieval Psalters and Bibles. One of the more complex of these is the *Tripartitum psalterium Eadwinii* (c. 1150), which contains a triple-version Psalter (St. Jerome's), arranged in three columns. The version translated by the saint from the Hebrew occupies the center column; the *Psalterium gallicanum* and *Psalterium romanum* occupy the outer and inner columns, respectively. And, in addition, there are several glosses: a French gloss appears above each line of the center column (the translation from the Hebrew); the *Psalterium gallicanum* is flanked left and right by a gloss once attributed to Walafrid Strabo (d. 849), while the interlinear space is filled with a gloss by Anselm of Laon (d. 1117); and the *Psalterium romanum* has an interlinear gloss, transcribed, apparently, by two or perhaps three different hands. Glosses were gradually superseded as a tradition of translated Bibles (prose and verse) developed.

When glosses were incorporated into a text and were expanded from the translation of single words or phrases to elaborate explanation, analogizing, or other types of translative interventions, translation clearly moved beyond the boundaries of literality. A typical example is the digressive Old English *Phoenix* (late ninth century), in which the translator moves between translation of, and meditative interpretation upon, the *Carmen de ave phoenice* of Lactantius (d. c. 320). The source has been substantially expanded by the process, from 170 lines to 677.

Further modifications to the shape of source texts occurred when translation was married with compilation. An anonymous thirteenth-century translator in France translated all the known Classical Latin texts about Julius Caesar into the encyclopedic *Li Fet des Romains*. Subtle analogies between his own king Philip (later known as "Augustus") and the former Roman "emperor" reveal that his translation/compilation was conceived as a service to the Capetian monarchy and its subjects before the battle of Bouvines (1214).

Sometimes the translator's exegesis vied with the translation proper for the public's favor. In Raoul de Presles's translation of St. Augustine's *De civitate dei*, commissioned by Charles V of France (1364–1380) for the instruction of his subjects, a variegated commentary, derived from a multiplicity of sources, followed every chapter of the translated text—its modern equivalent would be the footnote. Its diverse information (etymological, mythological, historical, and even topical) ranged from the virginity of sibyls to the depravity of Nero, and the translator's explanatory commentary may indeed have been more interesting to his French public than the translated text.

The most individual products of Latin-vernacular translation were, however, those in which the source text was completely reshaped and reinterpreted for a new public. Translation then allied itself with creation and the resulting works took on a life of their own. Whereas the *Séquence de sainte Eulalie* (c. 880) maintained the rigorous structure of the Latin sequence, and the Icelandic *Klári Saga* (mid-fourteenth century) appears to have been directly translated from a (lost) Latin metrical romance, some translated works underwent real structural change. In those cases (frequently works of entertainment/instruction) the criterion of structural equivalence between source and derivative was subordinated to the criterion of structural appropriateness for a new target audience. Poetry then became prose (Lucan's *Bellum civile* was paraphrased as prose history in *Li Fet des Romains*); epic became romance (Virgil's *Aeneid* became the anonymous *Enéas* [c. 1160] or the *Eneide* [completed c. 1190] of Heinrich von Veldeke, the latter work deriving both from the French and the Latin, and Statius's *Thebaid* became *Le Roman de Thèbes*); sermons even became drama (the pseudo-Augustinian *Sermo contra Judaeos* featured as a processional act of *Le Jeu d'Adam*). Such flexibility was illustrative of the translative vitality of those formative centuries in which Western Europe was (re)discovering old/new worlds and recreating them enthusiastically for a receptive public.

Not all translators appended their names to their translations. Material translated for devotional purposes often remained anonymous even in later centuries (for example, the corpus of late medieval German *Historienbibeln,* which paraphrased [for Latin-illiterate nuns and lay brothers?] portions of the Old Testament and other scriptural passages together with chunks of patristic and popular narrative). Some categories of translators were almost never named individually: the clerical translators who worked singly or collectively inside monastic scriptoria to convert all manner of Latin writings into the vernacular (monasteries were thoughout the Middle Ages the repositories of a range of manuscripts from Terence to *materia medica*); the translators employed by the many translation schools and workshops throughout Europe (Toledo, with its heterogeneous mix of Mazarabi, Jews, and Muslims; Salerno; and the workshop of the Vadstena monastery, which took upon itself the task of translating international religious literature of all genres [usually Latin] into Swedish); the civil notaries who were an essential part of any medieval town's jurisdiction, accompanying judges, traveling with diplomatic embassies, and profoundly influencing serious prose writing (annals, chronicles, and historiography generally) by their notarial, administrative style; and the teachers and pupils of the cathedral and rhetorical schools.

On the other hand, translation was practiced from the earliest days by a variety of individual notables whose names remain associated with their products: King Alfred ("Alfred the Great," d. 899) translated works by Gregory the Great, Orosius, Boethius, St. Augustine, and also, perhaps, Bede; Notker Labeo (d. 1022), monk and teacher at St. Gall, translated Boethius, Martianus Capella, Aristotle, and Pope Gregory; the aristocratically born Marie de France (fl. 1154–89) produced *L'Espurgatoire St. Patrice* from Henry of Saltrey's *De purgatorio Sancti Patricii* (which generated at least four other Anglo-Norman and three Middle English versions); and scores of other authors (e.g. Chaucer, Dante, and Jean de Meun) proudly juxtaposed the titles of their translations and those of their original compositions (see Jean de Meun's prologue to his translation of Boethius's *De consolatione philosophiae,* in which he claims recognition not only as the author of the popular *Roman de la rose* but also as the translator of Vegetius's *De re militari,* Gerald of Wales's *Topographia Hibernica,* the letters of Abelard and Heloise, and Aelred of Rievaulx's *De spiritali amicitia*). Royal patrons (e.g. Charles V of France, Alfonso X of Castile, and Pere III of Aragon) also saw translation as a means of acquiring prestige and officially sponsored translators for political as much as for humanistic motives.

The *litteratus* (i.e. the Latin-literate) was of course capable of translation in either direction, *from* or *into* Latin, and there were multiple contexts that generated translations out of the vernacular. In the bilingual and trilingual chanceries, trained scribes, reinforced with word lists, glossaries, formularies, and grammars, daily converted documents into the language of preservation. In a civil context notaries were trained to prepare official documents, records, and transactions in Latin, and in this regard it is interesting to note that Latin was demanded not only by Christendom: Latinate wills were commissioned even in the unlikely context of medieval Spain's Jewish community. In the schools pupils learned translation as an important part of their rhetorical formation. Some kings (e.g. Henry II of England, 1154–89) and their courts were polyglot. And of course Latin was the vernacular of clerical communities for so many centuries that, in the case of bilingual texts, it is often difficult to determine whether the original was conceived in Latin or in the vernacular.

The range of major works that were translated into Latin from a preceding vernacular version was vast. They could be legal (a Provençal version of Justinian's *Codex, Les Coutumes de Beauvaisis*); philosophical (Ramon Lull's large opus, which contains many Catalan-Latin titles and, in addition, several works written initially in Arabic); hagiographic (St. Catherine of Siena's *Dialogo*); theological (Jean Gerson's Latin translations of his own or of his contemporaries' vernacular writings; the Latin translation by Christians of Maimonides's *Mishneh Torah*); historical (Jofré de Loaisa's chronicle of the kings of Castile was transposed from Castilian into Latin by Armand of Cremona); geographical (Marco Polo's *Livre de Marco Polo,* first transcribed in French while the explorer was in prison, was translated into Latin by an anonymous translator in the early fourteenth century). The Italian jurist Guido delle Colonne (d. after 1287) chose to make a French Troy romance accessible to those "qui grammaticam legunt" rather than to translate it into Italian. *Le Roman des sept sages,* Nicole Bozon's *Contes moralisés,* Wolfram's *Willehalm,* Hartmann's *Gregor, La Chanson de Roland,* and Dante's *Divina Commedia* were all transformed into Latin versions after initial appearances in the vernacular.

The translated material might serve as entertainment (Medieval Latin love poetry); as instruction (sermons, charms, spells, recipes, and *materia medica* [for which Latin was often used also as a mediating language between Arabic and a vernacular]); as stylistic training (the all-important "Hague Fragment" [980–1030], upon which the dating of vernacular epics hangs, was apparently a schoolboy exercise: a Latin prose rendering of a Latin verse epic that had in turn been translated from a vernacular epic!); or as a function of pragmatic literacy (for example, the recording of births, deaths, marriages, wills, and property transfers, or the conversion of a royal letter, ordinance, or similar pronouncement into a language suitable for archival preservation). Whatever its purpose, translation was ubiquitous in the Middle Ages. Whether pragmatically literal or creatively productive, it transcended genre and molded everyday life and thought. For translation had not yet become idiosyncratic recuperation. It was still a discourse between living languages, whether Latin or vernacular.

## Select Bibliography

J. Beer, *Early Prose in France: Contexts of Bilingualism and Authority* (1992) [HD1].

J. Beer, *A Medieval Caesar* (1976) [HD2].

J. Beer, ed., *Medieval Translators and Their Craft* (1989) [HD3].

J. Bellanger, *Histoire de la traduction en France: Auteurs grecs et latins* (1892) [HD4].

S. Berger, *La Bible française au moyen âge: Étude sur les plus anciennes versions de la Bible écrites en prose de langue d'oïl* (1884, r1967) [HD5].

J. Bonnard, *Les traductions de la Bible en vers français au moyen âge* (1884, r1967) [HD6].

N. Brooks, ed., *Latin and the Vernacular Languages in Early Medieval Britain* (1982) [HD7].

C. Buridant, "*Translatio medievalis:* Théorie et pratique de la traduction médiévale," in *Travaux de linguistique et de littérature* 21 (1983) 81–136 [HD8].

P. Chavy, *Traducteurs d'autrefois, moyen âge et renaissance: Dictionnaire des traducteurs et de la littérature traduite en ancien et moyen français (842–1600),* 2 vols. (1988) [HD9].

G. Contamine, ed., *Traduction et traducteurs au moyen âge: Actes du colloque international du C.N.R.S.* (Paris, 26–28 May 1986) (1989) [HD10].

R. Copeland, *Rhetoric, Hermeneutics, and Translation in the Middle Ages: Academic Traditions and Vernacular Texts* (1991) [HD11].

M.-T. d'Alverny, "Translations and Translators," in *R&R* 421–62 [HD12].

L. Delisle, *Le Cabinet des manuscrits de la Bibliothèque impériale,* 3 vols. (1868–81, r1969) [HD13].

P. Dembowski, "Learned Latin Treatises in French: Inspiration, Plagiarism, and Translation," in *Viator* 17 (1986) 255–69 [HD14].

R. Ellis, ed., *The Medieval Translator: The Theory and Practice of Translation in the Middle Ages* (1989) [HD15]; id., ed., *The Medieval Translator II* (1991) [HD16].

R. Ellis and R. Evans, eds., *The Medieval Translator 4* (1994) [HD17].

G. Folena, "Volgarizzare" e "tradurre": Idea e terminologia della traduzione dal Medio Evo italiano e romanzo all'Umanesimo europeo," in *La traduzione: Saggi e studi* (1973) 57–120 [HD18].

J. Hamesse and M. Fattori, eds., *Rencontres de cultures dans la philosophie médiévale: Traductions et traducteurs de l'Antiquité tardive au XIVe siècle. Actes du Colloque internationale de Cassino, 15–17 juin 1989* (1990) [HD19].

N. Henkel, *Deutsche Übersetzungen lateinischer Schultexte: Ihre Verbreitung und Funktion im Mittelalter und in der frühen Neuzeit, mit einem Verzeichnis der Texte* (1988) [HD20].

J. Herman, *Du latin aux langues romanes: Études de linguistique historique* (1990) [HD21].

D. Kelly, "*Translatio studii:* Translation, Adaptation, and Allegory in Medieval French Literature," in *Philological Quarterly* 57 (1978) 287–310 [HD22].

L.G. Kelly, *The True Interpreter: A History of Translation Theory and Practice in the West* (1979) [HD23].

R.H. Lucas, "Mediaeval French Translations of the Latin Classics to 1500," in *Speculum* 45 (1970) 225–53 [HD24].

T.W. Machan, *Techniques of Translation: Chaucer's Boece* (1985) [HD25].

A.J. Minnis, ed., *The Medieval Boethius: Studies in the Vernacular Translations of De consolatione philosophiae* (1987) [HD26].

J. Monfrin, "Humanisme et traductions au moyen âge," in *JS* (1963) 161–69; *id.*, "Les traducteurs et leur public en France au moyen âge," in *JS* (1964) 5–20; both repr. in *L'Humanisme médiéval dans les littératures romanes du XIIe au XIVe siècles*, ed. A. Fourrier (1964) 217–46 and 24–64 [HD27].

A. Quak, *Die altmittel- und altniederfränkischen Psalmen und Glossen* (1981) [HD28].

F.M. Rener, *Interpretatio: Language and Translation from Cicero to Tytler* (1989) [HD29].

I. Rosier, ed., *HGL* [HD30].

H. Stone, *Medical Translations in French before 1500* (1941) [HD31].

R. Wright, ed., *Latin and the Romance Languages in the Early Middle Ages* (1991, r1996) [HD32].

# INDICES

These two indices list authors and texts mentioned only in the bibliographies of the guide. References are therefore to the letter and number codes assigned to all bibliographical entries.

*Index I* includes ancient, late antique, medieval, and renaissance writers and translators and their works; anonymous works are listed by title. Antiquarian bibliographers and historians of religious orders (see chapter BC) are part of Index II. Medieval and renaissance authors are listed under their first names; hence—with apologies for whatever irritation this consistency may cause!—Abelard is to be found under "Peter" and Valla under "Lorenzo." Arabic names are usually indexed according to their latinized forms (Albumasar, Alcabitius, etc.), but when modern transliterations are used (e.g. Al-Bīrūnī), the article *Al-* likewise determines the alphabetical position of the name. Classical and patristic names are indexed in the form traditionally most familiar (Ambrose, Augustine, Cicero, Jerome, Ovid, Pliny the Elder, Virgil, etc.). Authors and texts in Index I are also cross-referenced to those secondary works and studies in whose titles they are specifically mentioned.

*Index II* is an alphabetical listing of modern authors and editors—including also compilers, translators, and the honorees of *Festschriften*—as well as of the titles (often abbreviated) of standard Latin dictionaries (see chapter CD), of almost all the reference and research tools mentioned in chapters BA–BH, and of any other modern works mentioned in the bibliographies without specific author or editor. Personal names are listed under the surname and compound names under the first part; names with prefixes (*Al-, D', d', Dal, De, de, Del, del, Della, de la, Di, di, Du, L', Le, von, von den/der,* but not *Van* or *Van de/den/der*) are inverted.

# INDEX I

## Ancient, Late Antique, Medieval, and Renaissance Authors and Works

# INDEX II

## Modern Authors, Editors, and

## General Works of Reference

Cameron, A. GB20, GB46, GB57, GB79, GL24, GN40
Campbell, J. GN40
Campbell, M.B. GS21
Campbell, T.P. GG23
Camus, C. GB25
Cange, C. Du Fresne, Sieur Du BF69, CD15, FE8, FM8
*Canterbury and York Society* BG21
Cantin, A. GR23
*CANTUS* BE29
Capaiuolo, F. BA6
Capelletto, R. CH13
Capitani, O. GP86
*Capitula episcoporum* BA86
Caplan, H. GM27, GM34
Cappelli, A. BD86, EF21
Capponi, F. EH35
Caprioli, S. DG21
Capua, F. di CF3, CF12, DC2
Cárcel Ortí, M. DE8
Carducci, G. GC44
Carey, H.M. EE68
Cargill, O. GG24
*Caritas: Étude sur le vocabulaire latin* BB55
Carlson, E. GM21
*Carmelitana bibliotheca* BC17
*Carmina medii aevi maximam partem inedita* BG41
Carmody, F.J. EE50, EE67, EG12–13
Carnes, P. BA50
Caroti, S. EE2, EE68
Carozzi, C. GT36
Carpentier, P. CD15
Carrara, M. GA41
Carruthers, M. GA93
Carter, F.E.L. DD21
*Cartusiana: A heuristic instrument* BC56
Carus-Wilson, E.M. FJ31–33, FJ46
Cary, G. GC64
Casa, A. Della CD9
Casagrande, C. GP38
Caspar, E. DF40, GO12
*Cassell's Encyclopaedia of World Literature* BC29
Casson, L. FF26
Castro, A. BB68
*Catalogue of Medieval and Renaissance Optical Manuscritps* BC76
*Catalogue of Romances* BC114
*Catalogue of Thomists, 1270–1900* BC71
*Catalogues (Les) de bibliothèques* BA90
*Catalogus translationum et commentariorum* BA13
*Catholic Dictionary of Theology* BD32
*Catholic Encyclopaedia* BD107
*Catholic University of America Patristic Studies* CC25
*Catholic University of America Studies in Medieval and*

*Renaissance Latin Language and Literature* CC26
*Catholicisme hier, aujourd'hui, demain* BD33
Cavallo, G. GA6, GC75
Cave, W. BC4
*Census of Medieval Latin Grammatical Manuscripts* BC30
*Centenary Guide to the Publications of the Selden Society* DG41
Cerasa-Gastaldo, A. DA64
*Cetedoc Index of Latin Forms* BE31
*Cetedoc Library of Christian Latin Texts* BE30
Chambers, E.K. GG25
Champollion-Figéac, J.-J. FF27
Chantraine, P. BF68
Chaplais, P. GO36
Charland, T.-M. GM9, GM39, GP54
Charlet, J.-L. CH10, GB14, GB23, GB58, GB80–81
Chartier, Y. DJ19
Chase, C. GL57
Chatelain, E. BB58
Châtillon, J. FB16
Chauvin, B. BC28
Chavy, P. HD9
Chaytor, H.J. GA99
*Checklist of Non-Italian Humanists* BC36
Chédeville, A. FM18
Cheetham, S. BD40
Cheney, C.R. DD138, DK21, EF20, GO52, GQ20
Chenu, M.-D. DH69–75, EE69
Cherewatuk, K. GO45
Cherubini, L. FC2
Chesne, F. Du FF30
Chevalier, J. BD51
Chevalier, U. BC32, GJ8
Chew, H.M. DL45
Cheyne, T.K. BD64
Chiaudano, M. DK15, DK22–23
Chibnall, M. GN12, GN15, GN30
Chickering, H. DD107
Chiesa, P. HB3
Chirat, H. CD21, DA10
Chiri, G. GC65
Chittenden, J. DI114
Chodorow, S. DF4
Chomarat, J. CH14
*Christianisme et formes littéraires de l'Antiquité tardive en occident* GB56
*Chronological English Dictionary* BF25
*Chronology of Eclipses and Comets, A.D. 1–1000* BF96
*Chronology of the Ancient World* BF97
*Chronology of the Medieval World* BF97
Ciccarese, M.P. GT1, GT14
Cipolla, C. BG59
*Cistercian Fathers Series* GU44

Clagett, M EB1–2, EB39, EB47, EC20–22, EC26, EC28, ED12, FA7
Clain-Stefanelli, E. FL11
Clanchy, M.T. DD53, DD139, GA94
Clarence Smith, J.A. DF5
Clark, J. GA54
Clark, J.R. EM4
Clark, W.B. EH19, EH36, GD16, GD35
Clarke, B. GC22
Clarke, F.P. HA12
Classen, P. HB24
*Classical Scholarship: An Annotated Bibliography* BA4
*Classics of Western Spirituality* GU45
*Classiques (Les) de l'histoire de France au moyen âge* BG22
*Clavis apocryphorum Novi Testamenti* BC46
*Clavis Gerberti* BG40
*Clavis patristica pseudepigraphorum medii aevi* BC80
*Clavis patrum graecorum* BC45
*Clavis patrum latinorum* BC37
*Clavis scriptorum graecorum et latinorum* BA11, BC74
*Clavis scriptorum latinorum medii aevi* BC68
Cleasby, R. BF59
Cleeve, B. BC27
Clémencet, S. DC6
Clément, J.-M. BB27, BC33, GT16, GU10
Clementi, A. FJ34
Clerck, P. De DB120
Closs, A. EJ29
Clover, H. GO29
Cobban, A.B. DL68
Codoñer, C. DA14
Coffman, G.R. AA2
Coggins, R.J. BD38
Cohen, G. GG6, GG42
Cohen-Mushlin, A. FH14
Coing, H. DG15, DG38
Cole, P. GP53
Coleman, J. GA95, GN31
Coleman, O. FD2
Coleman, R. EL19
Colgrave, B. CF1, GL16–19, GN3
Colker, M.L. GC57, GO37
*Collection de textes pour servir à l'étude et à l'enseignement de l'histoire* BG23
*Collections (Les) canoniques* BA99
Colledge, E. GU11
Colli, V. DG24
Collins, F. DL39
Collins, F., Jr. GG7, GG26
Collison, R. GV19
*Colophons de manuscrits occidentaux* BC34
Colvin, H.M. DL56–57, FC10, FC17, FC38
Comba, R. FM17

*Medieval Latin: An Introduction and Bibliographical Guide* was composed in Minion by Graphic Composition, Athens, Georgia; printed on 50-pound Natural Smooth and bound by Braun-Brumfield, Inc., Ann Arbor, Michigan; and designed and produced by Kachergis Book Design, Pittsboro, North Carolina.